THE ROUGH GUIDE TO

Argentina

There are more than one hundred and fifty Rough Guide titles
covering destinations from Amsterdam to Zimbabwe

Forthcoming titles include
Alaska • Copenhagen • Ibiza & Formentera • Iceland

Rough Guide Reference Series
Classical Music • Country Music • Drum 'n' bass • English Football
European Football • House • The Internet • Jazz • Music USA • Opera
Reggae • Rock Music • Techno • Unexplained Phenomena • World Music

Rough Guide Phrasebooks
Czech • Dutch • Egyptian Arabic • European Languages • French • German
Greek • Hindi & Urdu • Hungarian • Indonesian • Italian • Japanese
Mandarin Chinese • Mexican Spanish • Polish • Portuguese • Russian
Spanish • Swahili • Thai • Turkish • Vietnamese

Rough Guides on the Internet
www.roughguides.com

ROUGH GUIDE CREDITS

Text editor: Judith Bamber
Series editor: Mark Ellingham
Editorial: Martin Dunford, Jonathan Buckley, Jo Mead, Kate Berens, Amanda Tomlin, Ann-Marie Shaw, Paul Gray, Helena Smith, Orla Duane, Olivia Eccleshall, Ruth Blackmore, Geoff Howard, Claire Saunders, Gavin Thomas, Alexander Mark Rogers, Polly Thomas, Joe Staines, Lisa Nellis, Andrew Tomičić, Richard Lim, Duncan Clark, Peter Buckley, Sam Thorne, Lucy Ratcliffe, Clifton Wilkinson (UK); Andrew Rosenberg, Mary Beth Maioli, Don Bapst, Stephen Timblin (US)
Production: Susanne Hillen, Andy Hilliard, Link Hall, Helen Ostick, Julia Bovis, Michelle Draycott,
Katie Pringle, Robert Evers, Mike Hancock, Robert McKinlay, Zoë Nobes
Cartography: Melissa Baker, Maxine Repath, Ed Wright
Picture research: Louise Boulton, Sharon Martins
Online: Kelly Cross, Anja Mutić-Blessing, Jennifer Gold, Audra Epstein (US)
Finance: John Fisher, Gary Singh, Edward Downey, Mark Hall, Tim Bill
Marketing & Publicity: Richard Trillo, Niki Smith, David Wearn, Jemima Broadbridge, Chloë Roberts, Birgit Hartmann (UK); Simon Carloss, David Wechsler (US)
Administration: Tania Hummel, Demelza Dallow, Julie Sanderson

THE AUTHORS

Danny Aeberhard After graduating in 1991 with a history degree, Danny steered clear of insidious law and accountancy conversion courses, opting instead for the third way of TEFL teaching, and heading to Spain for a year, ostensibly to pick up the language. This was followed by several years of backpacking and leading tours throughout South and Central America and trying – in vain – to work out which Latin country he liked the best. Returning to the motherland, he has pursued his passion for the region by editing a guidebook to Cuba and has worked for Rough Guides in Switzerland and Provence.

Andrew Benson turned to writing *The Rough Guide to Argentina* after fourteen years working as a translator for international organizations, and occasionally as a journalist for Vatican Radio, in Brussels, Paris and Strasbourg, his adoptive city. Before that he lived in Athens, selling books for an English publisher. He has been based in France for the last decade and, despite liking it less every day, still prefers it to any other country.

Lucy Phillips developed a passion for Argentina through the novels of Manuel Puig and Julio Cortázar and first travelled to Argentina in 1991 where she fell in love with Buenos Aires, tango and Boca Juniors. She has returned as often as possible ever since, spending a year studying at the University of Buenos Aires while completing her degree in Hispanic Studies. Since graduating she has interspersed periods of employment at home with travel and work in Latin America, spending time in Brazil, Uruguay and Venezuela. She now lives in Brighton where she works as a writer and translator.

PUBLISHING INFORMATION

This first edition published November 2000 by Rough Guides Ltd, 62–70 Shorts Gardens, London WC2H 9AH.
Distributed by the Penguin Group:
Penguin Books Ltd, 27 Wrights Lane, London W8 5TZ
Penguin Putnam, Inc., 375 Hudson St, NY 10014, USA
Penguin Books Australia Ltd, 487 Maroondah Highway, PO Box 257, Ringwood, Victoria 3134, Australia
Penguin Books Canada Ltd, 10 Alcorn Ave, Toronto, Ontario, Canada M4V 1E4
Penguin Books (NZ) Ltd, 182–190 Wairau Rd, Auckland 10, New Zealand
Typeset in Linotron Univers and Century Old Style to an original design by Andrew Oliver.
Printed in England by Clays Ltd, St Ives Plc
Illustrations in Part One and Part Three by Edward Briant.
Illustrations on p.1 and p.695 by Robert Evers

The publishers and authors have done their best to ensure the accuracy and currency of all the information in *The Rough Guide to Argentina*. However, they can accept no responsibility for any loss, injury, or inconvenience sustained by any traveller as a result of information or advice contained in the guide.

Robert Penrush

THE ROUGH GUIDE TO

Argentina

written and researched by

**Danny Aeberhard, Andrew Benson
and Lucy Phillips**

**ROUGH
GUIDES**

We set out to do something different when the first Rough Guide was published in 1982. Mark Ellingham, just out of university, was travelling in Greece. He brought along the popular guides of the day, but found they were all lacking in some way. They were either strong on ruins and museums but went on for pages without mentioning a beach or taverna. Or they were so conscious of the need to save money that they lost sight of Greece's cultural and historical significance. Also, none of the books told him anything about Greece's contemporary life – its politics, its culture, its people, and how they lived.

So with no job in prospect, Mark decided to write his own guidebook, one which aimed to provide practical information that was second to none, detailing the best beaches and the hottest clubs and restaurants, while also giving hard-hitting accounts of every sight, both famous and obscure, and providing up-to-the-minute information on contemporary culture. It was a guide that encouraged independent travellers to find the best of Greece, and was a great success, getting shortlisted for the Thomas Cook travel guide award, and encouraging Mark, along with three friends, to expand the series.

The Rough Guide list grew rapidly and the letters flooded in, indicating a much broader readership than had been anticipated, but one which uniformly appreciated the Rough Guide mix of practical detail and humour, irreverence and enthusiasm. Things haven't changed. The same four friends who began the series are still the caretakers of the Rough Guide mission today: to provide the most reliable, up-to-date and entertaining information to independent-minded travellers of all ages, on all budgets.

We now publish more than 150 titles and have offices in London and New York. The travel guides are written and researched by a dedicated team of more than 100 authors, based in Britain, Europe, the USA and Australia. We have also created a unique series of phrasebooks to accompany the travel series, along with an acclaimed series of music guides, and a best-selling pocket guide to the Internet and World Wide Web. We also publish comprehensive travel information on our Web site:

www.roughguides.com

HELP US UPDATE

We've gone to a lot of effort to ensure that the first edition of *The Rough Guide to Argentina* is accurate and up-to-date. However, things change – places get "discovered", opening hours are notoriously fickle, restaurants and rooms raise prices or lower standards. If you feel we've got it wrong or left something out, we'd like to know, and if you can remember the address, the price, the time, the phone number, so much the better.

We'll credit all contributions, and send a copy of the next edition (or any other *Rough Guide* if you prefer) for the best letters. Please mark letters: "Rough Guide Argentina Update" and send to:
Rough Guides, 62–70 Shorts Gardens, London WC2H 9AH, or Rough Guides, 4th Floor, 345 Hudson St, New York, NY 10014.
Or send email to: mail@roughguides.co.uk
Online updates about this book can be found on Rough Guides' Web site at www.roughguides.com

ACKNOWLEDGEMENTS

The editor: Thanks to Kate for her unwavering support; to Nichola for patience above and beyond in preparing the maps – and to Maxine for stepping into the breach; to Rob for typesetting with skill and fortitude, and, of course, to everyone else in production; and to Carole Mansur and Russell Walton for proofreading.

Danny Aeberhard: To my editors: Judith, Chris and Kate; Argentine Embassy, esp. Bibiana; J. Mazower; R. Casamiquela, T. Prieto, Amit Thakkar and M.L. Rubina. Tourist office/national parks staff: esp. R. Leserovich; J.C. Landi; R. Gazzera; the Benaventes; J.J. Valera; M. Ocampo; Mirta; D. Martín; G. Soria; G. Martín; C. Bertonatti; G. Ramacciotti. Mark and Ale Pearson; Claudio Valencia and Cristina; M. García. Lhaka Honhat; Hoktek T'oi; J. Braunstein; María Luisa; Perla. Sr. Morando; I. Belver; S. Keim; A. Holzmann. Wonderful families: Argañaraz; Avilez; Barruco; Bravo; Brosio; Cramer; Deane; Gravino; Hernández; Lemos; Mauras; Murray; Nauta and Harry; Nikolic; Ochoa; Szlápelis; and Vega. Clery Evans; D. Berk, L. Canessa; Dante; J. Cerezo; Cholino; Sandra; Talo; Elmer Williams; "Simpsonsisters"; B. Johnson; J. Guzmán; Paulo Álvarez; Alec Quevedo; Billinghams; M. McGeorge; Haschi; Karo; Macarena; D. Hammel. Patty, for "Surf's up!" Lastly, two insuperable families: my own, especially John and Penny; and my surrogate one in Caballito – Kely, Anselmo, Silia and Raúl Kojnover.

Andrew Benson: Monica, Coco and David Browning, Peter Mackridge and Jackie Willcox, Debbie Sellman and Ben Rapp, Eric Kaiser and Renaud Lallement, Ferrante Ferranti, Theodore Carrère and Juan Durañona y Vedia, Marjan Groothuis and Walter Baumgartner, Jordi Ferrer i Gràcia, Carles Orriols and Olga Pena for putting me up and putting up with me. Gustavo Masieri, Walter Maldonado and José Durañona in Buenos Aires, Jorge Birkner and Julio Einhart at Las Leñas plus Michael Purcell Labrecque,

Andrés Carrillo and everyone at the turismo in Catamarca, Julia Bisio and Julita, Fabrizio Bogado and Osvaldo Braida in Córdoba, Enrique Wienhausen in Jujuy, Alejandro Arroyo in Malargüe, Osvaldo José Urueta in Mendoza, Aurélien Paris, and Frank and Haike in Salta, Raphael Joliat and María José in San Juan, David Rivarola and family in San Luis, Gabriel Bessone in San Rafael, María Valeria Sosa and Eugenia Beatriz Bonetto in Santiago del Estero, and the Pasqualini family, Juan Pablo Domínguez and Sisto Pondal in Tucumán, for their invaluable help. A special mention for Ignacio "Ralph" Litardo and his in-depth polo knowledge, and for Mike Fineberg and Virginia Prieto-Fineberg. And not forgetting Pablo Márquez and Mónica Taragano for their music.

Lucy Phillips: To my friends in Buenos Aires: Gastón Chillier, Roberto Reinoso, Mariana Obarrio, Pablo Stefanoni and Nadina, Pablo Ben, Analía and, above all, Andrea Baliño and Chola. Also thanks to Néstor Andrés Arrazola; Lucrecia; Gabriel Barletta; Juan Lewis; Gabriela and Roberto; Vanessa Halipi; Professor Heriberto Pezzarini; Mario and Javier; Ignacio Vulliez; Carolina Dentone; Daniela and Germán; Juan Luis Sabatini; Diego Tignino, Ruffo and the guardarques of Ernesto Tornquist; Elsa Güiraldes and Maxi; Ruli Cabral and "Conejo"; Adriana Giromini; Mauricio Weinberg; Víctor and Andrea; Macarena; The Secretaria Nacional de Turismo; Estancia La Rica; Pampa Cura; Pippo and Rosi; Cuencas del Plata; Residencial Noelia; Juan Catalano and Inés Perie; Tomás and Guillermina; Carlos Vaccarezza; Antonio Rinaldi; Raúl Feversani; Lucas Iturriza; Marita and family; María Rodríguez; Antonio Lubarry; Angel and Gabriela; Daniela in Santa Rosa and the guarda-parques of Lihué Calel. Thanks too, to Dr Charlie Easmon of the Hospital for Tropical Diseases. Most of all, thanks to Steve for putting up with everything.

CONTENTS

Introduction x

PART THREE CONTEXTS 695

LIST OF MAPS

MAP SYMBOLS

══•═ Railway	⬥ Waterfall	⊙ Statue
═══ Paved road	⚶ Spring/spa	♦ Museum
─── Unpaved road	⸬ Marshland	Ⓗ Hospital
----- Path/trail	↑ Palm trees	ⓘ Tourist office
— — Ferry route	✈ International airport	✉ Post office
∼∼∼ Waterway	✈ Domestic airport	✆ Telephone
––– Chapter division boundary	★ Bus stop	⌘ Golf course
▬•▬• International borders	Ⓜ Metro stop	■ Building
══ × × Provincial boundary	Ⓟ Parking	✚ Church
◆ General point of interest	⊕ Ferry/boat station	Cemetery
✝ Guardaparque HQ/Park Ranger HQ	⚑ Campsite	Pedestrianized area
✝ Church (regional maps)	⛺ Refuge	Park
⌂ Cave	◉ Accommodation	National park
⛰ Volcano	■ Restaurant/café	Glacier
⌁ Mountains	⚘ Vineyard	Saltlake
▲ Peak	⛷ Ski area	Beach
⚶ Viewpoint		

INTRODUCTION

Argentina is a vast country. It measures 5000km by 1500km and, even without the titanic wedge of Antarctica that the authorities are wont to include in the national territory, it ranks as the world's eighth largest state, immediately behind India. Thanks to its longitudinal position, standing between the Tropic of Cancer and the most southerly reaches of the planet's landmass, the country encompasses a staggering diversity of climates and landscapes. The mainland points down like a massive stalactite on the map, from the hot and humid **jungles of its northeast** and the **bone-dry highland steppes of its northwest** down through windswept **Patagonia** to the end-of-the-world archipelago of **Tierra del Fuego**, a territory that is shared with Chile. Across the broad midriff stretch Argentina's most archetypal landscapes: the mostly **flat pampas** grazed by millions of cattle – subtly beautiful scenery formed by horizon-to-horizon plains interspersed with low sierras, and punctuated by small agricultural towns, the odd ranch and countless clumps of pampas grass. These wide open spaces are among the country's best assets – despite its mammoth area its **population** of 33 million weighs in at far less than Spain's. This is a land with huge swaths still waiting to be explored let alone settled.

Like Chile to its west – with which it shares 5000km of grandiose Andean cordillera, several of whose colossal peaks exceed 6000m – Argentina is, for the most part, less obviously exotic than its neighbours to the north, and its inhabitants will readily (and rightly) tell you how great an influence Europe has been on their nation. It was once said that Argentina is actually the most American of all European countries, but even that clever maxim is wide of the mark. It's a country with a very special character all of its own, distilled into the national ideal of **Argentinidad** – an elusive identity the country's Utopian thinkers and practical doers have never agreed upon. Undoubtedly, the people of Argentina suffer from, but also encourage to an extent, some of the world's most sweeping generalizations, based mainly on the typical **Porteño**, or native of Buenos Aires. They suffer from a bad press in the rest of the continent, but you're bound to be wowed by their spontaneous curiosity and intense passion for so many things. On this score there's a lot of truth in the clichés – their passions *are* dominated by the national religion of **football**, politics and living life in the fast lane (literally, when it comes to driving) – but not everyone dances the **tango**, or is obsessed with **Evita**, or gallops around on a horse, **gaucho-style**. Whether thanks to their beauty, sense of humour or other charms, the locals will help to make any trip to the country memorable.

So aside from the people, why visit Argentina? First, because the huge metropolis of **Buenos Aires**, home to two-fifths of the population, is one of the most exciting, charming and fascinating of all South American capitals. It's an immensely enjoyable place just to wander about, stopping off for an espresso or an ice cream, or people-watching, or shopping, or simply soaking up the unique atmosphere. Its many barrios, or neighbourhoods, are startlingly different, some decadently old-fashioned, others thrustingly modern, but all of them oozing character. Added to that, Buenos Aires is the country's gastronomic mecca and boasts a frenzied nightlife that makes it one of the world's great round-the-clock cities. Elsewhere, cities aren't exactly the main draw, with the exception of beautiful **Salta** in the northwest, the beguiling river-port of **Rosario** – birthplace of Che Guevara – and **Ushuaia** which, in addition to being the world's most southerly city, happens to enjoy a fabulous setting on the evocatively named Tierra del Fuego.

Wildlife and adventure in the extensive **outback** are the real attractions outside of the capital. By hopping on a plane it's feasible to spot howler monkeys and toucans in

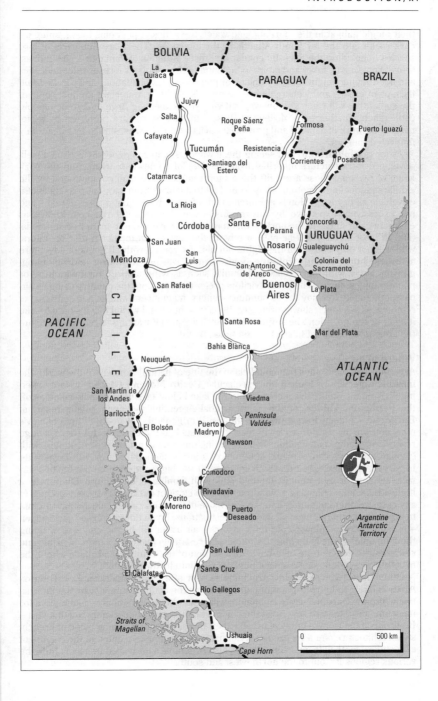

BOLIVIA

PARAGUAY

BRAZIL

La Quiaca

Jujuy

Salta

Roque Sáenz Peña

Formosa

Puerto Iguazú

Cafayate

Tucumán

Resistencia

Santiago del Estero

Corrientes

Posadas

Catamarca

La Rioja

Córdoba

Santa Fe

Paraná

Concordia

URUGUAY

San Juan

Rosario

Gualeguaychú

San Luis

Mendoza

San Antonio de Areco

Colonia del Sacramento

San Rafael

Buenos Aires

La Plata

C H I L E

Santa Rosa

Mar del Plata

Bahía Blanca

PACIFIC OCEAN

Neuquén

ATLANTIC OCEAN

San Martín de los Andes

Viedma

Bariloche

Península Valdés

El Bolsón

Puerto Madryn

Rawson

Comodoro Rivadavia

Perito Moreno

Puerto Deseado

San Julián

El Calafate

Santa Cruz

Río Gallegos

N

Argentine Antarctic Territory

Straits of Magellan

Ushuaia

Cape Horn

0   500 km

their jungle habitat in the morning, and watch the antics of penguins tobogganing off dark rocks into the icy South Atlantic in the afternoon. There are hundreds of bird species – including the majestic condor and three varieties of flamingo – plus pumas, armadillos, llamas, foxes and tapirs to be found in the country's forests, mountainsides and the dizzying heights of the altiplano or puna. Lush tea-plantations and parched salt-flats, palm groves and icebergs, plus the world's mightiest waterfalls are just some of the sights that will catch you unawares if you were expecting Argentina to be one big cattle-ranch. Furthermore, dozens of these vital biosystems are protected by a pioneering network of national and provincial **parks and reserves**, staffed by remarkably motivated rangers.

As for **getting around** and seeing these wonders, you can generally rely on a well-developed infrastructure inherited from decades of domestic tourism. And the challenge of reaching those areas off the beaten track is more than compensated by the exhilarating feeling of getting away from it all that comes from, say, not passing another vehicle all day long. Hotels are often much of a muchness, but a special treat – and not excessively expensive by any means – are the beautiful ranches, known as **estancias** – or fincas in the north – that have been converted into luxury accommodation. In most areas, you'll be able to rely on the services of top-notch tour operators, who will not only show you the sights but also fix you up with all kinds of adventure activities: **horse-riding**, **trekking**, **white-water rafting**, **kayaking**, **skiing**, **hang-gliding**, along with more relaxing pursuits such as **wine-tasting**, **bird-watching** or photography **safaris**. While some visitors prefer to whiz about the country using an air-pass, others like to enjoy the astounding scenery, magnificent wildlife and sensation of remoteness at a much slower pace. Argentina is so huge and varied that it's hard to take it all in in one go – don't be surprised if you find yourself wanting to return to explore the areas you didn't get to see the first time around.

Where to go

Argentina has many sites that could claim the title of natural wonders of the world: the majestic waterfalls of **Iguazú**, the spectacular **Perito Moreno Glacier**, whose towering sixty-metre walls calve icebergs into the lake below, fascinating whale colonies off the **Península Valdés**, or the quintessential Argentine mountain holiday-resort of **Bariloche** – indeed **Patagonia** and the south in general. Yet many of the country's most noteworthy sights are also its least known, such as the **Esteros del Iberà**, a huge reserve of swamps and floating islands offering unforgettably close-up encounters with cayman, monkeys, capybara and hundreds of brightly plumed birds; or **Antofagasta de la Sierra**, an amazingly remote village close to the biggest **crater** on the Earth's surface, set amid frozen lagoons mottled pink with flamingos; or **Laguna Diamante**, a high-altitude lake reflecting a wondrous volcano straight out of a Japanese woodcut. In any case, weather conditions and the sheer size of the country will rule out any attempt to see every corner or even all the main destinations. If you do want to see each region – broadly corresponding to our ten chapters – air travel will be the only way of fitting them in, unless time is no object. But climatic restraints make it far more sensible and rewarding to concentrate on a particular section of the country, and that's where the excellent network of long-distance buses comes into its own.

Other than if you're visiting Argentina as part of a South American tour, **Buenos Aires** is likely to be your point of entry, as it has the country's only *bona fide* international airport. Only inveterate city-haters will resist the capital's charm. Not a place for museum fans – though several of the city's art collections are certainly worth a visit – BA is one of the world's greatest urban experiences, with its intriguing blend of French-style architecture and a vernacular style that includes houses painted in the colours of a legendary football team. From the city, also Argentina's unrivalled transport hub, the various regions fan out to the north, west and south.

Due north stretches **El Litoral**, a region of subtropical riverine landscapes sharing borders with Brazil and Paraguay. Here are the photogenic Iguazú waterfalls, and the much-visited Jesuit Missions whose once noble ruins are crumbling into the tangled jungle, with the notable exception of well-preserved **San Ignacio Miní** set among manicured parkland. Immediately to the west of El Litoral stretches the **Chaco**, one of Argentina's most infrequently visited regions, a place for those with a dogged interest in **wildlife**, especially birdlife and endangered species of mammals; but be prepared for often fiercely hot conditions, a poor tourist infrastructure and a long wait if you want to see some of its rarer denizens. Tucked away in the country's landlocked **Northwest**, the historic cradle of present-day Argentina, bordering on Bolivia and northern Chile, is the polychrome **Quebrada del Toro** which can be viewed in comfort from the **Tren a los Nubes**, one of the world's highest railways. Even more colourful is the much photographed **Quebrada de Humahuaca**, a fabulous gorge winding up to the oxygen-starved Altiplano, where llamas and their wild relatives graze on straw-like pastures. In the **Valles Calchaqúes**, a series of stunningly beautiful valleys, high-altitude vineyards produce the delightfully flowery torrontés wine.

West and immediately south of Buenos Aires is pampa, pampa and more pampa. This is where you'll still glimpse signs of the traditional **gaucho culture**, most famously celebrated in the charming town of **San Antonio de Areco**. Here, too, you'll find some of the classiest **estancias**, offering a combination of understated luxury and horseback adventure activities. On the Atlantic coast are a string of fun beach resorts, including long-standing favourite **Mar del Plata**. While the farther west you go, the larger the Central Sierras loom on the horizon: the mild climate and bucolic woodlands of these ancient mountains have attracted Argentine tourists since the late nineteenth century, and within reach of **Córdoba**, the country's vibrant second city, are some of the oldest resorts on the continent. Both the city and its hinterland contain some wonderful **colonial architecture**, including the well-preserved Jesuit estancias of **Alta Gracia** and **Santa Catalina**. In the **Cuyo**, farther west still, with the highest Andean peaks as a splendid backdrop, you can discover one of Argentina's most enjoyable cities, the regional capital of **Mendoza**, also the country's **wine capital**. From here, the scenic **Alta Montaña** route climbs steeply to the Chilean border, passing **Cerro Aconcagua**, now well-established as a dream challenge for mountaineers from around the world. Just to the south, **Las Leñas** is a winter resort where a lot of skiers end up on the pages of the continent's glamour magazines, but the nearby black-and-red lava-wastes of **La Payunia**, one of the country's hidden jewels, are all but overlooked. Likewise, **San Juan** and **La Rioja** provinces are relatively uncharted territory, but their marvellous mountain-and-valley landscapes will reward exploration, along with their less known but often outstanding wineries. Their star attractions are a brace of parks: **Parque Nacional Talampaya**, with its giant red cliffs seen on many a poster, and the nearby **Parque Provincial Ischigualasto**, usually known the **Valle de la Luna** on account of its intriguing moonscapes.

Whereas neighbouring Chile takes up a mere sliver of the continent's Southern Cone, Argentina, like a greedy bedfellow hogging the blankets, has the lion's share of the wild, sparsely populated expanses of **Patagonia** and the archipelago of **Tierra del Fuego**. These are lands of seemingly endless arid steppe hemmed in for the most part by the southern leg of the Andes, a series of volcanoes, craggy peaks and deep glacial lakes. An almost unbroken chain of national parks along these Patagonian and Fuegian cordilleras make for some of the best trekking anywhere on the planet. Certainly include the savage granite peaks of the **Fitz Roy sector** of the **Parque Nacional Los Glaciares** in your itinerary but also the less frequently visited monkey-puzzle forests of **Parque Nacional Lanín** or the trail network of **Parque Nacional Nahuel Huapi**. These regions exert an irresistible lure on many visitors, and in addition to the fabulous scenery, they offer excellent opportunities for fly-fishing and adventurous horseriding, with the famous sheep estancias as a base. For wildlife enthusiasts the **Peninsula Valdés** is a must-see: famous above all else as a breeding ground for southern right whales, it and the nearby coast also sustain enormous colonies of elephant seals, penguins and sea-lions. If you have a historical bent, you may like to trace the region's associations with early seafarers such as Magellan and Drake in the **Bahía San Julián** or Fitzroy and Darwin in the beautiful **Beagle Channel** off Ushuaia. Ancestors of the Tehuelche, one of the many remarkable indigenous cultures wiped out after the Europeans arrived, painted the wonderful collage of handprints and animal scenes that adorn the walls of the **Cueva de las Manos Pintadas** in Santa Cruz Province. Finally, you might like to track down the legacy of outlaws like Butch Cassidy who lived near Cholila, or of the **Welsh settlers** whose influence can still be felt in communities like **Gaiman** and **Trevelin**.

When to go

Since you're unlikely to flit from region to region, you could probably manage to visit every part of the country at the optimal time of year. Roughly falling in September to November, the Argentine **spring** is perfect just about everywhere except parts of the south, where icy gales may blow, while **autumn** (March and April) is great for the wine-

AVERAGE MONTHLY TEMPERATURES (°C) AND AVERAGE MONTHLY RAINFALL (MM)

AVERAGE TEMPERATURES (°C)

The figures below denote the average highest and lowest daily temperatures.

	Jan	Feb	March	April	May	June	July	Aug	Sept	Oct	Nov	Dec
Asunción	35/22	34/22	33/21	29/18	25/14	22/12	23/12	26/14	28/16	30/17	32/18	34/21
Bahia Blanca	31/17	29/16	26/14	22/11	17/7	14/4	14/4	16/4	18/7	22/9	26/12	29/15
Buenos Aires	29/17	28/17	26/16	22/12	18/8	14/5	14/6	16/6	18/8	21/10	24/13	28/16
Esquel	26/11	25/11	21/8	17/6	12/2	8/-1	7/-2	11/-1	14/2	19/5	21/8	23/9
Mendoza	32/16	31/15	28/13	23/8	18/5	15/2	15/2	17/3	21/7	24/10	28/12	31/14
Punta Arenas	14/7	14/7	12/5	10/4	7/2	5/1	4/-1	6/1	8/2	11/3	12/4	14/6
Santa Rosa	34/15	32/14	28/12	24/8	19/3	15/0	15/3	18/1	20/4	24/8	28/11	32/14
Santiago del Estero	36/21	34/20	32/18	28/15	24/11	21/7	21/7	24/8	28/12	31/15	33/18	34/19

AVERAGE RAINFALL (mm)

	Jan	Feb	March	April	May	June	July	Aug	Sept	Oct	Nov	Dec
Asunción	140	130	109	132	117	69	56	38	79	140	150	158
Bahia Blanca	43	56	64	58	31	23	25	25	41	56	53	48
Buenos Aires	79	71	109	89	76	61	56	61	79	86	84	99
Esquel	5	8	8	10	20	20	15	13	10	8	5	8
Mendoza	23	31	28	13	10	8	5	8	13	18	18	18
Punta Arenas	38	23	33	36	33	41	28	31	23	28	18	36
Santa Rosa	71	71	71	31	25	18	15	18	28	76	64	76
Santiago del Estero	86	76	76	33	15	8	5	5	13	36	64	104

harvest in the Cuyo and the red and orange hues of the beeches down south. Above all, you're best off not being in the far south in the coldest months(April–Oct), or in the Chaco and some lowland parts of the northwest in the height of **summer** (Dec–Feb). On the other hand, summer's the only time to climb the highest Andean peaks and the most reliable time of year to head for Tierra del Fuego. Buenos Aires can get unbearably hot and sticky in midsummer and may come across as somewhat bleak in **mid-winter** (July and Aug) – though that's when you should aim to be in the skiing resorts. A final point to bear in mind: the **national holidays** are roughly January, Easter and July, when transport and accommodation can get booked up and many resorts are packed out.

PART ONE

THE

BASICS

GETTING THERE FROM THE USA AND CANADA

There are surprisingly few flights to Argentina from the US, but you should be able to find a fairly convenient direct flight to Buenos Aires. Several airlines offer daily non-stop flights, including American Airlines, United and Aerolíneas Argentinas, the Argentine national airline. Typical Apex fares start at US$860/1160 from New York/Newark in low season, US$745 from Miami, and US$1180 from Chicago. Flying times to Buenos Aires are around eleven hours from New York and Chicago, and nine from Miami. There's even less choice if you're flying from Canada, with Canadian Airlines offering the only direct flight into the country – from Toronto via São Paulo (with connections from other major Canadian cities). You'll find a considerably more flexibile itinerary if you look for connecting flights with a US carrier. Direct flights from Toronto take around thirteen

hours and prices start at CAN$1625 in low season; via Vancouver, the journey time is around eighteen hours, and deals start from around CAN$1865.

SHOPPING FOR TICKETS

The cheapest deals around are generally the **Apex** fares offered by all the airlines. They're not desperately flexible, though, and come with several restrictions: you need to book and pay for your ticket at least 21 days before departure, your trip needs to be a minimum of seven days and a maximum stay of three months, and if you can change your schedule at all, you are likely to be penalized heavily for doing so. It's also worth remembering that some cheap return fares offer no refunds or only a very small percentage refund if you need to cancel your journey, so make sure you check the restrictions carefully before buying a ticket.

It's worth looking out for special **promotional offers** or booking through a specialist flight agent if you want to cut your costs still further. **Consolidators**, who buy up blocks of tickets from the airlines, sell on at heavily discounted rates; **discount agents** offer special student and youth fares as well as a range of other travel-related services such as travel insurance, car rental, and tours. Some agents specialize in **charter flights**, which may be cheaper than anything available on a scheduled flight, but these are the least flexible deals available: departure dates are fixed and withdrawal penalties are high – check the refund policy. If you travel a lot, **discount travel clubs** are an option worth considering – for an annual membership fee you can get cut-price deals on things such as car rental as well as your flights.

AIRLINES

Aerolíneas Argentinas (US ☎1-800/333-0276; Canada ☎1-800/688-0008; www.aerolineas. com.ar). Daily non-stop flights from New York and Miami with connections from other major cities in the US and Canada.

American Airlines (☎1-800/433-7300; www.americanair.com). Daily non-stop service from Miami and New York with connections from other major cities in the US and Canada.

Canadian Airlines (Canada ☎1-800/665-1177; US ☎1-800/426-7000; www.cdnair.ca). Daily flights from Toronto via São Paulo with connections from other major Canadian cities.

United Airlines (☎1-800/538-2929; www.ual.com). Daily non-stop service from Miami and New York with connections from other major cities in the US.

DISCOUNT AGENTS, CONSOLIDATORS AND TRAVEL CLUBS

Airtech, 588 Broadway, Suite 204, New York, NY 10012 (☎212/219-7000 or 1-800/575-8324; *www.airtech.com*). Stand-by seat broker; also deals in consolidator fares and courier flights.

Airtreks.com, 442 Post St, Suite 400, San Francisco, CA 94102 (☎1-800/350-0612; *www.airtreks.com*). Round-the-World and Circle Pacific tickets. The Web site features an interactive database that lets you build your own RTW itinerary.

Council Travel, Head Office, 205 E 42nd St, New York, NY 10017 (☎212/226-8624 or 1-800/226-8624; *www.counciltravel.com*). Nationwide specialists in student travel, with branches all over the US including San Francisco, Los Angeles, Boulder, Washington DC, Chicago and Boston.

STA Travel, 10 Downing St, New York, NY 10014 (☎212/627 3111 or 1-800/777-0112;

www.sta-travel.com); plus branches nationwide. Worldwide discount travel firm specializing in student/youth fares; also student IDs, travel insurance, car rental, train passes and so on.

TFI Tours International, 34 W 32nd St, 12th Floor, New York, NY 10001 (☎212/736-1140 or 1-800/745-8000). Consolidator.

Travel Avenue, 10 S Riverside, Suite 1404, Chicago, IL 60606 (☎1-800/333-3335; *www.travelavenue.com*). Discount travel company.

Travel Cuts, 234 College St, Toronto, ON M5T 1P7 (☎416/979-2406 or 1-800/667-2887; *www.travelcuts.com*). Canadian discount travel organization, with branches in Calgary, Edmonton, Montréal, Vancouver and Winnipeg.

Unitravel, 11737 Administration Drive, St Louis, MO 63146 (☎314/569-0900 or 1-800/325-2222). Consolidator.

TOUR OPERATORS

4th Dimension Tours, 7101 SW 99 Ave, Suite 106, Miami, FL 33173 (☎1-800/343-0020; *www.4thdimension.com*). South American tour specialist, who will organize an itinerary tailored to your needs.

Abercrombie & Kent International, Inc., 1520 Kensington Rd, Oak Brook, IL 60523 (☎630/954-2944 or 1-800/323-7308; *www.abercrombiekent.com*). Upmarket South America packages plus independent travel service.

Anglatin, Ltd, 132 E Broadway, Suite 218, Eugene, OR 97401 (☎541/344-7023 or 1-800/485-7842; *www.anglatin.com*). Offers three-day city tours of Buenos Aires from US$199 per person (land only).

International Gay Travel Association, 4331 North Federal Highway, Suite 304, Fort. Lauderdale, FL 33308 (☎1-800/448-8550; *www.iglta.org*). Trade group with lists of gay-owned or gay-friendly travel agents, accommodation and other travel-related businesses.

Mountain Travel Sobek, 6420 Fairmount Ave, El Cerrito, CA 94530 (☎1-888/MTSOBEK; *www.mtsobek.com*). Trips to Chile that often include Argentina, such as their seventeen-day "Trekking the Paine Circuit" from US$3490 (land only).

Questers Worldwide Nature Tours, 381 Park Ave South, New York, NY 10016 (☎1-800/468-8668; *www.questers.com*). Offers a variety of nature tours including a twenty-day land-only trip through Patagonia, the Andean Lakes and Tierra del Fuego, which begins with a city tour of Buenos Aires.

Safaricentre, 3201 N Sepulveda Blvd, Manhattan Beach, CA 90266 (California ☎310/546-4411 or 1-800/624-5342; rest of US ☎1-800/223-6046; in Canada ☎1-800/233-6046; *www.safaricentre.com*). Wide range of packages, including a four-day cruise of the Patagonian lakes.

Saga Road Scholar Tours, Saga International Holidays Ltd, 222 Berkeley St, Boston, MA 02116 (☎1-800/621-2151). Adventures for senior travellers, including "South American Odyssey" – eighteen nights starting in Brazil and ending in Peru, with stops in Argentina and Chile along the way.

Wilderness Travel, 1102 Ninth St, Berkeley, CA 94710-1211 (☎510/558-2488 or 1-800/368-2794; *www.wildernesstravel.com*). Trips through Argentina and Chile, including a 21-day one around Patagonia.

If Argentina is only one stop on a longer journey, you might want to consider buying a **Round-the-World** (**RTW**) ticket. Some travel agents can sell you an "off-the-shelf" deal, which is by far the cheapest, but tailor-made deals are well worth considering. For US$1700 you can fly from

New York to London, Cape Town, Buenos Aries and Quito; while a Circle Pacific deal from Los Angeles via Auckland, Sydney, Buenos Aires and São Paulo costs from US$2300. However, if time is limited and you want to cover large areas of the country, it might be worth considering buying an **air pass**. Available through Aerolíneas Argentinas, the pass includes up to three internal flights along with your standard return ticket. For more on this, see p.24.

Whatever type of ticket you go for, be aware that all fares are **seasonally adjusted**: the most expensive periods are July and August and the Christmas and New Year period. Note also that flying on weekends, with some airlines, may add around US$60/CAN$90 to the round-trip fare; price ranges quoted here assume mid-week travel, are round-trip, and exclude **airport taxes**, which are usually around US$60/CAN$90.

SPECIALIST TOUR OPERATORS

If you're pushed for time, but want to get the most out of your trip to Argentina, you might want to consider contacting one of the specialist tour operators in the box on p.4. As well as providing off-the-peg deals, and group tours, some of these agencies can tailor an itinerary to your exact needs. Most basic packages, particularly the ones covering Patagonia, offer combined tours of Chile and Argentina.

GETTING THERE FROM THE UK AND THE REST OF EUROPE

Buenos Aires has long been one of the most expensive destinations for flights from the UK and the rest of Europe. Fortunately, prices have become more competitive in recent years and look set to drop further. Fares currently start at around £300 in low season, ie in spring and autumn, rising steeply to around £600 in the high season, namely around the end of the year and during the northern summer. Anyone with loads of time and good sea legs might like to arrive the old-fashioned way, by ship. This is usually quite expensive and less stylish than it sounds, but it's the perfect option for those who can't face a thirteen-hour flight.

FLIGHTS FROM THE UK

Around a dozen airlines offer regular **scheduled flights** from London to Buenos Aires, most of them via continental Europe, the US or Brazil, often with connecting flights to other airports in the UK, but with hardly any via Ireland. Routes via the US are often the most competitive, but take longer as you have to change planes or even stop overnight in the US.

The cheapest deals are through specialized or discount **flight agents**, who will track down the best fares, find onward flights and fix you up with domestic air passes. You can also book direct with the airlines, but don't expect to get any bargains this way: most companies will only quote their standard fares, which are generally much higher than those they sell to consolidators or flight agents. Finally, you may find some bargains in the weekend editions of most national newspapers, in travel magazines and through London's *Time Out*. Teletext and the Internet are other sources of information, especially for last-minute deals. Try *www.flightfinder.com*.

In addition to fares, bear in mind also the **routings** that the various airlines take – times of departure and arrival, the choice and number of stopovers, and length of time you have to spend in transit (stopovers in some US airports are uncomfortably long) can all have as much bearing on your decision as the price of the ticket.

AIRLINES AND ROUTINGS

Aerolíneas Argentinas (☎0845/601 1915; *www.aerolineas.com.ar*). Daily flights from London Gatwick and Heathrow to Buenos Aires via Madrid, in conjunction with Iberia Airlines. An Argentina air pass costs less if you fly out with them (see p.24).

Air France (UK ☎0845/0845 111; Ireland ☎01/814 4060; *www.airfrance.fr*). Flies daily from London Heathrow, Birmingham, Dublin and Manchester via Paris and São Paulo.

American Airlines (UK ☎0345/789789; Ireland ☎01/602 0550; *www.aa.com*). Daily flights from London Gatwick and Heathrow via Miami or New York.

Avianca (UK ☎0990/767747; Ireland ☎01/667 5713; *www.avianca.com.co*). Colombia's main airline, flying from London Heathrow to Bogotá, where you often make an overnight stop, then on to Buenos Aires.

British Airways (UK ☎0845/773 3377; Ireland ☎0141/222 2345; *www.britishairways.com*). Five flights a week from London Gatwick to Buenos Aires: the only carrier offering highly convenient non-stop flights between the two cities. Booking through central reservations is very expensive; it's cheaper to go through the subsidiary company, British Airways Travel Shops (see p.7). The "Visit Argentina" air pass

is available with a BA flight, but costs more than with Aerolíneas (see p.24).

Iberia (UK ☎020/7830 0011; Ireland ☎0990/341341; *www.iberia.com*). Non-stop daily flights from Madrid to Buenos Aires, with connections from London Gatwick and Heathrow, Manchester and Dublin. One free stopover allowed with some fares.

KLM (☎0990/750900; *www.klm.nl*). Three flights a week from Amsterdam via São Paulo, with connecting flights to and from a dozen airports across the UK, including Manchester, London Heathrow, Stansted and London City Airport.

Lufthansa (UK ☎0345/737747; Ireland ☎01/844 5544; *www.lufthansa.co.uk*). Flies daily from London Heathrow or Stansted, and from Dublin, all via Frankfurt.

Swissair (☎020/7434 7300; *www.swissair.com*). Flies four times a week from London Heathrow via Zurich and São Paulo.

United Airlines (☎01426/915500; *www.ual.com*). Two flights a day from London Heathrow, via Chicago or New York. Stopovers may be possible with some fares.

Varig Brazilian Airlines (UK ☎020/7287 1414; Ireland ☎0845/603 7601; *www.varig.com.br*). Daily from London Heathrow via Rio or São Paulo, with stopovers possible en route.

If you're in no hurry, you may choose to incorporate an **extended stopover** in your journey. Most of these are free, but some can cost an additional £20–50. Stopover cities include Amsterdam, Atlanta, Bogotá, Boston, Chicago, Dallas, Frankfurt, Madrid, Miami, Newark, New York, Paris, Rio de Janeiro, São Paulo, Washington and Zurich. Another option for breaking up your trip is to get an **open-jaw** ticket available with some of the airlines. These deals allow you to fly into Buenos Aires, but out of another South American city such as Santiago, Rio or Lima. For **Round-the-World** tickets Star Alliance (Variig and other airlines around the world) offers the best deals, always flying via São Paulo but fairly flexible otherwise; RTW deals start at £1160 in the high season, but some off-the-shelf deals can be excellent value.

If you plan to cover large areas of Argentina in a short time, it can be a good idea to invest in an **air pass** which you must buy with your ticket to

and from Argentina (see p.24). An alternative that can be useful if you're travelling around two or more South American countries is the **Mercosur Pass**, covering Argentina, Brazil, Chile, Paraguay and Uruguay, and using several national carriers; its rules are quite restrictive though. To qualify you must buy the pass in conjunction with a flight from outside the Mercosur area, and you must visit at least two countries within it, say Brazil and Argentina. The maximum number of flight coupons is eight per person and the price is based on the total mileage covered within the Mercosur area: from $225 for up to 1900 miles and $870 for 7201 miles or more. The pass is valid for a minimum of seven days and a maximum of thirty.

BY SEA

You can still reach Buenos Aires from Europe **by sea** but the possibilities are extremely limited. Passenger-carrying cargo vessels of the Grimaldi Line sail from Tilbury and Southampton

FLIGHT AND DISCOUNT AGENTS

Apex Travel, 59 Dame St, Dublin 2 (☎01/671 5933). General budget fares agent.

British Airways Travel Shops, 156 Regent St, London W1R 6LB (☎0845/606-0747); 1 Fountain Centre, Fountain St, Belfast BT1 6ET (☎01232/326566); with branches throughout the UK. A subsidiary of British Airways, but classed as a travel agency and so able to offer special discount fares.

Campus Travel, 52 Grosvenor Gardens, London SW1W 0AG (☎0870/240 1010; www.campustravel.co.uk), with branches nationwide. Student/youth travel specialist, with outlets also in YHA shops and on university campuses.

Flight Finders International, 13 Baggot St Lower, Dublin 2 (☎01/676 8326). Helpful and reliable discount fare outlet.

Joe Walsh Tours, 69 Upper O'Connell St, Dublin 2 (☎01/872 2555); 8–11 Baggot St, Dublin 2 (☎01/676 3053); and 117 Patrick St, Cork (☎021/277959). Former rock-guitarist, now long-established, efficient specialist in discount flights.

Journey Latin America, 12–13 Heathfield Terrace, Chiswick, London W4 4JE (☎020/8747 8315; www.journeylatinamerica.co.uk); and 51–63 Deansgate, Manchester M3 2BH (☎0161/832 1441; www.journeylatinamerica.co.uk). Knowledgeable and helpful staff, good at sorting out stopovers and open-jaw flights. Also does package tours.

The London Flight Centre, 131 Earls Court Rd, London SW5 9RH (☎020/7244 6411); 47 Notting Hill Gate, London W11 3JS (☎020/7727 4290); and Shop 33, The Broadway Centre, Hammersmith Tube, London W6 9YE (☎020/8748 6777). Discount flights around the world.

Major Travel, 28–34 Fortress Rd, London NW5 2HB (☎020/7393 1060). Reliable discount agent, often with very low fares to Buenos Aires.

North South Travel, Moulsham Mill Centre, Parkway, Chelmsford, Essex CM2 7PX (☎01245/608291). Friendly, competitive travel agency, offering discounted fares worldwide – profits are used to support projects in the developing world.

Scott Dunn South America, Fovant Mews, 12 Noyna Rd, London SW17 7PH (☎020/8767 8989). Very good South American specialist, offering low-cost fares and helpful advice.

South American Experience, 47 Causton St, London SW1P 4AT (☎020/7976 5511; www.sax.mcmail.com). Mainly a discount flight agent but also offers a range of tours, plus a very popular "soft landing package", which includes a couple of nights' accommodation and airport transfer on arrival.

STA Travel, 38 Store St, London WC1E 7BZ (☎020/7361 6262; www.statravel.co.uk), with branches nationwide. Worldwide specialist in low-cost flights and tours, with special discounts for students and under-26s.

Trailfinders, 42–50 Earls Court Rd, London W8 6FT (☎020/7938 3366); and 4–5 Dawson St, Dublin 2 (☎01/677 7888); with branches nation-wide. Long-established flight agent offering a wide range of cheap fares.

Usit Now, Fountain Centre, College St, Belfast BT1 6ET (☎01232/324 073); and 19 Aston Quay, Dublin 2 (☎01/602 1777 or 677 8117); with branches across Ireland. Student and youth specialist, though other customers are also welcome.

to Brazil via Hamburg, Antwerp, Le Havre and Bilbao, then on to Buenos Aires for £1000 (out-bound only). German shipping lines – often con-tainer ships with room for passengers – also sail to various South American ports, including Buenos Aires, from Felixstowe, Hamburg, Antwerp, Le Havre and Bilbao, and cost around £1500 each way. Another route (round trip only) starts in Liverpool and sails round the whole of South America, calling at Buenos Aires, return-ing to Europe via the Panama Canal. For infor-mation and bookings call Strand Voyages, Charing Cross Shopping Concourse, Strand, London WC2N 4HZ (☎020/7836 6363, fax 7497 0078; www.strandtravel.co.uk).

PACKAGES AND ORGANIZED TOURS

Travelling under your own steam in Argentina can be complicated and daunting, especially if you speak no Spanish or are pushed for time. In that case, or if you want to avoid a lot of organization, you might like to book up with one of the several **specialist tour operators** – such as Journey Latin America or South American Experience – who will either put you on a ready-made **package** tour or, for considerably more money, **tailor** one to your own requirements. Don't forget that a number of Argentinian firms also cater for foreigners; mak-ing use of their services, either purchased once in Argentina or pre-booked, may work out to be a

SPECIALIST TOUR OPERATORS

Andes, 93 Queen St, Castle Douglas, Kirkcudbrightshire DG7 1EH, Scotland (☎01556/503929 fax 504633; *john@andes.com*). Tour company specializing in climbing, including 25-day guided routes up Aconcagua and 22-day ones up Fitz Roy. Also offers Southern Patagonian Icecap skiing expeditions (21 days) and arranges bespoke itineraries for small groups with trekking or biking options.

Austral Tours, 120 Wilton Rd, London SW1V 1JZ (☎020/7233 5384). Small company offering tailor-made itineraries and some brochure packages to South America. Especially good at organizing special-interest holidays, based around wine tours, fishing, trekking and archeology.

Blue Green Adventures, 28 Lingfield Rd, London SW19 4PU (☎020/8947 2756). The leading specialist in horse-riding expeditions in Patagonia and the Lake District, mostly on ten-day tours.

Dragoman, 98 Camp Green, Debenham, Stowmarket, Suffolk IP14 6LA (☎01728/861133; *www.dragoman.co.uk*). A range of South American overland trips, including a new line with all accommodation in hotels rather than in tents. Regular slide shows in London.

Encounter Overland, 267 Old Brompton Rd, London SW5 9JA (☎020/7370 6845; *www.encounter.co.uk*). One of the longest-established companies going; its programme includes a Patagonian tour taking in Ushuaia.

Exodus, 9 Weir Rd, London SW12 0LT (☎020/8675 5550; *www.exodustravels.co.uk*). Well-run, small-group trekking holidays in southern Argentina and Chile, plus a number of overland trips that include Argentina in the itinerary.

Guerba Expeditions, Wessex House, 40 Station Rd, Westbury, Wiltshire BA13 3JN (☎01373/826611). UK branch of Canadian GAP Adventures, whose tours include a three-week tour of southern Argentina and Chile.

Hayes & Jarvis, Hayes House, 152 King St, London W6 0QU (☎020/8222 784). This well-known operator offers tours of Patagonia and the Lake District plus a few days seeing the sights in Buenos Aires.

Jagged Globe, The Foundry Studios, 45 Mowbray St, Sheffield S3 8EN (☎0114/276 3322, fax 276 3344; *expeditions@ jaggedglobe.co.uk*). Well-established climbing company offering Aconcagua expedition (24 days), which includes the option to try the Polish Glacier route.

Journey Latin America, 12–13 Heathfield Terrace, Chiswick, London W4 4JE (☎020/8747 8315; *www.journeylatinamerica.co.uk*). Long-established company offering a range of unescorted packages, adventure holidays, small-group trips with a tour leader, and tailor-made itineraries; one overland trip crosses from Santiago in Chile, to Buenos Aires, with an

less expensive option, and possibly less "touristy" than the tours offered by some of the British-based operators. Most of these companies are based in Buenos Aires and are listed on p.148. Some of the trips on offer entail long overland tours in jeeps or trucks, normally as part of a South

optional add-on to Iguazú, in northeast Argentina. Fairly expensive, but of a very high standard.

Sunbird, PO Box 76, Sandy, Beds SG19 1DF (☎01767/682969; *www.sunbird.demon.co.uk*). Experienced operator running escorted ornithological tours of Argentina (16–31 days), centring on Patagonia, with other options to Iguazú and Calilegua.

OTT Expeditions, South West Centre, Suite 5B, Troutbeck Rd, Sheffield S7 2QA (☎0114/258 8508, fax 255 1603; *info@ottexpeditions.co.uk*). Experienced climbing specialist offering a 24-day expedition up Aconcagua.

Scott Dunn South America, Fovant Mews, 12 Noyna Rd, London SW17 7PH (☎020/8767 8989). Specializes in putting together tailor-made holidays, and also offers a useful three-night accommodation package for your arrival in Buenos Aires.

South American Experience, 47 Causton St, Pimlico, London SW1P 4AT (☎020/7976 5511; *www.sax.mcmail.com*). Organizes flights, tailor-made packages, local excursions (such as to tango shows), estancia holidays and a fourteen-day tour including the penguin colonies at Valdés, and offers an excellent "soft-landing package", which includes three nights' accommodation and airport transfer on arrival.

Top Deck Travel, Top Deck House, 131–135 Earls Court Rd, London SW5 9RH (☎020/7370

4555). Group holidays in southern Argentina and Chile, plus a range of overland expeditions in South America.

Travelbag, 15 Turk St, Alton, Hampshire GU34 1AG (☎01420/541007; *www.travelbag-adventures.co.uk*). Long-established world travel company offering small group (14 people or fewer) expeditions to Argentinian and Chilean Patagonia.

Wildlife Worldwide, 170 Selsdon Rd, South Croydon, Surrey CR2 6PJ (☎020/8667 9158, fax 8667 1960; *www.wildlifeworldwide. com*). Sixteen-day Patagonia tour, including Valdés, Ushuaia and Chile's Torres del Paine; plus short options to Esteros de Iberá and Iguazú.

World Expeditions, 4 Northfields Prospect, Putney Bridge Rd, London SW18 1PE (☎020/8870 2600; *www.worldexpeditions. com.au*). UK branch of the very professional Australian tour company, offering a range of trekking, climbing and photographic tours in Argentina and Chile, plus adventure cruises to Antarctica.

Worldwide Adventures Abroad, Unit H/04, Staniforth Estates, Main St, Hackenthorpe, Sheffield, Yorkshire S12 4LB (☎0114/247 3400; *www.adventures-abroad.com*). Culturally sensitive tour operator specializing in small group expeditions. Several tours to Argentina and Chile, concentrating on Patagonia. Also Antarctic cruises and Iguazú Falls package.

American adventure tour covering several countries. A number of UK-based and Argentine companies also run various **special interest journeys**, treks o͏̈ on mountain-climbin ͏ing or flora an

GETTING THERE FROM AUSTRALIA AND NEW ZEALAND

Not surprisingly, the best deals to Argentina are offered by Aerolíneas Argentinas and Lan-Chile in conjunction with Qantas and Air New Zealand, either direct to Buenos Aires or via a stopover in Santiago. To get to other destinations in Argentina, such as Río Gallegos, Ushuaia and El Calafate, you're looking at either an add-on fare or air pass from either of these two cities. There are also plenty of flights via the USA, but only United Airlines is scheduled through to Buenos Aires – other airlines tend to offer much more time-consuming and expensive routings, as each sector has to be costed separately. Round-the-World tickets that include Buenos Aires, and Circle America fares, are also quite expensive, but can be worthwhile if you have the time to make the most of a few stopovers.

In **Australia**, most flights to Argentina leave from Sydney, though there's also a couple a week out of Brisbane and Melbourne. The most direct route to Buenos Aires is shared between Aerolíneas Argentinas and Qantas via Auckland while Air New Zealand/Lan-Chile's routings are a little more long-winded, flying via Auckland, Papeete, Easter Island and Santiago (as flying time is around twenty hours you may want to take advantage of the one free stopover allowed each way). From **New Zealand**, as from Australia, your best bet is with Qantas, Aerolíneas Argentinas or Air New Zealand/Lan-Chile. You can also travel **via the US** with United Airlines, who fly to Buenos Aires from Sydney and Auckland via either Los Angeles or San Francisco, and Miami.

If you plan to do a fair amount of travelling within Argentina (or to other South American countries), think about buying an **air pass** with your main ticket. These passes offer substantial savings, but can be bought only outside South America with your international ticket. See p.24 for more information.

FARES

In general, **fares** depend on the duration of stay, rather than seasons – although prices for flights

AIRLINES

Aerolíneas Argentinas (Sydney ☎02/9283 3660; Auckland ☎09/379 3675). Two flights a week from Sydney to Buenos Aires via Auckland: onward connections to all Agentinian provincial capitals and major South American gateways.

Air New Zealand (Sydney ☎13/2476; Auckland ☎ 7000 or 09/357 3000). Several flights a week from ane, Melbourne and Sydney to connect with Lan-Chile via Easter Island

Island and Santiago – you may have to overnight in Santiago on some flights. Onward connections to major Argentinian cities.

Qantas (Sydney ☎13/1211; Auckland ☎09/357 8900 or 0800/808767; www.qantas.com.au). Code-shares with Aerolíneas Argentinas to provide an additional two flights a week to Buenos Aires from Melbourne via Auckland.

United Airlines (Sydney ☎13/1777; Auckland ☎09/379 3800; www.ual.com). Daily service from Sydney to Buenos Aires via Los Angeles or San Francisco and Miami.

Varig Brazilian (Sydney ☎02/9321 9179; land ☎09/379 4455). Several flights a week to Buenos Aires via Río.

FLIGHT AGENTS

Anywhere Travel, 345 Anzac Parade, Kingsford, Sydney (☎02/9663 0411, *anywhere@ozemail.com.au*).Worldwide fare discount agent close to the airport.

Budget Travel, 16 Fort St, Auckland, plus branches around the city (☎09/366 0061 or 0800/808040). Established air fare discounter.

Destinations Unlimited, Level 7, FAI Building, 220 Queens St, Auckland (☎09/373 4033). Worldwide fare discounts plus a good selection of brochures.

Flight Centres, Australia: 82 Elizabeth St, Sydney, plus branches nationwide (☎02/9235 3522, nearest branch ☎13/1600; *www.flightcentre.com.au*). New Zealand: 350 Queen St, Auckland (☎09/358 4310; *www.flightcentre.com.au*), plus branches nationwide. Friendly service with competitive discounts on air fares plus wide range of travel brochures.

Northern Gateway, 22 Cavenagh St, Darwin (☎08/8941 1394; *oztravel@norgate.com.au*). Discount fares.

STA Travel, Australia: 855 George St, Sydney; 256 Flinders St, Melbourne; other offices in state capitals and major universities (nearest branch ☎13/1776, fastfare telesales ☎1300/360960; *www.statravel.com.au*). New Zealand: 10 High St, Auckland (☎09/309 0458, fastfare telesales ☎09/366 6673; *www.statravel.com.au*), plus branches in Wellington, Christchurch, Dunedin, Palmerston North, Hamilton and at major universities. Fare discounts for students and under-26s, student cards and travel insurance.

Student Uni Travel, Level 8, 92 Pitt St, Sydney (☎02/9232 8444), plus branches in Brisbane, Cairns, Darwin, Melbourne and Perth. Student/youth discounts and travel advice.

Thomas Cook, Australia: 175 Pitt St, Sydney (☎02/9231 2877; *www.thomascook.com.au*); 257 Collins St, Melbourne; plus branches in other state capitals (local branch ☎13/1771; Thomas Cook Direct telesales ☎1800/801002). New Zealand: 191 Queen St, Auckland (☎09/379 3920; *www.thomascook.com.au*). Discounts on fares, travellers' cheques, bus and rail passes.

Trailfinders, 8 Spring St, Sydney (☎02/9247 7666); 91 Elizabeth St, Brisbane (☎07/3229 0887); Shop 3, Hides Corner, Lake St, Cairns (☎07/4041 1199). Independent travel advice, good discounts on fares.

travel.com.au (☎02/9262 3555; *www.travel.com.au*). Online worldwide fare discounter.

Unit Beyond, cnr Shortland St and Jean Batten Place, Auckland (☎09/379 4224 or 0800/788336; *www.usitbeyond.co.nz*), plus branches in Christchurch, Dunedin, Palmerston North, Hamilton and Wellington. Student/youth travel specialists.

(and everything else) soar during Christmas and the New Year period. Cut-off points via the Pacific are 35 days, 45 days, 90 days, 6 months and a year; via the US they are 21 days, 45 days and 180 days. Whatever kind of ticket you're after, your first port of call should be one of the **travel agents** listed in the box above; they can fill you in on all the latest fares and any special offers currently available. If you're a student or under 26, you may be able to undercut some of the prices given here; STA is a good place to start.

On **direct routes** you should be able to get a return fare for A$/NZ$2050 for visits of less than 35 days. If you want to stay longer than this you'll be looking at fares from A$/NZ$2080 for 45 days, A$/NZ$2300 for 90 days and A$/NZ$2920 for 6 months. Special offers with Aerolíneas Argentinas and Lan-Chile sometimes bring fares down as low as A$/NZ$1899 for stays of up to 35 days, though your plans will need to be fairly flexible to take advantage of these last-minute bargains. Flights via the US on United Airlines are from A$/NZ$2399 for 21 days, A$/NZ$2499 for 45 days and A$2699 for a 180 days.

RTW AND CIRCLE TICKETS

The choice is limited and most fares are mileage based, making routes via South America more expensive than other **Round-the-World** options, but in comparison with the fares and routings of standard return deals to Argentina, they are still definitely worth considering. Some sample itineraries include starting from either Melbourne, Sydney or Brisbane, flying to Auckland, Papeete, San Francisco and London, making your own way to Paris from there, then flying to Buenos Aires on the way back home. Star Alliance allows you to take in US, European and Asian destinations as well as South America from A$/NZ$2700, for a maximum of 29,000 miles, and up to A$/NZ$3700 for 39,000 miles.

SPECIALISTS AND TOUR OPERATORS

Adventure Associates, 197 Oxford St, Bondi Junction, Sydney (☎02/9389 7466 or 1800/222141; *www.adventureassociates.com*). Offers individually tailored adventure and special interest holidays.

Adventure Specialists, 69 Liverpool St, Sydney (☎02/9261 2927). Overland specialist. Agents for Encounter Overland's five- and nine-week expeditions.

Adventure World, Australia: 73 Walker St, North Sydney (☎02/9956 7766 or 1800/221931), plus branches in Brisbane and Perth. New Zealand: 101 Great South Rd, Remuera, Auckland (☎09/524 5118). Agents for a wide range of international adventure travel companies who offer tours of Argentina, including Explore.

Australian Andean Adventures, 33 Imperial Arcade, Pitt Street Mall, Sydney (☎02/9235 1889). South American trekking specialists.

Contours Travel, 1/84 Williams St, Melbourne. (☎03/9670 6900). Specialists in tailored packages and eco-tours.

Earthwatch, 126 Bank St, South Melbourne, Vic 3205 (☎03/96826828; *www.earthwatch.org*).

Organizes volunteer work overseas on scientific and cultural projects.

IT Adventures, Level 4, 46–48 York St, Sydney (☎1800/804277). Extended overland camping/hostelling expeditions through Argentina. Agents for Kamuka and Tucan.

South America Travel Centre, 104 Hardware St, Melbourne (☎03/9642 5353 or 1800/655051). Specialist in tailor-made trips to Argentina.

South American Adventure Travel, 132 Wickham St, Fortitude Valley, Brisbane (☎07/3854 1022). Independent and group travel specialists.

Silke's Travel, 263 Oxford St, Darlinghurst, Sydney (☎02/9380 5835 or 1800/807303; *www.silkes.com.au*). Specially tailored packages for gay and lesbian travellers.

The Surf Travel Co., Australia: 2/25 Cronulla Plaza, Cronulla Beach, Sydney (☎02/9527 4722 or 1800/687873; *www.surftravel.com.au*). New Zealand: 7 Danbury Drive, Torbay, Auckland (☎09/4738388; *www.surftravel.com.au*). A well-established surf travel company that can arrange air fares and accommodation as well as give the lowdown on Argentina's best surf beaches.

A better option if you want to go only to South America is Air New Zealand/Aerolíneas Argentinas' 90-day **Circle America Fare** for around A$/NZ$2990; which allows stopovers in LA, Miami, Caracas, Rio, São Paulo, Montevideo, Buenos Aires and Lima. You are allowed up to four free stopovers (extras at US$100 each), and you must travel in the same direction – no backtracking.

PACKAGES AND ORGANIZED TOURS

Package holidays are few and far between, and **organized tours** may seem a little expensive – but both are well worth considering, especially if your time is limited, you're unfamiliar with the country's customs and language, or you just don't like travelling alone. Specialist travel agents and operators such as Adventure World and Adventure Associates offer a range of itineraries from the fully packaged experience to shorter add-on tours that give you the flexibility

of combining independent travel with, say, a cruise through the Straits of Magellan and the Beagle Channel to Ushuaia (from A$1270/NZ$1500 per person twin share).

Adventure tours are worth considering if you want to cover a lot of ground or get to places that could be difficult to reach independently. Two good-value camping/hostelling expeditions which take you south through the magnificent scenery of the Lake District, Patagonia and the Moreno Glacier to Tierra del Fuego, then up the east coast via Argentina's marine wildlife reserves to bustling Buenos Aries, are Tucan's four-week *"Pure Patagonia"* round-trip from Santiago (from A$2020/NZ$2300) and Exodus's longer six-week "Gaucho Overland" from Santiago which spends an extra two weeks travelling through Paraguay, along Brazil's Costa Verde and on to Rio de Janeiro (from A$2740/NZ$3370). Most tours don't include air fares from Australasia, though specialists can usually assist with flight arrangements.

RED TAPE AND VISAS

Citizens of the USA, Canada, Australia, New Zealand, South Africa, Britain, Ireland and other Western European nations do not need a visa for tourist trips of up to ninety days – which can be extended by a further sixty days – at the time of going to press, but always verify this in advance with your local consulate, as the situation can change.

You will need a valid **passport** and will have to fill in a **landing card** on arrival and you will be given a stamp for stays of thirty, sixty or ninety days. Staple your duplicate of the landing card into your passport, next to your entrance stamp, as you'll need it to leave the country and police may check it. If you do lose it, it's rarely a serious problem, but you'll have to fill in a new form at the border control. On entering the country, you will also be given a **customs declaration form**. Duty is not charged on used personal effects, books, and other articles for non-commercial purposes, up to the value of $300. Make sure you declare any valuable electronic items such as laptop computers, as customs officers can be suspicious that you may be bringing them into the country to sell.

You can **extend your stay** for a further sixty days by presenting your passport to the main immigration department: **Dirección de Migraciones**, at Av. Antártida Argentina 1350, Retiro, in Buenos Aires (☎011/4312 3288 or 4311 4118).

Alternatively, you could try leaving the country (best to do so for at least 24 hours, perhaps by making the short hop to Colonia del Sacramento)

EMBASSIES AND CONSULATES

USA
Consulates: 229 Peachtree St, Kain Tower, Suite 1401, Atlanta, Georgia 30303 (☎404/880-0805, fax 404/880-0806; *atlar@att.net*); 205 N. Michigan Ave, Suite 4209, Chicago, IL 60601-5968 (☎312/819-2608, fax 312/819-2626; *argecchic@aol.com*); 3050 Post Oak Blvd, Suite 1625, Houston, TX 77056 (☎713/871-8935, fax 713/871-0639; *jel@mrecic.gov.ar*); 5055 Wilshire Blvd.Office. 210, Los Angeles, CA 90036 (☎323/954-9155, fax 323/934-9076); 800 Brickell Ave, Penthouse 1, Miami, FL 33131 (☎305/373-1889, fax 305/371-7108; *cmiam@earthlink.net*); 12 West 56th St, New York City, NY 10019 (☎212/603-0400, fax 212/541-7746; *argnyc@yahoo.com*).
Embassy: 1600 New Hampshire Ave, NW, Consular Section, Washington DC 20009 (☎202/238-6400, fax 202/238-6471).

CANADA
Consulates: 90 Sparks St, Suite 910, Ottawa, Ontario K1P 5B4 (☎613/236-2351, fax 613/235-2659; *www.argentina-canada.net*); 2000 Peel St. 7th Floor, Suite 710, Montréal, Québec H3A 2W5 (☎514/842-6582, fax 514/842-5797); 1 First Canadian Place, Suite 5840, Toronto, Ontario M5X 1K2 (☎416/955-9075, fax 416/955-0868; *fctoro@mrecic.gov.ar*).

UK
Embassy: 65 Brook St, London W1Y 1YE (☎020/7318 1300, fax 7318 1301).
Consulate: 27 Three Kings Yard, London W1Y 1FL (☎020/7318 1340, fax 7318 1349).

AUSTRALIA
Consulate: Goldfields House, Level 13, Suite 1302, 1 Alfred St, Sydney, NSW 2001 (☎02/9251 3402).

NEW ZEALAND
Embassy: Level 14, 142 Lambton Quay, PO Box 5430, Wellington (☎4/4728 330; *enzel@arg.org.nz*).

and returning to get a fresh stamp. This usually works, but is frowned upon if done repeatedly, and the provision of an extra stamp is totally at the discretion of the border guards. Some people manage to stay for a year on tourist visas alone, by using a combination of these brief trips abroad and extensions (*prórrogas*).

When leaving the country, you must obtain an **exit stamp**. At certain controls (particularly in the north of the country, where there is a lot of cross-border Mercosur traffic), it is often up to you to ensure that the bus driver stops and waits while you get this – otherwise drivers may not stop, assuming that all passengers are Mercosur nationals, who don't need stamps. Not getting your proper stamps will leave you facing fines and considerable hassle later on in your trip. Be aware that in some places (for example, Clorinda), your Argentine exit stamp is actually given on the far side of the border, but check this with the driver.

Visas for work or study (both valid for a maximum of twelve months) must be obtained in advance from your consulate. **Students** will first need to obtain a letter from their proposed place of study, which offers a place on a course and has been legalized by the Argentine Ministry of Education. This must be presented to your respective consulate, along with medical and birth certificates and three photos. The visa costs approximately $100, plus around $50 for additional paperwork fees (processed in approximately a week). For a **working visa**, you can either get your prospective company to approach immigration in Argentina with the contract and arrange for an entrance permit to be sent to your respective consulate, or take your work contract, authorized by an Argentinian public notary, to the consulate yourself and the consulate will obtain the work permit from Buenos Aires. Expect the process to take at least a month. Work permits cost $200, and the visa itself another $100. Both student and working visas can be extended only in the Dirección de Migraciones (see above).

Visitors are legally obliged to carry their **passports as ID**. You might get away with carrying a photocopy, but don't forget to copy your entrance stamp and landing card as well. In the majority of cases, this is acceptable to police, but getting a copy certified by a public notary increases its credibility.

INSURANCE

A typical travel insurance policy usually provides cover for the loss of baggage, tickets and – up to a certain limit – cash or cheques, as well as cancellation or curtailment of your journey. Most of them exclude so-called dangerous sports unless an extra premium is paid: this could mean scuba-diving, white-water rafting, windsurfing and trekking, though probably not kayaking or jeep safaris. Read the small print and benefits tables of prospective policies carefully; coverage can vary wildly for roughly similar premiums. Many policies can be chopped and changed to exclude coverage you don't need – for example, sickness and accident benefits. If you do take medical coverage, ascertain whether benefits will be paid as treatment proceeds or only after you return home, and whether there is a 24-hour medical emergency number. When securing baggage cover, make sure that the per-article limit – typically under £500/$700 equivalent – will cover your most valuable possessions. If you need to make a claim, you should keep receipts for medicines and medical treatment, and in the event you have anything stolen, you must obtain an official statement from the police. Bank

and credit cards often have certain levels of medical or other insurance included and you may automatically get travel insurance if you use a major credit card to pay for your trip.

Travellers from **Britain** and **Ireland** would do well to take out an insurance policy before travelling to cover against theft, loss and illness or injury. Travel agents and tour operators are likely to require some sort of insurance when you book a package holiday, though according to UK law they can't make you buy their own (other than a £1 premium for "schedule airline failure"). If you have a good all-risks **home insurance policy** it may cover your possessions against loss or theft even when overseas. Many **private medical schemes** such as BUPA or PPP also offer cover-

age plans for abroad, including baggage loss, cancellation or curtailment and cash replacement as well as sickness or accident.

American and **Canadian** citizens should also check that they're not already covered. Canadian **provincial health plans** usually provide partial cover for medical mishaps overseas. Holders of official student/teacher/youth cards are entitled to meagre accident coverage and hospital in-patient benefits. Students will often find that their student health coverage extends during the vacations and for one term beyond the date of last enrolment. **Homeowners' or renters' insurance** often covers theft or loss of documents, money and valuables while overseas, though conditions and maximum amounts vary from company to company.

ROUGH GUIDES TRAVEL INSURANCE

Rough Guides now offer their own travel insurance, customized for our readers by a leading UK broker and backed by a Lloyds underwriter. It's available to anyone, of any nationality, travelling anywhere in the world, and we believe it is the best-value scheme you'll find.

There are two main Rough Guide insurance plans: **Essential**, for effective, no-frills cover, starting at £11.75 for two weeks; and **Premier** – more expensive but with more generous and extensive benefits. Each offer European or Worldwide cover, and can be supplemented with a **"Hazardous Activities Premium"** if you plan to indulge in sports considered dangerous, such as skiing, scuba-diving or trekking. Unlike many policies, the Rough Guides' schemes are **calculated by the day**, so if you're travelling for 27 days rather than a month, that's all you pay for. You can alternatively take out **annual multi-trip insurance**, which covers you for all your travel throughout the year (with a maximum of sixty days for any one trip).

For a policy quote, call the **Rough Guides Insurance Line** on UK Freefone ☎0800/015 0906, or, if you're calling from outside Britain, on ☎(+44)1243/621046. Alternatively, get an online quote at *www.roughguides.com/insurance.*

INFORMATION AND MAPS

Since Argentina has very few tourist offices abroad, and embassies don't seem to see tourism as a priority, the two main sources of information before you go are the Internet (*www.turismo.gov.ar*) and private tour companies and operators. Your best bet for brochures or factsheets is one of the companies specializing in Latin America, such as South American Experience or Exodus (see pp.8–9). Nearly every aspect of life in Argentina seems to have its own Web site, with an incredible number dedicated to polo. You might like to buy maps before you go (see box, p.18), but a wider selection is on offer in Argentina itself.

TOURIST INFORMATION

The only European countries with **official Argentine tourist offices** are Germany and Italy; in the USA three overseas delegations can give you the lowdown: 12 West 56th St, in New York (☎212/603-0443, fax 212/315-5545); 5055 Wilshire Blvd, Suite 210, Los Angeles (☎213/930-0681, fax 213/934-9076); and 2655 Le Jeune Rd, Ph. 1, Miami (☎305/442-1366, fax 305/441-7029). The main **national tourist board** is, of course, in Buenos Aires (see p.75), and you should go there for maps of the country and general information about getting around. Piles of leaflets, glossy brochures and maps are dished out at national, provincial and municipal **tourist offices** across the country, which vary enormously in quality of service and quantity of information – from extremely professional, with all the latest com-

puter equipment, to dingy offices with a couple of rusty filing-cabinets. Don't rely on staff speaking any language other than Spanish; nor on the leaflets or lists of accommodation, campsites, museums and other facilities being translated into foreign languages. In smaller towns you may find that the **oficina de turismo** is attached to the municipalidad or town hall, and can provide nothing more than some basic advice.

Every province maintains a **Casa de Provincia** in Buenos Aires, where you can pick up information about what there is to see or do, prior to travelling. The standard of information you'll glean from them varies wildly, often reflecting the comparative wealth of a given province. Some of the *casas* have fairly in-depth archives and the busier of them should be able to provide you with detailed print-outs of accommodation and transport to various destinations under their jurisdiction. Notably helpful ones are Buenos Aires, Córdoba, Salta, Mendoza and La Pampa. Many also have a shop selling locally made arts and crafts. Getting the information you need can sometimes be a question of finding the right person – the Casas de Provincia are staffed by people from the various provinces and if you persist you may well be rewarded with some real insider knowledge. As well as the *casas de provincia* there are also several **shop-window tourist offices** in Buenos Aires run by major resorts, mostly those on the Atlantic seaboard (see box on p.17).

MAPS

Road maps can be obtained at bookshops and kiosks in all big towns and cities or at service-stations but are quite hard to find anywhere else. Many maps aren't up to date or contain a surprising number of errors: road numbers are sometimes wrong; barely passable tracks may be depicted as sealed roads or vice versa; and roads that have been there for years are missed out while routes that nobody has ever heard of are clearly marked. It's often a good idea to buy a couple of maps and compare them as you go along, always checking with the locals to see whether a given road does exist and is passable, especially with the vehicle you intend to use.

The really good news is that the clearest and most accurate map of the whole country is the one you can get free from the national tourist office in

TOURIST INFORMATION

CASAS DE PROVINCIA

Buenos Aires Av. Callao 237 (Mon–Fri 9am–3pm; ☎011/4371-3587).

Catamarca Av. Córdoba 2080 (Mon–Fri 9am–6pm; ☎011/4374-6891).

Córdoba Av. Callao 232 (Mon–Fri 10am–7pm; ☎011/4373-4277).

Corrientes San Martín 333, 4th Floor (Mon–Fri 10am–4pm; ☎011/4394-0859).

Chaco Av. Callao 322 (Mon–Fri 10am–4.30pm; ☎011/4372-5209).

Chubut Sarmiento 1172 (Mon–Fri 10.30am–5.30pm; ☎011/4382-8126).

Entre Ríos Suipacha 844 (Mon–Fri 9am–6pm; ☎011/4328-9327).

Formosa H. Yrigoyen 1429 (Feb & March Mon–Fri 9am–3pm; rest of year closes 1pm; ☎011/4383-0721).

Jujuy Av. Santa Fe 967 (Mon–Fri 10am–4pm; ☎011/4393-6096).

La Pampa Suipacha 346 (Feb Mon–Fri 9am–3.30pm; rest of year same days 9am–6pm; ☎011/4326-0511).

La Rioja Callao 745 (Mon–Fri 9am–6pm; ☎011/4815-1929).

Mendoza Av. Callao 445 (Mon–Fri 7am–5.30pm; ☎011/4371-0835).

Misiones Santa Fe 989 (Mon–Fri 9am–5pm; ☎011/4393-1211).

Neuquén Pte Perón 687, 1st Floor (Mon–Fri 9.30am–4pm; ☎011/4326–6812).

Río Negro Tucumán 1916 (Mon–Fri 10am–4pm; ☎011/4371-7273).

Salta Av. Pte Roque S. Peña 933 (Mon–Fri 10am–5.30pm; ☎011/4326-2456).

San Juan Sarmiento 1251 (Mon–Fri 9am–6pm; ☎011/4382-9241).

San Luis Azcuénaga 1083 (Mon–Fri 10am–5.30pm; ☎011/4822-3641).

Santa Cruz Suipacha 1120 (Mon–Fri 10am–5.30pm; ☎011/4325-3098).

Santa Fe Montevideo 373, 2nd Floor (Mon–Fri 9.30am–3.30pm; ☎011/4375-4635).

Santiago del Estero Florida 274 (Mon–Fri 9am–7pm; ☎011/4322-1389).

Tierra del Fuego, Santa Fe 919 (Mon–Fri 9am–5pm; ☎011/4322-8855).

Tucumán Suipacha 140 (Mon–Fri 9am–3pm; ☎011/4322-0564).

LOCAL TOURIST OFFICES

Mar del Plata, Av. Corrientes 1660 (☎011/4384-5658).

Pinamar, Florida 930 (☎011/4315-2680).

San Clemente del Tuyú, Bartolomé Mitre 1135 (☎011/4381-0764).

Villa Carlos Paz, Lavalle 623 (☎011/4322-0053).

Villa Gesell, Bartolomé Mitre 1702 (☎011/4374-5199).

Buenos Aires; it's called **Rutas de la Argentina** and has small but clear inset maps of twenty towns and cities as well as a 1:2,500,000 national map, the ideal scale for most travellers. Slightly more detailed but a tad less accurate is the mini atlas (*Atlas Vial*) published by **YPF**, the national petrol company and sold for $10 at their service stations. The **ACA** (Automóvil Club) produces individual maps for each province which vary enormously in detail and accuracy; the regional maps or route planners the club publishes may be enough for most travellers, especially since the provincial maps cost $5 each.

Glossy and fairly clear – but equally erratic – regional road maps (Cuyo, Northwest, Lake District, etc) are produced by Línea Azul under the generic name of **AutoMapa** and are often available at petrol stations and bookshops, as are the similar **Argenguide** series of maps, published by Argentum. These all cost around $8. Outside Argentina you can get hold of the user-friendly *Kevin Healey's Travel Map of Argentina* (though at 1:4,000,000 the scale's a bit small), and the *World's End Maps* of different areas of Patagonia, published by Zagier and Urruty (*zagiel@ciudad.com.ar*). Finally, there's a brilliant map of Buenos Aires, the **Insight Fleximap**, which is clear, reliable, easy to fold and waterproof.

The **street plans** distributed free of charge at tourist offices also range from the highly detailed to the impressionistic, and some of them are dominated by their private sponsors rather than

MAP AND GUIDE OUTLETS

As well as over-the-counter sales, most of the outlets listed below allow you to order and pay for maps by mail, over the phone and sometimes via the Internet.

USA AND CANADA

ADC Map and Travel Center, 1636 I St, Washington DC 20006 (☎202/628-2608).

Adventurous Traveler Bookstore, 245 South Champlain St, Burlington, VT 05401 (☎1-800/282-3963; *www.AdventurousTraveler.com*).

Book Passage, 51 Tamal Vista Blvd, Corte Madera, CA 94925 (☎415/927-0960; *www.bookpassage.com*).

The Complete Traveler Bookstore, 199 Madison Ave, New York, NY 10016 (☎212/685-9007; *www.completetraveler.com*); 3207 Fillmore St, San Francisco, CA 94123 (☎415/923-1511; *www.completetraveller.com*).

Distant Lands, 56 S Raymond Ave, Pasadena, CA 91105 (☎626/449-3220; *www.distantlands.com*).

Elliott Bay Book Company, 101 S Main St, Seattle, WA 98104 (☎206/624-6600; *www.elliottbaybook.com*).

Map Link, 30 S La Petera Lane, Unit 5, Santa Barbara, CA 93117 (☎805/692-6777; *www.maplink.com*).

Phileas Fogg's Books & Maps, 87 Stanford Shopping Center, Palo Alto, CA 94304 (☎1-800/533-FOGG; *www.foggs.com*).

Rand McNally, 444 N Michigan Ave, Chicago, IL 60611 (☎312/321-1751; *www.randmcnally.com*); 150 E 52nd St, New York, NY 10022 (☎212/758-7488); 595 Market St, San Francisco, CA 94105 (☎415/777-3131); 7988 Tysons Corner Center, McLean, VA 22102 (☎703/556-8688).

Sierra Club Bookstore, 730 Polk St, San Francisco, CA 94110 (☎415/977-5653; *www.sierraclubbookstore.com*).

Travel Books & Language Center, 4437 Wisconsin Ave NW, Washington DC 20016 (☎1-800/220-2665).

Traveler's Choice Bookstore, 2 Wooster St, New York, NY 10013 (☎212/941-1535; *tvlchoice@aol.com*).

BRITAIN AND IRELAND

Blackwell's Map and Travel Shop, 53 Broad St, Oxford OX1 3BQ (☎01865/792792; *www.blackwell.co.uk*).

Daunt Books, 83 Marylebone High St, London W1M 3DE (☎020/7224 2295); and 193 Haverstock Hill, NW3 4QL (☎020/7794 4006).

Easons Bookshop, 40 O'Connell St, Dublin 1 (☎01/873 3811).

Fred Hanna's Bookshop, 27–29 Nassau St, Dublin 2 (☎01/677 4754).

Heffers Map Shop, 3rd Floor, Heffers Stationery Department, 19 Sidney St, Cambridge CB2 3HL (☎01223/568467; *www.heffers.co.uk*).

James Thin Melven's Bookshop, 29 Union St, Inverness IV1 1QA (☎01463/233500; *www.jthin.co.uk*).

John Smith & Sons, 57–61 St Vincent St, Glasgow G2 5TB (☎0141/221 7472; *www.johnsmith.co.uk*).

The Map Shop, 30a Belvoir St, Leicester LE1 6QH (☎0116/2471400).

Newcastle Map Centre, 55 Grey St, Newcastle upon Tyne NE1 6EF (☎0191/261 5622).

National Map Centre, 22–24 Caxton St, London SW1H 0QU (☎020/7222 2466; *www.mapsworld.com*).

Stanfords, 12–14 Long Acre, London WC2E 9LP (☎020/7836 1321); Campus Travel, 52 Grosvenor Gardens, SW1W 0AG (☎020/7730 1314); British Airways, 156 Regent St, W1R 5TA (☎020/7434 4744); and 29 Corn St, Bristol BS1 1HT (☎0117/929 9966). Web site *sales@stanfords.co.uk*

The Travel Bookshop, 13–15 Blenheim Crescent, London W11 2EE (☎020/7229 5260; *www.thetravelbookshop.co.uk*).

AUSTRALIA AND NEW ZEALAND

The Map Shop, 16a Peel St, Adelaide (☎08/8231 2033).

Specialty Maps, 58 Albert St, Auckland (☎09/307 2217).

Worldwide Maps and Guides, 187 George St, Brisbane (☎07/3221 4330).

Mapworld, 173 Gloucester St, Christchurch (☎03/374 5399, fax 03/374 5633; *www.mapworld.co.nz*).

Mapland, 372 Little Bourke St, Melbourne (☎03/9670 4383).

Perth Map Centre, 1/884 Hay St, Perth (☎08/9322 5733).

WEB SITES

Buenos Aires *www.buenosaires.gov.ar* Tourism in the capital, with details of hotels, events and where to dance or watch tango.

Buenos Aires Herald *www.buenosairesherald. com* Condensed but interesting overview of local, national and international news in English and plenty of articles on culture and eating out.

Clarín *www.clarin.com.ar* This site operated by one of the country's main newspapers is painfully slow to download but is full of info on everything from politics to sport, or the two combined.

Disappeared persons *www.desaparecidos. org/arg* Speaks for itself: this site is an interface for finding out more about the human side of this harrowing episode in Argentina's history (see p.711).

Entertainment *www.xsalir.com* All the places to go out to in and around the capital: bars, discos, restaurants, concerts, sports meetings.

General information *www.grippo.com* Excellent and eclectic site with a variety of information on art, sport, current affairs, tourism (especially adventure or alternative tourism) and Perón and Evita.

Greenpeace *www.greenpeace.org.ar* Ecology campaigns in and around Argentina with special emphasis on whales.

Historical information *www.geocities.com/ Heartland/Park/6037/links.html* History, geography, culture, literature and more on this excellent site.

Link-up *www.wam.com.ar/tourism/homepage. htm* Multilingual site putting you in touch with tour operators catering for foreigners in Argentina.

La Nación *www.lanacion.com.ar* Extremely well-executed site set up by the country's leading conservative daily with up-to-date news, weather and information about the arts and media.

Pagina 12 *www.pagina12.com* Tries to beat *Clarín* for having the slowest site to download, but worth persevering for the outspoken newspaper's alternative and at times caustic opinion of national politics.

South American Explorers' Club *www.samexplo.org* Very useful site set up by the experienced non-profit-making organization aimed at scientists, explorers and all travellers in South America. Includes travel-related news, descriptions of individual trips, a bulletin and indexed links with other Web sites.

Tourism *escapeartist.com/argentina6/tournet. html* Tourism-oriented Web site covering mountaineering, Buenos Aires restaurants, eco-tourism and all kinds of other issues of topical interest.

Tourist info *www.mercotour.com* Reliable region-by-region site full of information on a variety of tourism-related issues from skiing to spas and adventure tours to farm holidays.

designed to steer you easily around a given town or city. Luckily, most urban areas, with their convenient grid-systems and publicly displayed maps, are difficult to get lost in and many locals are only too happy to give directions. Some cities produce **directories of services** that include detailed maps, with transport routes.

For 1:100,000 **ordnance-survey style maps** the Instituto Geográfico Militar at Av. Cabildo 381, Casilla 1426, in Buenos Aires, is the place to go (Mon–Fri 8am–1pm; ☎011/4576-5545, fax 011/4576-5509). The maps cost around $15 each but you might be able to get a photocopy for less; although these topographical maps – and the colour satellite maps sold here at similar prices – are great to look at and very detailed, they're not really very practical unless you're used to maps of this type.

COSTS, MONEY AND BANKS

Argentina has a relatively healthy economy, by South American standards, miraculously low inflation, and its currency, the peso, has been pegged to the dollar since the early 1990s. Although this parity has led to unprecedented economic and monetary stability, it has made exports increasingly difficult and resulted in a high cost of living and belt-tightening austerity for many Argentines. But if certain precautions are taken and a few tips are followed, a visit to Argentina needn't be prohibitively costly.

CURRENCY AND EXCHANGE RATES

The Argentine **peso**, divided into one hundred centavos, equals exactly one US dollar. In Argentina, and throughout this book, it's represented by the "dollar sign" ($). There has been off-and-on talk of **dolarización** (adoption of the US dollar as the official currency and legal tender), but political and popular resistance has so far stood in its way. Notes come in 2, 5, 10, 20, 50 and 100 peso denominations while 1 peso and 1 (rare), 5, 10, 25 and 50 centavo coins are in circulation. Sometimes people are loath to give change, as coins are in short supply, so it's a good idea to have plenty of loose change on your person; otherwise insist that they find change, if they want to do business. Ask for small denominations at banks if possible, break bigger ones up at places where they obviously have plenty of change (busy shops, supermarkets or post offices), and withdraw odd amounts from ATMs ($90, $190, etc) to avoid getting your cash dispensed in $100 bills only. In theory you can use **US banknotes** (in pristine condition only, and watch for fakes), but not coins or travellers' cheques, though some places take only Argentine money. ATMs often give you a choice of pesos or dollars and it might be a good idea to keep a stock of both, remembering that Argentine money is difficult to change outside the country, except in Uruguay, or border areas of Bolivia, Brazil and Paraguay, where it may be used as legal tender.

Although very worn or bedraggled notes are sometimes refused, there are no out-of-date notes or coins still floating about as in some other countries. In Tucumán and Catamarca provinces **bonds** (*bonos*) are still issued, and are totally useless anywhere else in the country. Steer clear of them if you can, but be aware that their face value is taken as the same in pesos within the two provinces. Counterfeit notes come into circulation from time to time, as in most countries, and many businesses are equipped with authentication devices for checking all paper money.

COSTS

Argentina will initially seem extortionately expensive to anyone arriving from the neighbouring countries, even Chile. Buenos Aires, in particular, is an expensive city and as a rule of thumb the further south you travel in the provinces the more your budget will be stretched, which means that Patagonia is not a place to travel around on a shoestring. That said, you can get by on less – albeit not much less – than you would in North America, Western Europe or Australasia, especially with some careful planning or, say, by camping and self-catering. **Accommodation** is certainly far more expensive than in Peru or Bolivia, but also more luxurious on the whole.

Eating out tends to be on the pricey side, too, but again at least the quantities are generous and quality is reliable; you can usually save money by having your main meal at lunchtime, when set menus (sometimes called *menú ejecutivo*) are really quite reasonable. You may want to avoid

EXCHANGE RATES
You can check current exchange rates and convert figures on *www.xe.net/currency*

the international fast-food chains, but the home-grown equivalents tend to be better, healthier and cheaper in any case. Snacks such as *lomitos*, often bumper sandwiches filled with real steak, or delicious *empanadas*, are far more satisfying than any cheeseburger, while pizzas are often unbeatable value. Picnicking is another option; local produce is often world class and an *al fresco* meal of bread, cheese, ham or salami with fresh fruit and a bottle of table wine in a great location is a match for any restaurant feast. Breakfast and drinks at cafés, especially in Buenos Aires, can be expensive, so it's often a good idea to avoid them if money's tight.

Long-distance **transport** will also eat up a huge chunk of your expenses and hitchhiking is not always an option. The enormous distances to cover are obviously an important factor to bear in mind, and you may have to budget for some internal flights. Look out for special deals once you're there, especially with the smaller private airlines (see also p.23). Buses vary greatly in condition and price from one category to another and some companies give student discounts, while others promote given destinations with special fares, so it's worth asking around. Remember, too, that the better companies usually give you free food and drink (of varying quality) on lengthy journeys which can more than compensate for a slightly higher fare. Spacious and modern buses offering *coche cama* comfort overnight enable you to save the price of a room and are worthwhile options for covering long distances over less interesting terrain. City transport, including taxis and *remises*, are far better value than in the UK or North America, and most cities are compact enough to walk around anyway. Airports and bus stations are rarely a long way from the centre of town, although mostly too far to walk.

Most places, especially hotels, restaurants and big stores, ask for a huge handling fee for credit-card payments (as high as 20 percent); so it's worth knowing that many businesses – and hotels in particular – will give you a fair-sized **discount for cash payments** (*efectivo* or *contado*) on the quoted price, though they may need prompting.

Roughly speaking, you'll need to reckon on spending at least $200 a week on a shoestring budget, $400 to satisfy creature comforts, by staying in mid-range accommodation and not stinting, while for $800 a week you can live in the lap of luxury. If you're **travelling alone**, you might need to add at least another ten to twenty percent to these prices. For advice on tipping, see the Directory on p.64.

IVA

IVA (*Impuesto de Valor Agregado*) is the Argentine equivalent of VAT or purchase tax and is usually included in the price displayed or quoted for most goods and services. The major exceptions are some hotels, which quote their rates before tax and, significantly, air fares and car rental firms. In the case of the last, this adds a huge supplement to already astronomical figures – IVA is currently a hefty **21 percent** and is added to everything except food and medicines. It is worth knowing that most foreigners can get IVA reimbursed on many purchases. This is worthwhile only for bigger transactions (over $100) and subject to all kinds of limits and complications: shops in the more touristy areas will volunteer information and provide the necessary forms. Finding the right place to go to have the final paperwork completed, signed and stamped and to get your money back, at your point of exit (international airports and ports), is a much taller order, though; ask for instructions when you check in, as you go through the formalities once you've been given your boarding pass.

CHANGING MONEY AND GETTING CASH

ATMs (*cajeros automáticos*) are plentiful in Argentina. Very few towns or even villages have no ATM at all, though you can sometimes be caught out in very remote places, especially in the Northwest, so never rely completely on them. Most machines take all credit cards or helpfully display those that can be used: you can nearly always get money out with Visa or Mastercard, or with any other cards linked to the Plus or Cirrus systems. LINK machines seem to cause a lot of foreigners problems, so maybe avoid them. Machines are mostly multilingual though some of them only use *castellano*, so you might need to have a phrase book or a Spanish-speaker handy. You may be offered a choice of pesos or dollars but whichever you withdraw try to avoid getting lumbered with only $100 notes by deliberately taking out odd figures such as $90 or $140. Trying to buy a drink, cigarettes or a postcard with a crisp $100 can be a frustrating ordeal and won't make you many friends.

Unfortunately **travellers' cheques** are not really a viable option. Fewer and fewer banks seem to accept them, none at all in some areas, and when they do they charge exorbitant commission and take ages to fill out all the paperwork. If you do insist on taking a stock of travellers' cheques (as a precaution in case your credit card goes astray) make sure they're in US dollars and are one of the main brands such as American Express – their own, not those issued by a bank with the Amex logo – and that your signature is 100 percent identical to that in your passport, down to the colour of the ink. Be scrupulously careful when countersigning the cheques, and you will be watched like a hawk as you do so. Travellers' cheques can't be used like cash nor can they be changed in many banks – **casas de cambio** tend to be a better bet. Their opening hours vary from region to region but on the whole they are open from 9am to 6pm, perhaps closing for lunch or siesta. A few are open on Saturday mornings but Sunday opening is virtually non-existent. Tourist offices should be able to tell you where you can change travellers' cheques, but be prepared for blank looks. Banks may also be able to give you a **cash advance** on your credit card, though again this may be expensive.

Another way of getting emergency cash is to **have money wired** to you. This is a speedy but terribly costly option and only to be resorted to when absolutely necessary. Western Union operates through all post offices in Argentina.

CREDIT CARDS

Credit cards (*tarjetas de crédito*) are certainly useful in Argentina, given that travellers' cheques are not that practical and in the light of the abundance of ATMs. They are good for dealing with emergencies, obviate the need to carry large sums of cash (especially for paying in expensive restaurants) and can be used to book rooms ahead, or as payment guarantees on car rental (for which they are indispensable). **Visa** and **Mastercard** are the most widely used and recognized, with **American Express** and **Diner's** lagging in third and a poor fourth place. You might have to show your ID when making a purchase with plastic and be warned that, especially in small establishments, the authorization process can take ages and may not succeed at all. A very practical and often more economical alternative is a **bank debit card**, which saves you having to sort out bills at the end of the month and helps to stop you overspending. You just put your holiday money into your checking account before leaving.

It's always a good idea to take out card **protection insurance** before your departure so that, if you lose your cards or they're stolen, you'll only have to call the insurance company. These schemes are available from most banks and tend to cost only £10/$15 a year, more than worth it especially if they will then wire funds to you. Otherwise make sure you have written down all your card numbers and an emergency telephone number so that you can block any lost or stolen cards; these particulars should be kept in a safe place apart from the cards themselves. Another precaution is to carry one card at a time and leave the others in a hotel safe or tucked away in the darkest recesses of your rucksack.

GETTING AROUND

Distances are immense in Argentina, and you are likely to spend a considerable proportion of your budget on travel expenses. Most people travel by bus, but a domestic air pass is often the best way of seeing a lot of the country if your time is limited. Car rental is useful in places, but too expensive for most budget travellers, unless they can share the cost; and in fact, many backpackers on a tight budget might be forced to hitch. Finally, most boat trips and some ferry crossings are incredibly scenic, and are well worth working into your itinerary if at all possible.

BUSES

By far the most common and straightforward method of transport in Argentina is the **bus**. There are hundreds of private companies, most of which concentrate on one particular region, although a few, such as TAC, run pretty much nationwide. Wherever possible, routes follow sealed roads, as even when these are not the shortest distance between two points, they are invariably the fastest and most comfortable. A high proportion of buses are modern, plush Brazilian-built models designed for long-distance travel, and your biggest worry will be what video the driver has chosen to "entertain" you with (usually subtitled Hollywood action flicks of the Stallone/Seagal/Schwarzenegger type, played with the sound either turned off or at thunderous volume). On longer journeys, snacks, and even hot meals, are served (included in the ticket price),

although these vary considerably in quality and tend towards sweet-toothed tastes. Some of the more luxurious services have waiter service and are usually worth the extra money for long night-rides: *coche cama* and *pullman* services have wide, fully reclinable seats; and *semi-cama* services are not far behind in terms of seat comfort. These services usually cost twenty to forty percent more than the regular *común* services. On the minor routes, you're more likely to encounter old-style buses, but most are decent quality with plenty of leg room.

Buying tickets is normally a simple on-the-spot matter, but you must plan in advance if travelling in peak summer season (mid-Dec to Feb), especially if you're taking a long-distance bus from Buenos Aires or any other major city to a particularly popular holiday destination, when you must often buy your ticket two to three days in advance. Before buying your ticket, check that you are indeed getting the service you want (locals will advise you of your best options). Be aware that some destinations have fast and slow services, and though virtually all services call into the bus terminal at intermediary town stops, this is not always the case: some drop you on the road outside the centre. Similarly, when heading to the capital, check that the bus goes to **Retiro**, the central bus terminal (see p.76). Prices for tickets rise considerably in peak season. It's always worth asking for **discounts**, especially if you're travelling as a group in low season, when your custom is at a premium, or if you have an ISIC or YHA card (some companies give 10–20 percent off). In a few places, you have to pay a small **terminal tax** in addition to the bus ticket ($0.50-1). There's usually some kind of **left-luggage office** ($1–2 per day) at most terminals, or, if you have a few hours to kill between connections, the company with whom you have your onward ticket will usually store your pack free of charge, enabling you to look around town unencumbered.

PLANES

Argentina's most important domestic airport by far is Buenos Aires's **Aeroparque Jorge Newbery** (for details about connections from here to its international terminal, Ezeiza, see p.76). There are connections from the Aeroparque to all provincial capitals and major tourist centres of the country, including Puerto Iguazú, Puerto Madryn/Trelew, and El Calafate. Most people who are keen to get an overview of Argentina's tremendous variety in a limited time will rely heavily on domestic flights to combat the vast distances involved (what takes an hour by plane might take twenty by bus) – and even if you're not pushed for time, it's always worth checking out prices, as some cut-price deals booked in advance can work out to be little more expensive than the bus. One of the best deals is the **"Visit Argentina" air pass** sold by Aerolíneas Argentinas and valid for domestic flights on Aerolíneas and its subsidiary, Austral. This pass must be bought in conjunction with your international flight, and it is not for sale within Argentina. Flights are awarded on a voucher scheme: if your carrier to Argentina is Aerolíneas the basic option (one to three coupons) costs $299; with any other airline it costs $339. Both variants can be supplemented by up to a maximum of eight coupons, each of which costs $105 extra. They're not so brilliant if you value flexibility ahead of a fixed itinerary: you have to nominate your flights in advance; you can stop only once per city; and you can make only one free change of route (additional changes cost $50 each). The pass is valid for up to two months.

If you're planning to stay longer in Argentina or want greater flexibility with your routes, you may be better off buying **individual tickets**. To keep prices down, ask for the *banda negativa* deals, where a percentage of seats are sold off at a **cut-price** rate. These sell out fast for the popular routes, so book as far in advance as is possible. The same is true for any ticket to holiday destinations at peak times. Service on the different domestic carriers varies considerably. Aerolíneas Argentinas is currently fairly run-down and is not renowned for its in-flight service, offering little more than a snack, even on longer flights to destinations such as Ushuaia (3hr 30min). Its partner airline, Austral, is suffering from an even more acute lack of investment and its fleet is outdated; and LAPA, which tends to be less expensive than Aerolíneas/Austral, is renovating its fleet but has had a dubious safety record in the past. Southern Winds, a new company based in Córdoba, has a good reputation and a modern fleet of aircraft, but charges high prices by comparison with its competitors (often twenty percent more). One of its strengths is that it has a good network of connec-

tions between provincial cities, which means you don't always have to go via Buenos Aires. Dinar is another dynamic airline that is rapidly garnering a significant share of the market, with its regional focus being around Salta and the Northwest.

The military also provides civilian services – the airforce's **LADE** is one of the cheapest methods of travel in the country, but there's limited availability on most flights and they're often heavily booked. Its flight routings are often convoluted, bearing some resemblance to a delivery round, although improvements have been made with the recent suspension of many services to smaller provincial destinations as part of an economy drive. In a similar vein to LADE, the navy operates a ridiculously cheap $10 **Aeronave** service from Río Grande to Ushuaia, but you can buy tickets only at the airport and won't know if you have a seat until the last minute.

Domestic **departure taxes** tend to hover at around $5 to $13 (check to see whether or not this has been included in the price before buying your ticket). Many smaller airports are not served by public transport, though some airline companies run shuttle services to connect with flights; otherwise, you're stuck with taxis, which can hit single travellers' budgets hard (most airports are 10-20km from town).

TRAINS

Argentina's **train network**, developed with British investment from the late nineteenth century and nationalized by the Perón administration in 1948, collapsed in 1993 with the withdrawal of government subsidies. Certain long-distance services were maintained by provincial governments, such as the one that links isolated rural communities between Viedma and Bariloche in Río Negro Province, but these tend to be slower and less reliable than buses. The city of Buenos Aires has a large and remarkably inexpensive network of trains that run to the suburbs, into its namesake province, and to the town of Santa Rosa in La Pampa Province.

You're far less likely to want to use Argentinian trains as a method of getting from "A" to "B", however, than you are to try one of country's famous **tourist trains**, where the aim is simply to travel for the sheer fun of it. There are two principal stars: *La Trochita*, the Old Patagonian Express from Esquel; and the *Tren a los Nubes*, one of the highest railways in the world, which climbs through the mountains from Salta towards the

Chilean border. A tinpot toy train runs from near Ushuaia in Tierra del Fuego into the nearby national park, but it has little in the way of an authentic feel and as a journey for its own sake is overhyped.

TAXIS AND REMISES

There are two main types of taxi in Argentina: regular urban taxis that you can flag down in the street; and *remises*, or minicab radio taxis, that you must book by phone or at their central booking booth. Urban **taxis** are fixed with meters – make sure they use them – and each municipality has its own rates (generally $0.10 per block, with a $2 minimum charge). Buenos Aires, like New York, is a city that seems to be suffering from a taxi plague of biblical proportions: you'll rarely have problems finding one, and if you follow a few basic precautions, you'll find them a handy way of negotiating the metropolis. For reasons of safety, if you need a cab from Retiro, get one at the official pick-up point, where you'll be issued with a destination ticket and the price. Also, when flagging down cabs on the street, make sure you ask a rough price before you get in and, to be on the safe side if you have luggage in the boot, wait until the driver has got out of the cab before you do. **Remises** operate with rates fixed according to the destination. They are less expensive than taxis for out-of-town and long-distance trips. Often, it makes more sense to hire a *remise* for a day than to rent your own car: it's often more economical, plus you save yourself the hassle of driving.

In some places, shared taxis or **colectivos** also run on fixed routes. *Remis colectivos* head between towns: they wait at a given collection point, each passenger pays a set fee, and the *colectivo* leaves when it has a car load (some carry destination signs on their windscreen, others don't, so always ask around). They often drop you at a place of your choice at the other end. *Taxi colectivos* drive up and down fixed routes within certain cities: flag one down and pay your share (usually posted on the windscreen).

BOATS, FERRIES AND HYDROFOILS

Boat and ferry services in Argentina fall into two broad categories: those that serve as merely a functional form of transport; and (with some overlap), those that you take to enjoy tourist sights. The two **ferry services** you are most likely to use

are the comfortable ones from Buenos Aires to Colonia del Sacramento in Uruguay (also served by the speedier hydrofoil, see p.159), which provide plenty of space for day-trippers to sunbathe and may entertain you with a game of bingo; and the much more spartan, functional Chilean ones that transport foot passengers and vehicles across the Magellan Straits into Tierra del Fuego at Punta Delgada and Porvenir (see p.689). There are also several practical river crossings throughout the Litoral region, connecting towns such as Concordia with Salto in Uruguay; Rosario with Victoria in Entre Ríos; Goya in Corrientes with Reconquista in Santa Fe; as well as numerous crossings from Misiones to neighbouring Paraguay and Brazil. Tigre, just to the northwest of the capital, tends towards the pleasure-trips end of the market, and offers boat trips around the Delta, to the Isla Martín García, and up to Villa Paranacito in Entre Ríos.

In Patagonia, most lacustrine **boat trips** are designed purely for their scenic value. Chief among these are the different options to behold the polar scenery of the Parque Nacional Los Glaciares near El Calafate at close quarters, especially the world-famous Perito Moreno Glacier. As popular is the Three Lakes Crossing from Bariloche through to Chile, a trip that can be truncated so as to access the Pampa Linda area of Parque Nacional Nahuel Huapi. Of other notable launches, one crosses San Martín de los Andes' Lago Lolog to access the interior of Parque Nacional Lanín; and a tourist passenger launch crosses the western end of Lago Viedma, linking Estancia Helsingfors with El Chaltén. Further south, there's also a new **catamaran service** that crosses the Beagle Channel from Ushuaia to Puerto Williams in Chile, a popular day-trip from Argentine Tierra del Fuego's provincial capital.

HITCHING

Hitching always involves an element of risk, but it can also be one of the most rewarding ways to travel – especially if you can speak at least elementary conversational Spanish. It is getting more tricky to hitch in Argentina: some truck drivers are prohibited by company rules from picking you up; others are reluctant as it often invalidates car insurance or you become the liability of the driver. And in general, it is not advisable for women travelling on their own to hitch, or for anyone to head out of large urban areas by hitching: you're far better off catching a local bus out to an outlying service station or road checkpoint and trying from there. In the south of the country, hitching is still generally very safe. In places such as Patagonia, where roads are few and traffic sparse, you'll often find yourself part of a queue, especially in summer. Always travel with sufficient reserves of water, food, clothes and shelter: you can get stranded for days in some of the more isolated spots.

DRIVING

You are unlikely to want or need a **car** for your whole stay in Argentina, but you'll find one pretty indispensable if you don't have the flexible itinerary necessary for hitching but nevertheless want to explore some of the more isolated areas of Patagonia, Tierra del Fuego, the Northwest, and Mendoza and San Juan provinces. It makes sense to get a group together, not just to keep costs down but also to share some of the driving, which can be arduous, especially on long stretches of unsealed roads. Approximately thirty percent of roads are paved in Argentina, but some of the less important of these routes are littered with potholes. In Buenos Aires, driving is not an entirely relaxing experience: do not expect much lane discipline, and plan your route in advance as the pace of traffic doesn't allow for dithering. In other areas – such as the Chaco – unsealed roads can be extremely muddy after rain, and after prolonged rainy periods roads can be impassable, even to 4WDs. Unless you're travelling on minor roads in mountainous areas or when you're likely to encounter snow, a 4WD is not usually necessary, but having a good clearance off the road is helpful on many unsurfaced roads. Outside major cities, most accidents (and often the most serious ones) occur on unsurfaced gravel roads - for information about safe driving on what is called *ripio*, see p.622.

Altitude can also be a problem in the high Andes: you may need to adjust the fuel intake. A common hazard in rural areas is livestock on the road. One thing worth noting: flashing your lights when driving is a warning to other vehicles *not* to do something, as opposed to the British system, where it is frequently used to signal concession of right of way. You can be fined for not wearing **seatbelts**, although most Argentines display a cavalier disregard of the law in this respect. There are almost no places that rent **motorbikes**, and unless you're an experienced rider, you should avoid taking these on unsurfaced roads: biking on

these requires a wearing degree of concentration, and you need to be careful of stones flicked up by passing cars.

To **rent a car**, you need to be over 21 (25 with some agencies) and to hold an International Driving Licence. Bring a credit card for the **deposit** and your passport. Before you drive off, check that you've been given insurance, tax and ownership papers. Check too for dents and paintwork damage, and get hold of a 24-hour emergency telephone number. Also, pay close attention to the small print, most notably what you're liable for in the event of an accident: excess normally doesn't cover you for the first $1500 if you flip the car, nor for the cost of a smashed windscreen or headlight – a particularly common occurrence if driving on unsurfaced roads. Another frequent type of damage is bent door hinges - be careful when opening doors that they're not slammed open by high winds. Car rental **costs** are far higher in Argentina than in Europe, Australasia or the United States, though prices are falling as competition heats up. The main cities offer the most economical prices, whereas Patagonia is where costs are highest. If looking just for an urban runaround, you can pick up a small car for about $40-50 a day (with the first 50km free), or a week's rental (with 1000km free) from about $330. A similar week's package in the south might cost $100 extra. Be careful to look for **unlimited mileage** deals if you're using it for more than just a runaround, as the per-kilometre charge can otherwise exceed your daily rental cost many times over. You can find some deals that offer this for under $100 per day for small hatchbacks such as a Fiat Uno or Daewoo Tico.

Organizing rental from your home country often proves a competitive option (local companies are listed in the main guide). Note, too, that diesel is much cheaper than petrol ($0.35 per litre, as opposed to just over $1 for super, and $0.80 for regular). Unfortunately, there are relatively few places in Argentina where you can rent a vehicle and drop it in another specified town without being clobbered with a relocation fee (often several hundred pesos). Book as early as possible if you're travelling in high season to Tierra del Fuego, El Calafate or other holiday destinations, as demand usually outstrips supply.

If you plan to do a lot of driving, consider a monthly or annual membership of the **Automóvil Club Argentino** (**ACA**), which has a useful **emergency breakdown** towing and repair ser-

CAR RENTAL AGENCIES

US
Avis ☎1-800/331-1084
Budget ☎1-800/527-0700
Dollar ☎1-800/800-6000
Hertz ☎1-800/654-3001

CANADA
Avis ☎1-800/331-1084
Budget ☎1-800/527-0700
Dollar ☎1-800/800-4000
Hertz ☎1-800/620-9620

UK
Avis ☎0870/6060100
Budget ☎0800/181181
Hertz ☎08708/448844

AUSTRALIA
Avis ☎13/6333
Hertz ☎1800/550067

NEW ZEALAND
Avis ☎09/526 4847 or 0800/655111
Hertz ☎09/309 0989 or 0800/655955

MOTORING ORGANIZATIONS

UK
Automobile Association ☎0800/444999
www.theaa.co.uk
Royal Automobile Club ☎0800/550055
www.rac.co.uk

AUSTRALIA
Australian Automobile Association
☎02/6247 7311

NEW ZEALAND
New Zealand Automobile Association
☎09/377 4660

vice and offers discounts at a series of lodges across the country, many of which are in need of an overhaul. You can join in Buenos Aires at Santa Fe 887, near Plaza San Martín (Mon–Fri 9am–7pm; ☎011/4311 5341), at the less conveniently located head office at Av. del Libertador 1850 (Mon–Fri 10am-6pm; ☎011/4802 6061), or at any of the ACA service stations.

BICYCLES

Most towns with a tourist industry have at least one place that rents **bicycles** (usually costing $10 to $15 per day) for visiting sights on half- and full-day trips. These excursions can be great fun, but remember to bring spare inner tubes and a pump, especially if you're cycling off sealed roads, and check to see that the brakes and seat height are properly adjusted. Argentina is also a popular destination for more serious cyclists, and expeditions along routes such as the arduous, unsurfaced RN40 attract mountain-biking devotees who often value physical endurance above the need to see sights (most sights off the RN40

lie a good way to the west along branch roads, which deters most people from visiting more than one or two). You will need to plan these expeditions thoroughly, and you should buy an extremely robust mountain bike and the very best panniers and equipment you can afford. Bring plenty of high-quality spares with you, which can be hard to come by out of the major centres; punctures and broken spokes are extremely common on unsealed roads. Be prepared to get extremely dusty, and plan your stages with great care, paying particular attention to how much **water** you're going to need. Wind is the biggest problem in places like Patagonia, and if you get the season wrong, your progress will be cut to a handful of kilometres a day. High altitude can have a similar effect. Keep yourself covered as best you can to protect from wind- and sunburn (especially your face), and do not expect much consideration from other vehicles on the road.

For more **information**, see *Latin America by Bike: A Complete Touring Guide*, by Walter Sienko (Mountaineers Books, US; 1993; $14).

ACCOMMODATION

Accommodation in Argentina runs the whole gamut from campsites and youth hostels to fabulously luxurious estancias and international five-star hotels. In the middle there is everything from characterful old colonial houses with balconies to dark and seedy hotels which lack so much as a window. The vast majority of places, however, are pretty anonymous, albeit acceptable, hotels with so little to distinguish one from another that when you find a place that stands out you feel like cheering. The main types of accommodation in Argentina are hotels – ranging from very simple establishments to international luxury hotels and including *posadas*, *hosterías* and B&Bs. But there are also *hospedajes* and *residenciales*, offering basic accommodation, often in a converted family house; estancias or luxury farm houses; youth hostels, which offer some of Argentina's best budget accommodation; *cabañas*, small chalet-style constructions popular in resorts; and campsites, common throughout the country and often with superb facilities. In trekking and mountain-climbing areas a convenient alternative to pitching your tent is provided by *refugios*: small and simple brick or wood constructions. You may like to consider house rental, available in many resorts and sometimes a surprisingly economical accommodation option, provided you are part of a reasonably sized group. Finally, an informal system of room rental is common in towns which receive occasional large numbers of tourists but which have insufficient hotels to cope with the seasonal demand. Argentinian hotels are categorized by a star system, based on facilities rather than standards and a hotel that has been awarded stars is referred to as *de categoría*. The ins and outs of this system are of very little interest to the traveller, however – the only thing you really need to know is that they are little indication of a hotel's desirability. There are many very attractive *hospedajes* and *residenciales* (not to mention estancias) which lack classification (*sin categoría*), while some of the one- and two-star hotels can be grim to say the least.

Accommodation prices are relatively high in Argentina, particularly in Patagonia. However, this often gets exaggerated by travellers used to the very low prices of some other Latin America countries and, in general, you can expect to pay less than you would in many European countries. As ever, you'll get the best deals if you're travelling as a couple or, even better, if there are three or four of you willing to share a room (triple, quadruple and even quintuple rooms are fairly

ACCOMMODATION PRICE CODES

The following codes refer to the cheapest rate for a double room in high season. Single travellers will only occasionally pay half the double-room rate; nearer two thirds is the norm and some places will expect you to pay the full rate. Note that in resort towns, there are considerable discounts out of season.

① $20 or less   ④ $45–60   ⑦ $100–150
② $20–30   ⑤ $60–80   ⑧ $150–200
③ $30–45   ⑥ $80–100   ⑨ Over $200

common). **Single travellers** on a budget who want more privacy than a youth hostel can provide will find things more expensive – many hotels don't have single rooms or offer a discount for single travellers. However, discounts can sometimes be negotiated, particularly if you are staying for a longer period and if you make it clear that you don't need a receipt. Always try to pay in cash as credit cards invariably entail a surcharge. A reasonable accommodation budget to set yourself is around $15 a night – single travellers will only sometimes get away with paying less, and while double rooms can be had for around $20, $30 is a more realistic figure to bear in mind.

HOTELS

Hotels in Argentina range from the exceptionally good to the terribly bad and, as already mentioned, the star system of grading them is not a reliable guide to quality. However, generally speaking, two stars and above guarantees you cable TV, air conditioning and a comfortable, if not necessarily attractive, room. Though few hotels in Argentina are downright dangerous, a general rule of thumb is that those around bus terminals tend to be drab at best and sleazy at worst. Male travellers probably won't feel any qualms about staying at these places, but women travelling alone may feel slightly uncomfortable. Some cheaper places are also popular with couples as an alternative to *albergues transitorios* (see below), though this in itself is not usually a problem. What you should be aware of, however, is that, at the lower end of the market, particularly in larger towns, a handful of places calling themselves hotels are actually more accustomed to dealing with prostitutes and their clients than tourists: this is usually pretty clear from a scout around the lobby area and the reaction to your request for a room. If in doubt about the security of a hotel, check with the tourist office or local businesses.

You can often tell by a hotel's name what kind of place to expect: the use of the term **posada** usually denotes a characterful places, often with a slightly rustic feel, but generally comfortable or even luxurious. In a similar vein, the term **hostería** is often used for smallish, upmarket hotels – oriented towards the tourist rather than the businessman. The term **hostal** is sometimes used too – but doesn't seem to refer reliably to anything – there are youth hostels called *hostales*

as well as high-rise modern hotels. A small but expanding category of hotel, particularly common around Buenos Aires, are **Bed and Breakfasts** (the English term is used) which tend to be chic, converted town houses with an exclusive but cosy atmosphere – they're not budget options, but generally offer far more attractive surroundings than standard hotels of the same price.

Finally, **Apart hotels** are basically small apartments with bedroom, living room and small kitchen. They're usually very well maintained and are often a much better deal than comparably priced conventional hotels.

RESIDENCIALES AND HOSPEDAJES

Residenciales and **hospedajes** are basically simple hotel-style accommodation, graded accorded to a different system (A, B or C is used instead of stars). Most are reasonably clean and comfortable and a few of them stand out as some of Argentina's best budget accommodation. Furnishings tend to the basic, with little more than a bed, perhaps a desk and chair and a fan in each room – though some are far less spartan than others and there is even the odd *residencial* or *hospedaje* with cable TV. Most places offer rooms with private bathrooms.

There's really little difference between the two names – indeed the same establishment may be described in different accommodation lists as both, or even as a hotel. The only real difference is that *hospedajes* tend to be part of a family house (though the atmosphere is that of a hotel rather than a lodging), but otherwise facilities are very similar to those of a *residencial*. Both *hospedajes* and *residenciales* have low prestige in Argentina and may not be recommended to tourists, but they're often far more welcoming and secure places than cheap hotels.

ESTANCIAS

A very different experience to staying in a hotel is provided by Argentina's **estancias**, as the country's large ranches are called. Guests stay in the *casco*, or farmhouse – which could be anything from a simple family home to an extravagant castle-like residence. The estancias are nearly always family run, the income from tourism tending to serve as a supplement to the declining profits earned from the land itself. Estancia accommodation is generally luxurious, and with a lot more character than hotels of a similar price;

for between $100 and $200 per person a day you are provided with four meals, invariably including a traditional *asado*; at working estancias you will have the chance to observe or join in ranch activities such as cattle herding and branding; and at all of them horseriding and often swimming are also included in the price.

You can book your estancia accommodation either by approaching individual estancias direct or through certain *travel agencies*, at no extra cost: the two main agencies are both based in Buenos Aires: Comarcas, Laprida 1380 (☎011/4821-1876; *comarcas@tournet.com.ar*) and José de Santis, Diag. Roque Sáenz Peña 616, 5th Floor (☎011/4342-8417).

YOUTH HOSTELS

Youth hostels are known as *albergues juveniles* or *albergues de la juventud* in Argentina. Avoid referring to them as simply *albergues* as this may be taken to mean *albergue transitorio* (short-stay hotels where couples rent rooms by the hour to have sex). There are two hostelling organizations in Argentina, somewhat in dispute with each other for "official" status, but both recognizing Hostelling International (HI) cards at their separate networks of hostels: the Asociación Argentina de Albergues de la Juventud (AAAJ) is at Talchahuano 214, 2nd Floor (☎011/4372-1001); and the more dynamic Red Argentina de Albergues Juveniles (RAAJ), is at Florida 835, 3rd Floor (☎011/4511-8712). In practice, both organizations have both good and bad hostels. In fact there are also a growing number of independent hostels which, particularly in Buenos Aires, are among the country's best. You won't need an HI card at these establishments. Accommodation is generally in **dormitories**, though most places also have one or two double **rooms**. Facilities vary from next to nothing to Internet access, washing machines, cable TV and patios with barbecue facilities.

Even if you do not have an HI card, it's unlikely that you'll be refused entry at the official hostels, but you should expect to be charged a couple of pesos more than the going rate for your accommodation.

CABAÑAS

If you fancy a break from the hotels, and especially if you are travelling as part of a group, self-catering **cabañas** make a good choice. Popular in resort towns, they are small, self-contained chalet-style buildings which can resemble miniature suburban villas with cable TV and microwaves, but are far more likely to be pleasingly simple and rustic wooden constructions. *Cabañas* can be very good value for money for small groups, and if you have been staying in a lot of hotels or doing some hardcore camping, they can be fun and relaxing places to take a break for a few days. A few of the simpler ones can also be a surprisingly affordable option for couples or even single travellers.

CAMPING

There are plenty of **campsites**, (called simply *campings*) throughout Argentina, with most towns and villages having their own municipal campsite, but standards vary wildly. At the major resorts, there are usually plenty of privately owned, well-organized sites, with facilities ranging from provisions stores to volleyball courts and TV rooms. Some sites are attractive, but mostly they seem to take the fun out of camping and you're more likely to wake up to a view of next door's 4WD than the surrounding countryside. They are, however, good places to meet other travellers and generally offer a high degree of security. There are also many simpler campsites, though at nearly all of them showers, electric light and barbecue facilities are standard. A campsite with no, or very limited, facilities is referred to as a *camping agreste*. In non-touristy towns, muncipal sites can be rather desolate and sometimes not particularly secure places: it's usually a good idea to check with locals as to the security of the place before pitching your tent.

HOUSE AND ROOM RENTAL

As well as conventional accommodation options you may also wish to consider **house rental** – a particularly popular option with monied Porteños summering at the major resorts, but also a pleasant (and not necessarily expensive) way to spend a week or so at a smaller resort. You can find house rentals through the classified sections of national newspapers and at accommodation agencies in the resorts. Also, particularly in the quieter places, impromptu notices spring up on houses saying *se alquila* ("for rent"), with a contact number or address. Tourist offices may also hold information on houses to rent. In towns which receive large numbers of tourists for festivals and other special events, there are usually plenty of families offering rooms to rent; lists of such accommodation are usually held by the local tourist offices.

HEALTH

Travel to Argentina doesn't raise any major health worries and with a small dose of precaution and a handful of standard vaccinations (tetanus, polio, typhoid and hepatitis A) you are unlikely to encounter any serious problems. A bout of travellers' diarrhoea is the most you're likely to have to worry about as your body adjusts to local micro-organisms in the food and water. It's also best to ease yourself gently into the local diet – sudden quantities of red meat, red wine, strong coffee and sweet pastries can be very unsettling for a stomach used to gentler repasts – and though tap water in Argentina is generally safe to drink, if sometimes heavily chlorinated, you may prefer to err on the side of caution in rural areas in the north of the country.

PHARMACIES AND MEDICAL TREATMENT

Argentinian **pharmacies** are a very useful first port of call for help with minor medical problems; staff are usually able to offer simple diagnostic advice and will often help dress wounds. You'll find a wider ranger of products and medicines available without **prescription** here than in many other countries and, while the brand names will undoubtedly be different, if you have the packaging of the product you're looking for, take it along so the pharmacist can find you the local equivalent. Medicines and cosmetic products are fairly expensive, however, so if you have room in your luggage, take plenty of supplies.

The easiest way to get treatment for more serious ailments is to attend the outpatients department of a local **hospital**, where treatment will usually be free. In Buenos Aires, the Hospital de Clínicas, José de San Martín, Av. Córdoba 2351 (☎011/4961-6001), is a particularly efficient place to receive medical advice and prescriptions; you can simply walk in and, for a small fee, make an on-the-spot appointment with the relevant specialist department – and English-speaking doctors can usually be found. For a list of English-speaking doctors throughout the country, contact the British, Australian, New Zealand, Canadian or US embassy in Buenos Aires.

DISEASES

Though your chances of contracting any of the following diseases are very low, they are sufficiently serious that you should be aware of their existence and of measures you should take to avoid infection. For up-to-date information on current health risks in Argentina check the Web sites *www.medicineplanet.com* and *www.cdc.gov*.

Chagas' disease is transmitted by a microscopic parasite, the *Trypanosome cruzi*, transported by a small beetle, the vinchuca or chinche gaucha. The parasite-bearing beetle bites its "victim" and then defecates next to the wound – and scratching of the bite thus causes the parasite to be borne into the bloodstream. The immediate symptoms – a fever, a hard swelling on the skin and occassionally around the eyes – last two to three weeks, are mild and may even be imperceptible; but the disease is treatable at this stage. In around twenty percent of untreated cases, however, potentially fatal cardiac problems caused by a gross enlargement of the heart can appear twenty or thirty years later, with no other symptoms suffered in between. Though it can be extremely serious, the disease isn't widespread and travellers should be aware of, but not unduly worried about, catching it. Contact is most likely to occur in poorer rural regions, particularly in dwellings with adobe walls. Where possible you should avoid camping in such areas and if you do sleep in an adobe hut, you should use a mosquito net and sling your hammock as far away from the walls as possible. If you suspect you have been bitten by a vinchuca you must avoid scratching the wound; bathe it with alcohol instead and get a blood test as soon as possible.

Cholera outbreaks are very rare, but there have been sporadic cases in the Northwest. If travelling in an area where there is an outbreak, you should exercise extreme caution with food, particularly shellfish (though this is pretty rare, anyway, in the main areas concerned) and drinking water. There is an immunization for cholera, but it's so ineffective as to be considered worthless by the World Health Organization.

Dengue fever is a viral disease transmitted by mosquitoes. The symptoms are a high fever, headache, and eye and muscular pain; it can be very debilitating but is rarely fatal except in the rare haemorrhagic strain. Dengue fever occurs in urban areas in the north of Argentina; there are regular public health campaigns aimed at avoiding outbreaks, principally by making sure that

MEDICAL RESOURCES FOR TRAVELLERS

USA

Centers for Disease Control, 1600 Clifton Rd NE, Atlanta, GA 30333 (☎404/639-3311; *www.cdc.gov*). Publishes outbreak warnings, suggested inoculations, precautions and other background information for travellers.

International Association for Medical Assistance to Travelers (IAMAT), 417 Center St, Lewiston, NY 14092 (☎716/754-4883; *www.sentex.net/~iamat*). A non-profit organization supported by donations that can provide a list of English-speaking doctors in Argentina, plus climate charts and leaflets on various diseases and inoculations.

International SOS Assistance, PO Box 11568, Philadelphia, PA 19116 (☎1-800/523-8930; *www.intsos.com*). Members receive pre-trip medical referral information, as well as overseas emergency services designed to complement travel insurance coverage.

Travel Medicine, 369 Pleasant St, Northampton, MA 01060 (☎1-800/872-8633; *www.travmed.com*). Sells first-aid kits, mosquito netting, water filters and other health-related travel products.

CANADA

Canadian Society for International Health, 1 Nicholas St, Suite 1105, Ottawa, ON K1N 7B7 (☎613/241-5785; *www.csih.org*). Distributes a free pamphlet, "Health Information for Canadian Travellers", containing an extensive list of travel health centres in Canada.

International Association for Medical Assistance to Travelers (IAMAT), 40 Regal Rd, Guelph, ON N1K 1B5 (☎519/836-0102). A non-profit organization supported by donations that can provide a list of English-speaking doctors in Argentina, plus climate charts and leaflets on various diseases and inoculations.

BRITAIN

British Airways Travel Clinic, 156 Regent St, London W1 7RA (☎0207/439 9584). No appointments necessary. For details of other clinics throughout the country, call ☎01276/685040.

Hospital for Tropical Diseases, Mortimer Market Centre, Capper St, off Tottenham Court

Rd, London WC1E 6AU (☎0207/388 8989). Travel clinic for vaccinations (including yellow fever); also stocks various first-aid items and anti-mosquito creams and devices. For advice on vaccinations and disease prevention, call ☎09061/337733.

---

stagnant water cannot collect. There is no vaccination against dengue fever, though the disease is treatable, and the best way to avoid the slim chance of infection is by covering up during the day (unlike malarial mosquitoes, the dengue mosquito bites during the day) and using mosquito repellent.

Hantavirus is a rare, incurable viral disease transmitted by long-tailed wild mice. It is present throughout the Americas (though not in the far south of Patagonia) and produces haemorrhagic fever and severe respiratory problems caused by the accumulation of liquid in the lungs. Initial symptoms are similar to influenza – with fever, headache, stomachache and muscle pain – and the fatality rate is around fifty percent. The virus is present in the excrement, urine and saliva of the mouse and is transmitted to humans through breathing in contaminated air, consuming contam-

inated food or water, or by being bitten by or handling a virus-bearing mouse. It cannot survive sunlight, detergent or disinfectant and the best way to avoid contamination is by being scrupulously clean when camping, particularly in rural areas. Recommended precautions are using tents with a proper floor, good fastenings and no holes; keeping food in sealed containers and out of reach of mice (hanging a knotted carrier bag from a tree is a standard precaution) and cleaning up properly after eating. If staying in a *cabaña* which looks as though it hasn't been used for a while, let the place ventilate for a good thirty minutes before checking (while covering your mouth and nose with a handkerchief) for signs of mouse excrement. If any is found, all surfaces should be disinfected then swept and aired. Despite the severity of hantavirus, you should not be unduly worried about the disease. In the unlikely case

Masta (Medical Advisory Service for Travellers Abroad) (☎0891/224100; *www.masta.org*). Efficient, automated service (calls charged at 60p a minute), offering tailor-made written health information on your destination by return of post. Be sure to speak clearly though, or you'll end up with information for Panama instead of Paraguay.

IRELAND

Travel Medicine Services, PO Box 254, 16 College St, Belfast 1(☎01232/315 220). Offers medical advice before you take your trip and medical help afterwards in the event of a tropical disease.
Tropical Medical Bureau, Grafton St Medical Centre, 34 Grafton St, Dublin 2 (☎01/671 9200);

Dun Laoghaire Medical Centre, 5 Northumberland Ave, Dun Laoghaire, Co. Dublin (☎01/280 4996, fax 280 5603; email; *www.iol.ie/-tmb/*). Offers medical advice before you make your trip and medical help afterwards in the event of a tropical disease.

AUSTRALIA AND NEW ZEALAND

www.tmvc.com.au has a comprehensive list of Travellers Medical and Vaccination Centres throughout Australia, New Zealand and Southeast Asia, plus general information on travel health. Addresses and telephone numbers for key centres are:

Adelaide 27–29 Gilbert Place (☎08/8212 7522).
Auckland 1/170 Queen St (☎09/373 3531).
Brisbane 6/247 Adelaide St, Brisbane (☎07/3221 9066).
Canberra Mezzanine Level, City Walk Arcade, 2 Mort St (☎02/6257 7156).
Christchurch 147 Armagh St (☎03/379 4000).
Darwin 5 Westralia St (☎08/8981 2907).

Hobart 270 Sandy Bay Rd, Sandy Bay (☎03/6223 7577).
Melbourne 2/393 Little Bourke St (☎03/9602 5788).
Perth 5 Mill St (☎08/9321 1977), plus branch in Fremantle.
Sydney 7/428 George St (☎02/9221 7133), plus branches in Chatswood and Paramatta.
Wellington Shop 15, Grand Arcade, Willis St (☎04/473 0991).

that there is an outbreak in the area you are visiting you will be well-informed by the local authorities of the virus's presence.

HIV and Aids cases have been climbing steadily in Argentina over recent years; latest figures estimate that around two percent of the adult population between 15 and 49 years carry the HIV virus. Some of the condoms sold in Argentina are of pretty poor quality, so it's wise to bring a reliable brand with you from home.

Malaria is a minor risk in Argentina and confined to low-lying areas of Salta and Jujuy provinces (Iruya, San Martín, Santa Victoria, Ledesma, San Pedro and Santa Bárbara), and the northern borders of Corrientes and Misiones (though not Iguazú) from October to May. Though the risk is low, it's certainly worth taking anti-malarial precautions if you are visiting this region. Fortunately, resistance to the standard anti-malarial drug Chloroquine has not yet been reported so you will not have to weigh up the pros and cons of taking the controversial drug Mefloquine. As with dengue fever, you should also guard against mosquito bites by covering up after dusk, using insect repellent and, where possible, mosquito nets and anti-mosquito coils or plug-ins, both of which are widely available in Argentina and often provided in hotel rooms.

Rabies is present throughout Argentina and if you are spending a long time travelling away from population centres or are likely to come into contact with wild animals, it's worth considering getting vaccinated before you go. The vaccine doesn't make you immune to the disease but it does buy you more time if you are bitten – in which case you will still need to receive a second vaccination.

Yellow fever is a very serious mosquito-borne viral disease which occurs in subtropical and tropical forested regions, particularly where there are monkeys. It's a very minor risk in the northeast of Argentina, but it is a wise precaution to invest in a ten-year vaccine for longer trips – and essential if you are travelling elsewhere in Latin America.

PUNA OR ALTITUDE SICKNESS

Altitude sickness is a potentially – if rarely – fatal condition encountered at anything over 2000m, but likeliest and most serious at altitudes of 4000m and above. It can cause severe difficulties – but a little preparation should help you avoid the worst of its effects. In many South American countries it is known by the Quechua word *soroche*, but in Argentina is most commonly, and confusingly, called **puna** (the local word for altiplano or high Andean steppes). You'll also hear the verb *apunar* and the word *apunamiento*, referring to the state of suffering from *puna*, whether affecting humans or vehicles (which also need to be adjusted for these heights)

First, if you're **driving** into the altiplano make sure that your vehicle's engine has been properly adjusted. All engines labour because of the low oxygen levels, and when you start walking you'll empathize, so don't try to force the pace and stay in low gears. To avoid the effects of the *puna* on yourself, don't rush anywhere, but instead walk slowly and breathe steadily – and make things easier on yourself by not smoking. Whenever possible, **acclimatize**: it's better to spend a day or two at around 2000m and then 3000–3500m before climbing to 4000m or more, allowing the body to produce more red blood corpuscles rather than forcing it to cope with a sudden reduction in oxygen levels. And make sure you're fully rested; an all-night party isn't exactly the best preparation for a trip up into the Andes. As for drinking, alcohol is also best avoided, prior to or during high-altitude travel, and the best thing to drink is plenty of still water – never fizzy because it froths over or can even explode at high altitudes – or tea. Eating, too, needs some consideration: digestion uses up considerable quantities of oxy-

gen, so snacking is preferable to copious lunches and dinners. Carry supplies of high-energy cereal bars, chocolate, dried fruit (the local raisins, prunes and dried apricots are delicious), walnuts or cashews, crackers and biscuits, avoiding anything that ferments in the stomach such as milk, fresh fruit and juices, vegetables or acidic food, as they're guaranteed to make you throw up if you're affected; the best – because it's the least acidic – form of sugar to ingest is honey. Grilled meat is fine, so *asados* are all right, but don't over-indulge.

Minor **symptoms** of the *puna*, such as headaches or a strange feeling of pressure inside the skull, nausea, loss of appetite, insomnia or dizziness, are nothing to worry about, but more severe problems, such as persistent migraines, repeated vomiting, severe breathing difficulties, excessive fatigue and a marked reduction in the need to urinate are of more concern. If you suffer from any of these, seek out **medical advice** at once and consider returning to a lower altitude. Severe respiratory problems should be treated immediately with oxygen, carried by tour operators on excursions to 3000m or more, as a legal requirement, but you're unlikely ever to need it.

SUNSTROKE AND SUNBURN

You should take the sun very seriously in all of Argentina. The north of the country is one of the hottest regions of Latin America in summer –temperatures regularly hit the 40 degree mark and the extended siestas taken by locals are a wise precaution against the debilitating effects of the midday heat. Where possible, avoid excessive activity between about 11am and 4pm and where you do have to be out in the sun, wear sunscreen and a hat. You should also drink plenty of liquids – but not alcohol – and always make sure you have a sufficient supply of water when embarking on a hike. Throughout the country, the sun can be extremely fierce and even people with darker skin should use a much higher factor sunscreen than they might normally: using factor 15 or above is a sensible precaution.

EATING AND DRINKING

Argentine food could be summed up by one word: "beef". Not just any beef, but the best in the world, succulent, cherry-red, healthy – and certainly not mad – meat raised on some of the greenest, most extensive pastures known to cattle. The barbecue or *asado* is an institution, every bit a part of the Argentine way of life as football, fast-driving and tango. But that's not the whole story. In general, you nearly always eat well in Argentina and you seldom have a bad meal, portions are always generous and the raw ingredients are of an amazingly high quality. Even so, imagination, innovation and a sense of subtle flavour are sometimes lacking, with Argentines preferring to eat the wholesome but often bland dishes their immigrant forebears cooked. The produce of Argentina's vineyards, ranging from gutsy plonk to some of the world's prize-winning wines, are increasingly available abroad; they make the perfect companion to a juicy grilled *bife de chorizo*. The quality of the wine is just beginning to be matched by some of the inventive *cordon bleu* cooking concocted by some daring young chefs at a few expensive restaurants across the country. Fast food is extremely popular but you can snack on local specialities such as *empanadas* and *lomitos* if you want to avoid the ubiquitous multinational burger chains.

Argentinians love eating out, even if that only means sharing a pizza in a shopping mall or grabbing a dozen *empanadas*, and in Buenos Aires

especially eateries stay open all day and till very late. By South American standards the quality of **restaurants** is high, with prices to match. If you eat à la carte you'll be hard put to find a main dish for under $10 but, as elsewhere in the continent, you can keep costs down by eating at the market, at a fast-food outlet (not necessarily McDonald's) or by making lunch your main meal (it's usually served from noon to 3pm), to take advantage of the *menú del día* or *menú ejecutivo* – usually good-value set meals for $8–10 all in. In the evening *tenedor libre* or *diente libre* restaurants are just the place if your budget's tight. You can eat as much as you like, they're usually self-service (cold and hot buffets plus grills) and the food is fresh and well prepared, if a little dull; most of Argentina's "Chinese" restaurants, many of them dazzlingly cavernous palaces with dozens of tables, offer this format but little in the way of real Chinese food. Watch out for hidden extras on the bill such as dishes not included in the set price, drinks, coffee, etc.

Cheaper hotels and more modest accommodation often skimp on **breakfast**: you'll be lucky to be given more than tea or coffee, and some bread, jam and butter, though the popular *media lunas* (small, sticky croissants) are sometimes also served. More upmarket hotels will go all out to impress you with their "American-style" buffet breakfast: an array of cereals, yoghurts, fruit, breads and even eggs, bacon and sausages, making it worthwhile getting up early and making it down to the restaurant. The sacred national delicacy *dulce de leche* (see box, p.42) is often provided for spreading on toast or bread, as is top-notch honey. **Tea** is often served in the afternoon – especially by anglophiles – with *facturas*, a variety of sticky pastries, a bulging box of which is frequently offered to hosts as a gift. Hardly any restaurant opens for **dinner** before 8pm, and in the hotter months – and all year round in Buenos Aires – few people turn up before 10 or 11pm. Don't be surprised to see people pouring into restaurants well after midnight; Porteños and Argentines in general are night owls and wouldn't dream of dining early.

If you're feeling peckish during the day there are plenty of **minutas** or snacks to choose from. The **lomito** is a nourishing sandwich filled with a juicy slice of steak, often made with delicious *pan árabe*

GLOSSARY OF FOOD AND DRINK

BASICS

aceite de maíz	corn oil	*mermelada*	jam
aceite de oliva	olive oil	*mostaza*	mustard
agregado	side order or garnish	*pan (francés)*	bread (baguette
ajo	garlic		or French stick)
ají	chilli	*pebete*	sandwich in a bun or
almuerzo	lunch		bread-roll
arroz	rice	*pimienta*	pepper
azúcar	sugar	*pimentón dulce*	paprika
carta/menú	menu	*plato*	plate or dish
cena	dinner	*queso*	cheese
comedor	diner or dining-room	*sal*	salt
cuchara	spoon	*sanduich*	sandwich (usually
cuchillo	knife		made with very
cuenta	bill		thinly sliced bread:
desayuno	breakfast		*sanduich de miga*)
harina	flour	*servilleta*	napkin
huevos	eggs	*taza*	cup
lata/latita	can or tin	*tenedor*	fork
manteca	butter	*vaso*	glass
mayonesa	mayonnaise	*vegetariano*	vegetarian
menú del día	set meal	*vinagre*	vinegar

CULINARY TERMS

parrilla	barbecue	*al vapor*	steamed
asado	roasted or barbecued;	*crudo*	raw
	un asado is a	*frito*	fried
	barbecue	*picante*	hot (spicy)
a la plancha	grilled	*puré*	puréed or mashed
ahumado	smoked		potatoes
al horno	baked/roasted	*relleno*	stuffed

MEAT (*CARNE*) AND POULTRY (*AVES*)

bife	steak	*filete*	fillet steak
bife de chorizo	prize steak cut	*jabalí*	wild boar
cabrito	goat (kid)	*jamón*	ham
carne vacuna	beef	*lechón*	suckling pig
cerdo	pork	*lomo*	tenderloin steak
ciervo	venison	*milanesa*	breaded veal
codorniz	quail		escalope
conejo	rabbit	*oca*	goose
cordero	lamb	*paletilla*	shoulder of lamb
chivito	kid or goat	*pato*	duck
chuleta	chop	*pavo*	turkey
churrasco	grilled beef	*pollo*	chicken
fiambre	cured meats – hams,	*ternera*	grass-fed veal
	salami, etc	*tocino/ beicon*	bacon

OFFAL (*ACHURAS*)

bofes	lights (lungs)	*chorizo blanco*	meaty sausage, not
corazón	heart		spiced like Spanish
criadillas	testicles		chorizo (*chorizo*
chinchulines	small intestine		*colorado*)

hígado	liver	orejas	ears
lengua	tongue	patas	feet or trotters
mollejas	sweetbreads (thymus gland)	riñones	kidneys
		sesos	brains
mondongo	cow's stomach	tripa gorda	tripe (large intestine)
morcilla	blood sausage	ubre	udder

TYPICAL DISHES (*PLATOS*)

arroz con pollo	a kind of chicken risotto	matambrito	delicious cut of pork, often simmered in milk until soft
bife a caballo	steak with a fried egg on top	milanesa napoletana	breaded veal escalope topped with ham, tomato and melted cheese
bife a la criolla	steaks braised with onions, peppers and herbs		
brochetas	kebabs	milanesa de pollo	breaded chicken breast
carbonada	a filling meat stew	mondongo	stew made of cow's stomach with potatoes and tomatoes
cazuela de marisco	a seafood casserole		
cerdo a la riojana	pork cooked with fruit		
fainá	chickpea dough traditionally served with pizza	pastel de papa	shepherd's pie
		provoletta	thick slice of provolone cheese grilled on a barbecue
guiso	basic meat stew, everything thrown in		
locro	stew based on maize, beans and meat, often including tripe	puchero	a rustic stew, usually of chicken (*puchero de gallina*), made with potatoes and maize or whatever vegetable is to hand
matambre relleno	cold stuffed flank steak (normally filled with vegetables and hard-boiled eggs, and sliced; literally means "hunger killer")	vittel tonné	the Argentine starter par excellence: slices of cold roast beef in mayonnaise mixed with tuna

FISH (*PESCADO*)

atún	tuna	manguruyú	river fish best grilled
boga	large, flavoursome fish caught in the Río de la Plata	merluza	hake
		pacú	firm-fleshed river fish
caballa	mackerel	pejerrey	popular inland-water fish
dorado	a large freshwater fish, with mushy flesh and loads of bones	pirapitanga	salmon-like river fish
		sábalo	oily-fleshed river fish
lenguado	sole	salmón	salmon
lisa de río	oily river fish	surubí	kind of catfish
manduví	delicious river fish with delicate, pale flesh	trucha (*arco iris*)	(rainbow) trout
		vieja	white, meaty fleshed river-fish

Continued overleaf

SEAFOOD (*MARISCOS*)

camarones	shrimps or prawns	*mejillones*	mussels
cangrejo	crab	*ostras*	oysters
centolla	king crab	*vieira*	scallop

VEGETABLES (*VERDURAS*)

aceitunas	olives	*morrón (dulce/rojo/verde)*	(sweet/red/green)
acelga	chard (a popular		pepper
	vegetable not	*palmito*	palm heart
	unlike spinach)	*palomitas*	popcorn
alcauciles	artichokes	*palta*	avocado
apio	celery	*papa*	potato
arvejas	peas	*papas fritas*	chips
aspárragos	asparagus	*perejil*	parsley
berenjena	aubergine	*pimiento*	green pepper
berro	watercress	*poroto*	bean
cebolla	onion	*puerro*	leek
champiñon	mushroom	*remolacha*	beetroot
chauchas	runner beans	*tomate*	tomato
choclo	maize or sweetcorn	*tomillo*	thyme
chucrút	sauerkraut	*zanahoria*	carrot
coliflor	cauliflower	*zapallo*	pumpkin
ensalada	salad	*zapallito*	gem squash – small
espinaca	spinach		green pumpkins
garbanzo	chickpea		that are a favourite
habas	broad beans		throughout the
lechuga	lettuce		country

FRUIT (*FRUTA*)

alcayote	spaghetti squash	*dátiles*	dates
almendra	almond	*damasco*	apricot
almíbar	syrup	*durazno*	peach
ananá	pineapple	*frambuesa*	raspberry
avellana	hazelnut	*frutilla*	strawberry
banana	banana	*higo*	fig
batata	sweet potato	*limón*	lemon
castaña	chestnut	*maní*	peanut
cereza	cherry	*manzana*	apple
ciruela (seca)	plum (prune)	*melón*	melon

while the **chivito** is made with a less tender cut; it was originally a Uruguayan term, used in Buenos Aires, but it also means kid, a speciality of the Central Sierras region. Other street food includes the **choripán**, South America's version of the hot-dog, but made with meaty sausages (*chorizos*), and at cafés a popular snack is the **tostado**, a toasted cheese-and-ham sandwich, usually daintily thin and sometimes called a **carlitos. Barrolucas** are beef and cheese sandwiches, a local variant on the cheeseburger, named after a Chilean president, and very popular in western Argentina, around Mendoza. **Milanesas**, in this context, refer to breaded veal escalopes in a sandwich, hamburger-style.

To ring the changes in your diet, you can tap into the variety of cuisines reflecting the mosaic of different communities who have migrated to Argentina over the decades. **Italian** influences on the local cuisine are very strong, and authentic

membrillo	quince	pera	pear
naranja	orange	pomelo	grapefruit
nuez	walnut	sandía	watermelon
pasa (de uva)	dried fruit (raisin)	uva	grape

DESSERTS (POSTRES)

arroz con leche	rice pudding	helado	ice cream
budín de pan	bread pudding	media luna (dulce/salado)	(sweet/plain)
crema	custard or cream		croissant
dulce de leche	thick caramel made from milk and sugar, a national religion (see box on p. 42)	miel	honey
		panqueque/crepe	pancake
		sambayón	zabaglione (custard made with egg yolks and wine, a popular ice cream flavour)
dulce	sweet in general; candied fruit or jam		
ensalada de fruta	fruit salad	torta	tart or cake
flan	crème caramel	tortilla/tortita	breakfast pastry

DRINKS (BEBIDAS)

agua	water	chopp	draught beer
agua mineral (con gas/sin gas)	mineral water (sparkling/still)	cidra	cider
		clericó	sangria made with white wine
botella	bottle		
cacheteado	Coke and red wine spritzer, very popular in Córdoba	Fernet	Italian-style digestive drink, popularly mixed with cola
café (con leche)	coffee (with milk)		
cerveza	beer	gaseosa	fizzy drink
cortado	espresso coffee "cut" with a little steaming milk (similar to macchiato)	jugo (de naranja)	(orange) juice
		lata	can
		leche	milk
		licuados	juice-based drinks or milkshakes
champán	sparkling wine, usually Argentine, or champagne	mate cocido	infusion made with mate, sometimes heretically with a "tea-bag"
chocolate/submarino	hot chocolate (often a slab of choc melted in hot milk, served in a tall glass)	té	tea
		vino (tinto/blanco/rosado)	wine (red/white/rosé)

Italian cooking, with a marked Genoese flavour, is available all over the country, but especially in Buenos Aires. **Spanish** restaurants serve tapas and familiar dishes such as paella while specifically **Basque** restaurants are also fairly commonplace. These are often the places to head for if fish or seafood takes your fancy. **Chinese** and, increasingly, **Korean** restaurants are to be found in nearly every Argentine town, but they rarely serve anything remotely like authentic Asian food and specialize in *tenedor libre* buffet diners, where one or two token dishes might be slightly more exotic, though more often than not they are Sino-American inventions, such as chow mein or chop suey, at times liberally spiked with MSG. **Japanese**, **Indian** and **Thai** food has become fashionable in Buenos Aires, where nearly every national cuisine from Armenian to Vietnamese via Persian and Polish is available, but such variety is almost unheard of in the provinces.

On the other hand, **Arab** or **Middle Eastern** food, including specialities such as kebabs and *kepe*, seasoned ground raw meat, is far more widespread, as is **German** fare, such as sauerkraut (*chucrút*) and frankfurters, along with Central and **Eastern European** food, often served in *choperías* or beer-gardens. **Welsh** tearooms are a speciality of Patagonia, where tea and scones are part of the Welsh community's identity.

PARRILLA, PIZZA AND PASTA

Parrilla, pizza and pasta are the mainstays of Argentine cuisine, whether at home or when eating out. The **parrilla** is simply a barbecue, the national dish, served at special restaurants known as parrillas. Usually there's a set menu, the **parrillada**, but the establishments themselves vary enormously. At many, especially in big cities, the decor is stylish, the staff laid-back and the crockery delicate, and the meat is served daintily on a platter. Elsewhere, especially in smaller, provincial towns, parrillas are more basic joints, where you're served by burly, sweaty-browed waiters, who spend all their time grilling and carving huge hunks of flesh and hurling them onto your plate. Sometimes it seems as if everything's being done to stop you ever getting your teeth into a juicy tenderloin. Traditionally you start off by eating the offal before moving on to the choicer cuts (for what you're chewing, see the box on p.36), but don't be put off – you can choose to skip these delicacies and head straight for the steaks and fillets. Either way, these places are not for the faint-hearted: everything comes with heaps of salads and mountains of chips. But the meat is invariably fabulous.

Mass immigration from Italy since the middle of the nineteenth century has had a profound influence on the food and drink in Argentina and the abundance of **fresh pasta** (*pasta casera*) is just one example of that. The fillings tend to be a little unexciting (lots of cheese, including ricotta, but seldom meat) and the sauces are not exactly memorable (mostly tomato and onion), and the pasta tends to be cooked beyond *al dente*, yet it's a reliable staple and rarely downright bad. Very convincing parmesan- and roquefort-style cheeses are both produced in Argentina, and are often used in sauces.

Pizzas are very good on the whole, though the toppings tend to lack originality. One popular ingredient will be unfamiliar to visitors – the palm-heart (*palmito*), a sweet, crunchy vegetable resembling something between asparagus and celery, is regularly used as a garnish. Argentine pizzas are nearly always of the thick-crust variety, wood-oven baked and very big, and meant to be divided between a number of diners. You might see some people liberally squirting ketchup or mayonnaise onto pizzas to liven them up, or perhaps Argentina's national condiment, *salsa golf*, a shocking-pink mixture of mayonnaise and tomato ketchup. Takeaway pizzerias are a thriving business all across the country.

BARBECUE BASICS

Asado (from *asar*, to roast) originally referred to a particular cut of beef, the brisket, meant to be slowly grilled or roasted, but now refers to the **barbecue** as a process and a rite; the Sunday *asado* is a sacrosanct male preserve, the pride of the true host, the length and breadth of the country. Since barbecues are an integral part of life in Argentina – and some of your best meals will be had at **parrillas**, restaurants specializing in barbecued food – it's good to know your way around the special vocabulary of beef-eating, especially as in Argentina beef isn't cut in the same way as in the rest of the world, although the cuts most resemble the British ones, sliced through bone and muscle rather than across them.

The first thing to note is that Argentines like their meat well done (*cocido*), and indeed some cuts are better cooked through. If you prefer your meat medium, ask for *a punto*, and for rare – which you'll really have to insist upon to get – it's *jugoso*. Before you get to the steaks, you'll be offered **achuras**, or offal, and different types of sausage. **Chorizos** are excellent beef sausages while **morcilla**, the blood sausage, is an acquired taste. Sometimes **provoletta**, slices of provolone cheese, grilled on the barbecue till they're crispy on the edges, will be on the menu. Otherwise, it's beef all the way.

After these "appetizers" – which you can always skip, since Argentine parrillas are much more meat-generous than their Brazilian counterparts – you move on to the **asado** cut, followed by the **tira de asado** (aka *costillar* or *asado a secas*) – ribs. There's not much meat on them but they explode with a meaty taste. Next is the muscly but delicious flank, or **vacío**. But save some room for the prime cuts: **bife ancho** is entrecôte; **bife angosto** or **lomito** is the sirloin (referred to as *medallones* when cut into slices); **cuadril** is a lump of rumpsteak, often preferred by home barbecue masters; **lomo**, one of the luxury cuts and often kept in reserve, is fillet steak; **bife de chorizo** (not to be confused with chorizo the sausage) is what the French call a *pavé*, a slab of meat, cut from either the sirloin or entrecôte. The **entraña**, a muscly cut from inside the beast, is a love-it-or-hate it cut, but aficionados claim it's the main delicacy in an *asado*. Rarely barbecued, the **peceto** is a tender lump of flesh often braised (*estufado*) and served on top of pasta, roasted with potatoes (*peceto al horno con papas*) or sliced cold for making *vittel tonné*.

Although mustard (*mostaza*) is usually available, the lightly salted meat is usually best served with nothing on it, but the traditional condiments are **chimichurri**, olive oil shaken in a bottle with salt, garlic, chilli pepper, vinegar and bayleaf, and **salsa criolla**, similar but with onion and tomato as well – everyone jealously guards their secret formulae for both these "magic" dressings.

VEGETARIAN FOOD

Asados are not for **vegetarians**, unless an evening of grilled cheese and salad appeals. Asian or Middle Eastern food (things like stir-fries, hummus and tabbouleh) may be the answer to vegetarians' prayers; in such a carnivorous land, real vegetarian food is very hard to come by and the phrase "*no como carne*" (I don't eat meat) is sometimes dismissed with a glib "*no tiene mucha*" (It doesn't contain much, referring to a pizza with a slice or two of ham on it, for example). That said, many locals are becoming aware of the health hazards of eating too much meat (an obsession with *ácido úrico* has become a nationwide mania), and health-food shops and "green" restaurants, some of them cooking very good food, are cropping up in towns and cities right across Argentina.

The other way to survive, apart from self-catering, is on a diet of omelettes, cheese *empanadas*, fondues or salads. **Vegans** will have a very hard time – veganism is unheard of in the country – and should be prepared for a constant battle of wits.

COCINA CRIOLLA

The nearest thing to a national cuisine is the traditional food based on local products such as maize, beans, peppers and squash, combined with European imports such as beef and pork, and known as *cocina criolla*. Not only is it delicious

and filling, it's also cheaper than other types of food and usually served in humble little *pulperías*. Indigenous fare has been adapted by the Spanish and other immigrants over the years to create a limited if distinctive selection of dishes.

Empanadas, associated with the Northwest but found all over the country, are turnovers or pasties that make excellent local-style fast-food and now come with a bewildering array of nontraditional fillings, including tuna, roquefort cheese and pineapple. They are either baked (Salta-style) or fried (more common in Tucumán, and Catamarca, known for its *empanadas árabes*, made with *carne picante* or *carne suave* – spicy or unspiced meat), but are invariably far smaller than their Chilean counterparts. The conventional fillings are beef, cheese and chicken. **Humitas** are made of steamed creamed sweetcorn, usually served in neat parcels made from the outer husk of corn cobs. **Tamales** are maize-flour balls, stuffed with minced beef and onion, wrapped in maize leaves and simmered. While the typical main dish, **locro**, is a warming, substantial stew based on maize, with onions, beans, meat, chicken or sausage thrown in. Less common but worth trying if you see it on the menu is **guaschilocro**, similar to *locro* but based on pumpkin.

DESSERTS

Although many meals end simply with fresh fruit, Argentines have a fairly sweet tooth and love anything with sugar, starting with the national craze, *dulce de leche*. Even breakfast tends to be dominated by sweet things such as sticky croissants (*media lunas*), delicious jams and honey or *chocolate con churros*, Andalucian-style hot chocolate with fritters, sometimes filled with *dulce de leche*. Ice cream, all kinds of cakes and biscuits including **alfajores** (maize-flour cookie sandwiches, filled with jam or *dulce de leche*, sometimes coated with chocolate), pastries called **facturas** and all kinds of candies and sweets are popular with Argentines of all ages. However, for dessert you'll seldom be offered anything other than the tired old trio of *flan* (a kind of crème caramel, religiously served with a thick custard or *dulce de leche*), **budín de pan** (a heavy, syrupy version of bread pudding) and fresh fruit salad (*ensalada de fruta*). And in Andean regions, you'll most likely be served *dulce vigilante*, a dessert consisting of a slab of a neutral, pallid cheese called *quesillo* and candied fruit such as sweet potato (*batata*), quince (*membrillo*),

---

DULCE DE LECHE

Dulce de leche, a sticky, sweet goo made by laboriously boiling large quantities of vanilla-flavoured milk and sugar until they almost disappear, is claimed by Argentines as a national invention, although similar concoctions are made in Brazil, France and Italy. Something called *manjar* is produced in Chile, but Argentines rightly regard it as far inferior. Argentina's annual production of *dulce de leche* could probably fill a large lake. The thick caramel is eaten with a spoon, spread on bread or biscuits, used to fill cakes, biscuits and fritters or dolloped onto other desserts such as *flan* and fruit salad. Some of the best flavours of ice cream are variations on the *dulce de leche* theme. Although some people still painstakingly make their own, most people buy it ready made, in jars. While all Argentines agree that *dulce de leche* is fabulous, there is no consensus on a particular brand: the divisions between those who favour Havana and those who would only buy Chimbote run almost as deep as those between supporters of Boca Juniors and River Plate, and foreigners are advised to maintain a diplomatic neutrality on the issue.

---

alcayote (a kind of spaghetti squash), pumpkin (*zapallo*) or lime (*lima*). *Panqueques* or crepes are also popular, stuffed with either apple (*manzana*) or the ubiquitous *dulce de leche*.

With such a large Italian community it is not surprising that good **ice cream** (*helado*) is easy to come by in Argentina. In fact the ice cream isn't good, it's superb, arguably the world's best. Even the tiniest village has at least one *heladería artesanal*, serving scoop upon scoop of ice cream of an amazing rainbow of colours to toddlers and grandparents and everyone in between. In cities, there are often dozens of different shops to choose from. The cones and cups are usually prominently displayed, with the price clearly marked. If you're feeling really self-indulgent you might like to have your cone dipped in melted chocolate (*bañado*). Some of the leading ice-cream makers offer an overwhelming range of flavours (*sabores*), including several variants of *dulce de leche*. Chocolate chip (*granizado*) is a favourite, and raspberry mousse (*mousse de frambuesa*) also takes some beating.

DRINKS

Fizzy drinks (*gaseosa*) are popular with people of all ages and are often drunk to accompany a meal, in this country where fewer and fewer people drink alcohol (even if wine consumption is relatively high) and drunkenness is regarded as a socially unacceptable, if minor, offence. All the big brand names are available, along with local brands such as Paso de los Toros whose fizzy grapefruit drinks (*pomelo*) are becoming increasingly popular. You will often be asked if you want **mineral water** with your meal – the carbonated versions often being referred to as *soda* – but you can ask instead for **tap water** (*agua de la llave*), which is safe to drink in most places (but best filtered in Buenos Aires and some other cities). Although little is grown in the country, good, if expensive, **coffee** is easy to come by in Argentina. In the cafés of most towns and cities – often trendy places where people gather to smoke, chat and watch the world go by – you will find very decent espressos, or delicious *café con leche* for breakfast (except in hotels); instant coffee is mercifully rare. The **tea** is usually made from teabags; grown in plantations in the northeast of the country, the tea is strong rather than subtle, and is served with either milk or lemon. **Herbal teas** or *yuyos* are all the rage, camomile (*manzanilla*) being the most common one. *Mate* is a whole world unto itself and is explained, along with the etiquette and ritual involved, in the box on p.43. **Fruit juices** (*jugos*) and milkshakes (*licuados*) can be excellent, especially in the areas where more exotic fruit are grown, but freshly squeezed orange juice is often sold at ridiculously high prices. Small cartons of apple juice, sold with a straw, are often good, but note the difference between juice and *néctar*: the latter are often very sweet juice-based drinks, some of which contain alarmingly little fruit.

Argentina's **beer** is more thirst-quenching than alcoholic and mostly comes as fairly bland lager. The Quilmes brewery dominates the market with ales such as Cristal, while Heineken also produces beer in Argentina. Mexican and Brazilian beers are commonplace but local brews are sometimes worth trying: in Mendoza, the Andes brand crops up all over the place while Salta's own brand is also good, and a kind of stout (*cerveza negra*) can sometimes be obtained in the

Northwest. Usually when you ask for a beer, it comes in large bottles (*tres cuartos*), meant for sharing, or in cans (*latitas*); a small bottle is known as a *porrón*. If you want draught beer you must ask for a *chopp*. **Wine** is excellent and not too expensive, though in restaurants the predictable corkage hikes the price up considerably. Unfortunately, most restaurants across the country still have limited, unimaginative wine lists, which don't reflect Argentina's drift away from mass-produced table wines to *vinos finos*, far superior single or double varietals of a quality that easily matches the best European and other New World wines (for more on wine, see the box on p.473). It is also difficult to buy wine by the glass, and half-bottles are all too rare. Cheaper wine is commonly made into **sangria** or its white-wine

equivalent, the **clericó**. Don't be surprised to see home-grown variants (*nacionales*) of whisky, gin, brandy, port, sherry and rum, none of which is that good. It's far better to stick to the locally distilled **aguardientes** or fire-waters, some of which (from Catamarca, for example) are deliciously grapey. There is no national alcoholic drink or cocktail, but a number of Italian vermouths and digestives are made in Argentina. **Fernet Branca** is the most popular, a demonic-looking brew the colour of molasses with a rather medicinal taste, invariably combined with cola, whose colour it matches, and consumed in huge quantities – it's generally regarded as the gaucho's favourite tipple. Indigenous peoples still make **chicha** from fermented *algarrobo* fruit or *piñones* (monkey-puzzle nuts) but this is difficult to obtain.

MATE

Mate is Argentina's national drink – though it's Uruguay's too – and on average people get through more of the stuff than coffee. Since pre-Hispanic times *mate* has been part of a ritual, but nowadays it's a daily custom, a simple and spontaneous act that brings people together. Complete strangers will often offer you some *mate*, which you might not like at first, as it can be quite bitter and has a sort of grassy aftertaste, but a refusal will be seen as a slight; anyway, it's a great way of meeting new people. The name *mate* (often spelled maté in English) comes from the Quechua *mati* or "vessel", referring to the native calabash in which it's traditionally drunk. In early colonial times the Church and Spanish Crown banned *mate*, but the colonizers went on drinking the bitter herb regardless and, as is usual with prohibited substances, it became even more popular as a result. There's even a Guaraní legend about how *mate* was "invented": once upon a time a poor old man offered a strange visitor, lost in the jungle, such generous hospitality that the guest's superior, Tupa the god of benevolence, rewarded him with the *mate* shrub and taught him how to make it into a drink.

Mateine is a gentler stimulant than the closely related caffeine, helping to release muscular energy, pace the heart-beat and aid respiration without any of the nasty side-effects of coffee, such as nervousness and insomnia. In the 1830s it even met with the approval of a wary Charles Darwin, who wrote that it helped him sleep. It's a tonic and a digestive agent, and by dulling the appetite can help you lose weight. Although its laxative, diuretic and sweat-making properties can be inconvenient, when they take effect at the wrong time and the wrong place, *mate* is very effective at purging toxins and fat, perfect after excessive *asado* binges.

If ever you do find yourself in a group drinking *mate*, it's just as well to know how to avoid gaffes. The *cebador* – from *cebar* "to feed" – is the person who makes the *mate*. After half-filling the *matecito* with *yerba*, the cebador thrusts the *bombilla* into the *yerba* and trickles very hot – but not boiling – water down the side of the *bombilla*, to wet the *yerba* from below, which requires a knack. If asked ¿*Como lo tomás?* answer *amargo* for without sugar, or *dulce* for sweetened; the latter's a safer bet if it's your first *mate* session, even if you don't have a sweet tooth. The *cebador* always tries the *mate* first – the "fool's *mate*" – before refilling and handing it round to each person present, in turn – always with the right hand and clockwise. Each drinker must drain the *mate* through the *bombilla*, without jiggling it around, sipping gently but not lingering, or sucking too hard (it's not milkshake), before handing it back to the *cebador*. Sucking out of the corner of the mouth is also frowned upon. A little more *yerba* may be added from time to time but there comes a moment when the *yerba* loses most of its flavour and no longer produces a healthy froth. The *matecito* is then emptied and the process started afresh. When the *cebador* has had enough, he or she "hangs the *mate* up". Saying "*gracias*" means you've had enough, and the *mate* will be passed to someone else when your turn comes round. The greatest honour comes when it's your turn to be *cebador*.

POST, PHONES AND EMAIL

Argentina's postal service, **Correo Argentino**, has improved vastly in reliability since privatization in the 1990s, but is still plagued by theft and loss. A smaller company, OCA, is fairly reliable but is of less use to foreign visitors as it serves only the domestic market. The telephone system is improving, both in terms of quality and price, though it has a long way to go to match services in North America, Europe and Australia; and Argentina is embracing the Internet – the network of coverage is expanding every year and finding places with public access is often easier than in Europe, North America or Australasia, since relatively few people own their own computer.

POST

Postal charges **to Canada and the US** are fairly high ($1.25 for postcards and letters up to 20g), and they're higher still to **Europe and Australasia** ($1.50); expect delivery times of one to two weeks, the quickest deliveries, unsurprisingly, being those out of Buenos Aires. **Express services** ($5.75 for 20g to the US, $6 to Europe) save a few days, but items are tracked only as far as leaving the country so it's worth spending the $2 extra to send them **registered post** (*certificado*) as well. You should send any important letters or packets registered, as this increases the likelihood of them reaching their destination (though registered items do also go missing), or use the expensive but more reliable special-delivery EMS packet service ($25 for 250g to the US, $27 to Europe).

Likewise, refrain from getting valuable items sent from home: normal post tends to come through fine, but any interesting-looking packet posted to you in Argentina should be sent registered. You are not permitted to seal envelopes with sticky tape: they must be gummed down (glue is usually available at the counter). It's worth noting that postal services in neighbouring Chile and Paraguay are both better value and more reliable, and that the Brazilian service is less expensive.

All post offices keep **poste restante** for up to a year. Items should be addressed clearly, with the recipient's surname in capital letters and underlined, followed by their first name in regular script, then "Poste Restante" or "Lista de Correos", Correo Central, followed by the rest of the address. Buenos Aires city is normally referred to as Capital Federal to distinguish it from its neighbouring province. Bring your passport to collect items ($1.50 fee per item). **American Express** also offers cardholders a mail collection service at their office in Buenos Aires. Address letters with your full name, followed by "Cliente de American Express".

For sending **packages within Argentina**, your best bet it to use the *encomienda* services offered by bus companies (seal boxes in brown paper to prevent casual theft by tampering). This isn't a door-to-door service like the post: the recipient must collect the package from its end destination (bring suitable ID). By addressing the package to yourself, this system makes an excellent and remarkably good-value way of reducing the weight in your pack whilst travelling, but be aware that companies usually keep an *encomienda* for only one month before returning it to its original destination. If sending an *encomienda* to Buenos Aires, check whether it gets held at the Retiro bus station (the most convenient) or at a bus depot elsewhere in the capital. Domestic rates for **letters** are reasonable ($0.75 for up to 150g), but the service is again quite slow – unsurprisingly perhaps, given the distances involved and the weak transport infrastructure. Calculate on a week for non-local letters to arrive.

TELEPHONES

Following privatization in the 1990s, Argentina's telecommunications system was carved in two: **Telecom** were the exclusive operators in the

---

GLOBAL CALLING CARDS

US AND CANADA
AT&T (☎1-800/222-0300) $10.12 for first minute, $2.92 thereafter.
Sprint (☎1-800/877-4040) $7.61 for first minute, $3.11 thereafter.
MCI (☎1-800/444-3333) $4.61 for first minute, $2.92 thereafter.

UK
BT Chargecard (☎0800/345144) £1.85 per minute.
Cable & Wireless (☎0800/096 1808) £1.90 per minute.

AUSTRALIA
Telstra Telecard (☎1800/626008)
A$1.20 connection, plus A$1.10 per minute.
Optus Calling Card (☎1800/557812) A$0.50 connection, plus A$0.85 per minute.

NEW ZEALAND
Telecom Calling Card (☎0800/26400)
NZ$2.80 connection, plus NZ$2.23 per minute peak rate, NZ$1.88 per minute off peak.

---

north of the country, **Telefónica** ran the south, and the two co-existed in Buenos Aires. As a consequence of these monopolies, Argentina suffered some of the world's most outrageous phone charges, especially for non-local domestic calls (over $1 a minute even for calls within the same province). Deregulation of the market in 2000 has seen the situation change, with the arrival of competition from foreign companies such as American Bell looking set to bring rates plummeting down.

One benefit of privatization is that it provided much-needed investment to improve the quality and extent of service, which is now generally good, although certain isolated rural areas still await their first phone line. Where there are no phones, the local radio station is your best bet for getting messages through in a hurry (see "Media", p.46). Virtually all phones have international access, and it is rare that you have a problem getting through.

By far the most common way to make calls and send **faxes** is from public call centres (*centros de llamadas*), known as **locutorios** (Telefónica) or **telecentros** (Telecom). You'll be assigned a cabin, and most have meters with which you can monitor your expenditure. Make as many calls as you want and then pay at the counter. Check all rates first before committing yourself to a chat, and ask for details of special international and domestic rates: there is usually a period of an hour or so in the day when calls are substantially **discounted** to prices well below normal off-peak rates (these sometimes differ to the discounted time on private lines). Off-peak rates generally start about 10pm for international calls and last till about 7am the next morning, and rates are usually fifteen to twenty percent less than peak

rates ($1.50 per minute to Europe as opposed to $1.80, slightly less for the US). When dialling locally, do not dial the area code, as there are areas where this confuses the computer and you can find yourself charged at provincial, not local, rates. Faxes are charged per sheet (normally $5 or $6 to Europe). Phone boxes on the street take coins or **phonecards**, which you can buy at kiosks or street vendors, but be aware that you usually pay more than the unit value of the card, and this surcharge varies, so shop around. In some of the more out-of-the-way places, **public telephones** take coins only ($0.10 coins upwards). The minimum local call charge is $0.25. For emergencies, some people carry an **international calling card**, billed to your credit card or home telephone account. However, rates for these cards are usually higher than direct-dial calls from the normal network.

Mobile or cell phones (celulares) are becoming increasingly popular, and call rates do not tend to differ much from land lines – but check first. One peculiarity to note about calling mobile numbers in Argentina is that you always need to use the **area code** in addition to the mobile number - and often you cannot contact an Argentine cell phone from outside of the country. Note also that rates for reverse-charge calls can be frighteningly high.

INTERNET SERVICES

Argentina is fast catching on to the **Internet**, and is one of the best developed of the Latin American countries in terms of using it as a business tool. However, prohibitive telecommunications charges and the fact that the majority of the population can't afford computers have retarded its spread amongst the public at large. Some outlying areas of the country are still not served by the Internet, while in some smaller places the service can be frustrating, with connections breaking off or downloading at a snail's pace, due to overcongested telephone lines. Having said that, most reasonably sized towns now have a public place for accessing the Internet, with rates varying considerably, from $3 to $8 an hour. Some places have Internet cafés or office rooms, but the telephone call centres are likely to be your first port of call. Not all places divide the hour, so check first. You can occasionally find free access in libraries and cultural centres. Try not to let Latin **keyboards** in this part of the world phase you: if you have problems locating the "@" symbol (called *arroba* in Spanish), hold the "Alt" key down and type 64; or in Chile, try the "Alt Gr" key and "2" simultaneously. If these don't work, ask. Printing off sheets is usually charged at $0.10 a sheet.

THE MEDIA

In terms of newspaper circulation, Argentina rates as Latin America's most literate nation, and it has a diverse and generally high-quality press. Its television is a rather chaotic amalgam of light-entertainment shows and sport; and its radio services tend to fall into one of two categories: urban mainstream commercial channels or amateur ones designed to serve the needs of local rural communities.

THE PRESS

In the past, the fortunes of the **press** in Argentina has varied greatly depending on the prevailing political situation. Overbearing state control and censorship characterized much of the twentieth century, typified by the Perón regime and the browbeating of the last era of military rule in the late 1970s, when, once Jacobo Timerman's *La Opinión* was closed down, the *Buenos Aires Herald* stood alone in refusing to let the issue of the disappeared slip off the agenda. The current situation is much more dynamic, and a resilient streak of investigative journalism provides a constant stream of stories revolving around official corruption. **Journalists** often take considerable risks in the process: one case that horified the nation was the brutal murder of a photojournalist, Cabezas.

Argentina's biggest-selling **national daily** is *Clarín*, which sells over half a million copies daily and over a million for its Sunday edition, which is packed with supplements, including an excellent cultural guide. The *Clarín* media group has a stake in several leading provincial dailies, such as the *Río Negro*, which are to a large extent reproductions of the mother paper but given a more local focus. *Clarín* also owns *Olé*, a paper dedicated solely to sport, with football taking up the lion's share. Second in importance to *Clarín* is *La Nación*, a broadsheet that was founded in 1870 by Bartolomé Mitre, a former Argentine president, and leans to the right of centre. It too prints a bumper Sunday edition. Unabashedly anti-establishment, *Página 12* is a paper with a distinct, trenchant style, a strong tradition of investigative journalism, and a particular penchant for harrying the ex-members of Latin military juntas who are guilty of crimes against humanity, especially the Argentine ones. One satirical cover it is fond of reproducing in this uncompromising crusade is a mugshot of whichever of these generals or admirals happens to be in the news superimposed onto the body of someone garbed in a prison uniform.

Argentina's **regional press** is also strong, though the quality varies enormously across the country. A handful of local dailies such as Mendoza's *Los Andes* and Córdoba's *La Voz del Interior* are every bit as informative and well-written as the leading national newspapers, and they contain vital information about tourist attractions, cultural events and travel news. The other advantage is they're often on the newsstands before the Buenos Aires-based titles arrive.

The *Buenos Aires Herald* is the continent's most prestigious **English-language daily** (dating back to 1876), with strong international news coverage and features from the international press, including Britain's *The Guardian*. In recent years, it has been headed by the astute author and commentator, Andrew Graham-Yooll. It is pitched at the highbrow end of the market and is well respected for the quality of its journalism but, unsurprisingly, it is still associated in the minds of many Argentines with the old-style Anglo-Argentine elite. It won international plaudits for its principled stand on human rights issues in the dark years of the last military dictatorship, but suffered during the Malvinas/Falklands war when distributors refused to stock it. Football coverage in its sports section focuses on British leagues rather than their Italian or Spanish counterparts. The *Herald* is reasonably widely available, but don't expect to find it outside major cities and tourist centres in the provinces.

Greatly admired for its independent investigative journalism is the **magazine** *XXII*, whose circulation is relatively minor due to its intellectual stance. More populist, but well worth checking out, is *Noticias*, a general-interest magazine that mixes well-researched investigative journalism features with a leavening of gossip and sport, and which includes a short section of international news. It takes particular delight in exposing alleged corruption within the circle of family and associates of ex-president Menem. Other magazines include *Gente* and *Caras*, which are glossies that form part of the tabloid press (*prensa de farándula*).

Newspapers and magazines are sold at **pavement kiosks**, usually found near the main square or bus terminals. In outlying areas, you pay a supplement (usually $0.20), and dailies often don't arrive till late in the day. International publications such as *Time*, *Newsweek* and *The Economist* are sold at the kiosks on Calle Florida in Buenos Aires, and you can normally track these down in other larger cities, although distribution can be erratic.

TELEVISION

Television in Argentina consists of a mix of football, soap operas (*telenovelas*), sport, chat shows, game shows and more football. For something a little more informative, try **TN**, one of the best channels in terms of heavyweight

news coverage (*telenoticias*), and you'll also find bulletins on **ATC**, **Telefé** and **Canal 13**. Cable TV is common in many mid-range hotels, and you'll pick up English-language news programmes such as **CNN** and, somewhat less commonly, the **BBC World Service**. **Fox** and **ESPN** cover worldwide sports, including baseball, NBA, and the English Premiership football. Syndicated foreign programmes on Argentinian terrestrial TV include two giants: *The Simpsons* and *The Teletubbies*.

RADIO

Argentina's most popular **radio** station, 100FM, plays a fairly standard formula of Latin pop; whereas Rock and Pop at 95.7FM veers, as its name would imply, towards Western music, especially rock and blues. Radio Mitre, at AM80, is owned by the Clarín group. The **BBC World Service** can be picked up on the following short-wave bands: in the morning on 6195kHz (49m band width), 15190 (19m) & 15220 (19m); during the day on 17840 (16m); and in the evening on 5975 (49m), 9915 (31m) and 12095 (35m). Broadcasts are also made on Radio Mania (AM 1670) and Radio Europa (FM 97.1).

Towns are blessed with a remarkable number of small-time radio stations, which are listened to avidly by locals, though they're rarely likely to appeal to foreign visitors. Should you ever lose anything or have documents stolen, these places are normally all too pleased to put out an appeal for you: indeed, this is usually your best chance of recovering your property. In rural areas, local amateur radio stations form a vital part of the community fabric, providing a message service that relays every conceivable type of salutation, appeal and snippet of gossip. You will hear everything from news of births and deaths, to people asking to be given lifts along little-transited routes. Messages normally go out twice a day (noon is a common time), and it is sometimes truly amazing how helpful and effective this seemingly rudimentary system can be.

OPENING HOURS, PUBLIC HOLIDAYS AND FESTIVALS

Most shops and services are open Monday to Friday 9am to 7pm, and Saturday 9am to 2pm. They may close at some point during the day for between one and five hours – as a rule the further north you go, the longer the midday break or siesta, sometimes offset by later closing times in the evening, especially in the summer. Supermarkets seldom close during the day and are generally open much later, often until 8 or even 10pm, and on Saturday afternoons. Large shopping malls don't close before 10pm and their food and drink sections (*patios de comida*) may stay open as late as midnight. Many of them open on Sundays, too. Banks tend to be open only on weekdays, from 10am to 4pm, but *casas de cambio* more or less follow shop

hours. However, in the Northeast, bank opening hours tend to be more like 7am–noon, to avoid the hot, steamy afternoons.

Museums are a law unto themselves, each one having its own timetable, but most close on Mondays. Legally, they are supposed to be free of charge at least one day a week; since that day varies you might like to plan your visits to different museums accordingly. Several Buenos Aires museums are closed for at least a month in the summer. **Tourist offices** seem to be forever adjusting their opening times, but the trend is towards longer hours and opening daily (some still close on Sundays). Don't bank on finding them open late in the evening or at weekends, especially off season or off the beaten track, though some have surprisingly long hours. **Post offices'** hours seldom vary from the standard 8am to 8pm on weekdays, with siestas in the hottest places, and 9am to 1pm on Saturdays, but check individual listings for exceptions. **Government offices** keep to an 8am to 5pm schedule, with a few variations.

PUBLIC HOLIDAYS

The list given in the box is of Argentina's **national holidays**, but some local anniversaries or **saints' days** are also public holidays when everything in a given city may close down, taking you by surprise. Festivals of all kinds, both religious and profane, celebrating local patrons such as Santa Catalina or

NATIONAL HOLIDAYS

January 1 New Year's Day (*Año Nuevo*).

Good Friday (*Viernes Santo*). The whole of *Semana Santa* or Holy Week, from Palm Sunday to Easter weekend, is a big event and traditionally a time when people go on the last vacation of the summer. Accommodation and restaurants stay open to take advantage of this. The Friday, and sometimes the Thursday, but not Easter Monday, are official public holidays.

May 1 Labour Day (*Día del Trabajo*).

May 25 May 1810 Revolution (*Revolución de Mayo*).

June 10 Malvinas Day (*Día de las Malvinas*). The anniversary of the unilateral treaty establishing

military rule by Argentina over the Falkland Islands in 1829 (only exercised briefly in 1982; coincidentally the South Atlantic conflict ended on June 10, 1982).

June 20 Flag Day (*Día de la Bandera*).

July 9 Independence Day (*Día de la Independencia*).

August 17 San Martín's Day (*Día de San Martín*). The anniversary of San Martín's death in Boulogne-sur-Mer, France, in 1850.

October 12 Columbus Day (*Día de la Raza*). Controversially commemorating the "discovery" of the Americas in 1492.

December 25 Christmas Day (*Navidad*).

the Virgin Mary, or showing off produce such as handicrafts, olives, goats or wine, are good excuses for much partying and pomp. In the Northwest, for example, there is probably a feast every day of the year somewhere (see box on p.408). In the Northeast the tropical mindset shows in the dedication to Brazilian-style carnival. Details of the more interesting fiestas are given throughout the text.

To avoid the old habit of "bridging the gap" between weekends and public holidays, some of the latter have been decreed movable feasts and are switched to the following Monday, but if they fall on Saturday or Sunday no day off in lieu is given. **Christmas Day** stays put regardless of when it falls.

In addition, although banks and government offices are closed on **Maundy Thursday** (*Jueves Santo*, the day before Good Friday), and

on December 8, the **Feast of the Immaculate Conception** (*Fiesta de la Virgen* or *la Concepción Inmaculada*), employers are allowed, confusingly, to insist that their employees work on those two "optional" holidays. **Museums** are often closed on those days and transport may be limited. **Banks** also close on December 31. Another important national festival (but not a bank holiday) is the **Día de la Tradición**, November 10, the climax of a week of gaucho parades, concerts and other celebrations (a sort of spring carnival), across most of the country. On the final working day before New Year's Day, ticker tape pours out of office windows in Buenos Aires' City district, and streamers are thrust into cars and bus windows, in the whole downtown area. Unless this is your idea of fun, this endearing custom makes it worth avoiding central Buenos Aires on that day.

CRIME AND PERSONAL SAFETY

Argentina is one of the continent's safest countries in which to travel and, as long as you take a few basic precautions, you are unlikely to encounter any problems during your stay. Indeed, you'll find many of the more rural parts of the country pretty much risk-free: people leave doors unlocked, windows open, and bikes unchained. More care should be taken in large cities and some of the border towns, particularly the northern ones, where poverty and easily available **arms and drugs make opportunistic crime a more common occurrence. Some potential pitfalls are outlined here, not to induce paranoia, but on the principle that to be forewarned is to be forearmed.**

By Argentine standards, **Buenos Aires** is currently suffering something of a crime wave, and incidents of violence and armed robbery (some by corrupt police officers out of uniform) are definitely on the increase. Porteños speak of these matters with mounting anxiety, and the De la Rua administration has vowed to make tackling crime and corruption a priority. It's sometimes difficult to know how much anxiety is due to a real increase in crime and how much to middle-class paranoia, but, in general, serious crime tends to affect locals more than tourists. Nevertheless, you should not take unofficial taxis from the airport and you're advised to be wary when taking a taxi from areas where serious money circulates (the new casino for example). Though Buenos Aires doesn't really have any "no go" areas, avoid walking around the quieter neighbourhoods after dark.

Taking some **basic precautions** will vastly reduce both the risk of you losing anything or of you getting into any situation you'd prefer not to be in. First, only carry what you need for that day, and conceal valuable items such as cameras and jewellery. Secondly, always try to look like you know what you're doing or where you're going, even if you don't: muggers and con-artists tend to pick on the less confident-looking tourists. Thirdly, if you're not sure about the wisdom of walking somewhere, play it safe and take a cab. Fourthly, always keep your bag secure – across your shoulders, rather than over just one – to cut out the chance of someone distracting you on one side whilst their accomplice snatches the bag from the other. Take especial care in markets and crowded places such as busy subway stations and bus terminals (particularly Retiro in the capital). Finally, beware of pickpockets operating on crowded urban buses and on Buenos Aires' underground. And in the rare event of being held up at gunpoint, don't play the hero. Locals warn that this is especially the case if your mugger is a kid, since they know that, as minors, they can't be jailed even if they shoot someone.

Theft from **hotels** is rare but, as anywhere else in the world, do not leave valuables lying round the room. Some hostels have lockers (it's worth having a padlock of your own), but in any case, reports of theft from these places are rare. Compared with other Latin American countries, you are extremely unlikely to have things stolen on **buses**, but it makes sense to take your day pack with you when you disembark for meal stops, and, particularly at night, to keep your bag by your feet rather than on the overhead rack.

Few of the more elaborate Latin American **scams** are practised here, but a weary one that still gets practised from time to time in places such as Buenos Aires is having mustard, ketchup, ice cream, mayonnaise or some similar substance "spilt" over you (often in the most unlikely of situations). Some "helpful" person (or persons) then offers to help clean it off, extracting your wallet or watch as payment. If this happens to you, push them off, get away from them fast and make as much noise as possible, shouting "thief!" ("*ladrón*!"), "police!" ("*policia*!") or for help ("*Socorro*!"). Note, too, that, though the police are entitled to check your documents, they have no right to inspect your money or travellers' cheques: anyone who does is a con-artist, and you should ask for their identification or offer to be taken to the police station (*gendarmería*). If you ever do get "arrested", never get into a vehicle other than an official police car.

Note that **drugs** are frowned upon in general. There is far more stigma here than in most European countries, for example, and Argentine society at large draws very little in the way of a line between "acceptable" soft drugs and "unacceptable" hard drugs. Drug use, particularly of marijuana and cocaine, is increasing amongst the younger generation, but you're very much advised to steer clear of buying or partaking yourself – the penalties are stiff if you get caught.

Women travellers are unlikely to experience any particular problems in Argentina: though you will receive plenty of male attention, it's very rarely threatening and far less likely to be backed up by the kind of aggressive drunkenness encountered in many European countries. A pervasive national custom is the *piropo*, a flattering comment made in the street, traditionally made by a man to a woman and often little more than a sharp intake of breath or a muttered exclamation, though sometimes far more elaborate and – occasionally – crude. Many, if not most, Argentinian women profess to enjoy receiving *piropos* and few find them offensive, but if they do irritate you, the best thing to do is simply ignore them.

It's always advisable to take photocopies of all important documents (passport with entrance stamp and entry card, airline tickets, insurance policy certificate and telephone numbers) in case of theft of the original: keep one with you, separate from the documents themselves, and leave another copy at home. And if you are unlucky enough to be the victim of a robbery (*asalto*) or lose anything of value, you will need to make a report at the nearest police station for insurance purposes. This is usually a time-consuming but fairly straightforward process. Check that the report includes a comprehensive account of everything lost and its value, and that the police add the date and an official stamp (*sello*). These reports do not cost anything.

EMERGENCY NUMBERS

Ambulance ☎107
Fire ☎100
Police ☎101

DISABLED TRAVELLERS

Argentina does not have a particularly sophisticated infrastructure for disabled travellers, but most Argentinians are extremely willing to help anyone experiencing problems and this helpful attitude goes some way to making up for deficiencies in facilities. There are also a couple of organizations based in the capital that can help you and several that can help you plan your trip before you leave home (see box below).

Things are beginning to improve, and it is in Buenos Aires that you will find the most notable changes: a recent welcome innovation has been the introduction of **wheelchair ramps** on the city's pavements – though unfortunately the pavements themselves tend to be narrow, are often littered with potholes or loose slabs and, especially in the microcentro, can become almost impassable due to the volume of pedestrians during peak hours. **Public transport** is less problematic, with many of the new buses that now circulate in the city offering low-floor access. For **accommodation**, the only sure-fire option for those with severe mobility problems are at the top end of the price range: most five-star hotels, including the *Marriott Plaza* and the *Sheraton* have full wheel-

---

USEFUL CONTACTS

USA AND CANADA

Directions Unlimited, 720 N. Bedford Rd, Bedford Hills, NY 10507 (☎914/241-1700). Travel agency specializing in customized tours for people with disabilities.

Mobility International USA, PO Box 10767, Eugene, OR 97440 (Voice and TDD: ☎541/343-1284). Information and referral services, access guides, tours and exchange programmes. Annual membership $25 (includes quarterly newsletter)

Twin Peaks Press, Box 129, Vancouver, WA 98666 (☎360/694-2462 or 1-800/637-2256). Publisher of the *Directory of Travel Agencies for the Disabled* ($19.95), listing more than 370 agencies worldwide; *Travel for the Disabled* ($19.95); and *Wheelchair Vagabond* ($14.95), loaded with personal tips.

UK AND IRELAND

Disability Action Group, 2 Annadale Ave, Belfast BT7 3JH (☎01232/491011). Information about access for disabled travellers abroad.

RADAR (Royal Association for Disability and Rehabilitation), 12 City Forum, 250 City Rd, London EC1V 8AF (☎020/7250 3222; minicom ☎020/7250 4119; *www.radar.org*). Provides brief lists of accommodation in Argentina; also offers good general advice for travellers with disabilities.

AUSTRALIA AND NEW ZEALAND

ACROD (Australian Council for Rehabilitation of the Disabled), PO Box 60, Curtin, ACT 2605, (☎02/6282-4333), and 24 Cabarita Rd, Cabarita, NSW 2137 (☎02/9743-2699). Provides lists of travel agencies and tour operators for people with disabilities.

Barrier Free Travel, 36 Wheatley St, North Bellingen, NSW 2454 (☎02/6655-1733).

Independent travel consultant, who will draw up individual itineraries catering for your particular needs.

Disabled Persons Assembly, PO Box 10, 138 The Terrace, Wellington (☎04/472-2626). Provides lists of travel agencies and tour operators for people with disabilities.

WEB SITES

www.access-able.com US-based site with scant information on Argentina but good general tips for travellers plus a forum where travellers can exchange information. Also links to other organizations and specialist tour operators.

www.sath.org The home pages of the US-based society for the advancement of travellers with handicaps, with plenty of tips on specific issues such as wheelchair access, visual impairment and arthritis – though no specific information on Argentina.

chair access including wide doorways and roll-in showers. Those who have some mobility problems, but do not require full wheelchair access, will find most mid-range hotels are adequate, offering at least spacious accommodation and lifts. In all cases, the only way of finding out if a place meets your particular requirements is to ring the hotel in person and make specific enquiries.

Outside Buenos Aires, finding facilities for the disabled is pretty much a hit-and-miss affair, although there have been some notable improvements at major **tourist attractions** such as the Iguazú Falls, where new ramps and catwalks have been constructed, making the vast majority of the falls area accessible by wheelchair. The **hostel associations**, Red Argentina de Albergues Juveniles and the Asociación Argentina de Albergues de la Juventud (for contact addresses, see p.30), can offer information on access at their respective hostel networks.

OUTDOOR PURSUITS

Argentina is a highly exciting destination for outdoors enthusiasts, whether you're keen to tackle radical rock faces or prefer to appreciate the vast open spaces at a more gentle pace, hiking or on horseback. World-class fly-fishing, horseriding, trekking and rock climbing options abound, as do opportunities for white-water rafting, skiing, ice-climbing, and even – for those with sufficient stamina and preparation, expeditions onto the Southern Patagonian Icecap. The Patagonian Andes provide the focus for most of these activities, most particularly the area of the central Lake District around Bariloche and El Calafate/El Chaltén, but Mendoza and the far northwest of the country, around Salta and Jujuy, are also worth considering for their rugged mountain terrain. If you're keen on any of the above activities (bar fishing, of course), ensure you have taken out appropriate insurance cover before leaving home.

RAFTING

Though it does not have the range of extreme options as neighbouring Chile, Argentina nevertheless has some beautiful **white-water rafting** possibilities, ranging from grades II to IV. Most of these are offered as day-trips, and range in price from $60 to $120. These include trips through enchanting monkey puzzle tree scenery on the generally sedate Río Aluminé, to the north of Junín de los Andes; along the turbulent and often silty Río Mendoza near

TOUR OPERATORS AND OUTFITTERS

Alessio Expediciones, C.C.33, Chacras de Coria, Mendoza (☎ & fax 0261/4962201; *aconcagua@alessio.com.ar*). One of the best local Aconcagua guiding outfits, used by many international groups.

Alquimia, Paseo Artesanal, Local "C", Junín de los Andes (☎02972/491355 or 02944/1561-0842). Small, enthusiastic agency that organizes climbing expeditions up Lanín and white-water rafting trips on the Río Aluminé.

Cumbres y Lagos Patagonia, Villegas 222, Bariloche (☎02944/423283). Offers white-water rafting trips on the Río Manso ($100 a day).

Estancia Huechahue, Junín de los Andes (*huechahue@jandes.com.ar*). Organizes horseriding trips.

Estancia La Maipú, Lago San Martín, Santa Cruz (☎011/4901-5591, fax 4903-4967). Organizes horseriding trips.

Fitzroy Expeditions, Lionel Terray 545, El Chaltén, Santa Cruz (☎ & fax 02962/49301; *troyexp@internet.siscotel.com*). Climbing, horseriding and trekking options, plus glacier iceclimbing and expeditions onto the Southern Polar Icecap.

Hostería Ayelén, Pasaje Arrayanes, Casilla de Correo 21 (☎ & fax 02972/425660; *charlesm@smandes.com.ar*). Experienced fishing guide, Charlie Muspratt, organizes bespoke fishing tours of the Lake District ($160 per day with transport).

the city of the same name, passing through barren mountain gorges; on the Río Manso in the Alpine-like country of the south of Parque Nacional Nahuel Huapi; and along the similar but less-visited Río Corcovado, to the south of Esquel. Esquel can also be used as a base for rafting on Chile's fabulous, world-famous Río Futaleufú, a turquoise river that flows through Chilean temperate rainforest and tests rafters, with rapids of grade V. You do not need previous rafting experience to enjoy these, but you should obviously be able to swim. Pay heed to operators' safety instructions, and ensure your safety gear (especially helmets and life jackets) fit well.

HIKING

Argentina offers some truly marvellous **hiking** possibilities, and it is still possible to find areas where you can trek for days without seeing a soul. Trail quality varies considerably, but many are difficult to follow, so always get hold of the best map available (for more information on these, see p.16) and ask for information as you go. Most of the best treks are found in the national parks – especially the ones in Patagonia – but you can often find lesser-known but equally superb options in the lands bordering the parks. Most people head for the savage granite spires of the **Fitz Roy** region around El Chaltén, an area whose fame has spread so rapidly over the last ten years, that it now holds a similar status to Chile's renowned Torres del Paine, not far away. Tourist pressures are starting to tell, however, at least in the high season (late-Dec to Feb), when campsites are packed and can become strewn with litter. The other principal trekking destination is the mountainous area of **Nahuel Huapi National Park** which lies to the south of Bariloche, centring on the Cerro Catedral massif and Cerro Tronador. This area has the best infrastructure, with a net-work of generally well-marked trails and mountain refuges. Though some trails become very busy in summer, there are plenty of them and you will always be able to find some less well-trodden ones. In the north of the country, some of the best trekking can be found in **Jujuy Province**, especially in Calilegua, where the habitat ranges from subtropical and cloudforest to bald, mountain landscape. **Salta Province** also offers a good variety of high mountain valley and cloudforest trails.

You should always be well prepared for your trips, even for half-day hikes. Good quality, **water- and windproof clothing** is vital for hiking in Patagonia and all other mountain areas: temperatures plummet at night and often with little warning during the day, and you put yourself at risk of exposure or hypothermia, which can set in fast, especially if you get soaked and the wind is up. Keep spare dry layers of clothing and socks in a plastic bag in your pack. **Boots** should provide firm ankle support and have the toughest soles possible (Vibram soles are recommended), as many types wear out with alarming rapidity on the stony trails. Gore-Tex boots are only waterproof to a degree: they will not stay dry when you have to cross peaty swampland. A **balaclava** is sometimes more useful than a woollen hat. Make sure that your **tent** is properly waterproofed and that it can cope with high winds (especially if you're trekking in Patagonia). You'll need a minimum of a three-season sleeping bag, to be used in conjunction with a solid or semi-inflatable foam mattress (essential as the ground will otherwise suck out all your body heat). Also bring high-factor **sunblock** and lipsalve, plus good **sunglasses** and headgear to cope with the fierce UV rays. Park authorities often require you to carry a **stove** for cooking. The Camping Gaz models that run on butane cylinders (refills are fairly widely available in *ferretería*

HIKING ROUTES

Please refer to the following pages in the Guide for further information on specific treks and trails:

hardware shops) are not so useful in exposed areas, where you're better off with a high-pressure petrol stove such as an MSR, although these are liable to clog with impurities in the fuel, so filter it first. Telescopic hiking poles save your knees from a lot of strain and are useful for balance. Miner-style head **torches** are preferable to regular hand-held ones, and gaffer tape makes an excellent all-purpose emergency repair tool. Carry a **first-aid kit** and a **compass**, and know how to use both, especially for the more isolated treks. And always carry plenty of **water** – aim to have at least two litres on you at all times. Pump-action **water filters** can be very handy, as you can thus avoid the hassle of having to boil suspect water.

Note also that, in the national parks, especially on the less-travelled and overnight routes, you should **inform the park ranger of your plans**, not forgetting to report your safe arrival at your destination – the ranger (*guardaparque*) will send a search party out for you if you do not arrive. See also the national parks section (p.59) for information on the low-impact trekking code.

You'd be advised to buy all your camping equipment before you leave home: quality gear is expensive and hard to come by in Argentina, and there are still relatively few places that rent decent equipment, even in some of the key trekking areas.

CLIMBING

For **climbers**, the Andes offer incredible variety – from volcanoes to shale summits, from the conti- nent's loftiest giants to some of its fiercest technical walls. You do not have to be a technical expert to reach the summit of some of these and, though you must always take preparations seriously, you can often arrange your climb close to the date through local agencies – though it's best to bring as much high-quality gear with you as you can. The climbing season is fairly short – November to March in some places, though December to February is the best time. The best-known challenge is South America's highest peak, **Aconcagua** (6962m), accessed from the city of Mendoza. Not considered the most technical of challenges, this peak nevertheless merits top-level expedition status as the altitude and storms claim several victims a year, some of whom are experienced climbers. Permission to climb must be obtained in advance from the Subsecretaría de Turismo in Mendoza, in person or through a tour company, and climbing fees are high (as much as $120 in peak season). Only slightly less lofty are nearby Tupungato (6750m), just to the south; Mercedario (6770m) just to the north, near Barreal in San Juan Province; Cerro Bonete (6872m) and Pissis (6779m) on the provincial border between La Rioja and Catamarca further north; and Ojos del Salado, the highest active volcano in the world (6885m), a little further north into Catamarca. The last three can be climbed from Fiambalá, where you're required to register with the police; but Ojos is most normally climbed from the Chilean side of the border. The most

---

USEFUL CLIMBING CONTACTS

ARGENTINA

Centro Andino Buenos Aires, Rivadavia 1255, Buenos Aires (☎011/4381-1566).

Offers climbing courses, talks and slide shows.

USA

American Alpine Club, 710 Tenth S, Suite 100, Golden, CO 80401 (☎303/384-0110, fax 384-0111; www.americanalpineclub.org). Annual membership costs $65, which includes free rescue insurance for peaks up to 6000m ($25 supplement for peaks up to 7000m), and a research service for specific articles or publications.

Club Andino Bariloche (CAB), 20 de Febrero 30, Bariloche, Río Negro (☎02944/422266; www.clubandino.com.ar). The country's oldest and most famous mountaineering club, with excellent specialist knowledge of guides and Patagonian challenges.

UK

British Mountaineering Council, 177–179 Burton Rd, Manchester, M20 2BB (☎0161/445 4747; www.thebmc.co.uk). Produces regularly updated and practical fact sheets on

mountaineering in Argentina (free for members, otherwise £6; membership £17). Excellent insurance services and book catalogue.

famous **volcano** to climb is the elegant cone of **Lanín** (3776m), which can be ascended in two days via the relatively straightforward north-eastern route. The two-day southern route involves tackling a heavily crevassed glacier and is for experienced climbers only.

Parque Nacional Nahuel Huapi, near Bariloche, offers the peaks of the **Cerro Catedral** massif and **Cerro Tronador** (3554m). And southern Patagonia has been a highly prized climbing destination ever since the Italian Salesian missionary, Padre de Agostini, published his *Andes Patagónicos* in 1941. One testing summit is **San Lorenzo** (3706m), which, from the Argentinian side, can best be approached along the valley of the Río Oro, although the summit itself is usually climbed from just across the border in Chile. Further south still are the inspirational granite spires of the **Fitz Roy** massif and **Cerro Torre**, which have few equals on the planet in terms of sheer technical difficulty and the grandeur of the scenery.

On all of these climbs, but especially those over 4000m, you must acclimatize thoroughly, and be fully aware of the dangers of **puna**, or **altitude sickness** (see p.34).

FISHING

As a destination for **fly-fishing** (*pesca con mosca*), Argentina is unparalleled, with Patagonia drawing in professionals and aficionados from around the globe. Trout, introduced mainly in the early twentieth century, form the mainstay of the sport, but there is also fishing for landlocked salmon and even Pacific salmon. The most famous places of all are those where the world's largest sea-running brown trout (*trucha marrón*) are found: principally the **Río Grande** and other rivers of eastern and central Tierra del Fuego, and the Río Gallegos on the mainland. The reaches of the Río Santa Cruz near Comandante Luis Piedra Buena have some impressive specimens of steel-head trout (sea-running rainbows or *trucha arco iris*), and the area around Río Pico is famous for its brook trout. The Patagonian **Lake District** – around Junín de los Andes, San Martín de los Andes, Bariloche and Esquel – is the country's most popular trout-fishing destination, offering superb fishing in delightful scenery.

The trout-fishing season runs from mid-November to Easter. Regulations change slightly from year to year, but **permits** are now valid countrywide. They can be purchased at national park offices, some *guardaparque* posts, and at fishing equipment shops, which are fairly plentiful – especially in places like the north Patagonian Lake District. Permits cost \$50, with permission to troll from boats \$20 extra. With your permit, you are issued a **booklet** detailing the regulations of the type of fishing allowed in each river and lake in the region, the restrictions on catch-and-release, and the number of specimens you are allowed to take for eating. Argentine law states that permit holders are allowed to fish any waters they can reach without crossing private land. You are, in theory at least, allowed to walk along the bank as far as you like from any public road, although in practice you may find that owners of some of the more prestigious beats try to obstruct you in this.

For more **information** on fly-fishing in Argentina, contact the Asociación Argentina de Pesca con Mosca, Lerma 452, (1414) Buenos Aires (☎011/4773 0821; *aapm@cvtci.com.ar*). Full details of fishing regulations are listed in an excellent illustrated **booklet**, *Nuestros Ríos y Peces* (in Spanish only), which is available from the Chaco tourist board.

In the north of the country, **sport fishing** for the powerful dorado is also very popular, and an international competition, the **Fiesta Nacional de Pesca del Dorado**, is held in mid-October off the Isla del Cerrito in Chaco Province (☎ & fax 03722/441033; \$150–200 entrant's fee). You do not need a permit to fish in **salt water**.

SKIING

Argentina's **ski resorts**, though not on the same scale as those of Europe or North America, attract mainly domestic and fellow Latin American tourists (from Chile and Brazil), as well as a smattering of foreigners who are looking to ski during the northern summer. Infrastructure is constantly being upgraded in the main resorts, and it's easy to find rental gear. The main skiing months are July and August (late July is peak season), although in some resorts it is possible to ski from late May to early October. Snow conditions vary wildly from year to year, but you can often find excellent powder snow. The most prestigious resort for downhill skiing is modern **Las Leñas**, which offers the most challenging skiing and once hosted the World Cup; followed by **Chapelco** near San Martín de los Andes (where you also have extensive cross-country options, plus views of Lanín), and the **Bariloche** resorts of **Cerro Catedral** and **Cerro Otto**, which are the longest-established in the country, and which are still perhaps the classic Patagonian ski centres, with their wonderful panoramas of the Nahuel Huapi region. Bariloche and Las Leñas are the best destinations for those interested in après ski, while **Ushuaia** is an up-and-coming resort, with some fantastic cross-country possibilities and expanding – if still relatively limited – downhill facilities. One of the advantages of skiing at Ushuaia is that the experience is enhanced by the wonderful scenic views of the rugged, forested Fuegian sierras and the Beagle Channel. Other, more minor resorts include the mountain bowl of La Hoya near Esquel (traditionally a late-season resort and good for beginners, see p.573); the tiny Cerro Bayo near Villa La Angostura; and isolated Valdelén near Río Turbio, with gentle runs on wooded hillsides right on the Chilean border. For updates on conditions and resorts, check out the Andesweb **Web site** (*www.andesweb.com*).

SPECTATOR SPORTS

Argentina suffers an incurable addiction to sport: its males go cold turkey at the thought of even one week without football, and you'll hear informed and spirited debate in bars on sports as diverse as rugby and the uniquely Argentine equestrian sport of pato. The country has few exports as prestigious and reliable as its polo and football players, but other sports have produced stars that have risen to conquer the world stage, typically delighting spectators with their flamboyance in the process – people such as Guillermo Vilas and Gabriela Sabatini in tennis, who reached their peak in the 1970s and 1980s, respectively; Carlos Monzón in boxing; and the legendary motor-racing driver, Juan Manuel Fangio.

PATO

The most curious of all Argentine sports is **pato** ("duck"), a sport that has its origins in the seventeenth century. The name comes from the original "ball": a trussed duck that the mounted teams would wrestle each other for, trying to secure possession and, with it, the honour of eating the unfortunate bird. It had to be banned in the nineteenth century due to the fact that the duck was rarely the only casualty: few holds were barred, and fierce gaucho brawls or horse accidents left many contestants dead. The sport was revived in the 1930s, but the duck is now symbolic: it has been replaced by a leather ball with six strap handles, and two teams of four riders compete to hurl it through a basket at either end of the 180-metre-long pitch. If you don't catch a live match, you may catch a televised game on one of the otherwise eminently missable rural farming channels. In November of each year, the national tournament is held in Palermo, Buenos Aires.

POLO

Of all the major sports played in Argentina, **polo** is the one you're likely to be the least familiar with. First played over two thousand years ago in Ancient Persia, the game became popular in the British Raj, and was adopted in Britain in the 1850s, when London's Hurlingham Club was founded. At first known as "hockey on horseback", it was soon called polo, from the Tibetan word for ball. Exported across the Atlantic to the United States in the 1870s, where the rules were changed, it began to be played on Argentina's estancias soon after and the **Buenos Aires Hurlingham Club** was established in the 1880s. By the 1920s Argentine teams were holding sway in the polo world; Argentina won the gold medal at the 1936 Berlin Olympics and have seldom been beaten internationally ever since. The country's *criollo* thoroughbreds – known as *petisos* – and champion *polistas* are exported worldwide; no leading polo team is complete without a troubleshooter from Argentina, proving that it's not just Argentine football players who earn lucrative livings as sporting mercenaries abroad. Ten-goal players (the top ranking) like Bautista Heguy, earn millions of dollars this way. In the country itself it's a game mainly for *estanceros* and wealthy families from Barrio Norte, but is nonetheless far less snobbish or exclusive than in Britain or the USA; there are some 150 teams and 5000 club members nationwide. One or two *polistas* are national heroes, worshipped as pin-ups and heart-throbs almost on a par with footballers and pop stars. Don't miss a chance to see an open championship match in the spring at the **Campo de Polo**, in Palermo, especially the final at the beginning of December. Even if the rules go over your head, the game is exciting and aesthetically pleasing to watch, with the galloping of athletic hooves over impeccably trimmed frescue and a virile ballet of horsemen waving sticks over their heads and whacking the ball the length of a huge green lawn.

For more **information** take a look at *www.polo.co.uk*. To find out more about matches and schools, should you want to learn to play, contact the **Asociación Argentina de Polo** at Hipólito Yrigoyen 636 (☎011/4331-4646).

RUGBY

Argentina has come to enjoy increasing levels of success on the rugby field. Rugby was introduced to Argentina in 1873, and the Argentine Rugby Union was founded in 1899. The country's national squad, the Pumas (founded in 1965), has gone from strength to strength in recent years, achieving their first defeat of England in 1990, and managing to secure fourth place in the 1999 Rugby World Cup. Although the game is popular in Buenos Aires city and province, many of the burliest figures come from Tucumán.

FOOTBALL

Football was introduced to Buenos Aires by British sailors in the 1860s, and by the end of the nineteenth century, amateur clubs had begun to spring up. In 1930, Argentina reached the first World Cup Final, before losing to the hosts, Uruguay, but with interest in the game booming, the domestic game turned professional in the following year. On the international stage, rivalry is hottest with Brazil. Argentina has twice won the **World Cup**: at home in 1978, and in Mexico in 1986. The 1978 World Cup was the most controversial of the competition's history: awarded during Isabel Perón's presidency, it became a political hostage of the country's military dictatorship, who saw in the tournament an opportunity to unite a riven nation and to demonstrate to the world the success of their regime. Money that was sorely needed for other projects (some $700 million) was spent on new stadiums and infrastructure projects, political opponents were rounded up, and despite growing international concern over human rights abuses, FIFA refused to change the venue. Argentina won the cup after a 3–1 victory over the Netherlands, among widespread reports that the Peruvian team was bribed to throw the match that led to Argentina reaching the final ahead of Brazil.

The domestic football scene is dominated by two colossi, **River Plate** and **Boca Juniors**. Both teams originated in the poor port area of Buenos Aires' La Boca, but have little else in common other than a shared hatred. Class divisions accentuate this rivalry. River Plate, founded by Englishmen in 1901, moved from La Boca to the more affluent area of Palermo in the north of the city, and it is traditionally the team of better-off Porteños. The team's kit is white with a diagonal

DIEGO ARMANDO MARADONA

The 1986 World Cup success was the defining moment in the career of **Diego Armando Maradona**, Argentina's most famous living sporting legend. Short, stocky, and blessed with a footballing genius that consensus places in the realms of that of Pelé, Maradona followed up his infamous "Hand of God" goal in the 1986 quarter-finals against England with a sublime goal that many regard as the greatest ever to bless the tournament, and did it wearing two different-sized boots since his right ankle was greatly inflamed by an injury he'd picked up earlier. Regrettably, his exquisite skills as a player were never matched by a corresponding ability to deal with the tectonic pressures of life at the top. During a spell playing in Italy, he became the darling of Napoli, but his time there ended in scandal, with a year's ban for cocaine abuse. Worse was to come, and he was expelled from the 1994 World Cup held in the USA, after a cocktail of ephedrine stimulants were detected in a urine sample. Many Argentines were outraged at the humiliation of their hero, and talked darkly of CIA conspiracies. For a large segment of the population, Maradona's skill excuses him all excesses, which are overlooked or forgiven as the behaviour of an archetypal *pibe* (a cheeky street rogue), and loyalty to the man runs deep, especially amongst those who support Boca, the Argentine team with which he is umbilically associated. For them, he represents a man of the people, who rose from the poor Villa Fiorito barrio to conquer the world.

red band, and their stadium, known as the Monumental or the Gallinera (Cock Pit), was the venue for the 1978 World Cup Final. Fans of Boca Juniors' (founded in 1905) are nicknamed the Xeneizes, which derives from the fact that the core of the club's early support came from Genovese immigrants, and the team has stuck loyally to its working-class roots. Their cauldron of a stadium, the Bombonera, is in the heart of La Boca, blocks away from El Caminito tourist street. The clash of these two arch rivals, known as the *superclásico*, is viewed with quasi-religious fervour and is given saturation coverage by the nation's media, both in the days leading up to the game and for the post-mortem afterwards. Neither team is completely satisfied about winning the championship if the season has been blighted by a defeat in the *superclásico*.

Boca are also notorious for their **barra brava**. Every team has a *barra brava* – organized mobs of fanatical supporters that are "sponsored" by the club with free tickets and transport to games. The *barras* have attracted fierce criticism in the press for their involvement in extortion rackets, drug dealing and political intimidation, and businessmen and corrupt politicos have been known to employ the *barras* as their hired heavies. Sporadic attempts at clamping down on the *barras* have had mixed success, but one significant prosecution resulted in José "The Grandfather" Barritta, a shady mafioso godfather figure who ran Boca's gang, being imprisoned for his role in the murder of two River fans in 1994.

Other important teams in the capital are Vélez Sarsfield; San Lorenzo, a team that has a nominal alliance with La Boca against River Plate and plays at the Nuevo Gasómetro Stadium; and **Racing Club**, who play in the deprived southern barrio of Avellaneda. Ignore the stench from the Riachuelo and head there to witness the extraordinary devotion of their fans, or *hinchada* (nicknamed the *Guarda Imperial*), universally acclaimed as the most fanatical of all, despite their team's lack of success on the field over the last thirty years and

numerous recent brushes with bankruptcy. Win or lose, the singing here is unbeatable. The strident antipathy that exists between Racing and local derby rivals, **Independiente**, comes close to the more famous feud between River and Boca. The city of Rosario has a similarly bitter clash, between **Rosario Central** (whose supporters are pejoratively known as *Los Canallas* – "riff-raff") and Newell's **Old Boys** (whose fans are called *Leprosos* – lepers). The only other cities that are represented by teams in the first division are Córdoba and La Plata.

If you can, be in Buenos Aires on a date that coincides with a crucial fixture for the national team: this is the best time to experience the full fervour of Argentina's passion for the game and, should the result go the right way, head to the **Obelisco** on Avenida 9 de Julio – the magnet for communal **celebrations**. Likewise, the Obelisco is the point of ritual homage for supporters of domestic clubs after league or cup success. Spectating at a domestic game can be an incredibly exciting experience. At present, the domestic footballing year is split into two separate championships: the opening one (*Apertura*), which is settled in December, and the closing championship (*Clausura*), which picks up after the summer recess and lasts until June. In January, some of the major teams from the capital decamp to Mar del Plata to play in a minor summer tournament. Seats (*platea*) at games cost about $20, but you'll get much more atmosphere on the **terraces** (*popular*, $10), though you should be aware that celebrations can get very rowdy: stand just in front of one of the crowd-control barriers so as not to get bowled over by the inevitable surge that follows a goal, and cede the very centre of the terrace behind the goal to the hard-core *hinchada*. Problems with crowd control are evidenced by the towering fences that surround most pitches. Also be aware that policing at the bigger games can get very heavy-handed: you may well be charged on horseback or baton-charged, so stay alert to avoid potential trouble spots.

NATIONAL PARKS AND RESERVES

The national parks of Argentina are one of the country's principal lures, encompassing the gamut of ecosystems and scenery that exist here, from arid dry chaco thornscrub to subtropical jungle, from high Andean peaks to Atlantic coastline. Though some parks were established purely for their fabulous scenery, many others – especially the more recently established ones – were created to protect examples of different ecosystems. In addition, some protect important archeological or geological sites. The parks vary in size from the minuscule botanical reserve of Colonia Benítez in Chaco Province, less than a tenth of a square kilometre in size, to the grand and savage Parque Nacional Los Glaciares in Santa Cruz, which covers some six thousand square kilometres.

These national protected areas fall into four different categories – **Parques Nacionales, Reservas Naturales, Reservas Naturales Estrictas**, and **Monumentos Naturales** – but the distinctions between them have little relevance to the tourist, although it is as well to be aware that a *monumento natural* is used to refer to individual species, such as the native Patagonian Andean deer, the *huemul*, as well as to places. More relevant to the tourist are the different degrees of protection that exist within the parks: strict scientific zones (*zonas intangibles*) that are not open to the general public, zones with routes of public access that are otherwise under full protection, and buffer zones where locals engage in certain limited forms of sustainable exploitation (such as forestry and the hunting of introduced species). The situation is complicated by the presence of indigenous communities in some parks, while in others there are enclaves of privately owned land which even *guardaparques* (rangers) must ask permission to enter.

The most famous **parks** of all are the subtropical **Iguazú** in the northeastern province of Misiones, with its famous waterfalls, and the great Patagonian parks that protect the lakes and subantarctic forests of the mountainous border with Chile – most notably **Nahuel Huapi**, by Bariloche in Río Negro Province, and **Los Glaciares**, near El Calafate in Santa Cruz, with its twin attractions of the Perito Moreno Glacier and the Fitz Roy trekking sector. **Lanín**, with its

famous volcano and monkey puzzle forests, **Los Alerces** and **Perito Moreno** (distinct from the glacier) are two other mighty Patagonian Andean parks, and in **Parque Nacional Tierra del Fuego** the Andes meet the Beagle Channel. One of the easiest national parks to access from Buenos Aires is **El Palmar**, in the province of Entre Ríos, a savannah plain studded with graceful native palms. Famous for its cloudforest are the northwestern mountain parks of **Baritú, Calilegua** and **El Rey**. Geologically fascinating are the spectacular canyon of **Talampaya** in La Rioja Province, and the **Bosques Petrificados** (Petrified Forests) in Santa Cruz.

In addition to the national parks, Argentina has an array of provincial **nature reserves** and protected areas, the most exceptional of which is the **Península Valdés** (see p.598), on the coast of Chubut near Puerto Madryn. Valdés is one of the country's leading tourist attractions and the most reliable of all destinations for seeing wildlife. Its marine mammals are the star attraction, principally the southern right whales which come to breed here. It is also one of the finest places to see the animals of the Patagonian steppe. Another good place for spotting this wildlife is at **Punta Tombo**, also in Chubut Province (see p.608). This reserve is most famous for sheltering the largest colony of Magellanic penguins on the continent. The **Esteros de Iberá** swampland in Corrientes Province (see p.318), is good for spotting cayman and capybara as well as a remarkable variety of wildlife. In Mendoza, the **Parque Provincial Aconcagua** was set up to protect South America's highest peak (see p.481), while **Ischigualasto** in San Juan protects a famous, desertified lunar landscape with bizarrely eroded geological formations.

INFORMATION CENTRES AND PARK ADMINISTRATION

The **National Park Headquarters** at Santa Fe 680 in Buenos Aires (Mon–Fri 10am–5pm; ☎011/4311-0303) has an information office on the lower ground floor, with introductory leaflets on the nation's parks, though some are occasionally out of stock. A wider range of free leaflets is often available at each individual park, but these are of variable quality and limited funding means that many parks give you only ones with a basic map and a brief park description. Contact the headquarters well in advance if you are interested in voluntary or scientific projects.

Nature enthusiasts would gain more from a visit to the **Fundación Vida Silvestre** than they would from a visit to the National Parks' headquarters in the capital. The Fundación, located at Defensa 245, 6∞, (1065) Buenos Aires (Mon-Fri 10am-1pm & 2-6pm; ☎011/4343-3778 or 4331-3631; *www.vidasilvestre.org.ar*), is a committed and highly professional environmental organization, and is an associate of the World Wide Fund for Nature (WWF). Visit its shop for back issues of its beautifully produced magazine, for books and leaflets on wildlife and ecological issues; as well as for information on its nature reserves. Birdwatchers should visit the headquarters of the country's well-respected birding organization, **Aves Argentinas/Asociación Ornitológica del Plata**, at 25 de Mayo 749, 2∞ "6", (1002) Buenos Aires Capital Federal (Mon-Fri 2.30-8pm; ☎ & fax 011/4312-1015; *aop@aorpla.org.ar*). They have an excellent specialist library ($5 per day for non-members) and a shop, and they organize morning outings once a month to the capital's prolific Costanera Sur marshland reserve (on weekends; $5), and **birding safaris** around the country (at prices far more accessible than most specialist overseas operators. A $50 annual membership for foreigners entitles you to their high-quality quarterly magazine, discounts on bird safaris, free access to the library, and the possibility of getting involved in scientific and conservation work.

Each national park has its own **Intendencia**, or park administration, although these are often in the principal access town, not within the park itself. An information office or visitors' centre is usually attached, and you can usually buy fishing licences here. Parks are often subdivided into more manageable units: the larger divisions of which are called **seccionales**, often with some sort of small information office of their own in the main building.

Argentina's **guardaparques**, or national park rangers, are some of the most professional on the continent: generally friendly, well-trained and dedicated to jobs that are demanding and often extremely isolated. All have a good grounding in the wildlife of the region and are happy to share their knowledge with those who express an interest, although don't expect them all to be professional naturalists – some are, but ranger duties often involve more contact with the general public than with the wildlife. You may need to register with the *guardaparque* before heading out on treks or to seek camping permits.

VISITING THE PARKS

All national parks have routes of public access, though many of the ones in more isolated areas – Baritú, Perito Moreno, and Santiago del Estero's Copo, for example – are not served by any public transport or even tour vehicles, and the only way of visiting is by renting your own transport. Most parks are **free** to visit, but in some of the more touristy ones, there's often a **fee** (usually $5 per visit), which is charged at the park gate. Scenic attractions such as the falls in Iguazú, Cerro Trondador and the Isla Victoria in Nahuel Huapi, or the Perito Moreno Glacier in Los Glaciares, thus serve to generate funds for less commercial parks that are still vitally important from an ecological perspective. In certain of the larger parks, such as Nahuel Huapi and Lanín, you are charged only to access the areas not served by a main public highway.

Camping is possible in virtually all parks, and sites are graded according to three categories: *camping libre* sites, which are free but have no or very few services (perhaps a latrine and sometimes a shower block); *camping agreste* sites, charging $2 per person, which are run as concessions and provide a minimum of hot water, showers, toilets, places for lighting a campfire, and usually some sort of small shop; and *camping organizado* sites, charged at about $5 per person, which have more services, including electricity and often some sort of restaurant. In some areas, Bariloche being the most obvious example, local climbing clubs maintain a network of **refuges** for trekkers and climbers. These range in quality from free places with ground space for sleeping bags but no services, to others costing up to $10 per person per night, with mattresses and meals available, and a small shop on site.

Always try to be **environmentally responsible** on your visit. Stick to marked trails, camp only at authorized sites, take all litter with you (don't burn it), bury all toilet waste and choose a spot at least 30m away from all water sources, and use detergents or toothpastes as sparingly as possible, choosing biodegradable options such as glycerine soap. Above all, please pay particular respect to the **fire risk** in all parks. Every year, fires destroy huge swathes of forest, and virtually all of these are started by hand: some deliberately, but most because of an unpardonable negligence. As ever, one of the prime culprits is the cigarette butt, often casually tossed out of a car window, but just as bad are campfires - both ones that are poorly tended and ones that are poorly extinguished. Woodland becomes tinder-dry in summer droughts, and, especially in places such as Patagonia, it is vulnerable to the sparks carried by the strong winds. Once started, winds, inaccessibility, and limited water resources mean that fires can turn into infernos that can blaze for weeks on end, and much fire-damaged land never regenerates its growth. Many parks have a complete ban on lighting campfires and trekkers are asked to take **stoves** upon which to do their cooking: please respect this. Others ban fires during high-risk periods. The most environmentally responsible approach is to avoid lighting campfires at all: even dead wood has a role to play in often fragile ecosystems. If you do need to light one, never choose a spot on peaty soil, as peat, once it has caught, becomes virtually impossible to put out. Choose a spot on stony or sandy soil, use only fallen wood, and always extinguish the fire with water, not earth, stirring up the ashes to ensure all embers are quenched.

WORK AND STUDY

Most English-speaking travellers seeking work in Argentina find themselves employment as English teachers. Traditionally there has been a slight bias towards teachers with a British accent, but there is such a demand for English language teachers in the country that those of other nationalities are unlikely to have difficulties in finding work. A TEFL certificate may be useful if you wish to work in a school, but often being a native speaker with a good standard of education is sufficient. Teaching can be a lucrative occupation here, and the highest rates are paid by large companies who offer up to $50 an hour for individual or small group classes. Informally, plenty of people set themselves up as private language teachers, advertising in the classified sections of local and national papers or on university or bookshop noticeboards. The downside of these informal arrangements can be finding yourself without work, and thus income, during the extended summer-holiday period – or left in the lurch when a student decides to cancel his or her classes. More financial stability – and a potentially more rewarding experience, since you get to mix with more locals – is offered by signing up for an official programme such as the Central Bureau for Educational Visits and Exchanges' Language Assistant programme, 10 Spring Gardens, London SW1A 2BN (☎020/7389 4169; *www.centralbureau.org*). Candidates for this programme should normally be aged between 20 and 30 and have completed at least two years of a degree or diploma course. The minimum language requirement is A-level Spanish and posts are for an academic year from early September to late May/early June: the level of responsibility can vary quite considerably from place to place.

Organized **volunteer programmes** are not particularly thick on the ground in Argentina, though you may have some success by approaching organizations which interest you directly. There are occasionally opportunities as a paying volunteer with the Earthwatch Institute, 57 Woodstock Rd, Oxford OX2 6HJ (☎01865/311600; *www.earthwatch.org*) on short environmental and archeological projects in Argentina. There may also be opportunities for volunteer work (only suitable for those with relevant experience or qualifications such as a degree in biology) within the national parks system: applications should be made, well ahead of time, to the national parks headquarters in Buenos Aires (see Nature Parks and Reserves, p.59).

Foreign university **students** may be able to enrol for courses in Argentina on presentation of an official letter from their own university. Academic standards in Argentinian universities are high: at the University of Buenos Aires in particular you will find lectures and courses given by many of the country's most respected writers, historians and analysts. Be prepared to find your classes taking place at any time between 7am and 11pm, though – the vast majority of Argentinian students work to subsidize their education (though public universities are still free, there are no grants for living expenses) and course timetables are consequently flexible enough to allow people to do this.

The only place where you'll find a significant number of **Spanish classes for foreigners** is in Buenos Aires. The best-value courses in the city are those at the University of Buenos Aires'

Laboratorio de Idiomas, 25 de Mayo 221, but are only really suitable if you're staying in the city for a while, since the courses usually run for several months. There are classes for learners or all abilities, including advanced and specialized week-long courses focusing on subjects such as pronunciation or current affairs. Other schools in Buenos Aires include Del Sur, at B. de Yrigoyen 668, 1st Floor (☎011/4334-1487; *www.delsur.com.ar*), and ILEE (Instituto de Lengua Española para Extranjeros), Av. Callao 339, 3rd Floor (☎011/4782-7173; *ileeovernet.com.ar*). Outside the capital, three of the best places to learn Spanish, in terms of quality of instruction and atmosphere, are Córdoba, Mendoza and San Rafael. Contact the Centro Cultural Anglo-Hispano del Oeste Argentino, Ortíz de Rosas 154, 5600 San Rafael, Prov. de Mendoza (☎02627/434688; *info@colegioargentino.com*); the IAIM, Rondeau 277, Mendoza Capital (☎0261/429-0269, fax ☎0261/424-8840; *info@iaim.com.ar*); or the Escuela Superior de Lenguas, Universidad Nacional de Córdoba, Secretaría de Extensión, ESL, Universidad Nacional, Av. Vélez Sarsfield 187, Córdoba (☎0351/433-1073; *secext@esl.unc.edu.ar*).

DIRECTORY

ADDRESSES These are nearly always written with the name only followed by the street number – thus, San Martín 2443; the only exception is with avenues, where the abbreviation Av. or Avda. appears before the avenue name – thus, Av. San Martín 2443. Pasajes (Pje.) and Bulevares (Bv.) are far less commonplace. The relatively rare abbrevi-

ation c/ for *calle* ("street"), is used only to avoid confusion in a city which has streets named after other cities: thus c/Tucumán 564, Salta or c/Salta 1097, Tucumán. If the name is followed by s/n (*sin número*), it means the building is numberless, frequently the case in small villages and for larger buildings such as hotels or town halls; we have not included the s/n abbreviation in this guide. Sometimes streets whose names have been officially changed continue to be referred to by their former names, even in written addresses. In most cities, blocks or *cuadras* go up in 100s, making it relatively easy to work out on a map where house no. 977 or a restaurant at no. 2233 is located.

BARGAINING There is no real tradition of haggling, although you can always try it when buying pricey artwork, antiques, etc. Expensive services such as excursions and car rental are obvious candidates for bargaining sessions while hotel room rates can be beaten down, off season, late at night or if you're paying cash (*efectivo*). But try and be reasonable, especially in the case of already low-priced crafts or high-quality goods and services that are obviously worth every centavo.

CONSULATES A very large number of countries from all five continents have embassies in Buenos Aires, mostly in the Barrio Norte, but in the provinces few countries maintain consulates. In the big provincial capitals you'll find diplomatic missions representing some other South American countries, along with those European countries with large communities in Argentina, especially Italy, Spain, Germany and Switzerland, plus the Netherlands.

EARTHQUAKES Seismic activity is very much a reality in western and, to a lesser extent, in north-western Argentina, since the Andes lie along one of the world's most unstable fault lines. Some of the planet's strongest ever quakes have hit the cities of San Juan and Mendoza over the last hundred and fifty years. Since then all buildings have been quake-proofed. It's unlikely that you'll find yourself in a violent tremor but, if ever you do, the first rule is not to panic. Don't use lifts or rush out into the street, whatever you do – this is how most injuries and fatalities are caused. Electricity supplies are programmed to go down if the quake is over five on the Richter scale.

ELECTRICITY 220V/50Hz is standard throughout the country. The sockets are two-pronged with round pins, but are different to the two-pin European plugs. Adapters will probably be needed and can be bought at a string of electrical shops along Calle Talcahuano, in Buenos Aires; some but not all of the multi-adaptors on sale at airports will do the trick, so check the instructions.

HOMOSEXUALITY The word that best sums up the attitude to gay men and lesbians in Argentina is ambivalence. Discreet relationships are quite well tolerated, but in this overwhelmingly Roman Catholic nation any "deviance", including any explicit physical contact between members of the same sex (let alone transvestism or overtly intimate behaviour) will be almost universally disapproved of, to say the least. Violent manifestations of homophobia are rare, however, especially now that the Church and the military have less influence on mores. Gay and lesbian associations are springing up in the major cities, notably in Buenos Aires, where nightlife and meeting places are increasingly open (see p.141), but rural areas still

do their best to act as if homosexuality doesn't exist. The same goes for even the most liberal-minded parents and, in this country where psychotherapy has become a pseudo-religion, don't be surprised to see analysts and "parapsy-chologists" advertising their "cures" – even in gay magazines. Arbitrary decisions by the myste-rious but powerful National Media Commission in recent months have resulted in raids at the offices of *NX*, the main gay and lesbian magazine (on sale in kiosks in downtown Buenos Aires and other big cities), because it printed pictures of "two men dangerously close to each other".

LAUNDRY Most towns and cities have a plenti-ful supply of laundries (*lavanderías* or *lavaderos*), especially since not everyone has a washing machine. Laverap is a virtually nationwide chain of laundries and is mostly dependable. Some of them also do dry-cleaning, though you may have to go to a *tintorería*. Self-service places are almost unheard of; you normally give your name and leave your washing to pick it up later. Laundry is either charged by weight or itemized, but rates are not excessive, especially compared with the high prices charged by hotels. Furthermore, the quality is good and the service is usually quick and reliable. One important word of vocabulary to know is *planchado* (ironed).

PHOTOGRAPHY Photographic film is not cheap and black-and-white and fast films, especially slides, are not always easy to lay your hands on, though standard film, of all brands, is widespread and reliable. Since fast film is recommended in places like the altiplano, bring a plentiful supply with you, and the same goes for all camera spares and supplies, which sell for exorbitant prices here even in the rare duty-free zones. Developing and printing are usually of high quality but are also quite expensive; slides aren't processed in that many places and black-and-white film won't always be accepted – outside Buenos Aires the situation is extremely erratic. A constant, how-ever, is that you should watch out where you take photos: sensitive border areas and all military installations, including many civilian airports, are camera no-go areas, so keep an eye out for signs and take no risks.

STUDENT CARDS These are not as useful as they can be in some countries, as museums and the like often refuse to give student discounts. Some bus companies, however, do give a 10–15 percent discount for holders of ISIC cards, as do certain hotels, laundries and outdoor gear shops, and even one or two ice-cream parlours. ASATEJ, Argentina's student travel agency, issues a booklet that lists partners throughout the country. The international student card often suffices for a discount at youth hostels in the country, though membership of the Youth Hostelling Association may entitle you to even lower rates.

TELEPHONE JACKS Argentina uses international standard telephone jacks (the same as those used in the USA), compatible with all standard fax and email connections.

TIME DIFFERENCES After some confusing experiments with daylight saving and even different time zones within the country, Argentina now applies a standard time throughout the year, nationwide: three hours behind GMT.

TIPPING Apart from the odd rounding up of taxi fares, for example, tipping is not common in Argentina. Restaurant bills increasingly include a percentage for service but any extra gratuity (*propina*) is discretionary. That said, Porteños have always traditionally tipped when eating or drinking out – recent austerity seems to have killed that custom off, or at least curtailed it.

TOILETS Occasionally central city squares include public toilets among their facilities, but otherwise public toilets or *baños* (men: *caballeros, hombres, varones* or *señores*; women: *damas, mujeres* or *señoras*), are very few and far between. The toilets in modern shopping malls tend to be spick and span and are often the best place to head for. In bars and cafés the toilets are usually of an acceptable standard and not all establishments insist that you buy a drink, though you may be made to feel you should (the legal position is unclear). It's worth knowing that toilet paper (carry your own), hot water and soap (*jabón*) are often missing. In bus stations, airports and large shops there is often an attendant who keeps the toilets clean and dispenses toilet paper (*papel higiénico*), sometimes for a small fee, usually $0.50. Note that, in rural areas or small towns, toilet paper must often be left in a bin rather than flushed down the pan, to avoid blocking the narrow pipes.

PART TWO

THE

GUIDE

CHAPTER ONE

BUENOS AIRES AND AROUND

F
ew journeys offer such a stunning introduction to a city as the aerial approach to **Buenos Aires**. The city – the third largest in Latin America, with around eleven million inhabitants – may not enjoy the dramatic scenery of, say, Rio, but what it does have is space; lots of it. Surrounded by the seemingly infinite pampa, Buenos Aires' sprawl is checked only to the northeast by the River Plate, an estuary whose great brown expanse in turn suggests a watery extension of these flattest and most fertile of lands. Just as impressive as this expansive vista, however, is the incredible regularity of the city's layout; with no geographical quirks to overcome, Buenos Aires is practically a blueprint for the strict grid system according to which the Spanish colonial administration built their New World cities.

On the ground, Buenos Aires initially seems to live up to this aerial impression of uniform vastness: the entire conurbation of **Gran Buenos Aires** covers some 1400 square kilometres, much of it taken up by nondescript suburbs, divided and subdivided by hectic motorways and flyovers. At the centre of the conurbation, however, sits the city proper or **Capital Federal** and, at its heart, you'll find a city on an eminently human scale. Buenos Aires is a city of **barrios** (neighbourhoods). In the downtown district these barrios merge somewhat – commerce and finance are the real defining boundaries of this area – but away from the city's compact core they assume strong individual identities. The strongest identity of all is worn by the highly idiosyncratic **La Boca**, the city's famously colourful southern port district and possibly the only place in the world where it's regarded as normal to paint houses, telegraph poles and trees in the colours of your football team. Adjoining La Boca to the north is the charming if occasionally crumbling cobbled neighbourhood of **San Telmo**, a bohemian mix of tango bars, antique shops and artists' studios. To the north of the city centre, there's the exclusive neighbourhood of **Recoleta**, synonymous with its fabulously aristocratic and ornate cemetery, and patrolled by designer-clad ladies-who-lunch and professional dog-walkers. In all there are 47 barrios in Capital Federal, forming a fascinating patchwork quilt of identities and provoking fierce loyalties in their inhabitants. For many people,

---

ACCOMMODATION PRICE CODES

The price codes used for accommodation throughout this chapter refer to the cheapest rate for a double room in high season. Single travellers will only occasionally pay half the double-room rate; nearer two thirds is the norm and some places will expect you to pay the full rate. Note that in resort towns, there are considerable discounts out of season.

① $20 or less	④ $45–60	⑦ $100–150
② $20–30	⑤ $60–80	⑧ $150–200
③ $30–45	⑥ $80–100	⑨ Over $200

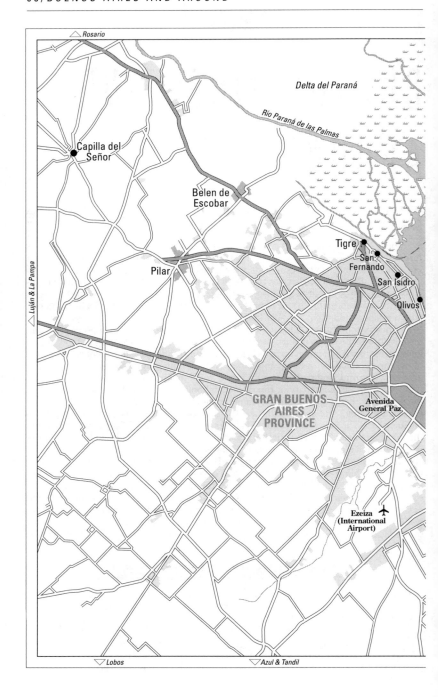

△ Rosario

Delta del Paraná

Río Paraná de las Palmas

Capilla del
Señor

Belen de
Escobar

△ Luján & La Pampa

Tigre
San
Fernando
San Isidro
Olivos

Pilar

GRAN BUENOS
AIRES
PROVINCE

Avenida
General Paz

Ezeiza
(International
Airport)

▽ Lobos

▽ Azul & Tandil

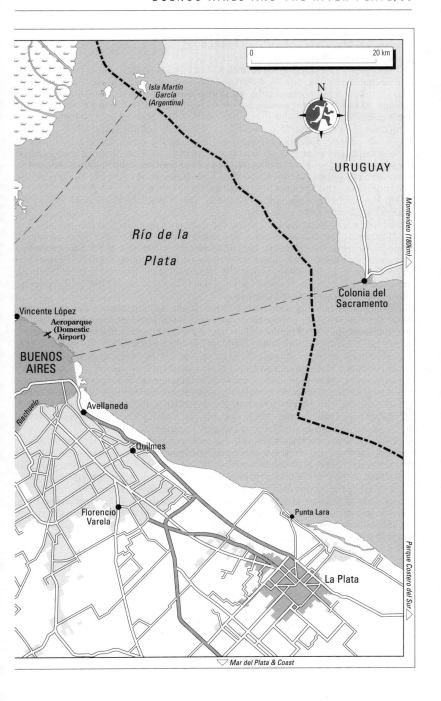

0   20 km

N

Isla Martín
García
(Argentina)

URUGUAY

*Río de la
Plata*

Montevideo (180km) ▷

Colonia del
Sacramento

Vincente López

Aeroparque
(Domestic
Airport)

BUENOS
AIRES

Riachuelo

Avellaneda

Quilmes

Florencio
Varela

Punta Lara

Parque Costero del Sur ▷

La Plata

▽ Mar del Plata & Coast

these neighbourhoods are Buenos Aires' best sights, more intriguing than the majority of the city's museums, churches or monuments and requiring nothing more than a bit of time and walking around to be enjoyed.

Even more important than divisions between barrios, though, is that between **north** and **south**. Ever since the city's elite fled the southern barrio of San Telmo in 1871, after a yellow fever epidemic, the north has been where you'll find Buenos Aires' monied classes, while the south is largely working class. This division of wealth shows itself clearly on the streets of Buenos Aires: the north is dominated by high-rise constructions and grand late nineteenth-century mansions and apartment blocks, whilst in the south low-rise buildings predominate, marking the area's much slower pace of development. The **centre** is perhaps best regarded as a kind of buffer zone between these two; no one feels out of place on busy pedestrianized Calle Florida or bookshop, cinema and café-lined Avenida Corrientes. Equally, the **west** of the city is a kind of neutral zone, largely middle class with pockets of both wealth and poverty.

For the tourist, all these areas of the city have something to offer. As well as the glamour of Recoleta, the main draw in the north are the city's best museums, and the landscaped parks, botanical garden and zoo of Buenos Aires' largest and greenest barrio, **Palermo**. The south is much more about soaking up the city's most traditional atmosphere while the centre is a kind of mixture of both these attractions, wrapped up in a sometimes hectic atmosphere but with plenty of welcoming cafés, bookstores and cultural centres to ease things along. The attractions of the west are scattered through various barrios and include one of the city's most enjoyable events, the Sunday **gaucho fair** in the outlying barrio of Mataderos.

Buenos Aires is one of Latin America's most culturally distinctive cities and there is both cliché and truth in its popular image as the home of tango, football and Evita. All make their presence felt on the streets, and no one witnessing the mass celebrations after a major football victory would doubt its importance in local life. Yet to sum up the city in terms of its most famous cultural icons would be to do an injustice to its diversity and subtlety. The city's elusive quality was perhaps best captured by Argentina's greatest writer, Jorge Luis Borges, who said it "inhabits me like a poem that I haven't yet managed to put down in words". Far less elusive, however, is Buenos Aires' linguistic identity; the heavily inflected, almost Italian-sounding Spanish of the city's inhabitants – liberally peppered with *lunfardo*, the capital's idiosyncratic slang – is one of the Spanish-speaking world's most instantly recognizable accents.

Above all, the capital is an immensely enjoyable place: one of the world's great 24-hour cities, it is perhaps one of the few where you'll find yourself with standing-room only on a bus in the early hours of a weekday morning. Whatever time you hit the streets, you'll find **Porteños**, as the city's inhabitants are known (from puerto, meaning port), in animated conversation over an espresso in one of the city's ubiquitous confiterías, or cafés. And unlike some of the continent's more Americanized cities, such as Caracas or São Paulo (and despite the ever-increasing traffic), Buenos Aires is still a great city to walk around. In addition, you'll find its central streets agreeably populated at most hours of the night: not only with revellers but with people walking their dog or nipping out for a coffee.

Around Buenos Aires are a number of worthwhile attractions. To the north lie wealthy suburbs such as Olivos, home to the presidential residence, leafy villa-lined **Vicente López** and **San Isidro** whose winding cobbled streets look down on the silvery brown waters of the River Plate. Beyond San Isidro, and only an hour from the city centre, you'll find one of the region's most beautiful and unexpected landscapes: the **Paraná Delta** where traditional wooden houses on stilts sit amongst lush subtropical vegetation. The Delta is reached via the town of **Tigre**, from where boat trips can also be taken to **Isla Martín García**, a former penal colony and now a nature reserve, as well as to the Uruguayan coast. Just across the River Plate, the Uruguayan town of **Colonia del Sacramento** makes an excellent overnight trip from Buenos Aires, as much for its laid-back atmosphere as for its stunning colonial architecture.

Some history

The first attempt to establish a settlement on the banks of the River Plate estuary took place twenty years after the region had been discovered by the Portuguese navigator Juan de Solís. In 1536, the Spanish aristocrat **Pedro de Mendoza** founded the settlement of **Nuestra Señora de Santa María del Buen Aire**, named after the patron saint of sailors – provider of the *buen aire*, or good wind. Mendoza's expedition was composed of 1600 men, three times the number that had accompanied Cortés in his conquest of Mexico sixteen years previously. To some extent, it was the very size of Mendoza's expedition that proved its downfall: they arrived too late in the year to sow crops and attempts to co-opt the native nomadic Indians into gathering supplies for the party proved understandably unsuccessful. With little foodstuff available to them, apart from fish, and under mounting attacks from a now hostile Indian population, the settlers were forced to abandon the settlement after five years – though not before many of them had starved to death or been killed by Indians (only eighteen months after its arrival, the party had already been reduced by two thirds). The remaining settlers fled upriver to Asunción del Paraguay, which had been founded by a section of Mendoza's party in 1537, leaving behind a granary and a few horses which soon multiplied on the fertile grasslands of the pampa. Forty years passed before an expedition led by **Juan de Garay** headed back down the Paraná River and, in 1580, **refounded the city**. This time around, the enterprise proved successful: provisions were now available from Asunción – where the settlers had encountered a more co-operative group of indigenous inhabitants and had managed to sow crops – and Santa Fe, founded by Garay on his way downriver. With cattle, cereal and horses available from these other sources, Garay's men did not need to resort to the co-ercive tactics employed earlier, and relations with the local Indians were more peaceful, if not entirely trouble free. Thus the tiny settlement began a period of slow but steady **expansion**. Nonetheless, its early growth was hampered by colonial restrictions on the flow of commerce to and from the River Plate region. The Spanish crown had supported the second founding of Buenos Aires primarily as a military garrison, and was anxious that the new settlement should not flourish as a port and thus allow non-Spanish goods to flood into its colonial markets. Buenos Aires protested bitterly to Spain throughout the seventeenth century, complaining that **trade restrictions** were impeding the city's growth. To some extent, however, it was colonial restrictions that sparked the ascendancy of Buenos Aires. Deprived of a stable source of imports and income, the city turned to **contraband** – primarily exporting silver from the mines of Potosí, in Upper Peru (now Bolivia) in exchange for slaves and manufactured goods from Portugal. The city's strategic location helped too: lying at the mouth of the River Plate, it was the logical point of entry for commerce from Europe, as well as being in a position to control trade with the Littoral provinces further up the Paraná and Uruguay rivers which merge in the waters of the mighty estuary.

By the mid-eighteenth century, Buenos Aires had 12,000 inhabitants, twice as many as any city in the interior. Trade relations with Spain also improved as crown policy switched from attempting to stifle commerce to competing with rivals by drastically increasing imports. Nonetheless, the Spanish grip on the New World was weakening. The last attempt to shore up the empire came with the **Bourbon reforms** of the late eighteenth century; in 1776 Spain gave the Argentine territories the status of Viceroyalty of the River Plate, with Buenos Aires as the capital. Trade was further liberalized with the introduction of the *comercio libre* (free trade) under which the old trading monopolies were abolished, along with various taxes. But though *comercio libre* marked an improvement on Spain's previous stranglehold on commerce, it proved to be misleadingly named. The aim was not to encourage all trade, but specifically that between the various colonies and Spain: foreign goods were only legally available as re-exports through Spain, and then with punitive tariffs applied to them. Yet in spite of these taxes, foreign goods were still sufficiently higher in quality or lower in price to ensure their dominance – either as re-exports or contraband. Spain's military conflicts with the British and the Portuguese during the late eighteenth century further weakened colonial commercial links – as Spain showed itself unable to keep its colonies supplied with goods. **Independence**, declared in 1816 and consolidated during the 1820s, freed the new capital from the last vestiges of colonial hindrance, but Buenos Aires maintained a rather tenuous grip over a country bitterly divided between unitarians and federalists. The real turning point came with the **federalization** of the capital in 1880, when the city was detached from the province and made federal capital of the republic. Combined with the driving back of the frontier to the south of Buenos Aires, through General Roca's infamous **Conquest of the Wilderness** in 1879, this ratification of Buenos Aires' special status paved the way for a period of phenomenal expansion.

Few cities in the world can have experienced a period of such astonishing growth as that which swept Buenos Aires between 1880 and 1914. Finally able to exploit and export the great riches of the pampa thanks to technological advances such as the steam ship and the railway and to massive foreign investment – most notably from the British – Buenos Aires leapt into the ranks of the world's great cities. European immigrants flocked to the capital, whose population doubled from 286,000 to 526,000 between 1880 to 1890, and by 1900 it was the largest city in Latin America with a population of around 800,000. The standard of living of its growing middle classes – the largest of any city in Latin America – equalled or surpassed that of many European countries, whilst the incredible wealth of the city's elite had few parallels anywhere. At the same time, however, much of the large working-class community – many of whom were immigrants – endured appalling conditions in the city's overcrowded *conventillos* or tenement buildings, in which up to ten people shared a room. And, though the city was becoming a byword for wealth and elegance, Buenos Aires was also earning a less glamorous reputation as the centre of **white slave traffic** from Europe. This sleazy side notwithstanding, Buenos Aires was still a city of grand ambitions. Remodelled along the lines of Haussmann's Paris in the 1880s – when the parallel avenues Santa Fe, Córdoba, Corrientes and the Avenida de Mayo were constructed, and interconnected by trams, buses and, in the early twentieth century, by Latin America's first underground railway – Buenos Aires had little cause to envy the capitals of the old continent. In 1926, both horrified and impressed by Buenos Aires' incredible dynamism, visiting French architect Le Corbusier felt compelled to describe the city as "a gigantic agglomeration of insatiable energy".

By the mid-twentieth century, however, this period of breakneck development had come to a close: the country as a whole was sliding into crisis and growth in the capital declined to match. In fact, since around 1950, the population of Capital Federal has remained more or less constant at around three million. The major addition to the cityscape during this period has been the construction of numerous high-rise apartment blocks, principally in the north and west of the city. In terms of the city's population, the legacy of European **immigration** remains (around ten percent of the city's population is European born), but the most recent influx of immigrants has been from Argentina's poorer provinces and neighbouring countries, many of whom settle in the capital's growing number of shanty towns. Euphemistically termed *villas de emergencia* in reference to their supposed temporary status, these shanty towns are more commonly and accurately known as **villas miseria**.

In stark contrast to these pockets of deprivation, the stabilization of the country's currency in the 1990s brought a new upsurge in spending by those who could afford it – and an infrastructure to match. Smart new shopping malls, restaurants and cinema complexes have sprung up around the city and are changing the way many Porteños live. Lofts, sushi bars and drive-in fast-food outlets have all become part of the city's identity, as have secure private housing estates (known as *countrys*) on the outskirts of the city. To some extent, this new Buenos Aires has prospered at the expense of the old city: the once bustling centre, for example, is no longer the major focus of cultural and social life. In spite of it all, though, Buenos Aires still feels like a fairly democratic place – the sharp and often shocking divisions of wealth that characterize many other Latin America cities are still far from being a defining feature of Argentina's capital.

BUENOS AIRES

BUENOS AIRES is a city which lends itself perfectly to aimless wandering. Though vast, it's mostly a very walkable place, and orientating yourself is made pretty straightforward thanks to the city's regular and logical grid pattern. The city is approximately triangular in shape and its boundaries are marked by **Avenida General Paz** to the west, the **River Plate** to the northeast and by its tributary, the **Riachuelo**, to the south. Holding the whole thing together is **Avenida Rivadavia**, an immensely long street (Porteños claim it is the longest in the world) which runs east to west for nearly two hundred blocks from Plaza de Mayo to Morón, outside the city limits. Parallel to Avenida Rivadavia run four major avenues, Avenida de Mayo, Corrientes, Córdoba and Santa Fe. The major north–south routes through the city centre are, to the east, Avenida L.N. Além – which changes its name to Avenida del Libertador as it swings out to the northern suburbs – and, to the west, Avenida Callao. Through the very heart of the centre runs the spectacularly wide Avenida 9 de Julio – an aggressively car-orientated conglomeration of four multi-lane roads.

The **city centre** is bounded approximately by Avenida de Mayo to the south, Avenida L.N. Além to the east, Avenida Córdoba to the north and Avenida Callao to the west. At its southeastern corner lies the city's foundational square, the **Plaza de Mayo**, centrepiece of the Haussmann-style remodelling that took place here in the late nineteenth century, and home to the governmental palace, the **Casa Rosada**. Within the centre lie the financial district, **La City**, and major shopping, eating and accommodation districts. It's a hectic place, particularly during the week, but from the bustle of **Florida**, the area's busy pedestrianized thoroughfare, to the *fin-de-siècle* elegance of **Avenida de Mayo** and the café culture of **Corrientes**, the area is surprisingly varied in both architecture and atmosphere. With the exception of the Plaza de Mayo and the Teatro Colón – Buenos Aires' world-renowned opera house – it's perhaps not so much the centre's sights that are the main draw but rather the strongly defined character of its streets, which provide a perfect introduction to the rhythm of Porteño life.

The **south** of the city – for many tourists and locals alike, its most intriguing area – begins just beyond Plaza de Mayo. It contains the oldest part of the city and its narrow, often cobbled streets are lined with some of the capital's finest architecture, typified by compact late nineteenth-century town houses with ornate Italianate facades, sturdy but elegant wooden doors and finely wrought iron railings. From the cultivated charm of **San Telmo**, setting for the city's popular Sunday antique market, to the passionate atmosphere of **La Boca** on match days, when the neighbourhood seems to drown in a sea of blue and yellow, the south offers an appealing mix of tradition and popular culture. It's also home to one of the city's most unusual green spaces, the unexpectedly wild **Reserva Ecológica**, which lies out to the east, beyond the chaotic rumble of lorries which trundle along the city's dock area.

The **north** of the city is generally regarded as beginning at Avenida Córdoba. Four of the area's neighbourhoods, **Retiro** and **Recoleta** – jointly known as Barrio Norte, plus **Palermo** and **Belgrano**, are renowned for their palaces, plazas and parks. They're the city's mostly wealthy garden barrios, swallowed up one after another as Buenos Aires expanded northwards, following the fatal epidemics that struck the south in the 1860s and 1870s, and as the city's population swelled. Set off against luxuriant native trees such as jacarandas and tipas, the architectural styles of the many aristocratic palaces are part Spanish and part British, but overwhelmingly French. Some are now open to the public,

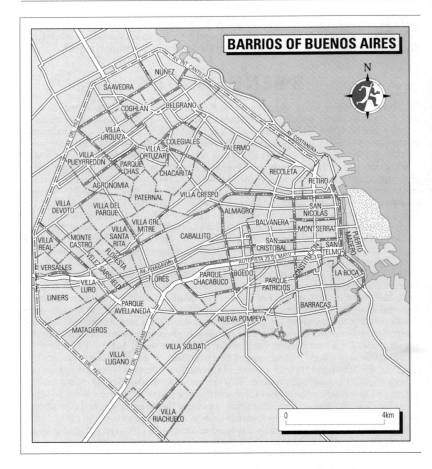

and this is where you'll find some of the city's finest **museums** – such as Retiro's Museo de Arte Hispanoamericano, Palermo's Museo de Arte Decorativo, and Belgrano's Museo de Arte Español. Despite opposition from the city elite, Evita is buried at **La Recoleta**, one of the world's most astonishing cemeteries, in terms of atmosphere and the sheer beauty of its tombs. Further north, incredibly wide avenues sweep past landscaped gardens, including a Japanese Garden, enormous parks, such as Parque 3 de Febrero, and some of the country's major sports venues, including the National Polo Field. Pockets of mid-nineteenth-century Buenos Aires are still left, the most atmospheric of all being **Palermo Viejo**, whose cobbled streets and single-storey houses contrast with the grandiose houses and high-rise apartment blocks that populate most of this side of the city.

Beyond Avenida Callao lies **the west**, an immense, mostly residential district which has its own commercial centre around the barrios of Caballito and Flores. There are only a small number of sights to see in this area, but two of the best of them are amongst Buenos Aires' most idiosyncratic offerings. No one with the remotest interest in tango should neglect to pay a visit to the shrine-like tomb of Carlos Gardel, the nation's most famous singer, in the huge cemetery of **Chacarita**, whilst the Sunday gaucho fair in the barrio of **Mataderos** offers the unforgettable sight of dashingly

dressed horsemen galloping through the city streets, as well as providing an authentic brew of regional cooking and live folk music.

Arrival and information

Buenos Aires is well served by numerous international and national **flights**. It is also a transport hub for the rest of the country, with frequent daily **bus services** to and from most towns and cities. Arriving by **train** these days is less common; the withdrawal of government subsidies to provincial rail services has left few long-distance connections to the capital. Additionally, there are **ferry** services from Uruguay (see p.159).

For **information**, head to the city's Secretaría de Turismo at Sarmiento 1551, 5th Floor (Mon–Fri 10am–5pm; ☎011/4372-3612, *www.buenosaires.gov.ar*), a useful port of call for specialized enquiries; otherwise the information on offer at the various **kiosks** in the city centre is more than adequate – the most useful of these is at Avenida Diagonal Roque Sáenz Peña and Florida (Mon–Fri 9am–5pm), but there are others in the Galerías Pacífico shopping centre on Florida and Córdoba (1st Floor; (Mon–Fri

10am–7pm, Sat 11am–7pm), in the Café Tortoni at Av. de Mayo 829 (Mon–Fri 2–6pm), and on the corner of Lamadrid and Caminito in La Boca (Fri, Sat & Sun 10am–5pm). All of them offer standard tourist leaflets and maps. Also look out for the free tango publications *El Tangauta* and *Buenos Aires Tango* and the excellent cultural **listings magazine** *Fervor de Buenos Aires*, available at all kiosks, but most reliably at the Avenida Diagonal Roque Sáenz Peña one. You can also pick up local information from the very well-organized **National Tourist Office** at Santa Fe 883 (Mon–Fri 9am–5pm; ☎011/4312-2232 or ☎0800/5550016). There are also **provincial tourist offices** within the capital, which are often useful places to head for help in planning travel beyond Buenos Aires; for further information on these, see p.17.

If you are spending more than a very short period in the city, a combined **street map and bus guide** such as Guía Lumi or Guía "T", widely available from central kiosks, is a pretty essential accessory. They're not cheap – although you can sometimes pick up special offers at bargain bookshops or from hawkers on the city's buses and subway trains – but for anyone keen to explore beyond the most obvious sites, or make full use of the extensive bus network, they're a worthwhile investment.

Arrival by air

All international **flights**, with the exception of a few from neighbouring Uruguay, arrive 35km west of the city centre at Ministro Pistarini Airport or – as it is actually referred to by everyone – **Ezeiza**, in reference to the outlying neighbourhood in which it is situated. In comparison with some Latin American airports, arriving at Ezeiza is a stress-free affair: touting for taxis is persistent but not overwhelming and the tourist information stand (daily 8am–8pm) is friendly and helpful, with good information on accommodation in the city. If you're determined to take a **taxi** into the city, ignore unofficial drivers who approach you – most of them have no desire to do anything more than earn a few pesos, but there have been a significant number of armed assaults involving phoney taxis (known locally as *taxis trucho*). Head instead for one of the official taxi stands and be prepared to make the first serious dent in your newly bought currency: a taxi or *remise* (a mini-cab) to the centre of town will set you back around $35. Considerably less expensive are the **tourist buses** run by Manuel Tienda Léon ($14) and San Martín ($11). Running every thirty minutes between 4am and 9pm, these buses are a quick and secure way to reach the centre of town. The buses drop you at the respective company's central office, both located in the downtown area – Manuel Tienda Léon is at Av. Santa Fe 790 (☎011/43150-0489), while San Martín is at Av. Santa Fe 1158 (☎011/4314-4747). A taxi from here to most hotels shouldn't set you back much more than $5. Alternatively, there's the **local bus** #86 which runs between Ezeiza and La Boca, entering the city via Rivadavia and continuing past Congreso, Plaza de Mayo and San Telmo; there's a seating-only service (*diferencial* $4), which leaves from the terminal car park, and a standard service, which takes considerably longer and takes standing passengers en route ($1.35), which leaves just beyond the entrance to the airport. Make sure you have change for the ticket machines, as notes are not accepted, and be warned that the standard service can become very full and bulky suitcases or backpacks may cause serious inconvenience for other passengers.

Buenos Aires' other airport is the **Aeroparque Jorge Newbery** – normally referred to simply as "Aeroparque" – situated on the Costanera Norte, around six kilometres north of the city centre. Most **domestic flights** and flights from Brazil and Uruguay arrive here. Local bus #33 runs along the Costanera past the airport and will take you to Paseo Colón, on the fringe of the microcentro. Alternatively, Manuel Tienda Léon runs a minibus service ($5). A taxi will set you back around $5.

Arrival by bus

If you are travelling to Buenos Aires by **bus** from other points in Argentina, or on international services from neighbouring countries, you will arrive at Buenos Aires' huge main long-distance bus terminal, known as **Retiro**, on Avenida Antártida and Ramos Mejía. There are good facilities at the terminal, including toilets, shops, cafés and left luggage. Unlike the majority of the country's bus terminals, Retiro is located very centrally and anyone with a reasonable amount of energy won't find it too strenuous simply to walk to hotels located in the Florida/Retiro area of the city. Taxis are plentiful and the Retiro subte station is just a block away, outside the adjoining train station (see below). There are also plenty of local buses leaving from the myriad stands along Ramos Mejía, though actually finding the one you want might be a rather daunting first taste of local bus transport. Bus #5 or #50 will take you to Congreso and the upper end of Avenida de Mayo, a good hunting ground for accommodation if you don't have anything booked.

Arrival by train

Few tourists arrive in Buenos Aires by **train** these days; the only long-distance services arriving in the capital are from Tucumán, Santa Rosa in La Pampa Province, Rosario and various cities in the province of Buenos Aires. Trains from the Atlantic Coast, Tandil and Sierra de la Ventana and La Plata, in the province of Buenos Aires, arrive at **Constitución**, in the south of the city at General Hornos 11 (Ferrobaires for Buenos Aires Province ☎011/4304-0038; Metropolitano Línea Roca for La Plata ☎011/4959-0783); those from Mercedes and Lobos in the province of Buenos Aires and Santa Rosa at **Once**, in the west of the city at Avenida Pueyrredón and Calle Bartolomé Mitre (TBA for Mercedes and Lobos ☎011/4866-5181; Ferrobaires for Santa Rosa ☎011/4861-0043). **Retiro** – actually composed of three adjoining terminals – is located on Avenida Ramos Mejía, just to the east of Plaza San Martín, and is the arrival point for trains from Rosario (TBA ☎011/4317-4407) and Tucumán (TUFESA ☎011/4313-8060). All three terminals have subte stations (Constitución, Plaza Miserere and Retiro, respectively) and are served by numerous local bus routes: #60 from Constitución to Avenida de Mayo, Plaza del Congreso and Avenida Callao; #9 from Constitución to Retiro, via Brasil, Piedras, Esmeralda and Avenida Santa Fe; #5 from Once along Calles Bartolomé Mitre and Libertad to Retiro; #86 from Once along Calle Hipólito Yrigoyen to Plaza del Congreso, Plaza de Mayo and San Telmo. For buses from Retiro see arrival by bus, above.

City transport

Buenos Aires may look like a daunting and chaotic city to get around, but it's actually served by an extensive, cheap and – generally – efficient **public transport** service. The easiest part of this system to come to grips with is undoubtedly the underground railway or **subte** which serves most of the city centre and the north of the city. Really to get around, however, you'll need to familiarize yourself with a few bus routes; **buses** are the only way to reach the outlying barrios or the south of the city. **Taxis** are also plentiful and reasonably priced.

The subte

The first in Latin America, Buenos Aires' undergound railway, or **subte** (short for *subterráneo*, or underground), was also one of the first in the world to be privatized: the network was taken over by Metrovías in 1994. It's a reasonably efficient system – you shouldn't have to wait more than a couple of minutes during peak periods – and certainly the quickest way to get from the centre to points such as Caballito, Plaza Italia or Chacarita. The main flaw in the subte's design is that it's shaped like a fork, meaning that journeys across town involve going down one "prong" and changing at least once before heading back up to your final destination. It can also become almost unbearably hot during summer, when the ventilation system expels blasts of sticky air at seemingly several degrees above the already steaming surroundings.

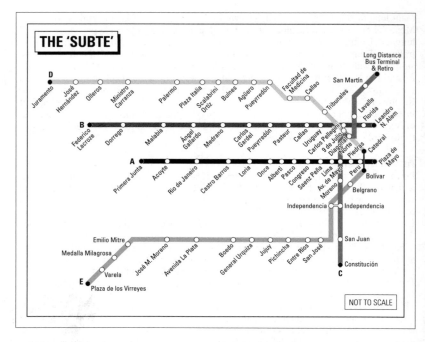

Using the subte is a pretty straightforward business. There are **five lines**, plus a so-called "premetro" system which serves the far southwestern corner of the city, linking up with the subte at the Plaza de los Virreyes, at the end of line E. Lines A, B, D and E run from the city centre outwards, whilst line C, which runs between Retiro and Constitución, connects them all. Check the name of the last station on the line you are travelling on in order to make sure you're heading in the right direction; note also that directions to station platforms are given by this final destination. You need to buy tokens (*fichas*) to use the subte; these cost $0.70 and are bought from the *boleterías* or ticket booths at each station – you don't need to have the right change to buy them. Unfortunately, the only thing you will save by buying *fichas* in bulk is your time, and there are no special deals for weekly or monthly travel.

Even if you use the subte only once during your stay in Buenos Aires, you really shouldn't miss the chance to travel on Line A, which runs between Plaza de Mayo and Caballito. It's the only line to preserve the network's original carriages and travelling in one of the rickety and elegantly lit wood-framed interiors is like being propelled along in an antique wardrobe.

Buses

Peak hours excepted, Buenos Aires' **buses** are one of the most useful ways of getting round the city – and indeed the only way of reaching many of the outlying barrios. The most daunting thing about them, from a tourist's point of view, is the sheer number of routes – almost two hundred bus routes wend their way around the capital's vast grid of streets. Invest in a combined **street and bus-route map** (see p.76), however, and you shouldn't have too much trouble. There's a $0.60 fare for very short journeys; all other trips within the city cost $0.70. Tickets are acquired from a machine, which gives

USEFUL BUS ROUTES

#5 from Retiro to the outlying barrio of Mataderos (but not the Feria de Mataderos) via Avenida Córdoba, Talcahuano, Avenida de Mayo and Rivadavia.

#17 for Recoleta from the centre via Brasil, Piedras and Esmeralda.

#24 for Plaza de Mayo and San Telmo (Plaza Dorrego and Parque Lezama) via Corrientes.

#29 to San Telmo and Boca from Olivos via Viamonte, Talcahuano, Corrientes and Bolívar.

#50 from Entre Ríos/Callao to Retiro via Corrientes.

#60 from Constitución to Tigre – the fastest routes are marked via Panamericano, the more picturesque via Bajo.

#86 from Boca to Ezeiza via Independencia, Perú, Avenida de Mayo and Rivadavia. Check that the bus has "aeropuerto" on the front as there are various alternative routings for the #86.

#126 for Feria de Mataderos via Além, Rivadavia, Bolívar and Carlos Calvo.

#140 from Puerto Madero along Avenida Córdoba (for Palermo and Palermo Viejo).

change for coins, though not for notes: as you get on you need to state your fare to the driver before inserting your money in the ticket machine. Once in Gran Buenos Aires, fares increase slightly – so if you're travelling beyond the city boundaries (to San Isidro, for example, or Ezeiza) it is easier just to state your destination. Despite sporadic traffic accidents involving *colectivos*, the bus system is a generally safe way of getting around the city – though, as always, keep your eyes on your belongings when buses are crowded. Many services run all night, notably the #5 and the #86. Argentinians are generally very courteous bus passengers and never hesitate in giving up their seat to someone who looks like they need it more – don't be shy of doing the same.

Taxis and remises
The sheer volume of black and yellow **taxis** touting their business on Buenos Aires' streets is one of the city's most notable sights and – other than during sudden downpours, when everyone in the centre of town seems to decide to take one at once – it's rare that it takes more than a few minutes to flag down a cab. The meter starts at just over $1 (charges increase at night) and you should calculate on a ride costing around $4 per twenty blocks. Taxis are a generally safe form of transport, though you should be aware of the existence of fake taxis, particularly in the vicinity of the financial district or Puerto Madero. Often working with an accomplice, these drivers generally take a detour, stopping at some deserted spot to relieve their passenger of valuables. If you're unlucky enough to be picked up by a phoney taxi, don't argue – guns are prevalent in Buenos Aires and you'd be foolish to encourage anyone to use one.

Remises are radio cabs, plain cars booked through an office (and therefore preferred by wary locals). Though not particularly economical for short journeys, they're cheaper than taxis for getting to the airport and you may prefer to book one for early-morning starts to either the bus terminal or Aeroparque. For names of *remise* companies, see listings (p.148).

Driving in Buenos Aires
Many of the world's major **car rental** companies and several national companies (see listings, p.148) operate in Buenos Aires, offering a range of vehicles, of which the most

economical is usually a Fiat Uno or Daewoo Tico. Be prepared to book some time ahead if you're planning to rent a car over a long weekend or holiday period. Given the excellent public transport system and the abundance of taxis, however, there's little point in renting a car simply to tour the city.

If you're a confident driver, you shouldn't find Buenos Aires too daunting to tackle by car – indeed, once you've got the hang of the street system, the city can feel like a straightforward place to zip around. With a few exceptions – notably Avenida 9 de Julio and Avenida del Libertador – the streets are one way, with the direction (which alternates street by street) marked on the street signs with an arrow. Traffic tends to move quickly, with split-second hesitation at green lights punished by a wall of impatient honking. Heavy congestion during the rush hour is the norm, however, and slows traffic down to a painful crawl.

The local technique for crossing the city's numerous traffic-lightless intersections at night is to slow down and flash your lights to warn drivers of your approach. Be prepared to give way if the other driver looks more determined and never take it for granted that a speeding bus will respect your trajectory: accidents involving buses regularly make the headlines.

Parking within the area bounded by Avenida Pueyrredón, Belgrano, Avenida Huergo and Libertador (known as the macrocentro) is controlled by parking meters (*parquímetros*) on weekdays between 7am and 9pm and Saturdays from 9am to 1pm. Tokens (*fichas*) can be bought from kiosks. Your other option is in one of the *estacionamientos*, or car parks, which are numerous throughout the city centre; look out for the flag-waving dummies marking the entrance. Hotel parking is generally only offered at mid- to upper-range establishments, costing around $10 to $15 per day. The area known as the **microcentro**, bounded by Avenida de Mayo, Avenida L.N. Além, Avenida Corrientes and Avenida 9 de Julio, is closed to private traffic between 7am and 9pm.

Accommodation

Finding **accommodation** in Buenos Aires is rarely a problem; almost half of all the hotels in the country are to be found in the capital, with prices ranging from $15 for a very basic double room with shared bathroom to $3000 for a luxury suite. However – with the exception of the city's excellent youth hostels – attractive accommodation can be difficult to find on a tight budget, particularly for the single traveller. Be warned that many hotel rooms, especially at the lower end of the market, face onto internal corridors, or may lack a window at all. A fan, or air conditioning, is pretty much an essential requirement in summer, and heating is a big plus in winter. **Discounts** can sometimes be negotiated, particularly if you are staying for more than a few days. Always try to pay in cash as credit cards invariably entail a surcharge. If you are planning on staying for some time, look out for *pensiones*, which offer monthly rates, starting at around $200 for a room with shared bathroom and kitchen facilities. You could also try the noticeboard at the Universidad de Buenos Aires' language faculty at 25 de Mayo 221, where Porteños offering rooms to foreigners often advertise; the classified section of the daily paper *Clarín*; or the back pages of specialist tango publications. There's also an excellent **Web site** – *www.bedandbreakfast.com.ar* – offering information in English on alternative accommodation in Buenos Aires, primarily in shared apartments, university residences and bed-and-breakfast type establishments. There are clear photos of the various options and a reservation system, as well as information on language courses.

Note that **breakfast** is not always included in the price of a hotel room, but in any case you'll probably get a better start to the day in a nearby confitería.

The centre

The biggest concentration of accommodation is to be found in the **city centre**, specifically on and around Avenida de Mayo, Congreso, and Corrientes. This area also has excellent transport links and is particularly handy if you're arriving on the local bus #86 from Ezeiza, which takes you along the southern side of the Plaza del Congreso. Avenida de Mayo is also well served by buses through the night (#5 from Retiro and Avenida Córdoba and #86 from San Telmo) and is probably one of the safest places to stay in the city. There are also accommodation options in the streets surrounding busy but pedestrianized Florida. The area is perhaps not the most atmospheric place to stay these days, but it's one of the best connected and handy for shopping and cinemas as well as transport.

Hostels

Che Lagarto Youth Hostel, Combate de los Pozos 1151 (☎011/4304-7618, *chelagarto@ hotmail.com*). Laid-back hostel run by a young team. A bit of a squash but very friendly and the owners are expert guides to the city's nightlife. The three-tiered bunk-bed dormitories take some getting used to; or you could try for the one double room. Be warned that the hostel can be pretty noisy, particularly when large contingents from the interior arrive. $8 per person.

V&S Youth Hostel, Viamonte 887 (☎ & fax 011/4322-0994; *hostelvs@vsyhbue.com.ar*). This fantastic new youth hostel is the most luxurious in Buenos Aires. Located in a stylish 1910 French-style mansion, it has a bar, giant TV and even a small gym. There's dormitory accommodation ($16 per person) and a beautiful double room with a balcony and private bathroom (book well in advance; $45), which must be one of the most desirable rooms in the city.

Hotels

Gran Hotel Oriental, Bartolomé Mitre 1840 (☎ & fax 011/4951-6427). Slightly spartan hotel, but clean and reasonably priced; all rooms have fan and central heating and there are two large rooms with balconies on the second floor. Breakfast included. ③.

Hotel Alcázar, Av. de Mayo 935 (☎011/4345-0926). Old hotel with lovely central staircase. Attractive, recently refurbished rooms all come with heating, a fan and private bathroom. Fifteen percent discount for extended stays (over ten days). ③.

Hotel Avenida Petit, Av. de Mayo 1347 (☎011/4381-7831). The rooms (with TV, telephone and clean, modern bathrooms) are adequate for the price, but the rather grim orange and brown interior could do with a bit of a facelift. ③.

Hotel Castelar, Av. de Mayo 1152 (☎011/4381-7873, fax 4383-8388). A Buenos Aires institution, this pleasant, old-fashioned hotel offers attractive rooms with big comfortable beds and good soundproofing for rooms overlooking noisy Avenida de Mayo. There's also a glamorous bar downstairs. ⑥.

Hotel Chile, Av. de Mayo 1297 (☎011/4383-7877). Recently refurbished, exceptionally friendly Art Deco hotel; some rooms with pleasant balconies overlooking a side street. Spacious rooms, all with central heating, air conditioning and TV. Includes breakfast. ④.

Hotel Claridge, Tucumán 535 (☎011/4314-2020). Recently refurbished, this centrally located luxury hotel is a bit lacking in character, despite the promise of its elegant sweeping entrance. Comfortable and spacious, if slightly bland rooms; some floors have non-smoking rooms. The hotel also has an outside pool and sunbathing area, currently slightly marred by the back view of crumbling nearby buildings. ⑨.

Hotel del Congreso, Hipólito Yrigoyen 2064 (☎011/4952-7728). Pretty, old-fashioned building with central patio. Rather basic rooms, many of them internal, but some with windows. ③.

Hotel de los Dos Congresos, Rivadavia 1777 (☎011/4371-0072; *hdoscong@hotelnet.com.ar*). Recently renamed (previously the *Mar del Plata*) this hotel runs some promotions which make its luxurious suites (the best of which have a spiral staircase and windows overlooking Congreso) an excellent deal. All rooms are a good size and are decorated in a clean, modern style with air conditioning, TV and minibar. Special promotions see twenty-percent reductions on all room prices. ⑥.

Hotel Europa, Bartolomé Mitre 1294 (☎011/4381-9629). Immaculately maintained hotel with pleasingly decorated and comfortable rooms; all with TV and private bathroom, some overlooking the street. One of best in its price range. ISIC discounts available. ③.

Hotel Gran Sarmiento, Sarmiento 1892 (☎011/4372-2764). Quiet hotel in an old-fashioned building. Small but well-kept rooms with telephone and private bathroom. ③.

Hotel Lyon, Riobamba 251 (☎011/4372-0100, fax 4814-4252). Elegant hotel on a relatively quiet street one block from Callao with exceptionally large suites. Breakfast included and parking available ($15 a day). ⑥.

Hotel Maipú, Maipú 735 (☎011/4322-5142). The old-fashioned *Maipú* is a bit scruffy but has reasonably comfortable rooms and is friendly and eternally popular with foreigners who have left behind a small library of travel guides and novels. Rooms are available with or without private bathroom. ②.

Hotel Normandie, Rodríguez Peña 320 (☎011/4371-7001). Old-fashioned building with light, well-maintained but rather characterless rooms, all with cable TV, telephone and minibar. Good location and well-priced parking ($7 a day). Breakfast included and possible discount for stays of more than five days if paying in cash. ⑤.

Hotel Nuevo Mundial, Av. de Mayo 1298 (☎011/4383-0011; *mundial@houseware.com.ar*). Beautifully old-fashioned hotel (vertigo sufferers might wish to avoid looking down on the stunning central stairwell), with some of the biggest and best balconies in Buenos Aires. Large and attractive rooms with air conditioning. The excellent buffet breakfast includes fresh fruit. Good discounts may be obtained with a bit of negotiating. ⑤.

Hotel Phoenix, San Martín 780 (☎011/4312-4845; *www.hotelphoenix.com.ar*). A pretty hotel in an elegant late nineteenth-century building, whose central wrought-iron stairwell is illuminated by light filtering through exquisite glass domes. Rooms are large and furnished with a mixture of antiques and modern facilities such as air conditioning and cable TV. Located just one block from the more exclusive end of Florida, the hotel is fairly quiet given its central location. Buffet breakfast. ⑥.

Hotel Premier, Corrientes 1455 (☎011/4371-3401). Pleasant, centrally located hotel with high-ceilinged, wood-panelled rooms, air conditioning and TV. Breakfast included. ④.

Hotel Roma, Av. de Mayo 1413 (☎011/4381-4921). A good deal, given its pleasant and central location, the *Roma* has some nice if slightly noisy rooms with balconies looking onto Avenida de Mayo. ② with shared bathroom, ③ en suite.

Hotel San Martín, Av. Callao 327, 1st Floor (☎ & fax 011/4371-6450). A comfortable and friendly – if very slightly scruffy – hotel. All rooms have TV and fan and some have balconies – although as always on Buenos Aires' busy central streets, this can be a mixed blessing. Breakfast included. ③.

Hotel Sportsman, Rivadavia 1425 (☎011/4381-8021; *sportsman@mixmail.com*). Budget hotel popular with foreigners. It's a characterful, rambling old building, though the interior is showing its age a bit. There's a range of rooms available, some with shared bathrooms; the nicest ones are the en-suite doubles at the front, which have balconies. All rooms have fans, some have TV and there are very basic shared cooking facilities. ②–③.

Nuevo Hotel Callao, Callao 292 (☎011/4374-3861; *hotelcallao@infovia.com.ar*). Recently refurbished, pleasant hotel with light, clean and attractive rooms, all with great balconies overlooking Callao. TV, fan and breakfast included. ④.

The south

There is not much in the way of accommodation in the **south**, though most of what there is can be found in the barrio of San Telmo, a magnet for many independent travellers for its cobbled streets and atmospheric buildings. Most places here are budget hotels or youth hostels. There are also plenty of hotels in the immediate vicinity of Constitución station, though it's generally worth going a bit further to find more agreeable accommodation.

Hostels

Albergue de la Juventud, Brasil 675 (☎011/4394-9112; *aaaj@hostelling-aaj.org.ar*). Buenos Aires' oldest youth hostel, located on the fringes of San Telmo, not far from Constitución train station. Spacious dormitories, terraces and a barbecue area. $12 with HI card only.

Buenos Ayres Hostel, Pasaje San Lorenzo 320 (☎011/4361-0694; *www.buenosayreshostel.com*). Newly opened San Telmo hostel. A smart modern place with bright, attractively decorated small dormitories and some double rooms. Agreeable communal space with cable TV, Internet access and laundry facilities, plus a terrace with a barbecue. $10 per person.

El Hostal de San Telmo, Carlos Calvo 614 (☎011/4300-6899; *elhostal@satlink.com*). Very well-located in one of the prettiest parts of San Telmo, this small hostel is friendly, well-kept and bordering on the luxurious: there's Internet access and a fax machine, a laundry, terrace and barbecue area. Most accommodation is in four-bed dormitories ($10 per person) but there is also a handful of very small double rooms ($20 per room).

Hotels

Gran Hotel América Larre, Bernardo de Yrigoyen 1608 (☎011/4307-8785). A stone's throw from Constitución station, this large and reasonably priced hotel shows its vintage by the wonderful old antique cash register at reception. Good-sized rooms, some of them a bit dark, but all well looked after with private bathroom. Ten percent discount for stays of more than three days. ②.

Hotel Bolívar, Bolívar 886 (☎011/4361-5105). Located in the heart of San Telmo, this hotel offers basic but perfectly acceptable rooms, the few with balconies are by far the most attractive. ①, ② with bathroom.

Hotel Los Tres Reyes, Brasil 425 (☎011/4300-9456). A new hotel in a great location just half a block from Parque Lezama. Rather frilly, but comfortable rooms with spotless private bathrooms. Breakfast included. ③.

The north

There are precious few bargains to be had to the **north** of the city centre, but for sheer luxury, Retiro and Recoleta are the neighbourhoods to head for, while there are a couple of extremely agreeable options in the further-flung barrios of Palermo Viejo and Colegiales.

Hostels

Recoleta Youth Hostel, Libertad 1216 (☎011-4812-4419; *recoletayouthhostel@libertel.com.ar*). Smart new hostel in an attractively modernized and spacious old mansion. Accommodation is in a mixture of dormitories and double rooms and there is a large terrace area and good facilities including TV and Internet access. $10 per person.

Hotels

Alvear Palace Hotel, Av. Alvear 1891 (☎011/4804-7777; *alvear@satlink.com*). Located in Buenos Aires' most aristocratic neighbourhood, Recoleta, the Alvear was once the choice of wealthy estancieros visiting the capital. Still one of the most stylish and traditional of Buenos Aires' luxury hotels, it offers well-appointed and tastefully decorated rooms and extras such as cellular phones, newspapers to each room and a private email address at the hotel. There are floors offering non-smoking rooms, and there's access to the hotel's business centre and gym. ⑨.

Hotel Alpino, Cabello 3318 (☎011/4802-5151). An oasis of peace in this noisy area, the *Alpino* has appealingly decorated, spacious rooms, plus large self-catering apartments. ⑥.

Hotel Ayacucho, Ayacucho 1408 (☎011/4806-0943). Housed in a smart French-style building, the rooms in this hotel are rather dowdy. That said, they are clean, comfortable and cooled by noiseless fans. ⑤.

Hotel Embajador, Carlos Pellegrini 1181-5 (☎011/4326-5302; *embajador@hotelnet.com.ar*). The comfortable if nondescript rooms in the *Embajador* have their own shower or bath and are well soundproofed – especially vital for those overlooking Av. 9 de Julio. ⑥.

Hotel Etoile, Pres. Ortiz 1835 (☎011/4805-2626, fax 4805-3613; *hotel@etoile.com.ar*). Modern, glitzy hotel with very large rooms, a swimming pool, sauna and Turkish bath, and fantastic bird's-eye views of Recoleta Cemetery. ⑨.

Hotel Gran Dorá, Maipú 963 (☎011/4312-7391, fax 4313-8134). Large, airy rooms and spotless marble bathrooms, in this central, business-oriented establishment. ⑦.

Hotel Guido, Guido 1780 (☎011/4812-0341). Very comfortable, tastefully decorated bedrooms, all en suite, in a stylish Recoleta building. ⑥.

Hotel Palermo, Godoy Cruz 2725 (☎011/4774-7342 or 4773-5133). Bright, cheerful place with basic bathrooms, TV, air conditioning, a good snack-bar and a very decent restaurant. ④.

Hotel Plaza Francia, E. Schiaffino 2189 and Av. del Libertador (☎011/4804-9631; *plafrancia@ impsat1.com.ar*). Slightly old-fashioned but immaculate hotel, with some rooms affording panoramic views of Recoleta. Avoid the noisy rooms overlooking Avenida Libertador, though. ⑧.

Hotel Recoleta Plaza, Posadas 1557 (☎011/4804-3471). Very smart hotel in a sumptuous palace, with enormous, luxurious rooms and a number of suites, plus faultless room service. ⑨.

Malabia House, Malabia 1555 (☎011/4833-2410, fax 4831-2102; *www.malabiahouse.com.ar*). An upmarket bed-and-breakfast, in a beautiful town house in the heart of Palermo Viejo, with no sign outside. The rooms are spacious, each is decorated differently and all have en-suite bathrooms. ⑦.

Marriott Plaza Hotel, Florida 1005 (☎011/4318-3000). Long-established luxury hotel recently taken over by the Marriott chain, who've given it a slightly corporate feel. Top-notch, very plush rooms with plenty of attention to detail; the nicest rooms have a stunnning view over Plaza San Martín. Elegant Thirties-style bar and good restaurant. ⑨.

Residencial Lion d'Or, Pacheco de Melo 2019 (☎011/4803-8992). Homely place, with a variety of pretty, spotlessly clean rooms, without TV and mercifully free of the kitsch decor found in similar places nearby. ②.

Sheraton Hotel, San Martín 1225 (☎011/4318-9000). High-rise hotel with glamorous views over the city from the front and slightly less glamorous – though still impressive – views over the port and railway tracks from the back. Neatly decorated modern and spacious rooms with all the trimmings you'd expect. Oriented towards the needs of business travellers; there's also an outdoor swimming pool, tennis courts and a gym. ⑨.

Zabala Home, Freire 1101 (☎011/4553-7472, fax 4554-1806; *zabala@arnet.com.ar*). Delightful B&B in a leafy part of Colegiales, not far from Belgrano's museums. Shared kitchens, bright, mostly en-suite bedrooms, and a charming family atmosphere. Long-term rates negotiable. ④.

Once and beyond

There are plenty of budget hotels – as well as one or two mid-range choices – in the streets surrounding **Once train station**. It probably wouldn't be anyone's first choice but is worth considering if you're on a budget and unable to secure accommodation elsewhere.

Hotels

Hotel Bahía, Hipólito Yrigoyen 3062 (☎011/4931-7198). Quiet and safe, with slightly rickety but adequate bedrooms. Shared and private bathrooms available; some rooms have TV. ②–③.

Hotel Galicia, Hipólito Yrigoyen 3072 (☎011/4931-9629). One block from Once train station. Despite the slightly seedy reception area, the rooms are clean if a bit scruffy. Shared and private bathrooms available. ①–②.

Hotel Metropolitan, Av. Boedo 449 (☎011/4932-7547; *www.hotelnet.com.ar/hotel/house.asp*). The *Metropolitan* markets itself as a budget hotel, but given its less than central location and not particularly inspiring rooms it doesn't seem to offer such a great deal. Nonetheless, it's a pleasant enough place in a quiet area of the city with more of a neighbourhood feel than the city centre. Rooms available with or without private bathroom. To get there, take bus #115 or #155, or the subte to Boedo station. Discount with ISIC card. ②–③.

The City Centre

A sometimes chaotic mix of grand nineteenth-century public edifices, cafés, high-rise office blocks and tearing traffic, the **city centre** exudes both frenetic energy and old-style elegance. Its heart is the **Plaza de Mayo**, a good place to begin a tour of the area, perhaps more for the square's historical and political connections than for its somewhat mismatched collection of edifices, which range from the regularly remodelled colonial **cabildo** and the stern Neoclassical **cathedral** to the square's most famous building, the striking pink **Casa Rosada** or government house. From the plaza, you can choose to head directly north and strike into the densely packed narrow streets of **La City**, where almost palatial banks and financial institutions loom over you, together with one of the city's finest churches, the **Iglesia Nuestra Señora de la Merced**, and a handful of modest museums. A gentler introduction to the area, however, would be to amble westwards from the plaza along the wide boulevard **Avenida de Mayo**, lined with a striking selection of tall Art Nouveau and Art Deco buildings. The avenue is even more notable, however, for its traditional restaurants and confiterías, of which the most famous is the supremely elegant **Café Tortoni**. At its western end, the Avenida de Mayo opens up into the long, thin Plaza del Congreso, named after and presided over by the very forbidding **Congress** building. From Plaza del Congreso, the logical route to follow is to head north along Avenida Callao until you hit one of the city's most famous streets, **Avenida Corrientes**. Nowadays not immediately striking unless you know its pedigree, Corrientes is famous for having been both the centre of the capital's nightlife and the hub of intellectual, left-leaning café society. Though there's less plotting going on there these days, it's still lined with bookshops, cinemas and cafés and is a great place for people-watching. A short detour north from Corrientes will take you to **Plaza Lavalle**, a lovely grassy square surrounded by various imposing and important buildings, such as the Palacio de Justicio – but most notable for its opera house, the **Teatro Colón**. Heading east from Plaza Lavalle, you'll run slap bang into the enormous **Avenida 9 de Julio** – the city's multi-lane central nerve. At its heart stands Buenos Aires' favourite symbol, the stark white **Obelisco** – a 67-metre stake through the intersection between 9 de Julio and Corrientes. Crossing over the avenue, you could head down Lavalle, a pedestrianized street famed for its cinemas, though suffering somewhat these days from competition from the city's new shopping centres and multiplex cinemas. Following Lavalle will bring you to the central section of **Calle Florida**, where you'll be swept along by a hectic stream of pedestrians past small shopping malls, book and record stores and regaled by a variety of street performances. To the east of Florida lies a grid of much quieter streets – home to some of the city's best bars – which lead down to Avenida L.N. Além, commonly referred to as "el bajo". To the east of el bajo lies the newly revamped **Puerto Madero** district, the city's newest barrio and a swanky assemblage of restaurants, loft and office space.

Plaza de Mayo

The one place that can lay claim to most of Buenos Aires' historical moments and monuments is the **Plaza de Mayo**. It's been bombed, filled by Evita's *descamisados* (literally "the shirtless ones" or manual workers) and it's still the site of the Madres de Plaza de Mayo's weekly demonstration – a reminder that the 1976–83 dictatorship may have gone but many of its crimes are still unaccounted for. The square itself is one of the most attractive in the city, largely thanks to its stupendous towering palm trees, which give the plaza a wonderfully subtropical feel, particularly when the whole place is bathed in evening sunlight. At its centre stands the pristine white **Pirámide de Mayo**. The monument was erected in 1811 to mark the first anniversary of the Revolución de Mayo when a junta led by Cornelio de Saavedra overthrew the Spanish viceroy Cisneros, declared Buenos Aires' independence from Spain and set about establishing the city's jurisdiction over the rest of the territory. The headscarves painted on the ground around the pyramid echo those worn by the Madres de Plaza de Mayo. For more on the Madres, see p.714.

As well as Evita, Maradona, Galtieri and Perón have all addressed the crowds from the balcony of the **Casa Rosada** (guided tours: Mon–Fri 11.15am & 2.15pm; $5; bring

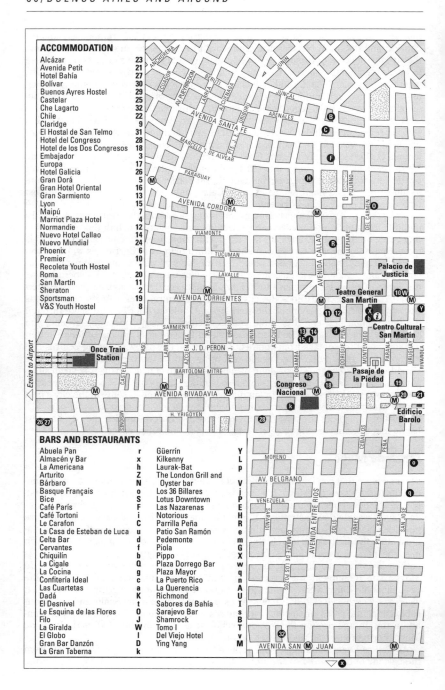

ACCOMMODATION

Alcázar	23
Avenida Petit	21
Hotel Bahía	27
Bolívar	30
Buenos Ayres Hostel	29
Castelar	25
Che Lagarto	32
Chile	22
Claridge	9
El Hostal de San Telmo	31
Hotel del Congreso	28
Hotel de los Dos Congresos	18
Embajador	3
Europa	17
Hotel Galicia	26
Gran Dorá	5
Gran Hotel Oriental	16
Gran Sarmiento	13
Lyon	15
Maipú	7
Marriot Plaza Hotel	4
Normandie	12
Nuevo Hotel Callao	14
Nuevo Mundial	24
Phoenix	6
Premier	10
Recoleta Youth Hostel	1
Roma	20
San Martín	11
Sheraton	2
Sportsman	19
V&S Youth Hostel	8

BARS AND RESTAURANTS

Abuela Pan	r	Güerrín	Y
Almacén y Bar	x	Kilkenny	L
La Americana	h	Laurak-Bat	p
Arturito	Z	The London Grill and	
Bárbaro	N	Oyster bar	V
Basque Français	o	Los 36 Billares	j
Bice	S	Lotus Downtown	P
Café París	F	Las Nazarenas	E
Café Tortoni	i	Notorious	H
Le Carafon	C	Parrilla Peña	R
La Casa de Esteban de Luca	u	Patio San Ramón	e
Celta Bar	d	Pedemonte	m
Cervantes	f	Piola	G
Chiquilín	b	Pippo	X
La Cigale	Q	Plaza Dorrego Bar	w
La Cocina	g	Plaza Mayor	q
Confitería Ideal	c	La Puerto Rico	A
Las Cuartetas	a	La Querencia	U
Dadá	K	Richmond	I
El Desnivel	t	Sabores da Bahía	s
Le Esquina de las Flores	O	Sarajevo Bar	B
Filo	J	Shamrock	T
La Giralda	W	Tomo I	v
El Globo	l	Del Viejo Hotel	v
Gran Bar Danzón	D	Ying Yang	M
La Gran Taberna	k		

CENTRAL BUENOS AIRES

△ Bus Terminal

0 _____ 500m

N

ARROYO

(A) Retiro Train
Station

Torre
Monumental

JUNCAL

❶

ARENALES

(D) ❸

(i)

AVENIDA SANTA FE

(G)

MAECELO T. DE ALVEAR

PARAGUAY

PLAZA
SAN
MARTIN

(E)

❹ Edificio
Kavanagh

(J) (K)
(L)

(N)
(P)

TTES SARGENTOS

Teatro
Nacional
Cervantes

(M) Galerías Pacífico &
Centro Cultural Borges

AVENIDA CORDOBA

(Q)

Aliscafos &
Buquebus Ferry
Terminal

✡ Sinagoga
Central

PLAZA
LAVALLE

❽

❼

(i) ❻

VIAMONTE

Teatro
Colón

(M)

9 DE JULIO

TUCUMAN

❾

LAVALLE

(T)

(M) CORRIENTES

Obelisco

(M)

(Z)

(c)

(a)

(U)

(M) Museo
Mitre

Correo
Central

SARMIENTO

Museo de
la Policia

(e) (M)

Catedral
Anglicana

Banco de
la Nación

Dique 4

(S) AVENIDA A. DAVILA

PTE. PERON

(g) Basílica de
Nuestra Señora
de la Merced

BARTOLOME MITRE

Catedral Metropolitana

RIVADAVIA

MITRE

❶❼

❷❷ (j)

❷❹ ❶❷❺

Casa
Rosada

(M) Museo de la
Casa Rosada

Buque Museo
Fragata ARA
Presidente Sarmiento

(M) ❷❸

AVENIDA DE MAYO

Cabildo

(M)

PLAZA
DE MAYO

(M)

Dique 3

H. YRIGOYEN

Parroquia de
San Ignacio Loyola

(M)

Museo de
la Ciudad

(n) Iglesia de
San Francisco

ALSINA

LIMA

MORENO

AVENIDA ROCA

Manzana de
las Luces

Museo Etnográfico
"Juan Bautista
Ambrosetti"

(M) AVENIDA BELGRANO

Basílica de
Santo Domingo

VENEZUELA

(P)

MÉXICO

PERU

CHILE

(r)

Pasaje
San Lorenzo

❷❾

Casa
Mínima

Dique 2

AVENIDA INDEPENDENCIA

(S)

❸❶

ESTADOS UNIDOS

Mercado de
San Telmo

(U)

CARLOS CALVO

(t)

❸❶

HUMBERTO 1

PLAZA
DORREGO

(V)

(w)

Pasase de la Defensa

Parroquia de
San Pedro
Telmo

(M) AVENIDA SAN JUAN

Dique 1

Buque Museo
Corbeta ARA
Uruguay

Reserva Ecológica Costanera Sur

your passport to leave at the entrance), the pink governmental palace that occupies the eastern end of the square. The present building, a typically Argentinian blend of French and Italian Renaissance styles, developed in a fairly organic fashion. It stands on the site of the city's original fort, begun in 1594 and finished in 1720. With the creation of the Viceroyalty of the River Plate in 1776, the fort was remodelled as the viceroy's palace. In 1862, President Bartolomé Mitre moved the government ministries to the building, remodelling it once again. The final touch to the building was added in 1885, when the central arch was added, unifying the facade. The palace's colour dates from Sarmiento's 1868–74 presidency. The practice of painting buildings pink was common during the nineteenth century, particularly in the countryside – you'll still see many estancias that have been painted this colour. The shade was achieved with the use of ox blood, for both decorative and practical reasons – the blood acted as a fixative to the whitewash to which it was added. For much of the latter part of the twentieth century the Casa Rosada was a rather muted rose colour. In 1999, however, the building was repainted in its current striking shade. The sudden switch provoked considerable debate: many Porteños were horrified by the new and strident colour, while those responsible for the change stood by their claim that it was based on a meticulous historical investigation of the building's original colour. Whatever the merits or otherwise of the building's new look – and despite claims from the manufacturer for the paint's indestructability – it seems almost certain that the combination of fierce sun and heavy pollution to which all buildings in Buenos Aires are subjected will result in the mellowing of the controversial shade.

On the south side of the building, a side entrance leads to the **Museo de la Casa Rosada**, Hipólito Yrigoyen 219 (Mon–Fri 10am–6pm; $1; ☎011/4344-3600), whose basement houses the remains of the old Aduana de Taylor, a customs building named after the British engineer who designed it in 1855. The main section of the museum is devoted to a collection of objects used by Argentina's presidents from 1826 to 1966, together with panels in Spanish and English providing a carefully neutral overview of Argentina's turbulent political history. It's mostly pretty staid viewing: the collection is composed largely of official photographs and medals but there are a number of slightly more idiosyncratic exhibits such as tango scores written in honour of political parties and politicians, including the rather unmusical-sounding *El Socialista*, written for the socialist Alfredo Palacios, elected to the Chamber of Deputies in 1904.

At the far end of the square from Casa Rosada is the **Cabildo**, the only civil building to have survived from colonial times. Despite Italianate remodelling at the end of the last century, its simple unadorned lines, green and white shuttered facade and colonnaded front, still stand in stark contrast to the more ornate public buildings that have been constructed around it. The interior of the Cabildo houses a small **museum** (Mon–Thurs & Sun 12.30–7pm) whose modest collection includes standards captured during the 1806 British invasion, some delicate watercolours by Enrique Pellegrini and original plans of the city and the fort. Though the exhibits themselves are of only minor interest, the interior of the building itself is worth a visit, in particular the upper galleries lined with a collection of architectural relics such as huge keys and sturdy wooden doors from the colonial period onwards. A small artisan **fair** (Thurs & Fri 11am–6pm) takes place in the patio behind the Cabildo. To the right is the columned facade of the **Catedral Metropolitana** (Mon–Fri 8am–7pm, Sat 9am–12.30pm & 5–7.30pm, Sun 9am–2pm & 4–7.30pm; free guided tours Mon–Fri 1pm, Sat 11.30am, Sun 10am), a sturdy and rather severe Neoclassical edifice. Like so many of Buenos Aires' churches, the cathedral took its final form over a period of many years; built and rebuilt since the sixteenth century, the present building was completed in the mid-nineteenth century. The twelve columns which front the entrance represent the twelve apostles; above them sits a carved tympanum whose bas-relief front depicts the arrival of Jacob and his family in Egypt. After a lengthy period of restoration, the interior of the cathedral, with its Venetian mosaic floors, gilded columns and silver-plated altar, is looking at its gleaming best – though by far the most significant feature of the interior is the solemnly guarded **mausoleum** to Independence hero, **General San Martín**.

La City

Immediately to the north of Plaza de Mayo and bounded to the west by Calle Florida, the north by Corrientes and to the east by Avenida L.N. Além you'll find Buenos Aires' financial district, **La City**. The district is no longer the scene of such frantic money-changing as happened during the period of hyperinflation in the late 1980s (when inflation reached 4000 percent per annum and supermarkets announced price changes over loudspeakers), but it's still a hectic place, its streets thronged with gesticulating bank workers and echoing to the sound of a thousand mobile phones. The narrow streets and endless foot traffic seem to conspire to stop you from looking up, but if you do you'll be rewarded with an impressive spread of robust grand facades crowned with domes and towers. The city was once known as the *barrio inglés*, in reference to the large number of British immigrants who set up business here. Indeed, the first financial institutions here were built in a rather Victorian style; it seems that the Porteño elite thought their houses should be French and their banks British. There's also an Anglican church here, the Doric-style **Catedral Anglicana de San Juan Bautista** (Sunday service in English at 9.30am), three blocks north of Plaza de Mayo, at 25 de Mayo 276: the church was built on land donated by General Rosas in 1830. Around the corner, at Reconquista and Perón, there's the **Basílica de Nuestra Señora de la Merced** (Mon–Fri 8.30am–7pm, Sat 6.30–8pm, Sun 11am–noon), one of the most beautiful and least visited churches in Buenos Aires – though it has been favoured by important political and military figures through the ages. Every inch of the Basílica's sombre interior walls is ornamented with gilt or tiles, creating an air of gloomy sumptuousness. Next door, on Reconquista, is one of the city's best-kept secrets, the **Convento de San Ramón**, at its heart a charming courtyard where, amid palm trees and birdsong, you can eat in the restaurant located under the *recova* or just take a break from elbowing your way through the madness outside. One block west, at San Martín 336, you'll find the small **Museo Mitre** (closed for refurbishment at the time of writing; phone for latest information, ☎011/4394-8240), housed in a discreet colonial residence, dwarfed by the towering buildings around it. The rooms, grouped around a central patio, offer a mixture of furniture of the epoch and official paraphernalia relating to Mitre's presidency. Opposite, the **Museo de la Policía** at San Martín 353, 7th Floor (Tues–Fri 1–5pm; free; ☎011/4394-6857) offers a peculiar mix of censoriousness in its galleries dedicated to gambling, illegal drugs, robbery and black magic. There's a whole array of ingenious devices used by criminals such as the *limosnera* (from *limosna*, meaning alms), a magnetic tool used for extracting coins from alms boxes, as well as the cape used in black magic practices by the sinister José López Rega (known as El brujo, or "the wizard", adviser to Isabel Perón and founder of the triple-A death squad (see Contexts, p.710). The gratuitously gory forensic medicine with its gruesome reconstructions of dismembered bodies is best avoided unless you've a very strong stomach.

Avenida de Mayo

Heading west from Plaza de Mayo takes you along one of the capital's most striking streets, the **Avenida de Mayo**. A wide tree-lined boulevard flanked with ornamental street lamps, the Avenida de Mayo offers a stunning vista which runs for ten blocks between the Plaza de Mayo and the Plaza del Congreso. The city's first high-rise structures were built along here in 1894 on an initiative of Torcuato de Alvear, then the city's mayor. Part of a project to remodel the city along the lines of Haussmann's Paris, the Avenida de Mayo is notable for its melange of Art Nouveau and Art Deco constructions, many of them topped with decorative domes, and ornamented with elaborate balustrades and sinuous caryatids – sculpted female figures used as an architectural support. Ever unimpressed with the city's European pretensions, Borges called it one of the saddest areas in Buenos Aires, yet even he couldn't resist the charm of its **confiterías** and traditional restaurants. Unfortunately, many of these have now closed, or have been converted into less elegant *bares al paso* (sparse cafés serving up quick coffees and snacks to passers-by). Nonetheless, those that remain – most notably the famous *Café Tortoni* (see below) – are among the street's undoubted highlights.

Just half a block west of Plaza de Mayo, at Avenida de Mayo 567, there's the magnificent, heavily French-influenced **La Prensa** building, with grand wrought-iron doors, curvaceous lamps and a steep mansard roof. The building now houses the city's culture secretariat but was originally built as the headquarters of the national newspaper *La Prensa*, which first went into circulation in 1869, founded by the influential Paz family. You can pop in to take a peek at the opulent interior – all ornamental glass and elaborate woodwork – or take advantage of one of the free guided tours organized by the city government next door (Sat 4 & 5pm, Sun 11am, 4pm & 5pm).

The avenue's next attraction actually lies underground. On the corner of Perú and Avenida de Mayo, you'll find **Perú station**, second stop on Line A of the subte. You'll need to buy a *ficha* to enter, but the station is well worth a visit: it's been refurbished with old advertisements and fittings by the imaginative Museo de la Ciudad (see p.96), to reflect the history of the line. Two and a half blocks west, at Avenida de Mayo 829, you'll find the **Café Tortoni**. The café has been going for over 150 years (prior to the construction of the Avenida de Mayo it was actually located in Calle Defensa) and is famous for its literary and artistic connections – notable habitués included the poetess Alfonsina Storni and the Nicaraguan poet Rubén Darío, as well as visiting celebrities such as the Italian playwright Luigi Pirandello. Inside, heavy brown columns and Art Nouveau mirrored walls create an elegant atmosphere, presided over by discreet white-coated waiters. The coffee's a little on the expensive side at around $2 a throw, but it comes served with heaps of atmosphere as well as a tiny dish of amaretti.

Four blocks up, on the other side of Avenida 9 de Julio, there's another famous confitería, but one with a very different atmosphere. The cavernous and rather spartan **36 Billares**, at Avenida de Mayo 1265, introduced the game of billiards to Argentina in 1882. There's still a popular billiards salon downstairs, as well as a games room at the back of the café where an almost exclusively male crowd passes the day playing chess, dice, pool and *truco*, Argentina's favourite card game. On the left-hand side of the street in the 1300 block stands the avenue's most fantastical building, the **Edificio Barolo**. Built in 1922, it was once the tallest building in Buenos Aires, and its rather top-heavy form – a jutting mass of protruding balconies – still towers above the street. All in all, it's a rather clumsy example of the plundering of styles that marked much of early-twentieth-century Argentinian architecture, but from the perspective of the twenty-first century it seems to embody the avenue's awkward, grandiose and slightly faded elegance.

Plaza del Congreso

At its western extremity, the Avenida de Mayo opens up to encircle the spindly **Plaza del Congreso**, a three-block long wedge of grass dotted with statues, a fountain and swooping pigeons plus a number of benches where you can take a break from the heavy streams of traffic which run around it. Its western end is presided over by the Greco-Roman **Congress** building (guided visits available in English, French and Spanish; enquire at Hipólito Yrigoyen 1864, to the south of the main entrance), inaugurated in 1906 and topped by a green copper dome which seems rather dwarfed by the palace's wide columned front. The square's most striking monument is the exuberant **Monumento a los dos Congresos**, a series of sculptural allegories atop heavy granite steps and crowned by the triumphant figure of the Republic. The monument was erected to commemorate the 1813 Assembly and the 1816 Declaration of Independence, made at the Congress of Tucumán. The plaza has traditionally been the final rallying point for many political demonstrations, with the monument acting as a magnet for political graffiti. At the centre of the square stands a greening bronze, somewhat rain-streaked version of Rodin's **The Thinker**. The whimsical building to the right of Congreso, on the corner of Rivadavia and Avenida Callao, used to house yet another famous confitería, **El Molino**, renowned for its elegant style and political clientele, as well as the decorative windmill which adorns its facade.

Avenida Corrientes and around

Four blocks to the north of Avenida de Mayo and connected to the Plaza del Congreso via Avenida Callao, you'll find **Avenida Corrientes**. Immortalized in several tangos and long the focus of the city's cultural life, it's a broad avenue which sweeps down to the lower grounds of "el bajo". It's not the street's architecture that is of note, however – it's mostly a mixture of nondescript high-rise blocks interspersed with older apartment buildings – but the atmosphere generated by the mix of cafés, bookshops, cinemas and pizzerias which line either side of the avenue. For years, cafés such as *La Paz*, on the corner of Corrientes and Montevideo (sadly recently remodelled as a faux Thirties-style "pizza café") and the austere *La Giralda* one block down, have been the favoured meeting places of left-wing intellectuals and bohemians – and good places to spot the Porteño talent for whiling away the hours over a single tiny coffee. Corrientes' **bookstores**, many of which stay open till the small hours, have always been as much places to hang out in as to buy from – in marked contrast to almost every other type of shop in the city, where you'll be accosted by sales assistants as soon as you cross the threshold. The most basic of them are simply composed of one long room open to the street with piles of books slung on tables with huge handwritten price labels. There are more upmarket places, too, such as the very swish *Gandhi* at 1743 and the leftish, alternative *Liberarte* at 1555. Almost as comprehensive as the bookstores are the street's numerous pavement kiosks, proffering a mind-boggling range of newspapers, magazines and books, on subjects from psychology to sex. One of the most idiosyncratic of them is the decorative **tango kiosko** on the corner of Corrientes and Paraná (Mon–Fri 9am–8pm, Sat 9am–6pm) where those who take their tango really seriously can pick up various historical and biographical works as well as records.

A recent addition to Corrientes is **La Plaza**, a pleasant, tree-lined pedestrian arcade with a handful of cafés, shops and a performance space. La Plaza lies on the southern side of the street between Rodríguez Peña and Montevideo. One block east, at Corrientes 1500 you'll find the glass front of the **Teatro General San Martín** (see p.145 for booking details); as well as the theatre itself, there's a small free gallery at the back of the building which often has some worthwhile photographic exhibitions, showcasing Argentinian photographers. In the same building is the **Centro Cultural San Martín**, which houses the Museo de Arte Moderno's Ignacio Pirovano Collection on the ninth floor. with a strong selection on Arte Concreto, Argentina's major abstract art movement (see p.748) as well as work by Belgian artist Georges Vantongerloo, a member of the famed De Stijl school and a major influence on the Arte Concreto movement.

Just off Bartolomé Mitre, three blocks south of Corrientes (between Montevideo and Paraná), the **Pasaje de la Piedad** is a late nineteenth-century narrow pedestrian street which makes a pleasant detour with its arched street lamps and grand three-storeyed houses with elegant porches and stately wooden doors.

Looking east along the avenue, you won't miss the **Obelisco**, a 67-metre tall obelisk which dominates the busy intersection between Corrientes and Avenida 9 de Julio. It was erected in 1936 to commemorate four key events in the city's history: the first and second foundings; the first raising of the flag in 1812 and the naming of

Buenos Aires as Capital Federal in 1880. Towering above the swirling traffic and neon signs, the Obelisco is the centrepiece of a breathtaking cityscape which, thanks to the postcard industry, has become Buenos Aires' most iconic image. Its giant scale and strategic location also make it a magnet for carloads of celebrating fans after a major football victory.

Plaza General Lavalle and the Teatro Colón

One block to the north of Corrientes, there's the **Plaza Lavalle**, sandwiched between Calles Libertad and Talcahuano. Slightly less famous than the Plaza de Mayo, Plaza Lavalle can nonetheless lay a claim to its own share of the city's history. Now practically synonymous with the Palacio de Justicia, which houses the Supreme Court and the Poder Judicial (the whole area is often referred to as Tribunales), the square began life as a public park, inaugurated in 1827 by a group of English immigrants and which, the following year, became the site of the city's first funfair. In 1857, the plaza was the departure point for the first Argentinian train journey, made by the locomotive *La Porteña* to Floresta in the west of the capital. The original locomotive can still be seen in the Complejo Museográfico in Luján (see p.220). Later in the same century, the plaza was also the scene of confrontations during the 1890 revolution, also known as the Revolución del Parque when a coalition led by Leandro Além, of the Unión Cívica Radical, ousted the then president Juárez Celman.

Stretching for three blocks, the plaza is a pleasant green space at the heart of the city – though somewhat marred by an underground garage. It is notable for its fine collection of native and exotic **trees**, many of them over a hundred years old. Amongst the pines, magnolias and jacarandas, there stands an ancient Ceibo Jujeño, planted by the city mayor Torcuato de Alvear in 1870, with stunning bright red blossom in spring. The southern end of the square is dominated by the grimy and rather over-the-top facade of the **Palacio de Justicia**. A loose and heavy-handed interpretation of Neoclassicism, heavily adorned with pillars, the building stands as something of a monument to architectural uncertainty. The needs of the busy lawyers who rush to and from the court are catered for by numerous stallholders who set up tables spread with pamphlets explaining every conceivable aspect of Argentinian law. At the centre of the plaza there's a long-running general secondhand **book market** (Mon–Fri 9.30am–6pm). On the eastern side of the square, between Viamonte and Tucumán, there's the handsome **Teatro Colón** (see p.145 for booking details), its grand but restrained French Renaissance exterior painted a muted pinky beige. Most famous as an opera house, though hosting ballet and classical recitals too, the Teatro Colón is undoubtedly Argentina's most prestigious cultural institution. Most of the twentieth century's major opera and ballet stars have appeared here, from Caruso and Callas to Nijinsky and Nureyev, whilst classical music performances have been given by the likes of Toscanini and Rubinstein. The Colón was inaugurated in 1908 with a performance of Verdi's *Aida* and is considered to have some of the best acoustics in the world. There are regular, very informative **guided visits** to the theatre (Mon–Fri 11am–3pm hourly, Sat 9am & noon; $5) in both Spanish and English. The tour takes you through the Italian Renaissance-style central hall, the beautiful gilded and mirrored Salón Dorado (allegedly inspired by Versailles) and the stunning auditorium itself, whose five tiers of balconies culminate in a huge dome decorated with frescoes by Raúl Soldi. Note the boxes on either side of the orchestra pit: known as *palcos de viuda* or "widows' boxes", they provided a discreet vantage point for women in mourning who were anxious not to miss out on their cultural outings – a grille protected them from the public's gaze. The tour also includes a visit to the theatre's workshops where you can see scenery in construction and examples of some of the extravagant footwear and costumes used by past performers.

At the far end of the plaza lies the **Teatro Nacional Cervantes**. The intricate exterior is an example of *plateresque* ornamentation, a richly ornamented Spanish architectural style, common in the early sixteenth century and named for its supposed similarity to fine silversmith's work. At Lavalle 785, there's the **Sinagoga Central de la Congregación Israelita de la República Argentina**. Buenos Aires' Jewish population is one of the largest in the world, and the central synagogue, built in 1932, currently serves over a million people. There is a small **museum** of Jewish history attached to the synagogue (Tues & Thurs 4–6pm; free, but bring ID).

Florida and around

Bisecting the lower reaches of Corrientes, and running between Avenida de Mayo and Plaza San Martín, you'll find pedestrianized **Calle Florida**. At the beginning of the century, Florida was famed as one of the city's most elegant streets – the obligatory route for an evening stroll and home to grand department stores such as Harrods, now remodelled and no longer linked to the London store. Though the northernmost end of the street is still an upmarket shopping district, the majority of the thoroughfare is now given over to small shopping arcades, clothes and bookstores. Nonetheless, it's still one of those central city streets that tourists and locals seem to feel obliged to keep walking up and down. The street sees something like one million people a day tramp its length, and cutting your way through its uninterrupted stream of north–south foot traffic requires a considerable degree of determination. As a matter of fact, this is probably Florida's most appealing quality; there's a lively buzz about the place and always a handful of street performers doing their best to charm passers-by into digging into their pockets.

Running parallel to Corrientes, one block to the north, **Lavalle** is another pedestrianized street, mainly noted for its cinemas: a blockbuster movie during the school holidays can produce impenetrable queues along Lavalle's length. Towards the northern end of Florida, the **Galerías Pacífico** shopping centre offers a glitzy bit of retailing within a vaulted and frescoed building constructed by Paris department store Bon Marché at the end of the nineteenth century. On the first floor, you'll find the entrance to the **Centro Cultural Borges**, (see p.144) a surprisingly large space offering a worthwhile selection of photography and painting exhibitions, from both Argentinian and foreign artists. As far as eating and drinking are concerned, fast-food outlets have established a firm foothold in Florida and Lavalle, although at least one vestige of Florida's more elegant past remains in the shape of the almost anachronistically traditional Richmond confitería at Florida 468, famed for its cakes, hot chocolate, and large, worn leather armchairs. There's also a chess and billiards room downstairs.

A couple of blocks west of Florida, at Tucumán 844, lies the spot where **Jorge Luis Borges** was born. For more on Borges, see the box on p.94.

Puerto Madero

Lying to the east of Avenida L.N. Além, and running north–south from Avenida Córdoba to Avenida Juan de Garay, on the fringes of San Telmo, **Puerto Madero** is Buenos Aires' newest barrio, and the only one occupying the east of the city. The port was constructed in 1882 and consists of four enormous docks running parallel to the River Plate and lined by sturdy red-brick warehouse buildings. Unfortunately, by the time the port was terminated, in 1898, it was already insufficient in scale to cope with the volume of maritime traffic and a new port (named simply the Puerto Nuevo) was constructed to the north. For most of the twentieth century, Puerto Madero sat as a redundant industrial relic, but in the 1990s it was transformed into a voguish mix of restaurants, luxury apartments and offices. The transformation of Puerto Madero has undoubtedly opened up a long-ignored space in the city, but it's a rather elitist development – good for a stroll, but created with little regard as to the potential of the dock

This city that I believed was my past,
is my future, my present;
the years I have spent in Europe are an illusion,
I always was (and will be) in Buenos Aires.

Jorge Luis Borges, "Arrabal", from *Fervor de Buenos Aires* (1921)

There's no shortage of literary works inspired by Argentina's capital city, but no writer has written so passionately about Buenos Aires as **Jorge Luis Borges**. Though he was born in the heart of the city, in 1898, it was the city's humbler barrios that most captivated Borges' imagination. His early childhood was spent in Palermo, now one of Buenos Aires' more exclusive neighbourhoods, but a somewhat marginal barrio at the turn of the century. Borges' middle-class family inhabited one of the few two-storey houses in their street, Calle Serrano, and, though his excursions were strictly controlled, from behind the garden wall Borges could observe the colourful street life which was kept tantalizingly out of his reach. In particular, his imagination was caught by the men who would gather to drink and play cards in the local almacén at the corner of his street. With their tales of knife fights and air of lawlessness, these men appeared time and again in Borges' early short stories – and, later, in *Doctor Brodie's Report*, a collection published in 1970.

Borges' writing talent surfaced at a precociously young age: at 6 he wrote his first short story as well as a piece in English on Greek mythology, and in 1910, when Borges was 11, the newspaper *El País* published his translation of Oscar Wilde's *The Happy Prince*. However, it was not until he returned from Europe in 1921, where he had been stranded with his family during World War I, that Borges published his first book, *Fervor*

area as a recreational space for all the city's inhabitants. A seemingly endless stream of over-sized themed restaurants line the docks – all too many of which seem to be North American chains or pastiches of traditional Argentinian parrillas.

A recent addition to Puerto Madero is the floating **casino**, opened in 1999 and the first in the capital since 1933, when a law was passed prohibiting gambling in the city or its environs. Maritime enthusiasts will want to visit the area's **museum ships**; at dique 1, there's the *Buque Museo Corbeta ARA Uruguay* (daily 10am–9pm; $1) – built in British shipyards and the Argentinian navy's first training ship. At dique 3, you'll find the *Buque Museo Fragata ARA Presidente Sarmiento* (Mon–Fri 9am–8pm, Sat & Sun 9am–10pm; $2), also built in British shipyards, and the Argentinian navy's flagship from 1899 to 1938.

The south

Described by Borges as "an older, more solid world" in his short story entitled *El Sur*, **the south** is Buenos Aires' most traditional quarter and one of the most rewarding areas of the city to stroll around. Immediately to the south of Plaza de Mayo, there's the barrio of **Montserrat**, packed with historic buildings, churches and two small but enjoyable museums, the **Museo de la Ciudad**, whose inventive displays of domestic trivia make a refreshing change from the city's more traditional museums, and the **Museo Etnográfico Juan Bautista Ambrosetti**, focusing on South America's indigenous population. Heading south through **Montserrat**, you'll find yourself amongst the cobbled streets and alleyways of **San Telmo**, where grand nineteenth-century mansions testify to the days when the barrio was Buenos Aires' most patrician. San Telmo

de Buenos Aires, a collection of poems marking his first attempt to capture the essence of the city. Enthused by his re-encounter with Buenos Aires at an age at which he was free to go where he wanted, Borges set out to explore the marginal corners of the city which, during his seven-year absence, had grown considerably. It was never the city's burgeoning modern centre that impressed Borges, however, nor indeed the landscaped parks of Palermo. His wanderings took him to the city's outlying barrios, where streets lined with simple one-storey buildings blended with the surrounding pampa, or to the poorer areas of the city centre with their tenement buildings and bars frequented by prostitutes. With the notable exception of La Boca, which he appears to have regarded as too idiosyncratic – and perhaps, too obviously picturesque – Borges felt greatest affection for the south of Buenos Aires. His exploration of the area that he regarded as representing the heart of the city took in not only the traditional houses of San Telmo and Montserrat, with their patios and decorative facades, but also the humbler streets of Barracas, a largely industrial working-class neighbourhood, and Constitución where, in a gloomy basement in Avenida Juan de Garay, he set one of his most famous short stories, *El Aleph.*

For a writer as sensitive to visual subtlety as Borges – many of his early poems focus on the city's atmospheric evening light – it seems particularly tragic that he should have gone virtually blind in his fifties. Nonetheless, from 1955 to 1973, Borges was Director of the National Library, then located at México 564 in Montserrat, where his pleasure at being surrounded by books – even if he could no longer read them – was heightened by the fact that his daily journey to work took him through one of his favourite parts of the city, from his apartment in Calle Maipú along pedestrianized Florida. As Borges' fame grew, he spent considerable periods of time away from Argentina, travelling to Europe, the United States and other Latin American countries – though he claimed always to return to Buenos Aires in his dreams. Borges died in 1986 in Geneva, where he is buried in the Pleinpalais cemetery.

is particularly worth visiting on a Sunday, when its central square, Plaza Dorrego, is the scene of a fascinating antiques market, the Feria de San Pedro Telmo. At the southern end of the barrio, there's the tranquil **Parque Lezama** – a good spot for observing local life at play, and home to the comprehensive **Museo Histórico Nacional**. Beyond Parque Lezama, and stretching all the way to the city's southern boundary, the Riachuelo, the quirky barrio of **La Boca** is another great place to spend a Saturday or Sunday, wandering its colourful streets and soaking up its idiosyncratic atmosphere. There's also a new and very good gallery here, the **Fundación Proa**. Alongside the river, to the southeast of the city centre, there's the spectacularly wild **Reserva Ecológica**, a newly created park filled with pampas grass and birds, alongside the city's old riverside avenue, the **Costanera Sur**.

Montserrat

Montserrat, also known as Barrio Sur, is the oldest part of the city and, together with neighbouring San Telmo, is one of the most interesting parts to explore on foot. A good starting point for delving into its grid of narrow streets and historic buildings is Calle Defensa, named in honour of its residents who slowed down the pace of British troops by pouring boiling water on them as they marched down it during the British Invasions of 1806 and 1807.

On the corner of Alsina and Defensa stands the eclectic, neo-Baroque **Iglesia de San Francisco** (Mon–Fri 6.30am–noon & 4.30–7pm, Sat 7.30–11am & 4.30–7pm, Sun 7.30–11am), one of the churches burnt by angry Peronists in March 1955 after the navy had bombed a trade union demonstration in Plaza de Mayo, killing several hundred people. The demonstration had been convoked to show support for Perón in his conflict with the Church, which stemmed largely from what the Church saw as his invasion of the religious sphere. Though the Church had supported Perón in the 1946 election, it began turning against him in protest at his political exploitation of charity and education, his appropriation of religious language to describe the Peronist movement and, in 1952, at the campaign for the canonization of Eva Perón. It was a conflict which proved a major factor in Perón's forced resignation in September of 1955. The church was restored, reconsecrated and officially reopened in 1967. An oak column from the original altarpiece, which was destroyed by the fire, is preserved in the adjoining Franciscan monastery.

Half a block west of the church, there's the **Museo de la Ciudad** at Alsina 412 (Mon–Fri 11am–7pm, Sun 3–7pm; $1, free on Wed). The museum is situated in a handsome private residence with a tiled entrance hall and high windows. It's an imaginative, though small, museum which has regularly changing exhibitions designed to illustrate everyday aspects of Porteño life. The wittily displayed objects are largely donated by locals around themes such as summer holidays. Beneath the museum, it's worth popping into the **Farmacia de la Estrella**, a beautifully preserved old pharmacy on the corner of Alsina and Defensa. The pharmacy was founded in 1834 and it boasts a gorgeously opulent interior of heavy walnut fittings, quirky old-fashioned medical murals and mirrors, finished off with a stunning frescoed ceiling.

Continuing south along Defensa, you'll find the **Basílica de Santo Domingo** (Mon–Fri 9am–12.30pm & 2–6pm, Sat 6.30pm, Sun 10.30am–12.30pm), an austere twin-towered structure, on the corner of Defensa and Avenida Belgrano. The basilica's glory is somewhat stolen by the grand elevated mausoleum to General Belgrano which dominates the tiled patio at the front of the church. The square on which the basilica stands was taken by the British on June 27, 1806, on which date the Roman Catholic cult was prohibited. In a gloomy corner at the far left-hand end of the church you can see the flags from English regiments captured by General Liniers and dedicated to the Virgen del Rosario when the city was recaptured two months later.

Taking up the block bounded by Alsina, Perú, Moreno and Bolívar – one block west of Defensa – is the complex of buildings known as the **Manzana de las Luces** or block of enlightenment (for guided visits, ask at Perú 272). Dating from 1662, the complex originally housed a Jesuit community, and has been home to numerous official institutions throughout its history. A series of tunnels run underneath the area, constructed for military purposes during the eighteenth century, they were also used for smuggling. The block currently encompasses the elite Colegio Nacional as well as Buenos Aires' oldest church, **San Ignacio** (Mon–Fri 8am–1.30pm & 5–8.30pm, Sat & Sun 8am–1.30pm), begun in 1675, on the corner of Bolívar and Alsina. As with many of Buenos Aires' churches, various later additions have modified San Ignacio's original construction, the most recent being the tower at the northern end of the church, constructed in 1850. Apart from the rather baroque Altar Mayor, the church's interior is fairly simple. One of its most notable icons is the beautiful seventeenth-century Nuestra Señora de las Nieves, which dominates the altar on the left-hand aisle.

The Museo Etnográfico Juan Bautista Ambrosetti

The **Museo Etnográfico Juan Bautista Ambrosetti** stands at Moreno 350 (Wed–Sun 2.30–6.30pm; guided visits Sat & Sun 3.30pm & 5pm; $1). Named after the museum's founder, this fairly small but interesting museum is part of the Universidad de Buenos Aires. To the right of the entrance there is a room containing a fairly eclectic collection, including bark costumes from Brazil, a feathered headdress from the Chaco and a Japanese suit of armour. Look out for the fantastic Bolivian costume made of jaguar skin and topped with a feline mask, used in religious rituals. The museum runs some good temporary exhibitions on mostly indigenous themes. There's also an informative permanent display on Tierra del Fuego. There are few objects as such, but some excellent panels recounting the history of the region, beginning with a list of expeditions that passed through the area between the sixteenth and eighteenth centuries. Given the remoteness of the region, it's a surprisingly extensive list, comprising scientists, explorers and pirates, and including famous names such as Drake, Edmond Halley and John Cook. There's a very interesting display on the indigenous inhabitants of Tierra del Fuego with panels recounting stories such as that of Jemmy Button, one of four Yámama Indians taken to England by Fitzroy in 1830, where he lived for a period in the unlikely surroundings of Walthamstow, East London. The initial interest in "civilizing" Fueginos was later replaced by a tendency to exhibit them in circuses in Buenos Aires and Europe: in 1882, for example, the Karl Hagenbeck Circus displayed a family of Alacalufs in a cage in Berlin and Paris.

San Telmo

It's impossible not to be seduced by the crumbling decorative facades and cobbled streets of **San Telmo**, one of Buenos Aires' most atmospheric neighbourhoods. A small, almost square-shaped barrio, San Telmo is bounded to the north by Avenida Chile, six blocks south of Plaza de Mayo, to the west by Calle Piedras, to the east by Paseo Colón and to the south by Parque Lezama. Like neighbouring Montserrat, its main artery is the narrow and attractive **Calle Defensa**, once the road from the Plaza de Mayo to the city's port. The barrio's appearance – all crumbling mansions and decaying luxury – is the result of a kind of reverse process of gentrification. When the city's grand mansions were abandoned by their patrician owners after the 1871 yellow fever epidemic, they were soon converted into *conventillos* (tenements) by landlords keen to make a quick buck from newly arrived immigrants who had little option but to put up with the often miserable and overcrowded conditions. The effect of this sudden loss of cachet was to preserve much of the barrio's original features: whereas much of the north, centre and west of the city was variously torn down, smartened up or otherwise modernized, San Telmo's inhabitants simply adapted the neighbourhood's buildings to their changing needs. It's still largely a working-class area – with pockets of severe poverty, particularly underneath the Autopista 25 de Mayo, one of several busy freeways that swoop into town – though the area's superb architecture has also attracted bohemians and artists, many of whom have studios here. San Telmo is one of Buenos Aires' major tourist attractions, particularly for its enjoyable Sunday antiques market, the **Feria de San Telmo**, which takes place in the neighbourhood's central square, **Plaza Dorrego**, and for its nightlife, which includes some of the city's more bohemian spots and best-known **tango** shows. It's also a great area for informal sightseeing – just wandering its streets and admiring the beautiful old houses, traditional bars and antique shops can fill an afternoon, and there's a thriving food market, the Mercado de San Telmo, in the block bounded by Defensa, Carlos Calvo, Estados Unidos and Bolívar. At the southern end of the barrio, the small, palm-lined **Parque Lezama**, containing the city's well-organized **Museo Histórico Nacional**, makes a restful spot to end a tour of the neighbourhood.

Defensa and around

Running south from Plaza de Mayo to Parque Lezama, **Defensa** is a narrow cobbled street running through the heart of San Telmo. On weekdays it's a busy thoroughfare, with buses tearing recklessly along it, but at the weekends you've plenty of space to stand back and admire the elegant mansions which still line the street, some of them converted into bars and antique shops. Just off Defensa, half a block south of Avenida Chile, you'll find one of the barrio's most charming streets. The **Pasaje San Lorenzo** is a small alley running for just two blocks to the east of Defensa. On it, at no. 380, stands the narrowest building in Buenos Aires: the **Casa Mínima**, a tiny two-storey house wedged between its neighbours – its 2.17 metre front just wide enough to accommodate a narrow wooden doorway and a wrought-iron balcony above it. The house was constructed by liberated slaves on a narrow slice of land given to them by their former masters. At the bottom of Pasaje San Lorenzo you'll find a cluster of **tango bars**, of which the most famous, on the corner of Independencia and Balcarce, is *El Viejo Almacén*, founded in 1968 by Edmundo Rivero, one of Argentina's most revered tango singers and renowned for his gruff style and *lunfardo* classics. From here, looking down to Paseo Colón, you can see the massive *Canto al Trabajo*, sculpted by Rogelio Yrurtia (see p.748) in 1907. A great mass of bronze, the sculpture is composed of a heaving mass of bodies hauling a huge rock and is executed in a more expressionistic style than the majority of Yrurtia's rather academic works. From here a stroll south along Balcarce and then west along Carlos Calvo will take you past a pretty parade of houses, including the Antiguo Tasca de Cuchilleros, constructed in 1840, which conserves its original doors and decorative grilles and now houses a restaurant. Back on Defensa itself, don't miss the lively **Mercado Municipal** between Carlos Calvo and Estados Unidos, a thriving city-centre food market.

Plaza Dorrego and the Feria de San Pedro Telmo

At the heart of San Telmo stands Plaza Dorrego. A tiny square, on the corner of Defensa and Humberto 1°, it's surrounded by some elegant two-storeyed mansions, most of them now converted into bars and antique shops. During the week, cafés set up tables in the square and locals play chess or cards at tables. On Sunday, it becomes the setting for the city's long-running antique market, the **Feria de San Pedro Telmo** (Sun 10am–5pm; buses #9, #10, #24, #28 and #86). Almost theatrically set up and overflowing with antique *mates*, jewel-coloured soda syphons, watches and old ticket machines from the city's *colectivos*, the stalls offer a fascinating hour or so's browsing. There are probably no real bargains to be had – the stallholders and habitués are far too canny to let a gem slip through their fingers – but among the market's quirky jumble you may find your own souvenir of Buenos Aires. After the stallholders have packed away their goodies on a Sunday evening, Plaza Dorrego is – weather permitting – the scene for a free **milonga** (tango dance). There's a refreshing informality to this regular event, frequented by tourists, locals and tango fanatics, that might encourage even those with only a rudimentary knowledge of tango to take the plunge.

There are also many **antique shops** clustered around Plaza Dorrego – the window display of Macramé, at Defensa 1065, with its picture of the ever-smiling Carlos Gardel, Argentina's most famous tango singer, nestled among old-fashioned gramophones, is famous enough to have appeared on postcards. Inside you can pick up sheet music for tangos from $2. The bars surrounding the plaza are tempting, too, but watch out for prices. The most traditional of them is the lovely *Plaza Dorrego Bar*, at Defensa 1098, well worth peeking into even if you're not stopping for a coffee.

Just around the corner from Plaza Dorrego, at Humberto 1° 340, stands San Telmo's church, the **Iglesia de Nuestra Señora de Belén** (daily 8am–noon & 4.30–8pm; free guided tours Sun 4pm), whose prettily eclectic facade, a melange of post-colonial, Baroque and Neoclassical influences adorned with statues resting in niches and topped with blue and white tiled bell towers. At Balcarce 1053, one block east of Plaza Dorrego, the **Viejo Hotel** is, as its name suggests, an old hotel, now converted into artists' studios and workshops and with a decent and reasonably priced restaurant.

Heading south from Plaza Dorrego, still along Defensa, you'll come to the **Pasaje de la Defensa**, at Defensa 1179. It's a converted nineteenth-century residence, with a typical tiled courtyard inside and stairs leading up to a gallery. The building now houses more antique shops and cafés. Half a block to the south, the old-world charm of San Telmo's most prettified quarter is rather abruptly curtailed by busy Avenida San Juan, where you will find the **Museo de Arte Moderno de Buenos Aires** at no. 350

(Tues–Fri 10am–8pm, Sat & Sun 1–8pm; $1, free on Wed), housed in an old tobacco factory. The museum has some interesting temporary exhibitions of national and foreign artists in its vast and well laid-out galleries – recent exhibitions have included a visiting show from France with excellent contemporary photographic works from the likes of Cristian Boltanski, Jean Marc Bustamante and the Mexican Gabriel Orozco. The museum also hosts avant-garde theatre and music events and sometimes shows Argentinian and international films in collaboration with the nearby **Museo del Cine** (Mon–Fri 1–7pm; free), around the corner at Defensa 1220. A small, friendly museum, the Museo del Cine runs temporary exhibitions on themes such as Argentinian film posters or Italians in Argentinian film.

Parque Lezama and the Museo Histórico Nacional

Heading south for another three blocks along Defensa will bring you to **Parque Lezama** (buses #24, #29, #86), one of Buenos Aires' most beautiful and underrated parks. Located on a bluff overlooking Paseo Colón, it is generally regarded as the site of the first founding of Buenos Aires by Pedro de Mendoza in 1536. The conquistador's statue looms over visitors as they enter the park from the corner of Defensa and Brasil whilst, on the eastern side, overlooking Paseo Colón, there is a bust of **Ulrich Schmidl**, a German mercenary solider who accompanied Mendoza on his founding expedition. Schmidl's chronicles of the trip, published as *Log of a journey to Spain and the Indies* (1567) – though more easily available in Spanish as *Viaje al Río de la Plata* – recount how the would-be settlers had to resort to eating rats, snakes, shoe leather and, in a few extreme cases, meat cut from the corpses of hanged men. The park is best visited in early evening when the sun filters through its tall palm trees, and the area becomes a hive of quiet activity, with children running along its urn-lined paths and groups of old men play cards or chess at stone tables. The park is also home to dozens of stray cats, probably attracted here by the delicious smell of *dulce de leche*, which occasionally drifts up from the Canale biscuit factory in nearby Martín García.

Lying within the park, though entered via Defensa 1600, there's the **Museo Histórico Nacional** (Tues–Sun noon–6pm; guided visits Sat & Sun 2pm; free), founded in 1887. It's housed in a magnifcent colonial building, painted an almost startling deep red and covered with elaborate white mouldings that look almost like piped icing. The building was constructed by Gregorio Lezama, from whom the park takes its name. Previously rather eclectic, the collection has recently been reorganized and enlarged. It's now a strictly chronological tour of Argentinian history; a well-organized and very accessible exposition of the country's past dating from the pre-Spanish period to 1950. There's an informative display on the first founding of Buenos Aires, including a plan of the first distribution of land in the new city by Juan de Garay. A high point of the collection is the absolutely stunning **Tarja de Potosí**, an elaborate silver and gold shield given to General Belgrano in 1813 by the women of Potosí (a silver mining town in Upper Peru, now Bolivia) in recognition of his role in the struggle for independence from Spain. Over a metre tall, it's a delicately worked and intricate piece covered with tiny figures symbolizing the discovery of America. The room dedicated to the dictator Rosas is worth a visit, too, with its portraits showing the amazingly theatrical bright red uniforms of his troops and depictions of *candombes*, African influenced dances held by the Afro-Argentines of Buenos Aires who, along with other members of the urban poor, were among Rosas' most devoted supporters.

Looking rather out of place amongst all the French- and Italian-influenced architecuture and cobbled streets, the exotic **Iglesia Ortodoxa Rusa** lies opposite the northern end of the park, at Brasil 313. A mass of colourful and curvaceous domes, it was the first Russian orthodox church in Latin America. Built in 1899, it contains many valuable icons donated by Tsar Nicolas II and brought from Russia as the empire was falling into decline. The interior can be viewed, but a sign at the entrance requests that you comply with strict dress codes; women should wear long skirts while men should not enter wearing shorts or hats.

La Boca

La Boca isn't Buenos Aires, it's simply 'La Boca.'

Extract from an article in *La Nación*, 1902

More than any other barrio in Buenos Aires, **La Boca** and its inhabitants seem to flaunt their unique qualities. Located in the capital's southeastern corner, this largely working-class riverside neighbourhood is known as the "República de la Boca" and one of the first things you may notice is the local habit of walking on the road rather than the pavement. This is probably in part because of the disastrous state of some of the pavements (many of which are raised because of frequent flooding), but many Porteños would claim that it is a typical example of boquenses' refusal to play by the rules. Local quirks aside, La Boca is most famous for its brightly coloured wooden and corrugated-iron houses. The district was the favoured destination for the many Italian immigrants who arrived in Buenos Aires in the last century, and the colours of the houses derive from the Genoese custom of painting their houses with the paint left over from their boats. La Boca's other claim to fame is its football team, **Boca Juniors**, who, much to the pique of fierce rivals, River Plate, are not only the country's most popular team but its most famous abroad, partly thanks to Diego Maradona, who was signed to the team in 1981 and returned again in the mid-1990s to an ecstatic welcome by Boca fans.

Named after the *boca* or mouth of the Riachuelo which snakes along its southern border, La Boca is an irregularly shaped barrio, longer than it is wide. Its main avenue is Avenida Almirante Brown which cuts through the neighbourhood from the southeastern corner of Parque Lezama to the towering iron **Puente Transbordador** or transporter bridge which straddles the Riachuelo. Apart from some excellent pizzerias, there's little to detain you along the avenue, however: the majority of La Boca's attractions are packed into the grids of streets on either side. By far the most visited area is the huddle of three or four streets around the **Vuelta de Rocha**, an acute bulge in the river's course, and the barrio's most famous street, **Caminito** lined with the most pristine examples of La Boca's coloured houses. A couple of blocks to the north of Caminito, there's the equally famous **La Bombonera**, Boca Juniors' football stadium. Skirting this southern end of the barrio is **Avenida Don Pedro de Mendoza**, where there are some good bars as well as an excellent new art gallery, the **Fundación Proa**. Much less visited than Caminito, but with a brash down-at-heel charm of its own is **Calle Necochea**, to the east of Avenida Almirante Brown. The street is home to La Boca's famously rowdy *cantinas* or popular restaurants – past their heyday but still a favourite destination for large group outings such as office parties or stag and hen nights. Nearby **Plaza Solís** offers a rather more ramshackle collection of coloured houses than Caminito, though one with a more authentic feel.

La Boca has gained an unfortunate reputation for being, if not unsafe, at least slightly risky for tourists. There's no need to be paranoid about visiting the area, but you should avoid wandering around the less touristy parts visibly touting a camera. The barrio is easily reached on foot from Parque Lezama or can be reached by **bus** #29 from Corrientes or Plaza de Mayo, #86 from Plaza de Mayo or #53 from Constitución.

La Bombonera

The true heart of La Boca, **La Bombonera** makes a good place to start your tour of the neighbourhood. Boca Juniors' stadium stands at Brandsen 805 (☎011/4362-2050), three blocks west of Avenida Almirante Brown (the #86 bus runs right past

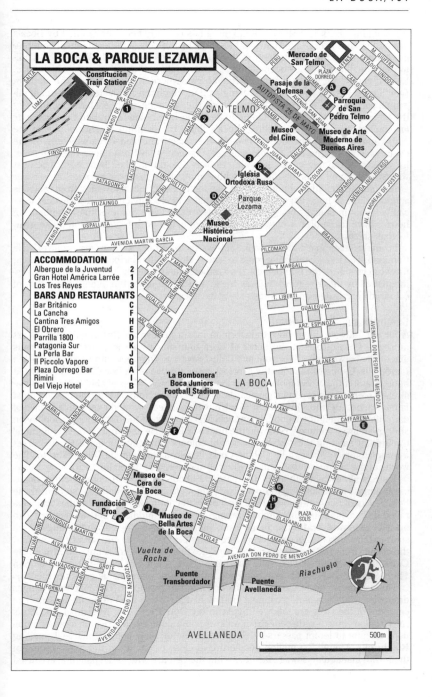

LA BOCA & PARQUE LEZAMA

Constitución
Train Station

SAN TELMO

Mercado de
San Telmo

Pasaje de la
Defensa

Parroquia
de San
Pedro Telmo

Museo
del Cine

Museo de Arte
Moderno de
Buenos Aires

Iglesia
Ortodoxa Rusa

Parque
Lezama

Museo
Histórico
Nacional

ACCOMMODATION
Albergue de la Juventud   2
Gran Hotel América Larrée   1
Los Tres Reyes   3
BARS AND RESTAURANTS
Bar Británico   C
La Cancha   F
Cantina Tres Amigos   H
El Obrero   E
Parrilla 1800   D
Patagonia Sur   K
La Perla Bar   J
Il Piccolo Vapore   G
Plaza Dorrego Bar   A
Rimini   I
Del Viejo Hotel   B

'La Bombonera'
Boca Juniors
Football Stadium

LA BOCA

Museo de
Cera de
la Boca

Fundación
Proa

Museo de
Bella Artes
de la Boca

Vuelta de
Rocha

Puente
Transbordador

Puente
Avellaneda

Riachuelo

N

AVELLANEDA

0   500m

the stadium). Built in 1940, La Bombonera has recently been remodelled by Boca's new millionaire president, Mauricio Macri (as historically significant bits of concrete go, rubble from the old stadium is Boca Juniors fans' own Berlin Wall). The stadium's name, literally "the chocolate box", refers to its particularly compact structure. Even if you're not lucky enough to catch a game here, it's free to visit the stadium (you'll need to take your passport along as ID), which attracts a steady stream of pilgrims, particularly at weekends. Just inside the entrance, there's a large painting by the famous local artist Benito Quinquela Martín (see below). Entitled the *Orígen de la bandera de Boca* (the origin of Boca's flag), the painting illustrates one of the club's most famous anecdotes. Though the exact date and circumstances of the event vary according to different sources, all agree that Boca chose the colours of its strip from the flag of the next ship to pass through its then busy port. The boat was Swedish, and thus the distinctive blue and yellow strip was born.

Around the stadium, a huddle of stalls and shops sell Boca souvenirs, from footballs and key rings to huge flags. This is a good place to pick up a cheap replica shirt (official versions in sports shops often cost upwards of $60). Some of the neighbouring houses have taken up the blue and yellow theme, too, with facades painted like giant football shirts.

From the stadium it's a short walk southwards to La Boca's other nerve centre: Calle Caminito. The most interesting route to take is along Calle Garibaldi, which runs along the western side of the Bombonera. It's a rather ramshackle but characterful street, distinguished by the overgrown railway tracks which run down the middle and a slew of coloured corrugated iron buildings along its sides.

Caminito and the riverfront

A former railway siding now transformed into a pedestrian street and open-air art museum, **Caminito** is at the heart of Boca tourism. It's a short street, which runs diagonally between the riverfront and Calle Olavarría. Together with much less visited Plaza Solís, Caminito contains the greatest concentration of La Boca's vibrantly painted houses, and if the street looks familiar on your first visit, it's probably because you've already seen it on one of many postcards. The street was "founded" by the barrio's most famous artist, **Benito Quinquela Martín**, who painted epic and expressive scenes of daily life in the neighbourhood. Quinquela Martín rescued the old siding from oblivion after the railway company removed the tracks in 1954. He encouraged the immigrants' tradition of painting their houses in bright colours and took the name for the street from a famous 1926 tango by Gabino Coria Peñaloza and Juan de Dios Filiberto. The words of the tango can be found on the wall at one end of Caminito.

There's almost something of the pastiche about Caminito these days: its houses seem almost too colourful, too perfectly photogenic. Nonetheless, the sight of these bold blocks of rainbow-coloured walls set off with contrasting window frames and iron-railed balconies is still absolutely stunning. Down the middle of the street, there's an open-air **arts and crafts fair** (daily 10am–6pm), dominated by garish paintings of the surrounding area. Tango musicians frequently perform along the street too. Around the corner from the southern end of Caminito, there's a wax museum, the **Museo de Cera de la Boca** at Del Valle Iberlucea 1261 (Mon–Fri 10am–6pm, Sat & Sun 11am–8pm; $3), a truly old-fashioned and rather gothic place that is great fun to visit.

The southern end of Caminito leads down to the riverfront. The Riachuelo bulges dramatically at this point, creating a kind of inlet known as the **Vuelta de Rocha**. The contours of the river are followed by **Avenida Don Pedro de Mendoza**, La Boca's riverfront avenue. A wide pedestrian walkway runs alongside the river in a rather ambitious attempt to tempt passers-by closer to the notoriously polluted and evil-smelling **Riachuelo**. Around 3.5 million people live in close proximity to the river – some of them with inadequate sewage facilities – but the vast majority of the pollution is caused by the six hundred or so factories which empty their waste directly into its water. A favourite Porteño anecdote, told with bitter resignation, is that of the Menem government's failed initiative to clean up the Riachuelo. In 1992, President Menem entrusted his hugely unpopular environment secretary María Julia Alsogaray with the task of cleaning the river in one thousand days. By 1995, Menem declared, he'd be out on his boat on the Riachuelo, drinking *mate*, fishing and – most improbably of all to anyone familiar with the river – swimming. By 2000, however, despite the investment of millions of dollars in the project and the fishing out of over a thousand tons of rubbish, the Riachuelo remains seriously polluted and no sightings of either Menem or Alsogaray in swimming costumes have been reported. Another less than picturesque feature of the Vuelta de Rocha are the rusting hulks of ships which jut out of its waters – rather like great dying beasts. In spite of all of this, though, there's actually something strangely majestic about the whole area. The view from Pedro de Mendoza is of a jumbled mass of boats, factories and bridges: directly south as you stand on Pedro de Mendoza, there's the largely industrial suburb of Avellaneda, while to your left there's one of Buenos Aires' major landmarks, the massive iron **Puente Transbordador** or transporter bridge, built in the early years of the twentieth century and now out of use. Next to the transporter bridge is Puente Nicolás Avellaneda – a very similar construction, built in 1939. This functioning road bridge is one of the major routes in and out of the city. Far below it, small rowing boats still ferry passengers to and from Avellaneda.

Away from the riverbank, the area around the bottom of Caminito hosts a craft market at weekends and there are a number of pleasant bars such as *La Perla* on the corner of Del Valle Iberlucea and Pedro de Mendoza where you can soak up a bit of local colour over a draught beer. Half a block south of the intersection between Caminito and Pedro de Mendoza, you'll find one of Buenos Aires' newest and best art galleries, the **Fundación Proa** at no. 1929 (Tues–Sun 11am–7pm; $3; ☎011/4303-0909; *www.proa.org*). Housed within a strikingly converted white mansion – all traditional Italianate elegance outside and bright modern angular galleries within – Proa has no permanent collection but hosts some fascinating and diverse exhibitions ranging from pre-Columbian Argentinian art to twentieth-century Mexican painting. The gallery is topped by a tiny roof terrace – one of the few places from which you can get a view over La Boca – where Buenos Aires' young and trendy come to hear DJs spinning dance tunes on Sundays from 5.30pm.

Further east along Pedro de Mendoza there's the long-established **Museo de Bellas Artes de La Boca** at no. 1835 (Mon–Fri 8am–6pm, Sat & Sun 10am–5pm, closed Jan; free). It was founded in 1938 by Benito Quinqela Martín, on the site of his studio, and houses many of his major works, as well as those of contemporary Argentinian artists. It's the perfect setting for a display of Quinquela Martín's work, since you can actually see much of his subject matter simply by peering out of the windows of the gallery. More than anyone, Quinqela Martín conveyed the industrial grandeur of La Boca, dedicating himself to painting scenes of everyday working life – perhaps somewhat in the spirit of a Lowry, albeit in a much more exuberant and uplifting style.

Necochea and Plaza Solís

Immediately to the left of Puente Nicolás Avellaneda, and running parallel to Avenida Almirante Brown, you'll find Calle **Necochea**, its high pavements lined with slightly shabby bars and restaurants. Once known for its lively and rather decadent nightlife, Necochea has the feel of a street which has known, if not better, at least more exciting days. Nonetheless, there is a certain seedy charm to the street, something that was not lost on film director Wong Kar-Wai, who set much of his 1997 film *Happy Together* here – the strange story of a gay Chinese couple who decide to try their luck in Buenos Aires after a failed road trip to Iguazú. For most Porteños, however, Necochea's most famous institutions are its **cantinas**. The food (pasta, chicken and seafood) is not so much the point at these fantastically gaudy restaurants as the unlimited wine and lively entertainment which accompanies it into the early hours. Traditionally chosen for celebrating special occasions, the *cantinas* had their heyday in the 1970s. Since then, a number have closed, including the most famous, *Spadavecchia*. Nonetheless, several remain (see p.133), mostly on the two blocks that lie between Brandsen and Olavarría, a couple of blocks north of the riverfront. The best way to experience the raucous fun of a *cantina* (usually open weekends and holidays only) is undoubtedly in a large group – though there's nothing to stop you going as a couple, you'll probably feel a little out of place.

One block east of Necochea, you'll find **Plaza Solís**, a little-visited area of La Boca. This spacious square was the neighbourhood's first public space and once its heart. Like Caminito, Plaza Solis is surrounded by examples of La Boca's colourful architecture. It's far less pristine than touristy Caminito, though, and, like Necochea, has not been spruced up for the visitors.

The Costanera Sur and the Reserva Ecológica Costanera Sur

Running along the eastern side of the city, beyond Puerto Madero, the **Costanera Sur** is rather misleadingly named these days. Built as a riverside promenade at the beginning of the twentieth century, this sweeping avenue, flanked by elegant balustrades, is now estranged from its *raison d'être*. A landfill project, begun in the 1970s with the intention of creating a new coastal freeway and civic centre, separated the avenue from the river by some 1.5km. It's still a pleasant place for a stroll, though, if somewhat rundown in patches. Efforts are being made, however, to restore it as a leisure facility and a new sunbathing area is being constructed near the entrance to the Reserva Ecológica (see below). Opposite this same entrance there's the flamboyant Fuente de las Nereidas, a large and elaborate marble fountain executed by Tucumán sculptress Lola Mora in 1902. The fountain depicts a naked Venus perched with her legs coquettishly crossed on the edge of a shell supported by two straining Nereids, or sea nymphs. Below this central sculpture three Tritons struggle manfully amongst the waves to restrain horses whose rearing pose seems to suggest arousal by Venus. The fountain was originally destined for the Plaza de Mayo, but this seductive display of female nudity was regarded as too risqué to be placed in such proximity to the cathedral.

Lying at the southern end of the Costanera, the **Reserva Ecológica**, Av. Tristán Achaval Rodríguez 1550 (April–Oct 8am–6pm; Nov–March 8am–7pm; free; ☎011/4315-1320) offers an unexpectedly natural enviromnent just minutes from the fury of downtown Buenos Aires. The reserve stretches for some 2km alongside the Costanera and is about 1.5km wide at its broadest point. At first encounter you might imagine this sizeable fragment of wild and watery grassland to be a strangely neglected remnant of the landscape that greeted Pedro de Mendoza as he sailed into the estuary. Its origins are far more recent, however. When the landfill project of the 1970s was abandoned in 1984, the seeds present in the silt dredged from the river and borne by the wind provided the basis for a rapid vegetation of the area. Birds and animals soon established themselves, too, and the area is now thriving. Indeed, the area was made a dedicated reserve as early as 1986, although a recent spate of arson attacks indicates that there are those who would prefer to see this prime piece of real estate developed.

Just inside the entrance to the park, there's a **visitor centre** with display panels on the development of the park, and an excellent series of leaflets helping you to identify the park's plant and animal life. The rangers also organize guided walks – occasionally at night. There are a number of trails around the reserve, a strange and wonderful park in which each turn of the corner offers a new juxtaposition of urban and natural, whether it is factory chimneys glimpsed through fronds of pampa grass or the city sky-line over a lake populated by ducks and herons. The park is most noted for its bird pop-ulation (over two hundred species visit over the year), particularly the aquatic species which inhabit its lakes: as well as various sub-species of ducks and herons, you may spot elegant black-necked swans, skittish coots, and the common gallinule, very simi-lar to the coot but easily distinguished by the way it propels itself through the water with a jerking back and forth of the head. Gliding above your head you may see the snail hawk, a bird of prey which uses its hooked beak to winkle freshwater snails out of their shells. The park is also home to small mammals and reptiles such as the coypu, an acuatic rodent, and monitor lizards, commonly called iguanas in Argentina. The park's vegetation includes willows and the ceibo, a tall tree with a twisted trunk whose bright red blossom is Argentina's national flower. By far the most dominant plant, how-ever, is *cortadera* or pampas grass, which grows up to three metres high. The park is also a popular cruising area for gay men on Sundays.

No **bus** goes directly to the the Costanera Sur and the Reserva Ecológica, but both the #2 (which goes along Avenida Belgrano) and the #111 from Paraguay and Maipú terminate at the intersection of Belgrano and Azopardo, from where it's a ten-minute walk or so past Puerto Madero and over the railway tracks to the Costanera.

The north

Buenos Aires' finest museums happen to be concentrated in its northern residential barrios of Belgrano, Palermo, Recoleta and Retiro, which stretch for kilometres along wide avenues beyond Avenida Córdoba. These museums contain the country's princi-pal collections of colonial art, Spanish art, folk art, decorative art, and plastic art since independence, while a couple are dedicated to two of Argentina's most original twentieth-century artists, Xul Solar and Rogelio Yrurtia. Like the rest of the city's bar-rios, all four have a distinctive character while being true to the city as a whole – broad-ly speaking a combination of extravagant elegance and an authentic lived-in feel per-vades each of them.

The two northern barrios nearest to the centre, **Retiro** and **Recoleta**, both have their chic streets, lined with boutiques, art galleries, and smart cafés where there seems to be a dress code even to order a quick beer; these desirable neighbourhoods are known collectively to residents as **Barrio Norte**. Part of this snobbery is due to the fact that parts of Retiro – especially the dockside fringes and the highly insalubrious bits near the city's biggest train station, also called Retiro – are just as down-at-heel as parts of the southern barrios, if not more so. **Recoleta** on the other hand is avoided on business cards almost out of superstition, as the name is associated primarily with the barrio's magnificent **cemetery** where, among other national celebrities, **Evita** is buried. Both barrios also share an extraordinary concentration of French-style **palaces**, tangible proof of the obsession of the city's elite at the beginning of the twen-tieth century with the idea that their fledgling capital city needed to resemble Paris for Argentina to become a world power. Many of these palaces can be visited and some of them house the area's opulent museum collections, but they are also sights in them-selves; wandering about the barrios' streets scrutinizing their finer details offers an interesting counterpoint to roaming in San Telmo or La Boca.

Palermo and **Belgrano**, farther north, are large districts composed by turn of high-rise apartment buildings, tree-lined boulevards, and little cobbled streets of villas and grandiose neocolonial houses. An inordinate number of Buenos Aires' best restaurants and many of its shopping meccas are located up here, so you're likely to be heading in this direction at least once during a stay. It's worth making a day of it to check out the beautiful **parks and gardens**, attend a game of polo or pato – Argentina's most idiosyncratic national sports – or to see another beguiling side of the city in, for example, Palermo Viejo's Plaza Julio Cortázar, a colourful square surrounded by lively cafés-cum-art-galleries.

Retiro

Squeezed between Avenida Córdoba to the south, dog-legged Calle Montevideo to the west, and the mostly inhospitable docklands, to the north and east, **Retiro** gets its name from a wild hermits' retreat or *retiro*, hidden among dense woodland here in the sixteenth century, when Buenos Aires was little more than a village. Today, it's surprisingly varied for such a small barrio: commercial art galleries (see p.143) and airline offices outnumber other businesses along the busy streets around the far end of Calle Florida, near the barrio's focal point, Plaza San Martín, while to the west of Avenida 9 de Julio lies a smart, quiet residential area. The northernmost swathe, however, is of far less interest to visitors. You're unlikely to venture to the sleazy **riverside** reaches of Retiro unless you're catching a boat to Uruguay, a bus to any South American destination, or a train to the northern suburbs, Tigre or the provinces; it's certainly unwise to linger hereabouts, especially after dark.

A lot of the architecture around the plaza, and in the relatively secluded area immediately to the northwest, shows how, from the 1880s to the 1930s, wealthy Porteños yearned for their city to be a New World version of Paris. Sometimes they took this ambition to extremes: the builders of Art Deco **Palacio Estrugamou**, at Juncal and Esmeralda, for example, actually had all of the materials, down to the windowpanes, shipped over from France, and the massive apartment building is locally famous for sporting a bronze copy of the *Victory of Samothrace* in one of its huge patios. Lots of private homes built in the barrio, around 1900, were designed by French architects as exact copies of Parisian *hôtels particuliers* or French chateaux, so as to indulge this Francomania, and many have survived the destructive urban planning of the 1930s and 1950s.

Lying at Retiro's aristocratic heart, **Plaza San Martín** is one of the city's most enticing green spaces. It's flanked by opulent patrician buildings such as Palacio San Martín, the former Foreign Ministry, and Palacio Paz, now a military museum, as well as one of Buenos Aires' top hotels, and the lavish Basílica del Santísimo Sacramento. Further outstanding examples of the barrio's palaces are clustered around **Plaza Carlos Pellegrini**, undeniably one of the city's most elegant squares, on the edge of the Retiro's affluent residential streets. In between the two plazas, Museo Isaac Fernández Blanco, a gem among the city's museums, contains an impressive collection of colonial silverware, furniture and paintings. It's housed in a neocolonial Peruvian-style mansion of the kind built in the early twentieth century by those rare Porteños who rejected the obsession with all things French.

For most Porteños, the barrio's name has become synonymous with the once grand but now rather decrepit **Estación Retiro**, on Avenida Dr Ramos Mejia. It's actually three stations in one, named after Generals Mitre, Belgrano and San Martín. Built by a British company in 1913, they still retain their original Edwardian-style features, such as the mosaic floors, Royal Doulton tiles, wrought-iron lamps and platform signs, alongside automatic ticket-machines, the only concession to modernity. An estimated million commuters pass through every weekday. Beyond the dingy stations, the state-of-the-art bus terminal, and the traffic-choked streets around them, Retiro subsides into an urban wasteland. Just north of the bus terminal, lurks one of the city's most notorious shanty towns, **Villa 31** or Villa del Retiro, whose tightly packed inhabitants survive in abject poverty. Despite the nearby police station and Air Force HQ, the area can be a pretty dodgy place to find yourself in, so don't let your curiosity get the better of you. These associations explain why the barrio's wealthier residents invariably talk of it as "Barrio

Norte", a much-used generic name for both Retiro and its northern neighbour, Recoleta. You can reach the barrio by **subte**; both San Martín and Retiro stations are on Line C.

Plaza San Martín

The leafy southern half of **Plaza San Martín** is a romantic meeting place, office-workers' picnic area, children's playground, and many people's arrival point in downtown Buenos Aires, since the airport shuttle-buses drop you off here, at the far eastern end of Avenida Santa Fe. The plaza was designed by Argentina's most important landscape architect, Frenchman **Charles Thays** (see box below), and created specially for a **monument to General San Martín** that was moved here in 1910 for the country's centenary. Aligned with Avenida Santa Fe, the imposing bronze equestrian statue – cast in 1862 it was Argentina's first – stands proudly on a high marble pedestal decorated with scenes representing national liberation. The Libertador points west, showing the way across the Andes. Magnificent though it is, the statue's overshadowed by the magnificent rubber-tree that stands before it, its weighty branches propped like the fingers of a great gnarled hand that has guarded several generations of shade-seekers. The plaza's lush lawns are a favourite sunbathing spot in the warmer months, but when it gets baking hot you can always cool down on a bench beneath the luxuriant palms, ceibos, monkey puzzles, lime-trees and acacias. In November the spectacular jacarandas, added by Thays' son, blush mauve with their trumpet-shaped blossom.

The more open, northern half of the plaza slopes down to Avenida del Libertador, one of the major arteries that runs through northern Buenos Aires all the way to Tigre. The **Monumento a los Héroes de la Guerra de las Malvinas** stands here, a sombre block of black marble inscribed with the names of Argentina's fallen during the conflict, its eternal flame partly symbolizing Argentina's persistent claim over the

---

CHARLES THAYS

The French botanist and landscape architect **Charles Thays** (1849–1934) travelled to South America in the 1880s to study its rich flora, particularly the hundreds of tree species. He settled in Argentina, where his services were in great demand, first in Buenos Aires and then in the provinces, before moving on to Uruguay and Chile. In the 1890s, municipal authorities across the country wanted their cities smartened up in time for the end of the century and later for the 1910 centenary celebrations. Also, like their European and North American counterparts, they realized that the country's fast-growing urban sprawls needed parks and gardens as vital breathing-spaces and recreational areas. Open plazas formerly used for military parades, or *plazas secas*, were turned into shady *plazas verdes*, "green squares"; Plaza San Martín, in Buenos Aires, and Plaza 25 de Mayo, in Catamarca, are among the best examples of Thays' transformations. He also designed the capital's botanical garden, officially named after him and where he's honoured with a handsome bronze bust, and the zoo – which he planted with dozens of tipas – as well as Palermo's Parque 3 de Febrero, Belgrano's Barrancas, Córdoba's Parque Sarmiento and Parque San Martín, Tucumán's Parque 9 de Júlio and, most impressive of them all, Mendoza's Parque General San Martín. Thays received countless private commissions, too, such as the garden of Palacio Hume, on Avenida Alvear in Recoleta, and the layout of the exclusive residential estate known as Barrio Parque, in Palermo Chico. Despite his French origins, he preferred the informal English style of landscaping; he also experimented with combinations of native plants such as jacarandas, tipas and *palo borracho* with Canary Island palms, planes and lime trees. In 1890, he was appointed director of city parks and gardens and, given the high regard in which he was held, Plaza Carlos Thays, alongside the city's monumental Law Faculty, is disappointingly barren, and definitely not the best example of landscaping the city has to offer.

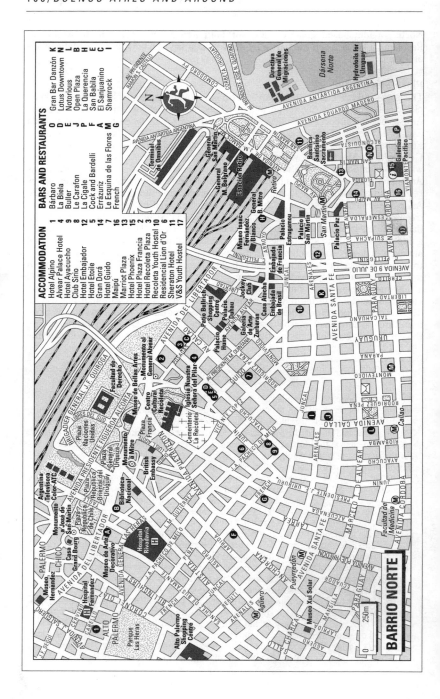

ACCOMMODATION

Hotel Alpino	1
Alvear Palace Hotel	4
Hotel Ayacucho	9
Club Sirio	8
Hotel Embajador	12
Hotel Etoile	5
Gran Dorá	14
Hotel Guido	7
Maipú	16
Marriot Plaza	13
Hotel Phoenix	15
Hotel Plaza Francia	2
Hotel Recoleta Plaza	3
Recoleta Youth Hostel	10
Residencial Lion d'Or	6
Sheraton Hotel	11
V&S Youth Hostel	17

BARS AND RESTAURANTS

Bárbaro	B	Gran Bar Danzón	K
La Biela	I	Lotus Downtown	N
Buller	J	Notorious	L
Le Carafon	P	Open Plaza	B
La Cigale	F	La Querencia	H
Cock and Bardelli	A	San Babila	C
Errázuriz	M	El Sanjuanino	I
Le Esquina de las Flores	G	Shamrock	
French			

BARRIO NORTE

South Atlantic islands. In the former Plaza Británica – **Plaza Fuerza Aérea Argentina** since 1982 – across the avenue to the north, however, is a symbol of the recent thaw in relations between Argentina and the UK. London's Big Ben was clearly the model for the seventy-metre **Torre de los Ingleses**, the Anglo-Argentine community's contribution to the 1910 centenary celebrations, but during and after the 1982 conflict there was talk of demolishing it, and it was officially renamed Torre Monumental. The landmark was smartened up for the millennium celebrations, though, and you can once again climb to the top for great views (Mon–Fri 9am–6pm; free). The clock-tower used to share the plaza with a statue of nineteenth-century British Foreign Secretary Lord Canning (see box, p.116).

Palacio San Martín

Immediately to the northwest of Plaza San Martín, at Arenales and Esmeralda, **Palacio San Martín** (guided visits: Thurs 11am & noon, Fri 3pm, 4pm, 5pm & 6pm, last Sat of month 11am, noon, 3pm, 4pm, 5pm & 6pm; free; ☎011/4819-8092) is a particularly extravagant example of the ostentatious palaces that many of the city's rich and famous commissioned in the early twentieth century. It was built in 1905 for one of Argentina's richest and most influential landowning clans, the aristocratic **Anchorena family** – who gave rise to the Argentine expression "as rich as an Anchorena". Matriarch Mercedes Castellanos de Anchorena and her sons, Enrique and Emilio, and their families lived here for twenty years, until the great Depression left them penniless. The enormous building is actually divided up into three subtly different palaces, sharing a huge Neoclassical entrance and ceremonial courtyard. Its overall structure is based on a nineteenth-century Parisian banker's mansion, with its slate mansard roofs, colonnades and domed attics, while the neo-Baroque interior is inspired by the eighteenth-century *Hôtel de Condé*, also in Paris. Fashionably Art Nouveau details were also incorporated, such as the ornate stained-glass windows and the flowing lines of the wrought-iron staircases.

After the palace and its accumulated treasures were hurriedly sold off in 1927, the State turned it into the Ministry of Foreign Affairs, International Trade and Worship. Since the 1980s, when the ministry moved out into larger premises, a shiny plate-glass monstrosity across Calle Esmeralda, the palace has been reserved for **state ceremonies**, and has been open to the public since 1999. It's still being restored as far as possible to its former appearance, and some of the original furniture and paintings have even been recovered, but the guided visits are above all a rare opportunity to witness the opulent interior of a Porteño palace. The enormous gilt mirrors, marble fireplaces, gleaming tropical wood furniture, giant chandeliers, collections of French porcelain and imposing family portraits are all on a grandiose scale. Yet they still look lost in the cavernous reception rooms and dining halls, with their polished parquet floors, inlaid wooden panelling and ceilings richly decorated with oil paintings.

Basílica del Santísimo Sacramento and Edificio Kavanagh

On the southeast flank of Plaza San Martín, at San Martín 1039, the **Basílica del Santísimo Sacramento** (Mass Mon–Fri 7am, 8am, 9am & 7pm, Sat 7am, 8am & 7pm, Sun & religious feasts 10.30am & 7.30pm) stands opposite the Palacio San Martín. The basilica was also built with some of **Mercedes Castellanos de Anchorena**'s considerable fortune, and she is buried there, in considerable style. Consecrated in 1916, it's still regarded as the smartest place to get married in Buenos Aires. It was designed by French architects, of course, with its white marble dome and five slender turrets; and it's no coincidence that it looks so much like Paris's Sacré Coeur, which was considered to be the pinnacle of church design in this Paris-obsessed city. Inside, the Byzantine style altarpiece is the work of an Italian artist, while the wooden confessionals, pulpit and doors are that of Flemish craftsmen. No expense was spared by the devout widow: red onyx from Morocco, marble from Verona and Carrara, red sandstone from the Vosges, glazed mosaic tiles from Venice and bronze from France were shipped across to decorate her monument to devotion. Down in the crypt and behind a protective grille, Mercedes Castellanos de Anchorena's **mausoleum**, an ostentatious yet doleful concoction of marble angels guarded by a demure Virgin Mary, seems unintentionally to denote the heiress's fall from wealthy grandeur.

The **Edificio Kavanagh**, next door to the basilica at San Martín and Florida, similarly sums up the social – and architectural – evolution in twentieth-century Buenos Aires. When it went up in 1935, it was, at 120m, the tallest building in South America, and the first on the continent to use reinforced concrete and to have integrated air conditioning. The two facades of its distinctive grid-iron shape – it's built in a wedge formed by the two streets – were hailed at the time by the American Institute of Architects as the world's best example of Rationalist architecture. Inhabited in the early years by many of the city's rich and famous, including Enrique Larreta (see p.126), it's no longer regarded as a desirable address and, although still impressive, it long ago lost its title as the city's tallest building.

Palacio Paz

Press baron José Paz, founder of daily *La Prensa* and related by marriage to the Anchorena family, wanted his Buenos Aires home to look like the Louvre. He therefore had the **Palacio Paz**, on the southwest side of Plaza San Martín at Marcelo T. de Alvear 745, built by a French architect who came up with the goods in 1902. The largest single house ever built in Argentina, it's an uncanny replica of the Sully wing of the Parisian palace, with its steeply stacked slate roofs in the shape of truncated pyramids, double row of tiny windows and colonnaded ground floor. The Prince of Wales dined there during his historic visit to the city in 1925, but the Paz family, like the Anchorenas, fell on hard times in the late 1920s and the palace was divided between the Círculo Militar, an officers' club, and the **Museo de Armas de la Nación** (Wed–Fri 3–7pm; $1), which now houses a large exhibition here of armoury, weapons and military uniforms, some dating back to the Wars of Independence.

Museo de Arte Hispanoamericano Isaac Fernández Blanco

Three blocks north and one west of Palacio Paz, at Suipacha 1422, is the **Museo de Arte Hispanoamericano Isaac Fernández Blanco** (Tues–Sun 2–7pm; guided tours in Spanish and English Sat & Sun 4pm; closed Jan; $1, free on Thurs), one of the city's cultural highlights. It's housed in the Palacio Noel, a stunning neocolonial house, built by architect Martín Noel, who shared it with his brother Carlos until 1947, when they donated it to the city. He built it in the 1920s, in a style imitating eighteenth-century Lima Baroque, as a backlash against his contemporaries' slavish imitation of Parisian palaces. With its plain white walls, lace-like window-grilles, dark wooden bow-windows and wrought-iron balconies, it's the perfect home for the superb collection of Spanish-American art on display inside. The flagstoned patio, which you cross to enter the house, and the Andalucian-style gardens to the side of it, decorated with Moorish-tiled benches, are usually an oasis of calm, but the silence was shattered in 1992 by the murderous bomb attack that tore apart the nearby Israeli Embassy. The museum's contents miraculously survived, but the house suffered structural damage and the repairs took seven years to complete.

Several private collections, including the Noel brothers' own collection of colonial art, and the art dealer Isaac Fernández Blanco's generous donation of paintings, were merged to form the present-day museum, which boasts a huge collection of colonial silverware. A strategically exposed masterpiece strikes you as soon as you walk in: a fantastic eighteenth-century silver sacrarium, embellished with a portrait of Christ on

THE CUSQUEÑA SCHOOL OF ART

The **Cusqueña School of Art**, named after the Peruvian city of Cusco, is generally regarded as the most prodigious in colonial South America. Its masters, especially active in the eighteenth century in and around the city, were gifted with an extraordinary ability to produce subtle oil paintings, mostly of religious, devotional subjects, that somehow combined sombre understatement with a startling vitality. Favourite subjects – as part of Counter-Reformation propaganda – were the Crucifixion, the Virgin Mary, San Francisco Solano and other founders of the religious orders that evangelized Spanish America, and the saints in general. Their highly valued work is partly derivative, with the main inspiration taken from fashionable Flemish, French and Italian engravings and woodcuts, though the influence of the great Spanish master Francisco Zurbarán (1598–1664) can be detected in the clear, austere use of colour, the solid forms and the frequent fusion of the mystical and the realistic. The bulk of their production has never left Peru, but several examples of this school's production can be found in churches and museums across Argentina, a reflection of the fledgling country's reliance on imported art in the early nineteenth century, to satisfy the demands of the landed aristocracy and emerging middle classes until local artists came to the fore.

a copper plaque, strikingly set off against purple velvet. This, and most of the remaining artefacts on display, all favourably presented and delicately lit, were produced in the seventeenth and early eighteenth centuries, in Peru or Alto Peru, today's Bolivia. Only when the upper and middle classes began to emerge in Argentina, in the late eighteenth century, was there any domestic demand for silverware and paintings. That demand was initially satisfied by artisans working in places such as Cusco and Lima, where a huge and prosperous industry had flourished since the earliest colonial times, or by Portuguese craftsmen brought down from Brazil.

High points of this huge and varied collection, on two floors, include finely wrought silver *mate* vessels, a set of brightly painted wooden figures from Ecuador, and a Luso-Brazilian silver votive lamp. Look out, too, for the polychrome furniture, including a particularly vibrant bedstead, the work of Bolivian craftsmen, in a naive adaptation of an early nineteenth-century Spanish bedroom. From the extensive display of anonymous Cusqueña paintings (see box above), a dramatic portrait of *Philip V*, an *Admiration of the Shepherds* and a *Virgin of Mercy Crowned by the Holy Trinity* stand out. Even more startling is a naked Mary Magdalene, concealing her breasts with her forearm, in a delicately coloured seventeenth-century painting by Peruvian artist Antonio Bermejo. Highly acclaimed temporary exhibits of colonial art from the rest of Latin America are regularly displayed in the museum annexe, to the right of the main entrance.

Plaza Carlos Pellegrini and its palaces

If there's any part of Retiro where local residents talk of "Barrio Norte" instead of using the neighbourhood's official name, then it's around **Plaza Carlos Pellegrini**. This elegant triangle is a focal point of Retiro's well-heeled, residential streets west of Avenida 9 de Julio, and near it you'll find a variety of spectacular buildings that have two main things in common: their meticulously French style and their exorbitant cost, both to build at the time and to live in nowadays. Between 1910 and 1925, the obsession with turning Buenos Aires into the "Paris of the South" reached fever pitch in this part of the city. **Carlos Pellegrini** was president in the 1890s and his many feats include founding the Banco Nación, still a major bank, and Argentina's influential **Jockey Club**; the latter's national headquarters occupies the massive honey-coloured stone hulk of the **Palacio Unzué de Casares**, on the north side of the plaza, at Av. Alvear 1345. Built in the severely unadorned *style académique*, it's alleviated only by its delicate wrought-iron balconies. Opposite, on the south side of the plaza, stands the **Palacio Celedonio Pereda**, named after a member of the oligarchy who wanted a carbon copy of the Palais Jaquemart-André in Paris. The Porteño palace, now occupied by the Brazilian Embassy, is a totally successful replica, Ionic columns and all, crowned by a huge slate-tiled cupola.

Directly east of the plaza, at the corner of Calle Cerrito, stands ivy-clad **Casa Atucha**, a soberly stylish Second Empire mansion by René Sergent, a French architect who never set foot in Argentina but designed dozens of houses here. Half a block north, at Cerrito 1455, *La Mansión*, one of the city's most expensive restaurants, now occupies the Palacio Félix Alzaga, the faultless duplicate of a Loire chateau, built in attractive red brick and pale cream limestone and topped off with a shiny slate mansard roof. In 1925, the French Embassy moved into the Louis XIV-style **Palacio Ortiz Basualdo**, just after the Prince of Wales was put up there, as the guest of the Argentine government. The magnificent palace, with its slightly incongruous detailing such as Art Nouveau balconies, monumental Ionic pilasters and bulging Second Empire corner-turret, mercifully escaped the fate of many similar buildings, demolished in the 1950s when Avenida 9 de Julio was widened, but had to be altered considerably to accommodate the highway. From Plaza Carlos Pellegrini, Avenida Alvear (see p.115) leads due northwest to Recoleta and its landmark cemetery.

Recoleta

Immediately northwest of Retiro and stretching all the way to Avenida Coronel Díaz, the well-heeled barrio of **Recoleta** is, for most Porteños, synonymous with the magnificent and highly elitist **cemetery** lying in its midst. Many visitors to the city make a bee-line there, if only to see the vault beneath which Evita's remains are buried, in one of the world's most remarkable burial grounds, along with Paris' Père-Lachaise, London's Highgate and Prague's Jewish Cemetery. Somehow not morbid, it presents an exhilarating mixture of architectural whimsy and a panorama of Argentine history, given that most of Argentina's great and good have been buried here since the country's independence. Recoleta wasn't always a prestigious place, though: until the end of the seventeenth century, its groves of Barbary figs were hideouts for notorious brigands. Franciscan monks then set up a **monastery** here around 1720, and monks flocked there to enjoy its peace and quiet, perfect for meditation or "recollection", hence the name. At the beginning of the nineteenth century, **Calle de las Tunas**, or "Barbary Fig Street", now called Avenida Callao, was laid out as a kind of early city ring-road, and some Porteños had weekend homes built along it. However, it wasn't until the cholera and yellow fever epidemics in 1867 and 1871 that the city's wealthy moved here from hitherto fashionable San Telmo. In 1885, Buenos Aires' first mayor, **Torcuato de Alvear**, had a wide avenue built to join the area to the rest of the city – the avenue was later named after him. The soil scooped out when creating the city's docks, at the end of the nineteenth century, was used for landscaping Recoleta's gardens and squares. Even though, over the past decade or two, many of its former residents have left for the cleaner air of the northern suburbs, a Recoleta address definitely still has cachet.

For the visitor, there's more to Recoleta than a cemetery, beginning with the gleaming white **Basílica Nuestra Señora del Pilar**, right next door to La Recoleta's gates: it's one of the capital's few remaining colonial buildings and most revered churches. Close by are two arts centres, the **Centro Cultural de Recoleta**, housed in the disused convent, and the **Palais de Glace**, a former skating rink and tango hall, currently used for a variety of cultural events. Not far away, the country's biggest and richest collections of nineteenth- and twentieth-century art are on display at **Museo Nacional de Bellas Artes**, while the **Biblioteca Nacional**, a controversial piece of modern architecture, houses a priceless set of antique books and is also the country's copyright library. Out on a limb, in the southwestern corner of the barrio, is the **Museo Xul Solar**, the former home of one of Argentina's most original artists; it contains a large collection of his intriguing paintings. Avenida Alvear is Buenos Aires swankiest street, along which you'll find more stately palaces, plus designer boutiques, swish art galleries and one of the city's most prestigious hotels. Recoleta's mainly a residential area, whose inhabitants – like Retiro's – prefer to say they live in "Barrio Norte". Scattered throughout the barrio, in among the blocks of grandiose apartment buildings, are a host of restaurants and bars, ranging from some of the city's most traditional institutions to trendy joints that come and go. A standing joke has it that the elite of Barrio Norte used to eat and drink at *Café de la Paix*, pray at the basilica and rot in the cemetery.

The subte skirts the southern edge of Recoleta, so for most destinations hop on a **bus**, such as #10, #37, #38, #41, #60 or #118. The Museo Xul Solar is the exception, just three blocks west of Agüero station on subte Line D.

La Recoleta Cemetery

La Recoleta Cemetery at Av. Quintana and Junín (daily 7am–6pm; 3rd Sun of month 7am–2.30pm; guided tours last Sun of month at 2.30pm; free) is an awe-inspiring place, exerting a magnetic attraction on locals and foreigners alike, principally because it's where **Evita** is buried. Created in 1822, in the gardens of the Franciscan monastery, after the monks were ejected by the city governor, it was extended to its current rhomboidal shape in the 1830s, and a grid pattern of streets and plazas, like that of the rest of the city, was introduced. Seen from high up, the cemetery's giant vaults, stacked along avenues inside the high walls, resemble the rooftops of a fanciful Utopian town, not unlike the ones you sometimes see in seventeenth-century engravings. The necropolis is a city within a city, a lesson in architectural styles and fashions, and Argentine history materialized in great monuments of dark granite, white marble and gleaming bronze, decorated with countless stone angels and statues of the Virgin Mary. In his poem *La Recoleta*, in the 1923 collection *Fervor de Buenos Aires*, Borges elegizes the cemetery and its beautiful graves with their terse Latin inscriptions and fateful dates, its mixture of marble and flowers, and its little plazas as cool as patios. Another Argentine writer, Martín Cáparros, was even more melancholy: for him, La Recoleta was a magnificent tribute to many great civilizations of the past – from Babylonian and Egyptian, to Roman and Byzantine – and its flamboyant architecture embodied the grandiose hopes of Argentina's heroes and historians that their country would become just as great. But in the end, he concluded, the only fatherland they managed to build was the cemetery itself.

Given the snobbishness surrounding the cemetery – its authorities treat it more like a gentlemen's club than a burial ground – it's hardly surprising that Porteño high society tried to prevent Evita's family from laying her to rest here. Even President Perón himself had to make do with second-best Chacarita Cemetery (see p.129). Nevertheless, her family's plain, polished black granite vault is now her final resting place, since Perón himself brought her embalmed corpse by plane from Milan and had her coffin slipped into the cemetery at night, in 1973, more than two decades after she died. Unlike many other graves, it's not signposted – the cemetery authorities are still uneasy about her presence – but you can locate it by following the signs to President Sarmiento's, over to the left when you come in, then counting five alleyways farther away from the entrance, and looking out for the pile of bouquets by the vault. Her full name, **María Eva Duarte de Perón**, and some poignant quotes from her speeches are inscribed on several bronze plaques, including a tribute from the union of taxi-drivers.

The cemetery, a haven of peace and quiet within its high walls, is a great place to wander, exploring its narrow streets and wide avenues of yews and cypress trees, where dozens of feral cats prowl among the graves. The tombs themselves range from simple headstones to bombastic masterpieces built in a variety of styles including Art Nouveau, Art Deco, Secessionist, Neoclassical, neo-Byzantine and even neo-Babylonian. The oldest monumental grave, dating from 1836, is that of **Juan Facundo Quiroga**, much-feared La Rioja caudillo and General Rosas' henchman. It stands straight ahead of the gateway, and you can't miss the sparkling-white marble statue of the *Virgen Dolorosa*, said to be a likeness of his widow. Alongside it, inscribed with a Borges poem, stands the solemn granite mausoleum occupied by several generations of the eminent Alvear family, including Torcuato de Alvear who, as city mayor, had the ceremonial portico of Doric columns added to the cemetery's entrance. As well as individual tombs and family vaults, La Recoleta contains a number of monuments, such as the magnificent **Panteón de los Guerreros del Paraguay**; up against the far-west corner of the cemetery, this is the mass grave of Argentine heroes of the late nineteenth-century War of the Triple Alliance against Paraguay, and is guarded by two bronze infantrymen. Over by the northwest wall, due west of the central plaza, is the **Mausoleo de los Caídos en la Revolución de 1890**, a huge granite slab smothered in commemorative bronze plaques, beneath a centenarian cypress tree. It's the tomb of several Radical party leaders, including founding father Leandro Além and Hipólito Yrigoyen, president of Argentina twice from 1916 to 1930. The remains of the 1960s Radical president Arturo Illia were interred in the same plot, beneath a moving bronze statue of a winged *Victory*, holding a "dying patriot in her arms" according to the inscription.

Despite La Recoleta's tradition for coffins to be stacked up in multi-generation family vaults rather than buried under separate gravestones, there's a long waiting list for a plot, and money and status in life count less than family ties. Most of the great artists, scientists, financiers and politicians buried here would not have been granted a space here without a resoundingly patrician surname like San Martín or Dorrego, Anchorena or Pueyrredón, Mitre or Hernández. The main exception is that of the military heroes, many of them Irish or British seafarers, who played a key part in Argentina's independence. As you wander around the cemetery, you'll see tombs engraved with names such as Juan Hunter and Guillermo Small, Cipriano Newton and James MacDonald. Admiral William Brown, an Irish sailor who became an Argentine hero after he decimated the Spanish fleet near Isla Martín Garcia (see p.156), at the beginning of the nineteenth century, and later defeated the Brazilian navy, is not buried here but has an unusual cenotaph memorial decorated with a beautiful miniature of his frigate, the *Hercules*, a highlight of the cemetery's central plaza.

Basílica Nuestra Señora del Pilar

Just to the north of the cemetery gates is the stark white silhouette of the **Basílica Nuestra Señora del Pilar** (daily 9am–7pm; guided tours Tues, Thurs & Sat 10.30am, Sun 2.30pm & 6.15pm; free). Built in the early eighteenth century by Jesuits, it's the second oldest church in Buenos Aires, and is effectively the parish church for the elite of Recoleta barrio, although until the 1930s it had been allowed to decay. The sky-blue Pas-de-Calais ceramic tiles atop its single slender turret were then painstakingly restored, along with the plain facade, using eighteenth-century watercolours as a guide. The interior was also remodelled, and the monks' cells were turned into sidechapels, each decorated with a gilded reredos and well-restored polychrome wooden saints. These include a statue of *San Pedro de Alcántara*, a *Christ of Patience and Humility*, a *Virgen de la Merced* and a *Casa de Ejercicios*, all attributed to a native artist known simply as "José". The magnificent Baroque silver altarpiece, embellished with an Inca sun and other pre-Hispanic details, was made by craftsmen from Jujuy. Equally admirable is the fine altar crucifix allegedly donated to the city by King Charles III of Spain.

Centro Cultural de la Recoleta and Palais de Glace

Immediately north of Basílica Nuestra Señora del Pilar, at Junín 1930, the **Centro Cultural de Recoleta** (Tues–Fri 2–9pm, Sat & Sun 10am–9pm; guided visits Sat & Sun 4pm; $1) is one of the city's leading arts centres. After its closure in the 1820s, the Franciscan convent was turned into a school, and later became an old people's home. Recycled in the 1980s, the building retains its former cloisters, but now houses a concert hall, the Anfiteatro Astor Piazzolla. There's also a theatre "El Aleph" – named after the Borges short story – a modern chapel-like building, painted garish pink. Several exhibitions are staged simultaneously in the various galleries; some are mainstream, others more avant-garde, but all have an emphasis on local talent. Subjects range from photographs of Buenos Aires cafés and fashion collections to retrospectives of Argentine sculpture or performance art. From the roof terrace you can enjoy views of the surrounding parkland and, more to the point, part of the cemetery.

Directly east, at Calle Posadas 1725, is the **Palais de Glace** (Mon–Fri 1–8pm, Sat & Sun 3–8pm), a distinctive circular *belle époque* building, that started life as an ice rink. From 1912 onwards it became a ballroom, hosting important galas including one for the Prince of Wales in 1925. Porteño trendsetter Barón de Marchi staged tango soirees there in the 1920s, after which the dance was accepted by local high society. The Palais' vast hall is now used for all kinds of art exhibitions and trade shows.

Between the two arts centres, **Plaza San Martin de Tours**, a grassy slope at the northern end of Avenida Alvear (see below), is shaded by three of the biggest rubber-trees in the city, an impressive sight with their huge buttress-roots, contorted like arthritic limbs. Another hundred-year-old rubber-tree, the famous Gran Gomero, shades the terrace of nearby *La Biela*, on the corner of Avenida Quintana, 100m west. One of the city's most traditional confiterías, it gets its name, meaning the "connecting-rod", from being the favourite haunt of racing-drivers in the 1940s and 50s; it was also the favourite target of Trotskyist guerrillas in the 1970s. Nearby, on Plaza Intendente Alvear, the grassy parkland to the north of Plaza San Martin de Tours, buskers and jugglers entertain crowds at weekends, while artisans sell high-quality crafts including *mates*, jewellery and ceramics, at stalls arranged along the wide paths.

Avenida Alvear and its palaces

Only five blocks in length, from Plaza Carlos Pellegrini to Plaza San Martin de Tours, **Avenida Alvear** is one of the city's shortest, but most exclusive, avenues. Along it, expensive art galleries – selling mostly conventional portraits and landscapes but also some avant-garde Argentine and foreign works – alternate with big-name international fashion boutiques. At the corner of Calle Ayacucho is the luxurious **Hotel Alvear Palace**, built in 1932 in French Art Deco style and recently restored. Opposite some elegant apartment blocks, in a single block between Calles Montevideo and Rodriguez Peña, stand three palaces that were home to some of Argentina's wealthiest landowning families at the turn of the twentieth century. The northernmost, behind a Charles Thays garden (see box, p.107) – with its luscious rubber-tree and a straggly palm – is the **Palacio Hume**. This perfectly symmetrical Art Nouveau house, embellished with intricate wrought-ironwork, was originally built for British rail-engineer, Alexander Hume, but was sold to the Duhau family in the 1920s, who staged the city's first ever art exhibition inside. The Duhau family also built the middle building, the **Residencia Duhau**, an austere grey imitation of an eighteenth-century French Neoclassical palace, with plain columns and an unadorned triangular tympanum. It's now used as a home for clergymen, like the third palace, the severely Neoclassical **Nunciatura Apostólica**, on the corner of Calle Montevideo. Built in 1909 by a French architect for a member of the Anchorena family, it was used as Marcelo T. de Alvear's official residence when he was president in the 1920s, and was lent to Pope John Paul II during both of his visits to Argentina.

THE MONUMENTS AND STATUES OF NORTHERN BUENOS AIRES

Throughout Retiro, Recoleta, Palermo and Belgrano you'll see dozens of **monuments** and **statues** dominating the green spaces, like an open-air museum of sculpture. Some of them were created by great artists, including **Rodin** and **Bourdelle**, others are lesser works, but as well as being decorative they relate the history of Argentina. When this part of the city was being landscaped at the turn of the twentieth century, the fashion was for great open squares with the statue of a famous person at the centre, not to everyone's liking. Borges once complained that "there wasn't a single square left in the city that hadn't been ruined by a dirty great bronze statue of someone or other."

The belligerent equestrian statue of **General San Martín** on Plaza San Martín started this trend, but in 1950, another, more placid bronze of the national hero was erected to mark the centenary of his death. It's opposite the Instituto Sanmartiniano, and depicts the Libertador serenely seated on a granite plinth, surrounded by his grandchildren. In front of Recoleta's Palais de Glace stands the extremely elegant equestrian statue, by Emile-Antoine Bourdelle, of a hatless **General Carlos M. de Alvear**, on a grey- and red-granite pedestal. Farther north, Plaza Mitre is dominated by a monument to **Bartolomé Mitre**, who founded the influential broadsheet *La Nación* in the mid-nineteenth century. A bronze Mitre sits astride a majestic mount, on a solid granite pedestal decorated with an extravagant set of white marble figures. Behind the square, next to the British Embassy, is the very green statue of **George Canning**. Lord Canning was British Foreign Secretary in the 1820s and instrumental in getting the South American nations' independence from Spain recognized by the rest of Europe. Previously next to the Torre de los Ingleses (see p.109), the ton of bronze was chucked into the River Plate at the height of the South Atlantic conflict, fished out several years later and moved to this "safer" position.

Farther west, the plazas named after Uruguay and Chile have statues of their respective national heroes as their focal points. The sandstone monument to **General Artigas** has an unfortunate fascist look about it, while a majestic bronze of **Bernardo O'Higgins** sits astride a rearing mount in a pastoral setting of huge tipas, pines, and a spreading ombú tree. At the corner of Plaza Sicilia, in Palermo, a marble and bronze statue of **President Sarmiento** by Rodin stands on the exact location of his arch-enemy Rosas' mansion. Opposite is a far more dramatic equestrian statue of **Juan Manuel de Rosas** himself. A surprisingly diminutive statue of **Manuel Belgrano** stands at the centre of Plaza Belgrano, in the barrio named after the inventor of the national flag.

One of the most recent additions is a statue of **Pope John Paul II**, funded by the city's Polish community, and positioned next to the Biblioteca Nacional in 1999. Below, in renamed Plaza Evita, previously Plaza Rubén Darío, is a bronze statue of **Eva Perón** – but not a very good likeness – unveiled by President Menem less than a week before his mandate ended in December 1999. Peronists saw this monument (incidentally the only one to a famous woman in the whole city) as a way of avenging Evita's ill-treatment at the hands of the oligarchy even after her death.

For Argentina's 1910 **centenary celebrations**, the country's major communities each donated a monument to their adoptive country. At the middle of Recoleta's Plaza Francia is a very Baroque marble monument representing Liberty, while Plaza Alemania is dominated by a huge monument that juxtaposes an effete white-marble youth, not unlike Michelangelo's David, standing coyly next to a sturdy ox, with three embarrassed-looking ephebes posing by a plough. On Plaza Italia, aptly at the heart of Palermo, is a pompous equestrian monument of Italy's national hero, and South American freedom-fighter, caustically dismissed by Borges as "just some greenish, rain-streaked horse and its **Garibaldi**". The busy rotunda at the junction of Avenida del Libertador and Avenida Sarmiento, due north, is taken up by the most glorious monument in the city, the **Monumento de los Españoles**, whose fine bronze sculptures symbolize the Andes, the Chaco, the Pampa and the River Plate. Its allegorical figures, including the dainty angel at the top, are sculpted from Carrara marble and are so dazzlingly white that the monument is often blamed for road accidents.

Museo Nacional de Bellas Artes

Argentina's principal art museum, the well-displayed **Museo Nacional de Bellas Artes** (Tues–Fri 12.30–7.30pm, Sat & Sun 9.30am–7.30pm; free; *www.startel.com.ar/ bellasartes/mnba*) is housed in an unassuming brick-red Neoclassical building at Av. del Libertador 1473, half a kilometre due north of Recoleta Cemetery. Like the barrio's architecture, the museum's contents – mostly nineteenth- and twentieth-century paintings and some sculpture – are resoundingly European, while the European influences on the Argentine art on display are clearly evident. On the ground floor is a modest but refined collection of mostly European art, while the upper floor galleries contain a selection of major Argentine artists, many of them influenced by European masters or even educated in Europe; it's an excellent introduction to Argentine art. Various additional spaces on both floors are used for temporary exhibitions (free) – some dedicated to Argentine artists, others more international.

In the **ground-floor** galleries, the Impressionists such as Degas, Monet, Pissarro, Renoir and Sisley are given pride of place, while Courbet, El Greco, Goya, Rubens and Zurbarán get a couple of paintings apiece as do later masters as varied as Chagall, Dubuffet, Modigliani, Pollock, Saura and Tàpies. Two untitled works by Argentine-born artist, Lucio Fontana, just to the right of the main entrance, are not his best works, but their position is a recognition of his international status. In a room by itself, the wide-ranging Hirsch bequest – left to the nation by the wealthy Belgrano landowners and art-collectors – includes some fabulous paintings, sculptures, furniture and other art objects, spanning several centuries and from all over Europe, including a retable from Spain and a Hals portrait.

Upstairs, *El baño* by Prilidiano Pueyrredón is clearly influenced by Bouguereau's *Toilette de Vénus*, displayed on the ground floor. The influence of Degas (*Deux danseuses jaune et rose*) on Valentín Thibon de Libian's *Fifí*, a ballerina putting on her tutu, is obvious. Lino Spilimbergo's *Terracita*, closely resembles de Chirico's *Piazza*, even though it was painted nearly twenty years later. Xul Solar's masterpiece *Predicador* could easily be mistaken for a Klee (see p.118). Raquel Forner, who painted *Retablo del dolor*, was actually a pupil of Othon Friesz, whose *Dans le jardin de l'Emir* is hanging downstairs. Only much later Argentine artists also on display here, such as Guillermo Kuitca and Juan Carlos Distéfano, managed to break away from this imitative tendency and create a provocative, groundbreaking movement of their own.

Biblioteca Nacional

About half a kilometre west, standing back from Avenida del Libertador at the top of a steep slope, is the **Biblioteca Nacional**, Agüero 2502 (Mon–Sat 8am–9pm, Sun noon–8pm; guided visits daily at 4pm, free; *www.bibnal.edu.ar*), Argentina's copyright library. It's built on the site of Quinta Unzué, the elegant palace where the Peróns lived when they were president and first lady. Argentina's rulers after the so-called Revolución Libertadora, which overthrew Perón in 1955, were petrified that the residence, where **Evita** died in 1952, would become a shrine, and had it razed to the ground. The government decided to build a library on the site, but political upheavals, financial scandals and disagreements over the design held up building work for over three decades; the library was finally inaugurated in 1992. It's a futuristic concrete edifice, built in the 1970s and 1980s, and stands at the top of a steep slope. Designed in the 1960s by three of Argentina's leading architects, Clorindo Testa, Francisco Bullrich and Alicia Cazzaniga de Bullrich, it's a kind of giant cuboid mushroom, complete with ribbed gills, perched on four hefty stalks. What you see is only the tip of the iceberg, though, since most of the five million tomes and documents housed inside – including a first edition of *Don Quixote*, a 1455 Gutenberg Bible and the personal collection of General Belgrano – are kept in huge underground rooms away from sunlight. Book-related **exhibitions** and recitals are frequently held in the Auditorio Borges or the Sala

Leopoldo Marechal. On the southwest side of the building are attractively landscaped gardens, with a café and terrace. On the other side, along Avenida del Libertador, the grassy park below the library has been symbolically renamed Plaza Evita, and is overlooked by a 1999 bronze statue of Eva Perón, the city's only monument to a non-fictional female figure (see p.116).

Museo Xul Solar

A dozen blocks west of the library, the **Museo Xul Solar** (Mon–Fri noon–8pm; guided visits Tues 3pm; $3) is at Laprida 1212 near the corner of Calle Mansilla. The museum is in the "Fundación Pan Klub", an early twentieth-century town house where, for the last twenty years of his life, eccentric Porteño artist Xul Solar (1888–1963) lived with his wife Lita and received countless visits from his great friend Borges, who often called by to borrow books from the enormous library. The house was remodelled in the 1990s and its design is as exciting as the display of paintings and other works by Solar. The space contains work spanning nearly five decades and is on several different levels, built of timber and glass, each dedicated to a period in the artist's career.

Two atypical oil paintings hang near the museum entrance, but Solar preferred watercolour and tempera, and the majority of the works use those media. Apart from the very Klee-like paintings, there's a set of "Pan Altars", multicoloured mini-retables designed for his "universal religions" – Solar once told Borges that he had "founded twelve new religions since lunch". Other curiosities include a piano whose keyboard he replaced with three rows of brightly painted keys with textured surfaces, created both for blind pianists and to implement his notion of the correspondence of colour and music. In some of the later works you can detect Solar's passion for linguistics and his plans for universal understanding based on his versions of Esperanto. His "Neocreole" – mixing Spanish, Portuguese, Guaraní and English – was to be a common language for all Americans, while "Panlengua" was a set of monosyllables based on arithmetic and astrology, Solar's "ideal universal language". Texts written in these languages are the inspiration behind the more child-like paintings.

Palermo

Palermo, in those days just some idle swamps skulking behind the fatherland's back.

J.L. Borges, Palermo de Buenos Aires, in *Evaristo Carriego*

Palermo stretches all the way from Avenida Coronel Díaz, the border with Recoleta, to Colegiales and Belgrano, to the north. Avenida Córdoba forms its southwestern boundary with Villa Crespo and Chacarita, while its main thoroughfare, Avenida Santa Fe, becomes Avenida Cabildo at its far northern end. Given that it's by far Buenos Aires' biggest barrio, it's not surprising that it isn't completely homogeneous. It's really several distinctive neighbourhoods rolled into one: Palermo Chico, Barrio Parque, Alto Palermo, Villa Freud, Palermo Viejo and Las Cañitas. Palermo takes its name not from the Sicilian city but from an Italian farmer, **Giovanni Domenico Palermo**, who in 1590 bought the flood plains to the north of Buenos Aires, drained them and turned them into vineyards and orchards, soon known as the "campos de Palermo". In the early nineteenth century, **Juan Manuel de Rosas** bought up the farmland and built a mansion, **La Quinta**, where he lived, with his family and a domesticated tiger, as president oversaw public works in the area, until his overthrow. The barrio began to take on its present-day appearance at the turn of the twentieth century, when its large parks and gardens were laid out. When **Borges** lived here in the 1920s much of it was still regarded as insalubrious, but more and more middle-class Porteños moved here over the following decade or two. It's now regarded as a distinctly classy barrio, and the

DOG-WALKERS

Along the wide avenues and in the many parks of Barrio Norte and Palermo, you'll often be treated to an impressive sight that's probably unique to Buenos Aires: the *paseaperros*, or professional **dog-walkers**. Joggers holding seven or eight prized pedigrees on leashes are surprising enough, but these dilettantes are rightly held in contempt by the beefy specialists who confidently swagger along in spite of being towed by twenty to thirty pet dogs, many of them bigger than they are. You can't help wondering how it is they don't get tangled up or lose one of the pack, but they never seem to. These invariably athletic young men are not paid just to take wealthy Porteños' Afghans, Dalmatians or Wolfhounds for a stroll, with inevitable pit stops along the way, but must brush and groom them, and look out for signs of ill-health, which is why many of them have veterinary training. Paid on average $100 a month per animal, they perform these vital duties every weekday – the dogs' owners usually manage the chore themselves at the weekends. The number of *paseaperros* on the streets is regarded as a litmus test of the prosperity of the northern barrios; fewer dog-walkers implies less money in circulation.

small red-light district around the train station, north of Palermo Viejo, is the nearest it gets to being seedy.

The bit of Palermo around Plaza República de Chile that juts into Recoleta is known as **Palermo Chico** and it contains some important museums. The **Museo de Arte Decorativo** and the **Museo de Arte Oriental** share an impressive French-style palace while the nearby **Instituto Nacional Sanmartiniano** is in a replica of the house where San Martín lived near Paris. Immediately to the north is **Barrio Parque**, an oasis of private mansions laid out by Charles Thays in 1912. A short way up Avenida del Libertador is the fourth of the area's museums, **Museo Hernández**, which among other things displays a huge collection of antique *mate* vessels. This area's verges and parks, such as **Parque Las Heras**, at the corner of Avenida Las Heras and Avenida Coronel Díaz, are the likeliest places to spot a typical Porteño sight, a professional **dog-walker** (see box above). Over to the west is a mass of shopping streets and apartment blocks called Alto Palermo and, to the west of that, a small patch of the barrio, centred on Plaza Güemes and its café *Sigi* (short for Sigmund), so chock-a-block with psychiatrists and psychologists that it's irreverently nicknamed "Villa Freud". Most of the city's estimated 15,000 analysts, a larger number than in New York, have their surgeries in Palermo. North of Villa Freud, **Palermo Viejo** is a traditional neighbourhood with lovely old houses along cobbled streets, but it's becoming an increasingly trendy place, with its funky cafés and avant-garde art galleries.

Much of the **north of Palermo** is taken up by parks and gardens, such as the **Botanical Garden** and **Zoo**, a **Japanese garden**, and Buenos Aires' Bois de Boulogne, the **Parque 3 de Febrero**. The country's first ever sports club, the **Buenos Aires Cricket Club** of all things, had its grounds in this area in the late nineteenth century and, later on, the first games of rugby, tennis, golf and football in Argentina were played on the same plot of turf. Near the **Campo Nacional de Polo**, or national polo ground, at the northern reaches of Palermo, is **Las Cañitas**, an extremely trendy zone of imaginative bars and restaurants, focused on the corner of Calles Báez and Arévalo. On the down side, the whole of northern Palermo suffers somewhat from its noisy proximity to Aeroparque, the city's busy domestic airport. Even so, plans to move all flights to Ezeiza Airport are bitterly opposed even by Palermo residents who like the convenience of having the airport on their doorstep.

Part of **subte** Line D runs underneath Avenida Santa Fe, one of Palermo's main arteries, and where appropriate the nearest station is indicated in the text. Otherwise, take one of the many **buses** that go up Avenida Las Heras and Avenida del Libertador, such as #10, #12, #37, #38, #41, #60 and #118.

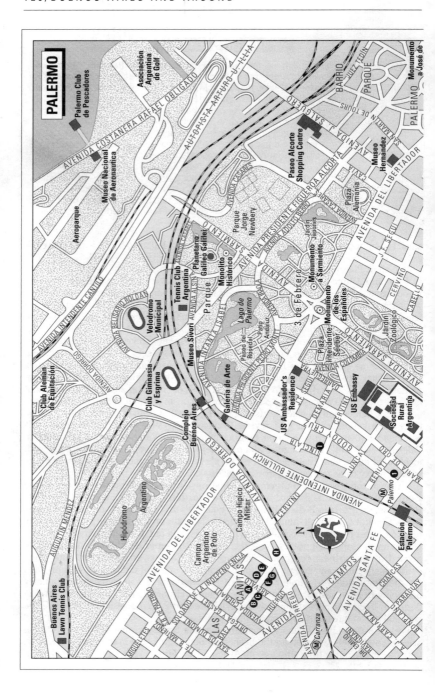

PALERMO

Buenos Aires Lawn Tennis Club

Club Aleman de Equitación

Complejo Buenos Aires

Club Gimnasia y Esgrima

Velodromo Municipal

Tennis Club Argentina

Museo Sívori

Galería de Arte

Hipódromo Argentino

Campo Argentino de Polo

Campo Hípico Militar

Aeroparque

Museo Nacional de Aeronáutica

Palermo Club de Pescadores

AVENIDA COSTANERA RAFAEL OBLIGADO

Asociación Argentina de Golf

AVENIDA INTENDENTE CANTILO

AVENIDA DORREGO

AVENIDA AUGUSTIN MENDEZ

AVENIDA DEL LIBERTADOR

Planetario Galileo Galilei

Monolito Histórico

Parque 3 de Febrero

Lago de Palermo

Paseo del Rosedal

Patio Andaluz

Monumento a Sarmiento

Monumento de los Españoles

Parque Jorge Newbery

Jardín Japonés

Plaza Alemania

Jardín Zoológico

Museo Hernandez

Paseo Alcorte Shopping Centre

AVENIDA CASARES

AVENIDA ADOLFO BERRO

AVENIDA PRESIDENTE FIGUEROA ALCORTA

AVENIDA SARMIENTO

AVENIDA DEL LIBERTADOR

BARRIO PARQUE

PALERMO

Monumento a José de

Monumento Intendente Seeber

Plaza Intendente Seeber

Plaza Italia

US Ambassador's Residence

US Embassy

Sociedad Rural Argentina

AVENIDA INTENDENTE BULLRICH

AVENIDA COLOMBIA

AVENIDA SANTA FE

Estación Palermo

M Palermo

M Carranza

LAS CAÑITAS

AVENIDA DEL LIBERTADOR

M. CAMPOS

A B C D E F G H

N

SANTA FE

CHARCAS

PARAGUAY

SOLDADO DE LA INDEPENDENCIA

CONCEPCIÓN ARENAL

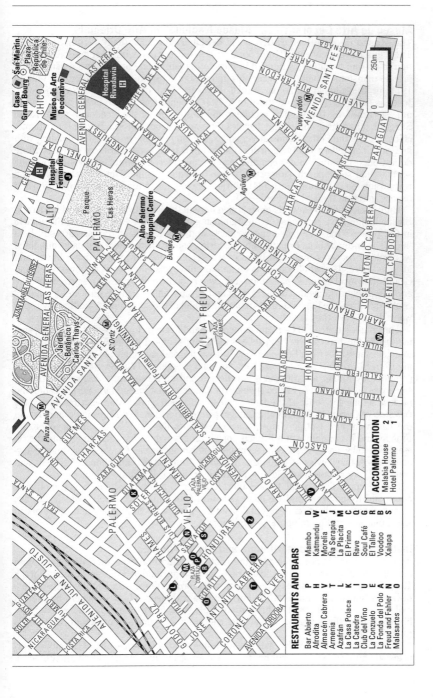

RESTAURANTS AND BARS

Bar Abierto	P	Mambo	D
Afrodita	H	Katmandu	W
Almacén Cabrera	V	Morelia	F
Armenia	T	Na Serapia	J
Azafrán	L	La Placita	M
La Casa Polaca	K	El Primo	C
La Catedra	I	Rave	Q
Club del Vino	U	Soul Café	G
La Conzuelo	E	El Taller	R
La Fonda del Polo	A	Voodoo	B
Freud and Fahler	N	Xalapa	S
Malasartes	O		

ACCOMMODATION

Malabia House	2
Hotel Palermo	1

Museo de Arte Decorativo and Museo Nacional de Arte Oriental

The **Museo de Arte Decorativo**, at Av. del Libertador 1902 (daily 2–7pm; $1, free on Tues; guided tours Mon & Thurs 5pm; *www.mnad/org.ar*), with its remarkable collection of art and furniture, is housed in Palacio Errázuriz, one of the city's most original private mansions, albeit of typically French design. The two-storey palace was built in 1911 for the Chilean diplomat Matías Errázuriz and his patrician Argentine wife, Josefina de Alvear, who lived there until 1937, when it was turned into a public museum. Designed by the French architect and proponent of the Academic style, **René Sergent**, it has three contrasting facades. The western one, on Sanchez de Bustamante, is inspired by the Petit Trianon at Versailles, the long northern side of the building with its Corinthian pillars, on Avenida del Libertador, is based on the palaces on Paris' Place de la Concorde, and the eastern end, where you enter, is dominated by an enormous semicircular stone porch, supported by four Tuscan columns. The coach house, now a restaurant and **tearoom** (see p.134), sits just beyond the monumental wrought-iron and bronze gates, in the style of Louis XVI.

High society was frequently entertained here in the Errázuriz days; García Lorca and Blasco Ibáñez gave readings, Arthur Rubinstein played and Pavlova danced *Swan Lake* in the palace's massive halls, and concerts and classical masterclasses are still held here. The **interior** is as French as the exterior, especially the Regency ballroom, lined with gilded rococo panels and huge mirrors, all stripped from a Parisian house and installed here. The whole house is on an incredible scale, not least the overwhelming Grand Hall, in a French Renaissance-style, where some of the museum's prize artworks are admirably displayed. The Errázuriz and Alvear family arms feature in its magnificent stone fireplace but next to it is a bronze model of the sculpture by Rodin they really wanted, but even they couldn't afford.

The couple's taste in **art** – Flemish furniture and French clocks, Sèvres porcelain, statues by Rodin, bronzes by Bourdelle – including a model of his Alvear monument in Recoleta, tapestries from Brussels, Gallé glassware, and paintings, old and modern, ranging from El Greco (*Christ bearing the Cross*) and Fragonard (*The Sacrifice of the Rose*) to paintings by Manet and Boudin – is reflected and preserved here. Errázuriz's private salon was decorated in Art Deco style by the Catalan artist Josep Maria Sert, creating the perfect setting for some of the later acquisitions, such as the Klimt-like *Portrait of the Countess of Cuevas de Vera*, by the Catalan painter, Hermenegild Anglada i Camarasa. In the basement is a Gothic chapel, transferred from the Chateau de Champagnette in France, and decorated with a French polychrome wooden chancel, dating from the fifteenth century, an early sixteenth-century Spanish alabaster effigy of a knight, and seventeenth-century Swiss stained-glass windows. Temporary exhibitions of ancient and contemporary art are also held down here, or in the garden in the summer.

On the upper floor of the palace, until it moves to a home of its own, is the pitifully cramped **Museo Nacional de Arte Oriental** (same hours; extra $1), which displays its hugely rich collection of oriental painting, porcelain, engravings and other art in small but outstanding temporary exhibitions.

Instituto Nacional Sanmartiniano and Barrio Parque

Across the Avenida del Libertador, the **Instituto Nacional Sanmartiniano**, at Rufino de Elizalde 2373 (Mon–Fri 9.30am–noon & 2–5pm; guided visits at 9.30am; library 10am–1.30pm; free) is housed in an accurate reproduction – on a slightly large scale – of Grand Bourg, the simple, white Parisian villa with green shutters, where he lived in exile from 1838 to 1848. The institution dates back to 1946 and boasts an extensive library and archives, telling you all you can possibly want to know about Argentina's founding father.

Immediately to the north, past the enormous *gomero histórico*, one of the city's characteristic hundred-year-old rubber-trees, and across wide Avenida Presidente Figueroa

Alcorta, lies **Barrio Parque**. This is a maze of untypically winding and curving streets laid out in 1912 by Charles Thays (see box, p.107). Each of the opulent houses in a variety of styles – Art Deco, neocolonial, Tudor, Secessionist, Flemish and Italian Renaissance – has its own landscaped garden, planted with jacarandas, magnolias, plumbagos or hibiscus. Oval Calle Ombú is the barrio's hub, from which several streets radiate like spokes; the two finest houses are the manor at Calle Ombú 2994 and the curious circular building at no. 3088.

Museo Hernández

About 200m west of the Instituto Sanmartiniano, in a rambling neocolonial house at Av. del Libertador 2373, you'll find the quaint **Museo Hernández**, also known as the Museo de Motivos Argentinos (Tues–Fri 2–7pm, Sat & Sun 3–7pm; $1; *www.naya.org.ar*). José Hernández, after whom the museum is officially named, wrote the great gaucho classic *Martín Fierro* (1872), a revolutionary epic poem that made *campo* or peasant culture respectable. The museum's permanent exhibition about the Argentine folk heritage is housed in two buildings separated by a shady patio. The first section is an impressive but unimaginatively presented display of mostly nineteenth-century rural silverware; the seemingly endless arrays of spurs, stirrups, saddles, knives and gaucho weaponry stand side by side with a large collection of fine silver *mate* ware, including a particularly splendid and unusual *mate* vessel in the shape of an ostrich. Many of the artefacts were donated by the Anglo-Argentine collector Carlos Daws. The second part, across the courtyard, comprises a number of beautiful ponchos, one of them woven in Birmingham, England, the inevitable reconstructed pulpería and other miscellanea related to gaucho customs and rituals. Finally, you can see an exhibition of contemporary crafts in the basement of the first building.

Palermo Viejo

Bounded by Avenidas Santa Fe, Córdoba, Juan B. Justo, and Raúl Scalabrini Ortiz – the latter still usually referred to by its pre-1982 name, Canning – atmospheric **Palermo Viejo** is the only area of Palermo that still has an old-fashioned Porteño feel to it, despite the fact that it's becoming increasingly fashionable to live there or to go shopping or for an evening out. The part of the city most closely linked to Borges, where he lived and started writing poetry in the 1920s, it has barely changed since he moved back there from Switzerland, aged 22. It's a compact oblong of quiet streets, most of them still cobbled and lined with brightly painted single- or two-storey neocolonial villas and town houses, many of them recently restored, some of them hidden behind luxuriant gardens full of bougainvillea and jasmine, a great place to stroll around at random. Part run-down, part gentrified, old-fashioned in places, increasingly trendy in others, it's a leafy district with a laid-back bohemian ambience, and many of its stylish houses with their ornate interiors have been converted into bars, restaurants and boutiques. Large communities from Poland, Ukraine, Lebanon and Armenia live there, alongside the larger Italian contingent and some old Spanish families, and they all have their shops and bars, churches and clubs, adding to the district's colour. The area also boasts a lot of outstanding restaurants, serving cuisines as varied as Mexican and Vietnamese, Polish and Armenian, and is fast attracting people away from more superficial districts such as Puerto Madero and Las Cañitas.

Palermo Viejo's official epicentre is **Plaza Palermo Viejo**, a wide, park-like square dominated by a children's playground and some huge lime trees. However, the barrio's cultural and social focal point is the nearby Plaza Serrano, also known as Plaza Racedo, but now officially named **Plaza Cortázar** after the Argentine novelist Julio Cortázar, who frequented this part of the city on his rare visits to Buenos Aires from his adoptive Paris in the 1960s. His surreal novel *Hopscotch* (published in English in 1966) is clearly set in the area. This lively plaza is now surrounded by trattorias, cafés and trendy bars, some of them doubling up as extremely active arts centres and galleries. The stretch of Calle Serrano leading due east from this plaza, to Avenida Santa Fe, has been officially renamed Calle J.L. Borges. The writer's 1920s home, a two-storey villa with its own mill, used to stand at no. 2135, but **Borges** pilgrims will have to make do with a commemorative plaque at no. 2108, inscribed with the words "A whole block of houses, far out in the country/Open to sunrises, rainshowers and south-easterlies./The similar block that lingers on in my barrio:/Guatemala, Serrano, Paraguay, Gurruchaga." – a stanza of his *Mythical Foundation of Buenos Aires*, from the early collection *Cuaderno San Martín* (1929). In the poem the colonial beginnings of Buenos Aires are narrated, with a slight twist: the city is founded not at today's microcentro but in the middle of Palermo.

The nearest **subte** stations to Palermo Viejo are Scalabrini Ortiz and Plaza Italia.

Botanical Garden and Zoo

The entrance to Buenos Aires' charming but dishevelled **Botanical Garden** (daily 8am–6pm; guided visits Sun 2pm; free) is at Plaza Italia, east of Palermo Viejo. Started at the end of the nineteenth century by Schubeck, the gardener to the royal courts of Bavaria, who died before getting very far, the layout was handed over to Charles Thays (see box, p.107) who completed the work in 1902. He divided it up into different areas representing the regions of Argentina, but few of the labels on the shrubs and trees are now legible. The garden is officially named after Thays, and he is honoured with a bronze bust alongside the great red-brick bulk of the city's Headquarters of Parks and Gardens, inside the garden, where he had his offices. Next to this stands a large **glasshouse** brought back from the 1900 Universal Exhibition in Paris, where it was part of Argentina's pavilion: this ethereal construction of wrought-iron and engraved crystal shelters the garden's less hardy botanical specimens such as orchids and cacti.

Borges was inspired to write a poem entitled *El jardín botánico*, in the *Fervor de Buenos Aires* collection (1923), and in another poem described the garden as "a silent dockyard of trees and the fatherland of all the city's walks". After decades of municipal neglect, much of the park is now sadly dank and overgrown, but its brighter grassy spots are popular with sunbathers – and the many feral cats, fed by a neighbourhood "cat lady". The part nearest the entrance has recently been renovated, and the first feature you see is a lush waterlily-pool around an elegant bronze statue of the *Ondina del Plata*, a demure river-nymph from a legend about the River Plate; she has a decidedly coquettish look about her. This Italianate part of the garden is dotted with a number of sculptures, including a white marble *Venus* copied from a Roman statue in the Louvre, an appropriately cobwebbed stone *Sophocles*, a bronze of a she-wolf with heavy dugs being suckled by Romulus and Remus – a centenary gift to the city from its Roman community, and *Saturnalia*, an enormous bronze ensemble of a rather low-key Roman orgy, intended to warn cityfolk against debauchery. Although these rather bombastic statues detract from the pastoral calm of the garden, it's still a shady haven of peace from the noisy avenues around.

With its entrance right next door on Plaza Italia, Buenos Aires' **Zoo** (Tues–Fri 10am–5pm, Sat, Sun & holidays 10am–3.30pm; $5) was also landscaped by Charles Thays, in the 1890s, and is of considerable architectural as well as zoological interest. Its monumental pavilions and cages, built around 1905, include a fabulous replica of the temple to the goddess Nimaschi in Bombay, a Chinese temple, a Byzantine portico and a Japanese pagoda. After decades of scandalous neglect under state ownership, it has been privately run and infinitely improved since the early 1990s. The entrance fee has shot up but the money has been properly spent on improving the animals' living conditions, which are now as decent as they can be in a zoo. It's a popular place for kids, of course, who particularly enjoy watching the seals, penguins and sea elephants. The big cat area – pumas, cheetahs, lions, jaguars and snow tigers – is another highlight; the sweet-toothed cat-lover Borges fondly wrote that the zoo "smelled of toffee and tiger", a description that still holds true, given the number of stands selling freshly caramelized peanuts and other sweets. Fauna from throughout the world, ranging from apes to zebras, is represented while a baby orang-utan is a proud newcomer. It's also the place to come and see the difference between guanacos, llamas, vicuñas and alpacas, the four native camelids.

Plaza Italia **subte** station is right by the entrance to both gardens.

Japanese Garden

Taking up part of Plaza Sicilia, immediately north of the zoo, the **Japanese Garden** has its entrance on Plaza de la República Islámica de Irán (daily: Dec–March 10am–7pm; April–Nov 10am–6pm; guided visits Sat 3pm & 4pm; $2, guided visits a further $1.50; *info@jardinjapones.com.ar*). The garden was donated to the city by Buenos Aires' small Japanese community in 1979, in readiness for a state visit to Argentina by the Japanese imperial family. The purr of traffic on all sides undermines any Zen within the garden's walls, but it's still relatively peaceful and is immaculately tended. The beautifully landscaped gardens, including a bonsai section and standing stones, and planted with handsome black pines and gingkos, are at their best in the springtime, when the almond trees are in blossom and the azaleas are out. Great shoals of huge coy carp kiss the air with their pouting mouths, in lakes crossed by typical red-lacquer bridges and zigzagging stepping-stones. A temple-like **café** serves green tea, sushi and some Argentine dishes, while the Japanese cultural centre, next door, puts on regular dance, music, theatre and craft displays.

Parque 3 de Febrero

A short way to the northwest, at the corner of Avenida del Libertador and Avenida Sarmiento, **Parque 3 de Febrero** is one of the biggest and most popular parks in the city. Designed by Charles Thays (see box, p.107) at the end of the nineteenth century, it was originally planned by environmentally conscious **President Sarmiento**. He chose the name, 3 de Febrero, as that was the date of the 1852 Battle of Monte Caseros when his arch-rival General Rosas was defeated and overthrown. After decades of neglect by the municipal authorities, the park has recently been cleaned up and its massive rubber-trees, palms and jacarandas, where parrots squawk, are surrounded by well-tended lawns. Although the wide pathways running along the banks of the boating-lake become overcrowded with joggers, cyclists and in-line skaters, at weekends and public holidays much of the park is relatively quiet. Near the southern entrance the **Jardín de los Poetas** is dotted with stone and bronze busts of major Argentine and international poets, including Borges, Uruguayan-born Enrique Larreta and Swiss-born Alfonsina Storni, the Mexican Alfonso Reyes, the Spaniard Federico Lorca, Miguel Ángel Asturias – the Guatemalan Nobel laureate who served as a diplomat in Buenos Aires – and Shakespeare. Nearby is an Andalucian patio, decorated with vibrant ceramic tiles and donated by the city of Seville, while alongside it an immaculate rose garden is a showcase for new and colourful varieties, amid immaculate lawns. At the northern end of the bridge over the boating-lake, at Av. Infanta Isabel 555, is the **Museo de Artes Plásticas Eduardo Sívori** (Tues–Sun & public holidays noon–6pm; guided visits Sat noon & 3pm, Sun 3pm & 5pm; $1, free on Wed). Regular temporary exhibitions of home-grown artists are held there – the museum, named for an Argentine painter (1847–1918), has a collection of some five thousand works. At the far eastern tip of the park, at Avenida Sarmiento, stands Saturn-shaped **Planetario Galileo Galilei** (daily 10am–6pm; guided visits Sat & Sun 3pm, 4.30pm & 6pm; $3). In the entrance hall, you can see an alarmingly huge metal meteorite, discovered in the Chaco in the 1960s (see p.369).

Belgrano

To the north of Palermo and the quiet residential barrio of Colegiales, **Belgrano** contains two of the finest museums in the city, plus three others of more specialized interest. Like most northern barrios, it's largely residential, apart from the popular sports venues and riverside bathing complexes in the north, and the lively shopping streets on either side of its main artery, Avenida Cabildo. Named after **General Manuel Belgrano**, hero of Argentina's independence, it was founded as a separate town in 1855, starting out as little more than an inn and a few houses. Over the next decade or two lots of wealthy Porteños built their summer or weekend homes there, and it became part of the city of Buenos Aires in 1887. Many Anglo-Argentines settled in the barrio in the late nineteenth century, when the British-built railways linked it to downtown, and it became popular with the city's sizeable Jewish community in the 1950s. More recently Chinese and Korean immigrants have settled in the so-called Barrio Chino, or Chinatown, a small area near Estación Belgrano C. Along with a Buddhist temple, there's an oriental supermarket and some Chinese restaurants.

Parts of Belgrano still have a rural feel, like western **Belgrano R** (for "residencial"), whose cobbled streets are lined with huge trees, Mock Tudor villas and neocolonial mansions. In the lyrics of a popular tango, *Fantasma de Belgrano*, a ghost wanders through the one-way streets, slipping through garlands of wisteria and bumping into a Viceroy on every corner, a wordplay on the barrio's street names such as Virrey Loreto and Virrey Arredondo. Over the past decade tall luxury apartment blocks have shot up, with private tennis courts and swimming pools amid neatly strimmed lawns. Much more downmarket is **Belgrano C** (for "comercial"), the central part of the barrio, whose nucleus lies at the junction of Avenidas Cabildo and Justamento. It's a heaving mass of shops, cafés and galleries, but it's also where the barrio's museums are situated.

The chief reason to visit Belgrano is to see two of the city's major art collections: the **Museo de Arte Español**, an incredibly rich set of Spanish paintings, furniture and religious artefacts, housed in a patrician villa, and the **Museo Casa de Yrurtia**, in a neocolonial house where the leading Argentine sculptor, Rogélio Yrurtia lived with his painter wife, Lía Correa Morales. Nearby **Museo Histórico Sarmiento** is full of the memorabilia of one of Argentina's key historical figures. Farther afield, the **Fundación Banco Francés** displays the unusual work of another sculptor, Libero Badii, while the **Museo Nacional del Hombre** contains a small but intriguing collection of native art from different parts of the country.

Juramento station, at the end of **subte** Line D, is close to all of the museums, except the last which is nearer to Olleros station, while plenty of **buses** run along Avenida Cabildo, including #41, #57, #59 and #60.

Museo de Arte Español

On the northern side of Plaza Belgrano, the **Museo de Arte Español** at Juramento 2291 (Mon & Thurs–Sun 3–8pm; guided visits Sun 4pm & 6pm; $2, free on Thurs; for English tours call ☎011/4783-2640) is housed in a well-restored, whitewashed colonial building with green doors. A huge ombú dominates the oasis-like garden, a profusion of magnolias, hydrangeas and agapanthus. Inside is a priceless collection of Spanish art, from the Renaissance to the early twentieth century, collected by the aristocratic Uruguayan exile, **Enrique Larreta**. In 1900 Larreta (1873–1961) married Josefina Anchorena, the daughter of Mercedes Castellanos de Anchorena (see p.109), and her dowry was a Greco-Roman villa, built in 1882 as a summer-house for the architects' parents-in-law, who lived there for ten years. Larreta had the house transformed into an Andalucian-style mansion, now the museum, with the help of his friend, the leading

architect and aesthete Martín Noel. From around 1900 to 1916, including a five-year stint as Argentina's ambassador in Paris, the dandyish Larreta spent a lot of time in Spain, with a preference for Avila where he set his novel, *La Gloria de Don Ramiro* (1908), a curious tale written in archaic Spanish. During that time he visited churches and monasteries, buying up artworks for his Belgrano home, most of them from the Renaissance – statues and paintings of saints, but also furniture, porcelain, silverware and tapestries, all of which are displayed in the magnificent setting of this house, which he bequeathed to the city.

One of the first **exhibits** you see – through the iron-grilled window by the entrance – is a Munch-like portrait of Larreta, with the ramparts of Ávila and swirling cloud as a backdrop, painted in 1912 by Spanish artist, Ignacio de Zuloaga. Around it are arranged his jacaranda writing desk and numerous personal effects. The five rooms of the single-storey building, arranged around the original Roman-style atrium, with terracotta tiles from a Spanish convent on the floor, contain several masterpieces. One of them is an early sixteenth-century retable, *La Infancia de Cristo*, delicately painted and decorated with gold leaf; it's thought to have once belonged to Randolph Hearst and is in immaculate condition. Equally marvellous is Correa de Vivar's *Adoration of the Magi*, a sixteenth-century painting from Toledo, in which a fine-featured Mary has a gold-leaf halo. Another is an altarpiece dedicated to *St Anne*, dating from 1503 and painted for a church at Sinovas, near Burgos, Spain. Its painstaking detail, vibrant colours and the haunting expressions of the holy family and other figures, with their fabulous headdresses, make it the finest work in the collection.

Museo Histórico Sarmiento

Nearby, on the northeast corner of Plaza Belgrano, the **Museo Histórico Sarmiento**, at Juramento 2180 (Mon–Fri 2–7pm; free; *mhs@mcmhs.gov.ar*) is housed in a Neoclassical building, with a splendid portico. Built in 1870, as city hall, when Belgrano was a separate entity, it served briefly as the seat of Argentina's government in 1880. In 1938, it was turned into a museum dedicated to **Domingo Sarmiento** (1811–1888), President of Argentina from 1868 to 1874. He took part in overthrowing President Rosas and, as president, emphasized the importance of education, introducing North American schooling methods he had discovered while serving as a diplomat in the United States. He is also highly regarded as a writer, best known for his work *Facundo: Civilisación y Barbarismo* (1845). The rather musty and highly eclectic display of Sarmiento memorabilia includes a large collection of Delft china, a bizarre articulated armchair he took with him into exile in Asunción, and a first edition of *Facundo*.

Museo Casa de Yrurtia

Three blocks to the north, at O'Higgins 2390, the **Museo Casa de Yrurtia** (Wed–Sun 3–6pm; free) is a beautiful single-storey Spanish-style house, built in 1923 by the leading sculptor, **Rogelio Yrurtia** (1879–1950). His work is displayed in the homelike rooms, along with that of other artists, and items of furniture and decoration collected from around the world. The artist intended the Baroque-inspired building, with a white facade set off by mustard doors and windows, to be home for him and his Dutch wife, but she died shortly after they moved in. He lived there for over twenty years with his second wife, Lía Correa Morales, the daughter of Yrurtia's mentor, Lucio Correa Morales, and herself an important painter. The courtyard, behind the house, is luxuriant with grape-vines, plane trees and a tall Canary Island palm.

The eleven rooms contain several of Correa Morales' still lives and landscapes as well as her portraits – many of her husband, and a large number of pieces by Yrurtia. The ceilings are just high enough to take the full-sized trial moulds of his monumental sculptures, some of which are city landmarks. These include the strangely homoerotic *Mausoleo Rivadavia* on Plaza Miserere, Once, *La Justicia* at the Palacio de Justicia, and the statue of Manuel Dorrego on Plazoleta Suipacha; the gigantic clay head of Moses, part of the mausoleum sculpture, is startlingly lifelike. Mostly, the couple's work fits well with the Kashmiri shawls, Chinese vases, Spanish cabinets and Delft china that decorate the rooms, while a Picasso, *Rue Cortot*, hangs discreetly on the wall of Room II. But sometimes the juxtaposition verges on the absurd: a ferociously prim *Virgen del Rosario*, an eighteenth-century painting from Cusco, ironically seems to have her eye on one of Yrurtia's bronzes, the torso and leg of a sinewy youth.

Fundación Banco Francés and Museo Nacional del Hombre

The neocolonial **Fundación Banco Francés**, at 11 de Septiembre 1888 and Echeverria (Mon–Fri 10am–6pm; free), is three blocks east of Plaza Belgrano, overlooking the Barrancas de Belgrano, the grassy knolls landscaped in 1910 by Charles Thays (see p.107), with huge shady tipas and a quaint bandstand. Once the home of Belgrano's founder, **Valentín Alsina**, and the seat of Argentina's government briefly in 1880, it now houses a small collection of works by the Argentine sculptor and painter **Libero Badii**, whose sculptures decorate Plaza Roberto Arlt, in downtown Buenos Aires.

Seven blocks south and one west, at Calle 3 de Febrero 1370, is the **Museo Nacional del Hombre** (Mon–Fri 10am–6pm; $1; guided tours by prior arrangement, ☎011/4784-3371). It's the showcase of the Instituto Nacional de Antropología y Pensamiento Latinoamericanos (INAPL), and its exhibits range from striking Mapuche silver jewellery and the colourful Chané animal masks made of *yuchan*, the Chané name for *palo borracho*, to archive photographs of the many ethnic groups wiped out by European invaders, and archeological finds, such as ceramics from the Northwest. The museum is disappointingly dusty and badly displayed, but the items themselves are worth seeing for the quality of the workmanship and the degree of preservation of the urns and vases.

The west

Bisected by the Avenida Rivadavia, itself flanked by high-rise blocks, **the west** of Buenos Aires is a vast, mostly residential area spreading out for some ten kilometres towards Avenida General Paz to the west. To the north, the barrio of **Chacarita** is best known for its eponymous cemetery where Juan Domingo Perón and Carlos Gardel are buried. The central barrio of **Caballito** is a mix of high-rise residential blocks and pretty cobbled streets: it's not a major tourist attraction but makes a pleasant half-day trip on weekends, both for the **tranvía histórico** (historic tramway) which runs through its prettiest section and for the popular **book and record market** held in the barrio's central park, Parque Rivadavia. West of Caballito, Avenida Rivadavia heads out towards the suburbs through the barrio of **Flores**, a largely modernized neighbourhood but with a sprinkling of *quintas* dating from its patrician past. The main reason to head beyond Flores is for the hugely enjoyable gaucho fair, the **Feria de Mataderos**, held on Sundays in the barrio of the same name and one of the best days out in the city.

Chacarita

Dominated by the railway lines which crisscross its heart, **Chacarita** takes its name from the days when the barrio was home to a small farm (*chacra*), run by Jesuits. Nowadays, the neighbourhood is synonymous with its enormous cemetery, less aristocratic than Recoleta, but containing the city's most-visited tomb, that of Carlos Gardel, Argentina's most famous tango singer. Lying at the northern end of Avenida Corrientes (subte station Federico Lacroze) the **Cementerio de Chacarita** (daily 7am–6pm; free) whose main entrance is at Av. Guzmán 780, covers a good third of the barrio; at one square kilometre, it's Argentina's largest cemetery. Much of the cemetery – which, unlike Recoleta, is still very much in use – is dominated by numbered streets, unremarkable graves and crosses and, to the right of the entrance, by enormous pantheons in which anonymous niches are stacked up like a great chest of drawers of the dead. Immediately facing the entrance, however, there's a section of grand mausoleums which come close to the Baroque splendour of Recoleta. This section makes a fascinating area to wander around: a grid of streets crisscrossed by diagonals and flanked by marble and polished granite tombs, often with decorative glass fronts through which relics such as bibles and candlesticks can be spied. By far the best sight in the cemetery, however, is the tomb of **Carlos Gardel**. Known as the *zorzal criollo* (creole songbird), Gardel became, in the 1920s, Argentina's tango superstar, making films in Hollywood and inspiring devotion for his distinctive voice and charismatic personality. As with so many icons, it was Gardel's early death – in a plane crash over Medellín in Colombia in 1935 – that ensured his legendary status: to this day the phrase *cada día canta mejor* (every day he sings better) is used to refer to the singer. Gardel's grave lies on the corner of streets 6 and 33, to the left of the entrance. It is topped by a life-sized statue of the singer in typical rakish pose – hand in pocket, hair slicked back and characteristic wide grin. Every inch of the surrounding stoneworks is plastered with plaques of gratitude and flowers, placed there by the singer's devotees for whom he has become a kind of saint. Many visitors also light a cigarette and place it between the statue's fingers. In comparison to Gardel's much-visited grave, **General Perón**'s final resting place is very restrained – a low-key family mausoleum on the corner of street 34, two blocks to the right of the entrance. At the centre of the cemetery, the Recinto de Personalidades is a collection of rather kitsch statues adorning the graves of some of Argentina's most popular figures, including the tango composer and accordionist Aníbal Troilo, the pianist Osvaldo Pugliese, the poetess Alfonsina Storni, the painter Quinquela Martín and the comedian Sandrini. Agustín Magaldi, who at the height of his popularity was second only to his contemporary, Carlos Gardel, as the nation's most-loved singer, is also famous for being Evita's first lover and the man she left her home town of Junín with to move to Buenos Aires.

Note that if you are taking photos for professional purposes, you must obtain permission at the cemetery's administrative offices (to the right of the entrance) where you may also be able to pick up a free map of the cemetery.

Chacarita lies at the end of subte Line B (Federico Lacroze station). The train station opposite the subte station is also the departure point for the **tren histórico**, a Sunday tourist service aboard a 1908 steam locomotive (☎011/4796-3618). It's an enjoyable two-hour or so journey in old-fashioned carriages to the tiny village of Fátima in the province of Buenos Aires, where lunch is provided, followed by a display of gaucho skills. Ticket prices range between $30 and $50, according to the vintage of the carriage you choose and whether you take lunch at a restaurant or a local estancia.

Caballito

An unassuming, mostly middle-class barrio, **Caballito** lies at the very centre of the city. It is centred on narrow **Plaza Primera Junta**, the last stop on Line A of the subte, while Avenida Rivadavia, flanked here by high-rise apartment blocks and small shopping malls, runs east–west though the barrio. To the southwest of the avenue, the barrio has a very different atmosphere, all quiet cobbled streets, lined with acacias, and small, ornate villas. This area of the neighbourhood is home to the humanities faculty of the **University of Buenos Aires**, at Puan 470, eight blocks southwest of the Plaza; the nearby confiterías (philosophically named *Platón* and *Socrates*) are packed with students discussing their studies over coffee. The best way of touring this area is aboard the old-fashioned tram, the **Tranvía Histórico** which leaves from the corner of Avenida Directorio and Emilio Mitre (Jan & Feb Sat 5–8.30pm, Sun 10am–1pm & 5–8.30pm; March–Dec Sat 4–7pm, Sun 10am–1pm & 4–7pm; free). To get to the departure point, follow Rivadavia two blocks west from Primera Junta station and then turn left into Emilio Mitre; the intersection with Avenida Directorio lies some six blocks to the south. Five blocks east of Plaza Primera Junta, you'll find Parque Rivadavia, wedged between Avenidas Rivadavia and Rosario. There an excellent secondhand **book market** here, busiest at weekends, and a good place to buy Argentinian literary classics or a well-worn tango score.

As well as the **subte**, you can get to Caballito on **bus** #5 or #86 from Congreso, both of which run past Parque Rivadavia and Plaza Primera Junta.

Mataderos

Lying just inside the boundary of Capital Federal, around 6km southwest of Caballito, **Mataderos** is a barrio with a gory past. For many years, people came to Mataderos to drink the fresh blood of animals killed in the slaughterhouses from which the area takes its name, in the belief that this would cure illnesses such as tuberculosis. The slaughterhouses have long gone, but Mataderos is still home to the **Mercado Nacional de Hacienda**, or livestock market, set back from the intersection of Lisandro de la Torre and Avenida de los Corrales, whose faded pink walls and arcades provide the backdrop for one of Buenos Aires' most fabulous events: the **Feria de Mataderos** (Sun from 11am; buses #36, #92 & #126; ☎011/4687-5602). A celebration of

Argentina's rural traditions, this busy fair attracts thousands of locals and tourists for its blend of folk music, traditional crafts and regional food such as *locro, empanadas*, and *tortas fritas*, mouthwatering fried cakes. You can also try your hand at regional dances such as the *chamamé* and *chacarera*. The undoubted highpoint, however, is the display of **gaucho skills** in which riders (many of whom work in the livestock market during the week) participate in events such as the *sortija* in which, galloping at breakneck speed and standing rigid in their stirrups, they attempt to spear a small ring strung on a ribbon – which, in terms of difficulty, must be somewhat akin to passing a camel through the eye of a needle.

Eating

Buenos Aires is arguably Latin America's **gastronomic capital**. As well as the excellent and ubiquitous **pizza** and **pasta** restaurants common to the country as a whole, the capital offers an ever increasing number of **cosmopolitan** cuisines, ranging from Turkish through Basque to Japanese. The city's crowning glory, however, for meat eaters at least, are its **parrillas**. At the top end of the range, there are restaurants offering the country's choicest beef cooked on an *asador criollo*, that is staked around an open fire. There are plenty of humbler places, too, where you can enjoy a succulent parrillada in a lively atmosphere. There are excellent restaurants throughout the city but, with a few exceptions, the centre and the south are best for the city's most traditional restaurants whilst the north is the place to head for if you're looking for more innovative or exotic cooking. **Puerto Madero**, the recently renovated port area, is knee-deep in big, glitzy themed restaurants, though – a couple of decent places notwithstanding – these are hardly the capital's most exciting eating options. You'll find a far more original crop of restaurants around the hugely popular and trendy **Las Cañitas** area in Palermo (subte station Ministro Carranza or buses #29 and #60 bajo) and, increasingly, in **Palermo Viejo**, where restaurants are given added charm by being located in elegant late nineteenth- and early twentieth-century constructions.

VEGETARIAN RESTAURANTS

It's not impossible to be a **vegetarian** in Buenos Aires, but it's not easy. There are a few vegetarian restaurants, but only a few, and most *platos del día* at cheaper restaurants include meat of some variety. Nonetheless, the situation is not as desperate as it might seem. Large salads with a healthy mix of ingredients are not too difficult to find on any menu and it's not unusual to come across *milanesas de soja* (breaded and fried soya); *a la napolitana* means it comes with cheese and tomato. Pasta *al pesto* or *al fileto* (with tomato sauce) is another possibility – also note that the stuffed pasta which is so popular in Argentina is more often filled with vegetarian options such as spinach, nuts and ricotta cheese than meat. Buenos Aires' trilogy of favourite pizzas, *napolitana* (with fresh tomato), *muzzarella* (mozzarella cheese and tomato) and *fugazza* (with onions), are meat free, as is the classic accompaniment, *fainá*, a pizza-shaped Genovese speciality made with chickpea dough, whose fairly bland but agreeable flavour is a surprisingly good complement to the more assertive pizza. Another standby is *tarta de acelga* or *espinacas* (spinach tart) and *tortilla española* (omelette with potato and onion). You needn't miss out on *empanadas* either; try *queso y cebolla* (cheese and onion) or *humita* (sweetcorn). If you do find yourself faced with a particularly meaty menu, it's always worth asking if the restaurant can fix you something else – Porteño waiters are generally amenable and used to dealing with fairly demanding customers. Of Buenos Aires' few dedicated **vegetarian restaurants**, two of the most established are *La Esquina de las Flores* and *Ying-Yang*, listed below.

Though most restaurants open in the evening at around 8pm, it's worth bearing in mind that most Porteños don't go out to eat much before 10pm, so unless you want a restaurant to yourself, you should probably do the same. Most restaurant kitchens close around midnight during the week, though at weekends many keep serving till the small hours. There are also plenty of confiterías and pizzerias that open all night, so you shouldn't have trouble satisfying your hunger at any time.

The centre

Arturito, Corrientes 1124 (☎011/4382-0227). An old-fashioned oasis reigned over by courteous white-jacketed waiters, Arturito is a Corrientes landmark, and its *bife de chorizo con papas* (rump steak and chips) is an unquestionably good deal at just $5.

Bice, Av. Alicia M. de Justo 192 (☎011/4315-6216). Style sometimes triumphs over content in Puerto Madero, but the excellent pasta and gnocchi at this highly regarded, if expensive, Italian restaurant will not disappoint.

Cervantes, Perón 1883. An old stand-by, and, with portions big enough for two, it's a great deal. Try the *peceto al horno con papas* (roast meat with potatoes). They also do huge salads.

Chiquilín, Sarmiento 1599 (☎011/4373-5163). A classic Porteño restaurant serving traditional dishes at moderate prices such as *pollo al verdeo* (chicken with spring onions) in a friendly and stylish atmosphere.

Las Cuartetas, Corrientes 838. A pared down pizza and *empanada* joint where you can grab a slice of pizza at the counter or while away a few hours after the cinema over a cold Quilmes.

El Globo, Hipólito Yrigoyen 1199 (☎011/4381-3926). Long-established, moderately priced, Spanish restaurant with a gorgeously old-fashioned interior, offering classic dishes such as *camarones al ajillo* (prawns with garlic) which are perfectly acceptable if rather lacking in Mediterranean flair.

Güerrín, Corrientes 1368. If you want a traditional Porteño pizza experience look no further than this Corrientes institution. The traditional order is a portion of *muzzarella* and *fainá* eaten at the counter and accompanied by a glass of sweet moscato. Some Porteños hold that the pizzas served in the proper dining area are a notch above the counter versions; however, all are inexpensive.

Parrilla Peña, Rodríguez Peña 682 (☎011/4371-5643). Excellent parrilla at a reasonable price in a bustling atmosphere. Avoid the downstairs tables if you want to prevent your clothes reeking of grilled meat.

Patio San Ramón, Reconquista 269. Generous, well-cooked and inexpensive food with daily specials such as *pollo al horno con puré de batata* (roast chicken with sweet potato puree). The real attraction, however, is the stunning location in the patio of an old convent where, among palm trees and birdsong, you might even forget that you're at the heart of Buenos Aires' financial district. Lunchtimes only.

Pippo, Montevideo 341 (☎011/4374-0762). Despite its fairly indifferent pasta and parrillada, *Pippo* has established itself as a Buenos Aires institution: it's worth paying this inexpensive, glaringly lit restaurant a visit just to catch a glimpse of Porteño dining in all its noisy, gesticulating glory. The thick *vermicelli mixto*, with bolognese sauce and pesto, is a good deal.

The London Grill and Oyster Bar, Reconquista 455 (☎011/4311-2223). A real slice of old Anglo-Buenos Aires, serving up traditional English dishes such as lamb with mint sauce in an elegant if rather stuffy atmosphere. Closed weekends.

Tomo 1, Carlos Pellegrini 525, in *Hotel Panamericano* (☎011/4326-6695). Considered by many to be Buenos Aires' best *haute cuisine* restaurant; an elegant but refreshingly unpretentious place where all the emphasis is on the exquisitely cooked food. There are lunchtime and evening set menus for around $50, offering dishes such as a terrine of zucchini with almonds and an à la carte menu, with a superb *magrets* of duck accompanied by pears and rosemary.

The south

Almacén y Bar, Cochabamba 1701, Constitución; subte station Entre Ríos or buses #6, #12 and #37. Upmarket *picadas* comprising Argentinian and imported cheeses, cured ham and shellfish, plus an excellent wine list. Closed Sat evening and all day Sun.

Basque Français, Moreno 1370, Montserrat (☎011/4304-4841). For over a hundred years, this restaurant has been serving up expertly cooked seafood such as squid, octopus and *fruits de mer*. Expensive but delicious, and more affordable if there are a few of you to share dishes. Closed Sun.

La Cancha, Brandsen 697, La Boca (☎011/4362-2975). A classic place to spend a weekend lunchtime – in the shadow of La Bombonera – Boca Juniors' legendary football stadium. Good fresh seafood including excellent *pulpo a la gallega* (octopus with oil and paprika) to share between two.

Cantina 3 Amigos, Necochea 1200, La Boca (☎011/4301-2441). Particularly garishly decorated Boca *cantina* offering the usual mix of pasta, chicken and seafood at moderate prices accompanied by loud cumbia and merengue. Evenings only (ring first).

La Casa de Esteban de Luca, Carlos Calvo 383, San Telmo (☎011/4361-4338). Housed in a famous eighteenth-century building once occupied by the poet and journalist Esteban de Luca, this popular San Telmo restaurant serves up typical Porteño dishes with an imaginative twist.

El Desnivel, Defensa 855, San Telmo. This popular, no-frills parrilla offers good food at rock-bottom prices. Closed Mon.

La Gran Taberna, Combate de los Pozos 95, Monserrat (☎011/4951-7586). A popular, bustling and down-to-earth restaurant just a block from Congreso. The vast menu offers a mixture of Spanish dishes, including a good selection of seafood, and Porteño classics as well as a sprinkling of more exotic dishes such as *ranas a la provenzal* (frogs' legs with parsley and garlic). Many of the dishes are large enough to share. Prices are very reasonable, too, and service is friendly, though it can be a bit slow during busy periods.

Laurak-Bat, Belgrano 1144, Montserrat (☎011/4381-0682). This moderately priced restaurant within Club Vasco has as its centrepiece an oak tree said to be descended from the "Arbol de Guérnica" planted by God, according to Basque tradition. On a more down-to-earth note, the restaurant offers Basque specialities such as *bacalao al pil-pil* (salt cod in a garlicky sauce) and serves complimentary sherry and tapas.

El Obrero, Caffarena 64, La Boca (☎011/4362-9912). With the Boca Juniors souvenirs on the walls, and tango musicians moving from table to table at weekends, the atmosphere at the hugely popular and moderately priced *El Obrero* is as much a part of the attraction as the simple home-cooked food. Closed Sun.

Parrilla 1880, Defensa 1665, San Telmo (☎011/4305-1746). A classic and extremely good parrilla joint right opposite Parque Lezama. The walls are lined with photos and drawings from the restaurant's famous and mostly bohemian clients and the very friendly owner passes from table to table making sure that everyone is happy. Prices are reasonable too. Daily until about 12.30am.

Patagonia Sur, Rocha 801, La Boca (☎011/4303-5917). Very smart place run by the leading Argentine chef, Francis Mallmann. The interesting menu combines French sauces with top-rate lamb, beef and seafood from Patagonia. Closed Sun evening.

Il Piccolo Vapore, Necochea 1190, La Boca (☎011/4301-4455). Lively Boca *cantina*, offering set four-course menu plus unlimited wine and soft drinks at $20–25 per head for small groups or $16 for groups of fifteen or more. Cabaret, live music and dancing take centre stage though. Evenings only (ring first).

El Puentecito, Luján 2101, Barracas (☎011/4301-1794). This hundred-year-old restaurant in the traditional barrio of Barracas is well worth a trip for the generous *puchero* (boiled meat and vegetables), parrilla and seafood. Best of all, it's open round the clock.

Plaza Mayor, Venezuela 1399. The trouble with many Spanish restaurants in Argentina is that they will seem inordinately expensive to anyone used to the cheap and delicious seafood available in Spain itself. Nonetheless, *Plaza Mayor* is one of the better places, offering excellent *merluza* (hake) and a pretty decent paella at moderate prices. The restaurant is also famous for its *pan dulce* (pannetone), for which queues regularly form around Christmas and New Year.

Rimini, Necochea 1234, La Boca (☎011/4302-6900). One of the oldest of Necochea's famous *cantinas*, serving up a *menú fijo* of the usual chicken and pasta for $15, plus lively music until 4am. Evenings only (ring first).

The north

Afrodita, Báez 121, Palermo (☎011/4772-6527). This newly opened restaurant in the phenomenally successful Las Cañitas area offers imaginative pasta dishes such as *ravioles de calabaza* (pumpkin ravioli) at moderate prices in a stylish atmosphere. Evenings only.

Almacén Cabrera, Cabrera 4399, Palermo (☎011/4832-4670); buses #140, #142 from Córdoba. An attractive restaurant – the building was a traditional almacén – serving above average pasta, chicken and parrillada at below average prices. Good service and attention to detail. Evenings only, plus Sun lunch.

Armenia, Armenia 1366 (☎011/4775-7494), Palermo Viejo. Delicious and authentic Armenian food, including smoked ham, boreks, kepe and falafel, served in simple surroundings.

Azafrán, Honduras 5143 (☎011/4832-6487), Palermo Viejo. Spanish dishes such as paella, plus a wide selection of tapas including chorizo and broad beans on Sundays only. Closed Mon.

Burmana, Av. del Libertador 2701, Olivos (☎011/4799-5347). Exotic surroundings, plus oriental music and belly dances. The Armenian and Middle Eastern specialities, such as tarama, lamb kebabs and kataif, are served with panache.

La Casa Polaca, J.L. Borges 2076, Palermo Viejo (☎011/4774-7621). The infectious good humour of the owner, who wanders from table to table, goes a long way to turning eating at *La Casa Polaca* into a memorable experience. There's piano music too and plenty of hearty Eastern European food.

La Cátedra, Cerviño 4699, Palermo (☎011/4777-4601). Classic Argentine restaurant in a beautiful neocolonial house, with some unusual twists – like fruit sauces – to a standard menu.

Club del Vino, Cabrera 4737, Palermo (☎011/4833-0048); buses #140 and #142. With a modern Argentinian menu including duck, lamb and seafood, this small and elegant restaurant shares the space with a music venue (tango and jazz) and a wine bar. Evenings only. Closed Sun.

Club Sírio, Ayacucho 1496, Recoleta (☎011/4806-5764). Every Argentine city has its Syrian club-restaurant but this palatial place is one of the best. Excellent mezze-style buffet. Belly-dancing Thurs–Sat. Closed all Sun.

Colbeh Melahat, Av. del Libertador 13041, San Isidro (☎011/4793-3955). Let the owners advise you what to have at Argentina's only Persian restaurant, but the lamb cooked in pomegranate juice is unforgettable. Closed Sun and lunchtime.

El Cook & Bardelli, French 2316, Recoleta. Traditional, extremely friendly Italian trattoria, serving traditional, home-made food, with an extensive drinks and wine list. Closed Sun lunch & Mon.

Errázuriz, Museo de Arte Decorativo, Libertador 1902, Palermo (☎011/4806-8639). Refined but unpretentious French-style cuisine in the elegant surroundings of the mansion's coach-house. Pleasant garden terrace, weather permitting. Lunch and dinner daily; afternoon teas on Sun.

La Esquina de las Flores, Avenida Córdoba 1587 (☎011/4813-3630). Reliable vegetarian and mac-robiotic restaurant serving up a variety of hot (including a good *carbonada de vegetales*, a vegetarian version of the popular criollo stew) and cold dishes. Closed Sat evening and all day Sunday.

La Factoria, Arribeños 2393, Belgrano. A converted warehouse is the atmospheric setting for this Uruguayan-run place, with gaucho waiters.

Filo, San Martín 975, Retiro (☎011/4311-0312). As much a place to be seen as to eat; the food in this trendy restaurant is nevertheless to be reckoned with. Imaginative pizza, pasta and salads and Italy meets Argentina in dishes such as Venetian mussel soup with Patagonian clams.

La Fonda del Polo, Báez 301, Las Cañitas (☎011/4772-8946). Traditional parrilla in thematic decor, popular with polo players and their supporters from the Campo de Polo.

French, French and Azcuénaga, Recoleta(☎011/4806-9331). Warmly decorated neighbourhood bar-cum-restaurant, serving excellent pasta, veal dishes and a wonderful panna cotta.

Freud & Fahler, Gurruchaga 1750, Palermo Viejo (☎011/4833-2153). The serrano hams hanging from the ceiling and bottles of Rioja lined up on the shelves are served at this atmospheric tapas bar, which also does a mean paella.

Green Bamboo, Costa Rica 5802, Palermo Viejo (☎011/4775-7050). Delicious pork, fish and seafood, perfumed with ginger, lemongrass, chilli and fish sauce, prepared by the cooks from the Vietnamese embassy, so it's genuine.

La Grispella, Virrey Loreto 3093, Colegiales (☎011/4553-7211). Traditional but not stuffy Italian trattoria serving excellent pasta and other dishes, rounded off with an unbeatable tiramisu.

Hsiang Ting Tang, Arribeños 2245 Palermo, (☎011/4786-0371). An upmarket place serving a wide range of Taiwanese dishes, in soothing surroundings. Try the pork sautéed in ginger.

Katmandu, Av. Córdoba 3547, Palermo (☎011/4963-1122). You can watch your *naan* being baked and your *rogan josh* being simmered in the kitchen of this top-rate restaurant, where you dine among Indian antiques. By the way, "Indian hot" really does mean vindaloo-style.

Lotus, Ortega y Gasset 1782, Belgrano (☎011/4771-4449). Undoubtedly the most authentic Thai food in town, served with a smile in temple-like decor complete with gilded buddhas. Green curries are fabulous.

Morelia, Báez 260, Las Cañitas (☎011/4772-0329). Busy, noisy but smart place, with young fashion-victim clientele but excellent thin-crust pizzas, the speciality being yummy *pizza a la parrilla*.

Ña Serapia, Las Heras 3357, Palermo; buses #10, #37. An unexpectedly traditional and rustic restaurant in the heart of upmarket Palermo, *Ña Serapia* styles itself as a pulpería and bar and serves delicious regional dishes including *locro* and *tamales* at very reasonable prices.

Las Nazarenas, Reconquista 1132 (☎011/4312-5559). Superb parrilla cooked gaucho-style on the *asador criollo*, where meat is staked around an open barbecue. Moderate to expensive.

La Placita, Serrano 1636, Palermo Viejo. Filling home cooking at this traditional *cantina*, a counterpoint to the trendy bars across the Plaza Serrano, and marred only by the glaring fluorescent-strip lighting.

Piola, Libertad 1078, Barrio Norte. (☎011/4812-0690; *www.piola.it*). Trendy, popular and lively Italian restaurant serving excellent pizza. Happy hour Mon–Fri 6.30–9.30pm, live jazz on Wed. Reservations advisable. Closed Sat & Sun lunchtime.

El Primo, Báez 302, Palermo (☎011/4775-0150). One of the few relative bargains to be had in swanky Las Cañitas. Popular parrilla offering traditional Porteño dishes with a bit of flair. You'll probably have to queue, but at least they serve you a glass of wine while you're waiting.

Rave, Gorriti 5092, Palermo. Interesting food combinations and endless list of cocktails served in an unusual decor dominated by giant pink tulips and appreciated by a trendy, gay-dominated clientele. Closed Mon lunch.

San Babila, Roberto M. Ortiz 1815, Recoleta (☎011/4801-9444). Reliable, traditional Italian trattoria, with no surprises on the menu but delicious food, especially the pasta and above all the carpaccio.

El Sanjuanino, Posadas 1515, Recoleta (☎011/4805-2683). *Empanadas*, *locro*, *humitas* and barbecued chicken, plus delicious goat's cheese with honey for dessert. No credit cards. Closed Mon.

Sarkis, Thames 1101, Villa Crespo; buses #140 and #142; ☎011/4772-4911). Excellent tabbouleh, *keppe crudo* (raw meat with onion – much better than it sounds), falafel etc at this popular restaurant serving a fusion of Armenian, Arab and Turkish cuisine. Close to one of Buenos Aires' nicest barrios, Palermo Viejo.

Soul Café, Báez 246, Palermo (☎011/4778-3115). Describing itself as a "boogie restaurant", the food's probably not the point for much of the clientele of this pioneering Las Cañitas venue. Dishes are of the punning variety with "Pumpkin Soulrrentinos" on the menu for $12. It's not a bad place to have a cocktail though, all in all, the place is a bit too artful really to have "soul". Evenings only. Closed Mon.

Todos Contentos, Arribeños 2177, Belgrano; buses #29, #60, #64 or train from Retiro. One of the best places to eat in Belgrano's Chinatown; a friendly Chinese/Taiwanese with a good selection of very filling noodle soups for around $6. Closed Mon lunch.

Xalapa, Gurruchaga and El Salvador, Palermo Viejo (☎011/4833-6102). The owners lived in Oaxaca for a while, and it shows through in the cooking, the most authentic Mexican fare in the city. Bring a fire-extinguisher, especially for the stuffed chillies. No credit cards. Evenings only. Closed all Sun.

Ying Yang, Paraguay 858, Retiro (☎011/4311-7798). Pioneering healthfood restaurant with a variety of inexpensive, wholesome – if slightly tired – vegetarian (and some fish) dishes. Closed Sun.

The west

El Mirasol, Boedo 136 (☎011/4864-5890); subte Castro Barros or bus #86. Pretty restaurant serving superior parrillada (including *entraña* and *colita de cuadril*, two of the tenderest and tastiest cuts) with a good selection of *achuras* (offal). Abundant plates of *papas a la provenzal* (fries with parsley and garlic), though some of the other portions can be a bit on the small side.

La Piurana, Corrientes 3516 (☎011/4863-3615). One of a small enclave of Bolivian and Peruvian restaurants near the Abasto shopping centre, *La Piurana* is a friendly, family-run restaurant offering specialities such as ceviche and *chifles* (fried plantains) at reasonable prices.

La Popular, Corner of Lavalle and Mario Bravo, Almagro; bus #26. Decorated in the style of a *fonda*, the walls and ceilings of this attractive restaurant are strewn with football flags from around the world (there's usually a game showing too). The meat is very good and there's also *verduras a las brasas*, a delicious and unusual dish of grilled peppers, tomatoes, cucumbers, squash and aubergines, for a reasonable $6 or so.

Tuñin, Rivadavia 3902, Almagro. One of the city's best, most popular pizzerias, serving an unforgettable *fugazzeta* and other classics, including a great tiramisu.

Cafés, confiterías and snacks

Abuela Pan, Bolívar 707, San Telmo. Homely vegetarian café and wholefood store offering a daily two-course menu for $6 with options such as wholemeal pasta, aubergine omelette and vegetarian *locro*. Open Mon–Fri 8am–6pm.

La Americana, Callao 83–99, centre. A Callao landmark, serving up juicy *empanadas* to be consumed standing up at metal counters.

La Biela, Quintana 598, Recoleta. Institutional confitería famed for its *lomitos* and tip-top coffee, served in the elegant bistro interior or, with a hefty surcharge, in the shade of a gigantic gum-tree on the terraces.

Le Carafon, Callao 1143, Recoleta. Wine bar with an extensive list of Argentine wines married with classic French bistro dishes such as *coq au vin*, in the plush salon of a tastefully converted town house.

La Cocina, Local 61–62, Galería Boston, Florida 142. This simple Catamarcan eatery (take out or eat at the tables outside) is regarded as having some of the finest *empanadas* in the city, with juicy, home-made fillings (vegetarian options available) and delicious pastry. They also do a great and unusually light *locro*.

La Conzuelo, Báez 207, Las Cañitas. Trendy tapas bar with a good wine list, if a little overpriced, all in an ultramodern setting, with a VIP salon with huge armchairs upstairs.

Del Viejo Hotel, Balcarce 1053, San Telmo (☎011/4362-0086). Popular lunchtime café for good inexpensive food served in this restored former hotel which now houses artists' workshops.

Freddo, Galerías Pacífico, Av. Córdoba and Florida. Buenos Aires' best ice-cream chain provides a compelling reason to descend to the basement of this shopping centre on a hot day – *dulce de leche* fans will be in heaven and the unusual *pomelo* (grapefruit) flavour is superb. Many other branches throughout the city.

La Giralda, Corrientes and Uruguay, Centre. Brightly lit and austerely decorated Corrientes café, famous for its *chocolate con churros*. A perennial hangout for students and intellectuals and a good place to observe the Porteño passion for conversation.

La Ideal, Suipacha 384, (☎011/4553-2466). It's not quite as famous as the *Tortoni*, but this confitería is just as beautiful and has a great tango salon upstairs.

Open Plaza, Av. Libertador 1800, Recoleta. Eclectic confitería, and a great place for brunch or afternoon tea. It has a fast-food section, an antique-silver store, and an elegant salon with newspapers.

La Puerto Rico, Alsina 422, Monserrat. One of the city's classic confiterías. Simple, elegant and timeless.

La Querencia, Esmeralda 1392 at Av. Libertador. A small restaurant specializing in *empanadas tucumanas*, which are excellent, and regional dishes such as *locro* and *tamales*. A good spot for a snack if you have an hour or two to kill in the vicinity of Retiro.

Sabores da Bahía, Esmeralda 965, Retiro. Tucked away at the back of the Fundación Centro de Estudos Brasileiros, this snack-bar-cum-café is one of the few spots in Argentina where you can get Brazilian snacks such as *coxinhas*, delicious fried dough balls filled with chicken, or the energy-giving drink guaraná. *Feijoada*, a rich Brazilian stew of beans and pork, is served on Friday. Mon–Fri 10am–8pm.

Drinking and nightlife

There's no excuse for staying in on any night in Buenos Aires: Porteños are consummate night owls and though **nightlife** peaks from Thursday to Saturday, you'll find plenty of things to do during the rest of the week too.

Venues are to be found all over the city, but there are certain key areas. The Costanera Norte and Las Cañitas in Palermo are where the city's young and wealthy go to strut their stuff. El bajo, as the streets around Reconquista and 25 de Mayo are known, offers a walkable circuit of trendy **bars** and restaurants as well as the odd Irish **pub**, while San Telmo harbours some eclectic and interesting bars in amongst the tango spectacles. However, if you really want to sample the full range of Buenos Aires' superb nightlife you'll have to follow the example of locals and move around a bit.

The daily paper *Clarín* and *Vía Libre*, *La Nación*'s Friday supplement, have topical listings sections. Also worth looking out for is the tiny magazine *wipe* (*www.wipe.com.ar*), given out in some bars or on sale in kiosks, which is particularly good for the trendy end of the city's cultural events and nightlife. Look out, too, for *La Otra Guía*, the listings sheet for the gay scene, and *El Tangauta* and *Buenos Aires Tango* for, of course, **tango**.

Bars and live music

Buenos Aires has some great **bars**, ranging from noisy Irish pubs to drop-dead cool places where the young and moneyed sip on cocktails. There are also plenty of places offering live music including jazz, tango and rock music, hugely popular in Argentina. For recitals by local bands, check the *Sí* supplement in *Clarín* on Fridays and the oppositionally named *No* supplement in *Página 12* on Thursdays.

Bar Abierto, J.L. Borges 1613, Palermo Viejo. Pizzas, sandwiches, snacks, drinks, coffee all accompanied by live music, lectures and performances, in a very 1990s setting – a converted almacén with contemporary paintings on the walls.

Bar Británico, Corner of Defensa and Brasil, San Telmo. Old men, bohemians and night owls while away the small hours in this traditional wood-panelled bar overlooking Parque Lezama. Open 24 hours.

Bárbaro, Tres Sargentos 415, Retiro. Cosy bar tucked down a side street, with regular live jazz.

Buller, Presidente Ortiz 1827, Recoleta. The shiny stainless steel vats and whiff of malt tell you that this brasserie brews its own excellent beer, running the gamut from pale ale to creamy stout, all served with hot and cold dishes.

Celta Bar, Sarmiento 1702. Attractive bar with big wooden tables, popular with a friendly and relaxed crowd – a good place for an early-evening drink. Also live music from tango to pop, and tango classics in the basement.

Café París, Rodríguez Peña 1032. One of Buenos Aires' coolest hangouts, a trendily decorated but refreshingly unpretentious bar attracting a hardcore of night owls after a hard night's clubbing. Daily from 8pm to very late (or very early, depending on how you look at it).

Café Tortoni, Av. de Mayo 825 (☎011/4342-4328). Buenos Aires' most famous café offers pure elegance. Live jazz and tango in La Bodega downstairs.

La Cigale, 25 de Mayo 722, Centre (*lacigale@netizen.com.ar*). One of Buenos Aires' hippest bars attracting a young crowd. Regular live music and DJs on Thursdays (free). Happy hour with two drinks for the price of one Mon–Fri 6–9pm.

Dadá, San Martín 941, Retiro. Small bar playing jazzy music. Kitsch decor, and good but pricey food.

El Samovar de Rasputín, Del Valle Iberlucea and Caminito, La Boca. Popular Boca venue for live blues and rock.

Jazz Club, Paseo de la Plaza, Corrientes and Rodriguez Peña. The best live jazz in the city, on Saturday nights. Laid-back smoky atmosphere, $15 cover charge includes a drink.

El Taller, Serrano 1595, Palermo Viejo (☎011/4831-5501); buses #140 and #142. Bars and restaurants have sprouted around it, but *El Taller* still has the best outside seating in one of Buenos Aires' prettiest plazas. It also hosts regular plaza events.

Gran Bar Danzón, Libertad 1161, 1st Floor, Retiro. Fashionable bar and restaurant with sharply dressed bar staff and a good, though rather expensive, wine list. Elegant but a bit soulless.

Kilkenny, corner of Reconquista and Paraguay, Centre. Rather too pristine to resemble a true Irish pub, the boisterous *Kilkenny* is nevertheless a favourite of visiting foreigners and Guinness-drinking Porteños. Irish stew on the menu.

Malasartes, Honduras 4999, Palermo Viejo. Funky, trendy Plaza Serrano hangout, with avant-garde art on the walls and serving reasonably priced drinks and snacks.

Mambo, Báez 243, Las Cañitas (☎011/4778-0115). Extravagantly tropical *Club Latino* with dinner-shows run Thursday to Saturday followed by disco. Expensive set menus $40–60 per head. Otherwise reasonably priced if limited menu. Salsa and merengue classes Mon–Thurs 7–9pm.

Notorius, Av. Callao 966. Friendly bar, selling CDs which you can listen to on headphones. There's also a great garden at the back where you can chill out over a cold beer.

Plaza Dorrego Bar, Defensa 1098. Most traditional of the bars around Plaza Dorrego, a sober wood-panelled place where the names of countless customers have been etched on its wooden tables and walls, and piles of empty peanut shells adorn the tables.

Sarajevo Bar, Defensa 827, San Telmo. Apocalyptically named and eclectically decorated bar offering quintessential San Telmo mix of poetry nights, tango and rock music. Popular with students and an alternative crowd.

Shamrock, Rodríguez Peña 1220, Recoleta. Irish bar with a Porteño touch. A good place to meet foreigners, but watch out for the darts board placed perilously close to the toilets. Happy hour 6–9pm.

Tobago, Alvarez Thomas 1368 (☎011/4553-5530). Off the beaten track in the barrio of Chacarita, this popular bar hosts regular live music, particularly jazz.

Voodoo, Báez 340, Palermo. One of the places to be seen in Las Cañitas; a lively bar with room to dance and comfy armchairs. Closed Mon.

Nightclubs

In terms of **nightclubs**, Buenos Aires towers over any other city in Argentina, with just about every taste in music catered for. A typical Porteño night out might begin with a pizza with friends around 10pm, followed by a few hours spent in a bar or confitería. Not until at least 2am, or frequently an hour or two later, would anyone dream of hitting a nightclub – from when it might take a good hour or so for your average clubber actually to ease him or herself onto the dancefloor. On the whole, Porteños are notably sober and, while drunkenness is not quite taboo, the levels of alcohol you will see being consumed are well below the European or North American norm. What this makes for – apart from a lot fewer hangovers – is a generally friendly and relaxed atmosphere where fights and aggression are extremely rare. **Music** tends towards the commercial dance variety, interspersed in some places with salsa or rock, though there are also a growing number of places playing more cutting-edge dance music mixed by Argentinian and foreign DJs of international standing. At the other end of the spectrum, **bailantas** are truly democratic events where the predominant music is home-grown *cumbia*, Argentina's favourite "tropical" sound – a very basic but infectious version of Colombia's famous rhythm. Cheaper, more alcoholic and far less trendy than the capital's swanky nightspots, *bailantas* can be slightly rowdy places and – if you don't know your way around or speak the language very well – you will probably feel happier going to one in the company of a regular.

Admission **prices** to nightclubs range from about $5 to $15 (though women enter free in some places, particularly *bailantas*), with prices at the top end often including a free drink. Be warned that some places operate a system whereby you are issued a ticket, which is stamped when you get your free drink, and which you must hand in on leaving the nightclub hours later or pay an exorbitant "fine" of around $100.

For more information and listings on **gay nightlife**, see p.141.

Ave Porco, Corrientes 1980, Centre. Consciously avant-garde club with a wild mix of music and a wild crowd. Thurs–Sat from midnight.

Buenos Aires News, Paseo de la Infanta Isabel, Palermo. Large and flashy complex of bars, dancefloors and a restaurant. Mainstream dance music and a smartly dressed, wealthy clientele.

Cemento, Estados Unidos 1234, Constitución. Long-standing favourite of Buenos Aires' long-haired youth, with beer and *rock nacional* the main ingredients.

Club 69, Corrientes 1218. Friendly club attracting a relaxed and diverse crowd. The DJs play a mixture of soul, funk and hip-hop. Open Thurs–Sun.

Comodor, Niceto Vega 5956, Palermo. It's a little early to say whether the adventurous music policy of this new and trendy club will pull in the crowds, but it's a cool space with an intimate dancefloor and a positively sleep-inducing chill-out zone. There's also a gallery space and a restaurant. Fridays is jungle and big beat, Saturdays house.

El Dorado, Hipólito Yrigoyen 947, Centre. Current favourite of Buenos Aires' growing legion of dance-music fans, with popular night on Friday.

Fantástico Bailable, Rivadavia and Sánchez de Loria, Once; subte Loria. The trendiest *bailanta* – and a good place for your first taste of the heady mix of non-stop dancing and full-on flirting that goes with the territory. Open Fri & Sat from midnight.

K-dos, Viamonte 865. A real after-hours club for a hip crowd, playing a mix of electronic sounds (mostly trance and techno) from 6am on weekends.

El Living, M. T. de Alvear 1540. Laid-back club in a rambling old building with two bars and a coffee stand and a long narrow dancefloor that gets very packed. Plays a fun, danceable mix of funk, disco and rock music. Open Thurs–Sat.

Maluco Beleza, Sarmiento 1728. Long-running Brazilian club, playing a mix of lambada, afro, samba and reggae to a lively crowd of Brazilians and Brazilophiles.

La Morocha, Dorrego 3307, Palermo; buses #29 or #60 bajo. Currently one of most popular mainstream clubs where an energetic crowd work up a sweat to dance on the main floor and jig about a bit to funk and rock music on a smaller floor next door. Friday and Saturday nights are packed.

Morocco, Hipólito Yrigoyen 851, Centre (☎011/4342-6046). Theatre, nightclub and (expensive) restaurant. Arty, alternative – and seemingly popular with transvestites. Tues poetry evening, Tues, Wed drum'n'bass.

Odeón, Av. Casares and Av. Sarmiento. Trendy dance music club. Open Fri & Sat.

Pacha, Costanera Norte and La Pampa. Big glitzy club, the atmosphere best described as "hip mainstream", attracting a lively crowd, including a sprinkling of Argentinian celebrities. Open Fridays and Saturdays from 1.15am, with DJs from 2am; hosts some of Argentina's most famous dance DJs.

Quibic, Viamonte 845, 4th Floor, Centre. Hip Sunday evening chill-out club in large apartment. Tiny dancefloor though most of the very cool crowd seem to prefer hanging out by the outdoor swimming pool. Sun 6pm–midnight. $8.

La Trastienda, Balcarce 460, San Telmo (☎011/4342-7650). Live music including rock, jazz and tango, salsa dancing on Saturday nights and massively popular salsa classes on Wed evenings at 8.30pm.

Tango

The most obvious face of **tango** in Buenos Aires is that of the tango *espectáculos* offered by places such as *El Viejo Almacén*. Often referred to by Porteños as tango for export, these generally rather expensive shows are performed by professionals who put on a highly skilled and choreographed display. The shows can be dazzling, but if you want to dance yourself – or would prefer to see the tango as a social phenomenon – you'd be better off heading to one of the city's dancehalls to experience the popular *milongas* (for more on these, see box on p.140). Note that the days, times and locations of *milongas* change frequently – a *milonga* refers to a moveable event rather than a specific venue, so it's advisable to consult the listings in *El Tangauta* and *Buenos Aires Tango*.

Bar Sur, Estados Unidos 299, San Telmo (☎011/4362-6086). One of San Telmo's most reasonably priced tango shows ($15 with unlimited pizza). The quality of the shows can vary but it's an intimate space where audience participation (singing and dancing) is encouraged towards the end of the evening. Mon–Sat 9pm–4am.

Casa Blanca, Balcarce 668, San Telmo (☎011/4331-4621). Daily tango shows from 10pm (except Sun) at this popular San Telmo *tanguería*. Admission is $40 with unlimited drinks, but cheaper tickets may sometimes be offered through the city's youth hostels.

Centro Cultural Torquato Tasso, Defensa 1575, opposite Parque Lezama (☎011/4307-6506). Friendly San Telmo neighbourhood cultural centre with tango classes (Mon 8pm, Wed 9pm, Thurs 8pm, Fri 7pm for children & 8pm), and *milongas* on Friday from 11pm and Sunday from 10pm.

El Chino, Beazley 3566, Pompeya (☎011/4911-0215); bus #46 from Constitución or taxi. *El Chino* is the eponymous owner of this atmospheric bar and parrilla in traditional Pompeya – probably the most authentic place to hear tango, sung by the talented staff and a crowd of locals and regulars. Fri & Sat from 10pm.

MILONGAS

Tango, the dance once regarded as the preserve of older couples, or merely a tourist attraction, has gained a whole new audience in the last few years, with an increasing number of young people filling the floors of social clubs, confiterías and traditional dancehalls for regular events known as **milongas**. The price of entry to a *milonga* varies, but is generally around $5 and in many cases classes are given first. Whilst the setting for a *milonga* can range from a sports hall to an elegant salon, the structure – and etiquette – of the dances varies little. Generally, it is divided into musical sets, known as *tandas*, which will cover the three subgenres of tango: tango "proper"; *milonga* – a more uptempo sound; and waltz, each of which is danced differently. Occasionally there will also be an isolated interval of salsa, rock or jazz. Even if you don't dance, it's still worth going: the spectacle of couples slipping almost trance-like around the dancefloor, as if illustrating the oft-quoted remark "tango is an emotion that is danced", is a captivating sight. Apart from the understated skill and composure of the dancers, one of the most appealing aspects of the *milonga* is the absence of class – and, especially, age – divisions; indeed most younger dancers regard it as an honour to be partnered by older and more experienced dancers.

The invitation to dance comes from the man, who will nod towards the woman whom he wishes to dance with. She signals her acceptance of the offer with an equally subtle gesture and only then will her new partner approach her table. Once on the dancefloor, the couple wait eight *compases*, or bars, and then begin to dance, circulating in an anticlockwise direction around the dancefloor. As the floor of a *milonga* will inevitably be full of couples, it's unlikely that you'll see the spectacular choreography of the shows, but what you will see is real tango, in which the dancers' feet barely seem to leave the ground. The woman follows the man's lead by responding to *marcas*, or signs, given by her partner to indicate the move he wishes her to make. The more competent she is, the greater number of variations and personal touches she will add – though the basic steps of the tango may not look very difficult, it entails a rigorous attention to posture and a subtle – but essential to avoid losing balance – shifting of weight from leg to leg. The couple will normally dance together until the end of a set, which lasts for four or five

Club Almagro, Medrano 522, Almagro (☎011/4774-7454); Medrano subte station. This sports centre in the barrio of Almagro is the setting for various *milongas* (Tues 10pm, Fri 11pm, Sat 11pm, Sun 10pm) – the Tuesday night dance in particular is rated by many serious tango dancers as the best *milonga* in town. Also classes most days.

Club Gricel, La Rioja 1180, San Cristóbal (☎011/4957-7157); Urquiza subte station or bus #126 from Bolívar. Small, friendly club holding *milongas* on Fridays from 11pm, Saturdays from 10pm and Sunday from 9pm. Also daily classes.

Confitería Ideal, Suipacha 384, 1st Floor (☎011/4326-1515). An oasis of elegance just a few blocks from busy Corrientes, the *Ideal* has a stunning salon which is undoubtedly one of the most atmospheric places to dance. Wed & Thurs 4pm, Fri 1pm; classic "La Milonga Ideal" Sat 9pm, Sun 3–9pm.

La Estrella, Armenia 1366, Palermo (☎011/4307-5357); bus #140 from Avenida Córdoba or #142 from bottom of Avenida de Mayo. Classes on Friday at 10pm followed by *milonga*, regarded as a classic.

Michelangelo, Balcarce 433, San Telmo (☎011/4328-2646). One of San Telmo's glitziest *tanguerías*, offering dinner and show from Tuesday to Saturday. Transport available to and from central hotels for $4. (8.30pm dinner, 10.30pm show; $65 with dinner, $45 with just drinks).

Niño Bien, Centro Región Leonesa, Humberto 1° 1462, Constitución (☎011/4496-3053); San José subte station. Classes Thursday 8.30–10.30pm and *milongas* on Thursday and Saturday from 11pm. Appears to be particularly popular with a growing number of foreign "tango tourists" but there are plenty of locals, too, and a great atmosphere. They also serve food.

Salón Canning, Raúl Scalabrini Ortíz (former Canning) 1331, Palermo (☎011/4832-6753). A classic venue, with *milongas* on Wednesdays from 8pm and Sundays from 9pm.

Señor Tango, Vieytes 1655 (☎011/4303-0231). Large and very professional *tanguería* in the quiet southern barrio of Barracas. Daily dinner and show from 8.30pm ($55 with dinner, $40 with just drinks).

melodies. Once the set is finished, it is good tango etiquette for the woman to thank her partner who, if the experience has been successful and enjoyable, is likely to ask her to dance again later in the evening.

Watching real tango danced is the kind of experience that makes people long to do it themselves. Unfortunately, a *milonga* is not the best place to take your first plunge; unlike, say, salsa, even the best partner in the world will find it hard to carry a complete novice through a tango. In short, if you can't bear the thought of attending a *milonga* without dancing, the answer is to take some **classes** – you should reckon on taking about six to be able to hold your own on the dancefloor. There are innumerable places in Buenos Aires offering dance classes, including cultural centres, bars and confiterías and, for the impatient or shy, there are private teachers advertising in the specialized publications *El Tangauta* and *Buenos Aires Tango*, distributed through various hotels, tourist offices, cafés such as *Gandhi* and *El Tortoni*, and kiosks in the centre of Buenos Aires. If you're going to take classes, it's important to have an appropriate pair of shoes with a sole that allows you to swivel (rubber soles are useless). For women, it's not necessary to wear heels but it is important that the shoes support the instep. At a *milonga*, however, a pair of supportive and well-polished heels is the norm, and will act as a signal that you are there to dance. Any woman going to a *milonga*, but not intending to dance, should make that clear in her choice of dress and footwear: go dressed to kill and you'll spend the night turning down invitations from bemused-looking men.

The following places offer classes only; for places offering *milongas* along with their classes, see listings on p.139.

Academia Nacional del Tango, Av. de Mayo 833, 1st Floor (☎011/4345-6967). Individual and group classes Mon, Wed & Fri 7.30pm, Tues & Thurs 5pm.

Centro Cultural La Florcita, Sarmiento 4106, Almagro (☎011/4865-8995). Classes Mon, Fri, Sat & Sun 9pm.

La Escuela del Tango, San José 364, 3rd Floor, Montserrat (☎011/4981-9626). Beginners: Mon, & Wed 6.30–8pm, Fri 6.30–8pm & 9.30–11pm. Intermediate: Mon, Wed & Fri 8–9.30pm. Advanced: Mon & Wed 9.30–11pm.

Tangoteca, Av. Alicia Moreau de Justo 1728 (☎011/4311-1988). A new Puerto Madero enterprise offering a slickly packaged and rather theatrical programme of tango shows every night, plus a theme bar, gift shop and classes.

El Viejo Almacén, Av. Independencia and Balcarce (☎011/4307-6689; *valmacen@starnet.net.ar*). Probably the most famous of San Telmo's *tanguerías*, housed in an attractive nineteenth-century building. Occasionally hosts nationally famous tango singers of the stature of Susana Rinaldi, otherwise slickly executed dinner and dance shows daily from 8.30pm. Transport available to and from central hotels. $40.

La Viruta, Armenia 1366, Palermo (☎011/4832-4105); bus #140 from Avenida Córdoba or #142 from bottom of Avenida de Mayo). Classes on Wednesdays at 10.15pm (improbably preceded by a rock dance class at 9pm) followed by a *milonga* an hour or so later. Food available.

Pan y Teatro, Muñiz and Las Casas (☎011/4924-6920). Open every day except Monday, this beautifully restored grocer's shop serves an original blend of Italian and criollo food and puts on shows. Tango on Friday evening.

Gay nightlife

Buenos Aires cannot yet be listed among the world's major gay destinations but the city now has a multitude of bars, restaurants and discos for gay men and lesbians. Although some other Argentine cities have a small **gay scene**, Buenos Aires' anonymity and trendiness have the same centrifugal effect as in most capital cities. Buenos Aires can be very cruisy, making its streets and parks likelier places for meeting people than bars or discos, where people tend to go out in groups of friends. News of events and venues can all be found in *NX* (*nx@netline.com.ar*), *Corazones Bizarros* or *La Otra Guía*, the three national gay and lesbian publications, easily available at downtown kiosks or in gay establishments. The long-established heart of gay Buenos Aires is the corner of Avenidas Pueyrredón and Santa Fe, near which several bars and discos cluster on Calle Anchorena, but the rest are scattered across the city. The standard entrance charge for discos is $15, but some pre-discos give you discount vouchers.

Boicot, Pasaje Dellepiane 657, Downtown. Women-only disco on Sat from 1am.

BsAs Mix, Anchorena 1119, Recoleta. A pre-disco open daily for drinks and a friendly chat from 7pm onwards.

Bunker, Anchorena 1170, Recoleta. For many this it the gay disco in Buenos Aires, with its blaring house and techno music and sweaty torsos. Mixed crowd. Open Fri–Sun, from midnight until daybreak.

Extremo, Luis María Drago 236, Palermo. Increasingly popular disco-pub. Women only on Fridays, men only on Saturdays.

Gasoil, Bulnes 1250, Palermo. Raucous atmosphere and late-night shows, with raunchy strippers baring all on Thurs and Sun. Open Thurs–Mon from 11pm.

IV Milenio, Alsina 934, Downtown. Very late-night disco. Mainly Latin and salsa music, and a laid-back mixed crowd. Fridays only.

Judas, Anchorena 1158, Recoleta. Café-bar, serving food and acting as a pre-dance pub in the evening. Shows at weekends, mostly drag-acts and strippers; karaoke on Sun.

El Olmo, Avenidas Pueyrredón and Santa Fe, Recoleta. Nondescript confitería but the best place to hang out late on Friday and Saturday night, for free entrance or discount vouchers and information flyers.

Oxen, Sarmiento 1662, Downtown. One of the newest and trendiest discos in town. Open Fri–Sun from midnight onwards.

Punto, Puan 311, Caballito (*www.59sex.com.ar*). Open Thurs and Sun from 10pm for parties, shows, fashion parades and other events. Consult the Web site for latest details.

Rosh, Cabrera 3046, Recoleta. Buenos Aires' only bar exclusively for women. Open Wed–Sun.

Sagas, Anchorena 1169, Recoleta. Open daily, with shows and games from 11pm till dawn, when breakfast is served. Strippers titillate the mixed crowd in the early hours.

Scream, Cerrito 306 and Sarmiento, Downtown (*www.cibergay.com/scream*). Café-bar open Thurs and Fri from 8pm, Sat and Sun from 10pm; shows in the early hours on Sat. Good Web site for news about shows and events.

Sitges, Av. Córdoba 4119 and Pringles, Palermo. Large, bright, trendy bar, attracting a mixed but invariably young crowd. Bursting at the seams from from 6pm Thurs to Sun, with late-night shows on Thurs and Sun.

The arts and entertainment

There's a superb range of cultural events on offer in Argentina's capital, ranging from avant-garde theatre to blockbuster movies and grand opera with a wealth of options in between. One of the best features of Porteño cultural life is the strong tradition of free events, including film showings at the city's museums and cultural centres and free tango recitals.

There are a plethora of **listings** in the entertainment sections of both *Clarín* and *La Nación*; the latter's Friday supplement, *Vía Libre*, is particularly good. Numerous independent listings sheets, including *Guía Inrocks* and *wipe*, are also available in bars, bookshops and kiosks throughout the city, whilst the city government produces an excellent booklet *Fervor de Buenos Aires*, with comprehensive details of festivals, film, theatre and music events, available from tourist offices. *Arte al Día* (☎011/4805-7672) is a monthly newspaper with details of art exhibitions at galleries and arts centres, available from newspaper stands.

You can buy tickets at discounted prices for theatre, cinema and music events, at the various centralized **ticket agencies** (*carteleras*) in the centre. Try *Cartelera*, Lavalle 835, local 27 (Mon–Fri 10am–10pm, Sat 11am–11pm, Sun 3–9pm; ☎011/4322-9263); *Cartelera Baires*, Av. Corrientes 1382, local 24 (Mon–Thurs 10am–10pm, Fri 10am–11pm, Sat 10am–midnight, Sun 2–10pm; ☎011/4372-5058); *Cartelera de Espectáculos*, Lavalle 742 (Mon–Fri 10am–11pm, Sat noon–midnight, Sun noon–11pm; ☎011/4322-1559); *Cartelera Vea Más*, Av. Corrientes 1660, Paseo La Plaza, local 26 (daily 10am–10pm; ☎011/4384-5319; *www.veamas.com*).

Cinemas

Porteños are keen and knowledgeable **cinema** goers and there are around one hundred cinemas in the city showing everything from the latest Hollywood releases to Argentinian films and foreign art-house cinema. Foreign films are always subtitled, though occasionally the original language soundtrack is slightly muted or muffled. Cinemas showing purely mainstream stuff tend to be concentrated on Lavalle; for a mix of mainstream films (both foreign and Argentinian) and art-house flicks head to Corrientes. To some extent though, these streets are losing out to the newer multiplex cinemas housed within the city's shopping malls, which offer excellent visuals and acoustics, though in a blander atmosphere. There are also numerous free film showings, held at the city's cultural centres and museums. Argentina has a strong national film industry and if your Spanish is up to it, look out for films by established directors María Luisa Bemberg, Fernando Solanas, Eliseo Subiela and Alejandro Agresti. In April, the city holds an **International Festival of Independent Cinema**, with an excellent selection of national and foreign films at venues throughout the city – it's a good idea to book ahead where possible as Buenos Aires turns into a city of cinephiles during this popular event.

The more interesting or unusual cinemas are listed below; for complete details of what's on, consult the listings sections of *Clarín* and *La Nación*.

Cosmos, Av. Corrientes 2046 (☎011/4953-5400). Buenos Aires' favourite art-house cinema reopened in 1999 after a lengthy closure with a showing of Eisentein's classic *Battleship Potemkin* – an old stand-by of the Argentinian Left.

Galerías Pacífico, Florida 753 (☎011/4319-5357). Most centrally located of the mall complexes; a smart four-screen cinema at the back of the shopping centre – no surprises on the programme, but a good place to catch up on mainstream movies.

Museo del Arte Moderno, Av. San Juan 350 (☎011/4361-2462). Free film showings (usually on Wednesdays at 6pm) in conjunction with the Museo del Cine, around the corner. A good place to see foreign and Argentinian classics.

Cultural Centres and Art Galleries

Buenos Aires' cultural centres are one of the city's greatest assets. Every neighbourhood has its own modest centre – good places to find out about free tango classes and the like – whilst the major institutions such as the Centro Cultural Borges and the Centro Cultural Recoleta put on some of the city's best exhibitions. They're always good places to while away an hour or two and generally offer a mixture of art exhibitions, film, cafés and Internet access. Buenos Aires also has some prestigious commercial **art galleries**, the majority of which are based around Retiro and Recoleta, particularly around Plaza San Martín and nearby Suipacha and Arenales. During the second week in May, the art fair **ARTE BA**, held in La Rural exhibition centre in Palermo, showcases work from Buenos Aires' most important galleries.

Belleza y Felicidad, Acuña de Figueroa 900. Very "in" art gallery – a small, independently run place exhibiting both Argentinian and foreign artists.

British Arts Centre, Suipacha 1333 (☎011/4393-0275). The place to head for if you're nostalgic for a bit of Hitchcock – regular film and video showings, also English-language plays by playwrights such as Harold Pinter.

Casa de la Cultura, Av. de Mayo 575. Regular free events such as recitals of works by Astor Piazzolla, Argentina's internationally renowned tango composer.

Centro Cultural Borges, Corner of Viamonte and San Martín (☎011/4319-5449). Large space above the Galerías Pacífico shopping centre, with several galleries showing a mixture of photography and painting, also a theatre. Daily 10am–9pm; $2.

Centro Cultural General San Martín, Sarmiento 1551 (☎011/4374-1251). Tucked behind the Teatro General San Martín with a varied selection of free painting, sculpture, craft and photography exhibitions, and an art-house cinema. Also hosts free tango recitals by the Orquesta de Tango de la Ciudad de Buenos Aires on Tuesdays at noon.

Centro Cultural Recoleta, Junín 1930 (☎011/4803-1040). One of the city's best cultural centres, constructed around a pretty patio with a number of art galleries showing an imaginative range of contemporary, mostly Argentinian work, an auditorium and theatre. Great café and roof terrrace, too. Tues–Fri 2–9pm, Sat & Sun 10am–9pm; $1; free guided visits Sat & Sun 4pm.

Centro Cultural Ricardo Rojas, Corrientes 2038 (☎011/4953-0390). Affiliated to the University of Buenos Aires, this friendly cultural centre offers free events including live music and bargain film showings, usually alternative/art house. Also a gallery space.

Fundación Federico J. Klemm, Marcelo T. de Alvear 626 (☎011/4311-2527; *admin@ fundacionfjklemm.org*). Famous for a cringe-provoking cable TV programme, which definitely falls into the "so bad it's good" category, Argentinian art maverick Klemm is a kind of wannabe Andy Warhol producing bizarre portraits of modern-day Argentinian celebrities in mythic poses. Klemm's work is probably a bit of an acquired taste but he's also a serious art collector with a seriously impressive collection and the gallery has works by Picasso, Rauschenberg and Mapplethorpe – to name just a few – as well as major Argentinian artists such as Berni, Kuitca and Xul Solar. Mon–Fri 11am–8pm.

Goethe Institut, Corrientes 319 (☎011/4311-8964; *www.goethe.de/hs/bue*). Has a good library for German and English books Also offers Internet access and has a cinema. Mon, Tues, Thurs & Fri 12.30–7.30pm, 1st Sat in month 10am–2pm.

Ruth Benzacar Gallery, Florida 1000 (☎011/4313-8480). Rather unexpectedly reached through an underground entrance at the end of Florida, this prestigious gallery has temporary exhibitions featuring international artists as well as Argentinian artists of the stature of sculptor Enio Iommi, one of the most important figures in the Asociación Arte Concreto-Invención, Argentina's major abstract art movement. Mon–Fri 11.30am–8pm, Sat 10.30am–1.30pm.

Theatre

Theatre is strongly represented in Buenos Aires. As well as the major theatrical venues where you'll find a good spread of international and Argentinian theatre, both classic and contemporary, the city is scattered with innumerable independent venues, with stages in bars and tiny auditoriums at the back of shopping centres. The standard of productions at these smaller venues varies wildly, but they're invariably enthusiastically attended and can be great fun. You'll find many of these independent theatres around Corrientes and San Telmo, well-publicized by flyers given out in the street as well as in bars and bookshops. Argentinian playwrights to look out for include Roberto Cossa, whose plays deal with themes of middle-class Porteño life and immigration, in a somewhat similar vein to Arthur Miller; Griselda Gambaro, whose powerful works often focus on the ambiguous power relations between victims and victimizers (with a clear reference to Argentina's traumatic past); and the idiosyncratic Roberto Arlt who offers a darkly humorous and sometimes surreal vision of modernity.

Andamio 90, Paraná 660 (☎011/4374-1484). Long-established theatre school, run by actress and director Alejandra Boero. Two auditoriums putting on a range of contemporary classics by playwrights such as Eugene O'Neill.

Babilonia, Guardia Vieja 3360, Almagro (☎011/4862-0683); subte station Carlos Gardel. Tucked down a rather uninviting street by the side of the Abasto shopping centre, this is one of Buenos Aires' most established fringe venues – a theatre-cum-bar that also hosts live music and attracts a left-leaning intellectual clientele.

El Galpón del Abasto, Humahuaca 3549, Almagro (☎011/4861-8764). Imaginative programme of fringe theatre, generally on Fridays and Saturdays from 11pm.

Teatro General San Martín, Corrientes 1500 (☎011/4374-9377; free information service ☎0800/333-5254; *www.teatrosanmartin.com.ar*). Excellent modern venue with several auditoriums. Varied programme which usually includes one or two Argentinian plays as well as international standards such as Pinter or Brecht. Also contemporary dance events, children's theatre and art-house cinema in the Sala Leopoldo Lugones. Theatre prices from $6; half-price on Wed.

Teatro Nacional Cervantes, Libertad 815 (☎011/4816-4224). Grand old-fashioned theatre with a broad programme of old and new Argentinian and foreign works.

Teatro El Vitral, Rodríguez Peña 344 (☎011/4371-0948). An attractive old mansion off Corrientes is the setting for this small independent theatre.

Classical music, opera and ballet

Argentina has some world-class classical performers, especially opera singers, such as tenor José Cura and soprano María Cristina Kiehr, but disappointingly little **classical music** is on offer in the city. Even so, an evening at the Teatro Cólon is a memorable experience, for both the opulent decor and enthusiastic audience. If you can, go to an **opera** rather than a ballet, as it's generally of a higher standard – though you should look out for appearances of internationally renowned Argentinian **ballet** star, Julio Bocca. The Buenos Aires Philharmonic also plays at the Teatro Cólon, and the Mozarteum Argentina is a season of free chamber-music concerts.

Teatro Avenida, Av. de Mayo 1222 (☎011/4381-0662). Stylish early twentieth century theatre, mainly a ballet and opera venue.

Teatro Coliseo, M. T. de Alvear 1155 (☎011/4816-6115). Major venue for ballet and classical music; also has occasional free recitals.

Teatro Colón, Libertad 621 (☎011/4382-5414). One of the world's great opera houses – acoustically on a par with La Scala in Milan. Opera, ballet and classical music from March to December. Buenos Aires' most glamorous night out. Tickets from $5 standing to more than $100 for boxes. Also free classical music recitals in the Salón Dorado from Tuesday to Friday (5.30pm).

Shopping and markets

Buenos Aires has the best **shopping** of any city in South America. It may not be cheap – few things are here – but you can find everything you want, including some highly original items to take home. Over the past decade or two, shopping malls have partly superseded small shops and street markets, but those in Buenos Aires are among the most tastefully appointed in the world – and lots of the good old-fashioned stores have survived. Several of the malls are housed in revamped buildings of historical and architectural interest, and contain not only fashion boutiques, perfume shops, computer stores and the like, but also modern cinemas and some upmarket fast-food joints and ice-cream parlours. On a practical level, they're air-conditioned and the places where you'll find that rarity in Buenos Aires, public toilets.

Buenos Aires prides itself on being a literary city, and its dozens of new and second-hand **bookshops** are a real pleasure; several already had salons and cafés when, just about everywhere else in the world, booksellers expected you to make your purchase and leave. A succession of shops selling books, and **records** – with an enormous selection of tango, jazz, classical, folk and rock – are strung along Avenida Corrientes between Avenida 9 de Julio and Avenida Callao. Others are along the stretch of Florida north of Avenida Córdoba, together with lots of other interesting shops, many of them in covered arcades or *galerías*. Contemporary **art**, including some intriguing landscapes and "gaucho art", is on sale at the scores of smart galleries – or *galerías de arte* – that throng Retiro. More galleries are scattered across Recoleta, with several along Avenida Alvear, but anyone looking for colonial paintings and antiques, along with Evita or Gardel memorabilia and other curios, should head for Plaza Dorrego and its colourful flea-market.

The city's **markets**, along with some of the *casas de provincia* (see p.17), are also where you'll find **handicrafts** and **artesanía**, sometimes at lower prices than at the specialized craft centres or *ferias*. Crafts may seem alarmingly expensive to anyone used to Peruvian or Bolivian prices, but remember that you are getting beautiful, unique pieces of ceramics or wooden masks or woollens made of alpaca wool at far better value than the mass-produced alternatives. Other typically Argentine goods include *mate* paraphernalia, polo wear, wine and world-class leatherware. Or take a jar or two of *dulce de leche* away with you to satisfy cravings.

Shopping malls

Abasto, Av. Corrientes 3200, Almagro. A converted food market, it now has giant-screen cinemas, design shops and an enormous fast-food area, all on a grand scale.

Alto Palermo, Av. Santa Fe 3251, Palermo. In an airy modern building, with dozens of shops on four levels, and a very good *patio de comidas*, including a *Freddo* ice-cream stall.

Buenos Aires Design Center, Plaza Intendente Alvear, Recoleta. Right next to the Centro Cultural de Recoleta, this mall is dedicated to shops selling the latest design goods, from Argentina and elsewhere.

Galerías Pacifico, Florida 750, microcentro. Fashion boutiques and bookstores in a beautiful building decorated with murals by leading Argentine artists, plus the Centro Cultural Borges at the top, and even a tourist information bureau on the first floor.

Paseo Alcorta, Figueroa Alcorta and Salguero, Palermo. A huge shopping complex, with several cinemas and the excellent Carrefour supermarket, great for buying wine.

Patio Bullrich, Libertador 750, Retiro. A recycled thoroughbred horse market, this is the king of all the city's shopping malls, with its leather stores and shops for buying polo wear.

Books, records and CDs

Corrientes is the traditional place to head for **books** and **records**, though there are also a number of secondhand stores on Avenida de Mayo, and various upmarket bookstores, with good foreign-language and glossy souvenir book sections around Florida, Córdoba and Santa Fe. If you're in town during April, don't miss Buenos Aires' hugely popular **Feria del Libro** (*www.el-libro.com.ar*), held at the Centro de Exposiciones on Avenidas Figueroa Alcorta and Pueyrredón which attracts staggeringly large numbers of people and provides a good opportunity for some serious browsing as well as the chance to meet famous authors or attend special events such as lectures on Borges or poetry recitals.

Alberto Casares, Suipacha 521 and Av. Alvear 1883, local 15. Good selection of Argentinian history and literary texts, strong on Borges, also secondhand books

El Ateneo, Florida 340. Classy Florida bookshop with a good selection of fiction and glossy picture books.

Gandhi, Av. Corrientes 1743 (*libros_gandhi@ciudad.com.ar*). Newly revamped and very glossy bookstore, offering an excellent range of fiction, non-fiction and periodicals, plus a coffee shop where you can browse your purchases.

Liberarte, Corrientes 1555. An emporium of the assorted interests of the Porteño left-wing intelligentsia. Loads of offbeat periodicals.

Librería del Ávila, Alsina 500, Montserrat. Sprawling bookshop with excellent section on Buenos Aires and Argentina in general and an eclectic selection of secondhand foreign-language books

Librería de Mujeres, Montevideo 370. Small feminist bookshop with a cybercafé.

Librería del Turista, Florida 937. Good selection of travel books.

Librería Hernández, Av. Corrientes 1436. Good place for browsing latest Argentinian publications with helpful and well-informed staff.

Librería Platero, Talcahuano 485. Decent selection of non-fiction on Argentina and big (though rather expensive) secondhand section. Provides a cheap worldwide delivery service.

Librerías ABC, Good foreign-language section (mostly German and English) and loads of travel books and guides.

Musimundo, Various outlets along Florida and throughout the city. Argentina's major record chain, stocking everything from foreign pop and rock to tango and folk music. Branches throughout the city.

Tower Records, Florida 700, also at Santa Fe 1883. Local branches of the US chain.

Zival's, Av. Callao 395 (*www.zivals.com*). Small but well-stocked book and record store with a strong selection of musical books and an excellent CD selection. The staff are a great source of knowledge on the best tango recordings.

Art and crafts

As well as at the weekly fairs in Recoleta and Mataderos, local **arts and crafts** are available at a number of stores in the city centre. A few of the better ones are:

CEPAR, Museo Hernández, Av. del Libertador 2373, Palermo. A wide range of textiles, musical instruments and masks made by the Wichi, Toba, Chiriguano, Mapuche and Pilagá peoples, along with criollo crafts from all over the country. Mon–Fri 9.30am–3pm.

Fortín, Santa Fe 1245. High-quality handmade leather goods, principally boots, jackets and bags.

Kelly's, Paraguay 431 (*www.milonga.com*). Colourful store selling a variety of ponchos (with examples from different provinces), ceramics and, of course, *mates*.

Marcelo Toledo, Av. Belgrano 887, Montserrat (*www.marcelotoledo.com.ar*). Silver vases, jewellery, cutlery and *mate* vessels made according to traditional designs with a modern flourish.

Plata Nativa, Florida 860, Retiro. Silver antiques and crafts, religious paintings and textiles.

La Querencia, Esmeralda 1018. Packed with upmarket gaucho and polo paraphernalia – everything from ornate silver *mates* to leather stirrups.

Outdoor equipment

As well as the outlets listed here, there are many camping and fishing shops along the 100 to 200 block of Calle Paraná, just off Corrientes.

Deporcamping, Santa Fe 4830 (☎011/4772-0534). Tents, backpacks, climbing equipment.

Duve, Mendoza 1679 (☎011/4784-4799; *www.escalada.com*). Mountaineering, trekking and camping equipment

Rupal, 11 de Septiembre 4555 (☎011/4702-9017; *rupal@satlink.com*). Tents, backpacks and sleeping bags and climbing equipment. Also rents out equipment.

Tribu, Av. del Libertador 6279, Belgrano (☎011/4788-6719). Factory outlet for major brands such as Timberland and Swiss Army knives. Mon–Sat 10am–8pm.

Listings

ACA Main office next to the tourist office at Santa Fe 887 (Mon–Fri 9am–7pm, Sat 8am–1pm).

Airlines Aerolíneas Argentinas, Perú 2 (☎011/4340-7777); Aeroperú, Av. Santa Fé 840 (☎011/4311-4115); Air France, Paraguay 610, 14th Floor (☎011/4317-4747); Alitalia, Suipacha 1111, 28th Floor (☎011/4310-9910); American Airlines, Av. Santa Fe 881 (☎011/4318-1111); Austral, Paraná 590 y San Martín 427 (☎011/4340-7777); British Airways, Viamonte 570, 1st Floor (☎011/4320-6600); Canadian Airlines, Av. Córdoba 656 (☎011/4322-3632); Cubana, Sarmiento 552, 11th Floor (☎011/4326-5291); KLM, Reconquista 559, 5th Floor (☎011/4312-1200); LAER, Maipú 935 P.B (☎011/4311-5237); LADE, Perú 714 (☎011/4361-0853); Lan Chile, Paraguay 609 (☎011/4311-5334); LAPA, Carlos Pellegrini 1075 (☎011/4819-5272); Lufthansa, Marcelo T. de Alvear 636 (☎011/4319-0600); Southern Winds, Florida 868, 13th Floor (☎011/4312-2811); Swissair, Av. Santa Fe 846, 1st Floor (☎011/4319-0000); United Airlines, Av. Madero 900, 9th Floor Torre Catalinas Plaza (☎011/4316-0777).

Airport Enquiries Ezeiza (☎011/4480-9538); Aeroparque (☎011/4773-1406).

Buses Retiro bus terminal is at Avenida Antártida and Ramos Mejía (☎011/4310-0700). Note that it's almost impossible to get through on the station's general information number. If you know the name of the bus company you want (usually available by calling the relevant *casa de provincia*; see p.17), you could call direct to check the timetable and, in most cases, make a reservation or credit-card purchase. Otherwise, you're probably best off visiting the terminal in person, where there is a useful information booth to help you make sense of the hundreds of *boleterías* or ticket counters.

There are often many different companies going to the same destination: apart from obvious differences such as timetables and prices, deciding factors may include availability of student discounts (rare but worth enquiring about) and type of service.

Car Rental AI Rent a Car International, M.T. de Alvear 678 (☎011/4311-1000; *rentacar@ssdenet.com.ar*); Avis, Cerrito 1527 (☎011/4326-5577); Budget Rent a Car, Santa Fe 869 (☎011/4311-9870); Dollar, Esmeralda 684, 8th Floor (☎011/4393-5454); Express, Carlos Pellegrini 1576, local 24 (☎011/4326-0338; *recova@express-rent.com.ar*); Hertz, Ricardo Rojas 451 (☎011/4312-1317), also at *Sheraton Hotel* (☎011/4313-2525) and Ezeiza (☎011/4480-0054); Localiza, Maipú 924 (☎011/4315-8384); Ezeiza (☎011/4480-0431); Aeroparque (☎011/4776-3993); Tauro, Posadas 1590 (☎011/4807-1002; *maxicar@movi.com.ar*).

Embassies and Consulates Australia, Villanueva 1400 (Mon–Fri 9am–1pm & 2–5.30pm; ☎011/4777-6580); Bolivia, Av. Belgrano 1670, 1st Floor (Mon–Fri 9am–2pm; ☎011/4381-0539); Brazil, Cerrito 1350 (Mon–Fri 10am–2pm; ☎011/4815-8737); Canada, Tagle 2828 (Mon–Thurs 8.30am–11.30am); Chile, San Martín 439, 9th Floor (Mon–Fri 9am–1pm; ☎011/4394-6582); Ireland, Suipacha 1380, 2nd Floor (Mon–Fri 9.30am–3.30pm); New Zealand, Carlos Pellegrini 1427, 5th Floor (Mon–Fri 9am–1pm & 2–5.30pm; ☎011/4328-0747); Peru, Av. Córdoba 1345, 11th Floor (Mon–Fri 9am–4pm; ☎011/4811-4619); UK, Dr Luis Agote 2412 (Mon–Fri 9am–1pm; ☎011/4803-7070); United States, Av. Colombia 4300 (Mon, Wed & Fri 8.45–10.30am); Uruguay, Ayacucho 1616 (Mon–Fri 9.30am–12.30pm; ☎011/4807-3040).

Exchange Buenos Aires is the only city in the country where you will find it relatively easy to change travellers' cheques, but it can still turn into a lengthy transaction. The majority of bureaux de change are located around the financial district; particularly along San Martín – rates are similar at all of them and opening hours are generally Monday to Friday 9am–6pm. Only a few open on Saturday morning. American Express, at Arenales 707, changes its own cheques commission free.

Hospitals Consultorio de Medicina del Viajero, Hospital de Infecciosas F.J. Muniz, Uspallata (☎011/4304-2386); Hospital Británico, Perdriel 74 (☎011/4304-1081); Hospital De Clínicas José de San Martín, Av. Córdoba 235l (☎011/4961-6001 or 4961-7575).

Internet There are an increasing number of places offering Internet access in Buenos Aires, though in comparison with some of the provincial towns, they tend to be rather expensive. However, prices are dropping all the time, and various places along Florida run competitive offers from time to time – watch out for leaflets given out in the street. Throughout the city, many *locutorios* provide Internet access. Cybercafés to try include Al Cyber, Chile 1202 (*www.alcyber.com.ar*); Cybercafé, Maure 1886 (*www.cybercafe.com.ar*); Goethe Institut, Corrientes 319 (Mon, Tues, Thurs & Fri 1–7pm; *www.siemens.cafe*); Las Vegas, Carlos Pellegrini 469 (*usatotal@aol.com*); Librería de Mujeres, Montevideo 370 (*www.sion.com/libreriamujeres*); and Web Café, Alto Palermo Shopping, 3rd Floor, Av. Santa Fe 3253 (*www.webcafe.com.ar*).

Laundry Via Suipacha, at Suipacha 722 (☎011/4322 3458); Laverap, at Av. Córdoba 466 (☎011/4312-5460), plus many others across the city.

Pharmacies Farmacia Porteña, on the corner of Paraná and Corrientes; Hiperfarmacia on Corrientes, just past the intersection with Callao. Both open 24hr.

Police Lavalle 451 (☎011/4322-8033) and Suipacha 1156 (☎011/4393-3333).

Post Office Correo Central, Sarmiento 189 (Mon–Fri 10am–8pm). As well as standard post and parcel facilities, there is a *poste restante* office on the first floor, which charges $1.50 per item. There are numerous smaller branches throughout the city, open from 10am to 6pm. Outside these hours, there are many post office counters within stationery shops (*papelerías*) and at kiosks.

Taxis and remises Ordinary taxis are plentiful throughout the city, though if you have any difficulty, there are a number of radio taxi firms: City Tax (☎011/4585-5544); Radio Taxi Pídalo (☎011/4932-2222); Taxi Ya (☎011/4953-4206). For longer journeys, booked ahead of time, your best option is a remise: A.C.A.R (☎011/4831-0715); Agencia Barrio Norte (☎011/4811-1334); Tres Sargentos (☎011/4311-4832).

Travel Agents and Tours Agreste, Viamonte 1636 (☎011/4373-4442) offers adventurous camping trips across the country to destinations such as the Saltos de Moconá and the Valle de la Luna. Buenos Aires Tur, Lavalle 1444, Office 16 (☎011/4371-2304), offers city tours of Buenos Aires, including tango shows, and visits to Tigre and nearby estancias. ASATEJ, Florida 835, 3rd Floor, is a young and dynamic travel agency, affiliated to STA Travel and offering the cheapest flight deals in the city – be prepared to wait as the office gets very busy. Lihué Expediciones, Maipú 926, 1st Floor (☎011/4311-9610), offers imaginative literary walks through the city, based around the writings of Borges, Cortázar and others.

AROUND BUENOS AIRES

For all its parks and tree-lined avenues, Buenos Aires is a predominantly urban place, as you'd expect of one of the world's biggest cities, and you might like to get away from the hectic ferment for a day or two. The **northern suburbs** of Vicente López, Olivos and San Isidro have clung to their villagey character, and are less than forty minutes away from central Buenos Aires by train, rather more by bus. Further north, the sub-tropical islets, steamy swamps and traditional stilted houses of the **Paraná Delta** could not be a more radical change from the capital – it's as if the Everglades extended just beyond the Statue of Liberty. This intriguing landscape, lending itself to water-related activities such as kayaking and water-skiing, is right next to **Tigre**, a riverside resort with a lot of historical associations and a colourful fruit market, only 30km north of central Buenos Aires. It's served by regular train and bus services, but a great way to visit both the northern suburbs and Tigre is by the scenic **Tren de la Costa**, which links **Olivos** to the **Parque de la Costa**, a popular theme-park. Tigre's also the departure point for launches to **Isla Martín García**, a sparsely populated island at the mouth of the Río Uruguay, once a political penal colony but now a nature reserve. The beautifully preserved Uruguayan town of **Colonia del Sacramento**, a former Portuguese colony and a short ferry-ride across the River Plate from Buenos Aires, is another popular day-trip destination. However, like Tigre, it really deserves an overnight stay at least, if you're to enjoy its laid-back atmosphere to the full.

The northern suburbs

Many Porteños believe that all civilization comes to an abrupt end as soon as you cross Avenida General Paz, the peripheral highway that separates the Federal Capital from the rest of Greater Buenos Aires. They're duly ignored by residents of leafy suburbs such as Vicente López, Olivos and San Isidro, where you can enjoy cleaner air and live at a relaxed pace. The highlight of **Vicente López** is an eccentric arts centre, the Museo Fundación Rómulo Raggio, while **Olivos**, well-known for housing the summer residence of Argentina's president, is worth stopping off for a stroll around the Puerto, a lively marina with lots of smart bars and cafés. An aimless walk around **San Isidro**'s picturesque historic quarter makes for a perfect, lazy afternoon. A disused commuter rail-track was reactivated in the 1990s as the **Tren de la Costa**, allowing you to stop off along the way between Olivos and Tigre's Parque de la Costa, and has become an attraction in its own right. For the energetic, an excellent cycle path, a rarity in Buenos Aires, runs alongside the rail tracks north from Barrancas station to San Isidro, and is an excellent way of getting around; it's also popular with roller-bladers. Bikes, blades and other equipment can be rented at various outlets en route, and these places also serve drinks and snacks. All three suburbs boast a multitude of restaurants to try out, along with the upmarket parrillas clustered around Puerto de Olivos.

Vicente López and Olivos

The first suburb you come to after crossing Avenida General Paz is **Vicente López**, a prosperous area of cobbled streets sloping down to the waterfront, lined with lush trees, pretty villas and well-tended gardens. It's especially worth a visit for the curious **Museo Fundación Rómulo Raggio** at Gaspar Campos 861 (Thurs–Sun 4–8pm; $2, free on first Sat of month; free guided tours; ☎011/4796-1456; *ffrraggio@smsi.com.ar*). An eclectic arts centre, it offers classes in tango, tae kwon do and ceramics in a purpose-built workshop, alongside Palacio Lorenzo Raggio, a splendid but heavily remod-

TREN DE LA COSTA

The scenic **Tren de la Costa** (daily 7am–5am; $2 each way; ☎011/4732-6300) runs from Olivos all the way north to Tigre, a 25-minute trip if you do it in one go. Although it's one of the most attractive transport options for getting to Tigre – it runs parallel to the waterfront, mostly through green parkland and past grandiose suburban mansions and villas – it's also made for stopping off on the way, at the nine restored or purpose-built stations along the route. Originally the state-run *Tren del Bajo* line which ran northwards from Retiro station, it was built in 1891, but fell into disuse in the 1960s. In 1995 the northernmost section reopened as a privately run scenic railway, with luxurious mock-Victorian electric carriages running smoothly and silently along electrified tracks.

To get to the southern terminal, **Estación Maipú**, first take a commuter-train from Retiro (see p.76) to Olivos' Estación Mitre, a thirty-minute journey. From there, a walkway takes you across Avenida Maipú to the very British-looking red-brick station and its ticket-offices. Should you want to return downtown by the direct train, buy a one-way ticket, valid for the whole day; you're entitled to break the journey at any station, and you don't have to go as far as Tigre. There's a train every ten minutes until midnight; hourly thereafter.

As well as hopping-off points for Olivos and San Isidro, many of these stations are attractions in their own right. **Estación Borges**, the nearest to Olivos' marina, is named after a nineteenth-century Uruguayan colonel, an ancestor of the poet; the building's striking brickwork has been carefully revamped and it's next to the recently restored Cinema Juan Carlos Altavista. Built right at the beginning of the twentieth century, it's one of the world's oldest movie-houses still in use. **Libertador** and **Anchorena** stations both boast shops, cafés and exhibition areas, while **Estación Barrancas** houses an antiques fair (Sat & Sun 10am–6pm) and gives access to the cycle-path which runs north to San Isidro. **Estación San Isidro**, with its upmarket shopping mall, is located conveniently near the suburb's historic quarter. North of here, you pass through four more riverside stations – **Punta Chica**, **Marina Nueva**, **San Fernando** and **Canal** – before arriving at the northern terminus, **Estación Delta**, close to Tigre's fruit market and opposite the entrance to the Parque de la Costa.

elled Neoclassical villa, partly inspired by Vaux-le-Vicomte chateau near Paris. The villa itself houses one of the biggest private collections of Argentine paintings and sculptures, while classical recitals and avant-garde plays, sometimes in English, are regularly held in the adjoining auditorium. The museum is two blocks west of Estación Vicente López on the commuter-line from Retiro and can be reached by **buses #161 and #168** – get off at Avenida Maipú and Gral Las Heras and walk four blocks east.

Some 2km north, up the inland highway Avenida Maipú and riverside Avenida del Libertador, is **Olivos**, where the heavily guarded parkland surrounding the neocolonial presidential palace stretches for over 1km between the two avenues. Just over 1km northeast of the residence is the **Puerto de Olivos**, an exclusive marina and yacht-club, where you can stroll and admire the boats. Catamarans head upstream from here to Tigre, leaving from the southern end of the harbour (Dec–March Sat 4pm, Sun & public holidays 3pm & 5pm; $6 return). Expensive parrilla **restaurants** *Nelly* and *El Muelle*, on the harbour-front, both offer succulent steaks, while the sailing-club, *Club Nautico Olivos*, 200m east of Olivos' commuter-line station, is open to everyone for a drink, but you must be smartly dressed. The **Tren de la Costa**'s Borges station (see box above) is three blocks west of *Club Nautico Olivos*.

San Isidro

Wealth and tradition ooze from the streets of **San Isidro**, one of Buenos Aires' most beautiful suburbs. Even the mighty Avenida del Libertador, a multi-lane highway back into the city centre, givesway to the barrio's old-fashioned elegance and winds through San Isidro's luxurious residences as a cobbled street. The suburb's newer commercial centre lies around the train station on Avenida Belgrano (frequent services from Retiro, Línea Mitre), but San Isidro's most interesting section is the **Casco Histórico**, centred around Plaza Mitre to the north of here – turn right out of the train station and follow Avenida Belgrano, bearing left along 9 de Julio.

With the exception of the beautiful colonial **Quinta Pueyrredón**, named after General Pueyrredón, who once inhabited it, it's not so much the individual buildings in San Isidro's Casco Histórico that are interesting – although many of them are extremely beautiful – but rather the overall harmony of this rambling quarter. The plaza itself is sited at the edge of a slope and behind its soaring neo-Gothic cathedral, built in 1895, worth popping into for its striking French stained-glass windows, are winding cobbled streets which lead to a couple of viewpoints – the **Mirador Los Paraísos** and the **Mirador Los 3 Ombúes**. From here you can see glimpses of the silvery chocolate waters of the River Plate steadily being invaded by the ever-expanding islands of the Paraná Delta. Were it not for this most un-European of views, these tiny vantage points, with their crazily looping stairs, might remind you of cobbled corners of Paris. Turn around at the Mirador Los 3 Ombúes, however, and the beautiful pink and green facade of the nineteenth-century villa, the **Quinta Los Naranjos**, with its suggestion of tropical abundance, will remind you once again of where you are.

Claiming the title of the oldest house in the north of Buenos Aires, the **Casa del General Pueyrredón**, at Rivera Indarte 48 (Tues, Thurs, Sat & Sun 2.30–7pm; ☎011/4512-3131) stands in the remnants of one of the lots distributed by Juan de Garay in 1580, when San Isidro was the site of numerous *chacras* or small farms. The building itself was originally built in 1790, and, in 1815, was bought by General Pueyrredón – a hero of the reconquest of Buenos Aires in 1806 and Supreme Director of the United Provinces of the River Plate from 1816 to 1820. His son, Prilidiano Pueyrredón, a distinguished painter and architect, inherited the house and added the beautiful Doric-columned gallery that runs along the northern side of the house. Now a Monumento Histórico Nacional and housing San Isidro's **Museo Histórico Municipal**, the building's classic colonial lines, punctuated by green shutters and centred around a patio, are enhanced by its splendid location: there are fantastic views of the river estuary from the garden. The garden's enormous carob tree (known as the *algarrobo histórico*), with its sprawling branches propped up on sticks, was the location of Pueyrredón's discussions with General San Martín on Latin American independence. The museum has a display of historical documents relating to the General's achievements but also features a series of rooms furnished in period style, containing many objects that belonged to the Pueyrredón family itself as well as some accomplished portraits by Prilidiano Pueyrredón. To get to the Quinta Pueyrredón, follow Avenida Libertador past the cathedral and turn left into Roque Sáenz Peña, some five blocks away. The Quinta is located on the right towards the end of the street.

San Isidro is a good point to jump off from the new **Tren de la Costa** (see box on p.150), which brings you right to the foot of Plaza Mitre. Though surrounded by a new and very smart shopping centre, the newly revamped station has somehow managed not to detract too much from San Isidro's charm, and the streets which run alongside the railway tracks make a pleasant place to stop for a bite to **eat** or a **drink**, all within earshot of the atmospheric tinkling of the railway crossing. *La Esquina del Bajo*, on the corner of Del Barco Centenera, has a good seafood, pasta and parrilla menu while *El Pino*, on Pedro de Mendoza, on the other side of the tracks, is a small friendly bar with tables on the pavement and is easily recognizable by the Basque flag displayed outside. As well as the train, **buses** #60 (bajo) from Constitución, via Callao, and #168 from Boca, go to San Isidro.

The Paraná Delta

One of the world's most beautiful and unusual landscapes, the exotic **Paraná Delta** lies just a few kilometres to the north of Buenos Aires' Avenida General Paz. In constant formation due to sediment deposited by the Río Paraná, the Delta region is a wonderfully seductive maze of lushly vegetated islands separated by rivers and *arroyos*, or streams, lined by traditional houses on *pilotes*, or stilts, which peep out from behind screens of subtropical vegetation. The Delta actually begins at the port of Diamante in Entre Ríos Province, some 450km to the northwest of the city, and its one thousand square kilometres is divided into three administrative sections. By far the most visited area, however, is the first section, most of which lies within an hour and a half's boat trip from the pretty town of **Tigre**, around 20km northwest of Capital Federal. The first section is a favourite weekend destination for Porteños but is also home to around three thousand islanders, and the area's infrastructure includes petrol stations along the river banks, schools, floating shops and even a mobile library. There are also a number of restaurants and hotels here. Beyond the first section, bounded by the wide Río Paraná de las Palmas, inhabitants and amenities are much more dispersed and though mains electricity has recently been installed in the first section, more isolated isleños still have to rely on electric generators and kerosene lamps.

The Delta can be visited on a day-trip, but it's also a great place to stay overnight for a break from the hectic pace of the city. A longer trip can also be made to **Isla Martin Garcia**, a former penal colony situated close to the Uruguayan coast some 40km to the northeast of Tigre. Though for many the Delta's biggest attraction is that it offers the chance to do not very much at all, its numerous waterways are also popular with watersports enthusiasts as well as devotees of more traditional rowing and fishing.

Tigre

TIGRE owes its poetic name to the jaguars – popularly known as *tigres* in Latin America – that inhabited the Delta region until the beginning of the twentieth century. The town sits on an island bounded by the Río Luján, the Río Reconquista and the Río Tigre and was first documented in 1635 under the name of El Pueblo de las Conchas, a small settlement which functioned as a defensive outpost against Portuguese invasions during the seventeenth century. One of the favoured summer retreats of the Porteño elite in the late nineteenth and early twentieth century, the town owes its sumptuous mansions and palatial rowing clubs to this period. During this time, the hectic social life revolved around events at the **Tigre Club**, home to Argentina's first **casino**, and the **Tigre Hotel**, whose clientele included Enrico Caruso and the Prince of Wales. The town's decline as a glamorous destination was in part a result of the closure of the Tigre Club's casino (closed in 1933 through a law which prohibited casinos in the vicinity of the capital) and in part a result of the growing popularity of Mar del Plata, 400km south on the Atlantic coast and ever more accessible thanks to the arrival of the railway and improved roads. The Tigre Hotel, a grandiose mock-Tudor construction, was demolished in 1940, although the elegant Tigre Club, to be reopened as a cultural centre, still stands at the apex of the island.

As a departure point for **excursions** to the **Delta** and the **Isla Martín García** (see p.156), the town itself is sometimes overlooked by tourists. At first sight, it's a bit of a hotchpotch of a place: a recent upsurge in investment in the area has brought new developments, many – such as a slightly twee train station and the mega Parque de la Costa – seem to have been built with scant regard for Tigre's distinctive architectural heritage. Don't be put off by your first impression, however – Tigre offers an appealing mix of faded glamour and day-trip brashness and the bars and restaurants around its recently refurbished riverside area provide perfect vantage points for an unhurried contemplation of the comings and goings of Delta life.

Arrival and information

Trains depart regularly for Tigre from Retiro station (Línea Mitre); the hour's journey costs less than one peso and terminates at Tigre's new **train station** on the riverbank, just to the south of Avenida Cazón. For a little bit more, you can take the new **Tren de la Costa** (see p.150) which drops you at the portals of the Parque de la Costa. An alternative, though time-consuming, option is to take the #60 (bajo) **bus** from Constitución station, which also stops along Avenida Callao and takes you into the centre of Tigre.

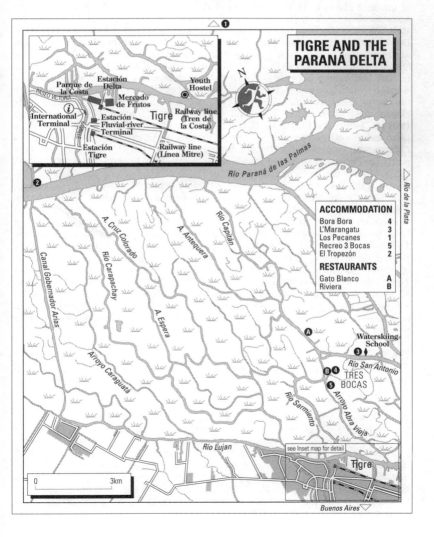

Tigre's helpful **tourist office** is on the western side of the Río Tigre, on the corner of Lavalle and R. Fernández (daily 10am–5pm; ☎011/4512-4498), where you can pick up some good leaflets and maps in Spanish and English. The tourist office also offers a number of tours to both Tigre and the Delta on Saturdays and Sundays.

Accommodation

There's very little **accommodation in Tigre**. However, there is a gorgeous bed & breakfast run by the Escauriza family at Lavalle 557 (☎011/4749-2499; $70). A fabulous old family house with enormous wood-floored bedrooms, huge balconies, a swimming pool in the garden and exceptionally friendly owners, the B&B is without a doubt one of the best places to stay in and around the capital. **On the Delta** itself, though, accommodation is fairly abundant, though it tends to be pricey. One of the most accessible places to stay – though lacking the wild charm of further-flung reaches of the Delta – is the area known as **Tres Bocas**, at the confluence of the Abra Vieja, Capitán and San Antonio rivers, a thirty-minute boat trip from the Estación Fluvial (Interisleña; $6 return trip). Tres Bocas is one of the few points on the Delta where you can disembark and wander for a considerable distance thanks to a public riverside path and wooden footbridges which cross from island to island. Accommodation here includes the *Recreo Tres Bocas* (no phone; ③), a crumbling old hotel, with few remnants of its elegant past when Perón, Evita and Gardel were all guests. Nearby *Bora-Bora* (☎011/472-8646, fax 4658-0551; ⑤, half board) is a slightly sterile, albeit comfortable place and also offers free canoes to guests. Further afield, hotels include the luxurious *I'Marangatu*, located on the Río San Antonio (☎011/4731-4752; ⑦, half board) whilst pretty *Los Pecanes*, on Arroyo Felicaria in the second section of the Delta (☎011/4728-1932), offers a two-night package for $120. The most atmospheric place to stay, however, is at the Delta's most famous hotel, *El Tropezón* (☎011/4728-1012; ⑥, full board), magnificently situated on the banks of the wide Paraná de las Palmas. A beautiful traditional building with a wide veranda, a bar stocked with half-century old aperitifs, and old-fashioned rooms, *El Tropezón* has had some famous guests, the most interesting being the Argentinian writer Leopoldo Lugones, who committed suicide there in 1938. The slightly gothic feel to the place is increased by the preservation of the writer's room in the state that he left it, down to the glass from which he drank the fatal dose of cyanide. *El Tropezón* can also be visited for lunch (ring first). Just downstream of Tigre, there's also a **youth hostel** on the Río Abra Vieja (☎011/4728-0396; weekdays $7, weekends $12), just a short hop across the river from the neighbouring locality of San Fernando (ring first to arrange transport), where there are no meals but you can do your own cooking. The hostel also has a campsite where you can pitch your tent for $5 a day.

The Town

Tigre lies along the western bank of the Río Luján, one of the Delta's main arteries, and the town is divided in half by the smaller Río Tigre, which runs north–south through its centre. A bridge joins the two halves, linking Avenida Cazón to the east with Avenida San Martín to the west. Riverside avenues flank both sides of the Río Tigre, while the broad Paseo Victorica runs along the Río Luján on the western side of town. A good place to begin a tour of the area is around the river terminal, the **Estación Fluvial**, on the eastern side of town, immediately north of the bridge over the Río Tigre. The point of contact between island and mainland life, the Estación bustles with activity, particularly at weekends, when holidaymakers and locals pass their luggage to the crew of the waiting boats, who pile it on to the roofs of the low wooden vessels. Many Porteños have weekend houses on the islands and a typical Sunday will see them departing en masse, loaded with the ingredients for the obligatory barbecue, and returning in the evening with a large sack of freshly picked oranges.

On the same side of the river as the Estación Fluvial – and well-signposted from the station – you'll find the **Parque de la Costa**, Vivanco 1509 (Wed, Thurs & Fri 11am–8pm, Sat & Sun 11am–9pm; $18; ☎011/4732-6300), one of Latin America's largest amusement parks, with an enormous and hair-raising aquatic roller coaster, carousels and amusement arcades. A couple of blocks to the west, alongside the Río Luján, there's a rather more serene attraction, the **Puerto de Frutos** (fruit market; daily 10am–6pm). A Tigre institution, the Puerto de Frutos has declined somewhat in importance since the days when fruit cultivation was the region's main source of income. At weekends crafts, in particular wickerwork – wicker grows in abundance in the Delta – are steadily taking over from fruit as the market's chief product.

The most enjoyable part of Tigre to explore on foot lies on the western side of the Río Tigre. Once over the bridge, follow riverside Avenida Lavalle north along the Río Tigre. At the intersection of the river with the Río Luján, Lavalle merges with Paseo Victorica, where there is a pretty riverside walk and plenty of bars and restaurants with views over the river. The **Museo Naval**, at Paseo Victorica 602 (Mon–Thurs 8am–12.30pm, Fri 8am–5.30pm, Sat & Sun 10am–6.30pm; $2) is housed in the old naval workshops and holds exhibits – such as scale models and navigational instruments – relating to general maritime history, as well as to Argentinian naval history from the British invasions of 1806 and 1807 to the Malvinas conflict. At the end of Paseo Victorica, you will find the **Tigre Club**. Built in 1900 by the French architect Paul Pater (who also designed Buenos Aires' fine French Embassy) it's a vast turreted and balustraded structure, influenced by grand European hotels of the same period. From here, the road curves round, merging with Avenida Liniers, which leads back towards the bridge. The avenue is flanked by fine, if sometimes slightly decaying, examples of the town's grand nineteenth-century mansions, interspersed with equally luxurious modern residences. Almost as impressive as the street's architecture are its giant trees whose powerful roots have turned the narrow pavement into a kind of pedestrian roller coaster. At no. 818, you'll find reconstructed colonial Casa de Goyechea, housing the **Museo de la Reconquista** (Wed–Sun 10am–6pm; free), surrounded by a lovely veranda and garden. The building was used as an overnight stop by General Liniers and his troops before launching their counterattack against the British invasions of 1806. The museum has an interesting display of documents and objects relating to the recapture of Buenos Aires, including a number of English caricatures from the time, satirizing the poor performance of British troops. There's also a section devoted to local history as well as the rise and fall of the Tigre Club and Hotel.

Eating and drinking

There are plenty of **restaurants in Tigre**; the best of them are located along Paseo Victorica. Options include *Don Manuel*, at no. 29, which offers home-made pastas and parrilla and has a glass-fronted terrace on the first floor; simple friendly *Don Ramón*, at no. 412, offers a similar menu, whilst at no. 135 there's *Y a mi que*, another parrilla with a lovely outside seating area both on the pavement and on the first floor. **On the Delta** itself, there are a number of eating options, including the rather swanky *Gato Blanco*, on the Río Capitán (☎011/4728-0390). One of the nicest places, though, is the simple and pretty *Riviera* (☎011/4728-0177) just by the jetty at Tres Bocas, one of the Delta's oldest restaurants.

Boat trips and activities

Tigre's Estación Fluvial, or River Terminal, lies on General Bartolomé Mitre, one block north of its main train station. From here, frequent regular passenger services, known as *lanchas colectivas*, run by various companies including Interisleña (☎011/4749-0900) and Delta (☎011/4731-1236), leave for all points in the Delta. On the opposite side of the river, at Lavalle 520, you'll find the international terminal from where boats depart for Uruguay and Isla Martín García. **Boats to Isla Martín García** are operated by Cacciola Turismo (Tues, Thurs, Sat & Sun at 8am; journey time 3hr; $28, including guided tour; $35 with lunch). Tickets are best bought in advance from their Buenos Aires office at Florida 520, 1st Floor (☎011/4322-0026). From the neighbouring terminal, there are regular sightseeing boats which are a good way to get an overall view of the Delta, and move slowly enough to take photographs en route.

As far as **activities** are concerned, there are various places **around Tigre** where you can practise watersports. Basic **kayak** courses and explorations of the Delta with specialized guides can be organized (☎011/4327-2854). There's a water-skiing school, run by Jorge Renosto, on the Río San Antonio (☎011/4542-3523) and also a wake-boarding school, run by South American champion Gabriela Díaz (☎011/4728-0031). **Rowing** enthusiasts may be able to join up for the day at one of the numerous clubs based around Paseo Victorica and Lavalle in Tigre.

Isla Martín García

With its quirky historical buildings, abandoned prison, airstrip and permanent population of only two hundred inhabitants, **Isla Martín García** seems to have walked off the pages of a children's adventure story. First discovered by Juan de Solís – and named after one of his sailors, who died during the expedition – on his pioneering trip to the Río de la Plata in 1516, the island has a rich history and unexpectedly varied terrain that make it an interesting excursion from Buenos Aires.

The island's location, between the east bank (now Uruguay), and Buenos Aires gave it an important strategic role. Most notably, it was used as a source of supplies by loyalist forces in Montevideo when they were held under land siege by Buenos Aires between 1812 and 1814. The loyalists were finally defeated by a naval squadron commanded by William Brown, an Irish-born lieutenant-colonel, who defeated loyalist forces on Martín García and blockaded Montevideo, making surrender to Buenos Aires inevitable. The capital's dominance over Montevideo was short-lived, however, as the Uruguayan independence hero José Gervasio Artigas, who had taken part in the early siege of the city, moved in to take control and declared an independent *Estado Oriental* (Eastern State), the foundation for Uruguay's subsequent independence in 1828. In 1886, the island came under the jurisdiction of the Argentinian Navy, who remained in control until 1970. In 1974, the island was declared a nature reserve in a pact signed by the Argentinian and Uruguayan governments. The two nations also agreed that, despite being much closer to the Uruguayan coast, Martín García should remain Argentinian on the condition that it continued to function as a nature reserve rather than a military base.

Strategic importance notwithstanding, it is as a prison that Martín García is best known – its most famous presidential prisoners being Yrigoyen, Perón and Frondizi. The island's **penal status** dates back to 1765; the first prisoners to be transported to the island were moved here from Buenos Aires' cabildo, as their habit of shouting obscenities at passing women there had made their complete removal from society desirable. The obvious isolation of the island aside, it's hard to think of a more appropriate site for a prison; though only a few kilometres from the Uruguayan coast, Martín García is separated from the mainland by a channel known as the Canal del Infierno, whose seven currents would have been a daunting prospect for any prisoner foolhardy enough to try to swim to freedom. These days, a handful of prisoners are still housed on the island under a regulation known as Rule 18, which provides for a period between internment and conditional liberty.

With a surface area of less than two square kilometres, Martín García can easily be seen in a day or two. The island has an underlying rock formation, giving it a greater height above the river (some 27 metres) than the low-lying sediment-formed islands of the Delta. Many of Buenos Aires' cobbles came from the old *canteras*, or quarries, in the southwest of the island. Given the island's small size, the terrain is surprisingly varied, ranging from sandy beaches and reed beds to jungly areas of thick subtropical vegetation. Of the island's equally varied fauna, which includes herons, deer and coypu, the most surprising inhabitants are perhaps the large monitor lizards which amble lazily about, occasionally losing a tail in scraps with local dogs.

At the heart of the island, around the sloping, leafy **Plaza Almirante Brown**, you'll find the island's civic centre, a small collection of pretty buildings housing administrative offices and the island's tiny post office. On the northeastern corner of the square, you'll see the crumbling ruins of the prison. One of the most fascinating buildings is the **Cine-Teatro**, along the street to the east of the square, a gem of decorative architecture whose original and elaborate facade is dominated by a central, rather bemused-looking gargoyle. Opposite is the **Museo Histórico**, housed in an old pulpería; its most unusual exhibit is probably the flowery china toilet that president Marcelo T. de Alvear insisted on being brought for his use while he was detained on the island in 1932.

A number of unsealed roads and paths lead around the island. Around the island's perimeter, a number of gun batteries overlook the river, constructed on President Sarmiento's orders at the beginning of the War of the Triple Alliance (see Contexts, p.706), though never used. On the eastern side of the island the so-called **Barrio Chino**, towards the old jetty, is a small collection of abandoned houses which seem to be in danger of being devoured by the surrounding forest. Beyond the island's airstrip, which runs north–south across the island, there is a small protected nature reserve, off limits to visitors.

Practicalities

Though the island is small, the length of the journey, combined with boarding procedures which mean you have to be at the jetty an hour before the departure time of either 4pm or 5pm, according to the time of year, means that you'll probably feel a little rushed if you visit on a day-trip. The most enjoyable way of seeing the island is to spend the night at either the island's **hostería** (packages arranged through Cacciola; $85 per person including return trip and all meals) or on its **campsite** ($3 per person) which also has some pleasant **cabins** or *albergues* (reservations advisable during busy periods; ☎011/4728-1808) for between $7 and $10 per person. Bring sheets and towels. There are a couple of simple restaurants on the island and you may be able to buy fish from locals to cook yourself.

Martín García's mosquitoes are possibly even more ferocious than the Delta's and a good repellent is a must, particularly if you venture into the forested region around the Barrio Chino.

Into Uruguay: Colonia del Sacramento

In terms of atmosphere, the historic Uruguayan town of **COLONIA DEL SACRAMENTO** is a universe apart from the hustle and bustle of Buenos Aires, but it's only a short boat-ride away, across the Río de la Plata, and is a popular day-trip or weekend destination with Porteños. A visit here offers an introduction, albeit fairly atypical, to Argentina's small neighbour, as well as an enticing blend of colonial history, museums and a laid-back ambience. Although Portugal officially ceded Nova Colônia do Sacramento, founded in 1680 by Manoel Lobo, to Spain in 1750, its Portuguese settlers resisted and the Spanish Viceroyalty took possession only in 1777, destroying part of the town in the process. Meanwhile Colonia was established as a prime smuggling centre, exploited mainly by the British, while the Spanish were busy building up their

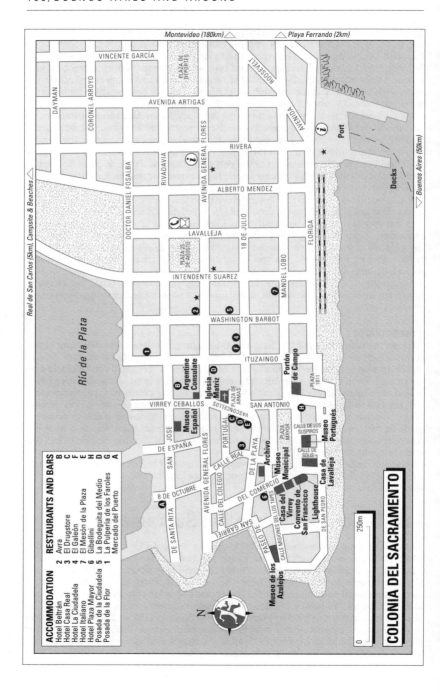

COLONIA DEL SACRAMENTO

Montevideo (180km) △   △ Playa Ferrando (2km)

△ Real de San Carlos (5km), Campsite & Beaches

Río de la Plata

▽ Buenos Aires (50km)

Port

Docks

VINCENTE GARCÍA

DAYMAN

CORONEL ARROYO

PLAZA DE DEPORTES

ROOSEVELT

AVENIDA ARTIGAS

DOCTOR DANIEL FOSALBA

RIVADAVIA

AVENIDA GENERAL FLORES

RIVERA

ALBERTO MENDEZ

LAVALLEJA

PLAZA 25 DE AGOSTO

18 DE JULIO

FLORIDA

INTENDENTE SUAREZ

MANDEL LOBO

WASHINGTON BARBOT

ITUZAINGO

Portón de Campo

PLAZA 1811

VIRREY CEBALLOS

Argentine Consulate

Iglesia Matriz

SAN ANTONIO

Museo Español

PLAZA DE ARMAS

VASCONCELLOS

SAN JOSE

DE ESPAÑA

PORTUGAL

CALLE REAL

PLAZA MAYOR

Museo Portugués

CALLE DE LOS SUSPIROS

AVENIDA GENERAL FLORES

CALLE DEL COLEGIO

DE LA PLAYA

Archivo

Museo Municipal

CALLE DE SOLIS

8 DE OCTUBRE

DE SANTA RITA

SAN GABRIEL

DEL COMERCIO

Casa del Virrey

Casa de Lavalleja

PASEO DE SAN PEDRO

CALLE MISIONES DE LOS TAPIS

Convento de San Francisco

Lighthouse

Museo de los Azulejos

ACCOMMODATION

Hotel Beltrán 2
Hotel Casa Real 3
Hotel La Ciudadela 4
Hotel Italiano 7
Hotel Plaza Mayor 6
Posada de la Ciudadela 5
Posada de la Flor 1

RESTAURANTS AND BARS

Avra B
El Drugstore C
El Galeón F
El Mesón de la Plaza E
Gibellini H
La Bodeguita del Medio D
La Pulpería de los Faroles G
Mercado del Puerto A

0   250m

N

colony in Buenos Aires. A stop was put to this when Uruguay was created in 1828, as a buffer state between Argentina and Brazil, both of which wanted its territory.

Colonia enjoys a superb location 180km west of Montevideo, perched on a diminutive promontory jutting into the great expanse of the Río de la Plata opposite Buenos Aires, and the warm light reflected off the bronze water, especially at dusk, further enhances the town's remarkable beauty. While its detractors complain that Colonia has been over-restored or that this once sleepy old town is now a playground for wealthy Porteños treating it like a suburb of Buenos Aires, it has managed to cling on to its charisma thanks to the sheer quality of its architecture – both old and modern – now protected by UNESCO. With its immaculate yet luxuriant parks and gardens, quiet cobbled streets and miles of beaches nearby, Colonia is a relaxing and well-tended place, without being sterile like some other "museum towns" around the world. Another asset is the warm welcome of the inhabitants: Uruguayans are among Latin America's friendliest peoples.

Arrival and information

With so many people in Buenos Aires wanting to enjoy the attractions of Colonia, **getting there** from the Argentine capital is no problem. The downside is that river crossings, especially in the high-speed catamarans and in peak season, are not cheap and seats tend to fill up quickly at weekends. If you can, go during the week – when there are fewer visitors and hotel rooms are considerably cheaper. Unless you're in a hurry, take the slower, slightly cheaper but more pleasurable ferry-boats, as you can go out on deck for some fresh air plus views of the Porteño skyline and the Uruguayan coast. There are plans afoot to build one of the world's longest bridges, spanning the 40km across the Río de la Plata between Punta Lara and Colonia, but there is opposition from ecologists as well as the ferry companies, and the project – which would be absurdly expensive to implement – is not likely to take off for some time yet, if at all.

Boats to Colonia depart from the two **ferry terminals** at Buenos Aires' Dársena Norte, at the far end of Avenida Córdoba. Ferry companies run a shuttle-bus between the docks and their Buenos Aires offices, and sometimes drop arriving passengers at their accommodation in downtown Buenos Aires; otherwise take a taxi to or from the rank just outside the terminal buildings. Either option is far safer than trying to jay-walk across the bewildering skein of busy roads and cross the overgrown rail-tracks in between the ferry terminals and downtown Buenos Aires, nor is it advisable to linger hereabouts, especially after dark. The crossing takes between forty minutes and three hours, and a return fare (Dec–March) costs from $30 to $65, including tax, with fares plummeting in the winter. Two companies run ferries, some of which take cars: Ferrylíneas, Maipú 866 (☎011/4314-5100), whose terminal is the one furthest from the city centre, and Buquebus, Patio Bullrich Shopping Center (☎011/4316-6500), which uses the modern terminal building nearer to the city. Ferrylíneas can also whisk you across the estuary on varyingly swift hydrofoils or catamarans, with competition from Alíscafos, which has offices at the docks only (☎011/4316-6500) and shares the Buquebus terminal; when you travel on these your luggage has to be checked in, airport-style, and there's sometimes a charge for excess baggage (usually over 30kg). Be sure to have your **passport** with you when buying your ticket and checking in – Australians and Canadians also require a **visa** for Uruguay – and arrive at least half an hour before the scheduled departure time. Remember to hold on to the insignificant-looking Uruguayan tourist-card, marked "Mercosur", for your return journey: people have been charged up to $50 when leaving Uruguay if they can't produce one.

Colonia's main **tourist office** is to be found in a rustic shed on the corner of General Flores and Rivera (Mon–Sat 8am–8pm & Sun 9am–5pm; ☎(+598)052/26141; *www.colonianet.com*), where the staff can give you a map and lots of leaflets. While you can change money on arrival in Colonia, you'll really only need Uruguayan pesos to buy stamps or make a telephone call – elsewhere you can pay with Argentine pesos or US dollars. The *peso uruguayo*, also depicted by the $ sign (in this guide shown as UR$), is currently worth about 9¢ (US), but many prices are displayed in dollars.

Accommodation

Hotels have become much more expensive over the past couple of years, partly because facilities have been upgraded to meet a more demanding clientele – even the most modest establishments have spruced up their interiors, installed en-suite bathrooms and whacked up the rates. The only truly budget option is to track down rooms rented unofficially in people's homes. Alternatively you can pitch your tent at the municipal **campsite** (☎(+598)052/24444 or 26938; UR$44), which boasts well-maintained facilities. It's located in a shady eucalyptus-grove 5km north of the historic town, near decent beaches and the Real de San Carlos, and offers double cabañas for UR$270–440 and some five-bed ones for UR$770. If you can, though, it's worth splashing out for at least one night in a colonial-style hotel with some charm, a reason in itself for coming to Colonia.

Hotel Beltrán, General Flores 311 (☎(+598)052/22955 or 21707). Grapevines adorn the enticing patio of this long-established and recently refurbished hotel. The rooms are cosily decorated, each one with a different theme, and the restaurant is excellent. ⑥.

Hotel Casa Real, Calle Real 170 (☎(+598)052/20753, fax 26303). Colonia's most luxurious hotel in a colonial house, with suites only, all done out in interior-design-magazine style, a Jacuzzi in every bathroom and a luxuriant patio. ⑨.

Hotel La Ciudadela, 18 de Julio 315 (☎(+598)052/21183). A reliable service, clean comfortable rooms, spotless bathrooms, and a friendly welcome from the knowledgeable owners. ④.

Hotel Italiano, Suarez 105 (☎(+598)052/22103). This laid-back family-run hotel is handily located between the port, the Plaza 25 de Agosto and the historic town. Despite extras, such as a swimming pool, garage and restaurant, the rooms are slightly overpriced. ⑤.

Hotel Plaza Mayor, Calle del Comercio 111 (☎(+598)052/23193). Housed in a colonial-style building, it combines atmosphere with comfort, plus sea views from upstairs rooms, and an attractive fountain-cooled patio. It's a favourite with Argentine honeymooners. ⑥.

Posada de la Ciudadela, Washington Barbot 164 (☎(+598)052/22683). One of Colonia's few remaining old-style, cheaper accommodation options, run by the grandmother of the owners of *Hotel La Ciudadela*. It's a bit dog-eared, but oozes character and the triples are particularly good value at $50. ③.

Posada de la Flor, Ituzaingó 268 (☎(+598)052/24476 or 27830). Each room in this tastefully decorated, colonial house, located on a very quiet street, is named after a flower, but the temptation to overdo the floral theme has been resisted. ⑥.

The Town

It's not difficult to find your way around Colonia's **Barrio Histórico**, confined to the far western end of the headland, bounded by the Río de la Plata on three sides. The best approach from the port and the nineteenth-century "new" town – focused on Plaza 25 de Agosto – is via Calle Manoel Lobo, which steers you through the ornately carved Portón de Campo, the only remaining colonial gateway in the fortified walls. Colonia is best seen early in the morning, before the day-trippers arrive, or at dusk, especially when there's a good sunset, which there often is. By opting for aimless wandering around the roughly cobbled streets, you'll get different perspectives of the old town, with its well-restored colonial and neocolonial buildings, some of which house museums, shops, hotels and restaurants, mostly clustered around the lush Plaza Mayor. Providing an interesting contrast, sleek-lined modern villas, many of them weekend retreats for rich Porteños, have been harmoniously slotted into vacant plots of land, where colonial houses had been allowed to collapse. There are seven museums in all, none of which takes very long to see, and in any case you can buy only a multi-entry pass costing UR$10, entitling you to visit all of them; on the other hand, the climb to the top of the lighthouse for a bird's-eye view is free. Out of town in either direction are miles of sandy beaches, though the best one is 2km east at Playa Ferrando. Along the sweeping bay to the north of Colonia, 5km away, is the white-elephant curiosity of **Real de San Carlos**, a dilapidated tourist complex built at the beginning of the twentieth century and now a ghostly but fascinating attraction.

Barrio Histórico

The **Plaza Mayor**, the heart of the **Barrio Histórico**, effectively doubles up as a botanical garden: its age-old fig trees, palms and cycads, draped with jasmine and bougainvillea, are enjoyed by insect-eating birds and shade-seeking humans alike. Since Colonia started out as a Portuguese settlement, it's logical to start with the **Museo Portugués** (daily 11.30am–5.30pm), housed in a late seventeenth-century house on the southern side of the square, at the corner of Calle de los Suspiros ("sighing street") – one of Colonia's most photographed streets with its ochre-walled houses, still roofed with the original terracotta tiles. Inside the museum an early colonial ambience has been recreated, with a display of domestic items, clothes and jewellery from Manoel Lobo's times. The town's beginnings are well explained, but in Spanish only. At the southwest corner of the plaza stands the **Casa Lavalleja** (daily 11.30am–5.30pm), dating from the same period. Once inside, you're transported to seventeenth-century Portugal, complete with a rustic kitchen, copper kettles, garlic-strings and all. A Colonia landmark, and the first thing you see when approaching by sea, is the pristine-white lighthouse or **El Faro** (Sat, Sun & public holidays 9am–noon), a few metres towards the waterfront from this corner of the plaza, and the views from the top take in the whole town. The sturdy lighthouse somehow looks as if it is shored up by the ruined walls of the late seventeenth-century **Convento de San Francisco**, never rebuilt after the Spanish bombardments in the early eighteenth century.

The two well-restored stucco-facaded colonial buildings on the west side of the plaza are the **Casa del Virrey** on the corner of Calle Misiones de los Tapes (daily 11.30am–5.30pm), housing furniture and paintings dating from the late eighteenth-century Spanish presence, and adjoining it to the south the **Museo Municipal** (daily 11.30am–5.30pm), home to an eclectic collection ranging from dinosaur remains dredged out of the estuary to an array of fancy lace fans once used by Colonia's high-society ladies. In the northwest corner of the plaza is the flinty facade of the **Archivo Regional** (daily 11.30am–5.30pm), with its small but informative collection of maps and parchments. A discreetly restored colonial building at the far western end of Calle Misión de los Tapes houses the **Museo de los Azulejos** (daily 11.30am–5.30pm). *Azulejos*, decorative glazed wall-tiles inspired by Moorish designs and found all over Portugal and southern Spain, are incorporated into Colonia's street-signs and some of its facades; the museum's small collection comprises varied and colourful samples of different styles.

From the eastern end of the Plaza Mayor, Calle San Antonio leads to the **Plaza de Armas** (or Plaza Manoel Lobo), dominated to the north by the gleaming white mass of the **Iglesia Matriz**, Uruguay's oldest church dating from 1680. Faithfully restored to the original design – it was severely damaged by an explosion in 1823, when gunpowder was being stored inside by the occupying Brazilian army – its immaculate facade and interior are stark but elegant. The whitewashed nave and arched aisles are set off by the dark jacaranda wood of the pews and doors, and museum pieces of religious art, including a seventeenth-century Portuguese retable simply decorated with scenes of the crucifixion. Next to the church, in the square, the ruins of the Portuguese Governor's house have been landscaped into a garden, where a bandoneon player often serenades passers-by. Across Colonia's main artery, Avenida General Flores, 100m northwest of Iglesia Matriz on the corner of Calle de España and Calle San José, is the **Museo Español** (daily 11.30am–5.30pm). A logical follow-on from the Museo Portugués, it contains furniture, paintings and costumes from the mid-eighteenth century, and panels in Spanish only – illustrated with Kokoschka-like portraits and landscapes – explaining Colonia's role in eighteenth-century rivalry between Portugal and Spain, with the British occasionally throwing a spanner into the works.

The Real de San Carlos

The **Real de San Carlos**, 5km to the north of the centre, is the remains of a once-grandiose entertainment complex named for King Charles III of Spain and built in the early twentieth century by Nicolas Mihanovic, an Argentine immigrant from what was then Dalmatia. It cost him a fortune to build the racecourse, now overgrown and used as a paddock, a Basque pelota frontón (still an impressively grandiose building, albeit rusting and crumbling away), a hotel-casino that lost its patrons when Argentina started levying prohibitive taxes on river crossings, and a Moorish-looking bullring that became useless when the Uruguayan government banned bullfights only two years after it was built. The abandoned buildings, apparently doomed to remain empty shells, are eery places but their weird appearance and the high quality of their original architecture make them worth seeing.

To get there, take one of the half-hourly COTUC **buses** from Avenida General Flores (UR$4).

The beaches

Another of Colonia's assets is its long sandy **beaches**, fringed with eucalyptus and pines. Ignore the water's unappealing muddy colour; it's perfectly clean and safe on this side of the estuary. From the Muelle Viejo, a rickety jetty at the end of Calle de España, you can charter **boats** ($5 per person, per hour) to the furthest beaches at the other side of the 10km arc of coastline that sweeps to the north. Some of these beaches are deserted during the week and remain quiet at weekends and, on the way, you can take a closer look at the wooded islets out in the estuary. Alternatively, take the Real de San Carlos bus along the waterfront, stopping at one of the popular beaches such as Playa Oreja de Negro, which has toilets, restaurants and kiosks. The best bathing areas within easy reach of Colonia are at Playa Ferrando, in a wooded setting 2km beyond the ferry-port to the east.

Eating and drinking

Colonia is all very low-key, so while the restaurants and bars are fine, there's nothing to do later in the evening. The food is mostly traditional Uruguayan fare: parrillas, pasta or pizza, the same familiar trio you find in Argentina. That said, new more adventurous places are cropping up all the time, and often a good atmosphere, with live music, makes up for the unimaginative cuisine.

Avra, Rivadavia 214. A delightful art gallery showing local artwork and crafts, plus a handful of tables where you can savour moussaka, souvlaki and stuffed vine-leaves or have real Greek coffee and baklava. Occasional wine-tastings and recitals.

La Bodeguita del Medio, Vasconcellos 163. Stylish place, with wooden tables, where fairly sophisticated dishes, especially by local standards, are served.

El Drugstore, Vasconcellos 179. Funky decor, smiling waitresses, live music at weekends, combined with fresh food at decent prices – with a view of the Iglesia Matriz thrown in. A couple of surprises on the menu, such as sushi or *lomo a la vodka*.

El Galeón, 18 de Julio and Ituzaingó. Barbecued meat in lavish quantities, and popular with large family groups on Sundays.

Gibellini, Paseo San Miguel 81. Restaurant-cum-bar with character, and a terrace. Fish and seafood top the menu, and you can drink tea there in the afternoon.

La Pulpería de los Faroles, Misiones de los Tapes 101. The surroundings are pleasant and the staff ultra-friendly. The cuisine is standard River Plate, with delicious fresh pasta – the ricotta ravioli are worth trying. Excellent local wines.

Mercado del Puerto, Santa Rita 40. No-nonsense food, snacks, *minutas*, pasta and steaks served on a terrace by the harbour, as the name suggests.

El Mesón de la Plaza, Vasconcellos 153 (☎(+598)052/24807). The elegance of the decor and attentive service are spoiled only by the atrocious muzak, but their wide-ranging menu is backed up by an excellent wine-list. A favourite haunt of upwardly mobile Porteños.

Listings

Banks Cambio Libertad, dockside. Cambio Viaggio, General Flores 350.

Bike rental Moto Rent, Virrey Cevallos 223 (☎(+598)052/22266).

Car rental Budget Gral Flores 91 (☎(+598)052/22939); Multicar, Manoel Lobo 505 (☎(+598)052/24893).

Consulate Argentina, General Flores 350 (☎(+598)052/22093).

Ferry companies Offices at the port: Buquebus and Alíscafos (☎(+598)052/22975 or 23365); Ferrylíneas (☎(+598)052/22919).

Left luggage At the ferry terminal (7am–9pm); free if you have a ticket to or from Buenos Aires.

Police ☎(+598)052/23347 and 23348.

Post office Lavalleja 226 (Mon–Fri 8am–6pm & Sat 8am–1pm).

Taxis Plaza 25 de Agosto (☎(+598)052/22920 or 22556).

Telephones Antel, Rivadavia 420 (Mon–Sat 9am–8pm & Sun 10am–6pm).

travel details

Buses to: Asunción (18 daily; 18hr–22hr 30min); Bahía Blanca (15 daily; 9hr); Bariloche (7 daily; 21–23hr); Carmen de Patagones (3 daily; 12hr); Catamarca (10 daily; 15hr); Chilecito (3 daily; 20hr); Clorinda (3 daily; 16hr–18hr 30min); Comodoro Rivadavia (daily; 26hr); Córdoba (hourly; 11hr); Corrientes (6 daily; 12hr); El Calafate (daily; 40hr); Formosa (7 daily; 14–15hr); Jujuy (hourly; 22hr); La Rioja (3 daily; 17hr); Las Grutas (3 daily; 14–15hr); Mar del Plata (20 daily; 7hr); Mendoza (1 hourly; 17hr); Merlo (6 daily; 12hr); Neuquén (14 daily; 15hr–16hr 30min); Paraná (30 daily; 7hr); Posadas (15 daily; 13hr); Puerto Iguazú (7 daily; 14hr 30min–19hr); Resistencia (18 daily; 12hr 30min–14hr); Rosario (frequent; 4hr); Salta (hourly; 22hr); San Juan (10 daily; 16hr); San Luis (9 daily; 12hr); San Rafael (4 daily; 13hr); Santa Rosa (17 daily; 8–10hr); Tucumán (10 daily; 15hr); Zapala (2 daily; 17–18hr).

Trains to: Bahía Blanca (1 daily; 13hr); Mar del Plata (7 daily; 6hr); Santa Rosa (Tues, Thurs & Sun 1 daily; 12hr); Santiago del Estero (3 weekly; 19hr); Tucumán (3 weekly; 23hr).

Flights to: Bahía Blanca (Mon–Fri 12 daily, Sat & Sun 5 daily; 1hr); Catamarca (1 daily; 2hr 30min); Córdoba (12 daily; 1hr 15min); Corrientes (3 daily; 1hr 20min); Formosa (2 daily; 1hr 45min–2hr); Jujuy (3 daily; 2hr 10min); La Rioja (5 daily; 2hr); Mar del Plata (4 daily; 1hr 15min); Neuquén (4 daily; 1hr 40min); Paraná (Mon–Fri 3 daily, Sat 1 daily, Sun 4 daily; 1hr); Posadas (Mon, Wed, Fri & Sun 5 daily, Tues & Thurs 4 daily, Sat 3 daily; 1hr 30min); Puerto Iguazú (5 daily; 1hr 50min); Rosario (7 daily; 50min); Salta (4 daily; 2hr); San Juan (10 daily; 1hr 50min); San Luis (2 daily; 1hr 30min); San Rafael (3 weekly; 1hr 50min); Santa Rosa (1 daily; 1hr 30min); Santiago del Estero (1 daily; 1hr 40min); Trelew (3 daily; 1hr 50min); Tucumán (6 daily; 1hr 50min); Ushuaia (daily; 3hr 30min).

CHAPTER TWO

THE ATLANTIC COAST AND THE PAMPA

Some thirty resorts dot the **Atlantic Coast** of Buenos Aires Province stretching from San Clemente in the north, to Bahía Blanca, nearly 700km south of the capital. Ranging in size from tiny Dunamar to the country's premier coastal resort, **Mar del Plata**, the resorts are generally characterized by wide sandy beaches, fringed by dunes. And with the exception of Mar del Plata, which has some interesting historical buildings and is a thriving city in its own right, the beach is the main reason to visit any of the towns along this stretch of coast. Most of the resorts are popular with families – **San Clemente**, **Miramar** and **Necochea** are notably so. Still family oriented, but attracting a younger crowd, too, **Pinamar** is the region's most upmarket resort – though bohemian **Villa Gesell**, to the south, makes for a more laid-back and enjoyable destination. Of all the resorts, though, Mar del Plata is the liveliest, with crowds in the city's numerous clubs and restaurants by night to match those that pack its beaches by day. If you simply hanker after peace and quiet, slightly more isolated spots such as sleepy **Mar del Sud** or **Dunamar**, set among pine forests, are worth checking out. **Bahía Blanca** in the far south of the province has a port but no beach; however there are connections from the town to the nearby coastal resorts of **Monte Hermoso** and **Pehuén-Có.** By far the busiest months to visit the coast are January and February, when you'll need to book accommodation – and public transport – in advance. November, December and March are good times to visit – though it's less lively at this time of year, the weather should still be good and prices will be a lot lower. March is traditionally the month when pensioners take their holidays. Some 260km to the northwest of San Clemente, but lying on the River Plate rather than the Atlantic Coast, is Buenos Aires' provincial capital **La Plata**. Often treated as a day-trip from Buenos Aires, La Plata marks the start of the coastal route south; the city was founded in the late nineteenth century on rationalist principales and houses one of Latin America's most famous museums, the Museo de Ciencias Naturales.

Inland, the province of Buenos Aires – covering some 307,000 square kilometres to the south and west of the capital – is dominated by the vast expanse of the **Pampa**, a

---

ACCOMMODATION PRICE CODES

The price codes used for accommodation throughout this chapter refer to the cheapest rate for a double room in high season. Single travellers will only occasionally pay half the double-room rate; nearer two thirds is the norm and some places will expect you to pay the full rate. Note that in resort towns, there are considerable discounts out of season.

① $20 or less	④ $45–60	⑦ $100–150
② $20–30	⑤ $60–80	⑧ $150–200
③ $30–45	⑥ $80–100	⑨ Over $200

region almost synonymous with Argentina itself. This is the country's heartland: birthplace of the **gaucho** and source of much of Argentina's wealth – the grain and beef produced by this incredibly fertile farmland constitute the bulk of the country's exports to the rest of the world. The pampa is certainly not Argentina's most dramatic landscape – its outstanding feature is its almost unremitting flatness – but this unbroken stretch of land and sky has its own subtle beauty. At any time the pampa's sheer limitless sense of space is mesmerizing, but in dramatic weather, or when an incredibly intense blue sky arches over the fields of ripe sunflowers, the pampa is transformed into a vibrant canvas covered with great sweeps of colour. This region is almost entirely cultivated and the province – the country's most populated – is dotted with strikingly similar towns whose main business is agriculture rather than tourism. A major exception, however, is **San Antonio de Areco**, lying just over 100km west of the capital. A charmingly old-fashioned town of cobbled streets and well-preserved nineteenth-century architecture, San Antonio de Areco stages Argentina's most important gaucho festival, the **Día de la Tradición**, held each November. Far less visited, though with a modest charm of their own, the lakeside towns of **Lobos** and **San Miguel del Monte**, both lying around 100km south of the capital, make possible stopovers on your way south – or overnight trips from Buenos Aires. Around Lobos and San Antonio de Areco and indeed throughout the province, you'll find some of Argentina's most traditional and luxurious **estancias** – great places to spend a night or two if you fancy a taste of the high life.

The pampa's most dramatic and unexpected region is the **Sierra de la Ventana** mountain range, lying 550km southwest of Buenos Aires. Offering a welcome change of scenery from the surrounding flat farmlands, the range is some six hundred million years old and contains the highest peak in the province, Cerro de la Ventana (1134m). Together with the popular resort of **Tandil** some 300km to the northeast, which is backed by a low range of hills, this region offers the best opportunities for activities such as horseriding, walking and camping in the province.

Heading southwest out of Buenos Aires, the RN5 is one of the major routes towards the south of Argentina. Although it is a largely unremarkable highway through cultivated lands, there are a couple of towns worth visiting along its way. For a mass display of religious devotion, head for **Luján**, some 70km to the west of Buenos Aires. The town is named after Argentina's patron saint, the Virgin of Luján, and her shrine here, housed in a vast neo-Gothic basilica, attracts around four million visitors a year. Just southwest of Luján lies the quiet and attractive town of **Mercedes**, whose authentic pulpería offers a glimpse into Argentina's gaucho past. The RN5 terminates at **Santa Rosa**, the modest provincial capital of La Pampa Province, which borders Buenos Aires to the southwest. La Pampa Province is smaller and far less populous than that of Buenos Aires and its scant network of roads seems designed to do little more than bear the traveller away from this little-visited region. Place names such as Arbol Solo ("solitary tree") conjure up an image of desolate lands punctuated by frontier settlements and to some extent this is a fair summary of this geographically transitional province, whose landscape merges with the humid pampa to the northeast and the Patagonian steppes to the south and climbs gradually to meet the foothills of the Andes to the west. The province's main tourist attraction is the **Parque Nacional Lihué Calel**, just over 200km southwest of the capital, whose low sierras add some drama to this otherwise gentle landscape.

As far as practicalities go, Buenos Aires is probably Argentina's easiest province to get around: its 307,000 square kilometres are dotted with towns and crisscrossed with roads and railways, making it pretty straightforward to negotiate using **public transport**. Bear in mind, though, that services to the coast are greatly reduced out of season. La Pampa Province, though much less populated and still with large areas untouched by tourism, is nonetheless well connected by routes running south from the capital into Patagonia. If you are planning on heading off the beaten track, note that many of the region's secondary roads are unsealed, and though easily negotiable in dry weather, they may become impassable after heavy rainfall.

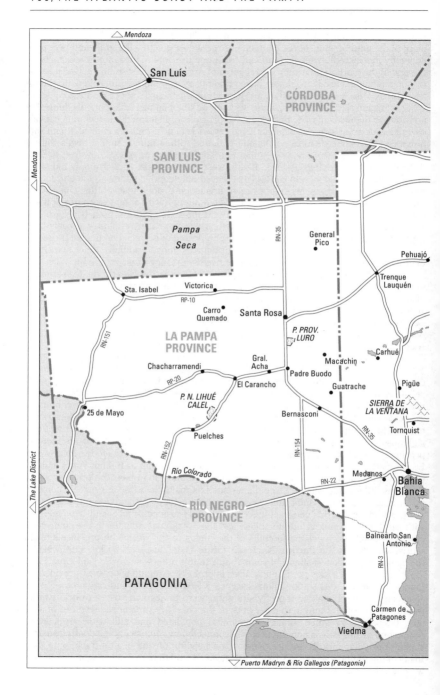

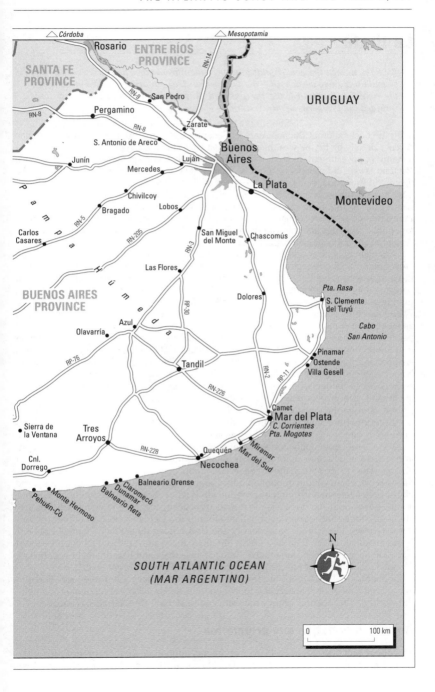

La Plata

We have named the new capital after the magnificent river that flows past it, and beneath this stone we deposit – in the hope that they remain eternally buried here – the rivalries, the hatred, the rancour and all the passions that have, for so long, impeded the prosperity of our country.

Speech made by Dardo Rocha, founder of La Plata, 1882

With the declaration of Buenos Aires as Federal Capital in 1880, the province of Buenos Aires – already by far the wealthiest and most powerful in the republic – was left without a centre of government. In 1881, the province's newly named governor, **Dardo Rocha**, a Porteño lawyer by profession, proposed that a new provincial capital be created in the vicinity of Ensenada, some thirty miles east of the federal capital. The new city's layout, based on rationalist concepts and characterized by an absolutely regular numbered street plan sitting within a five-kilometre square, was designed by the engineer and surveyor Pedro Benoit. An international competition was held to choose designs for the most important public buildings and the winning architects included Germans and Italians as well as Argentinians, a mix of nationalities reflected in the city's impressive civic architecture.

The country's first entirely planned city, **La Plata** was officially founded on November 19, 1882. Electric street lighting was installed in 1884 – it was the first city in Latin America to do so. The grand ambitions held for the new provincial capital can be gauged by the local writer José María Lunazzi's comment, made soon after the city's founding, that La Plata was the "Athens of America". Unfortunately, though, much of La Plata's carefully conceived architectural identity was lost during the twentieth century, as anonymous modern constructions replaced many of the city's original buildings. A particularly sad example was the loss of the grand Italianate **Teatro Argentino**, second in national importance after Buenos Aires' Teatro Colón, razed to the ground after a suspect fire in the 1970s and rebuilt as a massive octagonal concrete monolith. Nonetheless, enough of the city's original features remain for it to have made a recent serious bid to be declared a UNESCO World Heritage Site. Whether or not the bid is successful, the project will at least have had the positive effect of encouraging the preservation of the city's remaining architectural heritage – a symptom of this changing attitude is the recent completion of the city's imposing Gothic cathedral, over a hundred years after its foundation stone was laid.

La Plata was essentially conceived of as an **administrative centre**, and one might argue that it shows: indeed for many Argentinians the city is little more than a place you visit in order to carry out the dreaded and complicated *trámites*, bureaucratic procedures in which Argentinian public bodies seem to specialize. In terms of identity, the city suffers somewhat through its proximity to Buenos Aires, whose seemingly endless sprawl now laps at the outskirts of La Plata, practically turning the city which was created as a counterbalance to the capital into its suburb. La Plata is also an important **university town**: The city's first university, the Universidad de la Plata – founded in 1897 – was nationalized in 1905 and today the city's three universities – the Universidad Nacional de la Plata, the Universidad Católica de la Plata and Universidad Argentina de Abogacía (University of Law) attract students from all over the country.

La Plata's chief attractions are its pleasant city centre park, the **Paseo del Bosque** and – even though it is struggling to live up to its self-proclaimed reputation as one of the world's major natural history museums – the **Museo de Ciencias Naturales**.

Arrival, information and orientation

The nicest way to arrive in La Plata is at the beautiful *fin de siècle* **train station**, on the corner of avenidas 1 and 44, around ten blocks northwest of the town centre. Five

blocks southwest of the station is the **bus terminal**, on the corner of calles 4 and 42, with frequent buses from the capital, and most major cities throughout the country.

There isn't really a properly designated **tourist office** at present. However, the approachable tourism secretariat staff on the first floor of the building on the corner of Calle 50 and Avenida 13, on the western side of La Plata's foundational square, Plaza Moreno (☎0221/427-1535) will offer what help they can with accommodation, sightseeing and transport information. Printed information is scarce.

On paper, La Plata's **numbered grid layout** looks incredibly logical. The rationalist layout surpasses even the already regular Argentinian norm: the city is basically a kind of *mega cuadra*, or block divided into smaller blocks punctuated at absolutely regular intervals by diagonals and green spaces. The numbered calles become tree-lined avenues every six blocks and the two most important diagonals, 73 and 74, converge on central Plaza Moreno, the city's foundational square. In practice, however, things can go seriously awry when you hit one of the diagonals which regularly dissect the horizontals and verticals: the sudden convergence of similar-looking streets can be very disorientating. In fact, if you've a slightly dubious sense of direction you may find yourself wishing you'd laid a trail of string to remind yourself where you came from. Fortunately, the city is small enough that you're unlikely to go too far off track. If you grow tired of walking, the city's many taxis are probably a better deal than the rather expensive local buses.

Accommodation

La Plata's **hotels** mostly cater to a business clientele and to politicians. As a result, they are somewhat overpriced and rather uninspiring. Real budget accommodation is practically non-existent, but what there is is to be found mostly around the bus terminal and train station. Be warned, however, that some of these are used by prostitutes and their clients, which doesn't make for a very reassuring atmosphere. Safest is probably the *Hotel García* on Calle 2, between 42 and 43 (☎0221/423-5369; ③); all rooms have TV, fan and a private bathroom. Also close to the terminal is the rather dreary but adequate *Hotel Cristal* on Avenida 1, no. 620 (☎0221/424-1043; ⑤). Much better, though, is the friendly *Hotel Roga*, pleasantly located near the Paseo del Bosque on Calle 54 at no. 334 (☎0221/4219553; ④), with comfortable, well-equipped rooms with minibar and cable TV. Other possibilities include the *Acuarius* on Calle 3 at no. 731 (☎0221/4834765; ④) with attractive, unassuming rooms, and the centrally located *San Marco* on Calle 54 at no. 523 (☎0221/4229322; ⑤) with comfortable airy rooms. Note that you'll have to pay extra (around $10 a day) for parking at all hotels.

The City

La Plata's major points of interest lie between Avenida 1, which leads east from the train station to the **Paseo del Bosque**, where you will find the city's zoo, planetarium and the **Museo de Ciencias Naturales**, and Plaza Moreno, the central square. Just to the south of the Paseo del Bosque, there's La Plata's most successful modern building, the striking functionalist **Casa Curutchet**, built by the French architect, Le Corbusier. The hub of economic and administrative life is Avenida 7, particularly between Plaza Italia and Plaza San Martín; on the eastern side of the latter is the city's excellent cultural centre, the **Pasaje Dardo Rocha**, notable not only for its good contemporary art museum but also for it stunning interior and appealing café.

Plaza Moreno

La Plata's official centre is **Plaza Moreno**, a vast open square covering four blocks toward the southern end of the city. The city's foundation stone was laid in the centre of the square in 1882, together with a time capsule containing documents and medals relating to the founding of the city. The capsule was exhumed on the city's centenary, and a new one was buried in its place. There are a handful of theories floating around which claim that La Plata was founded according to a secret Masonic scheme and that when the documents buried in the time capsule were exhumed they would provide evidence. Sadly, the papers were too damaged to bear out the theory. The contents of the exhumed time capsule, though, together with a replica of its replacement, can be viewed in the **Museo y Archivo Dardo Rocha** (Mon–Fri 9am–6pm; free; ☎0221/421-1689) on the western side of the square, at Calle 50 no. 933, housed in the residence once occupied by La Plata's founder.

On the northern end of the square is the Germanic **municipalidad**, a broad white edifice dominated by a lofty central clock tower and elegant arched stained-glass windows. At the southern end is the vast and rather forbidding **Cathedral**. Designed by the French architect, Pedro Benoit, it's heavily neo-Gothic in style, with a pinkish stone facade and steep slate roofs. The foundation stone was laid in 1884 but the cathedral was not finally completed until 1932, with its two principal towers being finished as late as 1999. If the cathedral doesn't strike you as exactly beautiful from the outside, it is certainly tremendously imposing on the inside with its soaring, vertigo-inducing interior punctuated by austere ribbed columns. The **museum in the crypt** (Mon 9am–1pm, Tues–Sat 9am–6pm, Sun 9am–1pm & 3–7pm; $2, free on Tues) has more on the cathedral, including some excellent photographs documenting its construction.

Plaza San Martín and around

Avenidas 51 and 53 lead from Plaza Moreno to **Plaza San Martín**, the real hub of city life. This square is less imposing than Plaza Moreno, though it is also flanked by government buildings. At the northern end there's the **Casa de Gobierno**, a sturdy Flemish Renaissance building with a central slate-roofed dome; to the south you'll find the eclectic **Palacio de la Legislatura**, whose grand Neoclassical entrance sits slightly awkwardly on a more restrained facade. More interesting than these grand public edifices, however, is the **Pasaje Dardo Rocha**, on the western side of the square. This elegant pitched roof building, whose three-storeyed facade mixes French and Italian influences, was originally built in 1883 as the city's first train station. The Pasaje was remodelled in 1928, some twenty years after the station had been moved to its current site on the corner of Avenida 1 and Calle 44. The Pasaje now functions as an important **cultural centre** (daily 10am–8pm; free) comprising a small cinema and various art museums including the new **Museo de Arte Contemporáneo Latinoamericano**. The galleries are located around a stunning Doric-columned central hall, in which natural light (enhanced by a discreet modern lighting system) filters down through a high glass roof onto a vast sweep of black and white tiled floor. There's also a restaurant with a sun terrace, and a pleasant café, the *Café de las Artes*, with a collection of books and art catalogues for customers' use.

Five blocks west of Plaza San Martín, along Avenida 7, is the circular Plaza Italia where a small **crafts fair** is held at weekends.

The Paseo del Bosque and around

From Plaza San Martín, Avenida 53 heads north past the Casa de Gobierno. After four blocks you come to Plaza Rivadavia, separated by Avenida 1 from the **Paseo del Bosque**, La Plata's major green space.

Before entering the park, take a small detour along Boulevard 53, a short diagonal road branching off to the right of the plaza. Halfway along the street, on your right, stands **Casa Curutchet**. One of La Plata's least celebrated buildings but arguably one of its most significant, the Casa Curutchet is the only residence designed by Le Corbusier to have been built in Latin America. Commissioned by a local surgeon Pedro Curutchet in 1949, the house is a typical Le Corbusier construction, combining functionality with a playful use of colour and perspective. The building now houses the **Colegio de Arquitectos** of Buenos Aires Province and is open to visitors (Mon, Tues & Fri 8am–1pm; closed Jan; ☎0221/218032).

The park itself covers just over half a square kilometre. It's an attractive open space, dissected by various roads and with a pretty artificial lake where you can rent boats. Aside from the famous Museo de Ciencias Naturales (see below), the park's attractions include the city's old-fashioned **zoo** (Tues–Sun 9am–7pm; $2), complete with original enclosures dating from its foundation in 1907. The enclosures, though, are a little small for the larger exotic species such as the rhinoceros, but seem more appropriate for smaller native fauna such as the endangered grey fox. There's also a **botanical garden** within the zoo, with examples of most of Argentina's most typical trees, such as the ombú, the araucaria and the ceibo. There is also an **astronomical observatory** (Mon–Fri 8–10pm; guided visits Fri evenings), the **Teatro Martín Fierro**, an open-air theatre located just to the west of the lake, and, behind the train station, the city's racecourse.

The Museo de Ciencias Naturales

The first purpose-built museum in Latin America, and something of a relic in itself, the **Museo de Ciencias Naturales** (daily: winter 10am–6pm; summer 10am–7pm; $3) is a real treat for anyone with a fondness for old-fashioned museums. Curatorial policy, whereby each room is more or less autonomously organized, and a chronic shortage of funds make the museum somewhat patchy, but its highlights, together with its general ambience, are sufficient to make it well worth a visit.

The beautiful circular **entrance hall**, into which light filters through a glass dome, is hung with wonderfully old-fashioned oil paintings of animals such as the extinct mastodon, a huge elephant-like mammal. The first of the museum's 21 rooms, all chronologically ordered, lies immediately to the right of the entrance hall. The first section is devoted to **rocks and minerals**, including an example of a fossilized araucaria trunk from a petrified forest in the Patagonian province of Santa Cruz. The **palaeontological section** which follows contains a reproduction of the fossilized remains of the largest spider ever found: named the Megarachne Servinei Hünicken, the fifty-centimetre-long arachnid was found in Bajo de Véliz in San Luis Province and is some 290 million years old. There is also a reproduction of a diplodocus skeleton, donated to the museum in 1912 by the North American philanthropist Andrew Carnegie; the unusually complete original is housed in the Carnegie Museum in Pittsburgh. In the same room, you'll find the original skeleton of a neuquensaurus, or titanosaurus, a herbivorous dinosaur common in the north of Patagonia towards the end of the Cretaceous Period.

Room VI is dedicated to the beginnings of the **Cenozoic Period**, also known as the Age of Mammals, which extend from around 65 million years ago to the present day. It houses the museum's most important collection: the megafauna, a group of giant herbivorous mammals which evolved in South America at the time when the region was separated from the other continents. The room's impressive collection of skeletons includes the gliptodon, forerunner of today's armadillos; the enormous megatherium, largest of the megafauna which, when standing upright on its powerful two hind legs, would have reached almost double its already impressive six metres; the toxodon, somewhat similar to the hippopotamus, though unrelated; and the camel-like macrauchenia. The reconnection of North and South America began approximately three million years ago, allowing an interchange of species via the Panama isthmus. Both smaller and more successful, the North American fauna, which included the predatory sabre-toothed tiger, were the clear beneficiaries of the interchange and their incursion into South America, together with the arrival of man from the same direction, some 12,000 years ago, appears to have been a major factor in the extinction of the megafauna.

The **Latin American Archaeology** section is to be found **upstairs** along with the collection of objects from the northwest of Argentina. The first room to the left of the stairs has a large collection of ceramics, mostly from the pre-Columbian cultures of the Peruvian region: including a fine collection of brightly coloured Nazca pottery. In the second room the most notable pieces are the so-called *suplicantes* from the Condorhuasi-Alamito culture that thrived in Central Catamarca between about 200 and 500AD. These fascinating stone sculptures combine animal and human-like elements with more abstract details and represent fantastic, stylized beings. Their exact use is unknown, although it is thought that they had some kind of ceremonial or ritual function – perhaps being used for some kind of funerary practice, since the upturned faces are similar to those of the corpses found in funerary urns. Highly sophisticated and unique to the Condorhuasi, the *suplicantes* are among the most valuable pieces in the museum's collection.

Guided tours of the museum, well worth following if you have a reasonable grasp of Spanish, are available free of charge. It is possible to arrange guided tours in English, though you need to give considerable notice (two weeks) and will have to pay around $8 per person.

Eating and drinking

The bulk of La Plata's bars and restaurants are located around the intersection of calles 10 and 47, with favourite meeting places including *La Trattoria*, a **restaurant** and café whose tables command the best view of the to and fro of local life and, two blocks away, on the corner of 8 and 47, *La Esquina*, a popular spot for an evening beer. Other restaurants in the area include *Sardis*, on 48 between Diagonal 74 and Calle 10, and *Prego*, on 49 between Diagonal 74 and Calle 12, both serving good Italian food. For a slightly more unusual option, try the small bar serving Arab specialities on Diagonal 74 between calles 49 and 50.

One block west of Plaza San Martín there's La Plata's most famous – and most atmospheric – bar and restaurant, the classic *Cervecería Modelo* on the corner of calles 5 and 54. This bustling restaurant is perhaps the city's most popular meeting place, packed with office workers, couples and families. The restaurant's vast wood-panelled interior is hung with hams and the seemingly endless menu includes everything from hamburgers and liverwurst sandwiches to *bife de chorizo* and seafood. Prices are reasonable and there is a good selection of salads and filling starters for $2.50. The area harbours a number of other fairly upmarket restaurants, undoubtedly catering to expense-account diners, including the smart parrilla *La Alternativa*, diagonally opposite the *Modelo*, and with the unusual **vegetarian** option of grilled vegetables with cream cheese as well as standard carnivorous fare.

The laid-back **café-bar** *El Ayuntamiento*, on Avenida 1 between calles 47 and 48, is popular with students and has **live music** on Friday nights from about midnight, while there's always a hard core of night owls whiling away the small hours in the dimly lit classic *Bar Esquina San Juan*, on 55 and 7.

The Interbalnearia

The busiest section of the Atlantic coast is that lying between **San Clemente del Tuyú**, some 260km southeast of La Plata, and Mar del Plata, another 200km or so south. The many resorts in this section are connected by the RP11, known as the **Interbalnearia**, as it connects the region's balnearios or resorts. The route from La Plata runs southeast along RP36, which takes you through flat pampa landscape, dotted with cows and divided at intervals by tree-lined drives announcing the presence of estancias. Tall metal wind pumps, which extract water from beneath the surface of the land, inject a little drama into the scene, whilst giant cardoon thistles – a desiccated brown in summer – sprout in clusters like outsize bouquets. The RP36 joins up with the RP11 some 90km southeast of La Plata, which continues due south for another 100km before swinging east to San Clemente. On the coast, sand dunes predominate around **Pinamar** and **Villa Gesell**, whilst the first real hills surface just north of **Mar del Plata**, another 70km south of Villa Gesell.

San Clemente del Tuyú and around

SAN CLEMENTE DEL TUYÚ announces its presence with the sudden and somewhat incongruous appearance of tower blocks on the otherwise bare horizon of the pampa. Argentina's first beach resort is located just south of the point at which the River Plate officially ends and the Atlantic Ocean begins. Salt and fresh water mingle off the shore of San Clemente's wide, sandy beaches, turning the sea slightly brown but pleasantly warm. This is a family-oriented resort and, although it's a pleasant and friendly town, San Clemente is hardly Argentina's most exciting destination; it stands out mainly because of its proximity to one of Argentina's most visited tourist attractions, the **Mundo Marino Oceanarium**, and to the important natural reserves of the **Bahía Samborombón**.

The Resort
Although San Clemente's layout loosely adheres to the familiar Latin American grid system, it is made a little confusing by the semicircles formed by calles 2, 3 and 4 which loop off the **beachfront** Avenida Costanera. The main street, calle 1, is pedestrianized

during the evening and, with its numerous cheap restaurants and street theatre, becomes the focus of entertainment for families with young children, who zap away in the amusement arcades until the early hours. Close to the town, the beach is pretty drab: suitable for a spot of swimming and sunbathing, but not sufficiently enticing to keep you there for long. To the north and south there are some low dunes and at low tide the beach extends as far as Punta Rasa, around 15km north of town. When you've had enough of the beach, head for the pine-scented sandy walkways and dunes of the **Vivero Cosme Argerich**, Av. 111, a nursery and reserve at the southern end of the town. You can hire horses at the nursery entrance in the afternoon and, during the tourist season, the excellent **Teatro de la Mochila** puts on free plays at night – with neon scenery and puppets – for details, check with the tourist office.

Like many of the resorts along this stretch of the coast, San Clemente has an annual fishing competition: the **Fiesta de la Corvina Negra** (Festival of the Black Sea Bass – a local delicacy), held in early October: as well the competition itself there are a handful of related events ranging from the crowning of Miss Corvinita to an *asado* of the fish themselves. San Clemente's other major event is the **Encuentro Santosvegano de Payadores**, a celebration of local folklore held on the second weekend in February; the main attraction here is the *payada*, an improvised form of musical dialogue in which the participants often exchange good-humoured insults designed to demonstrate their superiority.

Mundo Marino and the port

South America's largest oceanarium and one of the few in the world to have killer whales, **Mundo Marino** (Jan & Feb daily 10am–10pm; March, Nov & Dec daily 10am–7pm; April–June & Aug Mon & Thurs–Sun 10am–6pm; July, Sept & Oct daily 10am–6pm; ticket office closes up to 3 hours before park; $7) is publicized the length and breadth of Argentina. San Clemente's biggest attraction may, however, turn out to be its biggest disappointment. The oceanarium's self-proclaimed conservation mission sits uneasily with the circus-like shows that constitute its primary attraction, whilst the sight of the majestic killer whale enclosed in a large swimming pool is frankly depressing. To be fair, the shows are the only way Mundo Marino can finance its activities and are hugely popular with visiting families, but unless you have small children to entertain, the whole thing is probably best avoided. To get to Mundo Marino, which lies around 10km northwest of the town centre, take local bus #500 or #532 from outside the service station on the corner of San Martín and Calle 1.

Just outside Mundo Marino and sitting rather uneasily next to its glitzy neighbour lies San Clemente's charmingly ramshackle **port area**, little more than a modest quay and gaggle of fishing boats. The main reason to visit the port is to try freshly caught grey mullet at any one of the friendly local restaurants, most of which have outside seating where you can watch your fish being prepared and cooked on the barbecue.

Practicalities

San Clemente's **bus terminal** is on Avenida Naval, between San Martín and Calle 25, eight blocks west of the centre. You should be able to pick up a map of the town from the terminal's tourist information kiosk; failing that, head for the very friendly **tourist office** (daily: Dec–Feb 8am–midnight; March–Nov 8am–4pm; ☎02252/430718), housed in a wooden cabin one block from the beach at the corner of Calle 2 and Calle 63.

Although it can be packed in high season, San Clemente is almost deserted for the rest of the year. Most **accommodation** options are within easy walking distance of the centre and the beach. One of the best is the friendly and spacious *Bellini*, Calle 21 no. 111 (☎ & fax 02252/421043; ③, single ①), which has its own parking and does good single rates. The *Frente al Muelle*, on the corner of Calle 16 and Calle 27 (☎02252/421218; ①, with breakfast), offers the best deal for those on a tight budget – though the rooms are basic and a bit dark, the hotel has an affectionate family atmosphere and is well-located, right by the beach. The *Splendid*, Calle 1 no. 2465 (☎02252/421316; ③), offers decent, slightly spartan rooms with private bathrooms and breakfast; the only drawback can be the noise from the nearby amusement arcade. The *Sur*, Calle 3 no. 2194 (☎02252/421137; ④), has very attractive and comfortable rooms; the best is at the front with a large balcony overlooking the street. Finally, it seems a little extravagant to go four-star in such a down-to-earth place as San Clemente, but you can do so at the *Fontainebleau* right on the Costanera at Calle 3 no. 2290 (☎02252/421187; ⑤). For campsites, try *Autocamping El Tala* at Calle 9 bis and Calle 72 (☎02252/421593), or *Los 3 Pinos*, at Av. 12 and Calle 74 (☎02252/430151). Both sites are several blocks from the beach, with barbecues, showers and provisions stores and charge $3 per tent plus $3 per person.

There are many cheap pasta and pizza **restaurants** on Calle 1, as well as parrillas, of which the best is probably *La Parrillita* between calles 2 and 3. *El Encuentro*, Calle 16 no. 42, serves good fried *empanadas*; *El Paellero Valenciano*, Calle 4 no. 2388, offers paella for two for $13; and *La Cheroga*, two doors along from *La Parrillita*, is the town's most popular **confitería**, serving delicious cakes. *Vadinho*, on the corner of Calle 18 and the Costanera, is one of the few **bars** for young people and attracts both locals and tourists.

Bahía Samborombón, Bahía Aventura and Reserva Campos del Tuyú

Some 20km northeast of San Clemente lies the southern end of the **Bahía Samborombón**, an immense bay bordered by protected wetlands. Visited by over one hundred and ninety species of migrating birds on their epic journeys between North America and Patagonia, the bay's most easterly point, **Punta Rasa**, is home to an Estación de Investigaciones Biológicas, where birds are ringed and their patterns of migration tracked. An excellent spot for bird-watching, Punta Rasa is most easily reached by taxi, though the bus to Bahía Aventura (see below) will take you to within 10km of the site.

To the west of Punta Rasa is **Bahía Aventura** (Jan & Feb daily 10am–8pm; March–June & Aug–Oct Fri, Sat & Sun 10am–6pm; July daily 10am–6pm; Nov & Dec daily 10am–7pm; $7; ☎02252/423000). Set in the grounds around Faro San Antonio, one of the oldest lighthouses on the Atlantic coast, Bahía Aventura is best described as a kind of educational theme-park, its well-kept walkways seemingly designed to keep nature at bay. The park does provide information at its visitor centre on the surrounding habitat, however, and its vegetation and wildlife, such as the espátula rosada or roseate spoonbill, a bird whose livid pink plumage outdoes even the flamingo. Look out, to, for cuis in the park, a small rodent common throughout Argentina. There are excellent views over Punta Rasa and the Bahía Samborombón from the top of the lighthouse. To get to the site, take bus #500 or #502 from Avenida San Martín.

This area is also home to one of the few remaining groups of pampa deer, native deer whose numbers were severely reduced with the introduction of agriculture to the region as well as by hunting and far outnumbered these days by the European red deer. A hundred or so of these deer are protected in the **Reserva Campos del Tuyú**, to the west of Bahía Aventura, but access is severely restricted and will probably only be conceded to those with conservation credentials. For more information, contact the Fundación Vida Silvestre in Buenos Aires.

Pinamar and around

PINAMAR, 80km south of San Clemente, takes its name from the surrounding pine forests, planted amongst dunes, by the town's founder, Jorge Bunge, in the 1930s. This attractive setting is somewhat overwhelmed, however, by the town's mix of high-rise buildings and ostentatious chalet-style constructions. Long the favourite resort of the Porteño elite, in the 1990s the town became almost synonymous with the high-living lifestyle of the Menem era and the exploits of the politicians and celebrities who holidayed here became a staple of gossip magazines such as *Caras* and *Gente*. In 1997, however, photo-journalist José Luis Cabezas was found assassinated on the outskirts of town after covering a society party. Though the major ramifications of the Cabezas case have been political, a side-effect has been to tarnish Pinamar's image and through the late 1990s the town struggled to recoup its lost cachet.

Despite all this, Pinamar remains a resort for Argentina's privileged. The spending power of its habitués is pretty evident along its main street, **Avenida Bunge**. A wide avenue flanked by glamorous boutiques and small shopping malls, Bunge runs east to west through the town centre, ending at the beachfront Avenida del Mar. Though the town itself has little to detain you, the **beach** is more attractive than San Clemente's, its pale sands littered with delicate shells and, to the north and south of the centre, bordered by high dunes. To the north of the centre lies an exclusive residential district set amongst pine forests where you can go **horseriding**; enquire at Palenque La Tradición, Av. Enrique Shaw and Juncal (☎0660/428035; $10 per hour). There are also various companies offering excursions by **jeep** to the most dramatic section of dunes, where you can try **sandboarding**. Try Werner Excursiones at Bunge 486 (☎02254/487951) or enquire at the *Liverpool* bar, Bunge 369.

To the south, Pinamar merges seamlessly with neigbouring **OSTENDE**, a much quieter resort, which in turn segues into down-to-earth **VALERIA DEL MAR**, which has been running a popular carnival for the last few years, with visiting carnival groups from Guayleguaychú and nationally famous bands such as Memphis La Blusera. The final resort on this stretch is **CARILÓ**, the most exclusive of resorts with bijou shopping malls and luxury holiday homes set amongst pine forests: accommodation here is predominantly timeshare or private rentals. The local Montemar bus from the corner of Bunge and Libertador in Pinamar connects all four resorts or you could simply stroll along the beach, which runs for some 10km without interruptions past all of them.

Arrival, information and accommodation

All long-distance **buses** arrive at the terminal on Avenida Shaw between Pejerrey and Lenguado, seven blocks north of Avenida Bunge. The **train station**, with a daily service from Buenos Aires (Constitución), is a couple of kilometres north of the town centre, just off Avenida Bunge; from here it's a short taxi ride into town, or there is a connecting bus service to the bus terminal. Pinamar shares an **airport** with Villa Gesell (☎02255/460418), some 25km south off the RP11.

With its glossy brochures advertising golf courses and estate agencies, the **tourist office** at Bunge 654 (daily 8am–8pm; ☎02254/491680; *municipalidad@telpin.com.ar*) is heavily geared towards Pinamar's wealthy visitors, but they do provide decent maps and guides of the resort; there's also a 24-hour multilingual touch-screen information post outside.

Hotels are plentiful, if generally expensive, **in Pinamar**: as in all resorts, reservations are advisable in high season. Discounts may be possible at the friendly and well-kept *Sardegna*, Bunge 1055 (☎ & fax 02254/482760; ⑥); each room has a television and telephone. The lovely *Posada Pecos* on the corner of Odiseo and Silenios (☎ & fax 02254/484386; ⑤) has an attractive, slightly rustic feel, with tiled floors and a bar with outside seating in a quiet area near the beach; after January prices go down considerably, particularly if you pay in cash. Pinamar's longest established hotel, attracting an older clientele, is the elegant *Playas* at Bunge and De la Sirena (☎02254/482236, fax 482226; ⑦), which has its own swimming pool. The ugly but luxurious *Algeciras* at Av. del Libertador 75 (☎02254/485550, fax 481161; ⑧) offers a presidential suite as well as swimming pool, sauna and a nursery. You'll find the area's most atmospheric hotel **in**

Avenue 9 de Julio, Buenos Aires

La Boca, Buenos Aires

Club de Pescadores, Río del Plata, Palermo, Buenos Aires

Café, San Telmo, Buenos Aires

Dog walker, Palermo, Buenos Aires

Mar del Plata, Buenos Aires Province

San Telmo market, Buenos Aires

Estancia, Buenos Aires Province

Gaucho breaking a wild horse, La Pampa

St Teresa, Cordoba

Pampas grass

Mina Clavero, Cordoba Province

Gaucho parrilla

Ostende; the *Viejo Ostende*, at Biarritz and Cairo (☎ & fax 02254/486081; ⑦), is a beautifully preserved reminder of the days when this pioneer resort hosted literary figures such as the Argentine authors Adolfo Bioy Casares and Silvina Ocampo as well as Antoine de St-Exupéry, author of *The Little Prince*. Rooms are simple but elegant and comfortable and the hotel has its own swimming pool. Breakfast, dinner and a beach tent at the hotel's balneario are all included in the price. There's also a nursery, making it a good choice if you're with small children.

Budget accommodation is practically non-existent in Pinamar – try the reasonable *Hospedaje Valle Fertil* on tree-lined Cangrejo between Centauro and Valle Fertil (☎02254/484799; ③), some distance from the beach. The *Bologna*, at Jason 497 (☎02254/482242; ④), has some pleasant rooms including three with large balconies. There is a large **youth hostel** in Ostende at Bme. Mitre 149 (☎02254/482908; $10 per person), which is a bit run-down, but well located on a quiet sandy street overlooking the sea; it has a huge kitchen and you can pitch tents in the small garden at the back. There are only a handful of **campsites** in Pinamar: Quimey Lemú lies just 250m north of the entrance to the town, along the RP11 (☎02254/484949; *www.pinamar.net/camping/quimey*), and is set in attractive wooded grounds with plenty of facilities from showers to shops. More convenient if you don't have your own transport is the small but well-located *Camping Saint Tropez*, at Quintana and Nuestras Malvinas (☎02254/482498), just north of the youth hostel. Both sites charge around $15 per pitch for up to four people.

Eating and drinking

The majority of **Pinamar's restaurants** are around Avenida Bunge and along the seafront. The most popular are large, *tenedor libre*-style parrillas such as *Cardo Azul*, Bunge 991; there's a vegetarian version, *El Vivero*, at Bunge and Libertador. There are a number of good restaurants specializing in freshly caught seafood, such as the bustling *Viejo Lobo* at Avenida del Mar and Bunge. The recently opened *Tulumei* at Bunge 64 is a small, friendly and prettily decorated place with a laid-back atmosphere, good music and imaginative cooking. Also excellent is the bustling *Sociedad Italiana*, Eneas 200, which does a mean spaghetti bolognese for $5. One of Pinamar's most traditional spots is the **teahouse** and restaurant *Tante*, opposite the Playas, on Avenida Bunge. The atmosphere here is a bit stuffy, but the cakes are exceptionally good; elaborate, mostly Germanic, savoury dishes are also served at lunchtime and in the evenings.

Nightlife is mostly centred around a handful of bars along Avenida Bunge and the seafront. There's a branch of Buenos Aires' trendy *Pizza Banana*, on Avenida del Mar and Tobías; a bright, modern and young place serving fast food as well as beers and with DJs at weekends. Pinamar's biggest nightclub is the *Ku* complex on Quintana and Nuestras Malvinas which houses a number of clubs playing everything from dance to rock and salsa; for $15 you can eat first and then enter any or all of the clubs. Pinamar's popular **casino** is at Júpiter and 1ro de Julio ($5 admission).

Villa Gesell and around

After slightly snooty Pinamar, the relaxed and vaguely hippyish feel of **VILLA GESELL** comes as a welcome relief. The resort carefully cultivates its laid-back image, much in the same way as Pinamar cultivates its exclusivity, and while it may not be the bohemian mecca it once was, Villa Gesell is still one of the more enjoyable places to sample Argentinian beach life. The town is named after its founder, Carlos Gesell, a mildly eccentric outsider of German descent. In 1931, Gesell bought a stretch of coastal land, largely dominated by still moving and seemingly useless sand dunes. After some experimentation Gesell managed to stabilize the dunes by planting a mixture of vegetation including tamarisks, acacias and esparto grass and began to sell lots, many of which were bought by Germans and Central Europeans escaping from the war. In the Sixties the resort became a particular favourite with young people and, though some high-rise construction has diminished the natural feel which first attracted them to the town, Gesell remains a firm favourite with parties of Argentinian youth holidaying away from the family.

Something of the bohemian feel that once distinguished Gesell can still be discerned in the small resort of **Mar Azul**, some 15km down the coast: in between the two lies the even smaller and notably tranquil **Mar de las Pampas**, a good spot to head for if all you want to do is relax. Beyond Mar Azul lies the **Faro Querandí**, a lighthouse set

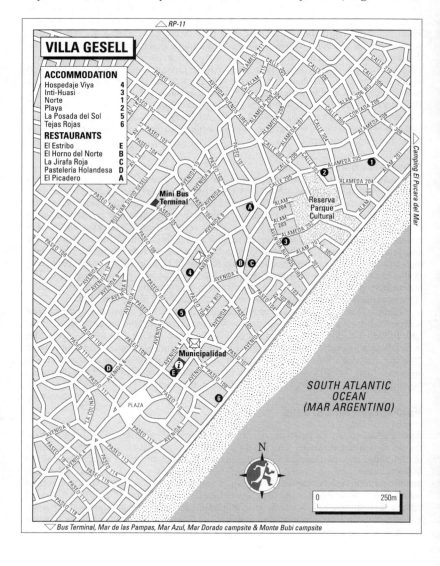

△ *RP-11*

VILLA GESELL

ACCOMMODATION
Hospedaje Viya	4
Inti-Huasi	3
Norte	1
Playa	2
La Posada del Sol	5
Tejas Rojas	6

RESTAURANTS
El Estribo	E
El Horno del Norte	B
La Jirafa Roja	C
Pastelería Holandesa	D
El Picadero	A

▷ *Camping El Pucara del Mar*

Mini Bus Terminal

Reserva Parque Cultural

Municipalidad

PLAZA

SOUTH ATLANTIC OCEAN (MAR ARGENTINO)

N

0   250m

▽ *Bus Terminal, Mar de las Pampas, Mar Azul, Mar Dorado campsite & Monte Bubi campsite*

amongst a reserve of dunes. Half-day trips to the lighthouse can be made with various companies in Villa Gesell.

The Resort

Villa Gesell is a friendly resort whose winding streets – many of them unsealed – do their best to defeat the order imposed by a complex system of numbered avenidas (which run parallel to the sea), paseos, calles and alamedas. The town's main street is Avenida 3, which is pedestrianized in the evening when it becomes the centre of the town's lively nightlife. To the west lies a pleasant residential district with houses set back from the roads, which are lined with high sandy banks.

At the northern end of the town, entered from Alameda 202, lies the **Reserva Parque Cultural**. Designed by Carlos Gesell, the park's wooded walkways offer welcome shade on hot days, and the dunes which separate it from the beach to the east are a particularly good spot for quiet sunbathing or picnicking. If you fancy something a bit livelier, however, head for one of Gesell's popular balnearios, such as Windsurf, El Agite, Pleno Sol or Cocoplum, which vie with each other every year to become the season's in spot. The balnearios are spread out along the length of the beach and lure regulars with the music from their bars – some of which even have Jacuzzis. Windy, on the beach at the bottom of Paseo 104 (☎02255/460430), runs a **windsurf** school.

Since the 1960s, Gesell has been a magnet for artisans and there's a good **artisan fair** selling a mixture of locally made crafts, jewellery and leather goods, every evening from about 8pm on Avenida 3 between paseos 110 and 112, in front of the central plaza. The town has a lively cultural life and of its numerous mini festivals, the most important is the **Fiesta Nacional Semana de la Raza en el Mar**, celebrated in mid-October with a procession of floats, followed by kayak competitions, several concerts and a giant paella. There are various places to **rent bikes** in town; try Casa Macca on Avenida Buenos Aires between Paseo 101 and Avenida 5 (☎02255/468013; $15 a day), or Rodados Luis on Paseo 107 between avenidas 4 and 5 (☎02255/463897; $12 a day). **Horseriding** is also popular, at schools such as the well-established Tante Puppi on Boulevard and Paseo 102 (☎02255/455533) which organizes rides in the woods and dunes or, more informally, from various points along Avenida 3 between Villa Gesell and Mar de las Pampas.

Arrival, information and accommodation

The town's main **bus terminal** (☎02255/477253) is some distance west of the centre, at Avenida 3 and Paseo 140; if you arrive here, you'll probably want to get a local bus (#504 which will drop you off close to central Avenida 3) or taxi to the centre. More central is the "mini terminal" at Av. 11 and Paseo 105 (☎02255/460940); many long-distance buses stop here before continuing to the main terminal. There are **left-luggage facilities** at the mini terminal (9am–2pm & 4–11pm). **Trains** from Buenos Aires (Constitución) travel as far as Pinamar, where there's a connecting bus service to the mini terminal, which also serves as a ticket office for the train station. Villa Gesell's **airport** (☎02255/460418) is 3km south from the turn-off to the town on the RP11, with daily flights from Buenos Aires and Rosario. A shuttle bus ($3) runs from the airport to the town dropping off at central hotels.

You'll find the most central **tourist office** at Av. 3 no. 820 (7am–midnight; ☎02255/463055; *www.gesell.com.ar*). There's another office at Av. Buenos Aires and the Paseo del Golf (daily 5–9am, 11am–3pm & 6pm–midnight; ☎02255/468596). Both have good maps and numerous leaflets on current events in the resort. You can change travellers cheques at the Fenix Tour bureau de change on Av. 3 no. 815 (Mon–Fri 10am–1.30pm).

The cost of **accommodation** varies considerably according to season, with some places doubling their prices from mid-January to mid-February, and some great deals available in March and December. There are plenty of *hospedajes* on Avenida 5, between paseos 104 and 107; one of the best is the charming *Viya* between paseos 105 and 106 (☎02255/462757; ③), with a pleasant garden and seating area and plain but very well-kept rooms. Another reasonably priced option is *Inti-Huasi*, next to the entrance to the park at Alameda 202 and Buenos Aires (☎02255/468365; ③), which also runs a cheap *tenedor libre* parrilla. Definitely the most unusual place is the very friendly *Posada del Sol*, Av. 4 no. 642 (☎ & fax 02255/465819; ⑤; closed April–Oct), which has a mini zoo in its garden in which ducks, flamingoes and rabbits wander freely. Rooms are small but attractive, comfortable and well-equipped; and the place is justly popular so reserve well in advance. The large *Tejas Rojas*, Costanera 848 (☎02255/462565, fax 462221; ⑦), has a beachfront location and a swimming pool; the hotel itself is a cool, tiled and spacious building. The *Playa*, Alameda 205 and 303 (☎02255/458027; ⑥), is Villa Gesell's oldest hotel and is set in wooded grounds in the quiet Barrio Norte with pleasant, simply decorated rooms. Nearby is the *Norte*, Alameda 205 no. 644 (☎ & fax 02255/458041; ⑤), with light, airy and comfortable rooms and a wooded garden.

The tourist office holds a complete list of Villa Gesell's numerous **campsites**, all of which are some distance from the centre. *El Pucara del Mar*, on Alameda 201 and Calle 313 (☎02255/458462), at the northern end of town, is open all year and has a beachfront location and plenty of services including shops, a restaurant and good showers. Some of the nicest sites lie amongst the dunes at the southern end of town: try *Mar Dorado* at Av. 3 and Paseo 170 (☎02255/470963), or *Monte Bubi* at Av. 3 and Paseo 168 (☎02255/470732), both with similar facilities to *El Pucara* and also open all year round. All campsites average around $15 per four-person tent.

Eating and drinking

There are a number of European-style **teahouses**, such as the lovely *Pastelería Holandesa*, on the corner of Av. 6 and Paseo 111, where the Dutch owner serves *Uitsmijter*, a kind of high tea of eggs, bacon, potatoes and salad, in the evenings. There are also plenty of good **restaurants**, including *El Picadero* on Av. 5 and Paseo 101, which serves good beer and *picadas* as well as cakes and sandwiches. *La Jirafa Roja*, a lively bar at night, does excellent versions of the old standby *lomito*, including *lomo de fuego* with red peppers and garlic or *lomo jirafa* with spring onions and mushrooms, and salads which you can make up yourself from ingredients including tuna, hearts of palm and apple. *El Horno del Norte* specializes in juicy *empanadas tucumanas* baked to order in a traditional oven outside and also offers Spanish specialities such as *callos a la madrileña*, tripe in a spicy sauce. The best **parrilla** in town is *El Estribo* – and at $9 for a *bife de chorizo*, it should be. For fast food, *Carlitos*, Av. 3 no. 814, is a Gesell institution while nearby *El Topo*, Av. 3 no. 978, with its landmark upside-down sign, sells wickedly good *churros* filled with *dulce de leche*.

You'll have no problem finding **nightlife** in Gesell; just follow the crowds to Avenida 3. Traditional bars along here include *Torino* at no. 424 and *La Nostalgia*, at no. 555, which offers live music (mostly blues and rock). *Catalina*, at Av. 1 no. 947, offers a classic Gesell mix of poetry recitals, home-made cakes and live music. *L'Brique*, Av. 3 between Buenos Aires and Paseo 102, and *Dixit*, housed in a futuristic-looking building in Paseo 106 just off Av. 3, attract a younger crowd. Finally, no self-respecting Argentinian beach resort would be without its **disco complex**; Gesell's, called *Pueblo Límite*, is out on Avenida Buenos Aires opposite the Secretaría de Turismo.

Mar de las Pampas and Mar Azul

The evocatively named **MAR DE LAS PAMPAS**, just south of Villa Gesell, is a haven of tranquil pine forests and pampas grass. The beach is not as deserted as you might expect since it is easily accessible from Gesell, but inland you can lose yourself along sandy tracks where the only sound comes from bird calls, the dunes acting as a barrier from the sounds of the beach. The village has only a couple of **hotels**: best is the *Posada El Granero*, Joaquín V. González (☎02255/479548; *elgranero@gesell.com.ar*; ⑥), a quietly luxurious place which also has a restaurant serving German food and Belgian beer.

MAR AZUL, further down the road, is currently enjoying the reputation for maintaining the spirit of Villa Gesell of the 1970s with musicians such as blues singer Celeste Carballo occasionally playing at local **pub** *Mr Gone* on Av. Mar del Plata and Calle 41. It also has more infrastructure, including a couple of **campsites**, the best of which is *Camping Mirage*, on Av. Mar del Plata and Calle 47, two blocks from the beach (☎02255/479502; closed April–Nov).

Both resorts could be reached on foot from Villa Gesell, either along the beach or via Avenida 3, but it's a pretty hefty walk. Alternatively, you could take the local **bus** which leaves on the hour from behind the bus terminal on Avenida 4 and passes through both resorts.

Faro Querandí

Thirty kilometres south of Villa Gesell lies the Reserva Dunícola, a wild landscape of shifting dunes and pampas grass, whose soaring centrepiece is the 56-metre high **Faro Querandí**. An elegant stone staircase spirals to the top of this lighthouse, from where there are stunning views of the surrounding coast. Various companies offer excursions here from Villa Gesell. The most competitively priced are those run by Empresa El Costero, Paseo 106, between avenidas 3 and 3 bis (9am–1pm; (☎02255/468989); they also have a kiosk in Paseo 110 bis, between avenidas 3 and 4 (9am–9pm; ☎02255/462158). The excursions last four to five hours, with around two hours spent at the lighthouse, cost $10 and there are three a day; the best is in the evening, when the lighthouse casts long shadows over the dunes. You'll need trainers or similar to climb the lighthouse and bring a swimsuit, too, if you fancy a dip. If you're returning in the evening, note that the temperature drops considerably once the sun goes down, so it's advisable to take some warm clothing.

Mar del Plata and around

Big, busy and brash, **MAR DEL PLATA** towers above all other resorts on Argentina's Atlantic coast. Around three million tourists holiday here every summer, drawn by the familiar charms of its busy beaches and lively entertainment. If the thought of queuing for a restaurant makes you shudder, Mar del Plata in the height of summer is best avoided, but if you prefer to mix your sunbathing and swimming with a spot of culture, nightlife or shopping, you'll probably find it one of Argentina's most appealing resorts. Despite some haphazard development, Mar del Plata is a solid and attractive city, favoured by the gentle drama of a sweeping coastline and hilly terrain and while its rather urban **beaches** may lack the wild charm of less developed strips of sand, they are fun places to hang out – good for a spot of people-watching as well as swimming and sunbathing. Mar del Plata is also the only resort really worth visiting out of season: while the city may breathe a sigh of relief when the last of the tourists leave at the end of the summer, it certainly doesn't close down – Mar del Plata has just over 500,000 inhabitants and its **port** is one of Argentina's most important.

The town was founded by Patricio Peralta Ramos in 1874, but it was Pedro Luro, a Basque merchant, who had the idea of turning the growing town into a European-style bathing resort three years later. As the railway began to expand into the province, previously isolated settlements such as Mar del Plata became accessible to visitors from the capital; the first passenger train arrived here from Buenos Aires in September of 1886. The subsequent opening of the town's first hotel – the luxurious **Hotel Bristol** – in 1888

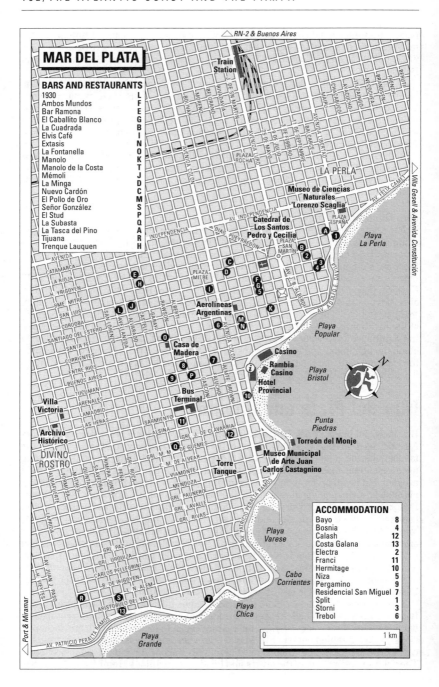

MAR DEL PLATA

BARS AND RESTAURANTS

1930	L
Ambos Mundos	F
Bar Ramona	E
El Caballito Blanco	G
La Cuadrada	B
Elvis Café	I
Extasis	N
La Fontanella	O
Manolo	K
Manolo de la Costa	T
Mémoli	J
La Minga	D
Nuevo Cardón	C
El Pollo de Oro	M
Señor González	S
El Stud	P
La Subasta	Q
La Tasca del Pino	A
Tijuana	R
Trenque Lauquen	H

ACCOMMODATION

Bayo	8
Bosnia	4
Calash	12
Costa Galana	13
Electra	2
Franci	11
Hermitage	10
Niza	5
Pergamino	9
Residencial San Miguel	7
Split	1
Storni	3
Trebol	6

was a great occasion for the Buenos Aires elite, many of whom travelled down for the opening on an overnight train.

The town's initial success aside, the richest of Argentina's very rich continued to make their regular pilgrimages to Europe. It took the outbreak of war in Europe to dampen Argentine enthusiasm for the journey across the Atlantic and to establish Mar del Plata as an exclusive resort. **Mass tourism** began to arrive in the 1930s, helped by improved roads, but took off in the 1940s and 1950s, with the development of union-run hotels under Perón finally putting Mar del Plata within the reach of Argentina's middle and working classes.

In the rush to reap maximum benefit from the resort's meteoric rise, laws were passed that allowed high-rise construction and led to the demolition of many of Mar del Plata's most traditional buildings. Today, with the notable exception of its landmark **casino** and **Grand Hotel Provincial**, the resort's coastline is dominated by modern high-rise developments. This uneasy mix makes for a weird and wonderful place: scattered here and there are quirky buildings, built in a decorative – even fantastical – style, known as pintoresco, an eclectic brew of mostly Norman and Tudor architecture. Indeed, in many ways this is still an intriguingly old-fashioned place, where people eagerly attend the latest show or queue patiently to go to a favourite restaurant and return, year after year, to the same hotel and the same beach tent. Above all, it's a place where people go to have fun, and it would be hard not to be affected by the atmosphere.

Away from the beaches, Mar del Plata has a number of modest but interesting **museums** and **galleries**: notably the charming Villa Victoria – an elegant wooden building once owned by Victoria Ocampo, one of Argentina's most famous writers, and now housing the city's cultural centre. The bustling **port area** is also worth a visit, not only for its colourful traditional fishing boats, but for a close encounter with the area's noisy colony of sea lions. If you're just looking for a spot of good living, Mar del Plata has some excellent bars and restaurants and – at the height of the summer – a non-stop nightlife.

South of Mar del Plata, the RP11 continues through a subdued landscape where wooded reddish-brown cliffs slope down to the creamy aquamarine waters of the Atlantic and arrives, after 40km, at the popular family resort of **Miramar**. The Interbalnearia finally peters out at the small and appealingly sleepy village of **Mar del Sud**.

Arrival, information and orientation

Mar del Plata is well-connected by public transport to most points in Argentina, particularly during the summer, when services increase dramatically. Its **airport**, Aeropuerto Camet (☎0223/478-0744), is around 8km northwest of the city centre along the RN2. Local bus #542 will take you from the airport into town, passing along Avenida Pedro Luro all the way to the seafront. **Trains** from Buenos Aires (Constitución) arrive at Estación Norte to the northwest of the town centre, at Luro and Italia (☎0223/475-6075), where you can still see the first train that brought passengers to Mar del Plata. Various local buses, including #511, #512 and #542, run between the station and the town centre. The bus terminal, at Alberti 1602, is right in the centre of things, and is a good point from which to start looking for reasonably priced accommodation if you haven't anything booked. If you are travelling by car, the most direct route from Buenos Aires is via the RN2, but this is also by far the busiest route during the summer and – thanks to hefty tolls – the most expensive. You'd be better off heading for the RP29 via Balcarce, a route which is longer by about 80km but much quieter and cheaper.

The main office for Emtur, Mar del Plata's **tourist information** service, is centrally located on the northwest corner of the old *Hotel Provincial* on the Boulevard Marítimo, opposite Plaza Colón (Mon–Fri 9am–8pm, Sat & Sun 9am–1pm & 4–8pm; ☎0223/495-1777; *www.argent.com.ar/emtur*). The information offered is rather minimal, but they can provide you with a good map of the resort, together with leaflets on the main tourist areas, and they will happily answer any specific questions you may have. For up-to-date information on Mar del Plata's lively calendar of entertainment check the **listings** in the local paper, *La Capital*.

Though Mar del Plata is a large city, **orientation** is fairly easy since both the sprawling coastline and the hills to the south of the centre make useful landmarks. The main square, **Plaza San Martín**, is connected to the seafront, six blocks to the southeast, by Avenida Pedro Luro. Running parallel to Luro, six blocks to the southwest, is Avenida Colón, which runs from the downtown area to the hilly streets of Stella Maris, where you will find most of the best examples of Mar del Plata's pintoresco architecture. Lying between Luro and Colón is the hectic **microcentro**, with the greatest concentration of shops, restaurants and hotels. Hugging the coast is a wide avenue officially called Avenida Patricio Peralta Ramos, but invariably referred to as the Boulevard Marítimo. Though the majority of Mar del Plata's attractions are within reasonable walking distance of each other, the combination of summer heat and hilly streets will probably make you glad to hop on a bus from time to time. Local buses are cheap and efficient and routes are well marked at bus stops. Useful routes include #551, #552 and #553, all of which run between Avenida Constitución – centre of the city's nightlife – Avenida Luro and the port; #523 also goes to Punta Mogotes and the Bosque. Taxis are easy to come by and relatively inexpensive: from the centre to Avenida Constitución, for example, costs about $6.

Accommodation

It's advisable to book ahead if you plan to stay in Mar del Plata during high season. Most of the **budget accommodation** is to be found around the bus terminal, although you can also find some good deals in La Perla, a pleasant barrio with hilly streets just to the north of the town centre. The only **hostel** in town is the *Pergamino*, Tucumán 2728 (☎0223/491-9872; $12 per person with HI card); more of a budget hotel than a hostel, it has bunk beds squeezed into small rooms, and things can be pretty cramped.

Costa Galana, Boulevard Marítimo 5725 (☎0223/486-0000, fax 4862020; *reservas@hotelcostagalana.com.ar*). One of Mar del Plata's newest luxury hotels, overlooking Playa Grande. Large, attractively decorated rooms with air conditioning; all with sea views. ⑨.

Hermitage, Boulevard Marítimo 2657 (☎0223/451-9081; *hermitag@lacapitalnet.com.ar*). A classically elegant hotel, almost lost amidst the surrounding modern buildings. Popular with visiting celebrities, the *Hermitage* has suitably luxurious rooms and an excellent location. ⑦.

Hostería Split, H. Yrigoyen 1048 (☎0223/495-3111). Croat-run hotel a couple of blocks from La Perla beach. Rooms have en-suite bathrooms. Breakfast not provided. ②.

Hotel Bayo, Alberti 2056 (☎0223/495-6546). This pretty hotel stands out from its rather dingy neighbours near the bus terminal. Private bathrooms and breakfast included. Closed Easter–Oct. ③.

Hotel Bosnia, Córdoba 1283 (☎0223/495-4281). Basic but reasonably priced rooms with television and fan, close to the beach. ③.

Hotel Calash, Falucho 1355 (☎0223/451-6115). On a quiet street near the centre, this friendly hotel has simple but light and attractive rooms with private bathrooms. There's also a 24hr café and an attractive shady seating area outside. ④.

Hotel Electra, 3 de Febrero 2752 (☎0223/495-0882). The rooms are very basic and a bit on the scruffy side, but the owners are friendly and offer one of the best deals in town for single travellers. ③, single ①.

Hotel Franci, Sarmiento 2748 (☎0223/486-2484). Centrally located and good-value hotel; rooms with TV and private bathroom; 24hr bar. ③.

Hotel Niza, Santiago del Estero 1843 (☎0223/495-1695). Sweet, old-fashioned hotel with pleasant, cool interiors, but basic rooms. Discounts may be available for single travellers if the hotel is not full. ③.

Hotel Storni, 11 de Septiembre 2642 (☎ & fax 0223/491-6200; *storni@argenet.com.ar*). Very close to La Perla beach. Ground-floor rooms are fairly simple – but all have TV and private bathrooms. Upstairs is more luxurious – all rooms come with a minibar and bathtub. Sea views are also available from some of the upstairs rooms. Friendly and efficient staff; seafood restaurant downstairs. Ground floor $35, otherwise ⑤.

Hotel Trebol, Corrientes 2243 (☎ & fax 0223/495-7251). Centrally located hotel with simple but pleasant rooms, all with private bathrooms. Breakfast included. ③.

Residencial San Miguel, Tucumán 2383 (☎0223/495-7226). Popular, central and with a lively atmosphere, thanks to the restaurant downstairs. Pleasant rooms with private bathroom. ③.

The City

Mar del Plata's official centre is **Plaza San Martín** but, on summer days at least, its true heart lies further southeast in the area surrounding central **Playa Bristol** and the **Rambla Casino**, a pedestrian promenade flanking the grand casino and Hotel Provincial. Aside from the beach itself, there's little in the way of sightseeing in the city centre, though just to the north, the barrio of **La Perla** is home to the town's Museo de Ciencias Naturales and the intriguing café and Mar del Plata landmark, **La Cuadrada**. If it's culture you're after, you'll need to head south for the steep streets of **Stella Maris**, where you'll find the Museo de Arte Juan Carlos Castagnino, or for the quiet residential area of **Divino Rostro**, where the main attraction is the **Villa Victoria** cultural centre and the Archivo Histórico Municipal. South along the coast, a visit to the port makes a fine way to end the day – both for the lively bustle of returning fishermen and for the majestic sea lions who have made their home at the port's southern end.

Plaza San Martín and the microcentro

Plaza San Martín, Mar del Plata's spacious central square, covers four blocks and is bounded by calles San Martín, 25 de Mayo, H. Yrigoyen and San Luis. The square's central statue of San Martín, executed by the sculptor Luis Perlotti, is slightly unusual in that it shows the general in old age. At the southern end of the square is the **Catedral de los Santos Pedro y Cecilia** (free guided tours Wed at 11am; meet at Mitre 1780), designed by Pedro Benoit, chief architect of the provincial capital La Plata. A fairly unremarkable example of late nineteenth-century neo-Gothic, the exterior is not particularly eye-catching, but it's worth taking a quick spin round the interior for its beautiful and decorative stained-glass windows. A lively *feria artesanal* takes place in the square in the evening.

To the immediate south of the square lies the hectic **microcentro**, dominated by pedestrianized **Calle San Martín**, which becomes a claustrophobe's nightmare in the evening when it is so packed that it becomes difficult to weave your way through the assembled mass of holidaymakers and street performers. Alternatively, follow Avenida Luro eight blocks northwest of Plaza San Martín to reach **Plaza Rocha** where, during the summer, there is a small **flea market** (Thurs–Sun 6–10pm) specializing in antiques, secondhand books, coins and stamps.

Playa Bristol and around

Some nine blocks to the southeast of Plaza San Martín lies **Playa Bristol**, Mar del Plata's most famous beach. Together with neighbouring Playa Popular, just to the north, these are the city's busiest beaches and in high season their blanket coverage of beach tents and shades is reminiscent of a strange nomadic settlement. At the centre of the bay formed by these two beaches you will find the **Rambla Casino** whose monumental red and white buildings, the casino and the former **Hotel Provincial**, vie with Buenos Aires' Obelisco as Argentina's most recognizable cityscape. Follow the bay round to the southeast and you will come to a promontory, known as Punta

Piedras, crowned by another of the city's landmark buildings, the **Torreón del Monje**. This "monk's tower" is a perfect example of Mar del Plata's peculiar brand of fantasy architecture, which at times makes the city look like a toy village; built as a folly in 1904 by Ernesto Tornquist, the tower looks a little overwhelmed by its neighbours these days, but you can still get a great view of Playa Bristol and the Rambla Casino from its confitería.

Some eight blocks southwest of Playa Bristol, and worth a detour, is the charming art gallery, the **Casa de Madera**, at Rawson 2250 (Tues–Sun 7–10pm; ☎0223/495-2317; *dabain@mdp.edu.ar*). Surrounded by a pretty garden, this white-walled and green-shuttered wooden building was constructed using prefabricated materials brought from Sweden in 1909, much like the better-known Villa Victoria (see p.187). The gallery has a good selection of paintings, prints and sculptures on display by mostly local artists; the building itself has recently been protected by the municipalidad.

La Perla

Heading north from Plaza San Martín takes you through the much quieter neighbourhood of **La Perla**. Perhaps the best attraction here is the stunning *La Cuadrada* café (see p.189), just one block from the Plaza on Mitre and 9 de Julio. Following Mitre another two blocks will bring you to La Perla **beach**, almost as busy as the central beaches but regarded as slightly more upmarket. One block to the south of Mitre there is a monument by Luis Perlotti to the poetess **Alfonsina Storni**, who committed suicide here in 1938. One of Latin America's most important poets, Storni had her first collection of poems published in 1916 and she reached prominence in the 1920s when she formed part of a group of writers, musicians and artists known as "La Peña", who gathered in Buenos Aires' famous *Café Tortoni*. In 1935 Storni was operated on for breast cancer and this, plus a subsequent series of suicides of close friends, including the writers Horacio Quiroga and Leopoldo Lugones, appears to have precipitated her own descent into depression: in October of 1938, Storni booked into a quiet hotel in Mar del Plata, one of her favourite cities, and sent a poem entitled *Voy a dormir* (I am going to sleep) to *La Nación* newspaper and, three days later, threw herself into the sea.

Following the coast around north brings you to La Perla's main square, the Plaza España, where you can visit the **Museo de Ciencias Naturales Lorenzo Scaglia** (Mon–Fri 10am–noon & 5–10pm, Sat & Sun 5–10pm; $2, free on Mon), which has a good collection of fossils from all over the world as well as a salt and freshwater aquarium.

Loma Stella Maris

Just to the southeast of Playa Bristol, the wide Avenida Colón begins to climb to the hill known as **Loma Stella Maris**. The area provides some good views over the city, particularly from the crest of the hill back down the impeccably straight Avenida Colón. It's also a pleasant place to wander around, if you're interested in Mar del Plata's pintoresco architecture – most of the major examples are in this neighbourhood. At Colón 1189, the imposing Villa Ortiz Basualdo, an exhuberantly turreted and half-timbered Anglo-Norman mansion, houses the **Museo Municipal de Arte Juan Carlos Castagnino** (Dec–March Mon, Tues & Thurs–Sun 5–10pm; April–Nov same days 4–9pm; $1). Local artist Castagnino, whose work forms the basis of the permanent collection, was born in Parque Camet in 1908 and painted colourful expressionist scenes of Mar del Plata, but it was with his illustrations for a bestselling version of *Martín Fierro*, published by Eudeba in 1962, that he struck commercial success. The museum is also notable for its elegant Art Nouveau interior, complete with the odd light-hearted detail such as the five extravagant flying ducks over the fireplace, and designed by the Belgian Art Nouveau designer Gustave Serrurier-Bovy. Serrurier-Bovy was a contemporary of Henry Van de Velde and much of his work in Europe was destroyed during

World War II: the villa's collection is one of the most complete still remaining. Temporary exhibitions generally focus on local and national artists.

Three blocks south of the museum, you can climb to the top of the bizarre, castle-like **Torre Tanque**, Falucho 995, an Anglo-Norman tower housing offices, from where there are great views over the city (Mon–Fri hourly 10am–1pm).

Divino Rostro

Lying some 3km south of Plaza San Martín is the leafy and well-heeled neighbourhood of **Divino Rostro**. The area is almost exclusively residential with little in the way of cafés or bars, but is worth the detour to see the **Villa Victoria** (daily: house 5–10pm; garden 11am–5pm; $2, free on Wed; ☎0223/4920569), at Matheu 1851. The site of some interesting exhibitions and events, the villa is an architectural curiosity in its own right. Built of Norwegian wood, it is a fine example of the prefabricated housing which the English took with them to their colonial outposts. It was imported by Francisca Ocampo, who had it shipped to Buenos Aires in 1911, and then transported by train to Mar del Plata. **Victoria Ocampo**, one of Argentina's most famous writers, and a great-niece of Francisca, inherited the house in the 1930s. From this time on, it became a kind of cultural retreat, visited by the various Argentine and foreign writers courted by Ocampo. In 1973, six years before her death, Victoria Ocampo donated the house to UNESCO – who promptly auctioned off most of its furnishings – and in 1981 it was purchased by the municipalidad. The bedroom is now the only room containing original furniture, donated back to the house by a private individual who had bought it at auction. However, the beautiful light and airy rooms still hint at the atmosphere of gracious living enjoyed by Argentina's elite at the beginning of the century. There are guided tours of the house (Spanish only), packed with anecdotes about Victoria Ocampo's life, but a little long for all but the most dedicated enthusiast.

The excellent **Archivo Histórico Municipal** (daily 4–9pm; $2; ☎0223/495-1200), at Lamadrid 3870, one block southeast of Villa Victoria, has plenty of interesting information on Mar del Plata's history. Within the archives are some wonderful early photos of the resort's elegant early days when the cognoscenti from Buenos Aires flocked to the *Hotel Bristol*, as well as copies of the strict rules enforced on bathers: single men could be fined or arrested for approaching within thirty metres of women bathers or for using opera glasses. A slightly unusual exhibit is the intricate carved wooden replica of the Duomo de Milan, carved by an Italian immigrant to the town.

To reach either the Archivo Histórico or Villa Victoria, take **bus** #591 from Avenida Luro or the Boulevard Marítimo and get off on the corner of Las Heras and Matheu.

The Port

After the Rambla Casino, Mar del Plata's favourite postcard image is the striking yellow fishing boats that depart daily from its **port**. In the early evening you can watch them returning to the Banquina de los Pescadores, when crates bursting with bass, sole and squid are hauled onto the quayside by the fishermen, mostly first- and second-generation Italians. At the far end of the wharf there is a colony of around eight hundred male **sea lions**. These can be observed from an incredibly close distance – only one metre or so – all year round, though the colony is much smaller in summer as large numbers head for the Uruguayan coast to mate. There are a number of good seafood restaurants around the port itself, as well as on the streets to the east.

Various **buses** head here, including #551, #552 and #553, all of which can be caught along Avenida Luro.

Eating, drinking and entertainment

There's a huge concentration of reasonable **restaurants** in the microcentro though if you want to avoid queuing you may prefer to head for the otherwise quiet streets bounded roughly by Avellaneda, Alberti, Independencia and Santiago del Estero, to the southwest of the microcentro, where there are some attractive small bars and restaurants.

For many visitors, Mar del Plata's **nightlife** is at least as important as its beaches – if you want to keep up with the locals you'll need both stamina and transport. The densest concentration of bars is along lively Calle Além, swamped by a young, affluent crowd during the summer, all intent on showing off their tan before heading to Constitución – an enormous avenue 4km north of the town centre which houses numerous clubs, none of which really gets going till well after 2am. You can reach Constitución on bus #551, which runs through the night; a taxi from the centre will cost you about $6.

Mar del Plata is also well catered for as far as **theatres** and **cinemas** are concerned; most of them are based around Avenida Pedro Luro, San Martín, Santa Fe and Independencia: major mainstream venues include the Teatro Colón, H. Yrigoyen 1665 (☎0223/494-8571); the Teatro Auditorium, Bv. Marítimo 2280 (☎0223/493-6001); and the Centro Cultural Pueyrredón, 25 de Mayo and Catamarca. There are also interesting theatrical and musical events at the more alternative **café-bars** *La Subasta*, Guemes 2955 (☎0223/451-2725); *Elvis Café*, Brown 2639 (☎0223/492-4529); and *La Minga*, Bolívar 2791 (☎0223/494-4406) – these are all good places to have a drink, too. Regular **folk music** shows take place at the Casa de Folklore, San Juan 2543 and the Casa de Salta, Libertad 3398.

Restaurants and cafés

1930, Avellaneda 2657. A slightly rustic place with a bustling, traditional atmosphere. Excellent and reasonably priced *picadas*, *empanadas* and *fugazettas*. Arrive before 9pm to get a good table and avoid queuing.

Ambos Mundos, Rivadavia 644. A popular place serving traditional Argentine fare and specializing in *puchero de gallina* (a light chicken stew with vegetables).

Cabaña del Bosque, Bosque Peralta Ramos. Mar del Plata's most famous café is located in a wooden building set in lush grounds within this residential district around 10km south of the city centre (take bus #526). The wildly exotic and rambling interior, decorated with fossils, carved wooden sculptures and stuffed animals, is worth a visit on its own, though the café's fantastic cakes are a pretty enticing attraction too.

El Caballito Blanco, Rivadavia 2534. A popular and consistently good restaurant in the centre, specializing in hearty German dishes.

El Pollo de Oro, Corrientes 2037. A *rotisería* offering a good choice of salads, *empanadas* and the like.

El Stud, Alberti 1975. This is one of the better restaurants in the vicinity of the bus terminal, offering simple but well-prepared standards such as grilled chicken and steaks.

La Fontanella, Rawson 2302 (☎0223/49405330). Named for its pretty fountain, *La Fontanella* specializes in *pizza a la piedra* as well as fish and pasta.

Manolo de la Costa, Castelli 15. Offering good sea views, the *Manolo de la Costa* does upmarket fast food such as pizzas and a delicious *brochette mixto*, a kebab of beef and chicken served with chips, salad and aubergine. Be prepared to queue in the evening. The sister branch at Rivadavia 2371 is busy, too, and a popular spot for *chocolate con churros* after a hard night's clubbing.

Mémoli, San Luis 2944 (☎0223/4915329). A stylish restaurant offering imaginative Italian cooking for around $10–15 a head.

Nuevo Cardón, Mitre 2047. A pleasant and spacious parrilla which does an excellent sizzling portion of *mollejas* (sweetbreads).

Trenque Lauquen, Mitre 2807 (☎0223/4937149). Mar del Plata's most famous restaurant, serving wonderful parrillada on traditional wooden tablas, at around $20 a head. It's not a budget option, but it does offer some of the best meat you're ever likely to eat. Book ahead.

La Tasca del Pino, Hipólito Yrigoyen y Balcarce. A new restaurant housed in a rather startling pink mansion. The menu includes adventurous, if slightly pricey, salads, fish and traditional Spanish dishes such as *patatas bravas*. A good place for a light meal or beer, especially at the outside tables.

Bars and nightclubs

Azúcar, Constitución 4478. One of Constitución's more relaxed clubs, playing salsa and merengue – though the slick hard core of salseros pretty much dance amongst themselves.

Bar Ramona, Castelli and H. Yrigoyen. A slightly posey but attractive bar, popular with the young and well-to-do.

Chocolate, Constitución 4445. Large, glossy club with the emphasis on commercial dance music.

Extasis, Corrientes 2044. Lively, predominantly gay bar.

La Cuadrada, 9 de Julio and Mitre. A café-bar and theatre that's worth a visit for its decor alone. Centred around a patio with a fountain and huge spreading palm tree, the interior is lavishly decorated with paintings, sculptures, antiques and wood carvings. It's a mesmerizing place to while away an hour or two and the food, though not cheap, is excellent and served with great style. They also do a fabulous breakfast.

Orbe, Constitución 4142. Constitución's only gay club with a friendly, mixed crowd. Open Fri–Sun.

Señor Gonzalez, Além, between Matheu and Quintana. One of Além's most popular bars – heaving with tanned bodies on summer evenings.

Sobremonte, Constitución. One of the Constitución's swishest complexes with themed bars ranging from mock Caribbean beach-bars to the laid-back Velvet Living Room, complete with pool table and Internet access. There are various dancefloors playing pretty standard dance music as well as a Mexican restaurant and a swimming pool.

Tijuana, Almafuerte, between Além and B. Yrigoyen. Alternative hangout to *Señor Gonzalez* around the corner – and in a very similar vein.

Listings

ACA Av. Independencia 3675 (☎0223/472-3059).

Airlines Lapa, Córdoba 1621 (☎0223/492-2112) and at the airport (☎0223/478-0333); Aerolíneas, Moreno 2442 (☎0223/472-7596).

Car rental Avis, Bv. Marítimo 2451 (☎0223/437850); Mardel Car, Moreno 2244 L.4 (☎0223/441310); Rent-A-Car International, *Hotel Dorá*, Buenos Aires 1841 (☎0223/491-1992); Unidas, Colón 3130, 10B (☎0223/425865).

Banks and exchanges There are many banks on Avenida Independencia, Avenida Luro (including Lloyds at 3101 and Citibank at 2983) and around San Martín. Exchanges include Jonestur at Luro 3191 and El Trébol at San Martín 2534.

Hospitals Hospital Interzonal Mar del Plata, Juan B. Justo 6800 (☎0223/477-0265).

Internet Krackers, Mitre 2069 (9am–2am; *www.krackers.com.ar*).

Laundry Laverap, Falucho 1572.

Post office The main office is at Luro 2460, on the corner of Santiago del Estero, offering all the usual facilities, plus a branch of Western Union; there are numerous other offices throughout the city.

Taxis Central Taxi (☎0223/472-4798); Mar del Plata Taxi (☎0223/482-4496); Tele Taxi Mar del Plata (☎0223/472-3688).

Travel agents and tour operators You'll find several travel agents in Galería de las Américas at San Martín 2648, including friendly Green Line (☎0223/492-2148), which offers city tours and trips to nearby towns such as Balcarce and Villa Gesell.

Miramar

Heading south from Mar del Plata, the first resort you come to is **MIRAMAR**, 40km further down the RP11. A largely modern town, it is much favoured by families and sells itself as a safe resort so insistently that you might start wondering what exactly is so dangerous about the other seemingly innocuous coastal towns. Miramar's regular grid of numbered streets is centred around **Plaza General Alvarado**, six blocks northwest of the beach. The even numbered streets run parallel to the beach. The town's gently curving bay is dominated by some rather grim high-rise buildings which tower over the central beaches. A series of stone breakwaters have been constructed to prevent the erosion of this stretch of the coast, creating a chain of calm inlets. The town's most attractive feature is the **Vivero Dunícola Florentino Ameghino**, half a square kilometre of forested section of dunes just to the south of the central beaches, where there is a nursery and barbecue area, and bicycles can be rented. In fact, cycling is popular throughout the town, which gives the place a relaxed, gentle pace. Though Miramar's not a bad choice if you want to spend a few days on the beach with children, there's otherwise little to recommend it.

The resort has two **bus terminals**: Rápido del Sud arrives from Mar del Plata at Av. 23, between calles 34 and 36, four blocks northwest of central Plaza General Alvarado; Costera Criolla buses, with connections to Buenos Aires and Necochea, arrive at Calle 30 and Diagonal Fortunato de la Plaza, one block to the north of the centre. Both terminals offer a left-luggage service. Miramar's **train station**, with services from Mar del Plata, Balcarce and Buenos Aires, is on Avenida San Martín, six blocks to the north of the centre. There's a helpful **tourist office** (daily 9am–6pm; ☎ & fax 02291/420190; *www.miramar-digital.com*) on the northern corner of Plaza General Alvarado. **Accommodation** is easy to find, with a wide choice of mostly one- and two-star places in the streets surrounding Plaza General Alvarado and the beachfront. For budget options near the terminals try the *Familia*, Av. 23 no. 1701 (☎02291/420671; ②, single ③); its rooms are rather gloomy and uninspiring but the single rate is probably the cheapest deal in town. Just across the road is the cheery *El Farol*, Av. 23, 1728 (☎02291/420937; ③, single ②; closed April–Nov), with more appealing, well-kept rooms. **Eating** options are plentiful, too, with most places again around Plaza General Alvarado and the seafront. Try the *Cantina Italiana* on Calle 21, between calles 32 and 34, which does hearty plates of pasta, or the busy *tenedor libre* parrilla *La Cascada* on Av. 26, between calles 17 and 19. Down on the seafront, try *El Muelle* on the corner of the Costanera and Avenida 37, towards the southern end of the beach, for good seafood.

Mar del Sud

A more interesting choice than Miramar if you want a complete break from the bustle of places like Mar del Plata is tiny **MAR DEL SUD**, 16km south of Miramar on the RP11. One of Argentina's least-developed beach resorts, Mar del Sud's chief attraction is its tranquil – to the point of soporific – atmosphere. Its **beaches** are far less frequented than those further north and, if you venture north or south of the small clutch of beachgoers grouped around the bottom of the grandly named Avenida 100, you won't have much trouble finding a stretch of beach to yourself. The town's pleasantly unassuming buildings are dominated by the crumbling faded-pink and ochre walls and steeply pitched roof of the **Boulevard Atlantic Hotel**, an elegant, French-influenced construction built in 1886. Away from the beach and the handful of hotels and restaurants, there's not much to the town apart from a few sandy roads flanked by telegraph poles, a favourite perch of sleepy owls.

Mar del Sud is reached via a local **bus** from Miramar, which leaves roughly every hour and a half from outside the Rápido del Sud terminal. The bus will drop you at any point in Mar del Sud before terminating at the bottom of Avenida 100. **Accommodation** is limited, but pleasant. Though the main section of the badly damaged *Boulevard Atlantic* is currently uninhabitable, there are some slightly musty but well-equipped apartments ajoining the hotel, with cooking facilities (☎ & fax 02291/491198; $7 per person). The only hotel on the seafront itself is the *Hostería Villa del Mar* on the corner of Av. 100 (☎02291/491141; ③; closed Feb–Nov), which has small rooms overlooking the sea. Friendly *Posada Miko*, at calles 15 and 98 (☎011/4752-6006; ②), is located two blocks from the beach and has comfortable, simple rooms. *Campsite La Ponderosa*, 400 metres from the beach and well to the west of the town centre, on the corner of Avenida La Playa (☎0223/4748759), is well equipped, with showers, a restaurant and shops. The town's few **places to eat**, including Croat restaurant *Makarska*, are mostly around the bottom of Avenida 100.

The southern beach resorts

Beyond Mar del Plata, the coast slopes round to the west and resorts are more widely spaced. The largest of these southern beach resorts is **Necochea**, favoured by families and with the region's widest beaches. Neighbouring **Quequén**, bereft of hotels but with a couple of campsites, offers quieter beaches and is also an important port. Some 140km further south lies the small town of **Claromecó**, separated by a small stream from the quiet wooded village of **Dunamar**. This area soaks up most of the tourism from southern Buenos Aires Province and – with the exception of ever so slightly snooty Claromecó – the resorts here have an unpretentious and relaxed feel. As ever, **fishing** is a popular activity on these beaches, and Necochea, which claims to have some of the best waves in Argentina, makes a good destination for **surfers**. The area is also an important cereal-producing region and away from the coast vast fields of sunflower, wheat and linseed mirror the immensity of the pampa sky, while grain elevators cluster around the edge of towns. There is no direct coast road linking Necochea with Claromecó; if you want to travel between the two resorts you'll have to make a detour inland via the agricultural town of **Tres Arroyos**, from where buses run to both places.

Necochea and Quequén

Separated by the Río Quequén Grande but governed by the same municipalidad, Necochea and Quequén make a slightly schizophrenic couple. The dominant partner is **NECOCHEA**, a sprawling town which took off as a tourist resort in the 1970s. It's particularly popular with families, thanks to its much publicized wide beaches and a large, attractive park. These qualities apart, though, the town's attractions are somewhat limited. Its biggest handicap is its disjointed layout: the town centre proper, known as the **centro viejo**, sits some 3km inland, well away from the bustle of tourist activity which is packed into a pretty charmless grid of streets down by the seafront. The **centro nuevo**, as this area is known, is centred on **Plaza San Martín** and pedestrianized calles 83 and 85, which run between the plaza and the seafront and are lined with amusement arcades and small shopping malls. The enormous **Parque Miguel Lillo** (6am–9pm) lies immediately west of the centro nuevo, alongside Calle 89, and contains, amongst other things, a lake, campsites, a go-kart track and the **Museo Histórico Regional** (Tues–Sun 9am–noon & 4.30–8.30pm) at the eastern end of the park, housed in a pretty, colonial-style building and containing a rather eclectic collection of exhibits and heavily labelled photographs showing Necochea's development.

Since 1996, Necochea's municipalidad has also had jurisdiction over neigbouring **QUEQUÉN** to the east, a much quieter and smaller town whose tranquillity is disturbed only by the lorries which rumble to and from its busy port, along Diagonal Almirante G. Brown. Quequén can seem a bit desolate – it's certainly not the place to be if you seek excitement – but in many ways it has a lot more character than its brasher neighbour. Once a rather upmarket resort, Quequén lost out to Necochea in the tourism stakes and its **beachfront** area remains a gentle, mostly residential strip given a quirky charm by a sprinkling of grand but rather dilapidated mansions standing on grassy lots.

Necochea's beachfront is a typically regimented and extremely busy stretch of sand dominated by tents and sunshades and lined with restaurants. To the north, close to the mouth of the Río Quequén, lies the quieter **Playa de los Patos**, flanked by low dunes and popular for fishing and surfing. There's a surf school here, La Escollera (classes daily 9am–1pm; $5). Quieter beaches still can be accessed in Quequén. An unsealed road hugs the coast here, taking you past the central beaches, less wide than Necochea's but still popular, to the aptly named **Bahía de los Vientos** ("Bay of winds"), where the hulks of shipwrecked boats rest on rocky outcrops. The beaches here are narrower and wilder and are a good place to head for for aimless strolling along the coast. To the south of Necochea, the beaches extend for some 30km; the most accessible of these undevel-

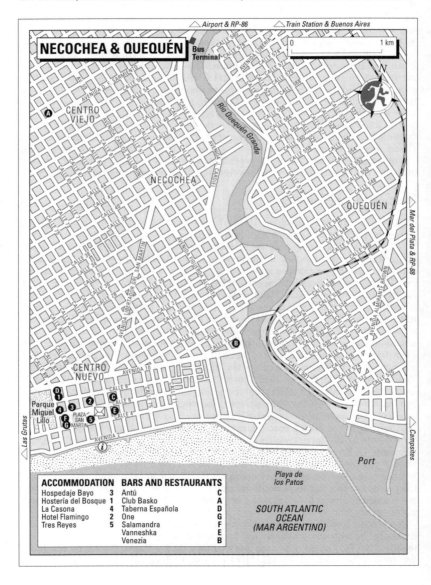

NECOCHEA & QUEQUÉN

Airport & RP-86   Train Station & Buenos Aires

Bus Terminal

0   1 km

N

CENTRO VIEJO

Río Quequén Grande

NECOCHEA

QUEQUÉN

Mar del Plata & RP-88

CENTRO NUEVO

Parque Miguel Lillo

Las Grutas

PLAZA SAN MARTÍN

Campsites

Port

Playa de los Patos

SOUTH ATLANTIC OCEAN
(MAR ARGENTINO)

ACCOMMODATION		BARS AND RESTAURANTS	
Hospedaje Bayo	3	Antú	C
Hostería del Bosque	1	Club Basko	A
La Casona	4	Taberna Española	D
Hotel Flamingo	2	One	G
Tres Reyes	5	Salamandra	F
		Vanneshka	E
		Venezia	B

oped rocky beaches is known as **Las Grutas**, backed by low cliffs and lying around 10km from the centre. Another 5km or so along the coast road you reach **Punta Negra** – so-called for its dark sand, and popular with divers. Finally, 30km south of town lies the attractively rocky **Cueva del Tigre**, a popular fishing spot. This last stretch of coast road is best tackled in a 4WD: if you have an ordinary car you can take an alternative route via Avenida 10, which runs along the north side of Parque Miguel Lillo.

Arrival, information and accommodation

Necochea's **airport**, served by daily flights from Buenos Aires, is 13km north of the town centre along the RP86. The municipalidad's **bus terminal** (☎02262/422470) is situated in Necochea at Av. 58 and Jesuita Cardiel, 3km north of the centro nuevo, so you'll need to take either a taxi or local bus #513 or #502 (to Necochea) or #511 (Quequén). **Trains** from Buenos Aires (Constitución), via Tandil, arrive at the train station in Quequén, on calles 563 and 580 (☎02262/450028). Local bus #512 runs between the train station and the bus terminal. The friendly **tourist office** (daily: 8am–8pm; ☎02262/438333), on the seafront in Necochea at the foot of Calle 83, produces an excellent and informative booklet listing everything from major attractions to the location of ATMs and the stakes at the town's defiantly Seventies-style casino.

At all but the height of the summer season you shouldn't find it difficult to get **accommodation** in Necochea – and prices are generally lower here than they are further north. Quequén has a couple of good campsites, but nothing else in the way of accommodation. One of Necochea's best budget options is the *Hospedaje Bayo*, Calle 87 no. 338 (☎02262/423334; ②), which has a nice interior patio, but the lack of fans can make the rooms a bit stifling in very hot weather. The rooms are simple, but all have a decent private bathroom. The very friendly *La Casona* on Calle 6, half a block from the park (☎02262/431871; ②), has parking, a central garden and good communal facilities. The comfortable, slightly basic rooms all have private bathrooms. The pleasant *Hotel Flamingo*, at Calle 83 no. 333 (☎02262/420049; ③), has attractively furnished rooms; best are the two rooms at the front with balconies overlooking the street. A television and minibar are available for a $3 supplement per person. The comfortable but rather characterless *Hotel Tres Reyes*, Calle 4 bis no. 4123 (☎02262/422011; ④), overlooks the plaza and, as well as standard doubles – all with private bathroom, TV, telephone and air conditioning – has large suites with two bathrooms and a living room. Parking and breakfast are included and discounts make it more affordable out of high season. Necochea's nicest hotel by far is the charming and friendly *Hostería del Bosque*, opposite the park at Calle 89 no. 350 (☎02262/420002; ④–⑤). The elegantly decorated rooms have big, comfortable beds and en-suite bathrooms; downstairs there is a lovely shady courtyard, set with tables and chairs for breakfast. The pretty building was once the summer-house of a niece of the Tsar of Russia who caused a scandal in Necochea in the 1930s by wearing trousers and smoking. There are many **campsites** in both towns, with a couple of the nicest in Quequén. *Monte Pasuvio*, off Calle 502 (☎02262/451652; $5 per person), is right by the beach in Quequén and has a snack bar, shady camping spots and a laid-back atmosphere. Friendly *Camping El Gringo*, also in Quequén, on Calle 519 (☎02262/425429; $5 per person) is more oriented towards families and has pitches in orderly wooded grounds with modern showers, a shop and various attractions aimed at appeasing restless kids, including a TV room. There are also some comfortable bungalows (4–6 people; $10 per person).

Eating and drinking

Finding a reasonably priced pizza, pasta or parrilla **restaurant** is easy in Necochea. Most of them are centred on Plaza San Martín and the surrounding streets. Particularly good value is the *tenedor libre* parrilla *Antú*, on Calle 6 no. 3974. The *Taberna Española* at Calle 89 no. 366 opposite the park is a nice spot to sit outside on a summer evening; the menu includes paella, *cazuela de mariscos* and a sweet but tasty version of traditional Argentine dish *pollo a la naranja* (chicken with orange). *Vanneshkha* at Calle 81 no. 258 offers filling sandwiches with a Danish influence; try their *Sandwich Copenhague* which comes with paté, pickled cucumbers, beef, salad, tomato and red peppers on home-made bread. They also do home-made hamburgers and sausages with sweet-and-sour potato salad. In the centro viejo, the restaurant inside the *Club Basko*, on the corner of calles 65 and 58, specializes in seafood as does the long-established and popular *Cantina Venezia* in the port, Calle 59 no. 259.

Nightlife in Necochea is rather quieter than in other resorts; local youth and tourists alike frequent **bars** such as *La Salamandra* and *One* in Calle 87 between calles 4 and 6 and *Casting* **nightclub** next door. During the summer, the various balnearios also have bars and nightclubs. The town's busy **casino** (daily 10pm–4am; admission $5), housed in a rather ugly 1970s concrete complex, is on the southern end of the seafront at Avenida 2 between calles 91 and 97. In the centro viejo, there's the elegant Art Deco Cine-teatro París, at Avenida 59 no. 2874 (☎02262/422273) and, in the centro nuevo, the Cine Ocean, Calle 83 no. 350 (☎02262/435672). Both show mostly mainstream **movies** – listings can be found in the local paper *Ecos Diarios*.

Claromecó, Dunamar and around

Warm currents from Brazil bring both exotic shells and stinging jellyfish to the waters of tranquil **CLAROMECÓ**. A small resort some 140km south of Necochea, Claromecó is known for hosting one of Argentina's most important fishing contests; the 24-hour **Fiesta de la Corvina Negra**. There is plenty of local fishing activity, too, and if you go down to the beach in the evening you may see fishermen going out with horses which they use to take nets out into the sea. The only downside to the excellent dune-fringed beach is that cars are allowed onto it, and at times the ample beach can look like a vast parking lot. Fortunately, the central section, overlooked by Claromecó's tall and spindly lighthouse, is reserved for bathers, and if you head out beyond the last of the cars, some 8km to the west, you will come to a stretch of beach known as the *caracolero* – a kind of exotic graveyard of large and beautiful shells, washed up from Brazil.

Lying to the west of Claromecó, on the other side of the Arroyo Claromecó, **DUNAMAR** is the more attractive of the two villages, bounded by forest, river and sea. There's not much to the place apart from sandy lanes and pine trees, but there are some pretty houses to rent and it's a good choice if you want to camp in a more natural environment.

There are two further balnearios on either side of Claromecó: Reta and Orense. Tiny **ORENSE** – also known as Punta Desnudez, with its distinctive rocky beach, is the smaller and wilder the two; both are surrounded by dunes and have a hotel or two and campsites.

Practicalities

Buses arrive at the terminal on Claromecó's main plaza (☎02982/480018), where there is a confitería and left-luggage facilities. There are a couple of direct services a day from Buenos Aires: if you are heading down the coast you will normally have to make a connection at Tres Arroyos, 70km inland, from where there are regular services to Claromecó. During the summer, there are also bus services from Tres Arroyos to Reta and Orense. Claromecó's small and friendly **tourist office** is on Calle 28 between calles 9 and 11 (☎02982/480001), half a block south of the bus terminal.

There's only a handful of **hotels** here, all in Claromecó – including *Residencial La Reserva* on Calle 7, between calles 24 and 26 (☎02982/480111; $10 per person). Most rooms are internal, but all have a private bathroom. Other options include the large and pleasant *Hotel Claromecó*, on the corner of calles 7 and 26 (☎02982/480360; ③) with simple but attractive rooms – try to avoid the slightly dingy rooms on the ground floor. The *Hostal Su-Yay* on Calle 11, just to the right of the bus terminal (☎02982/495809; *suyay@3net.com.ar*, ③) offers a snack bar and large, modern – if garishly decorated – rooms, some with a balcony overlooking the plaza. The nicest **campsites** are in neighbouring Dunamar – try *Los Troncos*, on the banks of the Arroyo (☎02982/480297; $3 per person), a simple, fairly rustic site with hot water, shops and barbecue facilities. You could also consider renting one of Dunamar's pretty houses, advertised by signs saying "se alquila" – calculate on these costing around $30 per day.

As far as **eating and drinking** go, there are a handful of parrillas on Calle 28 in Claromecó offering a *tenedor libre* service for around $8 per person. Popular in the evenings is *La Barra*, an upmarket bar on the seafront at the foot of Calle 26. In Dunamar, the friendly *Barlovento* is a lovely beach bar which serves *Frikadeller*, a Danish meatball dish, sells home-made preserves and has a small library of books.

San Antonio de Areco

Inland, and some 113km northwest of Buenos Aires is the charming town of **SAN ANTONIO DE ARECO**; if you visit only one pampa town during your stay in Argentina, this is the one to head for. The town is the recognized centre of pampa tradition with a popular gaucho festival, the **Día de la Tradición**, held in November, some highly respected artisans, and an extremely attractive and unusually well-preserved town centre. San Antonio also has a prestigious literary connection: the town was the setting for Ricardo Güiraldes' Argentinian classic, *Don Segundo Sombra* (1926), one of the first novels to celebrate the gaucho – previously regarded as a undesirable outlaw – as a symbol of national values.

The town's only real sights are a couple of museums. The most important of these, the heavily promoted Museo Gauchesco Ricardo Güiraldes, is actually a little disappointing, though it makes up for its rather run-of-the-mill collection with a spectacular collection of paintings by the Uruguayan artist, Pedro Figari. But what really makes San Antonio memorable is the harmonious architectural character of the town's centre; all cobbled streets and faded Italianate and colonial facades punctuated by elaborate wrought-iron grilles and delicately arching lamps. Another plus is the town's setting, on the banks of a tranquil river, the Río Areco. The riverside area is a popular picnicking spot and also has a number of attractive campsites.

Despite its modestly promoted status as a tourist destination, San Antonio has retained a surprisingly authentic feel. You may not find the town full of galloping gauchos outside the annual festival, but you still have a good chance of spotting estancia workers on horseback, sporting traditional berets and rakishly knotted scarves, or of coming across *paisanos* propping up the bar of a traditional establishment such as the *Boliche de Bessonart*.

The town's traditional gaucho atmosphere also extends to the surrounding area, where you will find some of Argentina's most famous estancias, offering a luxurious accommodation option to staying in Areco itself.

Arrival and information

Buses from Buenos Aires stop six blocks east of Areco's town centre, along Avenida Dr Smith. There's no terminal as such; ticketing and bus information are dealt with in *Bar Don Segundo*, on the corner of Segundo Sombra and Avenida Dr Smith. It's an easy and enjoyable stroll into town along Calle Segundo Sombra, which brings you to Areco's main square, Plaza Ruiz de Arellano. If you're carrying a lot of luggage – or heading for an estancia – pick up a taxi outside the terminals, though you will probably get better rates from a *remise* company such as Remis Auto Express (☎02326/452254), a couple of blocks south of the bus-stop, on the corner of General Paz and Alberdi.

The main **tourist office** is a short walk from the main square towards the river, on the corner of Arellano and Zerboni (Mon–Fri 9am–4pm, Sat & Sun 10am–8.30pm; ☎02326/453165). The information available is brief but useful and there is a good map of the town as well as a concise history, available in English as well as Spanish.

Accommodation

Though San Antonio is easily visited on a day-trip from Buenos Aires, staying overnight gives you the chance to explore the town at a more leisurely pace. Practically all **hotels** increase their prices on Friday and Saturday nights and on public holidays; you should calculate on paying up to $10 more for a double room at these times. The *Posada del Café de las Artes* at Bolívar 70 (☎02326/456371; *gonzalom@areconet.com.ar*; ③) has a few simple but charmingly decorated rooms with big old-fashioned beds and en-suite bathrooms: there's also an inviting garden area and a good café where the owners serve breakfast. Single rates are not usually available, but at quiet periods you may be able to get a room for around $25. The best option if you're on a tight budget is the simple but comfortable and well-kept *Hotel San Cayetano* on Segundo Sombra 515 (☎02326/456393; ②) – the entrance isn't very obvious but the hotel's owners run the kiosk next door, from where you can also gain access to the hotel. *Los Abuelos*, on Zapiola and Zerboni (☎02326/456390; ③), is a bit pricier than the *Posada* but is very friendly, and a good deal if you prefer a more modern hotel – there is a television and fan in each room, and free off-street parking. Some rooms also have balconies with views over the River Areco. The tourist office can provide information on **staying with families**, a particularly useful option during the Día de la Tradición celebrations, when accommodation can otherwise be hard to come by, and can also supply you with a full accommodation list. There are also several **campsites** within easy reach of San Antonio, including the spacious municipal site on the river bank to the northeast of the town centre; it charges $5 per tent (there's also a one-off $5 charge if you bring a car) and has a shower block as well as a small grocery store. There's a smaller site just across the river; run by friendly Miriam and her family (ask for directions to "Lo de Miriam"). It's a less orderly affair than the municipal site but has a very friendly family atmosphere. The site has showers and cooking facilities and costs $5 per tent. Some way out of town along the RP41 *Autocampamento Pago de Areco* is essentially a kind of classy caravan park where people rent small lots over periods of years. It has some good pitches by the river ($4 per person plus $4 per tent) but is only really accessible if you have your own transport or take a taxi. Take the RN8 east towards Buenos Aires and then turn left onto the RP41; after 1km there's a turning to the right, signposted for La Porteña – follow this unsealed road until it forks and then take the road to the right.

For more luxurious accommodation, there are a number of **estancias** in the countryside surrounding San Antonio de Areco (see p.199).

The Town

Areco's main square, the **Plaza Ruiz de Arellano**, lies some six blocks west of the bus terminals. It is named after José Ruiz de Arellano, whose estancia stood on the site now occupied by the town and who built San Antonio's founding chapel, the Iglesia Parroquial San Antonio de Padua, on the south side of the square. The original chapel, a simple adobe construction, was declared a parish church in 1730, and was rebuilt in 1792 and then again in 1870 in keeping with its growing importance. Of no great architectural note, the current version is nonetheless a pleasingly simple white construction,

---

ARTISANS

There are some excellent **artisans** working in San Antonio and a full list of *talleres*, or workshops open to the public, is available from the tourist office. Weaving and leatherwork are well represented and there are many silversmiths producing traditional items of *platería criolla*, typically Argentinian silverware which first emerged around 1750, when local craftsmen, who had previously been working according to Spanish and Portuguese traditions, began to develop a distinctive creole style. Fantastically ornate yet sturdy, in keeping with the practical use to which the items are – at least in theory – to be put, the style is most commonly used to produce gaucho knives (*facones*), belts (*rastras*), *mates* and stirrups. These are not items for everyday use, but are reserved for special occasions, notably the Día de la Tradición. Two of the most renowned silversmiths are Gustavo Stagnaro, whose workshop at Gral Paz 441 (some old street signs have it as G. Gastellú) has some fine examples of knives; and Juan José Draghi, at Alvear 345, whose work has been exhibited in the Museo de Motivos Argentinos José Hernández in Buenos Aires and who has produced pieces for various international figures, including the king and queen of Spain.

---

with clear Italian influences. The exterior is dominated by a sculpture of San Antonio himself, who stands within a niche clad with blue and white tiles which echo those of the church's small bell-shaped dome. Among the elegant *fin de siècle* residences that flank the square, is the Italianate **municipalidad**, to the north; originally a private residence it is painted a particularly delicate version of the pink that characterizes so many of Areco's buildings. On the northwest corner of the square stands a typically colonial two-storeyed construction known as the **Casa de los Martínez**, after the noted local family who once inhabited it. The building's handsome but rather plain green and white exterior is dominated by the original railings of a balcony which runs all the way around the first floor.

Heading west along the town's main drag, Segundo Sombra, will bring you to two buildings which have played an important role in the town's traditional social life. The first of these, the **Boliche de Bessonart**, on the corner of Segundo Sombra and Zapiola, is a rather dilapidated two-storeyed grocery store whose crumbling plaster work is steadily exposing the brickwork below. It's not for its architectural merit that the building is known, however, but for being San Antonio's most traditional meeting place: every evening at around 6.30pm a huddle of *paisanos* are to be found propping up the makeshift bar for a vermouth, a tradition which goes back to the time of Don Segundo Sombra, who was a regular customer, and beyond. A couple of blocks away, on the corner of Laplacette and Bolívar – follow Segundo Sombra one block out of town and then turn left into Bolívar – is the **Quinta Guerrico**, a typical early nineteenth-century construction with sturdy brick and adobe walls and a fine trellis-like iron balcony running along its first floor. The Quinta was built by Manuel José de Guerrico, grandfather of Ricardo Güiraldes, and the man who introduced the steam engine to Argentina. It was the scene of the first celebrations of the Día de la Tradición in the 1930s and was used, in 1969, as the backdrop for various scenes of the film version of *Don Segundo Sombra*. Just opposite the Quinta, you'll find one of Areco's most enjoyable restaurants, the *Almacén de Ramos Generales* (see p.199).

A block north of Plaza Ruiz de Arellano, along Valentín Alsina, is the **Centro Cultural Usina Vieja** (Mon–Fri 9am–3.45pm, Sat & Sun 10am–5pm; free). The restored building originally housed Areco's first electrical generator and has been declared a national industrial monument. Now housing a cultural centre the building also contains the **Museo de la Ciudad**, an eclectic collection – mainly supplied through local donations – of everyday items, from clothing to record players and even the town's old telephone switchboard; an exhibition of the works of local artisans; plus occasional temporary exhibitions, focusing mainly on subjects related to rural Argentine life. The permanent exhibit most likely to catch your eye is the huge metal sculpture *La Cautiva* by the local artist Perera: a startling but extremely accomplished work in which the traditional subject matter – a gaucho on horseback carrying away a young woman – sits uneasily with the work's almost aggressively modern execution, all exploding angles and pierced volumes.

Beyond the cultural centre, wide Calle Zerboni separates the town centre from the grassy banks of the Río Areco, popular for picnics and *asados* during good weather. Though most of San Antonio lies on the south side of the river, there is a small block of five by five streets to the north, which is connected with to rest of the town at its east and west extremities by two bridges. If you are travelling by car, you must cross via the **Puente Gabino Tapia**, to the right, but if you are on foot, cross straight over the simple brick **Puente Viejo**, which begins at the foot of M. Moreno, two blocks west of Alsina and leads to the Parque Criollo and the Museo Gauchesco Ricardo Güiraldes.

The rather scrubby **Parque Criollo** is less a park than a kind of exhibition ground, used during the Día de la Tradición as the setting for the main displays of gaucho skills. It also houses the **Museo Gauchesco Ricardo Güiraldes** (Mon & Wed–Sun 11am–5pm; $2). The entrance to the park and the museum is via the *Pulpería La Blanqueada*, once a staging post on the old Camino Real, which linked Buenos Aires with Alto Perú, and the setting for the first encounter between Fabio, the young hero of Güiraldes' novel, and his mentor, Don Segundo Sombra. The pulpería was closed in the 1930s but its original features have been retained, including the traditional bars which separated the owner from his customers – only trusted regulars were allowed access to the interior of the pulpería. The museum itself is a short distance away across the park. Housed in a rather drab 1930s reproduction of an old estancia, the collection is somewhat confused and mixes gaucho paraphernalia – *mate* gourds, silverware and boleadoras – with objects deemed to be interesting largely because of their famous owners – General Rosas' bed, W.H. Hudson's books, and so on. However, this all fades into insignificance next to the fantastic collection of works by Pedro Figari, a Uruguayan artist who settled in Buenos Aires in 1921 and worked with Güiraldes, one of the first people to appreciate Figari's talent, on the literary journal *Martín Fierro*. Figari was best known, though, for his dreamlike and deceptively primitive portrayals of gauchos, *candombe* (Afro-Brazilian religious rituals) and the distinctive urban and rural landscapes of the pampa. His paint-

---

DÍA DE LA TRADICIÓN

One of Argentina's most original and enjoyable fiestas, the **Día de la Tradición**, began in 1939, on an initiative of the then mayor of San Antonio de Areco, José Antonio Güiraldes. The Día de la Tradición itself is November 10 – the date of birth of José Hernández, author of Argentina's gaucho text par excellence, *Martín Fierro* – but the celebrations last for a week and are organized to run from weekend to weekend, generally from the second week in November. Activities, including exhibitions, dances, musical recitals and displays of traditional gaucho skills (*destrezas criollas*), run throughout the week, although the highpoint is the final Sunday, which begins with dancing and a procession of gauchos dressed in their traditional loose trousers (*bombachas*), ornamented belts (*rastras*) and wide-brimmed hats or berets. An *asado con cuero*, at which meat – primarily beef – is cooked around a fire with its skin on, takes place at midday in the Parque Criollo (you can eat as much as you like for around $15) and is followed by an extensive display of gaucho skills, including *jineteadas*, or Argentinian bronco riding.

Since 1971, the festivities have been supplemented by the Semana de la Artesanía Arequera, a display of local crafts. The Día de la Tradición celebrations attract thousands of visitors each year, and though many of them come for just one day, the town does become very busy and it's best to book accommodation in advance at this time.

ings, with their characteristic intense blue skies and flat mottled surfaces, seem to capture perfectly the almost hypnotic quality of the pampa landscape. The **museum shop**, close to the pulpería, is worth a visit for its small but superior collection of souvenirs, including local crafts, and a good selection of books including a criollo recipe book and an excellent illustrated history of the town.

Eating, drinking and nightlife

There are surprisingly few places to eat in San Antonio, but some of them are very good. The excellent **restaurant** *Almacén de Ramos Generales* at Bolívar 66 (closed Mon) is decorated in the style of an old grocery store with cosy, rustic seating, and its delicious traditional food is exceptional value: the *picada* alone, at a ridiculously cheap $3, would be enough for most people. The *asado* at *La Costa*, on the corner of Zerboni and Belgrano, is popular with the locals, as is the pasta at *El Colonial* on Zerboni and Alsina. The *Vieja Tortuga de Juan* on Alsina 60 offers simple home-made food and is a popular spot to listen to live folk music at weekends, when the place has an enjoyable buzz. If you've got a sweet tooth, don't miss *La Olla de Cobre*, a small chocolate factory and sweet shop at Matheu 433 (closed Tues), where you can try delicious handmade chocolates and *alfajores* before buying.

There are a handful of lively **bars** in town, mostly grouped a few blocks south of Plaza Arellano between General Paz and Além. The noisy *Gualicho*, popular with a very young crowd, is on General Paz between Alsina and Arellano, while the *Barril*, at San Martín 377, where there is occasional live music, attracts a slightly older clientele. The town's most popular **nightclub**, *Bronx* (Fri & Sat from 1am), is out on the corner of Segundo Sombra and Avenida Dr Smith.

Folk music and dancing is popular here and, as well as regular shows at the *Vieja Tortuga de Juan*, you may be able to catch one-off events at venues such as the municipalidad. Ask at the tourist office for details.

Estancias in and around San Antonio de Areco

The countryside around San Antonio is home to several of the province's most traditional **estancias**. Historic places in their own right, these estancias can make fantastic and luxurious places to stay. The closest of the overnight options to San Antonio is **La Porteña** (☎02326/453770, fax 454157; ⑨), named in honour of the Argentina's first steam locomotive, which was introduced to the country by Manuel José de Guerrico, grandfather of Ricardo Güiraldes, and the estancia's original owner. The estancia is still run by descendants of the novelist. The *casco* was built around 1823 and is a handsome whitewashed construction. Some publicity for the estancia states that the facilities include a polo school, although the owners stress that this is only for those already proficient in the sport. To get to *La Porteña* head southeast along the RN8 towards Buenos Aires, and turn left on to the RP41 just past the police post. After about one kilometre, turn right onto the unsealed road signposted to *La Porteña*. After a short distance the road forks; take the road to the left. Arguably the most luxurious of all San Antonio's estancias is **El Ombú**, Cuartel 6 (☎02326/4793-2454; ⑨). Its rooms are sumptuously decorated and a lovely tiled and ivy-covered veranda runs round the exterior of the building. As well as offering horseriding, the estancia has a small but well-maintained swimming pool and a games room. To reach *El Ombú* from San Antonio, head southeast along the RN8 towards Buenos Aires, and turn left on to the RP41 just past the police post. After about 5km you'll come to another intersection where there is an aerodrome: turn right onto the unsealed RP31, from where it is another 5km to the estancia. After rain, the road can become impassable: at such times, access is via the stud farm next door; ring *El Ombú* for details. **La Bamba** (☎02326/456293; *www.la-bamba.com.ar*; ⑨), a couple of kilometres beyond the turn-off for *El Ombú*, was famously used in Maria Luisa Bemberg's film *Camila* – the story of the ill-fated romance between Camila O'Gorman and a priest – and is one of Argentina's most distinctive estancias. The elegantly simple deep-rose facade of the *casco*, presided over by a *mirador*, or watchtower, is a particularly beautiful example of early eighteenth-century rural architecture. There are five double rooms in the main building, three of them en-suite, including one located in the watchtower itself, and four more rooms in various annexes. The Río Areco runs through the grounds, so guests can fish as well as ride, and there's a large swimming pool.

A less exclusive, but much more affordable, estancia experience is offered by **La Cinacina** in Areco itself; follow Bartolome Mitre five blocks west of the main plaza to the end of the street (☎02326/452773; *www.lacinacina.com.ar*). It offers a full day of *asado*, horseriding, and a display of gaucho skills for $30. The estancia also has a regular transport service from major hotels in Buenos Aires, with an English-speaking guide ($60 including return journey).

Lobos and San Miguel del Monte

The small towns of **Lobos** and **San Miguel del Monte**, connected by a 40km stretch of RP41, lie some 100km southwest of the capital. Though little visited by foreigners, they are popular weekend destinations for Porteños, primarily for their lakes where there are **camping** and **fishing** facilities, and good for overnight stops on your way south. Both are modest, old-fashioned towns; San Miguel is perhaps the prettier of the two, though Lobos has Argentina's only museum dedicated solely to Perón – who was born here – and, in the surrounding countryside, a couple of particularly attractive **estancias**.

Lobos

LOBOS is an old-fashioned country town with pretty, slightly crumbling houses and few pretensions to becoming a tourist destination. It is, however, the biggest town in the region, with some 30,000 inhabitants, and has a surprisingly lively nightlife that draws in people from the local towns and villages. The town's most famous son is Juan Domingo Perón, born here in 1895. The **Perón Museum** at Buenos Aires 1380, also known as Perón 482 (Wed–Sun 10am–noon & 3–6pm; free), first opened in 1953, but was closed by the military government in 1955 and again in 1976. It reopened in 1989 and though it lost some of its more important pieces, the museum still holds an interesting photographic archive and odd items of correspondence such as a love letter that Perón wrote to Evita when he was imprisoned on Martín García. One of the more curious items is the skull of famous gaucho and outlaw, Juan Moreira, who was killed by the police in a local pulpería, *La Estrella*, in 1874. The skull apparently fell into the hands of Mario Perón, Juan Domingo's grandfather, who used it as a paperweight.

To get to Lobos' quiet **lakeside area**, around 15km southwest of town – where there are picnic spots shaded by pines and eucalyptus – take the local bus which runs every couple of hours (6am–8.30pm) to the lake from the corner of Além and 9 de Julio, opposite the train station.

Practicalities

Lobos' **bus** and **train** terminals face each other on the corner of Hiriart and Além, around six blocks east of the town's central square, Plaza 1810. To get to the centre, follow Hiriart west until you hit Calle Buenos Aires and take a left for a couple of blocks to reach Plaza 1810. The municipalidad is at the southern end of Plaza 1810 and contains a friendly **tourist office** (Mon–Fri 8am–2pm, Sat & Sun 10am–4pm; ☎02227/431450).

There's not much **accommodation** in town, but the *Hotel de Julio*, 9 de Julio 241 (☎ & fax 02227/421465; ③) is well located with simple but decent rooms. If you prefer to stay around the lake (which can be a little desolate during the week), the hotel *El Pescador*, Av. Costanera and Calle 33 (☎02227/494114; ③), is a pleasant family-run place; while the best of the **campsites** is the *Club de Pesca*, although at $3 per person plus $5 for the tent it's a little expensive; you can also rent boats here or fish from the club's jetty. Upmarket accommodation is provided by nearby **estancias**: luxurious *La Candelaria*, RN205 at Km114 (☎02227/430180; ⑨), is distinguished by its extravagant turrets and towers – hence its local name, El Castillo. The all-inclusive price covers four meals, riding activities and use of tennis courts and a swimming pool. *Santa Rita*, A. Carboni (☎02227/495026; ⑨), located just beyond the tiny village of Carboni, is more low key – but its faded-pink *casco* is very pretty and, as well as horses, there is a small zoo of llamas, goats and ducks. You can arrive at the estancia by **train** from Buenos Aires (Constitución); the train tracks run right past the estancia and, with prior notice, you can arrange to get off in Carboni, from where the estancia's friendly English-speaking owners will pick you up.

In the town, *Tío Pipa*, Hiriart 18, is a good **restaurant** and parrilla; while *Emanuel* at 9 de Julio 130 serves **sandwiches** and **coffee**. There are no fewer than five **nightclubs**, which open until very late at the weekend: try *E–Mail* on Cardoner between 9 de Julio and Hiriart or *Tío Coco* on Suipacha between Perón and Albertini.

San Miguel del Monte

SAN MIGUEL DEL MONTE, or Monte, as it is affectionately known, might look like a glorified truck stop from the busy RN3 which runs past the town, but away from the bus terminal on the main road, it's a pretty and compact town which sits beside the Laguna de Monte. Originally known as the Guardia del Monte, the town was the point of departure for Rosas' first military expedition into the wilderness in 1833. His **Rancho de Rosas**, on the corner of calles Soler and Belgrano, is a thatched roof construction built and originally located on his nearby estancia and moved to the town in 1988. On one side of Monte's central **Plaza Alsina** is the town's distinctive mustard and white church, the **Iglesia San Miguel Arcangel**, finished in 1867 and still the town's tallest building; its interior contains works by artists such as Raúl Soldi, who also painted the interior dome of Buenos Aires' Teatro Colón. Plaza Alsina itself is heavily frequented in the early evening by local youths who buzz around its perimeter on motorbikes and bicycles.

The **Laguna de Monte**, Monte's lake, lies six blocks south of Plaza Alsina; follow Calle Bartolomé Mitre or Além. Covering some seven square kilometres, it's home to a variety of aquatic birds, including black-necked swans, as well as fish, including tararira and the highly prized pejerrey. The northern edge of the lake, flanked by the Costanera Juan Manuel de Rosas, is almost urban and dotted with parrillas and a couple of discos. The far side is wilder and you can camp there for free (though with no services). Organized campsites are located at the northern edge of the lake and **boats** can be rented at the Club de Pesca on the Costanera, a few blocks west of Mitre. You can walk all the way around the lake's 15-kilometre perimeter on a path or a road.

Practicalities

Monte's **bus** and **train stations** are on the corner of the RN3 and Avenida San Martín, which leads southeast to Plaza Alsina, a fifteen-minute walk. The **tourist office** is on the lakeside, on the corner of Fray F. Martínez and the Costanera, about eight blocks southwest from the plaza (Mon–Fri 7am–1pm, Sat & Sun 2–8pm; ☎02271/421138), though information is scant. Monte is particularly popular at the weekends, especially in summer, and prices for accommodation may rise at these times. The nicest **hotel** is the pretty green and white *Hotel del Jardín*, S. Petracchi and L.N. Além (☎02271/420019; ③), well located just on the corner of Plaza Alsina with rooms set around a central patio. A bit more expensive is the *Antigua Casona*, Santos Molina 419 (☎02271/420512; $45, breakfast $5 extra); the rooms are spruce and comfortable albeit rather frilly. Right by the lake, the *Hostería Laguna de Monte*, Av. Costanera and J.J. Sardén (☎02271/420687; ③), is an ugly modern building but with pleasant rooms, lake views, and outside seating; those checking out on Sundays can use their rooms until 5pm. For **snacks**, there are various confiterías around the central plaza and parrillas along the Costanera: *El Mangrullo*, ten blocks west from Mitre, along the Costanera, is particularly popular.

Azul and Tandil

A couple of hundred kilometres south of San Miguel del Monte, along RN3, lies **Azul**, essentially useful as a transport hub, but with some modest attractions in the surrounding low-lying hills, including Latin America's first Trappist monastery. **Tandil**, 70km southeast of Azul, is an attractive town of cobbled streets backed by gentle rolling hills, known as the Sierra de Tandilia, which are popular destinations for walking and riding trips.

Azul

Located in the centre of Buenos Aires Province, 300km south of the capital, **AZUL** is mainly useful as a transport hub, with around one hundred buses a day connecting the town with the rest of the interior and the coast. Architecturally, it's a bit of a mixed bag, though there are some attractive late nineteenth-century houses, which give Azul an elegant feel. Though there's little to detain you in the town itself, **excursions** can be made to some gently rolling sierras some 50km to the south, where there are a number of unusual sights including Latin America's first **Trappist monastery**. At Easter, the town plays host to an **Encuentro Internacional de Motos**, a motorbike rally which has attracted motorcyclists from all over Latin America and from as far afield as the US. The town owes its name (Azul means "blue") to the indigenous inhabitants of the region who called the stream along which they lived Callvú-Leovú, or "the stream of the blue country".

Plaza San Martín, Azul's main square, is noteworthy for its distinctive black and white Art Deco paving which gives the rather unnerving impression of walking on an undulating surface; it is surrounded by an eclectic mixture of buildings including the Neoclassical **Palacio Municipal**. Dating from 1886, the building's originally harmonious proportions were thrown somewhat out of kilter by the addition of a spindly watchtower. On the other side of the square stands Azul's cathedral, the neo-Gothic **Catedral Nuestra Señora del Rosario**, built in 1906. The cathedral's lofty central tower is echoed by smaller towers which descend on either side, creating a strong triangular shape.

On the corner of San Martín and Alvear is the **Museo y Archivo Histórico E. Squirru** (Wed & Thurs 8am–noon, Fri & Sat 4–8pm, Sun 4–9pm) which holds a good selection of Mapuche silverware; *mate* gourds and rifles as well as examples of traditional crafts which are currently being revived in Azul, including a typical pampa poncho, distinguished from other Argentine ponchos by its strong geometric design, predominantly black and white interspersed with a little red.

Continuing west along Calle San Martín will bring you to an attractive riverside walk along the Arroyo Azul. Head left along the river to reach the woody **Parque Municipal**

Sarmiento, distinguished by its many varieties of trees including lush magnolias and palms. Some distance further on lies Azul's vast **balneario municipal**, an artificially widened stretch of the Arroyo, good for a refreshing dip in hot weather.

Practicalities

Both the **bus terminal** and the **train station** are located on Cáneva, some twelve blocks east of Plaza San Martín. Azul's exceptionally helpful **tourist office** is at Av. 25 de Mayo 619 (Mon–Fri 8am–2pm, Sat 10am–1pm; ☎02281/431751), three blocks east of the plaza. Depending on resources, the staff may be able to accompany you around the town or to nearby attractions such as the monastery. There are plenty of **accommodation** options in town. The *Cervantes*, just a few blocks from the bus terminal at Cáneva 530 (☎02281/422581; ③), is a passable option if you arrive in the middle of the night, but otherwise it's nicer to stay nearer the plaza – try the *Roma*, Bolívar 543 (☎ & fax 02281/425286; ③), whose spotlessly clean rooms have fans, cable television and phone, or the *Argentino*, H. Yrigoyen 378 (☎02281/433988; ③), which is a little shabby but comfortable and includes breakfast. The best hotel in town is the three-star *Gran Hotel Azul* on Plaza San Martín (☎02281/422011; ⑤). The municipal **campsite** located on the banks of the Arroyo del Azul just beyond the balneario municipal is cheap and pleasant; be warned that it fills up with motorcyclists at Easter, here for the rally.

Azul's most enjoyable **restaurant** is *La Fonda*, San Martín 875. Terrific value for money and stylish with it, *La Fonda* has a daily-changing menu, rattled off to you by the friendly waiters; around six home-made dishes are offered, including excellent pasta, but best of all are the abundant and delicious *picadas* which are served free of charge before the meal and include olives, croquettes, aubergine, *empanadas* and salami. The same people also run *El Encuentro*, a parrilla on the corner of Roca and Uriburu. *Dime*, Perón 490, is another good choice for reasonably priced and well-cooked Argentine standards. Azul's most popular nightspot is *Shittó*, a **café-bar** on Yrigoyen between Uriburu and Burgos.

The Monasterio de Nuestra Señora de los Angeles and around

Some 50km south of Azul, along the RP80, the **Monasterio de Nuestra Señora de los Angeles** – Latin America's first Trappist monastery – lies in the region known as Boca de las Sierras, a gentle pass through Azul's low, undulating sierras. The monastery's Sunday Masses (10am) are popular with visitors as well as inhabitants of the surrounding area and the monks also accept guests for spiritual retreats. The **retreats** run from Tuesday to Friday, and from Friday to Tuesday, and reservations must be made in writing to the monastery: Monasterio Trapense, CC 34, (7300) Azul, Pcia de Buenos Aires. Women are accepted only in groups of four.

About 5km further along the same road, the tiny village of **PABLO ACOSTA** has a charming almacén, a traditional country store and bar.

There are no marked trails through the surounding **sierras** and exploring the area entails scrambling over rocks and pushing your way through shoulder-high pampas grass. Note also that the military has an explosives range, Fanazul, just to the north of the monastery and exploring the area unsupervised is not recommended. Check with Azul's tourist office for details of **accompanied visits** and other **excursions**, including **horseriding**.

Tandil

TANDIL, 70km southeast of Azul, is set amongst the central section of the range of hills known as the **Sistema de Tandilia**. The range begins some 150km to the northwest of Tandil, running southeast across the province to Mar del Plata, on the coast, and only rarely rising above 200m. Around Tandil, however, there are peaks of up to 500m. This is not wild trekking country, but Tandil's hills – somewhat reminiscent of the landscape of Wales or Ireland – are good for activities such as horseriding and mountain-biking, with various companies operating out of the town. Tandil also has the quirky distinction of being famous for something that's no longer there. For many years, the enormous **Piedra La Movediza** (literally "the moving stone") rested at an inconceivably steep angle on one of the town's many rocky outcrops, before finally smashing to the valley floor eighty years ago. Such is the fame of this 385-tonne rock, many Argentinians think it's still there and the place where it once stood remains one of Tandil's most-visited spots. The town's most famous remaining stone is the impressive but not quite so precarious **El Centinela**, a seven-metre high boulder perched upright on a small hill some 5km southwest of the town centre.

Rocks aside, Tandil is famed for its **Vía Crucis** procession (stations of the cross) each Easter, which ends at Monte Calvario, a small hillock topped by a giant cross to the east of the town centre. It's also a popular weekend destination and has a lively and enjoyable feel in the evenings, thanks to the bustle of holidaymakers and locals strolling around the town centre.

Arrival, information and accommodation

Tandil's modest **airport** (☎02293/424228) is a few kilometres west of town, along the RN226. The **bus terminal** (☎02293/432092) is around fifteen blocks east of the main square, at Buzón 650; there are usually plenty of taxis (☎02293/422466) waiting at the terminal to take you into town, or you could take local bus #503. The **train station** is at Avenida Machado and Colón, around twenty blocks northeast of the main square. The **tourist office**, at 9 de Julio 555 (☎02293/432073), is not terribly dynamic, but does publish a good map and maintains a list of families offering accommodation during the busy Easter period.

Popular for short breaks throughout the year, Tandil is absolutely inundated at Easter, when most **hotels** substantially increase their prices and are often fully booked up to a month beforehand. The nicest place in town is *Lo de Olga Gandolfi*, at Chacabuco 977, a few blocks north of the town centre (☎02293/440258; ③, with breakfast); it's a lovely rambling old building with a garden and parrilla. There are only a few rooms and the place is particularly popular with families, so if you'd like to stay you should try to reserve in advance. In the town centre, the *Austral*, at 9 de Julio 725 (☎ & fax 02293/425606; ③) is a very friendly hotel in a modern building. The en-suite rooms are equipped with TV and telephone; the hotel does not offer breakfast but there is an adjoining confitería. The *Hospedaje Helios*, at Gral Rodríguez 783 (☎02293/426747; ②) offers rather basic but clean and comfortable en-suite rooms – though none has outside windows. If it's not too busy, you may be able to get a single for half the price of a double room. Nearby is the *Hotel Cristal*, at Rodríguez 871 (☎02293/443970; ③), offering pleasant and fairly spacious rooms; parking is available for $5 a day. On the central square, there's the *Plaza*, at Gral Pinto 438 (☎ & fax 02293/427160; *plazah@necsus.com.ar*; ⑤), a three-star hotel with slightly sterile but comfortable air-conditioned rooms and restaurant; rooms at the front overlook the plaza. Overlooking the park, there's the pleasant and friendly *Hermitage*, at Av. Avellaneda and Rondeau (☎02293/423377; ④, with breakfast) with a terrace, restaurant and 24-hour bar. As well as the attractively furnished and spacious rooms, there are also some big apartments, holding up to six people, which can be a good deal: five-bed apartments are $75; six-bed apartments are $90. Parking $5 a day.

There are numerous **cabañas** on the outskirts of the town (the tourist office has plenty of leaflets), although you'll need your own transport to reach most of them. On Suiza, near the Sierra del Tigre reserve (see below), there's *Cabañas La Escondida*, (☎02293/430522 – ask for Jorge; $80 for four people, $90 for five), two well-equipped and upmarket cabins with their own swimming pool. More rustic in style are the

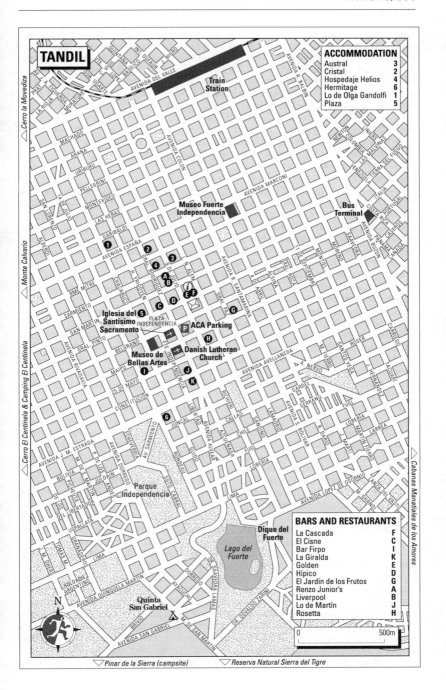

TANDIL

△ Cerro la Movediza

△ Monte Calvario

◁ Cerro El Centinela & Camping El Centinela

Train Station

Museo Fuerte Independencia

Bus Terminal

Iglesia del Santísimo Sacramento

ACA Parking

Museo de Bellas Artes

Danish Lutheran Church

PLAZA INDEPENDENCIA

Parque Independencia

Dique del Fuerte

Lago del Fuerte

Quinta San Gabriel

▷ Cabañas Manatiales de los Amores

ACCOMMODATION

Austral	3
Cristal	2
Hospedaje Helios	4
Hermitage	6
Lo de Olga Gandolfi	1
Plaza	5

BARS AND RESTAURANTS

La Cascada	F
El Cisne	C
Bar Firpo	I
La Giralda	K
Golden	E
Hípico	D
El Jardín de los Frutos	G
Renzo Junior's	A
Liverpool	B
Lo de Martín	J
Rosetta	H

0   500m

N

▽ Pinar de la Sierra (campsite)   ▽ Reserva Natural Sierra del Tigre

Cabañas Manatiales de los Amores, located in Villa Manantial; follow Avenida Brasil south from the bus terminal – at the end a road curves round to the right, from where the cabins are well-signposted (☎ & fax 02293/445701; $20 for two people, $40 for four). The *cabañas* are set in a quiet area at the foot of the sierras with basic cooking facilities inside and parrillas outside; conditions within the *cabañas* are pretty cramped. Tandil also has a number of **campsites**: *Camping El Centinela* lies 4km west of town along Avenida Estrada (☎02293/447061; $4 per tent); it's a quiet and attractive wooded site on the road out towards Cerro El Centinela with hot water round the clock and firepits. Log cabins also also available. On Avenida San Gabriel, to the southwest of the Lago del Fuerte (see below), there's the municipal campsite, *Camping Pinar de la Sierra* (☎02293/425370), in a pleasant location at the foot of the sierras.

The Town

Many of the streets in Tandil's attractive town centre are cobbled with stones quarried from the surrounding sierra. Its central square, **Plaza Independencia**, is located on the site of the old fort and is overlooked by the rather grand municipalidad and the **Iglesia del Santísimo Sacramento**. An imposing but somewhat ungainly building, the church was completed only in 1969, forty years after construction began. Best described as neo-Romanesque in style, it was inspired by Paris's Sacré Coeur – hence the unusual elongated domes which top the three towers. The streets surrounding the plaza, in particular 9 de Julio, have a pleasant bustling feel, particularly in the evenings, when they are filled with people out for a stroll, or sitting outside the cafés and ice-cream parlours. To the northwest of the plaza, on the corner of San Martín and 14 de Julio, is one of Tandil's oldest buildings, a simple, white construction which originally functioned as a staging post and which now houses the **Epoca de Quesos** – a kind of delicatessen and bar where you can try local specialities such as salami and cheese. At Chacabuco 357 half a block south of Plaza Independencia, the **Museo de Bellas Artes** (April–Nov 5–8pm; Dec–March 6–9pm; free; ☎02293/432067) puts on temporary exhibitions of works by local artists and has a permanent collection which includes minor works by Berni, Pettoruti and Quinquela Martín, three of Argentina's most famous twentieth-century artists.

To the south, Tandil's streets slope down towards **Parque Independencia**. The park's entrance, on Avenida Avellaneda, is marked by the twin towers of a mock Venetian palazzo while its central wooded hill is topped by a kitsch Moorish castle. A road snakes around to the summit of the hill, from where there's a clear view over the city – not a particularly stunning sight during the day but given a bit of drama at night when the strikingly regular streets of the town are lit up. There's a pleasant bar on the hill, the *Morisco*, which has occasional live music. Heading down the slopes of the park to the east will bring you to **Lago del Fuerte** and **Dique del Fuerte**, a large artificial reservoir built to retain the water which runs off the sierras. You may see the odd person swimming, but a dip in the lake's rather polluted waters is probably best avoided; head instead for the cleaner municipal swimming pools at the southern tip of the lake. Local **bus** #500 runs to the Dique from 9 de Julio.

To the north of the town centre, at 4 de Abril 845, is the **Museo Fuerte Independencia** (April–Nov 3–7pm; Dec–March 4–8pm; $1), a handsome old building housing a staggeringly large collection of artefacts donated by locals. Slightly disorganized, the museum is still a pleasant place to wander round with some interesting curiosities to be seen, such as the poncho worn by **Tata Dios**, a local *curandero* (healer) who was believed to have stoked a bloody revolt in 1871, launched by the disaffected native rural population – many gauchos amongst them – against recent European immigrant settlers. During the revolt, 36 land-owning immigrants were killed and Tata Dios was arrested and imprisoned for provoking the revolt. He was later assassinated in prison – the poncho on display in the museum has a (not terribly visible) blood stain. There's also a good selection of photographs showing the development of the town and some examples of the huge ox-drawn carts or *chatas* used to transport cereals around Argentina; the enormous wheels in the courtyard come from a *chata* and are the largest in the country.

The sierras

Opportunities for independent trekking in **Tandil's sierras** are somewhat limited as much of the area is privately owned. The highest peak here is the **Sierra Las Animas** (504m) to the southeast of the town centre, not far from the end of Avenida Brasil. It's a two-hour scramble over rocks to the top, but the peak lies on private land and you must obtain permission to scale it (ask at the tourist office). Much more visited however, and more accessible, is **Cerro El Centinela**, a small peak in the sierras topped by **El Centinela**, an upright seven-metre rock balanced on an unfeasibly tiny base. To get here, head southwest along Avenida J.M. Estrada, the continuation of Avenida Avellaneda. The signposted track to the Cerro lies to the left, some 5km out of town. There's a **confitería** at the base of the gentle trail which winds to the top; the array of tempting cakes is perhaps best dealt with on your way down. On the way up, a number of gaps in the vegetation afford views over countryside, as well as of the rock itself, which changes shape dramatically according to the angle from which you view it.

Perhaps the best way to explore the region is with the growing number of companies offering **adventure tourism** embracing a range of activities including trekking, riding, abseiling and mountain-cycling. Nido de Condores, Necochea 166 (☎02293/426519; *kron@necsus.com.ar*), organizes mountain-bike rides and trekking as well as walks that follow the old railway lines. If you fancy getting to know the sierras on horseback, contact Gabriel Barletta, Avellaneda 673 (☎02293/427225), who organizes adventurous half-day rides, and regularly takes groups swimming on horseback. Mountain bikes can be rented from Señor Rodríguez at Uriburu 1488 (☎02293/428669).

Several blocks southeast of the Dique del Fuerte, on the corner of Don Bosco and Suiza, lies the **Reserva Natural Sierra del Tigre** (9am–7pm, last entry 6pm; $2, plus $1 per car; ☎02293/423108), a privately run stretch of sierra of some 1.5 square kilometres where you can see indigenous species such as guanacos as well as exotic deer and antelope. The sierra is also home to the tiny marí marí frog, barely the size of a thumbnail and only found here and in Córdoba. The reserve's highest point is **Cerro Venado** (389m), an easy walk along the unsealed road that winds to the top, from where there are good views over the surrounding sierra. Near the entrance to the reserve there is a small zoo housing pumas, grey foxes and ñandúes.

Eating, drinking and nightlife

There are plenty of good **restaurants** in Tandil, most of them within a few blocks of Plaza Independencia. *La Giralda* and *Lo de Martín*, on opposite sides of the intersection of Constitución and General Rodríguez, both do good, reasonably priced parrillada: a generous helping of chorizo, *morcilla*, *chinchulines*, *tripa* and *asado* will set you back as little as $7 a person, though extras such as fries and salad can bump things up a bit. **Vegetarians** should head for *El Jardín de los Frutos*, at Maipú 392. The recently opened *Hípico* at Pinto 636 has a quietly elegant interior and serves up excellent basic pasta at lunchtime and more elaborate dishes such as lamb with mint in the evening; calculate on spending around $15 per person for two courses, plus a bottle of wine. *El Cisne* at Rodríguez 522 provides generous portions of standard Argentinian fare such as *milanesas*. There's a good *tenedor libre*, *La Cascada* at Pinto 736; and for takeaway meals *Rosetta*, at 9 de Julio 328, offers a fifteen percent student discount. For the best **ice cream** in town, follow the locals to *Renzo Junior's* on 9 de Julio between San Martín and Sarmiento.

On warm evenings, you'll find plenty of people sitting outside **bars** such as *Golden* on the corner of 9 de Julio and Pinto or *Liverpool* on 9 de Julio and San Martín; the latter's English-inspired interior comes complete with a red phone box and photos of England, though its waiter service is in the best Argentinian style. For something a bit more traditional, head for the *Bar Firpo* on the corner of 14 de Julio and 25 de Mayo; this charming and friendly place has a beautiful old-fashioned interior which recalls the days when almacenes also functioned as casual bars.

Most **nightclubs** in Tandil are out towards the lake, on Avenida Alvear, since licensing laws prohibit clubs in the centre of town. Established favourites include *Yamó*, at Alvear 410 and *Y Qué*, at Alvear 550; *Y Qué* attracts a slightly older crowd and sometimes has **tango** nights. In the town centre, you may be able to catch live music at the *Viejo Boliche* at 9 de Julio 425.

Listings

Car rental Lotus, 4 de Abril 1510 (☎02293/448007); Tandil Renta Car, 9 de Julio 391 (☎02293/445045). Both charge from $60 a day for the cheapest model, a Fiat 147.

Exchange There are plenty of banks and ATMs around Plaza Independencia and 9 de Julio. Jonestur on San Martín, between 9 de Julio and General Rodríguez, changes travellers' cheques (Mon–Fri 8.30am–1pm & 4.30pm–7.30pm, Sat 9.30am–12.30pm).

Hospital Hospital Municipal, Paz 1406 (☎02293/422010).

Internet Cybercafé Discovery, Belgrano 299 (daily 8am–1pm; $4 per hour; *alonsoma@formared.com.ar*).

Laundry Chacabuco 647.

Post office Correo Argentino, 9 de Julio 455.

Taxis Majestic, Sarmiento 193 (☎02293/427328), or one of the taxis outside the bus terminal (☎02293/422466).

Bahía Blanca and Sierra de la Ventana

The rugged **Sierra de la Ventana** mountain range, 550km southwest of Buenos Aires, is the principal attraction of southern Buenos Aires Province. Running from northeast to southwest for some 100km, the sierra's craggy spine forms an unlikely backdrop to the serene pampa and provides the best opportunities in the province for walking and climbing. The range is named after one of its highest points, the **Cerro de la Ventana**, a 1134-metre peak pierced by a small "window" or ventana; it's located within the **Parque Provincial Ernesto Tornquist**, which is bisected by the RP76, the main highway through the sierras. There are plenty of options for accommodation in the area: as well as a base camp within the park, there are three villages within striking distance of the range, with the **town of Sierra de la Ventana** offering the best options as well as the region's only tourist office. It lies around 30km southeast of the park entrance, along RP72, which branches off RP76. **Villa Ventana** is a quiet wooded village lying at the southern end of the park, just 5km from the park entrance; though it has little tourist infrastructure there's a good campsite and some *cabañas*. Finally, **Tornquist**, 25km west of the park, is primarily an agricultural town but offers a couple of hotels.

A daily bus service runs to Sierra de la Ventana from Buenos Aires, passing through Azul, but if you are making your way down the coast, the easiest way to reach the range is via the port city of **Bahía Blanca**, 687km southwest of the capital. Bahía Blanca is the most important city in the south of the province but of only limited appeal to the tourist. It is however a major transport hub, with numerous planes and buses to major towns in Patagonia and has one of Argentina's best museums, the outstanding Museo del Puerto, whose vibrant display of local history makes this otherwise unexceptional city well worth a detour. Back along the coast, the lively resort town of **Monte Hermoso** is the region's principal balneario, whilst nearby, but smaller, **Pehuén-Có** offers a more tranquil atmosphere, amidst dunes and pine forests.

Bahía Blanca

Sprawling out into the empty pampa like a disjointed patchwork quilt **BAHIA BLANCA** is not the most immediately appealing of cities. Though it's the economic and industrial centre of the south of Buenos Aires Province, with nearly 300,000 inhabitants, it has a rather subdued feel and many Argentinians regard it as not only a bit dull but as synonymous with the military: the country's largest naval base, Puerto Belgrano, lies 20km southeast of town and, during the 1976–83 military dictatorship, the city was the site of one of Argentina's most notorious torture and detention centres, known as "La Escuelita" and chronicled by one of its ex-detainees, Alicia Partnoy, in her book *The Little School: Tales of Disappearance and Survival in Argentina* (1986). Despite this somewhat negative image, the city shouldn't be written off altogether: its transport links with **Sierra de la Ventana**, resorts of the pampa region and major Patagonian cities are a practical plus and, once you head into town, you'll find a spread of handsome – if fairly typical – early twentieth-century architecture and enough modest attractions amongst its parks, museums and galleries to fill a day or so.

Five kilometres southwest of the centre lie the ramshackle but charming cobbled streets of **Puerto Ingeniero White**, a blend of hulking great industrial architecture and faded remnants of the days when its bars and *cantinas* were the raucous centre of social life for the then vibrant port area. At the heart of the area is the fabulous **Museo del Puerto**, an ingenious museum dedicated to recording the history, memories and even recipes of the port's largely immigrant population.

From Bahía Blanca it's an easy journey to the region's main beach resort, **Monte Hermoso** or the nearby, much smaller, village of **Pehuén-Có**.

Some history

Bahía Blanca was founded in 1828 as a fortified settlement on the southern fringes of the as yet unconquered pampa region. Its strategic location at the mouth of a large natural bay proved useful during General Rosas' first campaign against the indigenous inhabitants of the pampa in 1833, since provisions could be sent by ship from Buenos Aires, unloaded at Bahía Blanca and transported to Rosas' troops who were then mounting an attack on Argentina's indigenous inhabitants in the vicinity of the Río Negro, 200km to the south. After Rosas' bloodthirsty but inconclusive campaign ended, Bahía Blanca – still subject to sporadic Indian raids – dug in until General Roca's Conquest of the Wilderness in 1879 all but wiped out the region's remaining indigenous population. With the indigenous threat removed, Bahía Blanca finally dismantled its fortress and embarked on a period of rapid development. The arrival of the railway, in 1884, paved the way for the transformation of the previously isolated settlement into a thriving city with a major port in adjoining Puerto Ingeniero White from where grain was exported to Europe.

Bahía Blanca's glory years were in the early part of the twentieth century, when most of the imposing buildings on its main square, Plaza Rivadavia, were built. By the mid-twentieth century, however, a combination of factors including the declining importance of rail transport, thanks to the newly improved roads, and falling grain exports, due to rivalry from other ports such as Rosario and Quequén, had put a rather premature end to Bahía Blanca's ascendancy. The city's fortunes revived somewhat in the 1970s and 1980s with the development of the Polo Petroquímico Bahía Blanca, the largest petrochemical complex in the country, and the city still has, in Puerto Ingeniero White, the country's most important deep-water harbour.

Arrival, information and accommodation

Bahía's **airport**, the Aerostación Civil Comandante Espora (☎0291/486-0312) is about 15km east of the city; Austral provides a shuttle service to and from the airport. The

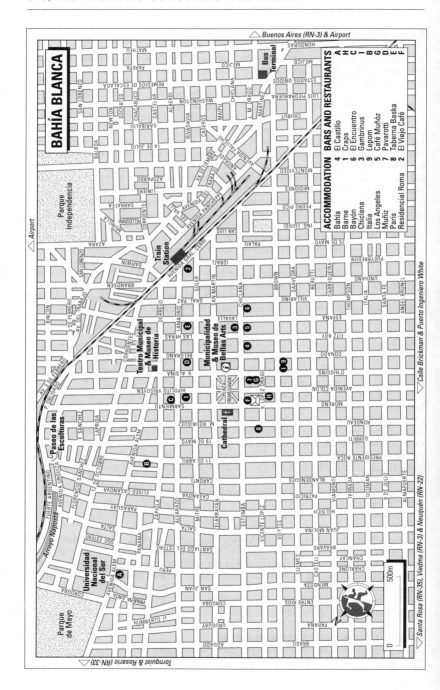

BAHÍA BLANCA

△ Buenos Aires (RN-3) & Airport

△ Airport

Parque
Independencia

Train
Station

Paseo de las
Esculturas

Teatro Municipal
& Museo de
Historia

Municipalidad
& Museo de
Bellas Arts

Cathedral

Parque
de Mayo

Universidad
Nacional
del Sur

Bus
Terminal

ACCOMMODATION	
Bahia	
Barne	
Bayón	
Chiclana	
Italia	
Los Angeles	
Muñiz	
Paris	
Residencial Roma	

BARS AND RESTAURANTS	
El Castillo	4
Craps	1
El Encuentro	6
Gambrinus	3
Lepom	9
Café Muñóz	5
Pavarotti	7
Taberna Baska	8
El Viejo Café	2

A
H
C — I
— B
G
D
E
F

▽ Calle Brickman & Puerto Ingeniero White

▽ Santa Rosa (RN-35), Viedma (RN-3) & Neuquén (RN-22)

△ Torquist & Rosario (RN-33)

500m

0

bus terminal is on Estados Unidos and Almirante G. Brown (☎0291/481-9615), a couple of kilometres east of the centre. Local buses #514 and #517 run to and from the terminal; before boarding you need to buy a card called a *tarquebus* (available from kiosks). A **taxi** to the centre will cost around $4. Bahía Blanca's **train station** is at Av. Cerri 750 (☎0291/452-1168), eight blocks east of the main square. The **tourist office** (Mon–Fri 7.30am–5.30pm, Sat 10am–1pm; ☎0291/455-0110; *www.bb.mun.gba.gov.ar*) is temporarily housed in the municipalidad on Plaza Rivadavia, the main square. Though the staff are very friendly, there isn't a great deal of printed information available.

There's a pretty unexceptional and slightly overpriced selection of **hotels** in town, largely catering to business travellers. A handful of budget hotels can be found opposite the train station, but the area is rather quiet and a bit run-down and you're better off heading to the streets around Plaza Rivadavia, where there's a reasonable choice of places. A slightly depressing feature of most of the hotels in Bahía is the shortage of rooms with exterior windows, particularly at the lower end of the price range. And, if you are bringing a car, bear in mind that you will have to pay extra for parking. There are two **campsites** on the outskirts of the town: *Camping Cala Gogo*, Sarmiento 4000 (☎0291/429511) and *Camping Balneario Maldonado*, Parque Marítimo Almirante Brown (bus #514 from bus terminal) which has a saltwater swimming pool ($5).

Bahía, Chiclana 251 (☎0291/455-0601). A pleasant and comfortable hotel with a confitería downstairs. Parking is in the nearby ACA garage at $6 a day. ⑤.

Barne, H. Yrigoyen 270 (☎0291/453-0864, fax 453-0294). A reasonable mid-range choice; the rooms in this hotel have televisions and fans and the price includes breakfast at the downstairs bar/confitería. ③.

Bayón, Chiclana 487 (☎0291/452-2504). A reasonable budget choice for the centre, although some of the interior rooms are very dingy. A few have private bathrooms. $28; singles with shared bathroom ①.

Chiclana, Chiclana 370 (☎0291/430436) Clean and comfortable, with a television in each room and breakfast included. ACA parking over the road for $6 a day. ④.

Italía, Brown 181 (☎0291/456-2700). One of the best hotels in town; all rooms have a window as well as a television and a private bathroom. There's also a restaurant downstairs, although breakfast is not included in the price of the room. ⑤.

Los Angeles, Chiclana 367 (☎0291/455-6668). Most rooms at this hotel are pretty uninspiring, if acceptably clean and comfortable: the two nicest rooms are at the front with windows onto the street. If you can persuade the friendly owner to rustle up a fan for you in summer (not all rooms have them) it's one of the best deals in the centre. Shared and private bathrooms available. ①.

Muñiz, O'Higgins 23 (☎0291/456-0060, fax 452-3833; *muñiz@hotelnet.com.ar*). An elegant hotel just half a block from Plaza Rivadavia. It has its own garage with parking for $5 a day. ⑤.

Paris, Rondeau 39 (☎0291/456-4818). Slightly smarter than the other budget hotels, with simple but attractive rooms all with their own TV. ③.

Residencial Roma, Av. Gral Cerri 759 (☎0291/453-8500). One of the best options near the train station: basic, clean rooms and very friendly owners. All rooms have a private bathroom. ②.

The City

Despite its straggling outskirts, Bahía's centre is compact, walkable and easy to find your way around. The main square is the distinguished **Plaza Rivadavia**, covering four blocks and bordered by an array of grand public edifices, largely constructed in the slightly ponderous vein of French Second Empire architecture favoured in Argentina at the beginning of the twentieth century – note the sharply pitched roofs and heavy ornamentation characteristic of this style. On the southeastern side of the square, at Alsina 65, you'll find the muncipalidad and, to the right of the main entrance, the tourist office and the **Museo de Bellas Artes** (Tues–Sun 4–8pm; free; ☎0291/455-0110 ex. 2126), with an interesting programme of temporary exhibitions.

The four blocks to the immediate southwest of Plaza Rivadavia were the site of Bahía Blanca's original fort, the Fortaleza Protectora Argentina: a maquette of the fort can be seen in the entrance to the **Museo Histórico Muncipal** (Tues–Sun 3–8pm; free; ☎0291/456-3117), which is located in the basement of the Teatro Municipal, at Dorrego 116, three blocks to the northeast of the Plaza. Housing a run-of-the-mill, if slightly eclectic, collection ranging from archeological remains from the area's indigenous inhabitants – Tehuelche, Querandí, Serrano, Araucano and Mapuche Indians – to pistols and cameras, the museum is worth a quick spin round, but not much more. The theatre itself is a refined, compact building, inaugurated in 1913, which offers a varied musical programmme of folk music, opera, jazz and tango as well as theatre and dance.

Just beyond the theatre, **Avenida Além** leads off to the left. A pleasant tree-lined avenue flanked by an interesting mix of architectural styles which hint at English, French and Italian influence but remain defiantly Argentinian, it is frequented by students from the nearby university. The imposing columned facade of the **Universidad Nacional del Sur** lies between San Juan and Córdoba; in front of the entrance is a pretty two-tiered **marble fountain** sculpted by Argentina's most famous female sculptor, Lola Mora. Despite the sinuous nymphs which encircle the fountain, the sculpture is saved from whimsicality by the boldness of its central motif – a huge, intricately detailed and fleshy bud. Just past the university is the entrance to **Parque de Mayo**, a pleasant leafy park, with a small café. The northeast side of the park leads to the **Arroyo Napostá**, a narrow stream, where you can take a leisurely stroll along a riverside path popular with runners and cyclists. Various simple arched bridges cross over to **Avenida Fuerte Argentino** where there are a number of good restaurants. Following the path to the east brings you to the **Paseo de las Esculturas**, a series of sculptures made using scrap metal, including tracks and pieces of carriages, salvaged from the railway in the early 1990s. Standing out amongst the pieces, all by local sculptors, is an abstract work by "Pájaro" Gómez, an appropriately bird-like design (pájaro means bird in Spanish).

Away from these modest attractions, there's little else to see in the centre of Bahía, though if you want to see a slightly idiosyncratic piece of architectural history you could head southwest from Plaza Rivadavia along Avenida Colón. After ten blocks you come to a bridge over the railway tracks and, on the other side to your left lies the dourly named **Calle Brickman**. Known as the **Barrio Inglés**, the street's semi-detached dwellings were built by the English railway companies to house their workers. Their red-brick facade stands out amongst the more traditionally Argentinian whitewashed and stuccoed buildings and, though their rather French shutters mean that they can scarcely be called typically English, the houses would not look entirely out of place in a south London suburb.

The Puerto Ingeniero White and around

Some 5km southeast of the city centre lies the port area of **Puerto Ingeniero White**. Here you'll find the truly original **Museo del Puerto**, on Calle Guillermo Torres (Sat & Sun: summer 4–8pm; winter 3–7pm; weekday mornings are officially reserved for school visits, but you may be able to see the museum by asking permission from the friendly staff; free; ☎0291/456-4157). Housed in the Great Southern Railway's old customs building, a brightly painted corrugated-iron construction, the museum has for its theme the everyday life of the port and its inhabitants. The collection is composed of a wonderfully eclectic mix of objects, all donated by locals and displayed with verve and humour by the museum's enthusiastic staff. The themed rooms include one dedicated to the sea where the lights suddenly dim for an impromptu simulation of a storm, complete with lightning and wind effects; and a reconstruction of a traditional barber's, complete with a sensor which triggers a recording of Carlos Gardel, Argentina's most famous tango singer. There are also beautiful old coloured photographs of immigrants to the town and an idiosyncratic collection of objects such as the Chilean poet Pablo Neruda's hat, acquired by one of Ingeniero White's inhabitants in exchange for his own hat. The museum also records the oral histories of the area's older inhabitants, publishing fragments in its inventive newspaper and booklets; and every Sunday the kitchens here become a centre of the community when it is transformed into a confitería, where you can try out the cakes made from recipes passed on by local residents, mostly Italian in origin. The museum is active in maintaining the tradition of the **Procession of San Silverio**, patron saint of the fishermen, which takes place on the third Sunday in November. During this typically Italian affair, a statue of the saint is carried out to sea in one of the port's traditional fishing boats before returning to celebrate a mass outside the Museo del Puerto.

The surrounding area is liveliest at weekends, particularly Sundays, when locals end a stroll in one of the neighbouring *cantinas*, or in the museum's confitería. During the week it can seem a bit of a desolate place, though its wooden and corrugated-iron constructions and cobbled streets give it the air of a faded La Boca, and thus a certain charm. Just to the north of the museum, along Guillermo Torres, you can see a well-preserved steam engine, taken out of service only in 1973. To the right, **Puente La Niña** straddles a vast expanse of now somewhat underused railway lines leading to the port terminal. On the other side of the tracks lies the poorer neighbourhood of **Boulevard**, separated from White not only by the bridge but by fierce rivalry between supporters of their respective **football** teams, Huracán and Comercial. To visit the **port** itself, walk to the southern end of Guillermo Torres and then left past the sign for Terminal de Bahía. To your left you may see a line of lorries waiting to unload their cargo; a seemingly simple task dramatically executed as huge trucks drive onto a kind of enormous stationary fork-lift truck and are then raised at a seemingly impossibly steep angle whilst the doors are opened and sunflower seed or grain is tipped out.

To get to Puerto Ingeniero White and the museum take **bus** #500 from Avenida Colón in the centre of Bahía Blanca and get off on the corner of Mascarello and Belgrano, which lies two blocks west of Guillermo Torres.

Eating, drinking and nightlife

Unusually for an Argentine town, decent **eating and drinking** options are a little thin on the ground in Bahía. In the area to the southwest of Plaza Rivadavia there's a handful of places to have a quick coffee or a leisurely breakfast: try *Café Muñoz* on the corner of O'Higgins and L.M. Drago, or *El Viejo Café* at Chiclana 47. The rather unfortunately named *Craps* on the corner of Drago and Colón is a traditional and elegant confitería with Internet access. For snacks, *El Encuentro*, Sarmiento 307, offers a bewildering selection of *empanadas* to take away including *mondongo* (tripe) and *ananá* (pineapple) as well as the more conventional beef and chicken. *Lepom*, 11 de Abril 450, just off Avenida Além, is one of the city's best ice-cream parlours. For something more substantial, welcoming *Gambrinus*, Arribeños 174, is a well-established German restaurant specializing in cold cuts, sandwiches such as liverwurst with pickled cucumber, and sausages served with potatoes or sauerkraut. *Pavarotti*, Belgrano 272, has a good à la carte menu with fresh fish and seafood and also offers quick lunches (*almuerzos rápidos*) for $8 during the week. For traditional **cantinas**, head to Ingeniero White, where you can get excellent seafood at places such as the long-established *Cantina Royal*, Guillermo Torres 4133 (☎0291/457-0348), or the *Cocinas del Puerto* (run by the Museo del Puerto; evenings only, closed Mon) housed in a pretty, brightly coloured corrugated-iron building. Also in Ingeniero White is the newly opened *Micho*, Guillermo Torres 3875 (☎0291/457-0346; closed Mon), on the site of an old Greek taverna, which explains the faded posters of Greece: their delicious rustic fish soup with fennel, leeks and shallots is slightly extortionate at $8 although the abundant bread and roquefort cheese provided on each table help to soften the blow. Alongside the river, you'll find **parrillas** such as *Estancia La Martina*, Fuerte Argentino 719 (☎0291/456-1808), which has outside seating, an *asador criollo* and offers *lechón* and *cordero* as well as beef for around $15 a head. Further up the road, *Zeta Pizzería* on the corner of Fuerte Argentino and Eliseo Casanova, is another pleasant place to sit outside. For Basque food, *La Taberna Baska*, Lavalle 284, is highly recommended.

As far as **bars** and **nightlife** are concerned, the town is a bit on the quiet side. There is, however, the university's lively *Club Universitario* on the corner of Além and San Juan, a good bet if you have a student card – and still worth a try if you haven't. Opposite the university is the friendly *El Castillo* pub, owned by Paraguayan Antonio, which has Mexican Tecate beer. There are a number of pubs and nightclubs on Fuerte Argentino on the other side of the Arroyo Napostá, including popular *La Barraca*, a pub at Fuerte Argentino 655 which also serves food and has pool tables, and *Bahía Bonita*, a trendy nightclub. Bahía also has a number of **cinemas** and **theatres**; try the Teatro Municipal for musical events or Cine Plaza, Alsina 166, and Cine Visual for mainstream Argentinian and foreign movies.

Listings

Airlines Austral, Las Heras and San Martín (☎0291/456-0561); Kaiken, San Martín 108, local 14, Galería Florida (☎0291/455-0963); Lade, Darregueira 21 (☎0291/453-7697); Lapa, Soler 68 (☎0291/454-6566); TAN, Alsina 569 (☎0291/455-2592).

Banks and exchanges There are plenty of banks with ATMs and dollar changing facilities on Chiclana and Rivadavia, including Lloyds Bank on the corner of Chiclana and Fitzroy. The only place to change travellers' cheques is Pullman at San Martín 171 (Mon–Fri 8.30am–5pm), which charges two percent commission and is also a bureau for Moneygrams, similar to Western Union, but slightly cheaper.

Car rental AT, Av. Colón 180 (☎0291/454-3944) and at the airport (☎0291/482-0737); Avis, Vieytes 74 (☎0291/450-1221); Bahía Car, at the airport (☎0291/456-4658); Dollar, Av. Colón 194 (☎0291/456-2526); Localiza, Av. Colón 158 (☎0291/452-8681).

Hospitals Hospital Municipal Leonidas Lucero, Estomba 968 (☎0291/455-8484).

Internet *Craps*, corner of Drago and Colón; Dinet, Além 180.

Laundry Laverap on corner of San Martín and Lavalle.

Post office Correo Central, Moreno 34 (Mon–Fri 8am–8pm, Sat 8am–1pm).

Monte Hermoso and around

Lying 85km east from Bahía Blanca, **MONTE HERMOSO** is the major resort for the far south of Buenos Aires Province. The beach here runs east to west and – consequently it and nearby Pehuén-Có are the only resorts in the province where the sun rises and sets over the sea. This geographical phenomenon and the town's hilly streets aside, there's little to distinguish Monte Hermoso from anywhere else on the coast. It's a passable place to get a taste of Argentinian beach life but has neither the buzz of bigger resorts nor the sleepy charm of quieter places, while its potentially attractive beach is somewhat marred by the dreary urban *costanera* which sprawls for several kilometres along the front. Monte Hermoso's **beaches** are washed by currents from Brazil – adding a few welcome degrees of warmth but also bringing tiny but potent jellyfish which can be a real nuisance, especially when they turn up en masse; you'll know when they're around as most bathers keep out of the sea. Those keen on archeology may be interested to know that three **archeological sites** have been discovered in the vicinity of the town: they consist of human footprints dating from around 5000BC that have been embedded in the sediment of the beach, formerly the site of a lake, some 6km along the beach to the west. More information on the sites can be obtained from the staff at the local **Museo de Ciencias Naturales** on the Avenida Costanera between Avenidas Patagonia and Dufaur (Dec–Feb daily 5pm–9pm; March–Nov Sat & Sun only, same hours); the museum itself consists of a pretty unremarkable collection of locally found dinosaur bones. The town's unusual lighthouse, the **Faro Recalado**, is an openwork structure towering seventy metres above the resort: beyond it lies the quiet, predominantly residential resort of **SAUCE GRANDE** – where there is a municipal campsite and less developed beaches, though little else. About five buses a day run to Sauce Grande from Avenida Faro Recalado, one block east of the bus terminal.

Practicalities

La Acción has a regular **bus service** to Monte Hermoso from Bahía Blanca; in addition there are a number of minibuses (*combis*) which run between the two towns. Combi Bus has an office at Faro Recalado 802 (☎02921/481713; from Bahía Blanca call ☎0291/454-4444), but picks up and puts down more or less where you want; the tourist office (see below) can provide information on other *combi* services. The centrally located **bus terminal** on Faro Recalado is two blocks from the beach and three blocks west of the town's main commercial street, Dufaur. There's a tourist information desk at the terminal (summer only) and left-luggage facilities. The main **tourist office** is around six blocks northeast at Intendente Majluf 700 (Dec–Feb 8am–10pm; March–Nov 8am–2pm; ☎02921/481123).

Accommodation is plentiful and mostly reasonably priced. The friendly *Hotel Plaza* on the corner of Faro Recalado and Patagonia (☎02921/481005; ②) has comfortable rooms and an adjoining restaurant, *Doña Pasta*. The *Hotel Romanos*, Av. Argentina 346 (☎02921/481122; ③), is very close to the bus terminal, but is not particularly good value unless you can get a room at the front with a balcony. The lovely *Appart Italia*, Faro Recalado 250 (☎02921/4815980), with high-ceilinged apartments and kitchen areas, is a good deal at $15 per person if there are a few of you. On the seafront, one of the best options is the quiet *D'Horizonte*, Juan D. Perón 675 (☎02921/481226; ③); run by a friendly family it also has a nice downstairs bar; rooms are slightly spartan but in good condition. There is a supplement of around $2 per person if you want a balcony with a sea view. There are a number of **campsites**, including *Las Dunas*, Av. Alvaro Soldani 257 (☎02921/482177; $5 per person), tucked in a wooded area behind the beach and the plush and highly organized *Camping Americano* (☎02921/481149; Dec–Feb pitches $4–$14, plus $4 per person; rest of year flat fee $5 per person), with numerous facilities including tennis courts, swimming pool, shops, restaurant and a beach bar, around 5km west from the centre. The site is a good hour's walk along the beach or there is a bus from Avenida Faro Recalado which also stops at Las Dunas on the way.

Restaurants include *La Brochette* on the corner of Dorrego and Río Paraná, which has a pleasant rustic atmosphere and a traditional *asador criollo* outside. The large *Cervecería Alemana*, Av. Argentina 129, has a limited *menú económico* at midday for $4: and good but more expensive seafood dishes. The *Pelicano* beach **bar** is a popular spot for watching the sun go down and does reasonable fast food and *picadas*, as well as serving Heineken and Corona beer to those who are tired of Quilmes. The trendy *Margarita* pub is a pretty bar perched up on a hill on the corner of Faro Recalado and Dorrego. Monte Hermoso's **casino** is at Pedro de Mendoza and Río Teuco (10pm–4am).

Pehuén-Có

A small and tranquil village, set amongst pine forests and low dunes, **PEHUÉN-CÓ**, some 20km south of Monte Hermoso, is one of the more attractive southern beach resorts. Its irregular, undulating streets are largely unsealed and the fine five-kilometre beach is separated from the village by dunes. Pehuén-Có is a good place just to relax for a few days – though if you fancy some gentle activity, there's horseriding, from Calle Fragata Sarmiento, to the east of the centre. Bikes can also be rented.

Fournier operates a daily **bus** service to Pehuén-Có from Bahía Blanca, dropping you on the corner of avenidas Almirante G. Brown and 9 de Julio, four blocks east of the resort's main street, Avenida San Martín. There are only a handful of **hotels** in the village; top of the range is the *Cumelcan*, down on the seafront at the end of Av. San

Martín (☎02921/497048; ③). A few blocks back from the beach you'll find the *Hospedaje Anay-Có*, Calle Fragata Sarmiento 839 (no phone; $25). There's a good municipal **campsite** in the village's small forestal reserve, the *Bosque Encantadó* which lies about ten blocks west of Avenida San Martín. Pehuén-Có's simple **eating and drinking** options are mostly based around Avenida Almirante G. Brown; try also *La Barraca* bar and restaurant on the beach one block west of the bottom of Avenida Almirante G. Brown.

Sierra de la Ventana and the Parque Provincial Ernesto Tornquist

Though lacking the soaring grandeur of the Andes, the **Sierra de la Ventana** is still impressive. Compared to the older and gentler Tandilia range to the northeast, these are proper mountains, with peaks tall enough to be shrouded with dark grey clouds in bad weather and to dominate the horizon for some distance. Formed principally from sedimentary rock during the Paleozoic Period, the range is notable for its intensely folded appearance and for its subtle grey-blue and pink hues – thrown into relief in late summer against the yellowing cultivated fields which surround the sierra. Most **walking** and **climbing** activities take place within a relatively small stretch of the sierras, lying between the villages of Sierra de la Ventana, Villa Ventana and Tornquist and mostly contained within the **Parque Provincial Ernesto Tornquist**, which covers some 67 square kilometres and lies to the north and south of the RP76. The park encompasses the most dramatic section of the sierras, including their undisputed star attraction, the **Cerro Ventana**, a 1134-metre peak pierced by a hole, formed by the collapse of a cave, that measures some eight by four metres. On clear days, the hole is visible from the road – although from this distance it appears a rather insignificant phenomenon; you'll get a much more rewarding view from the summit where the phenomenon lives up to its name (ventana means window in Spanish); its jagged edges framing a wonderful view of the surrounding sierra and pampa. Though the harsh, somewhat threatening, peaks of the sierra may appear rather barren, the parque also supports a surprising range of **wildlife** including pumas, foxes, guanacos, armadillos and vizcachas and the endemic copper iguana, named for its distinctive colour. The area around the foot of the sierras is also notable for being one of the last remaining tracts of original pampa grassland, roamed by herds of wild horses.

Lying just outside the park boundaries, 6km to the south of Villa Ventana, is the range's highest peak, **Cerro Tres Picos** (1239m). The peak is less dramatic looking than Cerro de la Ventana, but its height, combined with its distance from the nearest base, makes it a more substantial hike. Unfortunately, the route to the summit passes over private land whose new owners have somewhat curtailed access to the peak. You should check with the tourist office in Sierra de la Ventana before making the hike; it is possible that access will be allowed only via organized trekking excursions – try Geotur at Avenida San Martín 193 (☎0291/491-5355) in Sierra de la Ventana.

Long-distance **buses** from Buenos Aires, Azul and Bahía Blanca pass through the villages of Sierra de la Ventana and Tornquist. They will also drop you at the entrance to Villa Ventana or *Campamento Base*, both of which lie along the RP76. For return journeys to Buenos Aires, it's best to leave from Sierra de la Ventana or Tornquist, so that you can buy your ticket in advance; at busy times (Sun evening & Mon after long weekends) the bus is often full by the time it reaches Sierra de la Ventana. **Trains** also connect Sierra de la Ventana and Tornquist with Bahía Blanca and Buenos Aires. All **tourist information** for the region is dealt with at the tourist office in the village of Sierra de la Ventana. The easiest way of **getting around** the sierra is with your own transport; if you're relying on public transport you'll need to plan carefully: local service Expreso Las Sierras (2 daily) connects the village of Sierra de la Ventana with Tornquist, about 50km northwest, stopping more or less everywhere along the route, including both park entrances and the turn-off to Villa Ventana. Buses leave at 9am and 5pm from Sierra de la Ventana and noon and 7.30pm from Tornquist. Alternatively, you could catch one of the long-distance buses (3 daily) that pass through the villages or take a taxi – try Remis Avenida (☎0291/491-5307) or Radio-Taxi San Bernardo (☎0291/491-5031), both based in Sierra de la Ventana.

Parque Provincial Ernesto Tornquist

There are two **entrances** to the park. Approaching from Buenos Aires or Sierra de la Ventana, the first of these is around 22km from Sierra de la Ventana village, on the right-hand side of the RP76. This is where you'll find the **Centro de Visitantes**, with a good display of photos of the region's flora and fauna: on request slide shows can sometimes be organized. From the Centro de Visitantes you can also visit the **Reserva Natural Integral**, a strictly controlled sector of the park where herds of wild horses can be seen, and a number of caves can be explored. Visits to the reserve are made in your own vehicle, accompanied by a guide and generally leave around 3pm. Most of the park's **treks** are made from the other entrance, around 5km to the west, where there is a helpful *guardaparques'* post which can provide you with a sketchy map to the park's main attractions, as well as indications of distance, direction and estimated duration of the walks. A \$1 entrance fee is charged for hikes from this entrance. A well-marked trail to the summit of **Cerro de la Ventana** leads northeast from the *guardaparques'* post. Access is not permitted after noon to avoid walkers who get into difficulties getting stuck after nightfall, or during bad weather. For this reason, it's best to allow yourself a few days in the sierras to be sure of being able to scale the

Cerro. Though the climb to the summit (5hr return trip; access 8am–noon), undertaken by some 70,000 people a year, is not difficult, conditions can change dramatically and you'd be well-advised to follow the guidelines imposed. There are a couple of **short walks** worth trying around the same area: to the **Piletones** or rock pools, to the northwest of the *guardaparques*' post (2hr; access 8am–4pm), and to the **Garganta Olvidada**, a small waterfall closed in on three sides by jagged shelves of pinkish-grey rock which lies to the northeast (1hr; access 8am–5pm). More dramatic is the **Garganta del Diablo**, a gorge reached on a five-hour guided trek (Sat & Sun 9.30am from the *guardaparques*' post).

Campamento Base (☎ & fax 0291/4910067), a few minutes' walk west of the *guardaparques*' post, and recognizable from the road by its iron gate, is the best place to stay if you want to start out early for the park; as well as a shady **campsite** ($5 per person), the site provides **dormitory accommodation** ($8 per person) and some cabins for up to six people with wood-burning stoves and tables and chairs. You'll need to bring sleeping bags for all accommodation options. Cooking facilities and showers are provided and there is a small shop, though you're best off buying more substantial provisions in either Sierra de la Ventana village or Tornquist. For more luxurious accommodation, head for **Hotel El Mirador** (☎0291/4941338; ④, with breakfast; half and full board also available), just beyond *Campamento Base* on the way to Tornquist; it has some pleasant rooms overlooking the sierra as well as attractive and well-equipped wooden cabins with TV, telephone, fans and cooking facilities where you can do your own cooking. The cabins hold from four to eight people and start at $93 for four people with breakfast. The hotel also has a good restaurant and swimming pool. A few kilometres west along the RP76, towards Tornquist, good home cooking is on offer at the *Ich-Hutu* **restaurant** whose specialities include pasta, and rabbit with peppers and onions in escabeche, a delicious sour-sweet vinaigrette.

Sierra de la Ventana village

Away from its rather drab main street, Avenida San Martín, **SIERRA DE LA VENTANA** is a pretty, quiet little village with sandy lanes, and a good range of accommodation. Though there are some low sierras to the northeast, the village itself is pretty flat, dipping only slightly as the streets peter out towards the streams which practically encircle the village. There's little of note architecturally; nondescript modern buildings predominate although the colourful little train station, with its green iron roof and turquoise shutters gives a happy, holiday feel to the place, whilst, tucked away down leafy lanes, there are some quaint old-fashioned buildings which lend a more rustic air. Divided into several barrios and dissected by both a railway line and the Río Sauce Grande, the village has a rather disjointed layout. Its centre is really **Villa Tivoli**, which lies to the west of the railway tracks; here you'll find most shops and restaurants. By following San Martín east over the railway tracks, you'll come first to **Barrio Parque Golf**, a mostly residential area of curving streets and chalet-style buildings. More appealing is quiet **Villa Arcadia** to the north, separated from Barrio Parque Golf by a bridge over the Río Sauce Grande, and with some attractive accommodation. There are various swimming spots throughout the village, mostly to the north of Avenida San Martín, along the banks of the Río Sauce Grande.

Buses from Buenos Aires and Bahía Blanca arrive via Avenida San Martín and drop you at the small bus terminal on Avenida Roca (☎0291/491-5091), the last turning right off the main avenue before the railway tracks. The **train station**, also with services from Buenos Aires and Bahía Blanca (☎0291/491-5164), is at the intersection of Avenida Roca and San Martín. At Av. Roca 15, practically opposite the terminal, you'll find the friendly **tourist office** (daily 7am–1pm & 3–9pm; ☎0291/491-5303), with maps, accommodation lists and transport details for the area. There is a **post office** at Roca 195 (Mon–Sat 8am–noon), a Visa ATM at the Banco de la Provincia on San Martín 260, and a Laverap **laundry** on Güemes half a block north of San Martín. **Bicycles** are available to rent at Avenida Roca 142.

Good, if slightly expensive, **accommodation** can be found at the *Hotel Atero*, at San Martín and Güemes (☎ & fax 0291/491-5244; ③), within easy striking distance of the bus terminal; all rooms have a private bathroom and television and the hotel has its own restaurant and parking. The pretty and slightly gothic-looking *Hotel Alihuen* (☎0291/491-5074; ③, half board), is on the left at the end of Calle Tornquist, which runs northeast from Avenida San Martín towards the river: the rooms are rather basic but the hotel is set in lovely grounds and has a swimming pool. Top of the range is the comfortable but rather soulless *Hotel Provincial*, on Drago and Bahía Blanca, a couple of blocks south of Avenida San Martín (☎0291/491-5024; ⑦). Facilities include a tennis court, swimming pool and a casino. Quiet Villa Arcadia, on the other side of the river, has some of the best and least expensive accommodation in the village: basic but decent *Hotel Anay Ruca* on E. Rayces (☎0291/491-5191; ②) does good single rates ($13), whilst the enormous and attractive *Pillahuincó*, Av. Rayces 161 (☎0291/491-5151) is set in beautiful grounds and also has a campsite. *La Carolina*, a small **campsite** ($3 per person) opposite the railway tracks in Villa Arcadia – follow Avenida San Martín and bear left over the bridge – also has two great little *cabañas* with kitchen and bathroom for only $8 a person ($15 for one person). There are many other campsites around the village, including some free ones near the municipal pool, which lies north along Diego Meyer, the last road on your left before you reach the railway tracks in Villa Tivoli.

There are few **restaurants** in the village, although there's one very good parrilla, the *Rali-Hue* on San Martín 307, which does an excellent parrillada for two people ($9). The *Windmill*, at San Martín and Tornquist, serves some delicious home-made cakes, including a mouthwatering lemon pie. **Nightspots** are pretty thin on the ground, too, though there's a club popular with locals, *Casuhatí*, in Villa Arcadia, just opposite the bridge.

Geotur, at Avenida San Martín 193 (☎0291/491-5355), organizes **excursions** to nearby **Estancia El Pantanoso** ($7), where aromatic plants and herbs such as lavender and thyme are cultivated.

Villa Ventana

Some 18km northwest of Sierra de la Ventana village, and just off the RP76, lies **VILLA VENTANA**. The village is squeezed between two streams, the Arroyo de Las Piedras and the Arroyo Belisario, and its chief appeal lies in its dense forestation and rambling lanes. Laid-back to the point of lethargy, it makes a relaxing base for a day or two. Though small, the village has an elongated shape which makes a fair bit of walking inevitable. Orientating yourself, however, is fairly straightforward: the main thoroughfare, Avenida Cruz del Sur, runs north–south through the village from the access road and is crossed by secondary lanes which run roughly east to west for several blocks on either side. The village's perimeter is demarcated by calles Belisario and Las Piedras, which run alongside the two streams.

There are plenty of **cabañas** available for rent in the village, although they tend to be a bit on the expensive side. *Cabañas Explorar*, Gorrión and De Las Piedras (☎0291/491-0062; *explorar@teletel.com.ar*; ⑤–⑦) offers luxurious wooden cabins which sleep from two to eight people; all come with television and kitchen. The site also offers **excursions** into the sierras in jeeps or on horseback. The municipal **campsite** (☎0291/491-0014; $4 per person) is located on a pleasant woody spot by the river, where you can fish or bathe, and has good facilities including a grocery store. There are a number of teahouses in the village, including the lovely *Heidi* (daily 3pm–10pm; ☎0291/491-0020), whose scrumptious home-made cakes are well worth the trek to the southern end of Calle Curumalal. The friendly owner is also a good source of information on the surrounding area. There is a *locutorio*, the Cedro Azul (☎0291/491-0074; *villaluis@hotmail.com*), at the entrance to the village on the corner of Cruz del Sur and Canario. **Internet** facilities are available and the owner may be able to provide information on *cabañas* to rent.

Tornquist

A sleepy agricultural town, **TORNQUIST** is another possible stopover if you're heading to the sierras from Bahía Blanca. Its regular grid of streets is centred around an attractive wooded central plaza which is notable for being one of the few – possibly the only – squares in Argentina to have its church, the pretty red-tiled **Iglesia Santa Rosa de Lima**, at its centre rather than on one of the surrounding streets. The church's simple rough-stone construction and plain Gothic windows give it a Northern European feel – rather appropriately, since the church was built by the town's founder, Ernesto Tornquist, a businessman and landowner of German descent. A somewhat severe-looking statue of Tornquist, who died in 1908, stands at the entrance to the plaza. The other modest attraction here is a small artificial **lake** populated by ducks and geese.

All long-distance **buses** arrive at the La Estrella office on Calle Güemes, where you can also get details of local transport through the sierra region.The **municipalidad** lies on the northern side of the plaza, on Avenida Sarmiento (☎0291/4941075); there's no properly designated **tourist office** but you should be able to pick up a map of the town here. There are only two **hotels** in town: the *Hotel Central*, 9 de Julio 242 (☎0291/494-0035; ③, single ①), has a rather dingy entrance, but offers clean, comfortable rooms, with good showers; and the *Hotel San José*, Güemes 132 (☎ & fax 0291/494-0152; ③, single ②), a more appealing option with prettier rooms, TV and central heating. For **pizzerias** and **parrillas** head to Güemes, two blocks south of the plaza – one of the best is the pizzería, *Buon Piaccere*, on the corner of Güemes and 9 de Julio. There are telephone cabins on the corner of calles Tornquist and Bartolomé Mitre, one block south of the plaza, and a Banco de la Nación with an ATM on its southwestern corner.

Southwest from Buenos Aires

Heading **southwest from Buenos Aires**, towards La Pampa Province and Patagonia, the RN5 cuts through a swathe of pampa – some of Argentina's richest farmland, though generally of little interest to the tourist. You could quite comfortably head southwest without stopping at all, though there are three towns within the first 160km that could be treated as either brief stopovers or, in the case of the first two, as day-trips from Buenos Aires. At the very beginning of the RN5, **Luján**, 68km west of the capital, is Argentina's most important religious site, thanks to its vast basilica, built to house the country's patron saint, the Virgin of Luján. Some 30km southwest, **Mercedes** stands out thanks to its attractive town centre and authentic pulpería, largely untouched since the nineteenth century. **Chivilcoy**, an otherwise unremarkable agricultural town another 60km along the RN5, is worth visiting for its charming traditionalist museum, El Recreo. Beyond Chivilcoy, you'd be pushed to find much of interest in the rather dreary agricultural towns along the RN5, though if you do find yourself stuck, all of them offer a handful of hotels and restaurants.

Luján

Officially founded in 1755 on the site of a shrine containing a tiny ceramic figure of the Virgin, **Luján**, some 70km west of Buenos Aires, is now one of the major religious centres in Latin America. The **Virgin of Luján** is the patron saint of Argentina, Paraguay and Uruguay and the epic basilica erected in her honour in 1887 in Luján attracts around five million visitors a year. This soaring neo-Gothic edifice is one of the most imposing – though not perhaps one of the most beautiful – churches in Argentina. It's perhaps more interesting, though, as a huge machine dedicated to perpetuating the cult of the virgin, the centrepiece of a town which seems designed as a kind of antechamber to her sanctuary.

Luján also makes much of its almost accidental role in various events in Argentine **history**. In 1806, Viceroy Sobremonte stopped by when fleeing from the British invasions of that year and left the city's revenues in the building now known as the Casa del Virrey, before carrying on to Córdoba. The money was soon captured by the British, who took it to London, from where the money was never returned. Somewhat fittingly, the two leaders of the invasion, General Beresford and Colonel Pack, were later incarcerated in Luján's cabildo. Various documents and objects relating to these events are exhibited in the town's other major attraction, the vast **Complejo Museográfico Enrique Udaondo**, a kind of multiplex museum with an important historical section as well as Argentina's largest transport museum.

Away from the museums and the basilica, all grouped around the town's central square, Luján is pretty much like any other provincial town. It has its elegant early twentieth-century town houses and its slightly less elegant modern constructions. The town is actually quite large, with around 90,000 inhabitants, but its identity seems strangely subsumed by the Goliath in its midst. That said, Luján has a leafy riverside park, plenty of picnic spots and couple of decent campsites though its hotels and restaurants have little of the charm of nearby San Antonio de Areco (see p.195). A notable exception is the town's highly rated restaurant, *L'Eau Vive* which, in keeping with its location, is run by nuns.

If you want to get a real flavour of Luján in full religious swing, you should visit at the weekend, when seven or eight Masses are held a day – but, unless you want to take part, try to avoid visiting during the annual pilgrimages, when the town becomes seriously full. The major **pilgrimages** take place on October 5, when up to a million young people walk here from Buenos Aires; May 8, the day of the Coronation of the Virgin; and December 8 when smaller, informal pilgrimages mark the Day of the Immaculate Conception.

Arrival, information and accommodation

There are regular buses to Luján from Buenos Aires, arriving at Luján's **bus terminal** on Avenida Nuestra Señora de Luján 600 (☎02323/420040), a couple of blocks north of the town's central square, Plaza Belgrano. There are also frequent trains from Buenos Aires (Once), terminating at Luján's **train station**, a couple of kilometres southeast of the centre at Avenida España and Belgrano. The **tourist office** (Mon–Fri 8am–2pm; ☎02323/420453) is housed in a building known as the Casa de la Cúpula, which stands on the riverbank between Lavalle and San Martín, one block west of the Plaza Belgrano.

Though there are plenty of hotels in the city, decent, reasonably priced **accommodation** is pretty thin on the ground. The hotels around the bus terminal are mostly pretty seedy and not even a very good deal; you'd probably be better off heading to the streets to the east of the basilica, where there are a few acceptable mid-range options. One of the best places near the terminal is the *Biarritz*, on Lezica and Torrezuri 717(☎02323/421230; ④), one block south of the terminal. The simple but reasonable rooms all have air conditioning and cable TV; parking and breakfast are included. In the centre, the suggestively named *Eros*, on San Martín 129 (☎02323/420797; ④), is not, as you might imagine, an *albergue transitorio*. The hotel's rather cramped rooms are made even more cell-like by the lack of external windows, but they are very spruce and have a television and phone. Just round the corner, at 9 de Julio 1054, *La Paz* (☎02323/424034; ③) is one of Luján's oldest hotels, offering airy rooms with fans and

TV. There's also a pretty garden area overlooked by the towers of the basilica. Two blocks east of Plaza Belgrano, there's *Los Monjes*, at Francia 981 (☎ & fax 02323/430200; ⑤) with attractive decent-sized rooms, a good breakfast of croissants, cakes and fruit plus a swimming pool and free parking. Luján's newest hotel is the *Hoxon*, at 9 de Julio 760 (☎02323/429970 *hoxon@impsatl.com.ar*, ⑤). The rather flowery rooms may not be to everyone's taste but they are comfortable and the hotel has an outdoor pool, sunbathing area and a gym. Parking and a substantial breakfast are included and singles are priced at exactly half the double rate.

Some visitors to Luján set up camp informally around the river, but there are also a couple of organized **campsites** on the way out of town. Located just outside, on the RN7, *El Triángulo*, at RN7 Km69,500 (☎02323/430116; $4 per person), is a reasonable wooded campsite which has showers, security and a picnic area. *El Triángulo* is about five blocks northwest of the bus terminal; follow Avenida Nuestra Señora de Luján back out of town and turn left at the main access to the town – the campsite is just over the bridge, on the banks of the Río Luján, and charges $4 per person. Further afield there's *Huellas de la Naturaleza*, Camino a Carlos Keen Km0,800 (☎02323/434972; *huellas@abaconet.com.ar*), a kind of educational nature park with a very well-equipped campsite – complete with all the usual facilities, plus football pitches, swimming pools, volleyball courts and a restaurant at weekends – and **cabañas** for up to four people with kitchen and TV. There's a $6 entry fee to the park; *cabañas* are $45 with private bathroom, $35 without, while tents can be pitched for $8 per person per day (no entry fee required). *Huellas de la Naturaleza* is located just after *El Triángulo*, 800m along the first turning to the right off the RN7, signposted Carlos Keen. Local bus "El Pullmita" #305 from Luján's bus terminal (8 daily between 6am and 10pm) takes you to the park entrance; a taxi will cost around $4.

The Town

It would be perverse to visit Luján without taking a look at the Virgin – and, at busy times, all you need to do to get there is follow the flow. The town's main drag, the Avenida Nuestra Señora de Luján, rolls up like a Tarmac carpet to the door of the **Basílica**, at the far end of Luján's main square, Plaza Belgrano. The Avenida, which links the basilica with the bus terminal, three blocks north, is lined by stalls selling Virgin paraphernalia. Manned by official-looking white-coated vendors, the stalls get ever thicker on the ground as you head down the avenida and by the time you reach the basilica, the whole place seems awash with candles, clocks and key rings emblazoned with the Virgin's image. **Plaza Belgrano** itself is a wide, rather bare expanse of paving slabs adorned only by an equestrian statue of General Belgrano. Away from the plaza, such minimalism gets short shrift as the faux-colonial arcade which flanks Avenida Nuestra Señora de Luján slugs it out with the neo-Gothic basilica in a battle of architectural pastiches. The **Complejo Museográfico** is located in various mustard and white colonial buildings – most notably the cabildo – around the north and west of the plaza.

To the east of the basilica lies Luján's commercial and administrative quarter, centred on calles San Martín and Bartolomé Mitre, which connect Plaza Belgrano to **Plaza Colón**, site of the municipalidad. To the west lies Parque Ameghino, located on the banks of the Río Luján and containing restaurants, amusement arcades and picnic areas.

THE BASÍLICA DE NUESTRA SEÑORA DE LUJÁN

Begun in 1887 but not actually finished until 1937, the **Basílica de Nuestra Señora de Luján** (daily 7.30am–8pm; Mass Mon–Sat 8am, 9am, 10am, 11am, 5pm & 7pm, Sun 8am, 9am, 10am, 11am, 12.30pm, 4pm, 5pm & 7pm; guided visits hourly 10am–noon & 2–6pm; $3) is a mammoth neo-Gothic edifice, built using a pinkish stone quarried in Colón, Entre Ríos. A heavy, some might say heavy-handed, French influence is evident

– reflecting the nationality of the basilica's architect, Ulderico Courtois. In true Gothic style, everything about the basilica points heavenwards, from its remarkably elongated twin spires, which stand 106 metres tall, to the acute angles of the architraves surrounding the three main doors. At the very centre of the facade, a large circular or rose stained-glass window depicts the Virgin. Sixteen statues, representing the twelve apostles and the four evangelists, sit within niches to either side of the window.

Despite its imposing presence, it's what goes on inside the basilica that's most likely to catch your attention. Composed of a grand central nave, 30m long, and two lateral naves, the relatively restrained interior of the basilica simmers with hushed activity. Entering the place through one of the heavy bronze doors is a bit like stepping on to a religious conveyor belt as you get caught up in a seemingly endless stream of pilgrims, some on their hands or knees, others in wheelchairs, making their way to the **Camarín de la Vírgen**. Up to eight Masses a day take place in the basilica and the aisles are lined with confessional boxes, where privacy seems to have been abandoned as priests sit expectantly with their doors open, bathed in a pool of light. This public spectacle has probably come about in recognition of the symbolic nature of making a confession in Luján – although, given the steady flow of confessors, you might wonder if the busy priests haven't just grown bored of sitting in the dark. To visit the Virgin herself, simply follow the crowds along the aisles and up the stairs to the chamber behind the main altar.

The **crypt** below the basilica harbours reproductions of Virgins from all over the world, but particularly from Latin America and Eastern Europe: a rather quick-fire guided tour in Spanish (same hours as basilica; $2.50, combined ticket $4) explains the significance behind each icon.

A TINY MIRACLE: THE VIRGIN OF LUJÁN

In 1630, a Portuguese ship docked in Buenos Aires on its way back from Brazil. Amongst its cargo was a simple terracotta image of the Virgin made by an anonymous Brazilian craftsman. The icon had been brought to Argentina at the request of a merchant from Sumampa, Santiago del Estero, and, after unloading, it was transported by cart along the old Camino Viejo (now the RN8) towards the estancia of its new owner. The cart paused in the outskirts of Luján, from where, the story goes, it could not be moved. Various packages were taken down from the cart in an attempt to lighten the load – all to no avail until the tiny package containing the Virgin was removed. In the time-honoured tradition of miracles, this was taken as a sign that the Virgin had decided on her own destination. A small chapel was built and the first pilgrims began to arrive. Over the centuries, the Virgin has actually been moved, although according to legend it took three attempts and several days of prayers to move her the first time. In 1872, Luján's Lazarist order – a religious body founded in Paris in 1625 with the emphasis on preaching to the rural poor – was entrusted with the care of the Virgin by the Archbishop of Buenos Aires. In 1875, a member of the order, Padre Jorge María Salvaire, was almost killed in one of the last Indian raids on Azul. Praying to the Virgin, he promised that if he survived he would promote her cult, write her history and, finally, build a huge temple in her name. Salvaire survived and the foundation stone to the basilica was laid on his initiative in 1887.

The original terracotta Virgin is now barely recognizable: a protective bell-shaped silver casing was placed around the image in the late nineteenth century. Sky-blue and white robes were also added, reflecting the colours of the Argentine flag, as well as a Gothic golden surround, in keeping with the style of the new basilica. Only the hands and face of the original are now visible. Even if you don't visit Luján itself, you're likely to have seen her: the Virgin is the patron saint of public transport and stickers with her image can be seen on almost every bus's rear windscreen in Buenos Aires.

THE COMPLEJO MUSEOGRÁFICO ENRIQUE UDAONDO

The **Complejo Museógrafico Enrique Udaondo**, on the western side of Plaza Belgrano (Wed–Fri 11.15am–5pm, Sat & Sun 10.15am–6pm; $1) claims to be the most important museum complex in South America. However questionable that claim may be, it's certainly one of the continent's biggest. Its principal collections are those contained within the Museo Histórico Colonial, housed in the Casa del Virrey and the cabildo on the western side of Plaza Belgrano, and the Museo de Transportes, on the northern end of the plaza, between Avenida Nuestra Señora de Luján and Lezica y Torrezuri.

The **Museo Histórico Colonial** is rather misleadingly named, since its exhibits actually cover a much wider period. Though there are some notable pieces, the museum suffers from a confusing layout and lack of explanatory material; with the exception of the stunning collection of colonial silverware, you really need a certain familiarity with Argentine history to make sense of it all. There's a small display on Luján's history in the Casa del Virrey, but the museum's principal collection is accessed via the **Cabildo** next door, a two-storey galleried building dating from 1772. Amongst its other functions, the cabildo has served as a school and a prison, whose most notable inmate was General Bartolomé Mitre, incarcerated here in 1874 after his failed rebellion against the newly elected President Avellaneda. The leaders of the short-lived British invasion, General William Beresford and Colonel Dennis Pack, were also held in the cabildo after their surrender in August 1806. Trophies captured during the quashing of the invasion, notably the staff of the 71st Highland Regiment, are prominently displayed in the museum's first room, dedicated to the British invasions and immediately to your right as you enter. Beyond the entrance, an internal door leads onto a pretty courtyard with a marble well in the centre and an elegant wooden balustrade around the first floor of its green and white walls. No doubt it all looked a little less idyllic when the courtyard's cells, to the left as you enter, were actually occupied.

Beyond the patio, an outbuilding dedicated to the gaucho also includes a reconstruction of Ricardo Güiraldes' study in his estancia, *La Porteña*, on the outskirts of San Antonio de Areco (see p.199). The neighbouring **pavilion** houses a rather dry collection of photographs and documents relating to Argentina's presidents although if you've a fondness for political ephemera you might be interested in the cigarette packets and razorblades emblazoned with the image of Yrigoyen – Argentina's first Radical president, elected in 1916 after the introduction of universal male suffrage. Double back on yourself to return to the **main building**, where the museum continues with rooms dedicated to the Federal Period, with numerous examples of the *divisas federales* or ribbons, whose use was imposed by the bloodthirsty and theatrical dictator Rosas. Imprinted with variations on the slogan "death to the savage, disgusting and filthy Unitarists", the ribbons were worn to show loyalty to the Federalist cause and, presumably, to strike fear into the hearts of the Unitarists. Heading beyond these rooms brings you to one of the museum's high points: the Muñiz and Lezica collections of Hispanic art. The first of these is particularly impressive for its fine examples of silverware from Alto Perú. Most of the items, such as the huge votive lamp, were destined for religious use but there are domestic items, too: interestingly the extensive use of silver in Peru at this time was largely due to the prohibitive cost of porcelain. Look out for the stunning Mexican Rococo "Bedroom of the child Virgin with prophets, angels and cherubs", an intricate and delicate portrayal of the Virgin in bed constructed of silver, wood, wax, bone and cloth.

The **Museo de Transportes**, Argentina's largest transport museum, offers less a chronology of the evolution of transport than a display of some of Argentina's most historically significant planes, trains and carriages. The museum's two most important exhibits are *La Porteña*, Argentina's first steam locomotive whose first journey, between Plaza Lavalle and Floresta in Buenos Aires, took place in 1857; and the *Plus Ultra*, the hydroplane with which Ramón Franco, brother of General Franco, made the first crossing of the South Atlantic in 1926. The museum also has a large collection of carriages used by historical figures such as Belgrano and San Martín, including Rosas' Berlin carriage, painted a deep Bordeaux red – and allegedly pulled by horses of the same colour – in keeping with the tyrant's passion for that colour. There's also a staggeringly ornate horse-drawn funeral carriage dating from the late nineteenth century, as well as an example of the rather racy "Kaiser Carabela" motor hearse which replaced it. Two of the museum's more unusual exhibits are Gato and Mancha, the Argentine horses used by Tschiffely, a Swiss explorer who rode from Buenos Aires to New York in the 1930s, and preserved – albeit in a rather motheaten state – for posterity. Gato and Mancha were *caballos criollos*, Argentina's national breed, descended from the first horses brought by the conquistadores and characterized by a sturdy elongated body, a smooth gait and – as Tschiffely's trip demonstrated – an amazing hardiness. Tschiffely's book recounting the trip is available in English as *From Southern Cross to Pole Star* or in Spanish as *Gato y Mancha*.

Eating and drinking

There are plenty of **eating** options, mainly parrillas geared up to feed hungry pilgrims, on Avenida San Martín, whilst just beyond the entrance to Parque Ameghino you'll find *La Recova*, a restaurant offering pleasant outside seating and a simple, reasonably priced menu which includes pasta. *Berlín*, on San Martín between 9 de Julio and Francia, offers a rather underwhelming mixture of fast food and Germanic fare, principally sausages and sauerkraut, though you might find their wide selection of flavoured hot chocolates and cakes more inspiring; it's also a pleasant spot to sit for a drink in the evening. Luján's most famous restaurant is a long way out of the centre: *L'Eau Vive* at Constitución 2112 (☎02323/421774; closed Sun eve & all Mon), is fifteen blocks east along Avenida San Martín from Plaza Colón and most easily reached by taxi. The restaurant's main claim to fame is that it is run exclusively by nuns; and the cooking – a traditional European menu with an emphasis on rich meat dishes – is generally excellent. A reasonably priced tourist menu is available for $11.

Mercedes and around

Tranquil and cultured **MERCEDES**, 30km southwest of Luján, was founded in 1752 as a fortress to protect Luján from Indian attacks. It's a well-preserved provincial town, and easy to find your way around thanks to the numbered street system – odd numbered streets run north–south and even numbers east–west. Mercedes' main drag is Avenida 29; its main square, **Plaza San Martín**, which lies on the eastern side of Avenida 29, between calles 24 and 26, is not especially remarkable, despite its grand Italianate Palacio Municipal and large Gothic Basílica Catedral Nuestra Señora de Mercedes. It does, however, feel like a real hub of activity – especially in the evening, when locals fill the tables which spill out of its various inviting confiterías.

Aside from just wandering around the town itself, Mercedes' main draw is the **pulpería**, some twenty blocks north of Plaza San Martín, at the end of Avenida 29. Pulperías, essentially provisions stores with a bar attached, performed an important social role in rural Argentina and enjoy an almost mythical status in gaucho folklore. The sign outside Mercedes' pulpería, known locally as Cacho's place ("lo de Cacho"), claims it to be the last pulpería, run by the last pulpero – quite possibly a justifiable claim. The gloomy interior, which has hardly changed since the pulpería opened its doors in 1850, harbours a collection of dusty bottles, handwritten notices and gaucho paraphernalia: it doesn't require much imagination to conjure up visions of the knife fights which the current owner claims to have witnessed in his youth. To get to the pulpería, best visited in the evening for a beer and a couple of *empanadas*, take the local bus which runs towards the park from Avenida 29. A couple of blocks beyond the last stop, the road becomes unsealed and on the left-hand corner you'll see the simple white building, a sign saying pulpería painted on its side.

Mercedes' **bus terminal**, served by daily buses from the capital, is located to the south of the town centre from where it's a twenty-minute walk to Plaza San Martín. There's an infrequent local bus from the terminal to the centre, so if you don't fancy the walk you may be better off taking one of the terminal **taxis** (☎02324/433944). The very friendly **tourist office**, on the corner of Avenida 29 and Calle 26 (Mon–Fri 7am–7pm, Sat 10am–1pm, Sun 10.30am–1.30pm & 3–6pm; ☎02324/426738; *mercedesweb.com.ar*), doesn't have much in the way of printed information, but the staff are enthusiastic and knowledgeable, and can provide you with a slightly sketchy map of the town. **Accommodation** is not plentiful, but what there is is agreeable enough. A bit of nego-tiating may make the modern *Gran Hotel Mercedes* on the corner of Avenida 29 and Calle 16 (☎ & fax 02324/422528; ④) surprisingly affordable; the comfortable, slightly garish rooms have air conditioning and TV, while facilities include a large restaurant and bar area; or you could try the *Hotel Torino*, Calle 12 no. 644 (☎02324/420916; ③) with simple rooms around a central courtyard. There's a municipal campsite in the park on the edge of town; take any local bus from Avenida 29: note that Mercedes hosts a motorbike rally at the end of March, which is the only time you might have trouble find-ing space to pitch your tent here. **Eating** and **drinking** options include *El Aljibe*, on Calle 16 no. 542, a good parrilla in an attractive old town house, and *La Vieja Esquina*, a charming traditional bar on the corner of calles 25 and 28, which also sells deli-catessen produce. Of the confiterías around the plaza, good for coffee, sandwiches and *minutas*, one of the nicest is *La Recova*, the only building in the square to retain an old-fashioned arcade.

Some 15km back up the RN5 towards Luján, the small village of **TOMÁS JOFRE** is a popular weekend day-trip for Porteños, primarily for its traditional restaurants includ-ing the long-established *Silvano* (closed Mon & Tues) and *Fronteras*, with delicious home-made pastas including *sorrentinos* filled with mozzarella, ricotta and ham. A pop-ular souvenir is locally produced salami – Mercedes is the national capital of salami.

Chivilcoy and around

You wouldn't want to spend a lot of time in **CHIVILCOY**, some 60km south of Mercedes on the RN5, but the town is worth a brief detour for the beautifully restored **El Recreo**, a traditional almacén situated to the northeast of town on the old Camino Real, which provided access from Buenos Aires to the west of the province. The town itself, an important farming centre at the heart of the dairy belt, has a rather sprawling, industrial feel, though its centre is attractive enough and dotted with some quite pretty little plazas. Should you get stuck, there are at least a decent number of hotels and an estancia not far out of town.

Chivilcoy's absolutely regular grid of streets is centred around the town's most attractive feature, the particularly large and lush **Plaza 25 de Mayo**, eleven blocks southwest of the bus terminal, to which it is connected by Calle Pellegrini. The town's four major avenues – Soares, Ceballos, Sarmiento and Villarino – converge on the main square. Around fifteen **bus services** a day run from Buenos Aires and Mercedes to Chivilcoy. There's also one **train** a day from Buenos Aires (Plaza Once), arriving at Chivilcoy's train station, thirty blocks southeast of the plaza along Avenida Mitre. There are various **taxi** companies, including Remis Soares on the corner of Avenida Soares and the plaza (☎02346/433472). There's no tourist office, but the municipalidad, on the southwestern side of the plaza, may be able to rustle up a map.

Hotels, mostly catering to business travellers, are not hard to come by: one of the nicest in town is the *Iglesias*, Pueyrredón 115 (☎ & fax 02346/422322; ③), which has slightly erratic plumbing but is otherwise clean and comfortable with a television in each room, private bathrooms and a good breakfast. Alternatively, you could try the *Gran Hotel* at Sarmiento 125 (☎02346/430700; ⑤), which has a good restaurant and more upmarket rooms. The least expensive hotel is the *Centro*, Necochea 34 (☎02346/422444; ③), with simple but acceptable rooms, though you should find that rates are generally negotiable in all the hotels. Some 18km southeast of town, along an unsealed road off the RP30, is *Estancia La Rica* (☎02346/491246; ⑦, full board). All the more appealing for looking as though it could do with a lick of paint, the estancia has a long galleried *casco* and a surprisingly tropical garden, with a small swimming pool. Horseriding is also available. The estancia takes its name from the pretty nearby village of *La Rica* which, with its abandoned train station, exemplifies the declining fortunes of Argentina's rural settlements. To get to *La Rica*, or the "Estancia de López" as it is often referred to locally, you'll need to take a taxi from Chivilcoy.

As far as eating goes, Chivilcoy has a less convivial atmosphere than Mercedes. For drinks and snacks there's a pretty uninspiring bunch of **cafés** around the main plaza, the best of which is *La Perla*, on the corner of Villarino and 9 de Julio. For more substantial fare, *El Pino*, at Ceballos 157, offers a pleasant atmosphere and a reasonably priced menu with standard dishes such as grilled chicken with lemon; *Don Pedrín*, at Av. Soares 83, is a fairly similar affair. Out on the RN5, near the entrance to the town, there are a number of popular parrillas, dishing up hunks of meat to passing motorists and locals alike.

El Recreo

Essentially a private museum of ephemera and the rituals of provincial Argentine life, **El Recreo** is a carefully restored almacén and bar located just outside Chivilcoy, along the unsealed Avenida de la Tradición (formerly the Camino Real). The museum contains an enormous collection of old adverts, bottles and siphons, cigarette packets and matches as well as oddities such as a bottle casing made from a cow's udder. The museum's charm, however, lies less in its collection of objects than in the way the whole place has been put together to recreate a humble yet absolutely characteristic piece of Argentina's past. Surrounding El Recreo, there's a beautifully tended garden with a huge palm tree, roses and pomegranates and a stableyard, still in use. To gain access to the museum you'll need to arrange an appointment with the owner, Pampa Cura, who runs a leather and silverware shop on Pellegrini 75 (☎02346/422319) in the town centre. Entry is free, though contributions to the museum's upkeep are welcomed.

Santa Rosa and around

SANTA ROSA promotes itself as the gateway to Patagonia, and indeed the only real reasons to visit La Pampa Province's capital, at the southwestern end of the RN5, are to break a long journey to or from Patagonia, or to use it as a base from which to visit the **Parque Nacional Lihúe Calel**, the province's major attraction, dominated by low granite sierras. Parque Luro, 35km to the south, is much less wild than the national park but it offers a few gentle walks and opportunities for bird-watching. Santa Rosa is well connected to Buenos Aires, Neuquén, Bahía Blanca and Bariloche by public transport – but connections to the rest of the province from the town are less frequent and require a bit of planning.

The City

A rather squat modern city of around 80,000 inhabitants, **Santa Rosa** is sited on the western fringes of the wet pampa. Its predominantly flat and somewhat exposed position

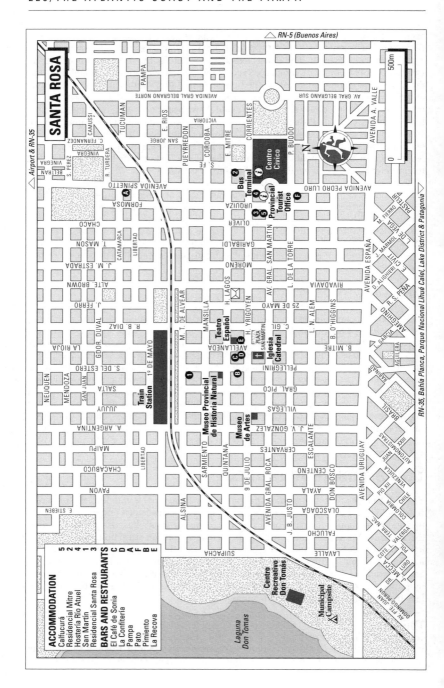

RN-5 (Buenos Aires)

SANTA ROSA

Airport & RN-35

500m

RN-35, Bahía Blanca, Parque Nacional Lihué Calel, Lake District & Patagonia

Centro Civico

Bus Terminal

Provincial Tourist Office

Train Station

Museo Provincial de Historia Natural

Teatro Español

Iglesia Catedral

Museo de Artes

Plaza San Martín

Centro Recreativo Don Tomás

Municipal Campsite

Laguna Don Tomás

ACCOMMODATION
Calfucurá   C
Residencial Mitre D
Hostería Río Atuel A
San Martín   F
Residencial Santa Rosa B

5
2
4
1
3

BARS AND RESTAURANTS
El Café de Sonia
La Confitería
Pampa
Pato
Pimiento
La Recova

E

means that it receives the full brunt of the pampa's harsh winters and its bakingly hot summers. It's primarily a business and administrative centre – albeit with a friendly, small-town feel – and offers little in the way of conventional sightseeing.

Santa Rosa has two centres, which lie some eight blocks apart. The recently constructed **centro cívico**, site of the province's governmental offices, lies immediately south of Santa Rosa's busy bus terminal; the surrounding streets are also where you'll find the majority of the town's hotels, and many of its restaurants. Apart from this, though, there's little to keep you in this area. Head west instead, across busy Avenida Luro, the town's main north–south axis, towards Santa Rosa's true town centre, which has a much more relaxed atmosphere. On the corner of Avenida Luro and Avenida General J.A. Roca, and well worth a visit, you'll find the **Mercado Artesanal** (Mon–Fri 7am–8pm, Sat 8am–noon), a regional crafts outlet run by the provincial government. The market sells leather goods and kitchen utensils carved from the reddish-brown caldén tree – whose distinctive spreading branches can be seen throughout the province. The outlet's most striking products, however, are the hand-woven pampa textiles dyed with vivid aniline dyes. More subtle hues are obtained from natural substances extracted from indigenous shrubs. One of the plants, piquillín, is also used to make syrup (*arrope de piquillín*).

Following Avenida Roca eight blocks west will bring you to Santa Rosa's other centre, around its main square, the **Plaza San Martín**. The plaza has the customary leaping equestrian statue at its heart; a slightly more unexpected sight is the bizarre **Cathedral** on its western side. Regarded, no doubt, as a daring piece of modernism when it was inaugurated, the honeycombed concrete facade sadly looks more like a contorted piece of novelty pasta. The plaza's most appealing characteristic is probably the pavement cafés on its northwest corner.

Santa Rosa's extremely modest museums are not worth going out of your way for, but if you're really stuck for something to do the old-fashioned **Museo Provincial de Historia Natural** at Pellegrini 180 (Mon–Fri 8am–5pm, Sat & Sun 6–9pm; ☎02954/422693), one block northwest of Plaza San Martín, bears a visit, if only to see what elusive species such as the mara or Patagonian hare actually look like; the museum also has a small collection of Indian artefacts as well as dinosaur fossils, discovered when the town centre was redeveloped in 1994. There is also a small art museum, most commonly known as the **Museo Verde**, at 9 de Julio and Villegas, three blocks west of the Plaza, with temporary exhibitions of local artists.

Arrival, information and accommodation

Santa Rosa's **airport**, with regular flights from Buenos Aires via Austral and Southern Winds is out on the RN35, a few kilometres north of the town centre. The **bus terminal** is at Av. Luro 365 (☎02954/422249) where a 24-hour information office (☎02954/422952) can provide you with maps, accommodation lists and left-luggage facilities. Across the road is the provincial **tourist office**, at Av. Luro 400 (Mon–Fri 7am–8pm, Sat & Sun 9am–noon & 4–8pm; ☎02954/425060), whose patient and helpful staff can provide information on the province's lesser-known regions and assist you in working out transport routes. Santa Rosa's **train station** (☎02954/433451), with three trains weekly to Buenos Aires, is on Alsina and Pellegrini, three blocks northwest of Plaza San Martín.

Accommodation in Santa Rosa is pretty nondescript, although it tends to book up fast. Most places are within a few blocks of the bus terminal and there are a few reasonable motels on the main roads in and out of the city – but these are only really accessible if you have your own transport. One block west of the terminal, *Residencial Santa Rosa* on H. Yrigoyen 696 (☎02954/423868; ③) is a spruce place with clean, comfortable rooms, some with a shared bathroom. The rooms in nearby *Hostería Río Atuel*, Av. Luro 356 (☎02954/422597; ③), have television, telephone and private bathroom; singles rates are rarely available here. Those travelling alone will get a better deal at the *San Martín*, opposite the train station on Alsina and Pellegrini (☎ & fax 02954/454802; ④), with similar, but larger, rooms to the *Río Atuel*, and with more facilities such as a laundry service, parking and single-room rates. Top of the range in Santa Rosa is the four-star *Calfucurá*, on San Martín 695 (☎ & fax 02954/423612; *calfuar@satlink.com*; ⑤), with comfortable modern rooms and a swimming pool. The hotel is easily recognizable by the nine-storey mural of the eponymous Indian cacique painted on its side. A typical example of the town's **motels** is *Motel Caldén*, 3km north of the bus terminal, on the RN5 (☎02954/424311; *motel@hotelescalden.com.ar*; ③); rooms have air conditioning and television and there is a sizeable swimming pool. Also, to the west of the town centre, there's the Centro Recreativo, a spacious though rather dreary-looking park on the banks of the Laguna Don Tomás which hosts the **municipal campsite** (☎02954/455358; $1 per tent) – though the campsite itself is mostly used for picnicking by day-trippers. The park, which redeems itself somewhat thanks to its sporting facilities, including a large swimming pool, is ten blocks west of Plaza San Martín along Avenidas Uruguay or Roca.

Eating and drinking

Eating out in Santa Rosa usually involves pasta, pizza and, above all, parrillada. Many of the parrillas are on the main roads in and out of the city, especially around the intersection of Avenida Circunvalación Ing. Santiago Marzo and Presidente A.U. Illia, to the east of the Centro Cívico. Reasonably central, and popular with the locals, is *Los Pinos* at Avenida Spinetto 815; whilst friendly *El Pato* at Avenida Luro 502 is handily located just a couple of blocks from the bus terminal and offers a *petit bife* if your appetite isn't up to a whole *bife de chorizo*. *Pampa*, at Catamarca 15, does satisfyingly large portions of pizza and pasta. In the centre, the new *Pimiento*, at Pellegrini 234, is Santa Rosa's fanciest restaurant, with a Mediterranean-style menu and a slightly self-consciously sophisticated interior.

The majority of Santa Rosa's **confiterías** are concentrated around Plaza San Martín, which has a lively atmosphere on summer evenings as groups assemble around tables set on the pavement around *La Recova* and *La Confitería*, both on the corner of Avellaneda and H. Yrigoyen. Santa Rosa's best **bar** is the bohemian *Café de Sonia*, at Quintana 79, between Avellaneda and Santiago del Estero, which has regular live bands at weekends and a good selection of jazz, blues and Brazilian CDs the rest of the week. There are a handful of **nightclubs**, mostly catering to a very young crowd, around Yrigoyen and 9 de Julio; try *El Sol* at Yrigoyen 49 or *Cádiz* at 9 de Julio 130. Santa Rosa's **cinema**, showing mainstream releases, is the Cine Don Bosco on the corner of Avenida Uruguay and Pico. It's also worth checking to see if there's anything on at the pretty Teatro Español, at H. Lagos 44 (☎02954/455325), notable for its rather baroque interior.

Listings

Airlines Austral, Rivadavia 256 (☎02954/422388); Southern Winds, at Swiss Travel, Pellegrini 219 (☎02954/427505).

Car rental Luro, Av. Luro 1459 (☎02954/424282). Cars and trucks for rental with 300km free per day.

Exchange There are several banks and ATMs in the streets surrounding Plaza San Martín; there's also the useful Banco de la Pampa ATM next to the tourist office on Avenida Luro. There's nowhere to change travellers' cheques in town, though dollars can be changed at most banks. Banking hours are 8am–12.30pm.

Hospital Av. Circunvalación and Raúl B. Díaz (☎02954/455000).

Internet Locutorio del Paseo. Av. S. Martín 730, on the corner of San Martín and Luro (*hrodrig@cpsarg.com*).

Laundry H. Yrigoyen, between Oliver and Garibaldi.
Post office Corner of H. Lagos and Rivadavia.
Taxis Radio Taxi Centro (☎02954/428682).
Travel agents Landers Viajes, Avellaneda 360 (☎02954/429109), has excursions to Lihué Calel, estancias and other towns in La Pampa.

Reserva Provincial Parque Luro

A gently rolling park of grassland and open forest, the **Reserva Provincial Parque Luro** (Dec–Feb Tues–Sun 9am–8pm; March–Nov same days 9am–6pm; $1) lies 35km to the south of Santa Rosa. Originally created as a preserve for hunting game, the park was bought by the province in 1965 and is now a haven for wildlife in a region where hunting is still widespread. Its seven and a half square kilometres are home to native pumas and ñandúes but you're actually much more likely to catch sight of red deer, imported from Europe for hunting at the beginning of the twentieth century. The park's other exotic inhabitant is the wild boar, though this surprisingly shy creature is harder to see. Though both species are now protected within the park, escapees have multiplied throughout the rest of the province where they once again face the business end of a rifle.

Over fifty species of **birds** visit the reserve, and on a quiet day you have a good chance of seeing many of them, including the white-browed blackbird, with its startling bright red breast; the brilliant white monjita and the fork-tailed flycatcher. Look out, too, for large flocks of the loro barranquero, a brightly coloured parrot, and noisy budgerigars, common in Argentina though often regarded as a nuisance for their ear-piercing squawk. Flocks of flamingoes also gather around the park's lake, the Laguna del Potrillo Oscuro; less welcome are the vicious mosquitoes which also hang out there.

On sunny weekends, the park is often dominated by picnicking day-trippers; if you fancy doing something a little more strenuous than eating, follow one of the short signposted **walks**. None of them takes more than half an hour or so; most worthwhile is the one to the **Punto Panorámico**, from where there are good views of the park. At the centre of the park lies the San Huberto residence, a clunky white mansion whose permanently closed green shutters lend it a rather spectral air. Known as **El Castillo**, the mansion was built by Pedro Luro, son of one of the founders of Mar del Plata and the park's creator. The mansion's still-furnished interior can be visited on regular guided tours; ask at the park's **Centro de Interpretación** where there are good photos of the reserve's wildlife. Past the information centre, a road leads round to a picnic area, where there is also a confitería. The park authorities are considering allowing camping in the park; but check with the tourist office in Santa Rosa before setting out with your tent.

Local **bus**, El Zorzal, goes to Parque Luro twice daily from Santa Rosa (8am & 1.30pm).

Parque Nacional Lihué Calel

A rather austere park, **Parque Nacional Lihué Calel**, 226km south of Santa Rosa, is dominated by the softly contoured granite sierras which run east to west across its 100 square kilometres. Formed through volcanic activity some 200 million years ago, the sierras emerge from a tract of wild open scrub, typical of the south of the province. Their slippery layers of ignimbrite rock retain hints of a violent origin in the cavities formed by the burst bubbles that pockmark their surface. The sierras help to retain water from the region's scarce rainfall and, it is claimed, to moderate La Pampa's fierce summer temperatures. As a result the park harbours a richer variety of vegetation than is found in the surrounding area. This phenomenon, referred to as a **microclimate**, was more succinctly described by the region's Indian inhabitants when they called the place the "Sierra of Life" (Lihué Calel means just that in the Araucanian language).

Despite its modest topography, Lihué Calel can be a stunning place: enhanced by the low light of sunrise or sunset, the intense reddish hues of the sierras glow against the surrounding countryside. In dull or rainy weather, however, scrub and rock merge gloomily with the threatening sky and the park can seem a bleak place indeed. A couple of days should suffice to see Lihué Calel: much of the park is off limits to visitors, although the part which has been made accessible contains its most scenic areas, including the highest peak, the **Cerro Alto** (590m).

The region's first inhabitants, hunter-gatherers, have left behind paintings in the park's **Valle de las Pinturas**. The meaning of these delicate geometric designs, some 2000 years old, is still unclear – indeed they may have been purely decorative. Though protected from the elements by overhanging rock formations, they have been damaged by vandalism and a barrier has been put up to stop you getting too close. In the nineteenth century, Lihué Calel was the last base of Namuncará, a famous Araucanian cacique, who finally surrendered to Argentinian forces in 1884, after various bloody battles. More recently, the park was an estancia; the unremarkable jumble of adobe ruins known as the **Casco de Santa María** is all that is left of the homestead, dismantled by the owners when the region was expropriated for the creation of the park.

As well as caldén trees and jarilla bushes, common throughout the rest of the province, the park harbours an unusual mixture of **vegetation** which includes both humidity-loving ferns and cacti. The most notable of the cacti is the particularly vicious Opuntia puelchiana, a silvery, densely spiked cactus more commonly known as traicionera or traitor. Until the recent discovery of examples in Mexico and the United States, it was thought that the traicionera was unique to the park; however, Lihué Calel still retains its claim to an endemic species in the delicate yellow flower of the margarita pampeana.

The star of Lihué Calel's varied **fauna** is undoubtedly the puma. Sadly, though, you've a very slim chance of actually seeing one of these shy and beautiful cats. Though park rangers claim to have enjoyed frequent sightings in the past, pumas appear to be in decline in the park and are only rarely seen these days. It seems likely that this is partly due to a shortage of their favourite meal, the vizcacha, a member of the chinchilla family: despite their size and ferocious claws pumas hunt fairly small prey. This is why, in the unlikely event of coming face to face with one, you are advised to make yourself as large as possible by standing with your arms raised. Slightly easier to see are grey foxes – who are occasionally to be found lurking around the campsite – and herds of guanaco, although picking out their well-camouflaged forms against the sierra requires a keen eye. Other species found in the park include ñandúes, armadillos and wild cats, whilst red deer and wild boar, unwelcome exotic migrants from Parque Luro, have also found their way into the park. You should also be aware that both the highly venomous and aggressive yarará and the similarly toxic, less aggressive coral snake are found in the park: accidental encounters with either of these reptiles can pretty much be avoided by not moving any stones or rocks and not venturing into undergrowth away from the paths.

Spring is perhaps the **best time to visit**, when the park's predominantly yellow flowering bushes (such as the jarilla) are in bloom and the air is heavy with their scent. Summer is good for bird-watching – around one hundred and fifty species can be seen in the park, including various types of buzzards, falcons, hummingbirds, the exquisitely coloured blue and yellow tanager, the yellow cardinal and the rufus-bellied thrush. However, it can also be very dry and hot at this time of year; despite the moderating effect of the microclimate, temperatures can still push 40°C. Milder temperatures make the park more bearable again in autumn, but although Lihué Calel receives only a few centimetres of rain a year, there can be days during March and April when it feels like all those centimetres are falling at once.

Practicalities

Lihué Calel is 226km south of Santa Rosa on the RN152, between General Acha (120km to the north) and Puelches (33km to the south). Transportes Unidos del Sud has a daily **bus service** (destination Neuquén) from Santa Rosa, which will drop you at the ACA Motel, 2km south of the park's entrance. If you plan to hitch, be aware that traffic on the road has decreased somewhat since the opening of the new Ruta de la Conquista del Desierto (RP20 & RN151), a more direct but extremely monotonous road to Patagonia.

There is a free **campsite** in the park itself, with showers and toilets. Bring your own food – the nearest stop for provisions (apart from some very basic items in the ACA Motel) is at Puelches – and a torch, as electricity is supplied only until 11pm. Without a tent, or your own transport, your only accommodation option is the grim *ACA Motel* itself (☎02952/436101; ③, single ②). Apparently suffering because of the diversion of traffic along the new route to the south, this so-called service station rarely has any fuel (nearest petrol stations are at Puelches and General Acha), and water, food and electricity supplies are all precarious. For general **information on the park**, contact Lihué Calel's *guardaparques*, who maintain a small visitors' centre (☎02952/436595).

travel details

Buses

Azul to: Buenos Aires (20 daily; 4–5hr); Mar del Plata (8 daily; 4hr).

Bahía Blanca to: Bariloche (2 daily; 12–14hr); Buenos Aires (15 daily; 9hr); Neuquén (9 daily; 7hr); Sierra de la Ventana (2 daily; 2hr 30min); Tornquist (6 daily; 1hr); Viedma (7 daily; 3–4hr).

Claromecó to: Buenos Aires (2 daily; 9hr).

La Plata to: Buenos Aires (every 30min; 1hr).

Lobos to: Buenos Aires (4 daily; 2hr).

Mar del Plata to: Bahía Blanca (7 daily; 6hr); Bariloche (2 daily; 20hr); Buenos Aires (20 daily; 7hr); Córdoba (1 daily; 18hr); Neuquén (4 daily; 12hr); Santa Rosa (2 daily; 11hr).

Miramar to: Buenos Aires (7 daily; 8hr); Mar del Plata (hourly; 1hr); Necochea (2 daily; 2hr).

Necochea to: Bahía Blanca (5 daily; 4hr); Bariloche (1 daily; 18hr); Buenos Aires (12 daily; 9hr); Mar del Plata (12 daily; 3hr); Neuquén (1 daily; 10hr); Tandil (5 daily; 3hr); Tres Arroyos (7 daily; 3hr).

Pinamar to: Buenos Aires (10 daily; 5hr); Mar del Plata (3 daily; 2hr).

San Clemente to: Buenos Aires (10 daily; 5hr).

San Miguel del Monte to: Buenos Aires (4 daily; 2hr); Tandil (3 daily; 3hr).

Santa Rosa to: Bariloche (2 daily; 13hr); Buenos Aires (17 daily; 8–10hr); Neuquén (15 daily; 7–8hr).

Sierra de la Ventana to: Azul (Mon–Fri & Sun 1 daily, none Sat; 4hr); Bahía Blanca (2 daily; 2hr 30min); Buenos Aires (Mon–Fri & Sun 1 daily, none Sat; 8hr).

Tandil to: Azul (7 daily; 2hr); Bahía Blanca (3 daily; 6hr); Bariloche (1 daily; 18hr); Buenos Aires (12 daily; 5hr); Chivilcoy (1 daily; 5hr); Mar del Plata (16 daily; 3hr); Neuquén (1 daily; 13hr); San Miguel del Monte (4 daily; 3hr); Santa Rosa (2 daily; 9hr).

Villa Gesell to: Buenos Aires (20 daily; 6hr); Bariloche (1 daily; 22hr); Córdoba (1 daily; 17hr); Mar del Plata (5 daily; 2hr).

Trains

Azul to: Buenos Aires (1 daily; 7hr).

Bahía Blanca to: Buenos Aires (1 daily; 13hr); Sierra de la Ventana (Tues, Wed & Sun 1 daily; 2hr 30min).

La Plata to: Buenos Aires (every 30 min from 4.30am to 1am; 1hr 15min)

Lobos to Buenos Aires (8 daily; 2hr).

Mar del Plata to: Buenos Aires (7 daily; 6hr).

Necochea/Quequén to: Buenos Aires (Mon–Fri & Sun 1 daily, none Sat; 11hr).

Pinamar to: Buenos Aires (1 daily; 5hr 40min).

San Miguel del Monte to: Buenos Aires (Mon, Wed & Fri 2 daily, Tues, Thur & Sat 1 daily; 2hr).

Santa Rosa to: Buenos Aires (Tues, Thurs & Sun 1 daily; 12hr).

Sierra de la Ventana to Bahía Blanca (Tues, Thurs & Sun; 2hr 30min); Buenos Aires (Tues, Thurs & Sun; 9hr 45min).

Tandil to: Buenos Aires (1 daily; 8hr).

Tornquist to: Buenos Aires (Mon, Wed, Fri & Sat 1 daily; 10hr 45min).

Villa Gesell (from Pinamar) to: Buenos Aires (1 daily; 5hr 40min).

Planes

Bahía Blanca to: Bariloche (1 weekly; 1hr); Buenos Aires (Mon–Fri 12 daily, Sat & Sun 5 daily; 1hr); Comodoro Rivadavia (Mon–Fri 1 daily; 1hr 40min); Neuquén (Mon, Tues & Thurs–Sun 1 daily, none Wed; 1hr 20min); Río Gallegos (Mon–Fri 1 daily; 2hr 15min); Río Grande (Mon–Fri 1 daily; 3hr 15min); Ushuaia (1 weekly; 3hr 15min).

Mar del Plata to: Buenos Aires (4 daily; 1hr 15min).

Necochea to: Buenos Aires (1 daily; 1hr 40min).

Santa Rosa to Buenos Aires (1 daily; 1hr 30min).

Tandil to: Buenos Aires (1 daily; 50min).

Villa Gesell to: Buenos Aires (6 daily; 1hr); Rosario (1 daily; 1hr 30min).

CHAPTER THREE

THE CENTRAL SIERRAS

The **Central Sierras**, also known as the Sierras Pampeanas, are the highest **mountain ranges** in Argentina away from the Andean cordillera. Their pinkish-grey ridges and jagged outcrops alternate with fertile valleys, wooded with native carob trees, and barren moorlands, fringed with pampas grass – a patchwork that's one of Argentina's most varied landscapes. Formed more than four hundred million years before the Andes and sculpted by the wind and rain, the sierras stretch across some 100,000 square kilometres, peaking at **Cerro Champaquí**, its 2884-metre summit often encircled by cloud. Irrigated by countless rivers and brooks, and refreshingly cool in the summer when the surrounding plains become torrid and parched, the highlands straddle the provinces of Córdoba and San Luis, each of which shares its name with its historic capital. The cities of **Córdoba** and **San Luis**, separated by the highest mountains, the Sierra Grande and Sierra de Comechingones, are very unlike each other: the former is a vibrant, thrusting metropolis as befits the country's second city, whereas modest San Luis is struggling to shake off its sleepy backwater image.

Colonized at the end of the sixteenth century by settlers heading south and east from Tucumán and Mendoza, the region's first city was Córdoba. The Society of Jesus and its missionaries played a major part in the city's foundation, at a strategic point along the Camino Real (or Royal Way), the Spanish route from Alto Peru to the Crown's emerging Atlantic trading-posts on the River Plate. Afterwards the Jesuits dominated every aspect of life in the city and its hinterland, until King Charles III of Spain had them kicked out of the colonies in 1767. You can still see their handsome temple in the city centre, among other well-preserved examples of **colonial architecture**. Also reminiscent of the Jesuits' heyday, Santa Catalina and Jesús María are two of Argentina's best-preserved **Jesuit estancias**, located between Córdoba city and the province's northern border, just off the Camino Real, promoted locally as the **Camino de la Historia**. Just north of Santa Catalina is one of the country's most beguiling archeological sites, **Cerro Colorado**, where hundreds of pre-Columbian petroglyphs decorate open-air galleries of red sandstone at the foot of cave-riddled mountains.

Northwest of the city of Córdoba is the picturesque **Punilla Valley**, along which are threaded some of the oldest, most traditional holiday resorts in the country, such as **La Falda** and **Capilla del Monte**, sedate towns with exclusive golf courses and genteel hotels. Many of the activities there are targeted at children but you can also indulge in demanding adventure pursuits such as hang-gliding – international championships are

---

ACCOMMODATION PRICE CODES

The price codes used for accommodation throughout this chapter refer to the cheapest rate for a double room in high season. Single travellers will only occasionally pay half the double-room rate; nearer two thirds is the norm and some places will expect you to pay the full rate. Note that in resort towns, there are considerable discounts out of season.

① $20 or less	④ $45–60	⑦ $100–150
② $20–30	⑤ $60–80	⑧ $150–200
③ $30–45	⑥ $80–100	⑨ Over $200

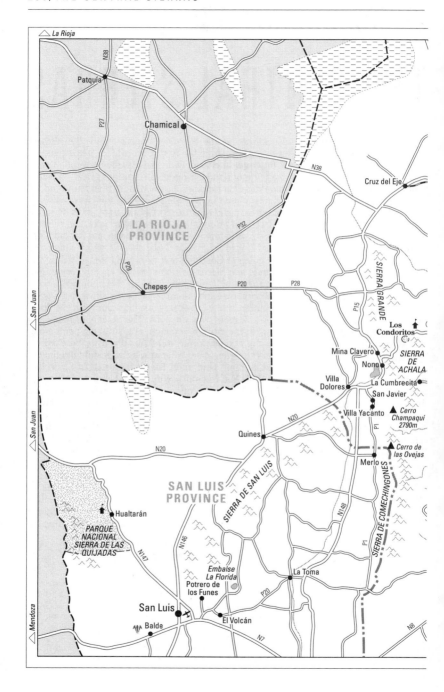

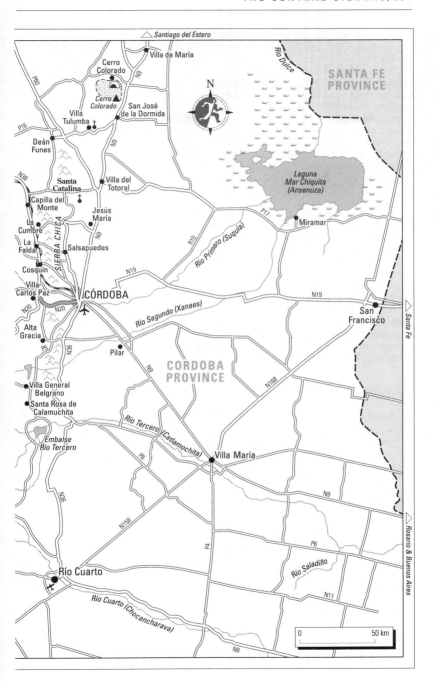

held annually near the Punilla resort of **La Cumbre**. At the southern end of the valley, not far from Córdoba city, are two nationally famous resorts: noisy, crowded **Villa Carlos Paz**, and quieter **Cosquín**, the latter known for its annual folk festival. Directly south of Córdoba, the **Calamuchita Valley** is also famed for two popular holiday spots, sedately Germanic **Villa General Belgrano** and much rowdier **Santa Rosa de Calamuchita**, from where alpine trails climb into the nearby Comechingones range, an excellent place to observe condors.

Peaceful almost to the point of being eerie is the hauntingly beautiful **Ruta de las Altas Cumbres**, a high mountain-pass that cuts through the natural barrier of the sierras. It leads to the more placid resorts of the **Traslasierra**, in western Córdoba Province, and some stunning scenery in the lee of Cerro Champaquí, which is easily climbed. Along this route lies Córdoba Province's only national park, the **Quebrada de los Condoritos**, whose dramatic, often misty ravines provide an outstanding breeding-site for the sinister yet magnificent **condor** and a habitat for a number of endemic species of flora and fauna.

Away to the south, just across the border in San Luis Province, **Merlo** is renowned for its fabled microclimate, but its real attraction is its splendid mountainside setting. San Luis city, the laid-back provincial capital, serves as a base for the **Parque Nacional de las Quijadas**, a dramatic red canyon that has yielded some prized dinosaur remains and is now home to guanacos and armadillos, and for one of the country's most modern spa resorts, at nearby **Balde**. Huge swathes of flat cattle-pasture stretch across the southern parts of San Luis Province, and eastern and southern Córdoba Province, too, and have none of the attractions of the sierras.

This relatively densely populated region is well served by **public transport**, especially along the Punilla and Calamuchita valleys, but you can explore at your own leisurely pace by renting a car or even a mountain-bike. Nearly everywhere is within striking distance from the city of Córdoba, which you could use as a base for day excursions, either on organized tours or under your own steam, given how easy it is to get around.

Córdoba

The bustling, modern metropolis of **CÓRDOBA**, Argentina's second city, guards some of the country's finest colonial architecture in its compact historic centre. Some 700km northwest of Buenos Aires and built in a curve in the Río Suquía, at its confluence with the tamed La Cañada brook, the city sprawls idly across a wide valley in the far northwestern corner of the pampa. The jagged silhouettes visible at the western end of its broad avenues announce that the cool heights of the **Sierras** are not far away; and it's in these, or in the lower hills nearer the city centre, that many of the million-plus Cordobeses take refuge from the sweltering heat of the valley.

As the capital of one of Argentina's largest and most populous provinces, Córdoba has a wide range of services on offer. It's reputed nationwide for its hospitable, elegant population, of predominantly Italian descent, and its people have a pronounced sense of civic pride, reflected in initiatives such as the country's first ever urban cycle-paths or the careful restoration of many of the oldest buildings. Another local trait is a caustically ironic sense of humour, sometimes bordering on the insolent, enhanced by the lilting drawl of the distinctive regional accent. Many people spend only an hour or two here before sprinting off to the nearby resorts, yet the city's plentiful accommodation and lively ambience make it an ideal base for exploring the area.

Some history

On July 6, 1573, **Jerónimo Luis de Cabrera**, Governor of Tucumán, declared a new city founded, at the fork in the main routes from Chile and Alto Peru to Buenos Aires,

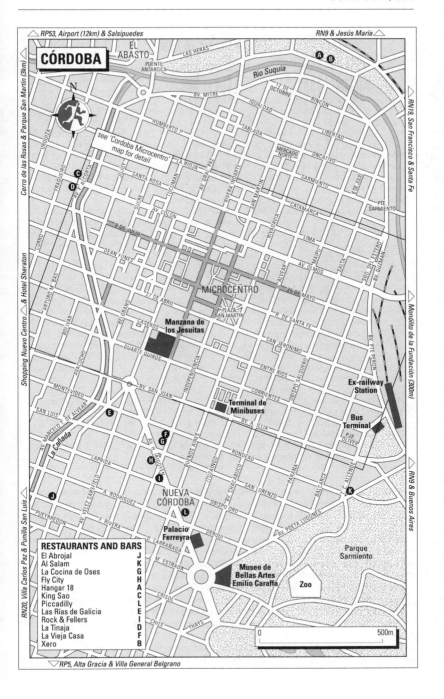

CÓRDOBA

EL ABASTO

RP53, Airport (12km) & Salsipuedes

RN9 & Jesús María

Cerro de las Rosas & Parque San Martín (3km)

RN19 San Francisco & Santa Fe

Shopping Nuevo Centro & Hotel Sheraton

Monolito de la Fundación (300m)

RN20, Villa Carlos Paz & Punilla San Luis

RN9 & Buenos Aires

Río Suquía

LAS HERAS
PUENTE ANTÁRTICA
BV. MITRE
12 DE OCTUBRE
IGUALDAD
RINCÓN
HUMBERTO I°
TABLADA
LIBERTAD
LA RIOJA
MERCADO NORTE
ONCATIVO
SANTA ROSA
TUCUMÁN
PAZ
AV. GRAL. PAZ
RIVERA INDARTE
SAN MARTÍN
SARMIENTO
6 DE JULIO
SUCRE
AV. COLÓN
CATAMARCA
PTE SARMIENTO
9 DE JULIO
RIVADAVIA
LIMA
DEÁN FUNES
MAIPÚ
AV. OLMOS
SALTA
SGO. DEL ESTERO
BV. GUZMÁN
27 DE ABRIL
MICROCENTRO
25 DE MAYO
PLAZA SAN MARTÍN
R. DE SANTA FE
Manzana de los Jesuitas
CASEROS
DUARTE QUIRÓS
SAN JERÓNIMO
BELGRANO
INDEPENDENCIA
ENTRE RÍOS
OBISPO SALGUERO
Ex-railway Station
MONTEVIDEO
BV. SAN JUAN
CORRIENTES
Terminal de Minibuses
Bus Terminal
SAN LUIS
BV. A. ILLIA
PJE. OLIVER
LAPRIDA
BUENOS AIRES
RONDEAU
PARANÁ
BALCARCE
A. RODRÍGUEZ
ITUZAINGÓ
CHACABUCO
SAN LORENZO
BALCARCE
T. DE ALVEAR
AV. VÉLEZ SÁRSFIELD
PUEYRREDÓN
F. RIVERA
NUEVA CÓRDOBA
OBISPO ORO
BV. PTE. PERÓN
AV. POETA LUGONES
Palacio Ferreyra
DERQUI
D. LARRAÑAGA
M. ESTRADA
Parque Sarmiento
Museo de Bellas Artes Emilio Caraffa
Zoo
CRISOL
CHILE
THAYS

see 'Cordoba Microcentro' map for detail

RESTAURANTS AND BARS

El Abrojal	J
Al Salam	K
La Cocina de Oses	G
Fly City	H
Hangar 18	A
King Sao	C
Piccadilly	L
Las Rías de Galicia	E
Rock & Fellers	I
La Tinaja	D
La Vieja Casa	F
Xero	B

0 — 500m

RP5, Alta Gracia & Villa General Belgrano

DEÁN FUNES

A local hero, whose name has been given to countless streets and squares across Argentina and to a town in the north of Córdoba Province, **Gregorio Funes** saved Córdoba from destruction at the hands of the anti-colonial Junta by cunningly siding with it in the early nineteenth-century dispute with the royalists.

Born in 1749 and educated for the priesthood, Funes showed early signs of the **radicalism** that would charcterize his later career. A year after his ordination in 1773, he sided with the progressive Rector of Córdoba University, Pedro Nolasco Barrientos, in his ideological battle with the city's pro-Jesuit clergy – although the Society of Jesus had been banished in 1767, its ideas continued to hold sway in the city. When the Church punished Funes with an obscure rural living, he managed to stow away on a ship to Spain. Once in Spain, he resumed his studies, proving to be a brilliant student and qualifying as a lawyer. By around 1785 King Charles III had caught wind of Córdoba's fresh ideas and anti-Jesuit stance, and, keen to inject some colonialist blood in the Argentine clergy, urged him to return to Córdoba. Back in his home city, and thanks to his academic qualifications and royal patronage, Funes had a meteoric career, becoming **Deán** and principal of the prestigious **Montserrat College** in 1804, and **Rector of the University** in 1808. Two years later, Déan Funes was the first in the city to hear news of the 1810 Revolution in Buenos Aires.

The Viceroy of the River Plate, de Liniers, a French-born aristocrat and a staunch royalist – his family had been guillotined after the French Revolution – was deposed by the independentists. He fled to Córdoba, where the city's pro-Spanish garrison and clergy refused to recognize the unilaterally declared "national" government. When the revolutionary Junta sent troops "to change their minds", Liniers fled to nearby Alta Gracia and, for a few weeks, tried to drum up support for the royalist cause, although by now the local aristocracy had come to terms with Charles IV of Spain's defeat by Napoleon. Back in Córdoba, having lost his royal protection, Deán Funes used his oratorical skills to persuade the city elders to welcome the Junta's envoys. The resisting royalists, including Liniers, were rounded up and executed. Shortly afterwards, in August 1810, **Juan Miguel de Pueyrredón**, the new Governor of Córdoba, made Funes his **Deputy** and Deán Funes' political career was crowned when he was elected to the **Constituent Assembly** to represent Córdoba in 1824, which he did until he died in 1830. Funes is honoured with a mausoleum in the entrance to Córdoba Cathedral.

Deán Funes left three major works – representing his main interests of law, the Church and Argentine history – the preamble of the 1819 Unitarian Constitution, an enlightened examination paper for would-be priests and a three-volume history essay, regarded as the **first written history of Argentina**.

and called it Córdoba la Llana de la Nueva Andalucía, after the city of his Spanish ancestors. Mission accomplished, Cabrera went east to oversee trade on the Río Paraná, leaving the city's new settlers to their own devices. The Monólito de la Fundación, on the north bank of the Río Suquía nearly a kilometre northeast of the Plaza San Martín, supposedly marks the precise spot where the city was founded and commands panoramic views. The first steps taken by the colonizers, mostly Andalucians like Cabrera, were to shorten the name to Córdoba de Tucumán, and move it to a better site, less prone to flooding, on the other side of the river. They prosaically rebaptized the river Río Primero ("first river") – the name Río Suquía was officially reinstated in the 1990s, as part of a general policy in the province to restore the pre-Hispanic names of rivers and lakes.

Almost from the outset the **Society of Jesus** played a crucial role in Córdoba's development, founding a college here in 1613 which was to become South America's second university, the Universidad San Carlos, in 1621, making Córdoba the de facto capital of the Americas south of Lima. The Jesuits' emphasis on education earned the city its nickname, *La Docta* (the "Learned"), and Córdoba is still regarded as a devoutly erudite kind of place – albeit politically progressive. Fertile farmland and nearby quarries made the pioneers' task easier and everything from climate to scenery made them feel at home. But while the Jesuits and other missionaries turned Córdoba into the cultural capital of this part of the empire, their presence resulted in the decline in numbers of the native population, whose nearby settlement was called Quisqui Sacate or "village of the narrow pass". Fierce in appearance, the indigenous **Sanavirones**, **Comechingones** and **Abipones** were really a peaceful lot, but they resolutely defended themselves from the invaders and, once conquered, they thwarted attempts by the Spanish to "civilize" them under the system of *encomiendas*. Devastated by influenza and other imported ailments, the indigenous population dwindled from several thousand in the late sixteenth century to a few hundred a century later. All that now remains of them – apart from a few archeological finds, such as rock paintings in nearby mountain caves – are the names of villages, rivers and the mountain range to the south of the city.

The Jesuits built their temple at the heart of the city in 1640, and for over a hundred and twenty years the Society of Jesus dominated life in Córdoba. King Charles III of Spain's order to expel them from the Spanish empire in 1767 inevitably dealt Córdoba a serious body blow. That, plus the decision in 1776 to make Buenos Aires the headquarters of the newly created Viceroyalty of the River Plate, might well have condemned the city to terminal decline had it not then been made the administrative centre of a huge *Intendencia*, or viceregal province, stretching all the way to Mendoza and La Rioja. By another stroke of luck, a forward-looking Governor, **Rafael de Sobremonte**, was appointed by Viceroy Vértiz in 1784. This aristocratic visionary from Seville expanded Córdoba to the west of La Cañada which, among other things, provided the growing city with secure water supplies. Sobremonte lived in a suitably patrician house, the oldest residential building still standing in the city and now the Museo Histórico Provincial. But the pivotal role played by Córdoba in the country's independence from imperial Spain was masterminded by **Gregorio Funes**, better known under his religious title of Deán (see box, p.240).Like so many Argentine cities, Córdoba benefited from the arrival of the British-built railways in 1870, its station acting as a hub for its expanding eastern districts. A period of prosperity followed, still visible in some of the city's lavishly decorated banks and theatres. By the close of the nineteenth century, Córdoba had begun to spread southwards, with European-influenced urban planning on a huge scale, including a French-style park, the **Parque Sarmiento**. This all coincided with a huge influx of immigrants from all over Europe and the Middle East, enticed by jobs in the city's flourishing economy, based largely on food processing and textiles industries.

A series of progressive mayors in the first half of the twentieth century gave Córdoba strong leadership when it emerged as one of the country's main manufacturing centres, dominated by the automobile and aviation industries, both now shadows of their former selves. The **Cordobazo**, a protest movement masterminded by students and trade unions in 1969 and partly inspired by Europe's May 1968 uprisings, brought considerable pressure to bear on the military junta and helped to trigger political change at national level. The city has always vehemently opposed the country's dictatorships, including the 1976–83 military regime, with mass demonstrations and civil disobedience and was also a hive of anti-Menemism, and, appropriately enough, produced Carlos Menem's successor, Fernando de la Rúa.

Arrival, information and city transport

Córdoba's international **airport** (☎0351/425-5804) is at **Pajas Blancas**, 13km north of the city centre. A regular **minibus** service privately run by TAS, the Travellers Airport Service (☎0351/156-521771 or 156-521775), picks passengers up and sets them down in the city centre and at a selection of hotels for only $3.50. A **taxi** ride to the microcentro will set you back $11.

The long-distance **bus station**, known as NETOC (☎0351/423-4199 or 423-0532), is at Boulevard Perón 300 (usually referred to by locals as Avenida Reconquista). Its impressive array of **facilities** on four levels includes banks and ATMs, a pharmacy, travel agency, telephone centre, restaurants, showers and dozens of shops, plus a supermarket on the top floor. Tickets for destinations throughout the country are sold in the basement, and advance booking is advisable during busy periods. NETOC is located several blocks to the east of the city centre, so you might need to take a bus or a taxi to get to and fro, especially if laden with luggage; stops for city buses and taxi ranks are close to the exit. Local buses serving some provincial destinations such as Santa Rosa de Calamuchita, Jesús María and Cerro Colorado, leave from the cramped **Terminal de Minibuses** behind the Mercado Sur market on Boulevard Arturo Illia, between calles Buenos Aires and Ituzaingó.

The city's main **tourist office** and the **provincial information service** are both located in the Recova del Cabildo (Mon–Fri 8am–8pm, Sat & Sun 9am–1pm & 3–7pm; ☎0351/433-1543 or 433-1549), on Plaza San Martín, at the corner of calles Deán Funes and San Martín; both hand out brochures, basic maps and flyers. Staff at the **information centre** in the bus station (☎0351/423-0532) are very helpful – they have stacks of **maps** and leaflets plus travel information and on-line accommodation details, but they cannot book rooms.

Informative, guided **walking tours** of selected downtown sights, lasting two hours, start from the city tourist office (daily 9.30am & 4.30pm, the latter in English upon request; $7; ☎0351/424-5758). Privately run *Banana Tours* (daily 11am; $5; ☎0351/423-3299) offers introductory **city tours**, in London-style red double-decker buses, starting from the Plaza San Martín opposite the Banco Nación.

The majority of the city sights are within easy reach of each other, in the microcentro, but you may want to use buses to reach some farther-flung districts, such as the **Cerro de las Rosas** where some of the best restaurants are to be found. **Buses** do not accept cash for fares, so you must first buy **tokens** (*cospeles*) costing $0.80 or multi-fare **magnetic cards** (*tarjetas*), costing $5 and $10, both available at kiosks and newsagents – and on the upper floor at the airport. In addition there are minibuses called *diferenciales*, requiring two *cospeles* instead of one. Buses #40–43 and #47, plus *diferenciales* #D1, #D1B and #D12B all run from the bus terminal to Cerro de las Rosas, via central Plaza San Martín.

Accommodation

Córdoba has plenty of centrally located and reasonably priced **hotels**. The more expensive establishments tend to cater for a business clientele and few have much charm or finesse, concentrating instead on facilities such as fax-machines and cable TV. Demand at the **budget** end of the market, however, is scantily met: as yet there's no youth hostel, the nearest being at Villa General Belgrano, 85km to the south. The **cheapest places**, some of them squalid, are mostly gathered at the eastern end of calles Entre Ríos and Corrientes, towards the bus station.

There's a passable municipal **campsite** ($3 per tent), offering free parking and a range of facilities, at Av. General San Martín, behind the Fair Complex, on the banks of the Río Suquía, 10km northwest of the city centre. The #31 bus from Plaza San Martín runs there.

Hotel Del Boulevard, Boulevard A. Illia 184 (☎0351/424-3718, fax 425-9188). Modern and airy, with spick-and-span rooms, plus lots of cooling marble. ④.

Hotel Dorá, Entre Ríos 70 (☎0351/421-2031). In a central location, offering a wide range of facilities including a swimming pool and garage, and big, smart bedrooms. ⑦.

Pensión Edith, San Jerónimo 322 (☎0351/424-8225). Rather neglected but, considering its location, surprisingly quiet. Basic, scruffy but clean rooms, some with bath. ①.

Pensión Entre Ríos, Entre Ríos 567 (☎0351/423-0311). A simple family-run B&B in the vicinity of the bus station; safe, clean and quiet with plenty of hot water. ②.

Hotel Felipe II, San Jerónimo 279 (☎0351/422-6185). Modern and well managed, with an attractive lobby, and comfortable, bright rooms. Cable TV, a large lift and airport bus transfer. ⑤.

Pensión Florida, Rosario de Santa Fe 459 (☎0351/422-8373). The rooms with air conditioning are also brighter and more appealing; others have fans only. The decor is plain and fresh, mattresses are firm, and the bathrooms functional. ②.

Hotel Garden, 25 de Mayo 35 (☎0351/421-4729). Well located, this welcoming and popular place has small, clean rooms, with fans and cramped en-suite bathrooms. No breakfast. ③.

Residencial Mi Valle, Corrientes 586 (no phone). A small, family-run place without much character but scrupulously clean, tidy and hospitable; most rooms have a bathroom. ②.

Hotel Panorama, Marcelo T. de Alvear 251 (☎0351/420-4000; *panorama@onenet.com.ar*). As the name suggests, the hotel enjoys fine views from its rooms, roof-garden and pool. Luxurious but understated bedrooms and en-suite bathrooms, with smart stainless-steel washbasins. ⑦.

Hotel Plaza International, San Jerónimo 137 (☎0351/426-8900). One of Córdoba's leading hotels, the *Plaza* is modern and efficient. The garish indigo blue cuboid exterior is off-putting, but the rooms are spacious, comfortable and stylish. There's also a gym and sauna. ⑦.

Hotel Quetzal, San Jerónimo 579 (☎0351/422-9106). Appealing with bright summery decor throughout, en-suite bathrooms, and ultra-friendly English-speaking staff. Avoid the street-facing bedrooms – otherwise it's quiet. ③.

Hotel Royal, Boulevard Presidente Perón 180 (☎0351/422-7155). The freshest-looking, least squalid of all the hotels near the bus terminal. Rooms are plain but comfortable. Breakfasts are generous. ③.

Hotel Sheraton, Duarte Quiros 1300 (☎0351/488-9000). Housed in a distinctive cylindrical tower, offering great views, this hotel lives up to the chain's standards in every way. It's a long way from the centre but near the Nuevocentro shopping mall and its cinemas. ⑦.

Hotel Sussex, San Jerónimo 125 (☎0351/422-9070). The rooms in this institution of a hotel are spacious and comfortable, some with wonderful bird's-eye views of Plaza San Martín, so don't be put off by the dusty exterior and dowdy lobby. ⑤.

Pensión Thanoa, San Jerónimo 479 (☎0351/421-7297). Clean, basic and quiet, with an attractive, flower-filled patio; a bit run-down but charming. ①–②.

Pensión Udine, Pasaje Tomas Oliver 666 (no phone). Very small, spartan but clean rooms; the pick of the places near the bus station. ②.

Hotel Windsor, Buenos Aires 214 (☎0351/422-9164, fax 422-4012). One of the few hotels with charm in this category, going for a resolutely British style complete with Beefeater doormen; in the classy new wing, rooms are more expensive, and the bathrooms are more modern. Sauna, heated pool and gym, plus pretentious *Oxford* restaurant. ⑦.

The City

Córdoba's more about soaking up atmosphere than traipsing around tourist attractions, and you can see most of the sights in the compact centre in a couple of days. The city's **historic core**, or microcentro, wrapped around the leafy Plaza San Martín, contains all the major **colonial buildings** that sealed the city's importance in the seventeenth and eighteenth centuries. Its elegant **Cabildo**, now housing the city museum, and **Cathedral**, the country's oldest still standing, are conveniently side by side, and the obvious place to kick off any visit. Nearby, beyond a handsome Baroque convent, the **Monasterio de Santa Teresa**, is a group of several well-preserved Jesuit buildings, including the temple and university, forming the **Manzana de los Jesuitas**, the Jesuits' block. East of Plaza San Martín, the eighteenth-century home of Governor Sobremonte (and the city's oldest standing residential building) has been turned into the **Museo Histórico Provincial**, which contains some outstanding colonial paintings; while some interesting examples of nineteenth- and twentieth-century Argentine art are on display in a splendid French-style house, the **Museo Municipal de Bellas Artes**, a couple of blocks northwest of the central plaza.

The city's regulatory Hispanic grid, centred on Plaza San Martín, is upset only by the winding **La Cañada** brook a few blocks to the west of the centre, on either side of which snakes one of the city's main thoroughfares, acacia-lined Avenida Marcelo T. de

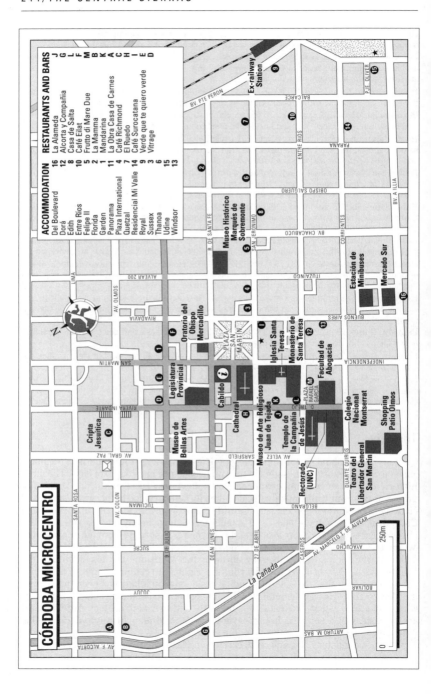

CÓRDOBA MICROCENTRO

ACCOMMODATION		RESTAURANTS AND BARS	
Del Boulevard	16	La Alameda	J
Dorá	12	Alcorta y Compañia	G
Edith	8	Casa de Salta	L
Entre Rios	10	Café Eilat	F
Felipe II	5	Frutto di Mare Due	M
Florida	2	La Mamma	B
Garden	1	Mandarina	K
Panorama	11	La Obra Casa de Carnes	A
Plaza International	4	Café Richmond	C
Quetzal	7	El Ruedo	H
Residencial Mi Valle	14	Café Surocatana	I
Royal	9	Verde que te quiero verde	E
Sussex	3	Vitrage	D
Thanoa	6		
Udine	15		
Windsor	13		

Museo Histórico Marqués de Sobremonte

Estación de Minibuses

Mercado Sur

Ex-railway Station

Oratorio del Obispo Mercadillo

Iglesia Santa Teresa

Monasterio de Santa Teresa

Facultad de Abogacia

Legislatura Provincial

Cripta Jesuitica

Museo de Bellas Artes

Cabildo

Cathedral

Museo de Arte Religioso Juan de Tejada

Templo de la Compañia de Jesus

Rectorado (UNC)

Colegio Nacional Montserrat

Shopping Patio Olmos

Teatro del Libertador General San Martín

La Cañada

PLAZA SAN MARTIN

PLAZA RAFAEL GARCIA

250m

Alvear, which becomes Avenida Figueroa Alcorta after crossing Calle Deán Funes. Street names change and numbering begins level with the cabildo, the city's point zero: for example, this is where Calle San Martín metamorphoses into Calle Independencia.

Boulevards San Juan and Presidente Illia mark the northern limits of **Nueva Córdoba**, a trendy neighbourhood awash with bars and restaurants and sliced through by diagonal Avenida Hipólito Yrigoyen, which leads from Plaza Vélez Sarsfield to the **Parque Sarmiento,** one of the city's open, green spaces, built on an isolated hill. Another even bigger park, **Parque General San Martín**, stretches alongside the leafy suburban neighbourhood of **Cerro de las Rosas**, on high ground to the northwest of the centre; head here to sample the restaurants or the fashionable nightlife.

Plaza San Martín

The **Plaza San Martín** has always been the city's geographical and social focal point. From dawn to the early hours, the square throngs with people, some striding purpose-fully along its diagonal paths, others sitting on the quaint benches and idly watching the world go by. Originally used for military parades, this leafy square was granted its recreational role in the 1870s when the Italianate cast-iron fountains were installed and semi-tropical shrubbery was planted: lush palm-fronds and feathery acacias, the prick-ly, bulging trunks of the *palo borracho* and, in the spring, the blazing display of pink *lapacho* and purple jacaranda blossom, whose fallen petals form a vivid carpet on the ground. Watching over it all is a monumental bronze **sculpture** of the Liberator him-self, victorious on a splendid mount and borne aloft on a huge stone plinth, unveiled in 1916 to mark the centenary of the declaration of independence.

The square's southern edge is dominated by the dowdy Banco Nación and the Teatro Real, now a cinema; along the eastern edge, more banks alternate with old-fash-ioned cafés. Wedged between shops and the modern municipal offices on the pedestri-anized northern side, sits the diminutive **Oratorio del Obispo Mercadillo**, all that remains of a huge colonial residence built for and inhabited by Bishop Manuel Mercadillo. He had the seat of Tucumán diocese moved from Santiago del Estero to Córdoba at the beginning of the eighteenth century, before becoming the city's first bishop. An intricate and rather flimsy-looking wrought-iron balcony protrudes over the busy pavement from the upper-floor former chapel. At ground level, the **Museo Gregorio Funes** (daily 9am–1pm & 4–7pm; free) sporadically hosts temporary exhi-bitions of icons, altarpieces and other religious artefacts.

THE CABILDO

Recumbent on the traffic-free western side of the square is the **Cabildo**, a sleekly ele-gant two-storey building whose immaculately white **facade** dates back to the late eighteenth century. Fifteen harmoniously plain arches alleviate this otherwise sober building, enhanced at night by impeccable lighting. Old-fashioned lamps hang in the **Recova,** a fan-vaulted colonnade held up by slender pillars, in front of a row of wooden doors alternating with windows protected by forged-iron grilles. On the pavement in front of the cabildo, as elsewhere in the historic city, a subtle trompe l'oeil device of mock shadows has been incorporated into the flagstones. The front of the building is further set off by a row of discreet Argentine flags and a delicate wrought-iron balcony jutting above the three central arches.

The original cabildo, or colonial headquarters, was built on this very spot at the end of the sixteenth century, but the present facade was added when the Marqués de Sobremonte became Governor-Mayor in 1784. Put to many different uses throughout its long history – law-court, prison, provincial parliament, government offices and police constabulary – nowadays the building and its inner courtyards are mainly used for exhibitions, official receptions, the occasional concert and regular summer tango evenings (*Patio de Tango*: Fri 11pm; $5); in cold or wet weather, the musicians and dancers take refuge in the Cripta Jesuítica (see p.249). Inside, the **Museo de la Ciudad** (Mon 4–9pm, Tues–Sun 9am–1pm; free) displays all kinds of **archeological** remains unearthed during restoration work on the cabildo in the 1980s. The museum's four rooms also contain other historical artefacts and exhibits about the city's past.

THE CATHEDRAL

Immediately to the south of the cabildo and completing the plaza's western flank, Córdoba's eighteenth-century **Cathedral**, Argentina's oldest if not its most beautiful, is part Baroque, part Neoclassical. Its most imposing external feature, the immense **cupola**, inspired by Salamanca Cathedral's, is surrounded by stern Romanesque turrets that contrast pleasingly with its Baroque curves. Even so, it now looks like a huge scorched meringue: the highly porous, pale cream-coloured stone has suffered badly from the ambient pollution and, scrubbed clean only a few years back, it has already begun to blacken again. The cathedral's **clock towers** are decorated at each corner with angelic trumpeters dressed in skirts of exotic plumes, like those worn by the Guaraní craftsmen who carved them. You enter the cathedral first through majestic filigreed wrought-iron gates, past Deán Funes' solemn black mausoleum to the left (see box, p.240), and then through intricately carved **wooden doors** transferred here from the Jesuit temple at the end of the eighteenth century. The first thing you notice is the almost tangible gloom of the interior: scant daylight is filtered through small, stained-glass windows onto an ornate but subdued **floor** of Valencian tiles, and the nave is separated from the aisles by hefty square columns designed to support the cathedral in the event of an earthquake, compounding the effect of almost oppressive melancholy. The ornate Rococo pulpit, in the left-hand aisle, momentarily lifts the otherwise oppressive atmosphere, as does the richly painted decoration of the **ceiling** and **chancel**. This was inspired by the Italian Baroque and Tiepolo's frescoes in particular, but executed in the early twentieth century by local artists of Italian origin, supervised by Emilio Caraffa, whose pictures are displayed at the Museo de Bellas Artes Dr Genaro Pérez (see p.249).

The cathedral's main altar is a dull early nineteenth-century piece, which replaced a Baroque work of art moved to Villa Tulumba, a tiny hamlet in the north of the province (see p.254). To the left, a minor altar is redeemed by a finely worked silver **tabernacle**, also dating from the early nineteenth century although some of its features are clumsily executed – the Lamb of God looks as if it's made of whipped cream while the Sacred Heart somewhat resembles a beetroot.

Monasterio de Santa Teresa

Immediately southwest of Plaza San Martín, across Calle 27 de Abril from the cathedral, lies a set of buildings dedicated to St Teresa, including the lavish pink and cream-coloured **Monasterio de las Carmelitas Descalzadas de Santa Teresa de Jesús**, completed in 1770. Of the working nunnery, only the soberly decorated **Iglesia Santa Teresa**, built in 1717, is open to the public (Matins: daily 8am) – the entrance is at Independencia 146. Founded by local dignitary Juan de Tejeda, great-nephew of St Teresa of Avila, the monastery was built out of gratitude for the miraculous recovery of one of his daughters from a fatal disease; after Tejeda's death, his widow and two daughters became nuns and never left the convent. It was designed by Portuguese architects brought over from Brazil, as can be seen from the typical ornate cross and gabled shape of the church's two-dimensional bell tower, like a cardboard cut-out stuck next to the main facade.

Housed in the northern side of the complex, in a part no longer used by the holy order, the **Museo de Arte Religioso Juan de Tejeda**, Independencia 122 (Wed–Sat 8.30am–12.30pm; $1), is entered through an intricate, cream-coloured Baroque doorway, typical of Portuguese craftsmanship, which contrasts with the pink outer walls. Informative guides, some of whom speak English, will show you around the partly restored **courtyards**, the garden of hydrangeas, orange trees, jasmine and pomegranates, and the rooms and cells of the former nuns' quarters. On display alongside all manner of religious artefacts and sacred relics, mainly of St Teresa and St Ignacio de Loyola, the founder of the Jesuits, are a very fine polychrome wooden statue of St Peter, a lavish silver-embroidered banner made for Emperor Charles V and some striking paintings from **Cusco** (see box, p.111). The nuns' devout asceticism and utter isolation is evident in their bare **cells**, lit only by ground-level vents, blocked off by forbidding grilles. Apart from these vents, the austere confessionals positioned against so-called communicating walls were the sisters' only means of communication with the outside world. Life for members of the Carmelite Order, still in residence next door, has barely changed.

The Manzana de los Jesuitas

Two blocks west and south of Plaza San Martín is the **Manzana de los Jesuitas**, a whole block, or *manzana*, apportioned to the Society of Jesus a decade after Córdoba was founded, as it began to play a dominant role in the fledgling city's religious, cultural and educational life. Set back only slightly from Plazoleta Rafael García, the **Templo de la Compañía de Jesús** was built by Felipe de Lamer in 1640 and is Argentina's oldest surviving Jesuit temple. The almost rustic simplicity of its restored facade, punctuated only by niches used by nesting pigeons, is a foretaste of the severe, single-naved interior, with its precious roof of Paraguayan cedar in the shape of an upturned ship – Lamer began his career as a shipbuilder in Antwerp. Fifty painted canvas panels huddled around the ceiling, darkened by time, depict the figures and legends of the Society of Jesus – at ten metres above ground level they're hard to make out without the aid of binoculars. Even more striking is the handsome Cusqueño altarpiece (see box, p.111) and the floridly decorated pulpit. The chapel to the right is dedicated to Our Lady of Lourdes and known as the Capilla de los Naturales: it was a roofless structure where the natives were graciously allowed to come and pray until the nineteenth century when it was covered and lined with ornate marble.

Around the corner on Calle Caseros s/n is the **Capilla Domestica**, the residents' private chapel and "gateway to heaven" – at least according to the inscription over the doorway. Its intimate dimensions, finely painted altarpiece and remarkable ceiling are in total contrast with the grandiose austerity of the main temple. The ceiling is a primitive wooden canopy, held together with bamboo canes and decorated with raw-hide panels which have been painted with natural vegetable pigments. Whereas the main temple is easily accessible, you have to ask the concierge to let you into the Capilla Domestica.

Twenty metres south from the temple, at Obispo Trejo 242, is the entrance to the two-storey **Rectorado** – or main headquarters – of the **Universidad Nacional de Córdoba (UNC)**, Argentina's oldest and South America's second oldest university, dating from 1621 and now attended by more than 80,000 students from all over the country. Venture beyond its harmonious cream- and biscuit-coloured facade and take a look around its shady patios, ablaze with bougainvilleas for most of the year; the libraries, open to the public (Mon–Fri 8am–9pm, Sat 8am–noon; free), contain priceless collections of maps, religious works and late fifteenth-century incunabula, along with the personal collection of Dalmácio Vélez Sarsfield, including the original manuscripts of his Argentine Civil Code, the country's first, on show in a special display-case. The heavily Neoclassical, sage green and cream building opposite, its balcony shored up by muscly atlantes, is the university's well-regarded **Facultad de Abogacía**, or Law Faculty.

Next to the Rectorado, and rounding off the trio of Jesuit buildings, is the prestigious **Colegio Nacional de Nuestra Señora de Montserrat,** founded at a nearby location in the city in 1687 but transferred to its present site in 1782, shortly after the Jesuits' expulsion; the building had been their living quarters, arranged around quadrangles. This all-male bastion of privilege finally went co-ed in 1998 despite fierce opposition from parents. The building's studiously neocolonial appearance – ostentatious salmon pink facades, a highly ornate doorway and grilled windows, and a pseudo-Baroque clock tower looming at the corner with Calle Duarte Quirós – dates from remodelling in the 1920s. Through the heavily embellished doors and the entrance-hall with its vivid Spanish majolica floor-tiles are the original Jesuit cloisters dating from the seventeenth century.

Teatro del Libertador General San Martín

The austere building a block southwest of the Colegio Nacional Montserrat, at Av. Vélez Sarsfield 317, is the Neoclassical **Teatro del Libertador General San Martín**, formerly known and still usually referred to as the Teatro Rivera Indarte. Of world-class calibre, with outstanding acoustics and an elegant, understated interior, it was built in 1887 and inaugurated four years later. Its creaking wooden floor, normally steeply tilted for performances, can be lowered to a horizontal position, and the seats removed, for dances and other social events.

Museo Histórico Provincial Marqués de Sobremonte

East of Plaza San Martín, at Rosario de Santa Fe 218, the **Museo Histórico Provincial Marqués de Sobremonte** (Tues–Fri 10am–1pm & 4–7pm, Sat & Sun 10am–1pm; $1; ☎0351/423-7687), is a well-preserved and carefully restored showpiece residence, the city's last private colonial house. Built at the beginning of the eighteenth century, it was the home of Rafael, Marqués de Sobremonte, between 1784 and 1796. As Governor of Córdoba he was responsible for modernizing the city, securing its water supplies and extending it westwards beyond La Cañada.

The unassuming exterior of the building, sturdily functional with thickset walls, is embellished by a wrought-iron balcony resting on finely carved wooden brackets, while delicate whitewashed fan-vaulting decorates the simple archway of the entrance. Guarding the door are two monstrous creatures, apparently meant to be lions, made of *piedra de sapo*, a relatively soft stone quarried in the nearby sierras. The calm, leafy **patio** is shaded by enormous jasmine bushes and pomegranate trees, supposedly planted when Sobremonte lived here.

Although only a few of the exhibits displayed on the ground floor belonged to the Marquess himself, most date from the period when he lived here. Best of all are an outstanding set of paintings of the **Cusco School** (see box, p.111), housed in the first two rooms on the right. Some of them, such as the *Triumph of King David* and a *Santa Rita de Cascia*, have been recently and very successfully restored, but the *Señor de los Temblores*, an unusual painting of Christ wearing a see-through lace skirt, is still in dire need of restoration. Another masterpiece is the portrait of Bishop Salguero de Cabrera, dated 1767 and painted not at Cusco but at Arequipeña. Dominating the adjoining **capilla azul**, or blue chapel, is a splendid cedar-wood altarpiece, naively decorated in vivid reds and greens, and in the following room is a lugubrious but moving *Ecce Homo*, Christ's half-shut eyes rolling heavenwards, and a fantastic *Descent from the Cross*, featuring a wonderfully contrite Mary Magdalene. In the remaining succession of ground-floor rooms are collections of porcelain, furniture and arms – much of which belonged to Sobremonte himself – such as a gleaming Portuguese jacaranda dining-table, miscellaneous portraits and piles of silverware. One room is taken up by a reconstruction of a late nineteenth-century **pharmacy**, with an inordinate amount of laxatives and suppositories. Another contains a fascinating collection of period **musical instruments**. Upstairs is a reconstruction of a **late nineteenth-century** Córdoba interior, dominated by a shocking pink four-poster bed and a huge family portrait of the fierce-looking Rosa Echegaray, a local dignitary, and her four intimidated grandsons.

Legislatura Provincial and around

One block west of the cabildo, the **Legislatura Provincial** (guided tours Mon–Fri 11am; free) squats at the corner of calles Deán Funes and Rivera Indarte. It's an extremely austere Neoclassical mass of a building designed by Austro-Hungarian architect Johan Kronfuss, but it's typical of the grandiose buildings that went up in Córdoba in the early twentieth century, when the city prospered – and wanted to look European. Built as the provincial parliament building, which was later moved to a modern headquarters in the west of the city, it's now used for civic ceremonies. The *Belle-époque* interior is lavishly decorated with imperious portraits of city dignitaries and paintings depicting the city's pivotal role in Argentina's independence. Half-hour guided tours, in Spanish only, are highly informative if rather automated.

The monumental Legislatura looks somewhat out of place among the colourful maze of shopping arcades, boutiques, cafés, fast-food joints and miscellaneous emporia, animated by a hubbub of shoppers, hawkers and the odd street-entertainer. This lively **commercial area**, stretching along the pedestrianized streets to the northwest of Plaza San Martín, is shaded by an elaborate system of pergolas, draped with bright bougainvilleas and vines. Over the past decade it has gradually lost out to the swish new shopping malls, such as Shopping Patio Olmos to the south on Plaza Vélez Sarsfield, or Nuevocentro Shopping at Duarte Quiros 1500, a dozen blocks west of the Manzana de los Jesuitas.

Museo de Bellas Artes Dr Genaro Pérez

To see some Argentine art from the nineteenth and twentieth centuries, head for the **Museo de Bellas Artes Dr Genaro Pérez**, a block west of the Legislatura Provincial at Av. General Paz 33 (Tues–Fri 9.30am–1.30pm & 4.30–9pm, Sat & Sun 10am–8pm; free). The municipal art gallery is housed in a handsome late nineteenth-century building, built to a French design for the wealthy Dr Tomás Garzón, who bequeathed it to the city in his will. Impeccably restored in the late 1990s, along with its fine iron and glass details including an intricate **lift**, the museum is worth a visit for its interior alone, an insight into how the city's prosperous bourgeoisie lived a century ago. Most of the paintings on permanent display belong to the **Cordobés School,** whose leading master was Genaro Pérez – after whom the museum is named – mostly brooding portraits and local landscapes, some imitating the French Impressionists. Other names to watch out for are those of the so-called **1880s Generation** such as Fidel Pelliza, Andrés Piñero and Emilio Caraffa, the last famous for his supervision of the paintings inside Córdoba Cathedral; while the **1920s Generation**, markedly influenced by their European contemporaries including Matisse, Picasso and de Chirico, is represented by Francisco Vidal, Antonio Pedone and José Aguilera. Temporary exhibitions, usually of local artists, are also held from time to time.

Cripta Jesuítica

One block east and one north of the Museo de Bellas Artes, where pedestrianized Calle Rivera Indarte intercepts the noisy, traffic-infested Avenida Colón, steps lead down into one of the city's previously hidden treasures. Beneath the hectic street lies the peaceful and mysterious **Cripta Jesuítica** (Mon–Sat 9am–1pm & 3–7pm, Sun 3–7pm; free), all that remains of an early eighteenth-century Jesuit noviciate razed to the ground during mid-nineteenth-century expansion of the city, and rediscovered by accident in 1989 when telephone cables were being laid under the avenue. The rough-hewn **rock walls** of its three naves, partly lined with bare brick, are a refreshing counterpoint to the cloying decoration of some of the city's other churches, and the space is used to good effect for exhibitions, plays, concerts and, in inclement weather, the Friday-night *Patio de Tango* usually held at the cabildo (see p.245).

Nueva Córdoba and Parque Sarmiento

South of the historic centre and sliced diagonally by its main drag, Avenida Hipólito Yrigoyen, **Nueva Córdoba** was laid out in the late nineteenth century. It was designed as an exclusive residential district, but many of Nueva Córdoba's majestic villas and mansions were taken over by bars, cafés, restaurants and offices, after the prosperous middle classes moved to the northwestern suburb of Cerro de las Rosas, where the air is cleaner, in the 1940s and 1950s. Architectural styles are eclectic, here, to say the least: neo-Gothic churches, mock-Tudor houses, Georgian facades and Second Empire mini-palaces. René Sergent, the architect of Buenos Aires' Museo de Art Decorativo, never set foot in Argentina (see p.285), but still managed to design one of Nueva Córdoba's finest buildings, the **Palacio Ferreyra**. Set in a large garden at the southern end of Avenida Hipólito Yrigoyen, it was built in 1913 in an opulent neo-Bourbon style, complete with Art Nouveau windows and doors. On the eastern side of the busy Plaza España roundabout is the **Museo Provincial de Bellas Artes Emilio Caraffa** (Tues–Fri 9am–1pm, 3–8pm, Sat & Sun 3–7pm; free), a ponderous Neoclassical pile inaugurated in 1916. It was designed by Johan Kronfuss, architect of the Legislatura Provincial (see p.248), and is named for the influential 1880s Generation artist who oversaw the decoration of the interior of the cathedral. Its airy galleries and shady gardens are used for temporary exhibitions, mostly featuring local artists.

Due east of the Plaza España stretches **Parque Sarmiento**, the city's breathing space. The centre of the park occupies high ground affording panoramic views of otherwise flat Nueva Córdoba and the surrounding city. The French landscape architect **Charles Thays** (see box, p.107) was called in to design this park for Córdoba, with the support of the 1880s Generation of painters. Work was completed by 1900, and included the boating lake with two islands and the planting of several thousand native and European trees. This huge open space, crisscrossed by avenues of plane trees, is where the city's main **sports facilities** are located, including an Olympic swimming pool, tennis courts and jogging routes. Córdoba's landscaped **zoo**, whose main entrance is at Rondeau 798 (☎0351/421-5625; daily 9am–6.45pm; $3, free for children), occupies part of the grounds. As well as native honey bears, jaguars, pumas and a giant serpentarium, the two hundred species include elephants, lions and hippopotamuses.

Cerro de las Rosas and Chateau Carreras barrios

The fashionable and prosperous northwestern suburbs of **Cerro de las Rosas** and **Chateau Carreras**, some 3km from the microcentro, are where many of Córdoba's best eating-places and trendiest nightclubs are located. Avenidas Figueroa Alcorta leads out of the El Abasto barrio, on the northern bank of the Río Suquía, becomes Avenida Castro Barros and eventually turns into **Avenida Rafael Núñez**, the wide, main street of Cerro de las Rosas, lined with shops, cafés and restaurants. Otherwise, it's a mainly residential area of shaded streets and large villas, built on the relatively cool heights of a wooded hill – the city's most desirable barrio since low-lying Nueva Córdoba lost its cachet in the 1940s and 1950s. Buses #40–43 and #47, plus *diferenciales* #D1, #D1B and #D12B from Plaza San Martín, run out here.

From the northern end of Avenida Rafael Núñez another avenue, Laplace, swings southwestwards and crosses a loop in the Río Suquía. On the peninsula formed by the river is the leafy district known as Chateau Carreras, named after a neo-Palladian mansion built in 1890 for the influential Carreras family. This picturesque building, painted the colour of Parma violets, save for a row of slender white Ionic columns along the front portico, houses the **Centro de Arte Contemporaneo** (Tues–Fri 9am–1pm & 2–6pm; Sat 8.30am–12.30pm; free). Uneven temporary exhibitions of contemporary paintings and photographs are staged here. The mansion is tucked away in the landscaped woods of **Parque San Martín**, another of the city's green lungs which, like Parque Sarmiento, was designed by Charles Thays (see box, p.107). Incidentally, the area immediately around the museum is regarded as unsafe and it's best not to linger here alone or after dusk. Just to the north of the park is the city's Fair Complex, while just across Avenida Ramón J. Cárcano, to the east, is Córdoba's massive football stadium, built for the 1978 World Cup finals. Along the avenue, just south of here, are clustered a number of the city's most popular nightclubs, most of them classy acts (see "Nightclubs", p.252). The direct bus to Chateau Carreras is the #31 from Plaza San Martín.

Eating, drinking and entertainment

Córdoba has a wide selection of **restaurants**, with something to please nearly all tastes, but cafés and bars are thin on the ground. The best places for eating and drinking are concentrated in trendy Nueva Córdoba and on the cooler heights of the Cerro de las Rosas. Most of the nightlife has moved to two outlying districts: El Abasto, a revitalized former warehouse district close to the centre on the northern banks of the Río Suquía, that buzzes with **bars**, **discos** and **live music venues**; and in the even trendier Chateau Carreras area, just south of Cerro de las Rosas, are a number of more upmarket **nightclubs** to choose from. One of Argentina's best **theatres**, the Teatro del Libertador General San Martín, puts on excellent dance and music, while the city's many **cinemas** screen a variety of films. The locals are split by allegiance to two of the nation's leading **football** clubs, Belgrano and Talleres, and the local derby is a highlight of the sporting calendar.

Restaurants

El Abrojal, Fructuoso Rivera and Belgrano (☎0351/428-2495). Good-value meals but the main reason to come is for the entertainment – regular, and brilliant, tango shows.

Alcorta y Compañía, Av. Figueroa Alcorta 43 (no phone). Ultra-fashionable decor, an unusual menu –highlights are the salmon with pink grapefruit and ginger followed by warm dates with chocolate ice cream – faultless wine-list, with all wines served by the glass, and discreet service.

Al Salam, Rondeau 711. Delicious hummus, tabbouleh, kebabs and baklawa at this atmospheric Middle Eastern restaurant, complete with hubble-bubbles and belly-dancers. Closed Mon.

Casa China, Av. Rafael Núñez 4580, Cerro de las Rosas. The only remotely authentic Chinese restaurant in the city, but mostly Sino-American fare such as chow mein, in a quaint red-lacquer décor with lots of paper lanterns.

Casa de Salta, Caseros 80. A taste of the Argentine Northwest, serving typical Salta dishes such as *locro* (maize-based stew) and delicious *empanadas*. Closed Sun.

La Cocina de Osés, Independencia 512. In an appealing neocolonial interior, with tasteful paintings and beautiful tiled floors, varied if predictable fish and meat dishes followed by scrumptious desserts, including *dulce de leche* pancakes.

Estación Victorino, Av. Rafael Núñez 4005, Cerro de las Rosas. An atmospheric café-bar in the Cerro de las Rosas, serving hearty meals and huge cocktails. A rusty locomotive and an old red British telephone box on the forecourt serve as landmarks.

Frutto di Mare 1, Av. Rafael Núñez 3812, Cerro de las Rosas (☎0351/481-5224). The menu at this stylish, Italian-influenced restaurant includes pasta with seafood, Caesar salad and crepe Suzette. Equally stylish sister restaurant, *Frutto di Mare 2*, is downtown at Caseros 67.

La Mamma, Av. Figueroa Alcorta 270 (☎0351/426-0610). Reliable and extremely popular, this traditional restaurant specializes in pasta and other Italian dishes such as osso bucco and tiramisu. Booking essential at weekends.

La Obra Casa de Carnes, Santa Rosa and La Cañada (☎0351/426-0612). One of several family-oriented restaurants in this neighbourhood: gargantuan quantities of luscious grilled meat are the house speciality.

Pizza Banana, Av. Colón 4450, Cerro de las Rosas. Pizzas, of course, plus ultra-fresh salads and pasta – with live music, fashion shows and even a disco at weekends.

Rancho Grande, Av. Rafael Núñez 4142, Cerro de las Rosas. Generous pastas and enormous barbecues served by trendy staff in a large barn-like structure, often rented out by parties.

Las Rías de Galicia, Montevideo 271 (☎0351/428-1333). At this swish restaurant you can choose from top-quality Spanish-influenced seafood, fish and meat dishes; the weekday lunchtime *menú ejecutivo* is great value at $9.

La Tinaja, Av. Colón 649. Self-service but high-quality food in a large and airy dining-room, with an indoor playground for children. Extensive wine-list and excellent desserts. Specialities include seafood, *asados* and pancakes. *Tenedor libre* $6 for lunch and $9 for dinner.

Verde que te quiero Verde, 9 de Julio 36. Appetising pizzas, quiches, soya burgers and fresh salads served by weight in cool surroundings; Córdoba's only vegetarian restaurant.

La Vieja Casa, Independencia 508. This extremely friendly *parrilla* offers juicy *milanesas* and other traditional fare, and the *budín de pan* is especially memorable. Attractive décor with a small patio. English spoken. Closed on Sun.

Zeta, Av. Rafael Núñez 4275, Cerro de las Rosas. Excellent pizzeria with a big terrace; the *Zeta* special is topped with mozzarella, bacon, red peppers and green olives.

Bars and cafés

La Alameda, Obispo Trejo 170. A slightly hippy ambience, with wooden benches to sit on. Reasonably priced food including great *empanadas* and *humitas*. Patrons leave scribbled notes and minor works of art pinned to the walls. Closed Sunday lunchtime.

La Cuadra, Av. Rafael Núñez 3880, Cerro de las Rosas. Crowded, lively bar, acting as a "pre-disco" for *Factory* nightclub (see below) and with a happy hour 7–8pm.

Eilat, 25 de Mayo. Stylish, quiet Art Deco café along this pedestrianized street, serving excellent breakfasts and great coffee.

King Sao, Colón 765. Very popular neighbourhood snack-bar serving beer and good coffee, plus cakes bursting with calories.

Mandarina, Obispo Trejo 175. Great décor in this trendy place with lots of atmosphere. Varied snacks include *rabas a la marinera*, tempura, *cazuela de calamar* and *fugazzas*.

Piccadilly, Av. Hipólito Yrigoyen 464. Welcoming British-style pub serving reasonably priced Argentine food.

Richmond, Av. Colón s/n, next to *Hotel Gran Astoria*. Old-fashioned café-bar, all wood-panelling and gilt mirrors; coffee laced with Tía María is the house speciality.

Rock&Fellers, Av. Hipólito Yrigoyen 320, Nueva Córdoba and Av. Rafael Núñez 4791, Cerro de la Rosas branches. These identical twins are trendy cocktail-bar-cum-restaurants and popular meeting-places, with live rock music most weekends. Student discount for drinks and meals.

El Ruedo, Obispo Trejo y 27 de Abril. Lively café-bar with music and a mixed clientele, serving fast-food snacks; closes relatively early, around 10pm.

Surocatana, San Jerónimo and Buenos Aires. One of the city's traditional café-bars, with old-fashioned wooden tables and chairs and a 1950s ambience.

Vitrage, 9 de Julio and Rivera Indarte 112. The best coffee in the city is served at this Italian-style *tavola calda*, offering an excellent-value *menú ejecutivo*.

Nightclubs

Carreras, Av. Ramón J. Cárcano s/n, Chateau Carreras. Large disco with "beach" decor plus eclectic music, ranging from country to golden oldies via latest hits, salsa and Argentine rock. Fri–Sun.

El Cólono, Av. Ramón J. Cárcano s/n, Chateau Carreras. Extremely fashionable "multi-space" for thirty-plus clientele, with restaurant, dance-floor, live shows, comedy and concerts. Fri–Sun.

Complejo Coco Walk, Av. Ramón J. Cárcano s/n. Lively, fun place with great music. Restaurant, bar and disco, attracting some of the city's glitterati. Fri–Sun.

Coyote. Av. Ramón J. Cárcano s/n, Chateau Carreras. Popular restaurant and discotheque done out in a tropical style with music to match. Fri–Sun.

Factory, Av. Rafael Núñez 3900, Cerro de las Rosas. Best disco in the neighbourhood in this small but classy joint in a discreet brick building with aluminium doors. Fri–Sun.

Fly City, Av. Hipólito Yrigoyen and San Lorenzo, Nueva Córdoba. One of the few discos left in the downtown area. Extremely popular, mostly frequented by under-25s. Fri–Sun.

Hangar 18, Av. Las Heras 118, El Abasto. Varied music and the odd show provide the entertainment at the city's main gay disco, with a mixed crowd, in a huge airy hangar, as the name suggests. Sat & Sun.

La Morocha. Av. Ramón J. Cárcano s/n, Chateau Carreras. Mostly Latino-style music keeps the young, sometimes business-suited, crowd boogying until dawn. Fri–Sun.

El Rey, Av. Ramón J. Cárcano s/n, Chateau Carreras. Upmarket nightclub where bright young things and professionals come to see and be seen; mostly dance music. Fri–Sun.

Villa Pancho, Av. Ramón J. Cárcano s/n, Chateau Carreras. Another complex with split-level restaurant and a huge disco, mostly playing *fiesta* and salsa. Fri–Sun.

Xero, Av. Las Heras 124, El Abasto. Best downtown discotheque, with a lively atmosphere and mostly Latin rhythms. Fri–Sun.

Listings

Airlines Aerolíneas, Av. Colón 520 (☎0351/426-7631); British Airways, Av. Colón 44 (☎0351/425-7486); Dinar, airport (☎0351/425-5804); Lan-Chile, Deán Funes 154 (☎0351/424-6060); LAPA, Av. F Alcorta 1181 (☎0351/426-3336); Southern Winds, Av. Colón 540 (☎0351/481-0808).

Banks The best for exchanging money are: Lloyds, Buenos Aires 93; Citibank, Rivadavia 104; Banco Mayo, 9 de Julio 137. ATMs everywhere, especially around Plaza San Martín.

Car rental Avis, Corrientes 452 (☎0351/426-1110); Dollar, Av. Chacabuco 185 (☎0351/421-0426); Hertz, airport (☎0351/481-6496) and at the *Sheraton* (☎0351/488-9050); Localiza, Humberto Primero 531 (☎0351/426-0240); Squire José, A. de Goyechea 2851 (☎0351/420-5131).

Consulates Bolivia, Barros 873 (☎0351/480-8690); Chile, Crisol 280 (☎0351/469-1944); Germany, A. Olmos 501 (☎0351/489-0826); Italy, Ayacucho 129 (☎0351/423-8854 & 421-1020); Netherlands, Chacabuco 716 (☎0351/420-8200); Paraguay, Gral Paz 73 (☎0351/423-7043); Spain, Chacabuco 875 (☎0351/469-7490); Uruguay, Obispo Salguero 638 (☎0351/468-4088).

Hospital Catamarca y Guzmán (☎0351/421-0243).

Internet CyberUNO, Duarte Quiros 201 (☎0351/4281849; *infor@pp1.net)*.

Laundry Laverap, Chacabuco 301, Belgrano 76 and R. Indarte 289.

Left luggage At bus terminal, open 24hr.

Pharmacy Taleb, Av. Hipólito Yrigoyen 398 or 25 de Mayo 15.

Post office Av. General Paz 201.

Taxis American Remis ☎0351/156-764456 or 464-5217; Taxi-Com ☎0351/464-0000.

Telephones Telecom, General Paz 36 and 27 de Abril 27, and *locutorios* everywhere.

The Camino de la Historia

The first 150km stretch of the RN9, running northwards towards Santiago del Estero from Córdoba city, is promoted by the provincial tourist authority as the **Camino de la Historia**, or History Route, coinciding as it does with part of the colonial Camino Real or Royal Way, the Spanish road from Lima and Potosí into present-day Argentina. This was the route taken by the region's first settlers, the founders of Córdoba city, and the **Jesuit missionaries** who quickly dominated the local economy and culture, building their estancias and funding their artistic output with slave labour employed on *encomiendas*, plots of land granted to colonizers. Eastwards from the road stretch some of Argentina's most fertile cattle-ranches, while to the west the unbroken ridge of the Sierras Chicas runs parallel to the highway. One of the country's finest Jesuit estancias, now the well-presented **Museo Jesuítico Nacional San Isidro Labrador**, can be visited at **Jesús María**, while beautiful **Santa Catalina**, lying off the main road to the north in a bucolic hillside setting, is still inhabited by direct descendants of the family who moved there at the end of the eighteenth century. Further north, in **Villa Tulumba**, a timeless little place well off the beaten track, the nondescript parish church houses a masterpiece of Jesuit art, the altarpiece that once adorned the Jesuits' temple and, later, Córdoba Cathedral, until it was moved up here in the early nineteenth century. As they developed their intensive agriculture, the Jesuits all but wiped out the region's pre-Hispanic civilizations but some precious vestiges of their culture, intriguing rock paintings, can be seen right up in the far north of the province, just off the RN9 at **Cerro Colorado**, one of Argentina's finest archeological sites.

Jesús María

Lying just off the busy RN9 50km north of Córdoba, **JESÚS MARÍA** is a sleepy little market town that comes to life for the annual Festival Nacional de la Doma y el Folklore, a gaucho fiesta with lively entertainments held every evening during the first fortnight of January. On the town's northern outskirts, near the amphitheatre where the festival takes place, is the Museo Jesuítico Nacional San Isidro Labrador (Mon–Fri 8am–noon & 2–7pm, Sat & Sun 2–6pm; $1), housed in the former residence and the *bodega*, or wineries, of a well-restored Jesuit estancia. Next to the missionaries' living quarters, and the adjoining eighteenth-century church, are a colonial *tajamar*, or reservoir, and apple and peach orchards – all that remain of the estancia's once extensive territory, which in the seventeenth and eighteenth centuries covered more than a hundred square kilometres. In contrast to the bare, rough-hewn granite of the outside walls of the complex, a sparkling white courtyard lies beyond a gateway to the right of the church. Its two storeys of simple whitewashed arches on three sides set off the bright red roofs, capped with the original ceramic tiles or *musleros*. These slightly convex roof-tiles, taking their name from *muslo*, or thigh, because the tile-makers shaped the clay on their legs, are common to all of the Jesuit estancias. The U-shaped *residencia* contains the former missionaries' cells, storehouses and communal rooms, now used for temporary exhibits and various permanent displays of archeological finds, colonial furniture, sacred relics and religious artwork from the seventeenth and eighteenth centuries, along with farming and wine-making equipment. The local wine, Lagrimilla, is claimed to be the first colonial wine served in the Spanish court – Argentina's earliest vineyards were planted here at the end of the sixteenth century.

Santa Catalina and Villa Tulumba

The RN156 to the west of Jesús María leads to Ascochinga where an easily passable trail heads north through thick forest to **Santa Catalina**, 20km to the northwest. Almost hidden among the hills, Santa Catalina is undoubtedly the finest Jesuit estancia in the region, an outstanding example of colonial architecture in the Spanish Americas. A sprawling yet harmonious set of early eighteenth-century buildings, it is dominated by its church, whose elegant pale grey silhouette and symmetrical towers suddenly and unexpectedly appear as you emerge from the woods.

On arrival, head straight for the little confitería, accessible through a narrow passageway to the right of the church; at least one member of the Díaz family should be on hand to serve you some delicious home-cured ham, open up the church and show you around the estancia. Indeed, the charm of this place is that it looks and feels so lived-in: it's the residence of direct descendants of Antonio Díaz, a mayor of Córdoba who acquired it in the 1770s, following the Jesuits' expulsion from the Spanish empire. The church itself ($1 donation) is dedicated to St Catherine of Alexandria whose feast-day is celebrated with pomp every November 25; the sternly imposing facade is reminiscent of the Baroque churches of southern Germany and Austria. Inside, the austere single nave is decorated with a gilded wooden retable, housing an image of St Catherine, and a fine carob-wood pulpit. The peaceful inner courtyards of the estancia, furnished with graceful wicker, leather and calfskin chairs, are shaded by magnolias and bougainvilleas and cooled by Italianate fountains. On the right-hand flank of the church, in a tiny walled cemetery, is the overgrown grave of the Italian composer and organist Domenico Zípoli, who died here in 1726.

The winding track that leads to Santa Catalina continues northeastwards for some 20km, to where the RN60 forks left from the RN9. Another 50km north by the RN9, at San José de la Dormida, a signposted road heads west to **VILLA TULUMBA**, 22km beyond, a tiny hamlet that's home to a Baroque masterpiece: you'll find the subtly crafted seventeenth-century tabernacle, complete with polychrome wooden cherubs and saints, and decorated with just a hint of gold, inside the parish church. Soon after Argentina's independence, Bishop Moscoso, a modernizing anti-Jesuit bishop of Córdoba, decided that the city's cathedral should have a brand new altarpiece, and asked all the parishes in his diocese to collect funds for it. The citizens of Villa Tulumba were the most generous and were rewarded with this tabernacle, which had been transferred to the cathedral from the city's Jesuit temple after the Society of Jesus was expelled from the Spanish empire by decree of King Charles III in 1767.

Parque Arqueológico y Natural Cerro Colorado

Nearly 120km north of Jesús María, at the far northern end of the Camino de la Historia, is the Parque Arqueológico y Natural Cerro Colorado (daily 9am–1pm & 2–6pm; $1). It's located next to Cerro Colorado village, 10km down a meandering dirt track off the RN9 to the west of Santa Elena. Drivers beware: there's a deep ford lurking round a bend, 1km before you enter the village, followed by another in the village itself.

CERRO COLORADO village, no more than a few houses dotted along the river bank, nestles in a deep, picturesque valley, surrounded by three looming peaks, the Cerro Colorado (830m), Cerro Veladero (810m) and Cerro Inti Huasi (772m), all easily explored on foot and affording fine views of unspoilt countryside. The main attraction, though, is one of the country's finest collections of **petroglyphs**, several thousand drawings executed between 1000 and 1600 AD which were scraped and painted by the indigenous inhabitants onto the pink rock face at the base of the mountains and in caves higher up. Compulsory **guided tours** ($1) leave several times daily from the *guardería* at the entrance to the village. Nearby is a tiny museum (daily 9am–6pm; free), with some photographs of the petroglyphs and native flora, though made slightly redundant by the guide who takes you round the petroglyphs, pointing out the many plant varieties along the way. Some of the petroglyphs depict horses, cattle and European figures as well as native llamas, guanacos, condors, pumas and snakes, but few of the abstract figures have been satisfactorily or conclusively interpreted – though you'll be offered convincing theories by your guide. The deep depressions, or *morteros*, in the horizontal rock nearby were caused over the centuries by the grinding and mixing of paints. Of the different **pigments** used – chalk, ochre, charcoal, oils and vegetable extracts – the white and black stand out more than the rest, but climatic changes, especially increased humidity, are already taking their toll, and many of the rock paintings are badly faded. Some of them have disappeared altogether: one drawing, representing the Sun God, was removed to the British Museum; all that remains is a gaping hole in the rock, high up on the Cerro, where it was hacked out. The petroglyphs are best viewed very early in the morning or before dusk, when the rock takes on blazing red hues and the contrast is at its strongest.

Several **buses** a day – Ciudad Córdoba, Cacorba, Río Seco and Córdoba-Mar del Plata – run from Córdoba to Santa Elena, 11km away; the only way to get to Cerro Colorado from there is on foot or by *remise*. There are **camping** facilities with river bathing in the village, and various rooms for rent but no tourist information – just ask around. The only **hotel**, as yet unnamed (③), is brand-new, modern and comfortable. Of the **places to eat**, the best is *Purinki Huasi* near the ford and stepping stones across the river, and serving reasonably priced grilled meats and sandwiches.

The Punilla Valley

Squeezed between the continuous ridge of the Sierras Chicas, to the east, and the higher peaks of the Sierra Grande, to the west, with a section of the RN38 toll-paying highway to La Rioja as its artery, the peaceful **Punilla Valley** stretches northwards for about a hundred kilometres from the horrendously noisy resort of **Villa Carlos Paz** – the "Gateway to the Punilla" – some 30km along the RN20 to the west of Córdoba. Punilla – whose name means "little *puna*" or highland plain – is Argentina's longest-established inland tourist area drawing a steady stream of visitors with its idyllic mountain scenery and fresh air, fun-for-the-family resorts, top-class hiking as well as opportunities for more adventurous pursuits, plus an especially amenable climate. For many years a community of Anglo-Argentines and artists from North America have also colonized the area, attracted by its mild weather, picturesque landscapes and tranquillity.

Tens of thousands of Cordobeses and Porteños migrate to the brash inland beach resort of **Villa Carlos Paz** every summer, in an insatiable quest for sun, sand and socializing – the town is renowned for its mega-discos and crowded bars. A short distance north and overlooked by a sugar-loaf hill, El Pan de Azúcar, is **Cosquín**, a slightly calmer place famed for its once-prestigious annual folk festival. The farther north you go, the more tranquil the resorts become: **La Falda**, **La Cumbre** and **Capilla del Monte** have all retained their slightly old-fashioned charm, while offering a high quality of services. Seldom overcrowded, they make for better bases from which to explore the mountains on foot, on horseback, or in a vehicle, or to try out some of the adventurous sports on offer.

Buses between Córdoba and Villa Carlos Paz are fast and frequent, running around the clock; many of them continue up the valley towards La Rioja and San Juan, stopping at all the main resorts along the way. Part of the late nineteenth-century passenger railway to Cruz del Eje has been revived as a scenic tourist attraction, the **Tren de la Sierra** (Dec–Easter Wed–Sun; ☎0351/482-2252). It leaves the station in Córdoba's Barrio Alto Verde at 10am, returning at around 4pm. A return to Cosquín costs $10, to Capilla del Monte is $22; the train also stops at La Falda and La Cumbre.

Villa Carlos Paz

VILLA CARLOS PAZ lies 35km west of Córdoba, at the southern end of the Punilla Valley and on the southwestern banks of a large, polluted reservoir, the Lago San Roque, filled by the Río San Antonio. It lies at a major junction, that of the RN20, which heads southwards to Mina Clavero and on to San Luis and San Juan, and the RN38 toll-road which goes northwards through the valley towards Cruz del Eje and La Rioja. Nationally famous, the resort is frequently compared with Mar del Plata (see p.181); it started out in the 1930s as the holiday centre for well-off Cordobeses for whom the Atlantic coast was too far away, and sandy beaches were built along the lakeside. People now whizz around the lake in catamarans and motorboats, or go water-skiing. In the town centre, dozens of tacky amusement arcades and entertainment theme-parks blare out loud music, while most of the bars and confiterías show video clips or offer karaoke. The town sprawls in a disorderly way around the lakeside, and the microcentro's main streets, avenidas Libertad, General San Martín, General Paz and 9 de Julio, head off in different directions, on the east bank of the river. Generally speaking, the western districts are greener, airier and more attractively built. The local population of 40,000 more than doubles at the height of summer, in January and February, when the 350 hotels and *hosterías* are all booked up and the dozen campsites are crammed full. Unless you like overcrowded holiday resorts with a raucous nightlife, there's nothing to detain you here.

Practicalities

Serving dozens of local, regional and national destinations, including Buenos Aires and Córdoba, the busy and cramped **bus terminal** is on Avenida San Martín, between calles Belgrano and Maipú. Right in front of it, the main **tourist information office**, at Av. San Martín 400 (9am–9pm; ☎03541/421624) will help you find a bed for the night; during peak periods this can be difficult, even though there are so many hotels, and many residents stand by the roadside advertising rooms for rent. Check them out before committing yourself, though they tend to be perfectly all right. Two lakeside **hotels** stand out from the huge crowd: *Hostería Hipocampus* at Brown 246, on the west bank (☎03541/421653; ③), with clean, plain rooms and a pleasant bar; and *Hostería El Ciervo de Oro* at Hipólito Yrigoyen 995, on the east bank (☎03541/422498; ⑤), in an appealing modern block, with a swimming pool, large terrace and smart, big rooms. Away from the water's edge, *Hostel Acapulco* at La Paz 75 (☎03541/421929; ②) is the most reliable budget accommodation. The best, least crowded **campsite** is outside town, at Bialet Massé 6km to the north; *Camping Domingo Funes* charges $3, and offers clean facilities and a confitería.

There are dozens of **places to eat**, mostly pizzerías, but the best is a Spanish-style *tasca*, *La Albufera*, at Av. General Paz, where many restaurants are located. *Il Gatto* at Av. Libertad and Belgrano, *El Dorado* at Av. San Martín 1500 and *La Casona* at San Martín and Gobernador Roca, are the three leading parrillas, each serving juicy steaks in a traditional decor. The most appealing **cafés** are *Angus*, at Av. San Martín 660 and *Hermitage*, at 9 de Julio 467. *Keop's*, at Rodriguez Peña and Séneca, and *Molino Rojo*, at Av. 9 de Julio and Calle C. Cuatiá, are the town's two most famous **discotheques**, each with a capacity of over five thousand, while *Khalama*, at Av. Estrada 113, is a little more intimate; as elsewhere, the popularity of nightclubs tends to be ephemeral.

Cosquín

Some 25km north of Villa Carlos Paz, the small bustling town of **COSQUÍN** nestles in a sweep of the river of the same name and in the lee of the 1260-metre **Pan de Azúcar**. It's one of the region's oldest settlements – dating from colonial times – and has been a holiday resort since the end of the nineteenth century, when the railway was built. The summit of the sugar-loaf mountain, affording panoramic views of the valley and mountains beyond, can be reached by a chairlift or *aerosilla* (daily: summer 9am–9pm; winter closes 7pm; $7 return). Just north of the town the Camino 6 de Septiembre climbs for 6km east to the station next to a bronze monument to Carlos Gardel, legendary tango singer. Alternatively, it's possible to walk to the top, about half an hour up a steep, winding path. Near the start of the Camino 6 de Septiembre, on the RN38, is the town's only worthwhile museum, the **Museo Camín Cosquín** (daily 8.30am–12.30pm & 2–9pm; closes 6pm in winter; $1), where you can learn more about the cultures of the indigenous Ayampitín and Ongamira peoples who inhabited the valley in pre-Hispanic times. The museum displays local archeological finds, such as ceramics, fossils and samples of semi-precious minerals; its shop sells some fine jewellery. Cosquín has always been associated with the **Festival Nacional de Folklore**, held every year in the second half of January, attended by folk artists, ballet troupes and classical musicians from across the country, but the festival has declined in quality in recent years. The festival takes place in the Plaza Próspero Molina (also known as the Plaza del Folklore Nacional), which is joined to the Plaza San Martín at the town's southern end by a stretch of the RN38, the Avenida San Martín.

The **bus station**, with half-hourly services to and from Córdoba and other Punilla resorts, lies one block west of Plaza San Martín at Presidente Perón s/n. The **tourist information office** is at San Martín 560 (Mon–Fri 8am–9pm, Sat, Sun & public holidays 9am–6pm; ☎03541/451105; *www.onenet.com.ar/cosquin*), five blocks north opposite Plaza Próspero Molina. The town has several **places to stay** (although resorts farther north have a much better choice), the best of which is the central *Puerta del Sol*, at Perón 820 (☎03541/451626; ⑤), with comfortable rooms with modern bathrooms. *Hotel*

El Lago, at General Paz 468 (☎03541/451542; ②), is far more downmarket, but enjoys riverside views and has plain, spotless rooms with bath. Cosquín's best-equipped **campsite** is the *San Buenaventura*, across the Zuviría bridge amid green fields (☎03541/423130); it charges $8 per tent and has modern sanitary facilities and a confitería. You eat very well at two **restaurants**, in particular: the *St Jean parrilla* at Avenida San Martín and Soberanía Nacional or, for excellent seafood, the *San Marino* at Av. San Martín 707.

La Falda and around

Twenty kilometres north of Cosquín, **LA FALDA** is today just another Punilla town, a peaceful place from which to explore the nearby mountains. In the early twentieth century, however, it was an exclusive resort, served by the newly built railway and luring the great and the good from as far afield as Europe. A major advertising campaign was conducted here by a German-run luxury hotel, **Hotel Edén**, now sadly dilapidated and an unusual tourist attraction (daily 9.30am–12.30pm & 3–7pm; guided tours $3). Located at the far eastern end of Avenida Edén, the magnificent holiday palace was built in the 1890s. Nearly all of Argentine high society stayed there in its 1920s' and 1930s' heyday, while the most famous international guests were the Prince of Wales and Albert Einstein. The hotel is now a relic rather than a monument, having never recovered after the state confiscated it from its German owners in the 1940s, but its grandiose design and opulent decor are still discernible in the ruins; the guided tours start with a drink at the bar, before taking you around the faded rooms.

The RN38 winds through the western side of the town as Avenida Presidente Kennedy; from it, Avenida Edén heads straight towards the mountainside to the east. The main reason to stop in La Falda, apart from relaxing, is to explore the nearby mountains on foot or on horseback, or to go on longer trips, some involving mountaineering, organized by a couple of professional outfits based here. Bird-watching, mountain-biking and photo-safaris are also on the agenda. For the less energetic the **Museo Arqueológico Argentino Ambato** (daily 9.30am–1pm & 3–8.30pm; $1), Cuesta del Lago 1467, at the east end of Avenida Edén near the former hotel, houses an outstanding and well-labelled collection of ceramics from the immediate area and the Argentine Northwest. Three blocks north, and well-signposted, at Las Murallas 200, the **Museo del Ferrocarril en Miniatura** (Nov–Easter daily 9.30am–8pm; rest of year Sat, Sun & public holidays only, same times; $1) is great for children, with model railways and old train carriages.

To reach nearby **Cerro Banderita** for exhilarating views of the valley, go to the far end of Avenida Edén and then, just past the railway museum, take Calle Austria as far as El Chorrito, a small waterfall among lush vegetation. This is the starting-point of the steep one-hour climb to the peak, which many people do on horseback, and then ride along the mountain-top. Of the longer routes, one of the most impressive takes you over the Sierras Chicas eastwards towards **Río Ceballos**; the views down into the Punilla valley from the peak at **Cerro Cuadrado**, 20km from La Falda, are stunning. To the west, past the Dique La Falda reservoir, a dirt track leads across the windswept but hauntingly beautiful **Pampa de Oláen**, where several well-preserved colonial chapels dot the moor-like landscape. The finest is the eighteenth-century **Capilla Santa Barbara** near Olaén, its simple, curvaceous white silhouette framed by gnarled trees; inside is equally stark, apart from some fine polychrome statues decorating the altarpiece.

Practicalities

La Falda's **bus station** is on Avenida Buenos Aires (☎03548/423186) just north of the intersection of avenidas Presidente Kennedy and Edén; all buses from Córdoba and

Carlos Paz to San Juan and La Rioja stop here. Next door at España 50, the enthusiastically staffed **tourist office** (daily 7am–9pm; ☎03548/423462) has stacks of information on accommodation and services. For hiring horses and renting motorbikes or mountain-bikes, try Casa Loza, at 25 de Mayo 460. Emotion at Av. Edén 475 is the best bet for bird-watching safaris, 4WD expeditions, mountaineering and other excursions. **Accommodation** ranges from the luxurious, large-bedroomed *Hotel Nor Tormarza* at Av. Edén 1063 (☎03548/422004; ⑦), through the very comfortable *Hotel Ollantay* at La Plata 236 (☎03548/422341; ④), to the inexpensive but pleasant *Residencial Achalay* at Victoria 294 (☎03548/422318; ①). *Hotel L'Hirondelle* at Av. Edén 861 (☎03548/422825; ③) has bright rooms and new bathrooms. The best-equipped **campsite** is the *Siete Cascadas* (☎03548/423869; $4 per tent), on the banks of the reservoir, due west of the bus terminal. Places to **eat** include *La Parrilla de Raúl* at Calle Buenos Aires 111 (☎03548/421128), and its twin establishment at Av. Edén 1002. *Il Nonno di Silmona* at Eucaliptos s/n (near the *Hotel Nor Tormarza*) serves slightly more sophisticated but inexpensive meals while La Falda's best pizzeria is the *America* at Sarmiento 199.

La Cumbre and around

LA CUMBRE, a small, leafy town, lying just east of the RN38, 13km north of La Falda, is a great spot for relaxing, fishing, exploring the mountains or participating in adventure pursuits. At over 1100m above sea level, it enjoys mild summers and cool winters, and it has been known to snow. Several trout-rich streams rush down from the steep mountains and gurgle through the town, among them the Río San Gerónimo that runs past the central Plaza 25 de Mayo. La Cumbre's prestigious golf club, its predominantly mock-Tudor villas and manicured lawns testify to the long-standing Anglo-Saxon presence. But despite the resort's genteel appearance it has become synonymous with **hang-gliding**; every March international competitions are held here. Cerro Mirador, the cliff-top launching-point for hang-gliding and parasailing, is near the ruined colonial estancia and chapel of **Cuchi Corral**, 10km due west of La Cumbre, worth visiting for the views alone whether or not you join in the lemming-like activities. Anyone with a literary bent will like the small museum at **El Paraíso**, in Cruz Chica, 2km to the north of La Cumbre (Dec–Easter daily 2–6pm; rest of year Sat, Sun & public holidays only, same times; $3; ☎03548/451160). The Spanish-style house, set in a beautiful garden, was home to the hedonistic Argentine writer Manuel "Manucho" Mujica Laínez, whose novel *Bomarzo* is regarded as an Argentine classic. Written in 1962, it was turned into an opera whose premiere at the Teatro Colón in Buenos Aires in 1967 was banned by the military dictatorship. As well as a delightful collection of the writer's personal effects is a specially cast iron door, his "gate to heaven", decorated with erotic figures, which leads to a room where it is said he held frequent orgies.

One of the province's most spectacular scenic routes, ideal for mountain-bikes, takes you along the **Camino del Pungo**. Beyond **Estancia El Rosario**, signposted from the golf course to the southeast of La Cumbre's centre, it climbs the mountainside and plunges into dense pine forest, before fording the Río Tiu Mayu. It then passes through luxuriant forest – eucalyptus, cacti, palms, firs and osiers – and crosses the summit of the Sierra Grande, before reaching Ascochinga, 41km away, and Santa Catalina (see p.254). A right-hand fork immediately before the Río Tiu Mayu takes you southwards along a roughly surfaced but spectacular road. At the end of the road, some 45km from La Cumbre, is the splendid eighteenth-century Jesuit chapel of **Candonga**, with its pristine walls, ochre tiled roof and rough-hewn stone steps. The majestic curve of its porch, the delicate bell tower and lantern-like cupola fit snugly into the bucolic valley setting, set off by a fast-flowing brook that sweeps through the pampas fields nearby. The delightful *Hostería Candonga* (☎0351/471-0683; ④) offers half or full board, including great *asados*.

Practicalities

La Cumbre's **tourist office** (daily 8.30am–7pm; (☎03548/451154) is in the train station – now used only by the Tren de la Sierra – where Avenida San Martín intersects Calle Caraffa, 300m southwest of the central square. Immediately to the south, the **bus station** is at Caraffa and General Paz; services to and from Córdoba and Capilla del Monte are half-hourly. Top-notch **accommodation** includes the upmarket *Hotel San Andrés* at Benitz and Monteagudo (☎03548/451165; ⑨), with excellent breakfasts and a swimming pool, and the charming *Hotel Victoria*, overlooking the golf course at Posadas and Moreno (☎03548/451412; $60), slightly old-fashioned but cosy, with excellent cuisine. Cheaper alternatives are the very comfortable *Hotel Los Cedros* at Argentina s/n (☎03548/451028; ④) and the basic but clean *Residencial Petit* (no phone; ②), near the bus terminal at Paz and Rivadavia. La Cumbre's excellent **campsite** is the *El Cristo* up near the Cristo Redentor statue, at Monseñor Pablo Cabrera s/n (☎03548/451893; $5 per pitch); tents may be rented for $6 a night. The two best **restaurants**, for trout and other specialities, are *La Casona del Toboso* at Belgrano 349 (☎03548/451436) and *La Bagubla* on the road towards the Estancia del Rosario (closed Easter–Nov). Better still, the dining-room at the *Hotel Victoria* serves set-menu gourmet dinners for $20.

Should you be tempted by **hang-gliding**, try Julio Verne (☎03548/421967), Extreme (☎03548/491677), Escuela de Aladelta (☎03548/452188) and the Club Andino (☎03548/492271). **Horses** can be hired from Cachito Silva, at Pasaje Beiró s/n (☎03548/451703) and El Rosendo at Juan XXIII s/n (☎0358/451688). Rent-a-Car is at Caraffa s/n (☎03548/451025).

Capilla del Monte and around

Lively **CAPILLA DEL MONTE** sits at the confluence of the Ríos Calabalumba and Dolores in the lee of bare-sloped Cerro Uriturco, at 1979m the highest peak of the Sierras Chicas, 16km north of La Cumbre. A well-heeled resort for Argentina's bourgeoisie at the end of the nineteenth century, as testified by the many luxurious villas, some of them slightly dilapidated, these days it attracts more alternative vacationers, as you can tell from the number of hotels and restaurants calling themselves *naturista*, or back-to-nature. The town has little to offer in the way of sights, but it serves as a good alternative base along the valley for treks up into the mountains or for trying out hang-gliding and other pursuits. Central Plaza San Martín lies only a couple of blocks east of the RN38, which runs through the west of the town, parallel to the Río de Dolores. From the plaza, Diagonal Buenos Aires, the busy commercial pedestrian mall, runs southeastwards to the quaint train station –these days used only by the seasonal Tren de la Sierra – on Calle Pueyrredón; it's claimed to be South America's only roofed street, an assertion nowhere else has rushed to contend. A number of safe bathing areas, or *balnearios*, can be found along the Río Calabalumba, such as Balneario Calabalumba, at the northern end of General Paz, and Balneario La Toma, at the eastern end of Avenida Sabattini.

Many visitors are drawn by the claims of **UFO sightings**, "energy centres" and the many local **legends**, as well as the fresh air, unspoilt countryside and opportunities for sports pursuits, such as trekking and fishing. One such legend asserts that when Calabalumba, the young daughter of a witch-doctor, eloped with Uriturco, the latter was turned into a mountain while she was condemned to eternal sorrow, her tears forming the river that flows from the mountainside. Incidentally, the **Cerro Uriturco** is well worth the climb (2–3hr to the top) for the grandiose views across the valley to the Sierra de Cuniputo to the west. The steep clamber up a well-trodden path starts near the Balneario Calabalumba, to the northeast of Plaza San Martín, and cuts through private property ($1). Only part of the climb is shaded, so preferably go early in the morning and take a supply of water with you.

A short drive out of town is the entrance to **Los Terrones** (daily 9am–dusk; $1), an amazing formation of multicoloured rocks on either side of a 5km dirt track. You can drive through Los Terrones quickly enough, but it's far better to walk along the sign-posted path which winds in between the rocks (a ninety-minute circuit), so you can admire the strange shapes, all gnarled and twisted, some of them resembling animals or human forms. To get there head 8km north of town, along the RN38, and turn off along the RP17 which climbs east into the heights of the northern Sierras Chicas; after 5km, near a house selling excellent palm-leaf baskets and trays, is the entrance to the site. Another 14km east, back on the RP17, along winding cliff-side roads that take you across the impressive Quebrada de la Luna, is **Ongamira**. Here strange caves and rock forma-tions sculpted by wind and rain in the reddish sandstone were painted with black, yel-low and white pigments by indigenous tribes some six hundred years ago; the pictures are of animals, human figures and abstract geometric patterns, and must be surveyed from a special viewpoint ($2 entrance), as the extremely friable stone is gradually crum-bling away and many of the pre-Hispanic rock paintings have already been lost. This road, affording magnificent panoramas, eventually leads on to Santa Catalina and Cerro Colorado (see pp.254–255).

Practicalities

Capilla del Monte's **bus station** is at the corner of Corrientes and Rivadavia, 200m south of Plaza San Martín; there are regular bus services down the valley to Córdoba and up to Cruz del Eje. The station building houses the dynamic **tourist information centre** (daily 8am–8pm; ☎03546/481903), whose eager staff have the details of dozens of guides and operators offering treks, horse-riding, hang-gliding and safaris into the nearby mountains. **Hotels** include the very pleasant *Hotel Principado* with its own river-beach and a large park, at 9 de Julio 550 (☎03546/481043; ⑤); the clean and smart *Hotel Petit Sierras* at Pueyrredón and Salta (☎03546/481667; ⑤); the plain but tidy *Hotel Las Gemelas* at L.N. Além 967 (☎03546/481186; ③), with its own health-food restaurant; and the bright *Hotel La Loma* at Pedro Frias 123 (☎03546/481138; ③). *Hostería Tercero Milenio* at Corrientes 471 (☎03546/481958; ③) is one of the many *naturista* places to stay, and its excellent health-food restaurant is open to non-guests. The town's best **campsite** is the *Calabalumba* on the river bank, near the bridge at the end of General Paz (☎03546/481341; $3 per tent). Most of the **cafés and restaurants** are strung along Diagonal Buenos Aires; *Entreplatos* at Buenos Aires 182 does a vegetarian set lunch for $5, *Il Formaggio* at Buenos Aires 106 specializes in pizzas and pasta, while meat-eaters will prefer *Camón* at Buenos Aires 247, which serves roast kid and suckling-pig, along with steaks. *Confitería City* at Buenos Aires 187 does very good cakes, while *Skorpios*, at Buenos Aires 178, has the best *lomitos* and serves real Irish coffee.

The Calamuchita Valley

Long established as one of Córdoba Province's major holiday destinations, and where many cityfolk have weekend or summer homes, the green **Calamuchita Valley** begins 30km south of Córdoba city at the Jesuit estancia town of **Alta Gracia** – a popular day-trip destination from Córdoba – and stretches due south for over 100km, between the undulating Sierras Chicas, to the east, and the steep Sierra de Comechingones range to the west. The fertile valley gets its Camiare name from Río Catlamochita, which flows down from the Comechingones peaks. In turn, the river which the colonizers pro-saically baptized Río Tercero, or "Third River", comes from the words *ktala* and *muchi*, the locally abundant native shrubs called *tala* and *molle* in Castilian. The vegetation that covers the valley-sides provides a perfect habitat for hundreds of varieties of birds. Two large and very clean reservoirs, Embalse Los Molinos in the north and Embalse Río

Tercero at the southern extremity of the valley, both dammed in the first half of the twentieth century for water supplies, electricity and recreational angling, give the valley its alternative name, sometimes used by the local tourist authority: **Valle Azul de los Grandes Lagos** or Blue Valley of the Great Lakes. It's believed that the area's **climate** has been altered by their creation, with noticeably wetter summers than in the past.

The valley's two main towns could not be more different: **Villa General Belgrano** is a chocolate-box resort with a predominantly Germanic population, whereas **Santa Rosa de Calamuchita**, the valley's rather brash self-styled capital, to the south, is youthful and dynamic but far less picturesque. Both are good bases for exploring the beautiful Comechingones mountains, whose Camiare name means "mountains and many villages". One of these villages, the quiet hamlet of **La Cumbrecita**, would not look out of place in the Swiss Alps and is the starting-point for some fine highland walks. All the villages offer a wide range of accommodation and some high-quality places to eat, making them ideal bases for anyone wanting to avoid big cities like Córdoba. Frequent **buses** and *trafics* run along the arterial RP5 between Córdoba and Santa Rosa de Calamuchita, some stopping at Alta Gracia.

Alta Gracia

Forty kilometres south of Córdoba and 3km west of the RP5, historic **ALTA GRACIA** lies at the northern entrance of the Calamuchita Valley. In the 1920s and 1930s, its rural, hilly spot between the city and the mountains made it popular with the wealthy bourgeoisie of Buenos Aires and Córdoba, who built holiday homes in the town – Che Guevara, surprisingly, spent some of his youth here, and revolutionary composer Manuel de Falla fled here from the Spanish Civil War. The original colonial settlement dates from the late sixteenth century, but in 1643 it was chosen as the site for a **Jesuit estancia** around which the town grew up – most of the other estancias in the province, like Santa Catalina and Jesús María, remained in open countryside. After the Jesuits' expulsion in 1767, the estancia fell into ruin but was inhabited for a short time in 1810 by Viceroy Liniers, forced to leave Córdoba by events following the Argentine declaration of independence (see box on Deán Funes, p.240). The **Museo Histórico Casa del Virrey Liniers** is housed in the Residencia, the Jesuits' original living quarters and workshops (Dec–Easter Tues–Fri 9am–1pm 4–8pm, Sat, Sun & public holidays 9.30am–12.30pm & 5–8pm; Easter–Nov Tues–Fri 9am–1pm & 3–7pm Sat, Sun & public holidays 9.30am–12.30pm & 3.30–6.30pm; $2, free on Wed; guided tours in English). Entered through an ornate Baroque doorway on Avenida Sáenz Peña, the beautifully restored building, with its colonnaded upper storey, forms two sides of a cloistered courtyard. Exhibits consist mainly of period furniture and art, mostly dating from the early nineteenth century, but the most interesting sections of the museum are the painstakingly recreated **kitchen** and the coyly named *áreas comunes*, or toilets, from which the waste was channelled into a cistern used to irrigate and fertilize the estancia's crops. The church adjoining the Residencia, in pitifully poor repair, forms the west side of the town's main square, **Plaza Manuel Solares**.

Directly to the north of the estancia are the peaceful waters of the **Tajamar**, or estancia reservoir, one of Argentina's earliest hydraulic projects, dating from 1659; it both supplied water for the community and served as a mill-pond. In its mirror-like surface is reflected the town's emblematic **clock tower**. Erected in 1938 to mark 350 years of colonization, the tower is decorated at each corner by a stone figure portraying the four major civilizations of Córdoba Province: native, conquistador, Jesuit missionary and gaucho. Avenida Sarmiento leads up a slope from the western bank of the Tajamar into **Villa Carlos Pellegrini**, an interesting residential district of quaint timber and wrought-iron dwellings, dating from when rich Porteños built summer-houses here in the fashionable so-called *estilo inglés*, a local interpretation of mock-Tudor. One of these, Villa Beatriz, at Avellaneda 501, was for several years in the 1930s home to **Ernesto "Che" Guevara**, sent here as an adolescent to benefit from the dry continental climate in the vain hope of curing his debilitating asthma. Another villa, Los Espinillos, nearby at Av. Carlos Pellegrini 1011, was the Spanish composer **Manuel de Falla's** home for seven years until his death on November 14, 1946. Now the **Museo Manuel de Falla** (Dec–Easter Tues–Fri 3–8pm, Sat, Sun & holidays 10am–noon & 3–8pm; Easter–Nov Tues–Fri 2–7pm Sat, Sun & holidays 10am–noon & 3–8pm; $1), exhibiting its piano and other personal effects, it affords fine views of the nearby mountains. Piano and other music recitals are given in the small concert hall in the garden.

Regular **buses** from Córdoba stop at the corner of avenidas Sarmiento and Vélez Sarsfield, and leave equally regularly for Villa General Belgrano. The municipal **tourist office** is in the clock tower at Luís Sáenz Peña and Calle del Molino (daily 9am–5pm; ☎03547/423455). Should you want to stay over, the town's best **hotel**, *La Posada*, is situated 100m west of the clock tower, at Av. del Tajamar 95 (☎03547/423804; ⑤). It has large, smart rooms with en-suite bathrooms, and enjoys lovely views of the mill-pond. The *Hotel Savoy* (☎03547/421125; ③) at Av. Sarmiento 418, near the bus-stop, is better value, though, with spotless rooms, all with shower. Up in the hills to the west, 5km along the road to Los Paredones, is *El Potrerillo de Larreta* (☎03547/423804; ⑦), an upmarket ranch-style hotel, with golf course, stables, beautiful rooms with mountain views and a gourmet dining-room. You can also fish in the Arroyo de los Paredones, which runs through the extensive grounds. The town's **campsite**, *Los Sauces*, in located in wooded Parque Federico García Lorca, half a kilometre west of the Museo Manuel de Falla. It costs $4 per person and has decent facilities. You eat best at Villa General Belgrano, but you could try **restaurants** such as the *Trattoria Oro*, at Av. España 18, on the corner of Plaza Manuel Solares; it serves reasonably priced fish, pasta and *empanadas*, and even features frog on the menu. Beer, snacks and German-style pastries are available at the *Stuttgart*, a couple of blocks east at Av. Belgrano 135.

Villa General Belgrano

Fifty kilometres south of Alta Gracia, along attractive corniches skirting the blue waters of the **Embalse Los Molinos**, and just a couple of kilometres west of the RP5 artery, is the demure resort of **VILLA GENERAL BELGRANO**. The unspoiled alpine scenery of its back country, the folksy architecture and decor, and the Germanic traditions of the local population all give the place a distinctly Mitteleuropean feel. Most of the townspeople are of German, Swiss or Austrian origin, some of them descended from escapees from the *Graf Spee*, a U-boat sunk off the Uruguayan coast on December 13, 1939. The older generations still converse in German, maintain a Lutheran outlook and read the local German-language newspaper, while souvenir shops sell cuckoo-clocks and tapes of oompah music. For many European visitors this will either seem a case of *déjà vu*, or a reassuring bit of home from home. Either way, Villa General Belgrano is an excellent base for the region if you'd rather avoid Córdoba itself, especially since the plentiful and varied accommodation ranges from the province's only official youth hostel to luxury hotels. However, if adventure sports such as kayaking, trekking and hang-gliding are what you're after, you're better off at Santa Rosa de Calamuchita, farther south.

Essentially a sedate place favoured by older visitors attracted by its creature comforts and hearty food – especially welcome in winter when it frequently snows here – Villa General Belgrano suddenly shifts up a gear or two during one of its many festivals. While the Feria Navideña, or Christmas festival, the Fiesta de Chocolate Alpino, in July, and the Fiesta de la Masa, a Holy Week binge of apple strudel and pastries, are all eagerly awaited, the annual climax is the nationally famous **Oktoberfest**, Villa General Belgrano's answer to the Munich beer festival held during the second week of October. Stein after stein of foaming Pilsener is knocked back, after which merry revellers stagger down Villa Belgrano's normally genteel streets to their hotels, while elderly ladies barricade themselves into their favourite tearooms and consume hefty portions of blackberry crumble until the whole thing is over.

Two streams, Arroyo del Molle and Arroyo La Toma, trickle through the town before joining Arroyo del Sauce, 1 km to the south. **Avenida Julio Roca**, the town's main drag, lined with shops, cafés, restaurants and hotels, many of them replicas of Swiss chalets or German beer-houses, runs south from oval Plaza José Hernández, where the Oktoberfest takes place. On the plaza stands the 1989 bronze memorial to the Battle of the River Plate, when the *Graf Spee* incident took place (see above). Frankly, the town's three museums – one containing some vintage carriages, another housing a jumble of pre-Hispanic ceramics and the third with an exhibit about UFOs, supposedly a common phenomenon hereabouts – are not worth the candle. The real attraction of Villa General Belgrano is its proximity to the Sierra de Comechingones.

Practicalities

Regular services from Buenos Aires, Córdoba and Santa Rosa de Calamuchita arrive at the small **bus terminal** on Avenida Vélez Sarsfield, five minutes northwest of Plaza José Hernández. Siete Lagos runs a shuttle minibus service three times a day to and from La Cumbrecita, and its bus-stop is on Avenida San Martín, 100m north of Plaza José Hernández. The extremely helpful, well-stocked **tourist office** in the municipalidad, Plaza José Hernandez s/n (daily 8am–1pm & 5–10pm; ☎03546/61215; *belgrano@vallecalamuchita.com*), is doing its best to give the town a younger, more modern image, with computerized information about accommodation, leisure activities and events. Youth and student discounts for many of these activities, operated out of nearby Santa Rosa de Calamuchita, have also been introduced. Banks and **ATMs** can be found along Avenida Julio A. Roca.

You're spoilt for choice when it comes to accommodation. Most of the **hotels** are on the expensive side, but they're nearly all of a high standard, spotlessly clean and comfortable; rooms are plentiful but book ahead in the high season, especially during one of the festivals. Try the Austrian-style *Hotel Edelweis*, at Ojo de Agua and Comechingones (☎03546/461317 or 461387; ⑥); the *Hotel Baviera*, at El Quebracho 21 (☎03546/461476; ④); or the *Hotel Nehuen*, at San Martín 17 (☎03546/461412 or 462267; ④). The excellent **youth hostel**, *El Rincón* at Calle Alexander Fleming s/n, fifteen minutes' walk northwest of the bus station and very laid-back (☎03546/461323, fax 461761; *cordoba1@hostels.org.ar*, ①), has dorms, rooms with private bath, and you can pitch your tent for $4. **Cabañas** are an excellent alternative to the hostel, especially for groups of four or five: try the very cosy *Cabañas Alpino*, at Julio Roca and 25 de Mayo (☎03546/461355; ②); the rustic but comfortable *Cabañas Bodensee*, at Julio Roca 343 (☎03546/462078; ②); or the attractive *Cabañas Sierras Chicas*, Julio Roca 127 (☎03546/461350; ②). The best **campsites** are along the RP5 a short way east of the town centre: the *San Jos* (☎03546/462496) and *La Florida* (☎03546/461298) are both spotless and set in beautiful wooded locations with swimming pools.

Not surprisingly, many of the town's plentiful **places to eat**, such as the *Tirol,* at Av. San Martín 125, offer German and Central European dishes such as goulash, sauerkraut, sausages and tortes. *Ciervo Rojo*, at Julio Roca 210, serves schnitzels and wurst, washed down with tankards of home-brewed beer; while *Café Rissen* at Av. Julio Roca 36 is the place to go for Black Forest gateau, strudel and fruit crumbles, served on gingham tablecloths; *Rissen's* excellent ice-cream parlour stands opposite.

Santa Rosa de Calamuchita

In 1700 a community of Dominicans built an estancia and a chapel dedicated to the patron saint of the Americas, Santa Rosa of Lima, after which nothing much else happened in **SANTA ROSA DE CALAMUCHITA**, 11km south of Villa General Belgrano, until the end of the nineteenth century. Then, thanks to its mountainside location on a wooded riverbank, and its mild climate, the place suddenly took off as a holiday resort, an alternative to its more traditional neighbour to the north. Now it's a highly popular destination, swamped by visitors from many parts of the country in the high season, and makes an excellent base for exploring the relatively unspoilt **mountains** nearby – on foot or on horseback. The main attraction of Santa Rosa de Calamuchita is the way that it's geared to all kinds of **outdoor activities** – from diving and kayaking to jet-skiing and flying. Notoriously less sedate than Villa General Belgrano but less spoilt than Villa Carlos Paz, from Christmas until Easter it throbs with disco music blaring from convertibles packed with holidaymakers from Córdoba and Buenos Aires, or through loudspeakers atop vans advertising nightclubs. The town's compact centre is built in a curve of the Río Santa Rosa, just south of where the Arroyo del Sauce flows into it. There's no main plaza but a number of busy streets run off the main Calle Libertad. You can take refuge from the hullabaloo in the beautifully restored Capilla Vieja, at the northern end of Libertad – the ruined estancia was demolished at the beginning of the twentieth century. It houses the **Museo de Arte Sacra** (daily, 9am–noon and 3–6pm; $1), where you can see a superb late seventeenth-century wooden Christ crafted by local Jesuit artisans, and other works of colonial religious art.

Practicalities

Since there's no **bus** station, regular services from Buenos Aires, Córdoba and Villa General Belgrano drop and pick up passengers at stops along Libertad. The energetic staff at the **tourist information office**, Güemes 13 (☎03546/429654; *munstarosa@ onenet.com.ar*) – a side street off Libertad two blocks south of the museum – dish out computer print-outs and glossy brochures on accommodation, activities and tour operators. **Accommodation** tends to be less expensive here and not necessarily less comfortable than in Villa General Belgrano, and includes the stylish *Hotel Yporá*, 1km outside town on the RP5 (☎03546/421233; ⑥); the charming, family-orientated *Hotel Santa Rosa*, at Entre Ríos 86 (☎03546/420186; ③); and the very clean and quiet *El Nogal*, at El Nogal 161 (☎03546/420145; ③). Budget options include the *Hospedaje Yuyos*, at Benito Soria 248 (☎03546/420888; ①), and the *Hospedaje Independencia*, at Independencia 64 (☎076554104; ①), both of which have small, plain but pleasant rooms, some with bath. Groups can always share a **cabaña**, such as the roomy, rustic ones at *Malike*, Calle Champaquí Sur (☎03546/420401; ②), and the charming *Villa Jupinda*, at Mendoza 148 (☎03546/420280; ②).

The town's best **restaurants** are the upmarket, Basque-influenced *Azkaine,* at Córdoba 538, the reliable parrilla *La Pulpería* at Libertad and Juana de Fernández, or *El Gringo*, an inexpensive pizzeria at Libertad 270. For **coffee and cakes** or a drink, try the friendly *Stone Age*, at Hipólito Yrigoyen 560, or the popular *Chaman Pub*, at Libertad and El Nogal, known for its delicious patisserie. When it comes to **nightclubs**, the two biggest and most sophisticated in town are the classy *New Stone*, at Cerro de Oro s/n, and *Sheik*, at Hipólito Yrigoyen 560, which attracts a younger, slightly rowdier crowd.

You can hire **horses** to cover the mountain trails from René Yedro, on Avenida Costanero (☎070395154), or rent **mountain-bikes** from Eduardo Medina, at Vélez Sarsfield 60 (☎03546/421675). **Motorbikes** and **buggies** can be rented all along Playa de Santa Rita. Half-day or full-day **treks** into the Comechingones are arranged by Dapa Turismo, Libertad 263 (☎03546/420047 or 420277), or Aquatrek (☎03546/483003), who can also rent you equipment for **water-sports** – jet-skis, kayaks or canoes – or arrange short **flights** in microlights for a spectacular bird's-eye view of the mountains and the valley. For anyone with a bit more time to spare, two- or three-day 4WD **safaris** into the mountains' remoter recesses, inaccessible by passenger car, are run by Alejandro Corrales at *La Olla* campsite, at the southern end of Calle Córdoba (☎03546/499600), and Juan Setemberg at *El Parador de la Montaña* (☎03546/420231). For **diving expeditions** in the summer, or advanced dives in nearby lakes for $20 per person, ask at *La Olla* campsite (or call ☎03546/483003).

La Cumbrecita and around

Around 35km northwest of Villa Belgrano along a winding scenic track, **LA CUM-BRECITA** is a small, peaceful alpine-style village, high up in the foothills of the Comechingones range. Benefiting from a mild microclimate and enjoying views of wild countryside, devoid of human settlements, it has developed as a relatively select holiday resort ever since it was built in the 1930s by Swiss and Austrian immigrants. To get there from Villa Belgrano, take Avenida San Martín, which leads north from Plaza José Hernández, and keep going until you reach the edge of town; from there the dirt-road swings in a westerly direction and climbs up through hills, from which you have sweeping views of the Río Segundo Valley.

Two paths wind their way through the village, parallel to the Río del Medio that cuts a deep ravine below. Paseo Bajo, the lower of the two, passes several cafés and hotels, and the mock-medieval Castillo, on the way to the Río Almbach, which flows into the Río del Medio north of the village; while the upper trail climbs the hill to the west of the village, cutting through the well-tended cemetery from where you can enjoy wonderful views of the Lago Esmeralda, and the fir-wooded mountains behind. Motor vehicles are banned from the whole village, but many people rent electric buggies to get around.

To cool off in hot weather, head for one of the *balnearios* along the clean Río Almbach, such as **Forellensee** – named for the plentiful trout in the stream – or **Grottensee** – named for its caves – both with bucolic settings and views up to the craggy mountain-tops. La Cumbrecita is also a perfect base for some of the region's most rewarding mountain walks, along well-trodden but uncrowded trails going up to 2000m or more. Signposted treks lasting between one and four hours each way head off to the eyrie-like *miradores* at Casas Viejas, Meierei and Cerro Cristal, while one of the most popular trails climbs from El Castillo, past Balneario La Olla, with its very deep pools of crystal-clear water created by the gushing waterfalls, to the summit of the unfortunately named Cerro Wank. From there, and from **Yatán**, a wild gorge three hours away on foot up a steep trail, impressive views of the valley are guaranteed and spottings of condors are frequent.

Villa Alpina, as its name suggests, is another Swiss-style hamlet, a four-hour walk away to the south, which can also be reached by direct road from Villa Belgrano and Santa Rosa de Calamuchita. It's the eastern base-camp for treks to the top of the region's tallest peak, **Cerro Champaquí** (2884m). This involves a long haul – at least eight hours' gentle climbing – but it's not especially difficult and you can always spend the night in the basic mountain-refuge at Puesto Dominguez, halfway up. Although this climb is by no means dangerous, it isn't signposted and is therefore best done with a local guide – ask in one of the village bars about hiring horses and guides, or enquire at the tourist offices in Villa Belgrano or Santa Rosa de Calamuchita.

Practicalities

Siete Lagos runs a shuttle **bus** service three times a day to and from Villa Belgrano, stopping at the entrance to the village, beyond which no motorized traffic is allowed. Ask at the tourist office in Villa Belgrano about transport to Villa Alpina, which is seasonal and highly erratic. A hut next to the bus-stop in La Cumbrecita serves as a tourist information office of sorts (Nov–April 9am–6pm; ☎03546/481070).

The best **hotels** in La Cumbrecita are the luxurious *Hotel La Cumbrecita* (☎03546/498405; ⑤) and comfortable *Hotel Las Verbenas* (☎03546/481008; ④), both charmingly Germanic, with great sunrise views on the eastern side, while the *Hospedaje Kuhstall* offers more basic rooms (☎03546/481015; ②). The only accommodation in Villa Alpina is an unofficial **youth hostel**, *Señor Escalante* (☎03546/420508; ②), with a very decent **restaurant**. It also has **horses** for hire and organizes **treks** into the Comechingones.

The string of generally excellent *confiterías* and **restaurants** along La Cumbrecita's Paseo Bajo mostly offer fondues, strudels and other Central European specialities, plus the odd steak. For meals, the *Bar Suizo,* at the south end of the village, leads the way, while the village's best cakes and pastries are served at *Conditorei Liesbeth*, right at the northern end of the Paseo Bajo, across the Río Almbach.

From Córdoba to Merlo

By far the most rewarding route from Córdoba to San Luis, the other provincial capital, is by the RN20 beyond Villa Carlos Paz, continuing along the RP1 via Merlo. The winding **Nueva Ruta de las Altas Cumbres** climbs past the **Parque Nacional de la Quebrada de los Condoritos**, a deep ravine where condors nest in cliffside niches, over a high mountain-pass, before winding back down a series of hairpin bends. The unspoiled, sunny valleys to the west of the high Sierra Grande and Sierra de Achala, crisscrossed by gushing streams and dotted with oases of bushy palm trees, are known as the Traslasierra, literally "across the mountains"; the capital of the Traslasierra, **Mina Clavero**, is a popular little riverside resort and minor transport hub. Several **buses** a day run between Córdoba and Mina Clavero, and can drop you at the ranger station of the national park.

Near Nono, a tiny village in the lee of the northern Comechingones, a short distance down the RN20, to the south of Mina Clavero, is the oddball **Museo Rocsen**, an eclectic jumble of artefacts, archeological finds and miscellanea. Not far from there, the RP1 forks off towards the bustling resort of **Merlo**, just over the border into San Luis Province, while the RN20 continues southwestwards towards San Luis city, across uninteresting countryside, via Quines. Forever vaunting its apocryphal microclimate, Merlo is above all a relaxing place from which to explore the nearby mountain trails or try out some adventurous pursuits. Along the RP1 to Merlo, in a long valley parallel to the Sierra de Comechingones, are the picturesque villages of **Yacanto** and **San Javier**, from where you can climb the highest summit in the Central Sierras, the majestic **Cerro Champaquí**. And from Merlo you can continue to **San Luis**, either south along the scenic RP1 and west by the RP20, or west along the RP5 and south by the RN148; buses tend to take the latter option, and both routes converge at La Toma.

Parque Nacional de la Quebrada de los Condoritos

About 60km from Villa Carlos Paz, just to the south of the RN20, is the **Parque Nacional de la Quebrada de los Condoritos** (daily 9am–6pm; no phone; *pncondor@ carlospaz.com.ar*), a misty canyon eroded into the mountains which gets its name from the baby condors reared in its deep ravines. It's the condors' most easterly breeding site.

You get there via the splendid **Nueva Ruta de las Altas Cumbres**, the section of the RN20 that sweeps across the **Pampa de Achala**, an eerily desolate landscape, ideal for solitary treks or horse-rides. For the first 15km or so, this road, which starts just

12km southwest of crowded Villa Carlos Paz, is quite narrow but several viewpoints have been built at the roadside. From them, you have unobscured views of the Icho Cruz and Malambo valleys to the northwest, the distant peak of **Cerro Los Gigantes**, at 2370m the highest mountain in the Sierra Grande, to the north, and the **Sierra de Achala** to the south; the views are framed by nodding pinkish *cortaderas* or pampas grass. Some 20km farther on, the bleak granite moorlands of the Pampa de Achala, reaching 2000m above sea level, are barren save for thorny scrub and a few tufty alpines. An even narrower mid-nineteenth-century mule-trail, the Camino de las Altas Cumbres, now the RP14, still winds along ledge-like roads almost parallel to the RN20, which superseded it in the 1960s, and makes for an even more pleasurable alternative route to the Quebrada, should you have your own vehicle and more time to spare. Condors, some with wing spans exceeding three metres, can be seen hovering majestically overhead.

Just after the derelict Hotel Cóndor, you reach the **Fundación Cóndor** (daily 9am–6pm; no phone; *pncondor@carlospaz.com.ar*), the *guardería* of the Parque Nacional de la Quebrada de los Condoritos. Here, the *guardaparques* will show you round an interpretation centre, with a small exhibition of striking photos of the park's flora and fauna, mostly condors and their young, of course. They can also give you information about the park and its rich wildlife, indicate the trails, supply important weather details – hazards include fog and thunderstorms – and they may even be available to accompany you and point out the flora and fauna on the way. The various **hikes** take between one and twelve hours; the longer ones are physically demanding as they take you down steep, sometimes slippery paths into the bottom of the canyon. All kinds of trees, shrubs and ferns can be spotted, even some endemic species such as rare white gentians, while the plentiful fauna includes various wild cats, a number of indigenous rodents, foxes and hares, and several snake varieties, including three never observed anywhere else. Birdlife is prolific but the stars are the condors themselves, especially their young; if you're lucky you might see condors and their chicks bathing in the water at the bottom of the gorge.

About 5km farther along the RN20 from the Fundación, a discreetly signposted track to the right leads to **Hotel La Posta** (☎03544/470873 or 470887; ⑤), a converted early nineteenth-century post-house where salt convoys on the way to Córdoba used to stop for a change of horses. Its remote location on the barren pampa lend it an almost eerie atmosphere, offset by the designer magazine interior, snug rooms, and the delicious food, including trout suppers (full board is available). **Horses** can be hired to explore the surrounding countryside, dominated by wonderful views of Cerro Champaquí.

Mina Clavero and around

Some 15km kilometres west of the Quebrada de los Condoritos, the RN20 begins to snake along narrow Corniche roads, down to Mina Clavero, which offer stunning views of the valley and a cluster of extinct volcano cones in the distance; the sheer cliffs and fissured crags look as if they might crumble into the wide plains below. Wedged between the Sierra Grande and the much lower Sierra de Pocho, to the west, is **MINA CLAVERO**, just 3km up the RP14, north of the junction with the RN20. A transport hub for routes between Córdoba, San Luis, Merlo and Cruz del Eje, at the northern end of the Punilla Valley, it's also a riverside resort. The place is noteworthy for little else, other than its attractive black ceramics, made at various workshops in and around the town; the metallic glaze on the vases, pots and animal figures, with a bluish sheen, is made from cow dung of all things.

Mina Clavero can become quite lively during the holiday season, especially in January and February, when people come to relax at the many *balnearios*, or bathing areas, along the three rivers that snake through the small town: Río Los Sauces, Río Mina Clavero and Río Panaholma. Of all the *balnearios*, the cleanest is the Nido de Aguila, set among beautiful rocks on the Río Mina Clavero 1km east of the centre, along Calle Corrientes. The nearby mountains lend themselves to a number of pursuits such as mountain-biking, horseriding, trekking and rock-climbing.

A compact place, it's not difficult to find your way around; the two main streets are Avenida San Martín, or the RP14, and Avenida Mitre, which forks off it at the southern end of the village. Just north of the town centre, the RP14 heads eastwards towards the Pampa de Achala (see above); for several kilometres along this dirt track you'll find the best **ceramics workshops**, which set up little stalls on the roadside; the best of all belongs to Atilio López, whose clearly signposted house is set among a lush garden some 5km east of the town.

Practicalities

Mina Clavero's **bus terminal** is along Avenida Mitre, next to the municipalidad; there are regular services from Córdoba, Merlo, San Luis, Mendoza and Buenos Aires. Seven blocks south, in the cleft of the fork with Avenida San Martín, is the **tourist information centre** (daily 8am–8pm; ☎03544/470171); as well as helping you with accommodation, it can provide information on local activities. Mina Clavero has a wide choice of **hotels** for such a small place, including the comfortable *Panaholma*, with spacious rooms, at Av. Mitre (☎03544/471020; ⑤); the French-run *Du Soleil*, with a good restaurant and smart rooms with modern bathrooms, at Avenida Mitre and La Piedad (☎03544/470066; ⑤); or the bright and airy *España*, at Av. San Martín 1687 (☎03544/470123; ③). The **campsites** are better at Villa Cura Brochero, 2km to the north: *El Buen Retiro and Sol y Río* are both located on Calle Ejército Argentino, and offer clean, attractive facilities at riverside settings for $3 per person. For **meals** the two best places are *Las Pircas* at El Paso de las Tropas s/n, serving pizzas and grilled chicken, while *Lo de Jorge* is a parrilla locally known for its excellent meat, at Poeta Lugones s/n.

Museo Rocsen

From the junction with the RP14, the RN20 heads due south through rolling countryside, in the lee of rippling mountains, whose eroded crags change colour from a mellow grey to deepest red, depending on the time of day. Their imposing peak, Cerro Champaquí, lurks to the southeast at the northern end of the Comechingones range, sometimes crowned by cloud. Some 10km south of Mina Clavero you reach the sleepy village of Nono, from where 5km along a good dirt road leading eastwards is one of the country's weirdest museums, **Museo Rocsen** (daily 9am–sunset; ☎03544/498065; *www.rocsen.org*; $4). The museum's pink sandstone facade is embellished with a row of 49 statues – from Christ to Mother Teresa and Buddha to Che Guevara – representing key figures who, according to the museum's owner and curator, Juan Santiago Bouchon, have changed the course of history. After many years as cultural attaché at the French embassy in Buenos Aires, Bouchon opened his museum in 1969, with the intention of offering "something for everybody". The result is an eclectic collection of more than ten thousand exhibits, from fossils and mummies to clocks and cars – even the proverbial kitchen-sink, a nineteenth-century curio. You're well advised to select what interests you from the useful plan you can pick up at the entrance, rather than to try and see everything. Another 3km towards the mountains, along a signposted track, is the area's best accommodation, the French-run *Hotel La Lejania,* (☎03544/498960; ⑦) with comfortable rooms in a secluded, pastoral setting, a private riverside beach, and delicious French and Tunisian cuisine on offer; the hotel also offers treks and horseriding in the mountains.

San Javier and Yacanto

Some 35km south of Mina Clavero, the RP1 towards Merlo branches off the RN20 and heads due south towards **SAN JAVIER**, another 12km away, and **YACANTO** just farther south, after which there's nowhere to stay before Merlo, across the border in San Luis Province. The straight road offers outstanding views of the northern Comechingones mountains to the east. If you're driving, watch out for the often treacherously deep *badenes* – these are very deep fords that suddenly flood after storms and, even when they're dry, the sudden drop and rough surface can damage a car's undercarriage or tyres.

San Javier and Yacanto are pretty little places, set amid peach orchards and vineyards, and are essentially bases for climbing to the 2884-metre summit of **Cerro Champaquí**, directly to the east. San Javier's municipalidad (☎03544/482041 or 482077) has information about **guides** to accompany you on the seven-hour hike to the top; ask for Gustavo Zerbinato. For **accommodation**, San Javier offers the comfortable *Hostería San Javier* (☎03544/482006; ③) or the plain but very clean *Hostería Casapueblo* (☎482038; ②), both near the main plaza. In Yacanto, just off the main road is *Hotel Yacanto* (☎03544/482002; ⑥), once luxurious, now slightly down-at-heel but offering tennis courts, a nine-hole golf course and horse rides into the mountains.

Merlo

MERLO, just over the border into San Luis Province, some 95km south of Mina Clavero and 280km southwest of Córdoba, is a charming resort whose main claim to fame is its **microclimate** – all local, provincial and national tourist literature is obsessed with it and the town's thriving holiday industry makes a lot of it, but the whole thing's rather exaggerated. That said, Merlo does enjoy a superbly sunny yet cool location, at around 1000m above sea level amid dense woodland. It lies in the western lee of the green-sloped Comechingones range and is overlooked by San Luis Province's highest peak, the **Cerro de la Ovejas** (2260m). The settlement was founded on January 1, 1797 by the Governor of Córdoba, Rafael de Sobremonte, who named it after the Viceroy of the River Plate, Don Pedro Melo de Portugal – Melo gradually became Merlo. **Sobremonte** gave his name to the town's shady main square at the northeast corner of which stands an attractive white Jesuit-built church, whose finest interior feature is its wonderfully rickety *quebracho* roof. Don't waste your time on the abysmal museums or the "main sight", a thousand-year-old **carob tree** known as *algarrobo abuelo*, 5km out of town. Instead make the most of the nearby mountains: adventurous pursuits such as hang-gliding, paragliding, horseriding, rock-climbing, trekking or rambling are all possible here.

Practicalities

Buses from Buenos Aires, Córdoba, Mendoza and San Luis drop passengers at Merlo's busy bus station, centrally located at the corner of calles Pringles and Los Almendros, one block south and east of Plaza Sobremonte. The **tourist office** (daily 9am–8pm; ☎02656/476078) at Coronel Mercau 605, at the junction with the RP5 to San Luis, ten minutes' walk to the south of the plaza, has plenty of leaflets and brochures plus a comprehensive list of places to stay. For information on the various sporting pursuits and activities, contact **tour operators** such as Valle del Sol at Av. de los Césares 2100 (☎02656/476009) and Villa de Merlo at Av. del Sol 100 (☎02656/475319).

Regardless of whether the microclimate is fact or fiction, in high season the place is inundated with visitors – during the summer, at Easter and in July you should book your **accommodation** in advance. There are plenty of central options but for peace and quiet, mountain views and quick access to surrounding countryside, stay at **Piedra**

Blanca, 3km to the north of Plaza Sobremonte; **Cerro de Oro**, 3km to the southeast; or **Rincón del Este**, 5km due east. In Merlo itself, *Hotel Algarrobo* at Av. del Sol 1120 (☎02656/475208; ③) is typical of the small, quiet hotels on offer. *Hotel Villa de Merlo* at Avenida del Sol and Pedernera (☎02656/475335; ⑥), a short way southeast of the centre, is a beautiful brick-and-timber construction, with charming rooms overlooking a large, well cared for garden, and a rustic dining-room. Up in Piedra Blanca, there's the quiet, secluded and well-appointed *Hotel Piedra Blanca*, Av. de los Incas 3000 (☎02656/475226; ④); or the family-run *Hotel Altos del Rincón*, at Av. de los Cesares 2977 (☎02656/476333; ④). Both have en-suite bathrooms. All of the **campsites** have excellent facilities and are in attractive settings in the foothills: *Cerro de Oro*, at Cerro de Oro, 3km southeast of Merlo (☎02656/477189), is brand new and has an attractive swimming pool; there's also the well-kept *Don Juan* (☎02656/475942; donjuan@merlo-sl. com.ar), 5km east of town at Rincón del Este. Nearer to the town centre is *Las Violetas* at Calle Chumamaya (☎02656/475730), also with a pool. Finally, the *Pensión La Llegada* at Sarmiento 405 (no phone; ②) is a decent, clean and simple place to stay.

There are dozens of **eating** options to choose from, offering everything from roast kid to staples like pasta and pizza. The extensive menu at reasonably priced *El Establo*, arguably Merlo's best restaurant, in a thatched hut at Av. del Sol 540, includes trout and frog, plus excellent *chivito*; while the speciality at *La Posta Monte Grappa*, at Av. del Sol 280, is kid in white wine sauce. For *asados* try *El Ciprés del Tornado*, 1km along the RP1 south of the town, opposite the airstrip. *Los Helados de la Abuela* at Becerra 558 serves Merlo's best ice creams. There are several **cafés** dotted around the main square, but the best are the laid-back *Comechingones*, at Coronel Mercau 651, and its smart rival, *Cunto,* at Coronel Mercau 625.

San Luis and around

SAN LUIS has always been a stopover on the colonial route between Santiago de Chile and Buenos Aires. Some 467km southwest of Córdoba it is known as the *Puerta del Cuyo*, or "Gateway to the Cuyo", the region centred on Mendoza which lies 280km to the west. The city's location at the southernmost point (*punto*) of the crinkly Sierras de San Luís, a dramatic backdrop of forever changing colour and sloping down to the flat, sandy pampa, earns its friendly inhabitants, the Sanluisinos, their nickname of "Puntanos". Running past the city to the south, the Río Chorrillos, no more than a trickle except in the spring, gives its name to the bracing *chorrillero*, the prevailing southerly wind that almost constantly sweeps the city clean. A friendly, cheerful little city, it's essentially a base for visiting one or two nearby attractions, exploring the sierras and soaking up the easy-going atmosphere. The microcentro is very compact, and the city has a villagey feel to it; high-rises are mercifully rare, with most people living in small houses and bungalows, lovingly tending their gardens and patios – cool havens perfumed with jasmine and garlanded with bougainvilleas.

San Luis was founded from Chile in 1594 by **Luis Jufré de Loaysa y Meneses**, an Andalucian grandee, officially as a tribute to King Louis of France; founding cities evidently ran in the family, as his father Juan had established San Juan. Until the *malones*, or Indian uprisings, were brutally crushed in the 1830s by **Juan Manuel de Rosas**, whose Conquest of the Wilderness campaign made him a local hero, San Luis never managed to control all of its hinterland and, whereas Córdoba was a flourishing Jesuit capital by the seventeenth century, San Luis did not come into its own until the very end of the nineteenth century, after the arrival of the railways.

San Luis holds few conventional attractions, but if you stop over at least you'll eat well; the eastern suburbs are favourite weekend haunts for their traditional *parrillas*. You can burn off the calories practising water-sports on one of the nearby lakes and reservoirs, a short distance to the east, on the banks of which are the picturesque resorts of **Potrero de los Funes, El Volcán** and **Trapiche**. There are also alternative places to stay, offering rural peace and quiet as well as the opportunity for sports activities. While in the San Luis area, you could relax at one of the country's most modern spa resorts, **Balde**, only 30km to the west, or take a longer trip to San Luis Province's main attraction, the **Parque Nacional Sierra de las Quijadas**. The highlight of the park's beautiful scenery is a huge canyon of orange-pink rock that turns cochineal red at sunset. Between San Luis and Merlo, to the northeast, stretch the **Sierras de San Luis**, mountains rich in metals, minerals and precious stones such as **onyx**, and the scene of a gold rush and intensive mining in the nineteenth century; today they're quiet and seldom visited, being less dramatic than the ranges to the north and east.

The City

Plaza Pringles – dominated by a statue of the eponymous Colonel, a local hero who fought alongside San Martín in the Campaign of the Andes – is the nerve centre of the city, complete with cafés, ice-cream parlours and shops, as well as a miniature park shaded by giant palm trees and subtropical shrubs. In the southeast corner of the square stands the Italianate **Cathedral**, built between 1880 and 1940. A fairly nondescript church, it is of note only for its unusual onyx fonts, one green, one grey, both extracted from quarries up in the Sierra de San Luis. The delightfully kitsch **electronic crib** (daily 10am–1pm and 6–8pm; $1) is accessible through a door to the left of the main entrance. Built by a local engineer, it is beautifully modelled and painted, and performs for five minutes by lighting up, while the various figures, apart from Jesus in his manger, whizz up and down, and different hymns and carols blare out from loudspeakers.

Three blocks south of Plaza Pringles, down busy, commercial Calle San Martín, is the city's other central square, **Plaza Independencia**. Here, you'll find the early eighteenth-century **Convento San Domingo** and its eye-catching white church, complete with handsome **Mozarabic facade** – an elegant, brick-edged horseshoe arch surrounded by intricate Moorish stucco, a style often found in Spain but seldom in Latin America. The convent is the oldest building in the city; founded by the Dominican Order, the first religious community to settle in San Luis, in its early years it frequently doubled up as a refuge for the city's population during the repeated attacks by natives.

Way up at the northern end of the city, seven blocks from Plaza Pringles, is the tiny **Museo Geológico**, housed in a tin hut on the university campus at Italia and Ejército de los Andes (Tues–Sun 11am–1pm & 6–10pm; $1). This interpretation centre is a useful prelude to a visit to the Parque Nacional Sierra de las Quijadas, over 120km from San Luis. It houses a small but fascinating collection of geological and archeological finds, mostly fossils, like those of strange tiny flying dinosaurs, unique to this region, and the model of a huge prehistoric spider, whose original is safely stored in Córdoba.

Practicalities

San Luis' tiny **airport** is 4km northwest of Plaza Pringles; the only way to reach the centre from here is by **taxi** ($4). Regular buses from Buenos Aires, Córdoba, Merlo, Mendoza and San Rafael arrive at the very basic **bus terminal**, six blocks north of Plaza Pringles. The provincial **information centre** (daily 8am–8pm ☎02652/423479) is wedged in the fork of avenidas Presidente Arturo Illia and San Martín close to Plaza Pringles and supplies only the most basic information, such as accommodation lists. Most of the banks around the main square have ATMs.

There's not much in the way of **accommodation** in San Luis: options range from hotels primarily aimed at commercial travellers – functional and pricey but cheaper at

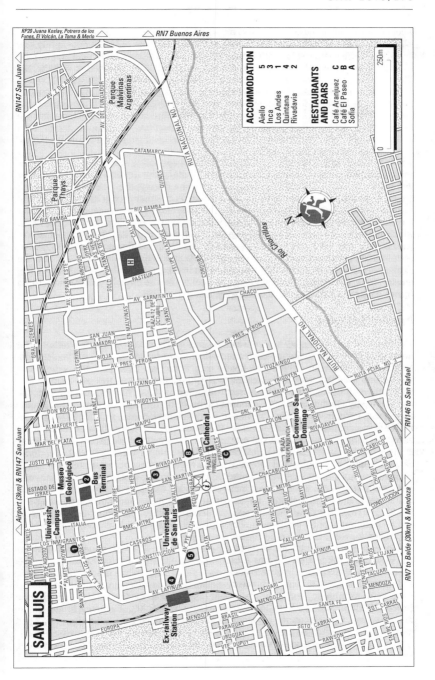

SAN LUIS

RP20 Juana Koslay, Potrero de los Funes, El Volcán, La Toma & Merlo

RN7 Buenos Aires

RN147 San Juan

Airport (3km) & RN147 San Juan

RN7 to Balde (30km) & Mendoza

RN146 to San Rafael

RUTA PCIAL NO 3

RUTA NACIONAL NO 7

RUTA NACIONAL NO 7

Río Chorrillos

Parque Malvinas Argentinas

Parque Thays

ACCOMMODATION

Aiello	5
Inca	3
Los Andes	1
Quintana	4
Rivadavia	2

RESTAURANTS AND BARS

Café Aranjuez	C
Café El Paseo	B
Sofía	A

0   250m

Museo Geológico

Bus Terminal

University Campus

Universidad de San Luis

Ex-railway Station

Convento San Domingo

Cathedral

Plaza Pringles

Plaza Independencia

weekends – to downmarket *pensiones* and *residenciales*. The city's most reputable hotel is the smart *Hotel Quintana*, at Av. President Illia 546 (☎02652/438400; ⑥); slightly less luxurious but far better value with its airy rooms and a fine swimming pool and terrace is *Hotel Aiello*, at Av. Presidente Illia 431, opposite (☎02652/425609, fax 425694; ④). The best budget options are *Pensión Inca*, at Bolívar 943 (☎02652/425243; ②), where you get a copious breakfast as well as cheerily decorated en-suite rooms; and *Pensión Los Andes*, at Ejército de los Andes 1180 (☎02652/422033; ①), much more basic but clean and comfortable. The only remotely decent rooms next to the bus terminus are the spotless but cramped ones at *Residencial Rivadavia*, Estado de Israel 1470 (☎02652/422437; ②). If you want to **camp** you should head out to Potrero de los Funes, El Volcán or Trapiche (see below).

While you're in San Luis be sure to try the local speciality, *chivito con chanfaina*, or roast goat with gravy. The best **places to eat** lie along the RP20 to the east, mostly in the leafy suburbs of Visitadores Médicos and Juana Koslay; the pick of a large bunch are *La Escondida* and *Raquel* (no phone), opposite each other on the RP20, just past the junction with the RN147. Apart from the *Hotel Quintana*'s expensive, chic restaurant the only downtown place worth trying is *Sofía*, at Colón and Bolivar (☎02652/427960), which specializes in Spanish-style fare and seafood, such as paella. The two most atmospheric cafés are *Aranjuez*, at Pringles and Rivadavia, a traditional café-cum-snack-bar with wooden panelling, and *El Paseo*, at Rivadavia and Artigas, a popular haunt for the city's students and youth, serving decent coffee in an appealing decor; both lay on live music – rock, folk or jazz – after midnight at weekends. The city's best nightclub, *Acqua Barra*, is 5km east of town in Juana Koslay, along the RP20.

Around San Luis

The artificial lakes located in deep valleys and surrounded by wooded hills to the **northeast** of the city make for good alternative places to stay and relax if you're stopping over in this area. The RP20 heads east from San Luis, past the suburbs of Visitadores Médicos and Juana Koslay, to a roundabout next to the golf course. The RP18, the road heading northwards past the suburb of Las Chacras, cuts through the narrow, bushy Quebrada de los Cóndores to reach the Embalse Potrero de los Funes, a reservoir 18km from the city. The village on its northern banks, **POTRERO DE LOS FUNES**, is a popular weekend retreat for Puntanos, many of whom have second homes here, and come for picnics or a sail on the lake. The most luxurious **accommodation** in the area, the government-run *Hotel Potrero de los Funes* (☎02652/495001; ⑦), dominates the southern banks, and offers spacious rooms, a decent restaurant and sports facilities – tennis, boats and water-skiing. Alternatively, ask around for rooms for rent. The **campsite** on the wooded west bank of the lake, *Camping El Potrero* (no phone), has a beach and clean facilities, for $3 per person, but the one 4km north along the RP18, *Camping Don Goyo* (no phone), has better facilities, including electric current and a restaurant, for $4 per person. Try *Comedor Yunka Taki* or *Comedor Minincó* in the village for roast kid and other delicious **meals**.

Due east of the roundabout by San Luis golf club, the RP20 continues eastwards to **EL VOLCÁN**, 18km from the city. A tiny village built along the Río El Volcán, on the north banks of Embalse Cruz de Piedra, it's a picturesque place nestling among fruit and walnut orchards. It boasts a brace of charming but modest, family-oriented **hotels**, both with swimming pools, a restaurant and sports facilities: *Hotel El Volcán* (☎02652/421337; ②) and *Hotel Villa Andrea* (☎02652/494009). *Camping El Volcán*, on the river-bank, with electricity, a restaurant and clean sanitary facilities, charges $3 per person. Farther still from the city, but amid even more pastoral scenery, is the tiny village of **TRAPICHE**, on the northern banks of the Embalse La Florida, 42km away from San Luis. To get there turn off the RP20 just before El Volcán, and take the northward

RP9 towards Quines. The village is built around a loop in the Río Trapiche which flows through a narrow, rocky gorge, from which refreshing **waterfalls**, such as Salto La Loma, near the municipal bathing-area or *balneario*, cascade into the crystal waters. The best **place to stay and eat** is *Hostería Los Sauces* at General San Martín s/n (☎02652/493027; ②), but you can also ask around for rooms and *cabañas*. The two **campsites** are the *Camping Municipal* at the southern end of the village (no phone) and *Tota Schmidt* at Junín s/n (no phone), from where you can also hire horses. Both have clean facilities and charge $2 per person.

Tiny **BALDE**, 30km **west** of San Luis on the R7, is a beautiful spa resort. Until 1999, the **hot springs** were a basic affair, just mineral water at 44°C bubbling into a pool. But then some enterprising locals gave the place a face-lift and *Los Tamarindos* (☎02652/442220; Tues–Sun 9.30am–9.30pm; reservations recommended), named after the nearby feathery tamarind grove, is now a state-of-the-art luxury **health centre** where, after a brief medical check-up, you can soak in spotlessly clean pools of crystalline hot and warm water, in tasteful surroundings with an understated Roman baths theme. You can use the pool for $5, while professional shiatsu and Swedish **massages** cost an extra $20. Although regular **buses** from San Luis to Mendoza stop at Balde, the health centre can arrange for you to be transported to and from the city centre in their **minibus** free of charge – just give them a call.

Parque Nacional Sierra de las Quijadas

Along the RN147 towards San Juan, some 125km northwest of San Luis, a left fork along a dirt road leads from the tiny village of Hualtarán to the entrance to the **Parque Nacional Sierra de las Quijadas** (dawn–dusk; free; *linux0.unsl.edu.ar/~quijadas/index.htm*). Covering an enormous area of the mountain range of the same name – *quijadas* means jaw-bones – it's San Luis Province's only national park and one of the youngest in the country, operational only since 1995. The centrepiece of its outstandingly beautiful scenery is the much photographed **Potrero de la Aguada**: a majestic canyon, 8km long, 6km wide and up to 300m deep, its giant red sandstone walls folded like curtains, castellated like medieval fortresses and eroded into strange shapes by millions of years of rain and wind. The canyon is best enjoyed at sunset, when the ochre cliffs and rock battlements turn the colour of blood oranges. The park served as the backdrop to Argentina's only Oscar-nominated film, Adolfo Aristarain's western-style *Tiempo de revancha* (released in English-speaking countries in 1992 as *A Place in the World*).

The park is also extremely rich in flora and fauna – guanacos and peccaries are plentiful and condor spottings frequent. It's also home to the pichiciego, a rare diminutive armadillo, and several endangered species of birds and reptiles such as the hawk-like crowned eagle and striking yellow cardinal, the boa *de las vizcacheras* and a species of land turtle; among gnarled quebrachos and carobs you can find the leafless chica shrub, unique to the region and now rare, and an endemic gorse-like plant, *Gomphrena colocasana*.

Geologists and paleontologists have had a field day over the past decade or two, unearthing fossils of plants and animals from the Cretaceous era, most of which are on display at the Museo Geológico in San Luis. This "Jurassic Park" is nonetheless a treasure-trove of the fossilized remains of dinosaurs, including those of a unique kind of pterosaurus, the pterodaustrus, – a flying dinosaur the size of a sparrow that lived here 120 million years ago. The **Loma del Pterodaustro** fossil-field, a thirty-minute hike from the entrance, is particularly rich in pterosaurus and pterodactyl remains still in situ. From Mirador Elda, the first of two vantage points you come to, with views towards the sierras, you have a choice of two trails: a physically demanding two-hour hike to see fossilized dinosaur footprints or a much easier path to the upper vantage point or *mirador*, with its exhilarating views across the crenellated Potrero de la Aguada.

Park practicalities

Most **buses** from San Luis to San Juan will drop you at Hualtarán. The *guardaparques* have a hut (daily 9am–6pm) at the northern edge of the tiny village, where the dirt track turns off the main road, which deserves a visit before heading into the park. The rangers will give you the **information** you need to get around, and possibly even a lift; they may guide you, for a small tip, or they can put you in touch with a guide – a wise precaution as the trails are not signposted and it's easy to get lost in the 150 square kilometres of reserve. Most of the park destinations, such as the two viewpoints, are accessible by vehicle along dirt tracks. Alternatively you could go on an **organized tour**. Although the tour operators in San Luis and Merlo run trips here, far better is the one organized by David Rivarola, an English-speaking geologist at San Luis University (☎02652/423789; *rivarola@unsl.edu.ar*). His regular weekend excursions, costing $35 per person, kick off at his university lab with an informal talk, followed by a quick visit to the city's Museo Geológico and then a hike around the park's main sites with a lively commentary, aiming to be at the Potrero de la Aguada in time for sunset. Right by the vantage point over the Potrero is a flat area where you're allowed to **camp** wild, but there's no other accommodation nearer than San Luis. Next to the camping area is a basic canteen-cum-store, *Don Enrique* (no phone).

travel details

Córdoba to: Alta Gracia (every 15min; 1hr); Buenos Aires (hourly; 11hr); Capilla del Monte (every 30min; 2hr); Catamarca (4 daily; 6hr); Cerro Colorado (2 daily; 3hr 30min); Chilecito (2 daily; 7hr); Jesús María (5 daily; 1hr 30min); La Rioja (5 daily; 6hr); Mendoza (7 daily; 9hr); Merlo (3 daily; 5hr); Mina Clavero (5 daily; 3hr); Rosario (6 daily; 6hr); Salta (4 daily; 12hr); San Juan (5 daily; 8hr); San Luis (8 daily; 7hr); Santa Rosa de Calamuchita (every 15min; 2hr 20min); Santiago del Estero (5 daily; 6hr); Villa General Belgrano (every 15min; 2hr).

Merlo to: Buenos Aires (6 daily; 12 hr); Córdoba (3 daily; 5hr); San Luis (4 daily; 3hr).

San Luis to: Buenos Aires (9 daily; 12hr); Córdoba (8 daily; 7hr); Mendoza (hourly; 3hr); Merlo (4 daily; 3hr); San Juan (3hr 30min); San Rafael (2 daily; 3hr).

Flights

Córdoba to: Bariloche (5 weekly; 3hr); Buenos Aires (12 daily; 1hr 15min); La Rioja (3 weekly; 1hr); Mar del Plata (5 weekly; 2hr); Mendoza (6 daily; 1hr 20min); Neuquén (1 daily; 2hr 30min); Rosario (5 daily; 50min); Salta (3 daily; 1hr 40min); San Juan (2 daily; 1hr 10min); Tucumán (2 daily; 1hr 20min).

San Luis to: Buenos Aires (2 daily; 1hr 30min); San Juan (1 daily; 40min); San Rafael (3 weekly; 40min).

CHAPTER FOUR

EL LITORAL

L ying either side of the Paraguay and Uruguay rivers and stretching from the lower reaches of the Paraná Delta to the Río Iguazú on Argentina's border with Brazil and Paraguay, **El Litoral** is a region defined by its proximity to water. The word *litoral* means shore and strictly speaking the region includes the provinces of Chaco and Formosa though the term is more commonly used to refer to the four provinces covered in this chapter: **Entre Ríos**, **Corrientes**, **Misiones** and **Santa Fe**. Collectively the first three are also referred to as Mesopotamia, in reference to the ancient region lying between the rivers Tigris and Euphrates, in modern-day Iraq.

The region's major attraction is the **Iguazú Falls** in Misiones, whose claim to the title of the world's most spectacular waterfalls has few serious contenders. First promoted as a tourist destination at the beginning of the twentieth century and described by a steady stream of superlative – but never quite adequate – adjectives ever since, the Iguazú Falls, or Cataratas as they are usually known, are the kind of natural phenomenon that countries build entire tourist industries around. Running a not very close second, in terms of number of visitors, **San Ignacio Miní** is one of the best-preserved ruins in the Jesuit Mission region which runs from Paraguay across Argentina to Southern Brazil – though some may find picking their way through nearby gothically overgrown **Loreto** and **Santa Ana** a more magical experience. Iguazú and San Ignacio aside, however, the littoral region is surprisingly little exploited in terms of tourism and as yet few travellers make the very worthwhile detours to two of Argentina's most unusual attractions: the strange and wonderful **Saltos del Moconá**, the world's most extensive longitudinal waterfalls, which spill for nearly 3km along the centre of a gorge dividing Argentina and Brazil; and the **Esteros del Iberá**, a vast wetland reserve stretching across the centre of Corrientes Province. Away from these dramatic interludes, the littoral is marked by gradual shifts in terrain or vegetation rather than major topographical accidents, though its riverine landscapes, which range from the caramel-coffee coloured maze of the Delta to the wide translucent curves of the Upper Paraná, have a seductive subtropical beauty that is perhaps the region's defining characteristic.

The two southernmost provinces of the region are Santa Fe, a large and elongated province to the west of the Paraná river, and Entre Ríos, a much smaller province

---

ACCOMMODATION PRICE CODES

The price codes used for accommodation throughout this chapter refer to the cheapest rate for a double room in high season. Single travellers will only occasionally pay half the double-room rate; nearer two thirds is the norm and some places will expect you to pay the full rate. Note that in resort towns, there are considerable discounts out of season.

① $20 or less	④ $45–60	⑦ $100–150
② $20–30	⑤ $60–80	⑧ $150–200
③ $30–45	⑥ $80–100	⑨ Over $200

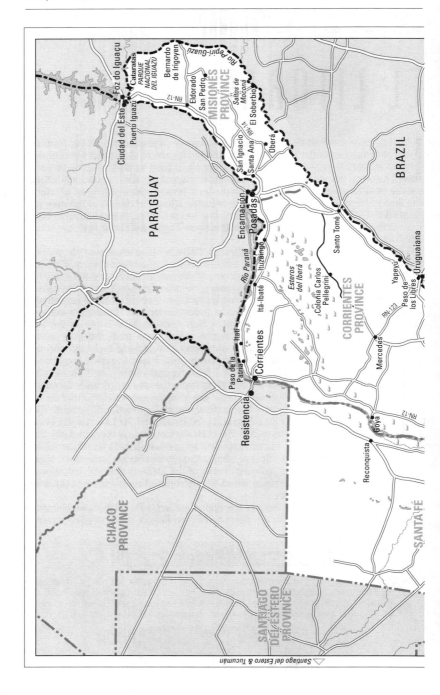

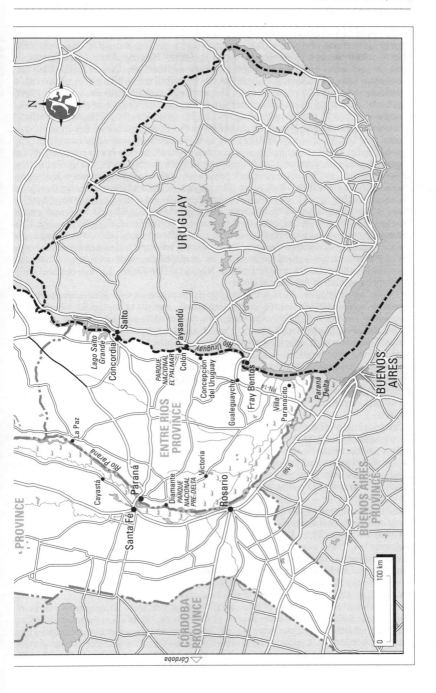

sandwiched between the Paraná and Uruguay rivers, hence its name. Santa Fe, a largely agricultural province with no national parks nor major resorts, does relatively little to attract tourists. However, city lovers will enjoy **Rosario**, home to a vibrant cultural life and some exquisite turn-of-the-century architecture, as well as the base for excursions onto the numerous islands which lie within a few kilometres of the city's handsome riverfront. North of Rosario, the provincial capital **Santa Fe** is a smaller and less lively city but has a handful of interesting historical buildings and museums and is a useful stopover for travellers heading north. This central section of Santa Fe Province is known as the *pampa gringa*, in reference to the large number of European immigrants that settled this part of Argentina in the nineteenth and early twentieth centuries. The far north of the province is far more arid and fiercely hot in summer, with a vegetation which merges with the Chaco, with which it borders to the north. Entre Ríos is perhaps the gentlest of Argentina's provinces, with a soothing verdant landscape characterized by low hills – little more than ripples on the landscape – known locally as *cuchillas*. A string of modest riverside resorts runs along the Río Uruguay here; best of them is the pretty town of **Colón** with a sleepy, old-fashioned port area and sandy beaches. The province's best attraction, however, is probably the **Parque Nacional El Palmar**, an enormous protected grove of dramatically tall yatay palms which dominate the surrounding landscape. On Entre Ríos' western border the pleasant provincial capital of **Paraná** makes a good stopover for its attractive riverside area or as a base for excursions to the recently created **Parque Nacional Pre-Delta**, the only national park to protect a section of the Paraná Delta.

To the north of Entre Ríos is the largely flat province of Corrientes; its most outstanding topographical feature is the extensive system of wetlands which runs through its centre. A 13,000-square-kilometre stretch of these lands is protected within the **Reserva Natural del Iberá**, a wonderful landscape of lakes, waterlilies and floating islands which offers outstanding opportunities for observing birds and animals. At the northwestern corner of the province, overlooking the Chaco coast, there's the attractive provincial capital **Corrientes**, whose historic centre is one of the best preserved in Argentina. The north of the province, bordered by the Río Paraguay, is dotted with small fishing resorts and is also the site of one of Argentina's major devotional centres, the village of **Itatí**, named for the Virgin housed here in a vast basilica.

A rogue finger of land jutting out in Argentina's northeastern corner, Misiones is one of Argentina's smallest but most distinctive provinces. What looks odd on the map makes perfect sense on the ground: Misiones' borders are almost completely defined by the wide Paraná and Uruguay rivers and one can even imagine that the province's central sierras have been formed through the land being compressed by neighbouring Brazil and Paraguay. Even the distinctive **red earth** found here ends abruptly – and for no apparent reason – on the border with Corrientes whilst the relentless torrent of water that hurtles over the falls at **Iguazú** must surely mark one of world's most dramatic and decisive frontiers.

Given its proximity to Iguazú, the rest of the province of Misiones is surprisingly under-visited. There is a well-established tourist corridor taking visitors from Iguazú to San Ignacio and from there to the capital city **Posadas** – a convenient and comfortable stopover, but hardly a major tourist destination – but away from these hubs, tourism is as yet little developed. In many ways, this adds to the province's appeal; getting to the isolated Saltos del Moconá is something of an adventure in itself.

The littoral region offers a fascinating mix of cultures. Throughout much of Misiones and along the western border of Corrientes, there's a significant Brazilian influence, whilst Paraguayan markets and food vendors are a common feature of the northern borders of Misiones and Corrientes. Misiones was also the centre of considerable immigration in the early twentieth century: the central city of **Obera** boasts of having fourteen different nationalities, including Ukranians, Swedes, Japanese and Germans. Finally, there's also a Guaraní influence, with small communities scattered through Misiones, though there's a more widespread indigenous influence in Corrientes, where some strikingly "primitive" beliefs and superstitions co-exist with a deep-seated Roman Catholic sentiment and a profound devotion to the cult of the Virgin of Itatí. This of cross-cultural influence is also echoed in the speech of inhabitants in some of the more rural regions where a mix of Guaraní and Spanish can be heard. Throughout the littoral region, isolated Guaraní words are a common feature of speech: you may hear a child referred to as a "gurí" or a woman as a "guaina". And Argentina's liveliest **carnival**, held in this region, is heavily influenced by Brazil, with major celebrations in Corrientes, **Paso de los Libres** and **Gualeguaychú** in Entre Ríos.

For most Argentinians, however, El Litoral means two things: **mate** and *chamamé*. The Litoraleños are fanatical consumers of Argentina's national drink, and their passion for the national infusion makes their countrymen look like amateurs. As well as the standard brew, typically drunk here without sugar from a wide-mouthed gourd, a cold version, *tereré*, drunk from metal cups, is popular in summer. **Chamamé** is perhaps Argentina's most infectious folk music, a lively danceable rhythm punctuated by a rather bloodcurdling cry, known as the *sapucay*. It is popular throughout the littoral region, but is best heard in Corrientes.

Note that summers are invariably hot and humid in the littoral region, with temperatures regularly reaching 40°C and above in the north. Consequently most business is done in the morning and the siesta is a serious and lengthy affair, with the streets not coming back to life until early evening. **Travel** around the region is relatively straightforward, with a steady stream of buses heading along the main arteries, NR12 and NR14, which run along the Río Paraná and the Río Uruguay respectively. All of the region's major cities – and a few of the smaller ones, too – also have an airport.

Rosario

Rosario, vital and crude, tough and tender: the true city of Argentina.

Waldo Frank

With one million inhabitants, **ROSARIO** vies with Córdoba for the title of Argentina's second city. To some extent, the city also regards itself as a worthy rival to Buenos Aires, 300km to the southeast. Geographically at least, the comparison holds: like the capital, Rosario is a riverside city and **port** and lies at the heart of an important agricultural region. Unlike Buenos Aires, however, whose back is pretty firmly to the water, Rosario enjoys a close relationship with the **River Paraná**; its attractive riverfront area runs for some 20km along the city's eastern edge, flanked by parks, bars and restaurants and, to the north, beaches. The city's trump card, however, is the splendidly undeveloped **delta islands** with wide sandy beaches which lie just minutes away from the city centre. Packed with locals during the sweltering summers that afflict the region, they give Rosario the feel of a resort town, despite the city's little-developed tourist industry. By far the most diverse and cosmopolitan city in the littoral region, Rosario is a fun stopover and worth considering as a destination in itself if you're a fan of city life: as well as a vibrant cultural scene – many of Argentina's most famous artists and musicians hail from the city – Rosario is noted for its lively nightlife, known as **la movida**.

Today, Rosario is a confident and stylish city which – despite the replacement of some fine old architecture with more modern buildings – retains a distinguished town

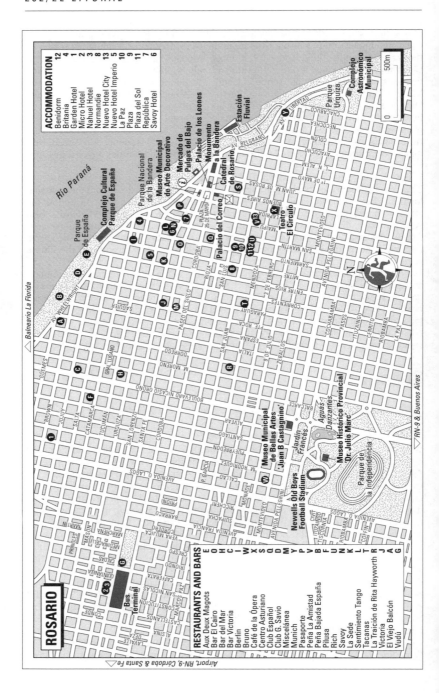

ROSARIO

ACCOMMODATION
Benidorm	12
Britania	4
Garden Hotel	1
Micro Hotel	2
Nahuel Hotel	3
Normandie	8
Nuevo Hotel City	13
Nuevo Hotel Imperio	5
La Paz	10
Plaza	9
Plaza del Sol	11
República	7
Savoy Hotel	6

RESTAURANTS AND BARS
Aux Deux Magots	E
Bar El Cairo	O
Bar del Mar	H
Bar Victoria	C
Berlin	I
Bruno	W
Café de la Ópera	X
Centro Asturiano	S
Club Español	Q
Club G. Savio	D
Miscelánea	M
Munich	Y
Pasaporte	P
Peña La Amistad	V
Peña Bajada España	B
Pilusa	F
Rich	U
Savoy	Z
La Sede	K
Sentimiento Tango	L
Tacanas	T
La Traición de Rita Hayworth	R
Victoria	A
El Viejo Balcón	G
Vudú	

Balneario La Florida

Río Paraná

Parque de España

Complejo Cultural Parque de España

Parque Nacional de la Bandera

Museo Municipal de Arte Decorativo

Mercado de Pulgas del Bajo

Palacio de los Leones

Monumento a la Bandera

Estación Fluvial

Parque Urquiza

Complejo Astronómico Municipal

Catedral de Rosario

Palacio del Correo

Teatro El Círculo

Museo Municipal de Bellas Artes 'Juan B Castagnino'

Jardín Francés

Aguas Danzantes

Museo Histórico Provincial 'Dr. Julio Marc'

Newells Old Boys Football Stadium

Parque de la Independencia

Bus Terminal

Airport, RN-9, Córdoba & Santa Fe

RN-9 & Buenos Aires

0   500m

centre. The city doesn't have the impressive ecclesiastical and colonial architecture of, say, Córdoba, but it has some particularly attractive examples of a rather more worldly architecture: the **stylish bars**, mansions and old department stores make it a rewarding city to simply wander around and *rosarino* life is conducted at a significantly less hectic pace than that of the capital. In terms of more traditional sightseeing, Rosario has a handful of worthwhile museums and galleries, notably the excellent **Museo de Bellas Artes J.B. Castagnino** and the **Museo Histórico Provincial**, both located in the city's major green space, the **Parque de la Independencia**. Its most famous sight, however, is the monolithic **Monumento Nacional a la Bandera**, a 70-metre marble paean to the Argentinian flag: General Manuel Belgrano created the flag in the city in 1812 and Rosario's official title is the "la cuna de la bandera", or the cradle of the flag.

As well as Che Guevara (born in an apartment block on the corner of Santa Fe and Urquiza), **rosarino celebrities** include the artists Antonio Berni and Lucio Fontana, three of Argentina's most popular singers – Fito Páez, Juan Carlos Baglietto and Litto Nebbia – and the cartoonist Roberto Fontanarrosa whose most famous creation, the luckless gaucho Inodoro Pereyra, is a staple of the back pages of the national newspaper, *Clarín*. Rosario's other key cultural icons are sporting: allegiances to two major teams – **Rosario Central** and **Newell's Old Boys** – divide the city with a fervour possibly greater than that provoked by River Plate and Boca Juniors.

Some history
Unusually for a Spanish-American city, Rosario lacks an official founding date. The city slowly grew up around a simple chapel, dedicated to the **Virgen del Rosario** and built in the grounds of an estancia in the late seventeenth century. The small settlement that began to grow up around the chapel became known as La Capilla del Rosario, and was granted the title "Ilustre y Fiel Villa" (loyal and illustrious town) in 1823. Despite Rosario's strategic location as a port for goods from Córdoba and the interior, early growth was slow: as in all the littoral region, Rosario's progress was hindered by Buenos Aires' stranglehold on the movement of trade between the interior and foreign markets through blockades of the River Paraná. With General Urquiza's freeing up of the rivers following the Battle of Caseros in 1852, Rosario was finally set on course for expansion and the city's population grew from 3000 in 1850 to 23,000 in 1869.

There was a further spur to growth in 1870 when the **Central Argentine Railway**, owned and largely financed by the British, was completed, providing a rail link between Rosario and Córdoba. By 1895 Rosario was Argentina's second city, with 91,000 inhabitants – many of them immigrants attracted by the promise of the by now flourishing port. By the early twentieth century, the city had an important banking district, with representatives from the world's major financial institutions and a growing number of industries. The legacy of this period of wealth can be seen on Rosario's streets today: the city has some of Argentina's finest late nineteenth- and early twentieth-century **architecture**, with an eclectic spread of styles ranging from English chalets to examples of Catalan modernism – a decorative early twentieth-century style incorporating elements of Moorish and Gothic architecture. Like Buenos Aires, Rosario also had its sleazy side: during the late nineteenth and early twentieth century, the city was a centre of white slave traffic with a notorious zone of **prostitution** known as the Barrio de Pichincha.

As in the rest of the country, the later twentieth century saw a decline in Rosario's fortunes as well as periods of intense political conflict – notably in May 1969 during the student uprising known as the *rosariazo*, provoked initially by the police shooting and killing a student in Corrientes during a protest at an unprecedented rise in prices at the university canteen. Rosario is also famous for being the birthplace of one of the twentieth century's greatest icons: **Che Guevara**.

Arrival, information and accommodation

Rosario's international **airport** lies around 10km northwest of the city centre, along the RN9 (☎0341/456-7997). There is no bus service to the centre from the airport – the half-hour taxi ride will cost around $10; alternatively you can take a taxi to the nearby neighbourhood of Fisherton, from where buses #115 and #116 run to the bus terminal.

Buses arrrive at Rosario's clean and attractive **Terminal de Omnibus Mariano Moreno**, some twenty blocks west of the city centre, at Santa Fe and Cafferata (☎0341/437-2384). There's a very helpful information kiosk which can provide you with a list of hotels and a map. **Left luggage** is charged at $1.70 for two hours. Before leaving the terminal, it's a good idea to buy a magnetic card (*tarjeta magnética*) which is used instead of money on the city's local buses. The cards are available from a kiosk towards the front entrance of the terminal and cost $1.20 for two journeys or $3 for five. Plenty of taxis pull up outside the front entrance or you can walk one block north along Cafferata to catch a bus (#116, #107) to the centre from San Lorenzo.

There's an extremely efficient **tourist information office** down by the riverfront, on the corner of Avenida Belgrano and Calle Buenos Aires (daily 8am–8pm; ☎0341/480-2230; *etur@rosario.gov.ar*). They produce an excellent map covering most of the city, as well as accommodation and restaurant lists. There is a smaller office in Parque de la Independencia, on the corner of Bulevar Oroño and Avenida Pellegrini (daily 8am–8pm; ☎0341/480-2233).

Rosario is adequately catered for as far as hotels go, though decent budget **accommodation** is pretty thin on the ground, while most of the more expensive places are pretty faceless. There's a clutch of hotels in the area around the bus terminal – which for once isn't particularly seedy – otherwise most hotels are located in the vicinity of Plaza 25 de Mayo, Rosario's central square and the main pedestrian street, Calle Córdoba. Discounts are often available at weekends.

Benidorm, San Juan 1049 (☎ & fax 0341/421-9368). Airy, clean and modern rooms, all with external windows, air conditioning and TV. ⑤, including breakfast and parking.

Britania, San Martín 364. Old and slightly chaotic hotel one block from the riverfront. Very basic rooms, but cheap and central. ② with private bathroom, ① with shared bathroom.

Garden, Callao 45 (☎0341/437-0025; *gardenh@citynet.net.ar*). An attractive modern hotel in a quiet area of town. Large, comfortable beds, air conditioning, and cable TV. Spacious bar area. ⑤, including breakfast and parking.

La Paz, Barón de Mauá 36 (☎0341/421-0905). Plain but adequate rooms with TV and private bathroom, some with balconies. ④, including breakfast.

Micro, Santa Fe 3650 (☎0341/439-7192). Dreary but passable hotel opposite the bus terminal, all rooms with private bathroom and air conditioning or fan. ③.

Nahuel Hotel, Santa Fe 3618 (☎0341/438-6807). A friendly, if unremarkable hotel, right opposite the bus terminal. Comfortable rooms with air conditioning, and TV. ③, including breakfast and parking.

Normandie, Mitre 1030 (☎0341/421-2694). Basic, slightly gloomy rooms with TV and private bathroom located around a central courtyard. Friendly staff, though, and good central location. Parking $5 a day. ③.

Nuevo Hotel City, San Juan 867 (☎ & fax 0341/404903). Centrally located hotel with basic, comfortable rooms – but few with external windows. Some rooms have fans, others have air conditioning – all have private bathroom. ④, including breakfast and parking.

Nuevo Hotel Imperio, Urquiza 1264 (☎ & fax 0341/426-2732; *himperio@satlink.com*). A bland Seventies construction grafted onto a venerable old hotel (part of the stunning but dilapidated Moorish interior survives but is not in use). A slick and spotless, if slightly overpriced, place with well-equipped rooms (facilities include cable TV and air conditioning), a bar and restaurant. Parking $8.50 per day. ⑤.

Plaza, Barón de Mauá 26 (☎0341/449-1122; *www.rosario.com.ar/plaza*). Spacious, clean but rather dull rooms with minibar, TV and air conditioning; there's also a pool and gym. ⑦.

Plaza del Sol, San Juan 1055 (☎0341/421-9899; *www.rosario.com.ar/plaza*). Sister hotel of the *Plaza* – a bit more expensive, but much more attractive rooms. Buffet breakfast and nice swimming pool. Parking $6 a day. ⑦.

República, San Lorenzo 955 (☎0341/424-8580). A modern block with large but depressingly ugly rooms – all the usual facilities, but no style. ⑤, including breakfast and parking.

Savoy Hotel, San Lorenzo 1022 (☎0341/480071). Beautiful and atmospheric old hotel with a sweeping marble staircase and a grandly anachronistic smoking room. Spotless rooms, with original wooden furniture and washstands; many rooms come with balconies. ④, ② with shared bathroom.

The City

Though Rosario is a large city, stretching for some 20km along the River Paraná, most points of interest lie within a fairly compact area and – with the exception of excursions to the city's popular balneario, **La Florida**, to the north – there is rarely any real need to take public transport. It's an easy city to find your way around, too, with streets following an exceptionally regular grid pattern, and the river itself making a useful reference point. Rosario's main square is the quiet **Plaza 25 de Mayo**, where you'll find the main post office, the cathedral and an excellent decorative arts museum, the **Museo de Arte Decorativo Firma y Odilio Estévez**. One block to the east lies the **Monumento de la Bandera**, which faces onto Rosario's main riverside avenue, the Avenida Belgrano. The southern end of Avenida Belgrano leads to **Parque Urquiza**, popular with joggers and walkers in the evening and home to the city's astronomical observatory. To the south and west of Plaza 25 de Mayo is Rosario's main commercial and shopping district, centred on the pedestrianized streets of San Martín and Córdoba. Beyond Calle Corrientes, Córdoba is known as the **Paseo del Siglo**, a stretch of street which is both home to some of Rosario's best-preserved architecture and the city's most upmarket shops and bars. The Paseo del Siglo ends at the **Bulevar Oroño**, an elegant boulevard which runs south towards Rosario's attractive park, the **Parque de la Independencia** where you will find most of the city's **museums**.

Plaza 25 de Mayo

Site of the first modest chapel built to venerate the Virgen del Rosario, the **Plaza 25 de Mayo** sits on the edge of the city before it slopes down to Avenida Belgrano and the river. The plaza itself is a pleasantly shady space laid out very formally around its central marble monument, the **Monumento a la Independencia**. Around the square lie a number of grand public buildings, including the imposing **Palacio del Correo** on the corner of Córdoba and Buenos Aires and, on the northeastern corner, the terracotta-coloured Municipal Palace, also known as the **Palacio de los Leones**, in reference to the majestic sculptured lions which flank the main entrance. To the south of the Palacio lies the **Catedral de Rosario** (Mon–Sat 7.30am–12.30pm & 4.30–8.30pm, Sun 7.30–1pm & 5–9.30pm), a late nineteenth-century construction in which domes, towers, columns and pediments are mixed to particularly eclectic effect. Inside, there's a fine Italianate altar carved from Carrara marble and, in the crypt, the colonial wood-carved image of the Virgin of Rosario, brought from Cádiz in 1773. At Santa Fe 748, you'll find the **Museo Municipal de Arte Decorativo Firma y Odilio Estévez** (mid-March to Dec Wed–Sun 5–9pm & 4–8pm; $1; *www.rosario.gov.ar/museoestevez*). Housed in a fantastically ornate mansion, whose facade reflects the early twentieth-century fashion for heavily ornamental moulding, the museum exhibits the collection of the building's former occupants, the Estévez family. It's a stunning display – every inch of the interior is furnished and ornamented with objects seemingly chosen to exemplify the wealth and taste of the owners, from Egyptian glassware and tiny Greek sculptures to Flemish tapestry and Limoges porcelain. There's a small but impressive **painting collection**, too, including *Portrait of a gentleman* by the famous French Neoclassicist Jacques

Louis David and a portrait of *Donna Maria Teresa de Apodaca et Sesma* by Francisco Goya, with typically piercing black eyes. At the back of the museum, there's a beautiful tiled patio with a central fountain, and an attractive café.

Monumento a la Bandera

Your first sight of the **Monumento a la Bandera** is likely to be through the gap between the cathedral and the Palacio de los Leones, from where the Pasaje Juramento, lined with marble sculptures by the Tucumán sculptress Lola Mora leads down to the monument itself. Finished in 1957 under the direction of the architect Ángel Guido, the Monumento a la Bandera is basically a huge allegorical sculpture based on the idea of a ship (representing Argentina) sailing towards a glorious future. Physically, it is divided into three sections: the so-called **Propileo**, a kind of temple-like structure within which burns an eternal flame commemorating Argentines who have died for their country; the **Patio Cívico**, a long, shallow rectangular flight of stairs leading away from the propileo; and, looming above everything, the **central tower** – a massive 70-metre block of unpolished marble whose crude lines seem particularly inappropriate in a city otherwise distinguished for its graceful architecture. It's well worth taking the lift to the top of the tower (Mon 2–7pm, Tues–Sun 9am–7pm; $1), from where there's a commanding **view** of the river and the city. The tower, unsurprisingly, is a magnet for patriotic suicide victims and the lift operators need little encouragement to recount the gory effects of falling onto the road below, though the recent erection of a barrier – after a Malvinas veteran threw himself off in 1999 – should prove a serious obstacle to any future attempts. Below the tower, there's a **crypt** dedicated to the creator of the flag, General Manuel Belgrano, and, below the propileo, there's the rather pointless and pompous **sala de banderas**, in which flags of all the American countries are exhibited, together with the national flower, the national anthem, the national shield and a sample of earth.

The Costanera

Stretching for some 20km from north to south, Rosario's **Costanera**, or riverfront, is one of the city's most appealing features, offering numerous green spaces and views over the River Paraná. Just to the east of the Monumento a la Bandera, you'll find this area's most central park, the **Parque Nacional de la Bandera**, a narrow wedge of grass lining the river. At the southern end of the park lies the **Estación Fluvial** (☎0341/448-3737) from where regular boat services run to various islands. On weekends you can **cruise** the river on the sightseeing boat, *Ciudad de Rosario* (Sat 5.30pm, Sun 3pm & 5.30pm; two-hour trip $5; ☎0341/425-7895). Around Av. Belgrano 500, which runs past the western edge of the park, there is a flea market, the **Mercado de Pulgas del Bajo**, every Saturday and Sunday evening, where you can browse through a selection of crafts, antiques and books. The park merges to the north with the **Parque de España**, where a cultural and exhibition centre, the **Complejo Cultural Parque de España** (☎0341/426-0941), has been imaginatively installed in some old nineteenth-century tunnels. The park is also the setting – in good weather – for a popular *milonga* on Sunday evenings.

Some fifteen blocks to the south of the Parque Nacional de la Bandera – follow Avenida de la Libertad which climbs the bluff just to the south of the Monumento – lies **Parque Urquiza**, a small park most notable for being the spot to go for an evening jog or stroll, ending up in the nearby *Munich* (see "Eating, drinking and nightlife", p.288). The park is also home to Rosario's astronomical observatory, the **Complejo Astronómico Municipal** (☎0341/480-2533), which consists of the observatory itself (Mon–Fri 9–10pm when skies clear; free); a planetarium (Sat & Sun at 5pm & 6pm; $2) and a science museum (Sun 6–8.30pm; $2).

Around 8km to the north of the centre lies Rosario's most popular mainland beach, **Balneario La Florida** (bus #101 from Rioja), packed on summer weekends, and with bars, restaurants and shower facilities. At the southern end of the balneario you'll find the **Rambla Catalunya** and Avenida Carrasco, lined with glitzy bars, restaraunts and nightclubs which, during the summer, become the focus of Rosario's famed *movida*.

Parque de la Independencia and museums

Dissected by various avenues and containing several museums, a football stadium – Newell's Old Boys, known affectionately as "El Coloso" – and a racetrack, the **Parque de la Independencia** feels like a neighbourhood in itself. The park was inaugurated in 1902 and is an attractively landscaped green space with shady walkways and beautifully laid out gardens such as the formal **Jardín Francés** just to the west of the main entrance on Bulevar Oroño. Just to the south of the entrance, there is a large lake which is the setting every evening for a rather kitsch but pretty spectacle known as the **Aguas Danzantes**, literally the "dancing waters": a synchronized fountain display complete with coloured lights and music (summer Mon–Thurs 8.30–11pm, Fri–Sun 8.30–midnight; winter Mon–Thurs 8.30–10pm, Fri–Sun 8.30–11pm). At Avenida Pellegrini 2202, a route which runs through the park, you'll find the **Museo Municipal de Bellas Artes Juan B. Castagnino** (Tues–Sat noon–8pm, Sun 10am–8pm; ☎0341/480-2542), regarded as the country's most important fine arts museum after the Museo de Bellas Artes in Buenos Aires. The museum has two permanent collections: European painting from the fifteenth to the twentieth century, with works by Goya, Sisley and Daubigny amongst others, and Argentine painting with examples from major artists such as Spilimbergo and Quinqela Martín as well as Antonio Berni and Lucio Fontana, both born in Rosario. The museum, arranged on two floors with large and well-lit rooms, also puts on some excellent temporary exhibitions – it's well worth looking out for exhibitions featuring local artists, who are producing some of Argentina's most interesting contemporary work. Also worth visiting is the **Museo Histórico Provincial Dr Julio Marc** (Tues–Fri 9am–5pm, Sat & Sun 2–5pm; free; ☎0341/472-1457), which lies to the west of the lake. A large and well-organized museum which has recently undergone some renovation, the Museo Histórico has a vast collection of exhibits spanning the whole of Latin America. Among its most notable collections are those dedicated to **Latin American religious art**, with a stunning eighteenth-century silver altar from Alto Perú which was used for the Mass given by Pope John Paul II when he visited the city in 1987, and some fine examples of polychrome works in wood, wax and bone, representing the famed Quiteña school. In the room dedicated to San Martín, look out for the strange navigational instrument known as an **astronomical ring**, used by San Martín during his famed crossing of the Andes: the piece's curiosity value lies in the fact that it was already somewhat archaic in San Martín's time. There's also an important collection of **indigenous American ceramics**, including some valuable musical pieces known as whistling glasses (*vasos silbadores*) from the Chimú culture of northern Peru and some stunningly well-preserved and delicate textiles. Parque Independencia can easily be reached on foot from the centre – it's a particularly attractive walk along the Paseo del Siglo and the Bulevar Oroño or you can take buses #129 and #123 from Rioja.

The river and islands

Known as the Alto Delta, the low-lying **islands** which sit off Rosario's coast actually fall under the jurisdiction of the neighbouring province, Entre Ríos. Like the islands of the Tigre Delta, in Buenos Aires, they have a subtropical vegetation fed by sediment from Misiones. The Alto Delta is far less developed than Tigre, however, and with the exception of **Chariguë**, where there is a small island settlement with its own school, police station and a handful of restaurants, the islands are largely uninhabited. If you can afford it, the best way of seeing the Delta is on an **excursion**; try Carlos Vaccarezza (☎0341/449-1921) or El Holandés (☎156-415880). Alternatively, there are various

---

FERRY SERVICES TO THE ISLANDS

From November to March, there are regular boat services from the Estación Fluvial to the various islands of Rosario's Alto Delta. Boat services run from 9am to dusk. Prices quoted are for return tickets. Out of season, services are less frequent.

Vladimir every 15min ($3.50)   **Aldea** at 9am, 11am and 5pm ($4)
Costa Esperanza every 15min ($3)   **Buenaventura** at 9am, 11am and 5pm ($4)
Oasis every 15min ($3)   **Charigüé** at 9am, 11am and 5pm ($4)

Additionally, there is a daily ferry service to the pretty town of Victoria, in Entre Ríos Province, leaving from Rosario at 2pm and arriving in Victoria at 6.30pm. The service returns from Victoria at 6.30am (Sun 9am). The ticket office, run by Expreso Delta (Mon–Fri 30min before departures, Sat & Sun 11am–2pm; ☎0341/424217, mobile 156-403469), is in the Parque de la Bandera, just to the north of the Estación Fluvial.

---

islands offering camping facilities, accommodation and restaurants which you can reach by one of the regular passenger services from the Estación Fluvial (see above), or by arranging to be picked up by the owners.

Isla Buenaventura (☎155-425607) directly to the east of Rosario, along the Riacho Los Marinos offers **accommodation** in well-equipped bungalows holding up to four people (Dec–March weekdays $40, weekends $70; rest of year, rates negotiable) with kitchen, private bathroom and fans. The friendly and ecologically minded young owners also offer guided walks into the island's wild interior as well as canoeing trips. You can also camp in the island's interior (no facilities). Some provisions can be supplied on the island, including fresh fish from local fishermen, but you should bring some provisions with you if you're planning on staying for a while. As well as the regular passenger service, you can arrange to be picked up by the island's owners ($30 return trip for up to four people). Just next door to *Isla Buenaventura*, there's an excellent **restaurant**, *La Aldea* (☎156-177402) where extremely fresh fish is cooked to order and can be eaten at one of the outside tables on the riverbank. Another option is the *Cabañas del Francés* (☎155-473045; *www.rosario.net.com.ar/cabfrances*; $50–$70 for five to seven people; twenty percent discount for two people or less) where there are attractive rustic-style *cabañas*, and a bar. There is no regular boat service to the *cabañas*, but the owner will pick up a party of up to five people from the mainland ($20 return).

If you just fancy spending a day swimming or sunbathing, head for **Vladimir**, just to the south of the Estación Fluvial where there are good sandy beaches and a couple of snack bars; be warned, though, that the sun can be very fierce and there is little or no shade – take a high-factor sun cream and sunshade. Not far north of the city, there is another good bar and restaurant, *Puerto Pirata* (daily 10am–10pm; ☎0341/156-174596) with great views over the river from its wooden terrace and a long strip of beach; to get there, take a bus to Granadero Baigorria, from where you can ring the owners to come and pick you up.

Eating, drinking and nightlife

Rosario has plenty of **restaurants** to suit all budgets, both in the city centre and along the costanera. As well as pasta, pizza and parrillada there are a number of excellent fish restaurants specializing in boga, dorado and surubí. What the city really excels in, however, are **bars** – there are so many stylishly revamped establishments around the city centre that you're pretty much spoilt for choice when it comes to drinking. The best spots for bar-hopping are just to the north of the centre, roughly between Santa Fe and Avenida Belgrano and, to the west, around the area known as the barrio de Pichincha, a notorious zone of prostitution at the beginning of the twentieth century, bounded by calles Ricchieri, Suipacha, Salta and Güemes. In comparison, Rosario's **clubs** are a little disappointing and in summer, when all the action moves to the Rambla Catalunya, a beachfront avenue at the northern end of town, you're pretty much limited to one or two very popular but pretty faceless mega-discos. A more interesting alternative might be to visit one of the city's popular *milongas*; Rosario has a hard core of **tango** enthusiasts and most nights of the week there is something going on – one of the most popular events in good weather is a regular Sunday evening *milonga* in the Parque España. Tango fans might be interested to know that Rosarinos are said to dance a slightly showier version of the tango than Porteños.

Cafés and restaurants

Aux Deux Magots, Entre Ríos 2. Spacious café-bar serving excellent coffee overlooking the river – a lovely spot for a leisurely Sunday breakfast.

Bar El Cairo, Santa Fe and Sarmiento. A classic old café famous for being a favourite haunt of Rosario's celebrated cartoonist Fontanarrosa.

Bar Victoria, Bulevar Oroño and Jujuy. Classic Rosarino bar. Traditional, mostly male clientele.

Bruno, Montevideo 2798. Long-established, family-run Italian restaurant serving excellent home-made pasta. Closed Mondays.

Club Español, Rioja 1052. Friendly restaurant housed in a beautiful old building with stunning decorative glass ceilings and an astonishingly elaborate facade. Simple daily menu ($7) includes a main course, dessert and wine and soda. Sunday lunchtimes are popular for Spanish specialities such as paella and tortilla.

Club G. Savio, located right by the river, at the end of Calle Paraguay; access via Calle Corrientes (☎0341/426-7157). Popular fish restaurant with lovely wooden terrace overlooking the river. Try the simple grilled *boga al limón*.

Munich, Av. L. Libertad 10. This large café and *cervecería* on the southern costanera is an almost obligatory early-evening pit stop for Rosarinos on their way back from a walk around Parque Urquiza – try the excellent draught lager. The outside tables are good for a spot of people-watching.

Pasaporte, Maipú and Urquiza. Stylish bar with outside tables on a pretty corner down near the riverfront. Coffee, alcoholic drinks and a large selection of filled crepes. Board games available.

Peña Bajada España, Av. Illia and España. Friendly and unpretentious fish restaurant on the costanera specializing in river fish.

Rich, San Juan 1031 (☎0341/440-8657). Rosario's most venerable restaurant, a lovely old-fashioned place with a vast mouthwatering menu which mixes traditional dishes such as *puchero* with more elaborate creations such as sea bass with champagne sauce or sirloin steak with shallots, mushrooms, bacon and red wine. Vegetarians can choose from dishes such as pasta with tomato pesto, cream and mushrooms, and asparagus omelette. It's a little expensive, but well worth it.

Savoy, San Lorenzo and San Martín. Definitely the best deal in town with plenty of fish, meat and pasta dishes for around $3. The spaghetti with home-made pesto and fresh parmesan for only $1.30 is unbelievably cheap and delicious. A good place for breakfast, too, with coffee and croissants for $1.

Señor Arenero, Av. Carrasco 2568. Big glitzy restaurant specializing in fish, in the popular Rambla Catalunya area.

Tacanas, Paraguay and Mendoza (☎0341/424-9797). Takeaway *empanada* joint (delivery service also available) with an imaginative range of fillings for Argentina's favourite snack; as well as traditional beef and chicken, there is tomato, mozzarella and basil, cheese and olives and mozzarella and mushroom.

Victoria, San Lorenzo and Pte. Roca. Pretty old-fashioned corner café-bar and restaurant with a sober wooden interior and tables on the pavement. Good-value *menú ejecutivo* with a main dish such as pork chops, a dessert and drink for around $5. Closed Sun lunch.

El Viejo Balcón, Wheelwright and Italia. One of the city's best parrillas, serving up all the usual cuts at an attractive riverside location.

Wembley, Av. Belgrano 2012 (☎0341/481-1090). Busy upmarket restaurant opposite the port. Daily specials such as salmon with capers though the most successful dishes are the more simply executed grilled river fish or parrillada.

Bars and nightclubs

Bar del Mar, Balcarce and Tucumán. Cool bar with aquatically inspired blue walls. Good selection of laid-back music and a trendy but friendly crowd.

Berlín, Pje Zabala 1128, between the 300 block of Mitre and Sarmiento. Regular cabaret and musical events from Thursday to Sunday at this popular bar.

Café de la Ópera, Laprida and Mendoza (☎156-422024). Beautiful café beneath the Teatro El Círculo, with cabaret events on Fridays and Saturdays from 10pm.

Catalinas, Av. Colombres 2600. *The* club in the summer; a big, mainstream disco along the Rambla Catalunya with outside bar area and a young, lively crowd.

Centro Asturiano, San Luis 644. Setting for popular *milonga* on Saturdays from 11pm – also tango classes at 10pm and salsa classes at 9pm.

Miscelánea, Pte. Roca 755. Setting for *Hot Club Rosario* – a club with live jazz performances embracing everything from big-band sounds to modern jazz. Jam sessions with invited musicians on Thursdays from 9.30pm to midnight.

Peña La Amistad, Maipú 1121 (☎0341/447-1037). A good spot to listen to folk music with the emphasis on *chamamé* and other littoral styles. Snacks such as *empanadas* and *tamales* are served. Fridays and Saturdays from 11pm.

Pilusa, Alvear and Catamarca. Attractive wood-panelled bar on a pretty corner of Pichincha. Good range of beers and also fruity non-alcoholic drinks.

Rancho, Av. Carrasco 2765. Popular summer bar along the Rambla Catalunya and a good place to pick up free invites for one of the area's clubs. Vast outside seating area and a range of beers, cocktails and fast food.

La Sede, San Lorenzo and Entre Ríos. Elegant and rather literary bar – a favourite meeting place for Rosario's artistic celebrities. Theatrical/cabaret evenings.

Sentimiento Tango, San Martín 580. A slightly down-at-heel but atmospheric tango bar attracting a handful of dancers every night except Monday. The atmosphere is anything but intimidating, which makes it a good place to take your first tango steps; classes Tues, Thurs, Sat & Sun from 9pm.

Teatro El Círculo, Laprida 1235 (☎0341/448-3784). As well as theatrical and musical events, Rosario's most famous theatre hosts a popular Wednesday night *milonga*.

Timotea, Av. Colombres 1340, just before Rambla Catalunya. Similar atmosphere to *Catalinas*; a swish mainstream disco attracting the tanned hordes of summer.

La Traición de Rita Hayworth, Dorrego 1170. Lively cultural bar named after a novel by Argentinian writer Manuel Puig, with a regular programme of alternative theatrical and musical events.

Vudú, Patio de la Madera, Av. Santa Fe. Located next to the bus terminal, this big techno club attracts a trendy crowd. Closed during the summer season.

Listings

Airlines Aerolíneas Argentinas/Austral, Santa Fe 1410 (☎0341/424-9332), and at the airport (☎0341/451-1470); Southern Winds, Mitre 737 (☎0341/425-3808) and at the airport (☎0341/451-6708; *swros@eldigital.com.ar*); Varig/Pluna, Corrientes 729, 7th Floor, office 710 (☎0341/425-6262) and at the airport (☎0341/451-2802).

Car rental Dollar, Paraguay 892 (☎0341/426-1700); Localiza, Córdoba 4199 (☎0341/435-1234); Olé, Gorriti 751 (☎0341/437-6517); Rent a Car Al, Sgto. Cabral 519 (☎0341/448-1936).

Internet access and telephones There are many *locutorios* in the centre, including Telefónica with Internet access at Urquiza 1275 (8am–midnight).

Laundries Both Tintorería Rosario, at San Lorenzo 1485 (☎0341/425-3620) and Lavandería VIP, at Maipú 654 (☎0341/426-1237) do a service wash for around $7 and will deliver to your hotel free of charge.

Pharmacies Farmacia Inglesa, Sarmiento 641; Farmacia León, Córdoba and España (24hr).

Post office The Correo Central, with all usual facilities plus a branch of Western Union, is at Buenos Aires and Córdoba, on Plaza 25 de Mayo (Mon–Fri 8am–8pm, Sat 8am–1pm).

Travel agent ASATEJ, Corrientes 653 (☎0341/425-3798).

Santa Fe

Capital of its namesake province and an important centre for the surrounding agricultural region, **SANTA FE** lies 475km to the north of Buenos Aires, along the banks of the River Paraná. A sizeable city of some 375,000 inhabitants, Santa Fe is of interest mainly as a stopover – although even on those terms the city loses out to the nearby and more appealing cities of Rosario and Paraná. Apart from a particularly hot and humid climate in summer, thanks to its low-lying riverside location, Santa Fe's main handicap is a rather sprawling and disjointed layout which makes getting to and from the city's modest attractions a bit of a slog.

Though Santa Fe is one of Argentina's oldest settlements – it was founded in 1573 by Juan de Garay in **Cayastá**, 80km to the north, and then moved to its current site in 1660 after repeated Indian attacks – careless development has made for a rather scruffy city in which unremarkable modern buildings largely overshadow the few remnants of a fine architectural heritage. What is left is largely grouped around the city's **centro histórico** where there are a handful of sights worth visiting: notably the seventeenth-century **Iglesia y Convento de San Francisco** and the well-organized **Museo Etnográfico y Colonial Juan de Garay** where there is a fine collection of artefacts recovered from the site of the original city of Santa Fe, at Cayastá. Also worth visiting is the zoo, the **Granja La Esmeralda**, to the north of the city centre, with a good selection of fauna native to the province.

Santa Fe is linked to Entre Ríos' provincial capital, **Paraná** (see p.296), by the **Túnel Subfluvial Uranga-Sylvestre Begnis** which runs for nearly 3km under the River Paraná.

Arrival, information and accommodation

Santa Fe's **airport**, with flights to many cities in the interior as well as Buenos Aires, is located at Sauce Viejo, seven kilometres south of the city along RN11 (☎0342/475-0386). The local bus marked "L" or "aeropuerto" runs between the airport and Calle San Luis in the city centre (45min–1hr). The **bus terminal** is situated on the corner of Avenida Belgrano and Hipólito Yrigoyen (☎0342/455-3908), just to the northeast of the town centre and within walking distance of most accommodation.

The helpful and friendly main **tourist office** is located in the bus terminal (daily 8am–10pm; ☎0342/457-4123; *www.santafeciudad.com.ar*). Staff can provide you with maps of the town as well as accommodation lists, and may agree to look after left luggage (there is no official left-luggage facility in the terminal). There is another smaller office at Boca del Tigre, on the corner of Dr Zavalia and J.J. Paso (☎0342/457-1862) at the southern entrance to the town and at Paseo del Restaurador, on the corner of Boulevard Gálvez and Rivadavia (☎0342/457-1881) to the north of the town centre. Due to the city's sprawling layout, you'll probably need to take the odd **bus** in Santa Fe: the standard fare is $0.75 or $0.50 within the centre, bordered by Gálvez, Rivadavia, Freyre and López.

Sadly, Santa Fe's **hotels** are an uninspiring bunch, with some particularly uninviting budget hotels in the immediate vicinity of the bus terminal – all right if you really don't mind where you sleep but otherwise best avoided. There are a couple of exceptions, but generally accommodation in Santa Fe is a little overpriced for what you actually get.

Castelar, 25 de Mayo and Falucho (☎ & fax 0342/456-0999). Pleasant, old-fashioned hotel whose exterior and lobby promise rather more than the slightly dreary rooms deliver. Parking and breakfast included, but it still seems rather overpriced. ⑤.

Colón, San Luis 2862 (☎0342/452-1586). Rather shabby rooms, but the hotel has a safe and friendly atmosphere. Air conditioning and parking included. ③.

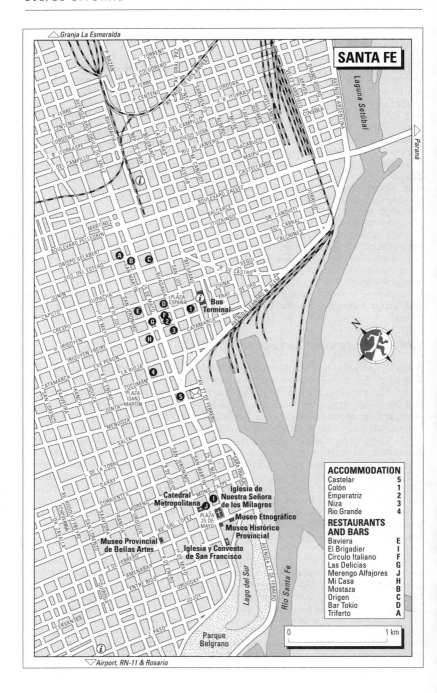

SANTA FE

ACCOMMODATION

Castelar	5
Colón	1
Emperatriz	2
Niza	3
Rio Grande	4

RESTAURANTS AND BARS

Baviera	E
El Brigadier	I
Círculo Italiano	F
Las Delicias	G
Merengo Alfajores	J
Mi Casa	H
Mostaza	B
Origen	C
Bar Tokio	D
Triferto	A

Bus Terminal

Catedral Metropolitana

Iglesia de Nuestra Señora de los Milagros

Museo Etnográfico

Museo Histórico Provincial

Museo Provincial de Bellas Artes

Iglesia y Convento de San Francisco

Parque Belgrano

Laguna Setúbal

Paraná

Lago del Sur

Rio Santa Fe

0   1 km

△ Granja La Esmeralda

▽ Airport, RN-11 & Rosario

Emperatriz Hotel, Irigoyen Freyre 2440 (☎ & fax 0342/453-0061). Definitely the best hotel in its price range and just about the only place in Santa Fe with any character: it's an unusual 1920s, Mudéjar construction – a Spanish architectural style combing Moorish and Gothic features – with arched wooden doors and a pretty tiled interior. There's a great triple room on the first floor with a small balcony and wooden floors. All rooms come with private bathroom, some with cable TV. The young owner is friendly and helpful. ③.

Hospedaje Los Aromos, (☎156-316561, ask for Mercedes). A pleasant alternative to staying in the centre of Santa Fe, *Los Aromos* is a pretty, old-fashioned building with a garden in Colastiné Norte, 4km out of town along the RP1. There are attractive three-, four- and five-person rooms, working out at just over $10 per person. To get here, take the "Servitur" or "Rincón" bus from Rivadavia (every 20min) and ask to be let off in Colastiné Norte; the *hospedaje* is around 200m to the west of the main road.

Niza, Rivadavia 2755 (☎0342/452-2047). Rather depressing-looking hotel with scruffy if adequate rooms – not a first choice but passable if all else fails. All rooms come with a fan and private bathroom; air conditioning can be had for $5 extra per night. Parking $5. ③.

Río Grande, San Jerónimo 2586 (☎0342/450-0700). Just about the best of Santa Fe's more expensive hotels; recently refurbished with spotless, comfortable rooms with cable TV, safe, minibar and air conditioning. Also some large suites with rather kitsch decor. Good buffet breakfast and courteous staff. ⑥.

The City

Santa Fe doesn't actually sit on the River Paraná but at the western extremity of a series of delta islands which separate it from the city of Paraná. Ships enter Santa Fe's important **port**, the most westerly port along the Paraná, via an access channel. The Río Santa Fe borders the southern end of the city, running north to feed into the **Laguna Setúbal**, a large lake to the east of the city, and bordered by the city's costanera which runs for some 5km from north to south. At the far northern end there is a balneario, while at the southern end lies the road bridge over the lake to Paraná, plus the remnants of the old suspension bridge, ripped apart by floods in 1983.

Santa Fe's mostly modern **downtown** area is centred around busy Calle 25 de Mayo, pedestrianized between Tucumán and Juan de Garay and lined with shops and confiterías. The quieter **centro histórico**, where you will find the majority of Santa Fe's older buildings, lies ten blocks to the south of Tucumán and is centred around **Plaza 25 de Mayo**. This is the most interesting area to explore on foot and you could while away an afternoon moving between its museums and churches, including the **Iglesia y Convento de San Francisco** and the **Museo Etnográfico y Colonial Juan de Garay**.

Five blocks to the south, you'll find the **Parque Belgrano** where there is a swimming pool and sunbathing area – though given that Santa Fe's busy ring road runs right past it you're just as likely to soak up carbon monoxide as the sun.

Plaza 25 de Mayo and around

Like the rest of the city, Santa Fe's main square, the **Plaza 25 de Mayo**, is an architecturally disjointed kind of place, with the styles of its surrounding buildings leaping from colonial through French Second Empire to nondescript modern. The square is somewhat unusual in having two churches. On the northern side stands the rather stark white **Catedral Metropolitana** (daily 8am–8pm), originally built in the mid-eighteenth century but subsequently modified to give it a simple Neoclassical facade crowned with domed and majolica-tiled bell towers. Little remains of the original building except the massive studded wooden entrance doors. On the eastern side of the square is the **Iglesia de Nuestra Señora de los Milagros**, its pleasingly simple and typically colonial facade looking rather overwhelmed by the more modern constructions around it. Built between 1667 and 1700, it is the oldest church in the province; it's well worth taking a look inside to see the fine carvings produced by Guaranís in the Jesuit Missions – most notably the impressive Altar Mayor, produced in Loreto.

On the southeastern corner of the square you'll find the **Museo Histórico Provincial Brigadier General Estanislao López** (March, April, Oct & Nov Tues–Fri 8.30am–noon & 3–7pm, Sat & Sun 4–7pm; May–Sept Tues–Fri 8.30am–noon & 2.30–6.30pm, Sat & Sun 3–6pm; Dec–Feb Tues–Fri 9am–noon & 5–8pm, Sat & Sun 5.30–8.30pm; ☎0342/459-3760). Housed in a cool late seventeenth-century colonial family house, the museum's collection comprises furniture, paintings, silverwork, religious icons and everyday items from the seventeenth century. There is a room dedictated to the famous caudillo of Santa Fe, Estanislao López, and a room of religious imagery with some notable carvings from the missions and paintings from the Cuzco school.

Three blocks to the east, at 4 de Enero 1510, there is the **Museo Provincial de Bellas Artes Rosa Galisteo de Rodríguez** (Tues–Fri 10am–noon & 4–8pm, Sat & Sun 4–8pm; ☎0342/459-6142), an imposing Neoclassical building with a large collection of Argentinian painting and sculpture from the likes of Spilimbergo, Petorutti and Fontana as well as a smaller selection of European painting with works from Delacroix and Rodin.

The Museo Etnográfico y Colonial Juan de Garay

One block to the east of the main plaza, at 25 de Mayo 1470, is the **Museo Etnográfico y Colonial Juan de Garay** (Jan & Feb Tues–Fri 8.30am–noon & 5–8pm, Sat & Sun 5–8pm; March & April Tues–Fri 8.30am–noon & 3.30–7pm, Sat & Sun 4–7pm; May–Sept Tues–Fri 8.30am–noon, Sat & Sun 3.30–6.30pm; Oct–Dec Tues–Fri 8.30am–noon & 3.30–7pm, Sat & Sun 4–7pm; ☎0342/459-5857; free). The bulk of the museum's well-organized and coherently displayed collection comprises pieces recovered from the site of **Santa Fe La Vieja** at Cayastá. The most commonly recovered pieces were *tinajas*, large ceramic urns – many of them in a surprisingly complete state considering they spent around 300 years under the ground – and delicate amulets in the form of shells or the *higa*, a clenched fist symbol, and used to ward off the evil eye. There's also a fine collection of **indigenous ceramics** with typical zoomorphic forms ranging from birds – especially parrots – and bats, to capybara, cats and snakes. Particularly attractive are the pieces in which the animal forms are moulded in such a way as to form a spout or handle. The arrival of the Spaniards had a significant impact on the pieces produced, both in the form (new shapes such as jugs began to appear) and in the design, with more floral and organic touches being introduced to the previously strongly geometric designs. At the centre of the museum there's a maquette showing the layout of Santa Fe La Vieja – it's interesting to note that when the city was rebuilt on its present site, the churches were rebuilt in the exact same location in relation to the centre.

The Iglesia y Convento de San Francisco

One block south of Plaza 25 de Mayo, at Amenábar 2557, lies the **Iglesia y Convento de San Francisco** (summer Mon–Sat 8am–noon & 4–7pm, Sun 9.30am–noon & 4.30–7pm; winter Mon–Sat 8am–noon & 3–6.30pm, Sun 3.30–6pm). Built in 1676, the church is notable for its incredible solid but rustic construction: the walls are nearly two metres thick and made of adobe, whilst the stunning and cleverly assembled interior **ceiling** was constructed using solid wooden beams of Paraguayan cedar, lapacho, algarrobo and quebracho colorado held together not with nails but with wooden pegs. The intricate dome at the centre of the church is a particularly impressive example of the application of this technique and also has a rather light-hearted touch: at the centre is suspended a beautifully carved pine cone. To your left as you enter the church is an ornate **Baroque pulpit** laminated in gold, which came from the original church at

Cayastá. Of the various icons around the church the most notable is that of **Jesús Nazareno**, immediately to your left as you enter. The beautifully detailed image was produced by one of Spain's most famous *imagineros*, or religious image makers, Alonso Cano, in 1650. It was presented to the church by the Queen of Spain, Doña María Ana de Austria, wife of Felipe IV, when the city was moved from Cayastá, in sympathy for the repeated Indian attacks.

One of the strangest relics in the church is to be found in the sacristy, a simple table scored by claw marks and known as the *mesa del tigre* ("the tiger's table"). According to a rather colourful tale, in 1825 a jaguar – known as *tigres* in Latin America – was washed up by a flood and found itself in the convent orchard. From there the animal sought refuge in the sacristy where it encountered its first victim, Brother Miguel Magallanes. Once the monk's body was discovered, a chase ensued with local bigwigs, monks and tracking dogs pursuing the jaguar. It was eventually shot in a small room off the convent cloisters, but not before it had attacked and killed two more monks and severely wounded another of the party of hunters.

Granja La Esmeralda

At Av. Aristóbulo del Valle 8700, some 6km north of the city centre, is the agreeable and ecologically minded **Granja La Esmeralda** (daily 8am–4pm; $1.50; ☎0342/469-6001), an experimental zoo dedicated to protecting and providing education about the province's native fauna. There are around seventy species of birds, animals and reptiles, including a large enclosure of the rare pampa deer. Other species include the puma, the tapir, the collared peccary, the guazuncho and the Aguará-popé or osito lavador. Bus #16 goes to Granja La Esmeralda from O. Gelabert and Castellanos, via the costanera and Barrio Guadalupe, or you could take the more direct #10 bis from Rivadavia.

Eating, drinking and nightlife

There are plenty of **restaurants** in Santa Fe, mostly within a few blocks of San Martín. *Origen*, at Av. Rivadavia, 3265, is a very good *tenedor libre* with plenty of fresh salads and parrillada amongst the dishes on offer. The *Círculo Italiano*, Hipólito Yrigoyen 2451, an elegant dining-room in the Italian community's social club, serves up fine pasta and also does a good-value *parrillada completa* with fries, salad and desert for $8.50. The stylish *El Brigadier*, at San Martín 1670, is housed in an old colonial building and does a good selection of well-prepared fish (both fresh- and saltwater) and meat; there is also a *menú promocional*, consisting of a starter, main course of pasta or chicken and dessert for $6.50. *Baviera*, at San Martín 2941, does basic well-prepared standards and is good for snacks at any time of the day. *Mi Casa*, San Martín 2777, is a popular *tenedor libre* parrilla. On the costanera, *El Quincho de Chiquito*, Ob. Príncipe 16, serves excellent grilled river fish and also has a small "museum" dedicated to the Argentinian boxer Carlos Monzón, who died in a road accident just north of Santa Fe in 1995.

Santa Fe's most famed gastronomic delights are the sweet snack *merengo alfajores* – a particularly tempting version of Argentina's favourite desert and produced in the city for 150 years; they can be bought from General López 2634. **Beer** is particularly good in Santa Fe, and locals ask for a *liso* – basically a draught lager served in a straight glass. A good place to try one is in *Las Delicias*, on the corner of San Martín and Hipólito Yrigoyen, a traditional confitería, serving good sandwiches and cakes. As far as **drinking** places goes, Santa Fe's liveliest bars are to be found around the intersection of San Martín and Santiago del Estero, all with tables on the pavement and a fun atmosphere on summer evenings: try *Triferto* at San Martín 3301 or *Mostaza* on Santiago del Estero and San Martín. For a totally different kind of atmosphere, head for the splendidly old-fashioned *Bar Tokio* (8am–10pm; closed Sun), on Plaza 25 de Mayo with snooker, pool and billiard tables and run by friendly Amelia, whose Japanese immigrant family have had the place for over 60 years.

Santa Fe isn't over-endowed with **nightclubs** but in the summer the nightclub to head for is *La Divina*, housed in a huge tent-like construction near the bridge leading to Paraná ($4) and playing a mixture of rock, salsa, Brazilian music and *cumbia*.

Listings

Airlines Austral, Lisandro de la Torre 2633 (☎0342/459-8400); Laer, Tucumán 2771 (☎0342/456-6100); Southern Winds, San Jerónimo 2656 (☎0342/456-5256).

Banks and exchange Lloyds and Citibank with ATM and dollar change facilities are on the corner of San Jerónimo and La Rioja. There are also several ATMs along San Martín. You can change travellers' cheques at TOURFE, San Martín 2500, on the corner of Tucumán and San Martín (Mon–Fri 7.30am–12.30pm & 4.30–7.30pm, Sat 9am–noon).

Car rental Annie Millet, 25 de Mayo 2786 (☎156-122003); Localiza, Lisandro de la Torre 2548 (☎0342/456-4480) and at the airport.

Internet access and telephones There are many *locutorios* around the city centre including "Llame Ya" at San Martín 2811, which also has Internet access.

Laundry Lavadero San Martín, San Martín 1786 (☎0342/458-2345), with free collection and delivery service.

Post office The central post office is at Av. 27 de Febrero 2331, around seven blocks southwest of the bus terminal.

Pharmacy Farmacia Roces Hipólito Yrigoyen 242.

Paraná and around

Lying 30km to the northeast of Santa Fe, to which it is linked by the subfluvial tunnel, **PARANÁ** is a far more appealing city than its neighbour. Favoured by a gentle hilly terrain and a lovely, pedestrian-friendly riverfront area, the city is, if not wildly exciting, at least a good place to chill out for a few days. As well as some fine sandy **beaches**, the city has a particularly attractive park, the **Parque Urquiza** whose shady walkways and thick vegetation provide welcome respite in the summer. Paraná's most famous landmark is its imposing heavily Neoclassical **Cathedral**, which dominates the city's main square. This is not a major sightseeing city but a couple of its museums are worth checking out: the **Museo Histórico Martiniano Leguizamón** has a well-presented section on the history of the region and a more interesting than usual collection of creole silverwork. while the **Museo de La Ciudad** is a friendly and accessible museum taking a more light-hearted look at the everyday life of the city.

Like Rosario, Paraná lacks a true **foundation** date: the area was simply settled by inhabitants from Santa Fe, who regarded the higher ground of the eastern banks of the Paraná as providing better protection from Indian attack. The city was declared provincial capital in 1822 and leapt to prominence as capital of General Urquiza's short-lived Confederación Argentina between 1854 and 1861 – during which period the city's major public buildings were constructed. Like most of Argentina, Paraná had its most significant period of growth in the late nineteenth century when the city received thousands of European immigrants. Today Paraná's population is around 250,000, making it the largest city in Entre Ríos Province.

Some 44km to the south of Paraná you can visit the **Parque Nacional Pre-Delta**, a small and little-developed national park protecting a typical delta environment of subtropical gallery forest and islands where aquatic birds and mammals can be spotted.

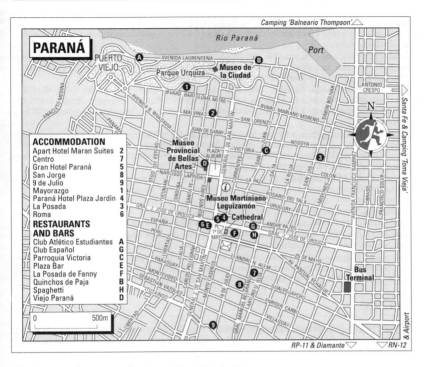

PARANÁ

Camping 'Balneario Thompson'

Río Paraná

Port

PUERTO VIEJO

AVENIDA LAURENCENA

Parque Urquiza

Museo de la Ciudad

ANTONIO CRESPO

N

Santa Fe & Camping Toma Vieja

Museo Provincial de Bellas Artes

Museo Martiniano Leguizamón

Cathedral

ACCOMMODATION
Apart Hotel Maran Suites   2
Centro   7
Gran Hotel Paraná   5
San Jorge   8
9 de Julio   9
Mayorazgo   1
Paraná Hotel Plaza Jardín   4
La Posada   3
Roma   6

RESTAURANTS AND BARS
Club Atlético Estudiantes   A
Club Español   G
Parroquia Victoria   C
Plaza Bar   E
La Posada de Fanny   F
Quinchos de Paja   B
Spaghetti   H
Viejo Paraná   D

0   500m

Bus Terminal

RP-11 & Diamante   RN-12

& Airport

Arrival, information and accommodation

Paraná's small **airport**, with daily flights to Buenos Aires (for other destinations flights leave from Santa Fe), is around 5km southeast of the city, along RN12 (☎0343/424-3320). Paraná's recently constructed and strangely confusing **Terminal de Omnibus** is at Av. Ramírez 2550, around nine blocks east of central Plaza 1° de Mayo (☎0343/431-5053). At the centre of the terminal there's a helpful combined bus information and **tourist office** (daily 8am–2pm & 4–8pm) with accommodation lists and maps. The central tourist office is at San Martín 637 (daily 8am–8pm; ☎0343/420-1661).

Paraná has possibly fewer **hotels** than Santa Fe but what there is is generally far more appealing and there are a couple of really attractive places. Budget places are thin on the ground and those that are in the vicinity of the bus terminal are not really sufficiently cheap to justify staying in this slightly dreary area. Paraná's most central **campsite**, the *Balneario Thompson* on the beach just to the east of the end of Avenida Francisco Ramírez (☎0343/420-1853; bus #1 or #6; $4 per tent), is best avoided – it's a scruffy, polluted and less than secure site. Far better is *Toma Vieja*, around 4km northeast of the centre, at the end of Avenida Blas Parera (☎0343/420-1821; two-person tent $4, plus $1 per person; four-person tent $5, plus $1 per person), a huge site with a large outdoor pool and views over the Paraná. Hot showers and electricity are provided and there is a grocery store just down the road but not on site. Bus #5 goes to *Toma Vieja* every hour from the terminal.

9 de Julio, 9 de Julio 674 (☎0343/431-9857). A friendly hotel in a quiet area of town. Pleasantly decorated rooms with private bathroom and fan. Bus #1 from terminal. Good singles deals available. Free parking. ③.

Residencial Centro, Belgrano 135 (☎0343/431-6860). Fairly centrally located hotel with small, mostly interior rooms which are scrupulously clean if a little claustrophobic. Private bathroom and fan. Parking available. ③.

Gran Hotel Paraná, Urquiza 976 (☎0343/422-3900; *www.hotelesparana.com.ar*). Smart modern block on the main square with its own restaurant, gym and parking facilities. Three categories of room, all with air conditioning and cable TV. ⑤–⑦.

Apart Hotel Marán Suites, Malvinas and Buenos Aires (☎ & fax 0343/423-5444; *maransuites@gamma.com.ar*). Attractive apartments decorated in clean, modern lines – each with its own kitchen and large balcony with views over Parque Urquiza. Air conditioning, cable TV and parking. ⑥.

Mayorazgo, Avenida Etchevere and Miranda (☎0343/423-0333). Paraná's most self-consciously luxurious hotel – an ostentatious and soulless block which towers over the costanera: the rather blandly decorated rooms are more inspiring for the great views over the river than anything else. Large and attractive outdoor swimming pool. ⑦.

Paraná Hotel Plaza Jardín, 9 de Julio 60 (☎0343/423-1700). Very attractive old-fashioned hotel right in the centre of town. Comfortable air-conditioned rooms grouped around a pretty courtyard. Cable TV and 24hr room service. Breakfast included. ⑤.

La Posada, San Luis 620 (☎0343/422-1281). The best hotel in town – a gorgeous, family-run place in an elegantly converted private house. Pretty wooden-floored rooms and a swimming pool. ④.

Roma, Urquiza 1061 (☎0343/431-2247). Friendly, family-run place with pleasant light rooms, some with balconies and a good central location. Private bathroom and fan. ③.

San Jorge, Belgrano 368 (☎0343/422-1685). The best of the cheaper places: a lovely old building with tiled floors, a small garden and kitchen facilities. There's a newer and slightly more expensive section at the back but the original front section has more style. ③.

The City

While Paraná is a pleasant place to wander round, there aren't any major sights and the city is probably best treated as a place to take a bit of a break from sightseeing. The city's main square is the **Plaza 1° de Mayo**, which lies some ten blocks inland. The single most outstanding building here is the **Cathedral**, built in 1887. It's a superficially handsome if somehow rather awkward Neoclassical edifice distinguished by an intense blue brick-tiled central dome and rather exotic, almost Byzantine bell towers. The plaza is connected, via pedestrianized Calle San Martín, with Plaza Alvear, three blocks to the north. On the southwestern corner of Plaza Alvear, at Buenos Aires 285, you'll find the **Museo Histórico de Entre Ríos Martiniano Leguizamón** (Tues–Fri 7.30am–12.30pm & 3–7.30pm, Sat 9am–noon & 5–8pm, Sun 9am–noon; ☎0343/431-2735). It's a large and mostly well-organized museum with two floors of exhibits. The upper floor is devoted to the history of Entre Ríos Province from pre-Columbian times to the twentieth century though the informative panels are sometimes more interesting than the objects themselves, which are often notable mainly for their illustrious owners. Downstairs, however, there's an excellent collection of creole silverwork – well worth a look if you haven't overdosed on such things already. Amongst the more interesting pieces are vicious-looking spurs known as *lloronas* – *llorar* means to cry; it's debated whether they were thus called for the sound they made when the horse was moving or for the fact that they made the animal "cry blood". There's also a fine collection of gaucho *facas* or knives, with inscriptions such as "do not enter without cause nor leave without honour". Look out, too, for the beautifully crafted *yesqueros*, elaborate early lighters formed by a stone and chain contraption – the last two creating a spark to light the tinder – made out of materials as diverse as silver and the tail of an armadillo. On the west side of the square, at Buenos Aires 355, is the **Museo Provincial de Bellas Artes Dr Pedro E. Martínez** (Tues–Fri 9am–noon & 4–8pm, Sat & Sun 5–9pm; free; ☎0343/431-2735). A slightly chaotic but attractive museum, housed in a fine old family mansion, it is mostly dedicated to Argentinian painting with a entire room given over to the Argentine impressionist Cesáreo Bernaldo de Quirós, and a pretty courtyard where sculptures vie with a collection of impressively contorted centenarian *palo borracho* trees.

Flanking Paraná's riverside, the **Parque Urquiza** is a 44-hectare park created on land donated by General Urquiza's widow, Dolores Costa de Urquiza. It is located on a fairly narrow but hilly stretch of ground which slopes up from Avenida Laurencena, Paraná's costanera, to the higher ground of the city. Designed, like so many of Argentina's parks, by the landscape gardener Charles Thays, it's a particularly attractive and verdant park traversed by serpentine walkways and with great views over the river. At its western end, there's a pretty neighbourhood called the **Puerto Viejo**, distinguished by its winding cobbled streets and handsome old-fashioned residences.

The real hub of Paraná life on summer evenings, the costanera itself, is lined with a handful of bars and restaurants and some good public **beaches**; you can also become a member for the day of various clubs, giving you access to the smartest beaches and facilities such as swimming pools and showers – one of the most reasonable is the *Paraná Rowing Club* (☎0343/431-2048) where day membership costs $5. On the costanera at the bottom of Avenida Vélez Sarsfield you'll find the modest but fun **Museo de la Ciudad** (Tues–Fri 8am–noon & 5–9pm, Sat 9am–noon & 5–9pm, Sun 5–9pm; ☎0343/420-1838). The museum provides information on the founding of the city, including a maquette of the early settlement, but its more interesting pieces are the quirkier bits of paraphernalia donated by local businesses and individuals: there's a display of objects from old pharmacies including a gruesome dummy with nails stuck in its head used to advertise Geniol aspirins and a special pair of glasses apparently used by a local dentist to hypnotise patients instead of using anaesthetic.

Eating, drinking and nightlife

Paraná feels like it should have more interesting **restaurants** than it does. However, there are enough decent places to eat to keep you happy for a day or two. In the centre try *Spaghetti*, on the corner of Urquiza and Belgrano, for pizza and pasta, or the venerable *Club Español*, at Urquiza 722, for good-value Spanish dishes. *La Posada del Fanny*, at Urquiza 843, is a pretty restaurant offering upmarket cooking but it also does lunchtime specials for around $5. There are a couple of excellent fish restaurants and parrillas down by the river, notably the *Club Atlético Estudiantes*, at the western end of the Avenida Costanera (☎0343/421-8699), and the highly rated if rather expensive *Quinchos de Paja* – named for its rustic thatched construction – on the corner of Avenida Laurencena and San Martín (☎0343/4231845). For **drinks and snacks** try the welcoming and classic *Viejo Paraná* on the corner of Buenos Aires and Rivadavia with pavement tables, or the upmarket *Plaza Bar* on the corner of San Martín and Urquiza. A few blocks northeast of the town centre, on the corner of San Juan and Victoria, the beautifully restored *Parroquia Victoria* bar is an old-fashioned wood-panelled building with an outside patio and a lively clientele, open until the small hours. There's a branch of Argentina's favourite ice-cream chain, *Freddo*, on the corner of Pazos and San Martín.

Paraná **nightlife** is liveliest in the summer when the trendy open-air *El Vasco* and the more mainstream *Parador*, playing *cumbia*, *marcha* and rock, open towards the northern end of Calle San Juan.

Listings

Airlines Aerolíneas Argentinas Corrientes 563 (☎0343/423-2425); Laer Buenos Aires 120 (☎0343/420-0810).
Banks and exchanges There are plenty of ATMs, around Urquiza and San Martín.

Car rental Best rates at local firm Maran, Illia 110 (☎0343/423-1707; *www.maran.com.ar*); also Localiza at Cervantes 177 (☎0343/423-3885) and at the airport.

Hospital Hospital San Martín de Paraná, Pte Perón 220 (☎0343/423-1607).

Internet Instituto de Informática, Av. Rivadavia 166 (Mon–Fri 8am–10pm, Sat 8am–8pm, Sun 4–9pm; $2.50).

Laundry Corner of Belgrano and Gualeguaychú; Las Flores, Cervantes 144.

Post office Correo Central on the corner of 25 de Mayo and Monte Caseros.

Travel agent Costanera 241, in the *Hotel Mayorazgo* (☎0343/423-4385), offers boat trips on the Paraná and trips to nearby towns such as Diamante and Victoria.

Diamante and the Parque Nacional Pre-Delta

Lying 44km to the south of Paraná, and 5km to the south of the small town of **Diamante**, the **Parque Nacional Pre-Delta** is one of the newer parks in the Argentine national park system and, as yet, has little in the way of a tourist infrastructure. Its 25 square kilometres of gallery forest, islands and streams mark the beginning of the vast Paraná Delta which stretches from here to Tigre, just to the north of Buenos Aires. Amongst the thick vegetation which lines the streams the most common trees are the *ceibo*, with Argentina's national flower, the *sauce criollo*, the *timbó blanco* and the laurel, whilst wildlife includes the coipu, the capybara and many birds amongst which one of the most striking is the park's emblem, the ringed kingfisher. To really see the park you need to take a **boat trip** as only a small section of it is accessible by foot alone. You may be able to arrange a trip with the *guardaparques*, who maintain an office in Diamante but are not always easily found in the park, although boat trips are officially handled by Davimar Turismo, in Diamante on the corner of Brown and Echagüe (☎0343/498-1132). In any case you should consult with the *guardaparques* before visiting, since accessibility depends on the level of the river: if it is either too high or too low then the park is barely worth visiting. At the Paraje La Jaula, at the northern end of the park, you are allowed to **camp**, though there are no facilities: be sure to pack a torch and insect repellent.

The Parque Nacional Pre-Delta is reached via **DIAMANTE**, with regular bus connections from Paraná. Diamante's **bus terminal** is on the corner of Avenida Sarmiento and Calle Belgrano, where there is also a friendly **tourist kiosk** (☎0343/498-1024). Just round the corner, at Sarmiento 407, you'll find the **guardaparques' office** (☎0343/498-3752) where you can get some basic information on the park and possibly arrange a boat trip. Without your own transport, the only way to the park is with a taxi – the journey will cost around $5.

Along the Río Uruguay

The first leg of the popular RN14, which runs from Ceibas, some 160km northwest of Buenos Aires towards Iguazú, is dotted with a string of towns which border the Río Uruguay. Languid and picturesque **Colón** is by far the most attractive of them, and has the most tourist infrastructure including numerous campsites right by its sandy beaches. It is also the most convenient base for making a trip to nearby **Parque Nacional El Palmar**. The **Palacio de San José**, once General Urquiza's luxurious residence, can be visited from the town of **Concepción del Uruguay** while **Concordia** lies within easy reach of the **Represa Salto Grande**, a large dam, where there are unexpectedly beautiful lakeside picnic spots and campsites. Concordia and Colón both have road links to Uruguay, as does **Gualeguaychú** – home of Argentina's most renowned carnival – further south. An unusual detour could be made by visiting **Villa Paranacito**, an island community at the heart of the Delta Entrerriano which can be reached either by bus or by a weekly boat from Tigre (see p.152).

Villa Paranacito

Dusty, sleepy little **VILLA PARANACITO** is the kind of place where you'll feel like you're on nodding terms with half the population soon after alighting at the tiny café which functions as the town's bus terminal. Situated on the easternmost tentacles of the vast **Paraná Delta**, this town of around 3000 inhabitants is the major population centre of the region known as the **Islas del Ibicuy**, a maze of low-lying islands that makes up Entre Ríos Province's southern tip. The region's first inhabitants were the Guaraní who gave their name to the region (*ibicuy* means "sandy area") and who apparently arrived in the Delta in search of their *tierra sin mal*, or land without evil: a terrestrial paradise inhabited by Ñandey, the female creator of the world. According to Guaraní legend this land was located to the east, close to the sea. The only evidence these days of these first inhabitants are shallow raised platforms of sand and earth which rise out of the islands' dense undergrowth. Known locally as *cerritos* they were constructed by the Guaranís to provide themselves with a vantage point from which to spot possible enemies and also to act as a defence against the floods which still regularly affect the region. The area's first white colonizers were Italians from Montevideo who arrived around the turn of the century looking for wood for charcoal, though the largest immigrant group these days is made up of those of central and northern European descent. The isolation and intricacy of the Ibicuy region also made it a favourite hideout for fugitives from nearby Buenos Aires and Montevideo as well as from the rest of the province of Entre Ríos. Many of the region's *arroyos* or streams still bear the names of the more famous of them.

Paranacito is the administrative centre for the Delta's many small **timber producers**, who sell their produce to the paper industry via the town's co-operative. It's a tranquil, down-to-earth kind of place, and while its waterside setting gives it a certain charm, the town itself is workmanlike rather than obviously picturesque. The best reason to visit Paranacito is to make use of its waterways, which are generally wider – and much less travelled – than those in Tigre, though fringed with the same subtropical vegetation. The quieter environment makes it a good place to spot **wildlife**: the white-necked heron and the neotropic cormorant are among the region's most common birds, whilst mammals include the capybara, the weasel, the nutria and, if you are very lucky, the marsh deer. Just a half hour or so from the town, the network of streams feeds into the vast quiet expanse of the **Río Uruguay**, from where the Uruguayan town of Nueva Palmira can just be spotted. Paranacito is also popular with **fishermen**, who fish for dorado in the summer and pejerrey in the winter.

Practicalities

Though only 150km from Buenos Aires, Villa Paranacito is not easy to get to via public transport. Without a doubt, the most romantic way to arrive is on the weekly boat from Tigre, which wends its way through the heart of the Delta region. Operated by Galofré, (☎011/4744-0571) the boat leaves at 7am on Saturdays, taking five hours to reach Paranacito and returns at midday on Sunday, arriving back in Tigre at around 5pm. Tata and Nuevo Expreso buses between Buenos Aires (and all points north) and Gualeguaychú can drop you at the junction (*empalme*) on the RN14, from where three or four buses a day make the 22-kilometre trip to the village ($2). There's a small bar at the junction selling refreshments and offering a bit of shade.

Paranacito's **tourist office** (☎03446/495222) is located just next to the bus terminal, though one of the most knowledgeable guides to the area is Mauricio Weinberg, who runs the youth hostel and campsite *Top Malo* (☎03446/495255; *topmalo@infovia.com.ar*) a couple of kilometres outside the town; ask the bus driver to let you off before Paranacito. Mauricio can also arrange fishing and sightseeing excursions – reckon on about $100 for a half-day fishing trip for four people – as well as horseriding and even flights at the local aerodrome. **Accommodation** at the hostel, located on a lovely riverside spot, is provided in comfortable wood cabins, with cooking facilities ($35 for four people, $25 to HI members). There are also individual lots, each one with its own parrilla, where you can pitch your tent for $10, plus $1 per person. Other options in the town include *Orlando Lisman's* bar and parrilla (☎03446/495269) on the main drag where spacious rooms for four with a kitchen cost $40. For more picturesque accommodation, the old-fashioned *Hostería Rose Marie* (☎03446/495204) is situated at the confluence of Arroyo Martínez and the Río Uruguay – transport can be arranged through the *hostería*'s owners.

Gualeguaychú

Apart from having a name that sounds like a tongue-twister followed by a sneeze, **GUALEGUAYCHÚ** (meaning "river of the large jaguar" or "calm waters" in Guaraní) is most notable for its **carnival**, generally regarded as Argentina's most important. During the months of January and February, the town is mobbed with people, particularly at weekends and Gualeguaychú's passion for processions is further given vent during October, when local high-school students take part in the **desfile de carrozas**, in which elaborate floats, constructed by the students themselves, are paraded around the streets. During the rest of the year – with the exception of long weekends – Gualeguaychú is a tranquil town with some handsome old buildings and a pleasant costanera and park. As a stopover, it stands out because of its decent accommodation and numerous campsites and is also just 33km from the southernmost **road crossing to Uruguay**, via the General San Martín international bridge which connects Gualeguaychú with Fray Bentos via Puerto Unzué.

Arrival and information

Gualeguaychú's **bus terminal** (☎03446/427987) is due to move from its central location on Bolívar between Mons. Chalup and 3 de Febrero to a new site on Boulevard Pedro Jurado and Avenida Julio Irazusta, some distance from the centre. If you are planning to travel directly to Iguazú from Gualeguaychú, note that buses to Iguazú don't enter town but are caught from Parador La Posta at Km 54 on the RN14 (☎03446/425095). There is a local car-rental office at Urquiza 1267 (☎155-73336) while bicycles can be rented on the corner of the Costanera and D. Jurado. The **tourist office** (daily: winter 8am–8pm; summer 8am–10pm ☎03446/423668; *www.gualeguaychu.gov.ar*) is on the Plazoleta de los Artesanos, Paseo del Puerto, down by the port. Their information leaflets are fairly sketchy, but the staff are helpful and it's a useful place to visit if you're having trouble finding accommodation. They can also offer information on the various *jineteadas* or rodeo events that are held in the vicinity at various times throughout the year, as well as on river excursions.

Accommodation

Gualeguaychú has probably the best selection of reasonably priced and attractive **accommodation** of the towns along the Río Uruguay and it's worth having a look around before settling on a hotel. You'll need to make reservations some time in advance if you plan to stay during carnival, and probably on long weekends, too, when many, if not most, places put their prices up. At these times, the situation is alleviated by the number of impromptu notices that spring up during these periods offering rooms to rent: look around in the vicinity of the costanera, particularly along San Lorenzo. There are numerous **campsites** in Gualeguaychú and the surrounding area; mostly located along the banks of the Río Gualeguaychú, or out towards the Río Uruguay. The two most centrally located are *Costa Azúl* (☎03446/433130), just to the north of Puente Casariego, and *La Delfina* (☎03446/423984), at the northern end of Parque Unzué, on the other side of

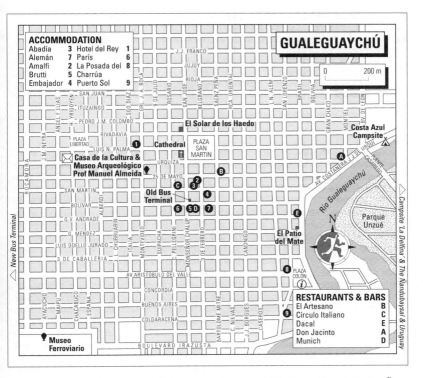

the bridge. Both charge around $8 for a two-person tent. The best, though, is the *Ñandubaysal* (☎03446/423298), located on an extensive site forested with ñandubay, a thorny plant typical of the region and whose fruit is a favourite of the ñandú – hence the name. The *Ñandubaysal* is located on the banks of the Río Uruguay, some 15 km east of the town. A local bus runs to and from the site in season.

The tourist office maintains a list of families renting rooms during carnival as well as an up-to-date price list of campsites, cabins and bungalows in the area.

Abadía, San Martín 588 (☎03446/427675). An attractive old building with some nice rooms, though none overlooks the street and there are no discounts for singles. ③.

Alemán, Bolívar 535 (☎03446/426153). Professionally run and centrally located hotel with well-equipped rooms. ④, including breakfast and parking.

Amalfi, 25 de Mayo 571 (☎03446/426818). One of the best of the cheaper hotels with some particularly spacious – though slightly dark – rooms at the front and a cheery, laid-back young owner. Cable TV. ②.

Brutti, Bolívar 591 (☎03446/426048). Friendly hotel right opposite the old bus terminal: the rooms are on the small side but pleasant. ③.

Del Rey, Luis N. Palma 788 (☎03446/433159). Very spacious rooms in an attractive building, run by helpful and friendly owners. Breakfast included and singles available for $15 during the week, $20 at weekends. ③.

Embajador, 3 de Febrero and San Martín (☎ & fax 03446/424414). Gualeguaychú's most luxurious hotel. The rooms are comfortable enough, though unless you make use of all the extras – free entrance to the adjoining casino, tennis courts and swimming pool, some distance from the hotel – it's not appreciably much better than cheaper accommodation. ⑤, ⑥ at weekends.

París, Bolívar and Pellegrini (☎03446/423850). Elegant hotel with various categories of rooms: most of them spacious. TV, fan and breakfast. ③.

La Posada del Charrúa, Av. del Valle 250 (☎03446/426099). A rustic name somewhat belied by the hotel's appearance, which is bland and modern. It is spick and span, though, and well located by the costanera, and includes parking. A little expensive, nonetheless, particularly as breakfast is not included. ③, ④ at weekends.

Puerto Sol, San Lorenzo 477 (☎ & fax 03446/434017; *puertosol@infovia.com.ar*). Far and away the nicest hotel in Gualeguaychú, the immaculate and friendly *Puerto Sol* has attractively decorated and very comfortable rooms, some looking onto the hotel's pretty interior patio. There's also a nice communal area with board games and a bar. The price includes breakfast. ⑤.

The Town

Gualeguaychú's two focal points are the streets surrounding its main square, **Plaza San Martín**, where the majority of hotels and shops are located, and – particularly in the summer – the **costanera**. On the northwestern corner of Plaza San Martín, you will find **El Solar de los Haedo** (April–Dec Wed–Sat 9–11.45am, Fri & Sat 4–6.45pm; Jan & Feb Wed–Sat 9–11.45am, Fri & Sat 5–7.45pm), officially Gualeguaychú's oldest building and housing a small museum. Built in a primitive colonial style, the simple whitewashed building opens onto a pretty garden planted with grapevines and orchids. Inside, the cool wood-floored rooms are filled with original furniture and objects belonging to the Haedos, one of Gualeguaychú's early patrician families. Amongst other exhibits, there's a beautiful Spanish representation of the Virgen del Carmen, made of silver and real hair; a number of fine pieces of French porcelain; and a collection of the satirical magazine *Caras y Caretas*, whose famous founder, José Alvarez, better known as Fray Mocho, was born in the house at Fray Mocho 135 in 1858. El Solar de los Haedo is also notable for having been occupied by Giuseppe Garibaldi in 1845, when he ransacked Gualeguaychú in search of provisions to assist General Oribe and his troops, who were under siege in Montevideo. A few blocks away the pretty Casa de la Cultura at 25 de Mayo 734 currently houses the **Museo Arqueológico Prof. Manuel Almeida** (Mon–Fri 7–9pm; free), containing a small collection of weapons – predominantly *bolas de piedra*, the stone balls favoured for hunting by Argentina's indigenous inhabitants – adornments and fragments of pottery made by the Chana and Guaraní and found locally. There is a local, rather dull, craft market, the Centro de Artesanos (Mon, Wed & Thurs 9.30am–noon, Fri, Sat & Sun 9.30am–noon & 4–7.30pm; closed Tues), on Chalup and San Martín, but Gualeguaychú's most original retailing experience is provided by the **El Patio del Mate** (open daily), on Gervasio Méndez down by the Costanera: a shrine to the Litoraleños' most pervasive habit, with *mates* carved out of every material imaginable – from simple and functional calabazas or gourds (generally regarded as the best material for *mates*) to elaborate combinations of hoof and hide, which are best described as examples of gaucho kitsch.

The **Costanera J.J. de Urquiza**, pretty quiet during the day and out of season, heaves with life on summer evenings when locals and holidaymakers indulge in an obligatory evening stroll or simply while away the hours on a bench accompanied by an equally obligatory *mate*. The southern end of the costanera leads to the **old port** and if you head down this way just before the October *desfile de carrozas* you will come across scenes of frenetic activity as students – many of whom barely sleep for the last few days – put the finishing touches to their floats, which are assembled in huge riverside warehouses. The port was the termination point for the old railway tracks, which reached Gualeguaychú in 1873. If you follow the tracks round along Boulevard Irazusta, you will come to the old railway station, now the open-air **Museo Ferroviario** or railway museum, where an old steam locomotive is displayed. Just next door is the Corsódromo, constructed in 1997, where up to 30,000 spectators pile in to watch Gualeguaychú's *comparsas* or processions during carnival.

On the intersection of Luis N. Palma and the costanera, the Puente M. Casariego leads to the **Parque Unzué**, bisected by the road which leads to the Ñandubaysal campground and the crossing to Uruguay.

Out along Urquiza, towards the RN14, the small farm **Itapeby** (☎03446/433423) offers educational tours of the establishment, pony rides and games for children and sells home-made produce. The farm (ring first) can be reached on the green Empresa Sarandí bus which leaves from Plaza San Martín.

Eating, drinking and nightlife

The majority of Gualeguaychú's tourist-oriented restaurants are down by the costanera. One of the most established places is the consistently good *Dacal*, on the corner of Andrade and the costanera, with a wide menu and a popular parrilla; the stylish *La Colina*, on the corner of the Costanera Sur and Avenida Parque, specializes in home-made pastas. *Don Jacinto* at Urquiza 52, on the corner of the costanera (closed Tues), specializes in seafood dishes such as prawns in garlic, but also does pasta and meat. In the centre, *Munich*, Bolívar 551, does good fresh food at reasonable prices, including daily specials such as dorado stuffed with orange, garlic, red pepper, nuts and herbs; while there is good pizza at *El Artesano* on the corner of 25 de Mayo and Mitre. A little further out, the down-to-earth *La Paisanita*, 25 de Mayo 1176, is popular with locals for parrilla and pasta. During the summer, the handsome *Círculo Italiano*, on the corner of Pellegrini and San Martín, functions as a restaurant – it tends to serve barbecued meat rather than Italian fare.

Like most littoral towns, Gualeguaychú is at its liveliest during the summer, when **nightlife** focuses on the area around the costanera. The town centre is somewhat lacking in enticing bars or even confiterías. Gualeguaychú's most popular nightclub is *Garage* on Rocamora and Bolívar, which plays a standard mix of dance music and *cumbia*. The town's **casino** (Mon–Thurs 10.30pm–3.30am, Fri 10.30pm–4am, Sat 6pm–4am & Sun 5pm–3am), somewhat in decline since the opening of new casinos in Buenos Aires and Tigre, is at 3 de Febrero 115, whilst the elegant French-style **Teatro Gualeguaychú** at Urquiza 705, inaugurated in 1914, still hosts various musical and theatrical events.

Concepción del Uruguay and around

Stuck between the more picturesque Colón and the livelier Gualeguaychú, **CONCEP-CIÓN DEL URUGUAY** – often referred to simply as Concepción or, rather confusingly, Uruguay – appears to have resigned itself to letting tourism pass it by. Concepción was the provincial capital on two occasions during the nineteenth century and was also the site of the first lay school in Argentina, founded by **General Urquiza** in 1848, and the town still enjoys the reputation of being the region's most cultured. There are a number of important educational establishments in the town and a handful of interesting historic buildings, though Concepción's main claim to fame is its proximity to the **Palacio San José**, built by General Urquiza, who is also buried in the town. The Palacio lies some 30km west of town, along the RP39.

Somewhat estranged from its own coast, which is several blocks from the centre, Concepción has less of a riverside feel than Colón, though a few kilometres north of town lies the slightly deteriorated **Banco Pelay**, a three-kilometre stretch of river beach with camping, swimming and sunbathing facilities.

The Town

Concepción's heart is the large and shady **Plaza Francisco Ramírez**, named after a local nineteenth-century caudillo who was splendidly referred to as the "Supremo

Entrerriano" or, less splendidly, "Pancho". At the eastern end of the square you can take a discreet wander around the courtyard of the **Colegio Superior del Uruguay Justo José de Urquiza**, site of Urquiza's first Colegio Nacional and retaining the elegant pink facade from its foundation in 1848; for guided visits to the interior, enquire at the entrance in 3 de Febrero. Next door to the Colegio lies another Urquiza project, the **Basílica Menor de la Inmaculada Concepción** (7am–noon & 4–8pm) where the General's remains are housed in a grand circular mausoleum, inspired by Napoleon's tomb. Apart from Urquiza's monumental piece of marble, upon which you can gaze from a circular viewing gallery in the church floor, the basilica is surprisingly austere inside: the result of damage done during repair work. Photos of the original elaborate interior can be seen in the **Museo Delio Panizza** (daily 9am–noon & 4.30–7.30pm; $2; guided visits available), at Supremo Entrerriano 58, an agreeably eclectic museum housed in a beautiful old colonial residence which once belonged to the poet Dr Delio Panizza. Panizza was clearly a collector in the widest sense of the word: amongst the museum's exhibits are such oddities as a tiny figure modelled in earth from Misiones by the writer Horacio Quiroga and a piece of piping from the Graf Spee. More conventional pieces include examples of creole silverwork, including a pair of vicious-looking spurs used by General Ramírez, paintings by the Argentine impressionist Quirós and a still-working French polyphone from the last century, which the museum's amenable staff may agree to demonstrate.

On the outskirts of town, just off the RN42, the privately run **Museo Yuchán** (daily: winter 10am–noon & 2–6pm; summer 4–8pm) houses a collection of contemporary objects made by some of Argentina's surviving indigenous groups, such as the Chané and the Wichi.

Practicalities

Concepción's **bus terminal** is around twelve blocks west of Plaza Francisco Ramírez: a taxi to the centre will cost you little more than $1. The **tourist office** (Mon–Fri 7am–1pm & 2–8pm; ☎03442/425820) is just a few blocks from the main square at 9 de Julio 844. At weekends an alternative information post functions on the way into the town, at Dr Elías 50. The information provided isn't vast, but they do provide a map and a useful accommodation and restaurant list. **Internet** facilities are available at Editcom, Moreno 105. For **tours** of local attractions, including the Palacio San José, try Turismo Pioneros, Mitre 908 (☎03442/427569).

You're not exactly spoilt for choice when it comes to **accommodation**, though there are a number of acceptable budget choices right in the town centre. The *Fiuri* (☎03442/427016; ②, with good singles discounts) is housed in an attractive old building at Sarmiento 779 and though the rooms are a bit shabby, they are spacious and have fans, and the staff are very helpful. Other similarly priced places are the slightly more spruce *Centro* (☎03442/427429; ②) at Moreno 130, and the friendly *La Posada* (☎03442/425461; ②) at Moreno 166. If you want to go a bit upmarket, try the old-fashioned but well-equipped *Grand* (☎ & fax 03442/25586; ⑤), on the corner of Eva Perón and Rocamora, which is probably the best hotel in town and can arrange various excursions, to places such as to the nearby estancia, Villa Teresa, as well as car rental. Price are reduced out of season. There are various **campsites** around the town, including a fairly basic municipal one at *Itapé*, at the southern end of the town and a much larger one at the Banco Pelay, both charging around $8 for a two-person tent. Alternatively, you could camp at the *Balneario-Camping Ruinas del Viejo Molino* (☎03442/425160; $10 per two-person tent), a 60-hectare complex on the site of an old water mill, with river beaches and sporting facilities. The campsite is some 15km along the RN14 towards Colón and can be reached by any bus heading north.

Palacio San José

When it was built in 1848 for General Justo José de Urquiza, the **Palacio San José** (Mon–Fri 9am–12.45 & 2–6pm, Sat & Sun 9am–12.45pm & 2–5.45pm; guided visits at 10am, 11am, 3pm & 4pm; $2), 33km west of Concepción off RP39, was perhaps Argentina's most luxurious private residence. Urquiza was caudillo of Entre Ríos in the early nineteenth century and became its governor in 1841. He was also the province's largest and wealthiest landowner, with a large *saladero* (meat-salting plant). Restrictions imposed by Buenos Aires on the provinces' freedom to trade, as well as their political authority, led Urquiza to revolt against the then dictator General Rosas, finally defeating him at the Battle of Caseros, outside Buenos Aires, in 1853. The lavishness of the palace seems clearly intended as a challenge to the Buenos Aires elite's idea of provincial backwardness. Designed by the Italian architect Pedro Fosatti – who also designed the Italian hospitals in Buenos Aires and Montevideo – and despite the typically colonial watchtowers which dominate its facade, the palace shows a strong Italian influence in the elegant Tuscan arches that are its strongest motif.

The entrance to the palace is located at the back of the building; to your right as you enter is a tiny **chapel** or oratory with spectacular frescoes by the Uruguayan n ineteenth-century academic painter Juan Manuel Blanes and an imposing three-metre high baptism font, entirely carved from Carrara marble. The palace itself lies to your left and its 38 rooms are laid out around two large courtyards. The first of these courtyards is the **Patio del Parral**, named for its grapevines, many of which were brought for Urquiza from France by the naturalist Eduardo Holmberg. A long, rectangular courtyard, flanked by an elegant wrought-iron pergola, the Patio del Parral was essentially the service section of the palace; to the right lies a large kitchen, which was the first in the country to have running water, while the rooms here were used by family members, officials and Urquiza's least important guests. To your left, as you enter the Patio del Parral, there is a room dedicated to the Battle of Caseros. The second courtyard is known as the **Patio de Honor** and the rooms here were occupied by Urquiza's most immediate family as well as by important guests such as General Bartolomé Mitre (later to become President) in 1860 and President Domingo Sarmiento in 1870. The courtyard is lined with arches that reflect those of the facade and are tiled with marble slabs specially imported from Italy. The most significant room within the Patio de Honor is the so-called **Sala de la Tragedia**, which was Urquiza's bedroom and the place where, on April 11 1870, he was assassinated by followers of the rival caudillo López Jordán. The bedroom was turned into a shrine by Urquiza's widow and traces of blood can still be seen on the door as well as bullets encrusted in the wall. Beyond the Patio de Honor lies an exotic, slightly unkempt **garden**, from where the Palacio's harmonious facade can best be admired.

During the high season, there are various **tour** companies offering trips to the Palacio San José from Concepción for around $12. Otherwise, a *remise* from Concepción's bus terminal will charge you around $18 for the trip, plus an hour or so's wait, or you can take any bus going towards Caseros and ask to be let off at the turn-off to the Palacio San José, from where it's a three-kilometre walk.

Colón

A small town popular for weekend breaks, **COLÓN** is the most appealing of Entre Ríos' resorts and, thanks to its lovely riverside setting and attractive hotels and restaurants, makes a good place to stop over for a day or two before heading on to **Parque Nacional El Palmar**, which lies 50km to the north. The town sits along the Río Uruguay and has a narrow strip of beach running for several kilometres alongside its attractive riverside avenue, the **Costanera Gobernador Quirós**, flanked by a pretty balustrade. The town's central square, Plaza Washington, where you will find the municipalidad, covers four blocks and lies ten blocks inland; far more elegant, however, is the smaller **Plaza San Martín**, to the east of Plaza Washington along Colón's main commercial street, Avenida 12 de Abril. By far the most distinctive district in town is the sleepy **port area**, a small but charming cobbled quarter lined with a clutch of pretty colonial-style buildings which slopes down to the riverbank, immediately to the north of Plaza San Martín. A few hundred metres from Colón's coast there are some lushly vegetated **islands** flanked with spectacularly pristine sandbanks; excursions to the islands in motorised dinghies can be made with *Ita I Cora* (☎ & fax 03447/423360, mobile 155-82204), who have an information stand on the corner of the costanera and Calle General Noailles, three blocks south of Plaza San Martín. Colón hosts an important craft fair, the **Fiesta Nacional de la Artesanía**, in February, with over five hundred exhibitors from Argentina, Latin America and Europe and various musical events. It is is also linked to the Uruguayan city of Paysandú, some 15km to the southeast, via the road bridge, the Puente Internacional General Artigas.

Practicalities

Colón's **bus terminal** (☎03447/421716) lies some fifteen blocks northwest of Plaza San Martín, on the corner of Paysandú and Sourigues. The busy **tourist office** (☎03447/421996) is down in the port area, two blocks north of the plaza, on the corner of the Avenida Costanera and Gouchón, and is a useful place to get accommodation information.

The town can be very busy for long weekends, so it's a good idea to book **accommodation** ahead of time. Easily the most attractive hotel is the stunning *Hostería del Puerto* (☎03447/422698, fax 03447/421398 *www.colonentrerios.com.ar/hosteria.html*; ④), a pretty, pink colonial building just one block from the port at Alejo Peyret 158. The huge, beautifully decorated rooms are located around a central courtyard; best rooms are upstairs with large balconies and a view over the river. Breakfast is included and there is a twenty percent discount during the week. A good option near the bus terminal is the *Hotel Paysandú* (☎03447/421140; ③), on the corner of Maipú and Paysandú, a spruce modern place with clean and comfortable rooms, parking and very friendly owners; breakfast is included. Ten blocks west of Plaza San Martín, the *Hotel Aridan* (☎03447/421830; ①) at General Alvear 57 is excellent value – the pleasant rooms all have TV, fan, and private bathroom. On the plaza itself, the attractive *Hotel Holimasú* (☎03447/421305; ③) offers decent rooms with private bathrooms, around a pretty courtyard; breakfast is included. A passable option is the *Nuevo Hotel Vieja Calera* (☎03447/423761; ③) at Bolívar 350, five blocks west of Plaza San Martín; rooms are well-equipped with TV, air conditioning and private bathrooms – though all are slightly gloomy; prices go up by two thirds on busy weekends. There are plenty of **campsites**, spread out along the length of Colón's beaches. At the northern end is the simple *Camping Municipal Norte* (☎03447/421917; $3 per person), on the beach at the foot of Calle Paysandú, with showers, electric light and barbecue facilities. Along the southern section of the costanera there is a long chain of campsites starting with the highly organized – and sometimes noisy – *Piedras Coloradas* (☎03447/421451; $8 per two-person tent), reached via the southern end of Calle General Belgrano; it has volleyball and basketball courts as well as the usual facilities. Beyond this site, the campsites have a slightly more rustic feel and the last of them, the relatively natural *Camping Agreste* (☎03447/421130; $3 per person), is an attractive wooded site popular for fishing.

There are some good **restaurants** in Colón, mostly located within a few blocks of Plaza San Martín. On the corner of Calles 12 de Abril and Alejo Peyret, the *Plaza* is a lively pizzeria and parrilla and is also a good place for a drink – either in its popular courtyard area or on the pavement tables which look onto the plaza. Another good choice is the *Viejo Almacén*, on the corner of Calles Urquiza and J.J. Paso, one block southeast of the plaza, a stylishly old-fashioned place which does excellent river fish – try the surubí with Roquefort sauce. There is good, very reasonably priced pasta at the long-established and homely *La Cantina*, on Alejo Peyret 79, which also does surubí and dorado and has outside tables on a quiet street. As far as **bars** go, the nicest place for a relaxed evening drink is outside *El Zaguán*, an attractive colonial-style building on Alejo Peyret between Gouchón and Chacabuco. Otherwise the main hub of activity is along Avenida 12 de Abril, an obligatory stop for locals on their evening stroll. Nicest of the slew of bars along here is the modern and lively *Moments*, between Lavalle and 3 de Febrero. Colón's main **nightclub** is *Mediterráneo*, housed in a distinctive white building along Alejo Peyret between Alberdi and Chacabuco where just about all of Colón ends up at weekends.

Parque Nacional El Palmar

As you head north from Colón along the RN14, the first sign that you are approaching **Parque Nacional El Palmar** is a sprinkling of tremendously tall palm trees towering above the flat lands which border the highway. This 85-square-kilometre park was set up in 1966 to conserve examples of the **yatay palm**, which once covered large areas of Entre Ríos, Uruguay and Southern Brazil. Intensive cultivation of the region almost wiped out the palm and the Parque Nacional El Palmar is now the largest remaining reserve of the yatay, as well as one of the southernmost palm groves in the world. Though the terrain itself is nondescript rolling grassland, the sheer proliferation of the majestic yatay – with many examples over 300 years old and growing up to 18 metres in height – makes for a wonderfully exotic landscape, rather like the backdrop to a 1960s dinosaur film. Bordering the Río Uruguay and its eastern fringe, the park is composed of **gallery forest**, dense pockets of subtropical vegetation formed as seeds and sediment are borne downstream from Misiones. It is best appreciated on an overnight stay – the rolling acres of palm forest are absolutely stunning in the evening light when their exotic forms sing out against the deepening blue sky and reddish gold of the earth. There are a number of well-signposted trails in the park, taking you both along the streams and through palm forests; the longer of these are designed for vehicles, though if you don't mind trekking along several kilometres of gravel road, there's nothing to stop you from doing them on foot. There are great views from **La Glorieta**, a gentle bluff from where you can take in the surrounding sea of palms. Wildlife in the park includes ñandúes, armadillos, foxes and capybaras and, particularly around the campsite, vizcachas and monitor lizards. **Guided walks** take place in the park, organized by Jorge Díaz (☎03447/493031); best are the night-time excursions, involving a fairly adventurous scramble through the gallery forest which flanks the river.

The entrance to the park lies some 50km north of Colón, along the RN14. There is a *guardaparques'* post at the entrance where you pay a $5 entrance fee and can pick up a map and information leaflet. It's a hefty ten-kilometre or so walk from the entrance to the visitor centre and campsite, though at all but the quietest times it should be possible to get a lift with someone else entering the park. The only place to stay within the park is at **Los Loros campground** (☎03447/493031; $6 per tent, plus $4 per person), a spacious and shady site with showers and a provisions store; the best pitches have a great view over the Río Uruguay. There is also a decent restaurant in the park, next door to the visitors' centre.

Concordia and around

With around 150,000 inhabitants, **CONCORDIA** is the largest town along the Río Uruguay and the second city of Entre Ríos after the capital, Paraná. Known as the Capital Nacional de la Citricultura, it lies at the heart of Argentina's orange-growing region which accounts for around a quarter of the country's total production of this fruit. It's a sprawling, pretty nondescript place – albeit with a handful of handsome late nineteenth- and early twentieth-century buildings – and only really of interest as a stopover either on your way north to Corrientes and Misiones or as a **border crossing** for travellers heading into Uruguay: Concordia is linked with the Uruguayan town of Salto, via the **Puente Internacional Salto Grand**e. The city's population expanded rapidly in the 1970s and 1980s with the arrival of the **Represa Salto Grande**, a huge dam and reservoir 18km to the north of town, and constructed jointly by Argentina and Uruguay. The project flooded a vast area of land on either side of the Río Uruguay, creating a 80,000-hectare lake, **El Lago de Salto Grande**. The southern end of the lake, where there are some beautiful inlets and wooded beaches, makes an easily accessible side-trip from Concordia if you have your own transport. Concordia has also recently opened some thermal baths which lie just to the north of the town centre.

Arrival, information and accommodation

Concordia's **airport**, the Aeropuerto Comodoro Pierrestegui, is some 12km north of the town centre, along Avenida Monseñor Rösch. Local bus #7 runs between the airport and the town centre. Tickets and timetables are available from the LAER offices at Pellegrini 538 (Mon–Fri 8am–12.30pm & 4–8pm, Sat 9am–1pm; ☎0345/421-1007). The **bus terminal** (left-luggage facilities $2) is fourteen blocks north of Plaza 25 de Mayo, on Juan B. Justo and H. Yrigoyen (☎0345/421-7235). Local bus #1 will take you from the bus terminal to the Plaza – catch it on Avenida Juan B. Justo. The helpful, if slightly chaotic, **tourist office** is located next to the cathedral, on the eastern side of Plaza 25 de Mayo, at Urquiza 636 (Mon–Fri 7am–10pm, Sat & Sun 8am–9pm; ☎0345/421-2137). If you are bringing your own car, enquire about the *tarjeta de turista*, a special permit which enables tourists to park free of charge in the city centre.

Accommodation is reasonably abundant, with a spread to suit all budgets within a few blocks of the centre. The *Hotel Salto Grande,* at Urquiza 581 (☎ & fax 0345/421-0034; *hotelsg@concordia.com.ar*, ⑤) is a smart modern block, with views from the higher floors over the plaza and the coast. There are various categories of rooms ranging from basic but comfortable *turista* to more luxurious *especial*, all with television and air conditioning; buffet breakfast and parking are included and there is also an attractive outdoor pool. The *Nuevo Hotel Colonial*, at Pellegrini 443 (☎0345/421-0097; ③) has simple attractive rooms with private bathrooms in a pretty, old-fashioned building. On the plaza, at Pellegrini 611, the crumbling, once grand *Hotel Colón* (☎0345/422-0373; ③) offers spacious if rather rickety wood-floored rooms, some with small balconies; good singles discounts. A couple of blocks away, the *Hotel Federico I*, at 1 de Mayo 248 (☎421-3323; ②), has a quiet location and pleasant rooms, some with balconies. Some way from the centre, near Playa Nébel, the *Hotel Betania*, on Coldaroli y Remedios de Escalada de San Martín (☎0345/431-0456; ②), is a family-style hotel with lovely sunny rooms around a pretty garden with its own swimming pool. On the shores of the Lago Salto Grande, the modern and upmarket *Ayuí Hotel and Resort* (☎0345/421-1112; ⑥) is set in wooded grounds and has luxurious, airy rooms with TV, air conditioning and mini bar. The hotel also has a swimming pool and tennis courts. There are a couple of pretty uninspiring **campsites** along Concordia's costanera including the free site *Los Sauces*, right by Playa Los Sauces, and the *Centro de Empleados de Comercio* on the corner of the costanera and Colón (☎0345/422-0080) which charges around $8 per pitch. If you have your own transport, try the lovely wooded beach site on the shores of the Lago Salto Grande, *Las Palmeras* (☎0345/421-8359; $10 per four-person tent). Facilities include a restaurant, provisions store and showers, though it can sometimes be closed, so call ahead or ask at the tourist office before setting out.

The Town

Concordia is centred on **Plaza 25 de Mayo**, a pretty, shady square with the obligatory monumental equestrian statue of San Martín as well as a particularly impressive example of the almost comically swollen *palo borracho* tree. To the east lies Concordia's main commercial district, centred on Calle Entre Ríos, which is pedestrianized for three blocks between Bernardo de Irigoyen and Catamarca. By following Entre Ríos seven blocks to the north you'll come to the town's most unusual building, the extravagant **Palacio Arruabarrena**, on the corner of calles Entre Ríos and 3 de Febrero. Built in 1919 by a local land-owning family, the Arruabarrenas, it's an impressive four-storey building with a strong French influence evident in the steeply pitched mansard-roof punctuated with elliptical windows. A sweeping marble staircase leads up to the grand loggia-style porch. Marble statues flank the entrance and also support a heavy pediment over the arched windows of the first floor. Though both the exterior and interior have suffered some quite severe deterioration over the years, it's still a fabulously exotic and decorative building. Inside you'll find the **Museo Regional de Concordia**

(Mon–Fri 7am–8pm; free), with a small and patchy collection of local exhibits but a very friendly staff and occasional temporary exhibits featuring, for example, local photographers.

Concordia's **riverside area**, centred around the Avenida Costanera, lies some twelve blocks to the southeast of Plaza 25 de Mayo. It's rather desolate out of season, though it hums with life on summer evenings as locals patrol the avenue by car and on foot. There's a busy beach here, the **Playa Los Sauces**, named for the willow trees which flank the edge of the sand. From the old port, which lies at the eastern end of Calle Sáenz Peña, small boats ferry passengers to and from **Salto** (Mon–Fri 8am, 10am, 12am, 3pm & 6.30pm, Sat 8am, noon, 3pm & 6.30pm, Sun 8.30am & 6pm; $4) – the journey takes around fifteen minutes, making it a quicker way to cross the border than via the road bridge. The ticket office on the quayside opens around fifteen minutes before departure.

A couple of kilometres to the north of the town centre lies **Parque Rivadavia**. It's a pleasantly hilly, if sometimes slightly unkempt, park, whose most unusual feature is a huge and rather gory wooden sculpture of Christ on the cross, carved by the sculptor Luis Javin Sissara and erected in 1999. At the eastern end of the park, overlooking the river, stand the ruins of the **Castillo San Carlos**, a grand residence built in 1888 by a French industrialist and banker, Eduardo de Machy. Machy and his family spent only a few years in the house, rushing somewhat mysteriously back to France in 1891. During the 1920s, the French aviator and writer **Antoine de St-Exupéry** was forced to make an emergency landing near to the house and became a friend of the family then inhabiting it. He included this anecdote in his collection of short stories *Terre des Hommes*, published in English as *Wind, Sand and Stars*. Unfortunately, despite the house's romantic past, it's in a bit of a sorry state these days – fire and general neglect have taken their toll and though you can wander freely round the building, there's little to see. There are some fine views of the river, though, as well as of the wild expanse of gallery forest which borders it. Close to the entrance, there's a sculpture of "The Little Prince", in homage to St-Exupéry. At the northern end of the park, there's a **botanical garden** (Mon–Fri 8am–6pm, Sat & Sun 8am–noon & 2–6pm; free) dedicated to conserving autochthonous plants and trees; look out for the strange spectacle of a yatay palm entwined by a strangler fig. To get to the park, take local bus #2 from Calle Pellegrini, which will drop you a block from the entrance.

Some 12km north of the town centre, along Avenida Monseñor Rosch (bus #7 from Calle Pellegrini), lie Concordia's **thermal baths** (daily 7am–1am; $2.50), a complex of six artificial pools with temperatures ranging from 33°C to 42°C.

Eating and drinking

Eating and drinking options in Concordia are adequate if not particularly inspiring. One of the best deals is the friendly *Yantar*, at Pellegrini 570, with good fresh standard Argentinian food and a takeaway next door. On the corner of Urquiza and Alberdi, *La Glorieta* is a popular, reasonably priced parrilla. *Portofino*, at Pellegrini 560, is an upmarket Italian serving excellent pasta. Down on the costanera there are a number of lively parrillas, busiest on summer evenings; one of the best is the spacious *Parrilla Ferrari* on the corner of the costanera and Calle Bolivia. There are several popular confiterías around the Plaza 25 de Mayo, including the glitzy air-conditioned *Cristóbal* with outside tables and live music at weekends. There are several bars with pool tables, including *La Barca*, frequented by a young crowd, on Calle Urdinarrain, between San Luis and Sarmiento. **Nightclubs** include the huge *Costa Chaval*, a young modern club in a recycled warehouse on the corner of P. del Castillo and Espino (Fri & Sat) and the friendly *Ezequiel*, on Av. Juan B. Justo (Fri only), just to the north of the bus terminal, popular with all ages. In the summer, the in place is the *Hostal del Río*, inside Parque Rivadavia, with an outside dancefloor (Fri & Sat).

El Lago de Salto Grande

Stretching some 144km north to south and up to 10km east to west, the **Lago de Salto Grande** is the largest artificial reservoir in Argentina. Its creation radically altered the surrounding landscape, flooding large areas and leading to the total rebuilding of the city of Federación, 60km to the north of Concordia. The reservoir's jagged coastline, composed of sandy bays and slender peninsulas, is, however, extremely attractive. You can't follow the entire perimeter of the lake but there are a couple of roads bordering its southern tip, just to the west of the international bridge to Uruguay. After the turn-off to the lake, left off the access road to the bridge, the road forks. The left-hand fork will take you past an abandoned railway station, complete with locomotive outside and then, always bearing right, to **Península Soler** where you'll find a **campsite** (see "Accommodation", above) and a lovely wild tree-fringed beach right at the tip of the peninsula where there are great views over the tranquil waters of the lake. At the southern end of the peninsula, a well-signposted road leads you to **Puerto San Rafael**, where boat excursions can be arranged with Señor Wdowiak (☎0345/421-5257; $60 per hour for up to five people). The right-hand fork leads to the slightly less wild **Península Casula**, where there are more beaches, a confitería and a **hotel** (see "Accommodation", above). You can reach the lake area by taking the international bus to Salto – ask to be let off at the access road to the lake. It's a three-kilometre walk from the road to the campsite and another couple of kilometres to the tip of Península Soler. The tip of Península Casula, known as Punta Viracho, lies about 3km from the road.

Corrientes and around

A sultry, subtropical city sitting on a bend in the Río Paraná, **CORRIENTES** is one of El Litoral's oldest and most attractive cities, founded in 1588 as an intermediary port along the river route between Buenos Aires and Asunción. The city's charm is derived largely from its slightly crumbling – but very pretty – centre, based around the city's main square, the **Plaza 25 de Mayo**. Here you'll find examples of traditional *correntino* colonial buildings with overhanging roofs supported on wooden posts interspersed with more elaborate late nineteenth-century Italianate architecture. The city's modest museums, most notably the original **Museo de Artesanía** where you can see fine examples of the province's distinctive crafts, are given added appeal by being housed in these traditional buildings. These central city streets make Corrientes a pleasant place to just wander around for a day or two. If you visit in summer, though, be aware that both temperatures and humidity can be very high. As a result, locals take the siesta very seriously, not emerging from indoors until dusk on the hottest days: if you must hit the streets on a summer afternoon, head for Corrientes' attractive **costanera**, curving for some 2.5km around the northwest of the city centre where native lapacho trees, with exquisite pink blossom in spring, provide a welcome bit of shade.

Corrientes is linked to Resistencia, the capital of Chaco Province, 20km to the west via the Puente General M. Belgrano, a suspension bridge across the Río Paraná. On the way to the crossing, 15km east of the city, is the charming old-fashioned village of **Santa Ana de los Guácaras**, with its pretty eighteenth-century chapel, traditional houses and numerous small lakes; it makes a good day-trip from Corrientes. Like many other littoral towns, Corrientes has an important **Carnival**, a very Brazilian-influenced affair held in the Corsódromo – a kind of open-air stadium specially constructed for carnival. A more locally authentic affair, though, is the **Festival del Chamamé**, a celebration of the region's most popular folk music with plenty of live music and dancing, held on the second weekend in December.

CORRIENTES

ACCOMMODATION
Grand Hotel Guaraní	4
Hospedaje San Lorenzo	7
Hostal del Pinar	1
Orly	3
Residencial sos	5
Sosa	6
Turismo	2

RESTAURANTS AND BARS
Las Brasas	E
La Cueva del Pescador	D
Milenium	A
El Solar	C
El Viejo Café	B

Arrival, information and accommodation

Corrientes' **airport**, the Aeropuerto Fernando Piragine Niveyro (☎03783/458340), lies some 10km northeast of the city, along the RN12. Austral runs a shuttle service from the airport to the city, to coincide with the arrival of its flights from Buenos Aires. The city's **bus terminal** (☎03783/442149) is around 4km southeast of Plaza 25 de Mayo, along one of the city's main access roads, the Avenida Maipú. Various local buses, including the #103, run between the terminal and the centre. A taxi from the terminal to the centre will cost around $5. Local buses from Resistencia arrive at a smaller bus terminal on the costanera, opposite the northern end of La Rioja, within walking distance of most accommodation. Corrientes' **tourist office** is centrally located in the heart of the city's shopping district, on the northeastern corner of Plaza Cabral, some ten blocks southeast of Plaza 25 de Mayo (daily 7am–9pm; ☎03783/442149). It is run by a friendly and helpful young staff, who can provide you with a decent map of the city

Corrientes' **hotels** are particularly oriented towards businessmen and while there are some good upmarket places, simple and pleasant residential accommodation is pretty thin on the ground. There are some cheaper hotels around the bus terminal but – unless you are literally just spending a night in transit – this area is too far away from everything to be a useful place to stay. Corrientes' particularly hot and humid summers make air conditioning almost a necessity – though a shady room with a good fan can be acceptable. There's a good **campsite**, with showers, electricity and barbecue facilities around 10km northeast of town at Laguna Soto, a pretty lake on the way to Santa Ana (see p.317). Local bus #109 from the terminal goes there every 10 minutes or so, taking about 45 minutes.

Gran Hotel Guaraní, Mendoza 970 (☎03783/433800; *hguarani@espacio.com.ar*). The smartest of Corrientes' upmarket hotels: a modern glass-fronted building with an attractive lobby and very inviting pool and bar area. There are several categories of rooms ranging from standard to VIP and two categories of suites; all have air conditioning and cable TV. ④.

Hostal del Pinar, Plácido Martínez 1098 (☎ & fax 03783/29726). Modern block facing the river with slightly bland but spacious rooms, with cable TV and good air conditioning. Small outdoor swimming pool. The very efficient staff speak some English. ④.

Hospedaje San Lorenzo, San Lorenzo 1136 (no phone). The best of the cheaper hotels, *San Lorenzo* is a friendly place offering basic, well-kept rooms on a quiet central street. Fans and private bathrooms. ①.

Residencial Sos, H. Irigoyen 1771 (☎03783/460330). Rambling old building with rather scruffy but acceptable rooms with fans. Shared and private bathrooms available. ①.

Sosa, España 1050. Large, slightly down-at-heel, but friendly hotel divided into old and new sectors. Rooms in the new sector (for which you pay more) are slightly better, and some have balconies, but the walls in particular in both sectors are shabby. ②.

Hotel Turismo, Entre Ríos 650 (☎03783/433174). An attractive old-fashioned hotel on a good location down by the costanera. Cool tiled floors and wooden furniture – though some of the rooms are showing their age a bit as is the very noisy air conditioning. There's a great outdoor pool. ④, includes breakfast.

The City

Corrientes is a reasonably compact city: all the major points of interest lie within the streets to the north of Avenida 3 de Abril, which runs east–west through the city towards Puente General Belgrano. The whole of this approximately triangular area is bordered to the northwest by the **Avenida Costanera General San Martín**. There are two centres: the Centro Histórico, with **Plaza 25 de Mayo** at its heart, lies to the north and is where you'll find most of Corrientes' historic buildings and museums, including the **Museo de Artesanía** and the **Museo Histórico**, while the Centro Comercial – of less interest from a sightseeing point of view – is centred on Plaza Cabral, some ten blocks southeast of Plaza 25 de Mayo and Corriente's main pedestrianized shopping street, Calle Junín.

Plaza 25 de Mayo and around

A lovely old-fashioned leafy square surrounded by some of Corrientes' most striking architecture, **Plaza 25 de Mayo** encapsulates the city's sleepy subtropical ambience. The square lies one block south of the costanera, to which it is linked by the narrow streets of Buenos Aires and Salta, the former in particular lined with fine examples of late nineteenth-century architecture. One of the most striking buildings on the square itself is the pretty pink **Casa de Gobierno**, on the eastern side, constructed in 1886 in the ornate Italianate style which replaced many of the older, colonial buildings at the end of the nineteenth century. Particularly attractive are the delicate filigree window grilles, best admired on the building's northern wall, along Fray José de la Quintana. Opposite the building, on the corner of Fray José de la Quintana and Salta, you'll find the **Museo de Artesanía** (Mon–Fri 8am–noon) and the Taller de Artesanos (Mon–Sat 7am–noon & 4–7.30pm). The museum is housed within a typical colonial Corrientes building; a low whitewashed residence constructed around a central patio flanked by a gallery, providing shade from the fierce summer sun. Inside you'll find an interesting selection of local crafts, including fine examples of leather, ceramics and basketwork.

Perhaps the most intriguing pieces, sold by craftsmen working in the workshops within, are the carvings of San La Muerte (literally "Saint Death"). These solemn little skeletons, carved of wood, gold or bone are carried around – or, in the case of the smallest figures, inserted under the skin – to ensure the bearer a painless death; they're a typical example of the popular cults, many of them inherited from the Guaraní, which co-exist in Corrientes with profound Roman Catholic beliefs. At the southern end of the square, there's the nineteenth-century **Iglesia de Nuestra Señora de la Merced** (daily 7am–noon & 4–8pm), housing a handsome hand-carved wooden retable, or altar screen, with twisted wooden pillars and rich golden inlay work.

Five blocks southeast of the Plaza, at 9 de Julio 1052, is the **Museo Histórico** (Tues–Fri 8am–noon & 4–8pm; free), in an attractively renovated old family house, dating from the nineteenth century. It's a fairly eclectic and not particularly well-organized collection covering various aspects of provincial history, though there is a fine collection of religious artefacts, including some Jesuit wood carvings.

Heading directly south from the square you'll come, after seven blocks, to the **Iglesia Santísima Cruz de los Milagros** (open by appointment only; ☎03783/ 427073), located at the southern end of the Plaza de la Cruz. Both the square and the church – an austere Italianate construction dating from 1897 – are named after Corrientes' first cross, brought by the Spaniards on the city's founding in 1588. The cross gained its epithet, the "Cross of Miracles", when, according to legend, it proved impervious to native attempts to destroy it with fire. A piece of the original cross is preserved as part of the altar within the church, while a replica of it can be seen in the Museo Histórico (see above).

The Costanera

Corrientes' attractively maintained riverside avenue, the **Avenida Costanera General San Martín** runs from the small **Parque Mitre**, at the northern end of the city, as far as the Puente General Belgrano. Lined with fine examples of native trees, it's a lovely spot on summer evenings, when the heat dissipates a little and locals leave the cool refuge of their homes to pack its promenades for a jog or a stroll, or simply sit sipping *mate* or *tereré* on stone benches. Just to the west of Parque Mitre, where there is a small beach, restaurants and a children's playground, you'll find the port buildings and the **Mercado Paraguayo** – a pretty standard fixture in northern Argentinian cities – selling all manner of cheap imported Paraguayan goods, from shoes to stereos. Buses from Corrientes to Resistencia also leave from here and unofficial taxis also tout for business along this section of the avenue. Beyond here, the wide avenue sweeps southeast, with various panoramic points jutting out over the river, from where there are views to the flat Resistencia coast. Beyond the eastern end of Carlos Pellegrini, 800m or so southeast of the Mercado Paraguayo, there's a number of popular parrillas, pizzerias and ice-cream parlours. At the intersection of the costanera and Junín, there's a small **zoo** (daily 9am–6pm; free), though its hopelessly inadequate enclosures are not the best place to see magnificent native species such as the puma, the yaguarandí or the capuchin monkey. A number of small beaches dot the costanera – they're fine for sunbathing, but you should avoid swimming here unless there is a lifeguard on duty (summer only; check with tourist office for details): the unexpectedly strong currents here gave rise to Corrientes' full name, San Juan de Vera de Las Siete Corrientes, "San Juan de Vera of the Seven Currents".

Eating, drinking and nightlife

Corrientes isn't over-endowed with interesting places to **eat** and **drink**, but there are a few good places both in the city centre (mostly around the *centro comercial*) and along the costanera. At San Lorenzo 830, there's an excellent buffet-style restaurant, *El Solar*, providing plenty of appetizing fresh salads, fruit juices and a variety of hot dishes. *La Cueva del Pescador*, on H. Yrigoyen and Mendoza, does well-prepared fresh fish and seafood dishes. Along the southern end of the costanera, between San Martín and Bolívar, there's a number of good parrillas with outside seating, including the popular *Las Brasas*. For snacks and coffees, there's the charming *Milenium*, a small bar on the corner of Salta and Fray José de la Quintana run by a friendly owner with a penchant for John Lennon. For a traditional café atmosphere, head for *El Viejo Café*, at Rioja 712. There are also plenty of fast-food joints along Junín and hamburger stalls and pizzerias along the costanera.

A popular **nightlife** option is a *chamamé* show held at various restaurants: *Parrilla El Quincho* on Av. Juan Pujol and Pellegrini and *La Peña Puente Pesoa* at the intersection of the RN12 with Avenida P. Ferrer (the continuation of Avenida 3 de Abril) both do a *tenedor libre* parrilla for $5 a head and live *chamamé* shows on Fridays and Saturdays from about 10pm. At *Peña La Rueda*, on Avenida Maipú and RN12, there are also *chamamé* shows ($5 entrance plus meal).

Listings

Airlines Lapa 9 de Julio 1261 (☎03783/431625).

Banks and exchange There are a handful of banks around the corner of 9 de Julio and Córdoba (all Mon–Fri 7–11.30am); El Dorado at 9 de Julio 1341 changes travellers' cheques (Mon–Fri 8am–noon & 4–8pm, Sat 8.30am–noon).

Car rental Localiza, San Juan 1163 (☎03783/434444), also at the airport.

Internet Ciberland, Pellegrini between Mendoza and Córdoba; Telecentro Taragui, La Rioja 842 (☎03783/432499; *alarc@arnet.com.ar*).

Post office San Juan and San Martín.

Pharmacy Farmacia Nueva Norte, C. Pellegrini 1399.

Taxis Remise VIP (☎03783/420015).

Telephones Telecentro Express, San Lorenzo 827 (daily 7.30am–midnight).

Travel agencies and tour operators Photographer Miguel Alvarez, 9 de Julio 1481 (☎155-57649), organizes tailor-made tours of the surrounding area, including Santa Ana, Mercedes and the Esteros del Iberá.

Santa Ana de los Guácaras

A tiny village of sandy streets, pockmarked with shallow lakes, **SANTA ANA DE LOS GUÁCARAS** lies 15km northeast of Corrientes. Founded in 1621, the village takes its name from its first inhabitants, Guácara Indians who lived and worked here in a *reducción* founded by Franciscan priests. The Guácaras and Franciscans also constructed the village's simple white chapel, a national historical monument. As well as the chapel, Santa Ana is notable for its fine examples of traditional Corrientes architecture – though what's perhaps most striking about the place is its sleepy unhurried atmosphere and natural setting amongst trees and lakes.

Santa Ana is built on an absolutely regular grid of seven by seven blocks, centred on the Plaza San Martín, a carefully tended central square filled with wonderful exotic plants. The **Capilla de Santa Ana** (daily 8am–noon & 5–8pm) stands at the southern end of the square. Built in 1765, it's a pleasingly simple white colonial construction. The interior is similarly ascetic, with whitewashed walls, red-tiled floors and sturdy wooden rafters and pews. The one ornamental note is provided by the carved wooden altar, with relatively restrained gilded mouldings and a central figure of St Ann carved by the Guácaras. Five blocks southeast of Plaza San Martín, there's another small square; along its western side stands an old locomotive **El Económico**, dating from the days when a sugar refinery functioned on the outskirts of Santa Ana. El Económico ran along a narrow-gauge railway, the first stretch of which was completed in 1892 between Santa Ana and San Luis del Palmar, some 15km to the southeast. Later extended into the interior of the province, the railway ran some 270km. In 1960, however, the train was taken out of service and the tracks dismantled.

Local **bus** #11 from the corner of Catamarca and 9 de Julio in Corrientes goes to Santa Ana. Buses return to Corrientes every hour between about 8am and midday and then every two hours between 3pm and 7pm. There isn't really a **tourist office** in Santa Ana, though the friendly staff in the municipalidad, on the northeastern corner of plaza San Martín (Mon–Fri 9am–noon & 4–7pm) are happy to answer questions about the village. There is no accommodation in the village either, though there are a couple of **campsites** nearby (see p.315). Bring food, too, if you're staying for more than an hour or two, as there's little more than a couple of grocery stores in Santa Ana.

The Reserva Natural del Iberá

Covering nearly 13,000 square kilometres (almost fifteen percent of Corrientes Province), the **Reserva Natural del Iberá** is a vast system of wetlands which offer some of the best opportunities for close-up observation of wildlife in the whole of Argentina. The reserve is composed of a series of lakes, *esteros* (marshes), streams and wonderful floating islands, formed by a build-up of soil on top of densely intertwined waterlilies. An elongated sliver running from the north to the centre of Corrientes Province, the reserve is bordered to the north by the RN12, to the east by tributaries of the Aguaypey and Miriñay rivers and to the west by tributaries of the Paraná. Its southern tip touches the RN123 which runs east–west from the border town of Paso de Los Libres, joining the RN12 some 150km south of Corrientes. For many years, the **Esteros del Iberá**, as the region is commonly known, was one of Argentina's wildest and least-known regions – a local legend even had it that a tribe of pygmies lived on the islands – harbouring an isolated community who made their living from hunting and fishing the area's wildlife. Since the creation of the reserve, in 1983, hunting in the area has been prohibited and many locals have been employed as highly specialized guides, or *baque-anos*, and park rangers, thus helping to preserve this unique environment. The ban on hunting has led to an upsurge in the region's abundant bird and animal population – which includes an amazingly diverse range of species, including caymans, capybaras, marsh deer, howler monkeys, boas, the rare-maned wolf and over three hundred species of birds. The wildlife has quickly become accustomed to the reserve's gentle stream of tourism, with the result that **boat trips** around the lakes and streams afford incredibly close contact with many of the species and provide excellent photo opportunities.

The reserve is best reached from the village of **Colonia Carlos Pellegrini**, a charming semi-rural settlement which sits beside one of the system's major lakes, the Laguna Iberá. Access to the village is from **Mercedes**, some 120km to the southwest, a pretty traditional town with a handful of good hotels.

Mercedes and around

Your first sight of **MERCEDES** is unlikely to impress; set amongst the flatlands of central Corrientes, some 200km southeast of the provincial capital, it appears as a sprawling modern settlement with little to tempt you into staying for more than an hour or two. Head into the centre, though, and you'll find an appealing little agricultural town given a distinctive flavour by a mix of old-fashioned adobe and galleried roof buildings and elegant nineteenth-century town architecture. The town is a real hub for local country life, too: horses and carts are a common sight on its streets and on Saturdays gauchos come to town, traditionally dressed Corrientes-style, with shallow, wide-brimmed hats, ornate belts and wide *bombachas* and accompanied by their wives in old-fashioned frilly dresses.

The town is built on a regular grid pattern and centred on **Plaza 25 de Mayo**, a densely planted square with little fountains. At its southern end stands the town's rather unusual church, the **Iglesia Nuestra Señora de las Mercedes**, a lofty late nineteenth-century red-brick construction. Avenida San Martín runs east–west along the northern side of the square, connecting with the bus terminal and the major access routes in and out of town. Along the southern side of the square runs Juan Pujol, an attractive street lined with some fine buildings and a number of good bars and restaurants. Three blocks to the east of the square, on the corner of San Martín and Batalla de Salta, there's a beautifully preserved example of the local building style: a low white-washed adobe-walled construction with a gently sloping red-tiled roof which overhangs the pavement, supported on simple wooden posts. The building houses the **Fundación Manos Correntinas**, a non-profit enterprise which functions as an outlet for locally produced crafts. The small but superior collection of goods includes basketwork, simple gourd *mates*, heavy woollens and hand-turned bone and horn buttons. The friendly manager is as happy for visitors to wander around the building as to purchase goods – so long as you sign her visitors' book. There are various other craft outlets throughout town: try the shops along San Martín and Pujol selling belts, gaucho knives, *mates* and the like – all with a sturdy utilitarian feel and far less gimmicky than the pieces on sale in more touristy towns.

Some 9km to the west of town, along the RN123, there is a roadside shrine to a popular local saint, the **Gauchito Gil**. A kind of nineteenth-century gaucho Robin Hood, the Gauchito Antonio Gil was persecuted and killed by the police and soon became the subject of local devotion. The shrine, erected on the spot where he was killed, presumably began life as a simple affair but such is the popularity of this figure that it has mushroomed into a vast complex of restaurants, campsites and souvenir shops. There is a kind of museum here exhibiting the offerings made to the Gauchito – including football shirts, wedding dresses and children's bicycles as well as more conventional rosaries. Simpler offerings, often made by passing motorists and bus passengers to ensure a safe journey, are ribbons and candles. The strangest thing about the place is the dominance of the colour red – apparently the colour worn by the Gauchito Gil; the groups of red flags on sticks stuck in the ground make the shrine look like the aftermath of a political demonstration after all the protesters have gone home.

Practicalities

Mercedes' **bus terminal** is six blocks to the west of Plaza San Martín, on the corner of Avenida San Martín and El Ceibo. There's a helpful information office here who can advise on transport and you can leave luggage at the terminal bar. Mercedes has no **tourist office** as such, but there's a helpful tourism and culture secretariat within the municipalidad, on the western side of Plaza San Martín (Mon–Fri 7am–1pm; ☎03773/420011), who can provide information on the town and a photocopied map. Internet access is available at the photography shop on the corner of Belgrano and Juan Pujol. There's an ATM at the Banco de Corrientes, on the corner of Pedro Ferre, three blocks west of Plaza San Martín.

Accommodation options in Mercedes are surprisingly good for a small provincial town. The best place is the gorgeous *Hotel Sol*, at San Martín a few blocks east of the Plaza (☎03773/420283; ③). It's a lovely old building with spotless and comfortable rooms – all of them en suite with TV and fans – set around a beautiful tiled courtyard filled with flowers. Another agreeable place is the *Hotel Ita-Pucú*, at Batalla de Salta 645, between Avenida San Martín and Juan Pujol (☎03773/1550-4388; ②). It's a friendly, family-run place in a traditional Corrientes galleried building with a pretty garden. The rooms are simple but pleasant; all have private bathrooms and fans.

Eating and drinking options are limited, but adequate. On the corner of the Belgrano and Juan Pujol, just west of Plaza San Martín, the excellent *Poravory* is a very pretty and upmarket little **café** serving fresh juices, good espresso coffee, sandwiches, cocktails and delicious home-made *alfajores*. It's also perfectly positioned for observing the bustle of local life along Juan Pujol. For more substantial dishes, the best place is *El Quincho*, housed within the Club Social, on the corner of Juan Pujol and Ferré, with well-cooked standards such as *milanesas*, pastas, steaks and chicken for around $4.

Colonia Carlos Pellegrini and the Esteros

The heart of the Reserva Natural del Iberá is the village of **COLONIA CARLOS PELLEGRINI** 118km northeast of Mercedes and accessed via the unsealed RP40. The journey there takes you through flat, unremarkable land, reminiscent perhaps of the African savannahs, but with little to prepare you for the wonderfully wild environment of the *esteros* themselves. The village sits on a peninsula, on the edges of the Laguna Iberá, a 53 square-kilometre expanse of water. The sparkling waters of the lake (*iberá* means "shining" in Guaraní) are spread with acres of waterlilies, most notably the striking mauve and yellow *aguapé*, and dotted with floating islands, known as *embalsados*. Access to the village is over a narrow bridge recently constructed on a raised mound of earth and rock. There's a small **visitor centre** immediately to the left before you cross the bridge with a small photographic display on the *esteros*. A short trail leads through a small forested area to the south of the visitors' centre; the densely packed mix of palms, jacarandas, lapachos and willows here is a good place to spot black howler monkeys who typically slouch in a ball shape amongst the branches or swing from tree to tree on lianas. The monkeys get their name from their low penetrating howl. Easiest to spot are the yellowish young, often ferried from tree to tree on the backs of their mothers. As the monkeys mature the females' fur turns brown whilst the males' turns black.

The village itself is composed of a small grid of sandy streets, centred on a grassy **Plaza San Martín**. There's a hospital, a school and a handful of grocery stores but otherwise little infrastructure: there's only one public phone, used by the whole village to receive calls, and nothing in the way of banking facilities so make sure you bring enough cash with you for your stay. The best **accommodation** in the village is provided by three *posadas*. Particularly well-located is the pioneering *Posada de la Laguna*, on a quiet lakeside spot at the eastern edge of the village (☎03773/1562-9532 or 9827; *www.habitantes.elsitio.com/ibera*; ⑤ half board, or $95 per person full board plus half-day boat trip). Run by Elsa Güiraldes, a descendant of the writer Ricardo Güiraldes, it offers pared-down luxury with a rustic feel; the elegant and spacious but simple en-suite rooms are situated in a galleried building whose veranda provides a good vantage point for observing the birds that gather around the lakeside. A couple of blocks west, there's the lovely *Posada Aguapé* (☎03773/1562-9759 or 011/4742-3015; *aguape@inter-server.com.ar*; ⑤, includes breakfast, or $95 per person full board with boat trip), another traditional building set in spacious grounds with very pretty en-suite rooms overlooking the lake. There's also a swimming pool and a cosy bar area. The newest *posada* is the *Ñanderetá*, towards the western end of the village (☎154-629536 or 011/4811-2005; *www.nandereta.com*; ⑤, includes breakfast, or $120 per person with full board and boat trip). It's a modern wood and stone construction, sitting within wooded grounds, with a sun terrace and pretty, brightly coloured en-suite rooms. The *posada* doesn't overlook the lake, but the owners have a separate stretch of lakeside land where they have installed a wooden watchtower from which you can take in the commanding views of the entire area. There are also two *hospedajes* in the village: best is the *Hospedaje San Cayetano* (☎03773/1562-7060; $10 per person) with simple but acceptable rooms with a shared bathroom. There's also the very basic *Hospedaje Guaraní* (☎03773/1562-9762;

①), a rather scruffy adobe-walled building, though with hot water and kitchen facilities and some en-suite rooms; the friendly owner also allows camping next door ($5 per two-person tent). Finally there's a municipal **campsite** immediately to the left as you enter the village ($4 per person); it's a pleasant riverside site with showers but is almost entirely bereft of shade.

Trips to the marshes are organized through the *posadas*, who take visitors out on small motor boats. Around the reed beds at the edges of the lake you may see snakes, such as the handsome yellow anaconda, its yellowish skin dotted with jaguar-like black patches and reaching up to three metres in length. Another common sight around the lakeside are chajás (southern screamers), large grey birds with a startling patch of red around the eyes. The birds frequently perch rather precariously on spindly trees around the lake, emitting a piercing yelp not dissimilar to the sound a small dog might make if you trod on it. Once on the water, the boats move swiftly across the centre of the lake, before cutting their engines to drift through the narrow streams which thread between the islands. This silent approach allows you an incredibly privileged view of the *esteros'* wildlife; turning a corner you suddenly find yourself amongst a wonderful landscape of waterlilies and verdant floating islands, the whole of it teeming with bird and animal life. Easiest to spot are the birds, most commonly neotropic cormorants, storks and herons. A striking, if rarer sight, is the elegant jabiru, a long-legged bird with a white body, bright red collar and a black head and beak. Amongst the smaller, non-aquatic birds that flit around the lake, look out for the boldly coloured scarlet-headed blackbird, a jet black bird which looks as though its head and neck have been dipped in a bucket of red paint.

As you approach the edges of the islands, seemingly static caymans suddenly slip into the water and observe you with their prehistoric eyes peeking above the water. Listen out, too, for the sudden splash of a capybara – one of the world's most unlikely aquatic mammals – diving into the water. On land, this large guinea pig-like mammal looks almost ungainly but they are incredibly graceful as they glide through the water with their eyes and nose skimming the surface. Most guides will take you onto the floating islands themselves; it's a particularly bizarre experience to feel the ground vibrating beneath your feet as you move. The islands are where the capybaras go to sleep and graze, giving you a chance to observe the adults and their young from a distance of only a few metres. As you approach them slowly, the animals seem to accept your presence and continue grazing lazily on aquatic plants, though freezing mid-mouthful at any sudden movement.

Another of the *esteros'* sights are the *garzales*, where hundreds of herons come to nest – a spectacular mass-gathering of this normally solitary bird. On the marshy lands and pastures around the more isolated extremes of the lake, you may spot the rare marsh deer, South America's largest deer, at home on both water and land. Rarest of all of the *esteros'* wild life is the endangered aguara-guazú or maned wolf, a reddish long-legged wolf which lopes through the vegetation, moving both legs on each side of its body at once.

Paso de los Libres and Yapeyú

North of Concordia, in Entre Ríos Province, the RN14 offer precious few interesting stopovers for those heading towards Misiones and Iguazú. In Corrientes Province, two possible options are provided by the border town of **Paso de los Libres**, lying some 250km north of Concordia and 369km south of Misiones' capital, Posadas. To the north is the sleepy and appealing village of **Yapeyú**, whose extremely modest tourist industry is built around its connections with the Jesuit missions and Independence hero General San Martín.

Paso de los Libres

A dreary and slightly seedy town, **PASO DE LOS LIBRES** is probably best avoided if you possibly can, though its good transport connections with towns along the RN14, with Mercedes for the Reserva Natural del Iberá, and with the Brazilian town of Uruguaiana, make it a useful transport hub, if nothing else. Traditionally a town where Brazilians come to buy cheap consumer goods, the recent devaluation of the *real* – making Argentina much more expensive for Brazilians – has hit Paso de los Libres hard and the town wears a slightly depressed air. Brazilian influence is strong here; you'll hear the latest Brazilian hits blaring out from shops in the town centre, whilst the town's popular **carnival** is dominated by samba rhythms.

The town is constructed on a grid pattern and sits on the banks of the Río Uruguay. The most attractive area is around the quiet central **Plaza Independencia**, whilst Colón, one block west, is the town's main drag, lined with an assortment of modest shops. Very limited **tourist information** can be had from the municipalidad, on the western side of Plaza Independencia (☎03772/425600). The town's small **airport** is around 5km northwest of the town centre, off the main access road into town. The **bus terminal** is a couple of kilometres southwest of Plaza Independencia, on Avenida San Martín immediately west of the international bridge to Uruguaiana (☎03772/425600). From here, your best way of getting into town is by taxi or one of the regular minibuses that depart from outside the terminal. Avoid the temptation to head along Avenida San Martín on foot: though it's only a short walk into town, this area is fringed by a shanty town which borders the river, and opportunistic muggings have been reported.

For the same reason, you're best off avoiding the handful of inexpensive *hospedajes* clustered around the terminal and heading into town for **accommodation**. The best hotel in town is the high-rise *Alejandro I*, on the corner of Pago Largo and Coronel López (☎03772/424102; ⑥), three blocks south of the plaza. Another good choice is the pleasant *Hotel Las Vegas*, at Sarmiento 554, one block east of the plaza (☎03772/423490; ③) offering attractive air-conditioned en-suite rooms with cable TV. At Coronel López 1091, the *Hotel Iberá* (☎03772/421848; ③) is no great shakes in terms of decor, but it's a simple, friendly place and is set to be revamped. All rooms have a TV and fan. Some eight blocks northwest of the plaza, the rather dingy *Hotel Uruguay*, at República del Uruguay 1252 (☎03772/425672; ②), is a passable budget option.

Paso de los Libres' scant **eating options** are mostly based around Colón and Madariaga, which runs along the western side of Plaza Independencia; best of the bunch is probably the simple *La Farola*, on the northwest corner of the square.

Yapeyú

A better choice for an overnight stay than Paso de Los Libres is the pretty riverside village of **YAPEYÚ**, some 60km to the north. The village was once an important Jesuit *reducción*, though it was largely destroyed in the early nineteenth century by the Portuguese army, leaving little more than blocks of stone, many of which formed the basis for the reconstruction of the village. Nowadays, the village is most famous for being the birthplace of the national hero **General San Martín** and Yapeyú is treated as a semi-obligatory patriotic stopover by Argentinians making the long road journey from Buenos Aires to Iguazú. The prestigious Mounted Grenadiers, who guard the Casa Rosada in Buenos Aires, also have a regimental quarters here.

Yapeyú's collection of unassuming buildings – many of them painted in the traditional colonial colours of mustard and white with green doors – sit on a grid of streets with the large **Plaza San Martín** at the centre. The square's centrepiece is a huge truncated arch, a monument to soldiers who died in the Falklands/Malvinas conflict: the idea is that the arch will be completed when the islands are regained by Argentina.

At the eastern end of the square, the mock-colonial **Templete Histórico Sanmartiniano** (daily 8am–6pm; free) is built around the foundations of San Martín's birthplace; in lieu of the remains of the hero himself (whose mausoleum is in Buenos Aires' cathedral) there is an urn containing the remains of San Martín's parents, moved here from their original resting place in Recoleta Cemetery. Slightly more interesting than this rather vacuous monument is the modest **Museo Sanmartiniano** (daily 7am–11pm; free), at the far southern end of the village, housed in the Grenadiers' regimental building, displaying a collection of documents, uniforms and items belonging to the San Martín family. There's a reconstruction of San Martín's bedroom in his house in Boulogne-Sur-Mer, where he died, and a couple of relics from the Jesuit mission, including a sturdy baptism font. More Jesuit pieces can be seen at the **Museo Jesuítico Guillermo Furlong** (Tues–Sun 8am–noon & 4–7pm; free; ☎03772/493013), on the south side of the plaza. The museum is laid out in the form of an *oga* (a Guaraní term for a collection of small huts) and contains various pieces of stonework from the missions, including a sundial: most interesting perhaps are the informative historical panels on the history of the mission region.

   Accommodation is limited but agreeable. The *Hotel San Martín*, on the south side of the plaza (☎03772/493120; ②), is a cosy little place in an old-fashioned building, with attractive en-suite rooms. Down towards the riverfront, northeast of the plaza, the *Hostería Yapeyú*, on the corner of Juan de San Martín and Paso de los Andes (☎03772/493053; ③), offers attractive self-contained *cabaña*-style accommodation. There's a pleasant grassy **campsite** at the southern end of town, again by the river ($5 per tent), offering hot showers and barbecue facilities; take insect repellent. On the southern side of the square, there's a friendly simple **restaurant**, the *Comedor El Paraíso*, where you can sit outside at tables.

Northern Corrientes

Primarily known in Argentina as a fishing region, the **northern Corrientes Province** offers a spectacular river landscape of pale sandy beaches which are gently lapped by the transparent waters of the glassy and deceptively calm Paraná, dotted with verdant wooded islands. The surrounding landscape is flat, marsh-pocked land with patches of neo-tropical forest where you can see howler monkeys and hummingbirds, whilst the river itself is so clear that it's easy to spot the abundant shoals of fish that attract fishermen from all over the country. The area's most famous town is **Paso de la Patria** – though unless you have a fondness for rowdy and beery fishing resorts, it's probably best avoided. **Itatí** is a far more modest village, dominated by its astonishingly grand basilica built to house the Virgin of Itatí, arguably as popular as the Virgin of Luján. Some 80km to the east lies the placid village of **Itá-Ibaté**, little more than a few sandy streets and a fine stretch of palm-fringed beach. The last resort along this section of coast is **Ituzaingó**, a popular weekend destination from Posadas and the location of one of Argentina's largest and most controversial dams, the **Represa Yacyretá**.

Paso de la Patria

Argentina's most famous fishing resort, **PASO DE LA PATRIA**, is something of a victim of its own success. This small town, 35km northeast of Corrientes via the RN12, attracts thousands of fishermen from Argentina and abroad for its **Fiesta Nacional del Dorado**, held in August. It's also a very popular weekend resort and over recent years has become a rather rowdy place with an increasing number of thefts reported from the town's holiday homes. Outside these busy times, though, it's a pleasant enough town of sandy streets flanked by rocky beaches, with a number of campsites and some good, more upmarket accommodation options. The town is spread out on a grid pattern for several kilometres along a curving riverfront. Most of the town's activity takes place around the eastern riverfront avenue, 25 de Mayo, where you'll find the municipalidad, the tourist office and a number of hotels. The western side of town, with a more relaxed, spread-out feel, is bordered along the riverfront by the winding Avenida Santa Coloma. There are small strips of sandy beach at both the east and western ends of town.

Long-distance **buses** arrive at the terminal on Catamarca and 8 de Diciembre, a couple of blocks south of the riverfront. There are also regular minibuses from Corrientes to Paso de la Patria which will drop you anywhere in town. The **tourist office** is at 25 de Mayo 518, east of the terminal along the riverfront (☎03783/494007). One of the best **accommodation** options is the attractive *Jardín del Paraná*, around six blocks west of the terminal on Avenida Santa Coloma (☎03783/494291; ④) with pretty en-suite rooms and an excellent restaurant. Serious fishermen stay at *Cabaña Don Julián*, at the far western end of Av. Santa Coloma (☎03783/94021; ④), where there are comfortable en-suite **rooms** with air conditioning, a good restaurant and a very professional team of fishing guides; English is spoken.

Itatí

Originally founded as a Franciscan mission in 1615, on the site of an existing Indian settlement, **ITATÍ** is a small village on the banks of the Paraná, some 70km north of Corrientes. Dominating the otherwise simple village is the vast **Basilica**, built here in 1938 to house the shrine of the Virgin of Itatí, who rivals in popularity Argentina's patron saint, the Virgin of Luján. The exact origins of this Virgin are unclear, but it appears that she was carved in the north of the Missions region and brought to the village by Father Luis de Bolaños, the village's founder.

Itatí consists of a small irregular grid of streets, many of them unsealed, and is centred on the **Plaza Fray Luis Bolanos**. The **Basilica** is on the western side of the square. It's a massive but compact structure, mixing classical and colonial features and dominated by a sturdy Doric-columned entrance and a huge slate-coloured dome, visible for several kilometres along the coast. Inside, it's fairly sparse, cavernous interior, illuminated by colourful stained-glass windows, sets off the central altar, above which stands the Virgin within an illuminated glass-fronted arch. Carved in walnut and timbó wood, the Virgin originally had strong Indian features, but was remodelled in the mid-nineteenth century, giving her a more European appearance. Behind the altar, an allegorical mural has a group of flute- and harp-playing Guaranís receiving the Virgin on the banks of the Paraná. The Virgin's chamber is on a mezzanine behind the altar, and is flanked by cabinets with tiny silver and gold offerings; mainly representing parts of the body, the beautifully detailed hands, hearts, lungs and eyes represent ailments for which the Virgin's help is sought.

Itatí is popular with pilgrims throughout the year, but the most picturesque gathering of devotees of the Virgin happens during the week of July 16 for the **Coronation**. On this date hundreds of thousands of pilgrims from all over Argentina and Paraguay converge on the village, including a traditionally dressed horseback procession from the nearby village of San Luis del Palmar.

Itatí's **bus terminal** is three blocks south of the main square, on Avenida de Mayo. Some long-distance buses also drop you at the intersection of the RN12 and the access road to the village, where you shouldn't have to wait long to pick up a minibus to take you the 8km into the village. There's no **tourist office**, but some information on the history of the village can be obtained from the municipalidad on the southeastern corner of the square (7am–1pm; ☎03783/1560-0990). There are also various booklets on sale in the shop beside the basilica. By far the best **place to stay** is at the *Estancia Nuestra Señora de Itatí*, some 15km east of the village via an unsealed road (☎03783/15663572;

$20 per person per day). An ecologically minded agricultural establishment dedicated to raising buffalo, the estancia offers spotless and comfortable modern *cabañas*, in a natural setting, with full cooking facilities. There's also a fantastic private beach, bordered by forest where you can spot howler monkeys. **Fishing trips** can also be arranged from the estancia (boga, surubí, pacú and dorado are all commonly caught), for around half the price charged by most places along this section of the Paraná. A *remise* from the terminal to the estancia will cost around $10. Accommodation in the village itself is rather drab. There are two **hotels**, of which the best is the *Hotel Antártida* at 25 de Mayo 250 (☎03783/93060; $15, including breakfast), offering large if very basic rooms with ensuite bathrooms. The hotel also has a restaurant and organizes fishing excursions on the Paraná for around $150 per day for four people with a guide (fuel not included). There's also a very basic *hospedaje* on the southern side of the square (☎156-63622; $12 per person, including breakfast; $20 for rooms for two to four people). There's also a rather rundown **muncipal campsite**, the Aba-Rapé ($1 per person), overlooking the river at the eastern end of the village. A better choice is *Cóctel*, on the riverfront near the centre of town on the corner of Castor de León, one block north of the plaza, offering barbecue and shower facilities with a kiosk on site.

Itá-Ibaté

Another 80km east along the RN12, you'll find **ITÁ-IBATÉ**. A pretty, quiet village of unsealed roads, it's primarily a **fishing resort**, and is particularly popular with Brazilian fishermen. Apart from fishing (boga, dorado and surubí are the most commonly caught species) there's very little to do here, but the lovely sandy beaches, unassuming atmosphere and good accommodation options make it a pleasant place to stop over for a night. The town is centred around a sandy central square, the Plaza San Martín, whose dominant feature is a little merry-go-round. Itá-Ibaté sits on a cliff above the Paraná (*itá* means rock and *ibaté* high in Guaraní) and winding paths lead down from the town to the **beach**, a couple of blocks to the north. The beach itself is a narrow strip of sand bordered by densely forested slopes, with views over the wonderfully clear waters of the river to some lush islands.

Itá-Ibaté doesn't have a bus terminal yet so **buses** drop you off on the eastern side of the plaza. There's excellent-value **accommodation** at the *Pensión El Hogar*, a couple of blocks north of the plaza, just off Calle Belgrano (no phone; $9 per person). This friendly, family-run place has large, basic but comfortable rooms for up to four people and sits just above the beach; bathrooms are shared. Around eight blocks to the east, again above the beach, there's *Cabañas Don Quico* (☎03781/495195), a spacious wooded site with well-equipped cabins for up to six people at around $15 per person and cheaper bunk-bed accommodation; tents can be pitched for $5 a day. Another few blocks to the east there's the smart *Barrancas de Itá-Ibaté* complex (☎03781/495058 or mobile 156-03476; ③) with hotel rooms and attractive two-storey alpine-style cabins for up to seven people ($80). The complex has an attractive confitería overlooking the river and tents can be pitched for $5 per person with access to barbecue facilities and bathroom. The cheapest place to pitch your tent is down on the beach at the bottom of Calle Islas Malvinas, seven blocks to the northeast of the plaza, ($3 per person), where there are basic toilet facilities and barbecues – mostly used by fishermen to cook their catch at the end of the day. **Eating** options within the town are very limited, but there's an excellent little café, *Bonjour*, within the kiosk on the eastern side of the square, doing good *empanadas* and more elaborate dishes in the evening when the handful of tables are lit by candles. The café's Porteño owner also makes excellent espresso coffee, an extremely rare commodity in the north of Argentina.

Fishing excursions are offered by both *Cabañas Don Quico* and the *Barrancas* complex: the cost is around $150 a day for up to four people, plus the cost of fuel. A slightly better deal is offered by Alfredo Secundino Haddad, who runs the fishing tackle shop on Av. San Martín, just south of the plaza (☎03781/495107 or mobile 156-08211) who offers a package for two people, including accommodation, meals and a day's fishing excursion with fifty litres of fuel for $100 per person or $160 for two people. The fishing season is winter and spring.

Ituzaingó and the Yacyretá Dam

When the heat all gets too much, Posadeños head for the river beaches of **ITUZAINGÓ**, some 220km east of Corrientes and 90km west of Posadas. Once a quiet little riverside village of some 5000 inhabitants, Ituzaingó grew rapidly with the construction of the nearby Yacyretá Dam, begun in 1983. At the peak of construction in 1986–87, the town's population mushroomed to 22,000. The population has now stabilized at around 15,000 with evidence of the previous surge provided by a rather dreary urban sprawl of low identical buildings which spread eastwards from the town's older centre towards the dam, some 12km to the northeast. On summer weekends, thanks to the influx of day-trippers, Ituzaingó has a lively holidaymaking feel. Outside these times, though, there's little to recommend it as a destination; even if you've a passion for dams, Yacyretá offers a far less dramatic spectacle than Brazil's Itaipu dam (see p.355).

Ituzaingó is, predictably, constructed on a grid pattern around **Plaza San Martín**. The oldest section of town is centred on Calle Centenario, four blocks to the west, which runs from the outskirts of town down to the port. The most central **beaches** lie a couple of blocks north of Plaza San Martín, though the best beach, wide sandy **Playa Soró** lies a couple of kilometres east of town; a frequent local bus runs here from Calle Corrientes. The town's **bus terminal** is on Avenida Centenario, ten blocks south of the port. Diagonally opposite the terminal, on the corner of Centenario and Avenida 9 de Julio, there's a very helpful **tourist office** (daily 8am–1pm & 2–7pm) with extensive lists of the full range of the town's accommodation from camping and *cabañas* to hotels and rooms in family houses. The most agreeable places to stay in town if you're travelling in a group are the **cabañas**, such as *El Balcón* (☎03786/1561-5744; *flialuna@itunet.com.ar*; $80 for six people) on the riverfront at the western end of town, on the corner of Catamarca and Pellegrini, with simple attractively decorated rooms, kitchens and balconies overlooking the river; there's also a swimming pool. There are few **hotels**: the most luxurious is the outwardly grim but comfortably fitted *Hostería Ituzaingó*, on Buenos Aires and Paso de los Pioneros, on the riverfront at the western end of town (☎03786/420577; ④), offering rather dreary but well-equipped rooms with air conditioning and TV. There's also a sun terrace overlooking the river, a swimming pool and a restaurant. More centrally located is the *Hotel Geminis*, at Corrientes 943 (no phone; ② with breakfast), with simple, slightly cramped en-suite rooms.

The Yacyretá Dam

A vast hydroelectric dam stretching between Argentina and Paraguay, the **Yacyretá Dam** is one of the most controversial features of the littoral region. As well as costing billions of dollars to construct, the 1700 square-kilometre reservoir created by the dam has flooded areas as far as 200km upstream and there are plans to relocate inhabitants of low-lying areas of Misiones' capital, Posadas, and of the Paraguayan city of Encarnación. Furthermore, water levels downstream of the dam have become unpredictable, while fish stocks upstream have declined as large species such as dorado seem reluctant to use the "lifts" intended to move them upriver. The project was first planned in the early nineteenth century: a bilateral agreement was signed in 1973 to give the go-ahead and work finally began in 1983, finishing in 1998 when the last of the project's massive twenty turbines was switched on.

Free **guided tours** are offered to the dam – providing little more than a long list of facts and figures and a peek over the side of the dam. The tours depart from the public relations office, on the corner of Ingeniero Carranza and Entre Ríos, about 1.5km east of the bus terminal (☎03786/420050). Tours run from Monday to Saturday at 9am, 11am, 3.15pm and 4.30pm, and on Sunday at 9am and 11am. You must bring a passport, as touring the dam involves crossing the Paraguayan border.

Posadas

If you arrive in **POSADAS** expecting your first taste of the jungle, you'll be sorely disappointed: Misiones' capital is sited on a rather bare patch of land bordering the Paraná, which – bar the red earth – has more in common with northern Corrientes than with the luscious emerald sierras of central and northern Misiones Province. The construction of a road link to Paraguay via the **Puente Roque González de Santa Cruz** in 1980 as well as the town's proximity to the massive Yacyretá Dam have led to a dramatic increase in Posadas' population and some local people lament the loss of a village atmosphere and complain of an increase in crime. It is certainly true that prostitution is a fairly evident phenomenon around Posadas' well-heeled centre at night, whilst contraband is undoubtedly as much a feature of Posadeño life as it is in all border towns, but the place still has far less of an edge to it than you might expect.

The first recorded settlement in the vicinity of modern-day Posadas was the **Jesuit Mission Nuestra Señora de Itapuá**, founded by Roque González de Santa Cruz in 1615. Due to disease, the mission was soon transferred to the Paraguayan side of the river and for the next couple of centuries the settlement progressed little until its strategic position was exploited during the War of the Triple Alliance when, under the name Trinchera San José, the town served as a supply post for Brazilian troops. In 1879 the fledgling city was renamed after **José Gervasio de Posadas**, who, in 1814, had become the first Supreme Director of the Provincias Unidas del Río de la Plata – a title somewhat longer than his reign, which lasted only until January of the following year. On the creation of the new national territory of Misiones in 1881, Posadas was left behind in Corrientes but in 1884 the neighbouring province and the national government were persuaded to redraw the boundaries and Posadas, by far the most important settlement in the region, became Misiones' new capital.

With around 250,000 inhabitants, Posadas is Misiones' most important city and is indeed an important urban centre for neighbouring Paraguay and Brazil as well as Corrientes. As far as tourism goes, it is primarily a **stopover city** and anyone intent on buying postcards of everywhere they go will have their work cut out for them in Posadas. This is not so much because the place is ugly – it's not – but more because it appears to do little to reap any benefit from the modest but nonetheless steady stream of tourists that passes through the town. The city clearly regards itself as a centre for business and administration rather than pleasure and while there's a handful of mildly interesting **museums**, there is little – bar the odd craft shop – specifically aimed at the holidaymaker. That said, Posadas is a pleasant and prosperous city with a lively feel. There are some attractive buildings tucked away among the centre's mostly modern constructions, though the only part of town that could lay a claim to being seriously picturesque is the old road to the port, known as the **Bajada Vieja**. Posadas has recently revamped its costanera, a sign that the city is starting to exploit its location, but if you really want to make the most of the river, you'd be better off heading up the road to San Ignacio, where you can pitch your tent with unbeatable views of the Paraná and the Paraguayan coast. The town hosts a lively provincial festival, known as the **Estudiantina**, which runs over three weekends in September. During the festival local schools prepare and perform dance routines – all with a strong Brazilian influence.

POSADAS

ACCOMMODATION
Andresito Guacurarí	6	Julio César	4	Residencial Colón	5
City Hotel	1	Le Petit	7	Residencial Misiones	3
Colonial	8	Posadas	2		

RESTAURANTS AND BARS
Bahía Bar	E
Del Cielo Pub	D
Glass	F
El Mensú	A
Mentecato	I
El Oriental	J
Los Pinos	B
La Querencia	G
Saint Thomas	C
Sociedad Española	H

Arrival and information

The quiet **airport**, where Posadas' main car rental agencies have stands, is around 7km southwest of the centre; bus #8 will take you right into town from here, or you could take a taxi which will cost around $10. Posadas' **bus terminal** (☎03752/454887 or 454888) is located around 4km south of the centre at the intersection of Avenida Santa Catalina and the RN12. It's a modern building with good facilities but, at the time of writing, no ATM machine. From the terminal there are numerous local buses (including #24, #25 and #21) heading into the centre; the taxi ride will cost about $5.

Posadas' friendly **tourist office**, at Colón 1985 (daily 8am–8pm; ☎03752/447539 or 0800/555-0297), has fairly decent maps of both the town and the province, though it doesn't have an awful lot of information on anything beyond the well-worn Posadas/San Ignacio/Iguazú groove. Be aware, when attempting to locate hotels and the like, that Posadas' streets have recently been renumbered and, confusingly, both systems are still in use. You will generally find that the address will be written as the new number, with the old number in brackets. Either may be used on the building itself. Note also that in Posadas, as in the rest of Argentina's subtropical region, business gets done in the morning: public offices – with the exception of the tourist office – open from 6.30am to 12.30pm, while banking hours are generally from 8am to 1pm.

Accommodation

The majority of people seeking **accommodation** in Posadas are businessmen and, as you would therefore expect, the majority of hotels are expensive and fairly bland. Nonetheless, there are a couple of worthy exceptions as well as a bargain **student hostel**, the *Andresito Guacurarí* at Salta 1743 (☎03752/423850) – a friendly and lively place mostly used for long-term accommodation by students at Posadas' university; there are cooking facilities and two-, three- and four-bed dormitories for $8 per person per night plus one double room with private bathroom for $20. There's also a very upmarket **cabin and camping complex**, *La Aventura*, on the riverbank towards the outskirts of town. Note that Posadas can be extremely hot and sticky during the summer, so you'll need to plan on spending more than your normal budget in order get air conditioning and other such comforts. Alternatively, you could hop over the border to Paraguay where you'll get a lot more for your pesos.

La Aventura, Av. Urquiza and Av. Zapiola ((☎03752/465555; *aventuraclub@arnet.com.ar*). Swish camping and cabin complex on the outskirts of town complete with good recreational facilities – including tennis courts – and a highly rated restaurant. The swimming pool is popular with locals during the summer. Buses #3 and #13 go to La Aventura from the corner of San Lorenzo and Sarmiento.

City, Colón 280 (☎03752/432400). A characterless block slap bang in the city centre – still it's a pretty good deal price wise: the rooms have TV and air conditioning and, from the upper floors, there are good views of the Paraná. ③.

Colonial, Barrufaldi 2419 (☎03752/436149). One of Posada's better hotels; a little off the beaten track in the vicinity of the old bus terminal, but worth making the trek – particularly as there are few comparably priced decent hotels in the centre itself. Includes breakfast, fan, TV and parking. Popular with travelling salesmen so reservations are advisable. ③.

Julio César, Entre Ríos 1951 (☎03752/427930 fax 420599; *hoteljcesar@cpsarg.com*). Posadas' most upmarket hotel – four-star comfort including a swimming pool and gym for only a little more than you pay at the *Posadas Hotel*. ⑥.

Le Petit, Santiago del Estero 1630 (☎03752/436031). Located on a quiet, tree-lined street away from the centre and by far the nicest hotel in its price range, this small, prettily decorated place has light and spacious rooms. Facilities include TV, telephone and air conditioning, and breakfast is provided, too. The friendly owner is also a good source of tourist information. Reservations advisable. ③.

Posadas, Bolívar 1949 (ex 272) (☎03752/440888, fax 430294; *hotelposadas@arnet.com.ar*). Rated as one of Posadas' best hotels, this centrally located place comes with all mod cons – nonetheless the rooms are rather cramped and uninspiring for the price. ⑤.

Residencial Colón, Colón 2169 (ex 485) (☎03752/425085). The *Colón*'s rooms are rather strangely located around the hotel's garage – however it's central, well-kept and perfectly adequate for the price. ③, includes parking.

Residencial Misiones, Félix de Azara 1960 (ex 382) (☎03752/430133). After the student hostel, this is just about the cheapest place in the centre of town: an old-fashioned hotel with rooms around a central patio. The whole family muck in with the running of the hotel and there's a friendly atmosphere, although some of the rooms are in serious need of an overhaul. ②.

The Town

Posadas' town centre is demarcated by four main avenues – Sáenz Peña, Guacurarí, Corrientes and B. Mitre, the last of which leads towards the international bridge. Within this area you will find the majority of hotels and points of interest. Just beyond Guacurarí, Calle Fleming, more commonly known as the **Bajada Vieja**, leads down to the port from where boats still take passengers over to Paraguay (see box on p.334). The main reason for heading further northeast is to visit the **Parque Paraguayo**, where there is a crafts market and the Museo Regional Aníbal Cambas, and the **costanera**, a popular hangout for local youth during the evening.

Plaza 9 de Julio and around

Posadas' central plaza is the **Plaza 9 de Julio**, flanked on San Martín by the early twentieth-century **Iglesia Catedral**, a work by the super-prolific Alejandro Bustillo, who designed Buenos Aires' Banco Nación, among many other buildings. The plaza's best-looking building, however, is the **Casa de Gobierno**, a sugar-pink Rococo construction on Félix de Azara. The building sits perfectly alongside the manicured subtropical splendour of the square itself, where there's a healthy selection of local vegetation, including pindó palms and lapacho, neatly displayed in densely packed flowerbeds which are like little urban squares of jungle. Throughout the town you will find examples of the bright red and yellow chivato tree, originally imported from Madagascar, as well as ficus trees whose enormous leaves provide welcome shade. Posadas' fancy new **municipalidad** is a couple of blocks away on Rivadavia and San Martín.

The city's **commercial centre** is concentrated on the streets to the west of the plaza, with Calle Bolívar in particular forming the hub of the clothes shops that make up much of the town's retail activity. There's usually a huddle of street traders, too, though for a real market atmosphere, you should head for the **mercado paraguayo** (daily 8am–6pm), located towards the port on the intersection of San Martín and Avenida Roque Sáenz Peña. Known locally as **"La Placita"**, this open and indoor market sells a vast range of electrical goods, toys, clothes and shoes, all imported from Paraguay.

A few blocks east of Plaza 9 de Julio, at San Luis 384, you will find the recently reorganized **Museo de Ciencias Naturales e Históricas** (July daily 8am–noon & 3–7pm; rest of year Tues–Fri 7.30am–noon & 2–8pm, Sat & Sun 9am–noon). The museum houses an interesting hotchpotch of local history, from the Jesuits and the Guaraní, the region's original inhabitants, to the colonization of the province in the late nineteenth and early twentieth centuries as well as natural history and ecology – with special reference to locally endangered species such as the yaguaraté, of which only a handful of examples remain in the Parque Uruguai provincial reserve. There is also a tiny **zoo** in the patio, inhabited chiefly by some very inquisitive monkeys, while fans of the slightly morbid will undoubtedly find something of interest in the **serpentarium**: as well as live snakes (principally yararás, the most common cause of snake bites in the province), there are pickled snakes, stuffed spiders and a very lifeless-looking human finger amputated with a machete because of a snake bite. The serpentarium is not all cheap thrills, though – there's also an informative section showing you how to deal with bites and, during July, a demonstration of **snake venom extraction** (Tues–Sun at 10am).

The Parque Paraguayo and the Museo Regional Aníbal Cambas

Some ten blocks northwest of the Plaza 9 de Julio, the small Parque Paraguayo is the location for a **craft market** (daily 8am–noon & 2.30–6.30pm), where you can see examples of Guaraní crafts – in particular basketwork made from local wild cane, and carved wooden animals. The far end of the Parque leads to the Anfiteatro Municipal Antonio Ramírez and, below, to the costanera whilst at the other end, housed in a handsome turn-of-the-century brick building, you will find the **Museo Regional Aníbal Cambas** (Tues–Fri 7.30am–noon & 3–7pm, Sat 9am–noon & 4–7pm, Sun 4–7pm; free) at Alberdi 600, loyally maintained by its friendly staff in the face of a fairly obvious shortage of funds. The museum's particularly unhealthy-looking collection of stuffed and pickled animals is not worth much of your time but there are some interesting and well-labelled exhibits in the **historical and ethnographical** collection, such as objects culled from the ruins of Jesuit missions and artefacts produced by the region's indigenous populations: the Guayaquí, the Chiripá, the Mbyá and the Guaraní. The latter are particularly strongly represented, with a large collection of clay funerary urns, known as *yapepo*, meaning hand-made in Guaraní. There are also a number of musical instruments, notably the *mimby*, a kind of wooden flute which was used by men and the *mimby reta*, similar but much smaller and used by women. The importance of music to the Guaranís is documented as far back as

Alvar Núñez Cabeza de Vaca's first incursion into the Paraná region when he noted that the Indians "received them covered in many-coloured feathers with instruments of war and music". At least one later observer, however, appears to have been unimpressed by the Guaranís' choreographical skills: "the movements of the dance are restricted to a sideways jump with the feet together such that, when the line of men jumps to the right, the line of women jumps in the same way to the left and the dance continues in this way, monotonously, for hours and hours on end." You can reach the museum on local buses, including #4 and #14 from Colón and Catamarca.

Eating and drinking

Bahía Bar, Bolívar 1911. Centrally located café-bar, good for reasonably priced snacks such as hamburgers and *lomos*.

Del Cielo Pub, San Martín between Junín and Ayacucho. Stylish *Del Cielo* is a nice spot to have a beer or a cocktail and does some good sandwiches – try the *lomito árabe*. There are also a couple of pool tables.

Dileto, Bolívar 1929. Sophisticated à la carte restaurant specializing in fish – try the delicious grilled surubí. Also pasta and steaks from about $6. Occasional live music. Closed Mon.

Glass, Corner of Bolívar and Colón. A favourite meeting place for Posadas' older crowd – a fairly traditional café overlooking the plaza and a good place to watch Posadeño life pass by on its evening stroll.

El Mensú, Coronel Reguera and Fleming (☎03752/434826). Regarded by some locals as the best restaurant in Posadas, *El Mensú* specializes in excellent home-made pasta and seafood and has a very good wine-list – plus the bonus of being on the corner of Posadas' prettiest street. Open every evening and midday also at weekends.

Mentecato, San Lorenzo 1971. A popular meeting spot with a lively pavement scene on warm evenings. Good for snacks too.

El Oriental, Junín 2168. Standard Argentine-Chinese restaurant – no great surprises but not a bad choice for a reasonably priced plate of rice or noodle dishes.

Los Pinos, Sarmiento and Buenos Aires. Popular pizza restaurant and confitería with a nice street-corner location. Also does takeaway food.

La Querencia, Bolívar 322. A bustling and stylish place that's a surprisingly good deal – particularly as you can easily share some of the dishes. Try their juicy *bife de chorizo* – shipped in from Buenos Aires as local beef is of poorer quality – and accompany it with fried *mandioca* for a local touch, or go for the excellent *galetos*, a kind of chicken and vegetable kebab. Closed Sun evening.

Saint Thomas, San Martín 1788, on the corner of Félix de Azara. Standard *tenedor libre* offering all you can eat for $7 and catering for vegetarians, carnivores and pasta fans.

Sociedad Española, Córdoba between Colón and Félix de Azara. Very popular lunchtime spot, which is not surprising as the basic two-course menu for $4.50 would possibly feed a small family. There are also more Spanish – and more expensive – dishes available à la carte.

Nightlife

Though it's a small provincial city, Posadas has a thriving **nightlife** which from Thursday to Saturday goes on till around 7am. As usual in Argentina, it's not worth going near a club until the early hours: most places don't open their doors until 1.30am. As well as home-grown rock and *cumbia*, the musical mix usually includes a bit of *marcha* – commercial dance – and Brazilian music, very popular in the littoral region. Prices vary from night to night, ranging from about $3 to $10.

El Ángel, Córdoba 1525. Very trendy and modern new club. Fri & Sat.

Lola, Avenida Corrientes and Centenario. Trendy and popular club, youngish crowd. Thurs, Fri & Sat.

Monterrey, San Lorenzo and San Martín. Large club with huge dancefloor. Pool tables downstairs. Thurs, Fri & Sat.

El Parador, Bolívar 524. Fri & Sat.

Listings

Airlines LAPA in the city (☎03752/426700), at the airport (☎03752/452600); Aerolíneas/Austral in the city (☎03752/435031), at the airport (☎03752/451104).

Banks and exchange The only official place to change travellers' cheques is Mazza Cambio at Bolívar 1932, who charge one percent commission and 25 centavos per cheque. They also change currency at good rates with no commission. There are plenty of banks along calles Bolívar, Félix de Azara and around Plaza 9 de Julio, most of whom will change money at good rates, without commission.

Books There are some excellent local publications – good for information on Misiones' nature reserves and the like – at the Librería Montoya on the corner of Ayacucho and La Rioja, while Liverpool Libros is, as the name suggests, a stockist of English-language books.

Car rental Dollar, Colón 1909 and at the airport (☎03752/435484; *dollar@infovia.com.ar*); Localiza, Colón 1933 and at the airport (☎03752/430901 or central reservations ☎0800/999-2999; *reservas@localiza.com.ar*). Localiza is currently the only car rental firm in Posadas to offer 4WDs.

Pharmacy Corner of Colón and Sarmiento (24hr).

Post office Bolívar and Ayacucho (Mon–Fri 8am–1pm & 2–8pm, Sat 8.30am–12.30pm).

Travel agencies and tour operators Abra Tours, Entre Ríos 1896 (ex 309) (☎03752/422221; *abra@misiones.org.ar*); standard San Ignacio and Iguazú tours as well as more unusual ones to Moconá (around $250 per person with accommodation) or fishing on the Paraná. Guayrá Turismo Alternativo, San Martín 1598, 1st Floor (☎03752/433415; *www.guayra.com.ar*). A new agency run by an enthusiastic young couple who specialize in more alternative tourism, including a visit to the Casa del Viento Verde, a small farm near Oberá, started by the first Japanese immigrant to Misiones.

Around Posadas: the Estancia Santa Inés

The **Estancia Santa Inés** (☎03752/436194, fax 439998 *staines@infovia.com.ar*), just outside Posadas, is run by descendants of Pedro Núñez, partner in the Núñez y Gibaja shipping company, one of the pioneers of the navigation of the Upper Paraná. The impressive outbuildings near the entrance testify to the family's former wealth and the scale of the operation: over a thousand workers were employed, primarily in the cultivation of *yerba mate*, and a private railway line connected up the estancia's extensive lands. The *asecadero* or drying house, from which the dry, slightly sweet smell of *mate* (vaguely similar to henna) emanates, is still in use and you can also visit the family's private chapel, containing handsome Jesuit wood carvings. The *casco* itself appears fairly modest on the outside, though it has a lovely old-fashioned and luxurious interior, but the estancia's trump card is its incredibly exotic setting: there is a mini-jungle just outside the front door where howler monkeys are regularly spotted and, a couple of kilometres away, a huge outdoor pool with a fantastically tall and shady bamboo-grove. You can wander among the *mate* plantations on horseback. Prices range from $25 for an afternoon (with tea) to just over $100 per person for accommodation plus full board (four meals and all activities).

The estancia is just off the RN105 (Km 8.5). Bus #30 from Posadas will leave you at the entrance, 2km from the *casco* – you can arrange for someone from the estancia to pick you up from here if you don't fancy the walk. Reservations for accommodation are essential.

Crossing to Paraguay: Encarnación and Trinidad

Treated by many Posadeños as a local discount store, **ENCARNACIÓN** is somewhat in the shadow of its richer Argentine neighbour. There's nothing on the scale of Ciudad del Este's crime, counterfeiting and consumerism, but Encarnación is still a place very much aware of its role as supplier of bargain goods and has a quite different feel to

MATE

The herby leaves used in making **mate**, Argentina's national beverage, come from an evergreen tree, *Ilex paraguayensis*, a member of the holly family that grows wild or in plantations in northeastern Argentina – especially in Misiones Province, in Uruguay, southern Brazil and Paraguay. Its spring flowers are white and insignificant, but it's the young leaves and buds that are of interest. They're harvested with machetes in the dry southern winter and used to make the *yerba* or *mate* herb. The preparation process for good *yerba* is every bit as complex and subtle as that for Darjeeling: first comes the *zapecado*, literally "opening of the eyes", when the *mate* leaves are dry-roasted over a fire, to prevent fermentation and keep the leaves green. The leaves are then coarsely ground – the *cancheo*, bagged and left to mature for nine months, though this is sometimes artificially accelerated to two months. A milling process results in either coarse *caá-guazú*, or "big herb", or the more refined *caá-mini*. Yerba is sometimes combined with other herbs (*yerva compuesta* or *con palo*), in a mountain blend using *hierbas serranas*, or mountain herbs, or flavoured with lemon essence, spearmint or cinnamon, though all such practices are frowned upon by serious *materos*.

The vessel you drink it out of is also called a *mate*, or *matecito*, originally a hollowed-out gourd of the climbing species *Lagenaria vulgaris*, native to the same region. It's dried, hollowed out and "cured" by macerating *mate* inside it overnight. These gourds are still used to this day and come in two basic shapes: the pear-shaped *poro*, traditionally used for sweet *mate* – some people always add a little sugar, but most cognoscenti disapprove of such things – and the squat, satsuma-shaped *galleta*, meant for *cimarrón*, literally "untamed", the name for unsweetened *mate*. Many *mates* are works of art, sometimes intricately carved or painted, and often made of wood, clay or metal – again, connoisseurs claim gourds impart extra flavour to the brew. *Mates* or *matecitos* make great souvenirs from all over the country, but especially the Northeast. The *bombilla* – originally a reed or stick of bamboo – is the other vital piece of equipment. Most are now straw-shaped tubes of silver, aluminium or tin, flattened at the end on which you suck, and with a bulbous or spoon-shaped protruberance at the other; this is perforated to strain the *mate* as you drink it. Optional extras include the *pava hornillo*, a special kettle that keeps the water at the right temperature. A thermos-flask is the latter-day substitute for this kettle, lovingly clutched by dedicated *materos* and replenished along the way at shops and cafés; "hot water available" signs are a common sight all over Argentina but especially in the littoral region and even more so across the border in Uruguay; a token sum is usually charged for the service.

Posadas. The town's original centre is known as the Zona Baja, a low-lying district down by the river which, since the building of the Yacyretá Dam, is living on borrowed time. It's a crumbling and rather chaotic district, where cut-price clothes spill out from shop fronts and street traders proffer bargains at anyone who looks as if they are there to spend money. There are also cheap electronic goods on offer, though you should be wary of the authenticity of these and buy from the more established businesses: if the deal looks too good to be true, it probably is.

Another good reason to come to Encarnación is to take advantage of much cheaper rates for **accommodation**: there is a clutch of decent hotels in the Zona Alta, of which one of the best is the *Cristal* (☎005971/202371; ②) at Mariscal Estigarribia 1157, whose large rooms, with TV, air conditioning and access to the hotel's swimming pool, are excellent value. There are some real bargain places in the vicinity of the bus terminal, though few of them are exactly inviting; one exception is the German-run *Viena* (☎005971/203486; ①), on P. J. Caballero.

Encarnación is also a useful base for visiting Paraguay's best-preserved **Jesuit ruins** at **Trinidad** (Mon–Sat 7.30–11.30am & 1.30–5.30pm; $1) and nearby **Jesús** (opening hours and entrance fee as Trinidad). Situated some 28km northeast of Encarnación,

---

RIVER CROSSINGS TO PARAGUAY AND BRAZIL

As well as the major road crossings at Posadas, Puerto Iguazú and Bernardo de Irigoyen, various small ferries take foot passengers and cars from towns and villages in Misiones across to the neighbouring countries. Times and availability may change, so it's as well to check before setting out.

TO PARAGUAY

Puerto Rico to Puerto Triunfo in Paraguay (Mon–Fri 8am–5pm, Sat 9–11am & 3–5pm; customs ☎03743/420044)

Puerto Maní to Bella Vista in Paraguay (Mon–Fri 8.30–11.30am & 2–5pm)

Posadas to Encarnación in Paraguay (Mon–Fri 8am–6pm; prefectura ☎03752/425044)

TO BRAZIL

Alba Posse to Porto Mauá (Mon–Fri 8am–11.30pm & 2–5.30pm, Sat & Sun 8–10am & 3.30–5pm; customs ☎03755/482014)

San Javier to Porto Xavier (Mon–Fri 8am–noon & 2–6pm, Sat 9–11am & 3–5pm; customs ☎03754/482000)

El Soberbio to Porto Soberbio in Brazil (Mon–Fri 8–11am & 1.30–5pm, customs ☎03755/495077)

Panambí to Veracruz in Brazil (Mon–Fri 7.30–11am & 1.30–5pm)

Trinidad is one of the most attractive of the Jesuit missions. The ruins occupy perhaps the most beautiful of all the mission sites, atop gently curving slopes from where there are stunning views across a rolling pastoral landscape, quite different from the jungle feel of Argentina's missions. The mission was one of the last to be founded, in 1706, though it grew rapidly and by 1728 Trinidad had a Guaraní population of 4000. The *reducción* raised large numbers of cattle and cultivated sugar and *mate*, whilst its craftsmen were noted producers of musical instruments such as harps and organs, which were exported throughout the region. Despite Trinidad's seemingly exposed site, the *reducción* remains surprisingly complete, with many fine details of **Guaraní Baroque carvings** still clearly visible on the richly hued sandstone walls. Particularly stunning are the ornate pulpit and frescoes within the *reducción*'s central church. Trinidad is little visited, which adds to the site's tranquil atmosphere, one of its most attractive features. **Jesús**, another 12km from Trinidad along a dirt track, is also relatively well-preserved, though the *reducción*, founded in 1685, was not quite such a splendiferous affair as its neighbour – and was in fact unfinished at the time of the Jesuits' expulsion in 1767.

Both Trinidad and Jesús are reached via the RN6, which runs between Encarnación and Ciudad del Este – any bus heading along this road will be able to drop you at Trinidad, while there are a couple of buses daily to Jesús, for those that don't fancy the trek from Trinidad.

Border practicalities

International buses to Encarnación from Posadas can be caught from the bus terminal or from various points in the town, including the corner of calles Ayacucho and La Rioja (every 15min 5.30am–midnight; $2). The journey into Encarnación is a fairly straightforward business; but, although you may be told that you don't need to obtain exit and entrance stamps if you are just visiting Paraguay for the day (and you may get away with it), you'd be well advised to make the effort to get off the bus when leaving and entering in order to put your documents in order. If, as is likely, the bus doesn't wait while you get your passport stamped, don't worry – hang onto your ticket and get back on the next one coming through. The journey back from Encarnación, which stops at various points along Juan León Mallorquín ($1.50 in guaranís or pesos, but not dollars) can be rather slower, as all passengers are required to get off the bus on entering Argentina as customs officials check their purchases. Encarnación's **tourist office** is on the corner of Tomás Romero Pereira and Antequera in the Zona Alta (Mon–Fri 7am–1pm); there is also an information post next to passport control on the bridge, where you may be able to pick up a map before heading into town. Encarnación's bus terminal (☎00 59 5071 202412) is located on the block enclosed by J. Memmel, Cabañas, Carlos Antonio López and Mariscal Estigarribia, Encarnación's principal artery.

The Jesuit Missions

After the *cataratas*, Misiones' major tourist attractions are the **Jesuit Missions** which lie to the north of Posadas. The largest of these, **San Ignacio Miní**, 60km to the north of Posadas, is also the best preserved in the whole of the mission region, which extended beyond the Paraguay and Uruguay rivers to Paraguay and Brazil, and also into the province of Corrientes. Far less well-preserved – and much less visited – are the ruins of **Santa Ana** and **Loreto**, to the south of San Ignacio, though these crumbling monuments, set amongst thick jungle vegetation, have a mysterious appeal of their own.

All three missions can be visited on a day-trip from Posadas, though it's well worth spending more than a day in San Ignacio. As well as the pretty village itself, there's a stunning area of forest and beaches to the southwest of the village with a good campsite and perhaps the finest stretch of river scenery in the whole littoral region. Accommodation is available in San Ignacio and Loreto.

Santa Ana

Heading northeast from Posadas along the RN12, the first mission site you come to, after approximately 40km, is **Santa Ana** (daily 7am–6pm; $1). Originally founded in the Tape region (see box on p.336) in 1633, Santa Ana was refounded, with a population of 2000 Guaranís, on its present site after the *bandeirante* attacks of 1660. At the entrance, accessed via a signposted unsealed road just to the south of the village of Santa Ana, there's a small display detailing the restoration work currently being undertaken at the site, with assistance from the Italian government. Like all the *reducciones*, Santa Ana is centred on a large central square, to the south of which stand the crumbling walls of what was once one of the finest of all Jesuit churches, built by the Italian architect Brazanelli whose body was buried underneath the high altar after his death in 1728. A lot of clearing work has been carried out on the site, yet the roots and branches of trees are still entangled in the reddish sandstone of the buildings around the plaza, offering a glimpse of the way the ruins must have appeared when they were rediscovered in the late nineteenth century. To the north of the church, on the site of the original orchard, you can still make out the water channels from the *reducción*'s sophisticated irrigation system.

Loreto

Some 12km to the north, the ruins of **Loreto** (daily 7am–6pm; $1) are even wilder than those of Santa Ana. This site, founded in 1632, was one of the most important of all the Jesuit missions, housing some six thousand Guaranís by 1733 and noted for its production of cloth and *yerba mate* as well as for having the missions' first printing press. Like Santa Ana, Loreto has a small visitors' centre at its entrance, reached via a six-kilometre

THE JESUIT MISSIONS

Known in Spanish as **reducciones**, the Jesuit missions were largely self-sufficient settlements of Guaraní Indians who lived and worked under the tutelage of a small number of Jesuit priests. The first Jesuit missions in Argentina were established in 1609, some thirty years after the order founded by San Ignacio de Loyola had first arrived in the region. Missions were first established in three separate zones: the **Guayrá**, corresponding to the modern Brazilian state of Paraná, bordered to the west by the Paraná and Iguazú rivers, to the south by the Iguazú and to the east by the sierras which run down Brazil's Atlantic Coast; the **Tapé**, corresponding to the southern Brazilian state of Río Grande do Sul, present-day Misiones Province and part of Corrientes Province; and the **Itatín**, least successful of the regions, lying between the Upper Paraná and the sierras to the north of the modern Paraguayan city of Concepción.

If the Jesuits were essentially engaged in the imperialist project of "civilizing" and converting the natives, they did at least have a particularly enlightened approach to their task – in marked contrast to the harsh, and ultimately unproductive, methods of procuring native labour that were being practised elsewhere in Latin America. Within the missions, work was organized on a co-operative basis, with those who could not work provided for by the rest of the community. Common land was known as *tupambaé*, whilst each family was also provided with a small parcel of land or *abambaé* on which they cultivated crops for their own personal use. Education and culture also played an important part in mission life with Guaranís being taught to read and write not only in Spanish but also in Latin and Guaraní, whilst music and artisanship were actively encouraged. The early growth of the missions was impressive, but then, in 1628 *bandeirantes*, or slave traders from São Paulo in Brazil, attacked, destroying many of the missions, and carrying their inhabitants off into slavery, leading the Jesuits to seek more sheltered areas to the west, away from the Guayrá region in particular. The mission population soon recouped – and then surpassed – its former numbers, and also developed a strong standing army, making it one of the most powerful military forces in the region. By 1650 there were twenty-two missions or *reducciones* in the Upper Paraná region, and thirty by 1700, with a combined population of around 50,000 Guaranís. The early *reducciones* mostly operated on a subsistence basis; however, in 1648, the Crown removed the order's previous exemption from

stretch of unsealed road (impassable after heavy rain) which branches off the RN12. Restoration work here is being carried out with the assistance of the Spanish government. Heading out from the visitors' centre to the *reducción* itself, it's actually difficult at first to work out where the buildings are. After a while, though, you begin to make out the walls and foundations of the settlement, heavily camouflaged by thick vegetation and lichen, upon which tall palms have somewhat fantastically managed to root themselves.

If you fancy staying the night in Loreto, try one of the attractive three-bed **dormitories**, with bathroom and kitchen facilities, available in the building opposite the visitors' centre ($10 per person).

San Ignacio and around

Considering it's home to such a major attraction, **SAN IGNACIO**, 60km northeast of Posadas via the RN12, is a remarkably tranquil place. Away from the huddle of restaurants and souvenir stands around the ruins themselves, the town has little in the way of a tourist infrastructure. There are, however, a number of worthwhile attractions to the southwest of the village.

San Ignacio is laid out on the usual grid pattern; it's a rather long thin shape, dissected east–west by broad Avenida Sarmiento and north–south by Bolívar. The western extremity is bounded by Avenida Horacio Quiroga. Heading south along the avenue for a kilometre or so, you'll come to the **Casa de Horacio Quiroga** (daily

taxes, and the missions began to develop trade with the rest of their territory. Their most important crop proved to be *yerba mate*, which had previously been gathered from the wild but was now grown on plantations for export as far as Chile and Peru; other products sold by the missions included cattle and their hides, sugar, cotton, tobacco, textiles, ceramics and timber. They also exported musical instruments, notably harps and organs from the Reducción de Trinidad in Paraguay.

By the end of the seventeenth century, the *reducciones* were amongst the most populous and successful areas of Argentina, and in the 1680s the Jesuits paid the Portuguese back for the earlier *bandeirante* attacks by sending some three thousand Guaraní soldiers to join forces with Buenos Aires in their attack on the Portuguese city of Colónia do Sacramento on the River Plate's eastern bank. By the 1730s, the larger missions such as Loreto and Yapeyú (see p.322) had over six thousand inhabitants – second only to Buenos Aires. Nonetheless, the mission enterprise was beginning to show cracks: a rising number of epidemics was depleting the population and the Jesuits were becoming the subject of political resentment. Settlers in Paraguay and Corrientes were increasingly bitter at the Jesuit hold over the "supply" of Guaraní labour and also at the Jesuits' domination of the market with Buenos Aires for *yerba mate* and tobacco. These tensions led to the **Comunero Revolt** of the 1720s and 1730s which culminated in a mass military invasion of the missions, followed by famine and kidnappings. Simultaneously, the previous climate of Crown tolerance towards the missions' almost complete autonomy was beginning to change. Secular absolutism became the order of the day with the accession of Ferdinand VI to the Spanish throne in 1746, and the Jesuits' power and loyalty began to be questioned. Local enemies of the missions took advantage of the new climate, claiming both that the Jesuits were hiding valuable silver mines within the *reducciones* and that foreign Jesuit priests were agents of Spain's enemies. In 1750, an exchange treaty between Spain and Portugal was proposed, according to which Spain would give up its most easterly mission in return for Colónia. The Jesuits and Guaranís put up considerable military resistance and the treaty was eventually abandoned in 1759, with the accession of Charles III. The Jesuits' victory proved a double-edged sword, however; the success of their resistance against the Crown only reinforced their image as dangerous rebels and, following earlier expulsions in France, Portugal and Brazil, the Jesuits were expelled from Argentina in 1767.

8am–7pm; $2; ☎03752/470130), a museum to the Uruguayan writer, who made his home here in the early twentieth century. Quiroga first visited the region in 1903 with his fellow writer Leopoldo Lugones, taking some of the first pictures of the then little-known ruins. Quiroga was famed for his rather gothic short stories, of which one of the best collections is *Cuentos de Amor, de Locura y de Muerte*, filled with morbid but entertaining tales of blood-sucking beasts hidden in feather pillows and demented, murderous children. Quiroga moved to San Ignacio in 1910, where the sultry tropical setting further fired his imagination, inspiring stories of sunstroke and giant snakes. The museum is composed of two houses; a replica of the first wooden house built by the writer, containing many of his possessions, including a typewriter, photographs and Quiroga's motorbike and a later stone construction also built by him. Though the buildings are pleasant to wander around themselves, much of the charm of the museum is derived from its wonderful setting, amidst thick vegetation in and out of which scuttle tiny lizards. At the back of the wooden house there's a small swimming pool built by the writer for his second wife (the first committed suicide, as did Quiroga himself in 1937). She later left him and, true to his gothic nature, Quiroga then filled the swimming pool with snakes. A number of the writer's publications are on sale in the small museum shop.

Continuing south past the museum, the unsealed road winds down for another 2km or so to the stunning **Puerto Nuevo** where there's a lovely strip of sandy beach and, best of all, a fantastic view across the curves of the Paraná to the Paraguayan coast – all rolling wooded slopes tumbling down to the water. Many Paraguayans cross daily to San Ignacio to sell produce at the town's market, and towards the end of the day you may see them heading back home in small rowing boats. Camping facilities are available at the beach (see below).

Another enjoyable trip from San Ignacio is to the **Parque Provincial Teyú Cuaré**, some 10km south of the village via a good unsealed road accessed from the southern end of Bolívar. It's a small but stunning park of less than a square kilometre, notable for its golden hued rocky formations, which jut out over the Paraná, and dense vegetation. The name Teyú-Cuaré, meaning "the lizard's cave", refers to a local legend which tells of a giant reptile that inhabited the region, attacking passing boats. Off the coast of the park lie a number of tiny islands, notably the Isla del Barco Hundido, whose name means "the island of the sunken boat". The park's most famous feature is its high rocky cliff, the **Peñón Reina Victoria**, named for its supposed similarity to the profile of the English queen. There is a wild **campsite** within the park.

En route to the park, there's a small **private reserve**, the **Osununú** (☎156-44937), a wonderful wild patch of forest managed by friendly Porota with some fantastic views over the river and islands and to the coast of the Parque Provincial. The reserve can be visited on a day-trip ($1), when horseriding can be arranged; tents can also be pitched and there are a couple of simple rooms to rent in Porota's house ($10 per person; bring food). The two-hour or so walk to Osununú should be avoided at midday as there's no shade en route; a *remise* from San Ignacio will cost around $7.

San Ignacio Miní

The most famous of all the *reducciones*, **San Ignacio Miní** (daily 7am–7pm; $2.50) was originally founded in 1610 in the Guayrá region (see box on p.336) in what is now Brazil. After the *bandeirantes* attacked the mission in 1631, the Jesuits moved southwards for thousands of miles through the jungle, stopping several times en route at various temporary settlements before finally re-establishing the *reducción* on its present site in 1696.

The ruins occupy some six blocks at the northeastern end of the village of San Ignacio: from the bus terminal head east along Avenida Sarmiento for two blocks and turn left onto Rivadavia. Follow Rivadavia, which skirts around the ruins, for six blocks and then turn right onto Alberdi, where you'll find the entrance to the site. At the entrance, there's an excellent **Centro de Interpetación Regional** (times as for site; ☎03752/470186) with a series of themed rooms depicting various aspects of Guaraní and mission life, as well as a detailed maquette of the entire *reducción*. A separate smaller museum contains many loose pieces garnered from the ruins, including decorative bits of walls, ceramic vessels and mortars.

Upon entering the settlement itself, along a wide grassy path, you'll come first to rows of simple *viviendas* or living quarters; a series of six to ten adjoining one-roomed structures, each one of which housed a Guaraní family. Like all the mission settlements, these are constructed in a mixture of basaltic rock and sandstone. Heading between the *viviendas*, you will arrive at the spacious Plaza de Armas, whose emerald grass provides a stunning contrast with the rich red hues of the sandstone. At the southern end of the plaza, and dominating the entire site, stands the magnificent facade of San Ignacio's **church**, designed, like Santa Ana's, by the Italian architect Brazanelli. The roof and much of the interior have long since crumbled away, but two large chunks of wall on either side of the entrance still remain, rising out of the ruins like two great Baroque wings. Though somewhat eroded, many fine details can still be made out: two columns flank either side of the doorway and much of the walls' surface is covered with decorative bas-relief sculpture executed by Guaraní craftsmen; most striking are the pair of angels which face each other high up on either side of the entrance whilst a more austere touch is added by the prominent insignia of the Jesuit order on the right-hand side of the entrance. Sadly, though, the visual impact of this imposing architectural relic has been somewhat diminished by the addition of wooden supports and crude scaffold steps between the two remaining sections.

To the left of the main entrance, you can wander around the **cloisters** and **priests' quarters**, where a number of other fine doorways and carvings remain. Particularly striking is the doorway connecting the cloisters with the church baptistry, flanked by ribbed columns with heavily moulded bases and still retaining a triangular pediment over the arched doorway.

Note that the best light for photographing the church is obtained in the morning, when the low light enhances its deep reddish hue.

Practicalities

Buses to San Ignacio all arrive at the western end of Avenida Sarmiento. It's not a terminal as such, but there's a kiosk here whose friendly owner may agree to look after left luggage for a few hours.

Accommodation options in the town are limited but agreeable. The largest hotel is the *Residencial San Ignacio* (☎03752/470047; ③), on the corner of San Martín and Sarmiento. It's a slick modern place with comfortable en-suite rooms, all with air conditioning. There's also an adjoining restaurant. Eternally popular with foreign travellers on a budget is the *Hospedaje Los Alemanes*, on Avenida Horacio Quiroga, 50m west of the bus terminal (☎03752/470362; $8 per person with shared bathroom). It's a pretty family house with basic but attractive rooms and access to kitchen facilities; tents can also be pitched for $3 per day. The friendly artist and writer couple, Juan and Inés, at San Martín 1291 (☎03752/470164; $10 per person) also sometimes rent a room in their house to foreigners; Juan's colourful geometric paintings inspired by the missions and the surrounding area can also be purchased here. Towards the outskirts of the village, *Hospedaje El Descanso*, at Pellegrini 270, around ten blocks south of the bus terminal (☎03752/470207; $10 per person) offers smart little *cabañas* with private bathrooms. The best **campsite** in town is at the *Club de Pesca y Deportes Acuáticos*, down at Puerto Nuevo (☎03752/1568-3411; $2.50 per tent plus $2 per person); tents can be pitched here on a bluff with an absolutely stunning view over the river and the Paraguayan coast. On Puerto Nuevo's beach itself, tents can be pitched behind the *cantina* ($2.50 per tent plus $1 per person).

Eating and drinking options are even more limited than accommodation; as well as the good restaurant in the *Residencial San Ignacio* there's a clutch of very similar large restaurants geared up for day-trippers around the entrance to the ruins. All of them serve snacks as well as more substantial dishes such as parrilla. One of the most popular is the *Carpa Azul*, with a swimming pool and shower facilities, at Rivadavia 1295.

Oberá and the Saltos de Moconá

East of Santa Ana, the RP103 heads towards the town of **Oberá**, the economic heart of central Misiones, and links the towns strung out along the Río Uruguay with the RN14 and the capital, Posadas. Some 170km to the east, the pretty village of **El Soberbio** lies in one of Misiones' most striking regions; at this border Brazil and Argentina sit like plumped up cushions on either side of the curvaceous Río Uruguay. El Soberbio is the main point of access for Misiones' unusual waterfalls, the **Saltos de Moconá**.

Oberá

OBERÁ, Misiones' second city, is an orderly modern settlement sitting amidst the province's gentle central sierras. The town was first settled in the early twentieth century by Swedish and then Swiss immigrants who had emigrated from their homelands to Brazil but stayed there for less than a generation. Many other nationalities followed, and today Oberá boasts of having fourteen different nationalities amongst its population of 40,000, including Ukrainians, Russians, French and Japanese. Despite a smattering of Russian Orthodox and Ukrainian churches – and Latin America's only Swedish cemetery – you probably wouldn't actually be that aware of Oberá's cosmopolitan mix on a brief visit. During the second week of September, however, the city runs an enjoyable **Fiesta Nacional del Inmigrante**, with a week-long programme of national dances, music and food. The fiesta takes place in the Parque de las Naciones, a large park out on the eastern side of town. The park is mainly notable for its collection of houses representing each of the communities which wear a rather desolate air during week but come to life at the weekend, when many of them open as restaurants, serving national dishes.

The fiesta aside, Oberá is a pretty unremarkable place, but its location does make it a useful **transport hub** for travellers moving between the west and east sides of Misiones, or following the scenic RN14 to or from Iguazú. There are good bus connections here to El Soberbio, Posadas, Santa Ana and Puerto Iguazú. The town also has one of Misiones' most attractive campsites just outside town at **Salto Berrondo**.

It's easy to find your way around town: the bus terminal lies just one block west of the wide Avenida Sarmiento which runs through the centre of town roughly north to south. Running diagonally east from Avenida Sarmiento, Avenida Libertad heads out towards the RN14. At the intersection of Avenida Sarmiento and Avenida Libertad stands the very austere modern Gothic **Iglesia San Antonio**, a pristine white church whose rather curious electronic chime is an insistent presence in the town centre. Two blocks southeast of the terminal there's Oberá's central square, the quiet and grassy **Plaza San Martín** which, unusually, is bereft of either a municipalidad (Oberá's is on the corner of Jujuy and Avenida Sarmiento) or a church. In the evening, there's more life around Plazoleta Güemes, which lies in front of the Iglesia San Antonio.

Eight blocks or so to the southeast of Plaza San Martín, the **Jardín de los Pájaros Wendlinger**, on the corner of Haití and Díaz de Solís, is a private collection of around two hundred species of birds including toucans and parrots – all kept in slightly cramped and shadeless conditions. There's also an **serpentarium** on the corner of La Paz and Villaguay, around twenty blocks southwest of the town centre along Avenida Sarmiento (Mon–Sat 8am–noon) where numerous snakes and spiders are kept and there are demonstrations of the extraction of Croxotin, used as a cure for cancer.

Practicalities

Oberá's **bus terminal** is right in the centre of town on the corner of José Ingenieros and G. Barreiro. There are toilets, left-luggage facilities and a rather dingy waiting room, though for a really offbeat way to kill time between buses, there's also a Museo de Ciencias Naturales (Mon–Fri 6.30am–noon & 1–7pm, Sat 7am–noon; free) with a particularly gruesome collection of stuffed and pickled animals including a two-headed cow from Santa Fe. The motheaten and insalubrious birds in particular make the "do not touch" signs somewhat superfluous. The **tourist office** is on the corner of Avenida Libertad and Entre Ríos, a couple of blocks east of the terminal (Mon–Sat 8am–9pm; ☎03755/421808; *mo@obernet.com.ar*); the very helpful staff can usually demonstrate the town's cosmopolitan roots by ringing around for interpreters when non-Spanish speaking foreigners turn up. **Internet** access is available at *Vital Informática*, Santa Fe 75 (*www.vitalinformatica.com.ar*; $5 hour).

Accommodation in Oberá is adequate but – with a couple of exceptions – a little on the drab side. Many commercial travellers pass through the town, meaning that accommodation is more likely to be booked up during the week than at weekends. The nicest place to stay in town is the *Miriam*, at Chaco 162 (☎03755/421626; ②), three blocks north of the bus terminal. It has three very attractively furnished rooms, including one exceptionally large triple with a spacious balcony. Breakfast ($2) is served on the pretty patio downstairs. Next best is the *Residencial Sewald*, at Chaco 300 (☎03755/421602; ③), a modern one-storey annexe to a family house, with modest but clean and pleasant rooms, all with private bathroom and fan. Parking is included. The most upmarket place in Oberá is the *Cabañas del Parque*, out in the Parque de las Naciones, on the corner of Ucrania and Tronador (☎03755/426000; ⑤). Looking more like suburban villas than typical *cabañas*, the *Cabañas del Parque* make up for their rather dreary exterior with rustic but comfortable interiors equipped with such luxuries as minibars, air conditioning, cable TV and telephone. There's also a large swimming pool in the grounds. One block west of the terminal, the very basic but friendly *Hospedaje Residencial Internacional*, at José Ingenieros 121 (☎03755/421796; $7 per person) has rather shabby rooms with no fan and shared bathroom, grouped around a central courtyard. There's a handful of midrange hotels around the town centre, all very similar in style with modern, slightly boxlike rooms, all with private bathrooms: try the *Hotel Vito I*, at Corrientes 56 (☎03755/421892; ②); the *Cuatro Pinos*, Avenida Sarmiento 853 (☎03755/425102; ②); or the *Premier*, 9 de Julio 1164 (☎03755/426171; ③). There's also an exceptionally well-maintained but pleasingly natural **campsite** at Salto Berrondo, 6km west of town along the RP103 towards Posadas ($2 entrance, plus $3 per tent; sometime free during quiet periods). The campsite's chief attraction is a gorgeous **waterfall**, the Salto Berrondo, which tumbles down into a lovely shady natural bathing pool. There's also an artificial swimming pool and a barbecue area and plenty of room to pitch your tent in picturesque surroundings. Local **buses** marked "Guaraní" or "Cementerio" go to Salto Berrondo, as do long-distance buses towards Posadas.

As far as eating goes, there's an exceptionally good Brazilian-style buffet **restaurant**, *New Vinicius*, on the corner of Avenida Sarmiento and Salta, with a cool, spotless interior and plenty of fresh salads as well as meat, fish and pasta. On the corner of Entre Ríos and 9 de Julio, *Juan Alfredo* offers good steaks, pastas and *milanesas* while the best parrillada is to be had out at Km 9 along the RN14, at *Los Troncos*, which does a *tenedor libre* for $5 a head.

The Saltos de Moconá

One of Argentina's strangest sights, the **Saltos de Moconá** are made up of nearly 3km of immensely powerful waterfalls which spill down the middle of the Río Uruguay, tumbling from a raised river-bed in Argentina into a 90-metre river canyon in Brazil. The falls – the longest in the world of this kind – are formed by the meeting of the Uruguay and Pepirí-Guazú rivers just upstream of a dramatic gorge. As the waters encounter this geological quirk, they once again "split", with one branch flowing on downstream along the western side of the gorge and one branch plunging down into the gorge. This phenomenon is visible only under certain conditions: if water levels are low, all the water is diverted into the gorge whilst if water levels are high the river evens itself out. Somewhere in between, however, the Saltos magically emerge as water from the higher level cascades down into the gorge running alongside, creating a curtain of rushing water between three and thirteen metres high. The incredible force of the water as it hurtles over the edge of the gorge before continuing downstream is perhaps best measured by its name – *moconá* in Guaraní means "he who swallows everything".

The Saltos de Moconá lie just over 80km northeast of the village of **El Soberbio**, via an unsealed road, and can be visited from both the Argentine and Brazilian (where the falls are known as Yucumã) sides. As with Iguazú the best view is from Brazil, although both excursions have their attractions – the Argentinian trip winning out in the adventure stakes. The first 40km of the Argentinian trip takes you through tobacco plantations and communities of Polish and German immigrants clustered around numerous simple wooden Lutheran, Adventist and Evangelical churches. Like many of Misiones' immigrants, the Poles and Germans of this region arrived in Argentina via Brazil and many of them use Portuguese as their first language. Despite the incredible lushness of this landscape, this is a region afflicted by considerable poverty, and the local small farmers carry out much of their work using old-fashioned narrow wooden carts, pulled by oxen. Various side-trips can be made en route, including to the **Salto El Paraíso**, 40km from El Soberbio, a gentle waterfall with swimming spots and camping facilities (see below) and to the simple **perfume distilleries** (*alambiques*) where locals extract essential oils – in particular the intensely lemon-scented citronella but also lemongrass and mint – from native plants.

Forty kilometres from El Soberbio the road strikes into the heart of an area of secondary forest, the last stretch of which is protected as the **Parque Provincial Moconá**. A small park of just 10 square kilometres, the Parque Provincial Moconá was created in 1988. As yet, little work has been done on registering the park's flora and fauna; sighted species of birds include the condor and the peculiarly noisy bare-throated bell bird. It also seems likely that the park is one of the last refuges of the rare yaguareté, whose presence has indeed been registered on the Brazilian side of the park. After 43km, you arrive at the *guardaparques'* post, from where there are a number of short trails through the forest. A trail of just over a kilometre leads to the edge of the Río Uruguay, from where – accompanied by a *guardaparque* or local guide and conditions permitting – you can embark on an adventurous wade across some 300m of knee-high water to reach the edge of the falls and peer up and down the length of the gorge.

The Brazilian trip (undertaken with an organised tour, see below) begins with a short river crossing from El Soberbio to **Porto Soberbo** – a one-horse town composed of little more than a dusty main street and a large general store selling everything from Guaraná, Brazil's national soft drink, to cowboy hats and tools. There are approximately 90km of mostly unsealed road between here and the falls – a bit of a bone-shaking but fascinating ride. The road curves up and down hills through wheat, manioc and soya fields, punctuated by tiny picturesque communities of blue and pink, or turquoise and red wooden houses, before arriving at the **Parque Estadual do Turvo**, just north of the town of **Derrubadas**. Created in 1947, the Brazilian park is far larger than its Argentine counterpart (its total extension is 17,491 hectares) and surveys of its wildlife have confirmed the presence of the rare yaguareté, the capuchín monkey, the tapir and over two hundred species of birds, including various different toucans. From the park entrance, 15km of unsealed road winds down through jungle before reaching the river where you traverse a wide bed of reddish-brown rock which takes you to within metres of the falls. A word of warning: by the time you reach the falls it will probably be around noon and the stretch of exposed rock can get very hot – remember to take some protection from the sun. Take a swimming costume, too – although you should never bathe in the river itself, due to incredibly strong currents, there are some lovely rocky pools on the Brazilian side of the river.

Practicalities

Before setting out for the Saltos, you should check the state of the river with the *gendarmes* who maintain a post nearby (☎03755/441001). Though the road is negotiable in good weather in an ordinary car, a 4WD is certainly preferable and the only option for periods when sections of the road are flooded. In any case, before setting out you should check with locals in El Soberbio as to the condition of the road and for precise directions as the Saltos are not signposted. If you are prepared to hang around in El Soberbio for a few days, it may be possible to catch a lift to the falls; vehicles do travel regularly to and from the site, taking provisions and sometimes school parties. **Transport** can also be arranged via the hostel within the park (see below). The easiest – if most expensive – option is to travel with an **organized tour**: a growing number of companies in Posadas and Puerto Iguazú are offering packages to the falls, though the pioneer in this field is Ruli Cabral, who manages the *Hostería Puesto del Sol* in El Soberbio (see below). Ruli organizes trips to both the Brazilian and Argentinian side of the falls, each taking the best part of a day and costing $180 per person for groups of one to three and $60 for groups of more than three people.

Within the Parque Provincial itself, just a few kilometres south of the Saltos, there is an excellent **hostel** and **campsite**, the *Complejo Turístico Moconá Naturaleza y Aventura* (☎ & fax 03751/470022; *jharriet@eldorado.dataco22.com.ar*) with six large dormitory rooms for $14 per person and pitches for $3 per tent. Tents can also be rented for $5 per person. The hostel can organize pick-ups from either El Soberbio or San Pedro, around 90km to the north of the Saltos via the unsealed RP21. The cost of a round trip (transport to hostel only) for a group of up to five people is around $60.

El Soberbio

The main gateway to the Saltos de Moconá, **EL SOBERBIO** lies perched on the banks of the Río Uruguay, some 170km east of Oberá, via the RN14 to San Vicente and then the RP13. The village's charm is derived not so much from its buildings, which are unassuming modern constructions, but from its gorgeously undulating setting, amidst lush sierras. There's also an intriguing **mix of cultures** – with sunburnt blond-haired Polish and German immigrants rubbing shoulders with Argentines of Spanish and Italian descent, all with a hefty dose of Brazilian culture thrown in. Locals have a refreshingly cavalier attitude to the idea of national boundaries, popping over to Brazil for Saturday-night dances and listening to Brazilian *música sertaneja* or *gaúcha* – infectious country music with a Brazilian swing – on the radio.

The town's **layout** is pretty easy to come to terms with: **Avenida Rivadavia** runs into town from the northwest and terminates at the small **ferry terminal** (for departures to Brazil see box on p.334) down on El Soberbio's riverfront. In the centre of the village, a few blocks back from the river, **Avenida San Martín** crosses Avenida Rivadavia and leads north towards the Saltos. A large grassy **plaza** lies at the intersection of these two streets.

El Soberbio's extremely modest **bus terminal** – little more than a corrugated-iron roof next to a bar – is right in the centre of town at the intersection of Avenida San Martín and Avenida Rivadavia. There's a sporadically open **tourist information** kiosk on Avenida Rivadavia as you head into town (☎03755/495133; ask for Miriam Dombrowski), and a handful of pretty decent places to stay. Pick of the **accommodation** is the *Hostería Puesto del Sol*, sited high above the village at the southern end of Calle Suipacha (☎03755/495161; ④). The large and attractively rustic rooms have French windows opening onto a veranda from where there are great views over the valley and the river. There's also a lovely outdoor pool and an outside bar/restaurant serving excellent home-cooked food for around $10 a head (also open to non-residents). Breakfast is included in the price. Make sure you bring a torch as the road down to the village is unlit at night. Down in the centre, on Avenida Rivadavia just east of the bus terminal, there's the modest *Hospedaje Rivadavia* (☎03755/495099; $8 per person), largely frequented by long-distance bus drivers and offering clean, functional rooms with private bathrooms. At Av. San Martín 800, on the way out towards the Saltos, you'll find the *Hostería Saltos del Moconá* (☎03755/495116; *www.hsm.ojb.net*; $15 per person) offering fairly plain but comfortable *cabañas* for up to four people. There's a good municipal **campsite**, *La Plata*, around 3km northwest of town off the RP13 towards San Vicente. Located on a lovely riverside spot, the site has toilets, electricity and barbecue facilities and costs around $3 per tent plus $0.50 per person. Forty kilometres out along the road to the Saltos, you can pitch your tent alongside the waterfall Salto El Paraíso, for a $2 entrance fee; there are as yet no facilities so bring all provisions. The Salto can be reached via local Empresa Juan bus on Tuesdays and Thursdays or on the daily bus to Puerto Paraíso from where it's an eight-kilometre walk.

There is one **bank** in El Soberbio, a sub-branch of the Banco Macro Misiones, but it has very restricted opening hours (Tues & Thurs 4–6pm), so you should bring enough money to cover all your expenses and avoid bringing large denomination notes since change always seems to be in short supply.

Iguazú Falls and around

Poor Niagara!

Eleanor Roosevelt

Composed of 250 separate falls and straddling the Argentina/Brazil border, the **Iguazú Falls**, or *cataratas*, as they are known in Argentina, are quite simply the world's most dramatic waterfalls. Set amongst the exotic subtropical forests of the **Parque Nacional Iguazú** in Argentina, and the **Parque Nacional do Iguaçu** in Brazil, the falls tumble for some 2km from the Río Iguazú superior over a cliff to the Río Iguazú inferior below. At their heart is the dizzying **Garganta del Diablo**, a powerhouse display of natural forces in which 70m of water per second hurtle over a semicircle of rock into the boiling river canyon below.

The first Europeans to encounter the falls were an expedition of Spaniards led by Cabeza de Vaca in 1542, who named them the Saltos de Santa María. Cabeza de Vaca had disembarked in Santa Catalina (Brazil) in order to investigate possible land and river links with the recently founded city of Asunción in modern-day Paraguay. Until the early twentieth century, however, the falls remained practically forgotten in this remote corner of Argentina. Tourism began to arrive in the early twentieth century, encouraged by the then governor of Misiones, Juan J. Lanusse. The first hotel was constructed in 1922, right by the falls, and by the mid-twentieth century Iguazú was firmly on the tourist map. Today the falls are one of Latin America's major tourist attractions with around 500,000 visitors a year entering the Argentine park and around twice that number entering the Brazilian park.

The falls are not the only attraction in the parks, though. The surrounding subtropical **forest** is packed with exotic animals, birds and insects and opportunities for spotting at least some of them are good. Even on the busy catwalks and paths that skirt the edges of the falls you've a good chance of seeing gorgeously hued bright blue butterflies as big as your hand and – on the Brazilian side – you will undoubtedly be pestered for food by greedy coatis. For a real close-up encounter with the parks' varied wildlife, though, head for the superb **Sendero Macuco**, a tranquil nature trail which winds through the forest on the Argentine side of the park. Commonly spotted species along here include various species of toucans, with their fantastically gaudy bills, and shy capuchin monkeys.

Conventionally, March to November is regarded as the **best time to visit** the park, when temperatures are not too high – although the combination of steamy heat, intense blue skies and sparkling spray in summer has a pretty undeniable appeal too. The rainy season runs from May to July, so you've a good chance of getting wet at this time, though the falls are at their most spectacular after heavy rain. Easter and July are best avoided if possible since around three thousand visitors a day visit the park at these peak times. The falls are worth visiting at any time of year, though; the only time in recent history when they've been known seriously to disappoint was in 1978 when the

Sheraton Hotel was opened within the park to coincide with Argentina's staging of the World Cup and visitors from all over the world were to be treated to a sight of the falls. However, most unco-operatively, the falls chose this time to dry up completely, following a severe drought in Brazil. Whenever you visit, you should allow yourself a few days' leeway to be sure of taking in the park's highpoint, the Garganta del Diablo, since if there is either too much or too little water then boats are unable to approach the viewing platform.

Unless you camp or stay in a hotel within the park (both Brazil and Argentina have one luxury hotel each in their respective parks), and discounting the inconvenient and slightly risky Paraguayan city of Ciudad del Este, there are two towns at which you can base yourself. On the Argentinian side, **Puerto Iguazú** lies approximately 18km northwest of the park and has a slightly sleepy small-town feel, whilst on the Brazilian side the much larger modern city of **Foz do Iguaçu** is some 20km northwest of the Brazilian entrance to the park. There are pros and cons of staying in both places. If you've been travelling for a while in Argentina then the novelty factor of staying in Brazil might win out: Foz is neither the most beautiful nor most exotic of Brazilian cities, but it'll still give you the chance to hear a different language, try some different food and sample some lively nightlife. On the negative side, there's undoubtedly more crime in Foz – this tends to be exaggerated by Argentinians but nonetheless you should be on your guard in the city. Puerto Iguazú, on the other hand, is a very low-key town, verging on the dull, but with a tranquil and largely secure atmosphere which belies both its proximity to such a major tourist attraction and its location in an area rife with corruption and contraband.

The Falls and the Parque Nacional Iguazú

The vast majority of the **Iguazú Falls** lie on the Argentine side of the border, within the Parque Nacional Iguazú. This side offers the most extensive experience of the falls, thanks to its well thought out system of trails and catwalks taking you both below and above them – most notably to the Garganta del Diablo. The surrounding forest also offers excellent opportunities to discover the region's wildlife. To round off your trip to Iguazú, however, you should also visit the Brazilian side. Though it offers a more passive experience of the falls, the view from here is more panoramic and photography opportunities are excellent.

The Parque Nacional Iguazú lies 18km southeast of Puerto Iguazú, along RN12. A bus runs to the park every hour from the bus terminal in town with the first one leaving at 7.30am and the last one returning at 8pm. The bus ($4 return) stops at the entrance to the park, where you have to get off and pay an entrance fee of $5, before it leaves you at the visitors' centre. To visit the Brazilian side, you will need to cross via the Ponte Presidente Tancredo Neves, the bridge that crosses the Río Iguazú between the two towns. There are international buses (companies Pluma, El Práctico, Itaipú and Nuestra Señora de Asunción) every 45mins from Puerto Iguazú to Foz do Iguaçu between about 6.20am and 7pm. Immigration formalities take place on the Brazilian side of the bridge, where you are given first an exit stamp for Argentina and are then stamped into Brazil. Standard wisdom amongst many travellers is that it's unnecessary to get either exit and entry stamps or visas when travelling between Argentina and Brazil for the day. However, the official line is that everyone, apart from Argentinians, Brazilians and Paraguayans, must acquire the necessary stamps and visas, even if crossing the border for only a few hours. In practice you may well get away without these formalities, but you're also setting yourself up for possible problems and it's worth taking the trouble to get stamped in and out. If you do cross several times between the two countries, make sure that you are given enough days when returning to Argentina to continue your journey as passport control frequently gives only thirty days here.

Once in Brazil, you can join the Brazilian Cataratas bus by getting off just east of immigration on the Brazilian side on Avenida das Cataras, the access road to the falls, but it's more straightforward (if slightly more time-consuming) to head into Foz itself and get on the bus there (see p.348). You'll need a small supply of the Brazilian currency, the *real*, both for the Brazilian Cataratas bus and for entrance to the park itself. Change can be obtained from the Micki kiosk in Puerto Iguazú's bus terminal or from various kiosks at Foz's terminal. There's also a change facility and an ATM machine just before the Brazilian entrance to the park. Note that at certain times of the year, Brazil may be one hour ahead of Argentina – don't forget to take this time difference into account, as it could be vital for making sure you catch the last bus back into town (7pm from park to Foz).

The Argentine side

Without a doubt, the best place to begin your tour of Iguazú is on the **Argentine side**. As you get off the bus within the park, you're greeted by the sound of rushing water from the falls, the first of which lies just a few hundred metres away. There's a **visitor centre** to the left of the bus-stop, where you can pick up maps and information leaflets. There's also a small but interesting museum here with photographs and stuffed examples of the park's wildlife. From the visitor centre, two well-signposted trails take you along a series of catwalks and paths past the falls. The best approach is probably to tackle the **Paseo Superior** first, a short trail which takes you through forest along the top of the first few waterfalls. For more drama, head along the **Paseo Inferior**, which winds down through the forest before taking you to within metres of some of the smaller but still spectacular falls – notably **Saltos Ramírez** and **Bosetti** – which run along the western side of the river. Around the falls, look out for the swallow-like *vencejo*, a remarkable small bird which, seemingly impossibly, makes its nest behind the gushing torrents of water. As you descend the path, gaps in the vegetation offer great views across the falls: photo opportunities are so numerous that you might want to remind yourself every now and then to put your camera down and just enjoy the experience of looking and listening to the falls. Even better, plan two days at the falls and spend just one of them looking round, returning to record the experience on film. Note that new catwalks have made **wheelchair access** possible to all of the Paseo Superior and much of the Paseo Inferior, although there is little room to turn round in many sections.

Along the lower reaches of the paseo, a regular free boat service leaves for **Isla San Martín**, a gorgeous high rocky island which sits in the middle of the river. Trails again take you round the island, through thick vegetation and past emerald green pools. There's a small sandy beach at the northern end of the island, though bathing here is permitted only in summer. From the departure point to Isla San Martín, Iguazú Jungle Explorer (☎03757/421600) also offers short **boat trips** taking you up close to the falls ($15), where the crew take special delight in getting you really soaked – though this impromptu shower is not quite compensation for the rather cursory nature of the excursion. The same company, which maintains an information post near the visitor centre, also organizes longer excursions combining jeep trips through the forest with boat trips along the rapids north of the falls.

To visit the **Garganta del Diablo**, you must return to the visitor centre and pick up the Cataratas bus (hourly, last bus 5.05pm; $1) for Puerto Canoas, some 4km southeast. From Puerto Canoas – so called because the first tourists used to make the trip to the edge of the Garganta by canoe – launches ($4) take you to the remains of a catwalk which ran all the way between the mainland and the Garganta before being destroyed by floods. Once on the catwalk, a small viewing platform takes you to within just a few metres of the staggering, sheer drop of water formed by the union of several immensely powerful falls around a kind of horseshoe. As the water crashes over the edge, it plunges into an dazzling opaque whiteness in which it is impossible to distinguish mist from water. If you're bringing your camera, make sure you've a bag to stash it away in as the platform is invariably showered with a fine spray from the falls. Once back on the mainland, you can simply return via the same bus, though a more interesting alternative if you have a few pesos left over is via one of the rowing boats that head back along the Río Iguazú Superior ($5). The 45-minute trip downstream offers a very different view of the river, passing through tranquil waters fringed with forest where, if you're lucky, you may even spot a caiman slipping into the water.

Heading west from the visitor centre, a well-marked trail leads to the start of the **Sendero Macuco**, a four-kilometre nature trail down to the lower banks of the Río

Iguazú, past a waterfall, the **Salto Arrechea** where there is a lovely secluded bathing spot. The majority of the trail is along level ground, through a dense area of forest. Despite appearances, this is not virgin forest. In fact, it is in a process of recuperation: advances in the navigation of the Upper Paraná – the section of the river that runs along the northern border of Corrientes and Misiones – in the early twentieth century allowed access to these previously impenetrable lands and economic exploitation of their valuable timber began. In the 1920s, the region was totally exploited and stripped of its best species and traversed by roads. Only since the creation of the park in 1943 has the forest been protected, allowing for the flourishing of species which can now be seen.

Today, it is composed of several layers of vegetation. Towering above the forest floor is the rare and imposing palo rosa, which can grow to some 40m and is identifiable by its pale straight trunk which divides into twisting branches higher up, topped by bushy foliage. At a lower level, various species of palm flourish, notably the pindó palm and the palmito, much coveted for its edible core, which often grows in the shade of the palo rosa. Epiphytes, which use the taller trees for support but are not parasitic, also abound as well as the guaypoy, aptly known as the strangler fig, since it eventually asphyxiates the trees around which it grows. You will also see lianas, which hang from the trees in incredibly regular plaits and have apt popular names such as *escalera de mono*, or "monkey's ladder". Closer still to the ground there is a stratum of shrubs, some of them with edible fruit, such as the pitanga, commonly used for fruit juice in Brazil. Ground cover is dominated by various fern species.

The best time to spot wildlife is either early evening or late afternoon, when there are fewer visitors and the jungle's numerous birds and mammals are at their most active: at times the screech of birds and monkeys can be almost cacophonic. At all times, you have the best chance of seeing wildlife by treading as silently as possible along the path, and by scanning the surrounding trees for signs of movement. Your most likely reward for quietness and vigilance will be groups of agile capuchin monkeys, with a distinctive black "cowl", like that of the monks they are named after. A rarer sight are the larger and lumbering black howler monkeys, though their deep growl can be heard for some distance. Along the ground, look out for the tiny corzuela deer. Unfortunately, you've little chance of seeing the park's most dramatic wildlife, large cats such as the puma and the jaguar or the rather doleful-looking tapir, a large-hoofed mammal with a short, flexible snout. Toucans, however, are commonly spotted; other birds that can be seen in the forest include the solitary black cacique, which makes its nest in the pindó palm, using the tree's fibrous leaves; various species of woodpecker and the striking crested yacutinga. Of the forest's many butterflies, the most striking are those of the *morphidae* family, whose large wings are a dazzling metallic blue.

The Brazilian side

You'll only need a few hours on the **Brazilian side**, but it's one of the best spots around the falls for photography – particularly in the morning – and provides you with a superb panorama of the points you will have visited in Argentina. The Parque Nacional do Iguazú lies around 20km southeast of Foz do Iguaçu. Buses stop at the entrance to the park, where an entrance fee of around $3 is payable (in *reals* only), before dropping you just outside the *Hotel das Cataratas* (see p.354). From here a walkway takes you high along the side of the river; it is punctuated by various viewing platforms from where you can take in most of the Argentine falls, the river canyon and the Isla San Martín. Along the path, stripe-tailed coatis accost visitors, begging for food. The 1.5km path culminates in a spectacular walkway which offers fantastic views of the Garganta del Diablo and of the Brazilian Santo Salto Maria, beneath the viewing platform and surrounded by an almost continuous rainbow created by myriad water droplets. Watch out for spray here and carry a plastic bag to protect your camera. At the end of the walkway you can take an elevator ($1) to the top of a cliff for more good views.

From a point opposite the hotel, **helicopter flights** are offered over the falls (7min, $60, minimum three passengers). The view from the helicopters is of course superb, but they're a noisy and intrusive presence in the surrounding area and seriously disruptive to the local wildlife: Argentina has banned the helicopters from flying over its side of the falls. A less controversial excursion is offered by Macuco Safari de Barco (☎045/574-4244), which maintains an information post inside the park, 3km north of the falls area. The hour-and-a-half excursion combines a jeep trip through the forest, followed by a short walk and a boat trip onto the rapids of the lower river area.

If you've not been lucky enough to see some of Iguazú's exotic birds at the falls themselves, head for the **Parque Das Aves**, 300m north of the park entrance (daily 8.30am–6.30pm; ☎045/523-1007; *www.foz-tropicana.com.br*), where walk-through aviaries allow for close encounters with some of the most stunning of them. The first of these is populated with various smaller species such as the noisy bare-throated bellbird, with a weird resonant call, the bright blue sugar bird and the blue-black grosbeak. For most people, though, the highlight is the bold and colourful toucans – almost comically keen to have their photo taken.

Puerto Iguazú

PUERTO IGUAZÚ is a strange kind of place. Potentially it's a far more attractive town to base yourself than Foz – its tropical vegetation and quiet streets seem more in keeping with the region than the high-rise concrete of the Brazilian city. Yet while the town's tranquil atmosphere provides a restful contrast to the goings-on just over the border, Puerto Iguazú really lacks anything that would make you want to stay there any longer than necessary. Consequently few tourists seem to do anything more than move between hotel, restaurant and bus terminal and the town wears a slightly resigned air. That said, it has a certain simple charm which can grow on you, and of the three border towns, Puerto Iguazú is the only one to have a really secure and accessible riverfront area from which you can take in the surrounding panorama.

Arrival and information

Puerto Iguazú's international **airport** lies around 20km southeast of the town, along the RN12 just past the entrance to the park. Aristóbulo del Valle (☎03757/420298) runs a bus service between the airport and the bus terminal. The **bus terminal** is on the corner of Avenida Córdoba and Calle Misiones; there's no official tourist information kiosk here, though there are plenty of private companies who tout for your custom as you get off the bus. The most helpful of the numerous kiosks offering **information** is probably the friendly *Agencia Noelia* (☎03757/422722) which also sells the tickets for the bus to the national park. There's a good restaurant in the terminal, a *locutorio* and a **left-luggage** service ($2 large bag, $1 small bag) which opens from 7am to 9pm; if you need to pick your bag up later, arrange with staff to collect the key for the luggage deposit from the toilet attendant.

Puerto Iguazú's **tourist office** is at Av. Aguirre 311 (Mon–Fri 7am–1pm & 2–8pm; Sat & Sun 8am–noon & 4–8pm; ☎03757/420800). They've very little in the way of printed matter, though, other than a pretty schematic map and unless you're attended to by a particularly helpful member of staff it's not a very useful port of call: most answers to practical transport and accommodation queries can be answered by the kiosks in the terminal. For more detailed information on the national park, its development and wildlife, there's a good library, the NEA at Av. Tres Fronteras (Mon–Fri 8am–4pm).

Accommodation

Puerto Iguazú has a good range of fairly priced **accommodation**, with some particularly good deals at the cheaper end of the price range. The greatest concentration of

ACCOMMODATION
La Cabaña	1
Hostería Los Helechos	6
Hostería San Fernando	2
Libertador	3
Residencial Bompland	4
Residencial Lilian	7
Residencial Noelia	8
Residencial Uno	9
Saint George	5

RESTAURANTS AND BARS
La Barranca	A
Blanco Paraiso	D
Charo	G
Jardín Iguazú	C
Pizza Color	E
Tío Querido	B
Las Vegas	F

hotels is around the bus terminal and this is certainly the most convenient area to stay for catching the bus to the falls as well as over the border to Brazil. There are also plenty of restaurants in this area. There are a couple of good options in the town centre proper, too, and some more luxurious hotels on the road out towards the national park. Reservations are a good idea at any time of year if you want to be sure of getting your first choice – during high season (July and Easter) they're a must. Note that you may get a better deal at some of the more expensive hotels by booking a package (with flight) from a travel agency in Buenos Aires. The best organized **campsite** is the large and well-equipped *Camping Viejo Americano* (☎03757/420190; $4 per tent, plus $4 per person), about 5km out of town along the RN12 towards the national park, with showers, provisions store, telephone and swimming pool. The campsite can be reached on the Cataratas bus or by taxi (around $3 from terminal). Within the park itself, there is a wild campsite, the *Camping Ñandú*, metres from Puerto Canoas. The site is not very well-publicized by the park authorities – and you are expected to notify the *guardaparques* if you plan on staying there. There are toilets at the nearby confitería but bring water, food and torches as well as insect repellent.

Hostería Los Helechos, Calle Paulino Amarante 76 (☎ & fax 03757/420338). Slick and well-maintained hotel on a quiet street near the bus terminal. Small but attractive rooms with TV and air conditioning. Excellent buffet breakfast with tropical fruit. Small swimming pool. ②.

Hostería San Fernando, Av. Córdoba and Guaraní (☎03757/421429). Friendly hotel right opposite the bus terminal. Simple, pleasant rooms all with fan. Breakfast included. ②.

Hotel Cataratas, RN12, at Km 4 (☎03757/421100; *www.fun.net/hoteis/cataratas-ar*). Spacious and quietly luxurious hotel on the way to the *cataratas*. Large outdoor swimming pool and small gym. Attractive rooms with big comfortable beds. ⑦.

Iguazú Grand Hotel, RN12, at Km 1640 (☎03757/498050; *juanfperesbreton@usa.net*). This is the place to stay for film-star glamour – a fabulously luxurious hotel with enormous suites supplied with everything from CD players to glossy picture books on Misiones. Landscaped outdoor pool and two very good restaurants. Weekends are reserved for high-rolling gamblers whom the hotel flies in from São Paulo and Buenos Aires to play at the adjoining casino. ⑨.

La Cabaña, Av. Tres Fronteras 434 (☎03757/420564; *lacabana@hostels.org.ar*). Quiet motel-style hotel affiliated to Hostelling International with comfortable if slightly musty rooms. $12 per person with HI card.

Residencial Bompland, Bompland 33 (☎03757/420965). Best budget choice in the centre of town; a simple but well-maintained and friendly hotel. All rooms with private bathroom and fan. Parking included. Good singles deals. ①.

Residencial Lilian, Fray Luis Beltrán 183 (☎03757/420968). Spotless light and airy rooms with good fans and modern bathrooms. ②.

Residencial Noelia, Fray Luis Beltrán 119 (☎03757/420729). Best deal in Iguazú, a friendly, family-run place largely catering to backpackers. Scrupulously maintained three- and four-bed rooms with fans and private bathroom and breakfast of toast, fruit and coffee brought to your room or the shady patio outside. $6 per person.

Residencial Uno, Fray Luis Beltrán 116 (☎03757/420529; *www.albergueuno.com*). Friendly if slightly down-at-heel youth hostel (affiliated to Hostelling International) with 75 dormitory beds and one double room for $20. Communal cooking and washing facilities. Check for curfew times as there have been reports of travellers being locked out at night. $8 per person.

Saint George, Av. Córdoba 148 (☎03757/420633). Best of Iguazú's mid-range hotels, a recently revamped and courteous hotel with some exceptionally light and attractive first-floor rooms with balconies overlooking the swimming pool. Good restaurant downstairs and buffet breakfast with fresh fruit included in room rate. ③.

Sheraton International Iguazú, Parque Nacional Iguazú (☎03757/420296; *www.iguazufalls.com*). Big, ugly modern hotel inside the national park – the crime of its construction compounded by the fact that you get a decent view of the falls from only a few of its rooms (for which you pay more). ⑦, ⑧ with view.

The Town

A small town of around 30,000 inhabitants, Puerto Iguazú sits high above the meeting of the Río Paraná and the Río Iguazú, at Argentina's most northern extremity. The town is bisected diagonally by **Avenida Victoria Aguirre** (named after one of the first tourists to the region, who donated $3000 for the construction of the first catwalk to the falls), which runs from Puerto Iguazú's modest **port** out towards RN12 and the national park.

You wouldn't exactly call Iguazú's **town centre** bustling, but most of what goes on goes on around the intersection of Avenida Aguirre, Calle Brasil and Calle Ingeniero Gustavo Eppens. From this intersection the Avenida Tres Fronteras runs west for some one and a half kilometres to the **Hito Tres Fronteras**, a vantage point over the rivers with views over to Brazil and Paraguay and marked by an obelisk painted in the colours of the Argentine flag. An alternative route to the Hito is via Avenida Aguirre, which forks right just before the town's triangular grassy plaza. From here, Avenida Aguirre snakes down through a thickly wooded area of town to the port area. You can then follow the pleasant Avenida Costanera, popular with joggers and cyclists and with fitness stations en route, left uphill towards the Hito.

Puerto Iguazú has a slightly unusual attraction on the outskirts of town. Some 4km along the RN12 towards the park, rustic signposts direct you to **La Aripuca** (8am–sunset; ☎03757/423488). An *aripuca* is an indigenous wooden trap used in the region to catch birds and La Aripuca is a giant replica of the trap, standing some 10m high and constructed out of 29 different species of trees native to Misiones Province (all obtained through unavoidable felling or victims of thunderstorms). Above all, La Aripuca is a kind of eco-symbol: the friendly German- and English-speaking family who constructed this strange monument hope to change visitors' conscience about the environment through educational tours designed to explain the value and significance of these trees. There are also plans to organize trips to the agricultural colony of Andresito, 60km east of Iguazú, and to run an adopt-a-tree programme.

Eating, drinking and nightlife

Puerto Iguazú doesn't have a particularly exciting range of **restaurants** and most of them seem fond of regaling customers with either television or live music – possibly to drown out the lack of atmosphere. Most of the better places to eat are grouped near the bus terminal. The *Jardín Iguazú*, on the corner of Avenida Misiones and Córdoba (daily 7am–1am), must be one of Argentina's better terminal restaurants, serving a mixture of parrillada, fish, Chinese food and fast food. The friendly staff are also pretty good at whipping up a quick takeaway sandwich for customers rushing for a bus. Iguazú's not the best place in Argentina for meat but there's reasonably priced parrillada in *Charo*, at Av. Córdoba 106, and *Tío Querido*, next door to the *Libertador* hotel on Calle Bompland; both restaurants also offer grilled river fish. There's a good restaurant inside the *Hotel Saint George*, offering a $6 *menú turístico*. The bright and modern *Pizza Color*, at Av. Córdoba 135, does excellent *pizza a la piedra* and good salads. The rather strange and clinical *Las Vegas Café*, at Av. V. Aguirre 250, nearly always seems to be empty but it's okay for a beer and fast food and has Internet access. You won't miss *Blanco Paraíso*, on Avenida Aguirre just south of the intersection with Calle Brasil: music from the *cumbia* bands that play nightly outside the restaurant dominates the centre of Iguazú. It's not a bad place to sit outside for a beer, though the food is rather overpriced.

For **drinking** and **nightlife**, the choice is even more limited – indeed many locals head over to Brazil for a good night out. There's a handful of bar-cum-nightclubs on Calle Brasil just before the junction with Aguirre; *Lautaro* has pool tables and a bar outside and upstairs there's a disco playing a cross section of music for a mostly young, local crowd. There's an older, more relaxed crowd at *La Barranca* pub along the Avenida Río Iguazú, just east of the Hito Tres Fronteras, a welcoming bar with good views over the river to Brazil and Paraguay and live music on Friday and Saturday nights – usually folk or Brazilian music. Iguazú's **casino**, along the RN12, is popular with locals and well worth visiting (☎03757/498000): even if you don't gamble you can pass the time in the large bar area and upstairs there are live bands, including some good Brazilian music. The casino also operates a free taxi service for customers to and from town.

Listings

Airlines Aerolíneas/Austral, Corner of Av. Aguirre and B. Brañas (☎03757/420168) and at the airport (☎03757/420915); LAPA, corner of Bompland and Perito Moreno (☎03757/422175).

Banks and exchange There are only two ATMs in Puerto Iguazú: at the Banco Macro Misiones, Av. Aguirre 330, and inside the Telecentro on Av. Aguirre and Calle Brasil. The only place to change travellers' cheques is Argecam, Av. Aguirre 562 (daily 7am–6.30pm; ☎03757/420273), which charges five percent commission and requires proof of purchase as well as a passport. You can also change travellers' cheques at Libres Cambio, on the Argentinian side of the international bridge, next to customs (daily 7.30am–10pm; ☎03757/422354).

Car rental Ansa International Rent a Car, *Hotel Esturión*, Av. Tres Fronteras 650 (☎03757/420100); Localiza, Av. Aguirre 271 (☎03757/422744); VIP Rent a Car, Av. Aguirre 211 (☎03757/420289).

Consulates Brazil, Av. Guaraní 70 (Mon–Fri 8am–2pm; ☎03757/421348).

Internet *Cafetería Las Vegas* and upstairs at Av. Victoria Aguirre 240 (*www.interiguazu.com.ar*).

Laundry Lava Rap Ljuba, corner of Misiones and Bompland.

Post office Puerto Iguazú's main post office is at Av. San Martín 780, though there's a more convenient branch inside the Telecabinas on the corner of Av. Aguirre and Calle Brasil.

Taxis Remises Centro, Gustavo Eppens 210 (☎03757/420907); Agencia Remise la Estrella, Av. Córdoba 42 (☎03757/423500).

Telephones There is a *locutorio* in the bus terminal and in the town centre there's Telecabinas on the corner of Av. Victoria Aguirre and Calle Brasil.

Tours and travel agents Sol Iguazú Turismo, Av. Aguirre 316 (☎03757/421147); Turismo Dick, Av. Aguirre 226 (☎03757/420778; *turismodick@interiguazu.com.ar*); Cuenca del Plata, Calle Paulino Amarante 76 (☎03757/421062; *cuencadelplata@fnn.net*); Caracol, Av. Victoria Aguirre 653

(☎03757/420064; *caracol.turismo@foznet.com.br*) and Aguas Grandes, Mariano Moreno 58 (☎03757/421140; *aguasgrandes@interiguazu.com.ar*) with French-, English- and Italian-speaking guides.

Foz do Iguaçu and around

A modern city, **FOZ DO IGUAÇU** faces its Argentine counterpart, Puerto Iguazú, across the Río Iguazú and is separated from the Paraguayan city of Ciudad del Este, 7km northwest across the Río Paraná, by the Ponte da Amizade bridge. Up until the Seventies, Foz had only around 30,000 inhabitants but its population soared with the construction of the Itaipu Dam (see p.355), reaching 150,000 by 1985. Today, the city has around 250,000 inhabitants and though the dam is still an important source of employment, the vast majority of the city's inhabitants are involved in tourism. But as well as servicing the hundreds of thousands of tourists who pass through the city on their way to the falls, Foz gains a lot of business as a retail outlet for Argentinians and Brazilians in search of bargain clothes and shoes. The town's growth is evident around the city's sprawling outskirts and in its scattering of high-rise buildings, but the city centre remains a fairly modest and compact area.

Foz is laid out on a fairly regular grid, with the main access route from Argentina being via the Avenida das Cataratas which heads into town from the southeast, joining up with Avenida Jorge Schimmelpfeng, off which the town's main drag, Avenida Juscelino Kubitschek (often referred to as Avenida JK – *jota ka*) runs northwards towards

Paraguay. The main shopping centre, where you'll also find plenty of banks, is Avenida Brasil, which runs parallel to Avenida Juscelino Kubitschek, one block to the east.

You'll hear a lot about the supposed danger of visiting Foz on the Argentinian side, but the central area around the local bus terminal and shops is relatively safe during the day, and the vast majority of the people are welcoming and friendly in a way that belies the volume of tourists they are accustomed to dealing with. You should, however, avoid heading down to the river below the bus terminal, where there is a shanty town.

Practicalities

Foz's local **bus terminal**, the arrival point for buses from Argentina, is at the intersection of Avenida Juscelino Kubitschek and Avenida República Argentina. From here, Transbalan buses leave approximately every forty minutes for the falls, (7am–6pm). The city centre is easy to walk around, though a taxi isn't a bad idea at night if you feel at all cautious. Be warned, though, that taxis are relatively expensive here. Foz's **tourist information** service is vastly superior to that of Puerto Iguazú, with excellent maps, transport information and accommodation listings doled out by friendly and helpful staff. There are various offices throughout the town; the Secretaria is at Rua Almirante Barroso 1300 (Mon–Fri 8am–noon & 4–6pm; ☎(00 55) 45/574-2196; *www.fozdoiguaçu.pr.gov.br*), while there is a 24-hour office on the corner of Rua Rio Branco and Avenida Juscelino Kubitschek.

Accommodation, ranging from campsites and youth hostels to five-star hotels, is abundant in Foz and, if the Brazilian *real* continues to fall, extremely good value. Close to the terminal, the decent *Hotel del Rey* at Rua Tarobá 1020 (☎(0055)45/523-2027; $18) offers clean, uncluttered en-suite rooms with good air conditioning and a tiny outdoor swimming pool. An excellent buffet breakfast is included. Favoured by backpackers, the *Pousada da Laura* at Rua Naipi 629 (☎(0055)45/574-3628; $10 per person) offers a friendly family atmosphere and simple rooms on a quiet street a few blocks southwest of the terminal. There's a good youth hostel, the *Paudimar*, at Rua Rui Barbosa 634 (☎(0055)45/574-5503; *paudimarcentro@fnn.com.br*; $10 per person with breakfast) in a converted hotel very near to the local bus terminal. It's a secure and very friendly place with hotel-style bedrooms, a kitchen and Internet facilities. The owners have arranged with local police so that travellers staying in the hostel can go out without a passport by showing one of the hostel's business cards. On Rua Xavier da Silva 1000 (☎(0055)45/572-4450; ②), the modern *Foz Presidente* has spacious rooms with big comfortable beds and an attractive outdoor swimming pool and sunbathing area. The fabulous *Hotel das Cataratas* (☎(0055)45/521-7000; *gegctr@tropicalhotel.com.br*, ⑦), inside the park itself, just metres from the falls, is a charming old building, with cool tiled floors and elegantly decorated rooms, which packs in all the style that the *Sheraton* on the Argentinian side lacks. There's a great outdoor swimming pool and an excellent restaurant. For **camping**, the excellent *Camping Club do Brasil* (☎(0055)45/574-1310; $10 per person) has a swimming pool, restaurant and laundry area, set in attractive forested grounds.

There are plenty of inexpensive buffet-style **restaurants** along Rua Marechal Deodoro. All along the route out to *cataratas*, there are various *churrascarias*, Brazil's version of the parrilla, specializing in *espeto corrido*, in which hunks of meat are carved onto your plate by waiters who pass from table to table. If you've been travelling for a while in Argentina, though, you're less likely to be impressed by the meat, much of it from the zebu – a kind of humped ox, originally from India, and far less appetizing than Argentina's famed beef – than by the buffet accompaniment of fresh salads, rice, beans and plantain. A typical example is *Rafain*, on Avenida das Cataratas, Km 6.5. The one real gastronomic highpoint in Foz is provided by the *Tempero da Bahia* at Av. Paraná 1419 (evenings only), which specializes in the exquisite cuisine of northeastern Brazil, with dishes such as *moqueca de peixe*, a delicious fish stew, flavoured with palm oil and coconut milk, and spicy *acarajé*, a fried bean mix with shrimp and hot pepper. There's outside seating overlooking a quiet street and excellent live Brazilian guitar music every night.

Itaipu Dam

Lying 10km north of Foz, the **Itaipu Dam** (*www.itaipu.gov.br*) is the world's largest hydroelectric project. Work began on the dam in 1974 and was completed in 1991 at the cost of $25 billion dollars and with the flooding of large areas upstream through the creation of a 1350 square-kilometre reservoir. Though it's a joint project between Paraguay and Brazil, Brazil uses the vast majority of the power generated by the Itaipu's eighteen generators.

Free **guided tours** (Mon–Fri 6 daily; 1hr) can be taken of the dam: it's true to say that once you've seen one dam you've seen them all – but if you're going to see one dam, you might as well make it Itaipu. The vast concrete edifice spanning the Río Paraná is so huge it's almost impossible to judge scale when you stand before it. Just as bewildering are the comparisons touted in the project's information leaflets: the amount of concrete used in the building of the dam is apparently enough to build 210 Maracana stadiums or a motorway from Lisbon to Moscow.

Buses #110 or #120 from Tancredo Neves (opposite the bus terminal) go to Itaipu – a journey of roughly fifteen minutes. If you go with a package tour then you will stay on your own bus to visit the dam; if you arrive independently you will be assigned to a bus.

travel details

Local buses

Colón to: Buenos Aires (12 daily; 5hr 30min); Concordia (9 daily; 2hr 15min); Corrientes (2 daily; 10hr); Córdoba (1 daily, not Wed; 11hr); Gualeguaychú (8 daily; 2hr); Paraná (9 daily; 5hr); Paso de los Libres (4 daily; 6hr); Rosario (1 daily, not Sat; 8hr); Santa Fe (6 daily; 6hr).

Concepción del Uruguay to: Buenos Aires (12 daily; 7hr 30min); Colón (24 daily; 45min); Concordia (2 daily; 3hr); Córdoba (Wed, Fri & Sun 1 daily; 10hr); Paraná (2 daily; 5hr); Paso de los Libres (3 daily; 6hr).

Concordia to: Buenos Aires (30 daily; 6hr); Córdoba (2 daily; 10hr); Corrientes (5 daily; 8hr); Iguazú (1 daily; 11hr); Paraná (15 daily; 4hr); Paso de los Libres (5 daily; 4hr).

Corrientes to: Buenos Aires (6 daily; 12hr); Concordia (1 daily; 8hr); Córdoba (1 daily; 14hr); Goya (6 daily; 3hr); Itatí (10 daily; 2hr); Ituzaingó (2 daily; 4hr); Paso de la Patria (18 daily; 1hr); Paso de los Libres (6 daily; 6hr); Posadas (9 daily; 5hr); Puerto Iguazú (1 daily; 10hr); Rosario (3 daily; 10hr).

Gualeguaychú to: Buenos Aires (21 daily; 3hr 30min); Colón (8 daily; 2hr); Concepción del Uruguay (1 daily; 1hr 15min); Concordia (6 daily; 4hr); Córdoba (1 daily; 7hr); Corrientes (3 daily; 12hr); Paraná (7 daily; 5hr); Rosario (4–5 daily; 8hr); Santa Fe (5 daily; 6hr).

Itá-Ibaté to: Corrientes (10 daily; 2hr 30min); Posadas (10 daily; 2hr 30min).

Ituzaingó to: Buenos Aires (6 daily; 13hr); Corrientes (13 daily; 4hr); Itá-Ibaté (6 daily; 1hr 30min); Posadas (20 daily; 1hr 20min).

Mercedes to: Buenos Aires (10 daily; 10hr); Corrientes (14 daily; 3hr); Goya (2 daily; 3hr); Paso de los Libres (4 daily; 2hr); Posadas (3 daily; 4hr); Resistencia (6 daily; 3hr 30min).

Oberá to: Alba Posse (5 daily; 1hr 30min); Bernardo de Irigoyen (1 daily; 5 hr 30min); Buenos Aires (3 daily; 14–16hr); El Soberbio (3 daily; 4 hr); Panambí (10 daily; 1hr); Posadas (36 daily; 1hr 30min); Puerto Iguazú (2 daily; 5hr 30min via the RN12 or 7hr 30min via the RN14); Resistencia (1 daily; 6hr 20min); Rosario (1 daily; 17hr); San Javier (3 daily; 1hr 45min).

Paraná to: Buenos Aires (30 daily; 7hr); Concordia (18 daily; 4hr); Córdoba (22 daily; 6hr); Corrientes (3 daily; 8hr); Diamante (every 30 min; 1hr); Paso de los Libres (5 daily; 6hr); Posadas (7 daily; 10hr); Puerto Iguazú (3 daily; 14hr); Rosario (25 daily; 3hr); Santa Fe (every 20 min; 50min).

Paso de los Libres to: Buenos Aires (15 daily; 9hr); Mercedes (4 daily; 2hr); Posadas (5 daily; 5hr); Puerto Iguazú (1 daily; 11hr); Yapeyú (5 daily; 1hr).

La Paz to: Paraná (5 daily; 2hr 30min).

Posadas to: Alba Posse (1 daily; 3hr); Bernardo de Irigoyen (1 daily; 5hr 30min); Buenos Aires (15 daily; 12hr 30min–14hr); Córdoba (5 daily; 15hr 30min–17hr 30min); Corrientes (2 daily; 5hr); El Soberbio (7 daily; 4hr 30min); Formosa (1 daily;

7hr); Goya (1 daily; 6hr 30min); Ituzaingó (20 daily; 1hr 20min); La Plata (6 daily; 13hr 30min); Oberá (15 daily; 1hr 30min); Panambí (1 daily; 3hr); Paso de los Libres (3 daily; 6hr); Puerto Iguazú (20 daily; 6hr); Resistencia (12 daily; 5hr 30min); Rosario (5 daily; 14hr); San Javier (14 daily 2hr 30min); Santo Tomé (2 daily; 2hr 15min); Tucumán (3 daily; 18hr).

Puerto Iguazú to: Buenos Aires (7 daily; 14hr 30min–19hr); Córdoba (2 daily; 22hr); Corrientes (1 daily; 10hr); La Plata (2 daily; 21hr); Oberá (2 daily; 5hr 30min via the RN12 or 7hr 30min via the RN14); Posadas (20 daily; 6hr); Rosario (Mon & Sat 1 daily; 18hr); Tucumán (1 daily; 24hr).

Rosario to: Buenos Aires (over 50 daily; 4hr); Concordia (3 daily; 7hr 30min); Córdoba (40 daily; 6hr); Corrientes (7 daily; 10–12hr); Resistencia (17 daily; 8–10hr); Posadas (5 daily; 15hr); Puerto Iguazú (1 daily; 18hr); Salta (9 daily; 16hr); Tucumán (24 daily; 12hr).

San Ignacio to: Posadas (9 daily; 1hr); Puerto Iguazú (13 daily; 5hr).

Santa Fe to: Buenos Aires (30 daily; 6hr); Cayastá (14 daily; 1hr 30min); Concordia (9 daily; 4hr 30min); Córdoba (21 daily; 5hr); La Gallareta (1 daily; 4hr 40min); Posadas (8 daily; 14hr); Puerto Iguazú (2 daily; 20hr); Resistencia (15 daily; 7hr); Rosario (5.30am–11pm hourly; 2hr 20min).

El Soberbio to: Posadas (7 daily; 4hr 30min).

Villa Paranacito to: Buenos Aires (20 daily; 2hr) Gualeguaychú (4 daily; 2hr).

International buses

Colón to: Paysandú, Uruguay (Mon–Sat 5 daily; Sun 2 daily; 1hr).

Concepción del Uruguay to: Paysandú, Uruguay (3 daily; 1hr).

Concordia to: Salto, Uruguay (Mon–Fri 4 daily; 1hr).

Corrientes to: Asunción, Paraguay (3 daily; 5hr).

Gualeguaychú to: Fray Bentos, Uruguay (Mon–Fri 5 daily; 1hr).

Posadas to: Asunción, Paraguay (1 daily; 6hr 45min).

Planes

Concordia to: Buenos Aires (2 daily; 1hr).

Corrientes to: Buenos Aires (3 daily; 1hr 20min); Posadas (Sun 1 daily; 45min).

Goya to: Buenos Aires (1 daily; 1hr 50min).

Paraná to: Buenos Aires (Mon–Fri 3 daily, Sat 1 daily, Sun 4 daily; 1hr).

Paso de los Libres to: Buenos Aires (Mon, Wed & Fri 2 daily; 1hr 25min).

Posadas to: Buenos Aires (Mon, Wed, Fri & Sun 5 daily, Tues & Thurs 4 daily, Sat 3 daily; 1hr 30min); Puerto Iguazú (Sun 1 daily; 35min); Resistencia (1 daily; 45min).

Puerto Iguazú to: Buenos Aires (5 daily; 1hr 50min); Córdoba via Buenos Aires (1 daily; 3hr 20min).

Rosario to: Bariloche (1 daily; 3hr 30min); Buenos Aires (7–10 daily; 50min); Córdoba (4–6 daily; 1hr); Mendoza (2 daily; 2hr 30min); Neuquén (1 daily; 3hr 20min); Salta (1 daily; 2hr 40min–4hr 20min); Tucumán (1 daily; 2hr 30min–3hr 30min).

Santa Fe to: Bariloche (1 daily; 5hr 30min); Buenos Aires (Mon–Fri 5 daily, Sat 2 daily, Sun 1 daily; 50min); Catamarca (1 daily; 4hr 30min); Córdoba (1 daily; 2hr); Rioja (1 daily; 3hr 50min); Mendoza (1 daily; 4hr); Río Cuarto (1 daily; 3hr 20min); Rosario (1 daily; 20min); Salta (1 daily; 4hr 15min); Santa Rosa, La Pampa (1 daily; 4hr 50min); Tucumán (1 daily; 4hr 10min).

CHAPTER FIVE

THE GRAN CHACO

One of Argentina's forgotten corners, the **Chaco** area in the central north of the country is a region of seemingly unending alluvial plains, covered with dry thornscrub in the west, and subtropical vegetation and palm savannah in the humid east. For those whose interest lies in classic sight-based tourism, the Chaco is an area to be crossed fast: it has little in the way of dramatic scenery, no impressive historical monuments, and the tourist infrastructure is not good – this is one of Argentina's poorest regions. Those with a specialist interest in **wildlife**, however, will find it more rewarding. In the sizeable remaining sectors not cleared for agriculture, it harbours an exceptional diversity of flora and fauna (see pp.718–729), making it worth your while to break your journey for a day or two as you cross the region. Here, adventurous nature lovers stand a genuine chance of sighting animals such as the capybara, caiman, howler monkey and perhaps even a giant anteater or a puma. Don't be fooled, though, by vast lists of elusive, endangered mammals pumped out by the reserves in their tourist literature – only the very luckiest or most patient observers will see a jaguar, maned wolf, giant armadillo, or mirikiná (nocturnal monkey). **Bird-watchers** should fare better: over 334 types of bird species have been recorded in the dry chaco; and **fishermen**, too, come from all over the world in search of sport fish such as the powerful dorado.

The **Gran Chaco** is the geographical term used to refer to the vast flatlands, over a million square kilometres in area, that cover the central watershed of Latin America, lying partly in eastern Bolivia and southwestern Brazil, but predominantly in western Paraguay and the central north of Argentina. In Argentina, it encompasses the heartland provinces of Formosa and Chaco, dealt with in this chapter; much of Santiago del Estero; the north of Santa Fe; and the eastern lowland slice of Salta – collectively sometimes referred to as the Gran Chaco Argentino. Three types of habitat characterize the Gran Chaco Argentino: low-lying **montane chaco** (*chaco serrano*), confined mainly to a transitional zone along parts of the southwestern fringe; and the two environments emblematic of the uniformly flat heartland, referred to normally as **wet chaco** (*chaco húmedo*) and **dry chaco** (*chaco seco*), although transitional areas exist between the two.

Wet chaco scenery is found near the major river systems of the Río Paraguay and the Río Paraná in the east, where the soils are rich in clay and rainfall can be as high as 1200mm a year, causing heavy flooding at times. It is characterized by palm savannahs;

ACCOMMODATION PRICE CODES

The price codes used for accommodation throughout this chapter refer to the cheapest rate for a double room in high season. Single travellers will only occasionally pay half the double-room rate; nearer two thirds is the norm and some places will expect you to pay the full rate. Note that in resort towns, there are considerable discounts out of season.

① $20 or less	④ $45–60	⑦ $100–150
② $20–30	⑤ $60–80	⑧ $150–200
③ $30–45	⑥ $80–100	⑨ Over $200

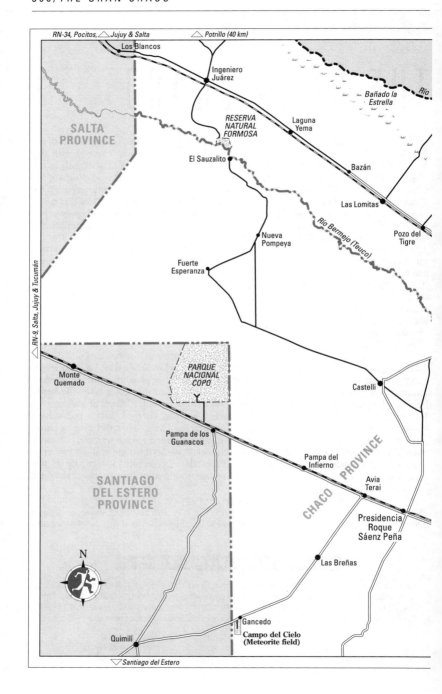

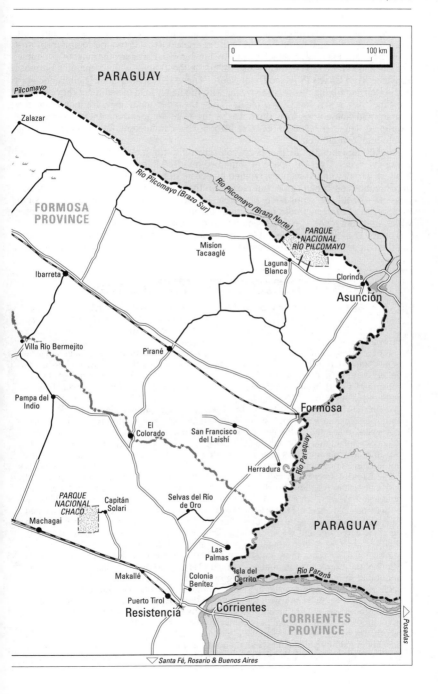

PARAGUAY

Pilcomayo

Zalazar

FORMOSA
PROVINCE

Río Pilcomayo (Brazo Sur)

Río Pilcomayo (Brazo Norte)

Misíon
Tacaaglé

PARQUE
NACIONAL
RÍO PILCOMAYO

Laguna
Blanca

Clorinda

Ibarreta

Asunción

Villa Río Bermejito

Pirané

Pampa del
Indio

Formosa

El
Colorado

San Francisco
del Laishí

Río Paraguay

Herradura

PARQUE
NACIONAL
CHACO

Capitán
Solari

Selvas del Río
de Oro

Machagai

PARAGUAY

Las
Palmas

Makallé

Colonia
Benítez

Isla del
Cerrito

Río Paraná

Puerto Tirol

Resistencia

Corrientes

CORRIENTES
PROVINCE

Posadas

Santa Fé, Rosario & Buenos Aires

0   100 km

remnant patches of riverine jungle; and plantations of sugar cane, soya, and fruit. Narrow strips are also found bordering the main rivers that cross the region from west to east: the Río Pilcomayo, which forms the border with Paraguay for most of its course; and the less erratic Río Bermejo – also called the Río Teuco – which separates Formosa Province from Chaco Province to the south. These rivers, after a fairly energetic start in the Bolivian highlands, seem to weary with the heavy load of sediment they carry by the time they reach the Chaco plains. They meander tortuously, frequently change course, and sometimes lose their way entirely. In some places they dissipate into swamps called *esteros* and *bañados*, or lagoons that can become saline in certain areas due to high evaporation.

Rainfall dimishes the further west you travel into the interior from the Paraná and Paraguay rivers. Over the space of some two hundred kilometres, the habitat gradually alters into dry chaco scenery, typified by dense thornscrub which is utilized to graze hardy, zebu-crossbreed cattle, but cleared in those areas where irrigation has made it possible to cultivate crops such as cotton. Historically, this zone was known to white explorers as *El Impenetrable*, less because of the thornscrub than for the lack of water, which only indigenous groups seemed to know how to overcome.

The RN11 is the region's most important artery, heading north from Santa Fe, joining the two provincial capitals, **Resistencia** in Chaco Province and **Formosa**, capital of

---

INDIGENOUS GROUPS OF THE CHACO

The Chaco is still home to several **indigenous cultures**, each with their own language and rich oral traditions. The main groups are the Komlek, the Mocoví, the Pilagá and the Wichí, with Chorote and Chulupí communities living in the eastern fringe of Salta Province. As in other colonized countries, missionary activity has tended to result in the loss of native systems of religion, although syncretic elements of folklore and superstition often underlie these groups' differing Christian faiths. Essentially, though these people wear Western dress, their way of thinking is often fundamentally different from consumerist Western society, viewing behaviour such as the amassing of personal goods as highly destructive of the well-being of the community. All indigenous groups face pressing social problems after having been treated as second-class citizens by the authorities for years, although some of these issues are being addressed by aid projects in certain areas such as the far northwest of Formosa. Rates of tuberculosis, venereal infections, infant mortality and chagas disease (see p.31) are some of the country's highest. In recent years, efforts have been made to provide bilingual education in schools, but funding is poor and results patchy.

The **Komlek** (frequently called **Toba**) came from the Guaraní group of peoples, and with a population of some fifty thousand they are one of the most numerous of the area's indigenous groups, living mainly in the central eastern band of Chaco Province, but also in Formosa Province, northern Santa Fe, and small communities in Salta Province and Buenos Aires. They took to the horse after contact with the Spanish, and became known for their fierce fighting ways, repelling Spanish attempts at conquest and expanding their territory over other indigenous groups in the interior of the Chaco. They are still known today as being more outspoken and less afraid of conflict than other groups. Many of the Komlek communities are in rural areas and others in barrios such as the one found in Resistencia, where people make a living from manual labour and crafts such as basket weaving, pottery, woodcarving and weaving. The Komlek have a rich musical tradition, playing instruments such as the *nvike*, a type of home-made violin.

The **Mocoví** people are found principally in the central south of Chaco Province and parts of Santa Fe, in communities around Villa Angela and Charata. Much less numerous than the Komlek, their population numbers between five and eight thousand, but only about half the population speak their native language, a tongue that belongs to the Guaycurú group, like that of the Komlek. The Mocoví are noted for their distinctive pot-

its eponymous province, before reaching the frontier close to both the **Parque Nacional Río Pilcomayo** and the historical centre of the region, the Paraguayan capital, **Asunción**. Resistencia and Formosa are unlikely to detain you for long, but they do provide the springboard for trips into the interior, along the two parallel arteries that strike out northwest – the RN16 and the RN81.

The most important interior road, the sealed **RN16**, runs from Resistencia to Salta Province, and is thus the route that all principal buses take across the Chaco. Detours off this route will enable you to visit the **Parque Nacional Chaco**, one of the best-preserved areas of wet chaco habitat; the new **Parque Nacional Copo** in Santiago del Estero Province, in the centre of the dry chaco; the **Campo del Cielo Meteorite Field** near Gancedo; and the **zoo** at Chaco Province's second town, Presidencia Roque Sáenz Peña, which serves as a rescue centre for some of the region's rarest species.

Further north, the **RN81** bisects Formosa Province. Sealed only in parts, the RN81 can be unpredictable to cross during the wet season, and though it can be crossed with public transport, most of the sites of interest lie just off the route and are difficult to access for those without their own transport. Chief amongst its attractions is the fascinating wetland environment of **Bañado La Estrella**, excellent for bird-watching, and best accessed from Las Lomitas. South of Ingeniero Juárez is the small **Reserva**

---

tery; and families buy what they can't grow by working in domestic service, forestry, or as seasonal farm-labourers.

The **Pilagá**, numbering approximately five thousand people, live in central Formosa Province. They make their living by a combination of settled agriculture and hunter-gathering, including fishing with home-made spears, known as *fijas*. In addition, some work as labourers on cotton plantations and in forestry. The Pilagá have no written language, although committees are currently trying to formulate a standardized alphabet.

The **Wichí** are the second most numerous group after the Komlek, with a population of perhaps twenty thousand, spread amongst communities in western Formosa, the northeastern fringe of Salta Province and along the Río Bermejo in the far northwest of Chaco Province. And of all the indiginous peoples, they are the nation that still relies on hunter-gathering for its economic and cultural life. Hunting these days is often with guns, where the Wichí can afford to buy them, but other more economical and more ancestral forms are still practised, such as fishing with different types of net: the use of the scissor net (*red de tijera*) involves remarkable skill, as fishermen dive into silty rivers, fishing blind underwater by sensing movement around them. The Wichí are famed as collectors of wild honey, collecting different types from twenty species of bee. They also depend for much of their diet on seeds of trees such as the carob and *chañar* – the latter has fruits somewhat like small dates. In addition, families cultivate small plots of beans, watermelons and maize and raise small herds of goats. A limited interaction with the market economy involves seasonal labour, and the sale of fish and beautiful handicrafts. The Wichí are especially famous for the beautifully woven *yica* bags made of a sisal-like fibre, prepared laboriously from the *chaguar*, a type of ground-growing bromeliad resembling a yucca plant. These are dyed with natural colours, some of them startlingly rich, obtained from a variety of plants. However, a constant problem for the Wichí, as with other indigenous groups, is finding markets for their produce.

The Wichí are perhaps the most egalitarian of all the cultures, partly due to the harshness of the dry chaco environment they make their home, as this impels them towards community co-operation. They are a quietly spoken people and have a philosophy that places strong emphasis on peaceful conflict resolution rather than violence. Internal community power structures have very little in the way of a hierarchy: caciques are not hereditary and they are more representatives of the community than leaders of it. Decisions are arrived at through consensus rather than democracy, which is rather an alien concept to the Wichí.

Natural Formosa, on the banks of the Río Bermejo, with an interesting mix of dry thornscrub and riverine forest.

The Chaco region records some of the highest **temperatures** anywhere in the continent during the summer months, often reaching 45°C. At these times, the siesta becomes even more sacred – nothing much moves between 11am and 3 or 4pm – and people survive by drinking chilled *tereré*. The best time to visit is from June to early Sept, when the heat is considerably less oppressive: although frosts are not unknown in June and July, daytime temperatures generally hover in the agreeable 20–24°C bracket. The **rainy season** generally lasts from October to May.

Some history

For some 7000 years, the Chaco was a melting pot of indigenous cultures from across the continent: **Arawak** peoples from the north, **Andean groups** from the west and nomadic tribes from the south. "Chaco" is a word taken to mean "place of hunting", as derived from the **Quechua** *chacú*, which was used to refer to a traditional system of hunting employed by the indigenous groups in the area. This co-operative method involved encircling a vast area on foot, and driving all animals therein to a central point, where pregnant females and babies would be let free and a quota of the rest killed.

In **colonial times**, the Spanish soon discovered that conquest here was not an attractive proposition. The region had no precious metals, and the indigenous groups were as hostile as the climate. Barring several short-lived incursions by the Jesuits in the seventeenth and eighteenth centuries, the only serious attempt at settlement was the colony of Concepción de la Buena Esperanza del Bermejo, founded in 1585 by Alfonso de Vera y Aragón. The Spanish tried to introduce the *mita* system of forced labour to produce cotton, a crop that was native to the area – according to the chronicler Oviedo, cotton cloth was used as money by tribes in the pre-Columbian era. The attempt backfired: press-ganged Abipone warriors revolted in 1632, destroying the colony. The site of the former colony, now known as Concepción del Bermejo, is found 75km north of Sáenz Peña, on the route to Castelli, but there's not much to see. After this, the Spanish opted for a **policy of containment** of the region, with some limited contacts through trade.

The inhospitable nature of the terrain meant that this was the last area to be incorporated into the **nation state of Argentina**, at the end of the nineteenth century. After the War of the Triple Alliance with Paraguay (1865–70) and the fixing of the frontier – in 1879, after the arbitration of President Hayes of the United States – the Argentine authorities sought to formalize control over its disputed northern border region by subjugating its indigenous inhabitants and opening it up to white settlement. However, it was only after the conclusion of the Campaign of the Desert in Patagonia that President Roca was at last in a position to focus military attention on the Chaco. During the 1880s, a series of short campaigns conducted from a chain of military forts brought most organized indigenous resistance in the region to an end, although in fact Chaco campaigns continued into the early twentieth century. Some of these were bloodless: when faced by the prospect of a pitched battle, the indigenous tribes tended to scatter, and withdrew across the border to Bolivia or Paraguay. The end result was the same: territory was ceded, and the indigenous groups became second-class citizens in their own land. The last indigenous uprising on Argentine territory occurred here: in 1919, a group of Pilagá destroyed Fortín Yunká, near the Paraguayan border, northwest of today's Parque Nacional Pilcomayo. Some isolated areas of the interior remained only nominally under the authorities' control as late as the 1930s. To this day, Formosa and Chaco provinces have one of the most numerous and diverse **indigenous populations** in the country, although the casual visitor is unlikely to have much contact with the major ethnic groups in the region – the Komlek (often called Toba), Pilagá, Wichí, and Mocoví (see box, p.361).

European settlers began to arrive in the region from the late nineteenth century, attracted by government land-grants and the prospect of exploiting the region's natural resources, especially its virgin tracts of quebracho forests, a tree prized amongst other things for its resistant, unrotting timber – *quebracho* means axe-breaker in Spanish. So began a period of dramatic **environmental change**, facilitated by the construction of railways into the interior, as millions of trees were felled by companies such as the English-owned La Forestal to provide sleepers for the world's railways, charcoal for Argentina's trains, posts to fence off the estancias of the south, and tannin for the world's leather tanneries. Land clearance paved the way for a cotton boom in the 1940s and 1950s, and cattle were introduced in their thousands to graze the scrub. In recent decades, the region has suffered from severe economic recession. Forestry resources have been massively depleted; the tannin industry is in crisis, following the introduction of artificial substitutes; and soil exhaustion, floods and competition from other areas of the world have hit the profitability of crops like cotton. Sustainable economic development still seems a long way off.

Resistencia and the route north

The easternmost strip of Chaco Province along the Paraná and Paraguay rivers is the steamy heartland of the wet chaco. Most of the original wet chaco forests and swamps have fallen victim to agricultural developments, and the land is now dedicated to the production of beef cattle and crops such as fruit, soya beans and sugar cane. The main highway through this region – albeit one that has few sites of tourist interest – is the **RN11**, which connects Santa Fe with **Resistencia**. This city is the starting point for trips along the RN16 to the Parque Nacional Chaco and the interior of the province (see p.367), as well as for excursions to the subtropical river island of **Isla del Cerrito** and the the botanical reserve of **Colonia Benítez**.

Resistencia and around

A humid and often roastingly hot city of 300,000 inhabitants, **RESISTENCIA** is Chaco Province's sprawling administrative capital and the principal gateway to the Chaco region. Despite its commercial importance, the city itself does not merit more than a fleeting visit. Known as the City of Sculptures, it is most famous for the civic statues that can be found on street corners and in parks throughout town, and for the remarkable cultural centre that inspired them, the **Fogón de los Arrieros** (see box, p.365). These statues are not works of art on a grand scale, but make a pleasant diversion as you wander the sweltering streets. Apart from that, Resistencia has only a handful of other sites worth checking out.

The town's vast main square, **Plaza 25 de Mayo**, is dotted with caranday palms and native trees; a neatly laid-out place occupying four whole blocks, the square is dominated by a statue of General San Martín and is host to a small artisans' market where you can buy Komlek ceramics. A couple of blocks to the southeast, the **Museo del Hombre Chaqueño**, (Mon–Fri 8am–12.30pm & 5–9pm, Sat 5–9pm; free), has a modest but clearly presented collection detailing provincial history, with information on the province's Komlek, Mocoví, and Wichí cultures; models of figures from Guaraní mythology; beautiful nineteenth-century silver *mate* gourds; and a small section on the War of the Triple Alliance, which embroiled the area in the 1860s. A more extensive archeological and ethnographical collection is housed in the **Museo de Antropología**, further to the southeast at Las Heras 727 (Mon–Fri 8am–noon & 4–9pm; free), with objects recovered from the ruins of the failed sixteenth-century Spanish settlement of Concepción del Bermejo on display. To the north of the centre,

△ Corrientes (15 km) & Isla del Cerrito (50 km)

RESISTENCIA

ACCOMMODATION
25 de Mayo	5
Bariloche	6
Colón	3
Covadonga	1
Illia	4
Royal	2
San José	8
Santa Rita	7

▽ Bus Terminal (3 km), Airport (5 km) & Santa Fé

natural history is covered by the **Museo de Ciéncias Naturales** at Pellegrini y Lavalle (Mon–Fri 8.30am–noon & 2–7pm; Sat & Sun 5.30–8.30pm; free). This collection is housed in the clean-cut nineteenth-century Estación Francesa train station, which served the region's timber and tannin industries during their heyday. A fruit and vegetable market is held in front of the station, on Avenida Laprida each Tuesday and Friday (6am–1pm).

The best place in the region to purchase indigenous crafts is the **Fundación Chaco Artesanal** at Pellegrini 272 (Mon–Sat 8am–1pm & 5–8pm, Sun 8am–1pm; ☎03722/459372, fax 423954), a smart, non-profit outlet which sells items such as smooth earthenware Mocoví nativity figures, rougher Wichí pottery, Komlek basketware and graceful *palo santo* figures of crucified Christs.

Arrival, information and accommodation

The city **airport** is 6km to the west of town. There's no regular bus service between here and the centre, but LAPA organizes a $3 shuttle service for its flights, with hotel pick-up; alternatively, pick up a taxi – prices vary considerably so bargain and ask around. The **bus terminal** (☎03722/461098) is at the junction of avenidas Malvinas Argentinas and MacLean, 4km southwest of Plaza 25 de Mayo. Bus #3 connects the two, leaving from the kiosk opposite the terminal (every 20–30min). A *remise* from here to the centre costs around $4. If you're heading straight to Corrientes, you might want to consider a *remise colectivo* as an alternative to the bus: they leave from the south side of Plaza 25 de Mayo at Alberdi ($1).

The municipal **tourist office** (Mon–Fri 8am–8pm, Sat & Sun 8am–1pm; ☎03722/458289) is in a bandstand-like booth on the Plaza 25 de Mayo; the staff are helpful, but it's badly stocked.

Most of the town's **hotels** are well located, within four blocks of the main square. The larger hotels usually offer a ten percent discount for cash payment, but ask first; those in the lower categories tend to charge extra for air conditioning. The nearest **campsite** to the city is *Camping 2 de Febrero*, Avenida Avalos 1100 (☎03722/458323), 1.5km to the north. Set in an attractive park near the Río Negro, the site has full services and a pool; take bus #9 from the plaza ($0.70).

25 de Mayo, Yrigoyen 83 (☎03722/422898, fax 440846). A well-sited, friendly, if neglected place, overlooking the main plaza. It's owned by the Chaco police. ④.

Residencial Bariloche, Obligado 239 (☎03722/421412). This guesthouse has an institutional feel, but it offers good-value rooms, some without external windows, for up to four people. Popular with local salesmen, it's at its busiest on weekdays. ②.

THE FOGÓN DE LOS ARRIEROS: ART IN "THE CITY OF STATUES"

Resistencia's **Fogón de los Arrieros** is a cultural foundation where a tongue-in-cheek bohemianism mixes quite naturally with a more serious artistic agenda, and is, as such, a testament to the energy and unconventional vision of its founding members – especially Aldo Boglietti, who set the ball rolling in 1943, and the sculptor, Juan de Dios Mena. Its name means "The Drovers' Campfire", and was intended to evoke a sense of transitoriness: like drovers who would meet up around the campfire to relate a story or join in song before moving on the next day, artists would come as friends to this meeting place, share their particular form of art, and then continue their journey.

The centre's fame spread quickly, so that, especially during its apogee in the 1960s and 1970s, it attracted an impressive list of major national and even international artistic figures. Fortunately for the Fogón, not everyone came to sing, and the walls are plastered by less transitory legacies. **Paintings** include the intense, energetic *Cuarteto de Cuerda* (*String Quartet*) by Julio Vanzo, as well as works by Chagall and Raúl Soldi. Demetrio Urruchua, Argentina's most famous **muralist**, left *Crisol de Razas* (*Crucible of the Races*) in 1954, intending to promote a pluralist spirit. Look out, too, for Dios Mena's appealing criollo **statues**, carved in *curupí*, a very light wood, and very much in the mould of Molina Campos caricatures. Eclectic curiosities range from a prisoner's shirt from Ushuaia to a Jíbaro shrunken head from Ecuador.

The idea for Resistencia's statues started with Aldo Boglietti, who saw the town becoming a kind of open-air museum: for him art had a vital role to play in enriching the region and he felt that it should be accessible and all-pervading, not just confined to stuffy museums. The concept of art as a tool for engendering civic pride has been amply demonstrated: Resistencia's citizens are very proud of their city's two hundred plus statues and graffiti is almost unheard of here.

The Fogón de los Arrieros is located at Brown 350 (☎03722/426418), between López y Planes and French. Visits are sometimes possible in the morning (Mon–Sat 8am–noon; $2 donation), but it's more reliably open in the evening (Mon–Fri 9pm–11pm; $2), when you will be able to have a drink at its cosy bar. Best of all, try to catch one of the **events** – concerts, poetry recitals, etc – staged once or twice a week in the main salon or the patio (usually Sat 10pm). Academic conferences are sometimes given (Thurs eve), and there are often tango lessons too (Wed & Fri 9pm–midnight).

Colón, Santa María de Oro 143 (☎ & fax 03722/422861). Pleasant if poorly lit rooms for up to five people. Breakfast is included. ④.

Covadonga, Güemes 200 (☎03722/444444, fax 443444; *hotcovad@hotelnet.com.ar*). A well-run establishment with smart rooms and comfy beds. English is spoken. Facilities include fax and email services, a pool, gym and sauna. ⑥.

Royal, Obligado 211 (☎03722/443666, fax 425486). A reasonable mid-range hotel, with spruce if somewhat bland rooms. Facilities include a squash court. ⑤.

Residencial San José, Arturo Frondizi 306 (☎03722/426062). Basic rooms with private bathrooms. Air conditioning costs $10 extra. ②.

Hospedaje Santa Rita, Alberdi 311 (☎03722/459719). A family-run establishment that offers some large rooms, but with fans rather than air conditioning. ②.

Eating, drinking and nightlife

Resistencia generally has a poor choice of **restaurants**. There are a few exceptions, however, of which *Catering* in the Club Social on Obligado 43 y Alberdi (closed Sun eve & Mon lunch) is the best. It serves a three-course menu with a half bottle of wine ($12), pricey starters, parrillas, and pastas from $5. Also good is *Charly*, Güemes 213 (☎03722/429491; open till midnight, closed Sun eve), which has delicious *mollejas al champagne* ($10), pastas ($5–9), and *surubí* dishes ($11.50), complemented by a wide selection of wines. It also runs the *rotisería* round the corner at Brown 71 (dishes for $9/kilo). *Sei Tu* is a fine **ice-cream parlour** on the corner of Güemes and Yrigoyen.

For **nightlife**, the bar at *El Fogón* (see box, p.365) is excellent for bohemian conversation; or catch a folkloric show at the *Peña Nativa Martín Fierro*, 9 de Julio y Hernández (☎03722/423167; Fri from 9pm), where they also serve parrilla meals. *Drink's* [sic], Güemes 183, is a café-cum-bar with a varied choice of beers, whose sedate ambience is ideal for chatting (open round the clock at weekends). Less restrained is *El Nuevo Café de la Ciudad*, Yrigoyen y Pellegrini (7am–3am, later at weekends), which acts as a café during the day, and a bar at night, and is popular with a young crowd.

Listings

Airlines Aerolíneas & Austral, Rawson y J.B. Justo (☎03722/445550 or 445553); LAPA, Pellegrini 100 (☎03722/430201).

Banks and exchange Scotiabank, J.B. Justo 164; Banco de Galicia, Mitre y Santa Fe; HSBC, J.B. Justo 151; Banco Francés, J.M. Paz 66. Exchange at El Dorado, J.M. Paz 50.

Car rental Gold, Pío XII 165 (☎ & fax 03722/428497).

Hospital 9 de Julio 1101 (☎03722/425050 or 427233).

Police Gendarmería Nacional, Julio Roca (☎03722/421658).

Post office Sarmiento y Yrigoyen (Mon–Fri 7.30am–8pm, Sat 8am–12.30pm).

Taxis ☎03722/424163, 428470 or 426865.

Travel agencies For flights, contact El Dorado, J.M. Paz 50 (☎ & fax 03722/435680). Agencies offering trips to the interior of the province include Quiyoc, Padre Cerqueira 19, 1°"B" (☎03722/433043); and Sudamericana, Pellegrini 207, 1° (☎03722/440810).

The Reserva Natural Estricta Colonia Benítez and Isla del Cerrito

The RN11, the stretch of highway that runs north from Resistencia to Formosa, passes through scenery that's a mix of dense thickets of *monte*, interspersed with rough savannah cattle pasture spiked with caranday palms, and fields of crops such as rice and soya. Have your documents ready, as police checkpoints exist along the road, controlling the main route to and from Paraguay. The best detour along the route is to the **Reserva Natural Estricta Colonia Benítez**, a tiny reserve, less than a tenth of a square metre in size, that is used for scientific study. In this small reserve, nature trails take you through three types of habitat: tall gallery forest, open cactus scrub, and wetlands. To get there, take the RN11 to Km1018, 15km north of Resistencia, and then turn east down a signposted six-kilometre dirt road. The Colonia Benítez **bus** runs here from the terminal in Resistencia (Godoy or Puerto Tirol).

Some 51km to the northeast of Resistencia, at the confluence of the Paraguay and Paraná rivers and reached by turning off the main road to Corrientes just before the Puente Belgrano, is the **ISLA DEL CERRITO**, a lush, subtropical reserve and holiday spot where locals go to fish, swim, barbecue, and otherwise relax. It is more of a wetland promontory than a true island, and it makes for an enjoyable day or half-day trip from the capital. The attractive, pavilion-style architecture seen today was constructed in 1924, when the Isla became the site of a leper hospital, an institution that eventually closed in 1968.

Aside from weekends – when the resort is packed with city folk – the place is very tranquil, and your most likely disturbance is going to be from the chattersome parrots in the ceibo trees. For splendid views of the rivers, climb the tower of the charming **Iglesia de Virgen del Pilar** on the hill (usually open in the afternoon); and to learn about the Isla's role in territorial struggles in the nineteenth century, visit the tiny, informative **Museo de la Isla** (Tues–Fri 9am–noon & 5–7pm, Sat & Sun 9am–noon & 3–6pm; donations). The Isla is famous for its fishing, above all for the powerful fighting fish, the dorado: every year in mid-October, anglers come to try their luck in the **Fiesta Nacional de Pesca del Dorado** (for information ☎ or fax 03722/441033; entrance costs $150–200 per person). For shore fishing, the best spot is where the muddy Río Paraguay flows into the clearer, greater Paraná.

A Burlatur **bus** leaves from outside the Banco Hipotecario on Resistencia's Plaza 25 de Mayo for Isla del Cerrito twice daily (5.30am & 12.30pm; returning 8.30am & 6pm; $1.50) and can drop you off anywhere along the resort's one road: you're best off alighting near the church. Groups can also take a *remise colectivo* from Resistencia, from the same departure point as the buses ($3.50 per person). **Accommodation** in the excellent *Hostería del Sol* behind the church (☎03722/496268; with air conditioning; ③) is pleasant and good value, with airy rooms sleeping up to four people. They serve ample **meals**, including a $5 eat-all-you-like *surubí* buffet (11.30am–3pm & 8.30pm–midnight). You can **camp** on the sward by the Río Paraná in front of the main boulevard that connects the promontory with the point (☎03722/496208; $3); or for free a little further south along the river, beneath the promontory (no services).

West of Resistencia: the RN16

The RN16 sheers straight through Chaco Province, running northwest from Resistencia. At one point it clips the northeastern corner of Santiago del Estero Province, and further on it reaches Salta Province. Unlike the RN81 through Formosa Province, it is paved all the way and is thus the route taken by all trans-Chaco buses. Dedicated naturalists can spend a few days trying to track down the region's fauna in one of two national parks on the route – **Parque Nacional Chaco** in the humid east and **Parque Nacional Copo** in the heart of the dry chaco – whilst the less dedicated can opt for a safer, easier bet at the zoo in **Presidencia Roque Sáenz Peña**. A sidetrip to the south takes you to the **Meteorite Field** of Campo del Cielo near Gancedo.

The first 163-kilometre section of the route, from Resistencia to Sáenz Peña, sees a gradual transition in the **scenery**, and the environment becomes progressively less green as humidity declines. The RN16's only toll ($5) is collected from vehicles heading beyond Makallé, 37km northwest of Resistencia. Soon after this is the turn-off north to Capitán Solari and the Parque Nacional Chaco. Further along the RN16, you pass a string of small agricultural settlements to the north of the road. The land has been cleared in places to plant banana groves, and caranday palms grow in the drier land between streams and reed- and lily-beds. The semi-dry chaco as you approach Sáenz Peña is characterized by vast flat areas of cotton plantation, and the tough, spruce-green *itín* plants that grow in dense thickets like overgrown gorse bushes. West of Sáenz Peña, the scenery becomes drier still, and cultivation gives way to scrub used for cattle grazing.

Parque Nacional Chaco

The **Parque Nacional Chaco** (☎03725/496166; $5 entrance), within easy striking distance of Resistencia, conserves a mix of threatened wet- and semi-dry chaco habitat around the banks of the Río Negro. In quick succession, you can pass from riverine forest to open woodland, palm savannah and wetlands. The park is relatively small: its 150 square kilometres are too restricted a space to provide a viable habitat for the largest Chaco predator, the jaguar, but mammals such as giant anteaters, honey anteaters, maned wolves and tapirs do still inhabit the park, even if your chances of seeing them are slight. You've a better, if still slim, chance of seeing a puma, and considerably less chance of sighting capybara, coatimundis, deer, howler monkeys or the two types of peccary that also inhabit the area. Birdlife, however, is plentiful and easy to spot. All of the areas open to visitors can be seen if you spend one or two nights in the park. The winter months of June to August are the best time to visit, since it's not stiflingly hot and humid, there are few biting insects, and many of the deciduous trees lose their leaves, so you've more chance of seeing wildlife.

Arrival and information
The turn-off to the park is 56km west of Resistencia along the RN16, from where the paved RP9 heads 40km north to the scrappy hamlet of Capitán Solari, 6km from the park headquarters. If coming from Resistencia, your best bet is to take the twice-daily Marito Tours **minibus** from Calle Vedia 334 (☎03722/422000; $6), which will drop you off at the park headquarters ($5 extra per group); the tours leave Resistencia at 8am and 7pm, returning at 5am and 4pm – arrange pick-up from the park in advance. You can also take the regular **bus** from the terminal in Resistencia ($5) to the second stop in the village; there are three buses a day back to the city. Getting the remaining 6km to the park is an easy but fairly haphazard affair: the municipality may help arrange a lift; or ask around for a *remise* (arrange the price first, as it can range from nothing to $10 per trip) or for Sr Lobera's house on the main street as he may take you in his Marito Tours minibus. If you have to walk to or from the park in rainy weather, it's easier to tackle it barefoot, due to the heavy clay soil.

Entrance to the park costs $5. There's a very pleasant (free) **campsite** next to the administration, with showers, toilets and drinking water. With permission from the *guardaparques*, you can **hire horses** from a friendly *baqueano* guide, Sr Mendoza, who lives just outside the park boundaries – it's a good method of visiting Laguna Panza de Cabra especially and is excellent value at $4 an hour). There's no **food** to buy in the park, and little in Solari, so bring supplies from Resistencia. You must bring insect repellent, sunscreen and a hat, especially in summer. There's no accommodation in Solari itself.

The trails
If you visit between October and May, try to time your walks as close to dawn or sunset as possible to avoid the humidity and fierce heat – temperatures regularly exceed 40°C – and to maximize your chances of seeing the wildlife. The terrain is flat, but don't underestimate your need for water – carry at least two litres per person. A board by the park headquarters displays the trails, which are also marked on a pamphlet available from the *guardaparque*.

A good introduction to the park is the well-shaded, nature-trail loop that leads from a suspension bridge behind the park headquarters (1.5km; 40–50min). But the most popular walk is the one to the lookouts at the ox-bow lagoons of **Laguna Carpincho** and **Laguna Yacaré**, with a deviation to see an enormous quebracho, El Abuelo, which is an estimated 500 years old. From the base camp at park headquarters, it's 6km direct to Laguna Yacaré (1hr 15min–1hr 30min), to which you must add half an hour if you make the detour to see El Abuelo, signposted to the left approximately 25 minutes from camp. With prior permission from the *guardaparques*, you may continue 4km northwards from Laguna Yacaré to the **Tranquera Norte** (North Gate) that marks the park boundary.

A longer walk (9km; 2hr 15min–2hr 45min each way) is to **Laguna Panza de Cabra**, a swamp that is choked with camalote waterlilies and which offers excellent bird-watching opportunities. Leave the campsite along the Laguna Yacaré trail, to find the trail's start, which is signposted fifteen minutes' walk away. Turn left here, and then take the left-hand peel-off immediately after the signpost. Soon you come to a sharp right-hand bend at a wire fence, and thereafter you enter open quebracho woodland, badly burnt out on one side of the path by a fire in 1999. Follow the path around to the right as you leave the woodland to reach the Laguna. You can **camp** here, but there are no facilities.

Presidencia Roque Sáenz Peña

Just over 100km further along the RN16, past the turn-off to Parque Nacional Chaco, lies **Presidencia Roque Sáenz Pena**, Chaco Province's second city, and an unattractive place. It is only worth stopping here to visit the **Complejo Ecológico Zoo**, on RN95 (daily dawn–dusk; $1), the best bet for viewing the endangered beasts of the Chaco, including a maned wolf, jaguars, pumas, tapirs, honey anteaters, bare-faced curassows, giant anteaters and, on occasion, giant armadillos. This zoo fulfils an important educational role in an area where ecological consciousness is sometimes acutely lacking. Though poorly funded, it does an excellent job too at rescuing, releasing or housing wounded or impounded specimens that are the victims of road traffic accidents, fires, illegal hunting and unscrupulous animal trading. A surprising side to its activities, given its un-Andean siting, is its captive breeding programme for condors, which has seen Chaqueñan-reared birds sent to Mérida in Venezuela to be successfully reintroduced into a country where they had hitherto died out.

The **bus terminal** is in the centre of town: the fast *remises colectivos* that run to and from Resistencia ($10 per person) stop here as well as the buses. To get to the zoo from the bus terminal catch urban bus #2. From the terminal, head a block south along Calle Moreno to Calle 17 (also called Superiora Palmira), then turn right and walk for six blocks until you reach the **tourist office** (daily 7.30am–1pm & 3–9pm; ☎ & fax 03732/421587) on the corner of Calle 10. One block further is the main commercial artery, Avenida San Martín (Calle 12), where you'll find the city's banks. El Dorado, at Belgrano 379, is the town's only exchange. For **accommodation**, *Residencial Mura*, Belgrano 589 y Calle 13 (☎03732/420764; ②), has pleasant, spacious rooms, some with bathrooms, and some inexpensive singles. *Hotel Presidente*, Superiora Palmira 464 (☎ & fax 03732/424498; ④), cash only), is heavy on the chintz, with a gloomy downstairs, but comfortable enough. The spacious municipal campsite is on the route from the bus station to the zoo, on Avenida de los Imigrantes/Calle 9 ($10 donation requested per tent). The town is the cotton capital of Argentina, and for ten days in late April to early May it hosts the **Fiesta del Algodón**, with modest parades and the election of a Cotton Queen.

The Campo del Cielo Meteorite Field

At Avia Terai, 35km northwest of Sáenz Peña on the RN16, the RP94 branches southeast through monotonous scenery towards Santiago del Estero. It's not worth a special trip, but if you're passing through anyway, stop to see the famous **Campo del Cielo Meteorite Field**, a place that's fascinating historically, but fairly drab to see. The largest and most accessible meteorite is called El Chaco, which lies 10km from the cotton-processing, agricultural town of Gancedo (the nearest town; 129km from

Avia Terai). The turn-off is 2km to the southwest of town, opposite a cotton plant (signposted "*Meteorito*" and "*Aerolito*"). Head south for 7km down a decent dirt road, and turn off left for the remaining 1km.

An estimated four to six thousand years ago, an asteroid shattered on impact with the earth's upper atmosphere, sending chips plummeting earthbound, to impact into a fifteen-kilometre band of the Chaco landscape. This cataclysmic spectacle and the subsequent bush fires that would have been triggered must have terrified the local indigenous occupants of the area. By the time the Spanish first arrived in South America, the Komlek knew this area as *Pigüen Nonraltá* – meaning the Field of the Heavens, or Campo del Cielo in Spanish. They venerated the curious stones that had come from the sky and whose surface, when polished, reflected the sun.

Mysterious legends reached Spanish ears, arousing an insatiable curiosity for anything that smacked of precious metal, and even sparking illusions of the fabled City of the Caesars. In 1576, Hernán Mexía de Miraval struggled out here hoping to find gold but, instead, he found iron. The biggest expedition of all came in 1783, when the Spanish geologist and scientist, Miguel Rubín de Celis, led an expedition of two hundred men to find out if the **Mesón de Fierro** – a 3.5m long curiosity and the most famous of the meteors – was in fact just the tip of a vast mountain of pure iron. When they dug below, they were mortified to find only dusty earth. The latitude was recorded, but since there was no way of determining its co-ordinate of longitude, the Mesón de Fierro was subsequently lost. Since it has never been found again, it's probable that the indigenous inhabitants reburied their sunstone.

The largest of the meteorites you can see today, **El Chaco**, has been reliably estimated to weigh 33,700kg, making it the second biggest in the world. It, too, has aroused the avarice of speculators. In 1990, a local highway cop foiled the plot of an American, Robert Haag, to steal El Chaco and sell it on to a private US collector – or, according to some rumours, to NASA. Haag was released on $20,000 bail but fled the country. Back home in the States, he became known as "Meteorman", and was allowed to enjoy his notoriety. Since 1997, El Chaco has been protected by a provincial law. This hasn't stopped local pranksters debasing it with graffiti, but at least the perpetrators were thoughtful enough to spray it a suitably cosmic neon green.

Parque Nacional Copo

Pressed into the far northeastern corner of Santiago del Estero Province is **Parque Nacional Copo**, the best remaining chunk of prime dry chaco habitat left in the country and the only area of protected land in the Argentine Chaco big enough to provide a sustainable habitat for some of the region's most threatened wildlife: in particular, jaguars, giant armadillos, and the elusive Wagner's peccary. Giant and honey anteaters also inhabit the park, as do bird species such as the threatened crowned eagle, the greater rhea and the king vulture.

Baking hot in summer, and frequently parched, it's a huge expanse of some 1140 square kilometres, with 550 square kilometres of provincial reserve attached to the west. The habitat is mainly open woodland and bush scrubland that's crossed by dry paleowatercourses, and with areas of rough grassland in the places where cattle are grazed. The current plan is to round up and evict the estimated four hundred cattle in the park by 2006. In the southeast sector, forestry was practised until the mid-1950s, so the spiny understorey is much denser and thicker than you'll find in the more mature dry chaco woodland, especially that in the north and east of the park, where the trees are up to twenty metres high. Temperatures can rise as high as 45°C between December and February, and a more tolerable 7–23°C between July and August, the best time to visit.

Copo was granted national park status only in 1999, and as yet the infrastructure is virtually non-existent, although a headquarters is planned. It can be visited from the dusty roadside settlement of **PAMPA DE LOS GUANACOS**, on the RN16, 155km from Sáenz Peña and 318km from Resistencia. Trans-Chaco **buses** stop here: either at the YPF fuel station on the RN16 or on the main street that runs parallel to it, some four blocks north, across the railway tracks. If you need **to stay** a night in Pampa de los Guanacos, try *Comedor Gerardo Rascaeta*, a diminutive roadside eatery next to the YPF that offers rooms (☎03841/491006; ② with shared bathroom, $10 extra with private one and air conditioning). **Access to the park** is by a well-maintained, but unsealed, road that runs north off the RN16 from opposite the Escuela Islas Malvinas, 15km west of Pampa de los Guanacos. Another track runs along the eastern border of the park, heading north from the RN16 where it crosses the provincial border with Chaco Province, a similar distance east of Pampa de los Guanacos and before you get to Río Muerto. **Park information** can be obtained from the amiable *guardafauna*, Sr Hugo Raimondo Almaraz, at the municipalidad, on the main street that runs parallel to the RN16, some four blocks north, across the railway tracks, or at his home, on Calle Güemes (☎03841/491036 or 156-70429). At the time of writing, there was no organized method of visiting the park, but Sr. Almaraz will help to charter transport if you don't have your own vehicle. Renée Omar Esperguin (☎156-70254) and Héctor Nery Caballero (☎156-70977) know the park well and may be able to **organize a tour** – neither have a fixed itinerary or price, so arrange details before departing. Whichever way you travel, bring plenty of water (there's no drinking water in the park), all the food you'll need, and emergency supplies of fuel – and make sure you advise the *guardafauna* of your plans. Rainfall can make the tracks within the park impassable, so you could get bogged down at certain times of year. **Camping** is allowed in the park, but there are no recognized sites or facilities.

Formosa and the northeast

Formosa Province is dominated by its eponymous capital city, which is second in importance to Resistencia in the Chaco region, but really a place only to pass through. It is overshadowed as a destination of tourist interest by two sites further north: the internationally significant wetland site of **Parque Nacional Río Pilcomayo**, on the border with Paraguay, and, across the border, the neighbouring country's own capital, **Asunción**, which is the historical and spiritual heart of the whole region.

FORMOSA itself seems a town pressed flat by the heat. Few buildings rise above a single storey, and many exhibit the grey mouldy stains of subtropical decay. Situated on a great dog-leg bend in the Río Paraguay, it acts as a **port** for the entire province. Though not a particularly attractive place, it's given a pink facelift when the lapacho trees flower in spring, the best time to see it. The main commercial district is concentrated within a block or two either side of the **Avenida 25 de Mayo** east of the Plaza San Martín. This boulevard leads down to Calle San Martín by the port, where, for three days over a November weekend, the **Fiesta Nacional del Río** is held – a modest event, with *chamamé* folk music concerts, water sports, and parades. Inexpensive merchandise – knick-knacks, clothes, *mate* gourds, fishing gear and electronics – is sold at the **Mercado Paraguayo**, clustered along the three blocks of Calle San Martín running south from the port; but of more interest is the **Casa de la Artesanía**, a non-profit organization based at San Martín and 25 de Mayo (Mon–Sat 8am–12.30pm & 4.30–8pm), the best outlet for Formoseñan indigenous crafts. It stocks a good selection of Wichí *yica* bags, Pilagá woollen carpets, tightly woven Komlek *carandillo* and *tortora* basketwork, plus *palo santo* carvings and *algarrobo* seed jewellery. Just north of the port is the attractive, restored, peach and grey train station – sadly, the train line, which crosses Formosa Province to Embarcación in Salta is nowadays used exclusively by the petroleum industry. A block inland from here, on the corner of 25 de Mayo and Belgrano, is the pink, hacienda-style **Museo Histórico** (Mon–Fri 8am–noon & 3.30–6.30pm, Sat 8am–noon; free), housed in the 1885 former residence of General Ignacio Fotheringham, the Southampton-born first Governor of what was then Formosa Territory. It is an eclectic and poorly organized collection, only worth visiting if you have time to kill; exhibits include a stuffed Swiss bear, Komlek artefacts, plus information on early exploration of the river systems of the Pilcomayo and Bermejo.

Arrival, information and accommodation

The city's **airport** lies just off the RN11, some 6km southwest of the town centre. Buses #4, #9, and #11 run between the two. Arriving in Formosa from the southwest, you'll be welcomed by **El Cruce**, a white Meccano-style cross that's a common reference point. The **bus terminal** is to the east of here on Avenida Gutnisky, a multi-laned thorough-fare that changes its name to Avenida 25 de Mayo before it reaches the Plaza San Martín, the start of the town centre and nearly 2km from the terminal. Buses #4, #9, and #11 ($0.60) head into the centre of town: upon reaching the Plaza San Martín, they take Calle Uriburu, which runs one block to the south of Avenida 25 de Mayo on its way down to the port, and return along Calle España, one block the other side of the main drag. A *remise* into the centre costs $3–4 (many charge for luggage, so check first). There's a small **tourist office** at the bus terminal (Mon–Fri 8am–noon & 4–8pm, Sat 8–noon; ☎03717/450777), and a much better one on Plaza San Martín, at Uriburu 820 (Mon–Fri 7.30am–1pm & 3–8.30pm; ☎03717/420442 or 425192), with helpful staff and an accommodation list for the entire province.

There isn't much to thrill you in terms of **accommodation**. *El Extranjero*, Av. Gutnisky 2660 (☎03717/452276; ②), is a friendly budget option and very conveniently sited, opposite the bus terminal. The most comfortable, modern places are the *Colón*, Belgrano 1068 (☎ & fax 03717/420719; ③, with breakfast), whose prices include free use of a sports complex and pool, 5km away (free shuttle bus); and the *Casa Grande*, González Lelong 185 (☎ & fax 03717/431573 or 431406; ⑤), a more attractive little complex whose well-equipped rooms have kitchenettes, and whose facilities include a pool, garden, business centre and gym. There are several uninspiring *residenciales* in the centre, including the *Cascabel*, at Belgrano 1033 (no telephone; ①); and the *España*, Belgrano 1032 (☎03717/430973; ②). For those with tents, the *Camping Banco Provincia de Formosa* (☎03717/429877; $5 per person), off the RN11, two blocks west of El Cruce as you head out of town, has an Olympic-sized swimming pool.

Eating, drinking and entertainment

The influence of Paraguay is felt in the **food** here, with *chipas* – dry hardbread rings made of mandioca flour – being sold on the street, and *sopa paraguaya* – a savoury maize cake, not a soup – being sold in some restaurants. *Borí borí*, a Paraguayan chicken soup with little balls of maize and cheese, is served on Wednesday lunchtimes at *El Copetín "Yayita"*, Belgrano 926 y Uriburu – the best place in town for a keenly priced feed; its $1 *licuados* and its lunchtime menus ($2–2.50) are particularly good value. *El Fortín*, Mitre y Saavedra (☎03717/439955), serves good fish and wines; a basic *milanesa de surubí* will set you back $3, or try the *lomito relleno Don Santiago* ($6.50) stuffed with ham and cheese. *Raíces*, at 25 de Mayo 65 (☎03717/427058; Mon–Sat till midnight, closed Sun eve), is a popular place serving good portions of *surubí* and pastas from $5, while *Il Viale*, at 25 de Mayo 287, is open for burgers and snacks (6am–3am). The town's **casino**, at San Martín y España, is open 24 hours. It puts on a **folklore show** (Thurs–Sat nights) and has a confitería for snacks.

Listings

Airlines Austral, 25 de Mayo 601 (☎03717/429314 or 429392); LAPA, 25 de Mayo 211 (☎03717/435979 or 435713).

Banks Banco de Boston, 25 de Mayo 317; Banco de Galicia, 25 de Mayo 160; Banco Francés, España 218.
Car rental MAS Autos, 25 de Mayo y Julio Roca (☎03717/436010).
Consulates Paraguayan, 25 de Mayo, between Deán Funes and P. Patiño (Mon–Fri 8am–1pm). However, if you need a visa, it's best to get it in Buenos Aires, as they take 4–5 days to process here.
Hospital Hospital Central, Salta 545 (☎03717/426194).
Internet 25 de Mayo 245 ($6/hr divisible); 25 de Mayo 798 on plaza.
Pharmacy San Luis, Saavedra y Moreno (open 24hr).
Police Saavedra 325 (☎03717/429000 or 426189).
Post office 9 de Julio y Uriburu.

Clorinda

The RN11 runs north of Formosa through more classic wet chaco scenery: open savannah with caranday palms, interspersed with extensive reed beds and clumps of horsetail pirí plants. Situated in a cotton- and banana-growing area 113km northeast of the capital is the steamy border town of **CLORINDA** – a place where you'll want to spend as little time as possible. You'll need to pass through, however, if you're heading for the Parque Nacional Río Pilcomayo (see below) or Asunción in Paraguay (see. p.375). If you do need to make an **overnight stop**, there are a couple of *residenciales* to choose from: *San Martín*, at 12 de Octubre 1150, some ten minutes' walk from the bus terminal, is clean and fresh (☎03718/421211; ①); otherwise try *Residencial 12 de Octubre* nearby at no. 1173 (☎03718/425533; ①). There's also the *Hotel Embajador*, opposite the terminal on San Martín (☎03718/422264; ②), though the place is in sore need of a facelift and replumbing.

To get **to the national park** from Clorinda, you have three options: a bus from the terminal ($3–4); a *remise* ($35; leaves from Buenos Aires y San Martín, two blocks up from the terminal); or a *remise colectivo* (last one usually leaves about 6–7pm; $3 to first turn-off, leaving 5km left to walk; $6 to Laguna Blanca sector park entrance; $5 to Laguna Blanca village), which departs from Calle José Cancio, three blocks further up San Martin.

Parque Nacional Río Pilcomayo

The 519-square-kilometre **Parque Nacional Río Pilcomayo** was created in 1951 to protect some of the best remaining subtropical wet chaco habitat. Rainfall in the park averages 1200mm annually, and extensive areas are subject to seasonal flooding, but in the winter months the park is prone to droughts. The park's importance as a wetland site has been recognized by it being protected under the international Ramsar Convention, which was designed to protect the planet's key wetland ecosystems – and its biological diversity has been safeguarded by a concerted campaign in the 1990s to get rid of most of the semi-wild cattle left by former settlers. In addition to swampy wetlands, it conserves some remnant gallery forest along the Río Pilcomayo, and large swathes of caranday palm savannah grassland studded by copses of mixed woodland (*isletas de monte*). The edges of these woodland patches are some of the most fruitful places for glimpsing the larger mammals that inhabit the reserve, including giant anteaters, honey anteaters, peccaries, deer, three types of monkey and puma. Capybara, the two species of cayman, and even tapir live in the wetter regions of the park. Jaguars are believed to be extinct here, bar the odd stray cat that swims across from Paraguay, but the maned wolf can, very occasionally, be found – indeed, this park offers one of your best chances of seeing one. Almost three hundred species of birds have been recorded here, including the bare-faced curassow and thrush-like wren, both highly endangered in Argentina. During March to October, the cooler, drier winter months, is the best **time to visit**; the average temperature from June to August is

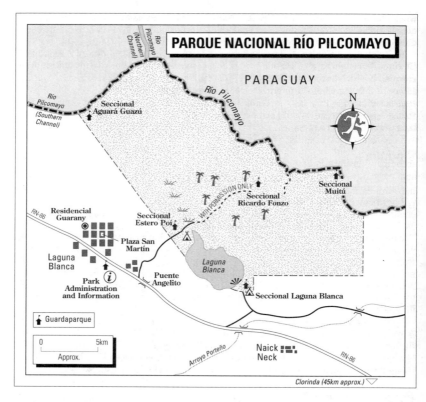

23°C. However, the heat in the park is regularly very fierce: always take a hat, plenty of drinking water and, in the rainy season, insect repellent against the mosquitoes and horseflies.

The park has **two entrances** – Estero Poí and Laguna Blanca sectors – both within striking distance of **LAGUNA BLANCA** village, 52km west of Clorinda. The **national park administration office** (Mon–Fri 7am–4pm; ☎ & fax 03718/470045) is on the RN86 at the entrance to the village, opposite the YPF fuel station. As well as being an information centre, this is the place you must head for to gain permission to explore the interior of the park on horseback or by 4WD. In the village, the hospitable *Residencial Guarany*, on San Martín (☎03718/470024; ②), has small, neat **rooms** grouped around a pleasant courtyard, and a good-value restaurant attached ($5.50 for a quarter chicken with salad). Arriving from Clorinda, *remises colectivos* drop you where you ask, while buses often do a loop of town, stopping at several points before getting to their main office. To get to Clorinda, Godoy **buses** leave from the corner of Alberdi and San Martín; Transportes Emmanuel from the white hut next to the Star Gym on San Martín; and VILSA from the Despensa Abuela María, across the street from YPF at Pueyrredón. *Remises colectivos* can be flagged down along San Martín or the main RN86.

Visiting the park

It's possible to **visit the park** as a day-trip from Clorinda or Laguna Blanca village, but it makes sense to stay at least one night so that you can take advantage of sunset and dawn, when it's cooler and you stand a better chance of seeing the wildlife. To get the most out of Estero Poí Sector you really need your own transport, be it a 4WD or horse – so if you don't, you're best off heading to the Laguna Blanca Sector, which is more compact.

The turn-off to **Estero Poí** lies 2km from Laguna Blanca village in the direction of Clorinda, from where it's 9km of dirt road to the *guardaparques'* house and adjacent free **campsite**, which has few facilities other than toilets, showers and drinking water – bring all your other supplies. An interpretation trail runs from the campsite through the adjacent scrub, and within easy walking distance is a pair of swamps, dominated by the attractive *pehuajó* reed with its banana-palm leaves, as well as bulrushes, horsetails, and the mauve-flowered waterlilies. Further into the park lie swathes of savannah grassland and the gallery forest of the Río Pilcomayo – relatively narrow and unimpressive as a river at this point, but good for spotting wildlife. One *baqueano* **guide** permitted to accompany visitors is Sr Cornelio Primera, an entertaining guy whose exceptionally loud voice does have an annoying tendency to give animals forewarning of your advance. He has steady **horses** ($30 a day for guide and horse), and will take you on a two-day trip (approx 64km) to the Río Pilcomayo, overnighting in an abandoned estancia, *Seccional Ricardo Fonzo*, 5km from the river. Sr Primera lives 500m down the turn-off from the RN86, in the second house on the right.

At Naick Neck, 12km east of Laguna Blanca village and 40km west of Clorinda, a dirt track leads to the **Laguna Blanca Sector**. Walking the 5km from the RN86 to the *guardaparques'* post takes between an hour and an hour and a half, depending on whether or not rain has turned the road to sticky clay. If coming by *remise colectivo*, it's worth paying the extra fare to get dropped at the entrance not the turn-off. Next to where the *guardaparques* live is a pleasant free **campsite**, shaded by carobs and palms, with drinking water and showers; be warned, it gets busy at weekends. You'll need to bring all your own food supplies. A 300-metre **nature trail** from behind the toilet block gives you a good chance of seeing the howler monkeys that wake you up at night; while an excellent boardwalk takes you from the campsite some 500m through first-rate reedbed marshland to several lookout points and a ten-metre **tower** on the shore of the shallow lagoon itself. You're permitted to swim here, but don't feed the fish: and be warned that you should swim with your shoes on, or piranhas might snack on your toes. The dense mass of greenery around the edges of the lagoon gives you an idea of what early explorers faced when trying to discover if river systems connected through to the Amazon or the Andes. There are excellent opportunities for **bird-watching** in this sector, but get up early at weekends or you'll be disturbed by other visitors.

Into Paraguay: Asunción

Anyone travelling in the Chaco area should view **ASUNCIÓN**, 45km north of Clorinda and the capital city of Paraguay, as an essential port of call. It is also makes an ideal staging post for those journeying between Misiones and the Argentinian Northwest. Though Asunción is a fairly scrappy city, set atop a low, curving rise on an inlet of the Río Paraguay, it has had a remarkable history that dates back to its founding in 1537. In a day's walking tour, you can easily stroll around most of the sights in the historic centre, the **minicentro**. The **Plaza de los Héroes** forms one quarter of the four-block main square, and here you'll find the ornate **Panteón Nacional de los Héroes** (daily 7am–5pm; free), a memorial to the heroes of Paraguay's highly militaristic past. Another quadrant of the square is called **Plaza de la Democracia**, where you'll find a daily handicraft fair, selling examples of Paraguay's superb, inexpensive *artesanía*. Other sights include the wedding-cake **Palacio de Gobierno**, the official Presidential residence, and originally built as a private residence by Paraguay's most famous dictator, Mariscal Francisco Solano López, in the 1860s; the **Casa de la Independencia**, with high-quality period exhibits focusing around the 1811 declaration of independence from Spain; and the **Museo Ethnográfico Andrés Barbero**, which preserves one of Paraguay's pre-eminent collections of artefacts from Paraguay's numerous indigenous groups and has a fine scholarly library. One highlight is a trip on Latin America's oldest working train, the **wood-burning steam engine** which puffs out to Luque and Areguá (Sat & Sun 7.30am & 9am; $1.25 return). This service is unpredictable: check times the night before at the point of departure: one block down the tracks from Plaza Uruguaya's historic Estación del Ferrocarril.

Arrival and information

The Silvio Pettirossi **Airport** is 15km northeast of the centre. Taxis cost $15, or you can take bus #30A into the centre (heading from the centre, it leaves from Calle Oliva; every 5min till 11pm; 40min; $0.30). The main **border crossing** connecting the Paraguayan capital with the Argentine Chaco is 4km north of Clorinda at the Puente Internacional Loyola (24hr). **Buses** leave Clorinda from 7am. Make sure the driver knows you are foreign so that he waits for you to complete all the necessary formalities – these are fewer and quicker for locals. Your **passport** must be stamped by both sets of immigration authorities: leaving Argentina you'll stop at the Paraguayan booth for both stamps; coming back, both are given on the Argentinian side. If bus timetables don't suit, take a *remise* from Clorinda to the border and then a minibus from the other side. *Remises* do not cross the bridge, leaving you a 500-metre walk. Change $10 at the border – more than enough to get a taxi from the terminal in Asunción to the centre. The Paraguayan **currency** is the Guaraní and there are around G3300 to US$1. Paraguay is an hour behind Argentina in the winter months.

Asunción's **bus terminal** lies some 5km to the southeast of the historical centre, at the corner of Avenida Fernando de la Mora and Avenida República Argentina. Local bus #8 runs from outside the terminal to one block from central Plaza de los Héroes (every 5–10min; 30min; $0.25); **taxis** to the centre cost $5 (make sure in advance that you don't pay extra for bags; 20min). The main **tourist office** is in the minicentro, at Palma 468 (Mon–Fri 7am–7pm, Sat 7am–1pm; ☎021/441530 or 494110, fax 491230; *ditur@infonet.com.py*). It has city maps, as well as some useful information on the whole country, including recommended day-trips from the capital.

Accommodation

Central **accommodation** options include the *Granados Park*, Estrella y 15 de Agosto (☎021/497921, fax 445324; ⑧), the plushest international-standard five-star, with fresh rooms, plenty of attention to detail, a swimming pool and gym, and *Il Mondo* international restaurant; *Asunción Palace*, Colón 415 (☎ & fax 021/492151 to 492153; ④), an elegant, colonial-style mid-range hotel with plenty of character, but located in an area that is rather dark and less than salubrious at night; *La Española*, L.A. Herrera 142 (☎021/447312, fax 449280; ③), an excellent-value, modern, mid-range option with attractive patio; and the *Sahara*, Oliva 920 (☎021/445935, fax 493247; ① with fan), an idiosyncratic institution that's favoured by budget tour groups and truckers, and which has a new section. Many inexpensive hotels lie within a couple of blocks of the bus terminal: try *Hotel 2000*, directly opposite at Fdo. de la Mora 2332 (☎ & fax 021/550776; ②), a spruce, value-for-money option with air conditioning and a swimming pool and garden patio.

Eating and drinking

Local street **foods** include *choripanes* (real sausage hotdogs); *sopa paraguaya* (a filling savoury maize cake flavoured with cheese); and *chipas* (dry mandioca-flour rings). Wash these down with *mosto* (ice-cold sugar-cane juice) or *tereré* (*yerba mate* mixed with wild herbs and served with iced water), both sold around the Plaza de los Héroes. For **restaurants**, first stop should be the *Lido Bar*, at Palma and Chile, a classic, time-honoured institution for rapid snacks on-the-go, which prepares colossal *milanesas napolitanas* and a local catfish speciality, *chupí de surubí*. *La Paraguayita*, at Brasilia and República de Siria (☎021/204497), is good bet for traditional Paraguayan fare; or there's upmarket international cuisine at *Il Mondo*, in the *Granados Park Hotel* at Estrella and 15 de Agosto (☎021/497921, fax 445324). Near the Plaza Uruguaya is the *Café Literario*, Mcal. Estigarribia 456 (☎021/491640; open till 2am on Fri & Sat), a cultured, quiet book café serving wine as well as coffee; while the *Chopería El Tren,* in the historic train station at Eligio Ayala y México, is a funky nightspot to eat and sink draught beer.

Listings

Banks and exchange Banks are open Mon–Fri 8.45am–12.15pm or 3pm. Banco do Brasil, Oliva y N.S. Asunción, changes all types of travellers' cheques with no commission. (Avoid the ABN ATM, at Estrella and Alberdi, which charges 5 percent commission on foreign cards.) American Express, Luis Alberto Herrera and Yegros. Good exchanges (typically open Mon–Fri 8am–4.30 or 5.30pm, Sat 8am–11am or noon) include Guaraní, Palma 449; Internacional Cambios, Palma 364; Alberdi, Alberdi 247; and Cambios Chaco, Alberdi 217. Note that 10 percent is sometimes deducted if your US dollars are soiled or ripped. Argentine pesos are valued at slightly less than US\$. Ask for bills smaller than G50,000 – even the G10,000 can be awkward to change at times. Moneychangers hang around the Plaza de los Héroes or outside the exchanges outside trading hours; these are generally fairly safe, but if in any doubt avoid using them.

Car rental Localiza, Eligio Ayala 695 (☎ & fax 021/446233); National, at Yegros 501 and Cerro Corá (☎021/492157, fax 445890; weekend rates from \$30, plus special deals on unlimited mileage).

Consulates and visas If you need a visa to enter Paraguay, get it in Buenos Aires, as they take 4–5 days from the Formosa consulate. Argentina, at España and Perú (☎021/212320, fax 211029); Canada, at Prof. Ramírez and Juan de Salazar (☎021/227207, fax 227208); Britain, Av. Boggiani 5848 (☎021/612611, fax 605007); USA, Mariscal López 1776 (☎021/213715, fax 213728).

Hospital Brasil y Fulgencio Moreno (☎021/204800).

Internet Cybershop, Estrella 474 (Mon–Fri 8am–10pm, Sat 8am–4pm; \$0.65 for 15min).

Pharmacy Farmacenter, at Estrella and 14 de Mayo (☎021/498371). Open 24hr.

Police ☎021/441111.

Post office Correo Central, Alberdi 130 (Mon–Fri 7am–7pm, Sat 7–11.30am). Encomiendas Paraguay, just round the corner on Paraguayo Independiente (Mon–Fri 7am–7pm), for sending packages (rates far cheaper than in Argentina). Packages must be inspected before sealing.

Taxis ☎021/311080 or 550116.

Across Formosa Province: the RN81

The RN81 runs northwest of Formosa, paralleling the petroleum industry railway that crosses the province in a line as straight as the barrel of a gun. For those with a specialist interest in wildlife – especially birdlife – the route gives access to the **Bañado La Estrella**, a fascinating wetland near Las Lomitas, 300km from Formosa, and to the tiny **Reserva Natural Formosa**, on the Río Bermejo near Ingeniero Juárez, 460km from Formosa. Otherwise, you should avoid it: if you're looking just to cross the Chaco region, head out along the much faster RN16 from Resistencia. You can cross the entire length of the RN81 through to Salta Province by public transport, but it will take you two days even in good weather. The route is paved only as far as **Bazán** (30km past Las Lomitas), after which it becomes very rutted and potholed and is very dusty in dry weather, especially when the north wind blows (usually in August). Heading west from **Ingeniero Juárez**, the *monte* scrub vegetation becomes increasingly degraded, especially after you cross the provincial border. Just over an hour from Juárez, you come to **Los Blancos**. From here, it's 60km (approx 1hr 40min) to **Pluma del Pato**, where you pick up the poorly maintained paved road, and then another 96km to the junction (*El Cruce*) where the RN81 joins the main north–south RN34.

Here the climate is noticeably more humid: make sure you have long-sleeved tops and long trousers on or you'll be a meal for the *gigenes* (small black bugs with a disproportionately powerful, itchy bite).

Buses pass regularly in both directions and can be flagged down (north to Tartagal and the Bolivian border at Pocitos; south to Embarcación, San Pedro de Jujuy and Salta). **Driving times** on unsealed roads in this area of the world are entirely dependent on rainfall. When it rains, many vehicles simply do not travel as they can't negotiate the mud, and the ones that do often take several times what the same journey would take in good conditions (if in doubt, call the Vialidad Provincial in Formosa; ☎03717/426040 or 426041). Rainfall causes major problems, however, only when it is sustained: the intense heat and, frequently, the winds soon dry the roads otherwise. Beware of cows on roads and truck road hogs.

Bañado La Estrella

From the city of Formosa, the scenery becomes progressively drier – scrub with the occasional, virulently green wetland. The land is used predominantly for grazing cattle and goats, but charcoal is also produced, and you'll see the ovens by the side of the road and in the baked earth compounds of villages. Some 45km north of the village of Las Lomitas on the unsealed RP28 is the **Bañado La Estrella**, the lung of the Formoseñan Chaco. A huge swathe of wetland swamp, it runs across the central north of the province, fed by the waters of the Río Pilcomayo, a river that loses its direction and dissipates into numerous meandering channels as it crosses the immense chaco plains.

The RP28 crosses the Bañado by means of a causeway, or *pedraplen*, several hundred metres long, which is usually just beneath the water line. At this point, the scenery looks like a Dalí painting: skeletons of trees swaddled in duckweed-green vines, as if the floodwaters had once covered them and then receded, leaving them snagged with weed; beneath their branches shines the mirror-smooth blue water, dotted with rafts of *camalote* – a water lily with an inimitable lilac flower. The place is a **bird-watcher's paradise**, with an assortment of species ranging from the hulking southern screamer to the delicate jacana. However, unless you take a trip with the *Portal del Oeste* hotel (see below), you'll have to content yourself with viewing from the road: there are no boats to rent, or any other type of infrastructure for that matter. The area is also used at times as a fishing ground for local **Pilagá fishermen** who hunt *sábalo* with homemade spears (*fijas*). Please refrain from taking intrusive photographs – these people are generally reluctant to be photographed, especially without permission. June or July are the **best months to visit**, as otherwise you'll have to contend with the various types of biting insects. Bring a good repellent if visiting during other months.

Minibuses from Las Lomitas and Formosa come in on Calle Salta and drop you off at their ticket offices on the town's other main street, Avenida Degem, with its squat *palo borracho* trees. VILSA minibuses stop at Tomy Tours (which is also the departure point for minibuses westwards to Los Blancos); and Independencia minibuses stop at their office nearby. The most comfortable **accommodation** in the area is found at *El Portal del Oeste* (☎03715/15616609 or 03717/430989; ④; no credit cards), 4km to the east of Las Lomitas on the RN81, with a swimming pool (Nov–Feb), meals ($10 menu) and excursions to the swamp for groups. Alternatively, you can stay in Las Lomitas itself: one block from the bus terminal is the *Hotel Las Lomitas*, Rivadavia y Jorge Newberi (☎03715/432137; ①, ②, with bathroom). It's fresh, tiled, cool and clean; all rooms come with fans, and air conditioning is $5–10 extra. To get to the Bañado La Estrella on public transport from Las Lomitas, catch one of the **buses** heading to Zalazar and disembark at the causeway: La Norteña leaves from Moreno y Belgrano (daily at 3.30pm, returning from Zalazar 6am; $4; ☎03715/432195); and Zorat leaves from the bus terminal (Mon–Thurs & Sun at 11.30am; $4).

Reserva Natural Formosa

The only reason for stopping in Ingeniero Juárez, 160km northwest of Las Lomitas, is to visit the tiny **Reserva Natural Formosa**, which lies 55km south of this drab, dusty town. One of Argentina's smallest national parks, the reserve was intended to safeguard two co-existing ecosystems: a section of extremely parched dry chaco and the threatened forest on the banks of the Río Bermejo (also called Río Teuco). This purpose has been dealt a great blow by a canal built to irrigate lands in the interior of the province, as it has divided the already tiny area – just 100 square kilometres – into two halves. The western half of the reserve has been effectively surrendered to the 120 settlers and their cattle, and the rest is not big enough to provide a realistic, safe habitat for some of the Chaco's most threatened species. Do not let the promotional literature fool you: the reserve has no jaguars and there hasn't been a sighting of a giant armadillo – the symbol of the park – in decades. There are pumas, however, and you might see a giant anteater or a honey anteater, though neither is common and you'll need some luck. You've a better chance of seeing deer, tortoises, reptiles, and rodents such as the vizcacha.

The six-kilometre, self-guided **nature trail** that leads from the *guardaparques*' house on the eastern side of the canal (follow the posts topped with yellow paint) is one of the most informative interpretation trails of any to be found in an Argentinian national park, although the accompanying leaflet, *Monte Adentro*, is in Spanish only. The trail is especially good for identifying the impressive quantity of individual plant species in the confusing mass of scrub vegetation, and it takes you past an ox-bow lake that's a favoured haunt of ducks and rosy spoonbills. In addition, the reserve offers welcome opportunities for swimming in the Río Bermejo, but beware – the lazy curves of this broad river can harbour surprisingly swift currents after summer rains. After dry spells you can almost ford it.

Practicalities

Minibuses from Las Lomitas drop you off at Tomy Tours in Ingeniero Juárez. Getting to the reserve from here without your own transport is not straightforward. You may be able to pick-up a **remise** if you ask around, or you could try to hitch a lift with the *Intendente* of the park (☎03711/420049). Little traffic heads that way otherwise. **Accommodation** in town can be found in the *Hotel Carfa*, on Salta (☎03711/420103; ②); while *Tomy Tours* on Avenida Degem (☎03711/420139; ①), has the least expensive rooms in town, all with shared bathroom. In the park itself, there's a **campsite** with showers and toilets. Depending on the disposition of the incumbent *guardaparque* – usually very amenable – you may be able to make use of the park's drinking water supplies, but it's safer to carry your own, and don't underestimate usage, as the park becomes extremely hot – as high as 45°C during the summer months. A helpful *baqueano* guide who lives next door to the *guardaparque* hires out horses for exploring the park further (prices are not fixed, but calculate on $20 per person for a dawn or evening tour of two to three hours).

travel details

Buses

Asunción to: Buenos Aires (18 daily; 18hr–22hr 30min); Clorinda (2–8 daily; 1hr 15min–1hr 45min); Córdoba (3 weekly; 22hr); Formosa (4 daily; 3hr 30min); Foz Do Iguazú (1 daily; 5–7hr); Resistencia (4 daily; 5hr 30min); Salta (daily; 16hr).

Capitán Solari to: Resistencia (5 daily; 2hr–2hr 30min).

Clorinda to: Asunción (Mon–Sat 8 daily, Sun 2 daily; 1hr 15min–1hr 45min); Buenos Aires (3 daily; 16hr–18hr 30min); Formosa (11 daily; 1hr 45min–2hr); Laguna Blanca (7–8 daily; 1hr); Resistencia (9 daily; 4hr).

Formosa to: Asunción (4 daily; 3hr 30min); Buenos Aires (7 daily; 14–15hr); Clorinda (11 daily; 1hr 45min–2hr); Córdoba (2 daily; 14–17hr); Corrientes (10 daily; 2hr 45min); Ingeniero Juárez (6 daily; 7–8hr); Jujuy (1 daily; 13–14hr); Laguna Blanca (7–8 daily; 3hr); Las Lomitas (7 daily; 3hr 30min–5hr); Posadas (1 daily; 6hr); Puerto Iguazú (1 daily; 10hr); Resistencia (15 daily; 2hr 15min); Salta (1 daily; 14hr); Santa Fe (5 daily; 10hr).

Ingeniero Juárez to: Formosa (6 daily; 7–8hr); Las Lomitas (6 daily; 3hr 30min–4hr); Los Blancos (2–3 daily; 2hr 30min).

Laguna Blanca to: Clorinda (7–8 daily; 1hr); Formosa (7–8 daily; 3hr).

Las Lomitas to: Bañado La Estrella (1–3 daily; 50min–1hr); Formosa (7 daily; 3hr 30min–5hr); Ingeniero Juárez (6 daily; 3hr 30min–4hr).

Los Blancos to: Ingeniero Juárez (2 daily; 1hr 15min); El Cruce junction (2 daily; 3hr).

Pampa de los Guanacos to: Resistencia (4 daily; 5hr 30min–6hr); Santiago del Estero (3 daily; 7–8hr).

Presidencia Roque Sáenz Peña to: Pampa de los Guanacos (4 daily; 3hr); Resistencia (13 daily; 2–3hr); Salta (2 daily; 10–11hr).

Resistencia to: Asunción (4 daily; 5hr 30min); Buenos Aires (18 daily; 12hr 30min–14hr); Capitán Solari (5 daily; 2hr–2hr 30min); Clorinda (9 daily; 4hr); Córdoba (3 daily; 13hr); Corrientes (15 daily; 30min); Formosa (15 daily; 2hr 15min); Gancedo (2 daily; 5–6hr); Jujuy (1 daily; 13–14hr); Mendoza (1 daily; 24hr); Pampa de los Guanacos (4 daily; 5hr 30min–6hr); Pocitos (1 daily; 19–20hr); Posadas (13 daily; 5hr); Puerto Iguazú (1 daily; 10hr); Roque Sáenz Peña (13 daily; 2–3hr); Salta (3 daily; 12hr); San Ignacio Miní (1 daily; 6hr); Santiago del Estero (3 daily; 10–11hr); Tucumán (2 daily; 13hr).

Domestic flights

Formosa to: Buenos Aires (2 daily; 1hr 45–2hr).

Resistencia to: Buenos Aires (3 daily; 1hr 20min).

CHAPTER SIX

THE NORTHWEST

A rgentina's **Northwest** is a region of startling contrasts and infinite variety: ochre deserts where flocks of llamas roam, charcoal-grey lava-flows devoid of any life form, blindingly white salt-flats and sooty-black volcano cones, pristine limewashed colonial chapels set against striped mountainsides, lush citrus-groves and emerald-green sugar plantations, impenetrable jungles populated by toucans and tapirs. Today regarded as a marvellously secluded, far-flung corner of the country, this region is in fact the birthplace of Argentina – a Spanish colony thrived here when Buenos Aires was still a wavering attempt to set up a trading-post on the Atlantic coast. One of these colonial cities, enticing and youthful **Salta**, is indisputably the region's tourism capital, with some of the country's best hotels and finest colonial architecture, matchless services and a well-earned reputation for hospitality. To the northwest of Salta you can meander up the harsh yet enchanting **Quebrada del Toro** on a safari or, for the slightly less adventurous, on the luxurious and poetically named **Tren a los Nubes**, or Train to the Clouds, one of the world's highest railways, which runs to the metal viaduct called Polverilla. Alternatively, you can head due east and north across the subtropical lowlands, where jungle-clad **cloudforests**, or *yunga*, poke out of the flat, fertile plains into the raincloud that gives them their name. Three of these *yungas* – **El Rey**, **Calilegua** and **Baritú** – are protected, along with their prolific flora and fauna, by National Park status.

By far the most accessible of the three cloudforest parks, Calilegua, is in Jujuy Province, one of the federation's poorest and remotest, shoved up into the far north-western corner of the country against Chile and Bolivia, where in the space of a few kilometres humid valleys and soothingly green jungles give way to the austere, parched Altiplano (known in northwestern Argentina as *puna*), home to flocks of flamingoes, herds of llamas, and very few people. **Jujuy**, the slightly oddball provincial capital, cannot rival Salta for its amenities or architectural splendours, but it's the best starting-point for exploring one of the country's most photogenic features, the many-coloured **Quebrada de Humahuaca**. Lying off the RN9 that swerves up this gorge and clambers ever higher to the Bolivian border at La Quiaca, are time-stood-still hamlets such as **Iruya**, **Cochinoca** and **Yavi**.

Further south, snaking mountain roads scale the verdant **Cuesta del Obispo** and the stark but vividly coloured **Quebrada de las Conchas** from Salta to the **Valles Calchaquíes**, dry, sunny valleys along which high-altitude vineyards somehow thrive,

---

ACCOMMODATION PRICE CODES

The price codes used for accommodation throughout this chapter refer to the cheapest rate for a double room in high season. Single travellers will only occasionally pay half the double-room rate; nearer two thirds is the norm and some places will expect you to pay the full rate. Note that in resort towns, there are considerable discounts out of season.

① $20 or less	④ $45–60	⑦ $100–150
② $20–30	⑤ $60–80	⑧ $150–200
③ $30–45	⑥ $80–100	⑨ Over $200

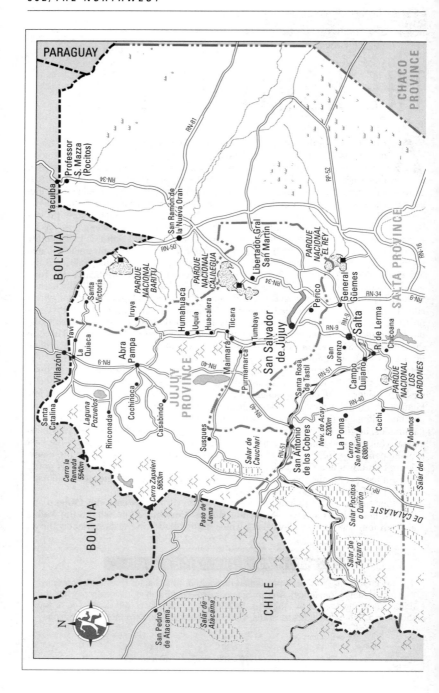

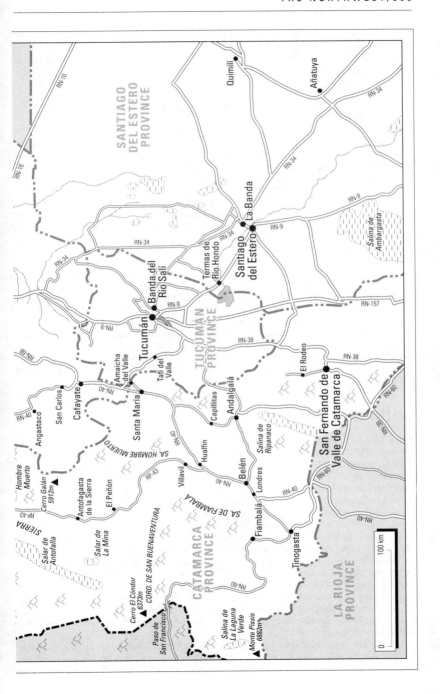

particularly around the airy regional capital of **Cafayate**. At the southern end of the valleys, one of the region's most thoroughly restored pre-Columbian sites, **Quilmes**, enjoys a fabulous mountainside location, while nearby **Tafí del Valle**, almost Alpine in feel, is the favourite weekend and summer retreat for the people of nearby **Tucumán**. Tucumán is the region's biggest metropolis by far and its commercial powerhouse; it sprawls across a brilliantly green valley where sugar cane, lemons and quinces grow in abundance, but like **Santiago del Estero** to the southeast, the country's oldest city, its attractions are too few to make you want to linger more than a day or two. The city of **Catamarca** to the south is no better endowed with sights, but the empty highlands to its northwest are staggeringly beautiful: noble landscapes that will tempt you to use up all your film or even sit down and paint. As you journey towards the sharp altiplanic atmosphere of the **Puna Jujeña**, via the transitional valleys, you could visit **Andalgalá**, surrounded by dramatic mountains, the charming, historic town of **Londres**, or **Belén**, the last justifiably famous for its textiles, particularly its handsome ponchos.

Higher still, on the way to remote and rarefied **Antofagasta de la Sierras** and beyond, desolate tracks take you past inhospitable salt-flats, the biggest **crater** on the Earth's surface and eternally frozen lagoons, in the shadow of **volcanic cones** the colour of tar, with the snowcapped ramparts of the Andes as a beguiling backdrop. This is a part of the world so remarkably unspoiled and thinly populated that you sometimes feel like the last, or better still the first, person alive. You would be very unlucky indeed not to spy **Andean wildlife**, in large numbers: flamingoes and condors, alpacas and vicuñas, grey foxes and vizcachas. Finally, as you head towards one of the most spectacular passes across the cordillera to Chile, the **Paso de San Francisco**, you could stop over and relax at the mountainside thermal springs of **Fiambalá**, the perfect antidote to the sometimes gruelling but always exhilarating experience of the Northwest.

Much of the Northwest region is accessible by **public transport** but organized tours or, even better, exploring in a 4WD are generally more rewarding ways of discovering the area, and at times are the only way of getting around. Should you choose to go it alone, take into account the mind-boggling distances involved, the challenging road and climatic conditions and, above all, the sheer remoteness of it all.

Salta and around

SALTA, historic capital of one of Argentina's biggest and most beautiful provinces, easily lives up to its well-publicized nickname of Salta the Fair (*Salta la Linda*), thanks to its festive atmosphere, handsome buildings and dramatic setting. In a region where the landscape and nature, rather than the towns and cities, are the main attractions, Salta is the exception proving the rule. Located at the eastern end of the fertile Valle de Lerma, nationally famous for its tobacco plantations, and bounded by the Río Vaqueros to the north and Río Arenales to the south, the city is squeezed between steep, rippling mountains, 1500km northwest of Buenos Aires; it enjoys a relatively balmy climate, thanks to its location at 1190m above sea level, making it the country's second highest provincial capital. In recent years, Salta has become the Northwest's undisputed tourist capital, and its top-quality services catering for the many visitors include a slew of highly professional tour operators, some of the region's best-appointed hotels plus a lively youth hostel, and a handful of good restaurants. In addition to a cable car and a tourist railway, its sights include the marvellous Neoclassical **Iglesia San Francisco**, an anthropological museum and a historical museum. A generous sprinkling of well-preserved or well-restored **colonial architecture** has survived, giving the place a pleasant homogeneity and a certain charm.

Many visitors to Salta speed around the city and then head off to the major attractions of the Quebrada del Toro (see p.398) – often on the Tren a los Nubes – and the Valles Calchaquíes (see p.419), perhaps staying over in Cafayate. But much closer to

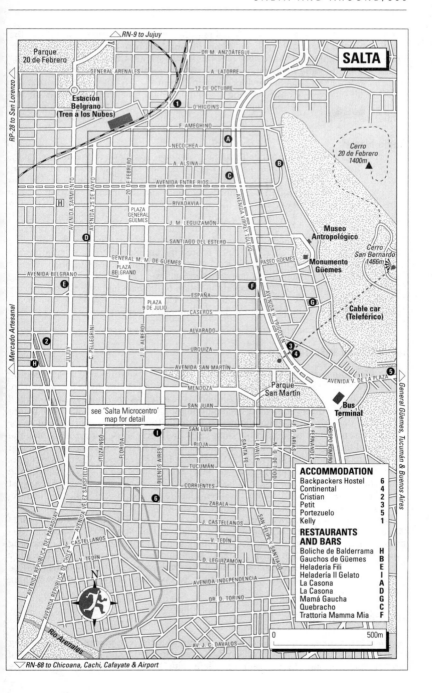

SALTA

Parque 20 de Febrero

RN-9 to Jujuy

DR M. ANZÓATEGUI
GENERAL ARENALES
A. LATORRE
12 DE OCTUBRE
O'HIGGINS
F. AMEGHINO
NECOCHEA
A. ALSINA
AVENIDA ENTRE RIOS
RIVADAVIA
J. M. LEGUIZAMÓN
SANTIAGO DEL ESTERO
GENERAL M. M. DE GÜEMES
PLAZA BELGRANO
AVENIDA BELGRANO
ESPAÑA
PLAZA 9 DE JULIO
CASEROS
ALVARADO
URQUIZA
AVENIDA SAN MARTÍN
MENDOZA
SAN JUAN
SAN LUIS
RIOJA
TUCUMÁN
CORRIENTES
ZABALA
J. CASTELLANOS
V. TEDÍN
D. LEGUIZAMÓN
AVENIDA INDEPENDENCIA
DR. D. TORINO
AV. J. C. DÁVALOS

Estación Belgrano (Tren a los Nubes)

RP-28 to San Lorenzo

AVENIDA SARMIENTO
AVENIDA 25 DE MAYO
20 DE FEBRERO

PLAZA GENERAL GÜEMES

C. PELLEGRINI
J. B. ALBERDI

Mercado Artesanal

JUJUY
ITUZAINGÓ
FLORIDA
BUENOS AIRES
AVENIDA REPÚBLICA DE PARAGUAY
AVENIDA REPÚBLICA DE CHILE
AVENIDA VELEZ SARSFIELD

Río Arenales

RN-68 to Chicoana, Cachi, Cafayate & Airport

Cerro 20 de Febrero 1400m

Museo Antropológico

AVENIDA VIREY TOLEDO
PASEO GÜEMES
Monumento Güemes

Cerro San Bernardo 1466m

AVENIDA H. YRIGOYEN

Cable car (Teleférico)

AVENIDA V. DE LA PLAZA

Parque San Martín

Bus Terminal

General Güemes, Tucumán & Buenos Aires

J. A. FERNÁNDEZ
G. ARIAS
M. G. TODD
LAVALLE
SANTA FE
SAN FELIPE SANTIAGO
OBISPO ROMERO

see 'Salta Microcentro' map for detail

N

ACCOMMODATION

Backpackers Hostel	6
Continental	4
Cristian	2
Petit	3
Portezuelo	5
Kelly	1

RESTAURANTS AND BARS

Boliche de Balderrama	H
Gauchos de Güemes	B
Heladería Fili	E
Heladería Il Gelato	I
La Casona	A
La Casona	D
Mamá Gaucha	G
Quebracho	C
Trattoria Mamma Mia	F

0   500m

hand are two other areas well worth visiting, the sub-tropical, jungle-clad hills to the north, around the tranquil weekend resort of **San Lorenzo**, perched on cool, sometimes misty heights, and the lowlands to the south, around **Chicoana**, an old gaucho stronghold in the **Valle de Lerma**, dripping with atmosphere and one of the gateways to the central valleys of Salta Province. Quite different to each other in feel, both make excellent alternatives for anyone trying to avoid big cities. An alternative excursion destination is the cloudforest national park of **El Rey**, to the east, though Calilegua, the similar park in Jujuy Province, is both more accessible and more rewarding.

Some history

Governor Hernando de Lerma of Tucumán, who gave his name to the nearby valley, founded the city of Salta on April 16, 1582, following the instructions of Viceroy Toledo, to guarantee the safety of anyone entering or leaving Tucumán itself. The site was chosen for its strategic mountainside location, and the streams flowing nearby were used as natural moats. In 1776 the already flourishing city was made capital of a huge Intendencia that took in Santiago del Estero, Jujuy and even the southern reaches of modern Bolivia, becoming one of the major centres in the viceroyalty. From 1810 to 1814 it was the headquarters of the Ejércitos del Norte and for the following seven years was where General Güemes posted his anti-Royalist forces, creating the now traditional red-poncho uniform for his gaucho militia. However, once Buenos Aires became the capital of the young country, Salta went into steady decline, missing out on the rest of the country's mass immigration of the mid- and late nineteenth century; the railway didn't arrive here until 1890. The belated urban explosion in the 1920s and 1930s has left its mark on the predominantly neocolonial style of architecture in the city.

Arrival and information

Salta's **El Aybal Airport** (☎0387/437-5111) is about 10km southwest of the city centre, along the RN51. Bus #22 ($3) runs between the airport and central Avenida San Martín; a taxi would set you back about $10. Aerolíneas Argentinas also runs a shuttle to and from its downtown office, meeting incoming flights and heading out one hour before scheduled departures. Regular flights arrive from Buenos Aires and several other domestic airports, as well as from Santa Cruz in Bolivia. Buses from all across the region and throughout the country use the scruffy but user-friendly **bus terminal** at Av. Hipólito Yrigoyen (☎0387/431-5227), just east of the Parque San Martín, five blocks south and eight east of central Plaza 9 de Julio. Bus #5 links the bus terminal with the **train station**, at Ameghino 690, via Plaza 9 de Julio. The only trains serving Salta apart from the privately run tourist train, the Tren a las Nubes (see box, p.399), are the infrequent goods- and passenger-trains to the Chilean border.

The excellent, dynamic and well-equipped provincial **tourist office** at Buenos Aires 93 (Mon–Fri 8am–9pm, Sat, Sun & public holidays 9am–8pm; ☎0387/431-0950) dispenses a free map and extensive accommodation information and offers free **walking tours** around city, taking in the main sights; some staff members speak English. Rather less impressive, but awash with useful brochures and leaflets, is the **city tourist office** further down Buenos Aires at the corner of Av. San Martín (daily 8am–9pm; ☎0387/437-3341).

Accommodation

As you'd expect of such a regional hub, Salta has a wide range of **places to stay**, ranging from one of the only boutique hotels in the country to a fun youth hostel, plus plenty of decent middle-range hotels and excellent-value *residenciales* in between. The

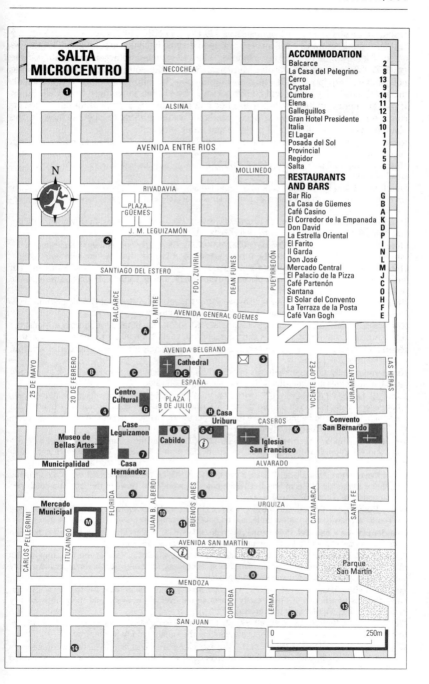

SALTA MICROCENTRO

ACCOMMODATION

Balcarce	2
La Casa del Pelegrino	8
Cerro	13
Crystal	9
Cumbre	14
Elena	11
Galleguillos	12
Gran Hotel Presidente	3
Italia	10
El Lagar	1
Posada del Sol	7
Provincial	4
Regidor	5
Salta	6

RESTAURANTS AND BARS

Bar Río	G
La Casa de Güemes	B
Café Casino	A
El Corredor de la Empanada	K
Don David	D
La Estrella Oriental	P
El Farito	I
Il Garda	N
Don José	L
Mercado Central	M
El Palacio de la Pizza	J
Café Partenón	C
Santana	O
El Solar del Convento	H
La Terraza de la Posta	F
Café Van Gogh	E

Backpackers Hostel is at Buenos Aires 930 (☎0387/423-5910; *backpack@hostels.org.ar*) and has double rooms as well as very cramped dorms. Facilities are not great but there's a very friendly, international atmosphere. Salta's enormous municipal **campsite**, *Casino* (☎0387/423-1341), in the Parque Municipal, 3km to the south of the centre, is a little noisy but well equipped, with a huge swimming pool, hot showers, balneario and a supermarket. It costs $3 per tent and $2 per person. The #13 bus runs there from Calle Jujuy. If you'd rather avoid the city, you'll also find a number of **fincas** and **estancias** in the surrounding countryside, offering accommodation ranging from the comfortable to the plain luxurious plus all kinds of pursuits and other services.

Residencial Balcarce, Balcarce 460 (☎0387/431-8135). A plain but pleasant *residencial*, with shared bathroom. ②.

Hostal del Cerro, Santa Fe 456 (☎0387/431-8572). Like most of Salta's cheaper establishments, it's small, friendly and basic but clean. ②.

Hotel Continental, Hipólito Yrigoyen 295 (☎0387/431-1083; *LU7OAJ@salney.com.ar*). Very Seventies decor in an outmoded way, but clean, comfortable and with great views of the *teleférico* and Cerro San Bernardo. ④.

Hotel Cristian, Islas Malvinas 160 (☎0387/431-9600). Very pleasant rooms, mostly quiet, with private bath, and fresh decoration. Large breakfasts. ⑤.

Hotel Crystal, Urquiza and Alberdi (☎0387/431-0738). Extremely old-fashioned, teetering on the dowdy, but everything works and the service is friendly. All rooms with en-suite bathroom. ⑤.

Hotel Cumbre, Ituzaingo 585 (☎0387/431-7770; *cumbre@salnet.com.ar*). Not luxurious, but smarter than most of the mid-range places, and modern plumbing. Large bedrooms, all with private bath. ⑤.

Residencial Elena, Buenos Aires 256 (☎0387/421-1529). Large bedrooms with en-suite bathrooms, in a Spanish-run guesthouse built around a leafy patio. ②.

Residencial Galleguillos, Mendoza 509 (☎0387/431-8985). One of the best budget pensions; the rooms are basic, but the breakfast is generous, and you could not want for kinder hospitality. ①.

Residencial Italia, Alberdi 231 (☎0387/421-4050). Clean, friendly place, with a handful of small but comfortable double rooms. ②.

Residencial Kelly, O'Higgins 440 (☎0387/422-4721). Convenient for the train station, it's small and basic but the rooms are more than adequate and very good value. ①.

Hotel El Lagar, 20 de Febrero 877 (☎0387/421-7943, fax 431-9439). A wonderful boutique hotel, where every whim is catered for and the decor forms an exquisite art collection; it's exclusive but not snobbish, and is undoubtedly one of the most luxurious, tastefully decorated hotels in the country. Rooms must be booked in advance. ⑦.

Hotel Petit, Hipólito Yrigoyen 225 (☎0387/421-3012). From the swimming pool and café terrace, and the rooms at the back, you get wonderful mountain views. Good service and plush rooms. ④.

Hotel Portezuelo, Avenida del Turista 1 (☎0387/431-0105; *hprtzelo@salnet.com.ar*). A modern inn-style hotel at the top of Cerro San Bernardo, enjoying wonderful views of the city. Top-notch service to match, and agreeable rooms. ⑥.

Hotel Posada del Sol, Alvarado 646 (☎0387/431-7290; *hpdelsol@salnet.com.ar*). Nothing special: the rooms are large, very comfortable, and all have bathrooms. ⑥.

Residencial La Casa del Pelegrino, Alvarado 351 (☎0387/432-0423). The best budget place in town – decent, clean and safe. Plenty of hot water for the shared shower. ①.

Gran Hotel Presidente, Avenida Belgrano 353 (☎0387/431-2022). One of the newcomers, this ultra-modern and slightly impersonal place has smart rooms, state-of-the-art bathrooms and a glitzy café, plus a stylish restaurant and swimming pool. ②.

Hotel Provincial, Caseros 786 (☎0387/432-2000; *hotel@salnet.com.ar; resev@hotelprovinc.com.ar*). One of Salta's best hotels, it's not exactly charming but everything works and the rooms are airy and comfortable; popular with tour groups. ⑦.

Hotel Regidor, Buenos Aires 10 (☎0387/421-1305). Charming place, with character, a rustic confitería and very pleasant rooms. Rooms overlooking the square tend to be noisy. ⑤.

Hotel Salta, Buenos Aires 1 (☎0387/431-0740; *hotelsalta@arnet.com.ar*). An institution; this hotel's comfort is in keeping with its architectural splendour, from the lovely majolica tiles and carved wood in the lobby, to the colonial-style rooms. The enormous and luxurious presidential suite is its pride and joy. ⑥.

The City

Salta's central square, **Plaza 9 de Julio**, is one of the country's most harmonious; on it stands the city's Neoclassical **Cathedral**, the snow-white **Cabildo** and a number of popular cafés. A couple of blocks to the west huddle some well-preserved eighteenth- and nineteenth-century houses, including the immaculately whitewashed Casa Arías Rengel, now home to the **Museo Provincial de Bellas Artes**. Two of the most striking sights in the city are the **Iglesia San Francisco**, an extravagant piece of neocolonial architecture, and the more subdued but equally imposing **Convento de San Bernardo**. All of these sights are concentrated in the square kilometre or so of microcentro and can comfortably be seen in a couple of days. Heavy traffic and pollution are something of a growing problem in Salta but getting around on foot poses no problems and it's hard to get lost, since the grid system is almost perfect in the microcentro; north–south streets change name at Calle Caseros; east–west streets on either side of avenidas Virrey Toledo and Hipólito Yrigoyen. **Taxis** are plentiful and cheap, while **buses** take coins not tokens, but you're unlikely to need either given the compactness of downtown Salta.

Plaza 9 de Julio

Surrounded on all four sides by graceful, shady *recovas* or arcades, under which several café terraces lend themselves to idle people-watching, **Plaza 9 de Julio** is a pleasant spot to while away an hour or two. The well-manicured central part of the square is

---

EARTHQUAKES AND THE FIESTA DEL MILAGRO

No earthquake as severe as those that destroyed the cities of Mendoza in 1861 and San Juan in 1944 has struck the Northwestern region of Argentina within recent history, but this part of the country lies along the same fault line that was answerable for that seismic activity and is prone to occasional tremors, some of them violent. The **Nazca plate**, beneath the eastern Pacific, and the southern **America plate**, covering the whole continent, are constantly colliding – a continuation of the tectonic activity that formed the Andean cordillera in the first place. To make matters worse, the Nazca plate is nudging its way beneath the landmass, an action that accounts for the abundance of **volcanoes** along the range; some of them are extinct, others lie dormant, but none in the Northwest is very active. A number of **earthquakes** of varying strength have rocked the Northwest of Argentina since the Europeans arrived, accounting for the repeated displacement of many settlements and the absence of colonial architecture in some of the oldest cities, such as Santiago del Estero. Salta still thanks its lucky stars for **El Milagro**, the legend according to which two sacred images have spared Salta the kind of destruction caused by seismic disasters. An image of **Christ** and another of the **Virgin Mary** were found floating in a box off the coast of Peru in 1592, exactly a century after the Americas were discovered by Columbus, and somehow ended up in Salta. Precisely one century later, on September 13, 1692, a series of tremors began to shake the city, damaging some public buildings and houses. During that night, a priest named José Carrión dreamed that if the images of Christ and Mary were paraded through the streets for nine days the earthquakes would stop and Salta would be spared for ever. Apparently it worked and, ever since, the **Fiesta del Milagro** has been a major event in the city's calendar. Festivities and religious ceremonies starting on September 6 reach a climax on September 15, when the now famous images are paraded through the city's streets in a massive, solemn but colourful procession.

a collection of palms and tipas, fountains and benches, plus a quaint late nineteenth-century bandstand.On the northern side of the Plaza at España 537, the cream-coloured **Cathedral** dates from 1882, the city's third centenary. It's an Italianate Neoclassical pile, of the kind found all over the region, with some well-executed interior frescoes – the one of the *Four Apostles* around the cupola is particularly fine. Inside, and immediately to the left of the entrance, is the grandiose Panteón de los Héroes del Norte, where General Güemes is buried. The Capilla del Señor del Milagro and Capilla de la Virgen del Milagro, at the far end of the left and right aisles respectively, house the sacred images that are the centrepieces of major celebrations every September (see box on p.389).

Opposite the cathedral, on the southern side of the plaza at Caseros 549, stands the white-facaded **Cabildo**. Originally built in the early seventeenth century, it took on its current appearance in the late eighteenth century, when the city became capital of the Intendencia. It underwent a face-lift that left its slightly lopsided structure – the two rows of graceful arches don't quite tally – essentially intact in the middle of the twentieth century, over a hundred years after it ceased to be the colonial headquarters. It now houses the highly eclectic **Museo Histórico del Norte** (Tues–Fri 9.30am–1.30pm & 3.30–8.30pm, Sat 9.30am–1.30pm & 4.30–8pm, Sun 9.30am–1pm & 4.30–8pm; $2), whose collections range from coins and eighteenth-century paintings through wooden saints and archeological finds to wonderful horse-drawn carriages parked in the atmospheric cobbled courtyards, amongst them an elegant nineteenth-century hearse. Of the religious art in the first two rooms, the moving *San Pedro de Alcantara*, by the eighteenth-century Altoperuvian artist Melchor Pérez de Holguin, stands out. Excellent temporary exhibitions, usually of regional art, are staged in the beautifully restored building but the superb views across the plaza from the upper-storey veranda alone make a visit worthwhile.

On the western flank of the plaza, at Bartolomé Mitre 23, the grandly named **Casa Cultural de las Americas** (Mon–Fri 8am–1pm 5–9pm; free) – used occasionally for art exhibitions, concerts or recitals – is a splendidly pseudo-Parisian, Academic-style building, complete with a mansard-roof and the regulation arcades, and its lavish interior is worth a lingering glance, even though the exhibitions aren't always up to much. Finally, diagonally opposite the cathedral at Buenos Aires 1, the **Hotel Salta** built in the 1930s is a fine example of the city's neocolonial architecture. Prestigious architects Asián y Ezcurra won a government competition to build Salta's official hotel and the resulting highly ornamented and perfectly symmetrical edifice is used for state visits even today. The Andalucian influence is enhanced by brightly coloured Moorish tiles in and around the lobby, while a rustic touch is provided by the rough-hewn stone walls and simple timber balconies.

Museo Provincial de Bellas Artes Arías Rengel

More colonial and neocolonial buildings are clustered in a few blocks to the west of Plaza 9 de Julio. Just 100m west of the cabildo is the **Museo Provincial de Bellas Artes Arías Rengel** at La Florida 20 (Tues–Sat 9am–1pm & 5–9pm, Sun 9am–1pm; $1). The pedestrianized street allows you an unrestricted view of its brilliant white facade, with its elaborate arched doorway and handsome green door. Erected towards the end of the eighteenth century, and virtually intact, albeit well-restored, it's the finest viceregal building left in the city. The home of Sergeant-Major Félix Arías Rengel, who conquered the Argentine Chaco and had the house built, it has splendid patios, full of lush trees and plants, while the fine interior details include verandas, bannisters and rafters of red quebracho timber. Occasionally putting on regional or national art exhibitions, the museum houses the city's rich fine art collection, ranging from paintings from Cusco to twentieth-century sculpture. Highlights are a *St Matthew* of the **Cusqueña school** (see box on p.111), an eighteenth-century polychrome *Asunción de* *la Virgen* from the Jesuit missions, a large painting of *The City of Salta*, painted in 1854 by Giorgio Penutti, and some fine engravings by nineteenth-century artists Basaldúa, Spilimbergo and Quinquela Martín. Contrasting effectively with the pristine museum building is the Casa Leguizamón next door, at Caseros and La Florida: constructed at the beginning of the nineteenth century for a rich merchant, it's painted a deep raspberry pink, and its plain two storeys are set off by fine detailing, a delicate wrought-iron balcony and zinc gargoyles. A few steps south is the **Municipalidad**, whose unusual twelve-columned oval patio is worth investigating, while opposite, at La Florida 97, is the **Casa de Hernández**, a typical corner-house with a chamfered angle – this idea of bevelled corners on city houses was "invented" by urban planners in mid-nineteenth-century Barcelona as a way of making pavements wider and was exported throughout the Spanish-speaking world. It is worth seeing in its own right as a typical neocolonial house, built around 1870, with a delightful patio at its heart, and the interior is being converted into the **Museo de la Ciudad** (Mon–Fri 9am–1pm & 4–8.30pm, Sat 9am–1pm; free), still at the fledgling stage but eventually destined to house artefacts and documents tracing the city's history.

Casa Uriburu, Iglesia San Francisco and Convento San Bernardo

Calle Caseros, a busy thoroughfare leading east from the Hotel Salta, takes you past a number of striking neocolonial buildings and a fine late eighteenth-century house, built to a simple design and with one of the most charming patios in the city: the **Casa Uriburu**, at Caseros 417, housing a museum of period furniture and Uriburu memorabilia (Tues–Fri 9.30am–1.30pm & 3.30–8.30pm, Sat 9.30am–1.30pm & 4.30–8pm, Sun 9.30am–1pm & 4.30–8pm; $1). Home to the influential Uriburu family, who produced two presidents of Argentina, its most impressive room is undoubtedly the reconstructed kitchen, with its polished copper and earthenware pots.

At the next corner, with Calle Córdoba, and taking up a whole block, stands a city landmark and one of the most beautiful religious buildings in the country, the **Iglesia y Convento San Francisco**: an extravaganza of Italianate neocolonial exuberance by architect **Luigi Giorgi**, displaying a text-book compliance with architectural principles combined with clever idiosyncrasies. The first thing that strikes you is the colour: pure ivory-white columns stand out from the vibrant ox-blood walls, while the profuse detailing of Latin inscriptions, symbols and Neoclassical patterns is picked out in braid-like golden yellow. Seen against a deep blue sky – virtually perennial hereabouts – the whole effect is stunning. While the main building, and the adjoining convent, were built in the middle of the eighteenth century, the facade and atrium were later additions, in keeping with the mid-nineteenth-century obsession with Neoclassicism. The church's most imposing feature is the slender **campanile**, towering over the low-rise neocolonial houses of downtown Salta and tapering off to a slender spire. Following the convention of three progressively smaller storeys on a plain base, each level is ornamented according to the classic Jesuit order of four styles of column: Tuscan, Ionic, Corinthian and Composite. The highly elaborate **facade** of the church itself, behind a suitably austere statue of St Francis in the middle of the courtyard, is lavishly decorated with balustres and scrolls, curlicues and pinnacles, Franciscan inscriptions and the order's shield, but the most original features are the organza-like **stucco curtains** that billow down from each of the three archways, nearly touching the elegant wrought-iron gates below. Inside, the decoration is subdued, almost plain in comparison, but the most eye-catching elements are the three eighteenth-century Portuguese-style jacaranda-wood **armchairs** in the presbytery. The **cloisters** of the convent sometimes shelter exhibitions of local arts and crafts.

Three blocks further east along Caseros, on a large, open square, stands another convent, the **Convento San Bernardo** and its relatively dull church, altered in the early twentieth century. Still a Carmelite nunnery and closed to the public, this sixteenth-century convent building is one of the oldest still standing in Salta, albeit heavily altered and restored over the centuries. The convent's sturdy limewashed facade, punctuated by the tiniest of windows and a couple of dainty lamps on simple iron brackets, contrasts pleasingly with the backdrop of chocolate-brown mountains, the stark plaza in front and two heavily ornate **Rococo-style doors**. The first, to the left, is the former entrance to the early nineteenth-century Bethlemite Hospital, now blocked off: framed by four Tuscan columns, it comprises an oval ox-eye and a curvaceous fan-shaped lintel, dripping with Baroque mouldings. A large Argentine flag flutters over the other convent entrance, further to the right, knocked through the wall in the middle of the nineteenth century. Its decoration is a carbon copy of the first, except it has spiralling columns on either side and, instead of a blind window, its centrepiece is a lavishly carved **cedar-wood door**, dating from 1762 and transferred from a patrician house elsewhere in the city. A smaller door, for daily use, has been cut into the enormous portal which is opened only for special processions.

Museo Antropológico Juan Martín Leguizamón and Cerro San Bernardo

Starting three blocks north of the Convento San Bernardo, and two east, across Avenida Hipólito Yrigoyen, tree-lined **Paseo Güemes** is the main thoroughfare of a leafy, well-to-do barrio crammed with later neocolonial houses; it climbs up towards a bombastic **monument** of General Güemes, Salta's local hero. Surrounded by a grove of eucalyptus, the bronze equestrian statue, dating from 1931, is decorated with bas-reliefs depicting the army which defended newly independent Argentina from several last-ditch invasions by the Spanish. Immediately behind it, where the streets begin to slope up the lower flanks of the mountain, is the modern **Museo Antropológico Juan Martín Leguizamón** at Ejército del Norte and Polo Sur (Mon–Fri 8am–1pm & 2–6pm, Sun 10am–1pm; $2). The varied collection could be better presented, and most of the explanations in Spanish are sketchy and inaccurate, but many of the items on display are well worth seeing. One highlight is a well-preserved **mummy** found on Cerro Lullaillaco, on the Chilean border, bearing signs that it may have been a human sacrifice, while the centrepiece of the extensive ceramics collection is a set of finds from Tastil (see p.400), along with a petroglyph known as the **Bailarina de Tastil**, a delightful dancing figure painted onto rock, removed from the *pukará* or pre-Columbian fortress to the safety of a glass case. A well-executed reconstruction of a pre-Columbian burial urn shows how the local climate preserved textiles and wood in perfect condition for centuries. Finally, the section on festivals and **carnival** includes photographs of celebrations in Iruya (see p.413) and displays examples of the so-called *máscaras de viejo*, the old-man **masks** worn during the ceremonies there, along with the distinctive Chané masks, animal and bird heads made of *palo borracho* wood, and the grotesque carnival masks from Oruro, Bolivia.

A steep path zigzags up the overgrown flanks of **Cerro San Bernardo** (1458m) immediately behind the museum, but you might prefer to take the **teleférico** or cable car from the base-station on Avenida Hipólito Yrigoyen, between Urquiza and Avenida San Martín, at the eastern end of Parque San Martín (Mon–Fri 9am–6.45pm, Sat, Sun & public holidays 9am–7.45pm; $3 each way; $2 for children). The smooth cable-car gondolas, running in a continuous loop, take you to the summit in less than ten minutes, and from them and from the small garden at the top you can admire panoramic **views** of the city and the snowcapped mountain range to the west; a **café** with terrace serves drinks and simple meals.

Eating, drinking and entertainment

Salta has plenty of **eating** places to suit all pockets, ranging from simple **snack bars** where you can savour the city's famous **empanadas**, to a couple of classy **restaurants**, where people dress up to go out for dinner. The most atmospheric **cafés** huddle together around the Plaza 9 de Julio, while the city's many lively **peñas**, informal folk-music clubs, also serve food and drinks, so you can kill two birds.

Restaurants

La Casona, Virrey Toledo 1017; and at 25 de Mayo and Santiago del Estero. Both branches, open round the clock, churn out a never-ending supply of *empanadas*, including the best cheese pasties in town.

El Corredor de la Empanadas, Caseros 117. Pleasant decor and a large patio are the settings for outstanding *empanadas*, *humitas*, *tamales* and other Northwestern dishes.

Don David, España 476. Roast kid and suckling-pig are the two high-cholesterol but delicious specialities at this institutional restaurant.

Don José, Urquiza 484 (☎0387/431-9576). Cheap and cheerful restaurant serving up home cooking in a laid-back atmosphere; the paintings on the walls are Don José's too.

La Estrella Oriental, San Juan 137. If you fancy a change from *empanadas* and steaks, this Middle Eastern restaurant can help out with hummus and lamb kebabs, rounded off with baklava.

Il Garda, San Martín 221 (☎0387/422-3266). Good, home-style Italian cooking in a traditional, easy-going restaurant overlooking the Parque San Martín.

Mamá Gaucha, Gurruchaga 225. A parrilla, serving gaucho-style steaks in a friendly ambience.

Mercado Central, La Florida and San Martín. A number of small stalls serving all the local fare at very low prices, great for a lunchtime snack.

El Palacio de la Pizza, Caseros 427. It lives up to its name, with the best pizzas in Salta by far. Also good *empanadas*.

Quebracho, Virrey Toledo 702. One of the best restaurants in the city, with reliable if predictable food, plus fish, unusual for Salta, all well served at reasonable prices.

Santana, Mendoza 208. An elegant establishment serving international cooking, which makes a change from the usual *locro* and *humitas*.

El Solar del Convento, Caseros 444 (☎0387/421-5124). Elegant surroundings, classical music and a free glass of champagne set the tone for this high-class restaurant, serving juicy steaks and providing an excellent wine-list. Salta's top restaurant, without a doubt.

La Terraza de la Posta, España 476. A family parrilla, ideal for children, with no-nonsense traditional food, such as *locro* and *humitas*, as well as tender steaks and the usual desserts.

Trattoria Mamma Mia, Pasaje Zorrilla 1. Delicious fresh pasta, pizzas, soups, grilled meats, tiramisu and a good wine-list.

Bars and cafés

Bar Río, Plaza 9 de Julio. An institutional bar, with fewer tourists than most around the square, despite the inexpensive drinks.

Casino, Mitre 331. Stylish café-bar, away from the tourist magnets of the plaza. Lots of locals drinking coffee or swigging beer.

El Farito, Caseros 509, Plaza 9 de Julio. Tiny *empanada* joint, dishing out piping-hot cheese and meat pasties all day long.

Heladería Fili, Av. Güemes 1009. One of the two best ice-cream places in town.

Heladería Il Gelato, Buenos Aires 606. The other of the two best ice-creameries in Salta.

Partenón, España 622 (*cafepartenon@ish.com.ar*). Internet access and the very camp pseudo-Hellenic decor make this café-cum-snack bar stand out from the gaggle of small eateries in this part of town.

Van Gogh, Plaza 9 de Julio. The best coffee in town, excellent cakes, quick meals, appetising snacks and the local glitterati are the attractions, plus live music late at weekends.

Peñas

Boliche de Balderrama, San Martín 1126 (☎0387/421-1542). One of the most popular *peñas*; well-known as a bohemian hang-out in the 1950s, nowadays it's a more conventional place, attracting tourists and local folk singers. Some nights an additional charge is added to the bill for the music.

El Rastro, San Martín 2555. One of the least known and therefore most authentic of all the *peñas salteñas*, with spurts of spontanous guitar in between large helpings of *locro*.

Gauchos de Güemes, Av. Uruguay 750 (☎0387/421-0820). One of the more touristy *peñas*, but it's still worth a try. Delicious food but be prepared for a music charge on top.

La Casa de Güemes, España 720. A mellow atmosphere combines with decent food and spontaneous music-making starting at midnight at the earliest.

La Casona del Molino, Luis Burela and Caseros 2500 (☎0387/434-2835). *Empanadas, locro, guaschilocro, tamales, humitas*, sangria and improvised live music much later on, all in an atmospherically tumble-down mansion.

Listings

Airlines Aerolíneas Argentinas at the airport (☎0387/424-1185), and at Caseros 475 (☎0387/431-1331); Lloyd Aéreo Boliviano, at the airport (☎0387/424-1181), and at Deán Funes (☎0387/431-0320); LAPA, at the airport (☎0387/424-2333), and at Caseros 492 (☎0387/431-7080); Southern Winds, at the airport (☎0387/424-1223), and at Buenos Aires 22 (☎0387/421-1188); Dinar, at the airport (☎0387/424-1185), and at Buenos Aires 46 (☎0387/431-0500); TAPSA at the airport (☎0387/424-2166).

Banks and exchanges Banco de la Nación, Mitre 151; Masventas, España 610. There's nowhere to change travellers' cheques, but there are plenty of ATMs.

Car rental MPC, Buenos Aires 8 (☎0387/431-7270 or 431-3402), for 4WD; Lopez Fleming, General Güemes 92 (☎0387/421-4143) for other vehicles.

Consulates Bolivia, Mariano Boedo 32 (☎0387/422-3377); Paraguay, Mariano Boedo 38.

Hospital San Bernardo, Tobías 69 (☎0387/432-1596).

Internet Partenón Café, España 622 (8am–midnight; *cafepartenon@ish.com.ar*).

Laundries Tía Maria, Av. Belgrano 236; Laverap, Santiago del Estero, 363.

Pharmacy Del Milagro, España and Mitre.

TOURS FROM SALTA

A comprehensive range of outfits offering a wide variety of highly professional **tours**, **expeditions** and other **activities** in the Northwest region are based in and around Salta city. The following is a selection of the best.

Apacheta Viajes, Buenos Aires 33 (☎0387/431-1622 or 421-2333; *apacheta@salnet.com.ar*). Conventional but reliably run guided trips to the Quebrada del Toro, Quebrada de Humahuaca, Cachi and the Valles Calchaquíes.

Ricardo Clark Expediciones, Caseros 121 (☎0387/421-5390; *yuchan@arnet.com.ar*). Specializes in natural history and bird-watching trips to Calilegua and El Rey national parks and to the Laguna de los Pozuelos. They also have concocted an original trip combining the Train to the Clouds (see p.399) with a 4WD trip to salt-lakes and flamingoes, with an optional extension to Quebrada de Humahuaca. Two other specials are a seven-day trek to the Nevado de Chañi (6200m) and an excursion to the Parque Nacional Los Cardones.

George Guevara, San Martín 353 (☎0387/156-39622). Reliable tours, including tailor-made packages, to Cafayate, Jujuy and elsewhere in the region.

Kallpa Tours, Hotel Portezuelo, Avenida del Turista 1 (☎0387/431-0105). 4WD tours to the Valles Calchaquíes and San Antonio de los Cobres plus horse rides in the Salta region.

MoviTrack, Buenos Aires 68 (☎0387/431-6749, fax ☎0387/431-5301; *www.movitrak.com.ar*). Safari a los Nubes, a far more flexible and adventurous alternative to the train, with an optional extension via Quebrada de Humahuaca, in a special vehicle giving all passengers panoramic views. In addition to safaris to Cachi, Quilmes and Cafayate, day-trips to Molinos and

Police Santiago del Estero 952 (☎0387/422-2286).
Post office Deán Funes 170.
Taxis Remises Sol (☎0387/431-7317) or Balcarce (☎0387/421-3535 or 431-5142).
Telephones Telecentro, Buenos Aires 170. Salta also has the usual plethora of phone centres citywide.
Travel agents see box, below.

San Lorenzo

Just 11km northwest of the centre of Salta along the RP28, little **SAN LORENZO** is part dormitory town, part retreat for many Salteños. Its slightly cooler mountain climate and lush vegetation lure many locals and visitors alike who want to escape from the big city. There's nothing to see there apart from spotlessly clean ceibo-lined avenues and patrician villas, but both the **accommodation** and restaurants make it an ideal alternative to staying downtown. *Hostal Selva Montana* at Alfonsina Storni 2315 (☎0387/492-1184, fax 492-1433; *wernerg@arnet.com.ar;* ⑤) is a wonderfully friendly place, in a German-style chalet, with very comfortable Alpine-style rooms, a swimming pool and delightful forest views. Less luxurious *Hostería Los Ceibos* at 9 de Julio and España (☎0387/492-1675 or 492-1621; ④) has smart rooms, swimming pool and other sports facilities, all in an attractive building. Slightly further away, but also on the luxurious side, are the *Casa de Campo Arnaga* at Aniceto la Torre (☎0387/492-1478; *tbuena@impsat1.com.ar,* ⑥) which offers bikes and horses, *asados* and guitar recitals, and British-style *Eaton Place* on the RP28 (☎0387/492-1347; ⑥), which also has horses for hire and very plush rooms, with classy service. San Lorenzo's best **restaurant** by far is *Lo de Andrés* at Juan Carlos Dávalos and Gorriti (☎0387/492-1600), with unforgettable *empanadas*, delicious *locro*, home-style *cazuela de cabrito*, fresh trout and excellent pasta, and friendly service to

Tilcara, an outing to Iruya and a five-day expedition to San Pedro de Atacama, Chile, they also arrange white-water rafting on the Río Juramento, through Aguas Blancas Expediciones.

Norte Trekking, Los Juncos 173 (☎0387/439-6957; *fede@nortetrekking. com*). Federico Norte and his experienced team can take you on a safari into the *puna*, on a two-day trip to the Valles Calchaquíes, or to the Parque El Rey. Norte Trekking also organizes longer tours to the Atacama Desert.

Gary Pekarek, Los Eucaliptos 595 ☎0387/439-2457; *gary@impsat1.com.ar*). Professional standard photo safaris and other trips all over northern Argentina, and further afield in Chile and Bolivia.

Martin Pekarek, España 45, Chicoana (☎0387/490-7009; *martinpek@ impsat1.com.ar*). Photo safaris, 4WD trips and river excursions, including floating trips, in the area around Chicoana where he's based and has a characterful hostelry.

Saltur, Caseros 485 (☎0387/421-2012, fax ☎0387/432-1111; *saltursalta@arnet. com.ar*). Their mostly conventional activities range from horse rides and 4WD tours to canoeing and fishing.

Tastil, Zuviría 26 (☎0387/431-0031, fax 431-1223; *tastil@ish.com.ar*). Well-run but mostly routine trips to the Salinas Grandes, Humahuaca, the cloudforest national parks, Laguna de Pozuelos and as far as Chile.

TEA, Buenos Aires 82 (☎0387/421-3333; fax 431-1722; *www.iruya.com/ent/tea/ cafayate.htm*). A wide range of tours to Iruya, the national parks and the Valles Calchaquíes.

Hernán Uriburu, J.M. Lequizamón 446 (☎0387/431-0605; *hru@salta-server. com.ar*). Excursions to Molinos, La Poma and other less visited routes. Horses for hire, bikes for rent and 4WD tours. Hernán is a highly experienced guide and a real character.

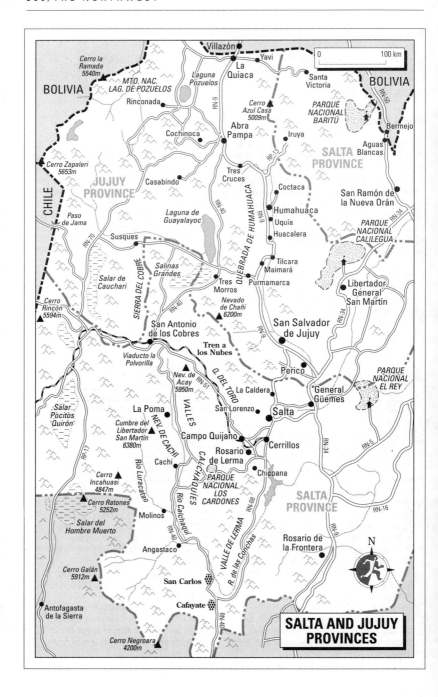

SALTA AND JUJUY PROVINCES

boot. Just along the road, at Juan Carlos Dávalos 1450, is *Confitería Don Sanca*, a charming place serving very decent tea.

Chávez runs hourly **buses** ($1) from the bus terminal in Salta, via the bus-stop at Avenida Entre Ríos and 20 de Febrero, to Camino de la Quebrada, San Lorenzo's main drag; but most hotels run a shuttle service or will give you a lift to and from the city centre.

Valle de Lerma

The sealed RN68 runs along the fertile **Valle de Lerma** to the south of Salta before climbing up the course of the Río de las Conchas to Cafayate, 180km away. This is an area of prosperous fincas, or ranches, some of which are great places to stay, amid green tobacco fields and cattle pastures. Throughout the densely populated valley, typical buildings include open-sided barn-like *secaderos* or tobacco-drying sheds, brick tobacco-kilns or *estufas*, and tiled-roofed *casas de galería*, long, low houses with colonnades along one side, some with straight pillars, others decorated with a row of mock-Gothic ogival arches.

The first small towns you come to, such as Cerrillos and El Carril, hold no attractions apart from the first examples of *casas de galería*, but **CHICOANA**, 50km south and 5km off to the west, at the gateway to the RP33 Cuesta del Obispo route to the Valles Calchaquíes (see p.419), is a quaint gaucho settlement, whose colourful **Encuentro Nacional de Doma** and **Festival del Tamal** coincide in mid-July. For several days Argentina's best rodeo-riders and horsemen show off their talents, risking life and limb to entertain an audience whose task it also is to judge the best *tamal*, traditional cornmeal parcels filled with chopped meat. Later on, in early August, the **Fiesta del Tobaco** is another excuse for festivities and the downing of large quantities of *Fernet con coca*. Chicoana's harmonious main square is surrounded by Italianate buildings – many of them ornamented with slender iron pillars – a fine well-restored colonial church and the splendid, tastefully restored *Hostería de Chicoana*, at España 45 (☎0387/490-7009; *martinpek@impsat1.com.ar*; ③), with plain but comfortable **rooms**, a courtyard inhabited by cats, dogs, an owl and other birds, none kept in captivity, and an excellent **restaurant**. The owner, Martín Pekarek, speaks perfect English and runs 4WD **tours**, horse rides, photo safaris and river floating trips in the surrounding area.

Other places to stay in the region include the *Finca Santa Anita* (☎0387/490-5050 or 431-3858; *clewis@salnet.com.ar*; ④), 25km south at **CORONEL MOLDES**, on the west bank of the huge Embalse Cabra Corral reservoir. There you can see tobacco being processed, in between swimming in the pool and organized horse rides. Nearby is the comfortable if basic *Hostería de Cabra Corral* (☎0387/490-5022; ③) on the RP17, while to the north of Chicoana, near the small town of **ROSARIO DE LERMA**, is the luxurious *Finca Puerta del Cielo* (☎156-830747; fax 0387/4317291; ⑦), also with horses, and famous for its round-the-bonfire *asados*. Nearby, along the RP33, is the oddly named *Finca Los Los* (☎0387/431-7258, 422-2959 or 421-5500; ⑥), where the food's excellent and the welcome very friendly. Just north of Rosario, at **LA SILLETTA** along the RP51 between Salta Airport and Campo Quijano, the starting-point of the Quebrada del Toro, the restful *Hotel El Manantial* (☎0387/439-5506 or 423-3615; *elmanantial@arnet.com.ar*; ⑦) provides hearty breakfasts, has horses for hire and will arrange to have you put on the Tren a los Nubes.

Rosario de Lerma, Chicoana and Coronel Moldes are all served by regular if infrequent **buses** from Salta.

Parque Nacional El Rey

Cloudforests are peculiar to southern Bolivia and northwestern Argentina, and the nearest one to Salta, nearly 200km by road from the provincial capital, is the **Parque**

Nacional El Rey: like the other cloudforest parks of the Northwest, namely the rather more accessible Calilegua (see p.417) and the extremely inaccessible Baritú (see p.418), it is an upland enclave draped in exuberant vegetation, sticking up from a low-lying plain, near the Tropic of Capricorn, and characterized by clearly distinct dry and wet seasons, winter and summer, but relatively high year-round precipitation. The peaks are often shrouded in cloud and mist – hence the name cloudforest – keeping most of the varied plant life lush even in the drier, cooler months.

Covering 400 square kilometres of land once belonging to Finca El Rey near the provincial border with Jujuy, the national park (9am–dusk; free) is perched at an average of 900m above sea level and nestles in a natural horseshoe-shaped amphitheatre, hemmed in by the curving **Crestón del Gallo** ridge to the northwest, and the higher crest of the **Serranía del Piquete**, to the east, peaking at around 1700m. A fan-shaped network of crystal-clear brooks, all brimming with fish, drains into the Río Popayán. The handsome **toucan** (*Ramphastos toco*) is the park's striking and easily recognizable mascot, but other birdlife abounds, totalling over 150 varieties.

The park's only access road is the RP20, branching to the left from the RP5 that leads eastwards from the RN9, near the village of Lumbrera halfway between Metán and Güemes. The RP20 fords several rivers, but cars will have no problem except during summer flash-floods. Since **public transport** to the park is non-existent and through-traffic very slight, the park's very difficult to visit without your own transport. **Guardaparques** at the park entrance can advise you on how to get around in your vehicle. The only **accommodation** option is to pitch your tent in the clearing in the middle of the park. A road of sorts follows the **Río Popayán** while more marked trails through the park are currently being planned to add to the two-hour climb from the rangers' station to **Pozo Verde**, an algae-rich lakelet where birds come to drink. If you have no vehicle – and even if you do – an organized trip is the best option. Two operators can be recommended: Norte Trekking, Los Juncos 173, Salta (☎0387/439-6957; *fede@nortetrekking.com*), can take you on an extremely informative and enjoyable safari to the park; while equally professional Ricardo Clark Expediciones, Caseros 121, Salta (☎0387/421-5390; *yuchan@arnet.com.ar*), specializes in natural history and bird-watching trips here.

Quebrada del Toro

Whether you travel up the magnificent gorge called the **Quebrada del Toro** by train – along one of the highest railways in the world (see box opposite) – in a tour operator's jeep, in a rented car or, as the pioneers did centuries ago, on horseback, the experience will be unforgettable, thanks to the constantly changing dramatic mountain scenery and multicoloured rocks. The gorge is named after the **Río El Toro**, normally a meandering trickle, but occasionally a raging torrent and as bullish as its name suggests, especially in the spring. It swerves up from the tobacco fields of the Valle de Lerma, 30km southwest of Salta, through dense thickets of **ceibo**, Argentina's national tree, ablaze in October and November with their fuchsia-red spring blossom, past **Santa Rosa del Tastil** and the pre-Incan site of **Tastil**, to the desiccated highlands of the Puna Salteña, Salta's Altiplano, focused on the ghostly mining village of **San Antonio de los Cobres**. Between this highest point and **Campo Quijano**, in the valley bottom, the RN51 road and the railway wind, loop and zigzag side by side for over 100km, joining two distinct worlds: the fertile, moist lowlands of Salta's populous central valleys, and the waterless highland wastes at over 3000m altitude.

A much cheaper and frankly more authentic experience than the Tren a los Nubes can be had by taking one of the **regular train services** from Salta to Socompa. A train currently leaves – theoretically, since the timetables chop and change – on Friday mornings and returns on Sundays, costing $30. For a long time, non-locals were discouraged from taking this train, seen as unwanted competition for the Tren a las Nubes, but now even the tourist information office in Salta dispenses the necessary details, and you no longer have to "coax" the crew with *mate* or cigarettes. In the past tourists were often allowed on only at Campo Quijano or even Rosario de Lerma, but that too seems to have relaxed. Above all, take provisions and very warm clothing and be prepared for delays or unexpected setbacks. In the winter, snow occasionally blocks the tracks and the journey may be curtailed. Whatever happens, this is a chance to get to know the locals better; you should also be able to make it to even higher altitudes and see more scenery farther up the track than if you take the tourist train. If you do make it to Socompa (3900m), it might just be possible to hop on a very basic freight

THE TRAIN TO THE CLOUDS

Travelling through the Quebrada del Toro gorge on the Tren as las Nubes, or **Train to the Clouds**, is an unashamedly touristic experience. The smart train, with its comfortable, leather-upholstered interior, shiny wooden fittings and spacious seats was custombuilt for this purpose; each coach has its own voluble steward, who will give you a running commentary in Spanish, while translations of all kinds of facts and figures are broadcast over loudspeakers in various languages, English included. As the train begins to climb into the gorge, coca-tea is brought round to help you combat *puna* or altitude sickness (see p.34). Facilities on board include oxygen and medical personnel, which you are unlikely to need, a dining-car where a decent set lunch costs $11, and even a post office.

Clambering from the station in Salta to the magnificent Meccano-like La Polvorilla Viaduct, high in the Altiplano, the train line was originally built to service the borax mines in the salt-flats of Pocitos and Arizaro, 300km beyond La Polvorilla. The viaduct lies 219km away from Salta, and on the way the train crosses 29 bridges and 12 viaducts, threads through 21 tunnels, swoops round two gigantic 360° loops and chugs up two switchbacks. The viaduct, seen on many posters and in all tour operators' brochures, is 224m long, 64m high and weighs over 1600 tonnes; built in Italy it was assembled here in 1930. The highest point of the whole line, just 13km west of the viaduct, is at Abra Chorrillos, 4475m. Rather disappointingly, the oft-related story according to which the late Marshal Tito, Socialist Yugoslavia's leader, worked on the construction in the 1920s, is apocryphal. At least two men by the common Yugoslav name of Josep Broz – the maverick statesman's real name – were on the contractors' pay-roll, but there's no evidence that either was the man destined to create the ill-fated republic after World War II. Brief stopovers near the Polvorilla Viaduct, where the train doubles back, and in San Antonio de los Cobres, allow you to stretch your legs and meet some locals, keen on selling you llama-wool scarves and posing for photos (for a fee). Folk groups and solo artists interspersed with people selling arts, crafts, cheese, honey and souvenirs galore help while the time away on the way down, when it's dark for the most part.

The trip, run by a company called Movitren, leaves Salta's Ferrocarril Belgrano station punctually at 7.05am – several times a week, during the high season, from April to October, with plans to extend the service throughout the year. The train returns to Salta at around 10pm, after a long, exhilarating but potentially tiring trip, and the journey costs $95, with no reductions. On some days, a cheaper trip ($50) leaves Salta at 8.30am but goes only as far as the Quebrada del Inca, where lunch is eaten at 2358m above sea level.Tickets for either route should be reserved in advance, especially during the most popular periods, such as July weekends, and can be bought in Buenos Aires at the Dinar offices, Calle Esmeralda 1008 (☎011/4311-2019 and ☎011/4311-4282), or at Movitren in Salta, at Calle Caseros 431 (☎0387/431-4984 or 431-4986).

The Ferrocarril Belgrano station is at Ameghino 690 (☎0387/421-3161), ten blocks due north of the central Plaza 9 de Julio, and can be reached by buses #5 and #13 from downtown, the bus terminal and the campsite.

train into Chile, but don't bank on it. If that's your aim, make sure you have Chilean pesos with you and expect a very long wait.

Many tour operators in Salta (see p.394) offer alternative, more adventurous but not necessarily cheaper **tours by road**, many of which ironically follow the train for much of the way, offering their passengers the chance to photograph the handsome locomotive and wave at it frantically, expecting passengers to reciprocate. Finally, Ricardo Clark Expediciones can meet you off the train when it stops at Polvorilla Viaduct, and guide you around the Altiplano in a jeep; although you miss out on the reverse train journey (single tickets are not available), and the folk show, you get the best of both worlds: the train ride plus a chance to explore the area more independently. Movitrak runs the best jeep safari excursions up the Quebrada del Toro, often combined with a return leg down the Quebrada de Humahuaca (see p.407).

Santa Rosa del Tastil and Tastil

The middle section of the Quebrada del Toro is a narrow valley, from which tall, cliff-like mountains loom, revealing strata of reds, purples, ochres and yellows that look their best in the early light. Along them run great walls of grey rock, like long battlements, and the whole landscape is spiked with tall **cardón cacti**. Intermittent stretches sport gigantic flint-arrowhead stone-formations jutting out of the bedrock. Tiny settlements of adobe houses, and their adjoining corrals of goats, perch on the bare mountainsides, and the Ruta Nacional and the railway, both clinging to the cliff-side, crisscross the river-bed several times and occasionally run alongside each other. Picturesque *chacras* or farmhouses are niched in the cliffs, and photogenic walled cemeteries, dotted with gaudy paper flowers, pepper the slopes beneath the stark Cerro Bayo (4250m). After parting ways temporarily with the rail track, the good dirt road continues to climb and, 75km from Campo Quijano and at 3000m above sea level, you reach minute **SANTA ROSA DE TASTIL**, with its tiny **museum** ($1), set beneath cactus-clad rocks and open when the curator feels like it. It contains a fine pre-Incan mummy and miscellaneous finds from nearby excavations, including arrowheads, plus some fine paintings of the region. If you're lucky he might also take you around the pre-Incan site, signposted 3km west, at **TASTIL** proper, the well-restored remains of one of the region's largest pre-Incan towns, inhabited by some 3000 people in the fourteenth century AD. The **mirador**, on once fortified heights commanding fabulous valley and mountain views, overlooks the clearly terraced farmland from which the people of Tastil eked their living. Nearly 35km beyond here the road runs above the railway before slipping through the narrow **Abra de Muñano** gorge and emerging into open, mountain-edge Altiplano, at over 4000km, entering the final run into San Antonio, after the junction with the RN40, south to La Poma (see p.402).

San Antonio de los Cobres and around

A major regional crossroads, just over 130km northwest of Salta by the RN51 – halfway to the Chilean border – and at a dizzying altitude of 3775m above sea level, **SAN ANTONIO DE LOS COBRES** is the small, windswept "capital" of an immense but mostly empty portion of the Altiplano, rich in minerals as its name ("of the copper") suggests and little else, except some breathtaking **scenery**. The **Salinas Grandes**, to the north of San Antonio de los Cobres, are among the continent's biggest salt-flats, a huge glistening expanse surrounded by brown mountains, snow-peaked volcanoes and sparse pasture for vicuñas and llamas. To the south, along an alternative route to the marvellous Valles Calchaquíes, **La Poma** is a typical Altiplano settlement, far more picturesque than San Antonio; it offers accommodation, albeit rudimentary, and acts as a

Iguazú Falls, Misiones Province

Banks of the River Paraná, Corrientes Province

Carpincho, Esteros del Iberá, Corrientes Province

Guaraní built Jesuit church at San Ignacio Miní, Corrientes Province

Dry tropical forest, Chaco Province

Talampaya, La Rioja Province

Flamingoes, Laguna de Pozuelos, Jujuy Province

Tumbaya, Jujuy Province

La Payunia, Mendoza Province

Casabindo, near Jujuy

San Francisco, Salta

possible base for exploring the valleys or heading across to Chile by the seldom used **Paso de Sico**, reached via the ultra-remote hamlet of Cauchari.

Most people only ever see San Antonio de los Cobres from its train station – the Tren a los Nubes makes a short halt here on its way back down to the plains, during which the blue and white Argentine flag is hoisted and the national anthem played. You won't be missing much if you don't hop off: the town's low houses (many of them built by the borax and lithium mining firms for their workforce in a highly utilitarian style) dusty streets and lack of vegetation make for a rather forlorn little town, not especially inviting and displaying few signs of the wealth generated by the valuable metals running in rich veins through the nearby mountains. Should you wish to get a bite **to eat** while you're here, *El Palenque*, on General Belgrano (☎0387/490-9019), a café serving soup-and-meat set meals for $3, will oblige. **Overnight stays** can be accommodated at the *Hostería de las Nubes* at Caseros 441 (☎0387/490-9059; ④); it's fairly basic but the plumbing and central heating work. Otherwise the *Hostería Los Andes* at Belgrano (no phone; ②) is the best value, offering plain but comfortable rooms, hot food and decent sanitation; if that's full, try *Hostería Inti Huasi* (☎0387/490-9035; ①), at Zavaleta and Avellaneda, or *Hostería Belgrano*, also on Belgrano (☎0387/490-9025; ①) – both are adequate for a night and supply masses of blankets. There's nothing in the way of tourist information here, but the police next to the train station can give you news about the state of the road or any weather hazards.

El Quebracho runs the twice-daily **bus service** between San Antonio and Salta; and there are services onwards to the Paso de Jama (see p.410).

North from San Antonio de los Cobres

Northwards from San Antonio de los Cobres, the RN40 starts its final, partly surfaced, run to Abra Pampa (see p.414), some 200km away. The RP75 branches off to the left 21km from San Antonio, eventually leading to Abra Pampa via Casabindo (see p.414) – 130km to the north – over very difficult terrain but through eerily dramatic Altiplano scenery, well worth exploring if you have plenty of time (and fuel supplies) while the main RN40 route veers northeast. Where it crosses the unmarked border into Jujuy Province, 60km farther on, across to the east you're treated to wonderful views of the snow-peaked Nevado de Chañi (6200m), an extinct volcanic cone poking above the brown slopes of the stark range where the Río El Toro has its thaw-fed source. To the north stretches the enormous glistening expanse of the aptly named **Salinas Grandes**, one of the country's biggest salt-flats and certainly the most impressive, ringed by mountains on all sides and beneath almost perennial blue skies. This huge rink of snow-white crystals, forming irregular octagons each surrounded by crunchy ridges, crackling like frozen snow under foot, acts as a huge mirror. The enormous expanses of salt, shimmering in the nearly perpetual blazing sunshine, often create cruel water mirages, though there are in fact some isolated pools of brine where small groups of flamingoes and ducks gather. This is a likely place for spotting vicuñas and llamas, too, flocks of which often leap across the road to reach their scrawny, yellow pastureland, or *tola*, on either side of the RN40. Way over to the north you can make out the dark bulk of Cerro Negro, a hill sticking out from the plain.

Some 13km before joining the RN52 Purmamarca to Susques road (see p.410), you pass the tiny hamlet of **Tres Morros**, with its simple but beautiful church – a typical Altiplano design with a plain facade and a single sturdy tower, all built in solid adobe that will resist all but the strongest earthquakes. The village also has a curious, walled graveyard, built on the gently sloping hill or *morro* – one of the three that gives the village its name – only a fraction full of graves, as if patiently waiting for dozens of future generations to die. No public transport comes along here so you'll either need your own transport or will have to go on one of the tours from Salta that takes in this route.

La Poma

From its junction with the RN51, just to the southeast of San Antonio de los Cobres, the unsealed and often poorly RN40 snakes its difficult way over the Abra de Acay, the world's highest mountain pass, at 4895m, a road often blocked by snowdrifts in the winter. Only 90km but sometimes several hours away, **LA POMA**, lying 5km off the Ruta Nacional near the Río Calchaquí, is a modern but pleasant village of adobe houses, built near the phantom-like ruins of La Poma Vieja, which was razed to the ground by a severe earthquake in 1930. La Poma lies in the shadow of the mighty **Cumbre del Libertador General San Martín**, whose 6380m summit is never without at least a tip of snow. Although it's far from luxurious, the comfortable *Hostería La Poma* (☎03868/491003; ②), on the main street, offering basic meals, will come in very useful if you've had a difficult trip down the pass or are contemplating crossing it. Fifty kilometres south, along one of the finest scenic routes in the region, with massive and imposing mountain peaks on either side, is Cachi (see p.420), the gateway into the Valles Calchaquíes proper.

Up to the Paso de Sico

To the west of San Antonio de los Cobres, the RN51 crosses both the railway and the provincial border between Salta and Jujuy provinces several times as it climbs steeply towards **Caucharí**, 68km away. About halfway there, it heaves itself over the Abra de Chorrillos pass, at an altitude of 4650m, marked by a sign and a traditional *apacheta* or cairn. From it you are treated to exhilarating views in all directions of the snowy Chañi, Acay and Cachi mountains, the plains around San Antonio and the lichen-yellow pastures of Campo Amarillo, grazed by sizeable flocks of camouflaged **vicuña**. Caucharí itself is a one-llama town at just below 4000m, comprising a quaint single-towered church, a house and a police station, the last before the border. To the north is the seemingly never-ending salt-flat, **Salar de Caucharí**, and the road continues to the frontier via the picturesque hamlet of **Catúa**, surrounded by spongy *bofedales* or bog-like pastures where alpacas and llamas munch away nonchalantly on slimy grass. The **Chilean border** at the **Paso de Sico**, 4080m and marked by a terse sign, runs through some out-of-this-world scenery: splashes of dazzling salt-flat picking their way through dusky **volcanoes**, whose perfect cones frequently surpass 5000m, with views across to the majestic **Volcán Llullaillaco**, 6739m, way across to the southwest.

There's no public transport across the pass, so you'll need your own vehicle, preferably a 4WD, to do this fabulous trip.

San Salvador de Jujuy

Just over 90km north of Salta by the direct, scenic RN9, **SAN SALVADOR DE JUJUY** – Jujuy for short – is indeed a peaceful place and, as the highest provincial capital in the country (1260m above sea level), enjoys an enviably temperate climate. It is the capital of the federation's most remote mainland province, a small but intensely beautiful and remote patch of land, ostensibly having more in common with next-door Chile and Bolivia than with the rest of Argentina, and little with Buenos Aires which lies nearly 1600km away. Dramatically located, Jujuy sits in a fertile natural bowl, with the fabulous multicoloured gorge of the **Quebrada de Humahuaca** (see p.407) immediately to the north, a major reason for heading in this direction in the first place. The Cerro de Claros (1704m) and Cerro Chuquina (1987m) loom just to the southeast and southwest, and the city is wedged between two rivers, the Río Grande and Río Chico or Xibi Xibi, both bone-dry for most of the year. That said, the place gives the impression of being on its uppers: the river-fronts are marred by concrete eyesores, the commercial

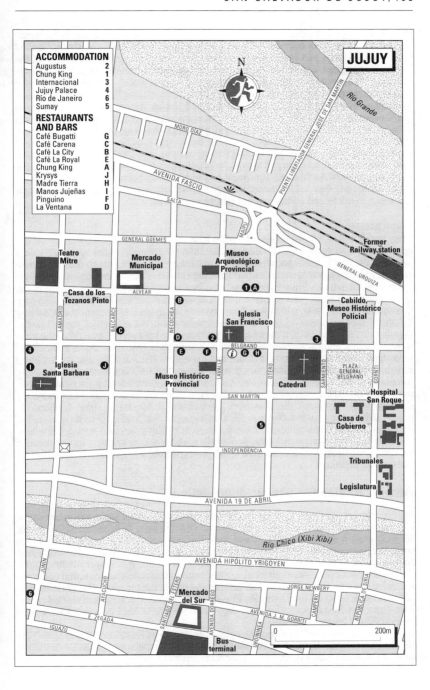

JUJUY

ACCOMMODATION
Augustus	2
Chung King	1
Internacional	3
Jujuy Palace	4
Río de Janeiro	6
Sumay	5

RESTAURANTS AND BARS
Café Bugatti	G
Café Carena	C
Café La City	B
Café La Royal	E
Chung King	A
Krysys	J
Madre Tierra	H
Manos Jujeñas	F
Pinguino	I
La Ventana	D

Río Grande

PUENTE LIBERTADOR GENERAL JOSÉ DE SAN MARTÍN

MORO DIAZ

AVENIDA FASCIO

SALTA

MAIPÚ

GENERAL GÜEMES

Former Railway station

GENERAL URQUIZA

Teatro Mitre

Mercado Municipal

Museo Arqueológico Provincial

Casa de los Tezanos Pinto

ALVEAR

Cabildo, Museo Histórico Policial

Iglesia San Francisco

LAMADRID

BALCARCE

NECOCHEA

BELGRANO

LAVALLE

OTERO

SARMIENTO

GORITI

PLAZA GENERAL BELGRANO

Iglesia Santa Barbara

Museo Histórico Provincial

Catedral

Hospital San Roque

SAN MARTÍN

Casa de Gobierno

INDEPENDENCIA

Tribunales

Legislatura

AVENIDA 19 DE ABRIL

Río Chico (Xibi Xibi)

AVENIDA HIPÓLITO YRIGOYEN

JUNÍN

AYACUCHO

E. ZEGADA

IGUAZÚ

SANTIAGO DEL ESTERO

Mercado del Sur

AVENIDA DORREGO

URDININEA

JORGE NEWBERY

AVENIDA J. M. GORRITI

CAMPERO

REPÚBLICA DE SIRIA

Bus terminal

0   200m

streets lack the buzz of Salta and Tucumán, and good hotels are few and far between. In *The Old Patagonian Express* (1978), Paul Theroux wrote about Jujuy that it "looked peaceful and damp; just high enough to be pleasant without giving one a case of the bends; it was green, a town buried, so it seemed, in lush depthless spinach". The gravelly river-beds, overgrown with lush vegetation though certainly not spinach, only add to the rather abandoned appearance, while Jujuy's outskirts spill along the riversides, sometimes in the form of shanty-towns. Scratch the lacklustre surface, though, and you'll unearth some real treasures, among them one of the finest pieces of sacred art to be seen in Argentina, the **pulpit** in the **Cathedral** – and the interior of **Iglesia San Francisco** is almost as impressive. A day or two in this slightly strange "world's end" kind of place will probably suffice; you'll soon want to start exploring the rich hinterland, its polychrome gorges and typical Altiplano villages of adobe houses. Jujuy is the ideal springboard for visiting the most accessible of the three cloudforest national parks, **Calilegua** (see p.417), or for the more adventurous and real nature enthusiasts the less accessible and utterly remote **Baritú** (see p.418).

Some history

Jujuy was founded, after a couple of earlier false starts thwarted by attacks by indigenous peoples, on April 19, 1593. Earthquakes, the plague and further sackings, culminating in the Calchaquí Wars, all conspired to hamper the city's growth during the seventeenth and eighteenth centuries and have deprived it of any of its original buildings. Even after the famous Jujuy Exodus ordered by General Belgrano at the height of the Wars of Independence – on August 23, 1812, he ordered the whole of the city's population to evacuate the city, which was then razed to the ground to prevent its capture by the Royalist commander – Jujuy continued to bear the brunt of conflict, sacked by the Royalists in 1814 and 1818. It then remained a forgotten backwater throughout the nineteenth century, and the railway did not reach it until 1903. Since the 1930s, its outskirts have spilled across both rivers and begun to creep up the hillsides, and it now has a sizeable immigrant population, mostly from across the Bolivian border to the north. Members of the largely indigent Bolivian community, drawn to Jujuy's relative prosperity, are spurned by many longer-term Jujeño residents. The province – and therefore the city, which lives off the province's agricultural production – have traditionally grown rich on sugar and tobacco, with a little copper and lead mining thrown in, but earnings from all these products have declined in recent years and forced farmers to diversify into other crops including fruit and vegetables. Tourism may be the solution for the city's economic woes but so far has been exploited only half-heartedly, with very little state assistance.

Arrival, information and accommodation

Jujuy's **airport**, Dr Horacio Guzmán (☎0388/491-1102), is over 30km southeast of the city, along the RN66 motorway, near Perico. TEA Turismo (☎0388/423-6270 or 156-857913) runs a shuttle service to and from the city centre for $7, while LAPA also transfers passengers free of charge. The **taxi** fare is around $25. The rudimentary **bus terminal**, at Iguazú and Av. Dorrego (☎0388/422-6299), just south of the centre, across the Río Chico, serves all local, regional and national destinations, and also runs a service to Chile. There's also a **left-luggage** facility at the terminal. For basic **tourist information**, head for the Dirección Provincial de Turismo at Belgrano 690 (Mon–Fri 7am–9pm; Sat, Sun & public holidays 8am–8pm; ☎0388/422-8153), two blocks west of central Plaza General Belgrano.

Apart from two excellent **campsites** near the city – *Los Vertientes* (☎0388/498-0030; $3 per person) and *El Carmen* (☎0388/493-3117; $2 per person) – Jujuy's limited but decent accommodation covers the range from squalid *residenciales*, best avoided, to a couple of top-notch five-star **hotels**. In between are one or two decent hotels and a few inexpensive pensions. Some 25km outside the city is an outstanding **finca** or ranch, with very comfortable rooms; although it's some way out of the centre, it's conveniently close to the airport.

Finca Los Lapachos, RP42, Perico (☎0388/491-1291). Definitely the place if you're looking for charm, luxury, peace and quiet, and an authentic finca experience, with horseriding and a beautiful swimming pool. The Leach family, who call this place home, would prefer that you book ahead instead of turning up on their doorstep. ⑦.

Hotel Alto la Viña, Pasquini López, La Viña (☎0388/426-1666; *lavina@mail.imagine.com.ar*). On the heights of La Viña, 4km northeast of the city centre, this recently refurbished hotel, with large comfortable rooms and a shady garden, commands fabulous views of the valley and mountains. Shuttle service to and from downtown. ⑦.

Hotel Augustus, Belgrano 715 (☎0388/423-0203). Extremely friendly place, with clean rooms, spacious bathrooms and good breakfasts. Snack bar serves delicious sandwiches and *lomitos*. ⑤.

Hotel Internacional, Belgrano 501 (☎0388/423-1599). A little bit kitsch in the reception area, this hotel overlooking the main square is nonetheless reliable, with bright rooms and cable TV. ⑤.

Hotel Jujuy Palace, Belgrano 1060 (☎0388/423-0433; *jupalace@imagine.com.ar*). One of the two top-range hotels actually in central Jujuy, this one has the edge in terms of stylish decor and charm. Professionally run, with a pleasant restaurant. ⑦.

Hotel Panorama, Belgrano 1295 (☎0388/423-0433). The other top-range downtown hotel, enjoying great views from its upper rooms, but not quite so characterful. Generous breakfasts in the stylish confitería, though. ⑦.

Hotel Sumay, Otero 232 (☎0388/423-5065). By far the best lower-range hotel, it's roomy, comfortable, and very popular, so book ahead. Can be noisy. ④.

Residencial Chung King, Alvear 627 (☎0388/422-8142). A slightly chaotic pension, but it's tidy at least and very welcoming. ②.

Residencial Río de Janeiro, José de la Iglesia 1356 (☎0388/422-3700). The cheapest place that can be recommended, it's a bit gloomy, but clean and safe. ①.

Residencial San Antonio, Lisandro de la Torre 993 (☎0388/422-5998). Small, modern and very close to the bus terminal – the only non-squalid place in the vicinity. ①.

Residencial San Carlos, República de Siria 459 (☎0388/422-2286). Basic, verging on the spartan, this friendly pension offers rooms with bath and cheaper ones without. ①–②.

The City

Jujuy is the most Andean of all Argentina's cities; much of its population is descended from indigenous stock, mostly mestizos, with a considerable influx of Bolivian immigrants in the last couple of decades. It's not a beautiful city, but the central streets have a certain atmosphere; women in brightly coloured shawls with their babies strapped to their backs huddle in groups and whisper in Quechoa; and two of the city's churches are remarkable, mainly for their colonial pulpits, which were crafted by indigenous artisans and are the most splendid of their kind in the whole country. **Plaza General Belgrano**, at the eastern extremity of the compact microcentro, was the colonial settlement's central square, Plaza Mayor, and is still the city's hub, partly occupied by craftsmen, mainly potters, displaying their wares. Planted with orange trees, it is dominated to the south by the French-style Neoclassical **Casa de Gobierno** (Mon–Fri 9am–noon & 4–8pm; free), with its slate mansard-roof, where the national flag donated to the city by General Belgrano, as a tribute to the Exodus, is proudly guarded. To the west stands Jujuy's late eighteenth-century **Cathedral** (Mon–Fri 7.30am–1pm & 5–9pm, Sat & Sun 8am–noon & 5–9pm), topped by an early twentieth-century tower and extended by an even later Neoclassical atrium. The exterior, painted a pale biscuit colour, is unremarkable, while the interior, a layer of painted Bakelite concealing the original timber structure, is impressively naive: a realistic mock-fresco of sky and clouds soars over the altar, while above the nave is a primitive depiction of the ceremony in which Belgrano awarded the Argentine flag to the people of Jujuy. Two original doors and two confessionals, Baroque masterpieces from the eighteenth century, immediately catch the eye, thanks to their profusion of vivid red and sienna paint, picked out with gilt, but the undisputed highlight – and the main attraction of the whole city – is the magnificent **pulpit**. Decorated in the eighteenth century by local artists, it easily rivals those of **Cusco** (see box on p.111), its apparent inspiration, with its harmonious compositions, elegant floral and vegetable motifs, and the finesse of its carvings. Its various tableaux in gilded, carved wood, gleaming with an age-old patina, movingly depict subjects such as Jacob's ladder and St Augustin along with Biblical genealogies from Adam to Solomon and from David to Abraham. One curiosity is the error in the symbols of the four **apostles**: Matthew and John are correctly represented by a human figure and an eagle respectively, but Mark, symbolized by a bull, and Luke, by a lion, are the wrong way round.

Not of quite the same calibre as the cathedral's, but very striking nonetheless, is the Spanish Baroque **pulpit** in **Iglesia San Francisco**, two blocks west at Belgrano and Lavalle; also inspired by the pulpits of Cusco and almost certainly carved by craftsmen in eighteenth-century Bolivia, it drips with detail, with a profusion of little Franciscan monks peeking out from row upon row of tiny columns, all delicately gilded. Although the church and separate campanile are built to the traditional colonial Franciscan design, in a neo-Baroque style, the church was built as recently as the 1930s.

Museums are not Jujuy's forte but the two that are worth a passing visit are conveniently located nearby. One block to the north of the church, at Lavalle 434, is the **Museo Arqueológico Provincial** (daily 9am–noon & 3–8pm; $1) with its diorama representing life in the region around 7000 BC and a small collection of locally unearthed mummies. One block to the south, at Lavalle 252, is the **Museo Histórico Provincial** (Mon–Fri 9am–1pm 4–8pm Sat 9am–noon 4–8pm; $1), in the Casa de Lavalle, housing an eclectic collection representing the city's more recent history, noteworthy for two seventeenth-century oil paintings by Cusco and a pre-Incan silver crown discovered at the *pukará* or pre-Incan fortress at Abra Pampa (see p.414), and famous for the perforated door through which the bullet that killed hero of the War of Independence, General Lavalle, on October 9, 1841, supposedly passed; Lavalle's assassination was a key event in the Argentine civil war between Federalists and Unitarists.

Three blocks west of the Casa de Lavalle at San Martín and La Madrid, is the stark, whitewashed **Capilla de Santa Barbara**, built in the late eighteenth century. Its style – despite heavy restoration – is similar to that of the typical Quebrada chapels that you find throughout the rest of the province: a plain thick-walled nave and a single squat tower. This chapel's extra tower was added in the nineteenth century. Inside is an outstanding set of religious paintings from **Cusco**, including a *St Barbara*, appropriately enough, a *St Stanislas*, and the *Lives of the Virgin and Jesus*. It's not always open so attending Mass (Sun 8am & 10am) is the surest way of gaining access.

Eating, drinking and nightlife

Jujuy is no gastronomic paradise but its **restaurants** will give you more than enough variety between local specialities and parrilladas. Apart from a couple of snazzy **bars**, sometimes hosting musicians, the nightlife is confined to a couple of out-of-town **discos** and the beautiful Italian-style theatre and opera house, **Teatro Mitre**, at Alvear 1009 (☎0388/442-2782), its gleaming white exterior and plush interior the result of recent refurbishment; classical concerts, as well as plays, are regularly staged here, and are usually of a high standard. For something a little more energetic, head for *Keops* (opposite *Hotel Alto la Viña*, Pasquini López, La Viña, 4km northeast of the city centre): this is the liveliest, most sophisticated **disco** in the city. Beautiful modern decor, loud but varied music, and a young crowd. (Open Fri & Sat. $10.)

Restaurants

La Candelaria, Alvear 1346. This is a very stylish parrilla, ten blocks or so out to the west of the city, serving mountains of meat until you burst. Heavenly desserts, too.

Chung King, Alvear 627. Filling, spicy food in very spartan surroundings, with TV for atmosphere, but it's an institution, serving regional specialities such as chicken pili-pili, *locro* and *chicharrón con mote*, fried pork with sweetcorn.

Krysys, Balcarce 272. Trout is the speciality on an otherwise not very inventive meat-dominated menu, but the service is impeccable.

Madre Tierra, Otero and Belgrano. Delightful, airy vegetarian lunch-only spot, serving an unbeatable menu at $7; even if you're not a vegetarian you'll find the fresh salads, meatless *empanadas* and delicious fruit juices a great change from the meat overdose. Closed Sun.

Manos Jujeñas, Senador Pérez 222. Absolutely fabulous Northwestern food, including memorable *locro* and delicious *empanadas*, accompanied from time to time by folk music. Incredibly friendly, too. Closed Sun lunch & Mon evening.

La Ventana, Belgrano 749. Old-fashioned place, with quaint wooden panelling, and specializing in pasta and *milanesas*, plus delicious puddings. Be prepared for slow service and be warned that it's closed at weekends.

Cafés and bars

Bugatti, Belgrano 683. Atmospheric café-bar, with live music most weekends.

Carena, Balcarce and Belgrano. Mellow confitería, serving snacks and acting as a community centre – concerts, seminars and group meetings are held here.

La City, Necochea 399. The pink walls and stylishly comfortable chairs tell you this is the chic place to come for a coffee or cocktail.

La Royal, Belgrano 766. Very pleasant café, livened up by local folk bands some Saturday nights.

Pinguino, Belgrano 718. This is Jujuy's best *heladería*, scooping out delicious ice cream by the bucketful; every flavour imaginable.

Listings

Airlines Aerolíneas Argentinas at the airport (☎0388/491-1106) and at San Martín 735 (☎0388/422-5414); Dinar, Senador Pérez 308 (☎0388/423-7100); LAPA, Belgrano 636 (☎0388/423-2244); LAB, Güemes 779 (☎0388/423-0699).

Banks and exchanges Quilmes, Belgrano 902, is the only bank in the city that will change travellers' cheques; for exchange, head to Banco de Provincia de Jujuy, Alvear and La Madrid; Banco Nación, Alvear 801. Several ATMs dotted around.

Car rental Noroeste (Thrifty reps), Hotel Augustus, Belgrano 715 (☎0388/422-5880).

Consulate Bolivia (the most helpful in the Northwest), Av. Senador Pérez and Independencia.

Hospital Pablo Soria, Güemes and Patricias Argentinas (☎0388/422-1256).

Internet Telecentro at Güemes and La Madrid.

Laundry Laverap, Belgrano 1214.

Pharmacies San Francisco, at Lavalle and Belgrano; Siufi, Alvear 1062.

Post office Independencia and La Madrid (Mon–Fri 8am–8pm, Sat 8.30am–12.30pm).

Telephones Telecom, Belgrano and Lavalle.

Tour company TEA, San Martín 128 (☎0388/423-6270 or 156-857913). Highly professional tours into Quebrada de Humahuaca and Puna Jujeña, plus smaller circuits near the city.

Quebrada de Humahuaca

Given the frequency with which it features in tourist literature, posters and coffee-table books, the intense beauty of the **Quebrada de Humahuaca** gorge comes as no surprise. Even so, it's an unforgettable and moving experience, taking you along some stunning, varied scenery, all the way up from the valley bottom, just to the northwest

A CALENDAR OF FESTIVALS IN THE NORTHWEST

Northwestern Argentina has maintained or revived dozens of pre-Hispanic festivals. There are also many religious and secular celebrations observed here that are a blend of indigenous and imported customs, so subtly melded that the elements are indistinguishable. **Carnival, Holy Week** and **saints' days** predominate among the latter.

The **first fortnight of the year** sees pre-Carnival revelries all along the **Quebrada de Humahuaca** (Jujuy), where carnival itself is a big holiday, and **January 6** is the date of processions in **Belén** (Catamarca) in honour of the Virgin Mary. In the **second half of January, Tilcara** (Jujuy) holds its annual bean-feast, followed by **Humahuaca**'s tribute to the Virgen de Candelaria, on **February 2**. Pachamama, the Mother Earth deity dear to the indigenous peoples, is feted on **February 6** in **Purmamarca** (Jujuy), and **Amaichá del Valle** (Tucumán) where festivities last a whole week. Cheese fans should head for **Tafí del Valle** (Tucumán) where the Fiesta Nacional del Queso takes place in early February.

Carnival is a boisterous time in **Santiago del Estero** and **Salta**, although it cannot be compared with the mardi gras festivities in the Northeast. The **Serenata Cafayateña** is a folk jamboree held on the weekend following Shrove Tuesday in **Cafayate** (Salta). **Londres** (Catamarca) hosts a lively Walnut Festival in early February, while **Fiambalá**'s Festival del Camino Hacia el Nuevo Sol takes place on **February 18 & 19**. The third Wednesday of the month is when the **Fiesta Nacional del Aguardiente** is held in **Valle Viejo** (Catamarca), while the third Thursday is dedicated to the hangover.

In **March** the Feria Artesanal y Ganadera de la Puna transforms normally quiet **Antofagasta de la Sierra**. **March 19**, St Joseph's day, is a red-letter day in **Cachi** (Salta), while a major pilgrimage, with night vigils and processions, converges on the tiny village of **Puerta de San José**, near Belén (Catamarca) on **March 18 & 19**.

of Jujuy, to the town of **Humahuaca** that gives the gorge its name, 125km north of the provincial capital; from there (see p.412) you can continue along the same road, crossing bleak but stunningly beautiful Altiplano landscapes, all the way to La Quiaca on the Bolivian border nearly 2000m higher, and 150km farther on. Although most day-trips along the gorge from Jujuy (and Salta) inevitably take you up and down by the same route, the RN9, you're actually treated to two spectacles: you'll have your attention fixed on the western side in the morning, and on the eastern flank in the afternoon, when the sun lights up each side respectively and picks out the amazing geological features: polychrome strata, buttes and mesas, pinnacles and eroded crags. What's more, the two sides are quite different, the western mountains rising steeply like abrupt cliffs, often striped with vivid colours, while the slightly lower, rounded range to the east is for the most part gentler, more mellow, but just as colourful.

Even if you go only as far as Humahuaca town itself, the case of most tours organized out of Jujuy and Salta, you get two dolly-shot views of multicoloured mountains, the highlight of which is the much photographed **Cerro de los Siete Colores**, overhanging the picturesque village of **Purmamarca** – from where a dramatic side-road takes you all the way across splendid Altiplano landscapes, via pretty little **Susques**, to the Chilean border at the Paso de Jama, high in the Andes. Like Humahuaca, Purmamarca has enough accommodation options to make it a possible stopover, especially if you are forging on towards Chile. Farther up the gorge, just outisde the village of **Maimará** and overlooked by oyster-shaped rock-formations in the mountainside, is one of the region's most photographed cemeteries. Two-thirds of the way to Humahuaca, the small town of **Tilcara** is worth lingering in, if only for its beautiful pre-Incan *pukará* or fortress; it too boasts a good range of lodgings, plus a fine archeological museum. Between Tilcara and Humahuaca the little village of **Uquia** boasts one of the finest churches along the gorge; in these parts the typical chapel design is utterly simple, a

Holy Week is a serious affair throughout the region but the highlights are: Maundy Thursday at **Yavi** (Jujuy), the pilgrimage to El Señor de la Peña at **Aimogasta** (northern La Rioja) and the procession of the Virgen de Punta Corral, from **Punta Corral to Tumbaya** (Jujuy). A week after Easter sees a minor performance of the momentous rituals in honour of the Virgen del Valle, in **Catamarca**.

May kicks off with Santa Cruz celebrations at **Uquía** (Jujuy), on **May 4**, while **May 25** is celebrated in **El Rodeo** (Catamarca) by a *destreza criolla* – or rodeo – and St John's Day, **June 24**, is a major feast throughout the region.

Late July is when **Catamarca** stages one of the country's biggest folk and crafts festivals, the Festival Nacional del Poncho. St James' Day, **July 25**, as you would expect, is a major holiday in **Santiago del Estero** but also in **Humahuaca**. Argentina's only bullfight, an unusual, bloodless and remarkable tradition, is the main event at Assumption celebrations held at **Casabindo** (Jujuy) on **August 15**. Santa Rosa de Lima is honoured at **Purmamarca** on **August 30**.

Salta's big feast thanks God for the Virgin of the Miracle during the nine days leading up to **September 15** while **Iruya** (Salta) holds a highly photogenic feast for Our Lady of the Rosary on the first Sunday in **October**. Still in Salta Province, in early October, it's **Cafayate**'s turn to honour the Virgin. Two Sundays later (usually around October 20), **La Quiaca** (Jujuy) holds its Fiesta de la Ollas or "Manca Fiesta".

All Souls' Day and the Day of the Dead, **November 1 & 2**, are important feasts all along the **Quebrada de Humahuaca** and especially in **Antofagasta de la Sierra**. The city of **Catamarca** attracts thousands of pilgrims for processions involving the Virgin del Valle, on **December 8**. **Angastaco** (Salta) hosts a gaucho festival in honour of the Virgin around the same time. Nativity plays and other Yuletide activities are popular throughout the Northwest but **Christmas** itself isn't associated with any special customs.

plain whitewashed facade, sometimes embellished with an arch, and a single squat tower, usually acting as a campanile. Many retain their straw roofs. From Humahuaca you could also visit the incredibly isolated and highly atmospheric hamlet of **Iruya**, if you really want to get off the beaten track. All of this stretch of the RN9 is accessible by regular **buses** from Jujuy, many of them also serving Salta.

Up to Purmamarca

As you climb the first stretch of the Quebrada, you soon leave the subtropical forest around Yala behind and enter an arid, narrow valley, gouged out by the Río Grande. The tiny village of Volcán, 40km from Jujuy, scarred by huge lime quarries, stands at 2000m; its name refers not to volcanic eruptions but to the frequent rock slides that sometimes block the whole length of the road after storms, referred to as *volcanes* as they can be violent. Only 7km further, you come to **TUMBAYA**, a tiny village with a handsome colonial church, the first of many along the Quebrada; the **Iglesia de Nuestra Señora de los Dolores y Nuestra Señora de la Candelaria** houses some fine colonial art, including a painting of *Nuestra Señora La Aparecida,* another of *El Cristo de los Temblores,* and a *Jesús el el Huerto*. Originally built at the end of the eighteenth century, it was partially rebuilt after two earthquakes in the nineteenth century and restored in the 1940s; its design is typical of the Quebrada, a solid structure clearly influenced by the Mudejar churches of Andalucia. The domed campanile is particularly elegant.

Purmamarca

Lying 4km west of a strategic fork in the RN9, 13km north of Tumbaya – at the start of the international route RN52, leading northwestwards towards Susques and the Chilean border – **PURMAMARCA** is a tiny, picturesque village at the base of the gorge of the same name, whose peace and quiet have been disrupted of late since traffic along the region's main trans-Andean route increased owing to stronger trading links with Chile. The main square is still a haven of tranquillity, though, flanked to the south by a pretty seventeenth-century church, the **Iglesia Santa Rosa de Lima**, built to the typically plain, single-towered design of the Quebrada. At the northeast corner of the plaza, the four graceful arches of the **Cabildo** embellish its otherwise simple white facade. The real attraction, though, is the famous **Cerro de los Siete Colores**, a dramatic bluff of rock overlooking the village. The mountain's candy stripes that give it its name range from pastel beiges and pinks, to orangey ochres and dark purple, though you may not be able to make out all seven of the reputed different shades. A signposted route, following an irrigation canal, takes you round the back of the village for the best views of the polychrome mountainside.

Purmamarca makes for a convenient stopping point on the route through the gorge, and has a surprisingly good choice of **accommodation**. Best of all, in a wonderful mountain-view location, but with triple-bed bungalows only, is the *Hostal La Posta* at Santa Rosa de Lima (☎0388/490-8040; fax ☎0388/490-8029; ③). Less attractive but quite comfortable is the *Residencial Zulma* at calle Salta s/n (☎0388/490-8023; ③). That leaves two basic, clean pensions, *Residencial Bebo Vilte* at calle Salta s/n (☎0388/490-8038; ①) and the slightly more appealing *Residencial Aramayo* at Florida (☎0388/490-8028; ②). On the main plaza, next to the cabildo, *La Posta* serves simple **meals**, **snacks** and **drinks**, and sells local crafts, in a rich red-ochre walled building. Frequent **buses** to Tilcara, Humahuaca and Jujuy leave from a block east of the main square.

Up to the Paso de Jama and Chile

Leading west from Purmamarca, the RP52 follows the Río Purmamarca and quickly climbs up the remarkable zigzags of the **Cuesta de Lipán**, one of the most dramatic roads in the region; this is the road towards the **Chilean border at Paso de Jama**, but is worth exploring if you have the time, as it crosses some of the country's most startling landscapes: barren steppe alternating with crinkly mountains, often snow-peaked even in the summer. Some 30km west of Purmamarca, just after the Abra de Potrerillos pass, you reach the road's highest point, at nearly 4200m, and enter majestic altiplanic landscapes: ahead you have open views to gleaming salt-flats and to the north, beyond the valley of the Río Colorado, the shallow, mirror-like **Laguna de Guayalayoc** glistens in the sun. Beyond the junction with the RN40 which runs north–south from San Antonio de los Cobres (see p.400) to Abra Pampa (see p.414), the pastures on either side of the road are home to considerable communities of vicuñas, the frail-looking, wispy-fleeced cousins of the llama. Where the road snakes between the **Cerro Negro** and the valley of the Río de las Burras, through the **Quebrada del Mal Paso**, it crosses the Tropic of Capricorn several times, before reaching **SUSQUES**, some 180km from Purmamarca. A minute but wonderfully picturesque village, formerly belonging to Chile, it's now where the Argentine customs point is located; expect lengthy clearance procedures, especially upon arrival from Chile. While waiting, take a look at the sumptuous church, with its delicate thatched roof and rough adobe walls, like those of all the houses in the village, and the naive frescoes on the inside. The very basic but clean *Hostería Las Vicuñitas* (☎490207 via operator; ①) is the only **accommodation**, and serves equally basic food.

From Susques, it's another 100km to the border crossing, at the **Paso de Jama**, where only a road sign tells you that you're leaving Argentine territory. This last stretch is trying and, given the altitude at well over 3500m, may give you *puna* symptoms (see p.34), as you first climb the **Cordón de Taire** – offering sweeping vistas back into the valley, from its peak at 4070m, and forward into the white expanses of the Salares de Olaroz and Cauchari – before descending into the plains, still at 3800m, following the RP70 southwards for 40km, and then negotiating the final ascent to the pass itself. The landscapes are fabulous, though: harsh desert-like plains relieved by unearthly volcanic cones and snowy Andean peaks at well over 5000m. On the other side of the border, a good sealed road swings down to the **customs post** at San Pedro de Atacama, 170km away.

Tramaca (☎0388/423-6438) runs **buses** from Salta, via Jujuy, Purmamarca and Susques to San Pedro de Atacama and on to Antofagasta and Arica, in Chile, twice or three times a week, leaving Jujuy at 8.30am, and arriving at San Pedro in the evening. In addition one or two buses daily serve Susques, run by Panamericano, Purmamarca and Línea Vilte; from there you could hop on the Tramaca bus to Chile.

Maimará and Tilcara

From Purmamarca, the RN9 continues to climb through the Quebrada de Humahuaca past coloured mountainsides, ornamented with rock formations like organ-pipes or elephants' feet with painted toes. One highly photogenic sight, conveniently visible from the main road, is the extraordinary cemetery at **MAIMARÁ**, 75km from Jujuy; surrounded by rough-hewn walls and a jumble of tombs of all shapes and sizes, and laid with bouquets of artificial flowers, it looks even bigger than the village it serves, and has been here for centuries. Behind it the rock formations at the base of the mountain resemble multicoloured oyster-shells. The various shades of reds, yellows and browns have earned the rocks the name La Paleta del Pintor, "the artist's palette".

Only 5km further on you are treated to your first glimpse from the roadside of the great pre-Incan *pukará* or fortress of **TILCARA**. Just beyond it is the side-road off to the village itself. At an altitude of just under 3000m and yet still dominated by the dramatic mountains that surround it, this is one of the biggest settlements along the Quebrada and the only one on the east bank; it lies just off the main road, where the Río Huasomayo runs into the Río Grande. The pleasant, easy-going village is always very lively, but even more so during **carnival**; like the rest of the Quebrada, it also celebrates **El Enero Tilcareño**, a religious and popular procession and feast held during the latter half of January, as well as **Holy Week**, and **Pachamama** or the Mother Earth festival, in August, with remarkable festivities, games, music, processions and partying, and accommodation is booked up in advance.

The impressively massive colonial church, **Nuestra Señora del Rosario**, stands one block back from the main square, Plaza C. Alvarez Prado, where you'll find the **Museo Arquelógico** (daily 9am–7pm public holidays 9am–8pm; $2; Tues free), on the south side of the square in a beautiful colonial house. Well presented, the collection includes finds not only from the region but also from Chile, Bolivia and Peru, such as a mummy from San Pedro de Atacama, anthropomorphic Mochica vases, a bronze disc from Belén, and various items of metal and pottery, of varying interest; the simple patio is dominated by three menhirs, including a very tall one, depicting humanoid figures, from the *pukará* of Rinconada, far up in the north of the province. Keep your ticket to visit the **pukará** (daily 9am–6pm; $2; Tues free) and the **Jardín Botánico de Altura**, both a kilometre or so southwest of the plaza. The University of Buenos Aires has long been working on the pre-Columbian fortress, one of the region's biggest and most complex, with row upon row of family houses built within the high ramparts, effectively a fortified town. It has reconstructed, with considerable success and expertise, many of the houses, along with a building known as La Iglesia or "church", thought to have been a ceremonial edifice no doubt used for sacrifices. The whole magnificent fortress is spiked with a grove of cacti and, with the backdrop of imposing mountains on all sides, it affords marvellous panoramic views in all directions. The garden, in the lee of the *pukará*, is an attractively landscaped collection of local **flora**, mostly cacti, including the hairy *cabeza del viejo* ("old man's head") and equally hirsute "lamb's tail" varieties. There are fabulous views of the *pukará* from its stone paths.

Practicalities

Frequent **buses** from Humahuaca and Jujuy stop at the main square. **Accommodation** is seldom hard to come by. *Albergue Malka*, a very well-run youth hostel, 400m up a steep hill, to the east of Plaza Alvarez Prado, at San Martín s/n (☎0388/495-5197; *malka@hostels. org.ar*; ①), commands sweeping views, is extremely comfortable and serves excellent breakfasts. The friendly owners run treks and 4WD tours in the area. Rather less charming but slightly more luxurious is the *Hotel de Turismo* at Belgrano 590 (☎0388/495-5100; *tilcahot@imagine.com.ar*, ③). Much more luxurious is *Casa de la Nona*, a traditional mountain-house at Belgrano 553 (☎0388/495-5068; *ccaliari@imagine.com.ar*; ⑤). Relaxed, cosy but a little run-down is *Villar del Ala* at Padilla 100 (☎0388/495-5020; *alvillar@ imagine.com.ar*, ⑥). Services include a swimming pool in the menagerie-garden and massages; also available for non-patrons are adventure pursuits such as mountain-climbing, 4WD tours and a five-day trek over the mountains to Calilegua (see p.417). At the budget end there are three basic but decent pensions: *Residencial El Antigal* (☎0388/495-5020; ②) at Rivadavia and Belgrano, which also has a picturesque tearoom that doubles up as a bar in the evening, *Residencial Esperanza* at Belgrano 335 (☎0388/495-5106; ①) and *Hospedaje Pukará* on Padilla (☎0388/495-5050; ②). *El Jardín* (☎0388/495-5128; $3 per person) is Tilcara's main **campsite**, well-run and in an attractive riverside location 1km to the northwest of the village. Apart from facilities provided by the hotels, the only **place to eat** is the *Ruta 9*, on the main road near the turn-off to the village. It serves cheap and cheerful meals based on local delicacies such as goat and trout.

Uquia

After a short, steep climb beyond the side-road from Tilcara, the RN9 levels off and crosses the Tropic of Capricorn – marked by a giant sundial monument built in the 1980s and meant to align with the noon shadow at the solstice, but curiously installed at the wrong angle by mistake – one kilometre south of **Huacalera**, a tiny hamlet dominated by its seventeenth-century chapel. If you're in need of somewhere to stay, *Hostería La Granja* (☎0388/426-1766; ③) is charming and comfortable. Otherwise forge on, past Cerro Yacoraite, a polychrome meseta to the west, streaked with bright reds and yellows, to picturesque **UQUIA**, just over 100km north of Jujuy. Also set against a vivid backdrop of brick-red mountains and surrounded by lush quebrachos, behind a delightful square, is seventeenth-century **Iglesia de San Francisco de Paula**, with its separate tower integrated in the churchyard wall, all painted pristine white, except the smart green door of the church. Inside, the simple nave directs the gaze at the fine **retable**, the original, with its little inset painted canvases. Nine beautiful and unusual **paintings**, again from the seventeenth century, line the walls: these are unique to Collao, Alto Peru, and depict warrior-like *ángeles militares*, or angels in armour, holding arquebuses and other weapons. Formerly they numbered ten, but one went missing while they were being exhibited in Buenos Aires, where the remaining nine were restored, excessively to some tastes –they seem to have lost their centuries' old patina. If the church is closed – which is likely – ask around for the old lady who keeps the key, a relic in itself and apparently the three-hundred-year-old original. Uquia has two **places to stay**: plain, simple *Cabañas El Molino* (☎0388/490515; ②), just outside the village, and the delightful *Hostería Uquia* at Güemes 222 (☎0388/490508; ④). After Uquia, along the final stretch before Humahuaca itself, you have views to the east of some very high mountains: Cerro Zucho (4995m), Cerro Santa Barbara (4215m) and Cerro Punta Corral (4815m).

Humahuaca and around

The main town in the area, **HUMAHUACA**, 125km north of Jujuy, spills across the Río Grande from its picturesque centre on the west bank. Its enticing cobbled streets, lined with colonial-style or rustic adobe houses, lend themselves to gentle ambling – necessarily leisurely at this altitude of just below 3000m. Most of the organized tours arrive here for lunch and then double back to Jujuy or Salta, but you may like to stay over, and venture at least as far as the secluded village of **Iruya**; it's also an excellent springboard for taking a trip up into the desolate but hauntingly beautiful landscapes of the Altiplano or **Puna Jujeña**.

If you're travelling by car, be prepared for local boys approaching you at the RN9 turn-off offering to guide you. They'll show you around the town for a small tip, but don't speak anything but Spanish. Most tours to and around the town aim to deliver you at the beautifully lush main square at midday on the dot, in time to see a kitsch **statue of San Francisco Solano** emerge from a niche in the equally kitsch tower of the whitewashed **Municipalidad**, give a sign of blessing, and then disappear behind his door. A crowd gathers, invariably serenaded by groups of folk musicians; the saint repeats his trick at midnight to a smaller audience. On the western side of the square, and far more impressive, is the **Cathedral**, the Iglesia de Nuestra Señora de la Candelaria y San Antonio, built in the seventeenth century and much restored since. Within its immaculate white walls is a late seventeenth-century retable, and another on the north wall by Cosmo Duarte, dated 1790, depicting the *Crucifixion*. The remaining artworks include a set of exuberantly Mannerist paintings of the *Twelve Prophets*, signed by leading Cusqueño artist Marcos Sapaca and dated 1764. Looming over the church and the whole town is the controversial **Monumento a la Independencia**, a bombastic concoction of stone and bronze, by local artist Ernesto Soto Avendaño, and built from 1940 to 1950. Triumphal steps lead up to it from the plaza, but the best thing about it is the view across the town and valley to the noble mountainside to the east. The twenty-metre high monument is topped by a bronze statue of an Indian in a ferociously warrior-like pose. Behind it, and far more appealing, framed by two giant cacti, is an adobe tower decorated with a bronze plaque, all that remains of Iglesia Santa Barbara, whose ruins were destroyed to make way for the monument.

Practicalities

Buses from Jujuy, Salta, La Quiaca and Iruya arrive at the small bus terminal a couple of blocks southeast of the main square, at Belgrano and Entre Ríos. Apart from the ordinary and overpriced *Hotel de Turismo* at Buenos Aires 650 (☎03887/421154; ④), **accommodation** in Humahuaca is on the basic side. The cheapest option, and just about commendable, is *Albergue El Portillo* at Tucumán 69 (☎03887/421288; *elportillo@cootepal.com.ar*, ①). The unofficial youth hostel, *Albergue Juvenil* at Buenos Aires 447 (☎03887/421064; ①), has some rooms with baths, and is passable. Slightly better, and clean, with hot water and also with some en-suite rooms are *Hostería Colonial* at Entre Ríos 110 (☎03887/421007; ②) and *Residencial Humahuaca* at Córdoba 401 (☎03887/421141; ②). Regional **food** is delicious and plentiful at *La Cacharpaya*, at Jujuy 295, and accompanied by live folk music, aimed at tourists, at the *Peña del Fortunato*, San Luis and Jujuy.

Iruya

Along the RN9, just 25km due north of Humahuaca, the RP13 forks off to the northeast and winds up a stunningly beautiful narrow valley, lined with vividly coloured rocks, into the mountainside at **Iruya**; this atmospheric hamlet seems loath to share its beautiful little church with the outside world. It fits snugly into the valley of the Río Iruya, in the far northwestern corner of Salta Province. Its fortified walls, cobbled streets, whitewashed houses with their smart blue doors and timeless atmosphere, accentuated by the rarefied air – at an altitude of 3900m – alone make it worth a visit, and you certainly feel a long way from the hectic streets of Jujuy or Salta. On the first Sunday of October, its **Iglesia de Nuestra Señora del Rosario y San Roque** – a typical Quebrada chapel built to the by now familiar Mudejar design – is the focal point for a wonderfully picturesque if weird festival, half-Catholic, half-pre-Columbian, culminating in a solemn procession of weirdly masked figures, some representing demons. Of all the Northwest's festivals and there are many (see box, p.408), this is the most photogenic, the most fascinating and the most mysterious. The only **place to stay**, should you really want to soak up this otherworldly atmosphere, is the very comfortable *Hostería de Iruya* (☎482-9152, via operator; ④), also justly reputed for its cooking – just as well as there are no restaurants. **Buses** take three hours to get here from Humahuaca; Empresa Mendoza (☎03887/421016 or 156-829078) runs a morning service most days, returning to Humahuaca in the middle of the afternoon.

Up to the Puna Jujeña

Due north of Humahuaca and the turn-off to tiny Iruya, the RN9, sealed only in parts, begins its long winding haul up into the remote **Altiplano** of northern Jujuy, known as the **Puna Jujeña**; this is a fabulously wild highland area of salt-flats, **lagoons** speckled pink with flamingoes, and tiny hamlets built of mud-bricks around surprisingly big Quebrada-style chapels: stocky thick-walled naves shoring up a single bell tower, still roofed with scrawny straw when well-preserved and some of them housing treasure-troves of colonial art. Some 30km north of Humahuaca, the RN9 enters the **Cuesta de Azul Pampa**, a dramatic mountain pass peaking at 3730m and offering unobstructed views across to the huge peaks to the east. Past the bottleneck of the Abra de Azul Pampa, where fords along the road sometimes freeze causing extra hazards, the road winds along to the bleak little mining-town of **Tres Cruces**, where there's a major *gendarmería* post – personal and vehicle papers are usually checked. Nearby, but out of sight, are some of the continent's biggest deposits of lead and zinc, along with silver mines, while overlooking the village is one of the strangest rock formations in the region, the so-called **Espina del Diablo** or "Devil's Backbone"; a series of intriguingly beautiful stone burrows, clearly the result of violent tectonic activity millions of years ago, ridged like giant vertebrae. This road continues all the way to the Bolivian border at **La Quiaca** – an ideal base for visiting the remote corners of the province, such as **Yavi**, and its superb colonial church, or **Laguna de los Pozuelos**, with its sizeable wildfowl colony. On the way you pass through the crossroads village of **Abra Pampa**, from where you can branch off to visit the picturesque villages of **Cochinoca** and **Casabindo**, with their fine churches and colonial art treasures.

Abra Pampa and around

ABRA PAMPA, 80km north of Humahuaca, lives up to its former name of Siberia Argentina, a forlorn village of llama-herdsmen living in adobe houses amid the windswept steppe planted with Siberian elms as windbreaks. This really isn't a place that you'd choose to spend the night, but should you need to, pick from one of the three suitably spartan **residenciales**: *Cesarito* at Senador Pérez 200 (☎491001 via operator; ①), *El Norte* at Sarmiento 530 (☎491315 via operator; ①), and *La Coyita* at Fascio 123 (☎491052 via operator; ①). Due southwest, the rough surfaced RP11 follows the Río Miraflores to **CASABINDO**, nearly 60km away, a tiny unspoiled village dwarfed by its huge church. Nicknamed La Catedral de la Puna, the **Iglesia de la Asunción** houses a collection of Altoperuvian paintings of *ángeles militares*, or angels in armour, similar to those in Uquia (see p.412). The church itself was built in the late eighteenth century to a Hispano-Mexican design and its several chapels are the theatre of major celebrations on August 15, the **Feast of the Assumption**, when plume-hatted angels and a bull-headed demon lead a procession around the village, accompanied by drummers. The climax of the festival is a bloodless corrida, a colonial custom known as the **Toreo de la Vincha**. The bull, representing the Devil, has a rosette hung with coins stuck on his horns and the Virgin's "defenders" have to try and remove it. Coca leaves and fermented maize are buried in another ceremony on the same day, as an offering to Pachamama, the Earth Mother, in a fusion of pre-Christian and Christian rituals; these are among the most fascinating and colourful of all the Northwest's festivals and well worth catching if you're here at the right time. The only **place to stay** in Casabindo is the very rudimentary *Albergue Casabindo* (☎491126 through the operator; ①). **COCHINOCA** is another unspoiled village, 22km along a numberless dirt track heading in a westerly direction from Abra Pampa. Its nineteenth-century church, **Iglesia de Nuestra Señora de la Candelaria**, shelters some fine colonial paintings and a magnificent retable. The alabaster windows were rescued from the colonial church destroyed in a major earthquake in the mid-nineteenth century, as was the *Lienzo de la Virgen de la Almudena*, an oil-painting depicting the construction of the original building, constructed on the same site in the late seventeenth century. Both Casabindo and Cochinoca are very hard to reach as there's no public transport, but are great destinations if you're looking to get well off the beaten track.

La Quiaca and around

LA QUIACA, almost 165km north of Humahuaca, is the largest settlement in the Puna Jujeña, a border town that has seen better days. Immediately to the north, the river of the same name, gushing through a deep gorge, forms the natural frontier with Bolivia, on the other side of which the twin town of Villazón thrives on cross-border trade, while La Quiaca stagnates because its shops are losing trade to cheaper stores in Bolivia. Although there's simply nothing to do in La Quiaca, except get used to the altitude – 3445m – and perhaps plan your trip into Bolivia, its accommodation makes it a possible base for exploring this farthest corner of Argentine territory, with side-trips easily made to nearby **Yavi**, with its unusual church, **Tafna**, also dominated by a chapel, and the **Laguna de los Pozuelos**. **Buses** from Jujuy and Yavi stop at the corner of Calle Belgrano and Avenida España; the latter is the final stretch of the main RN9 road, that comes to an abrupt end at the town's surprisingly grandiose football stadium, where Argentina's national team occasionally train to build up their stamina at high altitude. Usually sleepy, La Quiaca livens up a little on the third and fourth Sundays of October, when the **Manca Fiesta**, also known as the Fiesta de la Olla, or cooking-pot festival, is staged; ceramists and other artisans show off their wares, while folk musicians put on concerts. The best **place to stay** is the simple, clean and popular *Hotel de Turismo*, two blocks southeast of the bus terminal at Siria and San Martín (☎03885/422243; ③), while *Residencial Crystal*, at Sarmiento 539 (no phone; ②) has basic rooms leading off a stark courtyard, and serves the best food in town at very low prices.

Yavi

A good paved road, the RP5, leads east from La Quiaca, intended to lead to an airport that has yet to materialize. Across the rolling Siete Hermanos mountain range, 17km away along this road sits the village of **YAVI**, a totally unspoiled altiplanic village of sloping cobbled streets, adobe houses with flaking wooden doors, and a splendid working flour mill. From a mirador at the top of the main drag Avenida Senador Pérez, to the north of the village, you have a panoramic view, taking in the dilapidated but attractive eighteenth-century **Casa del Marqués de Tojo**, the erstwhile family home of the region's ruling marquess, the only holder of that rank in colonial Argentina; the house, on the Plaza Mayor, is a museum of sorts with erratic opening hours, and a motley collection of artefacts and junk. Next to it is the village's seventeenth-century church, **Iglesia de Nuestra Señora del Rosario y San Francisco**. Behind its harmonious white facade – ask around for the lady who keeps the key – is one of the region's best preserved colonial interiors, lit a ghostly lemon-yellow by the unique wafer-thin onyx-paned windows. Some of the church's treasures were stolen during the border conflict with Chile – when gendarmes left the village to guard Argentine territory – and were recently traced to a private collection in the United States. The ornate Baroque pulpit, three retables decorated with brightly coloured wooden statuettes of saints and a fine, sixteenth-century, Flemish oil painting that must have been brought here by early colonizers, look wonderful in the simple white nave. A couple of blocks north, the very comfortable **Hostería de Yavi** (☎03885/421288 or 482001; ④), with a welcome open fire in the sitting-room, offers half board only – not a bad deal, since there's nowhere else to eat and the meals are generous; it's run by the owners of the *hostería* in Uquia, who'll book ahead for you if you want. You can also **camp** across the *acequia* or irrigation channel from the church, but the site has no facilities. Guides – ask at the *hostería* – can take you on visits to local attractions, such as pre-Columbian petroglyphs and cave-paintings in the nearby mountains; the petroglyphs of human figures and animals, plus some mysterious abstract symbols, no oubt of religious significance, are nothing special but the walk there, through stunning Altiplano countryside, is worthwhile. La Quiaqueña runs frequent **buses** from La Quiaca, or you could try and hitch a lift from the market.

Tafna and Laguna de los Pozuelos

Heading west from La Quiaca on the RP5 takes you along parallel to the Bolivian border, past the northern tip of the steeply scarped Cordón de Escaya, to **TAFNA**, 20km away. This tiny settlement consists of three adobe houses and an enormous **colonial chapel**, whose ochre walls and towers, unusually two in number, and straw roof blend into the beige landscape; huge flocks of sheep and goats overrun the nearby colonial cemetery. Immediately to the west of Tafna, beyond the **Cuesta del Toquero**, a narrow pass lined with curious cobweb-like rock formations, you reach the crossroads and police checkpoint of Cieneguillas, from where you can continue another 30km along corrugated dirt track, to the tiny mountain-village of Santa Catalina, just to say you've been to the northernmost settlement in Argentina. Otherwise head south for 50km, through parched pastureland, dotted with farmsteads and corrals, to the entrance to the **Monumento Natural Laguna de los Pozuelos**, 150 square kilometres of protected land in a basin between the rippling Sierra de Cochinoca and Sierra de Rinconada. Access to the reserve is unlimited, but call in at the **guardería**, to the south of the lake, just off the road to Rinconada, if only for a friendly chat with the *guardaparques*; they'll also let you camp in the forecourt, if you need somewhere to stay. The lagoon itself, a couple of kilometres to the north, has shrunk in recent years, after a series of dry summers, but is still a considerable stretch of water covering 70 square kilometres, home to large flocks of Andean flamingoes and over thirty other varieties of wildfowl, including teals, avocets and ducks. Don't try and drive over the soft, spongy lakeside; the lake edge is a quagmire and the shy flamingoes take off in great clouds long before you get anywhere near them, forming long pink skeins streaked against the backdrop of dark brown mountains; instead walk from the reserve entrance, where a sign explains what fauna you'll see. You're also likely to see ñandúes scuttling away to find cover as you approach. **Buses** come out here every morning from Abra Pampa, 50km to the southeast, on their way to Rinconada, and return in the afternoon, just giving you time – three hours or so – to get to the lagoon and back.

Parque Nacional Calilegua and Parque Nacional Baritú

These cloudforests, or *yunga* jungles, like Parque Nacional El Rey further south (see p.397), are draped over high crags thrusting out of the flat, green plains of the subtropical lowlands; they are worth a visit for the dramatic scenery alone, but in addition incredibly varied fauna lives amid the dense vegetation. The biggest of the Northwest's cloudforest parks, the **Parque Nacional Calilegua**, is also the most accessible and best developed – it is the pride and joy of Jujuy Province – and within easy reach of San Salvador de Jujuy, though it might be better to stay in nearby **Libertador General San Martín**. Slightly smaller than Calilegua, **Parque Nacional Baritú**, away to the north in a far-flung corner of Salta Province, is far harder to visit, and therefore even less spoiled, than either of the other two national parks; the small town of **San Ramón de la Nueva Orán** can act as a springboard for getting there.

Parque Nacional Calilegua

Spread over 760 square kilometres, just south of the Tropic of Capricorn, in a province better known for its arid mountains, multicoloured valleys and parched altiplanic landscapes, the **Parque Nacional Calilegua** sticks up above rich fertile land where some of the country's biggest sugar farms stretch for kilometres. It's the setting for amusing anecdotes in Gerald Durrell's book *The Whispering Land*; his tales of roads cut off by flooding rivers can still ring true but his quest for native animals to take back to his private zoo cannot be imitated – the park's rich flora and fauna are now strictly protected by law. The land once belonged to the Leach brothers, local sugar barons of British origin, whose family donated it to the state to turn it into a national park in the 1970s. This was a shrewd business move: sugar plantations need a lot of clean water and the only way to keep the reliable supplies which run through the park free of pollution, uncontrolled logging and the general destruction of the fragile ecosystem was through the state regulations that come with national park status.

The park **entrance** (daily 9am–6pm; free) at Aguas Blancas is 120km from Jujuy city, along the unpaved RP83 which climbs westwards towards the hamlet of **Villa Grande** from the RN34, a few kilometres north of **Libertador General San Martín**. This uninviting small town, dominated by the huge Ledesma industrial complex – the world's biggest sugar refinery – and usually referred to as Libertador or LGSM on signs, is a possible stopover base for visiting the park (see below). For visits to the park, guides charge $3 per person an hour to take you around and point out the flora and fauna (see Contexts, p.718), which is certainly worth it. For exploring on your own, cars can make it along the main road, punctuated by numerous viewpoints, some offering splendid panoramas, as far as the **Mesada de la Colmenas**, near the other rangers' headquarters, but a 4WD will be required beyond there – the road continues its climb to the highest point, at 1700m, marked by the **Abra de las Cañas** monolith. You should certainly walk off the beaten track, well away from noisy trucks, if you want to have the slightest chance of spotting any of the wildlife. Trekking around Calilegua takes time and it's a very good idea to spend a night or two in the park. Morning and late afternoon are the best times to see animals and birds by streams and rivers. Seven trails of varying length and difficulty have been hacked through the dense vegetation, and it's worth asking the rangers for guidance; there aren't any maps.

The summits of the **Serranía de Calilegua**, marking the park's northwestern boundary, reach heights of over 3700m, beyond which lies arid altiplanic terrain. The trek to the summit of Cerro Amarillo (3720m) takes three days from the park entrance; the nearby shepherds' hamlet, **Alto Calilegua**, is certainly worth a visit. From there it's even possible to link up with **Tilcara** (see p.411), a three-day trek; some of the organized trips arranged in Salta and Tilcara itself, including horse rides, offer this amazing chance to witness the stark contrast between the verdant jungle below and the desiccated uplands.

Practicalities

At the park entrance, you'll find the **Intendencia** (☎03886/422046; *pncalilegua@ cooperlib.com.ar*), definitely worth a visit before you head in, for maps and extra information about the park; general **tourist information** about the area can be obtained at Confianza Turismo, Av. Libertad 350 in Libertador (☎03886/424527; *confianza@cooplib.com.ar*). **Accommodation outside the park** is to be found in **Libertador**, the nearest base to speak of. Best of all, and offering top-notch service and excursion possibilities, is the new and very plush *Posada del Sol* (☎03886/424900; ⑤), with inviting rooms arranged around an attractive courtyard and swimming pool, hidden away at Los Ceibos and Pukará. A little cheaper and rather less appealing, but clean enough, is the *Hotel Los Lapachos* at Entre Ríos 400 (☎03886/423790; ③). Alternative accommodation is available at the *Complejo Termal Aguas Calientes* spa resort (☎0388/156-50699), 30km northeast of Libertador, along the RP1 road that turns eastwards off the RN34 past the straggly village of Caimancito. Near the banks of the Río San Francisco in a bucolic setting, it offers excellent meals and clean rooms (②), camping ($3 per tent) or the opportunity to splash around in the various curative mineral pools for the day ($3). Barring the mosquitoes (bring repellent), this is an excellent place to rest, conveniently near Caliegua in an area rich in trails and scenery. Alternatively try the *Portal de Pedra* at nearby Villa Monte (☎0388/156-820564), across near the eastern border of Salta Province – gaucho traditions, fine countryside walks and excellent wildlife-spotting are the attractions, with the emphasis firmly on ecotourism. By far the best **place to eat** is in Libertador itself: *Del Valle* at Entre Ríos 793 is a restaurant serving plain but well-cooked meals at reasonable prices.

Buses from Salta stop at Libertador's terminal on Av. Antartida Argentina, 200m east of the RN34. Buses for Valle Grande, passing through the park, leave the terminal early in the morning, returning late at night – times vary – but you could also contact the Intendencia (☎03886/422046; *pncalilegua@cooperlib.com.ar*) to find out whether any timber trucks are going towards the park at a time convenient for you; there's no problem hitching a lift if there are. Buses from Salta to Orán sometimes stop at the *Club Social San Lorenzo*, near the park entrance, but otherwise hitching might well be the only way to get that far; the RN34 is a busy route. Announce yourself to the rangers at the park entrance, 8km from the RN34; nearby a camouflaged **campsite**, with basic facilities, has been cleared ($3 per person); for the time being, it's the only practical way of being **on site** early enough in the morning or late enough at dusk to be assured of spotting wildlife – though the voracious insects may deter you. If you get as far as **Valle Grande**, you could stay at either of the village's extremely basic **accommodation** options: *Albergue San Francisco* (no phone; ①) or *Albergue Valle Grande* (☎03886/461000; ①).

Like the other two parks, Caliegua is best visited in **spring** or **autumn** as the summer months – December to March or April – can see sudden cloudbursts cut off access roads and make paths much too slippery for comfort. At all times bring **insect repellent** since mosquitoes and other nasty bugs are also plentiful and virulent, especially in the warmer months. You may wish to visit the park on an **organized tour**; TEA, San Martín 128, Jujuy (☎0388/423-6270) can get you here and fix up accommodation; while Ricardo Clark Expediciones, Caseros 121, Salta (☎0387/421-5390; *yuchan@arnet.com.ar*) regularly runs expert bird-watching safaris to the park.

Parque Nacional Baritú and San Ramón de la Nueva Orán

Located in an isolated corner of northeastern Salta Province, the all but inaccessible **Parque Nacional Baritú** is one of the country's least visited national parks. Baritú's mascot is the red **yunga squirrel** (*ardilla roja*), but you will find most of the cloud-forest animal-life here, enjoying the relative seclusion. In addition to the typical flora (see p.718), the virgin vegetation includes large numbers of the impressive **tree-fern**, a dinosaur of a plant surviving from the Paleozoic era, whose reptilian scaly trunk and parasol of lacy fronds can reach five or six metres in height. Less pleasant is the *maroma*, a psychopathic parasite that ungratefully strangles its host tree to death.

A poor road, usually cut off in the rainy season, runs for 30km west from the customs post at Aguas Blancas on the Bolivian border, 50km north of **SAN RAMÓN DE LA NUEVA ORÁN**, a rather grandiose name for such an insignificant little town (it's usually shortened to Orán), and enters the park at the rangers' post known as **Sendero Angosto**, on the Río Pescado. Though of little interest in itself, Orán is the ideal base for visiting the all-but-inaccessible Baritú. **Accommodation** ranges from the fairly luxurious *Hotel Alto Verde* at Pellegrini 671 (☎03878/421214 ⑤), boasting air conditioning in all rooms and a fair-sized swimming pool, to the *Crillon* at 25 de Mayo 225 (☎03878/421101; ②) and *Colonial* on Pizarroy Colón (☎03878/421103; ②). Both are basic but have clean bathrooms and decent rooms. The alternative route means going into Bolivia, following the Río Bermejo in a northwesterly direction as far as Nogalitos, crossing the river and border at La Mamora and entering the park at Los Pozos, via an even more adventurous route for anyone who likes making life difficult.

Covering 720 square kilometres, the park has a geography that is complicated by a maze of *arroyos* and largely impervious high mountains: the steep Las Pavas and Porongal ranges both exceed 2000m while the park's southern reaches are dominated by the **Cerro Cinco Picachos**, at nearly 2000m. The lack of public transport, lack of on-the-spot facilities and the challenging terrain all but rule out individual travel and hardly any tour operators based in nearby towns seem interested in taking you there. Try contacting Hugo Luna at 9 de Julio 430 in Orán, or see if an operator in Jujuy or Salta will take you there: try TEA, San Martín 128, Jujuy (☎0388/4236270); or Ricardo Clark Expediciones, Caseros 121, Salta (☎0387/421-5390; *yuchan@arnet.com.ar*).

Valles Calchaquíes

Named after the Río Calchaquí, which has its source in the Nevado de Acay (at over 5000m) near San Antonio de los Cobres, in the north of Salta Province, and joins the Río de las Conchas, near Salta's border with Tucumán, the **Valles Calchaquíes** are a series of beautiful highland valleys, enjoying over three hundred days of sunshine a year, a dry climate and much cooler summers than the lowland plains around Salta. It can snow in winter, especially in July. The fertile land, irrigated with canals and ditches that capture the plentiful snowmelt from the high mountains to the west, is mostly given over to vineyards – among the world's highest – which produce the characteristic torrontés grape. The scenery is extremely varied and of an awesome beauty, constantly changing as you make your way along winding mountainside roads. Organized tours from Salta squeeze the visit into a day, stopping at the valleys' main settlement, the airy village of Cafayate, for lunch. However, by far the most rewarding way to see the Valles Calchaquíes is under your own steam, by climbing up the amazing **Cuesta del Obispo**, through the **Parque Nacional Los Cardones**, a protected forest of gigantic cardón cacti, to the picturesque village of **Cachi**; following the valley south through some memorable scenery via **Molinos** and **San Carlos**, on to **Cafayate**, where plentiful accommodation facilitates a stopover. The scenic road back down to Salta, sometimes known as the Quebrada de Cafayate but more accurately called the **Cuesta de las Conchas**, snakes past some incredible rock formations, best seen in the warm light of the late afternoon or early evening. All along the valleys, you'll see typical *casas de galería*: long, single-storyed houses similar to those in the Valle de Lerma (see p.397), some with a colonnade of rounded arches, others decorated with pointed ogival arches or straight pillars.

Regular **public transport** to Salta and Tucumán makes travelling around the valleys straightforward even without your own transport, though it is less frequent along the northern reaches around Cachi. **Organized tours** from Salta are your best bet if you have no transport of your own and don't have the time to hang around waiting for buses;

Apacheta Viajes, Buenos Aires 33 (☎0387/431-1622 or 421-2333; *apacheta@salnet.com.ar*); Ricardo Clark Expediciones, Caseros 121 (☎0387/421-5390; *yuchan@arnet.com.ar*); MoviTrack, Buenos Aires 68 (☎0387/431-6749, fax 431-5301; *www.movitrak.com.ar*); and Hernán Uriburu, J.M. Lequizamón 446 (☎0387/431-0605; *hru@salta-server.com.ar*) run a variety of tours to the valleys, some more specialized than others.

Up to Cachi

The northern Calchaquí settlement of Cachi sits 170km southwest of Salta, via Chicoana, in the Valle de Lerma (see p.397). To get there you go along the partly sealed RP33, a scenic road that squeezes through the dank Quebrada de Escoipe, before climbing the dramatic mountain road known as the **Cuesta del Obispo**, 20km of hairpin bends, offering views of the rippling Sierra del Obispo. These fabulously beautiful mountains, blanketed in olive-green vegetation and heavily eroded by countless brooks, are at their best in the morning light and should be seen if possible on the way up to, rather than on your way down from, the valleys; the best organized tours from Salta do just that. About 60km from Chicoana, just before you reach the top of the *cuesta*, a signposted track south leads down to the **Valle Encantado**, 4km away; this is a fertile little valley, set around a marshy lagoon, that becomes a riot of colour in September and October when millions of wild flowers burst into bloom, but it makes for a rewarding detour all year round; its cool temperatures and delightfully pastoral scenery make it a good place for a short rest, especially if you're driving. Foxes, vizcachas and other small animals are often spotted here. Back on the main road, 1km further on, is the **Abra Piedra del Molino**, a narrow mountain pass at 3347m, marked by the mysterious "mill-stone" that gives the pass its name; nobody knows how this perfectly circular stone got here, but the idea that it is a discarded mill-stone is probably apocryphal.

Some 20km west of the Abra Piedra del Molino, where the road forks to the left – an uninteresting short cut to Seclantás and the RN40 – the RP33 continues dead straight in a northwards direction, cutting through the **Parque Nacional Los Cardones**, an official reserve recently set up to protect the forest of cardón cacti that covers the dusty valley and creeps up the arid mountainside, mingled with the parasol-like *churquis* and other spiny trees typical of desert regions; there's no *guardería* and you can wander as you like among the gigantic cacti, many of them more than five metres tall. Cardones grow painfully slowly, less than a couple of millimetres a year, and their wood has been excessively exploited for making furniture, crafts and for firewood; it's now protected, so don't remove any specimens. Part of this road, known as the **Recta Tin-Tin**, 10km of straight-as-a-die roller coaster track, is well known for its optical illusion – the lie of the valley makes it look as though you're climbing when in fact you're going down (heading in this direction that is). At the tiny village of **Payogasta**, where the RP33 joins the RN40, you have a choice of road. You can either head north to explore the northernmost reaches of the Valles Calchaquíes; dramatic high mountains on either side and beguiling desert-like scenery accompany you all along the rough track to La Poma, 40km to the north (see p.402); or, especially if time is short or night is drawing in, you can head straight south for **Cachi**.

The picturesque village of **CACHI**, located at 2280m above sea level, is overshadowed by the permanently snowcapped **Nevado del Cachi** (6380m) whose peak looms only 15km to the west. The village is centred around the delightful Plaza Mayor, shaded by palms and orangetrees. On the north side stands the much-restored **Iglesia San José**, with its plain white facade, fine wooden floor and unusual cactus-wood altar, pews and confessionals. To the east, in a neocolonial house around an attractive whitewashed patio, is the **Museo Arqueológico Pío Pablo Díaz** (daily 8am–6pm; $1), displaying a run-of-the-mill collection of locally excavated items. Apart from that, there's little in the way of sights in Cachi; it's simply a place to wander, investigating the various local crafts, including ponchos and ceramics, or climbing to the **cemetery** for wonderful mountain-views and a panorama of the pea-green valley, every arable patch filled wth vines, maize and capsicum plantations. Farther afield, the scenic track to **Cachi Adentro**, 6km west of the village, leads from the end of Calle Benjamín Zorrilla and takes you through the fertile farmland where, in late summer (March–May), the fields are carpeted with drying paprika peppers, a dazzling display of bright red that features in the best postcards.

Practicalities

Buses from Salta (and local buses from various villages) arrive at Cachi's little unnamed square next to *Hotel Nevado de Cachi*, on Ruíz de los Llanos (☎03868/491004; ①), a good **place to stay**, with basic rooms, cactus-wood furniture but erratic hot water. Hill-top *Hostería ACA* at General Güemes (☎03868/491105; ③) is by far the village's most comfortable accommodation, but nearby *Hospedaje El Cortijo* (☎03868/491-034; ③), in a colonial house at the bottom of the hill, is incredibly good value. The only decent **place to eat** in Cachi itself is *El Jagüel* on Av. General Güemes (☎03868/491135) serving memorable *locro* and *empanadas*. Along the road to **Cachi Adentro**, a hamlet some 10km away into the mountains, and commanding stunning mountain views through a huge picture window, is the luxurious *Finca El Molino* (☎03868/491094 or 0387/4219368; ⑤), with very comfortable rooms and a designer interior. Further along the same road, with even better views and highly atmospheric, but sadly run-down, is hippyish *Hostal Samay Huasi* (no phone; ③), good value if you don't mind the lack of comfort.

From Cachi to Cafayate

The mostly unsealed RN40 from Cachi to Cafayate takes you along some stupendous corniche roads that wind alongside the Río Calchaquí itself, offering views on either side of sheer mountainsides and snowcapped peaks. It's only 180km from one to the other but allow plenty of time as the narrow track slows your progress and you'll want to stop to admire the views, take photographs and visit the picturesque valley settlements en route, oases of greenery in an otherwise stark landscape. **MOLINOS**, 60km south of Cachi, lies a couple of kilometres west of the main road, in a bend of the Río Molinos, and is worth the side-trip for a peek at its lovely adobe houses and the eighteenth-century **Iglesia de San Pedro Nolasco**, currently undergoing restoration; the expansive facade, topped with two sturdy turrets, is shored up with props. Opposite, in Finca Isasmendi, the eighteenth-century residence of the last Royalist governor of Salta, Nicolás Severo de Isasmendi, is the beautiful *Hostal Provincial de Molinos* (☎03868/494002; ⑤), well-furnished rooms around a shady patio. Even more luxurious accommodation is available at *Finca Luracatao* (☎0387/439-5371; full board only; ⑧), 2km west of Molinos.

At **ANGASTACO**, 40km away in the direction of Cafayate, and 2km down a side-road heading south, you'll find much more modest but clean, attractive **accommodation** in the *Hostería de Angastaco* on Libertad (☎03868/156-39016; ③). Just beyond Angastaco, the already impressive scenery becomes even more spectacular: after 10km you enter the surreal **Quebrada de las Flechas**, where the red sandstone cliffs form a backdrop for the flinty arrowhead-like formations on either side of the road that give the gorge its name. For 10km, weird rocks like desert roses dot the landscape and, beyond the natural stone walls of **El Cañón**, over 20m high, the road squeezes through **El Ventisquero**, the "wind-tunnel".

The oldest settlement in the valley, dating from 1551, picturesque **SAN CARLOS**, 35km further, straddles the RN40 itself; it's a wine-growing village and the several bodegas welcome visitors at all times, but do not provide proper guided visits. The nineteenth-century **Iglesia San Carlos Borromeo**, whose interior walls are decorated with naive **frescoes** depicting the life of St Charles Borromeo himself. The last stretch of the road to Cafayate threads its way through extensive **vineyards**, affording views of the staggeringly high mountains – many of them over 4000m – to the west and east.

Cafayate

Nearly 190km from Salta and little more than a village, **CAFAYATE** is the self-appointed capital of the Valles Calchaquíes and certainly the main settlement hereabouts. It's also the centre of the province's wine industry and the main tourist base for the area, thanks to its wide range of accommodation, and convenient location as a crossroads between Salta, Cachi and Amaichá (see p.432). Straddling the RN40, called the Avenida Güemes within the village limits, between the Río Chuschas, to the north, and the Río Loro Huasi, to the south, it's a lively, modern village, originally founded by Franciscan missionaries who set up *encomiendas*, or Indian reservations with farms attached, in the region. Apart from exploring the surroundings on foot, by bike or on horseback, or tasting wine at the bodegas (see box below), there's not actually a lot to do here; the late nineteenth-century **Iglesia Catedral de Nuestra Señora del Rosario** dominates the main plaza but is disappointingly nondescript inside. The **Museo de Arqueología Calchaquí**, one block southwest, at Calchaquí and Colón (daily 8.30am–9pm; $1), comprises one room piled with **ceramics** of the Candelaria and Santamaría cultures, including some massive urns, followed by another room cluttered with criollo antiques and curios. Two blocks south of the plaza, at avenidas Güemes and Chacabuco, is the feeble **Museo de la Vid y del Vino** (Mon–Fri 10am–1pm 5–8pm; $1), a motley collection of wine-related relics and photographs, in a defunct winery. About 2km south, on the RN40 to Santa María, you'll find the workshop and salesroom of one of the region's finest artisans: Oscar Hipaucha sells wonderfully intricate wood and metal boxes, made of quebracho, algarrobo and copper, at justifiably high prices. Way up to the north of the town, Cristofani makes elegant ceramic urns but most tend to be too big to make practical souvenirs.

THE CAFAYATE VINEYARDS

While Mendoza and, increasingly, San Juan are the names most associated with wines from Argentina, supermarkets and wine shops around the world are selling more and more bottles with the name Cafayate on their labels. These high-altitude vineyards, some of the highest in the world at around 1700m but thriving in the sunny climate, are planted with the malbec and cabernet varieties for which Mendoza is justly famous, but the local speciality is a grape thought to have been brought across from Galicia: the torrontés. The delicate, flowery white wine it produces, with a slight acidity, is the perfect accompaniment for the regional cuisine, but also goes well with fish and seafood. You can taste some excellent samples at *Vinoteca La Escalera*, San Martín, Cafayate, or see how the wine is made at one of the bodegas in or around Cafayate, where tastings and wine-sales round off each tour (Spanish only). Bodega Domingo Hermanos (daily 8am–noon & 2.30–6pm) is on 25 de Mayo, in the southern part of town, while prestigious Bodega Etchart (daily 9am–5pm) is a few kilometres along the RN40, in the direction of Santa María. Bodega La Banda (daily 9am–1pm & 3–7pm) lies to the north along the same road, while Bodega La Rosa (Mon–Fri 8am–12.30pm & 1.30–7pm), belonging to the prizewinning Torino family, is just along the RN68.

Practicalities

Frequent **buses** from Salta and less frequent ones from Cachi, via Molinos, plus daily services from Tucumán via Amaichá (see p.432) arrive at the cramped terminus just along Belgrano, half a block east of the plaza, or sometimes deposit passengers wherever they want to get off in the village. A kiosk (Mon–Fri 9am–8pm, Sat, Sun & public holidays 7am–1pm & 3–9pm) on the plaza dispenses **information** about where to stay, what to do and where to rent bikes or hire horses. A popular **folk festival**, the Serenata Cafayateña, is held here on the first weekend of Lent, when accommodation is hard to find. Otherwise, you're spoiled for choice when it comes to **accommodation**, starting with the unofficial but decent youth hostel at Av. Güemes Norte 441 (☎03868/421440; ①). *Hospedaje Familiar Basla* at Nuestra Señora del Rosario 165(☎03868/421098; ②), just south of the square, has basic rooms around a cheerful patio, while *Hotel Confort* at Av. Güemes Norte 232 (☎03868/421091; ③) lives up to its name. At the top end of the price bracket, *Hotel Asturias* at Av. Güemes 154 (☎03868/421328; *asturias@infonoa.com.ar;* ④) has a swimming pool, a reliable restaurant, and tasteful rooms decorated with beautiful photographs of the region. For **eating**, the choice is more limited. *Europa Centro* on the north side of the plaza is an excellent pizzeria with lots of atmosphere, enhanced by a resident Brazilian parrot, a black cat and a Dalmatian. Opposite is *Quijote* which specializes in regional cooking, as does the popular and well-priced *Carreta de Don Olegario* on the east side of the plaza. The ice creams at *Heladería Miranda*, on Av. Güemes half a block north of the plaza, are outstanding; try the wine sorbets.

The Quebrada de las Conchas

The RN68 forks off the RN40 only 2km of Cafayate, to the north of the Río Chuschas, before heading across fertile land, some of it given over to vineyards. It soon begins its winding descent, following the Río de las Conchas through the **Quebrada de las Conchas**, to the Valle de Lerma and onwards to Salta. The gorge is seen at its best on the way down, in the mellow late afternoon or early evening light; organized tours aim to take you down this way and you should follow suit if travelling under your own steam; leave plenty of time as down in the gorge you'll be tempted to make several stops, to admire the views and take pictures. At the northernmost part of the gorge you enter an invariably windy stretch, where you're better off inside your vehicle unless you want to be sandblasted; the result of frequent sandstorms is the formation of wonderful sand-dunes, **Los Médanos**, like gigantic piles of sawdust by the road. This is where the canyon proper begins, and the road snakes its way down alongside the river-bed. The majestic Sierras de Carahuasi – the northernmost range of the Cumbres Calchaquíes – loom behind as a magnificent backdrop, while in the foreground rock formations have been eroded and blasted by wind and rain to form buttresses, known as **Los Castillos**, or the castles, and a huge monolith dubbed **El Obelisco**. The reds, ochres and pinks of the sandstone make it all look staggeringly beautiful. Further on **La Yesera**, or "chalk quarry", is actually a strange group of eerily grey and yellow rocks exposed by millions of years of erosion, while a monk-like figure, skulking in the cliff-side, has earned the name **El Fraile**. Just off the road, about 50km from Cafayate, two semicircular ravines carved in the mountainside are called **La Garganta del Diablo** (Devil's Throat) and **El Anfiteatro**, while the animal-like figure nearby is **El Sapo** (Toad). Still passing through delightful scenery, you leave the stupendous canyon, spiked with cacti, behind you to enter the forested valley bottom. From La Viña, 100km northeast of Cafayate and just to the south of Embalse Cabra Corral, the enormous reservoir serving Salta, it's another 90km or so to the city, along the relatively busy RN68 highway.

San Miguel de Tucumán and around

In the humid valley of the Río Salí, in the eastern lee of the high Sierra de Aconquija, **SAN MIGUEL DE TUCUMÁN** is Argentina's fourth largest city, 1190km northwest of Buenos Aires and nearly 300km south of Salta by the RN9. It hasn't changed much, it seems, since Paul Theroux was there in 1978 and wrote, in *The Old Patagonian Express*, that it "was thoroughly European in a rather old-fashioned way, from the pin-striped suits and black moustaches of the old men idling in the cafés or having their shoes shined in the plaza, to the baggy, shapeless school uniforms of the girls stopping on their way to the convent school to squeeze – it was an expression of piety – the knee of Christ on the cathedral crucifix"; it still looks a bit like a European city caught in a time-warp. The capital of a tiny but heavily populated sugar-rich province, Tucumán is by far the biggest metropolis in the Northwest, the region's undisputed **commercial capital** and one of the liveliest urban centres in the country, with a thriving business centre, bustling, traffic-choked downtown streets, a youthful population and even a slightly violent undercurrent by Argentine standards. Tucumán certainly has a bois-terous image, perhaps partly since it's Argentina's rugby capital, but its confidence has been trimmed in recent years by a long-running political and economic crisis. Even Tucumanos themselves admit – they're known for their self-derision – that the city's people have a knack of "finding other people's property before it's lost", but you're unlikely to find Tucumán any more dangerous than other large city. Despite a heavy-duty nightlife that quietens down only on Mondays, it's not a place you're likely to spend long in, as attractions are in very short supply; the couple of museums worth see-ing, the **Museo Folklórico** and **Casa del Obispo Colombres**, are interesting enough, but the huge open space, where the latter is located, **Parque Centenario 9 de Julio**, needs a major face-lift. That said, some of the Northwest's finest scenery is within easy reach of the city and nothing can provide a more startling contrast than the steep ascent from the steamy lowlands, through the tangled mossy jungle of the Selva Tucumana, up to **Tafí del Valle** amid the bare mountains of the Sierra del Aconquija. An unusual museum, at **Amaichá**, and a restored pre-Incan fortress, at **Quilmes**, are the attractions in the far west of Tucumán Province, at the southern end of the Valles Calchaquíes, on the other side of the sierra. While these are included in classic day-trips from the city, you may wish to linger here – and stay over in Tafí or Quilmes, espe-cially when it's hot and sticky in the heaving city.

Some history

Originally founded in 1565 by Diego de Villarroel, Tucumán's first home was near the present town of Monteros, 50km southwest of the present city, but mosquitoes proved an intolerable nuisance, and the settlement was moved to its current drier spot in 1685. The etymology of the name Tucumán is something of a mystery; it is probably a cor-ruption of the Quechoa (see box opposite) for "place where things finish", a reference to the abrupt mountains that loom above the fertile plains, but may have been derived from the Kana word *yukuman* meaning "welling springs". For a while, the city flour-ished and its name was applied to a whole region of Spanish America corresponding to southern Bolivia and the northwestern quarter of today's Argentina; but the city was soon eclipsed by Salta and Córdoba, whose climates were found to be more bearable. Then, on July 9, 1816, the city hosted a historic Congress of Unitarist politicians at which Argentina's independence was declared from Spain. In the late nineteenth cen-tury, after the arrival of the railways and sizeable influxes of immigrants, from Italy mainly, along with thousands of Jews from central Europe, the city underwent the expansion that turned it into today's metropolis. British investment and climatic condi-tions favoured Tucumán's sugar industry, and most of the city's wealth, built up around

QUECHOA – THE LANGUAGE OF THE INCAS

Of all the country's regions, the Northwest now has the biggest concentration of native peoples, the largest single group being the 150,000-strong Kollas mostly in Jujuy Province, most of whom have kept their customs and language alive despite decades of Europeanization. Other ethnic groups in the Northwest include the Diaguitas, Toba, Wichí, Chané, Chorote, Tapiete, Chulupi and Zuritas. Until the Incan empire swallowed up the region only a century or so before the European invasion, the different groups – and even their distinct *ayllúes* or clans – spoke quite separate languages, that were mutually incomprehensible, but just as the Romans imposed Latin, so the Incas made **Quechoa** the lingua franca of their vast realms. Isolation from the rest of the country and uninterrupted cross-border contacts helped to keep the Quechoa language alive in Northwestern Argentina, and academic interest in this ancient heritage has recently been growing. Quechoa is now taught in local schools and even at universities. As a result, albeit artificially, Quechoa is undergoing a revival; by contrast, other non-European tongues such as Kana have died out, surviving only in local place names.

Quechoa (sometimes erroneously referred to as Quichoa) is subdivided into numerous dialects, and is spoken throughout Northwest Argentina, to the north and west of present-day Santiago del Estero. An oral language without a written form, it was adapted to the Roman alphabet by the colonizers, so its spelling roughly corresponds to the phonetic system of Castilian Spanish (*ch* is pronounced like the Spanish – and English – sound). Obviously totally unrelated to any Indo-European languages, Quechoa nonetheless follows most of the familiar rules of grammar, especially syntax and morphology, though it ignores any concept of gender or articles; its grammar is fairly regular and not too hard to learn. Although inevitably Quechoa-speakers now sprinkle their speech with many Spanish words, over the years Quechoa has managed to infiltrate Spanish: most famously, *cancha* – one word always on all Argentines' lips – meaning a sports field or stadium (especially for football), comes from the Quechoa word for "open field". Other familiar Quechoa words mostly relate to flora and fauna: llama, alpaca, condor, vicuña, guanaco, vizcacha, tuna, chañar and palta, plus the all-important term *puna*, referring both to the Altiplano and the altitude sickness you might suffer from up there. Otherwise topology is the main treasure-house of the indigenous peoples' tongues: Catamarca, Fiambalá, Jujuy, Humahuaca, Yavi and Cafayate all have names rooted in the pre-Hispanic past.

the end of the nineteenth century, accrued from this "white gold". A slump in international sugar prices and shortsighted over-farming have now forced local sugar-growers to branch out into alternative money-earners, such as tobacco and citrus fruit. Tucumán is now the world's biggest lemon-producing area but also grows mandarins, grapefruit and kumquats, and is still referred to fondly by the rest of the country as the "Garden of the Nation"; with a climate similar to that around Santa Cruz de la Sierra in Bolivia, much of the area has been given over to growing strawberries – with large numbers of Bolivian workers helping local farmers at harvest time. During the Dirty War of the 1970s military dictatorship, Tucumán and its hinterland were caught up in vicious fighting between the local government and the pro-Castro Ejército Revolucionario del Pueblo (ERP), in which the latter were all but wiped out under the ruthless command of General Antonio Domingo Bussi, the provincial governor.

Arrival, information and accommodation

Tucumán's international **airport**, Aeropuerto Benjamín Matienzo (☎0381/426-0121), is just 9km east of the centre of town. Tucumán is quite fog-prone and flights are sometimes inconveniently re-routed as far away as Santiago del Estero. A regular **minibus**

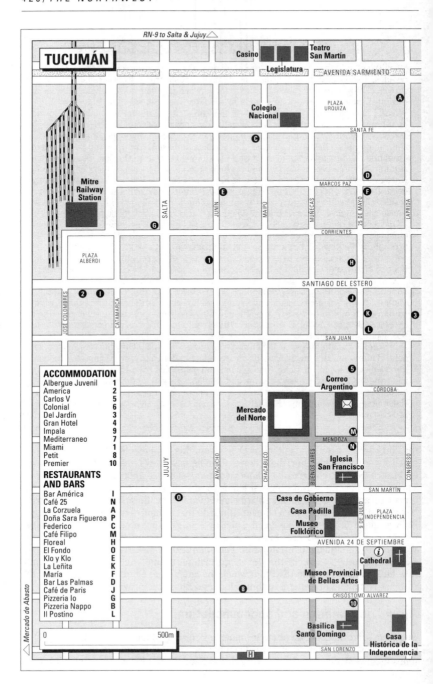

TUCUMÁN

RN-9 to Salta & Jujuy

Casino

Teatro San Martín

Legislatura

AVENIDA SARMIENTO

Colegio Nacional

PLAZA URQUIZA

SANTA FE

MARCOS PAZ

SALTA / JUNÍN / MAIPÚ / MUÑECAS / 25 DE MAYO / LAPRIDA

CORRIENTES

Mitre Railway Station

PLAZA ALBERDI

SANTIAGO DEL ESTERO

SAN JUAN

JOSÉ COLOMBRES / CATAMARCA

CÓRDOBA

Correo Argentino

Mercado del Norte

MENDOZA

JUJUY / AYACUCHO / CHACABUCO / BUENOS AIRES

Iglesia San Francisco

SAN MARTÍN

ACCOMMODATION

Albergue Juvenil	1
America	2
Carlos V	5
Colonial	6
Del Jardín	3
Gran Hotel	4
Impala	9
Mediterraneo	7
Miami	1
Petit	8
Premier	10

RESTAURANTS AND BARS

Bar América	I
Café 25	N
La Corzuela	A
Doña Sara Figueroa	P
Federico	C
Café Filipo	M
Floreal	H
El Fondo	O
Klo y Klo	E
La Leñita	K
María	F
Bar Las Palmas	D
Café de Paris	J
Pizzeria Io	G
Pizzeria Nappo	B
Il Postino	L

Casa de Gobierno

Casa Padilla

PLAZA INDEPENDENCIA

Museo Folklórico

AVENIDA 24 DE SEPTIEMBRE

Cathedral

Museo Provincial de Bellas Artes

9 DE JULIO

CRISÓSTOMO ALVAREZ

Mercado de Abasto

Basílica Santo Domingo

Casa Histórica de la Independencia

SAN LORENZO

CONGRESO

0   500m

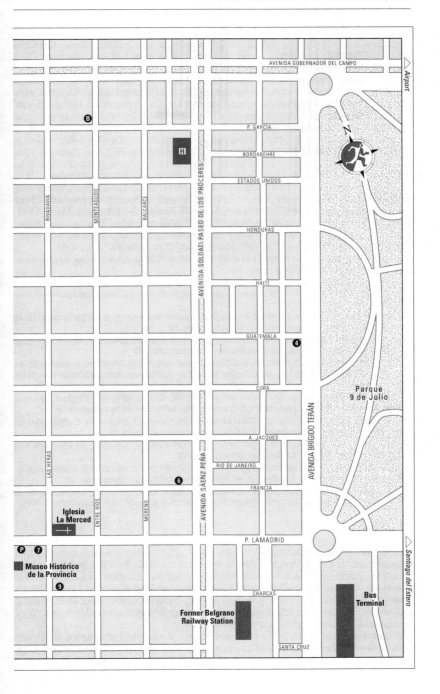

($2) runs to and from Plaza Independencia while a **taxi** will cost around $10. Tucumanos are justifiably proud of their modern and efficient **bus terminal** (☎0381/422-2221), at Brigido Terán 350, six blocks east and two south of Plaza Independencia. It has sixty wide-berthed platforms, a shopping-centre ("Shopping del Jardín") and supermarket, restaurants, bars, post office, telephone centres, left-luggage and even a hairdresser – but no working ATMs: try the supermarket for cash withdrawals. Most **city buses** run between the centre and the bus terminal, and you'll need a token (60 centavos) for each trip, on sale at all kiosks. Trains still run to and from Buenos Aires via Santiago del Estero from the **train station** (☎0381/431-0725) at Catamarca and Corrientes, but perhaps not for much longer. **Tourist information** is available at the provincial office at 24 de Septiembre 484 (Mon–Fri 7am–1pm & 5–9pm, Sat, Sun & public holidays 9am–1pm & 5pm–9pm), on Plaza Independencia. The branch at the **bus station** (same hours) can sometimes scrape a map together.

Tucumán has a wide range of **hotels**, although no really luxury ones. Many midrange hotels are conveniently clustered around the central Plaza Independencia. There are a number of decent **residenciales** and a **youth hostel**, the **Albergue Juvenil** (②), in a slightly run-down wing of the *Hotel Miami*, but no campsites. You may well prefer to do as the locals do – especially in the unbearable summer heat (Nov–March) – and stay in the cooler heights of Tafí del Valle (see p.431) or Quilmes (see p.433).

Hotel América, Santiago del Estero 1064 (☎0381/430-0810). Well-known for its bar, this hotel also has smart rooms, with bright bathrooms. ③.

Hotel Carlos V, 25 de Mayo 330 (☎0381/431-1666; *www.hotelcarlosv.com.ar*). Extremely well-run, with friendly reception, comfortable, classy rooms with reproduction furniture, and a decent restaurant. ⑤.

Hotel Colonial, San Martín 35 (☎0381/443-11523). Quaint but cosy place behind a neocolonial facade, it has a small swimming pool and pleasant rooms. ④.

Hotel Del Jardín, Laprida 463 (☎0381/431-0500). This very comfortable hotel, with a swimming pool and snack-bar, is very old-fashioned but has a certain charm. ⑥.

Gran Hotel, Los Próceres 380 (☎0381/450-2250). Aimed mainly at the conference- and business-market, this hotel is nonetheless worth trying for its fine location overlooking Parque 9 de Julio, large roof-top pool and all mod cons. Overpriced during the week, but cuts rates at weekends. ⑦.

Hotel Mediterráneo, 24 de Septiembre 364 (☎0381/431-0025 or 431-0080) Modern, spacious rooms, with air conditioning and cable TV. Room service and very friendly reception. ⑤.

Hotel Miami, Junín 580 (☎0381/431-0265). The part of the hotel not taken up by the youth hostel is not such good value, but the rooms are decent and everything works. ④.

Hotel Premier, Crisóstomo Alvarez 510 (☎0381/431-0381). An old-fashioned but efficiently run hotel, often crowded out with tours from Buenos Aires. ⑤.

Residencial Impala, Crisóstomo Alvarez 277 (☎0381/431-0371). Very clean, this modern *residencial* is more of a modest hotel, with its en-suite bathrooms and pleasant bedrooms. ③.

Residencial Petit, Crisóstomo Alvarez 765 (☎0381/421-3902). Of all the cheap *residenciales*, this is the only one that's not squalid; in fact it's spotless and appealing, though the rooms are tiny. ②.

The City

Despite its narrow, traffic-clogged streets and the slightly down-at-heel pedestrianized shopping area to the northwest of the centre, Tucumán lends itself to a gentle stroll and you could easily spend a full day visiting its few sights, including a couple of decent museums. As usual, orientation is simplified by the regular grid system; streets change name on either side of Avenida 24 de Septiembre, the street running past the cathedral, and change name twice as they go from west to east, first at avenidas Mitre and Além, and again at avenidas Avellaneda and Sáenz Peña.

Plaza Independencia is the city's focal point; a grove of native trees jostle with orange trees in the central area of the main plaza, each helpfully labelled, while a large pool with a fountain, a statue to Liberty, and a monolith marking the spot where Avellaneda's head was spiked, after his ruthless opponent Rosas had him executed in 1841, take up the rest. In the southeast corner of the square is the mid-nineteenth-century Neoclassical **Cathedral**, its slender towers topped with blue-and-white tiled domes. On the western side of the square, is the imposing, early twentieth-century **Casa de Gobierno**, pleasingly harmonious with its two rows of porticoes along the facade, topped with an elegant slate mansard-roof, and Art Nouveau detailing. Next to it, almost crushed by the tall buildings on either side, is the tiny facade of **Casa Padilla** at 25 de Mayo 36 (Tues–Fri 9.30am–12.30pm & 5.30pm–8.30pm, Sat 9.30am–12.30pm, Sun 5.30–8.30pm; $1), a typical elongated *casa chorizo* – literally "sausage house", the name given to city houses with a small street frontage but comprising several rooms one after the other – stretching back along four tiled patios, with a series of rooms filled with nineteenth-century curios, porcelain – including the striking, blood-red *sang de boeuf* variety – some Egyptian artefacts, period furniture and local paintings.

Much more interesting is the **Museo Folklórico** round the corner at Av. 24 de Septiembre (daily 9am–12.30pm & 5.30–8.30pm; $1). Its quaintly eclectic collection is housed in a beautiful neocolonial house, around an overgrown patio, and ranges from *mate* ware and textiles, including the typical local lace, known as "randas", to an exquisite set of traditional musical instruments, including the little banjoes or *charangos* made of mulita shell – a small species of armadillo – and *bombo* drums made of cardón cactus wood.

Two blocks south of the cathedral, at Congreso 151, is the **Casa Histórica de la Independencia** (daily 9am–1pm & 3.30–7.30pm; $2; free guided tours in the morning). Behind the gleaming white facade, between two grilled windows and mock-Baroque spiralling columns, the mighty quebracho doors lead into a series of large patios, draped with bougainvillea, jasmine and tropical creepers. This house, originally built for Francisca Bazán de Laguna, a leading Tucumán noblewoman, at the end of the eighteenth century, was where Argentina declared its independence from Spain and its first Congress was held. Most of it was demolished in the late nineteenth century, however – this replica was completed in the 1940s. Now a national monument, it houses a fine collection, spanning three centuries, of armoury, furniture, paintings, silverware and porcelain, while a rather kitsch but nonetheless interesting sound-and-light show in Spanish (July daily 8.30pm; rest of year closed Tues; $4; tickets from the tourist information office on Plaza Independencia) re-enacts the story of how the country gained its independence.

To the north of Plaza Independencia, Calle 25 de Mayo leads to the leafy, well-heeled barrio around Plaza Urquiza, past trendy boutiques and cafés, to a set of three Neoclassical landmarks, the **Casino**, **Legislatura** and **Teatro San Martín**. On the way, at the corner of Córdoba, you pass one of Argentina's most impressive **post offices**, built in the 1930s to a curious design that recalls the civic buildings of Renaissance Tuscany, complete with a castellated tower. Finally, seven blocks east of Plaza Independencia, is Tucumán's enormous **Parque 9 de Julio**, landscaped by Charles Thays in 1916. Long overdue for a far-reaching clean-up, and downright insalubrious in parts, the park itself would not be worth a visit, but for its highlight, the **Casa del Obispo Colombres**, in the western section, near the rose-garden. Built of adobe in the late nineteenth century, its two rows of seven elegant arches along a dazzling white facade are reflected in the oblong pool of its Italianate garden, the building houses the interesting **Museo de la Industria Azucarera** (Mon–Fri 8am–12.30pm & 2–7pm, Sat & Sun 7am–7pm), which traces the history and explains the process – and importance – of the sugar industry in the region, by means of photographs, diagrams and exhibits of items, some of them beautifully crafted, such as the set of ancient wooden sugar-cane presses and other impressive machinery.

Eating, drinking and nightlife

Tucumanos are *bons vivants* and there's an enormous range of places to eat, some trendy bars and cafés in downtown, especially up Calle 25 de Mayo, and a number of nightspots mostly located in the chic neighbourhood of **Yerba Buena**, three or four kilometres west of the centre, on slightly higher ground. **Discos** change name and location at the drop of a hat, so ask around.

Restaurants

La Corzuela, Laprida 866. *Locro* and *empanadas* are on the menu alongside juicy steaks and copious salads.

Doña Sara Figueroa, 24 de Septiembre 358. Hummus, tabbouleh and kebabs at this well-established Middle Eastern restaurant.

El Fondo, San Martín 848 (☎0381/422-2161). A traditional parrilla that gets very busy on Saturday nights when live music and stand-up comedians entertain the crowds.

Federico, Maipú 790. One of several gourmet establishments in the chic neighbourhood north of the microcentro; its professional service, elegant surroundings and delicious food make it an ideal place for a special occasion.

Floreal, 25 de Mayo 560 (☎0381/421-2806 or 421-6946). Considered by many to be the best in town, this stylishly decorated, intimate restaurant pulls out all the stops to serve out-of-the-ordinary, appetizing cuisine. Expensive, and booking is advised at weekends.

Il Postino, Córdoba 501 and 25 de Mayo. A reliable pizzeria, also serving good pasta, in a laid-back atmosphere.

Klo y Klo, Junín 665. Seafood and paella are the house specialities, along with fresh pasta; excellent value *menú ejecutivo* for $10.

La Leñita, 25 de Mayo 377. There's nothing special about this family-oriented parrilla, but the set menus are unbeatable value and the steaks are tender as can be.

La Nonna Petrucia, Muñecas 2677 (☎0381/427-3480). Some way out of town, this traditional Italian-style restaurant, with home cooking, is worth the long trek.

Pizzeria Io, Salta 602. Vying for the best pizza award, this place bakes its pizzas in a wood oven and shows more than usual imagination with the toppings.

Pizzeria Nappo, Monteagudo and Santa Fe. It may not be as imaginative as *Io*, but this pizzeria offers very good food and at slightly lower prices.

Bars and cafés

Bar América, Santiago del Estero. Opposite Plaza Alberdi and the train station, this lively bar occasionally puts on live music.

Bar Las Palmas, 25 de Mayo and Marcos Paz. Smart, sleek coffee-house and bar, and a good place for people-watching.

Café 25, 25 de Mayo and Mendoza. A favourite with business folk and functionaries, it serves top-notch coffee and has a lively atmosphere.

Café Filipo, 25 de Mayo and Mendoza. One of the busiest and most traditional of the downtown cafés, serving delicious sandwiches and other snacks.

Café de Paris, 25 de Mayo and Santiago del Estero. Don't be put off by the giant video screen outside; inside the atmosphere is warm and the coffee delicious.

María, 25 de Mayo and Marcos Paz. Its shady patio is very welcome in the blistering heat of summer; snacks, drinks and ice cream all on offer at this trendy bar.

Millennium, Av. Aconquija 1702, Yerba Buena. A popular, trendy pre-disco restaurant, bar and tearoom all rolled into one, with fashionable decor, in the cool heights of suburban Yerba Buena.

Nightclubs

Káiser, Junín 138. One of the few good downtown nightspots, with big fun-loving crowds and reasonably priced drinks; varied music including salsa. Closed Mon.

Makalú, Av. Aconquija s/n, Yerba Buena. All the clubs in Yerba Buena, out in the cool heights to the west of the city, are more upmarket than those in the city centre – and this is no exception. Entrance fee is $15 and drinks are pricey, but this is the friendliest of the lot and has the best music.

Listings

Airlines Aerolíneas Argentinas, 9 de Julio 110 (☎0381/431-1030); ALTA, Buenos Aires 196 (☎0381/430-7554); Dinar, 24 de Septiembre 508 (☎0381/452-2310); Lloyd Aéreo Boliviano, Buenos Aires 39 (☎0381/421-0647); Southern Winds, 9 de Julio 77 (☎0381/422-5554 or 422-0826); LAPA, Buenos Aires 95 (☎0381/430-2330 or 426-3900).

Banks Maguitur, San Martín 765 for travellers' cheques. There are several ATMs in the streets radiating from Plaza Independencia.

Car rental Avis, Congreso 76 (☎0381/430-0670); Dollar, Congreso 89 (☎0381/430-4629); Donde, Gobernador Gutierrez 1384, and at the *Gran Hotel* (☎0381/422-4716 or 428-2126); Movil Renta, San Lorenzo 370 (☎0381/421-8635).

Hospital Angel Padilla, Alberdi 550 (☎0381/422-1319).

Internet Tucumán BBS, Maipú and Santiago (☎0381/431-1960; *www.tucbbs.com.ar*).

Laundries Clean Shop, Mendoza 419 (☎0381/4229122); Marva, Santiago del Estero 694.

Pharmacy Karina, Córdoba 652.

Post office, 25 de Mayo and Córdoba.

Telephones Telecentro, Maipú 480. Lots of *locutorios* in the microcentro.

Travel agency Duport Turismo, Mendoza 720, Galeria del Rosario (☎0381/422-0000). For excursions to Tafí del Valle, Quilmes and Amaichá.

Tafí del Valle

TAFÍ DEL VALLE, 128km west of Tucumán by the RP307 – which turns off the RN38 at Acheral, 42km southwest of the provincial capital – makes a great day-trip from the city and its cool heights make it an ideal alternative stopover to Tucumán itself, especially in the summer when the city swelters. The dramatic journey lifts you out of the moist lowlands of eastern Tucumán Province, emerald-green sugar-plantations as far as the eye can see, up through the tangled mass of **Selva Tucumana** – ablaze with blossom from September to December – to the dry steppe of the highland valley that gives Tafí its name. As the RP307 snakes up steep jungle-clad cliffs, it offers fewer and fewer glimpses of the subtropical plains way below, where the sugar-fields look increasingly like paddyfields and the individual trees of the citrus orchards resemble the dots of a pointilliste painting. At 2000m, the road levels off and skirts the **Parque de los Menhires**, where a number of engraved **monoliths**, deceptively Celtic-looking in appearance – but in fact the work of the Tafí tribes who farmed the area around two thousands years ago, have been planted haphazardly on a hill overlooking **Embalse Angostura**, a large reservoir. The often snowy peak of extinct volcano **Cerro El Pelado**, 2680m, is mirrored in the lake's still surface. From here, the road hugs the eastern bank of the *embalse*, to reach Tafí del Valle itself, a sprawling village in the western lee of the Sierra del Aconquija, and sandwiched between the Río del Chusquí and the Río Blanquita, both of which flow into the Río Tafí and then into the reservoir. Although blue and sunny skies are virtually guaranteed year-round, occasionally thick fog descends into the valley in the winter, making its Alpine setting feel bleak and inhospitable. While Tafí is a favourite weekend and summer retreat for Tucumanos – the average temperature is 12°C lower than in the city – there's very little to do here except explore the surrounding mountains and riverbanks, but the trekking is very rewarding. Popular trails go up **Cerro El Matadero** (3050m; 5hr), **Cerro Pabellón** (3770m; 4hr), **Cerro Muñoz** (4437m; one day) and **Mala-Mala** (3500m; 8hr), but it's best to go with a guide, as the weather is unpredictable. The town's main streets, lime-tree-lined Avenida San Martín, and avenidas Gobernador Critto and Diego de Rojas

(Av. Perón on some maps), converge on the semicircular plaza, around which most of the hotels, restaurants, cafés and shops are concentrated. Across the Río Tafí, 1km from the Plaza, the **Capilla Jesuítica de la Banda** (Mon–Fri 10am–6pm, Sat & Sun 9am–noon; $1; guided tours), is a late eighteenth-century Jesuit building now housing archeological finds, mostly ceramic urns, from nearby digs, plus some items of furniture and modest paintings from the colonial period. Famous for its delicious cow's and goat's cheese, available at small farms and stalls all around the town, Tafí holds a lively **Fiesta Nacional del Queso**, with folk music and dancing and rock bands, in early February.

Practicalities

Buses from Tucumán, Santa María and Cafayate arrive at the terminal on the corner of avenidas San Martín and Gobernador Campero (☎03867/421025). Information can be gleaned from the **tourist office** on the southeastern edge of the main square (☎03867/421020; *www.tafidelvalle.com*), though they charge $4 for the admittedly comprehensive town map. In addition to the campsite, *Los Sauzales* (☎03867/421084; $3), at Los Palenques on the banks of Río El Churqui, **accommodation** is plentiful, but often booked up at weekends in the summer and during the cheese festival. *Hostería Lunahuana* at Av. Gobernador Critto 540 (☎03867/421330; ⑦) is quite luxurious but *Mirador del Tafí*, on RP307 to the east of the centre (☎03867/421219; ⑤), is better value, with very comfortable rooms and great views. *Hotel Tafí* at Av. Belgrano 177 (☎03867/421007; ④), south of the plaza, is simple and very peaceful. *Estancia Los Cuartos* on Juan Calchaquí (☎03867/421444; ③), offering horseriding, and *Hostería del ACA* at San Martín and Gobernador Campero (☎03867/421027; ③), are both excellent value, bright, clean and comfortable. Over to the west, *Hostería Castillo de Piedra* (☎03867/421199; ④) is a quaint stone castle-like building, with cosy rooms. At the budget end, *Hospedaje Celia Correa* at Belgrano 443 (☎03867/421170; ②) is best of all; basic but with private bathroom. The best **places to eat** are *El Portal de Tafí*, on Av. Diego de Rojas, *La Rueda*, on Av. Gobernador Critto, and *Rancho de Félix*, at Av. Diego de Rojas and Av. Belgrano, to the south of the plaza; they all serve local dishes plus parrilladas, in a cosy Alpine atmosphere. *El Parador Tafinista* on the corner of avenidas Gobernador Critto and Diego de Rojas dishes up hefty portions of pasta and grilled meat. For the best **tours** in the area, and farther afield, contact Bruno Widmer (☎03867/421076).

Amaichá

To get to the village of **AMAICHÁ**, you take the RP307 which zigzags northwards from Tafí, offering views of the *embalse* and the mountains – but be warned, low cloud often persists here, so you might be penetrating a blanket of thick fog instead – and heaves you over the windswept pass at Abra del Infiernillo, 3042m. From there, the road steeply winds back down, along the banks of the Río de Amaichá. It takes you through arid but impressive landscapes thickly covered with a forest of cardón cacti, with the Cumbres Calchaquíes to the east and the Sierra de Quilmes ahead of you, until you reach Amaichá itself. The peaceful, nondescript little place livens up during the **Fiesta de la Pachamama** in carnival week, when dancers and musicians lay on shows, while locals enact, in a kind of pre-Columbian Passion Play, the roles of the different pagan deities: Pachamama herself – Mother Earth, confused rather incongruously in the animist-Christian fusion with the Virgin Mary – as well as Ñusta, the goddess of fertility, Yastay, the god of hunting, and Pujllay, a faun-like sprite representing joyful festivity. Little stalls spring up along the main streets, selling food, drink and crafts. Together with a number of small eateries serving delicious *locro*, is the *Casa de Piedra*, where you can buy local crafts and something to eat all year around.

Just 200m along the road from the village centre, near the junction with the RP357, is the splendid new **Museo Geológico y Etnológico** (daily 8.30am–12.30pm & 2–6.30pm; $4). The brainchild of local artist Hector Cruz, it's actually several museums rolled into one, and it's worth a look to see the structure itself, built around fabulous cactus gardens and incorporating eye-catching stone mosaics, depicting llamas, pre-Hispanic symbols and geometric patterns. Each large room in turn displays an impressive array of local archeological finds, the well-executed reconstruction of a mine along with impressive samples of various precious and semi-precious ores and minerals extracted in the area, plus paintings, tapestries and ceramics from Cruz's own workshops, to modern designs inspired by pre-Columbian artistic traditions.

Beyond Amaichá, the RP307 veers westwards before running south to Santa María, in Catamarca Province, from where you can travel down to Belén (see p.447) and Andalgalá (see p.446), whereas the RP357, a straight well-surfaced road takes you northwestwards for 15km to the RN40, which heads north along the west bank of the Río Calchaquí towards Quilmes (see below) and Cafayate (see p.422). The regular **buses** from Tafí to Quilmes and Cafayate will drop you off by Amaichá's museum, but there are no lodgings to speak of here; if you're stuck or want to hang around during the fiesta, ask around for unofficial rooms to rent.

Quilmes

Just 3km north of the RP357-RN40 junction, 15km north of Amaichá, is the westward turn-off to the major pre-Incan archeological site of **Quilmes**, one of the most extensively restored in the country. **Buses** to Cafayate running along the RN40 will drop you at the junction, leaving you with the 5km trek along the dusty side-road to the **archeological site** (daily 9am–dusk; $2). Inhabited since the ninth century AD, the settlement of Quilmes had a population of over 3000 at its peak in the seventeenth century, but the whole Quilmes tribe was punished mercilessly by the Spanish colonizers for resisting evangelization and enslavement. Walls and many buildings in this terraced **pukará** or pre-Columbian fortress have been thoroughly, if not always expertly, excavated and reconstructed, and the overall effect is extremely impressive, especially in the morning light, when the mountains behind it are illuminated from the east and turn bright orange. The entrance fee also entitles you to visit the site **museum**, which contains some items found here, such as ceramics and stone tools, and displays more expensive modern crafts by Hector Cruz, who now owns the site and the luxurious *Hotel Ruinas de Quilmes* (☎03892/421075; ⑤), on the same grounds as the site – it offers llama rides, a decent confitería and very comfortable, spacious rooms, giving wonderful views of the site, affording you the opportunity to see them at their early-morning best.

Santiago del Estero and around

SANTIAGO DEL ESTERO is the easy-going capital of a dreary, flat and impoverished province of the same name in the transition between the Central Sierras and the Northwest, 150km southeast of San Miguel de Tucumán. For many people travelling from points south and east, it's the entrance to the Northwest region and, although you won't be tempted to linger for long, it has one good museum and some lively evening entertainment. Between Tucumán and Santiago del Estero, but in the latter's province, is the much-hyped spa resort of **Termas de Río Hondo**, where you might like to stop over to relax in a hot bath or fish for *dorado* in the nearby reservoir.

Francisco de Aguirre founded "the Noble and Royal City of Santiago del Esteco" – Argentina's oldest – on St James' Day 1553, after various false starts due to earthquakes, attacks by the indigenous inhabitants, repeated floods and petty administrative

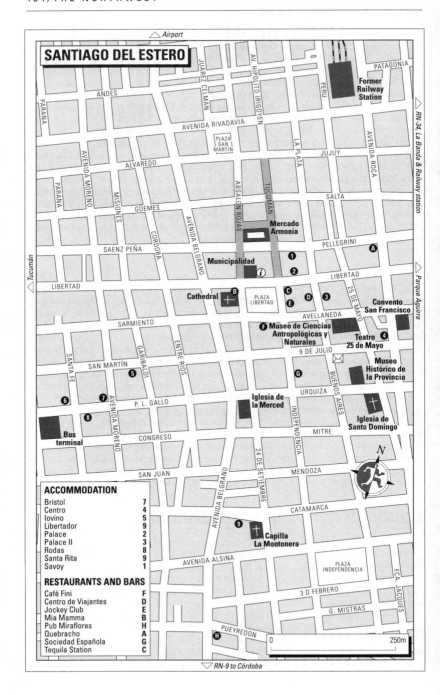

SANTIAGO DEL ESTERO

ACCOMMODATION

Bristol	7
Centro	4
Iovino	5
Libertador	9
Palace	2
Palace II	3
Rodas	8
Santa Rita	9
Savoy	1

RESTAURANTS AND BARS

Café Fini	F
Centro de Viajantes	D
Jockey Club	E
Mia Mamma	B
Pub Miraflores	H
Quebracho	A
Sociedad Española	G
Tequila Station	C

squabbles with officials in Chile. Aguirre's city was located at a relatively safe distance from the capricious Río Dulce and, in 1577, was made capital of the region of Tucumán, a home-base for founding the other major cities in Northwest Argentina. Over the years, it surrendered its religious and secular privileges to San Miguel de Tucumán, to Córdoba and, later, to Buenos Aires and, despite the nineteenth-century advent of the railways and large influxes of immigrants, never got its act together. Later floods and other natural disasters account for the paucity of colonial architecture in the modern city while poor planning, a series of criminally negligent caudillo governments (dominated by provincial strongmen more interested in nepotism than democracy) and acute administrative inefficiency have compounded Santiago's failure to hit upon an agricultural or industrial answer to its economic woes. Cotton remains the province's main crop, grown in nearby *bañados* or seasonally flooded plantations, painfully dependent on efficient irrigation, and on commodity prices. Today, Santiago is a scruffy, run-down place, many of its streets becoming quagmires when it rains, while the rest are riddled with potholes. Given the city's hot and sticky sub-tropical summers, the siesta is sacrosanct here, and even in the cooler winters life is lived at a slow, gentle pace. Still, it's a popular point of arrival in the region because of its laid-back ambience, and a good place to relax for a day or two before moving on, or simply to recover from the more hectic pace of city life in nearby Tucumán.

Arrival, information and accommodation

The **airport**, Mal Paso, is 6km northwest of the central Plaza Libertad, on Av. Madre de Ciudades (☎0385/422-2386). To get to the centre from here either take a **taxi** ($2) or the #19 bus. The abysmally run-down **bus terminal** (☎0385/421-3746) is at Pedro León Gallo 480, two blocks south and five west of Plaza Libertad. Buses run to most regional destinations and some further afield. Unless you are staying in a nearby hotel or *residencial*, hop in one of the many taxis – they're very inexpensive. *El Tucumano*, one of Argentina's few remaining passenger **trains**, runs between Retiro in Buenos Aires and Tucumán, and stops at La Banda, Santiago's twin city on the east bank of the Río Dulce. Connections are increasingly infrequent, however, down to twice a week in each direction at the last count (see listings). You can either hail a cab or catch a bus; #10, #14, #18 and #21 all link La Banda's station with central Santiago, most stopping near Plaza Libertad. Within the city you are unlikely to need transport other than to reach the campsite in the Parque Aguirre – any bus going along Avenida Libertad and marked with the park's name will get you there. For basic **information** – maps, accommodation details and little else – the city tourist office (☎0385/422-6777) and provincial tourist office (☎0385/421-4243) are conveniently located next door to one another, on the northern side of Plaza Libertad.

There's only a small selection of **accommodation** in town; the once prestigious *Gran Hotel* on Plaza Libertad is currently closed for refurbishment and the better hotels cater mainly for a business clientele, expensive for what they are and often booked up during the week, while some of the more modest ones double up as *albergues transitorios*. A bunch of *residenciales* are handily located near the bus station, but none of them is outstanding and some are downright squalid. Campers are well catered for, however, in the albeit mosquito-friendly Parque Aguirre: campsite *Las Casuarinas* has good facilities in a green location on the banks of the Río Dulce. It costs $3 to pitch a tent.

Hotel Bristol, Av. Moreno 667 (☎0385/421-8888). Worth the extra few dollars, this is possibly the best hotel in its category as it is bright, cheerful and fairly comfortable. ③.

Hotel Centro, 9 de Julio 131 (☎0385/421-9502). By far the best, and dearest, of the bunch; not really luxurious but efficient and comfortable, with decent rooms, all en-suite. ⑥.

Hotel Iovino, Av. Moreno Sur 602 (☎0385/421-3311). Perhaps the best of the cheap options in the vicinity of the bus station, it's at least clean if in need of refurbishment. ②.

Hotel Libertador, Catamarca 47 (☎0385/421-5766). Rather business-oriented, and the rooms are gloomy – lots of dark wooden panelling – but it's pleasant enough with a good dining-room. ⑥.

Hotel Palace, Tucumán 19 (☎0385/421-5766). The older, less comfortable and slightly cheaper of the two sister hotels, right next to the central square. ⑤.

Hotel Palace II, Buenos Aires 60 (☎0385/421-4919). The brighter, more attractive rooms here justify the few extra pesos when compared with the *Hotel Palace*. ⑤.

Hotel Savoy, Tucumán 39 (☎0385/421-1234). Undoubtedly the place to go for in the middle range. Very central, with clean rooms and pleasant bathrooms. ④.

Residencial Rodas, Pedro León Gallo 430 (☎0385/421-8434). The main asset of this shoddily run but safe joint is its location right next to the bus terminal. Breakfast is provided, but not especially recommended; if you can, eat elsewhere. ③.

Residencial Santa Rita, Santa Fe 273 (☎0385/422-0625). Probably the cheapest rooms in town: basic and gloomy but clean and safe. ②.

The City

Santiago's **grid system** is a slightly irregular one and not all of its thoroughfares run straight, starting with the dog-legged main drag, Avenida Belgrano, the city's north–south axis, divided into Avenida Belgrano Norte (N) and Sur (S); the main east–west street is Avenida Libertad. Being flat and compact, the city centre is easy to find your way around, however: leafy **Plaza Libertad** is the city's commercial and social hub. Some pleasant **cafés** line the square's south and east flanks, while the luxuriant trees and shrubs provide shade, especially welcome in December and January. The **Cathedral**, on the western side of the square, was inaugurated in 1877, and is the fifth to be built on the site of Argentina's very first cathedral. Its biscuit-coloured facade, in a rather self-consciously Neoclassical style, is instantly forgettable and the twin towers look out of proportion. Far more attractive is the **Jefatura de Policía**, usually erroneously referred to as the cabildo, because its white facade resembles the colonial cabildos of Buenos Aires and Córdoba, and easily the most striking building on the whole square: the lower storey is decorated by a series of elegant arches and the upper floor by a row of Ionic columns. The **Mercado Armonia**, one block north on Pellegrini, lies at the city's commercial hub, along pedestrianized Avenida Hipólito Yrigoyen. Housed in an impressive building dating from the 1930s, the market-stalls are heaped with bright fruit and vegetables, herbs and spices, local sweetmeats and other exotic produce, making it one of the city's highlights.

Two blocks east of Plaza Libertad, along Calle Avellaneda, immediately before the corner with Calle 25 de Mayo, stands the bombastic Neoclassical edifice housing not only the **Teatro 25 de Mayo**, but also, in the left wing, the **Legislatura Provincial** – torched by angry demonstrators in 1993 but since fully restored. In the same building, at Avellaneda 355, unscathed but in need of some updating, is the fascinating and potentially fabulous **Museo Arqueológico Emilio y Duncan Wagner** (Mon–Fri 7.30am–1.30pm & 2–8pm, Sat & Sun 10am–noon; $1; free guided visits). This is the collection of a French diplomat and his sons, whose main interests were the archeology, paleontology, ethnography and folklore of the Santiago region, and its rich pre-Columbian and post-colonial history. Strictly speaking an **anthropological museum**, it contains exhibits of local textiles and crafts as well as archeological finds. Ceramics are the mainstay, mostly vases, urns and figurines, tracing the artistic development of the Tonocote and Juríes tribes, from the primitive Mercedes period (300–700 AD) – mostly rather squat, unadorned pots – through the vividly coloured Suchituyoj period (800–1400 AD), with a predominance of zoomorphic figures such as snakes and owls representing the elements, to the more sophisticated designs, more elegant forms, very subtle pigment colours and richer glaze of the Averías period (110–1500 AD).

Nearby, on the corner of Calle 25 de Mayo and Avenida Roca, stands the grim neo-Gothic pile of **Iglesia San Francisco**, with its mushroom-grey facade; built at the end of the nineteenth century it has been restored recently but there's not much to be seen inside, except for an interesting map of the route taken by **San Francisco Solano** in the Americas. The Franciscan missionary, always depicted with a fiddle, apparently stayed in the city at the end of the sixteenth century and lived in a stark cell, though whether or not the *celda* on display inside the church is the original is the subject of local controversy; it may have been built much later on to attract prilgrims. A badly crafted marble statue of the saint – complete with violin – erected in 1910 to mark the tricentenary of his death, blights the small square in front of the church, while artefacts relating to the holy man and his order will be on display in the **museum**, next to the church, if ever the restoration work is completed. A block south and west at Urquiza 354, the **Museo Histórico Provincial** (Mon–Fri 7.30am–1pm & 2–8pm; $1) is housed in the oldest building still standing in the city, once belonging to the influential Díaz Gallo family. It dates back to the early nineteenth century and has a simple but appealing strawberries-and-cream coloured facade; the charming, slightly overgrown patios are oases of coolness, full of banana trees and showy shrubs, offering some respite from the noisy street outside. Inside is a predictable collection of religious and secular art, plus a miscellany ranging from fine antiques to junk, but a highlight is the silver collection, including a room packed with ex-votos, with figures of cattle and even a donkey. Opposite, the lopsided facade and flaking outer walls of **Iglesia Santo Domingo** do little to entice you in and its ghastly stained-glass windows and sinister interior do nothing to raise your spirits either. The church does contain an unusual curiosity, though: in the far right-hand corner, by the altar, a red-brick archway encases a rare **copy of the Turin Shroud**, visited by thousands of pilgrims every year.

Finally, huge, shaded **Parque Aguirre**, named for the city's founding father, lies one kilometre to the northeast of Plaza Libertad, a buffer between the city centre and the Río Dulce with its occasional floods and offering cool relief when the temperature soars. The city's campsite and balnearios, pleasantly refreshing if not especially attractive, are located there.

Eating, drinking and nightlife

There's not much in the way of choice when it comes to **restaurants** and **cafés**, but you're unlikely to be spending very long here, after all. At weekends, young Santiagueños like to let their hair down at their favourite **nightclub** and Santiago has a long folk tradition that has spawned a couple of lively joints, surprisingly full even on week-nights.

By far the most sophisticated place to eat is *Quebracho*, at Roca and Pellegrini; it's an excellent parrilla with an attractive decor: beautiful orange-ochre walls and a tented ceiling, plus professional service, complement the delicious if unimaginative food. The *Centro de Viajantes*, at Buenos Aires 37, dishes up decent, well-priced food, with friendly service in slightly drab surroundings, unfortunately made worse by the seemingly magnetizing TV. *Mia Mamma*, 24 de Septiembre 15, is an extremely reliable plaza-side parrilla, also serving pasta, as the name suggests, and fresh salads. The traditional *Sociedad Espanola*, at Independencia 236, prepares Andalucian specialities such as gazpacho, served in a charmingly antiquated atmosphere.

Heladeria Cerecet, at Av. Libertad and Córdoba, is one of several Italian-style ice-cream parlours, serving fantastic ice creams and sorbets in no-nonsense surroundings. *Tequila Station*, on the eastern side of Plaza Libertad, is a highly popular pizzeria, café and cyberspace, all rolled into one hive of activity. Next door, the *Jockey Club* is one of the more sedate cafés on the main square, with beautiful wooden tables and a clubbish atmosphere. *Miraflores*, at Av. Belgrano Sur 1370 (☎0385/422-3703), is a pub hosting live rock and folk gigs on various evenings throughout the week, climaxing at weekends with late-night partying and live music, and is a good place for finding out about discos. The *Peña Casa del Folklorista*, Av. Vargas s/n, puts on folk-music shows at weekends, aimed at locals and tourists alike, but retains an authentic atmosphere.

Termas de Río Hondo

Sprawling amid dull countryside 60km northwest of Santiago del Estero, along the RN9 towards Tucumán, **TERMAS DE RÍO HONDO** is South America's biggest spa resort and doggedly promoted as such by the provincial tourist board, but it's only worth interrupting your journey between Santiago del Estero and Tucumán if your muscles ache or you're a real fan of thermal baths. The hot springs were known to the indigenous peoples, who appreciated the waters' curative properties, but they were largely forgotten during colonial times. It was not until the arrival of the railways at the beginning of the twentieth century that Río Hondo was given a new lease of life. Nowadays, aside from the prospect of soothing **mineral waters**, Termas de Río Hondo is fairly downbeat, resting on its laurels as one of Argentina's major winter resorts, but fast losing its regular customers and failing to attract new ones because of a rather old-fashioned reputation, largely deserved. Even in the high season, March to September, the place doesn't exactly buzz, and frequent chilly, grey weather can make it quite unappealing. In July and August, the outside temperature often soars above 40°C, making a hot bath the last thing you'll want – it can feel like a sauna outside. In any case, this is no Baden-Baden, as the garish custard-yellow and rhubarb-pink **Casino** will attest, and the town's unkempt parks are in urgent need of some serious manicuring. Like the Black Forest resort, however, it's full of **shops** and **cafés** selling cholesterol-rich cakes, jams, liqueurs and ice cream, perfect for counteracting the beneficial effects of the spa. Nearby **Embalse Río Hondo**, a large reservoir, teems with the town's gastronomic delicacy, the dorado. Disappointingly, though, this much-vaunted fish has a rather mushy texture and not much flavour, so it's usually perked up with a variety of sauces, based on pepper or blue cheese.

Practicalities

The modern, open-plan **bus terminal**, serving much of the country, is rather inconveniently located some way to the north of the town, at Las Heras and España, but there is a more central bus-stop on the corner of the triangular Plaza San Martín, near the pedestrianized commercial centre – get on or off here rather than go all the way to the terminal. Most of the shops, cafés, restaurants and hotels are clustered around these streets or along Avenida Belgrano, across the large rectangular green wasteland on the far side of the main drag, Avenida Alberdi. The resort's helpful **tourist office** is at Caseros 132 (Mon–Fri 7am–1pm & 3–9pm, Sat, Sun & public holidays 7am–9pm; ☎03858/421721) and will supply you with a long list of **accommodation**. The place to stay is definitely the *Hotel Los Pinos* at Maipú 201 (☎03858/421043; ⑤), an institution with a decent restaurant, massage service and sauna and even an old-fashioned cinema. As at all hotels in the town, the bathrooms have steaming-hot thermal waters on tap; a relaxing soak just before bedtime will guarantee a rejuvenating night's slumber. Other accommodation includes the plain but clean *Hotel Semiramis* at Caseros 303 (☎03858/421416; ②) or the bland but decent *Hotel Petit Patric* at Mar del Plata 520 (☎03858/421030; ②), both of which offer en-suite bathrooms. For **food**, head for *La Casa de Rubén* at Sarmiento 65, which serves dorado and goat at reasonable prices. Should all its tightly packed tables be occupied, try *El Chivito* at Francisco Solano 158 or *La Cabaña de los Changos* on Alberdi (RP9), both nearly as good and serving similar food. The best place for a coffee and for watching the world totter past is the elegant *Jockey Club*, opposite the casino on Caseros.

San Fernando del Valle de Catamarca and around

The wedge-shaped province of Catamarca, immediately to the west of Tucumán and Santiago del Estero, is one of the country's poorest and most thinly populated. Nearly half of its population of a quarter of a million live in the quiet capital, **SAN FERNAN-DO DEL VALLE DE CATAMARCA**, often just called Catamarca, the smallest of all the Northwest's provincial capitals and the youngest, founded in 1683. A little over 230km south of Tucumán along the RN38 trunk road, and slightly less from Santiago del Estero along the RN64, the city lies at the end of a long, flat valley that gives it its name, loomed over by high mountains on all sides. The majestic, green-sloped Sierra de Graciana to the north climbs steeply to over 1500m; to the east, the Sierra de Anacasti, or Sierra del Alto, is higher still; while the stark, honey-brown Sierra de Ambato forms an all but impenetrable barrier to the northwest, peaking at Cerro El Manchao (4351m). With few sights of its own, Catamarca the ideal base for exploring the province's undeservedly ignored **hinterland**, mostly deserted Altiplano, with some of the most hauntingly dramatic scenery in the whole of Argentina. In the second half of July, the city hosts one of Argentina's major folk festivals, the **Festival Nacional del Poncho**, which is also a gathering for the region's outstanding artisans, along with some of the country's star folk musicians. It takes place every year in the third week of July, with bands such as Los Nocheros and Los Chalchaleros topping the bill. Nearby **El Rodeo** is a small, rambling town of weekend homes; its cool microclimate and rugged mountainside setting make it an agreeable excursion, especially to get away from the stifling summer heat in the city. The dramatic zigzags of the **Cuesta del Portazuelo** clamber up to the pampas-like summit of the Sierra de Ancasti, to the east of Catamarca, offering fabulous views of the city and surrounding valley. But the main reason for stopping over in Catamarca is to get your bearings before heading for the transitional valleys around Andalgalá, Belén and Londres, to the west. From there you can climb up to the almost disturbingly remote and staggeringly authentic Altiplano settlement of Antofagasta de la Sierra (see p.451), and its stark surroundings, or to the fabulous Paso de San Francisco, via the charming spa village of Fiambalá (see p.453).

Some history

The valleys of present-day Catamarca Province have been inhabited for some 10,000 years but the earliest known settlements date back only two millennia. The Calchaquí tribes of the **Diaguita** people, whose territory stretched north as far as San Antonio de los Cobres in Salta Province, built their villages and fortresses in the area around Belén and Pomán, and lived peacefully until they were dominated by the Incas in the late fifteenth century. Considerably weakened, they still managed to harass the Spanish colonizers enough to prevent them from establishing any major town in the area until after the Guerras Calchaquíes (see box, p.449), a drawn-out rebellion that kept the invaders on their toes until the late seventeenth century. Only on July 5, 1683, did the Governor of Tucumán, Fernando Mate de Luna, found the city of San Fernando, to be capital of the new province of Catamarca, established only four years earlier. When Buenos Aires became national capital, Catamarca felt the pinch more than most provinces and the government's decision to shelve a project to link it by rail to Chile dealt it a severe blow. Cotton and wool have earned it a meagre income over the past three centuries while agriculture in the fertile valley is mostly aimed at local self-sufficiency in staple products such as oil, meat and cereals. Sizeable gold, silver, cooper and bauxite deposits are exploited by multinationals.

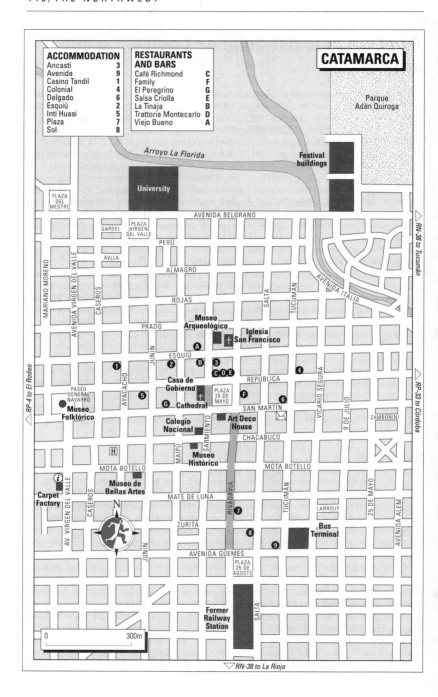

ACCOMMODATION
Ancasti	3
Avenida	9
Casino Tandil	1
Colonial	4
Delgado	6
Esquiú	2
Inti Huasi	5
Plaza	7
Sol	8

RESTAURANTS AND BARS
Café Richmond	C
Family	F
El Peregrino	G
Salsa Criolla	E
La Tinaja	B
Trattoria Montecarlo	D
Viejo Bueno	A

CATAMARCA

Parque Adán Quiroga

Arroyo La Florida

Festival buildings

University

PLAZA DEL MESTRO

AVENIDA BELGRANO

GARDEL

PLAZA VIRGEN DEL VALLE

PERÚ

AVLLA

ALMAGRO

ROJAS

MARIANO MORENO

AVENIDA VIRGEN DEL VALLE

CASEROS

PRADO

Museo Arqueológico

Iglesia San Francisco

JUNÍN

ESQUIÚ

AYACACHO

SALTA

TUCUMÁN

AVENIDA ITALIA

REPÚBLICA

Casa de Gobierno

PLAZA 25 DE MAYO

VICARIO SEGURA

9 DE JULIO

ZAMBONINI

Cathedral

SAN MARTÍN

PASEO GENERAL NAVARRO

Museo Folklórico

Colegio Nacional

Art Deco House

CHACABUCO

MAIPÚ

SARMIENTO

Museo Histórico

MOTA BOTELLO

MOTA BOTELLO

TUCUMÁN

25 DE MAYO

AVENIDA ALEM

Carpet Factory

AV. VIRGEN DEL VALLE

CASEROS

Museo de Bellas Artes

MATE DE LUNA

RIVADAVIA

LARROUY

ZURITA

Bus Terminal

JUNÍN

N

AVENIDA GÜEMES

PLAZA 25 DE AGOSTO

Former Railway Station

SALTA

RP-4 to El Rodeo

RN-38 to Tucumán

RP-33 to Córdoba

0   300m

RN-38 to La Rioja

Ruled for decades by dyed-in-the-wool caudillos, or local strongmen, but largely forgotten, Catamarca shot to the national headlines for all the wrong reasons in 1990. **María Soledad Morales**, a young student, was raped and murdered near a popular discotheque on the outskirts of the city. Their were rumours that relatives of people in very high places were allegedly involved, but predictably the affair was hushed up. Governor Saadi was eventually brought down by the scandal but it took a national outcry, demonstrations, sit-ins and the brave intervention of a nun, before two suspects, including the son of a local politician, were tried and sent to prison. *Caudillismo* – local rule by strongmen with a small but ruthless power base in the provincial capitals and little if any interest in democracy – still reigns in Catamarca, however. Saadi's successor has now been replaced – by his son. The spot where María Soledad's corpse was discovered, by the roadside of the Tucumán-bound RN38, near the RP1 turn-off towards Las Pirquitas, has become a grisly **shrine** piled up with offerings, photographs and candles, not just to her memory but to miscarriages of justice in Argentina as a whole. It makes for a rather gruesome tourist attraction, but many sightseers insist on having their photograph taken alongside the shrine, usually half-concealed by mounds of flowers. Many people believe that María has become a twentieth-century Difunta Correa (see p.504).

Arrival, information and accommodation

Catamarca's location in a narrow valley meant that its **airport**, Aeropuerto Felipe Varela (☎03833/437582 or 437578), had to be located 22km away to the south, on a service-road off the RP33, in the direction of San Martín. A **minibus** ($4) shuttles to and from the city centre, a much cheaper option than **taxis** which charge around $15 to $20. Apart from scheduled flights from Buenos Aires and La Rioja, useful and spectacular charter flights serve aerodromes around the province. Surprisingly inexpensive, they can cut journey time considerably for anyone in a hurry to get to Catamarca's stunning but inaccessible back country and are an experience in themselves. Catamarca has invested in a new **bus terminal** (☎03833/423415 or 423777), six blocks south and three east of central **Plaza 25 de Mayo** at Avenida Güemes and Tucumán. As well as a *locutorio*, restaurant and left-luggage office, it boasts shops selling everything from children's clothes to cactus-wood lampshades. Plenty of taxis wait outside.

Friendly staff at the provincial **tourist office** (daily 9am–1pm & 3.30–11pm; ☎03833/437593), on the corner of the so-called tourist block, at General Roca and Virgen del Valle, do their best despite the lack of resources and can supply a map of sorts and an accommodation list. **Accommodation** in Catamarca is thin on the ground, mostly aimed at the business traveller and especially limited at the lower end of the market, though a few of the cheaper *residenciales* are all right for a night or two. Usually you'll have no trouble finding a room, but for the Poncho Festival (late July) and the two pilgrimages to the Virgen del Valle, the week after Easter and, more so, from December 8 to 16, when over 30,000 people converge on Catamarca, hotels are booked up well in advance. The nearest **campsite** to the city is the municipal one at *La Quebrada*, 5km along the RP4, the road to El Rodeo. It's well-located, with a *balneario* on the banks of the Río El Tala, but can get extremely busy; and in the hotter, wetter months, from December to March, mosquitoes are also a problem. Facilities include a confitería and the charge is $6 per tent, per day. The #10 **bus** from the bus terminal, via the Convento San Francisco, runs there.

Hotel Ancasti, Sarmiento 520 (☎03833/431464). Tastefully renovated, this place leaves Catamarca's other hotels behind, with its stylish café-restaurant, well-equipped gym and sauna, bright bedrooms and modern bathrooms. ⑤.

Hotel Casino Tandil, Pasaje Carman (☎03833/430891). Boasting the city's casino, a popular pub-cum-disco, a fine dining-room and a large swimming pool in its garden, it has disappointingly plain rooms. ⑤.

Hotel Colonial, República 802 (☎03833/423502). Clean, efficient and friendly, with pleasant rooms and decent bathrooms. ③.

Hotel Inti Huasi, República and Junín (☎03833/435705). Modern and central, this hotel often fills up with tour operator clients. All rooms are en-suite with pleasant decor. ④.

Hotel Sol, Salta 1142 (☎03833/430803). Behind its off-putting exterior this establishment is clean and comfortable, as well as conveniently close to the bus terminal. ③.

Residencial Avenida Av. Güemes 754 (☎03833/422139). Friendly and clean if rather dog-eared, this *residencial* is handily located for the bus station. ②.

Residencial Delgado San Martín 788 (☎03833/426109). Basic but with private bathrooms and much more appealing inside than out. ②.

Residencial Esquiú Esquiú 365 (☎03833/422284). Charmless but fine for a night or two; avoid noisy street-side rooms. ②.

Residencial Plaza Rivadavia 278 (☎03833/426558). Spartan and just about commendable, this is the cheapest place in town that isn't squalid. ①.

The City

Orientation in mostly flat Catamarca, with its typical grid plan, poses no problems: the compact microcentro is bounded by avenidas Além to the east, Güemes to the south, Belgrano to the north, and Virgen del Valle to the west. In the long summer months, you'll soon get into the swing of taking a siesta to survive the blistering afternoon heat, which is why the shady vegetation of the city's epicentre, **Plaza 25 de Mayo**, is so welcome. A creation of Argentina's favourite landscape architect, Charles Thays (see p.107),

CATAMARCA'S ARTS AND CRAFTS

Catamarca's National Poncho Festival draws not only the country's major folk musicians but also its leading craftspeople from Catamarca Province, from the neighbouring provinces and from as far away as Patagonia and northeastern Argentina. The Catamarcan town of Belén is the country's self-styled Poncho Capital and some of the town's textiles, mostly made of llama, alpaca and sheep's wool, are works of art – and don't come cheap. While Salta produces its distinctive red ponchos and Jujuy has a preference for deep blue, the weavers of Catamarca go for natural tones, using the wool's blacks, greys, browns and whites, occasionally dying the yarn using vegetable pigments, ochre, yellow and maroon being the most frequent colourings. The best ponchos sell for at least $200–300. Catamarca's weavers, many of whose workshops can be visited – in Belén, Andalgalá, Fiambalá and elsewhere – also make rugs, blankets, bedspreads, shirts, jackets, sweaters, caftans and bags, while bonnets, hats, gloves, mittens and scarves are often knitted from the much-prized silky fleece of the elegant vicuña.

The ancient art of ceramics is also undergoing a revival throughout the Northwest, but some of the best can be found in and around Catamarca. Many indigenous artists have resuscitated ancient pre-Columbian designs, often using museum exhibits as their models, with a preference for geometric patterns, while other potters have taken inspiration from their ancestors to produce original art. Souvenir-hunters might also consider the high-quality leatherware, especially items related to horseriding, finely woven basket-ware, all manner of items made of cardón, the giant cactus, *Trychocereus pasacana,* that flourishes at altitudes of 2000–3500m throughout the region, or musical instruments. Instrument-makers in Catamarca, as well as in Jujuy, Purmamarca and elsewhere, still use ancient methods to fashion flutes and pipes out of native canes and twigs, to make animal-skin drums and to turn armadillo shells into the typical little ukeleles called *chorongos.* Tubes of cardón cactus filled with beans to make rain-sticks, or whole *mate* gourds, dried with their seeds inside and embellished with ornate, abstract patterns or naive etchings of llamas, pumas and other indigenous animals, make for unusual, easily transported mementoes.

the square is slovenly kept but its palms, orange trees, acacia-like tipas and pot-bellied *palos borrachos* are luxuriant. At the western end of the square stands the late nineteenth-century **Cathedral**, housing one of the most venerated images in the whole of Argentina. Hovering between brick-red and rich terracotta, depending on the light, the colour is the best thing about its unoriginal Neoclassical facade, but the blue-tiled cupolas are also striking. To the left of the cathedral is a passage leading to the **Camarín** (daily 7am–noon & 5–8pm; free), a specially built chamber where a hideously kitsch statue of the **Virgen del Valle** is kept, crowned by a priceless diamond-studded diadem. This Virgin appeared before locals in the nineteenth century, rather like the miracle of Lourdes, and ever since has been the subject of mass pilgrimages and devotion. The extravagant construction of white marble, gold and stained glass is served by a double staircase, to cope with the huge crowds who file past the Virgin on her feast-day on December 16. The other three sides of Plaza San Martín are lined with shops, cafés and restaurants, mostly built in a nondescript style, but on the southern side, at San Martín 543, you'll see a beautifully proportioned **Art Deco house**, and next to it a harmonious neo-Renaissance building, built in the style very much in vogue in Argentina at the end of the nineteenth century.

At Sarmiento 450, two blocks north of the cathedral, the **Museo Arqueológico Adán Quiroga** (Mon–Fri 7am–1pm & 3–8pm, Sat 9am–noon & 3–6pm, Sun 9am–1pm; $1) is potentially superb but its dusty, musty and dull presentation lets it down. In fact the museum comprises six sections, of which the archeological display is by far the best. It includes some exquisite black ceramics from the Aguada people, with some very fine abstract geometric detailing inscribed in paler pigments, typical of the so-called Middle Period (600–900 AD), which would look fabulous if properly exhibited. The intriguing ceramics of the earlier but by no means primitive Cóndor-Huasi, Ciénaga and Alamito cultures (500 BC–500AD) are also represented here, including animal and human figurines, urns, vases and pots, and intricate statues and statuettes, along with ancient mummies kept in antique fridges and some very fine carved stone. The other five sections – colonial history, natural history, iconography, philately and numismatology – respectively comprise little more than all-too-familiar jumbles of leather trunks and spurs, stuffed birds, mediocre statues of saints, dreary stamps and coins and Esquiú memorabilia.

One of the country's most curious religious relics is the shrivelled heart of **Fray Mamerto Esquiú** (the rest of his corpse is in Córdoba Cathedral) – a local hero, a revolutionary cleric and fiery orator famous for speeches in favour of the country's new constitution in the mid-nineteenth century – kept in a delicate glass case in the right-hand aisle of **Iglesia San Franscisco**, one block east of the museum at Esquiú and Rivadavia. The church was designed by Luigi Giorgi, the Italian architect of Salta's sumptuous Franciscan church. Far less exuberant in design and colour than Salta's, Catamarca's church nonetheless has a handsome late Baroque facade, painted pale salmon and off-white, and despite its antiseismic robustness – the previous church collapsed, along with many other buildings in the city, during a powerful earthquake in 1873 – manages to convey an airy elegance, contrasted with the fierce puce of the over-elaborate interior.

Way over to the west of the microcentro, at the far end of Calle Mota Botello, the **Feria Artesanal** (daily 8am–9pm; free) displays and sells some of the province's best traditional products ranging from delicious sugared walnuts and grape jelly, to some of the finest ponchos in Argentina (see box opposite), together with expensive jewellery made of rhodochrosite (see box, p.447) and musical instruments. You can also see attractive traditional rugs being woven on the looms in the showroom at the Fábrica de Alfambras, half a block south. Three blocks north, on the Paseo General Navarro, a mini-park at the western end of Avenida República, the **Museo Folklórico Juan Alfonso Carrizo** (Mon–Fri 8am–1pm & 3–8pm, Sat, Sun & public holidays 9am–noon & 4–8pm; free) is easily spotted thanks to the ostentatiously out-sized replica of the Virgen del Valle's diamond-studded crown above it. The extensive display of traditional Catamarcan objects includes some fine pottery, fascinating musical instruments (including *bombos* or large drums and *sikus* or reed-flutes), weaving-looms and brandy-stills.

Eating and drinking

Catamarca is no gastronomic highspot but it has a few **restaurants** worth trying, including those of *Ancasti* and *Casino Tandil* hotels. You'll find some fast-food joints along pedestrianized Calle Rivadavia while the **cafés** are grouped around Plaza 25 de Mayo. *Café Richmond*, at República 534, is a slightly old-fashioned but popular plaza café, serving excellent coffee and decent breakfasts. *El Peregrino*, San Martín 446, is one of the best cheap eateries, churning out traditional *empanadas*, good pasta and simple dishes, for as little as $4; while *Family*, at Rivadavia 640, is Catamarca's best pizzeria – it will never win prizes for originality, but the food tastes good and is cheap. At *La Tinaja*, Sarmiento 533, live music at weekends sometimes adds to the otherwise calm ambience at this reasonably priced parrilla, the best **restaurant** in the city, if only for its juicy meat. *Salsa Criolla*, República 542, dishes up traditional Argentine criollo food, as the name suggests, with an excellent-value *menú ejecutivo* for $8. *Viejo Bueno*, at Esquiú 480, is a dowdy but reasonably priced restaurant, with faded floral tablecloths, but serving excellent river fish, including delicious trout with roquefort. *Trattoria Montecarlo*, República 548, prepares Italian-style food, with lots of fresh pasta, best followed by the fresh fruit salad.

El Rodeo and Cuesta del Portazuelo

When the city blazes in the summer heat, locals head up to **EL RODEO**, a sprawling village of weekend homes, 37km north of Catamarca along the RP4, a scenic road that follows the El Tala Valley. El Rodeo boasts a pleasant microclimate, much cooler than Catamarca in the summer and snowy in the winter, and its rugged mountainside setting make it an agreeable excursion; delicious *locro* is served at the *Hostería Villafañez* on the main road where it bridges the Río Ambato, but there is nowhere of note to stay.

Another popular outing, organized by tour operators and no longer possible by public transport, takes you up the infinite zigzags of the **Cuesta del Portazuelo** to the grassy peaks of the Sierra de Ancasti, to the east of the city, off the RN38 Tucumán road. The giddying cliff-side roads afford ever more panoramic views, as does the hang-gliders' launch-pad among tufts of straw-like pasture atop the hill; the city of Catamarca is laid out like a map in the distance, and the views of the valley and the rows of different coloured mountains in every direction are breathtaking.

Andalgalá, Belén and Londres

Mysteriously overlooked by most visitors – no doubt because of the relative inaccessibility by public transport – Catamarca Province becomes utterly spectacular as you leave behind the populated eastern valleys and climb towards the lonely **Altiplano**. Across the barrier of the Sierra de Ambato from Catamarca city lies a transitional zone of dazzling **salt-flats**, rugged highland scenery and small hamlets whose inhabitants harvest walnuts, distil fabulously grapey *aguardiente* or weave rugs and ponchos for a living. Three historic villages, **Andalgalá**, **Belén** and **Londres**, serve as useful halts and are worth a longer stop if you're venturing further into this dramatic outback; the first two have the area's only accommodation to speak of.

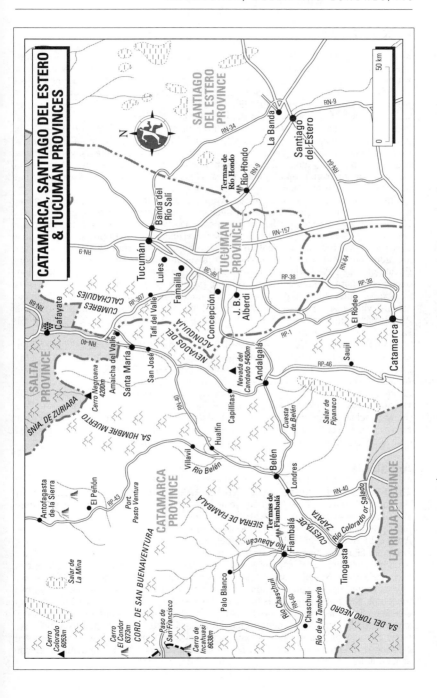

CATAMARCA, SANTIAGO DEL ESTERO & TUCUMÁN PROVINCES

Up to Andalgalá

Much of the joy of Andalgalá is in the getting there, and you have a choice of three spectacular approach routes. From Catamarca, it is most easily reached by travelling southwest along the RN38 for 70km, branching northwest along the winding **Cuesta La Sébila**, part of the RN60 that cuts through the southernmost tip of the mighty Sierra del Ambato, to El Empalme, 48km away. From there the RN46 heads due north, with open views to the west across the huge **Salar de Pipanaco**, a sugary-white salt-lake stretching for nearly 60km. It's worth branching off the RP46 onto the RP25, a good dirt road that edges you closer to the crinkled western flanks of the Ambato range, taking you through farming villages such as Pomán and Rincón, where olives, oranges, vines and walnuts flourish thanks to a sophisticated network of irrigation channels, dating from pre-Columbian times. This is the route taken by the regular but infrequent buses from Catamarca to Andalgalá.

The other approaches to Andalgalá, from Tucumán and Amaichá, take you along nail-bitingly dramatic *cuestas* – narrow mountain passes, with dozens of hairpin bends. Negotiating these narrow roller coasters of roads, with only the odd passing place shored up by flimsy stone walls that look more decorative than protective, requires absolute concentration and plenty of horn-blowing, but the views for any passengers are unforgettable. The route from Tucumán, along the **Cuesta de las Chilcas**, is a continuation of the RP365 which forks off the RN38 in a westerly direction at Concepción, over 60km south of Tucumán. After skirting the northernmost point of the Sierra de la Canela you enter the mountain pass, and twist and climb through forests of tall cacti to 1950m, with amazing views of the Salar de Pipanaco, to the south, and the valley of Andalgalá, to the northwest, before descending fast and entering Andalgalá from the east.

From the north, the **Cuesta de Capillitas** also slaloms among cacti, reaching an altitude of 3100m, in the western lee of the majestic Nevado de Candado (5450m). It's the final stage of the RP47, an initially decent track branching off the RN40, 62km south of Amaichá (see p.432), running alongside the stupendous crags of the Nevados de Aconquija and the Cerro Negro, before deteriorating into a trail as it takes you past the **rhodochrosite mines** at Capillitas, nearly 70km north of Andalgalá. Obstacles along the way include deep fords and dry river-beds, making a 4WD preferable, and since the area is prone to sudden blizzards from May to October, this route must be attempted only after a weather-check or asking at a police checkpoint along the way.

Andalgalá

The best thing about the village of **ANDALGALÁ**, 250km northwest of Catamarca by the shortest route, is its setting: dominated to the north by the hulking **El Candado** (5450m), nearly always crested with snow, by the Sierra del Ambato to the east and the Sierra de Belén to the west, it lies at a strategic crossroads, on the east bank of the Arroyo El Huaco. Middle Eastern in feel, with its many immigrants from Syria and Lebanon, laid-back cafés, busy streets and markets, and mountain setting, it makes a living from cotton, potatoes, olives, fruit and spices, such as aniseed and cumin, and from the **rhodochrosite mines**, (see box opposite) at nearby Capillitas. The nearby *pukará* or fortress and other pre-Incan sites have yielded up sufficient material for two museums, the better of which is the small **Museo Arqueológico** (Mon–Fri 8am–1pm & 5–9pm, Sat 9am–1pm; $1), at Belgrano and Mercado, a block south of the main plaza, with its shady plane and orange trees and cafés. Created with money from the Paul Getty Foundation the museum comprises a fascinating collection of well-preserved ceramics from the Belén, Santa María and Aguada cultures, including an unusual egg-shaped funerary urn.

RHODOCHROSITE

Rhodochrosite is a semi-precious stone, similar to onyx but unique to Argentina; it is mined only from a generous seam in the Capillitas mine, to the north of Andalgalá. Known popularly as the Rosa del Inca – and believed by the indigenous people to be the solidified blood of their ancestors – rhodochrosite is reminiscent of Florentine paper, with its slightly blurred, marble-like veins of ruby red and deep salmon-pink, layered and rippled with paler shades of rose-pink and white. Its rarity has made it Argentina's unofficial national stone. Some of it is sold in luscious blocks, suitable as paperweights or book-ends, while much of it is worked into fine jewellery, none of it cheap, or into animal and bird figures, many of them kitsch. If you're searching for rhodochrosite as an unusual keepsake, your best bet is in either Andalgalá or Catamarca city, where a number of artisans specialize in fashioning it.

Buses from Catamarca stop on San Martín one block north of the main square. Three blocks to the south, just before the market, is a fledgling **tourist information office** (daily 9am–1pm 4–8pm; no phone). Ask there about visits to the rhodochrosite mines at Capillitas. The Club Andino at San Martín 41 (☎03835/156-95716) offers trekking and adventure tourism in the nearby mountains. **Accommodation** is a choice between the overpriced but comfortable *Hotel del Turismo* (☎03835/422210; ③) with its decent restaurant, half a kilometre to the east of the centre, on Avenida Sarmiento, and the much more basic *Residencial Galileo* at Núñez del Prado 757 (☎03835/422247; ②). The **campsite**, *La Aguada*, just across the river to the west, charges $5 per tent.

Belén

Just 85km west of Andalgalá, along the mostly unsealed RP46 whose dullness is alleviated only by the Cuesta de Belén pass, the region's main settlement of **BELÉN** is squeezed between the Sierra de Belén and the river of the same name. Olive-groves, and plantations of capsicum – paprika-producing peppers – stretch across the fertile valley to the south. A convenient stopover, Belén offers the area's best accommodation and a couple of restaurants, and it's also a base for **adventure tourism** including trekking and horseriding. And since Belén promotes itself as the **Capital del Poncho** you might like to visit the many excellent *teleras* or textile workshops dotted around the town; they also turn out beautiful blankets and sweaters made of llama, vicuña and sheep's wool, mostly in natural colours. The wool is sometimes blended with walnut-bark, to give the local cloth, known as *belichas* or *belenistos*, its typical rough texture. As for **festivals**, every January 6 a pilgrimage procession clambers to a huge statue of the Virgen de Belén, overlooking the town from its high vantage point to the west, the Cerro de la Virgen.

On the western flank of its main square, **Plaza Presbítero Olmos de Aguilera**, shaded by whitewashed orange trees and bushy palms, and ringed by cafés and ice-cream parlours, stands the Italianate **Iglesia Nuestra Señora de Belén**, clearly inspired by the cathedral in Catamarca and designed and built by Italian immigrants at the beginning of the twentieth century. Its brickwork is bare, without plaster or decoration, lending it an unfinished but not displeasing look. Housed on the first floor of the Centro Cultural de Belén, at Lavalle and Rivadavia, one block south of the church, the **Museo Provincial Cóndor Huasi** (Mon–Fri 8am–noon & 5–8pm; $1) has one of the country's most important collections of **Diaguita** artefacts, but is poorly laid out. The huge number of ceramics, and some metal items, trace the Diaguitas' culture through all four archeological "periods": the Initial Period, 300 BC–300 AD, is represented by simple but by no means primitive pieces, often in the shape of squashes or maize-cobs; in the Early Period or Cóndor Huasi, 300–550 AD, anthropomorphic and zoomorphic ceramics predominate, including naive representations of llamas and pumas; the Middle or Aguada culture, 600–900 AD, produced some the museum's most prized pieces, such as a ceramic jaguar, of astonishing finesse; and the Late Period, from 1000 AD onwards, includes the so-called Santa María culture, when craftsmen produced large urns, vases and amphoras decorated with complex, mostly abstract geometric patterns, with depictions of snakes, rheas and toads.

Regular but infrequent **buses** from Catamarca, Salta and Santa María arrive at the corner of Sarmiento and Rivadavia, near the museum. For **tourist information** ask at the municipalidad, one block to the east. The best **place to stay** in the whole area is the *Hotel Samai* at Urquiza 349, one block east and south of the main square (☎03835/461320; ③). It's clean and warm, but certainly not luxurious. In the unlikely event that it's full, you can try the very basic *Hotel Gómez* at Calchaquí 141 (☎03835/461388; ①), or fall back on the overpriced and equally basic *Hotel Turismo* at Belgrano and Cubas (☎03835/461501; ②). Pick of the **restaurants**, all of which cluster around the main square, is *Parrillada El Unico*, housed in a rustic hut at Sarmiento and General Roca, one block north of the church. It serves excellent *empanadas* and does a great *locro*.

Londres

Fifteen kilometres west of Belén and even more charming since it shows no outward signs of modern-day life, with its partly crumbling adobe houses and pretty orchards, **LONDRES** lies 2km off the RN40 along a winding road that joins its upper and lower towns, on either side of the Río Hondo, a usually dry river that peters out in the Salar de Pipanaco. Known as the Cuna de la Nuez, or Walnut Heartland, the town celebrates the **Fiesta de la Nuez** with folklore and crafts displays during the first few days of February. Londres de Abajo, the lower town, is centred on Plaza José Eusebio Colombres, where you'll find the simple, whitewashed eighteenth-century **Iglesia de San Juan Bautista**, in front of which the walnut festival is held. The focal point for the rest of the year is Londres de Arriba's **Plaza Hipólito Yrigoyen**, overlooked by the quaint **Iglesia de la Inmaculada Concepción**, a once lovely church in a pitiful state of repair but noteworthy for a harmonious colonnade and its fine bells, said to be the country's oldest. As yet, there's no accommodation in the town but ask around, just in case someone has a room to let.

Londres' humble present-day aspect belies a long and prestigious history, including the fact that it's Argentina's second oldest city, founded in 1558, only five years after Santiago del Estero. **Diego de Almagro** and his expedition from Cusco began scouring the area in the 1530s, founded a settlement and named it in honour of the marriage between Philip, heir to the Spanish throne, and Mary Tudor: hence the tribute to the English capital in the village's name. Alongside the municipalidad, on the wall of which is a quaint fresco testifying to the town's glorious past, is the small but interesting **Museo Arqueológico** (Mon–Fri 8am–1pm; $1), displaying ceramics and other finds from the impressive **Shinkal ruins**. The ruins themselves lie 5km to the west (daily Dec–April 9am–1pm & 4–7pm; May–Nov 10am–5pm; $2); just follow the well signposted scenic road, next to the Iglesia de la Inmaculada Concepción. Amazingly intact, though parts of it are over-restored in a zealous attempt to reconstruct the fortress, it was the site of a decisive battle in the **Great Calchaquí Uprising** (see box opposite). After Chief Chelemín cut off the water supplies to Londres and set fire to the town, forcing its inhabitants to flee to La Rioja, he was captured and had his body ripped apart by four horses. Shinkal gives you an insight into what Diaguita settlements in the region must have looked like: splendid steps lead to the top of high **ceremonial mounds**, with great views of the oasis and Sierra de Zapata.

THE CALCHAQUÍ WARS

After the European invasions of this region in the late sixteenth and early seventeenth centuries, the autochthonous tribes who lived along the Valles Calchaquíes, stretching from Salta Province in the north, down to central Catamarca Province, stubbornly refused to be evangelized by the Spanish invaders and generally behave as their aggressors wanted; the region around Belén and Londres proved especially difficult for the invaders to colonize. Even the Jesuits, usually so effective at bringing the "natives" under control, conceded defeat. The colonizers made do with a few *encomiendas*, and more often *pueblos*, reservations where the Indians were forced to live, leaving the colonizers to farm their "own" land in peace. After a number of skirmishes, things came to a head in 1630, when the so-called **Great Calchaquí Uprising** began. For two years, under the leadership of Juan Chelemín, the fierce cacique of Hualfín, natives waged a war of attrition against the invaders, sacking towns and burning crops, provoking ever more brutal reactions from the ambitious new Governor of Tucumán, Francisco de Nieva y Castilla. Eventually Chelemín was caught, hanged, drawn and quartered, and various parts of his body were put on display in different villages to "teach the Calchaquíes a lesson", but it took until 1643 for all resistance to be stamped out, and only after a network of fortresses was built in Andalgalá, Londres and elsewhere.

War broke out once more in 1657 when the Spanish decided to arrest "El Inca Falso", also known as Pedro Chamijo, an imposter of European descent who claimed to be Hualpa Inca – or Incan emperor – under the nom de guerre of **Bohórquez**. Elected chief at an impressive ceremony attended by the new Governor of Tucumán, Alonso Mercado y Villacorta, amid great pomp and circumstance, in Pomán, he soon led the Calchaquíes into battle, and Mercado y Villacorta, joined by his ruthless predecessor, Francisco de Nieva y Castilla, set about what today would be called ethnic cleansing. Bohórquez was captured, taken to Lima and eventually garroted in 1667, and whole tribes fell victim to genocide: their only remains are the ruins of Batungasta, Hualfín and Shinkal, near Londres. Some tribes like the **Quilmes**, whose settlement is now an archeological site near Amaichá (see p.433), were uprooted and forced to march to Buenos Aires. Out of the 7000 Quilmes who survived a long and distressing siege in their *pukará*, or fortress, despite having their food and water supplies cut off, before being led in chains to Buenos Aires, where they were employed as slaves, only a few hundred were left to face a smallpox epidemic at the end of the eighteenth century, which successfully wiped out these few survivors.

The Puna Catamarqueña

The Altiplano of northwestern Catamarca Province – known as the **Puna Catamarqueña** (*puna* is the Quechoa word for Altiplano, which is of Spanish coinage), stretching to the Chilean border, is one of the remotest, most deserted, but most outstandingly beautiful parts of the country. **Antofagasta de la Sierra**, a ghostly but fascinating town of adobe-brick miners' houses and whispering womenfolk, is far flung even from Catamarca city in this sparsely populated region, but the tiny **archeological museum** is worth seeing for its fantastic mummified infant. Dotted with majestic ebony volcanoes and scarred by recent lava-flows, with the Andean cordillera as a magnificent backdrop, the huge expanses of Altiplano and their desiccated vegetation are grazed by hardy yet delicate-looking **vicuñas** while **flamingoes** valiantly survive on frozen lakes. This is staggeringly unspoiled countryside, with out-of-this-world landscapes, and a constantly surreal atmosphere, accentuated by the sheer remoteness and emptiness of it all; the trip out here is really more rewarding than the destination, **Antofagasta**, which is primarily a place to spend the night before forging on northwards, to San Antonio de los Cobres in Salta Province (see p.400), or doubling back down to Belén. As you travel, watch out for *apachetas*, little cairns of stones piled up at the roadside as an offering to the Mother Goddess, Pachamama, and the only visible signs of any human presence. Although a **bus** shuttles back and forth between Catamarca and Antofagasta twice a week, the surest way to get around is by 4WD, along the RP43, one of the quietest roads in Argentina; it's quite possible not to pass another vehicle all day. Take all the necessary precautions including plenty of fuel, and don't forget warm clothing as the temperature can plummet below -30°C at night in July.

In **Hualfín**, a tiny village where the RP43 branches northwestwards from the RN40, 60km north of Belén, you can find rooms for rent, if you need **accommodation**, but most people use Hualfín as their last **fuel-stop** before the long haul to Antofagasta de la Sierra; provisions can also be bought here. The village itself is famous for its paprika, often sprinkled on the delicious local goat's cheeses, and a fine **colonial church**, dedicated to Nuestra Señora del Rosario and built in 1770; ask for the key at the municipalidad to see the pristine interior adorned with delicate frescoes. Hualfín was also the birthplace and stronghold of Chelemín, the Calchaquí leader who spearheaded the Great Uprising in the 1630s (see box p.449). **Thermal springs** with rudimentary facilities, and slightly better ones 14km north at **Villavil**, are open from January to April only.

Up to Antofagasta de la Sierra

Between **Corral Quemado** and **Villavil**, the first stretch of the RP43 to Antofagasta de la Sierra, all of 200km from Hualfín to the northwest, takes you through some cheery if understated countryside, planted with vines and maize, with feathery acacias and tall poplars acting as windbreaks, and dotted with humble mud-brick farmhouses. Potentially treacherous fords at Villavil and, more likely, at **El Bolsón**, 10km farther on, are sometimes too deep to cross even in a 4WD, especially after spring thaws or summer rains; you'll either have to wait a couple of hours for the rivers to subside or turn back. Just over 70km from the junction at Hualfín, the road twists and climbs through the dramatic **Cuesta de Randolfo**, hemmed in by rocky pinnacles and reaching an altitude of 4800m before corkscrewing back down to the transitional plains.

Along this flat section, you're treated to immense open views towards the dramatic crags of the Sierra del Cajón, to the south, and the spiky rocks of the Sierra Laguna Blanca to the north. Impressive white **sand dunes**, gleaming like fresh snow against the dark mountainsides, make an interesting pretext for a halt. Down in the plain, the immense **salt-lakes** stretch for miles and this is where you'll probably spy your first **vicuñas** – the shy, smaller cousins of the llamas with much silkier wool – protected by the **Reserva Natural Laguna Blanca**. All along this road, with photogenic ochre mountains as backdrops, whole flocks of vicuñas graze off scrawny grasses, less timid than usual, perhaps because the flocks are so big and they feel the safety of numbers. You'll also see nonchalant llamas and shaggy alpacas and, if you're very fortunate, the ostrich-like suris or ñandúes, before they scurry away nervously. You could make a short detour to visit the shores of **Laguna Blanca** itself, a shallow, mirror-like lake fed by the Río Río and home to thousands of teals, ducks and **flamingoes**; it's clearly signposted along a track off to the north. A few kilometres on, the road then climbs steadily again up the often snow-streaked Sierra Laguna Blanca to reach the pass at **Portezuelo Pasto Ventura** (4000m), marked by a sign: this is the entrance to the Altiplano or *puna* proper. From here you have magnificent panoramas of the Andes, to the west, and of the great volcanoes of northwestern Catamarca, to the north, plus your first glimpse of wide-rimmed **Volcán Galan** (5912m), whose name means "bare mountain" in Quechoa. It's an incredible geological feature: some 2,500,000 years ago, in a cataclysmic eruption, blasting over 1000 cubic kilometres of material into the air, its top was blown away leaving a hole measuring over 45km by 25km, the largest known crater on the Earth's surface, or in the solar system as locals like to boast.

Delightful **El Peñón**, 135km from Hualfín, is the first Altiplano settlement you reach along the RP43: just a few gingerbread-coloured adobe houses, some proud poplar trees and an apple-orchard, surprising given the altitude. The village nestles in the **Carachipampa Valley**, which extends all the way to the Cordillera de San Buenaventura, to the southwest, and its striking summit, **Cerro El Cóndor** (6000m), clearly visible from here in the searingly clear atmosphere. Soon the chestnut-brown volcanic cones of **Los Negros de la Laguna** come into view, a sign that you're in the final approaches to Antofagasta. One of twin peaks, **La Alumbrera**, deposited enormous lava-flows when it last erupted, only a few hundred years ago. The huge piles of visibly fresh **black pumice** that it tossed out, all pocked and twisted, reach heights of ten metres or more. Like giant chunks of licorice or the broken up tyres of an outsize vehicle, they contrast starkly with the smooth volcanic mounds on the horizon and the serene white salt-lakes all around. Just before Antofagasta, the road swings round **Laguna Colorada**, a small lake often frozen solid and shaded pink with a massive flock of altiplanic flamingoes which somehow survive up here.

Antofagasta de la Sierra and around

Perched at 3440m above sea level, 260km north of Belén, **ANTOFAGASTA DE LA SIERRA** lies at the northern end of a vast, arid plain hemmed in by volcanoes to the east and south, and by the Cordillera, which soars to peaks of over 6000m, a mere 100km over to the west. With a population of under a thousand it exudes a feeling of utter remoteness, while still managing to exert a disarming fascination. It's a bleak yet restful place, an oasis of tamarinds and bright green alfalfa fields in the middle of the *meseta altiplanica* – a harsh steppe that looms above the surrounding Altiplano. Two rivers, Punilla and Las Paitas, meet just to the south, near the strange volcanic plug called **El Torreón**, adopted as the town's symbol. Named after the Chilean port-city, this is a tough town with a harsh climate, where night temperatures in midwinter drop as low as -30°C, accompanied by biting winds and a relentless sun during the day: its name means "home of the Sun" in the language of the Diaguitas. Salt, borax and various minerals and metals have been mined in the area for centuries and Antofagasta has the hardy feel of a mining-town, but most of its people are now subsistence farmers and herdsmen, scraping a living from maize, potatoes, onions and beans or rearing llamas and alpacas, whose wool is made into fine textiles. The people here are introverted and placid, hospitable but seemingly indifferent to the outside world.

The best views of the immediate surroundings can be enjoyed from the top of the Cerro Amarillo and Cerro de la Cruz, two unsightly mounds of earth that look like part of a huge building-site and dominate the town's humble streets of small mud-brick houses. The **Cerro de la Cruz** is the destination of processions held to honour Antofagasta's patron saints, St Joseph and the Virgin of Loreto, from December 8 to 10. In another sombre ceremony, the town's dead are remembered on November 1 and 2, when villagers file to and from the cemetery before a feast, talking in whispers so as not to disturb the spirits. And every March the town comes to life, for the **Feria Artesanal y Ganadera de la Puna**, a colourful event attended by craftspeople and herdsmen from all over the province. The only tourist attraction in the town is the beautifully presented **Museo Arqueológico** (Mon–Fri 8am–6pm; $1), recently created primarily to house a perfectly preserved, naturally mummified baby, found in the mountains nearby and believed to be nearly 2000 years old; surrounded with jewels and other signs of wealth, suggesting the child belonged to a ruling dynasty, it exerts a morbid fascination. The museum's other exhibits, few in number but of extraordinary value, include an immaculately preserved pre-Hispanic basket, the pigment colouring and fine weave still intact.

The **bus** from Catamarca will drop you in the main street. Apart from rooms in private houses, the only **accommodation** is near the municipalidad, at the extremely basic but scrupulously clean *Albergue Municipal* (☎03835/471001; ①), where you can also **eat**. Fuel can be bought at highly inflated prices from the municipalidad, but it's better to fill up before making this trip. Antofagasta has no tourist office; for visiting the immediate and farther-flung surroundings ask at the municipalidad for the town's most experienced guides, Catalino Soriano, Antolín Ramos and Jesús Vásquez.

Around Antofagasta de la Sierra

Unless it's cut off by winter snows, an alternative route to and from Antofagasta is the mostly unsealed and sometimes bumpy RP43 (in Catamarca Province, becoming RP17 in Salta Province), leading northwards to **San Antonio de los Cobres** (see p.400), 330km away via Caucharí. Therefore, Antofagasta could be visited as part of a gigantic loop, taking in vast, lonely yet dramatically memorable swathes of Salta and Catamarca provinces, but allow plenty of time and take far more provisions and fuel supplies than you think you'll need – in other words reckon on two or three days' food and several jerry-cans of petrol in reserve. The same road leads to the desolate, disorientatingly mirage-like landscapes of the great **Salar del Hombre Muerto salt-flats**, 75km to the north of Antofagasta and best explored using the services of a *baqueano* or guide. **Cerro Ratones** (5252m) and Cerro Incahuasi (4847m) form a breathtaking backdrop to the bright whiteness of the flats.

Within easy excursion distance of Antofagasta are a number of archeological and historical sites, such as the ruins at **Campo Alumbreras**, 5km to the south, and **Coyparcito**, 3km farther away. The pre-Columbian **pukará** or fortress on the flanks of the Alumbrera volcano, a few kilometres south of Antofagasta, and nearby **petroglyphs** (mostly depicting llamas and human figures) are also worth a visit; you'll definitely need the services of a guide to find them, and for the necessary explanations to make a visit worthwhile, but they are all open to the public at all times and no entrance fee is charged. Ask at Antofagasta's museum for archeological information and guided visits. The abandoned onyx, mica and gold **mines** in the region are another interesting attraction, while long treks on mule-back are the only way of seeing **Volcán Sufre** (5706m) on the Chilean border. If you want quieter recreation than climbing mountains or scrambling through disused mines you might care for a day's **trout fishing** at **Paicuquí**, 20km north of Antofagasta. In the crystal-clear streams you can catch delicious rainbow trout – apparently the streams used to swarm with fish but stocks are still at safe levels, albeit less plentiful than a few years ago. The **Río de los Patos**, another 70km north, is said to be a more reliable source of trout.

Up to the Paso San Francisco

The mostly sealed RN60, which starts way down in Córdoba, crosses the RN40 in Catamarca Province at Alpasinche, 90km south of Belén. It begins its gradual ascent towards the Chilean border at Tinogasta, a small town at the southern extremity of the province, overlooked by the imposing Sierra de Copacabana. From Tinogasta, El Cordillerano's buses (☎0387/420636 or 420314) go over the **Paso San Francisco** to Copiapó in Chile's Norte Chico about once a week, sometimes more often in the summer (Dec–March), and this is undoubtedly one of the most dramatic ways of entering Chile. The ruins of the Calchaquí *pukará*, or pre-Incan fortress, of Batungasta, a strategic Diaguita stronghold during the Calchaquí wars (see box, p.449), lie just off the RN60, 10km west of Tinogasta, in a beautiful gorge. The road to **Fiambalá**, the last settlement to speak of before the frontier, passes through lovely oasis countryside, with small, picturesque villages of adobe farmhouses such as San José, El Puesto and

Anillaco – the last not to be confused with Anillaco, La Rioja Province, the birthplace of former President Menem. The nearby **Termas de Fiambalá** are among the country's best located thermal springs, and are fabulous at night when the warm waters contrast with the fresh air and you can gaze up at the starry desert skies. From Fiambalá, the RN60 leads ever higher into the cordillera to the border; if driving make sure you fill up the tank and any jerry-cans you have, in either Tinogasta or Fiambalá, as there are no service stations after the latter. Be prepared for bad weather, too, and take passports, plus Chilean visas if necessary, your driving licence and all vehicle papers. The **pass**, at 4800m, is seldom cut off, but heavy snow can occasionally block the road in midwinter – though rarely for more than a couple of days. The journey takes you through the Cuesta de Loro-Huasi, with its weirdly beautiful sandstone formations, and the narrow gorge of Las Angosturas, past different species of cactus and extensive guanaco pastures. The sights on the other side of the frontier are even more spectacular: the turquoise waters of Laguna Verde, Cerro Ojos del Salado (6893m), the world's highest active volcano, the Cuesta Colorada, Parque Nacional Nevado de Tres Cruces and the Salar de Maricunga.

Fiambalá

Aptly meaning "deep in the mountains" in the native Kakano language, **FIAMBALÁ**, 50km north of Tinogasta, is near the olive-groves of the fertile Abaucán Valley, an area reminiscent of North Africa or the Middle East. It's a quiet oasis town of crumbling adobe houses, set among extensive vineyards, whose fruit is eaten fresh, dried as raisins, or fermented into very drinkable wine. Some of the locals are excellent **artisans**, specializing in weaving, and you can buy their work at various workshops around the village, including a crafts market just off the main square. In the town, on Calle Abaucán, just north of the Plaza Mayor, is the new, small **Museo del Hombre** (daily 9am–1pm & 4–8pm; $1) with an intriguing little collection, including two particularly well-preserved mummies and some striking stone sculptures. Two kilometres to the south, aside the RN60 from Tinogasta, stands the well-restored silhouette of **Iglesia San Pedro**, a colonial chapel built in 1702, set amid shady trees. During renovation, part of the reed roofing was left bare of plaster to reveal the construction. Chocolate-brown streaks from the mud and straw roof have attractively trickled down the curvaceous, impeccably whitewashed walls. A family living nearby has the key to the church, whose handsomely plain interior, decorated with **paintings of the Cusqueña school** (see box, p.111) of the Virgin, Infant Jesus and saints, is well worth seeing.

The town's other claim to fame is as a spa, and the **thermal baths** (daily 9am till late; $2) are perched in a beautiful, wooded mountain setting 15km to the east, at an altitude of over 2000m. The mineral spring gushes out at over 70°C but, by the time the water trickles down into the cascade of attractive stone pools, it cools to 30°C or so, very pleasant when the outdoor temperatures plummet well below freezing; in fact the baths are especially fun to relax in at night, when you can look up at the stars, wallow in the warm waters and listen to the campers singing fireside songs. You can **camp** by the pools, there are cabins to rent and even plans for an *hostería*, and the only way to get there is by taxi ($20 return fare, including waiting time).

Buses from Catamarca and Tinogasta, or to Chile, use the stop on Plaza Mayor. Some **tourist information** can be obtained at the municipalidad, 100m to the west, but the only place to **stay** is nearby, at the clean basic *Hosteria Municipal*, on Diego de Almagro (☎03837/496016; ②), whose rooms have their own bath; you're advised to book ahead. Excellent pizzas and other Italian-style **food** are on offer at the ultra-friendly *Pizzeria Roma*, calles Abaucán and Padre Arch, a couple of blocks north of the main square, should you want a change from the snacks and basic fare served at the *hostería*.

travel details

Buses

Catamarca to: Andalgalá (3 daily; 6hrs); Antofagasta de la Sierra (2 weekly; 13hr); Belén (2 daily; 5 hr); Buenos Aires (10 daily; 15hr); Fiambalá (2 daily; 6hr); La Rioja (6 daily; 2hr 30min); Salta (6 daily; 7hr); Tinogasta (every hour; 5hr); Tucumán (5 daily; 3hr).

Jujuy to: Buenos Aires (every hour; 22hr); Córdoba (10 daily; 13hr); Humahuaca (every hour; 3hr); La Quiaca (every hour; 7hr); Purmamarca (every hour; 1hr 15min); Resistencia (1 daily; 14hr); Salta (every hour; 1hr 30min); Tilcara (every hour; 2hr); Tucumán (10 daily; 5hr 30min).

Salta to: Buenos Aires (every hour; 22hr); Cachi (2 daily; 5hr); Cafayate (7 daily; 3hr); Córdoba (10 daily; 12hr); Jujuy (every hour; 1hr 30min); Resistencia (1 daily; 13hr); Santiago del Estero (10 daily; 5hr); Tucumán (10 daily; 4hr).

Santiago del Estero to: Córdoba (6 daily; 6hr); Roque Sáenz Peña (2 daily; 4hr); Termas de Río Hondo (10 daily; 1hr); Tucumán (10 daily; 2hr 30min); Tafí del Valle (8 daily; 3hr); Cafayate (3 daily; 7hr).

Tucumán to: Buenos Aires (10 daily; 15hr); Catamarca (5 daily; 3hr); Córdoba (6 daily; 8hr); Jujuy (10 daily ; 5hr 30min); Santiago del Estero (10 daily ; 2hr 30min); Tafí del Valle (6 daily; 3hr); Termas de Río Hondo (10 daily; 1hr 30min).

Trains

Tucumán to: Buenos Aires (3 weekly; 23hr).

Santiago del Estero to: Buenos Aires (3 weekly; 19hr).

Flights

Catamarca to: Buenos Aires (1 daily; 2hr 30min); La Rioja (1 daily; 30min).

Jujuy to: Buenos Aires (3 daily; 2hr 10min); Salta (1 daily; 20min).

Salta to: Buenos Aires (4 daily; 2hr); Jujuy (1 daily; 20min).

Santiago del Estero to: Buenos Aires (1 daily; 1hr 40min).

Tucumán to: Buenos Aires (6 daily; 1hr 50min).

CHAPTER SEVEN

MENDOZA, SAN JUAN AND LA RIOJA

A
rgentina's midwestern provinces of **Mendoza, San Juan** and **La Rioja** stretch all the way from the chocolate-brown pampas of **La Payunia**, on the northern borders of Patagonia, to the remote highland steppes of the **Reserva Las Vicuñas**, on the edge of the northwestern altiplano, more than a thousand kilometres to the north. They extend across vast, thinly populated territories of bone-dry desert dotted with vibrant oases where fertile farmland and the region's famous **vineyards** are to be found. To the west loom the world's loftiest peaks outside the Himalayas, culminating in the defiant **Aconcagua** whose summit is only a shade less than 7000 metres – a challenging but perfectly feasible climb – while further north is the second highest volcano on Earth, the extinct cone of **Monte Pissis** (6882m). The region's urban centre, the sophisticated metropolis of **Mendoza**, one of Argentina's biggest cities, is extremely well-geared to the tourist industry, as are **San Rafael** and **Malargüe**, further south, while the two smaller provincial capitals, **San Juan** and **La Rioja**, continue to be lethargic backwaters by comparison. In any case, the regional dynamics are not about towns and cities but the highly varied **landscapes** and **wildlife**. Ranging from the snowy peaks of the Andes to totally flat pampas in the east, from green, fertile valleys to dark barren volcanoes, and from sand dunes to highland marshes, the scenery includes two of the country's most photographed national parks: the sheer red sandstone cliffs of **Talampaya** and the nearby canyons and moonscapes of **Ischigualasto**. Pumas and vicuñas, condors and ñandúes, plus hundreds of colourful bird species, inhabit the thoroughly unspoiled wildernesses of the region, where some of the biggest known dinosaurs prowled millions of years ago. European settlers have wrought changes to the environment, bringing the grape vine, the Lombardy poplar and all kinds of fruit trees with them, but the thousands of kilometres of irrigation channels that water the region existed long before Columbus "discovered" America. Before the Incas and Spanish invaded, different tribes of the Amerindian Huarpe people eked a living by farming maize, beans and

---

ACCOMMODATION PRICE CODES

The price codes used for accommodation throughout this chapter refer to the cheapest rate for a double room in high season. Single travellers will only occasionally pay half the double-room rate; nearer two thirds is the norm and some places will expect you to pay the full rate. Note that in resort towns, there are considerable discounts out of season.

① $20 or less	④ $45–60	⑦ $100–150
② $20–30	⑤ $60–80	⑧ $150–200
③ $30–45	⑥ $80–100	⑨ Over $200

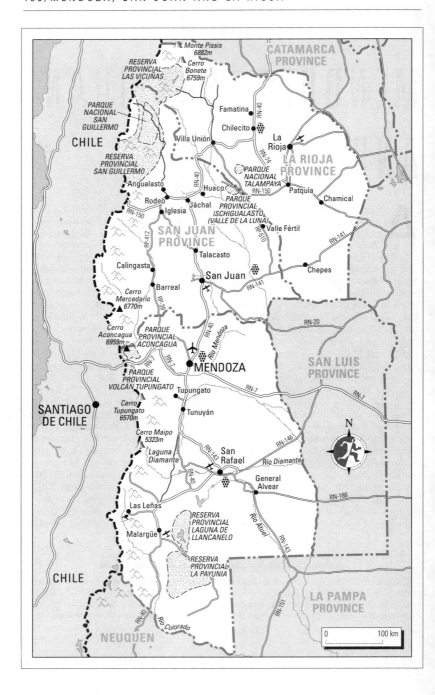

EL CUYO

Mendoza, San Juan and San Luis provinces are sometimes still referred to as **El Cuyo** and, more recently, with La Rioja thrown in, as El Nuevo Cuyo, a political entity set up to look after the region's commercial interests and international relations; while it's often dubbed *La Puerta del Cuyo*, or "gateway to the Cuyo", San Luis has closer geographical ties with Córdoba and is therefore covered with that province in Chapter Three. As for the region's name, purportedly derived from *cuyum*, meaning "sandy place", it still foxes modern linguists, who've found no trace of such a word in the native Huarpe language or any other indigenous vernacular – it's more likely that it comes from *xuyu*, a Huarpe word for river-bed. Whatever its origins, the first recorded use of Cuyo dates back to 1564 when the colonial Spanish authorities named one of the eleven Corregimientos, or administrative subdivisions, of Chile, with its capital in Mendoza. On August 1, 1776, El Cuyo, the only trans-Andean Corregimiento, was detached from the Chilean Capitanía and incorporated into the fledgling Viceroyalty of the River Plate, or proto-Argentina, but lasted only a decade as a separate entity before being swallowed up by the vast Córdoba Intendencia. Just after Argentina declared its independence, the Intendencia de Cuyo was revived under the leadership of General José de San Martín, but again was short-lived. Seven years later, in 1820, it fell apart and the provinces of Mendoza, San Luis and San Juan went their separate ways, until the Nuevo Cuyo came into being under a treaty signed by the four provincial governors – including La Rioja's – in 1988. You will often see the words Cuyo and Cuyano used by transport companies and other businesses, suggesting that a strong regional identity still lies behind this enigmatic name.

---

potatoes, herding llamas and hunting guanacos. Countless flowering **cactus** and the dazzling yellow *brea*, a broom-like shrub, add colour to the browns and greys of the desert in the spring. Winter sports can be practised at one of the continent's most exclusive resorts, **Las Leñas**, where the season is July to September. Other activities on offer are rock-climbing, mountaineering and white-water rafting and, if you're tempted by more demanding challenges, the ascension of Aconcagua or, better still, the **Mercedario** and **Tupungato** peaks.

MENDOZA PROVINCE

The southern half of this region is taken up by **Mendoza Province**, an area the size of Florida with enough attractions to occupy a whole holiday; it is the self-styled La Tierra del Sol y del Buen Vino, the "land of sunshine and good wine". Within its borders are some of the country's most dramatic mountain **landscapes**, where you can try out a host of adventure pursuits, from kayaking to hang-gliding. The urbane charms of its lively capital, the city of **Mendoza**, can satisfy yearnings for creature comforts after muscle-aching treks, tough climbs up into the Andes or an afternoon getting soaked while white-water rafting. Although Mendoza Province shares many things with the provinces of San Juan and La Rioja, to the north – bleak wildernesses with snow-peaked mountains as a backdrop, remarkably varied flora and fauna, an incredibly sunny climate prone to sudden changes in temperature due to the *zonda*, the scorching local wind, and pockets of rich farmland mainly used to produce beefy red wines – where it differs is the way it exploits all these assets. At national, not just regional, level Mendoza leads the way in **tourism** just as it does in the **wine industry**, combining professionalism with enthusiasm plus a taste for the alternative or avant-garde. Both industries come together for Mendoza city's nationally famous **Fiesta de la Vendimia**, or Wine Harvest Festival, held in early March, a slightly kitsch but exuberant bacchana-

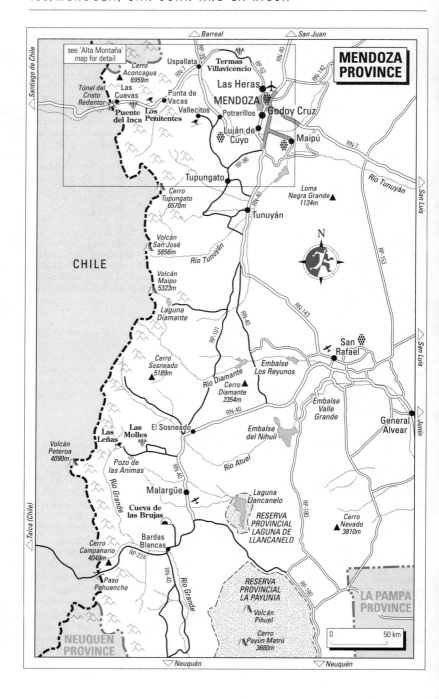

lia at which a carnival queen is elected from candidates representing every town in the province. For travelling purposes, Mendoza Province can be divided into three sections, each with its own base: the north, around the capital, has the country's biggest concentration of vineyards and top-class **wineries**, clustered around **Maipú**, while the scenic **Alta Montaña** route races up in a westerly direction towards the high Chilean border, passing the mighty **Cerro Aconcagua**, an increasingly popular destination for mountaineers from around the globe; not far to the southwest are the much more challenging **Vulcán Tupungato**, 6650m, and the remote **Laguna Diamante**, a choppy altiplanic lagoon in the shadow of the perfectly shaped **Vulcán Maipo**, which can only be visited from December to March. Central Mendoza is focused on the laid-back town of **San Rafael** where you can taste more wine, and where several tour operators offer excursions along the nearby **Cañon del Atuel**, usually taking in a beginner's-level session of white-water rafting. If skiing or snowboarding in July is your fantasy, try the winter-sports complex at **Las Leñas**, one of the world's most exclusive ski-resorts, where you'll be sharing pistes with South America's jet-set and northern-hemisphere giant-slalom champions. The third, least visited section, wraps around the southern outpost of **Malargüe**, a final frontier kind of place, promoting itself as Argentina's adventure tourism capital. Within easy reach are the mirror-like **Lago Llancanelo**, home to an enormous community of **flamingoes**, the charcoal-grey and rust-red lava-deserts of **La Payunia**, and a speleologists' delight, the karstian caves of **Caverna de la Bruja**. The province's dull, flat eastern fringe bordering on San Luis Province, and the instantly forgettable towns of General Alvear or La Paz, can be given a miss. Given that tourism is so developed in the province, it's possible to visit virtually all of these places by **public transport**, or on an organized tour, but to see them at your own pace and have many of them to yourself, consider renting a vehicle, preferably a 4WD since many of the roads are, at best, only partly sealed.

Mendoza and around

Home to nearly a million Mendocinos, **MENDOZA** is a mostly low-rise city, spread across a wide valley, that of the Río Mendoza, over 1000km west of Buenos Aires and less than 100km to the east of the highest section of the Andean cordillera – whose perennially snowcapped peaks are clearly visible from downtown. Its airy microcentro is less compact than that of most comparable cities, partly because the streets, squares and avenues were deliberately made wide when the city was rebuilt in the late nineteenth century (see below), to allow for evacuation in the event of *El Grande*, or a major earthquake. Another striking feature is that every street is lined by bushy sycamore and plane trees, providing vital shade in the scorching summer months and watered by over 500km of *acequias*, or irrigation ditches, forming a natural, outdoor air-cooling system. Watch out, though, when you cross the city's streets, as the narrow gutters are up to a metre deep and often full of gushing water, especially in the spring when the upland snows melt.

The centre of the late nineteenth-century urban layout is the park-like **Plaza Independencia**, the size of four blocks, where you'll find the city's modern art museum. Near its corners lie the four orbital squares, **Plazas Chile, San Martín, España** and **Italia**, each with its own distinctive character. Museums are not Mendoza's forte, but the **Museo de Ciencias Naturales y Antropológicas** is worth a visit. It's located in the handsomely landscaped park, **Parque General San Martín**, which slopes up a hill to the west of the microcentro and commands views of the city and its surroundings. One of the country's finest green spaces, with its avenues of planes and palms, its boating-lake, its manicured rose-garden, and a zoo, it's also the venue for the city's major event, the **Fiesta de la Vendimia**, held every March. Where Mendoza really comes into its own is as a base for some of the world's most thrilling **mountain-climbing** opportunities; treks and ascensions can be organized through a number of specialized operators in the city. In quite a different vein, you could also go on a **wine-tasting tour** of the many **bodegas** in or near the city, some traditional, some state-of-the-art. Mendoza's leading restaurants serve seafood from the Pacific coast or delicious local produce accompanied by the outstanding local wines, another reason for making the city your base for exploring the region's spectacular countryside. Within easy reach to the south of the city are two small satellite towns, **Luján de Cuyo** and **Maipú**, where in addition to the majority of the wineries you'll find a couple of museums, one displaying the paintings of Fernando Fader – a kind of Argentine van Gogh – and the other about the region's wine industry.

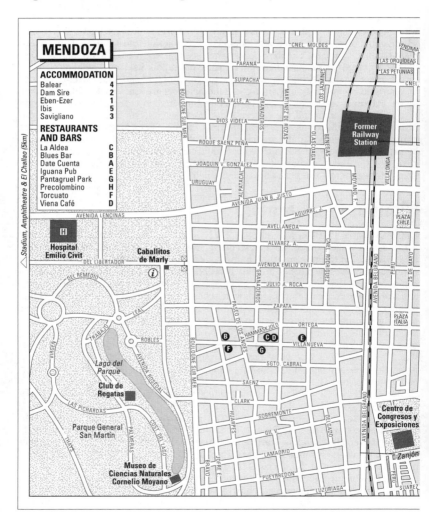

Some history

Mendoza started out as part of the **Spanish colony of Chile**, even though Santiago de Chile lies across a high, snowy mountain pass at nearly 4000m above sea level – until this century the only way across the forbidding barrier of the Andes. Despite the obstacles, in 1561 García Hurtado de Mendoza, Captain-General of Chile, sent over an expedition led by Pedro del Castillo to found a colony from which to civilize the indigenous Huarpes; Castillo founded a town and named it after his boss. Soon flourishing, Mendoza continued to be ruled from across the Andes, while its isolation enabled it to live a life of its own. The extensive network of pre-Hispanic **irrigation canals** was exploited by the colonizers, and their **vineyards** soon became South America's most productive. By 1700, the city's merchants were selling barrel-loads of their wine to Santiago, Córdoba

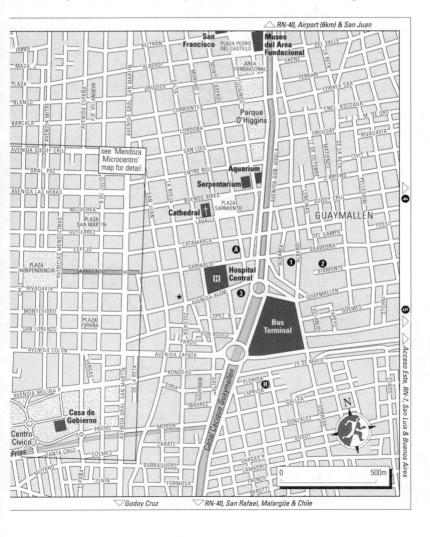

and Buenos Aires. After the Viceroyalty of the River Plate was created in 1777, Mendoza was incorporated into the huge **Córdoba Intendencia**. Mendocinos are still proud of the fact that San Martín's Army of the Andes was trained in and near their city before thrashing the Spanish Royalist troops at the Battle of Maipú, Chile, in 1818.

Suffering from its relative isolation in the newly independent Argentina, Mendoza stagnated by the mid-nineteenth century, but worse was to come. Three hundred years after its foundation, as night fell on March 20, 1861 – Holy Week – an **earthquake** smashed every building in Mendoza to rubble, and some 4000 people, a third of the population, lost their lives. Although it's believed to have been less powerful than the earthquake that was to hit nearby San Juan in 1944, at an estimated 7.8 on the Richter scale this was probably one of the worst ever to have hit South America. Seismologists now believe that the epicentre lay right in the middle of the city, just beneath the surface, explaining why the damage was so terrible and yet restricted in radius. Pandemonium ensued, God-fearing Mendocinos seeing the timing – the city's anniversary and Eastertide – as double proof of divine retribution. Thousands of refugees relied on charity from the rest of the nation, Europe and especially neighbouring Chile, but remarkably a new city was quickly built, overseen by the French urban planner **Ballofet**, who designed wide streets, open squares and low buildings for the new-look Mendoza. The city's isolation was ended soon afterwards with the arrival of the British-built railways in 1884. Another tremor in 1985 left some people in the suburbs homeless and claimed a dozen lives, and the earth continues to shake noticeably at frequent intervals, but all buildings in modern Mendoza are safely earthquake-proof, so there's nothing to be alarmed about.

The core department of Capital is home to only 120,000 people, but during the twentieth century Gran Mendoza or "Greater Mendoza" swallowed up leafy suburbs such as **Chacras de Coria** and **Las Heras**, and industrial districts, such as Godoy Cruz. Wine, petrochemicals, a thriving university and, more recently, **tourism** have been the mainstays of the economy in recent years. The effects of Chile's fast-growing economy have spilled over onto Mendoza's prosperity, and the long-neglected cultural, political and commercial ties between the city and Santiago, dating back to colonial times, have been revived over the past twenty years.

Arrival, information and city transport

Officially called Aeropuerto Internacional Ing. Francisco J. Gabrielli, but known popularly as "Plumerillo" after the suburb where it's located, Mendoza's modern and efficient little **airport** (☎0261/430-7837, 430-6484 or 448-7128) is only 7km north of the city centre, just off the RN40. As well as some shops and a bank, there's a cafeteria in the terminal. There are regular domestic flights, including several daily to and from Buenos Aires, as well as a couple of flights a day to and from Santiago de Chile. **Taxis** or *remises* are in plentiful supply, and the trip to downtown will set you back $7. **Bus #68** takes you to the corner of Calle San Juan and Avenida Além, downtown, but in the opposite direction be sure to catch one that has an "Aeropuerto" sign in the windscreen. The airport's **tourist information office** (☎0261/430-6484) doesn't seem to be open very often.

Mendoza's modern, efficient and very busy **bus station** (☎0261/431-3001) is slightly drab despite its bright-sounding name, *Terminal del Sol*, but has plenty of facilities: a small **tourist information office** (7am–11pm), bank and ATM, cafeteria and snack bars, toilets and showers, several shops – including a supermarket, and a post office. There are buses to and from just about everywhere in the country, plus Santiago de Chile, Lima, Montevideo and a number of Bolivian cities. It's located due east of the microcentro, on the edge of the suburb of Guaymallén, at the corner of Av. Gobernador Videla and Av. Acceso Este (RN7). It's less than 1km from the city centre but if the fifteen-minute walk is too much, the "Villa Nueva" trolley-bus ($0.55) is a cheaper alternative to a taxi (about $2).

The city's three **tourist information centres** are located at: Edificio Municipal, 9 de Julio 500 (daily 9am–9pm; ☎0261/449-5185); San Martín and Garibaldi (daily 8am–8pm; ☎0261/420-1333); and Av. Las Heras 670 (Mon–Fri 9am–1.30pm & 4–8.30pm, Sat 9am–1pm, closed Sun; ☎0261/425-7805). All of them dispense leaflets, maps, flyers and brochures. The **provincial tourist office** is at San Martín 1143 (daily 8am–9pm; ☎0261/420-2656, 420-2357 or 420-2800), with lots of material on the rest of the province. Further proof of Mendoza's strength in tourism is the presence of three **sub-regional tourist delegations** in the city, including one for the market town of General Alvear which is trying to attract tourists to its rather dull eastern region. You'll get an especially warm welcome at the other two: the **Casa de Malargüe** at España 1075 (Mon–Fri 9am–8pm, Sat 9am–1pm; ☎0261/429-2515) and the **Casa de San Rafael** at Av. Além 308 (Mon–Fri 8am–1pm & 2–8pm; ☎0261/420-1475). Just inside the main gates of the Parque General San Martín is another tourist office (daily 9am–8pm), mainly dispensing information about the park and its many sights; it also houses the **Dirección de Recursos Naturales Renovables** (daily 8am–1pm and 4–8pm), the administrative office where you must apply for permits to climb Aconcagua.

For an easy introduction to the city, you could take a trip on the **bus turístico** (Jan–March 10am–6pm; $5) which stops at nineteen numbered halts around the city and has English-speaking guides on board; ask for details at the tourist office at Av. San Martín and Garibaldi, where the route starts. Otherwise a number of tour operators run city tours (see box, p.472). And for finding your own way around, there are plenty of **buses** and **trolley-buses** – the latter mostly serve the inner suburbs plus the bus station, and the complex numbering system is meant to have a certain logic, though what it is escapes most people; study the map displayed at each stop. You pay a flat $0.55 fare, except for much longer distances such as the airport ($1.10); a new magnetic-card system, **Mendobus**, was recently introduced but some buses still accept coins. The pre-paid cards, worth $2 or multiples of $5, can be bought at kiosks, tourist offices, the airport and the bus terminal.

Accommodation

Compared with many Argentine cities, Mendoza's very well off for places to stay: it has more than enough beds for its needs, except during the Fiesta de la Vendimia in early March, when they're in short supply. It already boasts several luxurious **hotels**, with a couple of top-class international chain hotels about to open. **Budget** lodgings are not hard to come by either, tending to be less squalid than elsewhere in this proudly clean city – most are conveniently close to the bus terminal. Mendoza also has two outstanding official **youth hostels**, plus an unofficial but commendable third one. Also ask at the tourist office for their list of rooms to rent in private houses. In the middle range are countless, largely nondescript but very decent, smaller hotels. Campers should head for the cool heights of El Challao, 6km to the northwest, where **campsite** *El Suizo* is located among shady woods, on Av. Champagnat (☎0261/444-1991; $4 per person). It has a swimming pool, a small restaurant and even an open-air cinema. **Bus** #110 runs out to El Challao from the corner of Salta and Avenida Além.

Hostels, hospedajes and residenciales

Hospedaje Zamora, Perú 1156 (☎0261/425-7537). A neocolonial villa with clean rooms around a leafy patio. Larger rooms, with four or five beds, and group discounts. Very popular with Aconcagua climbers. ②.

Hostel Balear, Mitre 998, San José, Guaymallén (☎02685/453-516; *calias@ucongres.edu.ar*). A very friendly unofficial youth hostel. It's only 2km from the city centre and easily reached by trolley-bus "Villa Nueva". ①.

Hostel Campo Base, Mitre 946 (☎0261/429-0707; *mendoza2@hostels.org.ar*). The youth hostel preferred by Aconcagua climbers, as the owners organize their own treks. Clean, friendly and very laid-

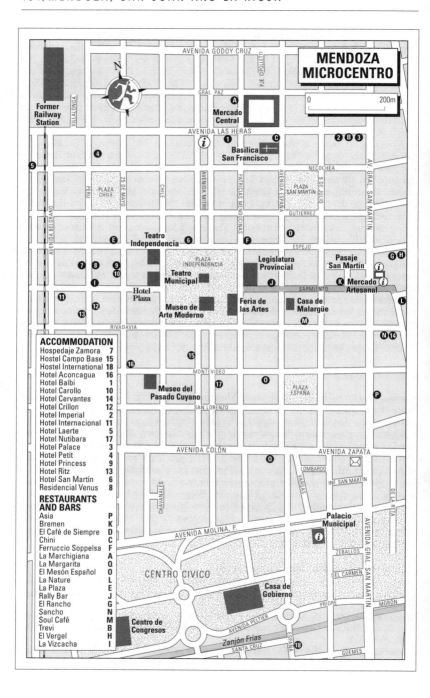

MENDOZA MICROCENTRO

0   200m

Former Railway Station

AVENIDA GODOY CRUZ
PJE CIPOLLETTI
GRAL. PAZ
Mercado Central Ⓐ
AVENIDA LAS HERAS
Ⓘ ❶ Ⓒ
Basílica San Francisco
❷ Ⓑ ❸
NECOCHEA
VILLALONGA
AVENIDA BELGRANO
PERU
PLAZA CHILE
25 DE MAYO
CHILE
AVENIDA MITRE
PATRICIAS MENDOCINAS
AVENIDA ESPAÑA
9 DE JULIO
PLAZA SAN MARTÍN
AV GRAL SAN MARTÍN
GUTIERREZ
Ⓔ
Teatro Independencia ❻
PLAZA INDEPENDENCIA
Ⓕ
Ⓓ
ESPEJO
Legislatura Provincial
Pasaje San Martín
Ⓖ Ⓗ
Ⓘ
❼ ❽ ❾ ❿
Ⓘ
Teatro Municipal
Ⓙ
SARMIENTO
Ⓚ **Mercado** Ⓘ **Artesanal**
Ⓛ
⓫
⓬
⓭
Hotel Plaza
Museo de Arte Moderno
Feria de las Artes
Casa de Malargüe
Ⓜ
RIVADAVIA

ACCOMMODATION
Hospedaje Zamora	7
Hostel Campo Base	15
Hostel International	18
Hotel Aconcagua	16
Hotel Balbi	1
Hotel Carollo	10
Hotel Cervantes	14
Hotel Crillon	12
Hotel Imperial	2
Hotel Internacional	11
Hotel Laerte	5
Hotel Nutibara	17
Hotel Palace	3
Hotel Petit	4
Hotel Princess	9
Hotel Ritz	13
Hotel San Martín	6
Residencial Venus	8

RESTAURANTS AND BARS
Asia	P
Bremen	K
El Café de Siempre	D
Chini	C
Ferruccio Soppelsa	F
La Marchigiana	A
La Margarita	Q
El Mesón Español	O
La Nature	L
La Plaza	E
Rally Bar	J
El Rancho	G
Sancho	N
Soul Café	M
Trevi	B
El Vergel	H
La Vizcacha	I

⓯
⓰
MONTEVIDEO
⓱
Ⓞ
PLAZA ESPAÑA
Museo del Pasado Cuyano
SAN LORENZO
Ⓝ ⓮
Ⓟ

AVENIDA COLÓN
AVENIDA ZAPATA
Ⓠ
LOMBARDO
INF. SAN MARTÍN
CHAVANALES
VARGAS
DE LA RETA
Palacio Municipal
Ⓘ
ZEBALLOS
AVENIDA GRAL SAN MARTÍN
AVENIDA MOLINA, P.
DEL CARMEN
MORON
CENTRO CÍVICO
Casa de Gobierno
PRIORE
Centro de Congresos
AVENIDA PELTIER
ESPAÑA
Zanjón Frías
⓲
SANTA CRUZ
GÜEMES

back atmosphere, but some of the dorms are slightly cramped. Lots of events, barbecues, parties and general fun. ①.

Hostel International, España 343 (☎0261/424-0018; *mendoza1@hostels.org.ar*). The most inviting of the three hostels, it has a bright patio, stimulating ambience, small dorms with private bathroom, an excellent kitchen, and fixes you up with tours and sports activities in the whole region. ①–②.

Residencial Dam Sire, Viamonte 410, San José, Guaymallén (☎0261/431-5142). Lovely, big rooms with bath, shared kitchen and a large terrace, in a quiet cul-de-sac. ②.

Residencial Eben-Ezer, Alberdi 580 (☎0261/431-2635). Very popular little family pension, so it's best to book ahead. You can negotiate the price for stays of a week or more. Shared bath. ②.

Residencial Savigliano, Pedro B. Palacios 944, Guaymallén (☎0261/423-7746; *savigliano@hotmail. com*). Peaceful, family-run, hostel-type place, in a pretty spotlessly clean house opposite the bus station. ②.

Residencial Venus, Perú 1155 (☎0261/425-4147). Well-maintained but with less neocolonial charm than some other *residenciales*, despite the plant-filled patio. Very clean. ②.

Hotels

Hotel Aconcagua, San Lorenzo 545 (☎0261/420-4499, fax 423-8338; *www.hotelaconcagua.com.ar*). Professionally run modern hotel, with small but comfortable rooms, with TV and minibar. A swimming pool, sauna and massage are welcome facilities. ⑦.

Hotel Balbi, Av. Las Heras 340 (☎0261/423-3500, fax 438-0626). Glitzy place with a lavish reception area, huge dining-room, and spacious rooms, with fresh decor. Swimming pool and terrace. ⑦.

Hotel Carollo, 25 de Mayo 1184 (☎0261/423-5666; *carollo@cpsarg.com*). Seventies interior with lots of leatherette; it has bright rooms, with air conditioning, and shares the swimming pool, patio and restaurant of its neighbour, the *Princess*. ⑤.

Hotel Cervantes, Amigorena 65 (☎0261/420-1782, 420-0131 or 420-0737, fax 420-1732; *www.hotel.cervantes*). Traditional-style, comfortable hotel, with pleasant rooms. Has one of the best hotel restaurants in town, the *Sancho* (see p.471). ⑤.

Hotel Crillon, Perú 1065 (☎0261/429-8494 or 423-8963, fax 423-9658; *www.hcrillon.com.ar*). One of the smartest, most charming hotels in its category, the *Crillon* has stylish furniture and new bathrooms. ⑤.

Hotel Ibis, Acceso Este 4241, Villa Nueva, Guaymallén (☎0261/426-4600, fax 421-4300). This rather anonymous chain hotel has smart, modern rooms, a swimming pool and up-to-date facilities including Internet access. ⑤.

Hotel Imperial, Gral Las Heras 88 (☎0261/423-4671). An old-fashioned but reliable hotel, with professional service and quiet, comfortable rooms. ④.

Hotel Internacional, Sarmiento 720 (☎0261/425-5606 or 429-1939; *hinternacional@lanet.com.ar*). All rooms have discreet air conditioning, lots of space and a minibar. A swimming pool and an enormous garage are two further assets. ⑥.

Hotel Laerte, J.L. Aguirre 19 (☎0261/423-0875). A typically non descript mid-range place, but the rooms are up to scratch, and the breakfasts are good value. ③.

Hotel Nutibara, Av. Mitre 867 (☎0261/429-5428; *nutibara@lanet.losandes.com.ar*). Rather dated but comfortable hotel, with large rooms, air conditioning, cable TV and efficient room service. Enormous swimming pool. ⑥.

Hotel Palace, Las Heras 70 (☎0261/423-4200 or 425-2969; *hpalace@slatinos.com.ar*). Chintzy furniture and very comfortable rooms, with newly installed bathrooms, so ignore the gloomy reception. ⑤.

Hotel Petit, Perú 1459 (☎0261/423-2099 or 429-7537; *petit@slatinos.com.ar*). Clean, airy rooms and bathrooms. Very Seventies decor, with candlewick bedspreads, but the young owners know the latest places to go at night. ③.

Hotel Princess, 25 de Mayo 1168 (☎0261/423-5666). Extremely smart rooms, with simple decor, and modern bathrooms. There's a swimming pool, too, and a part-shaded patio. ⑥.

Hotel Ritz, Perú 1008 (☎0261/423-5115). This place tries very hard to look British, and partly succeeds with its chintzy furnishing and plush fitted carpets. Air conditioning and reliable plumbing. ⑤.

Hotel San Martín, Espejo 435 (☎0261/438-0677, fax 438-0875). Pleasant if nondescript hotel with bright, airy rooms overlooking Plaza Independencia. Air conditioning, TV and garage. ④.

The City

Mendoza's sights are few and far between, but a couple of its museums are worth seeing, namely the **Museo del Pasado Cuyano**, which offers an insight into late nineteenth-century life for the city's richer families, and the **Museo de Ciencias Naturales y Antropológicas Juan Cornelio Moyano**, with a wide-ranging scientific exhibition. The latter is located in the magnificently landscaped **Parque General San Martín**, and it's the wide avenues, lively plazas and green parks that really make Mendoza. The ruins of colonial Mendoza's nucleus, where it was founded between the Guaymallén and Tajamar canals, to the northeast of the present-day centre, have been preserved as the **Área Fundacional**, where there's a small museum. The most impressive sight in the whole city, however, is the historic **Bodega Escorihuela** (see p.474), the outstandingly beautiful **winery** in Godoy Cruz, a southern suburb.

Mendoza has the most complicated **street-name system** of any city in Argentina. Streets that run north–south keep the same name from end to end, but those that run west–east avenues have up to four names within the city limits alone. From west to east, names change at Avenida Belgrano, Avenida San Martín and Avenida Gobernador R. Videla, the latter running along the Guaymallén canal, the city's eastern boundary. Beyond it lies the residential town of Guaymallén, part of Greater Mendoza, itself divided into several districts, where you'll find the bus terminal, a cluster of budget accommodation, a number of restaurants and a couple of wineries. On all street-signs is a useful number telling you how many blocks you are from the city's point zero, at San Martín and Sarmiento; 100 (O) means one block west, 500 (N) five blocks north. Paseo Sarmiento, a busy pedestrian precinct lined with loads of shops and cafés with terraces, joins Plaza Independencia, the city's centre-point, to Avenida San Martín.

For an overview of the city, to get your bearings, and to enjoy unobstructed views towards the Andes, preferably in the morning when the mountains are lit by the rising sun, you can take a lift up to the **Terraza Mirador**, on the roof of the **Palacio Municipal**, at 9 de Julio 500 (Mon, Wed & Fri 8.30am–1pm, Tues, Thurs & Sat 8.30am–1pm & 4–7pm; free).

Plaza Independencia

Four blocks in size, **Plaza Independencia** lies at the nerve-centre of the post-earthquake city and at the crossroads of two of Mendoza's main streets, east–west Avenida Sarmiento and north–south Avenida Mitre. Originally intended to be the administrative headquarters – which were built instead in the Centro Civico, four blocks to the south – it's the modern city's recreational and cultural focus, planted with shady acacias, magnolias, sycamores and other trees. It is also the setting for festivals, concerts and outdoor cinema-screenings, and both during the day and on summer evenings it bustles with life. During remodelling in 1995, monumental fountains, backed by a mosaic mural depicting the story of Argentina's independence, were installed, and beneath them is a late nineteenth-century bunker originally designed as an emergency hospital to deal with quake victims. It now houses the **Museo Municipal de Arte Moderno** (Mon–Sat 9am–1pm & 5–9pm, Sun 5–9pm; free), where temporary exhibitions of Argentine art are displayed. Along the eastern edge, a crafts fair is held at weekends. Just to the west of the central fountains stands a seventeen-metre-high steel structure, dating from 1942, on which a mass of coloured lights form the national coat-of-arms at night. Beyond it, along Calle Chile, are a number of prestigious buildings including, between Avenida Sarmiento and Rivadavia, the **Colégio Nacional Agustín Alvarez**, housed in a fine Art Nouveau quake-proof edifice of re-inforced concrete. Just north of it, on the corner of Sarmiento, is the illustrious 1920s **Plaza Hotel**, famous because the Peróns stayed there soon after meeting in San Juan. It's currently undergoing long-overdue refurbishment and is due to reopen in early

2001 as a five-star luxury hotel. Next door is the Neoclassical facade of the **Teatro Independencia**, one of the city's more traditional playhouses while, over on the eastern side of the plaza, is the **Legislatura Provincial**, built in 1889 but remodelled to take on its present grim appearance in 1918.

Plaza España

The small plaza that lies a block east and a block south of Independencia's southeast corner, called Plaza Montevideo until 1949, is now known as **Plaza España**. It's the most beautiful of all Mendoza's plazas – its benches are decorated with brightly coloured Andalucian ceramic tiles and the paths are lined with luxuriant trees and shrubs. Although Mendoza's population is of overwhelmingly Italian origin, the city's old, traditional families came from Spain, and they had the square built in the late 1940s. The mellow terracotta flagstones, picked out with smaller blue and white tiles, and the lily ponds and fountains set off the slightly creepy monument to the Spanish discovery of South America, standing at the southern end of the plaza. It comprises a *zócalo* or brightly tiled pedestal, decorated with scenes from *Don Quixote* and the Argentine epic *Martín Fierro*, along with Columbus's discovery and depictions of missionary work. At the centre of the plinth stand two female statues: one is a Spanish noblewoman clasping a book, the other a *mestiza*-looking woman, a Mendocina, holding a bunch of grapes. Dancing and folk music take place here on October 12, on **el día de la Hispanidad**, an international feast-day celebrating Spanishness.

Plaza Italia and Museo del Pasado Cuyano

Four blocks west of Plaza España's northwest corner along Calle Montevideo – an attractive street lined with plane trees and picturesque neocolonial houses with brightly coloured facades – is **Plaza Italia**, called Plaza Lima until 1900, but renamed when its Italian community built two monuments to their country of origin here. A monument in the south side of the square is a bronze statue of the mythical Roman wolf feeding Romulus and Remus, next to a marble Roman pillar. The main monument, to its west, in stone and bronze, represents La Patria, flanked by a statue of an Indian and a Roman philosopher. A frieze running around the monument, showing scenes of building, ploughing and harvesting, is a tribute to Italian immigrants whose hard labour helped build the new country. In November the park blazes with the bright red flowers of its tipas. In March, during the week leading up to the main celebrations of the Wine Harvest Festival, the plaza hosts the **Festa in Piazza**, a big party at which stalls representing every Italian region serve their local food specialities. The climax is an extravagant fashion parade.

Half a block east of the plaza's northeast corner is the **Museo del Pasado Cuyano** (Tues–Sat 9am–12.30pm; $1; ☎0261/423-6031) at Montevideo 544. It's the city's history museum, housed in part of an aristocratic late nineteenth-century mansion, the Quinta de los Civit. The adobe house, built to resist earthquakes, belonged to the family of Francisco Civit, Governor of Mendoza, and his son Emilio, who was a senator at the turn of the twentieth century and was responsible for many of Mendoza's civic works, including the great park. It contains a large amount of San Martín memorabilia and eighteenth-century furniture, artworks and weapons, all rescued from the earthquake rubble. The most valuable exhibit is a fabulous fifteenth-century polychrome **wooden altarpiece**, with a liberal dose of rosy cherubim, that somehow turned up here from Sant Andreu de Socarrats in Catalonia, and is now housed in the mansion's chapel.

Plaza San Martín and Plaza Chile

The square to the northeast of Plaza Independencia is the relatively nondescript **Plaza San Martín**; it's dominated by an early twentieth-century statue of General San Martín on a horse, looking towards the Andes he crossed with the Army of the Andes to defeat the Spanish. This square was previously called Plaza Cobo in honour of another local hero, the entrepreneur who introduced the vital Lombardy poplar to the region – the poplar not only acts as a windbreak, but its smooth, lightweight wood is also perfect for making fruit crates. Near its northwest corner is the city's only church of note, the **Basílica de San Francisco**, one of the first buildings to go up after the 1861 tremor. Its Belgian architect modelled it on Paris's Église de la Trinité, but its raspberry-pink and cream painted stucco make it look neocolonial rather than Neoclassical. This isn't the complete picture, either, as part of the structure had to be demolished after another quake in 1927, leaving the church looking a bit truncated. Despite its architectural shortcomings, it's locally venerated, since part of San Martín's family are buried in simple tombs inside. A special chamber up the stairs next to the altar (Mon–Sat 9am–noon; free) contains a revered image of *Our Lady of Carmen*, the patron saint of the Army of the Andes, along with San Martín's stylish rosewood staff, with a topaz hilt and a silver tip – it, too, has the status of a religious relic among the people of Mendoza, but if nothing else is a fine piece of craftsmanship.

The surrounding district is Mendoza's **"City"**, or financial barrio, whose opulent banks and insurance company offices are among the city's most impressive buildings, most built in a "British" style. The Banco de Galicia, the Banco de la Nación and the Banco de Mendoza, to name but three, were built in the 1920s and 1930s, the city's heyday. Lying on the eastern side of Plaza San Martín, diagonally opposite the basilica, the **Banco de Mendoza**, with its eight-sided lobby crowned with a huge stained-glass cupola, is certainly worth a look inside.

Four blocks west of Plaza San Martín is the least interesting of the four so-called orbital plazas, **Plaza Chile**. It got its name in recognition of Chile's assistance after the 1861 quake, and its centrepiece, shaded by towering palms, is a monument to the heroes of the two countries' independence, José de San Martín and Bernardo O'Higgins, seldom seen together in a sculpture – this is a 1947 piece by a Chilean artist. The plaza is shaded by an enormous *aguaribay* tree.

Área Fundacional

Built on the Plaza Mayor where the city was originally founded, 1km northeast of Plaza Independencia, is the **Museo del Área Fundacional**, at Alberdi and Videla Castillo (Tues–Sat 8am–8pm, Sun 2–8pm; $1.50; *museofun@impsat1.com.ar*). The modern building houses an exhibition of domestic and artistic items retrieved from the rubble, after the mammoth eathquake of 1861. It's built over part of the excavated colonial city foundations, which you can peer at through a glass floor. The exhibition relates the story of Mendoza's foundation and development before and after the great disaster. Nearby, across landscaped Plaza Pedro del Castillo, named for the city's founder, are the eerie ruins of the colonial city's Jesuit temple, popularly but erroneously known as the Ruinas de San Francisco. Immediately south extends a rather straggly park, the Parque Bernardo O'Higgins. At its southern end, you'll find the city aquarium and the **Serpentario Anaconda** (daily 9am–1pm 3.30–8pm; $2), a kind of large greenhouse with a varied and impressive collection of snakes, poisonous toads and spiders, some of them, disturbingly, native to the region.

Parque General San Martín

Just over 1km due west of Plaza Independencia by Avenida Sarmiento, on a slope that turns into a steep hill overlooking the city, **Parque General San Martín** is one of the most beautiful parks in the country. As well as large areas of open parkland, used for impromptu football matches and picnics, its four square kilometres contain the main football stadium, the amphitheatre where the grand finale of the Wine Harvest Festival is staged, a meteorological observatory, a monument to the Army of the

Andes, a rowing-lake, a tennis club, a hospital, the university campus, the riding club, an agricultural research centre, several restaurants, the best jogging routes in Mendoza, a rose-garden and an anthropological museum – in short, a city within the city.

First created in 1897 by **Charles Thays** (see box on p.107), it was extensively remodelled in 1940 by local architect, Daniel Ramos Correas. It contains over 50,000 trees of 750 varieties, planted among other reasons to stop landslides from the Andean foothills. The aristocratic Avenida de los Plátanos and Avenida de las Palmeras, lined with tall plane trees and Canary Island palms, and the romantic Rose Garden, with its 500 rose varieties and arbours of wisteria, are popular walks.

The main entrance is through magnificent bronze and wrought-iron gates, topped with a rampant condor, at the western end of Avenida Emilio Civit. They were not, as a popular legend would have it, ordered for Ottoman Sultan Hamid II, who couldn't pay the bill; the crescent motif in their fine lace-like design, lying behind the apocryphal anecdote, was simply a fashionable pattern at the time. The gates were ordered by the city authorities in 1910, to celebrate the country's centenary, and were made by the McFarlane ironworks in Glasgow. Just inside the park, next to a bronze bust of Thays, is the tourist information office (see p.463). A road open to traffic runs westwards from here, along the northern edge of the park, after going round the Caballitos de Marly, an exact reproduction in Carrara marble of the monumental horses in the middle of Paris' Place de la Concorde. From here you can rent a bike, take a horse and cart or catch a bus to the farthest points in the park. The nearby **Fuente de los Continentes** is a dramatic set of sculptures meant to represent the diversity of humankind, and a favoured backdrop for newly weds' photographs.

A good 2km west is the city's **zoo** (Tues–Sun 9am–6pm, $3; ☎0261/425-0130), one of the best in the country for its variety of animals and, more to the point, for the conditions in which they are kept. It's a landscaped forest of eucalyptus, aguaribay and fir trees, built into the lower slopes of the Cerro de la Gloria, from which also you get sweeping views of the city.

Another popular destination is the top of the Cerro de la Gloria, where there's an imposing 1914 monument to the Army of the Andes, the **Monumento al Ejército Libertador**, built for the anniversary of the Battle of Chacabuco. All cast in bronze, a buxom, winged *Liberty*, waving broken chains, leads General San Martín and his victorious troops across the cordillera. Around the granite plinth are bronze friezes depicting more picturesque scenes: the anti-royalist monk Luis Beltrán busy making weapons for the army, or the genteel ladies of Mendoza donating their jewellery for the good cause – these "Patricias Mendocinas", after whom a city street is named, were rumoured to have been particularly excited by the presence of so many soldiers billeted in the city; babies and infants sadly watch their valiant fathers head off to battle. Sometimes condors alight on the top of this grandiose monument.

At the southern tip of the park's one-kilometre-long serpentine rowing-lake, in its southeastern corner, is the **Museo de Ciencias Naturales y Antropológicas Juan Cornelio Moyano** (Tues–Fri 8am–1pm & 2–7pm, Sat & Sun 3–7pm; $2; ☎0261/428-7666). It's housed in an appropriate yacht-style building, designed in the 1930s by local architects who introduced German Rationalism to Argentina. The museum, named after the first Governor of Mendoza, who wanted the city to have lots of museums, is a series of mostly private collections of stuffed animals, ancient fossils, indigenous artefacts and mummies. The most interesting exhibits are a female mummy discovered at over 5000m in the Andes – along with a brightly coloured shawl, shrunken heads from Ecuador, and fossils or skeletons of dinosaurs unearthed near Malargüe in southern Mendoza. Sometimes temporary exhibitions about pre-Columbian civilizations or paleontological subjects are staged here.

Eating, drinking and nightlife

This is the prosperous capital of Argentina's western region, and the produce grown in the nearby oases is tip-top; as a result, Mendoza's many, varied and often highly sophisticated **restaurants** and **wine bars** are usually full, and serve some of the best food and drink in the country. Its bars are lively, it has a well-developed café-terrace culture and **nightlife** is vibrant, mostly concentrated in outlying places such as El Challao, to the northwest, Las Heras, to the north, and most fashionably Chacras de Coria, to the south. Unless you can find a discount flyer in a bar, you'll be paying the full whack of $15 to get into any of them.

Restaurants

Asia, San Martín 821. About the only Oriental restaurant worth mentioning in the city – it has a conventional *tenedor libre* buffet, but everything is fresh and tastes good.

Date Cuenta, Monte Caseros 1177. The best vegetarian restaurant in the city; bright decor and friendly staff are added bonuses to the food which is more imaginative than in most veggie places: stuffed vegetables, vegetarian *locro* and wonderful fruit dishes.

Don Mario, 25 de Mayo and Paso de los Patos, Guaymallén. An institutional parrilla, frequented by Mendocino families in search of comforting decor and an old-fashioned parrillada.

Lomo Loco, Av. San Martín Sur, 3001, Godoy Cruz. Trendy modern place, with an unappealing exterior, but inside it buzzes with youthfulness and the *lomitos* and *chivitos* are the best in town.

Francis Mallmann, Belgrano 1188, Godoy Cruz (☎0261/424-2698 & 424-3336). This ultra-chic wine bar and restaurant named after its chef, with fashion-model staff, swish decor and crystal wineglasses – rare in Argentina – is located next to the sumptuous Bodega Escorihuela and serves the bodega's fine wines with a balanced menu, including Patagonian lamb, trout from Malargüe and plums from General Alvear.

Mama Africa, Olavarria s/n, Lunlunta, Luján de Cuyo. As the name indicates, an African-themed restaurant – the decor is jungley and savannah-like, while the food is basically a parrillada dressed up to seem like camel or hippo; but it's fun and delicious.

WINE FESTIVAL

Mendoza's main festival is the giant **Fiesta de la Vendimia**, or Wine Harvest Festival, which reaches its climax during the first weekend of March every year. Wine seems to take over the city – bottles even decorate boutique windows – and the tourist trade shifts into top gear. On the Sunday before the carnival proper, the *Bendición de los Frutos* or Blessing of the Grapes takes place, in a ceremony involving the Bishop of Mendoza. During the week leading up to the grand finale, events range from folklore concerts in the Centro Cívico to Italian food and entertainment in the *Piazza Italia*. On the Friday evening is the Vía Blanca, a parade of illuminated floats through the central streets, while on the Saturday it's the *Carrusel*, when a carnival parade winds along the same route, each department in the province sending a float from which a previously elected beauty queen and her jealous entourage of runners-up fling local produce, ranging from grapes and flowers to watermelons and packets of pasta, into the cheering crowds lining the road. On the Saturday evening, the *Acto Central* is held in an amphitheatre in the Parque San Martín; it's a gala performance of song, dance and general kitschorama, compered by local TV celebs, eventually leading up to a drawn-out vote – by political leaders representing each department in the province – to elect the Queen of the festival. The same show is re-run, minus the election and therefore for a much lower entrance price – and less tedium – on the Sunday evening. The spectacle costs millions of pesos, and is a huge investment by the local wine-growers, but as it's attended by some 25,000 people it seems to be financially viable. It boasts that it's the biggest such festival in South America and one of the most lavish wine-related celebrations in the world. For more information contact the city's tourist office or Web site.

La Margarita, Colón 248. Chunky, succulent pizzas and fresh pasta in bright modern setting, with a big terrace, good music and friendly staff.

La Marchigiana, Patricias Mendocinas 1550 (☎0261/423-0751). This is *the* Italian restaurant in the city, run by the same family for decades. For a reasonable price you can eat fresh asparagus from the oasis, have delicious cannelloni, and finish with one of the best tiramisus in the country.

El Mesón Español, Montevideo 244. Wonderfully old-fashioned, intimate and atmospheric, this traditional Spanish restaurant serves specialities such as rabbit in a sherry sauce and Rioja wines.

La Nature, Garibaldi 63. Vegetarian and health-food restaurant serving run-of-the-mill, but totally fresh, appetizing food.

Pantagruel Park, Av. Arístides Villanueva 332. One of the best pizzerias in the city, dishing up an array of toppings on delicious crusts, until the early hours.

La Plaza, 25 de Mayo and Espejo. A traditional parrilla housed in beautiful neocolonial surroundings, with an extensive wine-list, all reasonably priced.

Precolombino, Florida 490, Dorrego, Guaymallén. As the name suggests it specializes in traditional Andean dishes such as *tamales*, *locro* and *empanadas*, plus all kinds of modern adaptations of traditional pre-Hispanic fare. Great atmosphere and frequent live music.

Safari Inn, Los Pescadores 2073, Las Heras. Another of the city's more imaginative restaurants, serving mock-African food in a jungle-like decor. Tropical evenings laid on at weekends.

Sancho, Amigorena 65. Conventional meals such as *milanesas* and steaks, together with pasta and fish dishes, are on offer at this institutional establishment.

Torcuato, Av. Arístides Villanueva 650. This gourmet restaurant transforms the region's outstanding produce – meat, fish, vegetables and wine – into something resembling *haute cuisine*, at fairly high prices.

Trevi, Las Heras 68. You could be in Bologna or Genoa in this home-style northern Italian restaurant with old-fashioned, discreet service, dowdy decor and delicious food. The *menú ejecutivo* is one of the best-value lunches in the city at $8.

El Vergel, Catamarca 76. The third of the main vegetarian restaurants in Mendoza, it's an excellent place to come for a crisp salad, for vegetarian pasta or a delicious fruit tart.

La Vizcacha, Av. Sarmiento and Av. Perú. Extremely commendable parrilla, serving decent pasta as well as top-notch grills, in very pleasant surroundings.

Bars and cafés

La Aldea, Av. Arístides Villanueva 495. A lively pub-style bar that does great sandwiches and *lomitos*.

Blues Bar, Av. Arístides Villanueva 687. Atmospheric bar with live music – jazz, rock and tango as well as blues – at weekends.

Bremen, Paseo Sarmiento and 9 de Julio. As you'd expect, this German-style beer-house serves up large steins of foaming Pilsener and can rustle up a mean ham sandwich.

El Café de Siempre, Av. España 1241. Typical City café, frequented by sharp-suited business people working in the nearby banks and offices; good for people-watching, and excellent coffee to boot.

Chini, España and Las Heras. One of the best ice-creameries in the city, doing dozens of flavours, but the best are the range of *dulce de leche*-based ones.

Ferruccio Soppelsa, Belgrano and Emilio Civit, Espejo 299 and Paseo Sarmiento 45. This chain of *heladerías* run by the same Italian family for years is guaranteed to give you enough calories to run to the top of Aconcagua.

Iguana Pub, Av. Arístides Villanueva and Coronel Oloscoaga. Funky decor and good music, enormous cocktails and hunky sandwiches at this fun bar.

Mexicana, Palmares Open Mall, Ruta Panamericana 2650. Very popular meeting-place for young people, happy to make one Corona last all evening, with top-rate salsa music, and live bands at weekends.

Rally Bar, Paseo Sarmiento and Av. España. You can't miss this bar with its now slightly clichéd car chassis crashing through the fascia; good drinks, smart interior and a lively ambience, with a crowded terrace, graced with comfortable seats.

El Rancho, Galería Tonsa, Av. San Martín and Catamarca. One of the liveliest downtown bars, often used as a meeting-place. Now a city institution.

El Rincón Suizo, RN7, Luján de Cuyo. Swiss and Argentine food, the pretext for young people set on meeting up and having a great time.

Soul Café, Rivadavia and 9 de Julio. Fun little café, playing mostly soul music as the name suggests, and serving up delicious snacks.

Viena Café, Av. Arístides Villanueva 471. Arty little tea room-cum-snack-bar, with tiny patio, properly brewed tea, and a warm welcome.

Nightclubs

Aloha, Ruta Panamericana s/n, Chacras de Coria. Extremely fashionable disco, frequented by a thirties crowd. Best on Saturdays, but also open Friday and Sunday. Argentine music.

Let's Go, Ruta Panamericana s/n, Chacras de Coria. Mostly couples in their thirties, dancing the night away to an international repertoire.

Omero, Av. Champagnat s/n, El Challao. Tends to be busiest on Fridays; great atmosphere, eminently danceable music and a varied crowd.

Queen, Ejército de los Andes 656, Dorrego, Guaymallén (*www.queen_mza.com.ar*). The city's main gay nightclub, open all night Fri & Sat. Cocktails, shows and even an alternative Fiesta de la Vendimia in March.

Runner, Ruta Panamericana, Chacras de Coria. Techno and *marcha* music dominate at this trendy disco patronized mostly by the under-25s.

Shyriu, Av. Champagnat s/n, El Challao. This club comes into its own on Sundays, thereby completing a weekend of clubbing for those who absolutely must go out every night.

Listings

Airlines Aerolíneas and Austral, Paseo Sarmiento 82 (☎0261/420-4185 or 420-4170) and at the airport (☎0261/448-7320); Aeroflot, Catamarca 7 (☎0261/429-0196); Aeroperú, Mexicana, Pluna and Varig, Rivadavia 209 (☎0261/429-5898 or 429-3706); Air Canada, Air New Zealand and United, Espejo 183 (☎0261/423-4683 or 438-1643); Alitalia and Lloyd Aereo Boliviano, Morón 20 (☎0261/423-8206); American Airlines, Av. España 943 (☎0261/425-9078); Avant, Espejo 285 (☎0261/420-0199); Avianca, San Lorenzo 55 (☎0261/429-6077); British Airways and LACSA, San Lorenzo 55 (☎0261/429-2375); Cubana, Montevideo 21 (☎0261/423-4582); Dinar, Sarmiento 119 (☎0261/420-4520/1); Iberia, Rivadavia 180 (☎0261/429-5609); Kaiken, Rivadavia 209 (☎0261/438-0243); KLM, 9 de Julio 968 (☎0261/429-4984); LAN-Chile, Espejo 128 (☎0261/420-4302 or 448-7387); LAPA, España 1012 (☎0261/429-1061); Lufthansa and LAPSA, España 1057 (☎0261/429-6287); Southern Winds, Rivadavia 209 (☎0261/420-4827); TAN, VASP and Ecuatoriana, España 1008 (☎0261/434-0240); TAPSA, airport (☎0261/423-8889 or 448-7356).

Banks Boston, Necochea 165; Citibank, San Martín 1098; Exprinter, San Martín 1198; Río, San Martín and Montevideo; Maguitur, Av. San Martín 1203; Banco Mendoza, Av. San Martín and Gutiérrez. ATMs everywhere.

TOURS FROM MENDOZA

The most popular tours from Mendoza are the day-long round trip into the **Alta Montaña** (see p.477), going as far as the Cristo Redentor on the Chilean border when weather permits, and half-day **wine tours**, taking in two or more bodegas near the city. From December and March you can go on a day-trip to **Laguna Diamante** (see p.484), while the half-day excursion to **Villavicencio** (see p.483) is a favourite option throughout the year. Many tour operators also offer longer trips as far afield as La Payunia, Cañón del Atuel, Talampaya and Ischigualasto, but they're better visited from Malargüe, San Rafael, San Juan or La Rioja. Depending on the type of trip and the number of people travelling, prices range from $15 for a half-day to $40–50 for full-day tours, seldom including meals. For the more energetic, several operators organize **mountain-bike** tours in the foothills and **white-water rafting** on the Río Mendoza, west of the city, costing $30-70.

ARGENTINE WINE

While Argentina's earliest recorded vineyard is the late sixteenth-century one at Jesús María in Córdoba Province (see p.254), and the wines of Cafayate in Salta Province (see p.422) are deservedly becoming better known nationally and internationally, the heart of the country's wine industry has always been **Mendoza**. To the north, the provinces of **La Rioja**, whose wineries are concentrated around Chilecito and Anillaco (where former President Menem's family built their wealth and power on wine), and **San Juan** also produce great wines, as do isolated wineries as far south as **Río Negro**, commercializing their produce as Patagonian wines. Nonetheless Mendoza steadfastly remains Argentina's answer to Bordeaux – an apt comparison since its producers still look to France for inspiration, for names such as **Comte de Valmont**, **Pont l'Evêque** or **Carcassonne**, and for vinification methods – such as imitations of Sauternes, Beaujolais and Champagne. Three quarters of the country's total production comes from the province's vines, mostly concentrated in the oases that spread across the valley to the south of the city, centred on Maipú and Luján de Cuyo. **San Rafael**, the heart of the province, is another major wine-growing centre (see p.485).

Mendoza's vines were originally planted by **colonizers from Chile**, theoretically for producing communion wine. In recent years, prosperous Chilean wine-growers, who got their act together faster than the Argentines, have been buying up many of the vineyards in the Mendoza area. Whereas, in terms of popularity, Argentina's wines are beginning to catch up with Chile's, long established bestsellers in North America, Europe and the Far East, they're still far less known outside the country. However, some wine experts think that, within a decade, Argentina's vintages will outstrip those of its western neighbour, in terms of quality, reflecting the sunnier climate, cleaner air and richer soil.

The main reason for the improvement in Argentina's wines is that the domestic market has become much more demanding, in terms of quality, and the market share taken up by superior *vinos finos* and *reservas* has rocketed in the past decade or two. **Table wines** still dominate, often sold in huge *dama-joanas* – demijohn flagons – that people drag along to the vintners for a refill. These are sometimes marketed under usurped names such as *borgoña*, or Burgundy, and Chablis. But younger Argentines increasingly prefer fizzy drinks or beer with their daily meals, drinking wine on special occasions and often preferring the lighter **New Wave** wines such as Chandon's **Nuevo Mundo**.

Although the most attractive wineries to visit are the old-fashioned ones (see the box on bodegas on p.474), with atmospheric musty cellars crammed with ancient oak barrels, some of the finest wines are now produced by growers who've invested in the latest equipment, including mammoth stainless-steel vats, hygienic storage-tanks lined with epoxy resin, and computerized temperature controls. They tend to concentrate on making varietal wines, the main grape varieties being riesling, chenin blanc and chardonnay, for whites, and pinot noir, cabernet sauvignon and malbec, for reds – Argentine reds tend to be better than whites. Malbec is often regarded as the Argentine grape par excellence, giving rich fruity wines, with overtones of blackcurrant and prune, that are the perfect partner for a juicy steak. The latest trend is for a balanced combination of two grapes rather than just the one: for example, mixing malbec for its fruitiness and cabernet for its body, while toning down the sometimes excessive oakiness that characterized Argentine wines in the 1980s. Growers have also been experimenting with previously less popular varieties such as tempranillo, san gervase, gewurztraminer, syrah and merlot. Very convincing sparkling wines are being made locally by the *méthode champenoise*, including those produced by Chandon and Mumm, the French champagne-makers.

Unlike Chile, where most of the best wine is exported, Argentina consumes a lot of its premium wines. Mendoza's restaurants are beginning to be more ambitious, too, offering extensive wine-lists including older, more subtle wines – but beware of the exorbitant corkage charges. Wine-grower names to look for are **Bianchi, Chandon, Etchart, Graffigna, Navarro Correas, Norton** and **Weinert**.

Car rental Andina, Sarmiento 129 (☎0261/438-0480); Aramendi, San Lorenzo 245 (☎0261/429-1857); Aruba, Primitivo de la Reta 936 (☎0261/423-4071); Avis, Primitivo de la Reta 914 (☎0261/429-6403); Herbst, Chile 1124 (☎0261/423-3000); Localiza, Gutiérrez 470 (☎0261/444-9149); Thrifty, Colón 241 (☎0261/423-5640).

Consulates Bolivia, Garibaldi 380 (☎0261/429-2458); Brazil, Pedro Molina 497 (☎0261/438-0038); Chile, Emilio Civit 599 (☎0261/425-4844); Ecuador, Francisco Moyano 1597 (☎0261/423-3197); Germany, Montevideo 127 (☎0261/429-6539); Peru, España 603 (☎0261/429-6270); Spain, Agustín Alvarez 455 (☎0261/425-3947).

Hospital Hospital Central, José F. Moreno and Av. Além (☎0261/420-0600 or 420-0063).

Internet Café Country, J.V. Zapata 189; Cyb@rexpress, Espejo 264.

Laundry Angelita, Ituzaingó, 3092; Ariel, Av. San Martín 251; La Lavandería, San Lorenzo 338; LaveRap, Colón 547 and Mitre 1623; Lavandería Necochea, Necochea 733; Tahiti, Garibaldi 255.

Left luggage At bus terminal, open 24hr.

Pharmacies Del Aguila, Av. San Martín and Buenos Aires; Del Centro, Colón 457, José V. Zapata 271; Del Puente, San Martín 1288; El Mercado Av. Las Heras 301; Franco Andina, Av. San Martín 1221.

Police Patricias Mendocinas and Montevideo (☎0261/429-4444); Federal Police, Perú 1049 (☎0261/423-8710).

Post office San Martín and Colón (☎0261/424-9777).

BODEGAS IN OR NEAR MENDOZA

These are the most interesting wineries that can be visited in the Mendoza area, but bear in mind that some of those near San Rafael (see p.485) are also worth visiting. Bodegas **Chandon**, **Santa Ana**, **Peñaflor** and **La Rural** are often included in the tours organized by the city's many operators, but many of the following can be visited by public transport. They're concentrated in the eastern suburb of Guaymallén and in the two satellite towns of Maipú and Luján de Cuyo, about 12km to the south, but one of the most beautiful, **Bodega Escorihuela**, is only 2km south of the city centre, in Godoy Cruz. If you're planning your own trip, it's worth asking at a tourist office or call ahead to check times, to book a tour in high season, and to ask for an English-speaking guide if you need one – and where available. All tours and tastings are free, but you're pointedly steered to a sales area at the end of most visits. Try and see different kinds of wineries, ranging from the old-fashioned, traditional bodegas to the highly mechanized, ultra-modern producers; at the former you're more likely to receive personal attention and get a chance to taste finer wines. Some wineries have a restaurant on the premises, as Argentines wisely prefer to eat when they drink. Buses referred to can be caught at the bus terminal or along Avenida San Martín; for transport to Maipú and central Luján de Cuyo, see pp.476 and 477.

Chandon, Agrelo 5507, Luján de Cuyo (☎0261/490-9966). Tours Feb–Mar Mon–Fri 9.30am, 11am, 12.30pm, 2pm, 3.30pm & 5pm; Sat 9.30am, 11am & 12.30pm. Apr–Jan Mon–Fri 9.30am, 11am, 2pm & 3.30pm. One of the more modern bodegas, somewhat lacking in character but impressive all the same; the tours start with a video, end up at the salesroom and are on the slick side, but the wine tasting is excellent. Bus #380.

Domaine St Diego, Franklin Villanueva 3821, Maipú (☎0261/439-5557, fax 499-0414). Tours daily 10am–6pm, limited numbers. Small producer, specializing in Cabernet Sauvignon. One of the more intimate wineries in the region.

Escorihuela, Belgrano 1188 and Presidente Alvear, Godoy Cruz (☎0261/424-2744). Tours daily 9.30am, 10.30am, 11.30am, 12.30pm, 2.30pm & 3.30pm daily. This historic bodega, founded in 1884, is famous for its fantastic and enormous barrel from Nancy, a work of art in itself, housed in a cathedral-like cellar. The sumptuous buildings include an art-gallery, huge vaulted storage rooms stacked with aromatic casks, and

Taxis Mendocar (☎0261/423-6666); Radiotaxi (☎0261/430-3300); Remis Car (☎0261/429-8734); Radiomóvil (☎0261/445-5855); Mendoza Remis (☎0261/432-0582; ISIC reductions).

Telephones Fonobar, Paseo Sarmiento 23 (☎0261/429-2957); Teléfonos Mendoza, San Martín and Rivadavia (☎0261/438-1291); Sertel, San Martín and Las Heras (☎0261/438-0219).

Tour operators Argentina Rafting, Potrerillos (☎02624/482037; *arg_rafting@hotmail.com*); Aymará, 9 de Julio 983 (☎0261/420-0607; *aymara@satlink.com*); Betancourt Rafting, Río Cuevas and RN40, Godoy Cruz (☎0261/439-1949; *betancourt@lanet.com.ar*); Campo Base Adventures and Expeditions, Av. Mitre 946 (☎0261/429-0707; *www.campo-base.com.ar*, *info@campo-base.com.ar*); El Cristo, Espejo 228 (☎0261/429-1911, fax 429-6911); Exploradores, (☎0261/425-6181; *jasanchi@lanet.com.ar*); Holding, Av. España 1030 (☎0261/423-1352, fax 420-1577; *holdinviajes@arnet.com.ar*); Mendoza Viajes, Sarmiento 129 ☎0261/438-0480, fax 0261/4380605; *mdzviajes@lanet.losandes.com.ar*); Navegante EV&T (☎0261/429-1615); Ríos Andinos, Adolfo 965, Dorrego, Guaymallén (☎02685/404-334); Ritz, Perú 1008 (☎0261/423-5115); Sepean, Primitivo de la Reta 1088 (☎0261/420-4162); Travesías Andinas, Av. San Martín 1998 (☎0261/429-0029).

Luján de Cuyo

Immediately to the south of Mendoza are two satellite towns, the first of which, where the Guaymallén Canal meets the Río Mendoza, is **LUJÁN DE CUYO**. Lying just to the

a gourmet restaurant, *Francis Mallmann* (☎0261/424-2698 & 424-3336) – see p.470. One of the main attractions of Mendoza. Bus #T.

Giol ("La Colina de Oro"), Ozamis 1040, Maipú (☎0261/497-2592). Tours Mon–Sat 9am–6.30pm Sun & public holidays 11am–2pm. A wonderfully old-fashioned place, with its fair share of antique barrels – including one of the biggest in South America – alongside the **Museo Nacional del Vino y la Vendimia** (same times; free) and a decent restaurant, *La Cava Vieja* (closed Sun). Bus #160.

Lagarde, San Martín 1745, Luján de Cuyo (☎0261/498-011; *lagarde@impsat1.com.ar*). Tours Mon–Fri 10am, 11am, noon, 2.30pm & 3.30pm. It is a major producer, and the site is enormous, but well worth seeing. There's also an impressive vintage car exhibition.

Nieto Senetiner, Ruta Panamericana, Chacras de Coria (☎0261/498-0315). Tours Mon–Fri 10am, 11am, 12.30pm & 4pm. The 12.30pm tour is followed by a delicious lunch, which must be reserved in advance. Some of the finest wines are produced by this traditional winery.

Norton, RP15, Perdriel, Luján de Cuyo (☎0261/488-0480). Tours Mon–Fri 9.30am–5.30pm. A prize-winning producer, making top-class if slightly old-fashioned wines, it opens its doors less willingly than many other bodegas in the region, but is well worth the visit. Tours must be reserved in advance. Bus #380.

San Felipe ("La Rural"), Montecaseros s/n, Coquimbito, Maipú (☎0261/497-2013). Tours Mon–Fri 9am–5.30pm, Sat 10am–4pm & Sun 10am–1pm. Small and traditional, this magnificent bodega stands among its own vineyards. An interesting contrast with some of the more urban wineries. Bus #170.

Santa Ana, Roca and Urquiza, Villa Nueva, Guaymallén (☎0261/421-1000). Tours Mon–Fri 9.30am, 10.45am, noon, 2.30pm, 3.45pm & 5pm. One of the closest worthwhile bodegas, near the city centre, with an enchanting mix of old-style and ultra-modern. The tours are especially friendly, and English is spoken – not always the case elsewhere. Bus #20.

Viña El Cerno, Moreno 631, Coquimbito, Maipú (☎0261/439-8447 or 481-1567; *elcerno@lanet.com.ar*). Mon–Fri 9am–5pm and at weekends, provided you call first. One of the most satisfying boutique wineries, in a small traditional country house with a tiny vineyard. The Malbec and Chardonnay are delicious and the tour highly personalized and enthusiastic. Weekend barbecues are laid on for anyone genuinely interested in buying a few bottles.

west of the Ruta Panamericana, or RN40, it's part residential, part industrial, with its huge brewery and some of the city's major wineries. The northern district, known as Carrodilla, 7km south of downtown, is an oasis of colonial Mendoza that survived the 1861 earthquake. Here you'll find the **Iglesia de la Carrodilla**, usually included in the city's wine tours. Built in 1778, it's now a museum of seventeenth- and eighteenth-century religious art (daily 9am–noon & 3–6pm; free), as well as the parish church. The naive frescoes depict scenes of grape harvesting, and the church's main relic is an oak-wood statue of the *Virgin and Child*, which is the star of the religious processions that precede Mendoza's Fiesta de la Vendimia in March. Artistically, the finest exhibit is the moving *Cristo de los Huarpes*, an exceptional piece of *mestizo* art carved out of quebra-cho wood in 1670 by local Indians.

The western district of Luján de Cuyo is called Chacras de Coria, a leafy suburb of European-style villas, golf courses and more bodegas, including one of the best wine-producers, Nieto Senetiner. It's also full of outdoor parrillas, bars and nightclubs, frequented at weekends and in the summer by Mendocinos. On its eastern edge, in a rural area called Mayor Drummond, at San Martín 3651, is Mendoza's **Museo Provincial de Bellas Artes Emiliano Guiñazú**, also known as the **Casa de Fader** (Tues–Fri 8.30am–1pm & 2–6.30pm, Sat & Sun 2.30p–7pm; $1). It's housed in a grandiose red sandstone villa, built in a style influenced by Art Nouveau at the end of the nineteenth century for Emiliano Guiñazú, an influential landowner and socialite, and is set off by a luxuriant garden of cacti, cypresses, magnolias and roses, among which Neoclassical marble statues lurk. In the early twentieth century **Fernando Fader**, an adoptive Argentine born of German parents in Bordeaux, moved to Mendoza with his engineer father, who worked on local hydroelectric projects. Having heard that Fader had been to art school in France, Guiñazú commissioned him to decorate the house interior. Fader's **Impressionistic murals** – especially appealing are the frescoes of tropical vegetation painted on the walls of the bathroom, alongside luxurious Art Nouveau tiles – are the main attraction here. His paintings, well-executed if strongly influenced by van Gogh, and at times by Monet, dominate the museum's collection of nineteenth- and early twentieth-century Argentine art. Temporary exhibits are staged from time to time.

Take **bus** #200 from downtown Mendoza to get here.

Maipú

The self-styled Cuna de la Viña, or Birthplace of the Grapevine, **MAIPÚ** is Mendoza's other small satellite town, lying some 15km southeast of Mendoza via the RN7. Founded in 1861 by the Mercedarian monk Fray Manuel Apolinario Vásquez and Don José Alberto de Ozamis as a new site for the destroyed Mendoza, it quickly became the centre of wine-making in the region, and is where the bulk of the city's **wineries** are located today. The wine-growing district, to the north of the town's centre focused on leafy Plaza 12 de Febrero, is called Coquimbito, where green vineyards alternate with dusky olive-groves. The wineries themselves range from small family bodegas, where you can chat with the owners and taste wines produced in tiny quantities and sometimes not yet available on the market, to the huge Bodega La Rural, at Montecaseros, where you'll also find Mendoza's **Museo del Vino** (Mon–Fri 9am–7pm, Sat 9am–1pm, Sun & public holidays 4–8pm; free; ☎0261/497-2090), a summary explanation of the region's wine industry housed in a fabulous Art Nouveau villa, with elegant fittings and detailing, including some delicate stained glass – the venue far outstrips the contents. The guided visits to the bodega take you round the whole wine-making process, but the most impressive part is the old cellar, where a humungous late nineteenth-century oak-cask from Nancy, is the star feature. Finely decorated in an Art Nouveau style, it's only surpassed by the giant barrel at Bodega Escorihuela, Godoy Cruz (see p.474). Next door is *La Cava Vieja*, a gourmet restaurant where you can sample the bodega's finest wines together with the region's other delicious produce, including freshwater fish, olives and fruit. For more on the **bodegas** in this area, see the box on p.474.

Buses #150, #151, #170, #172, #173 and #180 all go to Maipú, taking slightly different routes, from downtown Mendoza.

Alta Montaña

The Andean cordillera, including some of the world's tallest mountains, loom a short distance west of Mendoza, and its snow-tipped peaks are visible from the city centre almost all year round, beyond the picturesque vineyards and fruit orchards. You'll want to head up into them before long, even if you don't feel up to climbing the highest peak in the Americas, **Aconcagua**, ironically out of sight behind the high precordillera – the scenery is fabulous, and skiing, trekking and highland walks are all possible, or you can simply enjoy the views on an organized excursion. The so-called **Alta Montaña route**, the RN7, is also the international highway to Santiago de Chile via the upmarket Chilean ski-resort of Portillo. The tunnel under the Andes is one of the major border crossings between Argentina and Chile, blocked by snow only on rare occasions in July and August. The old mountain pass is no longer used but can be visited from Mendoza, weather permitting, to see the **Cristo Redentor**, a huge statue of Christ, erected as a sign of peace between the old rivals, and for the fantastic mountain views. As the road climbs up into the mountains beyond **Uspallata**, you pass some dramatic scenery, a variety of colourful rock formations including the pinnacle-like **Los Penitentes**, near a small ski-resort. A sulphurous thermal spring, **Puente del Inca**, is a popular stop-off point, and is also near the **Aconcagua** trailhead, base camp and muleteer-post. On the way you can stop at the spa-resort of **Cacheuta**, the pretty village of **Potrerillos** or, in winter, ski at **Vallecitos**, a tiny resort catering for a younger crowd than at the exclusive Las Leñas in southern Mendoza Province. An alternative to the direct RN7 route to Uspallata is via **Villavicencio**, a highland source, famous for its crystal mineral waters and a grandiose former hotel. The long route crosses some deadly dull desert plains but the **Caracoles de Villavicencio**, between it and Uspallata, is one of the region's most magnificent corniche roads. Farther south is the picturesque summer resort of **Tupungato**, the gateway to the fabulous but little-visited **Parque Provincial Tupungato**, dominated by the soaring volcano of the same name. These roads are covered in their tours by most of Mendoza's travel operators, but most places are also accessible by local **buses**. Should you prefer a **guided excursion** try one of the following: Aymará, 9 de Julio 983 (☎0261/420-0607; *aymara@satlink.com*); El Cristo, Espejo 228 (☎0261/429-1911, fax 429-6911); Holding, Av. España 1030 (☎0261/423-1352, fax 420-1577; *holdinviajes@arnet.com.ar*); or Ritz, Perú 1008 (☎0261/423-5115).

Cacheuta, Potrerillos and Vallecitos

To reach the RN7 Alta Montaña road from Mendoza, you must first head south along the RN40, and turn westwards 15km south of the city, beyond the Río Mendoza and Luján de Cuyo. The small town of **CACHEUTA** lies 27km along the RN7; the older road further north is now blocked by a huge reservoir which flooded the valley in the 1990s. This area makes an ideal alternative to Mendoza as a place to stay, if you want to avoid big cities. Cacheuta itself is a pleasant small spa-resort, with its modernized hotel, *Hotel Cacheuta* (☎02624/482082; ⑦), with plain but very comfortable rooms and a health centre, the **Centro Climático Termal Cacheuta**, with individual baths and large swimming pools in an artificial grotto (daily 9am–7pm; $5; ☎02624/482082); the baths

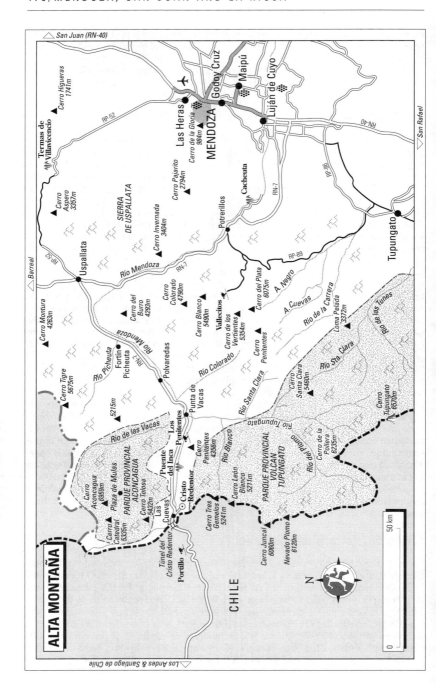

ALTA MONTAÑA

are open to non-residents for $10. Nearby *Hostería Mi Montaña*, just to the west of Cacheuta proper, serves delicious roast kid and ham sandwiches made with home-cured *serrano* and home-baked bread, as well as teas and drinks. You can also camp here, at either *Camping Termas de Cacheuta* (☎02624/482082; $4 per person) or *Camping Don Domingo* (☎0261/422-5695; $4 per person), 4km to the west along the RN7.

There are more campsites and a luxury hotel, the *Gran Hotel Potrerillos* (☎02624/482010, fax ☎02624/482004; ⑥) at **POTRERILLOS**, in a valley 10km north-west of Cacheuta. The hotel has beautiful rooms, a swimming pool, a top-rate restaurant, tennis-courts and sweeping views across the picturesque valley. The masses of poplar trees picking out the many oases turn vivid yellow in March and April, while the views up to the precordillera are fabulous: the colours form a blurred mosaic from this distance. A number of adventure-tour operators are also based in Potrerillos, including Argentina Rafting Expediciones (☎02624/482037; *arg_rafting@hotmail.com*), who run exciting **white-water rafting** trips down the Río Mendoza when the weather allows. The best place to eat, apart from the hotel, is at *Armando*, on the main street. From Potrerillos a good, partly sealed track leads southwest to Vallecitos, 25km away.

Some 25km west of Potrerillos, via an unnumbered track, **VALLECITOS** is a relatively inexpensive, traditional ski-resort, nestling in the Valle del Plata, in the lee of the Cerro Blanco, at an altitude of around 3000m. Popular with students and young people in general, it can be reached easily from Mendoza, but there is **accommodation** if you want to stay over. Its six pistes range from a nursery slope to the challenging "Canaleta". The ski centre itself (☎0261/431-1957 or 431-2713) is open daily from July to September, snow permitting, and equipment can be rented at the Refugio Esquí Club Mendoza and the Refugio San Antonio, where you'll also find professional instructors. To stay over there's the pleasant *Hostería La Canaleta* (☎0261/431-2779; ②), with bunk-beds and private bath, the more functional *Hostería Cerro Nevado* (no phone; ②), which also has a restaurant and bar, and the *Refugio San Antonio* (no phone; ①), with shared baths and a canteen. During the ski season there are **buses** to and from Mendoza.

Uspallata

The Sierra de Uspallata, which blocks Mendoza's view of Aconcagua, was described in the 1830s by Charles Darwin in the *Voyage of the Beagle*: "Red, purple, green and quite white sedimentary rocks, alternating with black lavas broken up and thrown into all kinds of disorder, by masses of porphyry, of every shade, from dark brown to the brightest lilac. It really resembled those pretty sections which geologists make of the inside of the earth."

USPALLATA itself, a village 54km north of Potrerillos by the RN7, has been an important crossroads between Mendoza, San Juan and Chile for centuries. Since its amazing scenery was chosen by Jean-Jacques Annaud to shoot his epic film *Seven Years in Tibet*, starring Brad Pitt, it has been firmly on the map, but in any case its cool climate, plentiful accommodation and stressless ambience make it an ideal alternative to busy Mendoza as a place to stay. It lies in the valley of the Río Uspallata, a fertile strip of potato, maize and pea fields, vineyards, pastures and patches of farmland where flocks of domesticated geese are kept. The fantastic backdrops that are the Sierra de Uspallata to the east and the barren Cerros de Chacay to the northwest, soaring mountains and totally unspoiled valley scenery, made it an obvious alternative to the Himalayan uplands around Lhasa. Like so many settlements around the region, there's really not very much to do here, but at 1850m it could act as an ideal acclimatization stop for anyone intent on climbing Aconcagua. While you're here you could visit the unusual **Bóvedas de Uspallata** (free access at all times), late eighteenth-century furnaces a short way to the north of the village used for smelting iron mined in the nearby mountainside. Famously the ovens were used by the patriotic monk Fray Luis Beltrán to make cannons and other arms for San Martín's army. The base is an adobe rectangle but the whitewashed domed cupolas of the ovens make the building look like a North African mosque.

The focal point of Uspallata is the junction of the RN7 and Las Heras, where frequent **buses** – including those run by the Uspallata company – arrive from Mendoza and head towards Puenta del Inca and into Chile. For **somewhere to stay**, nearby at Las Heras s/n is the *Hotel Viena* (☎02624/420046; ②), with pleasant rooms, private bath and cable TV. Closer to the junction, with nicer rooms, enormous modern bathrooms and a confitería, is the *Hostería Los Cóndores* (☎02624/420303; ③); the buffet breakfast is excellent and they also offer horseriding and treks into the nearby mountains. Some way to the south, lying just off the RN7, is the more luxurious *Hotel Valle Andino* (☎02624/420033; ⑤), which has spacious rooms, tennis courts and a pleasant sitting-room. *Café Tibet* near the junction serves good coffee and snacks amid a gallery of photos of Brad Pitt in his role as the unbearable Himalayan explorer. The best **place to eat** is the *Parrilla San Cayetano*, also near the junction; it's a popular stop-off for coach trips and buses to and from Chile, but despite the frequent crowds the food is good.

Up to Los Penitentes

From Uspallata the RN7 swings round to the west and rejoins the Río Mendoza, whose valley it shares with the now disused rail line all the way to its source at Punta de Vacas. You are following an ancient Inca trail; in the mountains to the south several mummified corpses have been found and are displayed in Mendoza at the Museo de Ciencias Naturales y Antropológicas Juan Cornelio Moyano (see p.469). The scenery is simply fantastic: you pass through narrow canyons, passing close by the Cerro del Burro (4293m) and the Cerro División (4603m), to the south, while the rugged ridges of the Cerros del Chacay culminate in the Cerro Tigre (5700m) to the north. Stripes of different coloured rock – reds, greens and yellows caused by the presence of iron, copper and sulphur – decorate the steep walls of the cordillera peaks, while the vegetation is limited to tough highland grass and *jarilla*, a scruffy gorse-like shrub gathered for firewood. The road climbs a gentle slope, passes through a series of tunnels, takes you through the abandoned hamlet of Polvaredas and past the police station at Punta de Vacas, at 2325m above sea level; the latter is only of interest if you are driving a goods truck across the border into Chile, while the main customs post is farther on at Los Horcones. Some 65km from Uspallata is the small ski-resort of **LOS PENITENTES** or more properly Villa Los Penitentes – the "penitents" in question are a series of strange pinnacles of rock, high up on the ridge atop Cerro Penitentes (4356m), towering over the small village of typical, brightly coloured ski-resort buildings to the south. The pointed rocks are thought to look like cowled monks, of the kind that traditionally parade during Holy Week in places such as Seville, hence the name. The resort's 21 pistes vary from nursery slopes to the black Las Paredes, with most of the runs classified as difficult and the biggest total drop being 700m. The modern ski-lifts also run at weekends in the summer, so you can enjoy the fabulous mountain and valley views from the top of Cerro San Antonio (3200m); the fissured peak looming over it all is the massive Cerro Leña (4992m).

The Los Penitentes resort has an office in Mendoza at Paso de los Andes 1615, Godoy Cruz (☎0261/427-1641). As well as a ski-school, a rental shop, a supermarket and a hospital, the resort is made up of several types of **accommodation**. In addition to a number of *apart-hotels* run by the resort, there's also the extremely comfortable *Hostería Los Penitentes* (☎0261/427-1641; ⑤), usually booked by the week, or the *Hostería Ayelén* (☎0261/427-1123, fax 427-1283; *ayelen@lanet.losandes.com.ar*; ⑦), which is more luxurious and can be booked by the night. A far more modest but still pleasant alternative are the **cabañas** run by Gregorio Yapurai (☎0261/430-5118) at nearby Puente del Inca (see below). The horseshoe-shaped La Herradura building houses both a pleasant confitería and the Ski-Life disco for après-ski.

Puente del Inca

Just 6km west of Los Penitentes is **PUENTE DEL INCA**, a compulsory stop for any-one heading along the Alta Montaña route and also near the track that leads north towards the Aconcagua base camp (see below). At just over 2700m, this natural **stone bridge** features on many a postcard, but is still especially impressive to visit, if only because you can walk across it. Formed by the Río de las Cuevas, it nestles in an arid valley, overlooked by majestic mountains; just beneath the bridge are the remains of a once sophisticated spa-resort, built in the 1940s but swept away by a flood. The ruins, the bridge itself and the surrounding rocks are all stained a nicotine-yellow by the very high sulphur content of the warm waters which gurgle up nearby from beneath the earth's surface. You can buy drinks and snacks at the many stalls, which among other souvenirs sell all kinds of objects that have been left to petrify and yellow in the mineral springs: shoes, bottles, hats, books, ashtrays and statues of the Virgin Mary have all been treated to this embellishment, and are of dubious taste, but the displays make for an unusual photograph of the site. Only 4km west of Puente del Inca is the dirt track that leads into the Parque Nacional Aconcagua.

There are only a couple of possibilities for **accommodation**, both popular with Aconcagua climbers: the fairly luxurious *Hostería Puente del Inca* (☎02624/420222; ④), which has some dormitory-style rooms at much lower rates; and the *Refugio La Vieja Estación* (☎0261/432-1485; ③), which has basic bunk-beds and shared bath.

Aconcagua

At 6959m, **Cerro Aconcagua** is the highest peak in both the western and southern hemispheres, or outside the Himalayan range. Its glacier-garlanded summit dominates the Parque Provincial Aconcagua, even though it is encircled by several other moun-tains that exceed 5000m: Cerros Almacenes, Catedral, Cuerno, Cúpula, Ameghino, Güssfeldt, Dedos, México, Mirador, Fitzgerald, La Mano, Santa María and Tolosa, some of which are easier to climb than others, and many of which obscure views of the great summit from most points around. The five glaciers that hang around its faces like icy veils are Horcones Superior, Horcones Inferior, Güssfeldt, Las Vacas and Los Polacos. For many mountain purists, Aconcagua may be the highest Andean mountain but it lacks the morphological beauty of Cerro Mercedario to the north or Volcán Tupungato to the south. Nevertheless, ever since the highest peak was conquered by the Italian-Swiss mountaineer Mathias Zurbriggen in 1897 – after it had been identified by German climber Paul Güssfeldt in 1883 – it has been one of the top destinations for expeditions or solo climbs in the world. In 1934, a Polish team of climbers made it to the top via the glacier now named after them; in 1953 the southwest ridge was the route successfully taken by a local group of mountaineers; while in 1954 a French team who had successfully conquered Cerro Fitz Roy made the first ascent of Aconcagua up the south face, the most challenging of all – Plaza Francia, one of the main base camps, is named after them. In recent years, given its relatively easy ascent and the high degree of organization on offer, it has become a major attraction, and more than two thousand visitors reach the top every season – namely December to early March. Like most of the region's toponyms, the origins of the name Aconcagua are anyone's guess, but the favourite explanations are that it comes either from the Huarpe words *Akon-Kahuak* or "stone sentinel" or, less poetically, from the Mapuche *Akonhue*, "from the beyond". The discovery in 1985 of an Incan mummy – now in the Museo del Área Fundacional, Mendoza (see p.468) – at 5300m on the southwest face suggests that it was a holy site for the Incas (and no doubt for the pre-Incan peoples too) and that ceremonies including burials and perhaps sacrifices took place at these incredible heights.

The three most important requisites for climbing Aconcagua are fitness, patience and acclimatization, and unless you're an experienced climber, you shouldn't even consider going up other than as part of an organized climb. Of the three approaches – south, west or east – the western route from the Plaza de Mulas (4230m) is the easiest and known as the Ruta Normal. More experienced climbers take either the Glaciar de los Polacos route, with its base camp at Plaza Argentina, reached via a long track that starts near Punta de Vacas, or the very demanding south face, whose Plaza Francia base camp is reached from Los Horcones, branching off from the Plaza de Mulas trail at a spot called Confluencia (3368m). The Ruta Normal is not too tough and most of it is just a steep path up which even motorbikes and bicycles have been ridden, but the two biggest obstacles are coping with the altitude and the cold. Temperatures can plummet to -40°C at night even in the summer, and fickle weather is also a major threat. Expeditions always descend when they see tell-tale milky-white clouds shaped like the lenses of eye-glasses, known as *el viento blanco*, which announce violent storms. Not only should you be fit but you must also carry plentiful supplies of food and, even more importantly, fuel. Over a hundred people have died climbing Aconcagua, and in 1999 the perfectly preserved body of a 1960s climber from Norway was lifted from a glacier. Frostbite and altitude sickness (see p.34) are the main health hazards, but proper precautions can prevent either. In any case allow at least a fortnight for an expedition, since you should acclimatize at each level and take it easy throughout the climb; most of the people who don't make it to the top fail because they try to rush it. Given the huge amount of supplies needed to make the ascent most people invest in a mule (see "Practicalities" below). For more details of the different routes, advice on what to take with you and how to acclimatize, consult the Aconcagua Web site (*www.aconcagua.com.ar*) or the excellent *Bradt Guide to Backpacking in Chile and Argentina*. For more specialist information, especially for serious climbers who are considering one of the harder routes, the best publication is R.J. Secor's *Aconcagua, A Climbing Guide* (1994) while the South American Explorers' Club also produces a reliable Aconcagua Information Packet.

Practicalities

Unless you are having everything arranged by a tour operator, the first place you need to go to is the **Dirección de Recursos Naturales Renovables** (daily 8am–1pm & 4–8pm), whose offices are just inside Mendoza's Parque General San Martín, near the monumental gates (see p.468); not only can you get good maps of the park here but also this is where you must apply for compulsory permits to climb Aconcagua in the first place. These cost $30 for foreign trekkers inside the park (valid for a week) or $80 to climb the mountain (valid for three weeks). In January, the most popular month as it coincides with Argentine holidays and is when the weather is usually most settled, the climbing permit costs $120. Don't be surprised to hear that Argentine nationals have paid less – they are officially charged half price. To get to either Los Horcones or Punta de Vacas, you can get the twice-daily **buses** from Mendoza, run by Uspallata or get off a bus to Santiago de Chile. It's definitely preferable, though, whether trekking or climbing, to go on an **organized trip**, if only because of the treacherous weather – local guides know the whims of the mountain and its sudden storms. Several outfits in Mendoza specialize in these tours, including Campo Base Adventures and Expeditions at Av. Mitre 946 (☎0261/429-0707); Aconcagua Trek at Güiraldes 246, San José (☎0261/424-2003); Aymará Viajes at 9 de Julio 983 (☎0261/420-0607); Fernando Grajales, José Moreno 898 (☎0261/429-3830; grajales@satlink.com); and Rumbo al Horizonte at Caseros 1053, Godoy Cruz (☎0261/452-0641). Mules are in short supply and heavy demand and so they're not cheap; current prices are around $120 for the first mule to Plaza de Mulas, though prices are lower if you hire several (only viable if you're in a group). Fernando Grajales and Aconcagua Trek are the two main outfits dealing in mule-hire. If you need **somewhere to stay** near the base camps, the only possibilities are at Puente del Inca (see above) or at Las Cuevas (see below). Most people camp at the Plaza de Mulas – that's the only way to overnight up on the mountain-trail – and the hotels' hot water and meals are invariably welcome after the climb.

Las Cuevas and Cristo Redentor

It's just 15km from Puente del Inca, via the customs post at Los Horcones, to **LAS CUEVAS**, the final settlement along this Alta Montaña road before the **Túnel Cristo Redentor** – a tunnel under the Andes into Chile (Nov–March daily 6am–10pm; April–Oct 8.30am–8.30pm; passport and vehicle documents required; no perishable foodstuffs or plant material allowed into Chile). At 3112m, Las Cuevas is a bit of a ghost town, a feeling enhanced by the rather grim Nordic-style stone houses, one of which is an anonymous confitería serving decent hot food and snacks. The *Hostel Refugio Paco Ibañez*, popular with Aconcagua climbers, is run by Hostel Campo Base in Mendoza (☎0261/429-0707; ①). From January to March, but usually not for the rest of the year because of snowfalls or frost, you can drive up the several hairpin bends to the **Monumento al Cristo Redentor**, an eight-metre-high, six-tonne statue of Christ as the redeemer. It was put here in 1904 to celebrate the so-called May 1902 Pacts, signed between Argentina and Chile, under the auspices of British King Edward VII, to determine once and for all the Andean boundary between the two countries. Designed by Argentine sculptor Mateo Alonso, the statue was made from melted down cannons and other weapons, in an ironic reversal of Fray Luis Beltrán's project a hundred years before (see p.480). Nearby is a disused Chilean customs post, but the nearby Paso de la Cumbre is no longer used by international traffic. The views towards Cerro Tolosa (5432m), immediately to the north, along the cordillera and down into several valleys, are quite staggering; make sure you have something warm to wear, though, as the howling winds up here are bitterly cold. When the road is open, most Alta Montaña tours bring you up here as the grand finale to the excursion; would-be Aconcagua conquerors often train and acclimatize by clambering to the top on foot.

Villavicencio

You often see **VILLAVICENCIO**, a spa-resort 50km northwest of Mendoza, without actually going there – the ubiquitous bottles of mineral water from its springs, which you'll find in the region's supermarkets and restaurants, carry an excellent likeness on their labels. To get there, however, you take the sealed RP52 from Mendoza, which crosses some flat dusty plains before climbing over a thousand metres to the tiny settlement, at 1800m above sea level. Its curative springs were exploited by the indigenous peoples and not rediscovered until 1902. When Darwin stopped there in 1835 he dismissed it as a "solitary hovel bearing the imposing name of Villa Vicencio, mentioned by every traveller who has crossed the Andes", but admitting there was "a nice little rivulet". The 1941 *Gran Hotel*, still being refurbished after years of protracted work, but certainly no hovel, was frequented by the wealthy of Mendoza and Buenos Aires in the 1940s and 1950s when Villavicencio became a smart spa-resort. The hotel owners have announced several reopening dates over the last five years, but it's still closed; you can just visit the small confitería, and have sandwiches and a drink. Beyond it a good dirt road covers the 38km to Uspallata, offering stunning views of the Mendoza valley and its oasis, from viewpoints such as El Balcón, 10km west of Villavicencio. The road's legendary 365 hairpin-bends – in reality there are something like twenty – earn it the nickname *Ruta del Año*, or One Year Road. It's also known as the "Caracoles de Villavicencio", literally snails of

Villavicencio, referring to the tightly spiralling bends of the pass. About 8km west, where the road straightens, is a commemorative plaque to Darwin's passage here in 1835 – curiously, his name has been Hispanicized to Carlos. Just before Uspallata, the RP39 towards San Juan Province turns off to the north. **Buses** run by Jocolí link Mendoza to Villavicencio three times a week. This circuit is popularly visited on a tour organized from Mendoza, usually as a half-day trip (see p.472).

Tupungato and Parque Provincial Tupungato

Now that Aconcagua has become almost a victim of its own success, anyone looking for a challenging mountain-trek or climb with fewer people crowding the trails and paths should head for the better-kept secret of Cerro Tupungato, an extinct volcano peaking at 6800m. Its Matterhorn-like summit dominates the **Parque Provincial Tupungato** which stretches along the Chilean border to the south of the RN7 at Puente del Inca, but is most accessible from the town of **TUPUNGATO**, reached from Mendoza via the RN40 and RP86, a journey totalling nearly 80km. There's nothing to see in the small market town, apart from some attractive Italian-style single-storey houses from the end of the nineteenth century, but this is where you can contract guides to take you to the top of the mighty volcano. Ask at the tiny **tourist office** (daily 7am–1pm; ☎02622/488097) on the main street, Av. Belgrano 348. You'll need plenty of time as the treks last between three and fifteen days, depending on how long you're given to acclimatize at each level – the longer the better. The virgin countryside within the park is utterly breathtaking, completely unspoiled and unremittingly stark, so take plenty of film with you. Apart from the companies recommended for Aconcagua, which also arrange tours to Tupungato (see p.482 above), you might also check out Rómulo Nieto at the *Hostería* of the same name, at Almirante Brown 1200 (☎02622/488029; ②). Not only does he arrange reasonably priced tours, but you can stay here in the small, plain but comfortable rooms. Alternatively you could **stay** at the *Hotel de Turismo*, Av. Belgrano 1066 (☎02622/488007; ③), which is nothing special but a little more spacious, with more modern bathrooms. There's also a very decent **campsite** on Calle La Costa, with barbecue facilities and clean toilets and showers, charging $5 per person. The best **place to eat** is the *Valle de Tupungato*, at Av. Belgrano 542, while *Pizzeria Ilo*, at Av. Belgrano and Sargento Cabral, serves up an excellent margarita and delicious *pasta casera*. **Buses** run fairly regularly from Mendoza and arrive at Plaza General San Martín.

Laguna Diamante

Some 220km southwest of Mendoza, the altiplanic lake called **Laguna Diamante**, amid its own provincial reserve of guanaco pasture and misty valleys, is the destination of one of the least-known but most unforgettable excursions from the city. The source of the Río Diamante that flows through San Rafael, the lake is so called because the choppy surface of its crystalline waters suggests a rough diamond. One reason for its relative obscurity is that weather conditions make it possible to reach Laguna Diamante only from mid-November to the end of March, when blizzards often blocking the road for the rest of the year. There's no public transport so a **guided tour**, either from Mendoza or San Rafael, is the only option. Two companies specialize in this destination: Exploradores, (☎0261/425-6181; *jasanchi@lanet.com.ar*), and Holding, Av. España 1030, Mendoza (☎0261/423-1352, fax 420-1577; *holdinviajes@arnet.com.ar*). Since it's in an area under military control, near a strategic point on the Chilean border, take your passport.

At Pareditas, 125km south of Mendoza by the RN40, the RP101 forks off to the southwest; the drive down is one marvellous long dolly-shot of the Andean precordillera and, if weather is bad in the valley, don't be put off as the sun shines every day, almost, at

Laguna Diamante. The RP101 is a reliable unsealed road that follows Arroyo Yaucha through fields of gorse-like *jarilla* and gnarled *chañares*, affording views of the rounded summits of the frontal cordillera. At Estancia El Parral you can take on provisions, camp – as long as you ask permission – and hire horses to trek through the unspoiled countryside. Afterwards, the road enters the Cañón del Gateado, through which the salmon-rich Arroyo Rosario flows past dangling willows. At another fork in the road, 20km on, the track to the left eventually leads to El Sosneado, while the right fork heads for the Refugio Militar General Alvarado, the entrance to the **Reserva Provincial Laguna Diamante**, where a friendly soldier will take down everyone's particulars for security and personal safety reasons. As the road twists and climbs across the Pampa de los Avestruces you'll catch your first sight of **Cerro Maipo** (5323m), the permanently snow-capped volcano that straddles the international frontier. The spongy plateau of khaki bofedales, drained by numerous streams that keep the valley bottom, Vegas del Yaucha, bright green for the grazing guanacos, averages 4000m above sea level, so you might start noticing some *puna* symptoms (see p.34).

Nestling beneath the Cordón del Eje, a majestic range of dark ochre rock, and towered over by the snow-streaked Maipo opposite – a perfect cone worthy of a Japanese woodcut – this ultramarine expanse of water is constantly buffeted into white horses by strong breezes and its waves noisily lap the springy, mossy banks. Icy blue mountain rivers twist across the unspoiled landscape stretching as far as the eye can see to the meringue-like Andean peaks on the horizon, in stark contrast with the chunks of dark charcoal moraine piled up in the foreground like the debris from a giant barbecue. The silence is broken only by the howl of the wind or the occasional plop of a *puna*-free trout. An off-the-track site along the banks of the brook makes a wonderful picnic spot, protected from howling gales by the moraine, with an unbeatable backdrop. Rangers at the **guardería**, which you pass on the final approach to the lagoon, can offer some information on the reserve and its wildlife, and appreciate a cigarette or sharing a *mate*.

San Rafael and around

Via the RN40 and RN143, the small city of **SAN RAFAEL** is some 230km south of Mendoza, and is the de facto capital of central Mendoza Province; it's now a kind of mini-Mendoza, complete with wide avenues, irrigation channels along the gutters and scrupulously clean public areas. The town was founded in 1805 on the banks of Río Diamante on behalf of Rafael, Marques de Sobremonte – hence the name – by militia leader Miguel Telles Meneses. Large numbers of Italian and Spanish immigrants flocked here at the end of the nineteenth century, but the so-called Colonia Francesa expanded further when the railway arrived in 1903. Favoured by French immigrants during the nineteenth century, San Rafael built its prosperity on vineyards, olives and tree-fruit, grown in the province's second biggest oasis, and its industry has always been agriculture-based: fruit preserving, olive oil and fine wines. In all, there are nearly eighty **bodegas** in San Rafael department, most of them tiny, family-run businesses, some of which welcome visitors. Tourism has been a big money-spinner over the past couple of decades, especially since adventure tourism has taken off. The **Cañon del Atuel**, a short way to the southwest, is one of the best places in the country to try out white-water rafting. The nearby cordillera also offers opportunities for safaris, and excursion options include the **Laguna Diamante** (see above). Accommodation is one of San Rafael's fortes and you could use the town as a base for exploring the southern parts of the province, centred on Malargüe, where good places to stay are harder to come by.

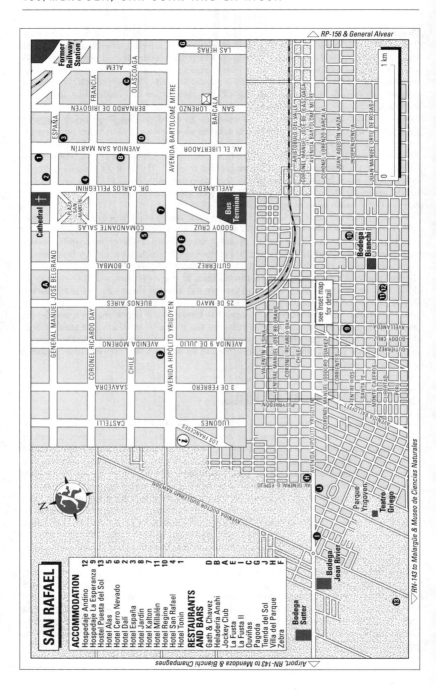

SAN RAFAEL

ACCOMMODATION
Hospedaje Andino	12
Hospedaje La Esperanza	9
Hostel Puesta del Sol	13
Hotel Alas	5
Hotel Cerro Nevado	6
Hotel Dali	2
Hotel España	3
Hotel Jardín	8
Hotel Kalton	7
Hotel Millalén	11
Hotel Regine	10
Hotel San Rafael	4
Hotel Tonin	1

RESTAURANTS AND BARS
Gath & Chavez	D
Heladería Anahi	B
Jockey Club	A
La Fusta	E
La Fusta II	I
Ouviñas	C
Pagoda	G
Tienda del Sol	J
Villa del Parque	H
Zebra	F

RP-156 & General Alvear

1 km

Former Railway Station

Cathedral

PLAZA SAN MARTÍN

Bus Terminal

See Inset map for detail

Bodega Bianchi

Parque Yrigoyen

Teatro Griego

Bodega Jean Rivier

Bodega Sutter

RN-143 to Malargüe & Museo de Ciencias Naturales

Airport, RN-143 to Mendoza & Bianchi Champagnes

Arrival and information

San Rafael's small **airport**, serving Buenos Aires three times a week, is 5km west of the town centre, along the RN143 towards Mendoza. There are no buses so just hop into a taxi ($3) if you don't fancy the long hike into town. The **bus terminal** – buses arrive here from Mendoza, Malargüe, San Juan and places farther afield – is wedged in between calles Almafuerte and Avellaneda, at Coronel Suárez. It's surrounded by shops and cafés, and is extremely central, so you shouldn't need transport to get anywhere. The very helpful **tourist information office** is at the corner of avenidas Hipólito Yrigoyen and Balloffet (daily 8am–9pm, ☎02627/424217) and can give information about tour operators, provide you with a map and fix you up with somewhere to stay.

Accommodation

San Rafael has no shortage of **places to stay**, ranging from basic refuges to luxurious *apart-hotels*, while one of the country's best youth hostels lies in very attractive grounds just outside the town. The best **campsite** hereabouts is *Camping El Parador*, on the Isla Río Diamante, 6km to the south of the centre; it has excellent facilities, is in a beautiful wooded location and charges $6 per tent per day.

Hospedaje Andino, Coronel Campos 197 (☎02627/421877). This small, family-style place has some very attractive, spacious rooms with impeccable bathrooms, plus a common kitchen for guests. ③.

Hospedaje La Esperanza, Avellaneda 263 (☎02627/422382). The cheapest commendable accommodation in the town other than the youth hostel; the rooms are functional but clean. ②.

Hostel Puesta del Sol, Deán Funes 998 (☎02627/434881; fax 02627/430187; *mendoza3@hostels.org.ar* or *puestaso@hostels.org.ar*). One of the newest and most beautiful hostels in the country, with modern facilities, a huge swimming pool amid landscaped grounds, and a lively atmosphere. ②–③.

Hotel Alas, Comandante Salas 51 (☎02627/422732). Compared with the wackily rustic reception decorated with enticing photos of regional sights, the rooms are rather dull, but they're decent and clean, all with their own bath. ④.

Hotel Cerro Nevado, Hipólito Yrigoyen 376 (☎02627/428209). This spotlessly clean place has a pleasant restaurant, but avoid streetside rooms as they're noisy. ③.

Hotel España, San Martín 292 (☎02627/424055). The breakfast room is very appealing, but the bedrooms are nondescript; avoid the so-called "colonial" section where rooms are slightly cheaper but quite grotty. ③–④.

Hotel Jardín, Hipólito Yrigoyen 259 (☎02627/434621). Very comfy rooms, all en suite, arranged around a lush patio shaded by an impressive palm tree. ④.

Hotel Kalton, Hipólito Yrigoyen 120 (☎02627/430047). The best hotel in San Rafael, with faultless service, spacious, enticing rooms, modern bathrooms and tasteful decor. ⑤.

Hotel Millalén, Ortiz de Rosas 198 (☎02627/422776). Modern hotel, with pleasantly understated rooms, sparkling bathrooms and unfussy decor. ⑤.

Hotel Regine, Independencia 623 and Colón (☎02627/421470 or 430274; *regine@infovia.com.ar*). All the rooms are well-furnished and charming, while the rustic dining-room serves reliably good food; there's also a beautiful garden dominated by a ceibo tree. ④.

Hotel San Rafael, Coronel Day 30 (☎02627/430128). An extremely smart place with very stylish but unpretentious rooms, lovely bathrooms and a very good restaurant. ⑥.

Hotel Tonin, San Martín 327 (☎02627/422499). Access to the rooms is along a weird maze that takes you through the garage, but once found they're very pleasant, with modish stainless-steel washbasins in gleaming bathrooms. ④.

The City

San Rafael has a flat, compact centre that lends itself to a gentle stroll, but otherwise there aren't any sights to speak of – the town is essentially a base for visiting the surrounding area. The main drag with most of the shops, cafés and many of the hotels, a continuation of the RN143 Mendoza road, is called avenida Hipólito Yrigoyen west of north–south axis Avenida General San Martín, and Avenida Bartolomé Mitre to the east. Streets change name either side of both axes and, while they follow a strict gridiron pattern across the city, whole sections are at an oblique angle, such as Avenida Balloffet that leads south towards the Río Diamante, a wide river that marks the town's southern boundary. Two blocks north of Avenida Hipólito Yrigoyen and one west of Avenida San Martín is the town's main square, leafy and peaceful **Plaza San Martín**, dominated by the modern cathedral.

To fill an hour or so with something cultural, take a taxi or a bus marked "Isla Diamante" from Avenida Hipólito Yrigoyen to the **Museo de Historia Natural** (daily 7am–1pm & 2–8pm; $1); Isla Diamante is a large island 6km to the south of the town centre, in the middle of the river of the same name. Housed in a very unprepossessing modern building, it is a working museum with research labs. The ground floor is cluttered with masses of bedraggled stuffed birds, moth-eaten foxes and lumps of rock, but on the upper floor you'll find some poorly displayed but fabulous Pre-columbian ceramics, the best of which are statues from Ecuador; there's also a small collection of crafts from Easter Island. As well as some particularly fine ceramics from northwestern Argentina, you'll see a mummified child dating from 40 AD and a gorgeous multi-coloured leather bag decorated with striking, very modern-looking geometric designs, found in the Gruta del Indio in the Cañón del Atuel.

Eating, drinking and nightlife

Good **restaurants** are fewer and farther between than good hotels in San Rafael, but one or two stand out. In addition there are a couple of atmospheric bars and two fun discotheques, all some way out of town towards the west.

Restaurants, bars and nightclubs

La Bodega, Hipólito Yrigoyen 5469. Discotheque for the under-35 crowd, with mixed music and a lively atmosphere.

Megadisco Il Castillo, Toledano 700. Extremely popular nightclub for a slightly younger crowd, with lots of house and techno.

Gath & Chavez, San Martín and Olascoaga. Very smart cocktail bar doubling as a café and tearoom.

Heladería Anahi, Chile 20 and San Martín. San Rafael's best ice cream.

Jockey Club, Belgrano 330. Good old-fashioned service and hearty food, with a very good-value *menú turista* at lunchtime for $8.

La Fusta, Hipólito Yrigoyen 538. By far the town's best parrilla, serving succulent steaks and full parrilladas at very reasonable rates; local wines recommended.

La Fusta II, Hipólito Yrigoyen and Beato Marcelino Champagnat. Sister restaurant to the above in ultra-modern surroundings with fine decor and a large terrace.

Ouviñas, Hipólito Yrigoyen 1268 and Olascoaga 177. Both branches of the town's best pizzeria also serve pasta and other Italian fare in no-nonsense surroundings.

Tienda del Sol, Hipólito Yrigoyen 1663. One of a cluster of trendy, post-modern bars, serving cocktails and other drinks at slightly inflated prices.

Villa del Parque, Hipólito Yrigoyen 1530. Another in the group of popular places to be seen and a great place to people-watch.

Zebra, Hipólito Yrigoyen 245. San Rafael's most popular bar-cum-café in the centre of town.

Cañon del Atuel

The **CAÑON DEL ATUEL** is San Rafael's main attraction, a beautifully wild canyon linking two man-made lakes along the Río Atuel, to the southwest of the town. Visits

BODEGAS IN AND AROUND SAN RAFAEL

Mendoza is undeniably Argentina's wine capital, but San Rafael is also a major wine centre that doesn't always get much of a look-in. Its wineries are among the finest in the country, and several of them open their doors willingly and very professionally to visitors. The following is a selection of the best.

Valentín Bianchi, Ortiz de Rosas and Comandante Torres (☎02627/422046). Beautiful town-centre bodega, using fairly old-fashioned techniques, and with a small museum. Mon–Fri 9.15am, 10.15am, 11.15am, 2.30pm, 3.30pm & 4.30pm.

Champañera Bianchi, Hipólito Yrigoyen s/n (☎02627/435353). Ultra-modern sparkling wine production unit, housed in a post-modern steel-and-glass building 4km west of the town centre, which makes an interesting contrast with the old downtown bodega; excellent sparkling wines made according to *méthode champenoise*. Mon–Sat 9am–1pm & 3–7pm.

Jean Rivier, Hipólito Yrigoyen 2385 (☎02627/432675, fax 432675; *jrivier@satlink.com*). Friendly small winery, founded by Swiss winemakers; their tip-top wines include an unusual Cabernet Sauvignon-Fer blend. Delicious

Chardonnays, too. Mon–Fri 8–11am & 3–6.30pm; Sat 8–11am.

Simonassi Lyon, 5km south of San Rafael by RN143, at Rama Caida (☎02627/430963; *s-lyon@satlink.com*). Guided visits Mon–Fri 9am–noon only at this family-run, prize-winning winery, housed in an attractive farmhouse.

Bodega y Champañera Rafael Salafia, Hipólito Yrigoyen 5800 (☎02627/430095). Traditional winery making both delicious Malbecs and Cabernets, and sparkling wines using the *méthode champenoise*. Personalized welcome. Mon–Fri 9.30am–3.30pm.

Suter, Hipólito Yrigoyen 2850 (☎02627/430135 or 421076). Slightly mechanical guided visits every half hour, but you're given a half-bottle of decent wine as a gift. Traditional-style winery. Mon–Fri 8am–8pm; Sat & public holidays 9am–7pm.

begin at the reservoir farthest away, the **Embalse del Nihuil**, reached along the winding RP144 mountain-road towards Malargüe, up the Cuesta de los Terneros to the 1300-metre summit, which offers stunning views of the fertile valley below; and then via the RP180 which forks off to the south. The lake, nearly 100 square kilometres in surface area, lies 92km southwest of San Rafael, its turquoise waters popular with windsurfers – boards can be rented at the Club de Pescadores, lying just off the road on the north-eastern banks of the *embalse*. The partly sealed RP173 then squeezes in a northeasterly direction through the narrow gorge whose cliffs and rocks are striped red, white and yellow, contrasting with the beige of the dust-dry mountainsides. Wind and water have eroded the rocks into weird shapes that stimulate the imagination: tour guides are fond of attaching often convincing names like "The Nun" or "The Toad" to these strange rock formations. The road then passes a couple of dams, attached to power stations, before swinging round the other reservoir, the **Embalse Valle Grande**. Among these blue-green waters are more weird rock formations, one of which does indeed look like the submarine its nickname suggests. From the high corniche roads that skirt the lakeside you are treated to some staggering views of the waters, dotted with kayaks and other boats, and the steep mountains beyond.

At the northern end of the reservoir you'll find two confiterías, *Lago Chico* and *Portal del Atuel*, both of which serve decent snacks and drinks. Near here starts the stretch of the Río Atuel used for white-water rafting. Raffeish, at República de Siria 296, San Rafael (☎02627/424456), are the most reliable operators, and they have an office here. Otherwise book a white-water rafting session through your tour operator. Trips last an hour, along an easy stretch for beginners, or a couple of hours or more, taking in a tougher section of the river, for more experienced rafters; take swimwear as you get soaked. The scenery along the way is charmingly pastoral along the more open parts and staggeringly beautiful in the narrower gorges, making the experience unforgettable. Farther downstream Hunuc Huar is a wonderful crafts workshop run by an indigenous family, specializing in very fine ceramics, set in an idyllic garden. San Rafael is only 25km away by the same RP173 road. Unless you have your own transport you'll have to get to the canyon on an **organized tour**; the best operator in San Rafael is Bessone Viajes at Av. Hipólito Yrigoyen 423 (☎02627/436439; *bessone-viajes@cpsarg.com*).

Las Leñas

To Argentines, **LAS LEÑAS** means chic; this is where the Porteño jet-set come to show off their winter fashions, to get photographed for society magazines, and to have a good time. Skiing and, increasingly, snowboarding, is all part of it, but as in the most exclusive Swiss and American winter resorts, the *après ski* is just as important if not more. In addition to rich Porteños, wealthy Brazilians and Colombians also come here to sport the latest in ski-wear and dance the night away. More seriously, many ski champions from the northern hemisphere head down here during the June to October season, when there's not a lot of snow in the US or Europe; the Argentine, Brazilian and South American skiing championships are all held here in August, while other events include snow-polo matches, snow-rugby, snow-volleyball and fashion shows. But even though Las Leñas is a playground for the rich and famous, it's nonetheless possible to come here without breaking the bank; you could stay in the least expensive accommodation, or overnight elsewhere nearby, such as in El Sosneado or Malargüe (see below), travelling here for the day. Las Leñas is also trying to branch out into summertime adventure travel, making the most of its splendid upland setting, with some amazingly beautiful trekking country nearby.

The road to Las Leñas heads due west from the RN40 Mendoza to Malargüe road, 28km south of the crossroads settlement of El Sosneado. It climbs past the ramshackle spa-resort of Los Molles, and the weird **Pozo de las Ánimas**, a set of two well-like depressions, each several hundred metres in diameter, caused by underground water erosion, with a huge pool of water in the bottom. The sand-like cliffs surrounding each lake have been corrugated and castellated by the elements, like some medieval fortress, and the ridge dividing the two looks in danger of collapse at any minute. The resort of Las Leñas lies 50km from the RN40, a total of nearly 200km southwest of San Rafael. If you are booked at the resort you might get a transfer from Mendoza or San Rafael, otherwise you either need your own transport or, during the ski season, take the daily **bus** run by TAC from Mendoza, a seven-hour journey.

This is no Gstaad or St Moritz but the Valle Las Leñas resort has made an effort to come up with inoffensive architecture and aesthetically it compares well with many European ski-resorts. When there is snow (the 1998 season was disastrously dry) the skiing is excellent, and the craggy mountain-tops, of which Cerro Las Leñas is the highest (4351m) and Cerro Torrecillas (3771m) the most daintily pinnacled, make for a breathtaking backdrop. The whole area covers more than 33 square kilometres, with 33 pistes, ranging from several gentle nursery slopes to a couple of sheer black runs, so you can get away from the crowds; cross-country and off-piste skiing are also possible. An early start definitely pays off, as most people need much of the morning to recover from all-night discoing. Instruction in skiing and snowboarding is given in several languages, including English; the equipment-rental service is pricey but of tip-top quality, and the twelve lifts are state-of-the-art – again rides aren't cheap, with day passes costing as much as $46 in the height of the season (August).

The ski-village's **accommodation** varies considerably in price, and ranges from the utterly luxurious to the functional. The *Hotel Piscis* (⑨) has a beautiful swimming pool, plus jacuzzis, saunas, comfortable rooms with piste views, its own equipment for rent, including special boot-warmers, and a charming bar called *Allegro*. Much farther away from the central village, and therefore rather quieter, is the *Hotel Aries* (⑦), which has a modern gym, very tastefully decorated rooms and impeccable service. Back in the village the *Hotel Escorpio* (⑧) boasts an excellent restaurant with a terrace, rooms with great views and very pleasant bathrooms. At the *Hotel Acuario* (⑥), rooms are very comfortable and there is a parrilla restaurant. The *Club de la Nieve* (④), housed in an Alpine-style chalet, has its own reasonable restaurant and spacious, functional rooms. Other more economical accommodation (③) can be found at the so-called "dormy houses", *Laquir, Lihuén, Milla* and *Payén*, all grouped at the edge of the village. Booking is organized centrally through Las Leñas resort at Reconquista 559, Buenos Aires (☎011/4313-1300, fax 4315-0270; *www.laslenas.com*). Budget accommodation is also available at the *Hostal El Sosneado*, (☎02627/471971; ①), nearly 80km away; it has very clean, simple rooms, central heating and a small restaurant. Excursions, including horse rides, are arranged throughout the year. For **eating** at the ski-village, there's the confitería and popular meeting-place *El Nuevo Innsbruck*, which serves beer and expensive snacks on its terrace with piste views. *Bacus* is an on-piste snack-bar, while *Elurra* serves lunch and is accessible by the Minerva chair-lift. *La Cima* is a pizzeria by day and a more chic restaurant by night, while the *Hotel Piscis'* luxury restaurant, *Cuatro Estaciones*, is the place to be seen for dinner; a strict dress code applies. Rather more informal, if still expensive, and serving delicious, huge-portioned fondues and raclettes with the best Argentine white wines, is the *El Refugio*, in the central Prámide building. Apart from the Casino, for **nightlife** you have a choice between *Ufo Point*, a funky bar-cum-disco, *Base Zero*, where you can also get food, and *Disco Ku*, with the best music in the village; some people hang around till dawn.

Malargüe and around

MALARGÜE is a small, laid-back little town, lying 186km south of San Rafael by the RP144 and RN40. The biggest settlement in the far southern portion of Mendoza Province, it serves as a possible alternative base to San Rafael for exploring this part of the province. At 1400m above sea level, the town enjoys warm summers and cool winters, and snow is not unknown. The self-styled Capital Nacional de Turismo de Aventura, or National Capital of Adventure Tourism – a slight exaggeration, although it does have one of the most dynamic tourism policies in the whole country – Malargüe is a good spot for exploring some of the least known, but most spectacular landscapes in Argentina, let alone Mendoza Province, as well as for dabbling in a spot of fishing; as yet, however, accommodation is the weak link in the chain, with less variety and quality than in San Rafael.

While it's run-of-the-mill in appearance, the town's undeniable asset is its location, near some of the most beautiful mountain scenery along the cordillera and within day-trip distance of the black and red pampas of **La Payunia**, a nature reserve where flocks of guanacos and ñandúes roam over lava-flows. Far nearer to hand – doable as half-day outings – are some remarkable underground caves, the **Cueva de las Brujas**, and **Laguna Llancanelo**, a shining lagoon flecked pink with flamingoes and crammed with other aquatic birdlife. You could also consider staying here in order to go skiing, for a day at least, at the exclusive winter sports resort of **Las Leñas** (see p.490) – although public transport in the area is virtually non-existent. Now that national and multinational firms seem to have lost interest in the nearby deposits of petroleum and uranium, and ever since farming was blighted in the early twentieth century by a massive volcanic eruption of ash – from Volcán Desabezado Grande (3830m), across the border in Chile – tourism has become a major industry, and the town's couple of tour operators are of a very high quality. An extra special treat is one of the various flights offered at the aerodrome; for $200 an hour for three to four people, these give you either amazing bird's-eye views of the black lava-flows – an unusual way of seeing the Laguna Llancanelo, on which the flamingoes look like confetti – or heart-stopping close-ups of the cordillera summits.

The Town

The core of the town lies either side of the RN40, called Avenida San Martín within the town's boundaries, a wide rather soulless avenue along which many of the hotels are located, as well as a couple of cafés, the bank and telephone centres. **Plaza General San Martín** is the focal point, with its benches shaded by pines and native trees, but it's nothing to get excited about. Being totally flat and compact, however, the town is extremely easy to find your way around, and in any case, its handful of attractions are clustered together at the northern reaches, beyond the built-up area. Conveniently close to the tourist office, the beautiful landscaped **Parque del Ayer**, or "Park of Yesteryear", is planted with pines, cypresses, willows, acacias, dog-roses, pyracanthus and native retamos. Various sculptures and items such as old hay-carts are dotted among the vegetation, but Malargüe's pride and joy is the splendid, new **Centro de Conferencias** (daily 10am–8pm; free; guided visits), subtly plunged underground in the middle of the garden. Its beautiful post-modern design, incorporating some fine workmanship including superb stained glass, is certainly impressive, as is the wonderful auditorium with its perfect acoustics and smart red seats. It all begs the question, however, what use the place is going to be put to, apart from showing it off to passing visitors. One answer is that it will complement the **Centro Pierre Auger**, planned to occupy a space opposite; this centre, named after a French physicist who discovered the energy-producing potential of cosmic rays, will be built with international funding and UNESCO backing as the southern hemisphere element in a worldwide project to harness the rays. It's due for completion in 2001. On quite a different level, just along from the park, three blocks north of Plaza San Martín, is the **Molino de Rufino Ortega**, a handsome thick-walled adobe flour-mill now converted into an exhibition centre (daily 10am–7pm; free). When Volcán Descabezado, across the border in Chile, exploded in 1932, the ash fall-out destroyed all of the wheat fields and rendered the surrounding farmland all but useless. Next to the mill, housed in a fine colonial building with a delightfully overgrown patio, is the **Museo Regional** (Tues–Fri 9.30am–7.30pm; Sat, Sun & public holidays 9am–noon 4–8pm; $1). The collection is a haphazard jumble of ammonites, guanaco leather, clay pipes for religious ceremonies, a mummified corpse, jewellery, dinosaur remains and even a set of vehicle registration plates dating from the 1950s, when the town was temporarily renamed Villa Juan Domingo Perón.

Practicalities

Buses from Mendoza, San Rafael and Neuquén go all the way to the bus terminal at Esquibel Aldao and Fray Luis Beltrán, four blocks south and two west of central Plaza San Martín, but will also drop off and collect passengers at the plaza en route. Malargüe's excellent **tourist office** (daily 7am–10pm; ☎02627/471659; *turismun@ slatinos.com.ar*), in a fine rustic building on the RN40 four blocks north of the plaza, has loads of information on what to see and do, and on places to stay, tour operators and fishing in nearby rivers. **Accommodation** is relatively limited and less good value than in San Rafael. The *Hotel Portal del Valle,* RN40 Norte (☎02627/471294; ④), has a small indoor pool, a sauna, bar and decent restaurant and organizes excursions; rooms are modern and very pleasant. Next door is the *Río Grande Hotel* (☎02627/471589; ⑤), with tastefully decorated rooms in a British style, very friendly owners and delicious food in the restaurant. The *Hotel de Turismo*, at Av. San Martín 224 (☎02627/471042; ③), has functional rooms and a busy confitería. If you stay at the smart *Hotel Rioma*, at Fray Inalicán 68 (☎02627/471065; ③), you get a fifty percent discount on ski-lifts at Las Leñas. *Hotel Llancanelo*, at Av. Rufino Ortega 158 (☎02627/470689; llancane@slatinos.com.ar, ③), has attractive double and triple bedrooms; the Alpine-style, pine-clad bar-cum-confitería serves very decent food. The only real budget accommodation is to be had at the awfully cramped but clean *Refugio del Juan* at Batallón N. Creación 462 (☎02627/156-75554; ①). Otherwise you could **camp** at *Camping Polideportivo* in Capdeval and Esquibal Aldao (☎02627/470691; $4) or in a wonderful setting at Castillos de Pincheiras, 27km southwest of the town. All of the **tour operators**, offering excursions in the region to places like La Payunia and Cueva de las Brujas, are of a very high standard. Check out Karen Travel at San Martín 1056 (☎02627/470342); Huarpes del Sol at Illesca 222 (☎02627/1558-4842); and Cari-Lauquen Turismo, at San Martín 85 (☎02627/470025), all of which can also fix you up with a vehicle, preferably a 4WD. If you are interested in one of the fabulous **flights** in a small passenger plane, contact the Aeroclub Malargüe, just to the south of the town along RN40 (☎02627/471600). *Café Ondas*, at Av. San Martín 500, and *Quinto Viego*, at no. 355, are the town's main meeting-places, both offering breakfasts, coffee and evening drinks. Apart from the *Hotel Río Grande*, the best place **to eat** in town is *La Posta*, an excellent parrilla serving goat and trout, at Av. Roca 374. For the best trout, though, head out of town to El Dique, 8km west of Malargüe, where at the trout farm *Cuyam-Co* (☎02627/411102) you can even catch your own fish if you want. It is then perfectly cooked and served with an excellent local rosé. You can pitch your tent at the nearby shady campsite for $2 a person. Fishing is charged at $7 an hour.

Reserva Faunística Laguna de Llancanelo

Spring is by far the best time to come to the **Reserva Faunística Laguna de Llancanelo**, an easy half-day trip from Malargüe, since that's when you're likely to see the largest numbers of waterfowl, as many species come here to nest. But throughout the year the shallow saline lagoon's mirror-still waters in the middle of a huge dried up lake-bed make for a fantastic sight. You'd be very unlucky not to spot flocks of flamingoes, at times so huge that whole swathes of the lake's surface are turned uniformly pink. Other species of birds that frequent this special habitat include black-necked swans, several kinds of duck, grebe and teal, gulls, terns and curlews. Parts of the reserve are out of bounds all year, while access to others is restricted to non-critical seasons. The park is patrolled by *guardaparques* and it is best to go on an organized tour from Malargüe, as you'll get more out of visiting the lagoon with someone who knows the terrain and the fauna. Preferably come very early in the morning or in the late afternoon and evening, when the light is fabulous and the wildfowl more easily spotted. Access to the reserve is via the RP186 road which branches east off the RN40 some 20km south of Malargüe; it's then another 20km to the reserve entrance, near the shallow cavern known as the Cueva del Tigre.

La Cueva de las Brujas

The **Cueva de las Brujas** is a marvellous cave that plunges deep into the earth at an altitude of just under 2000m, just 73km southwest of Malargüe, 8km off the RN40 along a marked track. To get there you climb over the scenic **Cuesta del Chihuido**, which affords fantastic views of the Sierra de Palauco to the east, in a region of outstanding beauty, enhanced by sparse but attractive vegetation. This area is covered by a thick layer of marine sedimentary rock, through which water has seeped, creating underground cave systems, such as the Cueva de las Brujas. The name, literally "witches' cave", is thought to be linked to local legends that it was used as a meeting-place for sorcerers. The Cueva lies within a provincial park, and a small *guardería*, manned by a couple of *guardaparques*, stands nearby; they have the key to the pad-locked gates that protect the grotto ($3). It's compulsory to enter with a guide, and the best option in any case is to go on an organized tour from Malargüe. Take pocket torches, though miners' helmets are also supplied – but don't rely on their batteries; a highlight inside the cave is experiencing the total darkness by turning out all lights and getting used to the spooky atmosphere. Las Brujas is a Karstian cave, named after Karst in former Yugoslavia, and it's filled with amazing rock formations, including some impressive **stalactites and stalagmites**; typically they have been given imagi-native names such as the Virgin's Chamber, the Pulpit, the Flowers and the Crystals. Water continues to seep inside, making the walls slippery as though awash with saliva, and the whole experience is like accompanying an endoscope on its exploration of someone's throat. Although the tourist circuit – as opposed to the speleologists' much longer route – is only 260m long and never descends more than 6m below the surface, the experience is memorable. Wear good walking shoes and take a sweater as the difference in temperature between inside and out can be as much as 20°C.

Just 5km west of the side-road to the caves is the turn-off to the **Paso Pehuenche**, a mountain pass across the cordillera into Chile some 80km away. At 2500m, this pass is hardly ever blocked by snow and is becoming a major route between the two countries.

La Payunia

The highlight of any trip to southernmost Mendoza Province, yet overlooked by most visitors because it is relatively difficult to reach, **La Payunia**, or the Reserva Provincial El Payén, is a fabulously wild area of staggering beauty, sometimes referred to as the Patagonia Mendocina. Dominated by Cerro Payún or Payén (3690m) and inactive Volcán Payún Matrú (2900m), it is utterly unspoiled apart from some remnants of old fluorite and manganese mines plus some petrol-drilling derricks, whose nodding-head pump-structures are locally nicknamed "guanacos", after the member of the llama fam-ily they vaguely resemble in shape. Occasionally you will spot real guanacos, some-times in large flocks, standing out against the black volcanic backdrop of the so-called **Pampa Negra**. This huge expanse of lava in the middle of the reserve was caused by relatively recent volcanic eruptions, dating back hundreds or thousands of years rather than millions, as is the case of most such phenomena in the region. "Fresh" trails of lava debris can be seen at various points throughout the park, and enormous boulders of ignaceous rock are scattered over these dark plains, also ejected during the violent vol-canic activity. The only vegetation is flaxen grass, whose golden colour stands out against the treacle-coloured hillsides. Another section of the reserve is the aptly named **Pampa Roja**, where reddish oxides in the lava give the ground a henna-like tint. The threatening hulk of Volcán Pihuel looms at the western extremity of the reserve – its top was blown off by a particularly violent explosion that occurred when the mountain was beneath the sea.

The approach to the park from Malargüe is farther along the RN40 from the Cueva de las Brujas. After crossing the Río Grande at Bardas Blancas, you travel another 100km or so, following the river valley and the golden expanse of the Pampa de Palauco. The road crosses the river again at a tightly narrow gorge, called La Pasarela, or the footbridge, where the waters quickly cooled a lava-flow thousands of years ago and created a rock formation that looks as brittle as charcoal. The park's volcano cones soon loom into view and the entrance to the reserve is via a side-turning to the east, at a place called El Zampal. There isn't really any viable alternative to one of the excellent day-trips run by Karen Travel, San Martín 1056, Malargüe (☎02627/470342).

SAN JUAN AND LA RIOJA

San Juan and **La Rioja** provinces share some of the country's most memorable landscapes, range after range of lofty mountains alternating with green valleys of olive-groves, onion fields and vineyards. Forming the northern half of Argentina's midwestern region, they're often regarded as the poorer cousins, in every sense, of Mendoza Province, and certainly neither of their capitals could be called sophisticated; rather, they give the impression of being resigned to backwater status, even though La Rioja was Carlos Menem's power base from where he was propelled to the Casa Rosada. To take one example, the provinces' **bodegas** continue to take a back seat to those of Mendoza and San Rafael, even though their wine can be just as good. One advantage of this relative seclusion is that you have more space to yourself and are usually treated with more spontaneous hospitality than is sometimes the case further to the south. **Tourism** has not quite got off the ground here, a fact that may present some drawbacks – transport and other facilities are sometimes below par, when not lacking entirely. But as long as you see this as a challenge rather than an obstacle, you can still discover some of the country's most breathtaking scenery in both provinces. The small southeastern corner of the region should be bypassed or given short shrift, however: it's a horrendous, flat area of dusty gorse and drab salt-flats.

To say that both provinces are sparsely populated is a gross understatement: outside the capital, La Rioja's density rate barely reaches one inhabitant per square kilometre while San Juan, where the equivalent ratio is around three, is on average half as densely populated as Mendoza Province. If these statistics seem too abstract, you'll soon understand what they mean in practice; leaving the cities behind to scout around the outback, you'll experience a real sense of setting off into uncharted territory, a sensation heightened by the often challenging terrain. Mostly unpaved roads frequently peter out into tracks barely passable in the hardiest jeep, and the weather conditions are equally inclement in summer, when sudden downpours sweep bridges away, or winter, when frequent squalls unpredictably turn into blizzards. This inhospitable nature offers up fantastic opportunities for alternative tourism, though the all but empty roads tend to rule out hitchhiking as a way of getting around.

About halfway between the dizzy heights of the Andean cordillera – many of its peaks exceeding 6000m along this stretch – and the tediously flat *travesías* in the easternmost fringe of both provinces, rises the **precordillera**, lower than the main range but still a respectable 4000m or more above sea level. Club-sandwiched between it and the two rows of cordillera – known as main and frontal ranges, a geological phenomenon unique to this section of the Andes – are successive chains of stunningly beautiful valleys. The higher ones over 1500m above sea level are known as the *valles altos*, of which **Valle de Calingasta** is an outstanding example. The two provinces can boast four transcendent landscapes that have been awarded official protection status. In San Juan Province, the highly inaccessible **Parque Nacional San Guillermo** pairs off neatly with the **Reserva Provincial Vicuñas**, across the boundary in La Rioja: respectively they give you a sporting chance of spotting wild pumas and vicuñas, along with a host of other Andean wildlife, amid unforgettable landscapes. Farther east is a duo of far better publicized parks: **Parque Nacional Talampaya**, with vertiginous red cliffs that make you feel totally insignificant and – only 70km to the south – its unidentical twin, **Parque Provincial Ischigualasto**, more commonly referred to as the Valle de la Luna, an important dinosaur graveyard in a highly photogenic site of extraordinary beauty. Often visited on the same day – which is a bit of a rush – the former is better seen in the morning light, while the latter's lunarscapes are dazzling at dusk.

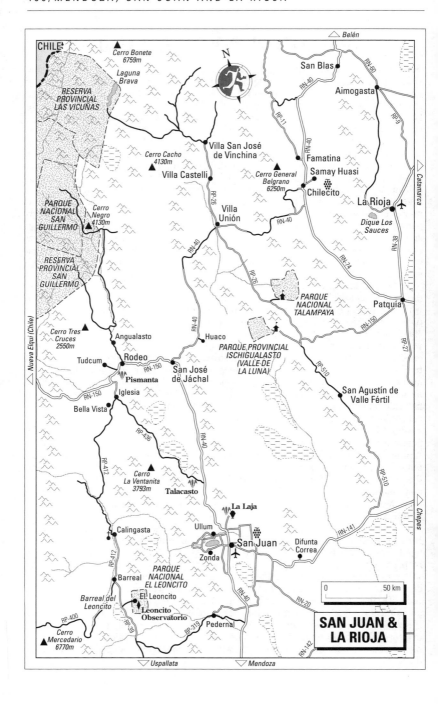

San Juan and around

Some 165km north of Mendoza and nearly 1150km northwest of Buenos Aires, the city of **SAN JUAN** basks in the sun-drenched valley of the Río San Juan, which twists and turns between several steep mountain ranges. Understandably, the city revels in its pet name, Residencia del Sol. In some of its barrios it has rained only a couple of times over the past decade, and the provincial average is under 100mm a year. When it does rain, it's usually in the form of violent storms, as savage as the *zonda* wind that occasionally stings the city and shortens people's tempers (see box below). All this sunshine – more than nine hours a day on average – and the generally mild climate quickly ripen the sweetest imaginable grapes, melons and plums, irrigated by pre-Columbian canals and ditches, that have helped the city and its mainly Spanish and Middle Eastern immigrant population to prosper over the years. But nature is also a foe: periodic tremors, some of them alarmingly high on the Richter scale, remind Sanjuaninos that they live along one of the world's most slippery seismic faults; the Big One is dreaded as much here as in California but, as they do there, people just live their lives, trusting the special construction techniques of the city's modern buildings. One of South America's strongest recorded earthquakes, around 8.5 on the Richter scale, and Argentina's worst ever, flattened the city in 1944, claiming over ten thousand lives – indirectly helping to change the course of Argentine history (see "Some history" on p.499).

With hardly a building more than half a century old, San Juan is a modern but attractive city, yet it's also quite conservative and, compared with its much bigger rival, Mendoza, seems to drag its feet somewhat. Around a third of a million people live in Greater San Juan, but in the compact microcentro, rebuilt according to the model already implemented in Mendoza after its own catastrophic quake, everyone seems to know everyone else. Broad pavements, grand avenues and long boulevards shaded by rows of flaky-trunked plane trees lend the city a feeling of spaciousness and openness. None of the sights amounts to much, but San Juan is a comfortable starting point for touring some of the country's finest scenery. The topography of San Juan Province – shaped like an arrowhead pointing north from its capital – alternates between splendidly fertile valleys, such as Calingasta and Iglesia, and some of Argentina's noblest mountains. Destinations close to the city include the man-made **Embalse de Ullum** and oasis landscapes to the west, the archeological museum and thermal springs at **La Laja**, to the north, and the mind-bogglingly grotesque pilgrim site of **Difunta Correa**, 60km to the east.

THE ZONDA EFFECT

Like the rest of the Cuyo, but especially so, San Juan is prone to the *zonda*, an almost legendary dry wind that blows down from the Andes and blasts everything in its path like a blowtorch. It's caused by thermal inversion arising when wet, cold air from the Pacific is thrust abruptly up over the cordillera, suddenly forced to dump its moisture mostly in the form of snow onto the skyscraper peaks before helter-skeltering down the other side into the deep chasm between the Cordillera Principal and the precordillera, which acts like a very high brick wall. Forced to brake, the *zonda* rubs against the land like tyre-rubber against tarmac, and the resulting friction results in blistering temperatures and an atmosphere you can almost see. Mini tornadoes can sometimes also result, whipping sand and dust up in clearly visible spirals all along the region's desert-like plains; the Cuyo's answer to the *foehn*, mistral or sirocco, ripping people's nerves to shreds, the *zonda* can be one of the world's nastiest meteorological phenomena. Although it can blow at any time of year, it's most frequent in the winter months, particularly August, when it can suddenly hike the temperature by ten to fifteen degrees in a matter of hours.

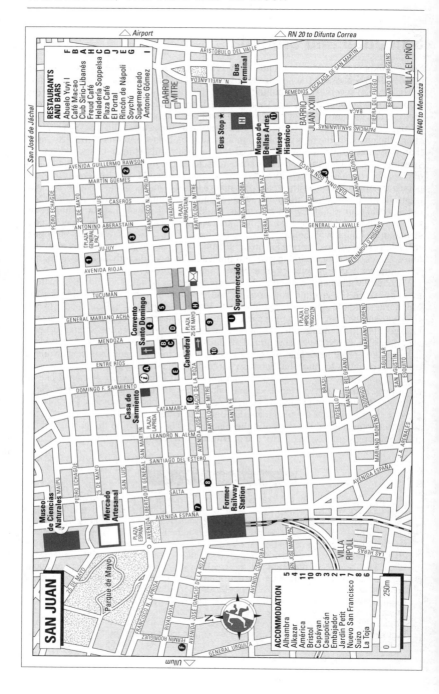

SAN JUAN

RESTAURANTS
AND BARS

Abuelo Yuyi I   F
Café Macao   B
Club Sirio-Libanés   A
Freud Café   C
Heladería Soppelsa   D
Plaza Café   J
El Portal   E
Soychú   G
Supermercado
Antonio Gómez   I

ACCOMMODATION

Alhambra   5
Alkazar   4
América   11
Bristol   10
Capayán   9
Caupolicán   3
Embajador   2
Jardín Petit   1
Nuevo San Francisco   7
Suizo   8
La Toja   6

Some history

The city was founded by the Spanish aristocrat, Juan Jufré, as San Juan de la Frontera, on June 13, 1562, during an expedition from Santiago de Chile, and since then has had a persistently troubled history. In 1594 the settlement was washed away by floods and in 1632 was again destroyed, this time under attack by natives. The Battle of Bermejo, the following year, was an uprising by the indigenous inhabitants, brutally put down by Juan Adaro de Irazola, sent from Santiago; seventeen natives were hanged on the Plaza Mayor to set an example. Later San Juan found itself at the heart of the country's Civil War in the middle of the nineteenth century: San Juan's progressive leader, Dr Antonino Aberastain, was assassinated by troops loyal to General Juan Saa, the federalist Governor of San Luis. In 1885 after the railways reached the city, which had remained a backwater for most of the century, it started attracting traditional Basque, Galician and Andalucian immigrant communities. With Mendoza, the city shares a terrible history of seismic shocks: several violent earthquakes struck the city in the 1940s, but the strongest of all, attaining around 8.5 on the Richter scale, hit San Juan on January 15, 1944. It flattened the city and killed more than 10,000 people; during a gala held in Buenos Aires shortly afterwards to raise funds for the victims, a relatively unknown officer, Juan Domingo Perón, met an equally obscure actress, Eva Duarte, and the rest is the stuff of musicals and Hollywood blockbusters. Quakes have continued to trouble the city regularly, the most severe being the 7.4 tremor epicentred on nearby Caucete on November 23, 1977, which left sixty-five dead and hundreds wounded.

Arrival, information and accommodation

Las Chacritas **Airport**, small but functional, is 12km east of the city, just off the RN141 (☎0264/425-0487); a taxi or *remise* to the centre from here will cost around $10. The city's user-friendly, spacious **bus station**, with regular services all over the province, region and country, is eight blocks east of the central Plaza 25 de Mayo, at Estados Unidos 492 sur (☎0264/422-1604). En-Pro-Tur, the **provincial tourist office**, is at Sarmiento 24 (daily 8.30am–8.30pm; ☎0264/422-7219), next to a mighty 200-year-old carob tree. The staff are extremely helpful and can propose excursions to major sights, such as Ischigualasto (see p.506). You won't be needing city transport, but all **buses** to nearby destinations such as Zonda or La Laja leave from stops alongside the bus station.

San Juan has no youth hostels, but most of the inexpensive **residenciales** are clean and comfortable. A whole crop of middling **hotels**, nothing special but pleasant enough, should meet your needs for the short time you're probably going to stay here, but if you want some creature comforts, there's one snazzy five-star establishment with all mod cons. Campers will go west to the **campsites** at Zonda and, if that's full, Ullum. Zonda's campsite, *Camping Municipal Rivadavia*, on the RP12 opposite the race track, has a swimming-pool and very decent facilities, charging $3 per person. Ullum's, *Camping El Pinar*, is within the grounds of the Parque Sarmiento, along the RP14, just before the Dique Nivelador. Set amidst a refreshing wood of pines, cypresses and eucalyptus, it has a bathing area, a canteen and well-kept facilities. It also costs $3 per person.

Hotels

Hostal Suizo, Salta 272 sur (☎0264/422-4293). An odd mixture, with a rather chaotic entrance and twee bedrooms, in an unsurprisingly Swiss style; good value though. ③.

Hotel Alhambra, General Acha 180 sur (☎0264/421-4780). Medium-sized rooms, each with bath, in this old-fashioned but well-run establishment, with friendly staff. ④.

Hotel Alkazar, Laprida 84 este (☎0264/421-4961 or 2 or 4965). This is San Juan's only luxury hotel to date; albeit on the impersonal side, it does have extremely smart, well-kept rooms, with ultra-modern bathrooms, and sweeping views across the city. Swimming pool. ⑦.

Hotel América, 9 de Julio 1052 este (☎0264/421-4514). Pleasant, traditional, small hotel, popular with foreign visitors, so call first to reserve. All rooms have en-suite bathroom. ④.

Hotel Bristol, Entre Ríos 363 sur (☎0264/421-4629). If you don't mind the dazzling predominance of orange in the decor, this bright, clean place is just the ticket; modern bathrooms. ④.

Hotel Capayán, Mitre 31 este (☎0264/421-4222 or 422-5442). The reception is strangely located in the basement, but the rooms are comfortable, albeit slightly old-fashioned. ⑤.

Hotel Jardín Petit, 25 de Mayo 345 este (☎0264/421-1825). Small, functional rooms with bath, and a bright patio overlooked by the breakfast room. ④.

Hotel Nuevo San Francisco, Av. España 284 sur ☎0264/422-3760). Extremely reliable place, with smart, pleasant rooms, new bathrooms, and friendly service. ③.

Residencial Caupolicán, Av. Libertador General San Martín 441 este (☎0264/421-1870). Cats roam around the lush patio, along which basic but clean rooms are aligned, most with their own bath. A communal kitchen for guests. ②.

Residencial Embajador, Av. Rawson 25 sur (☎0264/422-5520). This friendly if basic place is extremely popular, so book ahead. ②.

Residencial La Toja, Rivadavia 494 este (☎0264/422-2584). This *residencial* has cramped but very clean rooms and offers a friendly welcome. ②.

The City

The total area of San Juan city, girdled by the Circunvalación, the city ring-road, is extensive but easy to find your way around as the grid is fairly regular and the streets don't change name. In all directions from the point zero, the intersection of Calle Mendoza and Avenida San Martín, the cardinal directions are added to the street name; for example, Avenida Córdoba oeste or este, or Calle Tucumán norte or sur. **Plaza 25 de Mayo** is the epicentre, surrounded by cafés with terraces and some shops, plus the *Club Español*, on the northern side, a city institution but not the best place to eat or drink. The controversial **Cathedral**, too modern for many tastes, on the northwest edge of the plaza, has a fifty-metre brick campanile that takes its inspiration from the tower of St Mark's in Venice. It was built in the 1970s and its practical purpose is to provide a high viewpoint over the city. You can climb almost to the top of the **bell tower** (daily 9am–1pm 5–9.30pm; $1) – which plays a Big Ben chime, and the Argentine national anthem for special occasions – for panoramic views of the city and the surrounding countryside.

Two blocks west and one north, opposite the tourist office, is the only museum of any interest in the city, the **Museo Casa de Sarmiento** (Tues–Fri 8.30am–1.30pm & 3–8pm, Mon & Sat 8.30am–1.30pm; $1; guided tours half-hourly, in Spanish only) at Sarmiento 21 sur. The house where Sarmiento, Argentine president and Renaissance man, was born on February 15, 1811, was only slightly damaged in the 1944 earthquake, thanks to its sturdy adobe walls and sandy foundations, and has since been restored several times, to attain its present gleaming state – for the Sarmiento centenary in 1911 it was declared a national historic monument, Argentina's first. It's a beautiful, simple whitewashed house built around a large patio, with a huge rubber-tree. The rooms contain an exhibition of Sarmiento relics and personal effects, plenty of portraits and signs of sycophancy, echoed by the gushing commentary of the guides who steer you round.

Of San Juan's several other museums, only three have any potential whatsoever: the **Museo de Bellas Artes Franklin Rawson** and **Museo Histórico Provincial Agustín Gnecco**, both in the same building at General Paz 737 este (Tues–Sun 9am–1pm; free), seven blocks east and three south of Plaza 25 de Mayo; and the **Museo de Ciencias Naturales** (Mon–Sat 9am–12.30pm; $2), housed in the former train station at avenidas España and Maipú, seven blocks west and five north of the central plaza. The first two contain rather motley collections of paintings and antiquities, respectively. The art collection, named after the unimaginative nineteenth-century painter Franklin Rawson, includes work by him, plus some more interesting pictures, including a portrait of a chillingly tight-lipped widow by Prilidiano Pueyrredón. Major

Argentine artists Berni, Spilimbergo, Petorutti and Raquel Forner (see Contexts, p.748) are all represented here but not at their best. Among the thrown-together exhibits at the Museo Histórico is a set of coins, lots of nineteenth-century furniture and some criollo artwork, including spurs, stirrups and *mate* vessels. The Museo de Ciencias Naturales contains an incipient, state-of-the-art exhibition focusing on the remarkable **dinosaur skeletons** unearthed at Parque Provincial Ischigualasto (see p.506). You can see the scientific workshop, where the finds are examined and analyzed, while the collections of semi-precious stones extracted from the province's mines are for once imaginatively displayed, using modern techniques.

A lot is made by the local tourist authorities and tour operators of the cell where General San Martín stayed in 1815, part of a well-restored seventeenth-century Dominican convent, **Convento de Santo Domingo** at Laprida 96 oeste, two blocks east of the Casa de Sarmiento (Mon–Sat 8.30am–12.30pm; $1; free Feb 25, San Martín's birthday). The cloisters were wrecked by the 1944 quake, but the cell was almost intact, taken as a further sign of the Libertador's sainthood. The stark cell contains some of the hero's belongings, but that's all.

You could round off your exploration with a visit to one of the city's bodegas. None of them is anything like as well organized as those in Mendoza Province, but the most alluring in San Juan is the **Antigua Bodega Chirino** at Salta 782 norte (Mon–Sat 8.30am–12.30pm & 4.30–8.30pm; free; ☎0264/421-4327), housed in a beautiful brick reconstruction of the pre-quake winery, and its red and white wines are among the best in the province.

Eating, drinking and nightlife

San Juan has a wide range of **places to eat**, including one of the region's best vegetarian restaurants – so good it can be recommended for non-veggies too. You can also find excellent Middle Eastern, Spanish and French cuisine in addition to the usual pizzerias, parrillas and *tenedor libre* joints. Most of the best places are in the western, residential part of the city, away from the microcentro. **Café** life is all part of the *paseo* tradition, imported lock, stock and barrel from Spain, but later in the evening most Sanjuaninos seem to entertain themselves in their gardens, round a family *asado*. You'll also find a couple of decent **discos**, mostly in the outskirts.

Restaurants

Abuelo Yuyi, Av. José Ignacio de la Roza and Urquiza, and Fermin Rodriguez. Two branches of the most popular pizzerias in town, offering delicious thick-crust pizzas with a variety of toppings.

Club Sirio-Libanés, Entre Río 33 sur. The Arabesque coffee-room, with its majestic chairs, is more impressive than the dining-room, but the *mesa fria*, or mezze, is excellent; the local wine-list is also very good.

Antonio Gómez, Supermercado, General Acha and Córdoba. Stupendous paellas and other Spanish fare at this extremely popular market-stall. Lunchtime only.

El Hostal de Palito, Av. Circunvalación 284 sur (☎0264/423-0105). This is one of the best parrillas in town, with a delightful garden-terrace.

Las Leñas, Av. San Martín 1670 oeste. Cavernous dining-room often packed out with large parties; delicious meat.

La Nonna María, Av. San Martín 1893 oeste and P. Moreno. Top-quality pizzeria, serving wonderful creations cooked in wood ovens.

Rigoletto, Paula A. de Sarmiento 418 sur. Cosy atmosphere and friendly service, as well as delicious pizzas and pasta.

Rincón de Nápoli, Rivadavia 175 oeste. Traditional Italian-style trattoria serving pasta and meat dishes.

Soychú, Av. José Ignacio de la Roza 223 oeste. Delightful vegetarian restaurant serving fabulous dishes, in a bright, airy space; office workers flock here, taking food away, too, so come early.

Wiesbaden, Av. Circunvalación s/n norte (☎0264/426-1869). Some of the best food in town at this German-style beer-garden and eatery; freshwater fish is a speciality.

Bars, cafés and nightclubs

Aruba, Rioja and Maipú. Disco with a bar and confitería attached, playing mostly salsa and other Latin rhythms.

Café Macao, Laprida and Mendoza. The nearest thing to a Santiago de Chile-style "café con piernas" this side of the Andes; top-rate coffee.

C@sino, Cybercafé, Rivadavia 12 este. Lively bar-café, which is also the city's most reliable cyberplace.

Costa Salguero, Colón and Benavides. Salsa and other dance all week long at this funky nightclub.

Freud Café, Plaza 25 de Mayo. An establishment on the terrace-rich eastern side of the main square; coffee, drinks, lots of gossip and football chat.

Heladería Soppelsa, A. José Ignacio de la Roza 639 oeste and Mendoza 163 sur. Undoubtedly the best ice cream in the city.

Plaza Café, Plaza 25 de Mayo. Another institutional café on the central plaza; snacks and small meals, while you watch the world go by.

Listings

Airlines Aerolíneas Argentinas, Av. San Martín 215 oeste (☎0264/427-4444); Lufthansa, Entre Ríos 24 norte (☎0264/421-4038); LAPA, Av. José Ignacio de la Roza 160 este (☎0264/421-6039); TAN, Av. José de la Roza 278 este (☎0264/429-0010); Southern Winds, Av. José Ignacio de la Roza 288 este (☎0264/420-2000).

Banks Cambio Santiago, General Acha 52 sur, for travellers' cheques and exchange. Stacks of ATMs all over town, especially around Plaza 25 de Mayo.

Car rental Localiza, Av. Rioja 1187 sur (☎0264/421-9494); Renta Auto, Av. San Martín 1593 oeste (☎0264/423-3620).

Hospital Hospital Rawson, General Paz and Estados Unidos (☎0264/422-2272).

Internet C@sino Cybercafé, Rivadavia 12 este (☎0264/420-1397; *cafecasino@arnet.com.ar*).

Laundries Fast, Sarmiento and 9 de Julio; Laverap, Rivadavia 498 oeste.

Left luggage At the bus terminal (24hr).

Pharmacies Echegaray, Av. Rioja and Santa Fe; San José, Av. Córdoba and España.

Police Entre Ríos 466 sur (☎0264/4214521).

Post office Av. José Ignacio de la Roza 259 este (☎0264/422-4430).

Telephones *Locutorios* all over, several clustered around Plaza 25 de Mayo.

Tour operators Fascinatur, Ramón y Cajal 232 norte (☎0264/422-7709; *fascinatur_dahu@arnet.com.ar*); Gringo de Lara, Rivadavia 230 oeste (☎0264/423-1974, fax 0264/427-6873).

Around San Juan

Around San Juan you'll find wildly different sights that can be visited either on a short trip from the city, or on your way somewhere else – after all, you'll want to sprint off into the unspoiled wildernesses and high valleys of San Juan Province before too long. To the west you can go wine-tasting at **Zonda** or windsurfing on the **Dique de Ullum**, in a bone-dry valley, dotted with oases; at **La Laja** to the north is an archeological museum whose prize exhibit is a magnificent Incan mummy; to the east, the shrine to the **Difunta Correa** is the most concrete example of how Amerindian legends and Roman Catholic fanaticism have melded together in one belief. Farther to the northeast is **San Agustín de Valle Fértil**, one of the most agreeable towns in the region, near beautiful polychrome mountains, and the perfect base for visiting two of the region's big draws: **Ischigualasto** and **Talampaya** (see p.505). Finally, in the warmer months, along the

RN40 to the south, near the border with Mendoza Province, you'll see beautiful fruit stands, on which melons and watermelons are arranged in geometric patterns. From this road, a track cuts across a dust bowl before crossing the precordillera to the **Valle de Calingasta** (see p.509).

Zonda and the Dique de Ullum

In Quechua, the name **Zonda** means high sky, and the valley of that name to the west of San Juan, reached along the RP12, seems to enjoy blue skies nearly every day of the year. Vineyards and olive-groves alternate with lush fields of camomile that become snow-white in the spring – all watered almost entirely with irrigation channels that distribute the ice-melt from the Andes; the only blot on the landscape is the huge cementworks which belches clouds of dust high into the atmosphere. The air around here is so dry it tingles. The road soon enters a narrow gorge, formed by the crinkly Serranía de Marquesado; partly landscaped with native and European trees, the open Parque de Zonda, which nestles in the gorge by the roadside, includes a **Jardín de los Poetas**, also permanently accessible, where verses of Argentine poetry are inscribed on the rock-face. The most noteworthy piece of graffiti is a quotation by Sarmiento who passed through in 1840, on the way to his Chilean exile imposed by his arch-enemy Rosas – his words, "Ideas cannot be killed", were written in French so that Rosas' followers wouldn't understand them. Near the El Zonda racing track, 15km from the city you'll see a sign for the **Cavas de Zonda** (daily 9am–noon and 4pm–6pm; ☎0264/497-2148). It claims to be South America's only wine cellar to be housed in a natural cave; in the cool tunnel drilled into the cliff-side the temperature is up to 40°C lower than outside, ideal for storing some of Argentina's finest ciders and sparkling wines, the latter marketed as champagne; you're taken on a tour of the cellars before tasting a selection of the wines, which includes a rich Malbec. **Bus** #23 from San Juan's bus terminal runs to Zonda on a regular basis.

Just to the north of Zonda, but reached directly from San Juan by the RP113 and RP14, the **Dique de Ullum**, a large reservoir, is the city's vital water source, but it's perennially ultramarine waters are also used for non-polluting water-sports such as windsurfing, fishing and swimming – when the *zonda* blows, surfers race along at incredible speeds and the conditions can even be quite dangerous, especially for the inexperienced. Several clubs and associations rent out boards and other equipment, and give instruction; try the Club Náutico de Vela y Remo, Playa Bahía Los Turcos or the Complejo Bahía Las Tablas (no phone), all located on the east bank of the reservoir. The surrounding mountains are excellent for rock-climbing and hiking; if you decide to give either of these activities a go, take lots of water – at least two litres – as the hottest part of the day can be brutal here. **Bus** #29 comes out here from the city.

La Laja

Some 25km to the north of San Juan, by the RN40 and a minor road that zigzags through vineyards, **LA LAJA** is a tiny hamlet that's little more than a chalk quarry, some thermal springs and an archeological museum. The last, the **Museo Arqueológico de La Laja** (Mon–Fri 9.30am–5pm, Sat & Sun 9.30am–5.30pm; $2), run by San Juan University, is worth the trek not for its unappealing reinforced concrete building, but for the collection of mummies preserved inside. The highly academic presentation takes you through the pre-history and history of the provinces' cultures, from the so-called Cultura de la Fortuna (10,000–6000 BC), of which we just have a few tools as evidence, to the Ullum-Zonda civilization of the Huarpes people, whose land was invaded first by the Incas in the fifteenth century and then by colonizers from Chile in the sixteenth century; a number of digs near the city of San Juan have uncovered a treasure of ceramics and domestic items, displayed here in rather ramshackle glass cases.

Inside, the museum's highlights are a set of mummified bodies dating from the first century BC to the fifteenth century AD, and the most impressive of all was discovered in 1964 – interesting photographs of the expedition are also displayed – at over 4500m in the cordillera, northern San Juan Province. Kept in an antiquated fridge is **La Momia del Cerro el Toro**, probably the victim of an Incan sacrifice; the body is incredibly well-preserved, down to her eye-lashes and leather sandals. Other items worth a mention are a 2000-year-old carob-wood **mask**, some fine **basketwork** coloured with natural pigments, and a jointed **wooden condor** with malachite feathers, a masterpiece attributed to the late Angualasto culture – fourteenth to fifteenth century. The museum has no guides, but if you press the red button in each of the rooms you're treated to a commentary in Spanish, with all the intonation of the speaking clock. Outside, the Amerindians' habitat, including igloo-shaped stone huts and half-submerged burrows, has been reconstructed in a landscaped garden.

You can relax afterwards in the **Baños Termales La Laja** (daily 9am–9pm; $2), right next to the museum. There's a confitería and changing rooms, plus a scrupulously clean swimming pool, with mineral water at 35°C–40°C; for an extra $2 you can use the cabins for thirty minutes – the maximum recommended as the waters are highly sulphurous. **Bus** #20 goes out to La Laja from San Juan's bus terminal five or six times a day.

El Santuario de la Difunta Correa

Some 65km east of San Juan, **El Santuario de la Difunta Correa**, is both a repellent and an intriguing place. All around Argentina you'll come across mini Difunta shrines, sometimes little more than a few bottles of mineral water heaped at the roadside – and easily mistaken for a particularly bad bout of environmental pollution. But the original shrine is here in San Juan Province. To get there go past the airport, beyond which a couple of rather dreary satellite towns, including Caucete, badly damaged in the 1977 earthquake, are strung along the RN141 towards Chepes and La Rioja. The landscape then turns into desert-like plains, complete with sand dunes, though the most impressive aren't visible from the main road; to the north, the reddish Sierra Pie de Palo ripples in the distance, relieving the monotony. Suddenly, in the middle of nowhere, amid its own grim complex of hotels, confiterías and souvenir shops and on top of a small hill, is Argentina's answer to Lourdes.

The story goes that, during the Civil War in the 1840s, a local man Baudilio Correa was captured, taken to La Rioja and killed; his widow Deolinda decided to walk to La Rioja with their baby boy to recover Baudilio's corpse. Unable to find water she dropped dead by the roadside, where a passer-by found her, the baby still sucking from her breast. Her grave soon became a holy place and lost travellers began to invoke her protection, claiming miraculous escapes from death on the road. The story is believed to be Amerindian in origin but has been taken over by the Roman Catholic Church in a country where the borderline between religion and superstition is very faint. The Difunta Correa – *difunta* meaning deceased – is now the unofficial saint of all travellers, but especially bus- and truck-drivers, and thousands of people visit the shrine every year, over 100,000 of them during Holy Week alone, many of them covering part of the journey on their knees; national truck-drivers' day in early November also sees huge crowds arriving here. Some people visit the shrine itself – where a hideous statue of the Difunta, complete with sucking infant, lies among melted candles, prayers on pieces of paper and votive offerings including people's driving-licences, the remains of tyres and photographs of mangled cars from which the occupants miraculously got out alive – while others just deposit a bottle of mineral water on the huge collection that is creeping along like a small-scale replica of the Perito Moreno glacier (see p.653). Vallecito runs regular **buses** out here, but unless you're really curious, it's only worth the short stop you get on the bus route from San Juan to La Rioja.

Parque Provincial Ischigualasto and Parque Nacional Talampaya

San Juan and La Rioja provinces boast two of the most photographed protected areas in the country. In San Juan, the **Parque Nacional Ischigualasto** is better known as Valle de la Luna – Moon Valley – because of its eerily out-of-this-world landscapes and apocryphal legends. The province has jealously resisted repeated attempts to turn it into a national park, and this is probably a godsend, since the provincial authorities are doing an admirable job of providing easy access and looking after the fragile environment. President Menem made sure, on the other hand, that his native province of La Rioja got its first national park while he was in office. **Parque Nacional Talampaya** is another vulnerable biotope, home to several rare varieties of flora and fauna, including condors, but it's best known for its giant red sandstone cliffs, which are guaranteed to impress even the jaded traveller. While the latter is closer to the La Rioja town of Villa Unión (see p.514), both parks are within reach of the delightful little town of **San Agustín de Valle Fértil**, high in the mountains of eastern San Juan Province. Most visitors take in both parks in the same day, though each merits a longer visit; in any case it is wise to go to Talampaya in the morning, when the sun lights up the coloured rocks and illuminates the canyon, while Ischigualasto is far more impressive in the late afternoon and at sunset in particular. Then you can make it back to Valle Fértil before nightfall. Another possibility is a gruelling but rewarding day-trip from San Juan, or even La Rioja. Public transport can get you to these destinations but it is erratic and your own vehicle is preferable.

San Agustín de Valle Fértil

Set among enticing mountainside landscapes, some 250km northeast of San Juan, by the RN141 and mostly unpaved RP510, and about 100km south of the entrance to Ischigualasto, the oasis town of **SAN AGUSTÍN DE VALLE FÉRTIL** is the best place to spend the night in eastern San Juan Province. It prospered in the nineteenth century thanks to the gold, iron and quartz lines, and marble quarries in the mountains nearby, but has now turned to tourism as a source of income, to supplement meagre farm earnings. The fertile valley that gives it its name – sometimes it's referred to simply as "Valle Fértil" – is a patchwork of maize fields, olive-groves and pasture for goats and sheep – and the local cheese and roast kid are locally renowned. Valle Fértil's raison d'être for the traveller is as an alternative base for visiting the twin parks of Talampaya and Ischigualasto; although it's logistically less helpful than staying at Villa Unión, for example, since it's better to visit Talampaya in the morning and Ischigualasto in time for sunset, the facilities in Valle Fértil knock Villa Unión's into a cocked hat. It's also much more attractive, built around a mirror-like reservoir, the Dique San Agustín; cacti and gorse grow on its banks, and a small peninsula juts artistically into the waters.

Buses from San Juan (3 daily) and La Rioja (2 weekly) arrive at Mitre and Entre Ríos. The **tourist office** (Mon–Fri 7am–1pm & 5–9pm, Sat 8am–1pm; no phone) at Plaza San Agustín is extremely helpful, and can fix you up with guides and transport both to Ischigualasto and to other less dramatic sites in the nearby mountains, including pre-Hispanic petroglyphs; note that there are no ATMs in the town. The best **place to stay** is the comfortable *Hostería Valle Fértil* on a hilltop overlooking the Dique, at Rivadavia (☎02646/420015; ⑤–⑥). It has a decent restaurant, delightfully modern, bright rooms – the more expensive ones with lake views – but the bathrooms are cramped. Both *Hospedaje San Agustín* at Rivadavia and Juan Rojas (☎02646/420004; ②) and *Hospedaje*

Los Olivos at Santa Fe (☎02646/420115; ②) are basic, lackadaisically run pensions, but their clean rooms are fine for a night. There are two **campsites**: the *Campismo Municipal* (☎02646/420192) on the banks of the Dique charges $8 per tent, but *Camping Valle Fértil* (no phone), at the lower end of the road leading up to the Hostería Valle Fértil, at $10 per tent, has more appealing toilets and showers, and is generally better kept. Apart from the restaurant at the *hostería*, the best **places to eat** are the traditional parrillas *Los Olivos* and *Rancho Criollo*, both a block south of Plaza San Agustín.

Parque Provincial Ischigualasto

Just under 100km north of Valle Fértil, the **Parque Provincial Ischigualasto**, also known as the Valle de la Luna, or Moon Valley, is San Juan's most famous feature by far, yet even in the high season it is big enough not to be swamped by visitors. Covering nearly 150 square kilometres of astonishingly varied terrain, it can be visited only in a vehicle, whether your own, that of your tour operator or a vehicle rented for the duration from the park authorities, though don't count on the latter – you might be put with other visitors who can squeeze you into theirs. For the scientist, Ischigualasto's importance is primarily as an archeological site and a rich burial ground of some of the Earth's most enigmatic inhabitants, the dinosaurs, models of which litter the park. For geologists, the park is unique as all stages of the 45-million-year Triassic era are represented in its rocks. Most visitors, however, come simply to admire the spectacular lunar landscapes, which give the park its popular nickname, and the much publicized and alarmingly fragile rock formations – some have already disappeared, the victims of erosion and the occasional flash floods that seem to strike with increasing frequency. **Cerro El Morado** (1700m), a barrow-like mountain shaped like an Indian lying on his back according to local lore, dominates the park to the east.

Another of the park's attractions is the wealth of flora and fauna. The main plant varieties are the native broom-like brea, three varieties of the scrawny jarilla, both black and white species of algarrobo, the chañar, retamo and molle shrubs, and four varieties of cactus. Animals that you are likely to spot here are criollo hares, Patagonian hares, the vizcacha, the red fox, armadillos and small rodents, plus several species of bat, frog, toad, lizard and snake. Condors and ñandúes are often seen, too, while guanacos may be spotted standing like sentinels atop the rocks, before scampering off. This is a desert valley, in between two ranges of high mountains, the Sierra Los Rastros to the west and Cerros Colorados to the east. For a long time under the sea, as witnessed by the mollusc and coral fossils found in the cliff-sides, the whole area has been eroded by water and especially by wind in the course of millions of years, while sections, built of volcanic ash, have taken on a ghostly greyish-white hue. A set of red sandstone mountains to the north acts as a perfect backdrop to the paler stone formations and clay blocks, all of which are impressively illuminated in the late evening. The landscapes have often been compared with national parks in the US Southwest, such as Bryce Canyon.

Tours follow set **circuits**, beginning in the more lunar landscapes to the south; a segmented row of rocks is known as El Gusano (The Worm); a huge set of vessel-like boulders, including one resembling a funnel, is known as El Submarino; a sandy field dotted with cannon-ball shaped stones is dubbed the Cancha de Bolas (The Ball-court), but Aladdin's Lamp, precariously balanced on a pinnacle, was knocked over by a violent storm in 1998. Panoramic outlook points afford stunning views of ghoulish, empty landscapes of oceans of hillocks, bearing signs of different levels of water millions of years ago. These are the typical moonscapes, but they look uncannily like the famous landscapes of Cappadocia, with their Gaudiesque pinnacles and curvaceous mounds. Then you head north, where sugary white fields are scattered with petrified tree-trunks and weird and wonderful rocks. One famous formation, painfully fragile on its slender stalk, is **El Hongo** (The Mushroom), beautifully set off against the orange sandstone cliffs behind. Again visitors will be reminded of the canyons of New Mexico and Utah. This whole tour needs at least a couple of hours to be done at all comfortably; be warned that sudden summer storms can cut off the tracks for a day or two, in which case you may not be able to see all the park.

Park practicalities

The **guardería** (daily 9am–dusk), manned by ultra-friendly *guardaparques*, lies at the entrance to the park, along a well-signposted lateral road, off the RP510 at Los Baldecitos. You must pay $5 per person, which entitles you to a guided tour. While you can **camp** for free next to the visitors' centre (which has a few photographs and sketchy information about the park's geology and wildlife), most people stay at either Villa Unión or, preferably, Valle Fértil (see above). You could also come on an **organized tour** from San Juan. Fascinatur at Ramón y Cajal 232 norte (☎0264/422-7709; *fascinatur_dahu@arnet.com.ar*) is by far the best operator in the city. Triassic Tour at Hipólito Yrigoyen 294 sur, San Juan (☎0264/423-0358), specializes in trips to the park, as their name suggests. As for **public transport**, the infrequent Vallecito bus from San Juan to La Rioja could drop you at Los Baldecitos, about 5km from the park entrance. The optimal time of day for visiting the park is in the mid- to late afternoon, when the light is the most flattering. That way you also catch the mind-boggling sunsets that illuminate the park, turning the pinkish orange rock a glowing crimson, which contrasts with the ghostly greyish white of the lunarscapes all around. If you want to see both Ischigualasto and Talampaya in the same day, go to the latter first.

Parque Nacional Talampaya

The entrance to **Parque Nacional Talampaya**, known as the Puerta de Talampaya, is 55km down the RP26 from Villa Unión (see p.514), and then 12km along a signposted track to the east. Coming from the south, it's 93km north of Ischigualasto and 190km from Valle Fértil. The park's main feature is a wide-bottomed canyon flanked by 180-metre-high, rust-coloured sandstone cliffs, so smooth and sheer that they look as if they were sliced through by a giant cheese-wire. Another section of the canyon is made up of rock formations that seem to have been created as part of a surreal Gothic cathedral. Added attractions are the presence of several bird species, including condors and eagles, as well as rich flora and some pre-Columbian petroglyphs etched on the natural walls of rock. The park's name comes from the indigenous people's words *ktala* – the locally abundant *tala* bush – and *ampaya*, meaning dry river-bed.

Talampaya's cliffs appear so frequently on national tourism promotion posters or in coffee-table books, you think you know what you're getting before you arrive. But no photograph really prepares you for the belittling feeling you get when standing at the foot of a massive rock wall, where the silence is broken only by the derisive caw of a pair of condors flapping around their ledge-top nest. Even the classic shots of orange-red precipices looming over what looks like a Dinky-toy jeep, included for scale, don't really convey the astonishment. The national park, covering 215 square kilometres, was created in 1997 at President Menem's instigation – he is a Riojano after all – to protect the canyon and all its treasures. Geologically it's part of the Sierra Los Colorados, whose rippling mass you can see in the distance, to the east, along with the giant snow-capped range of the Sierra de Famatina, to the north. These mountains were all formed over 250 million years ago, during the Permic Period, and have gradually been eroded by torrential rain and various rivers – among them the Río Talampaya, along whose sandy bed you drive during the visit – which have exploited a series of geological faults in the rock, and the reason why the cliffs are so sheer.

Just to the south of the entrance to the canyon, huge sand dunes have been swept up by the strong winds that frequently howl across the Campo de Talampaya to the south.

The higgledy-piggledy rocks at the foot of the cliffs host a gallery of white, red and black **rock paintings**, made by the Ciénaga and Aguada peoples who inhabited the area around a thousand years ago. The pictures include animals such as llamas, suri and pumas, a stepped pyramid, huntsmen and phallic symbols, and the nearby ink-well depressions in the rock are *morteros*, or mortars, formed by decades of grinding and mixing pigments. You'll also see a huge *tacu* or carob tree, thought to be over 1000 years old. From here you enter the canyon proper, following tracks ploughed through the sandy river-bed; round the first gentle curve, you reach the so-called **jardín botánico**, or more accurately the *bosquecillo* – thicket – a natural grove of twenty or so different native cacti, shrubs and trees, all clearly labelled in Latin and Spanish. They include algarrobos, retamos, pencas, jarillas and chañares, all identified so you'll recognize them out in the countryside; occasionally grey foxes and small armadillos lurk in the undergrowth and brightly coloured songbirds flit from branch to branch. Nearby, and also clearly signposted, is the **Chimenea** (chimney), or the *Cueva* (cave), or the *Canaleta* (drainpipe), a rounded vertical groove stretching all the way up the cliff-side; guides revel in demonstrating its extraordinary echo which sends condors flapping as it ricochets off the rock face. Some 150m further along, the cliffs disintegrate somewhat, especially where the mostly dry river-bed of the Río de la Apolinaria meets that of the Río Talampaya, ripping down some of the rock whenever there's a storm. These rock formations, too, have been given imaginative names, mostly with a religious slant, but many of them do fit. *El Pesebre* is a set of rocks supposed to resemble a nativity scene, while appropriately nearby are **Los Reyes Magos**, the Three Kings, one of them on camelback. A partly hollowed out feature jutting out from the wall has been dubbed *El Púlpito*, while at the corner of the canyon a cluster of enormous needles and pinnacles is known as *La Catedral* – the intricate patterns chiselled and carved by thousands of years of erosion have been compared variously with Albi Cathedral or the facade of Strasbourg Cathedral, both in France and built of a similar red sandstone. Across another wide riverbed is a separate set of massive rock formations, known as **El Tablero de Ajedrez**, or the Chessboard, complete with rooks, bishops and pawns; a 53-metre-high monolith, resembling a cowled human figure is *El Cura*, the priest, or *El Fraile*, the monk, depending on who you ask; maybe *El Rey*, the king, is more appropriate. Continue up the fast narrowing canyon, down which trickle rivulets of spring water, wriggling with tadpoles in the spring, and you pass **El Pizarrón**, or the blackboard, fifteen metres of flat rock face of darker stone etched with more suris, pumas, guanacos and even a seahorse – more pre-Columbian petroglyphs showing that the peoples who lived here a thousand years ago had some kind of contact with the ocean. To reach the **Ciudad Pérdida**, another outcrop of monoliths, natural standing stones and cliffs so architectural in appearance that it has been dubbed the Lost City, you need to return to the main RP26 highway, travel down 6km, and turn off east along a separate track. This is the least-visited part of the park, and in any case is rather less impressive than the towering cliffs of the main canyon.

Park practicalities

The **guardería** is staffed throughout the year and is located at the end of the trail off the RP26, at the Puerta de Talampaya (daily 9am–5pm; $5; no phone). To get to the park without your own transport or without going on an **organized tour** from La Rioja or San Juan, you can be dropped off on the main road by the buses from Villa Unión (the nearest town to the park; see p.514) to La Rioja and Valle Fértil, or take the regular bus from Villa Unión to the village of **Pagancillo** 27km north of the park entrance. There you can stay at the basic but clean *Cabañas Adolfo Páez* (☎03825/470397; ②); the owner might even take you to the park and guide you around. It's also possible to **camp** in the open, next to the *guardería*, but bear in mind that it's often windy and can get extremely cold at night for much of the year. There's also a confitería serving basic, reasonably priced snacks and small meals. Whatever the rangers tell you, you are allowed to use your own vehicle, but you need a 4WD and must take a guide. Alternatively you can negotiate a fee to use one of their pick-up trucks, which give you an open-air view of the canyon as you drive along – but best avoided if it's windy. Three main circuits are on offer: the standard tour lasts 90 minutes and costs $35 per person, basically covering the canyon as far as the "Chessboard"; the second takes twice as long, costs $70 per person and adds on the upper river valley and goes off in search of wildlife in a nearby wood; while the third takes at least one hour more and you get the Ciudad Pérdida thrown in – it costs $110 per person. Avoid the midwinter when it can be bitterly cold, the middle of the day in the height of summer, when it can be unbearably hot, and the day after a storm, when the park is closed because of floods. The best time of day by far to visit is soon after opening, when the dawn light deepens the red of the sandstone; in the afternoon and evening the canyon is shaded and the colours are less intense.

Valle de Calingasta

Whatever your map tells you there is no RP12 road from San Juan via Zonda to Calingasta. The only routes to the marvellous fertile **Valle de Calingasta** are much longer detours than the old road: either south along the RN40 from San Juan to Villa Media Agua, nearly 50km away; from here the RP319 heads west across a dusty plain, through Pedernera, and up over a mountain pass before joining the RP412 south of **Barreal**, the main tourist centre in the valley. The alternative is to approach from the north, via Iglesia (see p.511), but that's a much longer route. Near the quiet, pleasant little town of Barreal, amid fields of alfalfa, onions and maize, with a stupendous backdrop of the Sierra Frontal, snowcapped for most of the year, is the **Complejo Astronómico El Leoncito**, one of the world's most important space observatories. The strange sand-flats of the **Barreal de Leoncito**, also just a few kilometres south of the town, are used for wind-car championships. To the east of the town is a series of mountains, red, orange and deep pink in colour, known aptly as the **Serranías de las Piedras Pintadas**. In the town of **Calingasta** itself the only sight is a fine seventeenth-century **chapel**. To the southwest of Barreal, the RP400 leads to the tiny hamlet of Las Hornillas, the point of departure for adventurous treks and climbs to the summit of **Cerro Mercedario** (6769m), said by many mountaineers to be the most satisfying climb in the cordillera.

Barreal and around

At an altitude of 1650m above sea level, the small oasis town of **BARREAL** enjoys a pleasant climate, alongside the Río de los Patos, at the southern extreme of the bright green strip of land that is the Valle de Calingasta. Since it is the only settlement in the valley with any infrastructure, it is the tourist base for visiting the immediate environs. The views across to the west, of the cordillera peaks such as the majestic **Mercedario** – with its two glaciers Caballito and Ollada – El Polaco, La Ramada and Los Siete Picos de Ansilta, seen across a beautiful plain, shimmering with onion and maize fields, are superb, while across to the east you can climb up into the coloured mountainside, or up to the **Cima del Tontal**, which affords wide-ranging views across to San Juan city. Just to the south is the Barreal del Leoncito, a great plain in the middle of which is a strange sand-flat whose windswept expanse lends itself to the exhilarating sport of wind-car racing. Up on nearby hills are two space **observatories**, among the most important in the world because of the outstanding meteorological conditions hereabouts – more than 320 clear nights a year on average. Barreal also makes a good base if you want to conquer one of the Andes' most challenging yet climbable mountains, the Cerro Mercedario itself (6769m).

Barreal town has no monuments or museums, but is pleasant enough to wander around. The central square, Plaza San Martín, is the focal point, at the crossroads of Avenida Presidente Roca and General Las Heras. **Buses** from Mendoza and San Juan stop here. For **places to stay**, apart from the municipal **campsite**, at Los Enamorados, in a leafy location, with standard facilities ($8 per site), you could try *Cabañas Doña Pipa* at Mariano Moreno s/n (☎02648/441004; ②), in pleasant grounds. The very basic *Pensión Jorge* at Av. San Martín s/n (☎02648/441048; ①) also serves snacks and simple meals; the rooms are arranged around an airy courtyard. The plain but comfortable *Hotel Barreal* at Av. San Martín s/n (☎02648/441114; ③) has its own restaurant and a swimming pool, decent rooms and can organize fishing and other activities. Relatively luxurious *Posada Don Eduardo* in delightful grounds at Av. San Martín s/n (☎02648/441046; ④) has plain but atmospheric rooms around an old patio, and the best **restaurant** in town, serving unimaginative but well-cooked food. Otherwise you're stuck with the run-of-the-mill *Isidoro* at Av. Roca s/n. Expediciones Ossa, operating out of Cabañas Doña Pipa (see above), is the best bet for excursions in the area, and treks or climbs to **Mercedario**.

Around Barreal

Immediately to the south of Barreal along the western side of the RP142 is a huge flat expanse of hardened sand, the remains of an ancient lake, known as the **Barreal del Leoncito**, or the Pampa del Leoncito, or simply the Barreal Blanco. Measuring 14km by 5km, this natural arena, with a marvellous stretch of the cordillera as a background, is used for **wind-car** championships (*caravelismo* in Spanish), and if you want to try your hand as this sport – the little cars with yacht-like sails have reached speeds of over 130km per hour here – contact Gringo de Lara at Rivadavia 230 oeste, San Juan (☎0264/423-1974, fax 427-6873).

Some 20km down this road from Barreal is the turn-off eastwards up into the **Reserva Astronómica El Leoncito**, which enjoys national park status, and is symbolized by the *suri* or Andean rhea. Some 12km up this lateral is the entrance (daily 10am–noon & 3–6pm; free) where you must announce your presence to the *guardeparques*. You then go up a narrow canyon, past the colonial estancia building, to the Complejo Astronómico. There two observatories are located at 2500m, one of which, the **Observatorio Félix Aguilar** (☎0264/421-3653; *www.casleo.secyt.gov.ar*), is open to the public (guided visits at 10.15am, 11.15am, 12.15pm, 2.15pm, 3.15pm, 4.15pm & 5.15pm; free). Its huge white dome sticks out from the brown mountainside. Inaugurated in 1986, this observatory uses Brazilian technology, Argentine know-how and Swiss funds, with some input by the Vatican. The attractive building was built to resist earthquakes of 10 or more on the Richter scale, an absolute necessity in this area of violent seismic activity. The main telescope weighs nearly 50 tonnes and its 2.13-metre diameter mirror has to be replaced every two years. The guided tour, led by enthusiastic staff members (English spoken) takes you through the whole process; take warm clothing as the inside is refrigerated.

The scenic RP400 strikes out in a southwesterly direction from Barreal, to **LAS HORNILLAS** over 50km away. This tiny hamlet is inhabited mostly by herdsmen and their families amid pastureland and gorse-scrub, which is effectively the base camp for the mighty **Mercedario** which looms nearby. If you want to climb this difficult but not impossible mountain, regarded by many as the most noble of all the Andean peaks in Argentina, contact Expediciones Ossa, operating out of *Cabañas Doña Pipa* in Barreal. The nearby rivers are also excellent for fishing for trout; also ask in Barreal.

The mountainsides to the immediate east of Barreal, accessible by clear tracks, are a mosaic of pink, red, brown, ochre and purple rocks, and the so-called **Cerros**

Pintados or "Painted Mountains", live up to their name. Among the rocky crags, tiny cacti poke out from the cracks, and in the spring they sprout huge wax-like flowers, in translucent shades of white, pink and yellow, among golden splashes of broom-like brea shrubs. About 8km north of Barreal, another track heads eastwards from the main road, climbing for 40km past some idyllic countryside inhabited only by the odd goatherd or farming family, to the outlook atop the **Cima del Tontal**, at just over 4000m. To the east there are amazing views down into the San Juan valley, with the Dique de Ullum glinting in the distance, or west and south to the cordillera, where the peak of Aconcagua and the majestic summit of the Mercedario are clearly visible.

Calingasta

The small village that gives the valley its name is located 37km to the north of Barreal, along the RP412. On the eastern side you are treated to more painted mountainsides, striped red like toothpaste. A marked side-road, at the locality called Tamberías, halfway, leads to an unusual rock formation of pale sandstone, called the **Alcázar**, because it looks just like a Moorish castle, with towers and solid curtain-walls. **CALINGASTA** itself is a peaceful village, where the Río Calingasta flows into the Río de los Patos; its only attraction apart from its idyllic site is the seventeenth-century **Capilla de Nuestra Señora del Carmen**, a simple whitewashed adobe building, with an arched doorway and a long gallery punctuated by frail-looking slender pillars. The bells are among the oldest in the country – they are visible in the bell tower – and the iron ladder leading onto the roof is a work of art, too. From Calingasta it's getting on for 150km along the RP412 north to Iglesia, along a dry valley, with the occasional ford, with the Sierra del Tigre to the east and the Cordón de Olivares providing stupendous views to the west.

Valle de Iglesia

The **Valle de Iglesia**, named after its main settlement, **Iglesia**, a sleepy village of Italianate adobe houses, is a fertile valley, separated from the Valle de Calingasta by the dramatic Cordón de Olivares range of mountains. You can get there directly from San Juan via the RN40, which forks off to the northwest at Talacasto, some 50km north of the provincial capital. From there a mountain road, the RP436, snakes round the Sierra de la Invernada, before descending in free fall into the valley. Alongside the highest section of the road, the Pampa de Gualilán is covered with tufts of glaucous vegetation that forms a glacier-like landscape on the mountainside. The cliffs are riddled with the tunnels of disused goldmines. Portezuelo del Colorado, 130km from San Juan, is a pass at nearly 2900m, affording panoramic views of Iglesia, 40km to the northwest, and beyond. Iglesia lies nearly 150km north of Calingasta via the RP406 and RP412. Several villages succeed each other along the valley, including the thermal spa-resort of **Pismanta**, the small market town of **Rodeo** and the idyllic village of **Angualasto**, along the dirt track that leads to one of the country's youngest national parks, **San Guillermo**, the location in Argentina where you are most likely to spot pumas in the wild.

Iglesia and around

IGLESIA is a tiny village at the southern end of its eponymous valley, watered by various streams or *arroyos*. To the southwest, just 2km away, is the aptly named Bella Vista, a picturesque "suburb" of Iglesia made up of crumbling mud-brick houses. Here you will find the area's best **campsite**, *Camping Bella Vista* (☎02647/496036; $3 per person), in a beautifully landscaped location with basic but clean facilities. **Buses** drop you wherever you want in the village, but you'll have to make your own way to the campsite. Some 14km to the north is the farming village of **Las Flores**, amidst fields of alfalfa, lettuce, potatoes and beans; ask around for the delicious goat's cheeses and also for traditional weaver's workshops, which produce beautiful ponchos. About 6km to the northeast is the **Capilla de Achango**, an early eighteenth-century Jesuit chapel with a very simple whitewashed facade, a tiled roof and a wonderfully rickety bell tower. Inside, it is almost painfully simple, adorned only by a couple of ancient statues of saints. Also 6km from Las Flores, but to the northwest, is the spa-resort of **Pismanta**, really nothing more than a small, modest hotel, the *Hotel Nogaró Termas de Pismanta* (☎02647/497002; ⑤) where you can soak in the mineral waters that spurt out of the earth at 45°C. The hotel's rooms are plain but pleasant, and certainly the best to be had in the whole area, and you eat well at the **restaurant**. At Pismanta, the RP412 joins the RN150, which heads west to Chile across the Paso de Agua Negra at 4779m. The Chilean town of Vicuña lies over 260km away; the customs post lies just 3km west of Pismanta and you can also seek more information, as well as details of excursions in the Iglesia and Pismanta area at the **tourist office**, at the RP412/RN150 junction (daily 9am–6pm; ☎02647/493290).

Rodeo and around

The RN150 arches round the pleasant, easy-going market town of **RODEO**, 19km east of Pismanta, bypassing it completely. If you want to see the town, you must turn off onto its main street, Santo Domingo, which leads past the Plaza Mayor and the municipalidad to the **Finca El Martillo** (daily 9am–6pm), at the northernmost end. You can buy all kinds of wonderful local produce here, including herbs, fresh fruit and preserved fruit, including whole candied apples, and excellent jam and honey. Rodeo hosts one of the region's major folk festivals in the first half of March, the **Fiesta de la Manzana y la Semilla**, when you can try local specialities such as *empanadas* and *humitas*, and watch dancing and musical groups in the lakeside Anfiteatro, just off Santo Domingo at the heart of the town.

To the north of Rodeo, you can head off towards Angualasto and the Reserva San Guillermo (see below), while to the east the RN150 takes you past the turquoise waters of the **Embalse Cuesta del Viento**, favoured by windsurfers (ask at Finca El Martillo for access; you'll need your own equipment). The **Quebrada del Viento** is an impressive gorge, followed by a winding cliff-side road, carved out by the Río Blanco.

Angualasto and Parque Nacional San Guillermo

From Rodeo, the RP407 heads north, cutting through a ridge of rock, and sloping down into the fertile valley of the Río Blanco. The little village of **ANGUALASTO**, which has preserved a delightful rural feel, seemingly detached from the modern world, is set among rows of poplars, fruit orchards and little plots of maize, beans and other vegetables. It is proud of its little **Museo Arqueológico Luis Benedetti** (Tues–Sun 8am–1pm 3–7pm; $1), though you may have to ask around in the village to find someone with the key. Its tiny collection of mostly pre-Columbian finds include a remarkable 400-year-old mummified corpse, found in a *tumbería* or burial mound nearby. To the north the road follows the beautiful Río Blanco valley, fording it once – often impossible after spring or summer rains or heavy thaws – to the incredibly remote hamlets of Malimán and **El Chinguillo**, where the Solar family's delightful farmhouse (no phone; ③) provides the only **accommodation** hereabouts, as well as delicious *empanadas* and roast lamb. This is the entrance to San Guillermo, in a beautiful valley surrounded by huge dunes of sand and mountains scarred red and yellow with mineral deposits.

Since the beginning of 1999, part of the Reserva Provincial San Guillermo, in the far northern reaches of San Juan Province, has enjoyed national park status, with investment and loans by the World Bank and the Interamerican Bank for Reconstruction and Development. The **Parque Nacional San Guillermo**, on great heights to the west of the Río Blanco valley, is home to a huge variety of wildlife. Guanacos and vicuñas abound, along with suris or ñandúes, eagles, condors, several different kinds of lizards, foxes and all kinds of waterfowl, including flamingoes, which match the seams of jagged pink rock that run along the mountainsides like a garish zip-fastener. Above all, this is a part of Argentina where you are almost guaranteed a rare spotting of a puma; for some reason the pumas living here are less shy of humans than elsewhere and often approach vehicles; extreme caution is recommended, as these powerful machines of feline muscle are effective mankillers. The highest peaks, at well over 4000m, are permanently snowcapped, and the weather is capricious. There is no *guardería* as such, and no entrance fee as yet, but *guardeparques* patrol the territory, mostly to prevent hunting. Even with your own vehicle – a 4WD is a necessity – this is a difficult trip, especially because of the dangerous fords, so go on a guided tour, with someone who knows the terrain. By far the best operator in San Juan is Fascinatur, Ramón y Cajal 232 norte (☎0264/422-7709; *fascinatur_dahu@arnet.com.ar*).

RN40 from San José de Jáchal to Villa Unión

The section of the RN40, Argentina's longest road, that stretches for 145km northeast from the sleepy little town of **San José de Jáchal**, in San Juan Province, to **Villa Unión**, in La Rioja Province, passes through some outstanding countryside, including the fertile farmland immediately to the north of the town, where you can see some beautiful early nineteenth-century flour-mills amid a landscape rather like that of North Africa or the Middle East. You then squeeze through the Cuesta de Huaco, a narrow mountain road that affords magnificent views of the virgin wastes and dust-dry valleys to the north. The little village of **Huaco** also boasts a delightful old mill. From there the road runs through a wide river valley, that of the Río Bermejo, bone dry for most of the time but suddenly and treacherously flooding over after storms. Beware of the many deep *badenes* or fords along the road; if they are full of water you should wait for the level to drop before attempting to cross and, even when dry, they can rip tyres or damage undercarriages if taken too fast. The dull town of Villa Unión is your destination, and it is no more than a dormitory for visiting the amazing Parque Nacional Talampaya (see p.507), or for going to see wildlife in the **Reserva Provincial Las Vicuñas**, in the far north of this region and in the middle of which is the beautiful **Laguna Brava**, an altiplanic lake of the sharpest blue. From Villa Unión you can get to Chilecito (see p.521) via the RN40 and the staggeringly beautiful Cuesta Miranda, or to the provincial capital of La Rioja (see p.515) via the RP26, past Talampaya, the RN150 and the RN38, a total journey of over 250km.

San José de Jáchal

The small town of **SAN JOSÉ DE JÁCHAL** lies 155km due north of San Juan by the RN40, in the fertile valley of the Río Jáchal, and was founded in the seventeenth century on the site of a pre-Columbian village; San José is 65km due east of Rodeo via the scenic RN150 (see above). Destroyed in a severe earthquake in 1894, it was rebuilt using mud-bricks in an Italianate style, with arched facades and galleried patios, focused on the Plaza Mayor. San José itself isn't much to write home about, but makes for a convenient stopover if you need a bed for the night, or you could have lunch here. During the first fortnight in November every year, it stages the **Fiesta de la Tradición**, a festival of folklore, feasting on local specialities, and music evenings. **Buses** from San Juan stop at the terminal four blocks east of the main plaza. A few **accommodation** possibilities exist but the only one that can be recommended is the *Plaza Hotel* at San Juan 546 (☎02647/420256; ④), which offers pleasant rooms with bath. The only decent place to eat is *El Chatito Flores*, which offers hearty, inexpensive food in very unexceptional surroundings at San Juan and Juan de Echegaray.

To the north of San José, the RN40 suddenly swerves to the east and the road continuing straight ahead, the RP456, cuts through San José's rural northern suburbs amid bucolic farmland, used to grow wheat, maize, alfalfa and fruit. With the stark mountain backdrops of the Sierra Negra to the east, Sierra de la Batea to the north and Cerro Alto (2095m) to the west, this dazzlingly green valley, dotted with adobe farmhouses, some of them with splendid sun-faded wooden doors, looks like the parts of Morocco in the lee of the Atlas. Canals and little ditches water the fields, using snowmelt from the cordillera and precordillera, as rain is rare here. At the beginning of the nineteenth century a number of **flour-mills** were built here, and they are now rightly historic monuments. Their pinkish-beige walls, wonderfully antiquated machinery and the enthusiasm of their owners make for a memorable visit. El Molino, the Molino de Pérez and the Molino de Reyes, all within a few hundred metres of each other on either side of the road, can all be visited, but the most rewarding is the extremely well-preserved **Molino de Sardiña** at the corner of calles Maturrango and Mesias. The charming owner will be delighted to show you around, but always appreciates a tip. Try to be here in the early evening when the warm light adds to the magically timeless atmosphere.

Huaco

Back on the RN40, the road hugs the Sierra Negra, before skirting the eerie little reservoir called Dique Los Cauquenes. Then you enter the Cuesta de Huaco, a narrow mountain road accurately described in a folksong as a place "where the reddish dawn lingers on the even redder clay of the mountainside". Deep-voiced crooner **Buenaventura Luna**, real name Eusebio de Jesús Dójorti Roco, was a highly popular star in the 1940s and 1950s, and he is buried in nearby **HUACO**. This is a small village, lying just off the main road, shaded by algarrobos and eucalyptus; it is no more than a cluster of picturesque mud-brick houses around a small square, but just before you get to the village you pass a splendid adobe **flour-mill**, similar to those to the north of San José. Built at the beginning of the nineteenth century, it belonged to the Docherty family, Irishmen who fought in the British army that invaded Buenos Aires, were captured and decided to settle in Argentina; Buenaventura Luna, poet and folksinger, was one of their descendants.

Villa Unión

The only thing to say about the small town of **VILLA UNIÓN**, in the parched Valle de Vinchina, 120km northeast of Huaco, is that it has a couple of places to stay and eat, when you may overnight before visiting the amazing canyon and rock formations of the Parque Nacional Talampaya (see p.507), 70km to the south. It's also a possible springboard for heading up to the staggeringly desolate Reserva Provincial Las Vicuñas, wrapped around the beautiful Laguna Brava (see below), and over 150km to the northwest. The town, formerly called Hornillos, received its name in the nineteenth century, in recognition of the hospitality of its people towards peasants thrown off a nearby estancia by the ruthless estanceros; today's town is utterly charmless, has no sights, offers no entertainments and doesn't even have an ATM to its name, though there is a bank on the featureless main square, Plaza Mayor. A couple of blocks east is the tiny **bus station**, serving La Rioja, Chilecito and Valle Fértil. You can obtain some information, for what it's worth, at the tourist office on the southeast corner of the Plaza Mayor. For **accommodation** you have a choice of two: one block east of the main plaza, *Hotel*

Noryanepat at Joaquín V. González s/n (☎03825/470133; ③) has decent rooms and cramped bathrooms, and seems to specialize in detachable toilet-bowls; *Hospedaje Doña Gringa*, with tiny but very clean rooms, a leafy patio and a laid-back atmosphere, is a few blocks north of the plaza, at Nicolás Dávila 103 (☎03825/470528; ①). The only place worth trying for something to **eat** is the *Pizzería La Rosa*, on the northwest corner of the plaza.

Reserva Provincial Las Vicuñas

Much easier of access than San Juan's Parque Nacional San Guillermo, immediately to the south, the **Reserva Provincial Las Vicuñas** is nearly 150km to the northwest of Villa Unión, via the RP26 and then a numberless track that twists and turns to the park's central feature, the volcanic lake of **Laguna Brava**. The main attractions are fabulous altiplanic scenery – most of its terrain is at over 4000m – the mountainous backdrop, and the abundant wildlife, mainly vicuñas, as the name suggests. Large flocks of the shy, smaller cousin of the llama, graze on the reserve's bofedales, the typical spongy marshes watered by trickles of run-off that freeze nightly. The best time to visit is in spring and autumn, since summer storms and winter blizzards cut off roads and generally impede travel. On the way to the reserve you pass through **VILLA SAN JOSÉ DE VINCHINA**, 65km north of Villa Unión, a nondescript village near which are six mysterious circular mounds, nearly 30m in diameter. Made of a mosaic of pink, white and purple stones, these **Estrellas de Vinchina** form star-shapes and are thought to have had a ceremonial purpose, perhaps serving as altars. Otherwise head on through the Quebrada de la Troya, a magnificent striped canyon, into the fertile Valle Caguay, dominated by the majestic cone of Volcán Los Bonetes. From here the road is best negotiated in a 4WD – in any case it is wise to visit the reserve on an organized tour from San Juan (see p.502). The track heads to the southern banks of the Laguna Brava, a deep blue lake 17km by 10km, whose high potassium-chloride levels make it undrinkable. When there is no wind the mirror-like waters reflect the mountains behind; when it's blowing a gale, huge waves can be whipped up. Other lakes in the reserve are the smaller Laguna Verde – a green lake as its name suggests – and the Laguna Mulas Muertas, often covered with pink flamingoes, Andean geese and other wildfowl. There's no public transport, no *guardería* and nowhere to stay: just you and the wilds.

La Rioja and around

LA RIOJA – or Todos los Santos de la Nueva Rioxa, as it was baptized at the end of the sixteenth century – is an indolent kind of town, built in a flat-bottomed valley, watered by the Río Tajamar, and nearly 1200km northwest of Buenos Aires and 517km northeast of San Juan. In the spring, the city is perfumed by the famous orange trees that have earned it the much-bandied sobriquet Ciudad de los Naranjos. In spite of the plentiful shade of luxuriant vegetation, the blistering summer heat is refracted off the brutally arid mountains looming to the west and turns the city, notoriously one of the country's hottest, virtually into a no-go zone even for its hardy inhabitants. At all times the place has a rough and ready, Wild West edge to it, and the heat seems to make people tetchy even when they've had their institutional siesta – everything shuts down from 1pm to 5pm. Yet La Rioja is not without its fashionable boutiques or cafés and the city's chic business people in sharp suits love to strut along the tree-lined streets, clutching mobile phones that chirp in competition with the omnipresent and vociferous cicadas. La Rioja is also pervaded by a palpable feeling of resentment at what is perceived as the city's treacherous neglect by former President Carlos

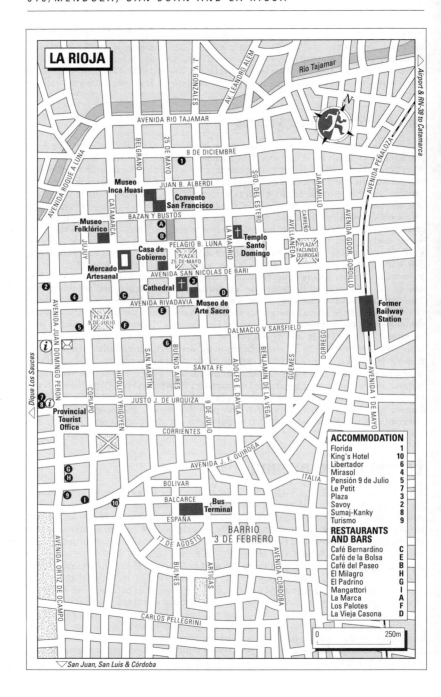

LA RIOJA

Río Tajamar

Airport & RN-38 to Catamarca

AVENIDA RIO TAJAMAR

8 DE DICIEMBRE

J. V. GONZALES

AV LEANDRO ALEM

BELGRANO

25 DE MAYO

SGO. DEL ESTERO

JARAMILLO

AVENIDA PEÑALOZA

JUAN B. ALBERDI

Museo Inca Huasi

Convento San Francisco

BAZAN Y BUSTOS

Museo Folklórico

PELAGIO B. LUNA

LA MADRID

AVELANEDA

CARREÑO

AVENIDA GODR. GORDILLO

Casa de Gobierno

PLAZA 25 DE MAYO

Templo Santo Domingo

PLAZA FACUNDO QUIROGA

Mercado Artesanal

AVENIDA SAN NICOLAS DE BARI

Cathedral

AVENIDA RIVADAVIA

Museo de Arte Sacro

Former Railway Station

DALMACIO V SARSFIELD

DORREGO

AVENIDA 1 DE MAYO

AVENIDA ROQUE A LUNA

CATAMARCA

JUJUY

AVENIDA JUAN DOMINGO PERON

PLAZA 9 DE JULIO

SAN MARTIN

BUENOS AIRES

SANTA FE

ADOLFO E. DAVILA

BENJAMIN DE LA VEGA

GUEMES

Dique Los Sauces

COPIAPO

HIPOLITO YRIGOYEN

JUSTO J. DE URQUIZA

9 DE JULIO

Provincial Tourist Office

CORRIENTES

AVENIDA J. F. QUIROGA

ITALIA

BOLIVAR

BALCARCE

Bus Terminal

ESPAÑA

BARRIO 3 DE FEBRERO

AVENIDA ORTIZ DE OCAMPO

17 DE AGOSTO

BULNES

ARTIGAS

AVENIDA CORDOBA

CARLOS PELLEGRINI

0   250m

▽*San Juan, San Luis & Córdoba*

ACCOMMODATION

Florida	1
King's Hotel	10
Libertador	6
Mirasol	4
Pensión 9 de Julio	5
Le Petit	7
Plaza	3
Savoy	2
Sumaj-Kanky	8
Turismo	9

RESTAURANTS AND BARS

Café Bernardino	C
Café de la Bolsa	E
Café del Paseo	B
El Milagro	H
El Padrino	G
Mangattori	I
La Marca	A
Los Palotes	F
La Vieja Casona	D

Menem, who hailed from the wine- and olive-growing centre of Anillaco, just 90km up the road. Not that people seem to be suffering too much; the city is by no means run-down – a smart hospital was recently opened, and the spick and span low buildings, some of them showcases of contemporary architecture, fronted by well-manicured gardens, radiate an impression of relative prosperity.

La Rioja is not a sightseers' city, but it is a good base for exploring the region and you'll certainly find enough to occupy a full day, not forgetting to do as the Riojanos do and take a full-length nap in the afternoon. Among the highlights are two of the country's best **museums** of indigenous art, one archeological and the other with a folkloric slant. Nearby, the **Quebrada de los Sauces**, named for the shady willows trailing in the **Dique de los Sauces**, a man-made lake, the city's reservoir, offers refreshing bathing and sports activities, acting as a vital safety valve during the most relentless heat waves. Unquestionably, the best time to come to La Rioja is when the orange blossom is out and the jacarandas are ablaze with their mauve flowers, from October to November, but whatever you do, avoid the midsummer when even the most avid sun worshippers will wilt or burn. Temperatures have been known to approach 50°C.

Some history

La Rioja came into being on May 20, 1591 when the Governor of Tucumán, Juan Ramírez de Velasco, a native of La Rioja in Castile, founded the city for King Philip of Spain, in its strategic valley location – in the lee of the mountain range that would later bear his name. Today's Plaza Mayor – officially Plaza 25 de Mayo but never called that by the Riojanos – coincides exactly with the spot he chose. Ramírez de Velasco had set out on a major expedition with an army of conquistadores and a dual purpose: to popu-late the empty spaces of the Viceroyalty and subdue the native Diaguitas, who had farmed the fertile oasis for centuries. La Nueva Rioxa, the only colonial settlement for leagues around, soon flourished and Ramírez de Velasco felt justified in boasting to his sovereign in a letter that it was "one of the finest cities in the Indies". For a long time chroniclers and politicians rhapsodized about the prosperous city, its fertile surround-ings and the heady scent of orange blossom. In the mid nineteenth century, future President Sarmiento even compared it to the Promised Land and the Río Tajamar to the Jordan; if we are to believe the various descriptions by visiting dignitaries and writers, La Rioja must have been a beautiful colonial city.

From it, mainly Franciscan missionaries set about fulfilling Velasco's other aim of converting the native peoples. Their convent and that of the Dominicans, one of the old-est in Argentina, both miraculously survived the earthquake that flattened most of the city in 1894. The Parisian-style Bulevard Sarmiento – now officially renamed Avenida Juan Domingo Perón – had just been completed, as part of the city's late nineteenth-century expansion scheme, when the tremor struck. The whole city was rebuilt, large-ly in a neocolonial style that was intended to restore its former glory. After long decades of neglect by the central government, La Rioja has not benefited as much as it hoped it would when Carlos Menem, scion of a major La Rioja wine-producing family of Syrian origins, was elected President in 1990.

Arrival, information and accommodation

La Rioja's small **airport** Vicente Almandos Almonacid is 7km east of town along the RP5 (✆03822/427239), and the only transport from it into town is by *remise* ($6). The seedy **bus terminal** is eight blocks south of the central Plaza 25 de Mayo, at España and Artigas (✆03822/425453), and serves the whole province including Chilecito and more distant destinations such as Mendoza, Córdoba, Catamarca, Salta and Resistencia. Nearby are some Formica-and-neon cafés and a souvenir shop or two. A taxi ride to the city centre will set you back about $2. The city's **tourist office**, called DiMuTur, is at Av. Perón 715, near the corner with Dalmacio Vélez Sarsfield (Mon–Fri 7am–1pm & 4–9pm, Sat & Sun 7am–1pm; ☎03822/427103); in addition to a list of hotels and *residenciales* staff can provide a list of rooms to rent, plus a map of the city. Two blocks down the road, at Av. Perón 401, the **Dirección General de Turismo** (☎03822/428839) has glossy leaflets and some rudimentary information about the rest of the province.

You're unlikely to want to stay very long in La Rioja, but it's good to know that it's not badly off for **accommodation**, covering the whole range with a few reliable options. Bed-and-breakfast style **casas de familia** (①–③), about which information can be obtained from the municipal tourist office, are the best bet at the budget end, while someone looking for a bit of luxury has a couple of hotels to choose from.

Hotel Libertador, Buenos Aires 253 (☎03822/427474). The hotel has a smart reception area and breakfast room: the rooms are clean and comfortable enough, though nothing special, and the plumbing is faulty. ④.

Hotel Mirasol, Av. Rivadavia 941 (☎03822/420760). Rather on the gloomy side, but the rooms are simple and pleasant, with functional bathrooms. ③.

Hotel Plaza, San Nicolás de Bari and 9 de Julio (☎03822/425215 or 425218). The hotel's neocolonial confitería is one of the places to be seen in La Rioja; everything is squeaky clean, almost clinically so, but the rooms are smart and the roof-top pool and terrace enjoy views of the cathedral and mountains beyond. ⑦.

Hotel Savoy, San Nicolas de Bari and Av. Roque de Luna (☎03822/426894). The decor is perfectly neutral in a rather boringly unimaginative way, but the place is friendly and the rooms are quite spacious, with decent bathrooms. ③.

Hotel de Turismo, Av. Perón 100 (☎03822/422065, fax ☎03822/436253). The more expensive rooms have TV, balconies, modern bathrooms and fine views of the mountains; the others, only slightly cheaper, are quite grim. Outdoor swimming pool and a reliable confitería; breakfasts are generous. ⑤–⑥.

King's Hotel, Av. Facundo Quiroga 1070 (☎03822/422122, fax 422754). The castle-like exterior gives way to a 1970s interior, complete with leatherette armchairs, but this large establishment has a kind of faded charm and shabby luxury about it. ⑦.

Pensión 9 de Julio, Copiapó 197 (☎03822/426955). A resident cat and leafy patio give some atmosphere to this basic pension, the only really budget establishment that can be recommended. Cramped but clean rooms. ②.

Residencial Florida, 8 de Diciembre 524 (☎03822/428583). Family-run place, with tiny rooms, but they all have bath. ③.

Residencial Le Petit, Coronel Lagos 427 (☎03822/427577). In a neocolonial building, slightly run-down, this friendly *residencial* allows you to do your own laundry and cooking; spacious but threadbare rooms. ③.

Residencial Sumaj-Kanky, Av. Castro Barros y Coronel Lagos (☎03822/422299). Avoid rooms on the avenue side, as the traffic's heavy at times, but otherwise this place is comfortable and clean, if basic; most rooms without bath, and those with cost a few pesos more. ②–③.

The City

La Rioja's microcentro really is small and all the places of interest are grouped around the two main squares, Plaza 25 de Mayo and, two blocks west and one south, Plaza 9 de Julio. On the west side of the former is the striking white Casa de Gobierno, built in a neocolonial style with a strong Andalucian influence, which contrasts with the **Catedral San Nicolás de Bari**, on the south of the plaza. This Neoclassical hulk of a church built at the beginning of the twentieth century in beige stone, with a huge Italianate cupola, neo-Gothic campaniles and Byzantine elements in the facade, is primarily the sanctuary for a locally revered relic: a seventeenth-century walnut-wood image of St Nicholas of Bari, carved in Peru. It's the centrepiece of two major processions, the first of which is the saint's day in July; the other is held on December 31 each year, when the statue is the joint star of the **Tinkunaku** – meaning "casual meeting" in Quechoa – joined in the procession by an image the Christ Child – the "Niño Alcalde"

– idolized as La Rioja's eternal guardian and mayor, which is kept at the Iglesia San Francisco. The ceremony represents St Francisco Solano's role in pacifying the indigenous inhabitants of the region in the late sixteenth century. The statue of St Nicholas is kept in a special *camarín* or shrine abutting the cathedral building and kept locked; to see it ask around for the key in the cathedral.

One block north of Plaza 25 de Mayo, at 25 de Mayo and Bazán y Bustos, is the **Iglesia San Francisco** itself, an uninspiring Neoclassical building visited by the saint when he was travelling around South America. The stark cell where he stayed, containing only a fine statue of the saint and a dead orange tree, said to have been planted by him, is treated as a holy place by Riojanos. Another block to the north is the **Museo Arqueológico Inca Huasi** (Tues–Sat 9am–noon; $1), set up in the 1920s by a Franciscan monk who was interested in the Diaguita culture – rather ironic, considering that the Franciscan missionaries did all they could in the seventeenth century to annihilate it. One of the pieces of art on display is a quite hideous seventeenth-century painting of the conversion of the Diaguita people by San Francisco Solana, but the rest of the exhibition is a fabulous collection of **Diaguita ceramics** and other pre-Columbian art. The dragon-shaped vase near the entrance is around 1200 years old; another later piece, inside one of the dusty cases, is a pot with an armadillo climbing it, while fat-bellied vases painted with, among other things, phalluses and toads – symbols of fertility and rain – line the shelves. Sadly, the quality of the items far outstrips that of the display techniques.

Far more impressive a museum is the **Museo Folklórico** at Pelagio B. Luna 811 (daily 8am–noon & 4–8pm; $1), especially since its renovation in 1999. Three blocks west of Plaza 25 de Mayo and two north of Plaza 9 de Julio, it contains the reconstitution of a nineteenth-century Riojano house, complete with furnishings, a bodega, gaucho paraphernalia and a kitchen. In the display on local mythology, a set of beautiful terracotta statuettes representing the various figures brings to life the whole pantheon, such as Pachamama, or Mother Earth, and Zapam-Zucum, the goddess of children and the carob tree – she has incredibly elongated breasts the shape of carob-pods. Zupay is the equivalent of the devil, while a series of characters called Huaira personify different types of wind. Opposite, on the corner of Pelagio B. Luna and Catamarca, is one of the region's best **craft markets** (Mon–Fri 8am–noon & 4–9pm, Sat & Sun 8am–noon); the *artesanía*, all of it local, is not cheap but of very high quality, especially the regionally famous *mantas* or blankets.

One block east of Plaza 25 de Mayo, the **Iglesia Santo Domingo** at B. Luna and Lamadrid is the only building of interest to have survived the 1894 earthquake, and is claimed to be the oldest building in Argentina – it dates from 1623. The extremely long, narrow and very white nave is utterly stark, apart from a fine altar decorated with seventeenth-century statuary, as is the simple whitewashed facade – but the carob-wood doors, carved by Indian craftsmen in the late seventeenth century, are one of the finest pieces of **mestizo art** in the whole country.

Eating, drinking and nightlife

Not as hard up as it sometimes likes to make out, La Rioja has several sophisticated places to have a drink or dinner – though the best of the rest are mostly pizzerias and simple confiterías. During heat waves a lot of locals go and cool down at the Dique Los Sauces (see p.521), where you can also have a meal or a snack, on the refreshing banks of the reservoir; better still, take a picnic.

Restaurants

Mangattori, J.F. Quiroga 1131. Outstanding Italian food, ranging from *insalata caprese* to a hefty *ossobuco*. In hotter weather you might just like one of their salads, followed by an ice-cream sundae.

La Marca, 25 de Mayo and Bazán y Bustos. You can eat as much as you want at this generous parrilla and you'll still be regarded as a small eater. Pig out on meat as the desserts are humdrum.

El Milagro, Av. Perón 1200. An old-fashioned parrilla with aproned gauchos tossing mammoth steaks onto your plate, accompanied with riojano wines.

El Padrino, Av. Perón and Peñaloza. Ferns hang from the ceiling in this modern bright parrilla where the cooks rustle up perfectly *al dente* pasta, plus roast kid, fish dishes and a gut-busting parrillada.

Los Palotes, Hipólito Yrigoyen 128 (☎03822/425900). One of the swishest restaurants in the whole region, with food to match, at reasonable prices. Not the usual fare, but imaginative dishes such as beef carpaccio, pasta with pork and orange, and spiced pears in wine. Served by trendy waiters and waitresses in a dark orange-ochre decor, with attention to detail. Reservations recommended at weekends.

La Vieja Casona, Rivadavia 427. Don't be put off by the lace curtains or the ghastly floral tablecloths. This is La Rioja's best parrilla, serving outstanding meat and delicious home-made pasta, with a wine-list from local bodegas.

Cafés and nightclubs

Café Bernardino, Rivadavia and Hypólito Yrigoyen. The service is a bit nonchalant, but the drinks and snacks are sophisticated, and the decor is resolutely late 1990s, all brushed metal and diffused lighting.

Café de la Bolsa, Rivadavia 684. A good place for people-watching, drinking a cortado or two, or grabbing a sticky *media luna* if your hotel breakfast left you hungry.

Café del Paseo, Pelagio B. Luna and 25 de Mayo. Part of a hacienda-style commercial complex, it has a large terrace, airy inside rooms and a range of drinks and snacks; the service is of the laid-back variety.

Fax, Av. San Francisco s/n. Lively disco open at weekends and especially popular in the summer; salsa and national rock dominate the music.

Heladería Estrellita, Pelagio B. Luna 101. Rainbow of flavours at the best ice creamery in town, where you usually have to queue up.

Moro, Av. San Fransisco s/n. La Rioja's trendiest nightclub, with a good variety of music, a young crowd and cool decor.

Listings

Airlines Aerolíneas Argentinas, Belgrano 63 (☎03822/426307); Lapa, San Nicolás de Bari 516 (☎03822/435281), Southern Winds, Pelagio B. Luna 457 (☎03822/460200).

Banks Exchange but no travellers' cheque service at Banco de Galicia, San Nicolás de Bari and Buenos Aires; Banco de la Nación, Pelagio B. Luna and Belgrano; Nuevo Banco de la Rioja, Rivadavia and San Martín. Plenty of ATMs around Plaza 25 de Mayo.

Car rental in *King's Hotel*, Av. F. Quiroga 1070 (☎03822/422122); La Rioja Tour, J.V. González 327 (☎03822/433888).

Hospital Hospital Presidente Plaza, San Nicolás de Bari Este 97 (☎03822/427814).

Internet Arnet 25 de Mayo 311 (☎03822/420666; *lario@arnet.com.ar*).

Laundry Lavaseco Super Jet, Dalmacio Vélez Sarsfield 750.

Left luggage At the bus terminal (24hr).

Pharmacy Plaza, Pelagio B. Luna 497.

Police Av. Perón 1274 (☎03822/427403)

Post office, Av. Perón 756 (☎03822/428522).

Taxis, Radio Taxis (☎03822/431222); Remis La Rioja (☎03822/424404).

Telephones, Telecom, Plaza 25 de Mayo, with Internet access.

Tour operators, Elysses Turismo, Pelagio B. Luna and 25 de Mayo, Paseo San Ignacio, (☎03822/434871); Uno Turismo, Pelagio B. Luna 362 (☎03822/432997); Yafar, Pelagio B. Luna (☎03822/423053). Tours to Talampaya, Ischigualasto and Chilecito.

Dique Los Sauces

Avenida San Francisco leads westwards out of the city and, as the RN75, eventually leads to Aimogasta in the north of La Rioja Province. Along a narrow valley formed by the Sierra de Velasco, with its violet, red and ochre rocks, is the Quebrada de los Sauces, in which a reservoir, **Dique Los Sauces**, was built at the end of the nineteenth century. Slightly higher than the city and cooled by the water and the willows that surround it – *sauce* means willow – its banks have become the Riojanos' weekend and summer resort, only 16km away from the city. You can picnic here, eat and drink at the lakeside bar, or have a meal at the nearby *Club Sírio-Libanés*, where you can get delicious mezze and kebabs. Near the dam a signpost shows to way to El Morro, or **Cerro de la Cruz** (1680m), up a steep twelve-kilometre road best tackled in a 4WD or, if on foot, during the coolest part of the day. The views from here of the mountains, valley and city are amazing; nearby is a launching-pad for hang-gliding and paragliding, used for international competitions because the weather conditions are so reliable. If you're tempted, contact the Asociación Riojana de Vuelo Libre at San Nicolás de Bari 1 (☎03822/422139).

Buses to Sanogasta stop at Los Sauces, but whatever you do don't catch any marked "Los Sauces" – confusingly, this refers to San Blas de los Sauces, a God-forsaken village at the northern tip of La Rioja Province, which the buses reach via Bazán to the north of the city.

Chilecito and around

La Rioja Province's second city, **CHILECITO**, is an old mining-town in a beautiful mountainside setting, some 205km by road from La Rioja city – but less than 70km west as the crow flies. It was founded in the early eighteenth century as Santa Rita de Casia, but the present name derives from the fact that most of the miners who worked in the gold mines in the early nineteenth century came from across the border. In the middle of that century, La Rioja's government moved here because of harassment from Facundo Quiroga, Rosas' right-hand man – Sarmiento, one of Rosas' fiercest opponents is still something of a local hero for taking part in Rosas' overthrow. One of Chilecito's two self-styled names, the Cuna del Torrontés, or birthplace of the torrontés, refers to the **wineries** based here, one of which can be visited, though the torrontés grape produces more subtle wines further north in Salta Province; the other, La Perla del Oeste, literally the "pearl of the west", is harder to justify, though the city is the only settlement in the province with any charm, despite its scruffiness. The city's **museum** contains a collection of archeological and other items spanning the area's history since the Stone Age, and the early twentieth-century **mine installations** just outside the town are also intriguing. But best of all is the cultural centre in an early nineteenth-century finca at **Samay-Huasi**, a short way to the east, which also makes for an idyllic place to stay. A longer trip, for which you need your own transport – though buses to Villa Unión take you there – is along the fabulous **Cuesta de Miranda**, a sinuous, parapet-like mountain pass across the Sierra de Famatina that reaches 2025m above sea level, some 50km west of Chilecito, on the RN40 road towards Villa Unión. The Río Miranda snakes through a deep gorge, hemmed in on both sides by multicoloured cliffs and peaks, striped red, green, blue and yellow with oxidized minerals and strata of volcanic rock.

To get to Chilecito from the provincial capital, you first head south down the RN38, and switch back in a northwesterly direction, taking the RN74, followed by the RN40, along a narrow valley. To the west stretch the Sierras de los Colorados, Sierra de Vilgo, Sierra de Paganzo and Sierra de Sañogasta, reddish and purplish cliffs and crags that form a dramatic backdrop for the fertile valley, with its olive-groves, walnut-groves and vineyards. To the east is the impenetrable barrier of the Sierra de Velasco – which is why it's such a long detour to get from La Rioja to the central valleys of La Rioja Province. To the northwest stretches another formidable wall of mountains, the majestic Sierra de Famatina, which peaks at Cerro General Manuel Belgrano (6250m), permanently snow capped; this is the highest outcrop of the Andean precordillera. Several **buses** a day also take this route between La Rioja and Chilecito.

The Town

Built on the southern banks of the often bone-dry Río Sarmientos, **Chilecito** itself is centred on Plaza Domingo Faustino Sarmiento, built in the mid-nineteenth century as the heart of the new Villa Argentina; its enormous plane trees, Judas trees, ash trees and palms provide welcome shade when the summer sun is at its strongest; the Judas trees are covered with powder-pink flowers in October. All around are huddled most of the town's restaurants, cafés, hotels – and a service-station. Few of the buildings – least of all the dreadful concrete Iglesia Sagrado Corazón de Jesús built in the 1960s, on the southern side of the square – are of any interest. Instead, head west four blocks to the Molino San Francisco at J. Ocampo 63 which houses the **Museo de Chilecito** (Nov–April Tues–Sun 8am–noon & 2–8pm; May–Oct Tues–Sun 8am–noon & 2–4pm; $1), a motley but interesting assemblage ranging from mineral samples from the nearby mines to all kinds of arts and crafts, indigenous, colonial and contemporary. The attractive building itself, an eighteenth-century flour mill, is a partly whitewashed, robust stone building, surrounded by huge cart-wheels. One block north and west, at La Plata 646, is the **Cooperativa Vitivinifrutícola Riojana** (tours at 8am, 10am & 12.30pm; free; ☎03825/423150) where you can visit the wineries and fruit-drying sheds, and taste the produce, including the refreshingly flowery torrontés wine, and succulent walnuts and raisins. About 2km southeast of the centre, past the abattoir along the RN40, is the Cable Carril La Mexicana, where you'll find the **Museo del Cablecarril** (daily 7am–1pm & 2–8pm; free), housed in the disused cable-car station dating from 1903. The display about mining isn't exactly scintillating, but the German-built installations – a bit like a nineteenth-century pier stranded in the middle of South America – are impressive; a massive crane made of spruce-timber and old ore-wagons still sit next to the station which is built on dainty stilts. The cable car, which was in use until 1929, was the second longest in the world; the route stretched nearly 40km up to the huge mine in the Sierra de Famatina, at an altitude of nearly 4500m above sea level.

Practicalities

Buses, several times daily from La Rioja, less frequently from Córdoba, Villa Unión and Buenos Aires, arrive at the tiny **bus station** one block north and west of Plaza Sarmiento, at La Plata and 19 de Febrero. Chilecito's rudimentary **tourist information office** is half a block north of the plaza, at Castro y Bazán (Mon–Fri 7am–1pm & 3–9pm, Sat, Sun & public holidays 8am–9pm; ☎03825/422688). The best **place to stay** hereabouts is at Samay-Huasi, but you could try the *Nuevo Hotel Bellia* at El Maestro 188 (☎03825/422181; ②), which has clean rooms with bath arranged around a stable-style patio. ACA-owned *Hotel Chilecito* three blocks east of the centre at Timoteo Gordillo 101 (☎03825/422201; ④) is the nicest place to stay in town, with plain, clean rooms, an airy confitería and views of the foothills. For **places to eat** you're pretty much restricted to *Parrilla Quincho* at Joaquín V. González, which serves incredibly juicy steaks and flavoursome *empanadas* and is a good place to watch the *paseo* on Plaza Sarmiento, and the *Club Árabe*, at Castro Barros 88, where you can have delicious mezze accompanied by local wine. *Café Keops* on the southeast corner of Plaza

Sarmiento has reasonably priced coffee, drinks and snacks. The most reliable **ATM** is at the pink neocolonial Banco Nación on the northwest corner of the plaza.

Samay-Huasi

Just 3km east of Chilecito is the British-built finca – or estancia – of **Samay-Huasi**, now belonging to the University of Plata, and housing the **Museo Samay-Huasi** (Tues–Sun 7am–8pm; $1; ☎03825/422629). At the beginning of the twentieth century this was the rural retreat of an eminent Riojano jurist, poet and mystic, Joaquín V. González, who founded the University of La Plata, and was particularly interested in Argentina's pre-Columbian history. The Quechua name means house of rest, and the mock-Etruscan doorway to the estate bears a Latin inscription which translates as "nothing and nobody shall disturb my peace". It's still a tranquil place, amid a luxuriant oasis-like garden and surrounded by steep rocky outcrops. The main rooms of the neocolonial house, draped in bougainvillea, remain as it was when González lived here, complete with his furniture, paintings and personal effects. The adjoining bodega has been converted into a museum, with portraits and landscape oil-paintings by Argentine artists on the ground floor – some good, some excellent – and a varied collection of insects, stuffed birds, local crafts and bits of minerals in the cellar. This is a great place **to stay**; the outhouses have been converted into simple rooms, with shared baths – but book ahead as it often fills with university groups, especially during the vacations (☎03825/422629; ③).

travel details

Buses

Chilecito to: Buenos Aires (3 daily; 20hr); Córdoba (2 daily; 7hr); La Rioja (4 daily; 3hr).

La Rioja to: Buenos Aires (3 daily; 17hr); Córdoba (1 hourly; 5hr); San Juan (7 daily; 6hr); Catamarca (7 daily; 2hr); Chilecito (4 daily; 3hr); Villa Unión (2 daily; 5hr); Salta (7 daily; 11hr); San Juan (7 daily; 6hr); Valle Fértil (2 weekly; 4hr).

Malargüe to: Mendoza (3 daily; 4–5hr); San Rafael (2 daily; 2hr 30min); Neuquén (2 daily; 10hr).

Mendoza to: Buenos Aires (1 hourly; 17hr); Córdoba (7 daily; 9hr); General Alvear (3 daily; 4hr 30min); La Rioja (7 daily; 8hr 30min); Las Leñas (June–Sept 2 daily; 4hr 30min); Los Penitentes (6 daily; 4hr); Malargüe (3 daily; 4–5hr); Neuquén (2 daily; 12hr); Río Gallegos (1 daily; 40hr); Salta (7 daily; 19hr); San Rafael (1 hourly; 3hr 15min); San Juan (1 hourly; 2hr 20min); San Luis (1 hourly; 3hr 40min); Santiago de Chile (4 daily; 7hr); Uspallata (6 daily; 1hr 40min); Valparaíso, Chile (4 daily; 8hr 30min).

San Juan to: Buenos Aires (10 daily; 16hr); Córdoba (5 daily; 8hr); La Rioja (7 daily; 6hr); Mendoza (1 hourly; 2hr 20min); San Rafael (2 daily; 5hr 30min); Valle Fértil (3 daily; 4hr); Barreal (2 daily; 5hr); San José de Jáchal (5 daily; 3hr 30min).

San Rafael to: Buenos Aires (4 daily; 13hr); General Alvear (3 daily; 1hr 20min); Las Leñas (June–Sept 3 daily; 2hr 40min); Malargüe (2 daily; 2hr 30min); Mendoza (1 hourly; 3hr 15min); Neuquén (2 daily; 12hr); San Luis (2 daily; 3hr).

Flights

La Rioja to: Buenos Aires (5 daily; 2hr); Catamarca (1 daily; 30min).

Mendoza to: Buenos Aires (12 daily; 1hr 50min); Córdoba (6 daily; 1hr 20min); Neuquén (1 daily; 1hr 30min); San Juan (2 daily; 30min).

San Juan to: Buenos Aires (10 daily; 1hr 50min); Córdoba (2 daily; 30min); Mendoza (2 daily; 30min).

San Rafael to: Buenos Aires (3 weekly; 1hr 50min).

CHAPTER EIGHT

NEUQUÉN AND THE PATAGONIAN LAKE DISTRICT

O ne of Argentina's most popular holiday destinations, the **lake district** of central and **northwestern Patagonia** is famous for the great network of easily accessible national parks that spreads itself along the cordillera. This is a land of immense glacial lakes, thick forests, jagged peaks and extinct volcanoes, which was controlled, until a little over a century ago, by the Mapuche. The lake district comprises the southwest of Neuquén, western Río Negro, and the northwestern corner of Chubut.

Shaped like a fish's tail and bigger than Portugal, **Neuquén Province** is Patagonia's most northwesterly region: its eastern half is a level plain, while the west is dominated by the Andes and parallel mountain ranges; and whereas the mountains in the north of the province are harsh and dry, in the south they are covered in dense Andean forest. The eastern and central region look much like any chunk of inland Patagonia, but here the huge expanses of parched steppe and *meseta* hide deposits of fossils and fossil fuels. The area is very important in paleontological terms – every few years, it seems, the bones of ever more gigantic **dinosaurs** are discovered. You can check out this legacy in the museum at **El Chocón** or in the museums of **Neuquén**, the province's namesake capital. Centred on **Chos Malal**, the little-visited north of the province is a zone of transition, much more akin in scenery to Mendoza and the Cuyo than to the rest of Patagonia. At this latitude, the mountains are harsh and barren, typified by the spiky Cordillera del Viento around the mining region of **Andacollo** and the hump-backed **Volcán Domuyo**. The great Patagonian Andean forests that are so magnificently represented in **Parque Nacional Lanín** in the south of the province are little in evidence, although the most northerly vestiges of the Patagonian *Nothofagus* forests can be found here at the beautiful **Lagunas de Epulafquen**.

ACCOMMODATION PRICE CODES

The price codes used for accommodation throughout this chapter refer to the cheapest rate for a double room in high season. Single travellers will only occasionally pay half the double-room rate; nearer two thirds is the norm and some places will expect you to pay the full rate. Note that in resort towns, there are considerable discounts out of season.

① $20 or less	④ $45–60	⑦ $100–150
② $20–30	⑤ $60–80	⑧ $150–200
③ $30–45	⑥ $80–100	⑨ Over $200

South of Andacollo, at the mountain resort village of **Caviahue**, you find the first significant groves of **araucaria**, or monkey puzzle tree, growing on the harsh basalt soils of Volcán Copahue. Flanking sparklingly clear waterfalls, these groves are much more impressive than the over-hyped thermal springs of Caviahue's sister resort, **Copahue**. Further south, against the cordillera, are the most majestic of the *araucaria* forests. From Paso Pino Hachado down into the north of Parque Nacional Lanín you have some phenomenal opportunities to trek, ride horses or mountain-bike past the trees that the indigenous Pehuenches considered to be sacred beings, daughters of the moon. Check out the **Pehuenia circuit** around Lagos Aluminé, Moquehue, and Ñorquinco, or access Quillén or the Aigo Mapuche community of **Rucachoroi**, in the northern sector of Parque Nacional Lanín is a wild area, popular with fishermen but otherwise much less disturbed than the rest of the vast park system in the Patagonian Lake District. Access this zone via Junín de los Andes or the uninteresting steppe town of Zapala.

Both **Junín de los Andes** and the scenic resort of **San Martín de los Andes** provide good bases for exploring the better-known central and southern sectors of Parque Lanín. Junín is more convenient of the two for investigating the area around the park's remarkable centrepiece, extinct **Volcán Lanín**, a fairytale snowcapped cone of 3776m. A mecca for aspiring climbers as well as their more experienced counterparts, the easiest route – physically challenging but technically fairly straightforward – is from the northeast: head with your gear for one of the Andes' most scenic passes, **Paso Mamuil Malal** near **Lago Tromen**. The classic views of the volcano are to be had from the **Lago Huechulafquen** and **Lago Paimún** area to the south, however. The region's volcanic activity can be witnessed at the hot springs not too far south: the **Termas de Epulafquen**; and the ones near **Lago Queñi**, at the western end of San Martín's wonderful **Lago Lácar**. San Martín is at the northern end of the scenic **Seven Lakes Route**, a gorgeous drive past forested mountain lakes to Villa La Angostura, from where you visit the **Parque Nacional Los Arrayanes**, formed to protect a captivating wood of myrtle trees at the end of the Peninsula Quetrihué. This tiny park is surrounded by a goliath: **Parque Nacional Nahuel Huapi**, which is perhaps the most famous, and one of the most visited, of all Argentina's national parks. It is very popular with Argentine holidaymakers, who pack out towns such as the archetypal Patagonian holiday resort, Río Negro's **Bariloche**, every year both in summer and for skiing in winter. They come to experience the Alpine flavour of this "Switzerland of Argentina" – a comparison that does, in a few places at least, bear out, although neither the scale of the park nor the urban planning nearby is remotely Swiss. The park has a well-developed infrastructure of trails and refuges for **trekkers**, who will love the **Cerro Catedral** region just to the south of Bariloche. Another base for trekking is **El Bolsón**, an alternative hangout to Bariloche in more than one sense of the word, with a hippy tradition that sets it completely apart from its brasher big-town neighbour.

Further south, in the province of Chubut, the major holiday destination is the **Esquel** region. From here, you can visit another classic Patagonian park, **Parque Nacional Los Alerces**, which has some exceptional lakes and is the best place to see threatened, majestic **alerce** trees, some of which are thousands of years old. To the north of the park is Cholila, where you'll find the famous cabin built by **Butch Cassidy**, while to the south is the engaging **Trevelin**, which still preserves something of its Welsh roots. The last highlight of the area is one of Argentina's two timeless trains: **La Trochita**, which rattles and hoots its way through the steppe between Esquel and El Maitén on a precarious narrow-gauge track.

Central and eastern Neuquén

Central and eastern Neuquén Province is a zone most visitors travel through fairly fast on journeys through to the cordillera or the coast. It is an area of desertified *meseta*

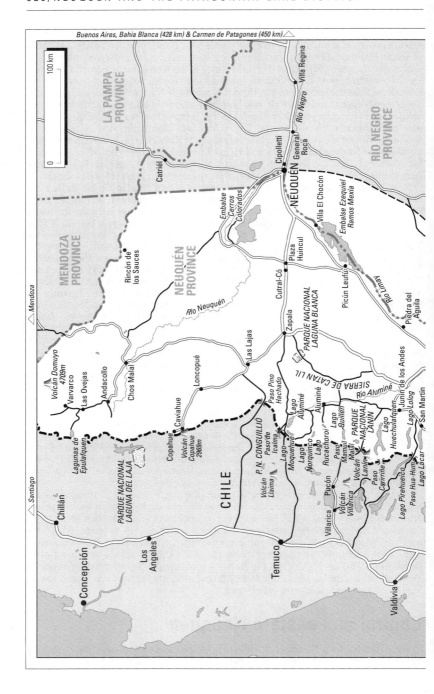

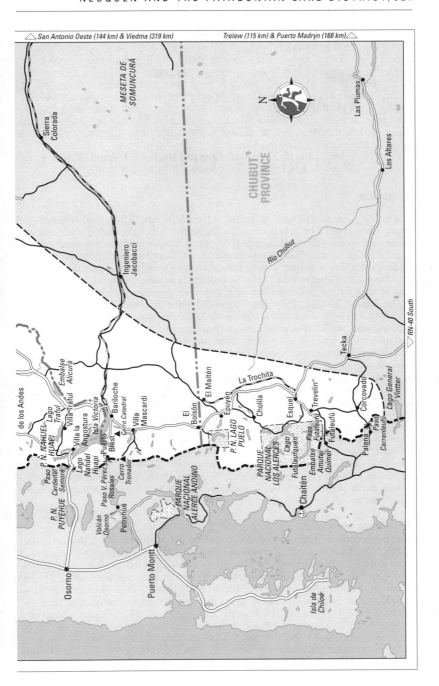

and steppe, cultivated in places along the river systems of the Limay and Neuquén. Its wealth lies primarily in energy production: this region has the most important reserves of natural gas and petroleum in the country, and is also Argentina's major exporter of thermal and especially hydroelectric energy, with massive reservoirs such as Pichí Picún Leufú, Ramón Mexía and Chocón forming much of its southern border with Río Negro Province. Though you won't want to tarry long, there are several points of interest that make worthwhile stopping points, most of which relate to dinosaurs. Both the bustling provincial capital, **Neuquén**, and the village of **El Chocón** have world-class paleontology exhibits in their museums, and the latter has some truly remarkable dinosaur footprints in situ by the lake.

For wildlife lovers, the highlight is the **Parque Nacional Laguna Blanca**, a shallow lake in the *meseta* near **Zapala** that is renowned for its waterfowl.

Neuquén

The bustling city of **NEUQUÉN** is sited at the confluence of the rivers Neuquén and Limay, whose waters unite to become the Río Negro. With a population of 250,000, this plains metropolis is Patagonia's largest city and functions as the commercial, industrial and financial centre of the surrounding fruit- and oil-producing region. It is not a particularly attractive or touristy place – a place to pass through rather than stay in – but it does have a couple of worthwhile museums and is a useful transport hub. The city is best avoided during December and February when it can get very hot.

The **Museo Municipal**, Av. San Martín 280 (Mon–Fri 8am–6pm, Sun 4–8pm; free; ☎0299/442-5430) has displays of indigenous exhibits, dinosaurs and Pleistocene mammals including parts of a 10,000-year-old megatherium excavated within the city limits. The town's best museum, however, is in the north of town on the university campus. The university is built on top of fossil deposits – some of them 85 million years old – that provide remarkably convenient fieldwork for the paleontology students here, some of whom can be seen at work in the **Museo de Geología y Paleontología**, Buenos Aires 1400 (Mon–Fri 9am–5pm, Sat & Sun 4–8.30pm; for half-hour guided tours in English, call in advance ☎0299/490300; $2.50; guided tours a further $1). A varied collection includes important first examples of new species and the smallest herbivorous dinosaur ever discovered: the sixty-centimetre gasparinisaurus cincosaltensis. Take bus #9 or #10 heading up Avenida Argentina (direction "Universidad"), which drops you three blocks to walk west of the site.

Mapuche ceramics, weavings and woodcarving can be bought at the non-profit cooperative, **Artesanías Neuquinas**, at Roca 155 (Mon–Fri 8.30am–12.30pm & 4.30–8.30pm, Sat 9.30am–1pm; ☎ & fax 0299/4423806). Finest-quality woollen ponchos will set you back over $1000, but a delicately carved willow flower is much more accessible at around $2.50.

Arrival and orientation

Neuquén's **airport** (☎0299/444-0446) is 5km west of town off the RN22, and is connected by two buses to the terminal: Turismo Lanín and #11 (every 40min; 30–40min; $0.90); a taxi will set you back around $10. The airport has a tourist information desk (Mon–Sat 8am–8pm, Sun closed in the morning; ☎0299/444-0072). By land, the main RN22 bisects the south of town and is called Avenida Félix San Martín to the east of the main drag, **Avenida Olascoaga**, and Dr T.L. Planas to the west. The **bus terminal** is at Mitre 147, two blocks north of Félix San Martín, and a block and a half east of the central boulevard. A spate of thefts has been reported at the bus terminal, so take extra care. To use Neuquén's urban buses, you must buy a ticket in advance from any kiosk ($0.65).

The very helpful main **tourist office** (daily 8am–8pm; ☎0299/442-3268, fax 443-2438; *turismo@neuquen.gov.ar*) is at Félix San Martín 182, two blocks down Calle Río Negro from the bus terminal. It has an excellent **map** of the town plus information on the whole province, including a good regional road map.

It's fairly easy to find your way round town: you'll find everything you need in the **microcentro**, which effectively comprises the area to the north of the RN22, three blocks on either side of the central boulevard. Where it crosses the obsolete railway tracks, three blocks north of the RN22, this boulevard's name changes from Avenida Olascoaga to **Avenida Argentina**. All of Neuquén's other north–south streets likewise change names as they cross the railway. Streets that run east–west change name as they cross the central boulevard. Do not confuse Félix San Martín (the RN22 to the east of Olascoaga), with Avenida San Martín, running west from Avenida Argentina to the Museo Municipal, one block north of the railway tracks. Unusually for an Argentinian town, Neuquén has no central square and, stranger still, only the merest scrap of a Plaza San Martín. If anything rates as the central square, it would have to be the partially landscaped park on either side of the railway tracks.

Accommodation

The best hotel options are listed below, but if you are stuck – hotels are busier in the week and it's well worth booking in advance – head for the area around avenidas Olascoaga and Argentina, where there are a string of unspectacular, mid-range places. The city's free municipal **campsite**, by the Río Negro, is poorly maintained and not considered to be very safe – instead, head for *Camping Butaco*, Obrero Argentino and Copahue (☎0299/440-0228), where you can pitch your tent for $5 per person; take a *remise* from the centre ($4), or a *remise colectivo* ($0.80) heading to Cipolletti and get off at Lázaro Martín to make the twenty-minute walk south.

Alcorta, Alcorta 84 (☎0299/442-2652, fax 442-7045). Clean and comfortable, though the service can be a little brusque. ②.

Apart Hotel Casino, Alcorta 19 (☎0299/442-3593, fax 447-1634). Reasonable self-catering apartments for up to five people ($100). ⑤

Del Comahue, Av. Argentina 377 (☎0299/442-2439, fax 447-3331). The classiest hotel in town, bang in the centre. Exemplary service for a four-star; popular with businessmen, and always busy: reserve in advance (especially Dec–Feb & July). It also has the best restaurant in town. ⑦.

Hospedaje Pani, Félix San Martín 238 (☎0299/442-2287). The least expensive option for single budget travellers. Friendly staff, but down-at-heel, gloomy rooms – some of which lack windows or have unsafe locks: check first. ②.

Hostal del Caminante, RN22 Km 1227 (☎0299/444-0118, fax 444-0119). Some 15min drive west of the centre, past the airport. Relaxing villa in pleasant grounds. Tennis court, pool and sauna. ⑥.

Residencial Belgrano, Rivadavia 283 (☎0299/448-0612). This pleasant *residencial* is well worth reserving in advance. The downstairs rooms are cooler in summer. ②.

Residencial Inglés, Félix San Martín 534 (☎0299/442-2252). Not as close to the bus terminal as some budget options, but by far the best of the bunch, run by charming family who speak some English. The spick-and-span rooms hold up to five people; there's a pleasant garden area too. ②.

Hotel Suizo, Carlos Rodríguez 167 (☎ & fax 0299/442-2606). Swiss in nature as well as name: spotlessly clean, fully functional and tastefully simple. Some rooms with bathtub. ④.

Eating and drinking

Restaurant Familiar Alberdi, Alberdi 176. An excellent old-style place popular with locals, especially at lunchtime. Try one of the *platos del día*, such as stuffed *zapallitos* with mashed potato ($4.50). Open till 11.30pm; closed Sun.

La Barca, Ministro González 26. A 24hr café-cum-bar serving snack food. The nightlife buzz comes late on Saturday, after midnight (no entrance fee; drinks $4).

1900 Cuatro, on the first floor of the *Hotel del Comahue*, Av. Argentina 377 (☎0299/442-2439). Imaginative and appetizing meals. Pastas start at $8, but you're better off going for a trout dish or the $18 menu. Keenly priced wine-list includes local specialities.

Las Antorchas, Diagonal Alvear and Av. San Martín (☎0299/443-4354). An excellent, stylish, and expensive parrilla.

Listings

Airlines Aerolíneas/Austral, Santa Fe 52 (☎0299/442-2409); LADE, Almirante Brown 163 (☎0299/443-1153); LAPA, Av. Argentina 30 (☎0299/448-8335); Southern Winds, Av. Argentina 237 (☎0299/442-0124).

Banks and exchanges Banco de la Provincia, Av. Argentina 13 (April–Nov 8am–2pm; Dec–March 7am–1pm) changes travellers' cheques and gives cash advances on Visa and Mastercard; Cambio Olano, J.B. Justo 97 (Mon–Fri 8.30am–1pm & 4.30–8pm, Sat 9am–12.30pm) change all travellers' cheques, though for a higher commission than the banks, and Chilean pesos as well as all other foreign currencies.

Car rental Ai Rent a Car, Perticone 735 (☎0299/443-4714); Avis, J.J. Lastra 1196 (☎0299/443-0216); Rent a Car, Av. San Martín 837 (☎0299/443-7875).

Consulate Chilean, La Rioja 241 (☎0299/442-2727).

Laundry Inside Casa Tía supermarket, at Olascoaga and Félix San Martín.

Hospitals Hospital Regional Neuquén, Buenos Aires 421 (☎0299/449-0800); Hospital Bouquet Roldán, Tte. Planas 1550 (☎0299/443-1328). Policlínico ADOS, Av. Argentina 1000, is a private clinic with some English-speaking doctors (☎0299/442-4110; $10 consultation fee).

Internet and telephone Telecom, Av. Argentina 147 and 25 de Mayo 20 ($6 per hour, divisible).

Pharmacy Farmacia Andina, Rivadavia 275 (Mon–Sat 24hr; ☎0800/666-5174).

Police Jefatura, Richieri 775 (☎0299/442-4100); ☎101 for emergencies.

Post office Correo, Rivadavia and Santa Fe (Mon–Fri 8am–8pm, Sat 9am–1pm).

Travel agents Cambio Olano, J.B. Justo 97.

Routes south and west of Neuquén: the dinosaur belt

The area to the south and west of Neuquén is one of the world's richest hunting grounds for **dinosaur fossils**. The RN22 slices west from the provincial capital through pretty bleak, level scenery towards Zapala (see p.531), passing the depressed Siamese oil towns of Plaza Huincul and Cutral Có. You won't want to stay in either, but it's worth stopping briefly to see the **Museo Carmen Funes** on Plaza Huineul (April–Nov Mon–Fri 7am–8pm, Sat & Sun 3.30–7pm; Sept–March Mon–Fri 7am–8pm, Sat & Sun 5–9pm; $1). Here you can look at a gargantuan thigh bone of the argentinosaurus huinculensis (until 1999, the biggest dinosaur ever discovered, with an estimated length of 40m and weight of 75 tonnes – as much as fifty elephants); and a frighteningly true-to-life reconstruction of the giganotosaurus (see below), created by a local sculptor, María del Carmen Gravino, who worked on the dinosaur models for the film *Jurassic Park*. Gravino lives at Río Negro 540 (☎0299/496-7658), and usually has smaller, equally exquisite pieces for sale. The museum sells limited-edition prints by Oscar Campos, another local artist who's famous nationally, depicting wildlife scenes with photographic realism.

The RN237 splits off the RN22 and heads southwest to Bariloche, paralleling the series of hydroelectric reservoirs along the Río Limay. Sited on the banks of the most important of these, the Embalse Ezequiel Ramos Mexía, is a little oasis in the steppe: **VILLA EL CHOCÓN**, 72km from Neuquén. You can't miss the turn-off – it's guarded by a life-size giganotosaurus. El Chocón is a trim, purpose-built company town originally built to house the workers on the vast neighbouring dam, whose turbines supply up to thirty percent of the country's electricity at any one time. Stop here to visit the **Museo Ernesto Bachmann** (daily 7am–7pm; $1), which displays the virtually complete, hundred-million-year-old skeleton of a giganotosaurus, discovered 18km away, in 1993. This fearsome beast puts even tyrannosaurus rex in the shade: it measured a colossal 14m long, stood 4.7m tall, and weighed an estimated nine-and-a-half tonnes. Bibliophiles will enjoy a visit to El Chocón's library, the **Biblioteca Patagónica** (☎0299/490-1114), dedicated exclusively to Patagonia and run by a dedicated local historian.

Further along the RN237, 5km southwest of the turn-off to El Chocón, a second turn-off takes you to the **Parque Cretácico**, where you'll find some huge, astonishingly well-preserved **dinosaur footprints** near the reservoir's edge. Not realizing what they were, fishermen used some of these in the past as barbecue pits for their trout. They resemble the prints of a giant rhea, but were probably left by an iguanadon – a ten-metre long herbivore – or some kind of bipedal carnivore. Other kidney-shaped prints are of four-footed sauropods, and smaller prints were probably left by three-metre long teropods. Claudio Bighetto runs half-day **tours** to all these sites as well as the dam ($10; English spoken; ☎ & fax 0299/490-1243).

There's an extremely pleasant **campsite** near El Chocón, *Club Chocón Lauquén* (☎156-323737; $3 per tent plus $1 per person; $2 one-off car charge). It has tennis courts and an excellent swimming pool (open Dec–March). *La Terraza* is a sunny **restaurant** overlooking the reservoir; it serves delicious *empanadas de trucha* at $6 per dozen.

Zapala and the Parque Nacional Laguna Blanca

ZAPALA, 150km west of Neuquén, is a useful base for exploring the **Parque Nacional Laguna Blanca**. The112-square-kilometre park lies some 33km southwest of town. Set on a high *meseta*, 1276m above sea level in the middle of desertified steppe, the wild lake at the park's centre is an important breeding ground and staging post for migrating **waterfowl**, a fact that has led to its protection by the international Ramsar Convention.

The species for which the park was originally established is the black-necked swan, up to two thousand of which nest here between August and September; but you'll also see flamingoes, several species of coot and duck, as well as less common species such as the silvery grebe. In all, almost 120 species of birds have been registered in the park.

Surrounding the lake, the steppe is rumpled by bald, rounded hills and, from the west, it's overlooked by a range that remains snowcapped into December. The far side of the lake is ringed by a steep scarp, the Barda Negra, which offers the water birds some shelter from the winds. Visit the lagoon in the morning if possible, as it's far less windy.

Practicalities

Buses arrive at Zapala's **bus terminal** on the corner of Etcheluz and Ejército Argentino. The park's **information office** is two and a half blocks east of the terminal at Zeballos 446 (Mon–Fri 8am–noon & 3–6.30pm). If you're lucky you may be able to catch a lift out to the park with the *guardaparque*. If not, Radio Taxi Lihuén opposite the terminal will run you there for around $25 (☎02942/430300).

Hitching into the park is possible – the RP46 passes right by the lagoon and the park office – but not advisable out of high season. You can **camp** for free, but bring water and provisions, and there are no facilities – not even toilets – and it can get very cold here, so come prepared. For more comfort, you could stay in Zapala and make a day-trip into the park. The best budget **accommodation** is to be found at the town's *CIRSE*, six blocks northeast of the terminal at Italia 139 (☎ & fax 02942/431891; ①); this is a police officers' hotel with clean rooms for up to four people. Two blocks east of the terminal are the *Coligueo*, Etcheluz 159 (☎02942/421308; ③), with rooms for up to five people, and the pleasant *Pehuén*, Etcheluz and Elena de la Vega (☎ & fax 02942/423135; ③), which is clean, quiet and hospitable. *Hue Melén*, Almirante Brown 929 (☎ & fax 02942/422414; ⑤) is Zapala's largest hotel and is generally very good, though the hot water takes a while to flow. Its restaurant serves an $11 two-course meal (closed Sun afternoon and Mon).

Northern Neuquén

The wild and arid region of **northern Neuquén** is an area that few foreign tourists ever visit. The top destination here is the area around **Volcán Copahue**, with its twin resorts of **Caviahue** and **Copahue**. The volcanic hot springs here are overrated, but walks amongst stands of *araucaria* to spectacular cascades are certainly not. Further

---

THE MAPUCHE

Knowing themselves as the people (*che*) of the earth (*Mapu*), the Mapuche were, before the arrival of the Spanish in the sixteenth century, a loose confederation of tribal groups who lived exclusively on the western, Chilean side of the cordillera. The aspiring conquistadors knew them as Araucanos (a word that derives from a Hispanic corruption of Ragko, the Mapuche name for a river in central Chile), and feared them for being indomitable and resourceful warriors. Eventually, the Spanish were forced to abandon attempts to subjugate this fiercely proud nation, opting instead for a policy of containment, but their encroachments into Araucania sparked a series of Mapuche migrations eastwards into territory that is now Argentina. These invasions, in turn, displaced ethnic groups such as the northern Tehuelche, and, in time, Mapuches became the dominant force in northern Patagonia to the east of the Andes, and became a group whose cultural and linguistic influence spread far beyond the areas they actually controlled.

Four major Mapuche tribes had established territories in Argentina by the eighteenth century: the Picunches, or "the people of the north", who lived near the arid cordillera in the far north of Neuquén; the Pehuenches, or "the people of the monkey puzzle trees", dominant in the central cordillera and whose staple food was *piñones*; the Huilliches, or "the people of the south" (also called Manzaneros; see p.559), of the southern cordillera region based around Lago Nahuel Huapi; and the Puelches, or "the people of the east", who inhabited the river valleys of the steppe. These groups spoke different dialects of Mapudungun, a tongue which belongs to the Arawak group of languages. Lifestyles were based around a combination, to varying degrees, of nomadic hunter-gathering, rearing livestock and the cultivation of small plots around settlements of *rucas* (family homes that were thatched usually with reeds). Communities were headed by a *lonco* or cacique, but the "medicine-men" or *machis* also played an influential role.

The single most important way in which the arrival of the Spanish influenced Mapuche culture was the introduction of cattle and the horse. Horses enabled tribes to be vastly more mobile, and caused hunting techniques to change, with the Mapuche adopting their trademark lances in lieu of the bow and arrow. As importantly, the herds of wild horses and cattle that spread across the Argentine pampas became a vital trading commodity.

Relations between the Mapuche and the Hispanic criollos in both Chile and Argentina varied: periods of warfare and indigenous raids on white settlements were interspersed with times of relatively peaceful co-existence. By the end of the eighteenth century, the relationship had matured into a surprisingly symbiotic one, with the two groups meeting at joint *parlamentos* where grievances would be aired and terms of trade regulated. Trade flourished: criollo mule trains would leave Chilean towns for Neuquén three or four times a year, laden with spurs, beads, cereals, tobacco and clothing which the whites would trade for salt, cattle, horses and Mapuche weavings. Tensions increased after Argentina gained its independence from Spain, thanks to the increasingly expan-

north, the scenery around the market town of **Chos Malal** becomes more reminiscent of the Cuyo and Mendoza than Patagonia. Exploring the mountainous area around **Andacollo** to the west of here is not easy, even if you have your own transport (a 4WD is recommended). Roads are very dusty, and if driving, watch out for livestock on the roads, particularly herds of the ubiquitous, long-haired **angora goats**.

Chos Malal

Strategically sited near the confluence of the rivers Neuquén and Curi Leuvú, **CHOS MALAL** is the oldest surviving white settlement in Neuquén. It acted as the provincial capital from its founding in 1879 – when General Uriburu stationed the Fourth

sionist policies of the nation state, and the fact that the herds of wild cattle and horses that sustained cross-Andean commerce were diminishing fast. The Mapuche resisted the military campaign that the dictator Rosas organized against them in the early 1830s, but their independence was finally crushed by Roca's Campaign of the Desert. The military humiliation of the Argentine Mapuche nation was completed with the surrender, in 1885, of Valentín Sayhueque, dynastic head of the Manzaneros. Following that, Mapuche communities were split up, forcibly relocated and "reduced" onto reservations, often on some of the most marginal lands available. For years they were effectively ignored by the nation state, and were often subjected to considerable prejudice.

Nevertheless, today the Mapuche remain one of Argentina's principal indigenous nations, with a population of some 40,000 people who live in communities dotted around the provinces of Buenos Aires, La Pampa, Chubut, Río Negro and, above all, Neuquén. The link with the land is still of vital importance to most communities, and most families earn their livelihood from mixed animal husbandry – principally of goats, but also of cattle, horses and sheep, from which wool is obtained for weaving items such as ponchos and belts. Mapuche are to be found working in a variety of rural positions, some employed on a salaried basis, but more frequently on a casual basis: on estancias, for the national parks, on afforestation projects, or fighting forest fires. Some title-holding communities have opened up quarries or mines on their land. Increasingly, Mapuche communities are setting up tourist-related projects. These include opening campsites; establishing points of sale for home-made cheese or *artesanía* such as their finely woven woollen goods, distinctive silver jewellery, ceramics and woodcarving; offering guided excursions; or receiving small tour groups – visitors are invited to share a few *mates* and eat *tortas fritas* (wedges of fried dough) with a Mapuche family. When visiting Mapuche communities, especially outside a tourist environment, remember that cameras can be a tourists' worst enemy at times: use them sensitively, and always ask permission first.

Today Mapuche culture is not as visibly distinct in Argentina as it is in Chile. In Argentina, you will not find elderly women dressed day-to-day in old-style traditional outfits as you might in the markets of Chile's Temuco, even if traditional colours are still popular, especially blue – a colour which represents the sky and purity. Political organization is also less developed east of the Andes than to the west but, nevertheless, the Mapuche are one of Argentina's best-organized groups in this sense, especially in Neuquén, where Mapuche concerns in the areas of land rights, health, education and transport links to markets are at least being addressed, albeit with patchy success. The Nguillatún – a religious ritual which aimed to root out evil and ensure good harvests – is still practised in some Argentinian Mapuche communities, though they're now often somewhat shorter than they were in historical times. On rare occasions these days, certain individual white people are invited to attend, but usually these ceremonies are exclusively Mapuche affairs. After decades of being in steep decline, there is some evidence too that there may be a reawakening of interest in such ceremonies. The *rehue* at Ñorquinco (see p.542), for example, stood neglected from 1947 until the year 2000, when the first Nguillatún in fifty years was held, with Mapuche delegations from both sides of the border attending.

Division of Roca's troops here during the Campaign of the Desert – to 1904. You'll need to pass through here if heading to the Andacollo region, but there's little to see. The main site lies in the northwest of town, overlooking the Plaza San Martín – there, on a landscaped rocky outcrop, stands the first military **fort** of the area, a protected historical monument that dates from 1887. It comprises the surprisingly informative little **Museo Olascoaga** (Tues–Fri 7.30am–1pm & 2.30–8.30pm, Sat & Sun 2.30–8.30pm; free), with a fine analysis of the Campaign of the Desert in the region, and the **Torreón**, a whitewashed tower and lookout point, with good views of the broad Río Curi Leuvú valley. Early November is a good time to visit: the **Fiesta del Chivito** (Kid Festival) is held then, during which you can sample the area's fabulous roast goat.

The **bus terminal** is in the southeast of town. To get to the centre from the terminal, head one block southwest along Calle Neuquén and turn right onto Sarmiento. Ten blocks along from here you get to the Plaza San Martín, where there's a **tourist office**, at Calle 25 de Mayo s/n (Mon–Fri 8am–3pm). The best-positioned **hotel** is the *Hotel de Turismo*, San Martín 89 (☎ & fax 02948/422472; ③), with simple and clean rooms. Two and a half blocks southeast of the plaza is the decent *Hospedaje Lemus*, Lavalle 17 (☎02948/422082, fax 421133; ②), which has good singles prices and free *mate*, and the comfortably equipped *Hostería Anlu*, Lavalle 60 (☎02948/422628; ③), with air conditioning and free covered parking. Opposite the bus terminal is *Residencial Don Daniel*, General Paz 1124 (☎02948/421707; ②), whose rooms can get stuffy. They also serve pizzas and cheap snacks. The municipal **campsite** is three blocks northeast of the main plaza, by the bridge over the Río Curi Leuvu, on the route to Andacollo. *El Viejo Caicallén*, General Paz 345 (☎02948/421373; closed Sun) serves a filling **parrilla** for two with salad and chips ($20) and home-made pasta ($8).

Andacollo and around

ANDACOLLO itself is a dusty mining-town set by the silty Río Neuquén, in a rugged bowl of infertile beige mountains. It acts as a base for adventurous trips into the cordillera to the north and west, but you'll need your own transport. Its sister town of **HUINGAN-CÓ** is 5km away, in a fold of the mountains at the foot of the dramatic **Cordillera del Viento**, a range that is both higher at this point (almost 3000m) and older than the parallel Andes. Huingan-Có is characterized by its plantations of pines, so it's perhaps not surprising to find a tiny museum dedicated to trees, the **Museo del Arbol y de la Madera** (Mon–Fri 8am–4pm; ☎02948/499059), run by Sr Isidro Belver, a man with infectious enthusiasm for, and an encyclopedic knowledge of, the area. The museum's collection of cross-slices of different regional trees includes one from a cypress felled by wind in nearby Cañada Molina that is more than 1200 years old.

The **bus** from Chos Malal drops you by the YPF fuel station in Andacollo at Valvarco and Nahueve, outside *Hostería La Secuoya*, (☎ & fax 02948/494007; *ordonezc@ neunet.com.ar*; ③), which has good, fresh rooms, but is usually full. In fact, there's very little **accommodation** in Andacollo, so if you're planning on staying here it's best to book in advance. The good municipal **campsite** (☎02948/494050; $2 per person; closed April–Nov) is 1km past the village, just after the bridge over the Río Neuquén (the bus heading from Chos Malal to Las Ovejas will drop you here). The site has a swimming pool and a shop.

Excursions from Andacollo

The most interesting trip from Andacollo is to the **Lagunas de Epulaufquen**, 134km from Chos Malal, a pair of Andean lakes that have been made into a protected nature reserve where ninety species of birds have been recorded. Lago Superior is particularly beautiful, with a Hollywood dreamland backdrop: a deeply notched cliff face, a series of shelving platforms of tousled low Andean woodland, and a small waterfall. The lake's startling turquoise colour is best seen in the morning. The area was also the site of the 1832 battle in which the last Spanish Royalists were defeated, thus liberating the continent from Spanish rule once and for all. A raggle-taggle gang led by the four Pincheira brothers and comprising deserters, royalists, bandits and indigenous groups had been conducting raids as far away as Carmen de Patagones on the coast since 1819. They were tracked to their hideout here and defeated by the Chilean military hero, Manuel Bulnes. **Camping** along the lakeshore is free, but you'll need to bring all your own supplies.

A second excursion takes you to **thermal springs** on the bald slopes of humpbacked **Volcán Domuyo** – at 4702m, officially the highest peak in Patagonia. This trip is more rewarding for the spectacular views of the bleak and barren scenery than for the springs themselves. You'll need a 4WD to cover the difficult terrain. En route, you pass through the village of **LAS OVEJAS**, where **rooms** are available in *Rotisería El Ciervo*, Cleomedes Vera s/n (☎02948/481021; ②, with shared bathroom). From here it's 25km to the hamlet of Vavarco, where the beige Río Vavarco splices dramatically with the turquoise Río Neuquén. Further on is the **Cajón del Atreuco** and **Los Bolillos** – bizarrely eroded formations of sandy volcanic toba stone, similar to those found in Cappadocia in Turkey. You arrive at the hot springs, 36km from Vavarco, at the isolated **Termas Domuyo** complex, which rents **cabins** with kitchen and cooking utensils (☎0299/481576; closed April–Nov; $450 for up to eight people; book in advance); bring good sleeping bags and non-perishable food. **Camping** and drinking water here is free.

Termas Domuyo also acts as the centre of operations for **climbers** who hope to reach the summit of **Domuyo** (2–3 days; altitude sickness is a real possibility: see p.34). The attendant hires out horses and acts as a guide ($10 per horse, plus $10 for guide). To get to the base camp, head back to the Los Tachos/El Humazo turn-off 2.5km before the complex. From there, it's half an hour by car to where the track ends, and then two and a half hours by horse. From the base camp, you can climb to the summit and get back down again in a day.

Caviahue and Copahue

The region around the resorts of **Caviahue** and **Copahue** is a provincial reserve, established principally to protect the country's northernmost stands of well-spaced **araucaria** woodland that grow on the slopes of the domed, shield volcano, **Volcán Copahue** (2953m), the summit of which marks the border with Chile.

CAVIAHUE is a small, spread-out town of tin-roofed houses set at altitude in a bowl of low hills, on the shores of **Lago Caviahue**, also known as Lago Agrio (Bitter Lake), due to its sulphurous waters. The peeled aridity of the slopes here is broken by groups of araucaria, which are reflected picturesquely in the lake whenever the sky is its usual clear diaphanous blue. When the wind is not up, the place gets pleasantly warm. Highly recommended are the walks to a series of exquisite **waterfalls** in the neighbourhood, especially the **Siete Cascadas** route along the Arroyo Agrio: this has entrancing scenes of cascades plunging over columned basalt rock, and flanked by prehistoric araucarias. The initial section of the route (approximately 45min) is well marked, and takes you past four or five falls, including the stunning Cabellera de la Virgen (25m) and up to the Cascada del Gigante (8m), set by a clump of *ñire* trees. To see all seven falls, it's best to go by horseback ($5–40). Northeast of Caviahue, 16km away and sign-posted 2km to the left of the RP27, is the **Salto del Agrio**, an impressive seventy-metre fall that plunges off a basalt terrace. Caviahue has some **skiing** in winter, but it's better for scenic cross-country options (16km of trails) than downhill (5km of pistes).

Tiny **COPAHUE**, whose name means "place of sulphur" or "place where you collect water" in Mapudungun, is 19km from Caviahue, further up the volcano's slopes and above the tree line. The Mapuche have long praised and sampled the health-giving qualities of its **thermal springs** and mineral mud baths, hyped in tourist brochures as being "the best in the world". Today's reality is that it's a depressing, huddled assemblage of overpriced 1960s hotels frequented by more than their fair share of hypochondriacs – a kind of "last resort" resort for those whose health has given way faster than their wallets – though the swirling clouds of steam rising from its pools and the amphitheatre setting gives the place some atmosphere. A $12-million investment in thermal under-street heating (the only system of its kind in the world) means the resort can remain open year-round. The central feature is the **Complejo Termal** (daily 7am–noon & 5–9pm), where you pay separately to try a multitude of different saunas, hydro-massage tanks, swimming baths and mud baths. You must pay for a doctor's consultation – which usually entails a wait of an hour or two – before trying any, however, and the treatments are at rip-off prices. Laguna Verde (cold) is free, but it's hardly appealing; the next cheapest deal is Laguna del Chancho ($5).

Between January and March, you can **climb** Volcán Copahue, which takes over seven hours (5hr outward climb; 2hr 30min return). The crater is interesting, since glacial ice often reaches right to the crater lake, despite the water being thermally heated to between 20°C and 70°C. This climb can also be done from Caviahue in a similar time. The tourist office in Caviahue should be able to recommend a guide: try Daniel Maniero, who has an office in the Complejo Termal itself (☎02948/495000); he is highly qualified and charges $40 per person to go halfway in a 4WD followed by a two-hour climb to the top, or $35 to make the journey by horse.

Practicalities

In Caviahue, Centenario **buses** stop at the Vi-Car café and fuel station, by the lake front, on the RP26 through town; El Petroleo stops a couple of blocks away at Mapuche s/n. From Caviahue, buses continue through to Copahue in summer only (Dec–Feb). A *remise* between the two resorts costs $10. Set on the slope four blocks back from the lakeshore in Caviahue is the **tourist office**, Bungalows 5 & 6 (☎02948/495144, fax 495036) where you'll find information on horseriding and walks.

As for **accommodation**, half or full board is compulsory in many places in high season. **In Caviahue**, the most luxurious place is the large *Apart Hotel Lago Caviahue* fronting the lake (☎ & fax 02948/495074; ⑥), with optional full board in high season. *Hotel Caviahue*, 8 de Abril s/n (☎ & fax 02948/495044; ⑤), imports thermal waters for its bathing rooms and offers discounts from Easter to December. *Camping Hueney* ($5per person; closed April–Nov) has fairly basic services – just a confitería and some toilets – but a pleasant siting, 3km out of town on the route to Copahue. **In Copahue**, the least expensive options are *Bravo Departamentos*, Ducloux s/n (☎02948/495028; $50 for a four-person self-catering apartment; closed March–Oct); *Hostería Pino Azul* (☎ & fax 02948/495071; no cards; ⑥, with full board; closed Easter–Nov); and the friendly but rudimentary *Hotel S.U.P.E*, Coronel Duclaud s/n (☎02948/495005; ⑥, with full board), which offers a bed and no board rate out of season. Comfortable *Valle del Volcán*, Ducloux 120 (☎ & fax 02948/495048; *copahue@valledelvolcan.com*; ⑦, with half board; closed June–Oct), is one of the few modern places, with luxuries such as satellite TV in the rooms, but little choice of menu for its full-board status. You can **camp** opposite the *Pino Azul* (☎02948/495071; hot water; closed Easter–Nov).

Parque Nacional Lanín

The most northerly of Patagonia's great national parks, **Parque Nacional Lanín** was formed in 1937 and protects 3790 square kilometres of Andean and sub-Andean habitat that ranges from barren, semi-arid steppe in the east to patches of temperate Valdivian rainforest pressed up against the Chilean border. To the south, it's joined to its sister park, the even more colossal Nahuel Huapi, while it also shares a boundary with Parque Villarica in Chile.

The park has three trademark features. The first is the presence of various Mapuche communities who live in and around the park (see box, p.532). The second is its geographical centrepiece – the fabulous cone of **Volcán Lanín**, rising to 3776m and dominating the scenery around. This volcano, and the central sector of the park around Lagos Huechulafquen, Paimún and Tromen, is best reached from **Junín de los Andes**. The park's other trump card is a species of tree – the araucaria, or *pehuén* (see box, p.539). Araucarias exist in isolated stands as far south as Lago Curruhue Grande, but are especially prevalent in the northern sector of the park around Quillén, Rucachoroi and Norquinco, and their range extends past the park's northern boundary: an area known as the **Pehuenia region**. It's not the easiest area of the park to get around, but tourism is less in evidence and it has some excellent treks. Most people gain access to this region via Zapala (see p.531) or Junín.

Parque Lanín's lakes drain eastwards, with the exception of Lago Lácar, which drains into the Pacific. This southern sector of the park and the famous **Seven Lakes Route** through the north of Parque Nacional Nahuel Huapi towards Villa La Angostura and Bariloche are covered in the section on **San Martín de los Andes** (pp.549–557). San Martín is by far the most scenic of the two principal towns for accessing the park, but is more expensive than its low-key rival, Junín.

As well as the araucaria, other species endemic to the region are the *roble pellín*, with leaves not unlike those of the oak, and the *raulí*, both types of deciduous *Nothofagus* southern beech, and often found together. The *raulí* does not extend much north of Lago Quillén. The park also protects notable forests of *coihue*, as well as *ñire*, *lenga*, *maniú*, *radal* and, in the drier areas, cypress. Flowers such as the *arvejilla* purple sweet pea and the introduced lupin abound in spring, as does the abundant, flame-red *notro* bush. Fuchsia bushes grow in some of the wetter regions.

As for fauna, the park reputedly protects a population of *huemules*, although their status is precarious. You have a very slim chance of seeing a pudú, the tiny native deer, a puma or a *gato huiña* wildcat. Better chances exist of spotting a coipu or a grey fox, but some of the likeliest creatures you'll come across are the ones introduced for hunting a century ago: the wild boar and the red deer that roam the semi-arid steppes and hills of the eastern margin of the park. Involuntarily, the latter species especially makes an important contribution to the local economy, as foreigners and Porteños pay significant sums for shooting rights. A common bird which has been introduced to the region is the California quail; the male of the species has a distinctive frontal plume on its head. One thing worth avoiding is any small black spider: black widows do inhabit the park, although they're not common.

The wettest places in the park (over 4000mm rainfall a year) are Añihueraqui at the western end of Lago Quillén and Lago Queñi. The park can be covered in snow from May to October, but it can snow in the higher mountain regions at almost any time of year. The **best time to visit** is in spring (especially Oct–Nov) – or autumn (March to mid-May), when the deciduous trees adopt a spectacular palette, particularly in the Pehuenia area; the contasts of rusts, golds and dark greens is irresistible. Trekking is possible between late October and early May, although the season for some of the higher treks is shorter, usually from December to March. January and February see an influx of Argentine holidaymakers, who come to Lanín to fish and camp, but in general, you've more scope here than in Nahuel Huapi to escape the crowds, even in high season. Take care when camping in forests of mature *coihue* trees, as the branches have a reputation for breaking off easily in windy weather.

The Araucaria Heartland: Northern Lanin and the Pehuenia Circuit

The northern sector of Parque Nacional Lanín and the adjoining Pehuenia region further north is one of the least developed and most beautiful areas of the Argentinian Lake District. This "forgotten corner" of Mapuche communities, wonderful mountain lakes, basalt cliffs and araucaria forests has largely escaped the commercial pressures found further south in the park system, although locals and recent settlers are fast waking up to its potential, and tourists are arriving in ever increasing numbers. Infrastucture links are still fairly rudimentary (though improving every year, so check before setting out), and having your own transport is a boon. Otherwise, you'll need to take a taxi, or hitch – best done along those roads that branch off the RP23 to the lakes

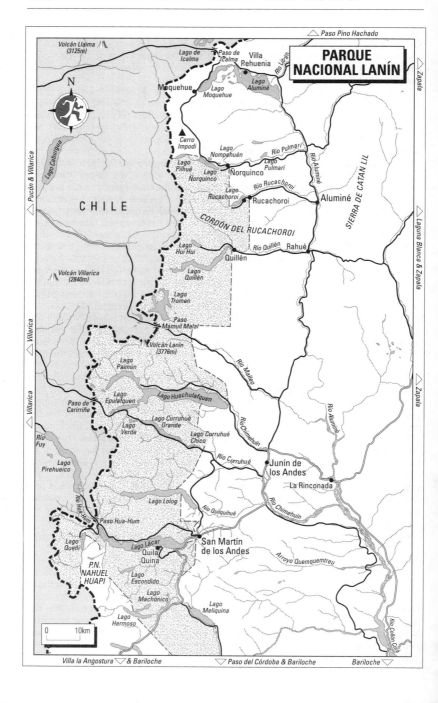

PARQUE NACIONAL LANÍN

of Quillén, Rucachoroi, and Ñorquinco, as well as the stretch between Ñorquinco and Moquehue. This latter stretch forms one of the legs of the only logical road circuit found here, the **Pehuenia Circuit**, which links **Villa Pehuenia** on the northern bank of Lago Aluminé with tiny **Moquehue**, at the southwest tip of the eponymous lake, and passes along **Lago Ñorquinco**, the northernmost boundary of the park. Most people finish or start the circuit in **Aluminé**, the region's most important settlement, though itself not much more than a village.

The lack of convenient road routes acts as encouragement to **trek**: you can make your own circuits by hiking through the park's heartland, linking any or all the stages from Villa Pehuenia south to Quillén. The sections described here take a north–south route, with the exception of the one from Quillén, which heads in the opposite direction. Each stage – Villa Pehuenia, Moquehue, Ñorquinco, Rucachoroi and Quillén – can be completed in a full day, but look at a minimum of five days rather than four to complete the whole route, not including transport to the trailheads. For the last three mentioned, you should carry all the food you need – though you can top this up in Ñorquinco and Rucachoroi – and you must register with the *guardaparque* before setting out on any of them, reporting your safe arrival at the other end. The *guardaparque* will inform you of the latest conditions, which is especially important in early or late season: you must cross several mountain ranges that top out at 2000m and branch eastwards from the cordillera, and snowfalls can obscure the path over the passes. If it's not safe, the *guardaparque* will refuse permission for you to trek. All of the stages

THE ARAUCARIA, OR MONKEY PUZZLE TREE

The **araucaria** is more commonly known as the **monkey puzzle tree**, one of the world's most distinctive and beautiful trees. They're found only in the cordillera of Neuquén Province and at similar latitudes across the border in Chile, growing on impoverished volcanic soils at altitudes of between 600m and 1800m. The species is a prehistoric survival that has been around for more than two hundred million years. The ones you see today are descendants of those that survived the great cataclysm that flattened the forests of the Bosque Petrificado in Santa Cruz, 150 million years ago.

Araucarias grow incredibly slowly, but they can live to over a 1000 years of age. Young trees grow in a pyramid shape, but after about a hundred years, they start to lose their lower branches to assume their trademark umbrella appearance. Mature specimens can reach 45m in height, and their straight trunks are covered by panels of thick bark that give the tree some resistance against fire. The female trees produce huge, head-size cones filled with fawn-coloured pinenuts called *piñones*, some 5cm long, and rich in proteins and carbohydrates.

Known to the Mapuche as the *pehuén*, the tree was revered as the daughter of the moon. Legend has it that there was a time when the Mapuche, though they adored the *pehuén*, never ate its *piñones*, believing them to be poisonous. This changed, however, during a terrible famine, when their god, Ngüenechén, saved them from starvation by sending a messenger to rectify this misconception and to teach them both the best way of preparing these nutritious seeds (roasting them in embers or boiling), and of storing them (burying them in the earth or snow). *Piñones* thus came to form the staple diet of tribes in the area (principally the Pehuenches, who were named because of their dependence on the tree) and, ever since, the Mapuche have revered them.

The tree was introduced into Europe in the eighteenth century as an ornamental species, and the English name "monkey puzzle" dates from soon after. Quite why it gained this sobriquet is not certain, as no monkeys live in its native habitat. One theory is that, perhaps in some ornamental menagerie, monkeys who climbed along the branches, sliding over the smooth spirals of interlocking leaves which covered them, found themselves faced with unforgiving ranks of prickly plates when they turned to go back – a kind of "lobster-trap" effect.

bar the one linking Rucachoroi and Quillén can be done by **mountain bike**, for which the terrain is ideal.

There's tremendous scope for other outdoor activities here, including **rafting** through the scenic gorge of the Río Aluminé and **horseriding**. Those especially keen on the latter might like to contact Paso Ancho, C.C. 10, Las Lajas (fax 02942/499220; *larminat@posoancho.com*), an adventure activities outfit whose speciality is a seven-day expedition on horseback from Paso Pino Hachado to their base at little-visited Lago Pilhué ($595 with airport transfer from Neuquén).

The RP23 to Aluminé

The **RP23** runs parallel to the turbulent waters of the Río Aluminé, carving its way through arid rocky gorges on its way from Junín to **Aluminé**, and then continues on to Lago Aluminé and the turn-off to Villa Pehuenia, passing groves of araucaria trees growing along the river's upper reaches. To the east, parallel with the valley, lies the **Sierra de Catan Lil**, a harsh and desiccated range that's older and higher than the neighbouring Andes. At **RAHUÉ**, 16km south of Aluminé, a branch road leads to Quillén, 29km away (see p.544). Rahué itself is nothing more than a couple of houses by a road junction and an enthusiastic **tourist office** (mid-Nov to April daily 8am–8pm).

ALUMINÉ itself is a tiny place built by the river, and has a gentle pace of life. For a week in March it celebrates the **Fiesta del Pehuén** to coincide with the Mapuche harvest of *piñones*, with displays of horsemanship, music and *artesanía*. Its main claim to fame is as a summer **rafting centre**: organized trips are run by Agencia Amuyén, General Villegas 348 (☎ & fax 02942/496368; $60 for five passengers). They also rent mountain bikes. A branch road heads west from the village to Rucachoroi and (28km away) the *guardaparque* post (see p.544). There is no public transport heading that way, you'll need to book a taxi (☎02942/496398 or 496179; $20–25).

Aluminé's **bus terminal** is on Avenida 4 de Caballería, half a block from Plaza San Martín, where you'll find the **tourist office**, at Cristian Joubert 321 (daily 8am-6pm; ☎02942/496001, fax 496154). Just about everything else you need is within a block or two of the plaza. *Hotel Pehuenia*, at junction of RP23 and Capitán Crouzeilles (☎ & fax 02942/496340; ⑤), is a resort **hotel** not entirely in keeping with the rest of the village. Its rooms are comfortable, if a little twee, and half have river views. The hotel rents out mountain bikes and arranges horseriding. *Hostería Aluminé*, Cristian Joubert 336 (☎02942/496174, fax 496347; ③), is a clean, straightforward ex-ACA hotel with apartments for up to six people. Sometimes they'll rent a room with shared bathroom for as low as $10 per person. The **restaurant** here is a good place to try soup of *piñones* (the famous araucaria pinenuts), and main courses are very reasonably priced ($4–8). Good value, too, is *Hostería Nid-Car*, Cristian Joubert 559 (☎02942/496131; ③), which also serves meals. Cheaper still is the free and agreeable municipal **campsite**, by the river, 1.5km north of town. Aluminé also has a YPF **fuel station** – one of the few in the area.

Villa Pehuenia

VILLA PEHUENIA is a young, friendly and fast-growing holiday village set amongst araucaria trees, on the shores of pristine Lago Aluminé. *Cabañas* are the boom industry here, springing up in both the main part of the village and on the lumpy, tree-covered peninsula that juts into the lake's chilly waters. In places, the steep basalt sides of the peninsula make great **diving** perches if you can tough out the water temperature. To the north is Volcán Batea Mahuida, a mountain that has a minuscule ski-resort.

The *Ruca Pehuén* mini-supermarket has some of the least expensive **accommodation** in the village (☎02942/498024; ⑤), with one quadruple for $40. *Camping Lagrimitas* (☎02942/496337; $5 per person plus $1 per tent; one $50 apartment for five people) has some fantastic, tranquil pitches beneath monkey puzzles by the lake shore.

On the peninsula, twenty minutes' walk from the main village or reached by Yumbel and Ruca Antú minibuses, you'll find *Eyén Lihué* on the hill ($48dbl with breakfast). Rooms are snug and peaceful, and snacks are served in the **restaurant**. A little to the left is *Cabañas Caren* (☎155-801227; ⑤), which rents well-designed luxury cabins with a fully equipped kitchen for up to seven people ($130). Its personable owners speak English and Italian. Next door is *Hostería Al Paraíso* ($70dbl, charged per person), another enjoyable place which serves meals of roast goat and trout ($12).

Moquehue and its lake

Villa Pehuenia is connected to the pioneer village of **Moquehue** by an unsurfaced road (23km) that runs around the northwestern shores of **Lago Moquehue**, Lago Aluminé's sibling. The two lakes are joined at La Angostura by a narrow, five-hundred-metre channel of the most captivating turquoise waters. Just west of La Angostura, a turn-off leads 4km to the **Paso de Icalma** (1303m), the pass closest to Temuco in Chile. A mere 30km past the border, you can access the Parque Nacional Conguillío, centred on imposing **Volcán Llaima** (3125m).

MOQUEHUE is a loose confederation of farmsteads set in a broad pastoral valley at the southwestern end of its lake, and overlooked on both sides by splendid ranks of rugged, forested ranges and **Cerro Bella Durmiente**, so named because the summit looks like the profile of a sleeping beauty. As yet, there's none of the contrived feel that comes from an excess of holiday *cabañas* that feature in nearby towns, and most residents have deep roots here. There are some excellent walks nearby: one short leg-stretch (35min one way) leads to an attractive **waterfall** in mystical mixed araucaria woodland; while longer ones include a hike up Cerro Bandera (2hr one way), with excellent views to Volcán Llaima. Jaime Ulloa is a knowledgeable and charming guide for hikes and horseriding ($50 per day). He rents **rooms** at *La Flor del Quillahue* (☎0299/493-3347 for messages; $40 for up to four people), fifteen minutes' walk to the east of the police **checkpoint** that lies on the main road to Ñorquinco. Just north of the checkpoint is the excellent-value *Hostería Bella Durmiente* (☎02942/496172; ③; reserve in advance in Jan), a wonderfully authentic, wood-built guesthouse, commanding soothing views of the scenery around. The friendly owner sells home-made bread and tarts, as well as pizzas or chicken **meals** ($7–10), and beautifully made craft items. She also runs a fine rural **campsite** close to the lake ($4.50 per person).

AROUND THE LAKE

Rather than take the road along the western shore of **Lago Moquehue**, you can make a gorgeous **day hike** around its southeastern side, through lands belonging to the Puel Mapuche community. You pass several Puel farmsteads as well as several diminutive, secluded lakes and beautiful woodland of *ñire, radal, notro*, araucaria and *coihue*. From Pehuenia, head west along the road to Moquehue until you get to the Puesta Sanitaria and La Angostura (25min). Past the tree nursery here, turn left and walk to the footbridge (10min) over the delightful narrows. Immediately on the other side is *El Puente* **campsite** (an alternative option to staying in Villa Pehuenia). Continue on the main track, ignoring a faint trail to your right. You pass an inlet of Lago Aluminé on your left, and then the road climbs upwards alongside an attractive gorge. You come to a small **hut** where the rough road forks (30min). Take the right-hand fork, usually blocked by a barrier: here the local Mapuche charge motorists a toll ($2) and sell *artesanía* in summer. Walkers are allowed to continue for free, but are asked to respect the environment by not lighting fires or littering. Also respect the locals' right not to be photographed.

Just past the hut is a tranquil wooded lagoon, Cari Laufquén. Another 35 minutes brings you to a Mapuche farmstead between a pair of shallow lagoons – the larger is called **Pichún**; the smaller **Laguna Verde**. Twenty minutes further on, there's a larger lake, **Matetué** (ignore the names if using the IGM map, as they've been wrongly placed). The track forks: take the left-hand fork, as the other runs down to the house you can see by the lake. This left fork, a cart track, curls around the lake to another farm, marked by a few Lombardy poplars and a proud araucaria. At the private gate in the fence, the main track ends. A path hugs the outside of the fence and disappears into woodland, but follow this for only about 30m past the gate, where you dog-leg back away from the fence up a horse trail.

In about ten minutes you enter some fine mature mixed woodland, and in another ten the uphill climb brings you onto a plateau, from where the path drops steeply to an exquisite, abandoned homestead by **Lago Moquehue** (ignore a left-hand fork on your way down). There's a fine **beach** here, but better ones slightly further on. Follow the wire fence left (southwest) to pick up the path, and after ten minutes you come to a tiny scoop of a beach by a ruined hut. This is a tempting place to camp free, but you need permission to do so. Ten minutes further on, along the larger neighbouring strand, you reach the mouth of the crystalline **Río Blanco**, which you'll need to ford.

The last section of the walk from Río Blanco to Moquehue (2hr–2hr 30min) follows a clear path, but involves some dips and climbs, as you scout around the steep banks that line the lake shore. The path heads along the beach before clipping woodland and cutting across the gap between the mainland and a jutting promontory hill. You pass some tremendous stands of giant *coihue* and, in places, araucaria. After about an hour, you cross the first of three reasonably sized brooks, spaced at ten-minute intervals. Soon after negotiating the last brook you come across a sign marked "Reserva Araucaria", and then rejoin a proper track at *Camping Trenel*. From here it's around ten minutes to *La Flor del Quillahue* in Moquehue, and the same again to the checkpoint and the main part of the scattered village.

Lago Ñorquinco and around

From Moquehue, a wide dirt road runs 31km to **Lago Ñorquinco**, the northern border of Parque Nacional Lanín and 1060m above sea level. There's no public transport along this route and hitching isn't easy as there's little traffic. On the way there are good views of peaks along the Chilean border and mountainsides half-clad in araucaria. **Cerro Impodi** (2100m) is an impressive silvery-grey massif of bare rock halfway along the route. South of Impodi is a gushing waterfall on the eastern side of the road and then some stunning, sheer **basalt cliffs** topped by araucaria, at the foot of which runs the Arroyo Remeco. Much of this region formed the focus for a heated dispute in the 1990s, when Mapuche groups tried, unsuccessfully, to reclaim land that had been ceded to the private Pulmarí Corporation and which passed into government hands during the Perón administration.

At the west end of Lago Ñorquinco is a signposted turn-off to a free national park **campsite** (no services), from where a track runs around the south of the lake to a *gendarmería* post – this is the most direct link to both the trek described below and the *guardaparque* post. Alternatively, stay on the main road and pass small **Lago Nompehuén**, which is good for fishing, to get to *Eco Camping* (☎156-61356; $5 per person; closed mid-April to mid-Nov), a beautiful lakeside site run on commendably rigorous environmental lines that outclasses almost anything else in the country. In peak season (Jan & Feb) you can rent bikes and hire horses from here; they also sell fishing permits. An hour's walk east of *Eco Camping* takes you past the scattered houses of Ñorquinco settlement to the bridge over the Río Pulmarí; or, if you can bear the cold and the water level is low enough (generally Nov–April), ford the river where it drains the lake, to the picnic spot on the other side (no camping here). This cuts off a loop of almost 4km if you're not interested in seeing the *rehue*, a Mapuche altar, described below.

From the Pulmarí bridge there are two routes. From here, it's 32km to the slightly busier RP23, and another 20km to Aluminé. On the way, 1.5km from the bridge, is another national park **campsite** ($2 per person); and on the side of the road past the park gate is a **monument** to one of the last battles of the Campaign of the Desert. Alternatively, take the track heading west to the *Seccional Ñorquinco* **guardaparque post** (35min). Shortly past the cattle grid, you can detour left, uphill along another track, to see the only surviving **rehue** in situ in Argentina. It's about twenty minutes away, in the middle of a small grassland plateau, up above the basalt cliff. The *rehue* is a cypress post, carved crudely into the shape of a man, and badly weathered. It stood unused from 1947 until the year 2000, when the first Nguillatún prayer ceremony in fifty years was held here, with Mapuche delegations from both sides of the border attending (see p.533).

The *guardaparque* will inform you of other walks in the area, including a one-hour route that visits three waterfalls, and ones in the well-preserved Lago Pilhué area by the Chilean border.

ON TO LAGO RUCACHOROI

There's a beautiful full-day's trek from Lago Ñorquinco to **Lago Rucachoroi**, taking you past some of the best mixed araucaria forests you can access. It's best to start the walk early (preferably by 7am), to avoid having to climb the pass in the midday heat. The IGM map #3972-23 "Lago Ñorquinco" (1:100,000) covers the region, but it is well overdue for an update. The stage between the Ñorquinco *guardaparque* post and the *gendarmería* along the shore of the lake is fairly flat and easy to follow, but it involves crossing many small streams (1hr 15min). You pass splendid examples of *coihue*; araucaria, *roble pellín* and *ñire* as well as a beautiful waterfall. For the last twenty minutes or so the scenery is more open: past a beach that's bordered by a profusion of lupins in spring, and then through *caña colihue* growth that's spiked by skeletons of trees. This is the evidence of a great **fire** that devastated the area in the late 1980s. Finally you arrive at the two buildings of the *gendarmería*. From here, head round the south side of the *gendarmería* shed to pick up the trail. The next stage takes you to the start of the **pass** (1450m; 2hr from *gendarmería*), which runs between Cerro Liuco (1964m) to the west, and **Cerro Clucnú Chumpirú** (2192m) to the east.

After around ten minutes, the trail zigzags up a brief slope and as far on again, there's a patch of open grassland (*pastizal*). Do not head straight on across this small pampa, but take the narrower track that veers diagonally to the right (westwards) across it. This takes you to a firebreak trail alongside the **Río Coloco**. After 25 minutes, you can look down upon a spectacular thirty-metre **waterfall** that plunges over a basalt cliff. Ten to fifteen minutes further on you find a low semicircular ridge of stones where the fire bulldozer left its last moraine. Look for the small, red, circular tin plate that marks where a trail cuts up left through a *caña coihue* thicket for a short stretch, before it rejoins a proper track. Soon you enter a stand of araucaria, and the path ahead is blocked by several of these fallen titans (victims of the fire).

In this woodland (about 1hr 30min from the *gendarmería*), you come to a deep ditch cut in the sandy soil by a stream. Do not cross by the tempting fallen araucaria bridge, but look to your right and find the rough path that drops down sharply through the mixed lenga and araucaria forest before it crosses the stream. The undergrowth here is of parrilla wild currant and holly. Five minutes past the first stream, you cross a second one and then the path starts to climb. The next twenty minutes are the hardest part of the walk, but not too difficult, as long as the *caña coihue* hasn't invaded the path too badly. The terrain levels off and you come to the **pass** at an amphitheatre of marshy grassland (*mallín*). Here you're likely to hear the vociferous chattering of austral parakeets (*cachañas*) searching out *piñones*. It can snow up at the pass as late as early December.

The next stage takes you across the pass and down through mature lenga and araucaria forest on the other side (50min). Twenty minutes will take you past the *mallín*. You must cross and recross the stream that meanders through it, following the red stakes. Enter the forest and enjoy some of the most enchanting scenery of the walk before dropping down the hillside at a good rate, following a broad track – a real buzz if you are following the trail by mountain bike. Cross a tributary burn that flows into the main stream, the Arroyo Calfiquitrá. Half an hour past the *mallín*, you leave the forest behind, entering the broad, grassy **Calfiquitrá Valley**, where the path flattens out.

The three-hour stage from leaving the forest to the head of **Lago Rucachoroi** (1200m above sea level) is fairly easy walking and is not hard to follow. However, it involves having to cross or ford (depending on the time of year) several streams, including the Calfiquitrá twice in the next fifteen minutes. Follow the ox-cart track into upland summer pasture for Mapuche cattle and goats, then cross a tributary stream, the Pichi Quinquín, and ford the icy Calfiquitrá (bigger by this point). You then pass through two typical Patagonian wire gates (be sure to shut them properly), before fording the Calfiquitrá again – it can be over knee-deep at this point. You reach a scenic shepherd's hut (*puesto*) on your right (1hr 45min after leaving the forest), which has a rustic wooden corral. Cross the small tributary streams here, and continue down the valley, passing another couple of *puestos* away to your right. You will have to cross several other shallow rivulets and finally one broad stream (approximately 2hr 40min from the forest). Another twenty minutes brings you to the head of the lake. Here there's a gorgeous but exposed **campsite**, the *Camping Punta del Lago* (no facilities; free). A few minutes' walk to the north, the exquisite coils of the Arroyo Calfiquitrá loop through the meadows before flowing into the lake. Don't be surprised if you see llamas grazing in the surrounding area (see box on p.545).

There's a second free campsite, *Lago Rucachoroi*, 45 minutes from *Punta del Lago* along the dirt road. **Cars** are permitted as far as *Punta del Lago*, so you may catch a lift. *Lago Rucachoroi* has a kiosk run by a Mapuche family (open Dec–Feb; sells goat meat, beer, biscuits and *artesanía*), but no other services. Around ten minutes further on is the *Seccional Rucachoroi* **guardaparque** post.

Rucachoroi

RUCACHOROI is the centre of the Aigo Mapuche community, and with a population of around 700 it is one of the most important in Argentina. This is a farming settlement strung out for several kilometres on either side of the RP18, with little in the way of a real centre, and not much of a definite beginning or end. Its western farmsteads lie within the park boundaries. Bordering the region to the south is the **Cordón Rucachoroi**, with peaks over 2100m. A trail leads from behind the *guardaparque* post here to Quillén, but it's not advisable to try it outside the summer season (Dec–March) as snow can render the path invisible in places. Consult the *guardaparque* about conditions, and ask him or her to draw a sketch map.

Rucachoroi's only **shop** lies 5km east of the *guardaparque* post and sells succulent home-made chorizos that are ideal for barbecuing. Nearby is an outlet selling **artesanía** made by the locals. There is no accommodation in town, but you can camp near the lake (see above). To get here, other than on foot, you'll need to hitch, or catch a **taxi** from Aluminé (☎02942/496398 or 496179; $25).

Quillén and its lake

The tiny settlement of **QUILLÉN** has the atmosphere of a very scenic ghost town, set in dreamy wooded scenery near the eastern tip of **Lago Quillén**. No more than a handful of estancia buildings, it once depended on the sawmill that operated here, but it is now a private specialist fishing lodge. The name derives from the Mapuche word *quellén* – their name for the wild strawberries that grow in the region. It has no shops or facilities other than a **public phone** (no international calls) where you can call for a

A POLITIC BALANCE

The area now forming Parque Nacional Lanín was once the heartland of the Mapuche, being the centre of the Pehuenches and their forebears, who depended heavily on the collection of *piñones* (pine nuts from the araucaria). Lanín, more than any other Argentinian park, is where the park authorities must engage in a highly complex trade-off between the right of the area's indigenous inhabitants to continue their lifestyle, and the need to protect a sensitive ecosystem. Several Mapuche communities, notably the Aigo of Rucachoroi and the Curruhuinca of Lago Lácar, are allowed access to the park either to gather pine nuts or for summer pasture for their goats and cattle. Overgrazing in certain areas has led to pioneering projects to try and find a balance that meets both needs. In Rucachoroi, a few volunteer Mapuche families have, since 1998, been raising llamas. Llamas' hooves cause less damage to the soil than those of cattle or goats, and they nibble the shoots of plants rather than rip up the roots, as does the voracious, destructive goat. The experiment has aroused interest in the community, although it remains to be seen whether the Mapuche embrace it on a wider scale.

taxi to take you into Aluminé (☎02942/496398 or 496179 for taxi; $25); there's no public transport.

Some 3km beyond the fishing lodge along the northern bank of the Río Quillén are the buildings of the **guardaparque** post. For information, knock on the door of the main building (8am–10pm), and if no one is in, try one of the neighbouring houses. You must register here for the walk to Rucachoroi (see below).

The **lake** itself, shaped like an attenuated arm and with an elbow bend, is bordered by some of the park's very finest Andean-Patagonian forests and is one of the most beautiful in the region. It's a deep green colour when still, but often gets very windy in the afternoon, when its colour darkens. At the top of a high ridge on the southern shore, a distinctive phallic rock sticks up at the sky: chastely called Ponom on maps, its real spelling is *panan*, the Mapuche word for penis. In the distance, the summit of Volcán Lanín can be seen poking above an intervening mountain range. There are great views of this from the lovely lake-shore **campsite**, *Camping Quillén* (with showers and shop; $2 per person), less than 1km west of the *guardaparque*'s house. A tranquil free site, *Camping Pudú Pudú* (no facilities), is some 5km further down the track.

Apart from the Rucachoroi trek, there are two principal **trails**, both of which take the road that forks inland from near the *Pudú Pudú* campsite (4WD access only), heading for **Lago Hui Hui**, a wild lake hemmed in by an amphitheatre of forest-clad hills and dotted with a couple of small islands. The first option is the walk through to the lake (6km from *Pudú Pudú*; 3hr return). At the low pass, you come to a flat pampa and a long line of old tree trunks laid end-to-end, which used to act as a corral for oxen. Up above is the **Cerro de la Víbora** (1720m), a mountain whose rocky summit resembles the broad head of a snub-nosed viper. The lake is just past an old disused *guardaparque*'s hut, over a wooden bridge.

The second trail makes for a two-day return hike (10hr each way; return along same route) to the **Añihueraqui** *gendarmería* post, at the far western end of Lago Quillén, by the Chilean border. You'll need prior permission from the *guardaparque* and the Quillén *gendarmería* post, as you'll need to camp at Añihueraqui. Añihueraqui is one of the wettest regions of the park, with annual rainfall in excess of 4000mm, and on the way you pass through superlative wet temperate forest. This hike is best done later in the summer (Jan–March), as you need to ford a fine fishing stream, the **Arroyo Hui Hui**, which can be more than waist-high outside these months. Take the track towards Lago Hui Hui, but turn off left (west) at the field just before the abandoned *guardaparque*'s hut.

Take care here, as the turn-off is not at all clearly marked. Further on, it is also often overgrown with *caña colihue*.

Sadly, walking around the lake is impossible unless you get permission from both the *guardaparque* and the fishing estancia, as they control access to private land on the southern shore.

QUILLÉN TO RUCACHOROI TREK

The trek from Quillén to Rucachoroi crosses the **Cordón Rucachoroi**, whose highest summit, **Cerro Rucachoroi**, is 2296m above sea level. It gives excellent views of mountains such as **Cerro de la Víbora** and **Cerro Mesa** to the northwest, as well as the unmistakable cone of **Volcán Lanín** to the southwest. You also pass through patches of araucaria woodland. It takes about nine to ten hours in total, and should only be tackled in summer (Dec–March), as snowfall can obscure parts of he trail in winter: verify the current state with the *guardaparque*. You should leave early (7am) to avoid having to climb to the pass during the heat of midday, and bring plenty of water with you. Be sure to bring at least a **sketch map** from the *guardaparque* or, better still, ask for him or her to mark the route on the IGM map #3972-23 "Lago Ñorquinco" (1:100,000). The beginning of the trek is described below, followed by a rough outline of the rest of the route.

The trail starts behind, and to the right of, the main, old-style Quillén *guardaparque* building. Pick up a stick along the way for moral support just in case you meet any farm dogs further on. After five minutes you come to a gate across the road. Beyond this, head along the track to a farm (35min), surrounded by bald earth and calafate bushes that have been ravaged by herds of goats. Go through the farm, bearing slightly to the right, and ford the **Arroyo Malalco**: ask a member of the Lefiman family here to point out where to cross. The water at the crossing is knee-high for much of the year.

At the small red stake on the far side, turn left (if you come to a wire fence at any point, it means you've gone too far to the right: retrace your steps to the river). Follow the red stakes until you reach some *coihue* trees. You then turn away from the river and cut right to start a stiff climb up the mountain spur which lies between two valleys (around 2hr). This is the toughest stretch of the route. Past some araucaria woodland the path zigzags its way up the slope through scrubby vegetation as you approach the tree line, before levelling off and heading for the first pass, which lies near the head of the right-hand valley. More red stakes mark the route across a boggy *mallín* on the other side. The path climbs again and you must cross a boulder field, keeping a sharp lookout for more red stakes, until you get to the lower second pass. Near the pass, a cairn marks a detour left to the Lagunas Las Mellizas (less than 1hr one way; return along the same route). From the pass, you drop into the valley of Lago Rucachoroi and meet the road that leads east to the *guardaparque* post (see p.544).

Junín de los Andes and around

Though not as attractive as its neighbour, San Martín de los Andes (see p.549), **JUNÍN DE LOS ANDES** is better placed for making trips to the central sector of Parque Nacional Lanín (see p.536 for general information on the park), especially for exploring the **Lago Huechulafquen** area and if you plan to climb Volcán Lanín itself. In addition, it is a convenient starting point for trips to **Aluminé** and the less-visited northern zone of the national park (see p.540). Junín is also less expensive than touristy San Martín, both in the summer and as an alternative winter base for skiing at Chapelco (see p.553).

Set in a dry, hilly area of the steppe at the foot of the Andes, Junín is a spruce little town with well-tended gardens and a relaxed atmosphere. It's popular with fishermen, since the Río Chimehuín that flows along the east side of town and other rivers in the region are popular with trout. The few sites of interest in town are all within a couple of blocks of the main square, the **Plaza San Martín**, and can be seen in an hour or two. The **Paseo Artesanal** on the east side of the square is a cluster of boutiques selling a selection of crafts, amongst which Mapuche weavings figure heavily. The tiny **Museo Mapuche** (Dec–Feb Mon–Fri 8am–noon & 3–8pm; free), Ginés Ponte 541 has Mapuche archeological artefacts and a few dinosaur bones on display; while opposite is the tall, Alpine-style tower of the **Santuario de la Beata Laura Vicuña**, also called by its old name of the Iglesia Nuestra Señora de las Nieves. Extensively remodelled and reopened in time for the millennium celebrations, this splendid church is dedicated to Junín's most famous scion, the beatified Laura Vicuña, and rates as the most original and refreshing church in Argentine Patagonia. Its airy, sky blue interior is suffused with light, and its clean-cut lines are tastefully complemented by the bold use of panels of high-quality Mapuche weavings, with strong geometric designs and natural colours – altogether a thoroughly satisfying hybrid of styles and cultural influences. Laura Vicuña herself, famed for her gentleness, was born in Santiago de Chile in 1891. She studied in Junín with the Salesian sisters for four years, and died here, aged just 13, in 1904.

A good time to visit is mid-February for the **Fiesta del Puestero**, with gaucho events, folklore music in the evenings, *artesanía* and *asados*.

Arrival and information

The RN234, called Boulevard J.M. Rosas for this stretch, cuts across the western side of town, and all you'll need is to the east of this. The **bus terminal** is found one block to the east, at Olavarría and F.S. Martín. Continue east along Olavarría for two blocks and turn right (south) for one block along Calle San Martín to reach the main square, Plaza San Martín, where all life centres. Diagonally opposite, at Padre Milanesio and Coronel Suárez, is the **tourist office** (daily: April–Nov 8am–9pm; Dec–March 8am–10pm; ☎ & fax 02972/491160; *turismo@jandes.com.ar*). Part of the same building acts as an excellent **park's information office** for Parque Nacional Lanín; you can buy the Paso Verde here (see p.567). Chapelco **airport** (☎02972/428388) lies halfway between Junín and San Martín and is shared by the two towns; it's 19km out of Junín (*remise* into town $16); there are no facilities for arrivals, though a small tourist office does open to meet incoming flights.

Banco de la Provincia, San Martín and Lamadrid, changes Amex travellers' cheques and gives advances on Visa and Mastercard. Chab, Don Bosco 532 local C, has expensive Internet access (Mon–Fri 9am–1pm & 2–9pm, Sat 9am–1pm; $5 per half hour, but with full office facilities). Alquimia, Paseo Artesanal, local C (☎02972/491355 or 156-10842; *alquimia@jandes.com.ar*), is a recommended **travel agency** which sells flights and organizes professional day tours in the region, including one to Lagos Huechulafquen and Paimún with a visit to a Mapuche community ($35). They specialize in adventure tourism (such as climbing Lanín and rafting on the Río Aluminé) and rent excellent climbing equipment.

Accommodation

Hotel tariffs rise slightly in summer, when it's worth reserving a little in advance. There are a couple of **campsites** within easy reach of the centre: *Municipal*, at the eastern end of Coronel Suárez, is a pleasant, shady site by the larger channel of the Río Chimehuín ($5 per person); and *Camping Mallín Laura Vicuña*, by the river, at the foot of Ginés Ponte (☎ & fax 02972/491149; ($4 per person), which is welcoming but lacks shade. The latter's single-room cabins ($40 for four people) with modest kitchens are good value.

Residencial El Cedro, Lamadrid 409 (☎ & fax 02972/492044). One of the most comfortable places, with good breakfast included in room rate and colour TVs in all rooms. Evening meals also served. ③.

Residencial Marisa, J.M. Rosas 360 (☎ & fax 02972/491175). Conveniently just round the corner from the terminal. A neat, amiable place, and not too noisy, despite some rooms facing the main road. ②.

Hostería Chimehuín, Coronel Suárez and 25 de Mayo (☎02972/491132). A rare gem, combining excellent value with a distinct personality that engenders great loyalty amongst its regular guests, especially fishing aficionados. A fine home-made breakfast is included in the price. Book at least two weeks in advance in summer. ③.

Posada Pehuén, Coronel Suárez 560 (☎02972/491569). One and a half blocks east of the main square, this peaceful place has its own garden. Two-course evening meals for $10. Reserve three weeks ahead in high season. ③.

Estancia Huechahue (☎02972/491303 *huechahue@jandes.com.ar*). A peaceful estancia some 30km out of town on the RN234, with fantastic horseriding opportunities and a knowledgeable English owner.

Restaurants and bars

Ruca Hueney at Padre Milanesio y Coronel Suárez (☎02972/491113) is a good first port of call. Trout is its speciality ($12–15 for a huge portion), but it serves Arabic food on Sundays (keppe $6) and has inexpensive tourist menus. Its well-chosen wine-list is accessibly priced. Visit *Tandil*, Coronel Suárez 431, for superb home-smoked venison and trout as well as scrumptious savoury *empanadas*. *Roble Bar*, Ginés Ponte 331, is the town's most happening pub, and serves snacks from 11am; while *Winners*, at Antártida Argentina y J.M. Rosas, is a disco playing a mix of tropical and dance music, but is worth trying out only in high season (open in season Wed, Fri & Sat, from 0.30am; $5 entrance).

Lago Huechulafquen and around

Two roads head west from near Junín into the lake district around **Lago Huechulafquen**. Just to the south of town, the RP62 takes you to the **Termas de Epulafquen** (also called Termas de Lahuen-Có): a collection of small circular thermal and mud pools up to 2m in diameter to the southeast of Lago Epulafquen. The hottest pool, Pozo Central, reaches temperatures of 65°C. To walk around all the pools takes about 45 minutes. Agencies in Junín charge $30 for a day-trip to the pools, passing Lagos Curruhué Chico and Curruhué Grande, Lago Verde and the ancient black **lava-flow** (*escorial*) of Volcán Achen Ñiyeu on the way. Or you can make your own way here and pitch a **tent** at *Camping Termas de Epulafquen*, 64km from Junín. The RP62 continues to **Paso Internacional Carirriñe** (open summer only), a Chilean border crossing.

The second road, the RP61, branches off the RN234 just north of Junín and skirts the northern shores of **Lago Huechulafquen** on its way to beautiful, boomerang-shaped Lago Paimún. Huechulafquen, the park's largest lake, is an enormous finger of deep blue water, 105km long, that extends into the steppe. The mouth of the Río Chimehuín at the lake's eastern end is a notable fly-fishing spot. At the park gate, you'll be charged $5 entrance. On the north shore, there are plenty of spots to **camp** for free, as well as organized sites with facilities, run by the Raquithué and Cañicul Mapuche communities: *Bahía Cañicul* is about halfway along the lake at Km 54, while *Raquithué* is 1km further on to the west.

At the western end of the lake is the settlement and jetty of **PUERTO CANOA**. From here, you can look up at the fantastic, crevassed **south face** of Volcán Lanín, a popular photo opportunity. A seven-hour trail leads from behind the *guardaparque* post here to the climbing refuge halfway up the mountain, where you can overnight before returning along the same route. Also from Puerto Canoa, a fun **boat trip** on the catamaran José Julián leaves for a circuit that includes Lagos Huechulafquen, Paimún, and Epulafquen, where you'll see the solidified lava river of Volcán Achen Ñiyeu ($15). At Puerto Canoa, **stay** at *Hostería Huechulafquen* (☎ & fax 02972/426075; *lafguen@smandes.com.ar*; closed March–Oct), a snug fishing lodge in full view of Lanín, 55km from Junín. Its **restaurant** is open to the public at lunch, and the cuisine has central European influences. Just beyond is *Hostería Paimún* (☎02972/491211, fax 491201) in a delightful spot on the shore of Lago Paimún.

The eastern end of Lago Paimún is fairly bucolic farmland, dotted with Mapuche smallholdings. The further west you go, the more forested the scenery becomes, with beautiful woods of *raulí*, *roble pellín* and *coihue*. Its northern shores have beaches of dark volcanic sand. You can hike around the lake in three days: it's not too strenuous, although the path is difficult to follow in places, so ask for information at Puerto Canoa's *guardaparque* post or the one 8km along Paimún's northern shore. To complete the loop, you'll need to make use of the **rope-pull ferry** across the narrows at La Unión, the place where the two lakes join.

CROSSING TO CHILE: PASO MAMUIL MALAL AND LAGO TROMEN

One of the most scenic border crossings anywhere in the continent, the **Paso Mamuil Malal** (also called **Paso Tromen**; 1253m; open 24hr all year) lies at the northeastern foot of **Volcán Lanín** and connects Junín de los Andes with the Chilean resort town of **Pucón**, a favourite backpackers' haunt, 72km from the frontier. Volcán Lanín's capacity to cause awe and respect has not altered much since the days when the indigenous Mapuche tribes of the region believed it to be the abode of Pillán, the brooding guardian deity of nature. Legend has it that a local tribe, the Huanquimil, was one day hunting huemules on the slopes of the mountain. This affront incensed the deity, who proceeded to spew lava and ashes, trapping the hunting party in a cave. Pillán was only appeased when Huilefun, the beautiful daughter of the *lonco* (cacique), was offered for sacrifice. She was swept up in the talons of a condor, who flew up on high and dropped her, alive, into the crater's black maw.

North of Junín, turn off the RP23 onto the RP60, a superb panoramic route through the valley of the Río Malleo. After crossing the national park boundary, you pass through a fine grove of araucaria and come to the Argentine immigration post and *guardaparque*'s house. You can pitch a **tent** here at *Camping Lanín* (☎ 02972/426005, fax 428282; $2 per person). Out of season (Dec–Easter), you won't have to pay, but there are no services and the shop is closed. You pay at the *Lanín* site shop if you want to stay at the more peaceful *Camping Tromen*, 3km to the north (no showers; latrine only) on the shores of **Lago Tromen**, a beautiful greenish lake with beaches of volcanic sand.

Two kilometres beyond the *guardaparque*'s house is the customs post, and 16km further on you'll find its Chilean counterpart.

San Martín de los Andes and around

A very pleasant place just to hang out, **San Martín de los Andes** is the most convenient base for exploring the southern sector of Parque Nacional Lanín (see p.536 for general information on the park), especially the zone around **Lagos Lácar** and **Lolog**. The park's central sector is also easily accessible (see Junín, pp.546–547). San Martín is the northern terminus of the famous **Ruta de Los Siete Lagos** (see p.553), which heads into the north of the contiguous Parque Nacional Nahuel Huapi before reaching Villa La Angostura, from where you can link through to Bariloche.

San Martín de los Andes

One of the most beautiful of all Patagonian towns, **SAN MARTÍN DE LOS ANDES** is a small resort of chalets and low-key architecture set in a flat, sheltered valley at the eastern end of **Lago Lácar**, compressed between steep-sided slopes that are covered in native cypress (*ciprés de la cordillera*) and forestry pine. In spring, the introduced broom (*retama*) daubs the scenery on the approach roads a sunny yellow. Expansion

CLIMBING LANÍN

The **Lanín Volcano** (3776m) – meaning "choked himself to death" or "died of suffocation" in Mapudungun – is now believed to be extinct. It is a good mountain to climb: easy to access and yet retains the balance between being possible for non-expert climbers to ascend while still representing a real physical challenge. The most straightforward route is from Tromen. The heavily glaciated south face is a much fiercer option that's suitable only for experienced climbers. There's a refuge here at 2300m, some seven hours' hike from the *guardaparque* station at Puerto Canoa. For more information, consult the Club Andino Junín de los Andes (☎02972/491637).

The route **from Tromen** takes two to three days, as long as the weather – which, as ever in Patagonia, can turn extremely nasty – doesn't close in. There is a slight danger of altitude sickness towards the top (see p.34) and you must have a fairly good level of fitness to attempt the climb, especially if you go for the two-day option, which involves a very tiring second day that includes the summit push plus a complete descent of the mountain. Climbing in a guided group costs $140–150 per person: one good agency to book with is Alquimia in Junín (leaves with a minimum of six people or an addtional supplement must be paid). They also rent the all the essential mountaineering gear: good boots; warm, waterproof clothing; helmet; ice-axe; crampons; torch or, better still, a miner's headlamp; and a cooker. UV sunglasses; high-factor sunblock; matches and an alarm clock are likewise essential. Optional items are gaiters (especially in later summer when you have to negotiate volcanic scree); black bin liners (for melting snow in sunny weather); candles; a radio (*handi / handy*) and emergency whistle. You are unlikely to need a compass or climbing rope, but an incense stick will help to counter pungent refuge odours. There is no really reliable official map – ask at the tourist office in Junín for a photocopy of the "Ascensión del Centenario" sketch map, which is much more useful.

You'll need to register for the climb at the Lago Tromen **guardaparque's office** (8am–6pm, or knock at door at respectable times thereafter), and the *guardaparque* checks your equipment. Depending on your experience and his or her permission, you can make the climb solo, but it is not advised. You'll need to start the climb by 1pm at the latest. It will be necessary to acclimatize for a night in one of the three free refuges on the mountain. The *guardaparque* will assign one to you, and will try to accommodate your preference. In high season, get to Tromen early, as all refuges might otherwise be full (about fifty people in total). You may just be able to persuade the *guardaparque* to let you pitch a tent in one of the few (exposed) pitches by the refuges, but this is not really a good idea and they're generally loathe to grant permission. The first of the refuges, **Refugio RIM**, sleeps fifteen to twenty people. Its big advantage is that it has meltwater close by (Jan & Feb; if climbing outside high summer, you'll need to melt snow for water anyway). You may prefer to try for the smaller **CAJA**, further up the slope, especially if you plan to make the final ascent and total descent in one day, as this saves you half an hour's climb in the early morning. CAJA sleeps six comfortably – up to ten at a squeeze. The **VIM** refuge has pleasant tables and chairs, but is the lowest down the slope. It's the largest of the three, sleeping up to thirty people.

here has been rapid, but – with the exception of the hideously out-of-place *Hotel Sol de Los Andes* that overlooks town – by no means as uncontrolled as in its much larger rival resort, Bariloche; and whereas Bariloche caters for the young party crowd, San Martín has deliberately set itself up for a more sedate type of small-town tourism, pitching for families rather than students.

There is little to do in town itself, bar shopping, sunning yourself on the small beach by the lake, or popping in to the tiny **Museo de los Primeros Pobladores** (Tues–Fri 10am–7pm, Sat & Sun 3–8pm; $1) on the main square, which has exhibits on archeology and skiing. In winter, especially July and August, hotels pack out with

Argentines coming to **ski** at the nearby resort of **Chapelco**, one of the country's best (see p.553).

El Trabún (meaning the "Union of the Peoples") is the main annual **festival**, held in early December in the Plaza San Martín. Local and Chilean musicians hold concerts (predominantly folklore), and big bonfires are lit at the corners of the square to prepare *asados* of lamb and goat.

Arrival and information

Chapelco **Airport** lies 25km away in the direction of Junín de los Andes. Caleuche minibuses connect the airport with the town (☎02972/422115 for hotel pick-up, $8). The **bus terminal** is scenically located in the southwest of town, across the road from Lago Lácar and the **pier**, handy for the tourist launches across the lake. From the terminal, walk one block northwest along Juez del Valle or Díaz and turn right along the main avenue, San Martín. Five blocks up gets you to the Plaza San Martín, in the heart of town, sandwiched between the main drag and Avenida Roca, to the northwest (left). Pretty much everything you need is found along these two avenues, or the parallel street on the other side of Avenida San Martín, Villegas.

On the main square, you'll find the efficient and willing staff at the **tourist office**, (mid-Dec to Easter 8am–10pm; rest of year 8am–9pm, ☎ & fax 02972/427347 or 0800/4447626337; *munitur@smandes.com.ar*). They can provide decent town maps and will lend a hand if you can't find a room in high season: when all rooms in town are full, they're permitted to provide a list of *casas de familia*. The **Intendencia of Parque Nacional Lanín** is found on the Plaza San Martín at Emilio Frey 749 (Mon–Fri 8am–1pm). Here you can get maps, leaflets and information on trekking as well as buy the Paso Verde (see p.567). They also sell fishing permits, as do all the fishing shops in town –Aquaterra, at Villegas 788, also rents camping equipment. You can rent **bikes** at H.G. Rodados, San Martín 1061.

Accommodation

During the peak summer and skiing seasons it is essential to **reserve rooms** as far in advance as possible: you'll always get something if you just turn up, but your choice will be limited. Some hotels have three or four price brackets, with the ski season often more expensive than summer. Out of season, rooms can be as much as half price There's one **hostel** in town, the *Puma*, Fosberry 535 (☎02972/422443, fax 428544; *puma@smandes.com.ar*, $11 HI members, otherwise £13); a small, well-scrubbed, modern place, with a couple of double rooms (③), kitchen and washing facilities. For **camping**, there's a choice of three sites: the *ACA* site, at Av. Koessler 2175 (☎ & fax 02972/429430; closed Easter–Nov; $5 per person), popular with families; the *Amigos de la Naturaleza* ($5 per person), about 7km on the road to Junín; and *Camping Lolen* ($5 per person), a lakeside site with superb views, run by the Curruhuinca Mapuche community, 4km southwest of town and 1km off the main RN234, down a very steep track to Playa Catritre.

Cabañas Los Notros, Juey del Valle 1076 (☎02972/428245). Self-catering cabins for up to six people, adjacent to the bus terminal and overlooking the lake. $150 high season for up to six people; ⑤, low season only.

Hostería Hueney Ruca, Obeid and Coronel Pérez (☎02972/421499, fax 428528). With a garden and free parking; all rooms have a private bathroom, and breakfast is included in the price. Rooms for up to six people. ⑤.

Hostería Ayelén, Pasaje Arrayanes, Casilla de Correo 21 (☎ & fax 02972/425660; *janetdickinson@smandes.com.ar*). Commanding one of the finest hotel views in Patagonia, this place is owned by an English-speaking couple who know the area intimately. There are only three rooms, so reserve as far in advance as possible. Prices include an excellent breakfast and dinner is an optional extra. Pick-up from the airport or San Martín is free to those stopping for more than one night. Organized fishing trips, horseriding and trekking can be arranged. ⑤.

Hotel Caupolicán, San Martín 969 (☎02972/427658, fax 427090). Comfortable three-star in the centre of town. Facilities include a sauna. ⑦.

Hostería La Posta del Cazador, San Martín 175 (☎02972/427501, fax 422231). Close to the bus terminal, this place is kitted out in the style of a Tyrolean hunting lodge; large breakfasts and baby-sitter service provided. Close to bus terminal. ⑥.

Le Village Hotel, Teniente General Roca 816 (☎ & fax 02972/427020). Spacious three-star hotel in the style of a Swiss chalet, close to the main plaza. Rooms have all the usual facilities and a baby-sitter service is provided. ⑧.

Patagonia Plaza Hotel, San Martín and Rivadavia (☎02972/422280, fax 422801). Plush, brand-new and central, but understaffed and only Spanish is spoken. ⑨.

Residencial Casa Alta, Gabriel Obeid 659 (☎ & fax 02972/427456). Full of character, with home-ly, wood-panelled rooms for up to five people, most with private bathrooms. The personable, English-speaking owners allow use of their impressive private library. Closed mid-Sept to Nov & Easter–June. ④.

Residencial Los Pinos, Almirante Brown 420 (☎02972/427207). An excellent family-run residence, with inexpensive rooms and shared bathroom for single budget travellers. Breakfast is included in the price of the room. Pleasant garden. Closed May & June. ③.

Eating, drinking and nightlife

There's a good selection of **places to eat** in town, most staying open till midnight. There's little else in the way of **nightlife**, however. Options include the *Casino Magic*, at Villegas and Elordi – with a dated, Seventies feel, but good for cheap eats late at night – and *Zoo*, at Elordi 950 (midnight–6am; $5 cover) – a nightclub open daily in season and playing a wide mix of music.

Avataras, Teniente Ramayón 765 (☎02972/427104). Pride of place in town goes to this ambitious venture: an exquisite menu with a select choice of gourmet foods from around the world, in a sympathetically lit venue. Thai, Morrocan and Indian offerings, with freshwater fish sushi on Fridays. Main courses from $12. Open from 9pm. Live jazz and blues on Thursdays.

Confitería Deli, Costanera and Villegas. Snacks and beers with a lakeside view.

De La Montaña, Roca 756. An excellent deli with a wide selection of cheeses and salami.

Ku, San Martín 1053 (☎02972/427039). Parrillas and pastas, with regional trout, venison and wild boar dishes. Expensive wine-list. Closed Tues.

La Tasca, Mariano Moreno 866 (☎02972/428663). Expensive but appetizing regional specialities and filling portions. Options include *ciervo mirtilo* – venison flambéed in a gin, cognac and blueberry sauce.

Panquequería El Amanecer de Carlitos, San Martín 1371 (☎02972/425990). An advertised three hundred varieties of sweet and savoury crepes – many vegetarian, and all surprisingly inexpensive (from $2.50) – served in this down-home place.

Pollo Track, San Martín 1373. Straightforward grill with the emphasis on value for money – massive hamburgers for $2.50.

Pulgarcito, San Martín 461 (☎02972/427081). This place specializes in inexpensive home-made pasta (from $5).

Pura Vida, Villegas 745 (☎02972/429302). Freshly prepared vegetarian quiches, bursting with flavour ($3), and trout and chicken for non-vegetarians.

Listings

Airlines Southern Wings, San Martín 881, local 4 (☎02972/425275); LAPA, San Martín 941 (☎02972/429357).

Banks and exchange Banco de la Nación, Avenida San Martín 687; Banco de la Provincia, Belgrano and Obeid; Andina Internacional, at Capitán Drury 876 (☎02972/428233).

Car rental El Sol, San Martín 461, Local 11 (☎ & fax 02972/421648, 24hr emergency hotline ☎421870).

Hospital Hospital Ramón Carrillo, San Martín and Coronel Rohde (☎02972/427211); private clinic at Centro Médico del Sur, Sarmiento 489 (☎02972/427148).

Internet and telephone Telefónica co-operative, Capitán Drury 761 (7.30am–12.30am; $7 per hour, divisible).
Laundry Lavavero, Villegas 939; Laverap, Capitán Drury 880, Villegas 972 or Belgrano 618.
Pharmacy San Jorge, San Martín 405 (☎02972/428842).
Police Gendarmería, Gral. Roca 965 (☎02972/427339).
Post office Roca 690 and Pérez 600 (Mon–Fri 8am–1pm & 5–8pm, Sat 9am–1pm); poste restante service.
Taxis Remises Andes (☎02972/422131).

Cerro Chapelco and the ski-resort

One of Argentina's prime ski-resorts, **CERRO CHAPELCO**, is 21km from town, in the Cordón del Chapelco, an offshoot range of the Andes that rises to almost 2400m. It has 29 ski pistes that descend a maximum of 750m in altitude, and which are served by a cable car and five chair lifts. There's a snowboard park, and floodlit night-time skiing, whilst by day you can enjoy views of Volcán Lanín.

In **summer**, it becomes an outdoor activity centre, especially good for those with young families. A $25 daily passport, sold by Chapelco Aventura, San Martín 876 and Elordi (☎ & fax 02972/427845) entitles you to a wide range of entertainments, including archery, horseriding, and mountain biking. Chapelco can be visited on a loop circuit from San Martín: take the turn-off just past the ugly *Hotel Sol de los Andes* that overlooks town, and return along the RN234.

The Ruta de los Siete Lagos

The **Ruta de los Siete Lagos**, or "Seven Lakes Route", is one of Argentina's classic scenic drives, passing as is does through thickly forested mountain valleys and giving access to many more than seven wild lakes. It connects San Martín de los Andes to Villa La Angostura, and Villa La Angostura with Bariloche. It is mostly paved, and the rest is due to be sealed, but the remaining unsealed section – between Lago Villarino and Lago Espejo at the time of writing – can get extremely dusty, especially in the summer. This considerably reduces the fun factor if you're thinking of cycling the route, as do the stones kicked up by vehicles, so you may want to check at the tourist offices at either end to see if works have been completed. Calculate on taking two days to cycle the whole route. There are fabulous **fishing** spots along the way, but buy permits before setting off.

The seven principal lakes by the roadside are, from north to south: Lácar, Machónico, Falkner, Villarino, Correntoso, Espejo and Nahuel Huapi. Leaving San Martín, you climb up into the mountains on the winding RN234, passing through *ñire* and *coihue* woods. Stop at the Mirador de Pil Pil to look back at the superb panorama of Lago Lácar. Further on you scout round the eastern shore of Lago Machónico, and soon after a detour west leads to **Lago Hermoso**, where you'll find the attractive, rustic *Lago Hermoso* campsite, in woodland by the lakeshore (mid-Dec to Feb, $3 per person), which sells provisions and has showers.

South of Lago Hermoso you cross the boundary between the two parks, leaving Lanín and entering Nahuel Huapi. Just to the north of **Lago Falkner** you pass **Cascada Vullignanco**, a twenty-metre waterfall to the west of the road. Lago Falkner – where all types of fishing are permitted – sits at the foot of Cerro Falkner to the south and Cerro del Buque (1952m). Right on the roadside here is the beautiful *camping agreste Lago Falkner*, which has a small shop and toilets but no shower ($2 per person, plus $2 per vehicle). Just beyond is *Hostería Lago Villarino* (☎02972/425274; ⑥, includes breakfast; closed June–Oct), which offers free pick-up from Bariloche or Chapelco Airport. It's an old-style lodge with intimate **rooms**, all with a fireplace, and bungalows for four to six people ($150–190). There are excellent horseriding opportunities in the vicinity, and it's possible to rent mountain bikes and fishing boats. Opposite Lago Falkner is **Lago Villarino**, another popular place for fishing, with Cerro Crespo as a picturesque backdrop.

South of the pass, just past the limpid waters of Río Pichi Traful, is Seccional Villarino (8am–11pm), where the *guardaparque* will give you information on recommended walks such as the three-hour trek up Cerro Falkner. Some 2km east of here, down a bumpy track, is a pleasant fisherman's **campsite** on the Brazo Norte of Lago Traful. Further down the main route is pint-sized **Lago Escondido**, the most enchanting of all the lakes. Demurely, it hides its emerald green charms in the forest – park up and walk the few metres to a viewpoint. South of here is the RP65 turn-off to Lago Traful (see p.555).

Beyond here you skirt the rocky northern shores of **Lago Correntoso**, and pass another detour to **Lago Espejo Chico**, which lies 2.5km northwest of the RN234, down a rutted dirt road. Here you'll find *Camping Lago Espejo Chico* ($2 per person), which has a shop and toilets but no shower or hot water, yet is one of the most charming and peaceful campsites of the route, and is popular with weekend campers. The Río Espejo Chico here is a gorgeous dolphin-blue colour. They rent boats (with outboard motor and guide; $15 an hour). A little further down the main RN234 you get your first views of **Lago Espejo**, the warmest lake in the park. Alongside the Seccional Espejo *guardaparque* post is a free campsite, by a beach that's good for swimming. Further on is a track that leads to the tidy, cosy *Lago Espejo Resort* (☎ & fax 02944/494583; mid-Dec to Easter; ⑦), set in a secluded site. They provide free transfers from Bariloche airport, and offer boat trips and hikes in the region. The RN234 ends at the T-junction a couple of kilometres further south. Here you can turn east along the paved RN231 to Villa La Angostura (12km away; see p.556), passing on the way the mouth of the stunted **Río Correntoso**, a world-famous fishing spot. Turning west takes you to **Paso Cardenal Samoré** (formerly called Puyehue), which is the region's most important, year-round border crossing into Chile, heading to Osorno (8am–8pm, 9pm in summer).

The Lago Lácar and around

Lago Lácar to the south and west of the city is best explored by combining boat or road trips with hiking. The unsurfaced RP48 runs for 46km along the northern shore of Lácar to **Hua-Hum**, at the far western end of Nonthué. Three kilometres further on is the **Paso Hua-Hum**, one of the most enjoyable of the Andean routes through to Chile, open all year round and leading towards the resort town of Villarica. Following the Río Hua-Hum northwest brings you to the slender, gorgeous Lago Pirehueico, which can be crossed only by the modest **car ferry** (minimum of ten passengers: Jan–Feb daily 10am, 3.30pm & 8pm; March & April Mon–Sat 10am & 5pm, Sun 2pm; May–Oct Mon–Sat 10am & 3pm, Sun 12.30pm; Nov–Dec daily 10am & 5pm; 2hr; foot passengers, $1, cars, including passengers $20). A bus service connects San Martín with the ferry (2hr; $5.50) and there are various campsites along the route.

To the southeast of Hua-Hum, 12km by dirt track, is the *guardapargue*'s post at **Lago Queñi**. The area around this lake is one of the wettest places in the Lanín National Park, and is covered with Valdivian temperate rainforest and dense thickets of *caña colihue*. The star attraction here is the enchanting **Termas de Queñi** – or hot springs, set in lush forest near the southern tip of the lake. The season for visiting the springs is generally from late September to early May: register with the *guardaparque*, and you can **camp** just past the post, on the other side of Arroyo Queñi. You can walk to the springs on an easy route from the campsite (3hr), or on a two-day trek around the lake and Cerro Chachín to Pucará, a settlement on the southern tongue of land where lakes Lácar and Nonthué meet. From here a track leads back to Hua-Hum, past the **Cascada de Chachín**, a thirty-metre waterfall on the south side of Lago Nonthué.

The Cascada de Chachín can also be visited on the Plumas Verdes **boat excursion** that leaves San Martín's pier and heads to Hua-Hum and back (leaves 8am, returns 6pm; some English-speaking guides; $30, plus $5 park entrance). Boats also leave San Martín's pier for **Quila Quina** on the southern shore of Lago Lácar (minimum of six passengers; 2.30–6pm; $10 one way, plus $5 park entrance). Quila Quila is an incongruous mix of agricultural smallholdings of the Curruhuinca Mapuche community and holiday homes. There's a beach and walks in the area, including one that runs west all the way to Pucará.

Lago Traful

Lago Traful is a pure, intense blue, like a pool of liquid Roman glass. It is a popular destination for fishermen trying to hook trout and the rare landlocked salmon, and is best accessed along the RP65, which follows its entire southern shore. The most beautiful approach is from the Ruta de los Siete Lagos, crossing the pass of El Portezuelo and heading through the **Valle de los Machis** (with its majestic *coihue* trees), beneath the heights of Pico Traful (2040m). The road levels out in mixed woodland of cypress, *radal*, *retamo*, *maitén*, and *espina negra*. If coming from the east, the steppe scenery looses its harshness the closer you come to the cordillera.

Halfway along the lake is **VILLA TRAFUL**, a loose assemblage of houses spread out along several kilometres of the shoreline. It's a rather twee place despite its beautiful setting, but there are several interesting hikes in the vicinity, and one particularly impressive lookout point: the **Mirador Pared del Viento** (or Mirador del Traful). Found 5km east of the village on the RP65, this is a precipitous rock face that survived the onslaught of the glaciers, and from the top you've superb views down its sheer seventy-metre face into the Mediterranean-blue waters below.

Set back from the village's main jetty is a **guardaparque post**, where they can provide you with information on local hikes – and you'll have to register with them before setting out. There are treks to various waterfalls, you can climb Cerro Negro (1999m) behind the village (7–9hr); or make a trip to Laguna Las Mellizas on the northern side of the lake to see indigenous rock paintings (15min to cross by launch; 5hr return walk on other side).

To the west of the village centre are two *hosterías* offering **rooms**: *El Rincón del Pescador* is well-appointed and has lakeside views (☎02944/479028, fax 479027; ⑦, for half board); *Villa Traful* (☎ & fax 02944/479005; ④, with breakfast; closed Easter to mid-Nov) is more homely and rents cabins all year ($100 for up to four people; $120 for six). *La Vulcanche* is a pleasant budget hostel and **campsite** close to the centre (☎02944/479061; *vulcanche@infovia.com.ar*; $12; camping $5 per person). It has a shop, serves snacks and offers guided excursions – English is spoken. More scenic for its setting, by the foot of the Mirador del Viento, is the free *Paloma Araucana* site (no facilities). Out of town to the west are two other lakeshore campsites: *Cataratas*, 10km away, has only basic services ($2 per person; closed Feb to mid-Nov); while *Puerto Arrayán* ($2 per person; closed Easter to mid-Nov), 15km from the village, is more attractively sited and more developed. It rents kayaks ($5 per hour) and boats with outboard motor ($50 per half day).

Inland from Villa Traful's YPF fuel station, is the place's most popular tearoom and **restaurant**, *Ñancú Lahuen* (☎02944/479017), serving high-quality chocolates and cakes, as well as pasta and trout, although the touristy African thatch seems somewhat incongruous, especially when listening to tango.

Parque Nacional Los Arrayanes

A park within a park, **Parque Nacional Los Arrayanes** was created to protect the world's best stand of myrtle woodland, the **Bosque de los Arrayanes**, which is found at the far tip of the **Península Quetrihué**, the narrow-necked peninsula that juts out into Lago Nahuel Huapi from **Villa La Angostura**. Quetrihué, in Mapudungun, means "place of the *arrayanes*", and the peninsula is a legacy from the glaciation of the Pleistocene era, as its rock proved more resilient to erosion than that which surrounded it. It is now covered with dense forests of *coihue*, *radal*, and uncommon species such as *palo santo* (different to the species found in the Chaco) with rich, glossy foliage and an ashy grey bark. These forests provide cover for native fauna and introduced species such as the red deer.

The **arrayán** is a slow-growing tree that is characterized by its flaky, cinnamon-coloured, paper-like bark and amazing trunks, which look rather like barley-sugar columns in churches. It can reach heights of up to 15m and lives for three hundred years (although some specimens here may be as much as 600 years old), and it only grows close to cool water. Its canopy is made up of delicate glossy clusters of foliage, and in late summer, it flowers in dainty white blossoms, with the edible bluey-black berries maturing in autumn.

The famous **Bosque** can be reached by hiking or cycling the trail from La Villa (12km one way), or by boat from La Villa or Bariloche. Boulevard Nahuel Huapi terminates in La Villa with the stretch that connects the two bays on either side of the peninsula's narrow neck: **Bahía Mansa** ("Peaceful Bay"), on the eastern side, is where you'll find the **Intendencia** of the park and the Puerto Angostura **jetty** for boats to the Bosque; and Bahía Brava ("Wild Bay") on the western side, which is used only by fishing boats. The park entrance is halfway between the two.

If you're **hiking**, count on a five- to six-hour round trip (2hr 15min one way). Start early to enjoy the wildlife of the peninsula and to get to the myrtle forest by 10am (before the arrival of the first boat). The first twenty minutes, when you climb steeply to the lookout, is by far the hardest part. If you go by mountain bike (3–4hr return trip), you'll have to push it up this initial section. A **boat trip** lasts approximately two and a half hours. In January and February they get very busy, so book in advance – try Martín Raúd's El Paisano (☎155-53940), with an office on Calle Pilquén (the small street parallel to Boulevard Nahuel Huapi where it links the two bays); he takes only twenty passengers, guides in English, and you have more time at the wood than with other operators. The Bosque is open till 6pm, and there's a *guardaparque* post and a *cafetería* there.

When seen from the lake, the Bosque doesn't look much different from the surrounding forest – it's when you're underneath the canopy that its magic envelops you. The rumour that Walt Disney took his inspiration for the forest scenes in *Bambi* from this enchanted woodland is not true (he actually took it from photographs of birch forests in Maine), but that doesn't much matter, as it certainly feels that way: walk around the 600-metre **boardwalk** at your leisure whilst the contorted corkscrew trunks creak against each other in the breeze and the light plays like a French Impressionist's dream, and you'll see why.

Villa La Angostura

Spread haphazardly along the northern shore of Lago Nahuel Huapi, **VILLA LA ANGOSTURA** is a relaxed but expensive holiday town that caters mainly for better-off Argentinians. Though the area has plenty of outdoor possibilities, the main reason for overnighting here is to see the Bosque de los Arrayanes in the Parque Nacional Quetrihué. From here too, the Ruta de Los Siete Lagos heads north to San Martín de los Andes (see p.549). In winter, there's **skiing** on the slopes of Cerro Bayo, 10km to the northeast of the village.

The town is actually divided into two main settlements: **El Cruce** ("The Crossroads") is the first you'll come across, being built around the main RN231 – called Avenida Siete Lagos at its western end and Avenida Los Arrayanes, the main commercial street, from Bariloche to the east – while **La Villa** is next to the national park entrance, 3km south down the Boulevard Nahuel Huapi spur road. These three roads converge on the ACA service station in El Cruce. The **bus terminal** is a block west of ACA, on Avenida Siete Lagos.

Across the road from the terminal at no. 93 is the **tourist office** (daily 8am–9pm; ☎ & fax 02944/494124; *munivla@cybersnet.com.ar*), one of Patagonia's best. Even if it's closed when you arrive, consult the useful display window for all accommodation possibilities, prices and locations. Inside, it has excellent leaflets on walks and excursions in the area (an abbreviated version available in English). One recommended walk is to Mirador Belvedere (a lookout point that can be reached by car) and the Cascada Inacayal, a delightful fifty-metre waterfall. You can rent **bikes** at Ian, Topa Topa 102 ($10 for 6hr). **Internet** access is available at CybersNet, Belvedere 173.

The best **accommodation** in La Villa is at *Hotel Angostura*, Nahuel Huapi s/n (☎ & fax 02944/494224; *hotel-angostura@cybersnet.com.ar*, ⑥), a comfortable, family-run establishment with calming lakeside views and a good restaurant. Boats from its jetty head to the Bosque de Los Arrayanes. In El Cruce there are three *residenciales* offering rooms for up to four people with breakfast: friendly, clean *Nahuel*, by the YPF, is 400m west of the terminal down Avenida Siete Lagos (☎ & fax 02944/494737; ③) and spotless *Río Bonito* is two blocks northwest of the terminal at Topa Topa 260 (☎02944/494110; ④); neither offers good singles rates – for these you'll need to head for the plain *Don Pedro*, four blocks from the terminal at Belvedere and Los Maquis (☎02944/494269; ③). Pleasing cabins are available to rent at *Cabañas Lihuén* (☎02944/494564; *lihuen@nieveuen.com.ar*, ⑦), in a fine natural setting on the shores of Lago Correntoso, 4km to the west of town. The most convenient **campsite** is *Camping Unquehué* (☎02944/494688; $6 per person), 500m west of the bus terminal on Avenida Siete Lagos. *Camping Cullunche* (☎02944/494160; $5 per person) is the closest to the **port**, but is not the easiest to find, 2km down a signposted northwest turn-off from Boulevard Nahuel Huapi on the way to La Villa (approximately 3.5km from the terminal).

Bariloche

Approaching from the north, you can appreciate the mountain backdrop of the holiday capital of Argentinian Patagonia, **BARILOCHE**, or San Carlos de Bariloche, to give it its full title, spread along the dry southeastern shores of Lago Nahuel Huapi. It banks up against the slopes of Cerro Otto, behind which rear the spiky crests of the Cerro Catedral massif, but this view is obscured the closer you get to town. Everything in town faces the lake, Northern Patagonia's heavyweight: an impressive expanse of water that can seem like a benign Mediterranean one moment and a froth of seething whitecaps the next, lashed by the icy winds that sometimes whip off it into town.

The town's life-blood is tourism, with 700,000 visitors arriving annually, most of whom are Argentinian. As well as families, this is a place of pilgrimage for the nation's students, who flood here in January and February. They don't necessarily come in search of the mountain experience, but often end up having one, pushed out of town by the inflated high-season prices of hotels and clubs. The area's main attraction is a large one: the Parque Nacional Nahuel Huapi that surrounds town, although in winter, it's specifically the **ski-resort** of Cerro Catedral nearby – one of the country's most important. For five days in August, Bariloche celebrates the **Fiesta Nacional de la Nieve**, with ski races, parades and a torchlit evening descent on skis to open the season officially, as well as the election of the Reina Nacional de la Nieve, or Snow Queen.

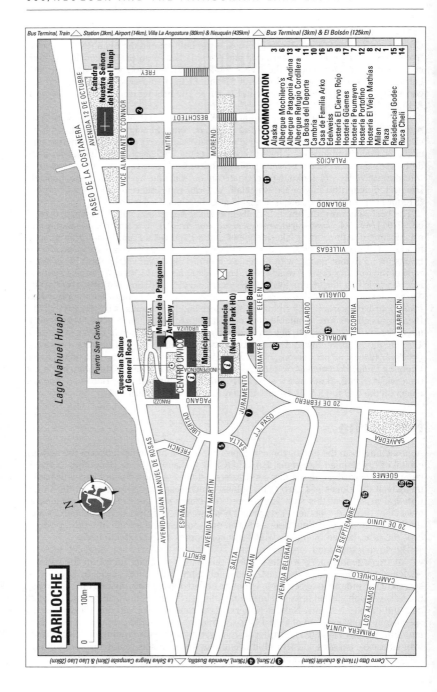

Bus Terminal, Train △ Station (3km), Airport (14km), Villa La Angostura (80km) & Neuquén (435km) △ Bus Terminal (3km) & El Bolsón (125km)

BARILOCHE

0 — 100m

Lago Nahuel Huapi

Puerto San Carlos

Equestrian Statue
of General Roca

Museo de la Patagonia
Archway

Municipalidad

CENTRO CIVICO

Intendencia
(National Park HQ)

Club Andino Bariloche

Catedral
Nuestra Señora
del Nahuel Huapi

ACCOMMODATION

Alaska	3
Albergue Mochilero's	6
Albergue Patagonia Andina	13
Albergue Refugio Cordillera	4
La Bolsa del Deporte	11
Cambria	10
Casa de Familia Arko	16
Edelweiss	5
Hostería El Ciervo Rojo	9
Hostería Güemes	17
Hostería Peumayen	7
Hostería Portofino	12
Hostería El Viejo Mathias	8
Milan	2
Plaza	1
Residencial Godec	15
Ruca Cheli	14

At peak times of year, you may find that the excesses of commercialization and crowds of tourists will spoil elements of your visit. Nevertheless, the place does work well in giving remarkably painless access to many beautiful, and some genuinely wild, areas of the cordillera and, out of season, the town is still big enough to retain some life.

Some history

Before the incursions of either Mapuche or white settlers, the Nahuel Huapi area was the domain of the Poyas, the Vuriloches, the Pehuelches, and the Puelches, who navigated on the lake. These groups used the region's mountain passes to conduct trade with their western, Mapuche counterparts. The discovery of these routes became an obsession of early Spanish exporers in Chile, many of whom were desperate to hunt down the fabulous wealth of the City of the Caesars that was rumoured to exist in these parts. Early expeditions were frustrated and knowledge of the passes' whereabouts reverted to being a closely guarded indigenous secret until the late seventeenth century.

The history of white presence in the region really begins with the Jesuit father, **Nicolás Mascardi**, who was despatched by the Viceroy of Perú and Chile to found a **mission** in the area in 1672. The job proved too tough, in the end, even for the Jesuits: the indigenous tribes despatched Mascardi and several subsequent fathers – this time to meet their maker – and, in 1717, destroyed the mission once and for all. Past experience of Spanish slaving expeditions, such as the one conducted by Juan Fernández in 1620, probably had much to do with this hostile attitude. Fearing the image of the Virgin, however, they apparently wrapped it in horsehide and hid it in the forest nearby, where it was recovered by another Jesuit father and taken to Chiloé and then Concepción. Sadly, the Virgin of Nahuel Huapi disappeared in the mid-nineteenth century. The local indigenous groups took one seventeenth-century Jesuit introduction more to their hearts than the Virgin: the humble apple or *manzana*. Used for brewing *chicha*, wild apples became so popular here that the region's Mapuche tribes became known as **Manzaneros**. It was this confederation that was led by the renowned cacique, **Sayhueque**, last of the Mapuches to surrender to the Conquest of the Desert.

After the defeat of the indigenous groups, permanent white settlement became a possibility. Modern Bariloche has its roots in the arrival of German settlers from southern Chile around the turn of the twentieth century, but was a small town of only a few thousand until the creation of the national park in 1937. Since then, in many ways, it has become a liability for the park, causing it numerous headaches such as forcing it to cede the area to the west to development. In recent decades, the population has skyrocketed, and the town is now a major urban centre of some 100,000. Lack of planning restrictions has meant that the homogeneity of its original architecture – a local style heavily influenced by the mountain regions of Germanic Europe – has long since been swamped by a messy conglomerate of high-rise apartment blocks, a fact often bemoaned by its long-term residents.

Arrival and information

Bariloche's **airport** (☎02944/422555) is 14km to the east of town. A shuttle bus runs in to town (daily: 9.30am–5.30pm; $3), returning from outside the Aerolíneas/Austral office at Quaglia 238, and then picking up LAPA and SW passengers from the corner of Mitre and Villegas (9am–6pm; first service Mon 6.30am, Tues–Fri 7.30am; $3). A *remise* into the centre will cost about $10. The main **bus terminal** is next door to the **train station** (☎02944/423172), 3km east of the city centre along the main RN237, here known as Avenida 12 de Octubre. The best local buses for the centre are #10, #20 and #21 (every 15–20min; 10min; $1), running along Calle Moreno and dropping you at the corner of Calle Morales near the **centro cívico**; a cab to here will cost around $5. Buses to the terminal leave from Elflein and Quaglia.

The **tourist office** is located in ridiculously cramped quarters in the centro cívico (daily 8am–9pm; ☎ & fax 02944/426784 or 423122; *securismo@bariloche.com.ar*). It has copies of the free monthly listings magazine for the Bariloche area, *Agenda Cultural*; also worth having is a copy of the *Guía Busch*, which has good maps of the area. In addition, staff have a list of *casas de familia*; and information on horseriding, as well as wind-surfing and diving. Just to the south of the tourist office are two other useful places for information: the Club Andino Bariloche, 20 de Febrero 30, which is a vital port of call for trekkers; and the **Intendencia** of the Parque Nacional Nahuel Huapi, Av. San Martín 24 (8am–4pm; ☎02944/423111), which has pamphlets on all the sectors of the park, sells the ten-day park pass (the Paso Verde; see p.567), and fishing permits ($10 per day in Patagonia), as well as up-to-date information on changes of status of the park's camp-sites. Their free *Trekking de Bajo Impacto* leaflet has a handy colour map of the central trekking zone, but is insufficiently detailed to be of use for route-finding.

Most of what you'll need in town can be found in the commercial area to the east of the **centro cívico** – sandwiched between the lake and Calle Elflein – plus the hilly Belgrano barrio to the southwest, which is useful for accommodation. Avenida 12 de Octubre from the terminal runs along the lake front, past the cathedral and the elevated centro cívico park, where its name changes to Avenida Juan Manuel de Rosas. Further west this becomes **Avenida Bustillo**, which runs through the western suburbs and is the start of the Circuito Chico (see p.563). Running inland from the centro cívico, Calle Morales is the street which acts as the division for street names on an east–west axis: do not confuse the Vice Almirante O'Connor, which runs parallel with 12 de Octubre with John O'Connor, to the east of the cathedral.

For those with cars, a rather complicated **parking** scheme operates in the heart of the city (restrictions apply basically from Elflein and Avenida San Martín to the lake). After the first day in town, you must purchase a "Codigo de Barras" sticker from any kiosk, which works in conjunction with tickets for the time you need ($4 for 6hr; $8 for 10hr). Fix them in the back windscreen of your vehicle on both sides. You can move your car as often as you like within the time allotted.

Accommodation

During peak periods – mid-December to February, Easter, and July and August – it's best to reserve accommodation in advance. For great deals, you'll need to come out of season – though there are a few good hostels, **accommodation** is generally quite expensive. There is one **campsite** within easy reach of town: *La Selva Negra*, Bustillo Km 2.95 (☎02944/441013; $8 per person) has all the usual facilities.

Hotels

Hotel Cambria, Elflein 183 (☎ & fax 02944/430400). Modern, business-like mid-range hotel, though the bathrooms are on the small side. ④.

Hotel Edelweiss, San Martín 202 (☎02944/426165, fax 425655; *reservas@edelweiss.com.ar*). A cultivated five-star hotel in the downtown area with lakeside views. All rooms come with private bath, plus there's an excellent restaurant and indoor pool. Attentive service, with English spoken. ⑨ in winter, ⑧ in summer.

Hostería El Ciervo Rojo, Elflein 115 (☎ & fax 02944/435241; *ciervorojo@mailcity.com*). One of the best mid-range options. A tastefully remodelled and centrally located town house which successfully fuses modest old-style charm with modern comforts. Light and airy rooms, with continental breakfast included in the price. ④.

Hostería El Viejo Matías, Elflein 47 (☎ & fax 02944/434466). Friendly if basic and somewhat stuffy *hostería*; most rooms with en-suite bathrooms and breakfast included in the price. Low season deals are good value (①). ③.

Hostería Güemes, Güemes 715 (☎02944/424785, fax 435616). Simple, clean two-star lodging. Some rooms with private bathrooms, and use of large living room for all. ③.

Hostería Longuimay, Longuimay 3672, Barrio Melipal (☎02944/443450). Nicely appointed chalet-style hotel with an intimate feel, located not far from the Cem Otto Chairlift. Take bus #10 to Av. Bustillo km 3.8.

Hostería Portofino, Morales 435 (☎02944/422795). All rooms have private bathroom in this family-run place; the one drawback is that the lighting is poor. ③.

Hotel Milan, Beschtedt 120 (☎02944/422624, fax 420247). A smart, modern hotel near the lakeside. Some rooms hold up to five people. ⑤.

Hotel Plaza, Vice Almirante O'Connor 431 (☎ & fax 02944/424100). Nothing flashy, but good value for its lakeside location and a simple breakfast is included in the price – served in the dining-room which has panoramic views over the lake. Popular with students, particularly in the winter. ③.

Ruca Cheli, 24 de Septiembre 275 (☎ & fax 02944/424528; *rucacheli@ciudad.com.ar*). Comfortable, well-run place. ⑥, including breakfast.

Hostels

Alaska, Lilinquen 328 (☎ & fax 02944/461564; *alaska@bariloche.com.ar*). Well-equipped and homely place with kitchen, laundry and bike rental. Buses #10, #20 or #21 to Av. Bustillo Km 7.5. $10 HI member, otherwise $12.

Albergue Patagonia Andina, Morales 564 (☎02944/422783; *elalbergue@bariloche.com.ar*). A popular and pleasant hostel in the centre, though the double rooms are cramped. Facilities include Internet access, kitchen, laundry and luggage store; dorm beds $10, rooms $24.

Albergue Refugio Cordillera, Bustillo Km 18.6 (☎02944/448261; *cordiller@bariloche.coml.ar*). A pleasant hostel some fifteen minutes' drive from town. There'a a kitchen and shop on site, and it's possible to rent bikes. Buses #10 or #20 from the station or the centre (every 15min). $10 per person HI member, otherwise $12.

La Bolsa del Deporte, Elflein 385 (☎ & fax 02944/423529; *bolsadep@bariloche.com.ar*). Inexpensive dorm accommodation and use of a kitchen. $10.

Casa de Familia Arko, Güerres 691, Barrio Belgrano (☎02944/423109). Lodging offered by helpful, multilingual couple who have exceptional regional historical and mountaineering knowledge. There's a luggage store, a kitchen, and space in the garden for tents. $12.

The Town

The **centro cívico**, dating from 1939, as the centrepiece of town. It's a noble architectural statement of permanence: an ensemble of buildings constructed out of timber and local greenish-grey stone that are grouped around a plaza and which resolutely face the lake. The Alpine design is the work of Ernesto de Estrada, who collaborated with Argentina's most famous architect, Alejandro Bustillo, in the development of a style that has come to represent the region. In the centre of the main plaza, around which these buildings are grouped, is an equestrian **statue** of General Roca, whose horse looks suitably hang-dog after the Campaign of the Desert. On the lake shore in front of the plaza is the **Puerto San Carlos**, where boats depart for various excursions across Nahuel Huapi (see p.565). Of the attractions around the plaza, the most interesting is the **Museo de la Patagonia** (Mon & Sat 10am–1pm, Tues–Fri 10am–12.30pm & 2–7pm; $2.50), which rates as one of the very best museums in Patagonia. Look out for the caricature of Perito Moreno as a wet-nurse guiding the infant Theodore Roosevelt on his trip through the Lake District in 1913. Superb, too, are the engraved Tehuelche tablet stones that experts speculate may have been protective amulets – they may have had an unknown ceremonial or medicinal function, and are not found in Chile; Aónik'enk painted horse hides and playing cards made of guanaco skin; one of the Mapuche's famous lances; and Roca's own uniform. Informative booklets are on sale for $2.50, but only the one on the Campaign of the Desert is translated into English. On the lake shore to the east of the museum is the **Catedral Nuestra Señora del Nahuel Huapi**, designed by Bustillo; its attractive stained-glass windows illustrate Patagonian themes such as the first Mass held by Magellan.

Running due east from *centro cívico* is Bariloche's main commercial street, the busy **Calle Mitre**. Here you will find ice-cream parlours, shops selling regional smoked specialities, and the much-lauded palaces devoted to chocoholics. Fenoglio, Mitre 301, also has a factory at Av. Bustillo Km 1.2 (Mon–Sat 9am–12.30pm & 3.30–8pm; ☎02944/422170). Just to the north of Mitre, at Moreno and Villegas, is the Paseo de los Artesanos, the place to buy regional handicrafts.

Restaurants

El Boliche de Alberto, Villegas 347 (☎02944/431433) and Bustillo 8800 (☎02944/462285). The juiciest and largest parrillas in town, with steaks at around $10: prepare to gorge yourself.

El Viejo Matías, Elflein 47 (☎ & fax 02944/434466). A cheerful, no-frills eatery. *Tenedor libre* of parrilla with salads and dessert for $12.

El Viejo Munich, Mitre 102 (☎02944/422336). Coffees and gateaux in the hunting-lodge tearoom on the ground floor; popular with a more mature age group. Restaurant options include goulash ($9), sausages and sauerkraut, and fondue.

Familia Weiss, Palacios and O'Connor (☎02944/435788). A perennial hit with visitors. Try *ciervo a la cazadora* (venison in a creamy mushroom sauce; $13) or a *picada* selection of smoked specialities. Evening shows range from salsa to cheesy Julio Iglesias covers. Open 8am–3am.

Friends, Mitre and Rolando. Open 24hr, so perfect for night owls. Burgers for $4, pizzas for $7, and beers and spirits from $2.50.

La Bohemia, Moreno 48 (☎02944/423182). A "piano restaurant", with a relaxed, nostalgic ambience and excellent food, ranging from seafood to mixed grills. A $5 *plato del día* is served at lunchtimes in high season. Live tango and jazz on Fri and Sat (from 9.30pm).

La Marmite, Mitre 329 (☎02944/423685). No bargain, but recommended for its regional and Swiss specialities, especially its fondues. Intimate, old-fashioned setting. Closed Sun lunch.

La Tavola, in the *Hotel Edelweiss*, San Martín 202 (☎02944/426165). High-class cuisine: prawns on saffron with a creamy champagne sauce ($16.50), fondue for two ($22).

Rock Chicken, Quaglia 283 and San Martín 88. A value-for-money fast-food joint, one branch of which is always open in the "dead phase" of the afternoon, when other restaurants are closed. Open late (6am).

Vegetariano, Elflein and Morales. Pleasant atmosphere, and well-prepared vegetarian and fish dishes.

Bars and clubs

1970 Pub, Mitre 641 (☎156-05555). Variable quality, but with live music on Fridays and Saturdays. Closed Mon.

Pub de la Luna, Bustillo Km 7.5. A friendly crowd with lively music.

Rocket, J.M. de Rosas 424 (☎02944/431940). Over 21s only, Saturday night for over 25s. State-of-the-art effects and dancefloor.

Grisu, J.M. de Rosas 574 (☎02944/422269). Mixed Latin and pop music. $4 drinks.

Genux, J.M. de Rosas 420 (☎02944/426254). Playing Latin tunes and packed with tourists; open till breakfast – which is served at 7am.

Listings

Airlines Aerolíneas/Austral, Quaglia 238 (☎02944/423091, fax 422548); LADE, Quaglia 238, local 8 (☎02944/423562); LAPA, Villegas 121 (☎02944/423714); Kaikén, Palacios 266 (☎02944/420251); Southern Wings, Villegas 145 (☎02944/423704, fax 423704).

Banks and exchange Bank hours vary depending on season: April–Nov 9am–2pm; Dec–March 8am–1pm. Banco de la Nación, Mitre 178; Banco Francés, San Martín 336; Banco de Galicia, Moreno 77. Cambio Sudamericana, Mitre 63.

Car rental Annie Millet, Quaglia 161 (☎02944/434543); Bariloche Rent A Car, Moreno 115, 1° (☎ & fax 02944/427638); Dollar, San Martín 491 (☎ & fax 02944/430358); Lagos, San Martín 82

(☎02944/428880); Localiza, San Martín 463 (☎02944/424767); Sur, Mitre 340, Local 58 (☎02944/429999).

Consulate Chilean, J.M. de Rosas 180 (☎02944/422842 or 423050).

Hospital Pento Moreno 601 (☎02944/426100).

Internet Cyber Café, Quaglia 220 ($6 per hour, divisible); Telecom, Mitre and Rolando (8.30am–midnight; $5 per hour divisible).

Laundries Lavadero Brujitas, Belgrano 21; Laverap, Elflein 251.

Pharmacies Del Centro, Rolando 699; de Miguel, Mitre 130.

Police *Centro cívico* (☎02944/422992, 422772 or 423434).

Post office Correo, Moreno 175 (Mon–Fri 8am–8pm, Sat 8.30am–1pm).

Taxis Autojet, España and French (☎02944/422408); Remises del Centro, Rolando 268 (☎02944/427200).

Telephone Telecom, Mitre and Rolando (8.30am–midnight).

Travel agencies Ecos del Sol, Elflein 89, 1 (☎ & fax 02944/433830); Transitando lo Natural, 20 de Febrero 28 (☎02944/424531, fax 428995); Cumbres y Lagos Patagonia, Villegas 222 (☎02944/423283); Turisur, Villegas 310 (☎02944/426109); Catedral Turismo, Mitre 399 (☎ & fax 02944/425444).

The Circuito Chico

Bariloche's most popular excursion is along the **Circuito Chico**, a 65-kilometre road circuit along the lake shore to the west of town. You could join one of the organized tours (4hr) or visit the highlights on public transport. **Buses** (3 de Mayo) leave from the terminal and from Moreno and Rolando: #20 for Puerto Pañuelo and Llao Llao and #10 for Colonia Suiza.

The initial part of the circuit is disappointing: as you drive along Avenida Bustillo you'll pass a stream of twee boutiques, hotels, restaurants, workshops and factory outlets for cottage industries. It's good for buying regional produce ranging from woollen sweaters to preserves, smoked trout and meats, ceramics, chocolates and woodcarvings, but for very little else. The best sights of the circuit lie at its westernmost end. Before you reach **Puerto Pañuelo** – where boats depart for excursions to the Isla Victoria, the Bosque de los Arrayanes, and Puerto Blest (see p.567) – you pass a tiny neat chapel, the **Capilla San Eduardo** (10am–1pm & 2–5pm; closed Thurs), on your left-hand side. Built with cypress and tiled with *alerce* shingles, it was designed by Estrada under the supervision of Bustillo. Across from the chapel is the magnificent sight of the **Llao Llao**, Argentina's most famous hotel (☎02944/448530, fax 445781; *llaollao@datamarkets.com.ar*, ⑨). Guarding the neck of the peninsula from its verdant knoll, it is sited like some palatial country chateau, backed up by a centurion guard of mountains. Yet despite the hotel's size, Alejandro Bustillo's alpine design sits harmoniously with the scene. The original building – made in the Canadian style of enormous cypress logs and roofed with *alerce* tiles – tragically burnt down soon after completion in 1939. The forests were plundered again, and the hotel reopened in 1940. State-owned until 1991, the place itself is now owned by a private company and can be visited as part of a **guided tour** (Thurs only; book in advance; ☎02944/445709). For guests, facilities include an indoor pool, gym, tennis courts, conference rooms, a fine restaurant – *Los Césares* – with superbly cooked regional cuisine (main courses $14–30), and a diminutive but beautiful eighteen-hole golf course. Not quite so grand, but plush nonetheless, the *Hotel Amancay*, overlooking *Llao Llao* at Av. Bustillo Km 24.8 (☎02944/448344, fax 448348; *amancay@bariloche.com.ar*, open Jan & Feb only, reserve three weeks in advance) has views to rival those of its exclusive neighbour.

The wildest scenery of the circuit is found along the road that runs through the forested sector beyond *Llao Llao*. It brings you to the *Cadena del Sol* hotel at Bahía López (☎02944/448005; *csol@hotelnet.com.ar*, ⑥) – a bulky place in a scenic location, opposite the domineering bluff of Cerro López (2075m). It has a restaurant and its rooms are comfortable but, in low season, the place can be rather too quiet. The last point of call on the circuit is **Colonia Suiza**, originally settled by Swiss immigrants. There's nothing in particular to see here, but it's a good place for gorging yourself on Sunday lunch. The local speciality is a mixed meat-fest called *curanto*, traditionally prepared with hot stones: try the one at *Lo de Nora/Curanto Emilio Goye*, with lamb, sausages, pork, sweetcorn, potatoes, *matambre*, pumpkin and chicken (eat-all-you-like for $18, with wine, salads and dessert; arrive for 1.30pm; reserve on ☎02944/448250).

Cerro Catedral and the Circuito Grande

Some 20km south of Bariloche is **Cerro Catedral**, named after the Gothic spires of rock that make up this craggy massif's summits (2405m). In summer, the village of **VILLA CATEDRAL** at the foot of the bowl (just over 1000m) is the starting point for several fantastic treks, and you can take a cable car and then a chair lift to reach *Refugio Lynch* near the summit (1870m; $16). Views from here and from the ridge above are superb. In winter, the village serves the main ski-resort, with an infrastructure that includes hotels, restaurants, and shops offering ski rental. There are 67km of pistes, and descents of up to 4km in length. July and August are the busiest months to visit, with a day pass costing as much as $40. Buses (3 de Mayo) leave from Moreno 470 in Bariloche; alternatively, you could take a half-day organized trip to the village (4hr 30min; $13).

The so-called **Circuito Grande** is a loop of 240km that takes you up past the rock formations of the Valle Encantado ("Enchanted Valley") of the Río Limay, on to the Mirador del Traful and Villa Traful (see p.555), past Lagos Correntoso and Espejo, and then returns via Villa La Angostura. A more tiring day-trip is the famous Ruta de los Siete Lagos (Seven Lakes Route; see p.553) to San Martín de los Andes, which involves either 360km of driving if returning via the Paso Córdoba, or 460km on the paved route returning via Junín and La Rinconada. The lake section is being paved, but calculate on at least a twelve-hour day ($34). If you can form a group, it's better to rent a car for this than to take a tour (ensure you get unlimited mileage), but you'll want to share the driving. Alternatively, arrange an itinerary with a *remise* taxi. If you use public transport, the Ko-Ko bus from the terminal goes to San Martín by the Seven Lakes Route during the summer (☎02944/425914; it goes via La Rinconada in winter, 4hr 30min); or Albus (☎02944/421689) goes via the Seven Lakes Route (daily, 6.30pm; $17), unless conditions are bad, in which case it goes via La Rinconada.

The Lake crossing to Chile

The **Cruce Internacional de los Lagos** or "Three Lakes Crossing" (not Sun), via the Paso Pérez Rosales to **Puerto Montt** in Chile, is one of the classic border crossings of the continent. The joy of this one- or two-day crossing is the scenery: if the weather turns sour or if you need to get to Chile fast, you'd be better to cross by the standard bus route via Paso Cardenal Samoré (see p.567). And in high season, the number of tourists can detract from the special wilderness character of the trip. The highlights are, of course, the lake cruises: Puerto Pañuelo to Puerto Blest; across peppermint **Lago Frías**; and across enchanting **Lago Todos Los Santos**, with wonderful views of **Volcán Osorno**, one of the cordillera's most shapely volcanic cones. On the two-day version you make the short climb to see the Cascada Los Cántaros, a waterfall on the northern side of Bahía Blest. On the Chilean side, the Saltos de Petrohué near the foot of Osorno are very beautiful, as are the views of Tronador from Peulla.

Crossings can be booked through Catedral Turismo, Mitre 399 (☎ & fax 02944/425444; *cattur@bariloche.com.ar*; $110 one way). With a bit of initiative, those on a budget can make a more affordable route by paying for certain boat stages and walking or cycling the land sections (bikes can be taken on the boats). Between September and April, the entire trip to Puerto Montt can be made in one or two days, with an optional overnight stop in **Peulla**. In winter (May–Aug), only the two-day option is possible. If you do the one-day tour, you'll leave Bariloche at 7am, and should arrive in Puerto Montt by 8pm.

Parque Nacional Nahuel Huapi

The mother of the Argentine national park system, **PARQUE NACIONAL NAHUEL HUAPI** protects a glorious chunk of the northern Patagonian cordillera and its neighbouring steppe. Its origins lie in the grant of 25 square leagues of land which Dr Francisco P. Moreno made, in 1903, to the national government, on the condition that it be safeguarded for the enjoyment of future generations. He had originally been given title to the land in recognition of the services he rendered to the Comisión de Limites, the body that presented Argentina's case with respect to fixing the international border with Chile. What started as the Parque Nacional del Sur grew to embrace its current 7100 square kilometres.

Most of the park falls within the watershed of **Lago Nahuel Huapi** (770m above sea level) and drains to the Atlantic. The lake's name comes from the Mapudungun for Isle (*huapi*) of the Tiger (*nahuel*) and refers to the jaguars that once, surprisingly, inhabited regions even this far south. Of glacial origin, it's a gigantic expanse of water, 557 square kilometres in area, and forms the centrepiece of the park, with its peninsulas, islands, and attenuated, fjord-like tentacles that sweep down from the thickly forested border region. Rainfall is heaviest by the border, in well-soaked places such as Puerto Blest and Lago Frias – the nucleus of the land donated by Moreno – where over 3000mm fall annually. This permits the growth of Valdivian temperate rainforest and individual species such as the *alerce*, found here at the northernmost extent of its range in Argentina. Other species typical of the subantarctic Patagonian forests also flourish: giant *coihues*, *lengas* and *ñire*, as well as the *maniú*, with yew-like leaves, and the oval-leaved *radal*.

A second important habitat is the high Alpine environment above the tree line (upwards of 1600m), including some summits that retain snow all year. The dominant massif of the park is an extinct volcano: **Cerro Tronador**, whose three peaks (Argentino at 3410m; Internacional at 3554m; and Chileno at 3470m) straddle the Argentinian–Chilean border in the south. Glaciers slide off its heights in all directions, though all are in a state of rapid retrocession. The "thundering" referred to in its Spanish name is not volcanic, but rather the echoing roar heard when vast chunks of ice break off its hanging glaciers and plunge down to impact on the slopes below. Rainfall decreases sharply as you move eastwards from the border: by Bariloche, annual levels are down to 800mm. Cypress woodland typifies the transitional semi-montane zone, and at the eastern side of the park you find areas of arid, rolling steppe, covered with *coirón* and *neneo*. Snow can occur into December and as early as March at higher altitudes: for this reason, it's not advisable to hike certain trails in the park outside the main high season. Average temperatures are 18°C in summer and 2°C in winter months. The strongest winds blow in spring, but these months otherwise make for a **good time to visit**, as do the calmer **autumn** months, when the deciduous trees wear their spectacular late-season colours.

The park has abundant **birdlife**, with species such as the Magellanic woodpecker, the green-backed firecrown, the ground-dwelling chucao, the austral parakeet, the upland goose (cauquén) and the thorn-tailed rayadito being some of the most frequently sighted. You'll hear mention of rare **fauna** such as the huemul and pudú, the huillín (a type of freshwater otter) and the monito de monte (a nocturnal marsupial

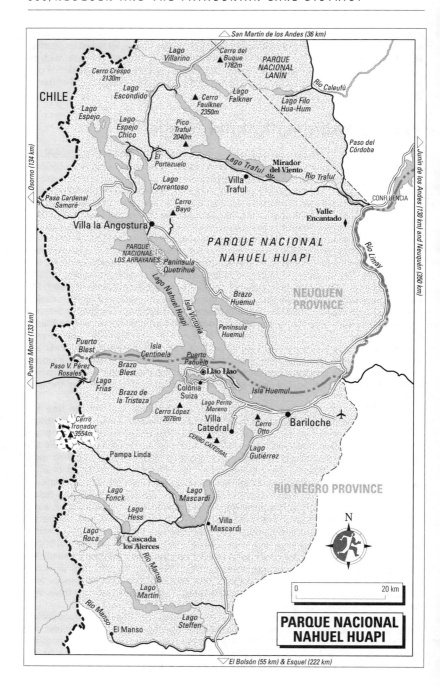

△ San Martín de los Andes (36 km)

Cerro del Buque 1782m

PARQUE NACIONAL LANÍN

Lago Villarino

Cerro Crespo 2130m

Río Caleufú

CHILE

Lago Escondido

Cerro Faulkner 2350m

Lago Falkner

Lago Filo Hua-Hum

Lago Espejo

Lago Espejo Chico

Pico Traful 2040m

Osorno (134 km) △

Paso del Córdoba

El Portezuelo

Lago Traful

Mirador del Viento

Río Traful

Junín de los Andes (130 km) and Neuquén (350 km) △

Lago Correntoso

Villa Traful

CONFLUENCIA

Paso Cardenal Samoré

Cerro Bayo

Valle Encantado

Villa la Angostura

PARQUE NACIONAL LOS ARRAYANES

Península Quetrihué

PARQUE NACIONAL NAHUEL HUAPI

NEUQUÉN PROVINCE

Río Limay

Lago Nahuel Huapi

Isla Victoria

Brazo Huemul

Península Huemul

Puerto Blest

Isla Centinela

Puerto Montt (133 km) △

Paso V. Pérez Rosales

Brazo Blest

Puerto Pañuelo

Llao Llao

Isla Huemul

Lago Frías

Brazo de la Tristeza

Colonia Suiza

Lago Perito Moreno

Cerro López 2076m

Villa Catedral

Cerro Otto

Bariloche

Cerro Tronador 3554m

CERRO CATEDRAL

Lago Gutiérrez

Pampa Linda

RÍO NEGRO PROVINCE

Lago Fonck

Lago Mascardi

Lago Hess

Villa Mascardi

N

Lago Roca

Cascada los Alerces

Río Manso

Lago Martín

0   20 km

Río Manso

Lago Steffen

El Manso

PARQUE NACIONAL NAHUEL HUAPI

▽ El Bolsón (55 km) & Esquel (222 km)

that lives in thick forest), although you have about as much chance of seeing one of these as you do of spying Nahuelito, Patagonia's version of the Loch Ness Monster. Animals that make their home in the steppe regions of the park (guanaco, armadillos, rheas and foxes) are more predictably seen. Of the introduced species, the most conspicuous are the **red deer** (ciervo colorado) and the **wild boar** (jabalí), which were introduced by hunt-loving settlers, and which have thrived ever since. The authorities issue shooting permits in an effort to cull numbers, and this continues to act as a source of revenue for the park. Noteworthy, too, is one other influx of shy, exotic species: that of American-based celebrities seeking to escape their own personality cults. Ted Turner, Albert Schwarzenegger, Madonna, Daniel Day Lewis and Sylvester Stallone are all rumoured to have bought private ranches in and around the park.

Information and accommodation

North to south, the park is divided into three zones. The **zone to the north** of Lago Nahuel Huapi centres around **Lago Traful**, but tends to be visited more for the Seven Lakes Route (see p.553), which runs north from Villa La Angostura, passes through spectacular forested mountain scenery, and enters the contiguous Parque Nacional Lanín before reaching San Martín de los Andes. *Guardaparques* stationed at points along the way are helpful when it comes to recommending treks in their particular sectors. In the far south of this zone is the main overland pass through to Chile – **Paso Cardenal Samoré** (formerly called Paso Puyehue; Argentinian immigration open 8am–8pm; Chilean side open 8am–7pm). The **central zone** is the one centred on Lago Nahuel Huapi itself, and embraces the "park within a park", Parque Nacional Los Arrayanes, on the Península Quetrihué (see p.556). Visits to this central zone are dependent, for the most part, on boat trips from Bariloche. One of these trips heads to **Isla Victoria**, the elongated, thickly forested island to the northwest. You disembark at Puerto Anchorena, situated on the narrow isthmus that joins the two halves of the island. From here trails lead to panoramic lookouts and past rock paintings that testify to the former presence of indigenous groups. Archeological excavations indicate that people made the island their home at least two thousand years ago. A chair lift runs up to the summit of Cerro Bella Vista for those not keen to walk.

At the western end of Brazo Blest is the outpost of **Puerto Blest**, surrounded by some of the park's most impressive forest. A short and scenic trail connects this with the north side of the bay, where a stepped walkway leads up past the **Cascada Los Cántaros**, a series of cascades in the forest. A dirt road runs south for 3km to Puerto Alegre at the northern end of tiny Lago Frías, and a launch crosses the lake daily to Puerto Frías, from where you can cross to Chile or hike south across the Paso de los Nubes towards Pampa Linda (see p.568).

The three most important **hosterías** in the area are the *Posada Lago Hess* near the Cascada Los Alerces (reservations in Bariloche at Morales 439; ☎ & fax 02944/462249; *piccino@bariloche.com.ar*); the upmarket *Hotel Tronador*, at the northwestern end of hook-shaped Lago Mascardi (☎02944/468127, fax 441062; ⑨, half board); and *Hostería*

THE PASO VERDE

The **Paso Verde** is a ten-day pass valid throughout the national parks of Nahuel Huapi, Lanín and Lago Puelo, which costs $10 and allows you to visit those sectors for which you'd otherwise be charged $5 per trip. In Nahuel Huapi, this means the Isla Victoria, Puerto Blest, and the southern sector that includes Tronador and the Cascada de los Alerces. It can be purchased at the Intendencia of Nahuel Huapi in Bariloche, the Intendencia of Lanín in San Martín de los Andes, and the park information office in Junín de los Andes.

Pampa Linda, at the base of Tronador (☎02944/442038; ⑤). There are also **campsites** at all major destinations: *Lago Roca* near the Cascada Los Alerces ($3 per person); *Los Rápidos* (☎02944/461861; $3 per person) and *La Querencia* (☎02944/426225; $5.50 per person) at Lago Mascardi; and *Pampa Linda* ($3 per person). Check, too, with the Intendencia in Bariloche as to the current status of the other authorized sites.

A useful Transportes RM **bus** connects Bariloche to Pampa Linda, leaving from outside the Club Andino Bariloche at Neumeyer 40 (summer daily 9am, returning 5pm; reserve in advance; $20). A 3 de Mayo bus departs from Moreno and Rolando and goes to Paraje El Manso at the extreme southwest corner of the park, by the park boundary (Friday 6am & 7pm; returns 8.40am & 9.30pm; $7.50).

Trekking in the park

Parque Nacional Nahuel Huapi is a famous and spectacular destination for hikers. The park's principal trekking region is the sector to the southwest of Bariloche, and the two most important points of interest are Cerro Catedral and the Pampa Linda area to the southeast of Cerro Tronador. An impressive network of well-run **refuges** makes life for the trekker much easier in this part of the world: you'll need a sleeping bag, but can buy **meals** and basic supplies en route and thus cut down on the weight you need to lug around on the longer circuits. Some refuges also have climbing equipment for rent. There are also authorized **camping sites**, but you need to get a camping **permit** from the Intendencia or any *guardaparque* in order to use them; the park has suffered a series of devastating **fires** in recent years, so restrictions have tightened up as regards free camping and you must now carry your own stove for cooking. Always inform the *guardaparque* or the person in charge of the *refugio* where you plan to trek to, and remember to confirm your arrival when you get to your destination.

Generally, the **trekking season** is between December and March, but you should always heed weather conditions, come prepared for unseasonal snowfalls, and check in advance with the *guardaparques* to find out which refuges are open. As a rule trails or *sendas* to refuges are well marked; the high mountain trails (*sendas de alta montaña*) are not always clearly marked, though, whilst the less-frequented paths (*picadas*) are not maintained on a regular basis, and close up with vegetation from time to time – one trail notorious for becoming overgrown is the swampy but otherwise popular one between Paso de Los Nubes and Lago Frías, in the far west of the park. Note that those keen on doing this trail will also need to budget for the boat crossings to Puerto Pañuelo or through to Chile.

In high season, refuges and trails in the more popular areas can get very busy. Popular day- or two-day hikes include ones to **Refugio Frey** in the Cerro Catedral area and Refugio Otto Meiling in the Pampa Linda area (both popular with climbers), but there are several options for longer treks, including ones of five days or more, such as the loop from Cerro Catedral through to Colonia Suiza. However, some sections – notably the one that links Refugio San Martín with Refugio Italia (also called Refugio Segre) – require proper mountaineering equipment and experience.

All prospective trekkers should visit the Club Andino Bariloche, at 20 de Febrero 30, in Bariloche. Their information office and shop is in the wooden hut alongside the main building (Jan & Feb 9am–1pm & 4–9pm; rest of year 11am–1pm & 6–9pm; ☎02944 422266). They sell a series of trekking **maps**: the standard one is the *Carta de Refugios, Sendas y Picadas* (1:100,000), which has been expanded into three larger-scale (1:50,000) maps. These maps are very useful and include stage times, but the route descriptions are in Spanish only, and not all topographical details are accurate. The park Intendencia has two free leaflets aimed at trekkers: *Area Pampa Linda* and *Trekking de Bajo Impacto*. They're useful in conveying broad options, but contain insufficient detail to be of much help on the ground. CAB also sells a slim volume, *Las Montañas de Bariloche* by Toncek Arko and Raúl Izaguirre, which has sections in English and German on suggested treks.

Keen hikers on longer stays in Bariloche may actually find it worthwhile to join CAB: ask if they're running any membership promotions. Those looking to join a guided group should ask about the cheap weekend hikes organized every second week (ask on Thurs).

El Bolsón and around

El Bolsón, to the south of Parque Nacional Nahuel Huapi, is a useful tourist centre with plenty of trekking opportunities in the neighbourhood. It also acts as the main access point for several attractions just across the provincial border in Chubut: the small **Parque Nacional Lago Puelo**, the Trochita steam train at El Maitén (see p.573); and two minor settlements close to the mountains – **Epuyén**, and **Cholila**, once home to Butch Cassidy. The 123-kilometre drive along the RN258 from Bariloche to El Bolsón should be done during the day for its excellent views. There are two routes from El Bolsón to Esquel (see p.573): the normal, faster route is the along the sealed RN258 and RN40; the more scenic route is via Cholila and passes through the north of the Parque Nacional Los Alerces (p.577).

El Bolsón

Set in the bowl of a wide, fertile valley, hemmed in by parallel ranges of mountains, straggly **EL BOLSÓN** was Latin America's first non-nuclear town, and a place famous in the 1970s as a hippy hangout. This legacy continues, although diluted by a more commercial ethos, and the town is a laid-back, welcoming place worth a day or two's stay. In summer, it's a popular place for young Argentinian backpackers, since it's far easier on budget travellers' wallets than nearby Bariloche. The municipality's strong environmental convictions mean that, in high season, tourists are given native tree seedlings to plant upon arrival, and fish fry to pop into the valley's Río Quemquemtreu or Río Azul. Spiritual life here is cosmopolitan, and you'll find Chinese Buddhist temples and a variety of practitioners of alternative paths. Unsurprisingly, UFOs and spirits (*duendes*) are also claimed to stop off regularly, being guaranteed an especially sympathetic reception on the last Saturday of February, when the town's main party, the **Hops Festival** (*Fiesta del Lúpulo*) is held. It celebrates the harvest of an important local crop, with music in the main square and an enjoyable, well-lubricated atmosphere. The **Farm Olympics** (*Olimpiades Agrarias*) is another off-beat festival worth checking out, held over four days in mid-February, with ox-races and other oddities.

To the east of town, on the wooded slopes of **Cerro Piltriquitrón** (2260m), is another unconventional and interesting site: the **Bosque Tallado** or Sculpted Forest. The sculptures, mostly crafted by local artists, are all left exposed to the elements.

Arrival, information and accommodation

Arriving from the north, the RN258 is called Avenida Sarmiento; from Esquel in the south it's called Avenida Belgrano. These two converge on the ACA fuel station that lies in the centre of town on Avenida San Martín, the avenue that forms the backbone of town. **Buses** drop you off at their respective offices, none of which is more than three blocks from Plaza Pagano, the main square. On the north side of the plaza, at the corner of San Martín and Roca, is the useful **tourist office**, bursting with promotional material (daily: mid-March to mid-Dec 10am–8pm; mid-Dec to mid-March 8am–10pm; ☎ & fax 02944/492604). They have two excellent free **maps** marking the positions of all hotels, restaurants and walks both in and around town, and sell a fun illustrated map in relief, the *Mapa del Bolsón de Dr Venzano* ($4), as well as a detailed magazine, *Guía Turística Comarca Andina del Paralelo 42*, which is worth buying if you're staying more than a day or two in the area and can read Spanish. They're also a useful source of information about trekking in the area, but better still is the Club Andino Piltriquitrón (CAP; ☎02944/492600), at Roca and Sarmiento.

As for **accommodation**, *La Posada de Hamelín*, Granollers 2179 (☎02944/492030; ③), is a homely well-kept guesthouse in the centre of town with rooms for up to four people, as does *Hotel Amancay*, San Martín 3217 (☎02944/492222; ③). *Hospedaje Salinas* (☎02944/492396; ②) is conveniently close to the Plaza Pagano at Roca 641. *Vamos al Bosque* is a great-value budget **hostel** 1.5km east of the centre, at Lomo del Medio on the road to Río Azul (☎155-59233; $5 per person). The well-run, HI-affiliated *Albergue El Pueblito* (☎02944/493560; *pueblito@hostels.org.ar*, $8 per person) is 4km north of the centre; take a Transporte Urbano bus to the bridge 3km out of town from where it's signposted, 1km down the Barrio Luján road. Another great hostel, the airy, ecologically minded *Albergue Gaia* (☎02944/492143; $8 per person), is 7km north of the centre; facilities include a kitchen, laundry and a swimming pool. To get there, take a Transporte Urbano bus to Km 118 of the RN258. Leafy *La Chacra* **campsite**, Belgrano 1128 (☎02944/492111; $5 per person), is the closest to the centre, less than fifteen minutes' walk down the RN258 in the direction of Esquel. It is situated behind a **brewery-restaurant**, where the aficionado owner serves up moreish fruity brews similar to those found in the Low Countries: raspberry, blackcurrant, cherry and a dark winter beer.

Eating, drinking and nightlife

El Bolsón is one of the few towns in Argentina where finding vegetarian food is not a problem. The valleys around are chock-a-block with smallholdings that produce crunchy organic vegetables, and fruits and berries for jams or desserts. Local honey and cheeses are also good. *Calabaza*, San Martín 2518, offers some appetizing vegetarian dishes, including cheese *milanesas*, omelettes, and pastas with local boletus (*hongo de pino*) and morelle (*hongo de ciprés*) mushrooms. It's open till late and is reasonably priced. Goulash at the brewery near *La Chacra* campsite (see above) costs $6.50. *Las Brasas*, Sarmiento and Pablo Hube (☎02944/492923), is a good parrilla, while north of town, off the road to the Mallín Ahogado waterfall (15min in *remise*; $7), is *El Quincho* (☎02944/492870), a fun place in the countryside where you can gorge on an eat-all-you-like lunchtime parrilla for $10 (Thurs, Sat & Sun; 2pm). Mouthwatering ice cream is scooped onto cones at excellent *El Bolsón*, San Martín 2526.

On Subida Tres Cipreses in the Villa Turismo suburb to the southeast is *Cabaña El Pitío* (☎02944/492723), which hosts medieval **music-and-dance shows** in high season (Thurs & Sat at 9.30pm).

Parque Nacional Lago Puelo

Situated in the northwest corner of Chubut Province, 19km south of El Bolsón, the relatively small **Parque Nacional Lago Puelo** (237 square kilometres) protects the area of rugged mountains, forests and pasture that surrounds the windswept, turquoise lake of the same name. In recent years, several fires in the region have damaged swathes of the native forest, but it still offers some excellent trekking possibilities. A few endangered huemules inhabit the remoter border areas of the park; and some 120 species of birds have been recorded here, including the resident Chilean pigeon (*paloma araucana*), a species that came close to extinction due to disease but whose numbers are now recovering.

There are incursions here of several tree species usually found only in Chile, such as the *avellano*, the *olivillo* and the *ulmo*, which flowers in later summer with large white flowers reminiscent of magnolia blooms. The park also protects *alerces* (see p.579) and groves of the water-loving *patagua* (or *pitra*), a species related to the *arrayán*.

The park can be accessed via either of two routes. A minor access road, 13km long, runs from El Hoyo de Epuyén, just to the south of El Bolsón, and reaches the lake at the mouth of the Río Epuyén, where there is a campsite ($2 per person). This is a good starting point for hikes south, but you'll need first to have visited the Intendencia on the main route. By far the most common access to the park is from El Bolsón itself, passing through the **Lago Puelo Village**, 3.5km north of the lake and outside the park boundary. Certain scheduled **bus** services from Bariloche and El Bolsón only go as far as the village (especially in the winter), so check first. It's $3 in a *remise* from the village to the park headquarters and pier (☎02944/499133 or 499068). A plethora of places in the area rent out **cabins**, of which *Puelo Ranch* (☎02944/499234; $90 for four people, $120 for six) and *Peuma Hue* (☎1560-3652; ⑤) are recommended. The *Hostal del Lago* (☎02944/499199), just outside the park gate, offers straightforward, good-value accommodation ②) as well as cheap *platos del día* ($4 for gnocchi).

Within the park, near the entrance, is the **Intendencia** (☎02944/499232, fax 499064), where you should stop for an excellent illustrated pamphlet on key bird species (Spanish only), a map marking authorized campsites, and useful trekking information. You must obtain a (free) permit here for all trekking and camping. Where the road ends at the north end of the lake, you have a choice of **campsites**: the *camping agreste* ($2pp) to the right of the pier, or the more developed *Camping Lago Puelo* (☎02944/499183; $5 per person) to the left. A little further round the shore from the *autocamping* is a beach popular with locals in the summer.

A new **boat** service crosses the lake to El Turbio (18km away), which is making it easier to trek in the Río Turbio area south of the park. At El Turbio there's a park ranger's post, a campsite and *hostería*. You could hike along the entire eastern side of the lake if you don't want to take the boat, although the path is poorly marked in places for the first section to Río Epuyén. From El Turbio, it's possible to make an expedition hike through to Cholila (see below), passing the spectacular ramparts of **Cerro Tres Picos** or Three Peak Mountain (2492m) beyond the park's southern boundary. Other hiking options from the Intendencia include the fairly flat Los Hitos trek to the border with Chile (18km return). This can be made into a five-day trek to the town of Puelo on the Pacific. Before setting out, check on the procedure at the Intendencia, and ask for information on where to cross the Río Azul if water levels are high.

Epuyén and Cholila

Just to the west of the main El Bolsón to Esquel road is the strung-out settlement of **EPUYÉN**, the main part of which is just by the turn-off. The more interesting section is some 6km away on the shores of **Lago Epuyén**. Parts of the picturesque mountain area around here were badly hit by forest fires in 1999, but it still makes a good base for trekking, especially if you're seeking to avoid better-known and busier centres such as El Bolsón. Proyecto Lemu (☎02945/499050; *lemu@red42.com.ar*), a committed ecological organization fighting for the protection of native Patagonian Andean forests and their promulgation through afforestation, is based in the town. One of their specific aims is to bring about the creation of an immense, protected biological corridor connecting the Parque Nacional Los Alerces to Parque Nacional Lanín.

On the shores of Lago Epuyén, at the base of Cerro Pirque, you'll find *El Refugio del Lago* (☎02945/499025, fax 499050; ④), a rustic **guesthouse** and campground ($4 per person) run by a multilingual French couple who organize fishing, trekking and horseriding expeditions in the area and prepare wholesome organic meals ($12).

You could be forgiven for thinking that the hamlet of **CHOLILA**, with its spectacular backdrop of savage peaks, was actually in Wyoming or Utah. It is located on prairie grasslands, 3km east of the junction of the RP71 and the RP15. The area's main tourist attraction lies 12km northwest of the village itself along the RP71. At El Blanco, there's a sign for *La Casa de Piedra* teahouse, down a farm track to your right. Fifty metres down this track, an even more basic cart track on your right (you may have to jump the

BUTCH CASSIDY AND THE SUNDANCE KID

Butch Cassidy, Etta Place and the **Sundance Kid** were fugitives together in the Argentinian frontier town of Cholila between the years 1901 and 1906, as attested by both Pinkerton and provincial records of the time. They fled to these distant parts because, at the beginning of the century, the American West was changing fast and the life of an outlaw was becoming far riskier: the territory had become more densely settled; the small, closely knit homesteading communities which had previously given shelter to the outlaws were disappearing; and the spread of the rail, telegraph, and telephone networks all served to counteract the advantages that a well-prepared relay of thoroughbred getaway steeds had once brought. Butch and Sundance had begun to weary of years of relentless pursuit, and had heard rumours that Argentina had become the new land of opportunity, offering the type of wide-open ranching country they loved so well, and where they could live free from the ceaseless hounding of Pinkerton agents and the certain threat of jail. In addition, the two had money to invest – the proceeds from the Winnemucca, Nevada bank robbery of 1900.

It appears that the *bandidos* were trying to go straight, even living under their real names – Butch as "George Parker" (an old alias derived from his name at birth, Robert Leroy Parker), and Etta and Sundance as Mr and Mrs Harry Longabaugh – and in this they succeeded, for a while at least. They were always slightly distant from the community and were evidently viewed as somewhat eccentric, yet decent, individuals. Certainly no one ever suspected they had a criminal past, let alone one that was to be made famous with the first of many films about the Wild Bunch, cinema's first ever cowboy film, *The Great Train Robbery*, hitting American cinemas in 1903.

Things were to change however. Various theories are mooted as to why the threesome sold their ranch in such a rush in 1907, but it seems as though the arrival of a Wild Bunch associate, the murderous Harvey "Kid Curry" Logan, following his escape from a Tennessee jail, had something to do with it. The robbery of a bank in Río Gallegos in early 1905 certainly had the hallmarks of a carefully planned Cassidy job, and a spate of robberies along the cordillera in the ensuing years have, with varying degrees of evidence, been attributed to the *bandidos norteamericanos*.

Cholila certainly became too hot for them: one account has a frontier police commissar come to visit the three with the intention of making an arrest. After offering the officer a whisky, the outlaws drew out their Colt revolvers, and began to shoot rocks that they'd thrown in the air, apologizing for firing in that manner, but saying, "it was to stop them from getting bored". Prudently, the officer decided to leave the arrest for a later date.

What happened to Cholila's outlaws next is a matter of conjecture. Etta returned to the States, putatively because she needed an operation for acute appendicitis, but equally possibly because she was pregnant, as a result of a dalliance with a young Anglo-Irish rancher. The violent deaths of Butch and Sundance were reported in Uruguay, and in several sites across Argentina and Bolivia. The least likely scenario is the one depicted by Paul Newman and Robert Redford in the famous 1969 Oscar-winning film. Bruce Chatwin in his travel classic *In Patagonia* proposes that they were shot by frontier police in Río Pico, to the south of Esquel (see p.622), but a convincing case is made in Larry Pointer's study, *In Search of Butch Cassidy*, that, whereas Sundance did indeed get killed in a separate incident in Bolivia, Butch returned to live under an alias in Washington State, dying in 1937 in a somewhat less cinematographic manner – in an old people's home, of rectal cancer.

fence) leads you towards a cluster of buildings nestled in a group of poplars. This is the site of the **cabin** of **Butch Cassidy**, who fled incognito with his partner, the **Sundance Kid**, to this isolated area of the world at the turn of the century when the detectives from the Pinkerton Agency were closing in on him in the United States. The Sundance Kid and his beautiful gangster moll, **Etta Place**, also lived here for a short while. The group of buildings, which were already in a lamentable state of repair when Bruce Chatwin visited in the 1970s, have degenerated still further – sheets of corrugated iron now roof them, the wood is rotting badly, and half the barn has collapsed. *La Casa de Piedra* teahouse, a much sturdier construction, is 400m further down the main track; its owners offer **rooms** as well as scrumptious Welsh teas (☎02945/498126).

Cholila's **bus terminal** is on the main square (☎02945/455900). Comfortable, roomy **lodging** is offered at the tranquil *Hostería El Trebol*, 2.7km from the terminal along the RP15 (☎ & fax 02945/498055; no credit cards; ⑦).

Esquel

For a place so close to the exuberant Andean forests of Parque Nacional Los Alerces, **ESQUEL**, 180km south of El Bolsón, can surprise you on arrival for the aridity of its setting. Enclosed in a bowl of dusty ochre mountains, it has something of the feel of a cowboy town, but a pleasant one nonetheless. Few sites of tourist interest exist in town, although there's the tiny, under-funded **Museo Indigenista**(Mon–Fri 8am–10pm, Sat & Sun 5–9pm; free), Belgrano 330, which has a small collection of artefacts from Mapuche, Tehuelche and pre-Tehuelche cultures. The reason why most people make the trip to Esquel, however, is to visit the nearby **Parque Nacional Los Alerces** (see pp.577–583), with the trip on the Trochita (see box) as the next biggest attraction.

Some 13km to the northeast is the **skiing** centre of **La Hoya**, which sometimes has later snow than larger, more challenging complexes such as Chapelco (see p.533), lasting on occasion into early October. It has eight lifts, is good for powder snow, and is promoted as a low-key family skiing centre.

LA TROCHITA: THE OLD PATAGONIAN EXPRESS

A trip on the **Old Patagonian Express** rates as one of South America's classic train journeys. This steam train puffs, judders and lurches across the arid, rolling steppe of northern Chubut, like a drunk on the well-worn route home, running on a track with a gauge of a mere 75cm. Don't let Paul Theroux's disparaging book *The Old Patagonian Express* put you off: travelling in this way has an authentic Casey Jones feel to it and is definitely not something that appeals only to trainspotters. You'll see guanacos, rheas, hares and even condors as you pass through the giant estate of Estancia Leleque, owned by the Italian clothes magnate, Benetton, Argentina's biggest landowner.

Referred to lovingly in Spanish as **La Trochita**, from the Spanish for narrow gauge, or *El Trencito*, it has had an erratic history. It was conceived as a branch line to link Esquel with the main line joining Bariloche to Carmen de Patagones on the coast. Construction began in Ingeniero Jacobacci in Río Negro Province in 1922, but it took 23 years to complete the 402km to Esquel. Originally, it was used as a mixed passenger and freight service, carrying consignments of wool, livestock, lumber and fruit from the cordillera region. The locomotives had to contend with snowdrifts in winter and five derailments occurred between 1945 and 1993, caused by high winds or stray cows on the track. Proving to be unprofitable, the line was eventually closed in 1993, but the Province of Chubut took over the running of the 165km section between Esquel and El Maitén soon thereafter, and its future now seems secure. *La Trochita* has matured into a major tourist attraction, but it is not only a tourist train: it is the only means of transport for locals living in isolated outposts along the line, and they use the train for free.

For most people, a trip on *La Trochita* means the half-day trip from Esquel to Nahuel Pan, 22km away (high season Mon–Wed, Fri & Sat 10am & 2pm; rest of year Sat only same times; 2hr; $15; moderately priced; restaurant car; further information on (☎02945/451403). For a more authentic experience travel with the locals on the **public service** (6hr 15min; $25) which covers the whole route once a week in each direction.

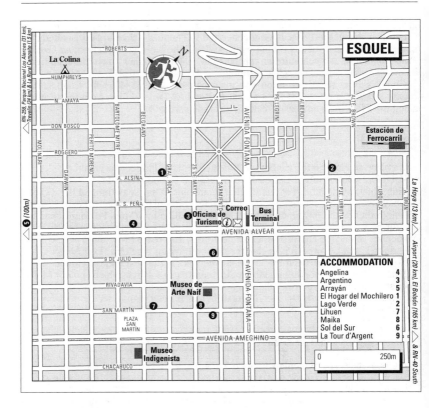

Arrival, information and accommodation

The town's **airport** is 21km east of the centre; Esquel Tours, Fontana 754 (☎02945/452704), runs minibus services between the two. The **bus terminal** is handily sited in the centre of town, on the corner of Fontana and the main boulevard, **Avenida Alvear**. The *La Trochita* **train station** (see box on p.573) is at Roggero and Brun, nine blocks northeast of the terminal. The proficient **tourist office** is 100m to the right of the bus terminal, just past the post office, at Av. Alvear y Sarmiento (March–Nov Mon–Sat 7.30am–8pm; Dec also Sun 9am–noon and 4–7pm; Jan & Feb daily 7.30am–0.30am; ☎ & fax 02945/451927; *turiesquel@teletel.com.ar*). They can provide you with information on specialist fishing and nature guides, and have a list of *casa de familia* lodgings. Ask too for leaflets on the park, especially the *Servicios Turísticos* one, which has a map of all the campsites and lodgings. Rent **bikes** at Coyote Bikes, Rivadavia 887 and Roca ($15 per day), or less expensively from Carlos Barria, Don Bosco 259 (☎02945/454443; $10 per day).

Overall, the standard of **accommodation** in Esquel is disappointing. Some hotels shut in low season (especially May, June, Oct & Nov), though others offer discounts. There are three **campsites** within easy reach of town, but none is particularly appealing: most central is the site attached to the *El Hogar del Mochilero* hostel (see below; $3 per person); alternatively there's *La Rural*, on RN259, 1km southwest of town ($5 per person); or *La Colina*, Darwin 1400 (☎02945/454962; $3 per person), which is basic and grubby, but cheap and has great views over town – though it's a steep climb to reach the site, which is off-putting. There is one official **hostel** in town: *El Hogar del Mochilero*, Roca 1028 (☎02945/452166; $5 per person), which is cramped but fun, and popular with young Argentine backpackers; in addition *Lago Verde* offers some hostel-price accommodation.

Argentino, 25 de Mayo 862 (☎02945/452237). Basic budget hotel popular with young party crowd. Noisy in the evenings due to pumping bar. ②.

Hostería Arrayán, Antártida Argentina 767 (☎02945/451051). A tidy place with personable atmosphere. Worth the extra walk from the centre. ③.

La Tour D'Argent, San Martín 1063 (☎ & fax 02945/454612). Decent mid-range hotel with good restaurant. ④.

Lago Verde, Volta 1081 (☎02945/452251, fax 453901; *lagoverd@hostels.org.ar*). Run by a hardworking family who speak English, this is a peaceful, welcoming home with spotless little rooms and a small garden, that honours a hostelling price ($11) for those with HI cards, but otherwise charges a standard hotel rate. Reserve in advance in high season. ②.

Residencial Angelina, Alvear 758 (☎02945/452763). Comfortable family-run place with buffet breakfast included. Closed April–June, Oct & Nov. ④.

Residencial Lihuen, San Martín 820 (☎ & fax 02945/452589). Fairly characterless, but reasonable place. No phone reservations in high season without pre-payment. ③.

Residencial Maika, 25 de Mayo and San Martín (☎02945/452457). Unattractive architecture, and gloomy insides, but clean. ③.

Sol del Sur, 9 de Julio 1086 (☎ & fax 02945/452189). Best of the three-stars, but fairly standard comfort and amenities. Spacious bathrooms; breakfast included. Mind the step by the lift. ⑤.

Eating and drinking

Many **restaurants** close between about 3pm and 7pm; last orders are generally around midnight. The best **bar** in town is in the *Hotel Argentino*, 25 de Mayo 862 (☎02945/452237); a $4 entrance is charged in season, when the dancefloor gets feisty, but you can cool off with a well-chilled Quilmes.

Cassis, Sarmiento 120 (☎02945/450576). The best cuisine in town, with succulent Patagonian specialities. From 9pm.

Don Chiquino, 9 de Julio 964 (☎02945/451508). Italian food in a cosy atmosphere. Always packed in season; brain-teasers to solve while waiting for your food.

El Lomo del Abuelo, Av. Alvear 1360. Popular for straightforward pasta, *milanesas* and pizzas, with the emphasis on value for money – most options under $6.

Fitzroya Pizza, Rivadavia 1048 (☎02945/450512). Tasty, though somewhat pricey, pizzas and hamburgers. Open till 1am in high season.

La Tour D'Argent, San Martín 1063. Cheap and filling tourist menus of pastas and chicken for under $5. More adventurous, appetizing à la carte selection includes trout with cheese and mushrooms ($13). Closed Tues lunch.

La Trochita, 25 de Mayo 633. A good bet for carnivores, with a parrilla on the go.

Listings

Airlines Huala (agent for Austral), Fontana and Ameghino (☎02945/453614); LADE, Alvear 1085 (☎02945/452124).

Banks Banco del Chubut, Alvear 1131; Banco de la Nación, Alvear y Roca (☎02945/452105); Bansud, 25 de Mayo 737.

Car rental Localiza, Rivadavia 1168 (☎02945/453276); Esquel Tours, Fontana 754 (☎02945/452704).

Hospital 25 de Mayo 150 (☎02945/451074 or 451224).

Internet Unifom, Rivadavia y Mitre ($6 per hour, divisible).

Laundries Laverap, Mitre 543; Marva, San Martín 941 ($8).

Pharmacies Dra. Bonetto, 25 de Mayo 468; Pasteur, 9 de Julio and Belgrano.

Police Rivadavia and Mitre (☎02945/450789 or 450001).

Post office Alvear 1192.
Swimming pool Natatorio, Alvear 2300.
Taxis ☎02945/452233; Remise La Terminal ☎02945/451222.
Telephone Bus Terminal; Su Central, 25 de Mayo 415.

Trevelin and around

The most Welsh of the cordillera towns, **TREVELIN** is a small, easy-going settlement which retains more of a pioneering character than Esquel, with several of that time's characteristic low brick buildings. Lying 24km to the south of its larger neighbour, it commands impressive views across the grassy valley to the peaks in the south of Parque Nacional Los Alerces. It was founded by Welsh settlers from the Chubut Valley, following a series of expeditions to this area of the world that began in 1885 with a group led by Colonel Fontana of the Argentine army and John Evans. Its Welsh name means "village of the mill", and the vital **flour mill**, a stalwart brick structure dating from 1918, now forms the main museum in town, the **Museo Regional Molino Andes** or **El Viejo Molino** (daily 11am–8.30pm; $2). The exhibits – mainly items from pioneer days – include a fascinating group photo of the 1902 plebiscite when the whole colony had to vote on whether it wanted to be Chilean or Argentinian: those who want to know more should read *Down where the Moon is Small* by Richard Llewellyn, which is evocative in its recreation of the pioneering years of the Welsh community here and of its relations with both the indigenous Mapuche and the Argentine authorities at this time.

The mill, though interesting, is outshone by the **Hogar del Abuelo** (Dec–Feb 9.30am–noon & 3–9.30pm; rest of year, knock at door; $2), the house of Clery Evans, granddaughter of the village's founder, John Evans. In the garden is the **Tumba del Malacara**, the burial place of his faithful steed. On one of the early Welsh explorations, El Malacara leapt heroically down a seemingly impossibly steep scarp, thus saving his master from the same grisly fate as befell his companions – butchered by enraged Mapuche warriors who were bent on reprisals against any whites, in the wake of an atrocity committed against their tribe during the Campaign of the Desert. The house attracts a steady stream of Bruce Chatwin pilgrims, as the story features in his classic travelogue, *In Patagonia*.

Welsh heritage is evoked in the celebration of a minor **Eisteddfod** (two days in the second week of October), and several **casas de té**, the best of which is *Nain Maggie*, at Perito Moreno 179 (☎02945/480232; 3–10.30pm; $10 for full tea).

Practicalities

The RN259 from Esquel arrives at the octagonal Plaza Coronel Fontana at the north end of town. Get off here if the bus driver is willing – otherwise, you will be dropped at the **terminal** at Libertad and Roca, four blocks south of the plaza on the main north–south avenue through town, Avenida San Martín. The **tourist office** is on the plaza (8am–10.30pm; ☎02945/480120; *trevelin@teletel.com.ar*), though it has a poor record in customer service it can provide a good **map** of the area.

The best **accommodation** in town is the snug *Hostal Casaverde* (☎ & fax 02945/480091; $12 per person), with laundry and kitchen facilities and a privileged view from its little hilltop up Calle Alerces; it's off Avenida Fontana, five- to ten-minutes walk from the plaza or terminal. *Hotel Estefania*, Perito Moreno s/n (☎02945/480148, fax 480445; ②; closed Sept & Oct) with inexpensive rooms for up to five. It also serves meals. For convenience alone, you can **camp** at the poor municipal *Camping Adventure*, on Ap Iwan, right by the west side of the plaza ($4 per person). A better option is *Camping El Chacay* ($4 per person) near the south end of San Martín – turn left one block beyond *Oregón* restaurant – with showers and a shop. Far more scenic and interesting, however, is *La Granja Trevelin* (☎02945/480120; English spoken), just off the RN259, 4km north of the village, 300m from the Río Percey. You can camp ($4 per person) or rent an inexpensive **cabin** ($40, sleeps four). There's a creative, artistic ethos here, with opportunities to try yoga or pottery using local clay; and macrobiotic food is served, including excellent home-made pasta. Another recommended place lies outside town: contact Gales Al Sur travel agency to take you to their *Refugio Wilson*, in the countryside 7km away. This funky, open-plan, cabin-style **refuge** has bunk-beds ($7 with your own sleeping bag), or you can camp ($5 per person). On Saturdays it acts as a local pub, with a great atmosphere but not conducive to sleep.

All types of fondues can be had at *Clery Fondue*, a cosy **restaurant** at the entrance to the village at Brown and Patagonia (☎068-281383), but if it's a slap-up parrilla you want, head to *Oregón*, near the southern exit of the village at San Martín and Laprida (☎02945/480408, fax 480215), where you can also rent cabins ($65 for up to five people); the bus to Futaleufú will drop you outside.

Nant y Fall and the Futaleufú and Carrenleufú/Palena border crossings

Nant y Fall (9.30am–5.30pm; $1), 19km from Trevelin, off the RN259 to Futaleufú, is a series of sparkling **cascades** which tumble over rock ledges in the midst of hillside *coihue* and cypress forests. There are fine views across the valley to the mountains of Parque Nacional Alerces from here, and in a couple of hours you can wander around the circuit and have time to bathe in the pools.

Beyond here two border crossings lead to Chile's beautiful Carretera Austral, the unsurfaced last leg of the Panamerican highway. They're useful for travelling through to the port of Chaitén, from where you can catch a ferry to the popular island of Chiloé. Buses run several times a week from Esquel, passing through Trevelin. Adjacent to the national park's southern boundary is **Paso Futaleufú** (Argentinian immigration open 8am–10pm). Some 10km from the border is the first Chilean settlement, appealing wood-built **FUTALEUFÚ**. This is a base for some of Patagonia's most spectacular **white-water rafting**, on the turquoise river of the same name.

The hamlet of **CARRENLEUFÚ** is 26km west of the pleasant, little-visited village of Corcovado, and its nearby pass connects through to the Chilean settlement of Palena, 8km past the border. Codao buses leave from Esquel and Trevelin for Carrenleufú. The Río Corcovado (called the Río Palena on the Chilean side) is noted for its Pacific salmon, and it also offers medium-grade rafting. To the south of Corcovado lies the wild scenery of Lago Vintter (also called Lago Winter).

Parque Nacional Los Alerces

Established in 1937, and part of the Pacific watershed, the 2630-square-kilometre **Parque Nacional Los Alerces** protects some of the most biologically important habitats and scenic landscapes of the central Patagonian cordillera. Its lakes are superb: famous for both their rich colours and their fishing; while most have a backdrop of sumptuous forests that quilt the surrounding mountain slopes. In the northeast of the park these lakes form a network, centring on **Lagos Rivadavia**, **Menéndez** and **Futalaufquen**, whose waters drain south to the dammed reservoir of **Lago Amutui Quimei**, and from here into the Río Futaleufú (also called Río Grande).

Los Alerces doesn't have any mountain peaks of the calibre or altitude of Volcán Lanín or Cerro Tronador in Nahuel Huapi (see p.565). Nevertheless, some of the two-thousand-metre ranges that divide the park are spectacular, with dramatic rock colorations and cracked and craggy summits such as those that can be seen in the **Cordón Situación**, whose peaks rise to 2300m. **Cerro Torrecillas** (2253m), in the north of the park, has the only glacier you'll witness, but patches of snow can last on the upper peaks into mid-summer. The peaks also seem to act as regular moorings for some remarkable high-altitude cloud formations.

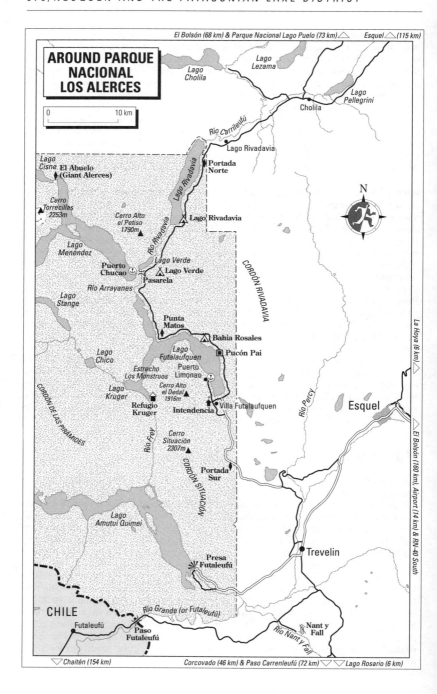

AROUND PARQUE NACIONAL LOS ALERCES

0   10 km

El Bolsón (68 km) & Parque Nacional Lago Puelo (73 km) △   Esquel △ (115 km)

Lago Lezama

Lago Cholila

Lago Pellegrini

Cholila

Río Carrileufú

Lago Rivadavia

Lago Cisne

El Abuelo (Giant Alerces)

Portada Norte

Cerro Torrecillas 2253m

Cerro Alto el Petiso 1790m

Lago Rivadavia

Lago Menéndez

Lago Verde

Puerto Chucao

Lago Verde

Pasarela

Río Arrayanes

CORDÓN RIVADAVIA

Lago Stange

Punta Matos

Bahía Rosales

Lago Futalaufquen

Pucón Pai

Lago Chico

Estrecho Los Monstruos

Puerto Limonao

Lago Kruger

Cerro Alto el Dedal 1916m

Refugio Kruger

Villa Futalaufquen

Intendencia

Esquel

Cerro Situación 2307m

Río Percy

CORDÓN DE LAS PIRÁMIDES

Río Frey

Portada Sur

CORDÓN SITUACIÓN

La Hoya (6 km) △

Lago Amutui Quimei

El Bolsón (160 km), Airport (14 km) & RN-40 South

Presa Futaleufú

Trevelin

CHILE

Río Grande (or Futaleufú)

Nant y Fall

Futaleufú

Paso Futaleufú

Río Nant y Fall

As in other parks in this region, vegetation alters considerably as you move east from the Chilean border into the area affected by the rain shadow cast by the cordillera. Up against the border, rainfall exceeds 3000mm a year: enough to support the growth of dense **Valdivian temperate rainforest** (*selva Valdiviana*), and most particularly the species for which the park is named: the **alerce**. Other species in the forests include *coihues, lenga, arrayanes, canelo, maitén* and *laurel*. The ground is dominated by dense thickets of the bamboo-like *caña colihue*, while two species of flower dominate: the orange or white-and-violet *mutisias*, with delicate spatula-like petals, and the *amancay*, a golden yellow lily growing on stems 50cm to 1m high. In contrast, the eastern margin of the park is much drier, receiving 300mm to 800mm of rainfall annually. Cypress woodland and *ñire* scrub mark the transitional zone here between the wet forests and the arid steppe near Esquel, on the other side of the Cordón Rivadavia.

The western two thirds of the park are off-limits, being designated a strict scientific reserve. This is the haunt of the endangered huemul, a species you're highly unlikely to see, except perhaps in winter when they come down from the heights in search of food; and the shy pudú, the smallest deer in the world, standing 40cm tall. Other frustratingly invisible denizens of the park include the gato huiña (a type of wildcat); the nocturnal comadrejita trompada (a species of marsupial); and the huillín (a type of otter). The non-native mink (*visón*), an escapee from a fur-farm in Cholila, has caused havoc amongst the wildlife, eating bird's eggs and capturing small mammals.

You'll need patience to see the Chilean pigeon (*paloma araucana*), now making a comeback from the verge of extinction, and the Des Mur's wiretail (*colilarga*), which secretes itself in clumps of *caña colihue*. More accommodating are the chattering austral parakeet (*cachaña*); waterbirds like the great grebe (*huala*); the dull-grey giant hummingbird (*picaflor gigante*), and its wee relative, the green-backed firecrown (*picaflor rubí*). At the other end of the scale, you may glimpse a condor. In mature woodland, listen out for the "thwack-thwack-thwack" of the Magellanic woodpecker, a powerful bird with a torpedo-shaped black body, white dorsal patch, and a scarlet flame of a crest on the male. **Anglers** try to hook introduced species – landlocked salmon; plus brook, rainbow and brown trout – but not the protected native species, such as the puyén grande and the perca criolla. If caught, these should be returned, preferably without removing them from the water – cut the line if necessary.

The **northeastern section** of the park is the most interesting for the visitor, especially around the area of beautiful **Lago Verde**, which works as a useful base for

THE ALERCE

Similar in appearance to the Californian redwood, the *alerce* or Patagonian cypress can reach heights of 45m and is one of the four oldest species of tree in the world. Its name in Mapudungun, *lahuén*, means "long-lived" or "grandfather", and certain individuals may live for as long as four millennia. They grow in a relatively narrow band of the central Patagonian cordillera, on acidic soils by lakes and only in places where the annual rainfall exceeds 3000mm, so are more common on the wetter Chilean side of the Andes than in Argentina. Growth is extremely slow (0.8–1.2mm a year), and so it takes a century for the tree's girth to gain 1cm in diameter.

From the late nineteenth century onwards, the tree was almost totally logged out by pioneers: the reddish *alerce* timber is not eaten by insects and does not rot, so was highly valued for building and especially for roof shingles. Other uses included musical instruments, barrels, furniture, telegraph poles and boats. In Argentina, the only trees to survive the forester's axe were the most inaccessible ones, or those like El Abuelo, whose wood was rotten in parts. In Argentina, a few stands exist north of Los Alerces, in Parque Nacional Lago Puelo and the Lago Frías area of Nahuel Huapi, and the trees that remain are generally well protected.

camping and trekking. The must-see of the park, irrespective of time or budgetary concerns, is the transcendental **Río Arrayanes** that drains Lagos Menéndez and Verde. A **pasarela** or suspension bridge, 34km from the Intendencia, gives access to a delightful hour-long loop walk that takes you along the riverbank to Puerto Chucao. Another highlight – unless the weather really closes in and for those whose budget allows – is the trip from Puerto Chucao across Menéndez to see **El Abuelo**, a titanic millennial *alerce*. The savage Lago Rivadavia area is the least visited of those accessed by the park's principal road, the **RP71**, but it's less handy than Lago Verde or Villa Futalaufquen as a centre of operations.

The south of the park is a subsidiary destination. The **Futaleufú hydroelectric complex** here was a controversial project from the 1970s, designed to provide power for the aluminium smelting plant at Puerto Madryn on the coast. Ironically, submerged in the depths of the expansive reservoir are *Cuide Los Bosques* signs, telling you to look after the forests.

Arrival and information

Los Alerces is fast getting more popular as holidaymakers explore further afield from the often saturated Bariloche area. Ninety thousand people a year visit, most from late November to late March or Easter, and the park gets extremely busy in January and February. Campsites at this time of year can be overcrowded and noisy, and many don't provide foreign tourists with the kind of "national park experience" they're looking for. If possible, visit the park off-peak. **Autumn** months are perhaps the best, as the deciduous trees put on a blaze of colour; but spring is also very beautiful, if subject to some fierce winds. Year-round access is possible, although the main route through the park, the RP71, can, on rare occasions, be cut off by snow for a day or so. If you come in winter, remember that many places close outside the fishing season (mid-Nov to Easter), so you'll have to be more self-sufficient.

Entrance to the park costs $5, and you have three points of access. Most people come from Esquel via the **Portada Sur** (Southern Gate; 33km from Esquel and 12km before Villa Futalaufquen), which misleadingly serves the central sector of the park. This route is the most practical as it heads to the park headquarters and the useful information centre (see below). The RP71 continues unpaved through the northeast corner of the park and exits it beyond the **Portada Norte**, by the headwaters of Lago Rivadavia near to Cholila (see p.571). Arriving along this route from the north is the most scenic way of entering the park, but it's a long way (55km) to the information centre. The third gate, **Portada Futaleufú**, is in the southeastern corner of the park, 14km from Trevelin and 12km before the dam.

Those who don't have their own transport can get around the park with Transportes Esquel, which has a twice-daily service along the RP71 in summer. Plans to pave the RP71 from the Futalaufquen lakehead to Rivadavia have been thwarted up to now by budgetary and environmental concerns: walk this road in summer and you'll get coated in dust from passing vehicles.

As with all Patagonian parks, there's a high risk of **fire** in summer, the dangers of which are exacerbated in windy weather. Only camp in designated sites, do not light campfires unless places are provided (*fogones*), and please be especially careful with cigarettes.

Set on manicured lawns alongside the bus stop in **VILLA FUTALAUFQUEN** is the Intendencia (☎02945/471020; open daily 8am–2pm); the **visitors' centre** here (daily: Easter–Nov 9am–1pm; Dec–Easter 8am–9pm) is staffed by volunteers who give information on hikes and fishing, and sell fishing permits. They'll give you a useful map marking all the myriad campsites and lodgings in the park, and up-to-date per person prices. There are a good range of services in the village – including a fuel station, post office and general stores – but it's much cheaper to pick up everything you need in Esquel. *El Abuelo Monje* on Calle Los Retamos (☎02945/471029; closed Easter to mid-Nov) serves the best **meals** in town, and is especially recommended for its filling $8 portion of roast lamb (*cordero*). Alternatively, try *El Lugar del Lago* on Calle Corcoren, a tearoom that serves trout meals for two ($18) and sells home-made bread, jam and cheese.

Accommodation

In season, you have a wide choice of **accommodation in the park**, especially along Lago Futalaufquen's eastern shore. Out of the fishing season, most establishments close. Those who don't want to camp must splash out heavily in private **hotels** or rent out a **cabin**, though these are geared towards groups of fishermen or whole families. Reserve in advance, especially in high season. Just over 4km north of the Intendencia, 400m beyond Puerto Limonao, is the *Hostería Futalaufquen* (☎02945/471008, fax 471009; ⑧; closed Easter–Sept), a solid, granite-block and log lodge designed by Bustillo. It's in an attractive setting by the lake, but the atmosphere is spoilt somewhat by the "ambient" piped music; the restaurant has a limited choice and is overpriced ($25 menu).

On the eastern shore of Futalaufquen from the Intendencia is *Hostería Quimei Quipan* (☎02945/454134; $140 cabin for six people), and unpretentious *Los Tepúes*, which has cabins holding up to seven people (☎02945/453622; ⑧), though it's set back from the lake shore. You can camp here, too – there are hot showers and a shop on site ($2.50 per person plus $1 per tent). Further on is *Pucón Pai*, at Km 10, which has camping with full facilities as well as accommodation in rather regimented, barrack-style buildings (☎02945/451425; ④); the *Tejas Negras* tearoom, which rents cabins all year (☎02945/471046; $160 for five); and *Hostería Cume Hue* (☎02945/453639; ⑦ full board), which is popular with fishermen. Just north of the park on the road to Cholila, *Cabañas Carrileufú* in Villa Lago Rivadavia is a much less expensive option, with cabins for up to six people ($70).

Los Maitenes (☎02945/451003; $3 per person plus $4 one-off tent charge; closed Easter to mid-Nov) is the closest **campsite** to Villa Futalaufquen (400m from the Intendencia) and is generally good, although packed. On the other side of the road before the Río Desaguadero is *Rahue-Calel*, a quieter place, but one that doesn't front the lake ($2 per person plus $1 for shower). As for free sites, avoid *Las Lechuzas* and head for lakeside *Las Rocas* (about 2km from the Intendencia), which is cleaner, quieter and smaller, though more exposed. About 14km from the Intendencia is *Bahía Rosales* – with a shop and hot water ($6 per person); it rents bikes, Canadian canoes and horses ($11 per hour) and is the starting point of the boat trip to Lago Kruger. It also has a cabin with kitchen facilities that holds up to six people (☎02945/471044; ④, $133 for six). At Km 21 is *Punta Matos*, a small free site with excellent views and fine swimming, while *Playa El Francés* is also free and has a good beach. There are several sites in the Lago Verde region, but the cheaper ones can get very crowded. A two-day maximum stay applies in *camping libre Río Arrayanes*, 2km before the *pasarela* footbridge. Just north of the *pasarela* are popular paying sites (one *agreste* and one *organizado*) at Lago Verde. Lago Rivadavia has organized and free sites at both northern and southern ends. *Bahía Solís* ($2 per person) is recommended and has fine fishing. Lago Kruger has a *refugio* and a campsite for trekkers and those arriving by boat (see below). See under Trevelin (p.576) for campsites in the south of the park.

El Abuelo

The most popular excursion in the park takes you to the far end of Lago Menéndez's northern channel to see **El Abuelo** ("The Grandfather", also named *El Alerzal*), a gigantic *alerce* 2.2m in diameter, and 57m tall. This magnificent tree is an estimated 2600 years old, making it more venerable than four of the five most important religions in the world (only Hinduism is older). It was already a sapling when Pythagoras and Confucius taught, but a mere hundred years ago it almost became roof shingles: only the fact that settlers deemed its wood to be rotten inside saved it from the saw. The **boat trip** to El Abuelo departs from Puerto Chucao, halfway round the Lago Verde/Río Arrayanes trail loop that starts at the *pasarela*, 34km from the Intendencia. You should count on thirty minutes to walk from the road, and you won't want to rush it. The morning boat (9am) is $10 cheaper than the afternoon one (1pm; $35) and, even better, it's usually less crowded. The excursion is guided, but in Spanish only: if you want an English translation, you'll need to organize a tour from Esquel rather than just turn up at the pier. Either way, you should book in advance – boats are generally full in peak season and go only when demand is sufficient in low season.

On the ninety-minute trip across the pristine blue waters of **Lago Menéndez** you get fine views of the Cerro Torrecillas glacier, which is receding fast and may last only another seventy years. To get to El Abuelo a three-kilometre trail takes you through dense Valdivian temperate rainforest (*selva Valdiviana*), a habitat distinguished from the surrounding Patagonian forests by the presence of different layers to the canopy, in addition to the growth of lianas, epiphytes, surface roots and species more commonly found in Chile. Here a mass of vegetation is engaged in the eternal struggle of the jungle: height equals light. In addition to the *alerces*, you'll see fuchsia bushes and myrtles (*arrayán*), with trunks like rough-chiselled cinnamon sticks that are cold to the touch. The introduced mink is the culprit for the fact that enchanting, aquamarine **Lago Cisne** has none of the birds it was named after – the black-necked swan (cisne de cuello negro).

Trekking in the park

There are 130km of public trails in the park, which are generally well-maintained and marked at intervals with red spots. For several you are required you to **register** with the nearest *guardaparque* before setting off (remember to check back in afterwards), and some – such as El Dedal – are not recommended in winter or for those under ten years old. In times of drought, some trails are closed, whilst others (El Dedal is one) must be undertaken only with a guide. Take plenty of water, sun protection, and adequate clothing as the weather changes rapidly and unseasonal snowfalls occur in the higher regions. Insect repellent is worthwhile, especially after several consecutive hot days in December and January, as that's when the fierce horseflies (*tábanos*) come out.

The **Sendero Autoguiado**, or Self-Guided Trail, with signs in Spanish about the native flora, is less than 200m long, and starts at the small white church on the road to Puerto Limonao. As for the pastoral five-hundred-metre **Pinturas Rupestres** circuit, the most difficult part is the spring-loaded gate at the beginning. You pass partially obliterated indigenous geometric designs painted about 3000 years ago on a hulk of grey rock that's surrounded by *caña colihue* and *maitén* trees. The lookout from the top of the rock affords a fine view. Longer walks include the **Cinco Saltos**, **El Cocinero** and **Cerro Alto El Petiso** in the north of the park, which is best accessed from Lago Verder and provides sterling views of the northern lakes. Another recommended trip is to the *refugio* and campsite at the southern end of **Lago Kruger**. This can be reached in a fairly stiff day's trekking, returning the same way or by launch the next day. However, it's better to make it into a three- or four-day excursion. You can break the outward-bound trek by putting up a tent by the beautiful beach at Playa Blanca (about 8hr from the Intendencia), but you must have previously obtained permission from the visitor's centre. Fires are strictly prohibited and there are no facilities.

The **El Dedal Circuit** is one of the most popular and convenient hikes in the park. It involves some fairly stiff climbs but is not particularly technical, and you'll be rewarded with some excellent panoramic views. Do it with a day-pack by basing yourself near Villa Futalaufquen or ask the visitor's centre to look after your rucksack. Calculate on taking some six to seven hours (4hr up and 2–3hr down). Register at the visitor's centre, and you're required to be back before 7pm. Take the "Sendero Cascada" (which runs up behind the visitor's centre) for approximately 35 minutes through thick *maitén* and *caña colihue*, then take the signposted right-hand branch where the path forks. Further up you enter impressive mature woodland. Approximately two to two and a half hours into the walk, you climb above the tree line into an area of open, flattened scrub on the hilltop. From here you have a panoramic view of the scarified, rust-coloured **Las Monjitas** range opposite. If it's *tábano* season, though, you'll want to keep moving rather than enjoy the view. Climb up to the ridge and follow this northwest towards the craggy El Dedal massif above you. Up here you'll see delicate celeste and grey-blue *perezia* flowers, and possibly even condors. Do not follow the crest too far up though: look out for a short right-hand traverse after some 300m. The path then levels off for 100m. Below you is gorgeous **Lago Futalaufquen**, whose turquoise body is fringed, in places, by a frill of Caribbean-blue shallows. Bear left across a slight scoop of a valley, and you'll come to the lip of an impressive, oxide-coloured glaciated cwm. From here, follow the thirty-degree slope down into the bowl. Normally, a stream at the bottom flows with good drinking water (the first you'll find in the two-and-a-half hours since leaving the Sendero Cascada). The path up the other side of the cwm is difficult to make out: choose the pale, broad band of scree and make the tiring scramble up the top of the ridge, which overlooks the *Hostería Futalaufquen* and Puerto Limonao. From the ridge, a poor path leads up left to the summit of **Cerro Alto El Dedal** (1916m), about forty minutes away; if weather conditions are not good, it's best avoided. Descending from the ridge, it's about ninety minutes to the road by the port's Prefectura and then another half hour back to the Intendencia.

travel details

Buses

Aluminé to: Junín de los Andes (1 daily; 3hr); Villa Pehuenia (1 daily; 1hr); Zapala (1 daily; 2hr 30min via Rahué, 4hrs 30min via Villa Pehuenia).

Andacollo to: Chos Malal (2 daily; 1hr 30min–2hr); Las Ovejas (2 daily; 1hr).

Bariloche to: El Bolsón (14 daily; 2hr); Buenos Aires (7 daily; 23hr); Córdoba (2 daily; 22hr); Esquel (1; 4hr 30min); Epuyén (5 weekly; 3hr); Junín de los Andes (1 daily; 4hr); Lago Puelo (3 daily; 2hr 20min); Mendoza (daily; 18hr 45min); Neuquén (12 daily; 5hr 30min–6hr); Puerto Madryn (daily; 14hr); Salta (2 daily; 39hr); San Martín de los Andes (2 daily; 6hr); Santa Rosa (3 daily; 15hr); Trelew (1 daily; 13–16hr); Villa La Angostura (3 daily in summer; 1hr); Villa Traful (4 weekly; 1hr 45min–2hr 30min).

El Bolsón to: Bariloche (14 daily; 2hr); Esquel (6 daily); Lago Puelo (5–10 daily; 30min).

Caviahue to: Copahue (1 daily in high season; 45min); Las Lajas (3 daily; 1hr 45min–2hr 15min); Neuquén (2 daily; 5–6hr); Zapala (2 daily; 3hr–3hr 15min).

Cholila to: El Bolsón (daily; 1hr 40min–2hr); Esquel (3 daily or 5 weekly depending on season; 2hr 30min–3hr 45min); Lago Puelo (2 weekly–daily; 2hr 45min).

Chos Malal to: Andacollo (2 daily; 1hr 30min–2hr); Las Ovejas (2 daily; 3hr); Neuquén (5 daily; 6hr); Zapala (5 daily; 3hr).

Copahue to: Caviahue (1 daily in high season; 45min).

Esquel to: Bariloche (1 daily; 4hr 30min); El Bolsón (6 daily; 2hr 30min); Cholila (3 daily or 5 weekly depending on season; 2hr 30min–3hr 45min); Trevelin (every 1–2hr; 30min).

Junín de los Andes to: Aluminé (1 daily; 3hr); Buenos Aires (3 daily; 20hr); San Martín de los Andes (6 daily; 1hr); Zapala (4 daily; 3hr)..

Las Lajas to: Caviahue (3 daily; 1hr 45min–2hr 15min); Chos Malal (2hr; 2hr)

Lago Puelo to: El Bolsón (5 daily; 30min); Cholila (2 weekly; 2hr 45min).

El Maitén to: El Bolsón (daily; 1hr); Esquel (4 weekly).

Moquehue to: Neuquén (3 weekly; 5hr 30min); Villa Pehuenia (5 weekly; 40min).

Neuquén to: Bariloche (12 daily; 5hr 30min–6hr0); Buenos Aires (14 daily; 15hr–16hr 30min); Caviahue (2 daily; 5hr–6hr); Chos Malal (5 daily; 6hr); Córdoba (2 daily; 18hr 30min); Mendoza (6 daily; 12hr–12hr 30min); Moquehue (1 daily; 5hr 30min); San Juan (2 daily; 12hr–12hr 30min); San Martín de los Andes (1 daily; 6hr); Villa Pehuenia (2 weekly; 5hr); Zapala (hourly; 2hr 30min–3hr).

Las Ovejas to: Andacollo (2 daily; 1hr).

San Martín de los Andes to: Bariloche (2 daily; 6hr); Junín de los Andes (6 daily; 1hr); Villa La Angostura (1 daily; 2hr 30min).

Trevelin to: Esquel (every 1–2hr; 30min).

Villa La Angostura to: Bariloche (3 daily in summer; 1hr); San Martín de los Andes (1 daily; 2hr 30min).

Villa Pehuenia to: Aluminé (1 daily; 1hr); Moquehue (5 weekly; 50min); Neuquén (3 weekly; 5hr); Zapala (4 weekly; 2hr 15min).

Villa Traful to: Bariloche (4 weekly; 1hr 45min–2hr 30min).

Zapala to: Aluminé (1 daily; 2hr 30min via Rahué, 4hr 30min via Villa Pehuenia); Buenos Aires (2 daily; 17–18hr); Caviahue (3 daily; 3hr 30min); Chos Malal (5 daily; 3hr); Copahue (3 daily, mid-Dec to Feb only; 4hr); Cutral Có (hourly; 1hr); Junín de los Andes (4 daily; 3hr); Moquehue (2 weekly; 2hr 45min); Neuquén (hourly; 2hr 30min–3hr); Plaza Huincul (hourly; 1hr); San Martín de los Andes (6 daily; 4hr); Villa Pehuenia (4 weekly; 2hr 15min).

International buses

Bariloche to: Osorno (3 daily; 4–5hr); Puerto Montt (3 daily; 7–8hr).

Trains

Bariloche to: Viedma (Tues & Fri 5pm; 16hr).

Esquel to: El Maitén (Thurs 11am; 6hr 15min).

El Maitén to: Esquel (Wed 2pm; 6hr 15min).

Flights

Bariloche to: Buenos Aires (3 daily; 2hr); Córdoba (1 daily; 2hr); Esquel (1 weekly; 30min); Mendoza (1 daily; 1hr 30min); Trelew (2 weekly; 1hr 15min).

Neuquén to: Buenos Aires (4–8 daily; 1hr 35min); Puerto Madryn (Fri 1.50pm; 4hr 30min); Río Gallegos (1 daily; 7–8hr); Trelew (1 weekly; 5hr); Ushuaia (1 daily; 7hr 30min–8hr 30min).

CHAPTER NINE

PATAGONIA

land of adventures and adventurers, of myths and fabulous reality – the only thing that parallels Patagonia's geographical immensity is the size of its reputation. As a region of contrasts and extremes it has few equals in the world: from the biting winds that howl off the **Hielo Continental Sur** (Southern Patagonian Icecap) to the comforting hearthside warmth of old-time Patagonian hospitality; from the lowest point on the South American continent, the **Gran Bajo de San Julián**, to the savage peaks of the **Fitz Roy massif** or **San Lorenzo**; from the sterile desert plains of the coastline to the astoundingly rich marine breeding grounds which abut them, among which the **Península Valdés** is the crowned king.

The term "Patagonia" was formerly used to refer to all lands on both sides of the Andes that lay to the south of the southernmost white settlement. On the Argentinian side this once signified, in effect, any land south of Buenos Aires, though as the whites gained control of increasing amounts of indigenous territory, so Patagonia's frontiers were pushed ever southwards. By the nineteenth century, the concept of Patagonia had begun to take on a more fixed location, one which is usually defined today as all lands to the south of Argentina's **Río Colorado** and Chile's **Río Bio Bio**. This chapter deals with all of Argentinian Patagonia, with the exception of Tierra del Fuego (see Chapter 000) and the northwestern Lake District (see Chapter Eight), and also includes a section on the deep south of mainland Chilean Patagonia.

The region's principal artery, the **RN3**, runs south from the historic town of **Carmen de Patagones** right across Patagonia to **Río Gallegos** and the border with Chile, providing access to the narrow fringe of Atlantic coastline plus the vast central steppe. This desiccated area, covered by tough *coirón* grassland and scrub, is grey and dusty for most of the year, except for brief periods when spring rains bring forth green shoots and isolated carpets of yellow flowers. The few poplar and willow trees that exist shelter sheep-farming estancias or cling to the banks of the rare rivers that run eastwards from the Andes. From these plains rise spectacular, eroded mesetas, punctuated by areas of genuine desert.

South of Carmen de Patagones, the principal highlight of Chubut Province is the fabulous wildlife reserve of **Península Valdés**, where rare marine mammals breed in their thousands between July and April. Nearby is the resort town of **Puerto Madryn** and, just to the south, the **valley of the Río Chubut**, where you can explore the cultural legacy of

---

ACCOMMODATION PRICE CODES

The price codes used for accommodation throughout this chapter refer to the cheapest rate for a double room in high season. Single travellers will only occasionally pay half the double-room rate; nearer two thirds is the norm and some places will expect you to pay the full rate. Note that in resort towns, there are considerable discounts out of season.

① $20 or less	④ $45–60	⑦ $100–150
② $20–30	⑤ $60–80	⑧ $150–200
③ $30–45	⑥ $80–100	⑨ Over $200

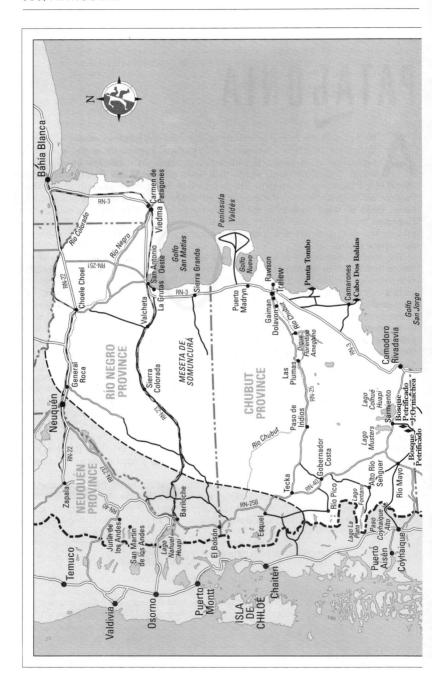

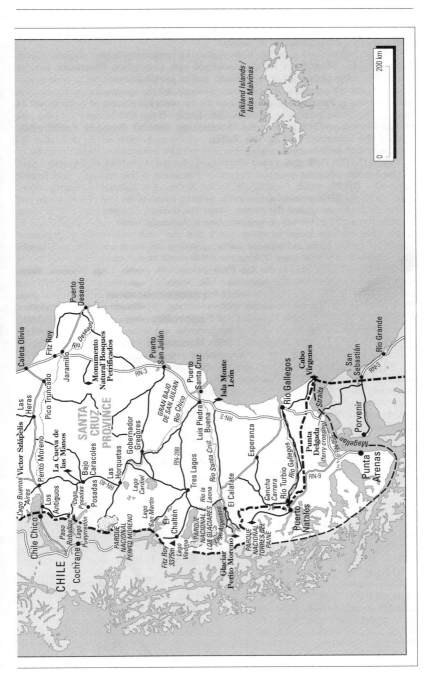

the Welsh pioneers in the villages of **Gaiman** and **Dolavon**, and at the town of **Trelew**, Welsh by name if less obviously by nature.

South of Trelew, up to a million birds nest at the continent's largest penguin colony, **Punta Tombo**. West of the region's industrial hub, **Comodoro Rivadavia**, lies the peaceful farming community of **Sarmiento**, and its petrified forests, set in eerie moonscapes. South of Comodoro, in Santa Cruz Province, are the spectacular porphyry cliffs of the estuary at **Puerto Deseado**, famous for its colourful colonies of seabirds and its playful Commerson's dolphins, while another detour off the RN3 brings you to the 150-million-year-old petrified trees of the **Monumento Natural Bosques Petrificados**. Passing the unhurried port of **San Julián** you come to sites where dedicated fly-fishermen with daily budgets ranging from $10 to $1000 come from around the globe, in particular the **Río Gallegos**, a river which meets the sea at the town of the same name.

The second principal artery of Argentine Patagonia is the famous – and largely unpaved – **RN40**, which runs parallel to the Andes, at a distance of roughly 90km. Detours off the RN40 provide access to the western fringe of the vast desert steppe and to the area right up against the Andes, where the scenery changes abruptly: in many spots here you'll find forests of southern beech. Although some places are difficult to reach, this western fringe is where you'll find the most impressive of Argentine Patagonia's great lakes and national parks, as well as the finest spit-roast lamb *asados* and some uniquely wild skies. Taking the RN40 south from Esquel brings you to the first-rate trout-fishing lakes in the **Río Pico** area and the mighty **Lago Buenos Aires**, with its useful border crossing point into Chile. South of Lago Buenos Aires you'll find the canyon of Río Pinturas, home to one of Argentina's most famous archeological sites, the **Cueva de las Manos Pintadas**, with its striking, 10,000-year-old rock art; west of here are the beautiful **Lagos Posadas** and **Pueyrredón**, lying in a largely unexplored area which contains the stately peak of San Lorenzo. Just to the south of here stretches the wilderness of **Parque Nacional Perito Moreno**, one of the most inaccessible of Argentina's national parks, with the aquamarine gem of Lago Belgrano and excellent trekking possibilities. Beyond here are two of the region's star attractions: the trekkers' and climbers' paradise of the **Fitz Roy** sector of the **Parque Nacional Los Glaciares**, accessed from El Chaltén; and the craggy blue face of the **Perito Moreno glacier**, regularly cited as one of the world's natural wonders, situated near the town of El Calafate. Between these two sites lie two gigantic lakes fed by the Southern Patagonian Icecap – **Lago Viedma** and **Lago Argentino**.

Finally, we cover the deep south of Chilean Patagonia around the area of Punta Arenas and Puerto Natales, including the spectacular **Torres del Paine** national park. In these southernmost latitudes, the lands are not quite as parched, and even the odd tongue of woodland begins to stretch away from the mountains.

The area's tourist infrastructure has expanded considerably over the last ten years, but it is still primitive in many areas: if planning to visit the lesser-known sites you'll need reserves of patience and flexibility, both in terms of time and style of travel. Barring a few exceptions, such as Carmen de Patagones, the region's **towns** are not tourist destinations in themselves. Set out on a uniform grid pattern, they are generally uninspiring, low-key places with little overriding architectural style, few sights, and little in the way of distinct character. Most are useful only as transport hubs or bases for tours in the surrounding area.

High season runs from December to the end of February, and it's important to book accommodation and other services in advance during this period. November is a pleasant month to visit, although the winds that scour Patagonia are at their most unremitting. The period from March to Easter can be one of the most rewarding in which to travel: most tourist services are still open, but you'll avoid the crowds, while the Patagonian forests along the Andean spine assume their autumnal colours and the winds are less incessant. **Close season** runs from Easter to around the end of October.

At this time, temperatures can plummet to –25°C, and many mountain roads become impassable. Public transport becomes extremely infrequent and there's very little tourist traffic, with the exception of those who visit Península Valdés to see the breeding of the southern right whales and sea elephants.

Though cheaper than in the early 1990s, Patagonia is still renowned for its **high prices**. For those with a healthy wad of pesos, the range of **accommodation** available reaches international standards of luxury in a few places, though for those on a tight budget there's little option but to hitch, camp and cut out the luxuries. Reasonably priced dormitory accommodation is available in the more popular spots, but elsewhere cheap options can be hard to find, particularly for singles.

Despite the distances involved, **driving** is relatively cheap, as fuel in the provinces of Chubut and Santa Cruz is subsidized by fifty percent. Be aware of the need for caution on the region's many gravel roads, however (see p.622). Visitors who have limited time, or who are less interested in getting an impression of the vast scale of the place, should try to make use of **domestic flights** to avoid some rather gruelling bus journeys. Airports at Trelew, El Calafate, Río Gallegos and Comodoro Rivadavia all have regular connections to the capital.

Some history

For over ten thousand years Patagonia was exclusively the domain of nomadic **indigenous tribes**, before the arrival in the sixteenth century of seafarers from Spain and rival European powers – Magellan and Drake both visited (and survived mutinies in) the bay of **San Julián**. The tales related by these early mariners awed and frightened their countrymen back home, mutating into myths of a godless region of giants where death came easy.

Two centuries of sporadic attempts to colonize the inhospitable coastlands only partially ameliorated Patagonia's unwholesome aura. In 1779, at a place some 1200 kilometres from Buenos Aires, the Spanish established **Carmen de Patagones**, which managed to survive as a trading centre on the Patagonian frontier. However, other early settlements all failed miserably: **Puerto de los Leones**, near Camarones, lasted a few months in 1535; **Nombre de Jesús**, by the Magellan Straits, struggled for a handful of desperate years in the late 1580s; **Floridablanca**, near San Julián, was abandoned after four years in 1784; and **San José** on the Península Valdés was crushed by a Tehuelche attack in 1810, after braving it out for twenty years. Change was afoot, nevertheless. In 1848, Chile founded Punta Arenas on the Magellan Straits, and in 1865, fired by their visionary faith in a benevolent Lord, a group of **Welsh Nonconformists** arrived in the Chubut valley. Rescued from starvation in the early years by Tehuelche tribespeople and Argentine government subsidies, they had managed to establish a stable agricultural colony by the mid-1870s.

In the late nineteenth century, Patagonian history entered a new stage with the introduction of **sheep**, originally brought across from the Falkland Islands/Islas Malvinas. The region's image shifted from one of hostility and hardship to that of an exciting frontier, where the "white gold" of wool opened the path to fabulous fortunes for pioneer investors. The transformation was complete within a generation: the plains were fenced in, roads were pushed from the coast to the cordillera, and the native Tehuelche found themselves driven from their ancestral hunting grounds onto marginalized lands that were unfit even for the hardy sheep that grazed the steppe in their millions. The populations of the northern hemisphere were clothed by Patagonian wool and fed by Patagonian mutton. Later, the region's confidence blossomed further with the discovery of oil, spurring the growth of industry in towns such as **Comodoro Rivadavia**.

Yet the boom caused by these two boons has collapsed in the last few decades. Jobs are being shed at an alarming rate in the oil industry, and hundreds of estancias, struggling to cope with a less and less viable market for wool and meat, closed or went bankrupt in the 1990s. The explosion of Volcano Hudson in Chile in 1991, which deposited ash over thousands of square kilometres of Santa Cruz Province and killed over a million head of livestock, was the final blow for many estancias. Swathes of land soon lay deserted, devoid even of sheep, and few were prepared to risk losing money in an area which seemed as uninviting to long-term investors as it had to the early Spanish settlers. Fortunately, there are signs that the worst of the crisis is over. The discovery of a major deposit of **gold** at Cerro Vanguardia near San Julián epitomizes this upturn, while a new-found confidence in the region's vast potential for **tourism** is spreading rapidly.

THE ATLANTIC SEABOARD AND THE WELSH HEARTLAND

A hostile, cliff-lined coast, countless hundreds of kilometres long, backed by an expanse of seemingly endless desolation – for at least three centuries after Magellan's voyage, this is what the word "Patagonia" conjured up in the imagination of the Western world. You may prefer to cover such vast distances by air, but if you're committed to discovering what Patagonia is really about, steel yourself for the overland crossing and arm yourself with a thick book – though preferably not one by the Argentinian novelist Roberto Arlt, who in 1934 said of Patagonia: "This landscape really winds me up. I'm already starting to regard it as a personal enemy. It's like a tiresome old windbag who keeps on saying the same thing."

Nowadays, you can drive all the way from the Río Negro to Río Gallegos in around 36 hours, though a more realistic estimate – depending on how much you like thorn-scrub steppe and desert – is to spend four or five days making the trip. This allows time to see the world-famous wildlife reserve at **Península Valdés**, usually accessed from the seaside town of **Puerto Madryn**; to investigate Patagonia's vaunted Welsh legacy in the towns and villages of the Chubut valley near **Trelew**; and to break the journey south with a stopover in beautiful **Puerto Deseado** or convenient **San Julián**, each with their own significant populations of marine wildlife and rich historical associations. If you have your own transport you might be able to fit in a side-trip to the petrified forests of the **Monumento Natural Bosques Petrificados** or those near **Sarmiento**, or (depending on the season) the penguin colony at **Punta Tombo**. The historic town of **Carmen de Patagones** is also worth a brief stop.

The Patagonian plains

The RN3 from Bahía Blanca reaches the north bank of the Río Negro at **Carmen de Patagones**, which for almost a century after its founding in 1779 acted as the gateway to Argentinian Patagonia. Crossing the river here you leave Buenos Aires Province and come to Carmen's uninspiring sister town, **Viedma**, the capital of Río Negro Province. At these latitudes, the Patagonian climate is still hot in summer (often well above 30°C), and you'll find ornamental palms and orange trees growing in these towns – somewhat unexpectedly, as the surrounding area away from the river comprises dry, wheat-growing plains. **South of the Río Negro**, the landscape becomes increasingly barren – there's little of interest to the tourist here, and most people travel the 425km to Puerto Madryn without stopping. If you want to break the journey, aim for the seaside resort of **Las Grutas** near San Antonio Oeste or make a detour from uninteresting Sierra Grande to the **Meseta de Somuncurá**, a bizarre landscape that is one of Argentina's oldest geological formations.

Heading **northwest from Carmen de Patagones,** following the course of the Río Negro, a fast, paved road takes you 550km to Neuquén. This route passes through irrigated farmland that provides a livelihood for towns such as Choele Choel, General Roca and Cipolletti. It's an area that's important from a regional and national perspective in terms of fruit production, though there's not much to see for the casual visitor.

Carmen de Patagones and Viedma

CARMEN DE PATAGONES is a slow-paced town with a small historical centre, attractively sited on a small hill on the northern bank of the **Río Negro**. Patagones was the symbolic gateway to Patagonia from its founding in 1779 to at least the Campaign of the Desert a hundred years later, and you can spend a pleasant couple of hours exploring this legacy. Across the water is the town's dull sister, **VIEDMA**. People living in Patagones say that the best thing about flat Viedma is the view of it from Patagones' main **Plaza 7 de Marzo**, and you certainly won't miss much if this is as close as you get. In the 1980s, President Alfonsín's government declared that Viedma was to be the future federal capital of Argentina instead of Buenos Aires. Needless to say, the plan bombed.

Founded by Francisco de Viedma, Patagones was the second of the strategic settlements created to fortify the Patagonian coast from the incursions of English and Portuguese pirates, and the only one to survive in the long term. The first families came direct from Spain, many from the Maragatería region of León in Old Castile, and inhabitants of the town are known to this day as *Maragatos*. Their first houses were **caves** excavated in the cliff face. Patagones' finest hour came on March 7, 1827, during the fledgling Argentine Republic's war with Brazil over the Banda Oriental (present-day Uruguay), when a force of local militiamen outwitted a far superior force of Brazilian troops who tried to storm the town in reprisal for raids on Brazilian ships. The two vast standards they captured can be seen in the Neoclassical **Iglesia Parroquial Nuestra Señora de Carmen** (8am–noon & 3–8pm) on the Plaza 7 de Marzo. Built between 1880 and 1885 and named after the settlement's protector Virgin, this twin-towered edifice was the first Salesian church in Patagonia and replaced the earlier fort church. Of the original fort, only the stone watchtower, the **Torre del Fuerte**, survives, now dwarfed by the neighbouring church. Dating back to 1780, it's Patagonia's oldest building. Patagones also has a well-presented and informative **Museo Histórico**, opposite the ferry to Viedma, at J.J. Viedma 64 (Mon–Fri 10am–noon & 2.30–4.30pm, Sun 5–7pm; free).

Practicalities

The **airport** for Patagones and Viedma lies 8km southeast of Viedma (no bus; $9 by taxi). Patagones' **bus terminal** is on Calle Barbieri, less than ten minutes' walk from the centre of town: turn left out of the terminal, walk three blocks northwest to Calle Bynon and turn left. This takes you past the Plaza 7 de Marzo and then downhill a couple of blocks through the old part of town to the pier from where the passenger **ferry** to Viedma departs (7am–10pm every 10min). The **tourist office**, on the main square at Bynon 186 (March–Nov 7am–8pm; Dec–Feb 7am–9pm; ☎02920/462053), has clear town maps.

Accommodation can be found in the straightforward *Hotel Pergaz*, Comodoro Rivadavia 348 y Irigoyen (☎02920/464104; ③); or, failing that, in the *Residencial Reggiani*, Bynon 420 (☎1560-8619; ②), which has fairly dark rooms. If these don't appeal, cross over to Viedma (take the half-hourly "La Comarca" bus from the terminal, or it's $3.50 by taxi), where two of the best options are the clean and well-kept *Residencial Río Mar*, Rivadavia y Santa Rosa (☎02920/424188; ②); and the *Hotel Austral*, by the ferry pier at 25 de Mayo y Villarino (☎02920/422615, fax 422619; ⑤), with good views across the river to Patagones.

Viedma to Puerto Madryn

The RN3 heads west from Viedma through level pasture that eventually gives way to the uniform, waist-high scrub so emblematic of Patagonia. This is where the Patagonian plains really begin, just as, on the coast, the region's characteristic cliffs start south of the mouth of the Río Negro. The RN3 hits the coast again near San Antonio Oeste, a fishing port on the Bahía San Antonio, in the far northeast corner of the Golfo San Matias. Some 18km southwest of here is **LAS GRUTAS**, one of Patagonia's main **beach resorts** due to the unusually warm and sheltered waters of its suntrap bay, and worth a quick detour if you have your own transport. The resort's glaringly white, Mediterranean-style houses and overpriced hotels are strung out along the arid coastal cliff, beneath which there's a swathe of fine sand – the cliffs themselves are riddled with tidal **caves** and make an ideal nesting site for noisy, burrowing parrots (*loro barranquero*). Avoid Las Grutas in high season (especially mid-Jan to mid-Feb),

THE TEHUELCHE

The name Tehuelche, meaning "Brave People", is derived from the language of the Chilean Araucanian groups. The Tehuelche actually consisted of three different tribal groups – the Gününa'küna, Mecharnúek'enk and Aónik'enk – each of whom spoke a different language but shared common bonds of culture and a similar way of life. Great inter-tribal parliaments were held on occasion to discuss trade or common threats to the community, but any alliances formed would be temporary and shifting, and sporadic warfare occurred between different tribes.

The Tehuelche's nomadic culture – centred on the hunting of the guanaco and the rhea – that Magellan and the first Europeans came into contact with had probably existed for well over three thousand years, but it was not static, and contact with Europeans soon brought change. By 1580, Sarmiento de Gamboa reported the use of the horse by indigenous Patagones around the Magellan Straits, and by the early eighteenth century it had become integral to Tehuelche life both for hunting and carrying. Intertribal contact and intermarriage thus became more regular, and hunting techniques evolved, with *boleadoras* and lances increasingly preferred to the older bow and arrow. The *boleadora* consisted of two or three stones wrapped in guanaco hide and connected by long thongs made from the sinews of rheas or guanacos. Whirled around the head, these were thrown to ensnare animals for dispatching at close quarters. *Boleadoras* are the only real physical legacy of Tehuelche culture in today's Argentina, and are still used on occasion by rural workers.

Women's life centred around their guanaco-skin shelters called *toldos* (or *kau*) – women were responsible for taking down the *toldo* and reassembling it whenever the group shifted camp – and around gathering firewood, cooking, preparing skins, sewing cloaks and caring for young children. Although women's workloads were definitely onerous, few observers spoke of men mistreating their womenfolk. The Victorian adventurer, George Musters (who in 1869–70 became the first white person to ride with them as a free man), reported that "The finest trait . . . is their love for their wives and children; matrimonial disputes are rare, and wife-beating unknown; and the intense grief with which the loss of a wife is mourned is certainly not 'civilized', for the widower will destroy all his stock and burn all his possessions." There was definitely an egalitarian streak in Tehuelche society: leadership was meritocratic, and there were no strict hierarchies. Caciques led groups of families, but territorial overlords in the manner of the Mapuche did not exist.

Tehuelche religious belief recognized a benign supreme God (variously named Kooch, Maipé, or Táarken-Kets), but he did not figure greatly in any outward devotions and was always rather distant in normal life. In contrast, the malign spirit, Gualicho, was

when it's overcrowded and prices skyrocket; out of season it's much more tranquil. The region is also famous for its excellent migratory marine **birdlife**.

From the San Antonio Oeste turn-off, the RN3 takes you 125km south to the ragged town of **SIERRA GRANDE**, a good starting point from which to reach one of the most isolated places in all Argentina, the **Meseta de Somuncurá**. A treeless expanse punctuated by bald, weirdly shaped mountains, this vast highland plateau makes even the surrounding Patagonian steppe seem overcrowded. Even if you have a good 4WD, it's not easy to explore yourself – tracks on the meseta are poor and it's better to take an organized tour, such as the long day-trip run by Turismo Güennaken, Calle 20 no. 461 (☎ & fax 02934/481149; Dec to early March only; $60) – you'll need to reserve one day in advance, and there's a four-passenger minimum. Budget **accommodation** in Sierra Grande can be found at the *Hotel La Terminal*, Güemes 230 (☎02934/481250; ①) – it's a bit gloomy, but the owners are very helpful and friendly. The more upmarket *Hostería Sierra Grande*, Calle 102 no. 381 (☎ & fax 02934/481016; ③) is well maintained and has central heating.

---

a much-feared figure who was the regular beneficiary of horse sacrifices and the object of shamanistic attentions. The idea of a Gualicho is the only spiritual legacy of the Tehuelche to have survived into the present, being recognized today not just in Argentina, but also in parts of Bolivia, Brazil, Paraguay and Uruguay. The greatest of the Tehuelche divine heroes was Elal, the being who created man, gave him fire, established the sacred relationships that exist both between the sexes and between man and beasts – he featured prominently in the rich seam of Tehuelche legends.

The decline of Tehuelche civilization came fast. In 1839, the French scientist Alcides d'Orbigny estimated that there were up to ten thousand indigenous people of all groups in Patagonia; Musters, in 1870, put the figure for the Tehuelche at 1500; while a 1931 census in the province of Santa Cruz (which had the greatest population of Tehuelche) recorded only 350. As with other indigenous tribes in the south, the causes for the destruction of this civilization are complex and interrelated. Wars with the *huincas* (white men) were catastrophic – above all the Campaigns of the Desert in the years following 1879 – and were exacerbated by intertribal conflicts between Tehuelche groups themselves and with the Araucanians. Contact with *huinca* civilization, even when conducted on a peaceful basis through trade, led to severe problems: diseases such as measles, smallpox and tuberculosis wiped out whole tribal groups, while exposure to a market economy destroyed the delicate environmental balance that had existed for millennia. Alcohol played a particularly destructive role, and the aura of fear and mystery that had once insulated the Tehuelche against *huinca* incursions was replaced by contempt as alcohol abuse led whites to replace one misconception (that of the "noble savage") with another (the "moral delinquent"). The pressure to settle ancestral Tehuelche lands, motivated by the huge profits to be gained from sheep farming, thus gained a spurious moral justification as part of a greater plan to "civilize the *indio*".

The remaining Tehuelche were pushed into increasingly marginal lands. Guanaco populations, which once numbered in the millions, crashed, and Tehuelche life, culturally dislocated and increasingly derided, became one of dependency. Many found the closest substitute to the old way of life was to join the estancias that had displaced them as *peón* shepherds. In this way, they were absorbed into the rural underclass that consisted mainly of poorer immigrants.

Whereas Mapuche customs and language have managed, tenuously, to survive into the twenty-first century, Tehuelche populations were much more fragmented geographically, and fell below that imprecise, critical number that is necessary for the survival of a cultural heritage. The last speaker of *Gününa'küna* died in 1960, and with him the pronunciation of the tongue, while the Aónik'enk tongue can be spoken, at least partially, by some half a dozen people, though it's extremely rare that two of these people actually meet, and most refuse point blank to speak it when they do, at least with whites present.

Puerto Madryn

Spread out along the beautiful sweep of the Golfo Nuevo bay, the neat town of **PUER-TO MADRYN** is promoted as a Patagonian **summer resort**, centred along a fun beachfront boulevard, though its real pull is as a base for trips to the ecological treasure trove of the Península Valdés – as such, it makes a pleasant place to stay for a couple of nights.

Arrival and information

The nearest **airport** is just north of Trelew, 60km to the south. If you're flying with LAPA or Aerolíneas Argentinas you can arrange for a $10 transfer (pay at the travel agencies Trelew Aereo or Argentina Vision respectively). The hourly Mar y Valle bus runs between here and the bus terminal; or you can take a *remise* taxi, though it will set you back around $45.

Madryn's **bus terminal** is located in one of the town's most attractive buildings, the old train station of 1889. From here, you can walk straight down Calle Roque Sáenz Peña for four blocks to reach the seafront. Turn right and the first-rate **tourist office** is a block and a half away, at Avenida Julio Roca 223 (Jan & Feb daily 7am–1am; March–Dec Mon–Fri 7am–2pm & 3–9pm, Sat & Sun 8.30am–8.30pm; ☎ & fax 02965/453504 or 452148). The helpful staff have good maps and leaflets in English, a list of houses for rent, and will help in emergencies if you can't find anywhere to stay. They also have a list of independent guides who speak foreign languages, and will furnish timetables for the **tides** in the area (useful if heading to Punta Norte in Valdés). Upstairs, you can watch **videos** on Valdés and scuba diving (some in Spanish only). Most of what you'll need in town is located within three blocks in any direction from the tourist office. Be careful not to confuse Calle 28 de Julio by the plaza with its near neighbour to the south, Calle 9 de Julio.

This region has interesting **diving** possibilities, with offshore wrecks and wildlife. Trips can be organized through the recommended Scuba Duba, at Boulevard Brown 893 (☎02965/452699); Patagonia Buceo, Balneario Rayentray (☎02965/452278); or numerous other outfits – expect to pay $45–60 per excursion. **Windsurfing** boards can be rented at Balneario Na Praia, Boulevard Brown and Perlotti ($10 per hour), while **sandboarding** on nearby dunes can be organized through Pablo at Hi Adrenaline, Humphreys 85 (☎02965/471475; board rental $10 per day). Pablo also rents **mountain bikes**, as does the *Backpackers* hostel at 25 de Mayo 1136 ($5 per hour or $15 per day; bring ID).

Accommodation

Madryn has a wide range of **accommodation** options, including a couple of good budget possibilities, especially out of season (from March to when the whales arrive in June), when most hotels offer substantial discounts. The nearest **campsites** are by the El Indio statue, round the bay (*colectivo* #2 from the terminal or the main square will take you to within easy walking distance); and the *Municipal Atlántico Sud*, 3.5km down Boulevard Brown (☎02965/455640; $3 per person) also has some hostel beds ($6 per person) and rents mountain bikes ($12 per day). *Automóvil Club*, 4km down Boulevard Brown (☎02965/452952; $16 for four people; closed Easter–Sept), is expensive unless you arrive with a carload.

Hotel Aguas Mansas, José Hernández 51 (☎ & fax 02965/473103, *aguasmansa@cpsarg.com*). Warm, pricey three-star near the beach, with comfortable rooms and a swimming pool. Singles are particularly expensive; $2 in *remise* from bus terminal. ⑥.

PUERTO MADRYN

▽ *Trelew (65km) & Península Valdés (100km)*

ACCOMMODATION

Aguas Mansas	2
Backpackers	5
Bahía Nueva	3
Centro	6
Gran Palace	10
Hipocampo	1
Huefur	7
Patagonia	4
Residencial Jos	13
Residencial Santa Rita	11
Tandil	12
Tolosa	9
Los Tulipanes	8

Albergue Huefur, B. Mitre 798 (☎02965/453224). Relaxed and recommended hostel, with free pick-up, plus laundry and cooking facilities. $7.50 per person.

Backpackers, 25 de Mayo 1136 (☎ & fax 02965/474426). YHA-affiliated hostel with two spacious four-bed rooms. It offers free pick-up from the terminal and has kitchen and laundry facilities, plus a pleasant garden. YHA members $10 (non-members $12).

Hotel Bahía Nueva, Roca 67 (☎ & fax 02965/451677 or 450045). A smart, modern hotel on the seafront with ample buffet breakfasts and covered parking. ⑥.

Hotel del Centro, 28 de Julio 149 (☎02965/473742). Budget hotel that's good value for its location (close to beach and plaza), though bathrooms are small and mattresses thin. It also has a quiet central patio. En-suite rooms cost fifty percent more. ②.

Hotel Gran Palace, 28 de Julio 400 (☎02965/471009, fax 452044). Two blocks from the bus terminal with plain, reasonable-value rooms, free parking and polite staff. ③.

Hosteria Hipocampo, Vesta 33 (☎ & fax 02965/473605). A decent mid-range option opposite the seafront, but quite a way from the centre. No single rates. ④.

Patagonia Hotel, Albarracín 45 (☎ & fax 02965/452103, *hotelpat@arnet.com.ar*). Apartments with basic kitchenette for two to five people. It's in need of an overhaul, but is friendly, central and has some great low-season offers. Free parking. ⑤.

Residencial Jos, Bolivar 75 (☎02965/471433). Cosy little guesthouse with good prices for singles, run by a charming couple. ③.

Residencial Santa Rita, Gob. Maiz 370 (☎ & fax 02965/471050). Hospitable guesthouse set in a well-tended garden, with comfortable, cheap rooms. Also offers Internet access ($8 per hour). ③.

Hotel Tandil, Juan B. Justo 762 (☎ & fax 02965/456152). No architectural wonder, but clean and friendly with triples and quadruples. Upstairs rooms have more spacious bathrooms. Basic breakfast included, and free, locked parking. ④.

Los Tulipanes Apart Hotel, Lewis Jones 150 (☎ & fax 02965/471840, *los-tulipanes@los-tulipanes.com.ar*). The best-value upper mid-range accommodation in town, with tasteful and luxurious self-catering apartments for two to four people, ideal for families. Also has Internet access ($5 per hour), a swimming pool and fine breakfasts. ⑥.

Hotel Tolosa, Roque Sáenz Peña 253, (☎02965/471850, fax 451141). A comfortable if uninspiring mid-range hotel. It has several rooms with handicapped facilities, but all at the more expensive end of the range. Free parking. ⑤.

The Town

Puerto Madryn was the site where the Welsh first landed in Patagonia in 1865, but it didn't develop until the arrival of the railway from Trelew in 1889, when it began to act as the port for the agricultural communities in the Chubut valley. Madryn has experienced very rapid growth since the 1970s, and now rates as one of the most important of Chubut's towns, with a population of 60,000. The **Golfo Nuevo** is best seen at the opposite ends of the day. Early in the morning, it can be as still and glassy smooth as a lake, while at sunset there's a glorious view of the wide arc of the gulf back to the lights of town from the **statue of El Indio** – placed here to mark the centenary of the arrival of the Welsh, and in homage to the native Tehuelche whose assistance ensured that the settlers survived. Just before it, a signpost points to **Punta Cuevas**, where lie the three-metre-square foundations of the very first houses built by the Welsh, just above the high-water mark.

Two blocks back from the tourist office is the well-kept and sunny central **Plaza San Martín**, with its mature eucalyptus trees, while to the north of town at D. Garcia and Menéndez is the **Museo Oceanográfico** in the elegant, turreted Chalet Pujol (Easter–Sept Tues–Fri 9am–noon & 4.30–8.30pm, Sat & Sun 3–7pm; Oct–Easter Tues–Sun 9am–noon & 4.30–8.30pm; $2). Here you can feel a whale's baleen and view photos of sea lion massacres and relics from Welsh pioneering days, including a Bard's Throne from the 1920 Eisteddfod. Climb the turret for good views over the bay.

THE WELSH IN PATAGONIA

In July 1865, 153 Welsh men, women and children who had fled Britain to escape cultural and religious oppression disembarked from their boat, the *Mimosa*, and took the first steps into what they believed was to be their Promised Land. Here they planned to emulate the Old Testament example of bringing forth gardens from the wilderness, but though the land around the Golfo Nuevo had the appearance of Israel, its parched harshness cannot have been of much comfort to those who had left the green valleys of Wales and just spent two deprived months on board ship. The omens were far from auspicious: on the very first day, a young man who had gone to climb a nearby hill to take a look around disappeared, never to be seen again.

The wheat they planted failed to prosper, and a lack of fresh water forced them to look further afield. Fired by Robert FitzRoy's descriptions of the valley of the Chubut river, they explored south and, a few months later, managed to relocate – a piecemeal process during which some groups had, in the words of one of the leading settlers, Abraham Matthews, to live off "what they could hunt, foxes and birds of prey, creatures not permitted under Mosaic Law, but acceptable in the circumstances, and legal, no doubt for He whose mercy is as infinite as his holiness".

The learning curve was proving steeper than any had imagined. Doubts and insecurities spread, with some settlers petitioning the British to rescue them and others seeking governmental permission to relocate in a more favourable area of the country. When all avenues of credit seemed closed, vital assistance came from the Argentinian

patch and colour variations; 23 have been tracked off Punta Norte using these distinguishing marks. One sad fact for those brought up on aquarium shows: the orca's lifespan in the wild is eighty to ninety years for a female, forty to fifty for a male; those Free Willies in captivity can expect a lifespan of closer to six. If you want to know more, contact Proyecto Orca (☎ & fax 02965/454723, *orcas@satlink.com*), a scientific organization based in Madryn dedicated to furthering study of this creature.

Sea lions were once so numerous on the peninsula that 20,000 would to be culled annually for their skins and blubber – a figure that equals the entire population found here today, despite almost thirty years of protection. They are the most widely distributed of the Patagonian marine mammals and their anthropomorphic antics make them a delight to watch. It's easy to see the derivation of the name when you look at a 300-kilogram adult male, ennobled by a fine yellowy-brown mane.

As beasts go, few come into the league of the southern **elephant seal** (*elefante marino*), a creature so large that Noah made him swim for it. Valdés is their only continental breeding ground and, as such, the only place you're ever likely to see them in the all-too-evident flesh. Weighing some three tonnes and measuring four to five metres, bull sea elephants mean business. Though the average size of harem that a dominant male can aspire to is between ten and fifteen females, some superstud tyrants get greedy. One macho male at Caleta Valdés amassed 131 consorts – apart from the tiring business of spreading his genes, he would have had to fight off love rivals too. October is the best month to see these noisy clashes of the titans, but be prepared for some gore, as tusk wounds are inevitable. Adult females, a fifth of the size of the vast males, are pregnant for eleven months of the year, giving birth to their pups from about mid-September. These "pups" weigh forty kilograms at birth, but then balloon on the rich milk of their mothers to weigh two hundred kilograms after only three weeks.

The elephant seal's most remarkable attribute, however, is as the world's champion deep-sea diving mammal. Depths of over a thousand metres are not uncommon, and it is reckoned that some of these animals have reached depths of 1500m, staying submerged for a breathtaking two hours.

the manuscripts left by pioneers and seek inspiration from what they pronounce to be the purity of the language that was preserved in Patagonia.

Trelew

TRELEW is second only to Comodoro Rivadavia as an industrial and commercial centre in the province of Chubut, though it's a more attractive place, with fewer high-rises and less heavy industry. It's also the self-proclaimed "Capital of the Penguin" – not because it has any of these birds (it isn't even on the sea), but due to its relative proximity to the famous penguin colony at Punta Tombo (see p.608).

Arrival, information and accommodation

Trelew's **airport** (which also serves Puerto Madryn) is situated 5km northeast from the town. There's a Banelco cash machine and a simple **tourist office** counter that opens for flight arrivals and dishes out maps of the town. *Remise* taxis cost $8 to Trelew (for details of getting to Puerto Madryn, see p.594). You'll find branches of all the major car rental agencies. Airport departure tax is $4. The **bus terminal** is within easy walking distance of the town centre. Mar y Valle buses head to Madryn via the airport every hour; 28 de Julio buses depart for Gaiman and Dolavon every half hour. and for Rawson every fifteen minutes. Trelew lies roughly equidistant between Buenos Aires and Río Gallegos (1430km and 1200km respectively), with buses either way costing about $50. The terminal has a café upstairs that does a reasonable *tenedor libre* but is otherwise fairly expensive. There's also a **tourist booth** (Mon–Fri 10am–1pm & 6–9pm, Sat

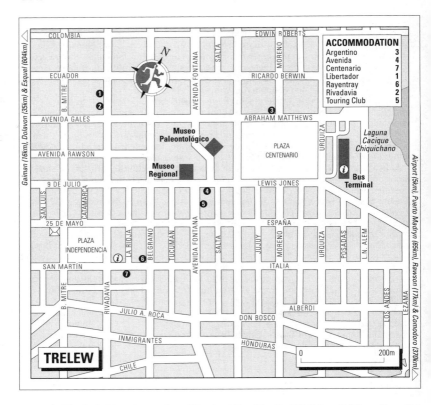

TRELEW

6–9pm). The helpful main **tourist office** is at San Martín 171 (Mon–Fri 8am–8pm, Sat 10am–1pm & 6–8pm; ☎ & fax 02965/420139).

Most **hotels** are open 24 hours, but phone in advance if arriving late. The hotels above the budget category usually offer a ten to twenty percent discount for cash payment.

Residencial Argentino, Moreno 93 (☎02965/436134). A basic hotel, but very close to the terminal. ②.

Hotel Avenida, Lewis Jones 49 (☎02965/434172). The least expensive lodging in town, and good for single budget travellers. Friendly and well situated but spartan; with shared bathrooms. ②.

Hotel Centenario, San Martín 150 (☎ & fax 02965/426111 or 420542). A fairly standard hotel with comfortable rooms. ⑥.

Hotel Libertador, Rivadavia 31 (☎ & fax 02965/420220 or 426126). None too stylish for a four-star, and with an overpowering smell of cleaner fluid, but warm rooms and friendly, efficient staff. Beds have well-sprung mattresses, and there's a bathtub in most rooms. ⑤

Hotel Rayentray, San Martín 101 (☎02965/434702, fax 435559). Very 1970s in style, but upper rooms have bathtubs and good city views. Also equipped with swimming pool, gym and sauna. ⑦.

Residencial Rivadavia, Rivadavia 55 (☎02965/434472, fax 423491). Clean, centrally heated rooms, with $50 quadruples. ② with shared bathroom; more expensive upstairs.

Hotel Touring Club, Fontana 240 (☎ & fax 02965/425790 or 433997). Take yourself back to the 1920s in this faded Art Deco historic monument. Rooms are centrally heated and comfortable, though they don't live up to the promise of the facade. Make full use of a bar as long as a football pitch and stocked with a terrifying array of dusty bottles of dodgy spirits. ③.

The Town

Trelew's name, in Welsh, means the "Village of Lewis", in honour of Lewis Jones, its founder. The settlement rose to prominence after the completion, in 1889, of the rail link to Puerto Madryn, which allowed easy export of the burgeoning agricultural yields. The railway has since disappeared, and the old station, on 9 de Julio and Fontana, is now used to house the **Museo Regional** (Mon–Fri: March–Nov 7am–1pm & 2–8pm; Dec–Feb 7am–1pm & 3–9pm; $2). One of two fine museums in Trelew, it contains some illuminating exhibits on the coexistence of the Welsh and the Tehuelche; a vast bellows for the local ironworks; some gruesome photos of the sea lion hunt at Punta Norte on the Península Valdés; and items on the Eisteddfod festivals. Across the road is the excellent modern **Museo Paleontológico Egidio Feruglio**, Fontana and Lewis Jones (Mon–Fri 8.30am–12.30pm & 1.30–8.30pm, Sat & Sun 1.30–8pm; $4), one of South America's most important paleontological collections, which claims to describe "300 million years of history" and contains rarities like beautifully preserved clutches of dinosaur eggs and skeletons from the region.

Trelew's urban centrepiece is its beautiful main square, the **Plaza de la Independencia**, with flourishing trees and an elegant gazebo, built by the Welsh to honour the centenary of Argentinian Independence. In the second half of October, the most important of the province's **eisteddfods** is celebrated, when two prestigious awards are made: the *Sillón del Bardo* (The Bard's Chair), for the best poetry in Welsh, and the *Corona del Bardo* (The Bard's Crown), for the best in Spanish.

Eating and drinking

Standard restaurant opening hours are from noon till 3pm and 8pm till midnight.

Comedor Universitario Luis Yllana, opposite the Eg3 fuel station on Rivadavia. Filling fare at student prices. Open 10am–8pm.

El Dragon, Belgrano 255. A greasy budget paradise; Chinese *tenedor libre* for $4.

Rancho Aparte, Fontana 236. An excellent *tenedor libre* of grill and salads, costing $6 at lunch and $8 in the evening. It has a large screen for football matches. Open till 1am; closed Mon & Sun lunchtime.

Touring Club, Fontana 240. Confitería and bar with touches of grandeur. Open 6am–2am.

Los Tres Chinos, San Martín 188. Another cheap *tenedor libre*, and better value than *El Dragon* in terms of quality.

TRIPS FROM TRELEW

The tourist office in Trelew has a good leaflet on the various Welsh chapels of the Chubut valley, and can fix up you up with an English-speaking guide ($90 per day). In season, Sur Turismo, Belgrano 330 (☎02965/434081 or 434550) arranges day tours of the **Welsh villages** ($15), the **penguin colony** at Punta Tombo (Sept–March; $30 plus $5 entrance), and Península Valdés (June–Dec; $40 plus $5 entrance), though you're better off organizing a tour to Valdés from Madryn. Other agencies such as Nievemar, at Italia 20 (☎02965/464114), offer similar services. Your alternative, especially useful for touring the Welsh villages, is to take a **taxi** with someone like the recommended Carlos Stigliani (☎02965/435352; approximately $110 to Tombo; $50 to the villages). Make sure you arrange an itinerary and agree on waiting times before setting out. One other trip for nature lovers is to **Playa Unión**, 6km past the dull provincial capital of Rawson, where you can take a boat trip to see the beautiful **Commerson's dolphins** (*toninas*; see p.616) in one of their northernmost haunts. "Capitán Tonina" (alias David Peralta) runs ninety-minute boat excursions from the pier at the **port** (☎02965/484799; $20; mid-March to mid-Jan). To get to Playa Unión, take the bus to Rawson's main plaza (every 15min), where you can catch a Transportes Bahía bus (every 15–30min) for the port.

El Viejo Molino, Avenida Gales 250. Renovated mill hosting concerts and cultural events, and a civilized place to enjoy a coffee, a Welsh tea ($9), or a few evening drinks.

Vittorio, Belgrano 351. A smart, formal café-bar serving long drinks ($5) and snacks. Open 7am–3am.

Listings

Airlines Aerolíneas Argentinas, 25 de Mayo 33 (☎02965/434549); LADE, Fontana 227 (☎02965/434944); LAPA, 9 de Julio and Belgrano (☎02965/423449); Kaikén, San Martín 146 (☎02965/421438).

Banks and exchange Lloyds, Belgrano and 9 de Julio. Bank hours are Mon–Fri 8.30am–1.30pm. Trelew is a poor place to change travellers' cheques: try Sur Turismo, Belgrano 330.

Car rental Avis, Paraguay 105 (☎02965/434634); Localiza, San Martín 88 (☎02965/435344); Rent a Car, San Martín 125 (☎02965/420898).

Post office 25 de Mayo and Bartolomé Mitre.

Supermarket Casa Tía, Rivadavia and 9 de Julio, five minutes' walk from the bus terminal.

Taxis Outside bus terminal or call ☎02965/435763, 435552 or 420404.

Telephone Julio A. Roca and Tucumán.

Gaiman and the Chubut Valley

The **Río Chubut** derives its name from the Tehuelche word *chupat*, meaning clean or transparent. The Welsh began irrigating the valley in 1867, and it was dammed a hundred years later to ensure a more predictable flow to the agricultural farm plots, whilst also generating electricity for industrial development. To the west of Trelew, the valley is broad, and flanked by low, brown, rounded hills.

Leaving Trelew, the RN25 strikes west for 16km, before coming to the most frequently visited of the Welsh villages, **GAIMAN**, lying amongst poplars trees in the irrigated centre of the valley and full of *casas de té* and other memorials to its Celtic heritage. Though you could be forgiven for missing the fact, the village doesn't rely totally on tourism, being a commuter suburb for Trelew, as well as having a productive market-gardening base and some light industry (including a seaweed-processing factory). Gaiman hosts mini **eisteddfods** in mid-September and the first week of May.

You can spend a pleasant hour or two wandering round the village's monuments: the attractive brick **Bethel Chapel** from 1914, next to its late nineteenth-century predecessor; the squat stone **Primera Casa** (First House), dating from 1874, and looking as if it had been transplanted from Snowdonia; the appealing little plaza with its early bust commemorating Christopher Columbus; the old railway station that now houses the **Museo Histórico Regional** (Tues–Sun 3–8pm; $1), with exhibits relating to pioneer life; and you can even walk through the abandoned three-hundred-metre long **railway tunnel** near the tourist office.

Gaiman's most individual and surprising monument has nothing whatever to do with tradition, Welsh or otherwise. **El Desafío** ("The Challenge"; daily 10–6pm; $5), on Almirante Brown, is a backyard where **tin cans** and plastic bottles have been recycled and reincarnated: "A place where rubbish is beauty, and perhaps even art." It's the work of a unique gentleman in his eighties, Joaquín R. Alonso. Floods periodically wreck his creations, but he enjoys the struggle with Mother Nature, and constantly remodels his patch. Recent constructions such as the tower he erected "in homage to myself" stand alongside wryly ironic mockeries of modern consumerist society: a pair of dinosaurs, the *Hot Rot Saurio* ("Vehicle which our parents used to use to go nowhere fast") and the *Motocicletas* ("Means of transport which normally leads to immobility, partial or total"). Leave your cynicism at the gate.

Eight kilometres to the south of the village is the **Parque Paleontológico Bryn Gwyn** (daily 4–8pm; $4), where there's a 1.5km circuit taking you past stratified fossil beds dating back some forty million years.

Practicalities

The 28 de Julio **bus** from Trelew stops outside the extremely helpful **tourist office** (April–July Mon–Sat 8am–3pm, Sun 3–7pm; Aug–March daily 8am–6pm; ☎02965/491152) in the Casa de Cultura on the corner of Rivadavia and Belgrano, one block up from the modest main street, Avenida Tello. They'll give you a useful **map** with a suggested walking tour, as well as other recommended circuits for those with more than a couple of hours to pass.

If you want **to stay** here, there are two decent choices. Firstly, the *Plas y Coed casa de té* on the main square (☎ & fax 02965/491133; ④ with huge breakfast) – the upstairs rooms with private bathroom are best, though nothing luxurious, and there's a spacious living-room for guests. Welsh, English and Afrikaans are spoken. Otherwise, try the *Hostería Gwesty Tywi*, at Miguel Jones 342 (☎ & fax 02965/491292, *gwestywi@infovia.com.ar*; ③, slightly more with private bathroom), an immaculately clean, flowery and perfumed bed and breakfast whose owners speak Welsh, English and Spanish. There's also an inexpensive **campsite**, *Los Doce Nogales*, across the river to the southeast, near the *Ty Té Caerdydd* teahouse.

The **casas de té** in Gaiman do a thriving trade – some of them are owned and run by descendants of the original Welsh settlers, and all serve similar arrays of cake, toast, scones and home-made jam ($10–12 per person). The most typical cake of all is the *torta negra* (Welsh black cake), which used to be given on weddings to be eaten on the first anniversary – the ones you'll come across on your plate should be a lot fresher. *Ty Nain*, H. Irigoyen 283 (closed May and June), is one of the most authentic, and bang in the centre, next to the plaza. Take your tea, surrounded by the mementoes of the owners' museum. *Plas y Coed*, Miguel D. Jones 123, was the first of the *casas de té* and is right on the square. Nearby is *Ty Cymraeg*, at Abraham Matthews 74, where a descendant of the pioneers serves teas in the original family home overlooking the river. For those who don't want to visit one of the *casas de té*, there's an excellent bakery, La Colonia, on Belgrano and Tello, and a rather pricey but good-quality **restaurant**, *El Angel*, at Miguel Jones 850.

Dolavon and the route west to Esquel

DOLAVON, 19km west of Gaiman, is the most authentically Welsh of all the villages and that which best preserves the character of an early pioneering settlement. It's a pleasant place to spend an hour wandering around amongst the original, whitened brick buildings and sense times gone by, enjoying the fact that there's not a teashop in sight. The **bus** from Trelew stops at the midget terminal, near the disused railway station, next to which is a charming stream, lined by weeping willows and curious irrigation waterwheels. In terms of specific sights there's little to see apart from the **Molino Harinero** at Calle Maipú 61 (Old Flour Mill; open afternoons and weekends; $1), where you'll be guided around by English-speaking student volunteers. Amazingly, the machinery is all original, and is still in working order. The only **accommodation** is a roadside motel by the YPF fuel station on the main road ($10 per person); there's also a free municipal **campsite** on the northern edge of the village.

Beyond Dolavon, the road traverses flat military-green thornscrub, punctuated by sandstone outcrops. The Chubut valley's impressive dam, the **Dique Florentino Ameghino**, lies 12km off the RN25 along a road that's paved till near the end, when it enters a series of tunnels hewn through the solid rock. The reservoir here makes a good picnic stop, and you can also swim, fish and admire the rugged red cliffs. Beneath the dam wall lies a pleasant little hamlet on the green, tree-covered floor of the valley, which contains a good **campsite** (☎02965/490329; $3 per person) and places **to stay**. Basic lodging can be found at *El Lago* (☎02965/436268 or 490314; ②), which also serves massive three-course *menús* with all-you-can-eat lamb *asados* for $12 per person. On Sundays, an El Ñandú bus makes a day-trip from Trelew, leaving at 9am and returning in the afternoon.

West of the turn-off to the dam, the road passes the soaring cliffs of some dramatic **rocky outcrops** and follows the course of the **Valle de los Mártires**, where John Evans's famous horse, Malacara, leapt down a precipitous bank, and thus saved his master from the grisly fate that had befallen Evans's companions at the hands of a band of pursuing Tehuelche (see p.592). At Tecka, the route joins the RN40, which heads 90km north from here to Esquel (see p.573).

South of Trelew

From Trelew it's around 360km south along paved road to Comodoro Rivadavia. En route, it's worth making two side-trips to the coastal nature reserves of **Punta Tombo** and **Cabo Dos Bahías**. Alternatively, the first reserve, 107km south of Trelew down the unpaved but well-maintained RP1, makes an easy day's excursion.

Punta Tombo

Punta Tombo is the largest single colony of penguins on the continent, with a population of more than a million birds. These black and white **Magellanic penguins** look less glamorous than their larger cousins, the king and emperor penguins – the yellow-throated birds that have so successfully cornered the brand image (very occasionally, a larger king penguin turns up accidentally at Tombo, far from its normal habitat in Antarctic waters). Nevertheless, it's an unmissable experience to wander around this scrubland avian metropolis amid an urban cacophony of braying, surrounded on all sides by waddling clowns as they totter about their business, unafraid of human visitors. The penguins nest behind the beach in scrapes underneath the bushes, eyeing you as you approach. Get too close and they'll indicate their displeasure by hissing or bobbing their heads from side to side like a dashboard dog – respect these warning signals and remember that a penguin can inflict quite a bite with its sharp bill.

Entrance to the reserve costs $5, and any time between August and early April is a good time to visit, although **November** is probably the best month of all, as there are plenty of young chicks. Check with the tourist office in Trelew if you are arriving in late

---

THE MAGELLANIC PENGUIN

The word "penguin", some maintain, derives from Welsh *pen gwyn* ("white head"), a name allegedly bestowed by a Welsh sailor passing these shores with Cavendish in the sixteenth century. In fact, a white head is not what you first associate with a Magellanic penguin, and it's far more likely that the name comes from the archaic Spanish for fat, *pingüe*. The birds were a gift to the early mariners, being the nearest equivalent of the day to a TV dinner.

Though they're slouches on land, in water these birds can keep up a steady 8km an hour, or several times that over short bursts. An adult bird stands 50–60cm tall and weighs a plump 5kg. Birds begin arriving at their ancestral Patagonian nesting sites from late August and, by early October, nesting is in full swing, with most females laying a brace of eggs. Parents share the task of incubation, as they do the feeding of the brood once the eggs start to hatch, in early November. By early January, chicks that have not been preyed upon by seabirds, skunks, foxes and armadillos make their first sorties into the water, and learn how to survive the depredations of sea lions. During the twenty-day February moult, the birds do not swim, as they lose their protective layer of waterproof insulation. At this time, penguin sites are awash with fuzzy down and sneezing birds. In March and April they begin to vacate the nesting sites. Although little is known of their habits while at sea, scientists do know that the birds migrate north, reaching as far as the coast off Rio de Janeiro, 3000km away. So much for the bird's polar profile.

March or April, as the reserve closes about then, and remember that there are no services, so tank up before you leave town. The countryside around the reserve is an excellent place to see **terrestrial wildlife**, such as guanacos, rheas, skunks, armadillos and, in particular, maras (the Patagonian hare).

Cabo Dos Bahías

The coastal reserve of **Cabo Dos Bahías** (entrance $5) has the only continental colony of the rare **fur seal** (an animal once hunted to the verge of extinction for its thick pelt), a healthy population of Magellanic penguins, and other marine wildlife. It also harbours plenty of steppe species, such as maras (Patagonian hare), ñandúes, and some surprisingly tame herds of guanacos. Situated 32km south of the tiny fishing port of Camarones, which lies 72km off the RN3, down the paved RP30, it can be reached by private car or on a long, 500-kilometre day-trip from Trelew.

Near Camarones is the spot chosen in 1535 by Simón de Alcazaba y Sotomayor for **Puerto de los Leones**, the base from which he planned to establish his governorship of the southern lands. Deaths from scurvy and a revolt put paid to the expedition, and Sotomayor was left buried in his domain. **Buses** reach as far as Camarones but leave from Trelew only (El Ñandú on Mon and Fri, 4pm, returns Mon 3pm & Fri 5.15pm; Robledo on Sat 4am, returns Fri 6pm). If you're coming from Comodoro, you'll need to hitch from the junction with the RP30.

Southern Chubut and northern Santa Cruz

Encompassing some pretty dreary towns and some of the most desolate scenery in the whole of the country, the region along this stretch of the RN3 does possess two natural gems: the **Río Deseado estuary** at **Puerto Deseado**, with its beautiful porphyry cliffs and tremendous opportunities to view photogenic wildlife at close quarters; and the tremendous trunks of fossilized araucaria monkey puzzles in the **Monumento Natural Bosques Petrificados**. In addition, the gentle agricultural town of **Sarmiento** inland has two different but equally interesting petrified forests nearby, the **Bosque Petrificado José Ormachea** and the **Bosque Petrificado Héctor Szlápelis**.

Comodoro Rivadavia

The largest of all Patagonian towns, with a population of 130,000, **COMODORO RIVADAVIA** is not a place you're likely to want to stay for longer than the time it takes to make your bus connection. Originally founded as a port to service the livestock industry, the town's fortunes were altered dramatically by the discovery of oil here in 1907, found accidentally whilst drilling for water. Recession has bitten deep in recent years, and hopes for an upturn now lie with the **Bioceanic Corridor**, 570km of upgraded road linking the town with the Pacific Ocean, at Puerto Aisén in Chile. This will be used to truck containers across the continent, thus obviating the need for slow ship passages around the Horn.

The centre of Comodoro, the **microcentro**, is sandwiched between the **San Jorge Gulf** and the bald, khaki-coloured ridge of **Cerro Chenque** (Tomb Hill), and virtually everything you need can be found in these few blocks. The best way of killing spare time is to visit the **Museo del Petróleo** (mid-March to mid-Dec Tues–Fri 8am–6pm, Sat & Sun 2–6pm; mid-Dec to mid-March Tues–Sun 8am–1pm & 6–9pm; $3.50) in the main northern suburb, Barrio Géneral Mosconi (take bus #6, #7 or #8 from the terminal). The ticket also gives free entrance to the **Museo Paleontológico** 20km north of town (Sat & Sun 2–6pm; Linea Astra from the terminal), but the collection here is not nearly as impressive as the one at Trelew. Otherwise, visit the resort town of **Rada Tilly**, 15km to the south, which has several kilometres of beach and is popular with the locals.

Practicalities

Comodoro has one of the region's busiest **airports** (☎0297/454-8355), 8km from the centre. *Colectivo* bus #8 connects it with the bus terminal, or it's $7 in a *remise* taxi; Austral, Kaikén and Aerolíneas airlines also operate a $3 transfer to and from hotels. The **bus terminal** is slap-bang in the centre. Leaving the terminal, walk one block towards Cerro Chenque to reach the main thoroughfare, Avenida Rivadavia, with the helpful **tourist office**, half a block away at no. 430 (daily: mid-March to mid–Dec 8am–5pm; mid-Dec to mid-March 8am–9pm; ☎0297/446-2376).

Comodoro is a good place to **rent cars** and 4WDs – try Dubrovnik (☎1559-23407) or Localiza (☎0297/446-0334, fax 447-3495), in the *Austral Hotel*. Unlimited mileage deals make good sense for day-trips to the petrified forests of Sarmiento (there are no car rental agencies in Sarmiento itself). The *Aónik'enk* travel agency, Rawson 1190 (☎0297/446-6768, fax 447-6349), runs excursions to Camarones, including a trip to see the fur seals at Cabo Dos Bahías, as well as trips to Monumento Natural Bosques Petrificados to the south (see p.614), and the José Ormachea petrified forest near Sarmiento (see p.611).

Restaurants include the cosy *Peperonni*, Rivadavia 619 (☎0297/446-9683), whose attentive staff serve a selection of interesting omelettes, and home-made pastas ($7–9); and a fun theme restaurant, *La Cueva de Butch Cassidy*, San Martín and España (☎0297/446-3725; open till late), which has an excellent $10 mixed grill *tenedor libre*, plus free live shows on Fridays and Saturdays after midnight, including tango. The *Lucania Palazzo* hotel restaurant serves an appetizing three-course menu for $16, as well as a fine dish of *merluza negra* (black hake; $14).

If stuck for budget **accommodation**, Calle Belgrano has a number of dives, catering more for locals than tourists; none is particularly welcoming. Ask for discounts with cash payment in the bigger establishments. The nearest **campsite**, *Amutui Mi Qui Mei Hue* (☎1562-42991; $2 per person plus $5 per tent) is 12km north on the RN3. The Línea Astra *colectivo* from the terminal leaves you at the gate.

Austral Hotel, Rivadavia 190 (☎0297/447-2200, fax 447-2444, *haustral@satlink.com*). The new part is slightly more expensive, but worth the extra price. ⑥.

Hotel Residencial Derby, San Martín 1046 (☎0297/446-2562). Fifteen minutes' walk from the terminal. A rudimentary budget option, but relatively friendly; rooms with (cramped) private bathrooms are more expensive, and they also have parking ($2–3). ③, or $8 per person if prepared to share.

Hospedaje 25 de Mayo, 25 de Mayo 989 (☎0297/447-2350). A clean, inexpensive guesthouse, close to the terminal, with a breezy courtyard area. Book in advance. ②.

Lucania Palazzo Hotel, Moreno 676 (☎ & fax 0297/446-0100, *reservas@lucania-palazzo.com*). Comodoro's smartest hotel: a competitively priced luxury four-star bang in the centre. It has vast suites with swimming-pool-sized jacuzzis, plus rooms for disabled guests. ⑦

Hostería Rua Marina, Belgrano 738 (☎0297/446-8777). A welcoming, good-value guesthouse, although some rooms don't have an outside window. ③.

Hotel Victoria, Belgrano 585 (☎0297/446-0725). A decent mid-range option close to the terminal, which has clean, if unstylish and fairly small, rooms, some with bathtub and sea view. It's open 24hr, and has covered parking ($5). ④.

Inland to Sarmiento

Heading inland from Comodoro, it's 150km along the paved RN26 (later becoming the RP20) to Sarmiento. The road cuts through hilly steppe country, covered in *duraznillo* bushes and the nodding heads of hundreds of oil wells, relentlessly probing the ground. The desiccated landscape changes as you approach Sarmiento, having been well irrigated by waters from the Río Senguer and the lakes it feeds, **Lago Colhué Huapi** and **Lago Musters**, the latter named after the famous English adventurer of the nineteenth century, Captain George Musters, who was the first white man to learn of its existence.

SARMIENTO itself is a farming community, originally founded by the Welsh, the Lithuanians and another famous immigrant group, the **Boers**, who fled here at the beginning of the twentieth century in an effort to escape the British after the Boer War. The town attracts relatively few tourists, despite the presence of the intriguing petrified forests of José Ormachea and Héctor Szlápelis nearby (see below), but it makes a very pleasant place to overnight, with a number of decently priced hotels and a good-natured, old-style ambience. The fine **Museo Regional Desiderio Torres** (April–Nov Mon–Fri 1.30–7pm; Dec–March Mon–Fri 9am–4pm, Sat & Sun 10am–noon; $1) has a sizeable collection of indigenous artefacts and dinosaur bones, plus displays of indigenous Mapuche and Tehuelche weavings. Over the second weekend in February, the inhabitants celebrate the three-day **Festival Provincial de Doma y Folklore**, with horse-taming and racing in the afternoon, and folk concerts in the evening at the Club Deportivo.

Practicalities

Sarmiento's main street – initially Avenida Regimiento de Infantería, later becoming Avenida San Martín – runs off the RP20 at right angles. ETAP **buses** stop outside their office on San Martín, whilst Don Otto buses pull into the ACA service station on the RP20, opposite the turn-off to the José Ormachea Petrified Forest. From here it's a two-kilometre walk into the centre, or take a taxi ($2). The helpful **tourist office** (April–Nov Mon–Fri 9am–1pm & 4–8pm, Sat & Sun 9am–1pm; Dec–March daily 8am–11pm; ☎0297/489-8220, fax 489-8268) is situated at the entrance to town at Regimiento de Infantería 25, just before the attractive stone water tower which marks the beginning of Avenida San Martín. They have a useful tourist map of the town centre and surrounding region. The Banco del Chubut, San Martín 756, buys and sells **Chilean pesos**.

For **accommodation**, *Hotel Ismar* at Patagonia 248 (☎0297/489-3293; knock at the back entrance if closed; ②, ③ with shower) is the best option: rooms are spotlessly clean and quiet, with comfortable beds, and it has good rates for singles too. *Los Lagos*, on Roca and Alberdi, has ground-floor rooms for up to four people (☎0297/489-3046, fax 489-3238; ③) and serves an all-day four-course menu in its restaurant for $10. Two basic cheapies for single travellers on a tight budget are the *Colón*, Perito Moreno 645 (☎0297/489-3057), an old-style hotel with shared bathrooms; and the musty but friendly *Residencial Sarmiento*, San Martín 899 (☎0297/489-3507; ②). **Campers** can pitch a tent for free behind the ACA service station (shower and toilet available), which isn't a bad option. Alternatively, there are several paying sites: the neighbouring *Club Deportivo*, by the main RP20, but screened off and well-sheltered by regimented poplars (☎0297/489-3103); or, 1.5km to the north of town, the riverside *Puente Traverso* (☎0297/489-3640 or 489-3630) and *La Isla* (☎0297/156-47975), which also has bungalows for four people ($20). *El Rancho Grande* is a good parrilla **restaurant** on the corner of Estrada and San Martín (closed Mon), with inexpensive house wine and side dishes.

Bosque Petrificado José Ormachea

Two kilometres from the centre of town, a clearly signposted dirt track off the RP20 leads 33km to the **José Ormachea Petrified Forest** (April–Sept 9am–6.30pm; Oct–March 8am–8pm; $5). Its warden, the jovial Señor Varela, offers information and helps with transport in his minibus ($18 return) – contact him by phone (☎0297/489-8407) or in person at Calle Uruguay 43 (early morning or late evening). El Valle *remise* taxi agency, Uruguay 378 (☎0297/489-8300), will run you out to the reserve for $30, with an hour's wait included.

This reserve has parallels with the Monumento Natural Bosques Petrificados in Santa Cruz Province (see p.614) in terms of the weird moonscape scenery, but its bands of "painted desert" soils are more striking. The **fossilized trunks** are by no means as gargantuan as those of the Santa Cruz site, but they are nevertheless fascinating for the manner in which they jut out from *barrancas* (ravines) and buttes of grey, sandy soil. Erosion processes are much more visible here. It's rather like walking around a sawmill, the ground covered by splinters of bark and rotten wood, except that these woodchips are approximately 65 million years old. Ownership of an area of the park is currently in litigation, and accompanied driving tours of it have therefore ceased, but you may be granted permission to go on foot to see the famous chunk of **hollow fossilized log**, about 15 minutes' walk from the main area. **Snacks** are served at the administration such as mouthwatering, home-produced chorizo sausages on homemade bread, or an excellent *asado de cordero* (groups only; try to order three days in advance; $14 per person). You're also allowed to **camp** here for free and use the bathroom facilities.

Bosque Petrificado Héctor Szlápelis

A similar but less accessible site, the **Héctor Szlápelis Petrified Forest**, lies further to the southwest. It's run in a typically old-style Patagonian way by a family with deep roots in the area. You can visit for free, but are asked to respect a few basic norms: seek permission first at the estancia; don't take "souvenirs"; and don't hunt. The bleak, impressively antediluvian scenery is reminiscent of the Badlands of Montana, studded with trunks projecting out of heavily eroded cliffs of ashy soil.

There are no facilities, so bring food and drink. Access is tricky and is only for those taking a tour or with their own transport – hitching can be very time-consuming. The forest is situated at the end of an eight-kilometre turn-off north from the old, unpaved section of the RN26, approximately 5km from the estancia, and signposted with a yellow sign. It's about 60km to the turn-off from the José Ormachea site: from the Ormachea administration, head back to the first T-junction, turn left for 3km, left again for another fifteen, and when you reach the RN26, head west for 24km. If coming from the west, take the RN26 from Río Mayo and continue for 30km after the junction with the RP18.

Caleta Olivia

CALETA OLIVIA, a coastal town of 40,000 inhabitants, makes an inauspicious introduction to the province of Santa Cruz. Never the most beautiful of towns, the place is made less attractive still by the sense of depression that's settled on it since the oil boom bottomed out in the 1990s, causing high levels of unemployment. It's all a far cry from the heady days of 1969, when the locals proudly raised **El Gorosito**, the thirteen-metre-high stucco statue of an oil worker that still dominates the town.

If you do find yourself having to **overnight** here, try not to get too confused by the mix-up of old and new street names. The *Granada* at San José Obrero 953 (☎0297/485-1512; ③) is the best of a poor lot in terms of less expensive lodgings, and is situated only two blocks from El Gorosito. More upmarket, but nothing special, is the three-star *Robert* (☎0297/485-1452, fax 485-2924; ⑤), right near El Gorosito, with two grades of rooms. The municipal **campsite**, a stony site on the Avenida Costanera by the beach, deems it prudent to offer 24-hour security, but is run by an amicable bunch.

Puerto Deseado

PUERTO DESEADO, a straggly but engaging fishing port on the estuary of the Río Deseado, is blessed with spectacular coastal scenery and some remarkable colonies of marine wildlife that thrive within sight of the town (see below). The town owes its name to the English privateer Thomas Cavendish, who baptized it **Port Desire**, in honour of his ship, when he put into here in 1586. At least one English expedition had less success here, and a sunken caravel from 1770, the *Swift*, was discovered in the port in 1982. Present-day Deseado has an easy-going atmosphere, a couple of unassuming but attractive squares, and a fine, porphyry-coloured former **railway station**, opposite the Salesian college. The **Museo Padre José Beauvoir** (Mon–Fri 9am–noon & 3–6pm, Sat & Sun 3–6pm; free, but you're asked to make a donation) in the Colegio Salesiano contains thousands of indigenous artefacts, but they are poorly displayed and the collection has been impoverished by numerous thefts. The **Museo Regional Mario Brozosky** by the seafront (Mon–Fri 10am–5pm; free) displays items brought up from the storm victim, the caravel *Swift*.

Practicalities

A bus service connects the town with Caleta Olivia, but Deseado's **bus terminal** is inconveniently sited at the far end of town. Try to disembark in the centre or, if leaving town, flag down the bus as it passes along Avenida España. The **tourist office** is at San Martín 1120 (Dec–Easter 9am–9pm; Easter–Nov 9am–4pm; ☎0297/487-2261, fax 487-2248, *turimo@pdeseado.com.ar*). The staff will give you a useful town plan. **Internet** access is available at CCI, San Martín 1131.

The cheapest **accommodation** is the clean *Albergue Municipal* (☎0297/487-0260; ②, or $8 per person in twelve-bed dorms), in the *gimnasio* on Colón and Belgrano, near the Museo Regional. The second of two *Residencial Sur* guesthouses, at Pueyrredón 367 (☎ & fax 0297/487-0522; ③), is friendly, with spruce if spartan rooms, and serves value-for-money four-course meals with wine for $15. *Residencial Los Olmos*, Gob. Gregores 849 (☎ & fax 0297/487-0077; ③, ④ en suite), is meticulously well-kept but smells of mothballs. Two upper-end hotels are *Isla Chaffers*, bang in the centre of town on San Martín and M. Moreno (☎ & fax 0297/487-2246; ⑤); and, occupying the bluff as you come into town, the better *Los Acantilados* (☎ & fax 0297/487-2167 or 487-2007), at España and Pueyrredón, whose comfortable rooms command fine estuary views. The municipal **campsite** (☎0297/487-0579), on Avenida Costanera Pedro Lotufo, occupies a large gravelly site facing the bay, and has trailers where you can sling a sleeping bag for $7.

Always full of locals, the best **restaurant** in town is *El Pingüino*, Piedrabuena 958 (closed Thurs), with prompt, cheerful service. The $6 *platos del día* are excellent value, and the $5 *pejerrey* is always extremely fresh. Other places worth checking out are the run-down *El Viejo Marino*, Pueyrredón 224 (closed Mon), with more seafood specialities such as *abadejo al jerez* (cod cooked in a sherry sauce; $8); *Puerto Cristal*, with as much atmosphere as an operating theatre, but cheap pastas and $9 grills (closed Wed); and *Galenos* pub and restaurant on Sarmiento and Ameghino (restaurant closed Sun–Tues), which serves a $15 three-course menu till midnight, and beers till 3am.

The Ría Deseado

Stretching 42km inland from Puerto Deseado is the **Ría Deseado** (Deseado Estuary), an astonishing sunken river valley, flooded by the sea. Opposite the town, its purple cliffs are smeared with guano from five different types of **cormorant**. Though all are striking, the prize must go to the dapper, morning-suited *cormorán gris* (red-legged cormorant), whose grey body sets off its yellow bill and scarlet legs. These birds are seen in few other places, and nowhere else will you get such a sterling opportunity to photograph them. The estuary also plays host to 100,000 penguins; small flocks of pure-white *palomas antárticas* (snowy sheathbills); several types of duck, including the crested duck; plus terns and oystercatchers. Mammals include a small colony of sea lions and an estimated twenty-five **Commerson's dolphins**, the playful and photogenic champion swimmers that frequently come right up to the boat. In December there's a slim chance of glimpsing southern right whales, migrating south from the Península Valdés.

Most **trips** round the estuary stop at the **Isla de los Pájaros** (Bird Island) so passengers can disembark and photograph the penguins. If the tide is high, they enter the **Cañon Torcida**, a narrow and steep-sided channel of the estuary. Tours, lasting around two hours, leave from the pier at the entrance to town (minimum four passengers; $25) and tend to depart at 10am and 3pm; morning ones are generally better for the light. In summer, later evening tours are also excellent. Arrange them with either Darwin Expediciones/Gipsy Tours (at their office on the pier or on ☎0297/1562-47554, fax 0297/487-2525), but choose their narrowboat as it's open-topped; or Los Vikingos, Estrada 1275. Gipsy Tours offers other interesting options, the most regular of which is the "Ruta de Darwin" day excursion ($65), retracing the journey made by the scientist in 1834 to the end of the submerged estuary valley (specify if you need an English-speaking guide).

The Monumento Natural Bosques Petrificados

The **Monumento Natural Bosques Petrificados** (sometimes called Bosque Petrificado de Jaramillo; 8am–8pm; free) is located down a branch road 50km off the RN3, some 256km from Puerto Deseado and 280km north of San Julián. It stretches the imagination to picture this blasted desert covered with luxuriant plant life, but a forest it once was – and quite some forest too. The sheer magnitude of the **fossilized trunks** here is astonishing, measuring some 35m long and up to 3m wide. They're strangely beautiful too, especially at sunset, when their rich, jasper-red expanses soak up the glow, as though they're heating up from within.

The primeval Jurassic forest grew here 150 million years ago – sixty million years before the Andean cordillera was forced up, forming the rain barrier that has such a dramatic effect on the scenery we know now. In Jurassic times, this area was still swept by moisture-laden winds from the Pacific, allowing the growth of araucaria monkey puzzle trees. A cataclysmic blast from an unidentified volcano flattened these colossi and covered the fallen trunks with ash. The wood absorbed silicates in the ash and petrified, later to be revealed when erosion wore down the supervening strata.

Surrounding the trunks is a bizarre **moonscape** of arid basalt *meseta*, dominated by the 400-metre-tall **Cerro Madre e Hija** (Mother and Daughter Mount). Guanaco roam around, somehow managing to find sufficient subsistence from what plantlife does exist. A two-kilometre trail, littered by shards of fossilized bark as if it were a woodchip path through a garden, leads from the administration past all the most important trunks.

Day-trips to the park can be organized with travel agents from San Julián, Comodoro or Puerto Deseado. **Hitching** off the RN3 is possible, mainly in summer, when up to thirty vehicles a day pass, but you'll need a tent and extra food in case you get stuck, since there's nothing to buy either at the junction or at the administration. Register at administration, and examine the fascinating fossils such as the araucaria pine cones in the **museum** room. Don't succumb to the temptation of picking up "souvenirs" from the park, and note that you're not permitted to pitch a tent in the park; the only **camping** nearby is at *La Paloma*, 24km before the administration (☎0297/4443503; $5 per person). Otherwise, the best option is to continue on to San Julián or Puerto Deseado.

The RN3: San Julián to Río Gallegos

Overland, the RN3 runs for 330km between San Julián and Río Gallegos, the provincial capital. This stretch has little of tourist interest, with the exception of San Julián itself. Nevertheless, you can break the tremendous distances into more manageable chunks by stopping at the fishing destination of **Luis Piedra Buena** or the coastal nature reserve at **Isla Monte León**.

San Julián

The small, relaxed port of **SAN JULIÁN** makes the most convenient place to break the enormous journey between Trelew and Río Gallegos. The town, treeless and barren to look at, is rich in historical associations, due to its oddly shaped, shingle-banked **bay**, which was one of the few safe anchorages along the Patagonian coast for early mariners. Sadly, there's next to no visible evidence of the town's history, though it is a good place to go on one of various **tours**, including an extremely convenient trip – indeed one of the best-value tours in all Patagonia – to view the **marine life** of the bay (see below) – highly recommended, especially if you're unable to visit Puerto Deseado. The penguins here live closer to human settlement than at any other site in the south, and they've been known to assert ancestral privilege, having been found walking the streets. Local radio has been known, not without irony, to put out appeals for qualified people to remove penguins from the town hall.

San Julián can rightfully claim to be the birthplace of Patagonia. In 1520, during **Magellan's** stay in the bay, the very first encounter occurred between the Europeans and the "giants" of this nameless land. As related by Antonio Pigafetta, the expedition's chronicler: "One day, without anyone expecting it, we saw a giant, who was on the shore of the sea, quite naked, and was dancing and leaping, and singing, and whilst singing he put sand and dust on his head . . . When he was before us he began to be astonished, and to be afraid, and he raised one finger on high, thinking that we came from heaven. He was so tall that the tallest of us only came up to his waist . . . The captain named this kind of people Pataghom." On Palm Sunday, April 1, 1520 Magellan celebrated the **first Mass** on Argentinian soil, near a site marked by a cross, down by the town's port. Magellan and **Francis Drake** both faced off mutinies in the bay, in moments of critical importance for their careers. Magellan exacted retribution on the ringleaders of his rebellion: one officer, Quesada, was beheaded, drawn, quartered and swung from a gibbet; and Magellan's treacherous, aristocratic second-in-command, Juan de Cartagena, was marooned on these coasts with only a troublesome priest for company. Drake beheaded the nobleman Thomas Doughty here in 1578, alongside Magellan's gibbet. Doughty, having been sentenced to death by Drake, proceeded to dine with his admiral: bizarrely, the two men drank toasts to each other and passed an evening of the utmost civility before the execution on the following morning.

Later, as part of Charles III of Spain's scheme to protect shipping routes along the Patagonian coast, Captain Antonio de Viedma founded **Floridablanca**, in 1780, though scurvy destroyed the colony within four years. Things turned around at the beginning of the twentieth century: sheep farming provided the impetus behind the founding of the modern port, and the petroleum industry contributed to the town's development. Although both these sectors have foundered catastrophically in recent decades, San Julián's luck has held, and the discovery of a major gold reserve at nearby **Cerro Vanguardía** has rescued it from recession.

One of the few traces of the past to be preserved went unnoticed for many years, right in what passes for the town's main square, until someone noticed that a paving slab he'd just walked on had been walked on before – by a dinosaur. The distinct, prehistoric prints of the **sauropod** (a crocodile-like reptile) were moved to the local **Museo Regional** on Rivadavia and Vieytes (early March to late Dec Mon–Fri 9am–1pm & 2–5pm; late Dec to early March 9am–1pm & 4–9pm; free). Regrettably, having survived mischances throughout millennia, the slab was cracked whilst being moved. The museum also houses a few relics from the Floridablanca settlement, though the scanty **ruins** of Floridablanca themselves, west of town, are currently off limits, since access has been denied by the new landowner. Check the latest situation with the tourist office.

Practicalities
San Julián lies 3km off the RN3, down a straight road that becomes Avenida San Martín, the town's main artery. The **tourist office** is at San Martín 1125 (mid-March to mid-Dec Mon–Fri 7am–2pm; mid–Dec to mid–March daily 7am–1am; ☎02962/452871, fax 452076) – service here is erratic.

There's more mid-range **accommodation** here than budget options. One of the least expensive places, especially for solo travellers, is *El Águila* at San Martín 525 (②), which has basic rooms with shared bathroom. *Argentino*, Saavedra 896 and Urquiza (☎02962/454414; ③), is a clean, functional place with shared bathrooms, and also serves three-course set lunches and suppers for $8.50. The breezy, seafront *Hostería Municipal*, 25 de Mayo and Urquiza (☎02962/452300 or 452301; ④), has good views of the bay from its upstairs rooms and an extremely helpful manageress, though the attached restaurant is overpriced, and its seafood less than fresh. The rooms at *Residencial Sada*, San Martín 1112 (☎ & fax 02962/452013; ④), are poorly lit, but bathrooms have bathtubs. *Bahía*, San Martín 1075 (☎02962/454028, fax 453145; ⑤), is by far the most upmarket option, having modern, well-furnished rooms with spacious bathrooms. Prices include a fine buffet breakfast. At the other end of the scale, the municipal **campsite** next to the bay is stony but clean (☎02962/452806; $3 per person), and gets very busy in January. The best seafood joint in town is *La Rural* **restaurant**, at Ameghino 811 near the museum (☎02962/454149; $7 for a main course). *Casa Lara*, San Martín and Ameghino, is an excellent, informal bar.

The Bahía de San Julián
The easiest tour from San Julián is also the best: a trip around the bay in a zodiac launch to see the most conveniently situated **penguin colony** in Patagonia, and a wide variety of flying seabirds. In addition, you stand a good chance of spotting the undisputed stars of the show, the **Commerson's dolphins**. Supermodels of the dolphin world, these beautiful piebald creatures haven't let vanity spoil their sense of fun and, apparently attracted by the sound of the outboard motor, they torpedo through the clear water to rollick in the bow wave, just inches away from the boat's passengers. You'll also be taken to the protected island of **Banco Justicia** (Justice Bank) to see the cormorant colonies (all four species: rock, olivaceous, guanay and imperial); plus other seabirds such as the dazzling-white snowy sheathbill, looking more suited to life in a dovecote than on stormy oceans.

Banco Justicia is thought by some to be the place of execution of the sixteenth-century mutineers, although others maintain it was **Punta Horca** (Gallows Point), on the tongue of land that encloses the bay, opposite the town. You're not allowed to disembark at either, though you are allowed to get off at the misleadingly named **Banco Cormorán** to photograph its Magellanic penguins up close. Trips last approximately ninety minutes, and leave regularly in season from next door to the Muelle Viejo on the seafront; alternatively, arrange your trip through Excursiones Pinocho, Brown 739 (☎02962/452856; minimum of two passengers; $15). In season, German and English commentary is given by volunteer biologists. The best month for seeing dolphins and cormorants is December (the period from Jan to early April is also good), but the guide, Señor Pinocho, will always give a scrupulously honest appraisal of your chances.

Another possible tour is to drive the **Circuito Costero** (Coastal Circuit), a 110-kilometre round trip along the mainland side of the turquoise bay, which has some lovely coastal views and passes the **tomb of Lieutenant Robert Sholl**, who died here whilst on board the *Beagle*, during FitzRoy's first expedition of 1828. If you don't have your own transport you can go in a *remise* taxi, or ask at one of two travel agencies: Turis Santa Cruz, San Martín 446 (☎ & fax 02962/452086); or Natural La María, San Martín 1125, which also arranges tours to the **nature reserve** on the spit of land opposite San Julián.

San Julián to Río Gallegos

Even the most ardent devotee of steppe scenery might be finding the RN3 a trifle tiring by now. The desolate monotony is lifted, briefly, by the **Gran Bajo de San Julián**, whose Laguna del Carbón – 105m below sea level – is the lowest point in the entire South American continent. Conveniently, the road passes the rim of this sterile valley, so you need only to get out of the car to see it.

COMANDANTE LUIS PIEDRA BUENA, to give it its full title, is a sleepy town 1km off the RN3, with little to detain visitors unless you've come specifically for the world-class **steelhead trout fishing** (licences available at the municipalidad, Ibañez 388, just down from the attractive bus terminal). The town is named after one of Argentina's most renowned nineteenth-century Patagonian explorers and mariners, the naval hero Piedra Buena, who was famed for his gentlemanly ways and determination to assert Argentinian sovereignty in the south. In 1859, he made **Isla Pavón** (the island in the jade-coloured Río Santa Cruz at this point) his home, building a diminutive house, from which he traded with the local Aónik'enk Tehuelches. To access Isla Pavón, a road drops off the main bridge over the river. You can visit a bare reconstruction of the house, the **Casa Histórica Luis Piedra Buena** (if closed, ask at the campsite for key; free). The island's **campsite** (☎02966/1523453; $7 per pitch) gets extremely busy in summer, but is otherwise pleasant, with plenty of poplars. There are two decent **hotels**: *El Alamo*, Lavalle and España (☎ & fax 02962/497249; ③), a well-kept establishment with a confitería; and *Huayén*, Belgrano 321 (02962/497010; ②), which is basic but friendly and clean.

Heading south from Piedra Buena, the Patagonian plateau continues with unabating harshness for 235km to Río Gallegos. A detour, 33km out of Piedra Buena, leads to **Isla Monte León**, a reserve that lies 23km down a poor unsurfaced road. The site is in the process of becoming Argentina's second coastal national park, and the cliffs here are very rugged, indented with vast caverns and rock windows. Colonies of sea lions, penguins, and three types of cormorant come here to breed between September and April. There are wild beaches and a free **campsite** (mid–Nov to mid–April) with a toilet block, but no other services.

Conveniently situated where RN3 joins the main Río Gallegos to Calafate road (30km west of Gallegos Airport) is the attractive tourist estancia, *Güer Aike* (☎02966/436127; ⑦; Oct–April). Rooms are homely and peaceful, with their original fittings, and the mature garden outside is the perfect place for eating the owner's delicious scones. If you have your own tackle, you can fish for a day in the famous waters of the Río Gallegos, 13km of which flows through the estate. For holiday stays specifically devoted to fishing, this place goes under the name of *Truchaike*, and arrangements must be made through Buenos Aires (☎ & fax 011/4394-3486 or 4394-3513). *Aike*, the Tehuelche word for "place" or "stopping point", is seen commonly in this area, leading to modern-day names such as *Truchaike* (Place of Trout) – there's even a *Ford Aike* in the city.

Río Gallegos

Few people hang around long in **RÍO GALLEGOS** (pronounced *RI-o ga-SHAY-goss*), heading out instead to Calafate, south to Ushuaia or northwards with as little delay as possible. Despite a surfeit of tourist offices, the town is well aware that it's not a tourist destination *per se*, though if you have time to kill here, all is not lost – there are a couple of little museums, one or two attractive early twentieth-century buildings, and a day excursion to the **penguin colony** at Cabo Vírgenes (see below).

One thing that does attract people to Gallegos from as far away as North America, Europe and Japan, is its incredible **fly fishing**. As with the Río Grande in Tierra del Fuego (see p.687), the **Río Gallegos** (the river that the town is named after) is the haunt of some of the most spectacularly sized, sea-going **brown trout** anywhere in the world. Take with you your licence, a guide (if you can afford one), and a camera for the glory shot, as it's considered particularly poor form to kill these leviathans.

Arrival and information

The **airport** is 5km west of the bus terminal, 7km from the town. A taxi into town will cost around $7; there are no buses to the town centre, though (peversely) you *can* take a bus to El Calafate, some 300km away. There's also an ATM, car rental offices for Riestra and Localiza (book in advance in summer), and a small **tourist office** desk that opens whenever a flight arrives.

From the **bus terminal**, situated near the edge of town on the RN3, it's best to take a cab the 2km into the centre; alternatively, buses #1 or #12 will drop you in Avenida Roca in the heart of town. The municipal **tourist office** has a tiny booth in the terminal (Mon–Fri 8am–10pm, Sat & Sun 10am–3pm & 5–10pm; ☎02966/442159). Gallegos has two main **tourist offices** in the centre, both extremely helpful and efficient. The provincial office is at Roca 863 (Easter–Oct Mon–Fri 9am–9pm; Nov–Easter Mon–Fri 9am–10pm, Sat & Sun 10am–10pm; ☎ & fax 02966/422702), which gives foreigners fifteen minutes of free **Internet** access and sells fishing licences. The municipal office is in the **Carretón** (Oct–Easter Mon–Fri 10am–7pm, Sat & Sun 9am–2pm & 4pm–8pm), the old pioneer wagon at the junction of San Martín and Roca. Look at the floor, constructed out of original boards from sheep-dip powder boxes made in England. The only place to buy or sell Chilean pesos is the El Pingüino *casa de cambio* at Zapiola 469 (Mon–Fri 9am–noon & 3–7.30pm, Sat 9am–1pm). They change any US-dollar travellers' cheques, plus various world currencies in cash.

Accommodation

If you're heading west, consider staying outside town at the *Güer Aike* tourist estancia (see p.617). For **campers**, there's *ATSA*, Asturias y Yugoslavia (☎2966/426219; $5 per tent plus $3 per person), in the *polideportivo* sports centre complex, near the bus terminal; those on a really tight budget can pitch a tent for free in the parking lot behind the San Cristóbal YPF, on the way west out of town.

Cirse, Avellaneda 485 (☎ & fax 02966/420329, fax 437881). Army officers' lodging house, but also open to the public, offering spotlessly clean en-suite rooms – excellent value, especially for solo travellers. It also has a good restaurant over the road. ①.

Colonial, Urquiza y Rivadavia (☎02966/420020 or 422329). A pleasant cheapie for Gallegos, not far from the centre, and good for singles ($15). Rooms have shared bathroom. ③.

Comercio, Roca 1302 (☎02966/420209, fax 422172). Uninspiring but decent mid-range hotel in the centre, with a confitería, cable TV and parking.

Santa Cruz, Roca 701 (☎02966/420601, fax 420603). Very central and clean, with cable TV, cramped bathrooms and a restaurant (see below). ⑤.

Sehuén, Rawson 160 (☎02966/425683). Gallegos' best hotel: a refreshing combination of bright, modern rooms and economical prices. It has en-suite bathrooms with bath and good shower. ④.

The Town

Gallegos, the provincial capital, is a bustling centre of commerce for the region, and the main shopping thoroughfare, **Avenida Roca**, is the focus of city life. **Plaza San Martín** is an attractive square with a fine equestrian **statue** of General San Martín and the quaint white and green Salesian **cathedral**, Nuestra Señora de Luján (daily 5–7pm), a classic example of a pioneer church made from corrugated iron, and originally built in 1899 with a labour force composed of displaced indigenous Tehuelche.

The **Museo de Los Pioneros** (daily 1–8pm; free), housed in a snug town house on the corner of Alberdí and Elcano, gives a good insight into life in the region a century ago – it's best to visit on weekdays, when two English-speaking ladies of Scottish descent will show you around. Apart from the usual collection of black and white photographs of pioneering families, there's a 1904 Victrola music cupboard on which the curators will play ancient, crackly discs. The **Museo Regional Molina**, San Martín and Ramón y Cajal 51 (Mon–Fri 10am–6pm, Sat & Sun 11am–7pm; free), hosts temporary exhibitions of contemporary art, along with displays of dinosaur remains and impressive reconstructions of pleistocene mammals such as a megatherium, rearing up in Godzilla pose.

For **tours** to the penguin colony at Cabo Vírgenes, stopping at *Monte Dinero* estancia, contact Escalatur, at Roca 998 or Alberdí 2 (☎ & fax 02966/422466 or 420001). Tours leave at 11am from the office on Roca, returning at about 7.30pm and cost $55, which includes lunch and the dog display at *Estancia Monte Dinero* (four passengers minimum; Oct–Easter). Otherwise, a *remise* taxi (☎02966/426850 or 422454) will set you back $150 for the round trip.

Eating and drinking

Most places open for lunch from noon to 3pm, and then again between about 7.30pm and midnight.

El Abuelo, San Martín and Comodoro Py. A fun café-bar with a pleasant ambience.

El Ancla, Magallanes 353 (also called *Sotito*; ☎02966/427305). Delicious à la carte seafood. Try the *cazuela de marisco* ($10) or the sea bass, *róbalo con roquefort* ($9).

Club Británico, Roca 935. Well-priced and imaginative food, served with formal style. *Pulpo en escabeche* (marinated octopus) is one of many dishes that will excite a jaded palate. Still the favoured hang-out for the declining community of those with British descent, the bar makes an excellent place to share a scotch and enjoy a chin-wag.

Díaz, Roca 1157 (☎02966/420203). A fine parrilla with large servings of *lomo* for $14, and a wide selection of salads.

El Dragon, 9 de Julio 27 (☎02966/429811). A place for a pig-out, with an eat-all-you-like Chinese buffet and meat grill ($9–10); sullen service. Closes 11pm

Gran Casona, Avellaneda and Magallanes, opposite the *CIRSE* hotel (☎02966/420329). Very competitively priced, with four-course set menus for $8 and cheap house wine. Open till 1am.

El Horreo, Roca 862 (02966/426462). A popular place bang in the centre, in the attractive Casa España. It has good wood-fired pizzas and Iberian dishes, including *pollo a la portuguesa* (chicken in a pepper sauce) for $8. The $10 *puchero* on Wednesdays is a speciality. Open till 1.30pm

Mónaco, Roca and San Martín. A 24hr *confitería*.

Cabo Vírgenes

Head south of Río Gallegos on the RN3 before turning left along the RP1, 15km out of town; 95km from the turn-off is the evangelical, bilingual Fenton family's *Monte Dinero* (☎02966/426923; ⑨ with full board), a working tourist estancia with comfortable rooms. Many furnishings were salvaged long ago from coastal wrecks, and there's a fascinating small family museum. Guests can arrange pick-up from Gallegos (minimum four passengers; $25 per person). Non-staying guests can arrange a three-hour visit to see excellent performances with pedigree Australian sheepdogs, combined with a delicious 1pm lunch made with wholesome, home-produced ingredients (reserve one day in advance; $22).

The Fentons also take guests on trips to the penguin colony and lighthouse at **Cabo Vírgenes**, 15km away. The cape, continental Argentina's most southerly point, was named by Magellan when he rounded it for the first time on the feast day of the Eleven Thousand Virgins, October 21, 1520. This bleak and inauspicious spot witnessed one of Patagonia's most miserable and tragic failures: Pedro Sarmiento de Gamboa's settlement of **Nombre de Jesús** ("Name of Jesus"), founded in 1584 and intended as a permanent base on the Magellan Straits to prevent a repetition of Drake's damaging Pacific raids of 1578–79. Of the 23 ships and 3500 settlers and soldiers that originally left Spain, only one ship, carrying three hundred people, reached this far. All bar one were to die either here or in the sister settlement of San Felipe (Puerto Hambre in Chile), killed partly in skirmishes with the local Tehuelche, but mostly by depression, disease, and starvation. No trace remains now, except for one shapeless concrete monument at the foot of the scarp on the Argentinian side, and a cross over the border in Chile.

The Argentine Navy (Armada Argentina) permits you to climb the **lighthouse** for an excellent view of the windswept coast. The 400-watt lightbulb throws its beam 40km out to sea. The **penguin colony** ($5 entrance) is a couple of kilometres further south: between October and April up to 160,000 birds come here to nest amongst the perfumed, resinous-scented *mata verde* scrub. There's a small information centre staffed by an amicable *guardafauna*, and a curious plastic podule acts as a hide from which to view the penguins without being lashed by the winds.

On to Punta Arenas and Tierra del Fuego

It can take up to a day to get from Río Gallegos to San Sebastían, the first settlement in Argentinian Tierra del Fuego, a journey which involves crossing two borders and the Magellan Straits. The **Monte Aymond border crossing** is 67km south of Gallegos. Formalities are fairly straightforward, but don't try to bring fresh vegetables, fruit or meat products into Chile, as they'll be confiscated. On the Chilean side, the road improves and heads to **Punta Arenas** (see p.658) and **Puerto Natales** (see p.661).

Alternatively, you can make for **Tierra del Fuego** by turning onto the RN257 at Kimiri Aike, 42km from the border. This takes you to the Primera Angostura (the First Narrows) of the straits, and the Punta Delgada **ferry** that plies across them. As early mariners knew, the currents here can be ferocious, but they're unlikely to be as disruptive to your plans as they were to seagoers in the past – only in extremely testy weather does the ferry not leave. Be prepared for a rough journey all the same. It leaves from 8.30am to 10.30pm, making the thirty-minute crossing every ninety minutes ($2 per person; $16 for a car). Whilst crossing history's most famous straits, look out for the attractive piebald Commerson's dolphins that frequent the seas here. Heading for Ushuaia, the road then crosses Chilean Tierra del Fuego to the border settlements of San Sebastián.

THE ANDEAN SPINE: THE RN40

The **RN40** – "La Cuarenta", as it is known to Argentinians – is at once more and less than just a road. Like Route 66 in the United States, it has its own ethos and is capable of evoking passions, inspiring songs and books, and causing arguments. It both attracts and deters visitors: some are drawn by the road's rugged mystique – a result of its inaccessibility and frequently poor condition – others are put off for the same reason. Though stretching from Salta in the northwest of Argentina all the way to Río Gallegos in the southeast, it is the southernmost section that is most famous. Aficionados praise the fact that it is still largely unpaved, whereas critics see this as the main factor delaying the influx of tourist dollars that would benefit an economically depressed hinterland.

Be that as it may, the RN40 *is* opening up to tourism. In the summer, newly prosperous Argentines, joined by some Brazilians and Chileans, are to be seen in increasing numbers as they take their 4WDs out of the city and put them to the test. In addition, there is now a **public transport** service (see box below), thus making it possible for those without their own vehicle to plan as dependable an itinerary as is possible in this part of the world.

The scenery is uniformly dry and desertified – but not at all uniform. Much of it is flat, over-grazed steppe covered with tussocks of *coirón* grass, compact clumps of the tough, spiky *neneo* plant, and punctuated by patches of scrub. Most brush looks fairly dreary and anonymous for most of the year, but some bushes liven up considerably in the spring: the thorny *calafate* (see p.648) blooms with a profusion of delicate yellow flowers, and the *lengua de fuego* produces gloriously bright orange flowers like clam shells. The *colapiche* is named for its tough green fronds, which resemble armadillos' tails, and you're sure to see the grey *senecio miser*, the robust *mata negra*, the slender-leaved *duraznillo*, and the aggressively spiked *molle*, peppered with spherical galls caused by a parasitic wasp/moth. You pass harsh mesetas, blasted rocky outcrops, patches of desert and the occasional river valley, usually accompanied by a green, boggy pasture and lined in places with emerald-green willows.

Along the whole route, the **Cordillera de los Andes** lies approximately 90km to the west, and it is here that most of the interest lies, centred on the region's lakes and national parks. Many areas of the range are completely barren, especially in the foothills, but in others, the mountain slopes are cloaked in southern beech woods, with only a narrow fringe of transitional scrubland separating forest from steppe. In these areas, you stand your best chance of seeing condors, and perhaps even a puma or a highly endangered huemul. Access roads run west from the RN40 to the mountains, but in virtually all cases you must return to it along the same track before continuing your journey.

A relaxed road tour will take four days, but to explore a couple of the little-visited spots near the Andes, aim instead to spend one to two weeks, more if you're an adventurous trekker. Between Esquel and the town of Perito Moreno, the RN40 passes through several uninspiring settlements, with the only diversion of any note being to the fishing lakes of the **Río Pico** area. From Perito Moreno, a road runs west along **Lago Buenos Aires** to the Chilean border at the orchard town of **Los Antiguos**, from where you can detour to Posadas before rejoining the RN40. South of Perito Moreno, the archeological site of **Cueva de las Manos** lies in the canyon of **Río de las Pinturas**, just to the east of the RN40. The next two western detours head to little-visited, wild areas that are excellent for trekking: the first to lakes **Posadas** and **Pueyrredón**; the second to the **Parque Nacional Perito Moreno**. Considerably further south, a turn-off heads to a

---

PUBLIC TRANSPORT ALONG THE RN40

For many years, the south Patagonian cordillera was a notoriously difficult one to explore unless you had your own transport or plenty of time to hitch. This has changed somewhat with the introduction of a **public transport service** along the RN40. From November to the end of March, Chaltén Travel operates a service between Los Antiguos and El Calafate ($68), passing Perito Moreno, Bajo Caracoles, Las Horquetas, Tres Lagos and *Hotel La Leona* (where it connects with the same company's service to and from El Chaltén; $15 extra). Buses leave on alternate days: running north–south on even-numbered dates and south–north on odd-numbered ones. For more information, call %02902/491833 or 492212.

SAFE DRIVING

Take especial care when **driving** along this stretch of road, as the combination of high crosswinds and poorly maintained gravel (*ripio*) roads makes it extremely easy to flip the car. In the first six weeks of 1999, there were ten overturns, eight of them on the stretch of road between Bajo Caracoles and Las Horquetas, and which involved four fatalities. To keep safe, do as the locals do:

Never exceed 70km/hr, even when road and weather conditions are good.

If swept out of the track, **do not brake** or swerve suddenly: change down gears and let the vehicle slow down before trying to steer back on course.

Watch out for poorly maintained sections: huge road-levelling wagons flatten *ripio* roads from time to time, but these improve conditions for a limited period only. You might need to drop to 20 or 30km/hr in the worst places.

Slow down in strong winds, especially crosswinds. At higher speeds, you're more susceptible to being blown out of the tracks into the dangerous loose gravel at the sides. Note, too, that 4WDs don't confer immunity, as wind gets underneath these high-clearance vehicles more easily.

Follow the most recently used tracks.

Always wear your seat belt.

Aside from the obvious desire to preserve life and limb, there is another reason to approach gravel roads with caution: most rental cars have a much higher excess in case of rolling the vehicle (usually around $1500), so any accident and it's more than just your roof or your pride that gets badly dented.

Always check your spare tyres are in good condition, and bring drinking water, sleeping bags, a torch, a good road map and a first aid kit. If you see a fellow road-user broken down or stationary at the edge of the road, do stop: in little-transited areas, even offering water or taking a message to the next town to raise help can be of vital importance. Secondly, *slow down* when approaching an oncoming vehicle or passing a slower road-user to avoid windscreen or headlight breakages.

---

similarly beautiful area around **Lago San Martín**. Beyond here is one of Argentina's highlights, easily accessible from El Calafate: the mountainous **Fitz Roy** area near the village of **El Chaltén**. Finally there's **El Calafate**, which, due to its nearby **Glaciar Perito Moreno**, is the major tourist destination in the province of Santa Cruz.

Esquel to Perito Moreno

Between Esquel (see p.573) and the town of Perito Moreno lie a few rather depressing transit towns with little to detain you, except for the detour to the fishing region of Río Pico in the Andean foothills. The RN40 is paved for the first 96km as far as **Tecka**, a drab settlement where you can refuel. Just south of the village, the RN65 turns off east towards Trelew and the Atlantic coast (see p.602).

Seventy kilometres south of Tecka by the Río Putrachoique, a consolidated road branches west off the RN40 to **RÍO PICO**, a **fishing** mecca in the damp pre-cordillera. Rich Americans pay up to $1000 a day to fish the lakes in the region for prize specimens of the elusive brook trout, which, ironically, here grows to sizes far exceeding those found in its native United States. Knowledgeable Señor Hugo López (contactable at *Kiosko Damian*, ☎02945/492045 or 1568-1538) sells permits and will assist those who want to fish the same waters much more economically. Chatwin fans can visit the cross that marks the grave of American bandits, **Wilson and Evans** – Chatwin claimed, rather dubiously, that these two were actually Butch Cassidy and the Sundance Kid. The cross is 2km up a heavily rutted track, which branches north off the road heading back to the RN40, about 4km east of Río Pico – a lone tree marks the junction, just before a small dip. Pass one gate, and continue up until the track is fenced off, where a small sign indicates the site of the grave, 100m to the left. **Accommodation** in the village is limited to Señor Aidar's lodgings on Mariano Moreno s/n (☎02945/492023; ②, bunk-beds $15 per person).

The RN40 splits the strung-out settlement of **GOBERNADOR COSTA**, 16km south of the Río Pico turn-off. Costa has a YPF **fuel** station with shop, but unless your visit coincides with the annual **Fiesta Provincial del Caballo** (usually the third weekend in Feb), when locals perform feats of gaucho horsemanship, you won't want to stop. **Accommodation** options include the clean, modern *Hostería Mi Refugio*, on Avenida Roca as you come into town (☎02945/491097; ②); rooms in charming Señora Gibbon's quiet home at San Martín 50 (②); or the municipal **campsite**, off Avenida Roca in the south end of town. Señor Brosio of Turismo Genoa, at J. Roca y Aguado (☎02945/491062), organizes horseriding, fishing and sightseeing trips to the Río Pico area in his minibus ($150).

Río Mayo and the border crossings

At a junction 54km south of Gobernador Costa, take the paved RP20 in preference to the much slower, unpaved RN40. The RP20 runs parallel to the Río Senguer before reaching a triangular junction where it peels off east towards the petrified forests near Sarmiento (see p.614) or west to rejoin the RN40 at **Río Mayo**, with its regimented, toytown military barracks. One weekend in the second half of January, Río Mayo hosts the **Festival Nacional de la Esquila** to find the region's premier sheep-shearer. The best **hotel** is the *Viejo Covadonga*, San Martín 573 (☎02903/420020; ①), where the older rooms hint of a bygone, more prosperous age of sheep farming.

Near Río Mayo are two **border crossings** heading to Coihaique in Chile: **Coihaique Alto** (April–Nov 9am–9pm; Dec–March 7.30am–10pm), and the busier **Paso Huemules**, on the new transcontinental route passing through Balmaceda (same hours). Both are fairly straightforward crossings. South of Río Mayo, the RN40 degenerates into an unsealed road that should be driven with care (see box opposite). After 112km, having crossed the **provincial boundary** from Chubut into Santa Cruz, it joins the paved RP43, which heads west for 12km to Perito Moreno.

Perito Moreno and around

With a whopping 3000 inhabitants, **PERITO MORENO** is the most populous town in this part of the world. It's a typically featureless, spread-out Patagonian settlement, built on a grid system, and is of use to the visitor only as a base for excursions to places such as the Cueva de las Manos (see p.627), or for its transport services: to Posadas, along the RN40, and to the Chilean border at Los Antiguos/Chile Chico. A wildlife refuge within town, the Laguna de los Cisnes – once the habitat of black-necked swans and flamingoes – is now all too frequently a swanless, dried-up reed bed, its precious water having been siphoned off for domestic and agricultural use.

Practicalities

The new **bus terminal** is sited to the north of town on the RP43, by the Eg3 fuel station. From here, cross the road and walk down Avenida San Martín to reach the centre of town in about ten minutes. The **tourist office** is at San Martín and Mariano Moreno (daily: Easter–Oct 8am–noon & 3–8pm; Nov–Easter 8am–9pm; ☎02963/432020, fax 432222). **Accommodation** is overpriced, especially for single rooms – if you're heading

TOURS FROM PERITO MORENO

The helpful staff at the ELAL travel agency, San Martín 1494 (☎ & fax 02963/432839), sell good-value tours in the area, most notably to the José Ormachea Petrified Forest in Sarmiento ($65 including lunch, entrance fee and guide) and the Cueva de las Manos ($55 including lunch, entrance fee and guide). Bring extra food and water. A recommended option is a trip to another area of great beauty and archeological interest, Arroyo Feo, 70km south of town. With its dramatic narrow canyon and important 9000-year-old cave paintings, it offers a wilder alternative to the Cueva de las Manos, and has good climbing possibilities. The agency also arranges specialist tours to less-visited areas of the cordillera: ask about the route along the rivers Jeinemeni and Zeballos south of Los Antiguos. Keen **trekkers** or **climbers** interested in exploring the San Lorenzo area to the south should contact Paco Sepúlveda at Juan Perón 1534 (☎02963/432306). An excellent guide, he charges a very reasonable $250 per person for a tough seven-day trek past San Lorenzo through to the Parque Nacional Perito Moreno, with transport to and from Perito Moreno town included.

to Chile, it's better to push on to Los Antiguos or Chile Chico across the border or, if you can afford it, try one of the nearby tourist estancias, *La Serena*, on the road to Los Antiguos, or *Telken*, to the south (see p.626). The only places in town that offer reasonable value for money are the homely bed and breakfast, the *Posada del Caminante* (☎02963/432204, fax 432203; ③) at Rivadavia 937, and the sociable municipal **campsite**, conveniently situated a few minutes' walk south from the centre along Avenida San Martín. The site also has a couple of **cabins** for hire ($5 per tent, plus $2 per person) – the cheapest option in town for those with sleeping bags but without tents.

Other hotels are only notable for the fact that they serve as offices and points of departure for the various **bus companies**: the *Santa Cruz* at Belgrano 1565 for La Unión buses to Los Antiguos (2 daily); the *Americano* at San Martín 1327 for the Sportman bus to Los Antiguos (2 daily) and El Chaltén (Wed & Sun 1 daily); the *Austral* next door for its Los Antiguos bus (1 daily). Transporte Lago Posadas runs to Posadas (Hipólito Yrigoyen) from Saveedra 1357 (Tues & Thurs 1 daily).

For those heading south, Perito Moreno is the best place until El Calafate to stock up on **food**. The Banco de Santa Cruz at San Martín 1493 gives **cash advances** on Mastercard with no commission, as does the Banco de la Nación nearby at no. 1385. This bank also accepts Visa, buys and sells US dollars at fixed rates, and changes US dollar travellers' cheques at good rates. If heading into Chile, change excess Argentinian pesos into dollars, as these get better rates across the border. If heading south, withdraw or change enough cash to last until El Calafate. None of Perito Moreno's **restaurants** is anything special, although the pizza place adjoining the *Hotel Austral* is open late and is popular with locals.

West to Los Antiguos

Leaving Perito Moreno, the paved and well-maintained RP43 sweeps towards the impressive expanse of **Lago Buenos Aires**, its ocean-blue waters in striking contrast with the dusty brown steppe surrounding it. At several points you can walk across the scrub from the road to the shore, but though it looks perfect for swimming, the temperature will douse your enthusiasm – it remains at an almost constant 10°C throughout the year. This vast lake was divided in half by the border commission in the early 1900s, and thus has two names: the Chileans call their half Lago General Carreras. The frontier marks an equally abrupt change of scenery, as the Argentinian meseta slopes upwards into the cordillera. The distinctive, ash-grey pyramid, **Cerro Pirámide**, dominating the north shore is not, as it would seem, a volcanic cone, although infamous

Volcán Hudson does lie in the range some 90km away behind it, out of sight. Some of the higher, snowcapped peaks that border Chile's Hielo Continental Norte (Northern Patagonian Icecap) are revealed by the broad U-shaped gap formed by the lake itself.

Sited by the lake shore, 30km out of Perito Moreno, in a tousled clump of poplars and willows, is the tourist estancia *La Serena* (✆ & fax 02963/432340; ⑥; Sept to early May). Buses to and from Los Antiguos stop at the entrance. Accommodation is in pleasant little bungalows with rooms for two to four people, and the multilingual Belgian owners prepare high-quality Patagonian and European cuisine using home-grown, organic ingredients – a three-course meal costs $25. Excursions in the area, including horseriding and fishing, are also available, but you're advised to book in advance.

Los Antiguos and around

The welcome sight of greenery as you approach the serene little town of **LOS ANTIGU-OS** is your first indication of the spring-like microclimate that exists in this area of the precordillera. High levels of sunshine and a sheltered position mean that, even at these southerly latitudes, it's an area well suited to fruit production, being famous for its succulent cherries, which are exported as far away as Europe. In early January, the crop is celebrated at the three-day **Fiesta de la Cereza** with music, dance, and fresh, cheap strawberries and cherries. Carnivores will enjoy the annual **Fiesta del Pueblo** held on February 5, if only for the vast orgy of free meat-eating that goes on.

The roadside into town is littered with **Tehuelche tombs**, little jumbles of blackened stones, now desecrated by artefact-hunters, that testify to the fact that this was one of the sacred places where the elderly would come to spend their last days once advancing age had made a nomadic life impossible – indeed, the town gets its name ("The Ancients") from this legacy.

The poetically sounding **Río Jeinemeni** (also spelt "Jeinimeni") has first-class salmon fishing. Running south from Los Antiguos, parallel to this river, is the stunningly scenic and desolate **RP41**. This road, just about the only Patagonian route that runs alongside the border with Chile, passes the angular form of Monte Zeballos (2743m), on its way to Lago Posadas, or Cochrane in Chile by way of the Paso Roballos. You'll need a high-clearance 4WD and to check road conditions at the *Gendarmería* on Avenida 11 de Julio before setting out (ask for the *informe de vialidad provincial*), as even in summer freak snowfalls or heavy rains may make it impassable. If you're fit enough, the route takes about three days by mountain bike in the summer.

Practicalities

Buses from Perito Moreno will drop you at their respective company's offices. The friendly, helpful **tourist office** at 11 de Julio 432 (Easter–Oct 9am–7pm; Nov–Easter 7am–10pm; ✆02963/491036, fax 491261) has a good photocopied map of the border route to Posadas and can help to organize **bike rental** ($20 per day or $5 for 3hr). Four-star **accommodation** can be found in the new *Hostería de los Antiguos* complex by the lakeside, with casino and sauna; or there's the unfriendly *Argentino* at 11 de Julio 850 (✆ & fax 02963/491132; ③ including breakfast). The excellent lakeside municipal **campsite** is a ten-minute walk from the centre (✆02963/491265; $2.50 per person) and also rents cheap **cabins** ($20 for six people; no bedding supplied), although in March these are likely to be booked up by local fishermen.

For **food**, the *Restaurante Andrada* on 11 de Julio serves snacks and tasty *empanadas*. The Banco Santa Cruz, at 11 de Julio 531, gives **cash advances** on Mastercard. Change excess Argentinian pesos to US dollars here if you're leaving for Chile. Arriving from Chile, you'll need dollars or Argentinian pesos in town: if stuck with Chilean pesos, try changing them with the cross-border transport companies.

Crossing the border to Chile Chico

Transporte Padilla and Acotrans minibuses run from the centre of town to the border. There are few border formalities, though remember you're prohibited from taking meat, fruit and vegetables into Chile. From Los Antiguos, it's 3km to Argentinian immigration; a further 12km across the Río Jeinemeini no-man's land to Chilean immigration; and then 4km to **CHILE CHICO**. This warmly welcoming little frontier town has excellent views across Lago Carreras and is a frequent jumping-off point for the verdant **Carretera Austral**, the single-track dirt road that is southern Chile's major artery. The **tourist office** (Dec–March Mon–Fri 9am–1pm & 2.30–6.30pm, Sat 10am–1pm & 2.30–6pm; no phone) is found in the Casa de Cultura on the main street. Out of season, ask at the municipality (☎67/411268 or 411359, fax 411355).

Argentine pesos and US dollars can be exchanged until late at the Casa Loly phone centre at Pedro Antonio González 25, fronting the square. From Chile Chico, a **ferry** (Dec–Easter daily; Easter–Nov every 2 days; 2hr 30min–3hr; US$4) crosses Lago Carreras to Puerto Ibañez, from where frequent buses leave for Coihaique. Acotrans minibuses run back to Los Antiguos. Several *casas de familia* offer basic **accommodation**, including *Residencial Aguas Azules*, at Manuel Rodríguez 252 (☎67/411320; ①). A more expensive alternative, with a cosy atmosphere and comfortable rooms, is the *Hostería de la Patagonia* (☎ & fax 67/411337 or 411591; open Dec–March; ①), on the road that links the immigration post to town. You can **camp** rough on the beach by the lake shore for free.

South of Perito Moreno

Follow the RN40 south of Perito Moreno to reach the turn-off to *Estancia Telken* (open Sept–April; Sept–April ☎02963/432079, fax 432303; May–Aug ☎011/4797-7216; ⑥, ⑤ with shared bathroom), renowned for the hospitable welcome offered by its owners. This is one of the best estancias to visit for a taste of what it means to live on a working ranch. As with other farms in the area, it was particularly hard hit by the explosion of Volcán Hudson in 1991 (see box below).

Further on, the RN40 descends through a moonscape valley of stratified "paleodunes", where paleontologists have excavated dinosaur skeletons. More basic than *Telken*, but also extremely friendly, is the *Casa de Piedra* (①; closed April–Oct), set in a clump of willows and surrounded by the marshy pastures of the Río Ecker Valley. You can **camp** at this pleasant spot ($2.50 per pitch), and the Sabella family sells *gaseosas*, beers and, occasionally, snacks. A highly recommended trip from here is to the dramatic, plunging canyon of the Río Pinturas and its Cueva de las Manos Pintadas, detailed below.

WHEN HUDSON BLEW

In early August 1991, Chile's Volcán Hudson erupted, sending a plume of ash and gases 18,000m up into the stratosphere. Due to the strength of the prevailing westerly winds, its effects were felt more keenly in Argentina than its homeland. Ash was deposited over a cone of land that, on the coast, stretched from Puerto Deseado to San Julián, while inland a crust of pumice formed like a scab on the surface of Lago Buenos Aires turning its waters grey. The RN3 from Buenos Aires was blocked in places by drifts of ash that reached depths of a metre and lasted for months, while even as far away as the Islas Malvinas/Falkland Islands, ash fell to depths of several centimetres. In all, over a million sheep died across the 25 million acres affected. For an already struggling sheep-farming industry, Hudson proved the last straw, as hundreds of estancias were bankrupted and abandoned, changing the face of the countryside for years.

South of *Casa de Piedra* along the RN40, weather permitting, the vast, recumbent hulk of San Lorenzo (see p.636) comes into view to the west – at 3706m the tallest peak in Argentinian Patagonia south of Volcán Lanín. Approximately 10km north of Bajo Caracoles, rough roads turn off west to Paso Roballos on the Chilean border, and east to the Cueva de las Manos, after which you reach the miserable settlement of Bajo Caracoles itself, only useful as a place to catch transport to Lago Posadas (Tues & Thurs 1 daily). There's a YPF **fuel** pump and the unfriendly *Hotel Bajo Caracoles* (☎02963/490100; ③), with an overpriced shop, a café, a **public phone** (the last one, if you're heading south, until Gobernador Gregores or Tres Lagos) and a couple of simple rooms. For $5, they may let you put up a tent.

The Cueva de las Manos Pintadas

The **Cueva de las Manos Pintadas** (Cave of the Painted Hands), one of South America's finest examples of rock art, can be approached either via 45km of *ripio* road from Bajo Caracoles, or, better, by walking or riding up the canyon it overlooks, the impressive **Cañón de Río Pinturas**. Hikes and horserides can be arranged from *Casa de Piedra* (see p.626), but whether you intend going on foot or on horseback, it is sensible to contract Señor Sabella to drive you to the trailhead at the canyon rim ($25 return). This saves a thirteen-kilometre hike or ride across the rolling pampa in each direction, and makes it a comfortable day-trip. You can drive to the trailhead by taking the first left-hand track as you leave the valley of the Río Ecker to the south, but ask permission first and remember to close all gates.

From the canyon rim, it's a spectacular two-hour walk to the cave paintings through scenery that would do any Arizonan Western proud: the path drops sharply to the fertile, flat valley bed, and stays to the right of the snaking river at all times, nestling up against imposing rock walls and pinnacles that display the region's traumatic geological history in bands of black basalt, slabs of rust-coloured sandstone and a stressed layer of sedimentary rocks that range in hue from chalky white to mottled ochre. Bring binoculars for viewing the wide variety of finches and birds of prey that inhabit the canyon, plus food, water, a hat and suncream.

Where the course of the Río Pinturas is diverted by a vast rampart of red sandstone, you start to climb the valley side again to reach the road and the entrance building to the protected area around the paintings (daily: May–Sept 8.30am–10pm; Oct–April 7am–10.30pm; $3), where there's a modest museum display. You can usually pitch a **tent** here free, but ask the *guardaparque*'s permission first.

The *cueva* itself is less a cave than a series of overhangs: natural cutaways at the foot of a towering ninety-metre cliff face overlooking the canyon below. From this vantage point, groups of paleolithic hunter-gatherers would survey the valley floor for game, though nowadays the view is partly spoiled by the ineffective and heavy-handed iron fence that attempts to keep tourists from etching their own twenty-first century graffiti on the rock. Even so, the collage of black, white, red and ochre **handprints**, mixed with gracefully flowing vignettes of guanaco hunts, still makes for an astonishing spectacle. Of the trademark 829 handprints, most are male, and only 31 are right-handed. They are all "negatives", being made by placing the hand on the rock face, and imprinting its outline by blowing pigments through a tube. Interspersed with these are human figures, as well as the outlines of puma paws and rhea prints, and creatures such as a scorpion.

The earliest paintings were made by the **Toldense** culture, and date as far back as 7300 BC, but archeologists have identified four later cultural phases, ending with depictions by early Tehuelche groups – notably geometric shapes and zigzags – from approximately 1000 AD. The significance of the paintings is much debated: whether they represented part of the rite of passage for adolescents into the adult world, and were thus part of ceremonies to strengthen familial or tribal bonds, or whether they were connected to religious ceremonies that preceded the hunt will probably never be known. Other tantalizing mysteries involve theories surrounding the large number of heavily pregnant guanacos depicted, and whether these herds were actually semi-domesticated or at least managed. One thing is for certain: considering their exposed position, it is remarkable how vivid some of the colours still are: the colours were made from the berries of *calafate* bushes, local mineral-bearing earth and charcoal, while guanaco fat and urine was applied to create the waterproof coating that has preserved them so well.

Posadas and around

Two hours' drive west of Bajo Caracoles, the seldom-visited area around turquoise **Lago Posadas** and lapis-blue **Lago Pueyrredón** is well worth the detour, but most places of interest around the lakes are accessible only to those with their own vehicle – it's difficult even to hitch due to the lack of traffic. The two lakes are famous for their dramatic colour contrast – most notable in spring – and are separated by the narrowest of strips of land, the arrow-straight **La Península**, which looks for all the world like an man-made causeway. It was actually formed during a static phase of the last ice age, when an otherwise retreating glacier left an intermediate dump of moraine, now covered by sand dunes, which cut the shallow lagoon of Lago Posadas off from its grander and more tempestuous neighbour. Pueyrredón is the better of the two for fishing – rainbow and brown trout of up to 8kg can be found at the mouth of the Río Oro.

The area's main village is listed on maps as **Hipólito Irigoyen**, but is usually referred to by its old name of **POSADAS**, from the neighbouring lake – though little more than a loosely grouped assemblage of modern houses, its inhabitants are amicable, and keen to promote the region. Two kilometres to the south of town, the low, rounded wedge of **Cerro de los Indios** lies beneath the higher scarp of the valley. Bruce Chatwin's description of this rock in *In Patagonia* is unerring: "a lump of basalt, flecked red and green, smooth as patinated bronze and fracturing in linear slabs. The Indians had chosen the place with an unfaltering eye for the sacred."

Indigenous **rock paintings**, some almost 10,000 years old, are to be found at the foot of the cliff, about two thirds of the way along the rock to the left. The famous depiction of a "unicorn" is rather faded; more impressive are the wonderful concentric circles of a hypnotic labyrinth design. The red splodges high up on the overhangs appear to have been the result of guanaco hunters firing up arrows tipped in pigment-stained fabric, perhaps in a vertical version of darts. However, the site's most remarkable feature is the polished shine on the rocks, which really do possess the patina and texture of antique bronze. There's also no ugly fence screening off the engravings and paintings here as there is at Cueva de las Manos, leaving the site's magical aura uncompromised.

Practicalities

In this village of about 250 inhabitants there is only one place to stay, *La Posada de Posadas* (☎ & fax 02963/490250; ④), with modern fittings in rooms for two or three people, cooking facilities and energetic showers; rooms without cooking facilities are slightly cheaper. The owner, Pedro Fortuny, works as a regional trekking and fishing guide, while his family runs the village's best restaurant in the old hotel, specializing in Mediterranean-style food (about $15 for a main course plus wine). The village has a YPF **fuel** station and a public telephone. The Transporte Lago Posadas *camioneta* leaves for Bajo Caracoles and Perito Moreno twice a week (Tues & Thurs). Five kilometres east of Posadas, the RP41 runs north towards the Chilean border at Paso Roballos, and Los Antiguos (see p.625).

Lago Posadas

Do not try to drive around the south shore of **Lago Posadas**, even though a road is marked on many maps: cars can easily get bogged down near the Río Furioso. Instead, take the route running around the north shore, which passes through a zone of blasted, bare humps, crisscrossed by lines of *duraznillo* bushes. Known as **El Quemado** ("The Burnt One"), it's one of the most ancient formations in Argentina, dating back 180 million years to the Jurassic age, and there are spectacular contrasts between minerals such as green olivina sandstone and porphyry iron oxides. A rudimentary track runs from here 57km to the Chilean frontier at Paso Roballos and north to Los Antiguos.

At the northwest end of Lago Posadas, the road swings left, running along La Península before following the south bank of Lago Pueyrredón. Beautifully located halfway along La Península, the estancia turística *Lagos del Furioso* (✆ & fax 011/4812-0959, *cramer@interlink.com.ar*; ⑦; Nov–Easter) rates as the most luxurious accommodation in the north of Santa Cruz. Purpose-built as a hotel, it doesn't provide the agrotourism opportunities of a working estancia, but the corresponding comforts are obvious: well-designed bungalows; a sauna; and an airy communal dining-room where freshly prepared cuisine of an international standard is served ($25 for three-course dinner without drinks), complemented by panoramic views of Lago Posadas and the striated Río Furioso canyon. The multilingual Cramer family owners know the area inside out and arrange excursions on foot or horseback as far as the Parque Nacional Perito Moreno.

Lago Pueyrredón and the Río Oro Valley

Ambitious engineers have somehow managed to squeeze a beautiful dirt road between the southern shore of this pristinely beautiful lake and the hills that press up against it, without having to resort to tiresome infill projects. This precarious arrangement is compromised only by the occasional spring flood (September is the worst month).

Just past the neat bridge over the Río Oro, a track wends its way up the mountainside and past the magnificent purple chasm of the **Garganta del Río Oro**. Further up the valley is a **campsite** ($6 per person; pay at *Los Ñires*) at a place across the river from *Estancia El Gaucho*, a place that specializes in mouthwatering home-grown herbal teas. Beyond the campsite, the *Estancia Los Ñires* offers lodging ($20 per person) and great possibilities for guided rough hiking in the wild frontier lands at the foot of **San Lorenzo** (for information, contact Señor Sar through *Hotel Bajo Caracoles* on ✆02963/490100). Pack horses are available for rent ($30 per day), and guides should be arranged well in advance ($150 per day for an English-speaking high-mountain guide).

At the moment, access is allowed onto this private land, but it is a sensitive issue: ask permission first at the estancia or from Señor Sar, and be conscious of the need for extreme environmental awareness – don't light fires or leave rubbish. Bring provisions and good camping gear, and prepare to get your hiking boots thoroughly soaked. To reach *Los Ñires* you must ford the fast-flowing Río Oro on foot, on horseback or by truck, but be careful after heavy rains – approximately twice a year (usually in spring or summer), floods make this crossing impossible for several days at a time. **Climbers** intending to ascend San Lorenzo from the (easier) Chilean side can cross from here to access Padre de Agostini's base camp, owned by the mountain guide, Luís Soto de la Cruz. Although it's not strictly legal, frontier guards tend to turn a blind eye to legitimate climbers crossing in this manner, but don't attempt to continue to Cochrane in Chile or to re-enter Argentina further south in the Parque Nacional Perito Moreno. The best **maps** available are those from the Instituto Geográfico Militar (#4772-27 "Cerro Pico Agudo" or #4772-33 y 32 "Lago Belgrano").

The RN40: Bajo Caracoles to Tres Lagos

The 380-kilometre stretch of the RN40 between Bajo Caracoles and Tres Lagos is the most rugged of all. High crosswinds and tiredness can make driving hazardous, so always keep your speed under control, and take breaks for coffee. The **Parque Nacional Perito Moreno**, accessed by a turn-off 100km south of Bajo Caracoles, is dealt with under a separate section (see p.632).

Las Horquetas

Continuing south along the RN40 from Bajo Caracoles brings you, after 107km, to **LAS HORQUETAS** (population 5). In blatant disregard of the three most important dictates for opening a successful retailing business – "location, location, location" – *Las Horquetas* sticks by the Patagonian motto of *"persever y triunfarás"* (persevere and you will triumph). Once a rip-off joint, this Baghdad Café of the RN40 is now run by a scrupulously fair family who provide a good-humoured service in difficult conditions. **Rooms** (②) with shared bathroom can get chilly and are basic, as are facilities (there's no flushing toilet, and the shower has to be heated in advance by generator – ask for *el generador*); the no-nonsense meals are excellent value (a $7 pasta will feed two); and emergency motoring services include tyre repair and a hand-held petrol pump. The best-maintained feature of this run-down place is the well-stocked **bar** – a famous meeting point for local Patagonian characters – and its welcome range of *caña quemadas* and pisco sours.

Around Gobernador Gregores

Fifty kilometres south of *Las Horquetas*, the RP25 branches east to San Julián on the coast, passing through **GOBERNADOR GREGORES**, whose services include a fuel station and two hotels: *San Francisco*, at San Martín 463 (☎02962/491039, fax 491038; ③, ④ en suite), and *Cañadón León* at Roca 397 (☎02962/491082; ③), with less expensive singles.

Continuing along the RN40, you pass the *Estancia La Angostura* (☎02962/452010, fax 452269; ⑥, breakfast included; Sept–May), 4km off the road. This is definitely a working estancia rather than a hotel, and accommodation is in unpretentious, rather uninspiring rooms in the family house – you'll get a real sense of the realities of life in the Patagonian interior, and the hard-working Kusanovic family will show you documents that trace a hundred years of history in the area. This is also a good place to try a typical regional dish that's rarely available to the tourist: *liebre al escabeche* (hare in escabeche; $20 for a three-course meal), which is prepared with a vinegar, carrot and onion marinade. Bird-watchers should keep their eyes open for possible sightings of the endangered, endemic hooded grebe (*macá tobiano*), which sometimes inhabits the pools of the attractive wetlands of the Río Chico that front the estancia.

The Kusanovic family also owns *La Siberia* (⑤ with shared bathroom, breakfast included; Nov–March), a roadside estancia 61km to the south which has less expensive accommodation and serves simple fare including, in season, good apricot tarts. It's situated above the shores of **Lago Cardiel**, a startlingly turquoise lake, named after a Jesuit priest who explored the area in 1745 – though saline, its waters contain a proliferation of three-kilogram brook and rainbow trout.

Tres Lagos

Beyond Lago Cardiel, the RN40 continues through one of its most desolate stretches before reaching the YPF **fuel station** at a junction on the outskirts of Tres Lagos. The

TOURIST ESTANCIAS OF SANTA CRUZ

Argentina is composed, in many people's minds, of a vast patchwork of immense *lati-fundias* presided over by their *estanciero* owners. Although this image is no longer as true as it once was, landowning is still deeply embedded in the national consciousness, and an opportunity to stay at an estancia provides an excellent glimpse into this important facet of Argentinian culture. The sheep-farming province of Santa Cruz is a perfect place to try this out. A group of estancia owners runs the **Estancias de Santa Cruz**, which produces an excellent booklet promoting their establishments, available from the head office at Suipacha 1120, Buenos Aires Capital Federal (☎ & fax 011/4325 3098 or 4325 3102, *estancias@interlink.com.ar*).

Room prices are generally too high for backpackers and budget travellers, although some places run campsites on their land. Also, though certain standards are uniform (for example, a commitment that the owner should attend to guests, provide home-grown produce, and apply environmental standards to water and waste disposal), establishments do vary widely. They fall into three broad categories. Firstly, the working estancias, where tourism is a needed to supplement income from the primary activity, sheep farming, and little or no changes have been made to upgrade facilities – a real insight into life on the estancias as it is, without cosmetic makeovers. Secondly come places whose main residence – the *casco antiguo* – offers ample comfort, and whose mainstay is a happy halfway house between tourism and raising livestock. A third group has now made a complete transition to tourism, often having invested heavily in tailor-made cabins or bungalows so as to meet all but the most demanding standards of comfort. These could reasonably be described as countryside hotels. This is not the complete picture, and one of the joys of travelling around the estancias is that each has its own indelible character. If you need help in choosing ones to suit your tastes, or have any queries, contact the helpful staff at head office.

YPF is the stop for the weekly bus between Luis Piedra Buena on the coast and El Chaltén (leaves Piedra Buena Fri; returns from Chaltén Sun); it's also the best place for hitching. You can pitch a tent for $2, and there are some reasonable bunks inside ($7 per person). Several roads converge at this junction, including the one to Lago San Martín (see below), but signposting is not particularly clear, so make sure you choose the right track.

The road leading due east from the YPF takes you 2km into the village of **TRES LAGOS**: not a place worth visiting in itself, but which has a free municipal **campsite**, shaded by cherry trees (take the first left and it's 100m down the road by a small stream). Other services include two tyre-repair places (*gomerías*), a supermarket, and a **public telephone** (the last heading north on the RN40 before Bajo Caracoles). Two **hotels** vie for custom: the tatty if friendly *Ahoniken* on the main street (☎02962/495018; ② with shared bathroom); and the clean if pricier *Sorsona's* to the left of the main street (☎02962/495033; ③). *Ahoniken's* restaurant serves pasta and *milanesas* at any time of the day or night, and prices are reasonable ($8).

South of the Tres Lagos YPF junction, the RN40 turns westwards and continues for 36km to the turn-off towards El Chaltén (see p.637).

Lago San Martín

From the Tres Lagos YPF station another gravel road, the RP31, strikes out west towards the area of **Lago San Martín**, 110km away. This lake, the most erratically shaped of all the major Patagonian lakes, with its glacial fjords stretching across the border into Chile like the tentacles of some gigantic ice-blue squid, is one of Patagonia's most isolated attractions. It was named after Argentina's national hero but, symbolically in an area that has had more than its fair share of entrenched patriotic wrangles over the placement of the frontier, it transmutes into Lago O'Higgins on the Chilean side, in honour of Chile's corresponding founding father. Ironically, these two great generals were contemporaries and friends who united to fight a common cause in the struggle for independence from Spain.

Fortunately, cross-border co-operation is increasing these days, and the region is opening up to tourism, especially now that Chile's **Carretera Austral** (a one-track dirt road) has reached its frontier settlement of **Villa O'Higgins**. Nevertheless, the area's climate can be inhospitable, and furious winds frequently lash the lake's surface, making navigation on its waters a perilous enterprise. The best **accommodation** is located on the southern shores of the lake at the *Estancia La Maipú* (in Buenos Aires ☎011/4901-5591, fax 4903-4967; ⑤, with low-season discounts of 20 percent; Oct–April). You can also stay in the old peon quarters here (bring your own sleeping bag) or camp (both options cost $12 per person). A **condor** breeding site (*condorera*) offers great opportunities to view these birds in the wild and the **horseriding** is first rate, with recommended trips of up to three days. Transport to and from Tres Lagos must be arranged in advance and costs $120 per trip.

The Parque Nacional Perito Moreno

Despite being one of the country's very first national parks, established in 1937, the **PARQUE NACIONAL PERITO MORENO** is one of the most isolated and least-visited of any in Argentina. This is not a "sightseeing" park in the way that Nahuel Huapi is, nor does it have the obvious mountain highlights of the Fitz Roy massif or Torres del Paine in Chile, even though the peak of San Lorenzo lies just to the north. The bulk of the park's forested mountain scenery lies in its western two thirds, which are reserved for scientific study, meaning that most of the area accessible to the public consists of harsh, arid steppe. Its tourist infrastructure is rudimentary, with the administration buildings lacking even public toilets for those who have made the considerable effort to get here. Nevertheless, what the park does offer – if you discount the whistling of the near-incessant westerly winds – is a peace and solitude that few other places in the continent can equal.

Though you can visit a lot of the park by car in a day or two, you could spend much longer trekking here without seeing everything. The park attracts hikers and naturalists who come to appreciate the starkly beautiful high pampa, virulently colourful lakes, the imperious snowcapped hulk of San Lorenzo, and the wildlife that thrives in the absence of man. Guanacos can be seen at unusually close quarters, and their alarm call, a rasping laugh, can be startling. The very luckiest visitors may glimpse an endangered huemul, a puma or a Geoffroy's cat (*gato montés*). Condors are plentiful, and other **birdlife** includes the Chilean flamingo; black-necked swans; four species of grebe (including, in the summer, the graceful, endangered hooded grebe, or *macá tobiano*); steamer ducks; *chorlito* sandpipers; upland geese (*cauquenes*); buff-necked ibises (*bandurrias*); Darwin's rheas (ñandúes); and the powerful black-chested buzzard eagle (*águila mora*). In the *lenga* woods, you may come across the austral pygmy owl, a surprisingly tame and curious bird that you can approach to within a couple of metres. One of the park's most biologically interesting features are its lakes: aggressive, introduced species of trout and salmon have devastated indigenous fish populations throughout Argentina, but the ones here have never been stocked with non-endemic species – they're now protected, and no fishing is allowed in the park. Nevertheless, it's thought that trout may have begun to appear in Lago Burmeister, having worked their way upriver. This is symptomatic perhaps of the fact that the park's era of isolation is coming to an end: whereas only ninety people visited in 1992, the number was approaching a thousand by the end of the decade.

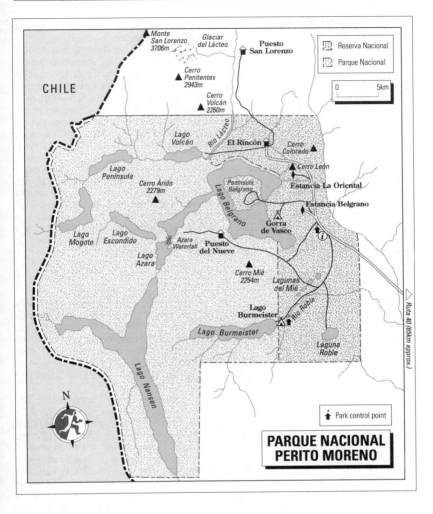

The sensitivity of this special area's environment should be respected at all times: do not light fires; do not remove any archeological artefact or any of the fossil ammonites; bury any toilet waste; and pack out all other rubbish. Walkers should note that, despite it being marked as a pass on several maps, it is strictly illegal to cross into Chile at Paso Cordoniz by Lago Nansen.

Arrival and information

Although the *ripio* roads into the park are reasonably well maintained, access can be guaranteed only from about the end of November to mid-March. After that, heavy snowfalls cut off the route on occasion: if travelling out of season, bring extra provisions in case you get stuck. Always bring warm, waterproof clothes, since the weather

changes moods like a spoilt child. Temperatures are bracing all year, and can drop to
−25°C in winter, even before the wind-chill is taken into account.

Unless you're a guest at *La Oriental* (see p.635), there's nowhere to buy fuel for
either your vehicles or your belly, so come well prepared. Cyclists attempting the trip
from the RN40 should be aware that there is no reliable water source along the 90km
branch road, so stock up either in Las Horquetas or Bajo Caracoles. Hitching both in
and out of the park is tricky – prepare for waits of days rather than hours. Visitors to *La
Oriental* can arrange a pick-up from Las Horquetas, although (especially where groups
are concerned) this is a racket, with a one-way price of $70 per person. Otherwise, ask
at the park office in Gobernador Gregores, San Martín 889 (☎02962/491477) to see if
you might be able to hitch in with a *guardaparque* on one of their infrequent trips to
town.

Ten kilometres from the entrance to the park is a tiny group of administration buildings (8am–8pm), where you are required to register and are given a (free) camping permit. You'll also be given a personal welcoming talk, leaflets on the trails and wildlife
(some in English), and there are creative educational displays in the small museum.
You can refill water containers, but there are no other facilities. Anyone planning to
head for the refuges at Puesto del Nueve and Puesto San Lorenzo must also register
here. Theoretically, you are not allowed to **camp** at the administration, although in
practice, latecomers can pitch tent for a night.

The southern sector

Six kilometres south of the administration you come across the **Lagunas del Mié**, a
series of shallow lagoons in the stark plateau of the pampas that are favoured by a rich
variety of feeding waterfowl. Near the first *laguna*, a signposted track to the left leads
south across the steppe to **Laguna Roble** (12km from administration), a sometime
summer haunt of the hooded grebe, but check at the administration to verify whether
the footbridge (*pasarela*) over the Río Roble has been reconstructed. A little further on,
another track branches right to join the path towards the Puesto del Nueve refuge and
Lago Azara (see p.635).

Otherwise, continue south to the gorgeous marine-blue **Lago Burmeister** – curiously, the only lake in the park that drains into the Atlantic rather than the Pacific –
squeezed into its wooded mountain valley, 16km from the administration. A well-sited
campsite lies in a stand of southern beech trees at the head of the lake, with a latrine
as its only facility. Windbreaks give protection from the persistent stormy gusts, and
this is the only place in the park where you are allowed to make fires (always extinguish
them well with water, not earth). The *guardaparque* stationed here will take you on a
guided walk across the Río Roble on the northern side of the lake to see the protected
rock paintings of guanacos and handprints – a legacy of the seasonal migrations of
groups of hunter-gatherers, some of which are believed to be 9000 years old, but most
are showing their age. The adjacent area is also blessed with rich deposits of marine
fossils.

The central sector

North of the administration, the road passes the *Estancia Belgrano*, and then forks left
towards **Lago Belgrano**, the most remarkable of the lakes accessible to visitors, with
one of the most intensely gaudy turquoise colours anywhere in Patagonia, and an
eccentric form like a ragged ear. After 8km, you'll come to a signposted side-track,
which runs south for 2km to the intimate *Gorra de Vasco* **campsite**, with space for but
one tent and a vehicle (no fires permitted; no toilet facilities). Otherwise, continue on
for 2km towards the scrub-covered **Península Belgrano** – to all intents an island,

except that Mother Nature has forgotten to cut its improbable umbilical attachment to the mainland. A leaflet in English is available from administration for a self-guided two-hour trail through the *mata negra* bushes, detailing facts about the behaviour of its graceful guanaco inhabitants.

A longer hike of two to three days can be made to the south of Lago Belgrano, but you must ask permission from administration first to use the old shepherd's refuge, **Puesto del Nueve**, as a base. From here, you can visit the ten-metre waterfall that drains Lago Belgrano and explore the region around beautiful **Lago Azara**, where you stand a slim chance of finding footprints or traces of huemules in the *lenga* forest. You may cook on the small stove in the refuge shed, but replace all firewood used.

Cerro León and La Oriental

Just to the north of *Estancia La Oriental* stands a cliff face that is stained by great white smears, indicating the presence of condors' nests. This **condorera** offers you the most realistic chance of sighting one of the giant birds, especially when the morning sun warms the rock face and the thermals start. You may like to climb **Cerro León**, 1434m, which affords excellent views of the heartland of the park, and which is one of the favoured habitats of a famous rodent: the *chinchillón gris* or *pilquín* (a type of vizcacha found only in Santa Cruz, and bearing some resemblance to a chinchilla).

The centre of operations for many staying in the park is the **tourist estancia** *La Oriental* (☎02962/452196 or 452445, fax 452235; ⑤; Nov–March), which has given up the struggle to survive as a purely working farm and has, somewhat reluctantly, embraced tourism. Fortunately for the owners, it occupies a privileged position not just scenically, but as the one place in the park where non-campers can stay. The rooms inside the house are more comfortable than the plain and rather draughty old peon quarters, now called the "Casa Patagónica" (which also contains cheap triples and quadruples). Facilities for **camping** are clean and pleasantly sheltered, but it's expensive, at $15 per tent, especially if you're on your own. They sell firewood (*leña*), but no provisions; fuel (*nafta* and *gasoil*) is sold to guests only; and there's radio contact with the outside world. Señora Lada cooks simple but hearty food ($20 for a three-course meal), and serves delicious scones. **Horseriding** from here is fantastic, and affordable by Argentinian standards ($15 for 3hr, plus $35 for a guide), especially if you can split the cost of the guide.

The northern sector

From *La Oriental*, take the pass between Cerro León and the La Condorera for a two-and-a-half-hour walk to the red-roofed *guardaparque*'s house at **El Rincón**, once one of the most isolated estancias in Argentina – you can **camp** here. Just before the buildings a track branches west towards the Chilean border. This is transitable by car for 3km, and from here it's a five-kilometre walk to the desolate shores of **Lago Volcán**, a milky-green glacial lake. Although a pass (Paso de la Balsa) is marked on some maps, to the west of here, this is not a legal frontier crossing and you will be detained if caught.

From El Rincón it's a stiff five- to six-hour walk to the **Puesto San Lorenzo** refuge; if you can speak Spanish, consult the helpful *guardaparque* about conditions ahead first. As a safety measure, you are required to register with him or at administration: say how many days you are planning to stay and inform them when you return. Take the winding track to the right of the house (traversible in a normal car for 5km, and then in a high-clearance 4WD), leaving the park's northern boundary. After one particularly tight hairpin down a small gravel scarp, you must ford two streams and pick up the track on the other side. Eventually you reach a bluff with a steep moraine scarp, which is far as you can get with a vehicle (9km from El Rincón).

From here, you have a fine view of the turbulent **Río Lácteo**, which you must keep on your left on the walk to the *puesto*. The track drops down the bluff, passes a windbreak that provides a sheltered spot for a tent, and then gives up entirely in the woods 200m beyond. From here on, there's always a temptation to drop down onto the flat gravel bed of the Río Lácteo, but resist this and stay high, at least until you have passed the huge, grey, alluvial moraine fan that pushes the khaki river waters far over to the right-hand (eastern) side of the valley. After this, the path drops down and wends its way through the marshy grassland that borders the gravel river valley. A little further on, the tin shack of the *puesto* is easily visible from a distance. The *puesto* is welcomingly decorated with the horned skulls of dead beasts and a supply of firewood and a rustic stove await inside, but remember to replace the wood you use so that it can dry off in time for the next trekkers.

With care, you can ford the Río Lácteo here. Beyond, a path leads west up the valley towards **Glaciar Lácteo** and the two-thousand-metre fortress wall of **San Lorenzo's southeast face**, one of the most "Himalayan" sights in the Patagonian cordillera – if you are lucky enough, that is, to catch this notoriously temperamental mountain in one of its more benevolent moods. Another path leads north from the *puesto* towards Cerro Hermoso and the fabulous northeast face of San Lorenzo, but this is for fit, experienced trekkers only, preferably with a guide (try Paco Sepúlveda from Perito Moreno; ☎02963/432306), as the path soon fizzles out and the weather can close in quickly – take a compass and the best map available (Instituto Geográfico Militar #4772-27 "Cerro Pico Agudo" and #4772-33 y 32 "Lago Belgrano").

El Chaltén and the Fitz Roy Massif

The RP23 turns off the RN40 35km west of Tres Lagos, running parallel to the northern shore of Patagonia's third largest lake, Lago Viedma (see p.645). From this position the **Fitz Roy Massif** rears up threateningly in the background.

The northernmost section of the **Parque Nacional Los Glaciares**, the Fitz Roy sector, contains some of the most breathtakingly beautiful mountain peaks on the planet. Two concentric jaws of jagged teeth puncture the Patagonian sky, with the 3445-metre incisor of **Monte Fitz Roy** at the centre of the massif. This sculpted peak was known to the Tehuelche as El Chaltén, "The Mountain that Smokes" or "The Volcano", due to the almost perpetual presence of a scarf of cloud attached in rakish fashion to its summit. It is not inconceivable, however, that the Tehuelche were using the term in a rather more metaphorical sense to allude to the fiery pink colour that the rock walls turn when struck by the first light of dawn. Francisco P. Moreno saw fit to baptize the pagan summit with the surname of the evangelical captain of the *Beagle*, who, with Charles Darwin, had viewed the Andes from a distance, after having journeyed up the Río Santa Cruz by whaleboat to within 50km of Lago Argentino. Alongside Monte Fitz Roy rise **Cerro Poincenot** and **Aguja Saint Exupéry**, whilst set behind them is the forbidding needle of **Cerro Torre**, a finger that stands in bold defiance of all the elements that the Southern Patagonian Icecap hurls against it.

Though not as extensive or as famous globally as Chile's Torres del Paine (see p.662), this area rivals it on most counts. Geologically, the two are in many ways sister parks, characterized by majestic spires of granite-like diorite, formed when the softer layers of rock that had covered these igneous intrusions eroded over the subsequent eighteen million years (twelve million in the case of Torres del Paine) to reveal their polished bones. The two massifs are afflicted by some of the most unpredictable – and frequently downright malevolent – weather you will come across, and many meticulously planned climbing expeditions have been foiled by the mountains' stubborn brew of sulky grey weather. When Darwin spoke of summits "occasionally peeping through their dusky envelope of clouds", he was conveying a generously pastoral effect that distance conferred.

Some 77km after the RN40 turn-off, you cross the tumultous meltwaters of the **Río de las Vueltas**. The park's information centre is a further 11km further on, and less than 1km past that, across the bridge over the Río Fitz Roy, lies the village of El Chaltén.

El Chaltén

Now that Fitz Roy is no longer a well-kept secret and an exclusive private paradise for climbers, the village of **EL CHALTÉN** has undergone a convulsive expansion. Established in 1985, this thriving tourist centre is regrettably showing signs of uncontrolled development, and whereas certain buildings have been built in a style sympathetic to the mountain surroundings, others would look more at ease in the beach resort of Mar del Plata. That said, the atmosphere in the village is pleasant and relaxed, with a friendly mix of young Argentinians and foreign visitors.

Rearing up on the opposite bank of the Río de las Vueltas is the curiously stepped, dark grey cliff face of **Cerro Pirámide**, while from the southern and eastern fringes of the village the tips of the park's most daunting peaks, Fitz Roy and Cerro Torre, can be glimpsed. Otherwise, in terms of specific sights, there is only the classically uncluttered Alpine **chapel** on the eastern edge of the village. Built by Austrian craftsmen with Austrian materials, it's a fitting memorial to the climbing purist, Toni Egger, as well as others who have lost their lives in the park.

More than most tourist centres, El Chaltén shuts up shop for the winter season. Between Easter and mid-October, many establishments are closed. Conversely, in high season, especially January, it is advisable to book accommodation in advance. As with most parks in Patagonia, autumn is a good time to visit: March and April are beautiful months, when the wind normally drops. The spring months of October and November are also good for avoiding the crowds, if not the winds.

Arrival and information

The **national park information centre** (8am–8pm; ☎ & fax 02962/493004), less than 1km before the village, is a necessary point of call where helpful young volunteers advise visitors of the park's regulations. Inside are wildlife exhibits, a message board, and a useful information book for climbers, all of whom must register here, as should anyone planning to stay at the Lago Toro refuge and campsite to the south. Fishing licences can be purchased at the desk here, or in the Mercado Artesanal in the village. Catch, if you can, one of the free slide shows (Wed; in English some Thurs; 8pm). The **tourist office** is in the Comisión de Fomento (Jan–March Mon–Fri 9am–8pm, Sat 3–8pm; ☎02962/493011), one of the first buildings on the right as you enter the village – helpful, but of less use than the national park's information centre.

Orientation is straightforward: Avenida M. Güemes is the main avenue you come in on across the bridge. Güemes finishes at the axis of Calle Lago del Desierto, and one block to the right is where Avenida San Martín begins – the only other main artery and the start of the RP23 northwards. Despite having a relatively small population, the village is quite spread out. Unless you ask otherwise, **buses** from Calafate will drop you off at their respective offices/hotels; it's better to try to get them to drop you off in the centre if that's where you plan to stay. Caltur buses start and finish at the *Fitz Roy Inn*; Chaltén Travel at the *Rancho Grande*; and Los Glaciares at the confitería *La Senyera del Torre*, at the junction of Avenida Güemes and Lago del Desierto – all these companies run daily services in season to Calafate, but there's only one service every five days out of season. The direct Burmeister service to Río Gallegos and its airport (Nov–Easter Tues & Fri) can be booked at Tur Aike on the corner of Avenida Güemes and Lago del

Desierto. A service runs in the summer months to the town of Perito Moreno and Los Antiguos for those who plan to cross into Chile at Chile Chico.

Chaltén has a YPF fuel station, and the confitería *La Senyera del Torre* acts as a post office, but there are no money-changing facilities or banks. For trekkers, the El Volcán hardware shop sells Calor camping gas, whilst the Mercado Artesanal on San Martín (mid-Nov to Easter) rents climbing and trekking gear, including tents and sleeping bags, as well as selling expensive but well-made Argentinian handicrafts. Fitzroy Expediciones (☎ & fax 02962/493017; *froyexp@internet.siscotel.com*), at Lionel Terray 545, rents harnesses and organizes both **trekking on Glaciar Torre**, teaching basic ice-climbing techniques (minimum two people; $60per person), and much more serious and expensive expeditions onto the continental icecap. In addition, they arrange **horse-riding** excursions to the Cerro Torre and Fitz Roy base camps (5–6hr) or Piedra del Fraile (8hr); horses can also be hired from Rodolfo Guerra near *Rancho Grande* or from *El Relincho* campsite. **Boat trips** ($60) aboard the *Huemul* to Glaciar Viedma and the *Estancia Helsingfors* (see p.646) can be organized.

Accommodation

Accommodation is to be found in the centre or on and around Avenida San Martín, to the north of the village. *Camping Madsen*, 1km from centre at the far north of town where Avenida San Martín ends, is the best of the free **campsites**, at the trailhead for Laguna Capri and with a scenic setting. It has no showers and only one latrine; you should only use fallen wood for fires. Two of the best paying sites are *Ruca Mahuida*, Lionel Terray s/n (☎ & fax 02962/493018; $6 per person), with 24hr hot water, showers and barbecue facilities; and *El Refugio*, San Martín s/n (Oct–April; $3 per person), next to Río de las Vueltas, with 24hr hot showers and barbecue facilities.

Albergue Patagonia, San Martín 493 (☎ & fax 02962/493019). The most homely of the YHA-affiliated hostels, run by a hard-working, genial crew (English and Dutch spoken). It has cooking facilities; a cheap laundry service; book exchange; luggage store; and a snug living-room with videos. It also serves hearty three-course meals ($10). YHA members $10 (non-members $12).

La Base, Lago del Desierto s/n (☎02962/493031). Some of the best-value rooms (for two to four people) in El Chaltén, several with rare mountain views. Its owners are hospitable; and it has kitchen facilities and free video showings in the attic sitting-room. Closed Oct some years. ④.

Cabañas Kalenshen, opposite *Fitz Roy Inn* on Lionel Terray (☎02962/493081 or ☎ & fax 02966/430515). Neat wooden cabins for two to six people at an affordable price, equipped with small gas cooker, pots and cutlery. ⑤.

Casa de Piedra, Lago del Desierto s/n (☎ & fax 02962/493015). Rents neat bungalows and rooms, with great beds, good private bathrooms and plentiful hot water – some rooms have the village's best views of the high peaks. Its knowledgeable geologist owner also works as a guide. ⑤.

Fitz Roy Inn, San Martín s/n (☎ & fax 02962/493062). Double rooms in a rather barrack-like building, with a garish green roof, plus less expensive, four-bed, hostel-type rooms with shared bathroom ($15 per person). Also has an expensive laundry service and acts as the agent for Caltur buses. Oct–April. ⑥.

Los Ñires, Lago del Desierto s/n (☎ & fax 02962/493009). Central, YHA-affiliated hostel, some of whose rooms have partial views of Fitz Roy. Open Oct–Easter. Cramped dorm beds (YHA members 10; non-members $12) and en-suite rooms for two to four people ⑤).

Posada Poincenot, San Martín 693 (☎02962/493022). Peaceful, spacious, cabin-style guesthouse run by a welcoming couple. It also has triples and quadruples, a laundry service, and serves a good-value three-course dinner ($10). Nov–March. ④.

La Quinta, 3km before the entrance to the village (☎02962/493012 or 011/4252-4279). Comfortable accommodation in this tourist estancia. Its owner is extremely knowledgeable about the region's history.

Rancho Grande, San Martín 635 (☎ & fax 02962/493005, *rancho@cotecal.com.ar*). A large, modern YHA-affiliated hostel with clean, clinical four-bed rooms, and one double (⑤). It has a lively bar/restaurant area ($12–15 for lunch or dinner), kitchen facilities, left luggage and a good laundry service, and you can pay with credit cards and TCs (no commission). It's also the agent for Chaltén Travel buses. Nov–Easter. YHA members $10 (non-members $12).

Eating

Provisions in Chaltén are expensive: Calafate offers much more in terms of price and selection (especially fruit and vegetables). Chaltén's best-value foodstores are the 2 de Abril **supermarket**, at the beginning of Avenida San Martín (try the fantastic home-made bread), and El Gringuito, a couple of blocks away on Calle Río de las Vueltas. The El Charito kiosk on Güemes offers the same fine bread and delicious, if expensive, home-made tarts.

   Restaurants are all fairly pricey. *Abuelo Emilio* on Calle Lago del Desierto, some-times called by its old name, *The Wall*, offers fine trout and *asados* served by its good-humoured owners in an intimate atmosphere by a roaring log fire. *Josh Aike*, in a fun, funky wooden cabin at the western end of the same street, cooks reasonable pizzas, and has well-chilled beers and slabs of chocolate. This is one of the only nightlife options in the village, along with the restaurant-bar area of the *Rancho Grande* youth hostel. *La Casita*, a cosy confitería opposite the *Fitz Roy Inn* on San Martín, makes a fine meeting-place and serves home-made pasta ($9) and cakes. The most imaginative menu in the village can be found at *Ruca Mahuida* on Lionel Terray, just off San Martín, with sur-prising options such as fondue and venison ragout ($12–16).

Trekking in the park

The area's claim to be the **trekking capital of Argentina** is justified, and the closer you get to the mountains, the clearer their beauty becomes. Early mornings are the best time for views and photography, both for the light and the weather, since the west-erly winds tend to pick up from about 11am, bringing the clouds with them. (Frustrated cameramen may wonder why on some days the clouds never seem to be swept from the summit of peaks such as Fitz Roy, despite there being blue sky all around and an obvious wind. In fact, the winds are actually *forming* the clouds: the air is chilled as it speeds over the rock, causing the moisture to condense. The clouds only disappear when the winds drop.)

   Adequate outdoor clothing is essential at all times of the year, as snowstorms are pos-sible even in midsummer. Unlike in Torres del Paine, one of the beauties of this park is that those with limited time, or who don't consider themselves in peak fitness, can still make worthwhile **day walks**, using El Chaltén as a base, and thus not have to lug around heavy rucksacks. For those who enjoy camping, the quintessential Monte Fitz Roy/Cerro Torre loop at the centre of the park makes a good three-day option, given good weather; the longer interlocking circuit to the north will add at least another two or three days. There are, of course, a variety of alternatives for those with more time, including the trek to Lago Toro and the Paso del Viento to the south. A certain degree of flexibility is desirable in all cases, due to the likelihood of the weather playing havoc with the views.

   The central loop can be done in either direction. The advantage of going anticlock-wise is that you avoid the steep climb up to Lagunas Madre y Hija from the valley, and you have the wind at your back when returning down that valley to Chaltén. However, the biggest gamble is always what the weather will be like around Cerro Torre, so if this most unpredictable of peaks is visible on day one, you might like to head for it first.

   The blanket **ban on lighting campfires** in the park must be observed, so if you need your food hot, please make careful use of gas stoves. Pack out all rubbish, and minimalize your impact on this highly sensitive environment by sticking to the marked trails; camping only where permitted; using only biodegradable detergents and being as sparing as possible in their use and the use of toothpaste; not going to the toilet near water sources; and burying all toilet waste.

The best trekking **map** available is the 1:50,000 *Monte Fitz Roy & Cerro Torre* published by Zagier & Urruty, on sale in village, which includes a 1:100,000 scale map of the Lago del Desierto area, but the topographical features are not always accurate, particularly as regards tree cover. The informative *Trekking in Chaltén and Lago del Desierto* ($10) by Miguel A. Alonso is also worth checking out.

El Chaltén to Laguna Capri, Campamento Poincenot and Fitz Roy

Your starting point is the house overlooking the *Madsen* campsite, at the northern end of Avenida San Martín. The path is clearly indicated, climbing up through the wooded slopes of Cerro Rosado and Cerro León, until the scenery opens out with views of Fitz Roy. About an hour into the trek, a turn-off left leads after a few minutes to the **campsite** at **Laguna Capri** – there are great views, but the site is rather exposed to the winds, and water from the lake should be boiled or treated. Better, if you have the time, to push on down the main path for another hour, crossing one stream just past the turn-off to Laguna Madre, and another brook, the Chorrillo del Salto, five minutes away. Pitch your tent at the **Campamento Poincenot**, named after one of the team of French climbers who made the victorious first ascent of Fitz Roy in 1952. According to the official story, Poincenot drowned whilst trying to cross the turbulent waters of the Río Fitz Roy before the assault on the mountain even took place, though another, darker rumour hinted that this was no accident, but the work of a cuckolded estancia owner, enraged by his wife's sexual infidelities with the dashing Gallic mountaineer. The campsite covers a sprawling area, set amongst *lenga* and *ñire* woodland on the eastern bank of the Río Blanco. Choose your spot well and you needn't have to get out of your tent to see the rosy blaze of dawn on the cliffs of Fitz Roy and its accompanying peaks.

From *Poincenot*, about an hour's climb brings you to an outstanding viewpoint. Follow the crisscrossing paths to the wooden bridge that spans the main current of the Río Blanco. A second, makeshift bridge takes you to the far bank, from where the path heads up through the woods, passing the ramshackle refuges of the **Río Blanco campsite** (exclusively for the use of climbers, and with no views of Fitz Roy peak), before pushing on past the tree line. The next section is tough going as the heavily eroded path ascends a steep gradient, but mercifully it's not long before you come to the top of the ridge, cross a verdant, boggy meadow and then climb the final hurdle: a moraine ridge that hides a breathtaking panorama on the other side.

You now stand in the cirque of the rich, navy-blue **Laguna de los Tres**, fed by a concertinaed glacier and ringed by a giant's crown of granite peaks, including Aguja St-Exupéry (named after Antoine de St-Exupéry, who drew on his experiences as a pioneer of Patagonian aviation when writing the minor classic, *Night Flight*), Cerro Poincenot, Fitz Roy and a host of other spikes. Climb the small rocky outcrop to the left for even more impressive views: you now stand on the ridge between the basins of Laguna de los Tres and Laguna Sucia, some two hundred metres below the level of the first lake. The **Glaciar Río Blanco**, hanging above Laguna Sucia, periodically sheds scales of ice and snow which, though they look tiny at this distance, reveal their true magnitude by the ear-splitting reports they make as they hit the surface of the lake. Although some people try to scramble down the scree slope to reach Laguna Sucia, this can be dangerous – you are better advised to retrace your steps and follow the path on the western (right-hand) bank of the Río Blanco (40min from the Río Blanco refuge).

The Lagunas Madre y Hija trail

From Campamento Poincenot there are two options. One is to cross the Río Blanco and follow the poorly marked and badly maintained path northwards along its western bank towards the Río Eléctrico and Piedra del Fraile (see p.643). Another is to take the trail

Llao Llao Hotel, near Bariloche, Río Negro Province

Caviàhue, Neuquén Province

La Trochita, Esquel, Chubut Province

Cordillera farmstead, Chubut Province

Windblown trees, Parque Nacional los Glaciares, Patagonia

Aguja Pollone, Fitz Roy area, Patagonia

Río Oro, Santa Cruz Province

Cueva de las Manos, Patagonia

Autumnal tree, Tierra del Fuego

Estancia Harberton, Tierra del Fuego

Ushuaia, Tierra del Fuego

past **Lagunas Madre y Hija** (Mother and Daughter Lagoons), which leads on to the Cerro Torre base camp (2hr 30min). To do this, you'll need to double back towards Laguna Capri a little way, before finding the signposted route.

The Laguna Capri path can be a little difficult to locate if you've come from Río Eléctrico in the north, since there are many misleading trails through the woodland at the back of the campsite. Don't succumb to the temptation of making your own path across the valley floor towards the eastern side of Laguna Madre, as the terrain is extremely boggy. If you're unsure, walk due south of the campsite to the Chorrillo del Salto stream and head east along its northern bank until you come to the bridge, where you'll pick up the path towards Laguna Capri and El Chaltén. The turn-off to Laguna Madre is five minutes away, on your right after crossing another bridge over a small stream.

The route past Lagunas Madre y Hija is not marked at all on some maps and is sig-nalled as closed on others. Neither is correct. In fact, it makes for gentle walking and is easy to follow, pushing through knee-high bushes and avoiding the swampy ground for the most part. Look out for upland geese (*cauquenes*), which like to graze by the lakeshore. The path curls round to the right, passing the far end of Laguna Hija, and continues through mixed pasture and woodland before coming to the lip of the valley of Río Fitz Roy. Here the path descends the steep slope and, if you look to your right, you may get your first glimpses of Cerro Torre through the *lenga* forest. Emerging from the trees, the slope levels out and you link up with the path from El Chaltén to *Campamento Bridwell*/Laguna Torre (see below).

Cerro Torre

A variety of paths lead out from El Chaltén towards **Cerro Torre** and **Campamento Bridwell** (also known as *Campamento Laguna Torre*). *Bridwell* is the closest campsite to the mountain for trekkers and also acts as the base camp for climbers. The trail that follows the course of the Río Fitz Roy is perhaps the toughest going and is poorly main-tained in places, although it does have some excellent views of the river gorge. A sec-ond trail leads out from behind the *La Base* hostel, but more scenic is the one reached by turning off Avenida San Martín by the Mercado Artesanal, picking up the clearly marked path at the base of the hill. This path climbs up past the eerie blackened skele-ton of a large *lenga* tree (now used as a monument to the dangers of cigarettes), on to some huge lumps of rock used by local climbers for bouldering, and then weaves through some hilly country before arriving, after a ninety-minute walk, at a viewpoint where you hope to catch your first proper view of Cerro Torre.

The path subsequently levels out along the Río Fitz Roy valley, in whose ragged stands of southern beech you're likely to come across wrens and the thorn-tailed rayadito, a diminutive foraging bird with attractive chestnut colouring and distinctive eye stripe that bounces around, seemingly oblivious to your presence. A signposted turn-off on the right leads to Lagunas Madre y Hija (see above), which you'll need to return to if hiking the central circuit in clockwise fashion. This path soon starts to climb up a steep, wooded hillside, before levelling out, running along the right-hand (eastern) side of the shallow lakes and continuing on to *Campamento Poincenot* (2hr from turn-off).

Sticking on the trail towards Cerro Torre, the path climbs to another viewpoint, before dropping down onto the valley floor – covered here in puddles that, in good weather, photogenically mirror Cerro Torre. The last section crosses a hill in the mid-dle of the valley and a small stream before eventually coming to *Campamento Bridwell* **campsite**, in woodland on the banks of the Río Fitz Roy. Though it occupies a beauti-ful site, it does get very busy (especially in January). The only good views of Cerro Torre from the campsite itself are to be had from a rocky outcrop at the back of the wood, where there's one extremely exposed pitch for a tent. Otherwise, follow the path

THE CERRO TORRE CONTROVERSY

Even members of the French team that first ascended Fitz Roy in 1952 thought that Cerro Torre was an impossible mountain. The altitude wasn't the problem – at 3102m, it wouldn't reach even halfway up some Andean peaks – neither was the type of rock it was made out of – crystalline igneous diorite is perfect for climbing. Rather, it was the shape: a terrifying spire dropping sheer for almost 2km into the glacial ice below, and the formidable weather, with winds of up to 200kph and temperatures so extreme that a crust of ice more than 20cm thick can form on vertical rock faces. Not only that, but the peculiar glaciers – "mushrooms" of ice – which build up on the mountain's summit often shear off, depositing huge blocks of ice onto unprotected climbers below.

In the late 1950s, the Italian Alpinist Cesare Maestri became the first to make a serious attempt on the summit. In 1959, he and the Austrian Toni Egger worked their way up the northern edge. Caught in a storm, Egger was swept off the face and killed by an avalanche of ice. Maestri somehow made it to the bottom, where he was rescued, disorientated and dangerously weak. Maestri announced that he had made it to the summit with Egger. The world, however, demanded proof – something that Maestri could not furnish. The camera, he claimed, now lay entombed with the unfortunate Egger in Torre's glacier.

Angered by the doubters, Maestri vowed to return. This he did, in 1970, and it was clear that he meant business. Among the expedition equipment lay his secret weapon: a compressor weighing over 150kg for drilling bolts into the unforgiving rock. Torre couldn't resist in the face of such a determined onslaught, and Maestri's expedition reached the summit, making very sure that photos were snapped on top. A stake had been driven through Torre's Gothic heart.

Or had it? The climbing world was riven by dispute. Were Maestri's tactics in keeping with the aesthetic code of climbing or had the use of a machine invalidated his efforts? Did this represent a true ascent? On top of this, Maestri's photos revealed that although he *had* reached the top of the rock, he had *not* climbed the ice mushroom – the icing that topped the cake. The monster would not lie down and die.

Enter Casimiro Ferrari, another Italian climber. Using guile where Maestri had used strong-arm tactics, Ferrari sneaked up on the beast from behind, attacking it from the Southern Patagonian Icecap. In the space of two days, Ferrari achieved his goal, and elatedly his team brought down photos of them atop the summit, ice mushroom and all.

So, almost thirty years on, who do people take as the first to climb the mountain? Toni Egger's body was recovered from the glacier in 1975, but no camera was found with him (he is now commemorated in the name of a jagged peak alongside Cerro Torre and a simple chapel in El Chaltén). The 150-kilogram compressor drill used by Maestri in 1970 still hangs in suspended animation near the top, a testament to his subjection of the mountain. And, despite the controversy at the time, the bolts drilled by Maestri are used to this day, forming the most common route to the summit.

Nevertheless, this irony is a bittersweet triumph for Maestri, who feels he has been cursed. In the 1990s, he reputedly voiced his hatred for the mountain, claiming that he wanted it razed to the ground. History has added its own weight to that of the doubters. The mountain has been scaled by routes of tremendous technical difficulty by modern climbers with modern equipment, culminating in the Slovenians Silvo Karo and Franc Knez's ascent of the south wall in 1988. No one, however, has ever been able to repeat the route that Maestri claimed he and Egger took in 1959.

alongside the river which brings you after five minutes to the terminal moraine at the end of **Laguna Torre**, a silty lake of glacial swill. On top of the moraine, you can gaze at the granite needles of Cerro Torre, **Torre Egger** (2900m), and **Cerro Standhardt** (2800m): a trio resembling the animated blips on a cardiograph that could, at that particular moment, well be your own. Here, too, you'll find a **cable crossing** of the river, used by climbers and groups that go ice-trekking on the **Glaciar Torre**. Although it looks easy enough to cross without a harness, be warned: a young German girl drowned here in 1998 after attempting to do just that. Gusts of wind down the valley can be sudden and fierce.

You can get closer to the mountain by walking for thirty minutes along the path which runs parallel to the northern shore of Laguna Torre to the **Mirador Maestri** lookout point. An expedition hut nearby contains moving commemorative dedications to climbers who never quite succeeded in their attempts on the various peaks (note that this is not a recognized camping spot). On certain maps, a route is marked that follows on from here round the great spur that comes down off the Fitz Roy massif. From the spur, you get jaw-dropping views of the entire east face of Cerro Torre and its glacier but, unfortunately, the terrain you must cross to get this far is unstable scree, especially around the gulches cut by meltwater streams, and should be attempted only by those with proper experience.

Río Eléctrico and Piedra del Fraile

The area to the north of Fitz Roy makes for rewarding trekking and can be linked to the standard circuit. Although much of this is private land, you are welcome as long as you observe the same regulations stipulated by the park and camp only in designated sites. If heading north out of El Chaltén along the RP23, you can take the bus for Lago del Desierto and get off right next to the bridge over the Río Eléctrico, which saves having to struggle for five to six hours against the prevailing winds that sweep down the valley from the north. With planning, you could walk to the **waterfall** of the **Chorrillo del Salto** first, and flag the bus afterwards as it passes. This plunging twenty-metre fall, framed by a moss-green cliff and adorned by the skeletons of drowned *lenga* trees, is an excellent picnic spot – it's a ten-minute walk off the RP23, approximately 3km past the *Madsen* campsite north of the village.

Beyond here is the park's northern boundary and, further up, the road makes a ninety-degree turn before passing *La Bonanza* **campsite**, a charming place right next to the Río de las Vueltas, where trees offer some shelter from the wind. About 4km further on (15km from Chaltén), a track turns off west to the *Hostería El Pilar* (☎ & fax 02962/493002; ⑥; Oct–April), one of Patagonia's most exquisite mid-range guesthouses, with an elegant wooden interior and a homely living-room with a central wood-burning stove. Home-made tarts are served in the tearoom, with its enviable view of the summit of Fitz Roy, and a three-course lunch will set you back $15. Rooms are snug and wonderfully peaceful, there is a neat little garden by the Río Blanco, and the owner is a knowledgeable mountain guide.

Less than 1km beyond the rickety Río Blanco bridge you come to the much larger one over the **Río Eléctrico**, a tempestuous river flowing through untamed mountain scenery. From this bridge, it's 23km to Lago del Desierto (see p.645). The path to Piedra del Fraile starts to the left of the bridge, although its first section is imperilled every time the river is in spate. Soon you peel away from the river and, following the fairly inconspicuous cairns, cross the flat gravel floor of the Río Blanco valley with its shallow rivulets. Littering the ground are attractive pieces of white crystalline granite covered by lacy black lichen growths. On the other side of the valley, the path joins the one heading south to Laguna Piedras Blancas and *Campamento Poincenot* (see below). Rather than turn south just yet, aim to the right of the ridge ahead, into the valley of the Río Eléctrico, where you enter an enchanting, sub-Antarctic woodland of *lengas*, interspersed with grassy glades. Cross a brook and fifteen minutes further on you come to a gate in a ragged fence with a sign to Piedra del Fraile, approximately forty minutes' gentle walk away.

At **Piedra del Fraile** you'll find the *Los Troncos* refugio and campsite, a picturesque place set alongside the swift-flowing Río Eléctrico and sheltered by a vast erratic boulder – the *piedra* of the name. The *fraile* (friar or priest) was Padre de Agostini

(1883–1960), a Salesian priest who was one of Patagonia's most avid early mountaineers and explorers. He was the first person to survey the area from a mountaineer's point of view, and chose this site for his camp, now sadly defunct. Bunks in the refuge huts cost $10 per person, or it's $5 per person to pitch a tent; a wood-fire is lit in the evenings to heat the hottest shower in Patagonia, with water temperatures that could serve for brewing *mate*. The cosy restaurant hut serves doorstep wedges of toasted sandwiches, unpretentious but filling meals ($15), and chocolate and alcohol.

Two worthwhile treks lead from here: the first a two-and-a-half-hour hike one way to the foot of the **Glaciar Marconi**, fording the Río Pollone and passing through the blasted scenery on the southern shore of Lago Eléctrico on the way. There are fine views of the northern flank of Fitz Roy, especially from the Río Pollone valley. Glaciar Marconi itself sweeps down off the **Hielo Continental Sur** (Southern Patagonian Icecap), and forms the most frequently used point of access for properly equipped expeditions heading onto this frigid expanse, by way of the windy **Paso Marconi** (1500m). Most of the icecap is actually in Chile, and estimates vary as to exactly how big it is, from 14,000 to 20,000 square kilometres. What is certain is that it forms the greatest icefield outside the polar circles.

The second hike involves much more of a climb – approximately 1200m in altitude – up to the **Paso del Cuadrado** (approximately 1700m). Walking times vary considerably on this stiff trek, but it's best to treat it as a day hike, allowing yourself approximately five to seven hours in total. From the camp, cross the small stream on the south side, walk through a wood with its climber's playground, and strike towards the gap between two streams, to the right of the wooded hillside. The path zigzags steeply up to where it levels out. You pass a large, erratic boulder with a tiny pool just above it. The path peters out further up, once it reaches the boulder scree zone. From here onwards you must make your own course, taking care not to turn an ankle as you climb slowly up the scree, and keeping the main stream to your right. When you reach the terminal moraine of the glacier, ford the river and work your way around the right-hand side of the col. Cross the exposed area of rock on your right and then make the tiring thirty-minute climb up the snow to the pass, which is not immediately obvious but lies in the middle of the ridge.

Expect a ferocious blast of wind at the top of the pass, but hold onto your headgear and look out at one of the most dramatic and vertiginous views you're likely to come across in Patagonia. Weather permitting, you look up at Fitz Roy's north face, across to the steeple of Cerro Torre, and down, across deeply crevassed glaciers, to the phallic peaks of Aguja and Cerro Pollone, named after Padre de Agostini's home village in the Italian Alps.

Heading back east from Piedra del Fraile, you may have difficulty locating the path that follows the Río Blanco valley south to **Laguna Piedras Blancas** and *Campamento Poincenot*. It's rather a lottery due to inadequate map topography and a number of false trails created by meandering cattle. Count yourself lucky if you do come across it, but otherwise do not despair: it's not serious. Upon leaving the woods and emerging into the valley plain of the Río Blanco, strike a bold right and keep close to the line of the trees you've just left. Eventually you'll pick up the line of under-ambitious cairns that mark the path: follow these until you come to the confluence of the Piedras Blancas stream and Río Blanco.

This area is strewn with chunks of granite any port authority would be proud to possess. It's worth making a short detour right (west) up this valley, scrambling across the boulder field, to see the **Piedras Blancas Glacier** tumbling into its murky lake, backed by a partial view of Fitz Roy (20–30min each way). Otherwise, ford the Piedras Blancas stream a little way up from where it meets the Río Blanco and cross the moraine dump to regain the trail. From this point it's less than an hour's walk along the deteriorated if fairly easy path to *Campamento Poincenot*, set back from the opposite bank of the Río Blanco and reached by a pair of bridges (see p.640).

Lago Toro and the Paso del Viento

South of the park's visitor's centre, a seventeen-kilometre trail leads to the valley of the Río Túnel and the silty glacial lake of **Lago Toro** (5–6hr). Register at the information centre and ascertain what conditions are like before picking up the path. It forms part of a more ambitious seven- to eleven-day loop that crosses the **Paso del Viento** (1550m) onto the treacherous continental icecap, and comes out over Paso Marconi to the north (see opposite), a route which is suitable only for organized, properly equipped expeditions – for more information, enquire at Fitz Roy Expediciones or the park administration.

Lago del Desierto

Lago del Desierto ("Lake of the Desert"), 37km to the north of Chaltén, is far less forbidding than its name suggests, being an alpine-style lake, surrounded by heavily forested mountains. The area has opened up to tourism considerably in the past few years, which in some ways is a shame, since its population of endangered huemules is bound to suffer from the influx. Day-trips are possible, allowing you to make the short walk from the southern end of the lake up to the **mirador** at **Laguna del Huemul**, with its excellent views of Fitz Roy. However, it's better to allow at least two days, so you can trek some of the longer trails. Lago del Desierto became one of the *causes célèbres* of Argentinian/Chilean **border disputes**, bringing the two countries to the brink of war in the 1960s. In 1995, an international commission awarded the area to Argentina, but the issue had repercussions: the Chilean military felt itself humiliated, and forcefully pushed territorial claims over the Hielo Continental Sur (Southern Patagonian Icecap) further south. Eventually, in 1999, the Argentine Senate ratified a treaty conceding sovereignty over a disputed chunk of land in the southeast of the Parque Nacional Los Glaciares, thus resolving the last outstanding border conflict between the two countries.

Practicalities

Los Glaciares runs a service here from El Chaltén (Oct–March daily), while Caltur buses leave the *Fitz Roy Inn* every two hours (Nov–March). En route to the lake, you pass the *Bonanza* campsite and *Hostería El Pilar* (see above), and then another campsite at the *Estancia Ricanor* ($5 per person), past the bridge over the Río Eléctrico. An eleven-kilometre trail runs along the eastern shore of the lake to the *Refugio Lago del Desierto* at the northern end, and this can be extended for another 13km to a more basic refuge at Laguna Diablo. A privately owned boat, *La Mariana*, (☎02962/493041) connects the two ends of the lake, running from the *Estancia Lago del Desierto* in the south, but it doesn't always run, due to disputes regarding the concession – check at the office on the corner of Avenida Güemes and Calle Río de las Vueltas in El Chaltén first. You can hike with guides through the mountain ranges to the east all the way to Lago San Martín (contact Fitz Roy Expediciones in Chaltén).

Lago Viedma and on to El Calafate

Just south of the turn-off to El Chaltén, the RN40 passes a track leading 2km to the *Estancia Punta del Lago* (☎02962/497442; closed April–Sept), owned by the great Italian climber Casimiro Ferrari, the first person indisputably to conquer Cerro Torre. The estancia lies on the shores of **Lago Viedma**, the lake named after the colonizer and explorer Antonio Viedma, the founder of Floridablanca and the first white man to see the lake: looking for wood to build his new settlement, he explored its shores in 1782, having been led to this "Laguna Grande" by Tehuelche guides.

Fifteen kilometres further on, RN40 crosses the **Río La Leona**, the sizeable, fast-flowing river that drains Lago Viedma. On the northern bank, a turn-off leads 7km to the tourist *Estancia La Leona* (☎02962/497442; ⑦, full board with drinks included; Oct–March), the home of the amiable Rojo family, and where there's excellent fishing. On the south side of the bridge is another of the RN40's famous original **wayside inns**, *Hotel La Leona* (② with shared bathroom; closed May–Aug), where you can enjoy a slice of the finest home-made lemon meringue and apple pies. A well-chosen selection of books about the area is for sale, and don't miss the opportunity to play the *Juego de la Argolla*, an old gaucho drinking game where you take turns to land a ring that's attached by a string to the ceiling over a hook mounted on the wall opposite: the first person to succeed wins a drink (try a sweet and inexpensive *Caña Ombú* or *Caña Quemada*).

Hotel La Leona marks the turn-off for two tourist estancias with tremendously privileged positions, occupying land on the southern shore of Lago Viedma (see below). Heading to El Calafate, the RN40 shadows the course of the Río La Leona, passing beneath some fascinating desiccated crags on the far side, before coming to Lago Viedma's bigger sister, Lago Argentino. Here the RN40 recrosses the Río La Leona at the point where it enters the lake, and soon crosses over the Río Santa Cruz, the river that drains this entire, massive basin. Five kilometres from this bridge, you come to the first stretch of paved road since Perito Moreno, from where the RP11 takes you the blessedly smooth and quick 32km into **El Calafate** (see below).

Lago Viedma's southern shore and the boat to El Chaltén

Turn off the RN40 at the *Hotel La Leona* to reach the **tourist estancias** on the southern shores of Lago Viedma. After 48km, you come to the extensive sheep-farming establishment of *Santa Teresita* (☎ & fax 02902/491732; ⑤, breakfast included; Dec–March) with rooms for up to five people in the old *casco* (administration building), and fantastic views of Fitz Roy and Cerro Torre.

At the westernmost end of the route, 73km from *La Leona*, is *Helsingfors* (☎ & fax 02966/420719 or 011/4824-3634, *landsur@internet.siscotel.com*; ⑨; Nov–Easter), whose prices include full board with the exception of drinks, plus one of several excursions per day's stay. The estancia itself is within the confines of the Parque Nacional Los Glaciares, and it is now dedicated solely to upper-end tourism. A *remise* taxi from Calafate costs $200.

The most popular excursion from *Helsingfors* is the **boat trip** in a modern sixty-seater launch, the *Huemul*, to watch **Glaciar Viedma** calve icebergs into its eponymous lake, and to explore a branch of the lake called the Canal Moyano (also called Canal Viedma). In addition, the *Huemul* runs right along the western edge of the lake, thus enabling you to get to El Chaltén by way of Puerto Bahía Túnel, and saving you a tiring trip around the lake by road. If making the $60 day excursion from Chaltén, the bus connection leaves confitería *La Senyera del Torre* at approximately 8.30am for Bahía Túnel, from where the *Huemul* departs. It then visits the glacier and Canal Moyano; stops at *Helsingfors* for an *asado* lunch ($20 extra), and returns to Chaltén for about 5pm.

El Calafate

EL CALAFATE (not to be confused with Cafayate in Salta Province) is the centre of the tourist network in the deep south of mainland Argentinian Patagonia, and is one of the country's most-visited tourist destinations, though this is due more to the town's outlying tourist attractions than the place itself. These offshoot attractions cluster around the tremendous bloated tuber of **Lago Argentino**, the greatest of all exclusively Argentinian lakes, and the third biggest in all South America, with a surface area of 1600 square kilometres – it's so deep that its temperature remains almost constant at 8°C year round. Catch it on a cloudy day and you could be looking at a tarnished expanse of molten lead, while when the weather is brighter the lake soaks up the light of the Patagonian sky to reflect a glorious hue of polarized blue. Most of the lake is surrounded by harsh, rolling steppe, but the scenery becomes more interesting around its western tendrils: transitional scrub and southern beech woodland press up on its shores, and the snow-capped mountains that fringe the Southern Patagonian Icecap rear up behind.

By any standards, the town isn't cheap, although it does offer some decent budget hostel accommodation and a couple of well-stocked, reasonably priced supermarkets.

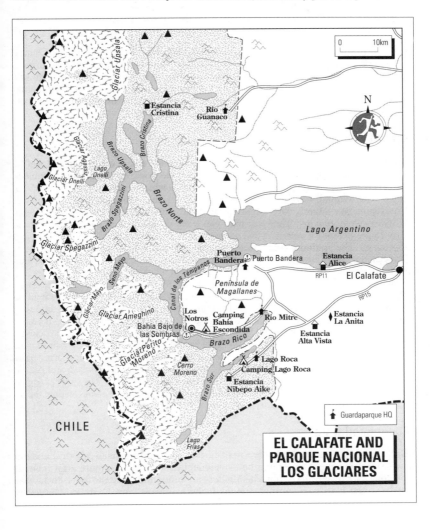

EL CALAFATE AND PARQUE NACIONAL LOS GLACIARES

THE CALAFATE BUSH

Calafate, the indigenous name for what is known in English as the box-leaved barberry (*berberis buxifolia*), is Patagonia's most famous plant. The bushes are protected by vindictive thorns, and the wood contains a substance known as *berberina* which possesses medicinal properties and is used as a textile dye. From late October onwards, the bushes are covered with exquisite little bright yellow flowers, while depending on where they're growing, the berries mature between December and March. Once used by the indigenous populations for dye, the fresh berries will stain your mouth a virulent purple; they're nowadays often used to make appetizing home-made preserves.

The oft-quoted saying is that "El que come el calafate, volverá" ("He who eats the calafate will return"), although other variants of this impute even greater, cupid-like powers to the berry. Those content to remain single should perhaps resist the temptation.

The best **months to visit** are those in spring and autumn (Nov to mid-Dec, and March to Easter/early April), when there's a nice balance between having enough visitors to keep services running but not too many for the place to seem overcrowded. High season's advantage is that you're sure to meet up with many friendly and exuberant Argentinian holidaymakers, but you're advised to book accommodation, and especially flights or car rental, well in advance.

Arrival and information

Calafate's international **airport** lies 15km east of town, and is connected to town by taxis. All **buses** stop at the terminal on Avenida Julio Roca, on the hillside one block above the main thoroughfare, Avenida Libertador, to which it's connected by a flight of steps. The helpful **tourist office** is situated in the terminal (daily: April–Oct 8am–10pm; Nov–March 8am–midnight; ☎ & fax 02902/491090 or 492884, *secturel-calafate@cotecal.com.ar*). They can help you track down a room in a *casa de familia* ($10–15 per person) if you can't find accommodation (a real possibility in January and February). The **national park information office**, at Libertador 1302 (Mon–Fri 8am–9.30pm, Sat & Sun 1.30–9.30pm; ☎02902/491005), has some useful maps, sell fishing licences, and will give you the latest information on campsites near the glacier.

You can withdraw **cash** with credit cards at the ATM at the Banco de Santa Cruz, Libertador 1285, and Banco de Tierra del Fuego, 25 de Mayo 40. Both the El Pingüino bus office in the terminal and Planet Patagonia, Libertador 958, change Chilean pesos, but the rates aren't great. Change excess Argentinian pesos into US dollars if you're heading into Chile, as you'll get a better deal here. For **bike rental**, try Cuatrociclón, Cte. Tomás Espora 20 (Sept–May 9am–10pm; ☎02902/493255), where they have sturdy 21-gear mountain bikes suitable for *ripio* roads ($9 for 2hr or $25 per day; bring passport for ID). The best **supermarkets** are Los Glaciares at Libertador 902, and Alas at 9 de Julio 59. Stock up here if heading for El Chaltén and the RN40. The town's biggest festival, the **Festival del Lago Argentino**, takes place in the week leading up to February 15, with music and a free *asado* on the final day.

Accommodation

High season runs from November until Easter. Prices are considerably reduced in low season, when the upper-end hotels suddenly become much more affordable. If you don't care to stay in the town itself, there are other options at the tourist estancias and near the glacier. **Camping** options include the pleasant *Camping Municipal*,

José Pantín s/n (☎02902/491829; $4 per person plus $4 per tent), with restaurant and shower block, conveniently located one block behind the YPF station at the entrance to town; *Jorgito*, Gob. Moyano 943 (☎02902/491323; $5 per person), in the garden of the owner's house; and *Los Dos Pinos*, 9 de Julio 358 (☎ & fax 02902/491271; $4 per person).

Hotels

Los Alamos, Gob. Moyano and Bustillo (☎02902/491144 or 491146, fax 491186, *posadalosalamos@cotecal.com.ar*). The most luxurious of the town's hotels, modestly posing as a *posada*, but with the feel of a village complex. It has wood-panelled rooms with bright bathrooms, an excellent restaurant, gardens, tennis courts and even a Lilliputian golf course. ⑧.

Apart Hotel Libertador, Libertador 1150 (☎02902/492080, fax 491511). Self-catering apartments in the style of a Spanish holiday resort; it's right on the main avenue, but rooms are peaceful. ⑦.

Frai Toluca Hotel, Perón 1016 (☎ & fax 02902/491773 or 491593, *fraitolucahotel@cotecal.com.ar*). Though rather graceless from the outside, its rooms offer three-star comfort, with views of the lake and town. ⑦.

Hostería Kalkén, Tte. Valentín Feilberg 119 (☎ & fax 02902/491073, fax 491036, *hotelkalken@cotecal.com.ar*). Pleasant en-suite rooms in a hotel with multilingual reception and a decent restaurant. ⑦. Closed May–Aug.

Kau Yatún Hotel, Estancia 25 de Mayo (☎02902/491259, fax 491260, *kauyatun@sminter.com.ar*). A well-appointed if rather expensive place set on its own grounds in the scrappy eastern edges of town (a free shuttle runs to the centre). It has an à la carte international restaurant and organizes tours, including balloon flights. ⑧. Closed mid-May to mid-June.

Hospedje Familiar Lago Azul, Perito Moreno 83 (☎02902/491419). The least expensive rooms in town, in the family home of the charming Echeverría couple, two of Calafate's original settlers. ② with shared bathroom; ③ in a cosy apartment with private bathroom and kitchen (ask for crockery).

Hotel Lar Aike, Libertador 2681 (☎ & fax 02902/491235, *hotellaraike@cotecal.com.ar*). A pleasant, airy, mid-range option, with friendly owners on the western outskirts of town.

Michelangelo Hotel, Gob. Moyano y Cmte. Espora (☎02902/491045). Heavy, 1970s log cabin-style architecture outside, but comfortable in, with plenty of piping hot water. ⑦. Closed May–Sept.

Hotel El Quijote, Gregores 1155 (☎02902/491017, fax 491103). Excellently sited modern three-star. Rooms come with minibar and TV, though beds are narrow. ⑦. Closed May–Sept.

Hostels

Residencial Buenos Aires, Buenos Aires 296 (☎ & fax 02902/491399). Helpful if rather crowded place close to bus terminal, with free luggage store and a cheap laundry service. In high season it opens an annexe at Julio Roca 1316, two blocks from bus terminal. $15 per person with shared bathroom, $7 per person with sleeping bag.

Ceirafate Hostel, 25 de Mayo and Gob. Moyano (☎02902/492212). A brand-new and fully-equipped hostel only blocks from the bus terminal, with kitchen, living room and Internet services. Accommodation is in four-bed dorms ($12) and doubles and triples from $30.

La Cueva de Jorge Lemos, Gob. Moyano 839 (☎ & fax 02902/491300, *jorgelemos@latinmail.com*). The cheapest place in town, centrally located and offering basic, refuge-style accommodation. Famous for its fun atmosphere, it has kitchen facilities, free luggage store and primitive bathrooms. Its mountain-guide owner is very knowledgeable about the area. $6 per person.

Albergue del Glaciar, Los Pioneros s/n (☎ & fax 02902/491243, off-season ☎ & fax 0488-69416, *hosteldelglaciar@datamarkets.com.ar*). Popular, YHA-affiliated hostel with clean, four-bed rooms, plus kitchen, free luggage store, free shuttle to and from bus terminal, a multilingual reception, e-mail and Internet access and a good-value restaurant. It also offers travel services, including recommended trips to the Moreno glacier. Also has more expensive private rooms with private bathroom (③–⑤) and floorspace for sleeping bags in the *refugio* ($6). Oct–March.

Lago Argentino, Campaña del Desierto 1050, one block south of bus terminal (☎ & fax 02902/491139). The hostel section has cramped, rather uncomfortable bunks ($9 per person), with communal showers; much better are the inexpensive en-suite doubles across the road (③). The owners are very helpful, and there's also a kitchen, laundry service and free luggage storage.

Estancias

Alta Vista (☎ & fax 02902/491247, in Buenos Aires 011/4343-8883, fax 6979, *altavista@cotecal.com.ar*). The most exclusive and expensive of the Santa Cruz tourist estancias, playing host to those seeking discretion and peace. Airy, intimate rooms with tasteful, restrained decor; non-intrusive, professional service; and a delightful garden filled with lupins. It serves simple, classically prepared regional cuisine. ⑨ ($514dbl) all inclusive. Oct to mid-April.

Nibepo Aike (☎ & fax 02966/422626 or 420180, *nibepo@internet.siscotel.com*). Sixty kilometres out of Calafate ($60 in *remise* taxi). ⑦. Oct–April.

Alice, also known as *El Galpón* (☎02902/491793, *info@elgalpon.com.ar*). On the way to Puerto Bandera, 21km out of Calafate. It also has an office in Calafate at Libertador 1015 that sells day excursions to see agricultural displays such as sheep-shearing. ⑦. Oct–April.

The Town

El Calafate is one of the few towns in the world which makes its living from ice – not that you're likely to find any in town, at least outside the bars. It's not a completely chilled-out place either: the main street is crowded with garish and often noisy souvenir shops and, in high season (above all in January and February), the place is invaded by everyone and their grandmother, come to marvel at the great glacier (*ventisquero*) that lies some 80km away.

If emerging from the RN40, arriving in Calafate seems like coming to suckle at Mammon's very breast; if you've flown in from Buenos Aires, you'll be surprised at just how modest and dusty the place is, sprawled under the umber ridge of its eponymous mountain (*cerro*). Apart from shopping or eating, however, there's little to do in town. The small **museum** (Mon–Fri 8am–noon & 2–8pm; free) in the Dirección de Cultura, Libertador 575, has the standard collection of pioneer family photos plus some indigenous artefacts, but isn't particularly inspiring.

A thirty-minute walk north of town along Calle Dr Bustillo, the bird reserve of **Laguna Nimes** has black-necked swans (the only two-coloured swan in the world), upland geese, Chilean flamingoes, the silvery grebe (*macá plateado*) and other species of dabbling waterfowl. Though suffering from the effects of pollution, it still makes for a pleasant spot for an evening walk. In winter, the lagoon is for skating.

Some 11km east of town, down a signposted track to the left (north) are the **Wualichu Caves** (also spelt Gualicho and Gualichu), home to some poorly preserved indigenous rock art and plenty of twentieth-century graffiti – the name comes from the

---

GETTING TO THE PERITO MORENO GLACIER

Guided day excursions to the glacier are offered by virtually all agencies in El Calafate, allowing for between two and three hours at the ice face, though many find this is too little to appreciate fully the spectacle. The one with the *Albergue del Glaciar* (see p.649) and the more expensive tour with Chaltén Travel ($40) are recommended. Several bus companies offer their own tours (book at the terminal), leaving every day, year round: Quebek and Interlagos (both $30) allow approximately four hours at the face, which is more than the average; El Pingüino ($25) is cheaper but has no guide and allows less time. Rather than have a fixed point of departure, all companies tend to drive round town collecting passengers from hotels. This can mean you have to get up much earlier than you need to, so try to arrange that you're the last pick-up or that you go to the office just before the bus leaves.

If you don't want to be restricted to a tour, you have four main options. Several private minibus operators run reasonably flexible transport-only services, where you phone up to arrange times and they collect you. Things work out best if you can form a group of four or so first. Try Santa Cruz (☎02902/491602; $24 return) or enquire at the tourist

malign spirit feared by the Tehuelche. If you cycle there, don't be tempted to go back along the lake shore, as some malign dunes will sap your spirit. Another option is to **hire a horse** from the gauchos at Casa Quinta, Bustillo s/n (on the way to Laguna Nimes; $30 per person for a 4–5hr trip); these guys also offer a three-day trip to the Sierra Baguales by the Chilean border for the amazing price of $70 (arrange a day in advance; food included, but bring a sleeping bag).

Eating and drinking

Restaurants tend to open from noon till 3pm, and then again in the evening from about 8pm to midnight or later. With a few exceptions, most are overpriced.

Restaurants

Bordeaux, Julio Roca and 1° de Mayo (☎02902/492118). Intimate place specializing in fondues for two or more ($22), with Swiss side dishes. Sept–April 5pm till midnight; off season weekends only.

Kau Kaleshen, Gob. Gregores 1256. A pleasant but expensive *casa de té* serving pricey speciality coffees ($6–7) and imaginative, home-made stuffed breads and cakes.

Michelangelo Hotel, Gob. Moyano and Cmte. Espora (☎02902/491045). Don't let the rather dreary restaurant decor put you off: dishes are well prepared and unexpectedly eclectic, and service is attentive. If you don't fancy the hare (*liebre*) with ginger root and rösti ($15), stick to the beef, lamb and trout dishes ($12–20).

La Posta, in the grounds of the *Los Alamos* hotel (☎02902/491144). Spacious dining-room looking out over the manicured setting. Exotic international menu, with an inventive range of sauces and sympathetic use of local ingredients – the rolled lamb with rose-hip sauce is excellent ($18). Well-chosen selection of Argentinian wines ($12–35).

Quincho Don Raúl, Libertador 1472. By far the best of the low-budget feeds, with a hands-on gaucho owner who isn't called Raúl, but who is otherwise the genuine article. All-day $5 *tenedor libre* and $12 *asado tenedor libre*. Worth the walk to the outskirts of town.

La Tablita, Cnel. Rosales 28, by the bridge into town (☎02902/491065). Serious-sized lamb or beef parrillas, all served with suitable dignity. Popular with locals and reasonably priced, except for the side dishes. Closed Wed lunch and June–Aug.

Tante Sonia, Gob. Gregores and 9 de Julio (☎02902/491343). Specializes in excellent-value seafood, served in an uncomplicated style. Good soups from $4, a rich shellfish *cazuela de marisco* costs $9, and main courses $4–10. Try the *lenguado* (sole) *al roquefort*.

office. Alternatively you could rent a car, or hire a *remise* taxi ($80 for two passengers; $100 for four), but agree on a waiting time before setting out, since drivers normally calculate on a two-hour stay. Alternatively, you could hitch. Remember that the glacier lies a long way from the park entrance itself (over 30km), in the event that your potential lift is only going that far.

Driving, you have two choices: either take the RP15 towards Lago Roca; or continue straight down Libertador along the RP11. The first route has the advantage of passing historical Estancia Anita and the tourist estancia of *Alta Vista*, with the shark-fin of Cerro Moreno (1640m) ahead of you in the background. In 1921, Estancia Anita saw one of Patagonia's most grisly episodes, when 121 men were executed here by an army battalion that had been sent to crush a rural strike and the related social unrest (for more information see Oswaldo Bayer's book *Los Vengadores de la Patagonia Trágica* or Chatwin's *In Patagonia*). A concrete monument by the roadside commemorates the victims. Turn right at the 30km mark, just after *Alta Vista*, and then left after another 12km to the park's main entrance. The second route is along a better-maintained road along the lakeshore; head along here for the tourist estancia *Alice* (see p.650), the park's main gate, and Puerta Bandera (see p.655), for boat trips to Upsala and other of the park's glaciers.

Bars

Don Diego de la Noche, Libertador 1603 (☎02902/491270). This rather cheesily named pub and restaurant is the only place in town with a lively nightlife buzz, especially in high season – but don't turn up till midnight. Moustachioed Don Diego himself frequently provides the live music. Food is served till late (5am), but is overpriced.

Casablanca, Libertador 1202 (☎02902/491402). An enjoyable place for pizzas and cool draught beer, with videos of the rupture of Perito Moreno glacier. Open till 1am.

Listings

Airlines Kaikén, 25 de Mayo 43 (☎02902/492072 or 491854), has a useful flight to Ushuaia, saving a painful and expensive overland journey, although departures can be subject to delays; LADE, Libertador 1080 (☎02902/491262).

Books and maps Planet Patagonia, Libertador 958.

Car rental Freelander, Gob. Paradelos 253 (☎02902/491437); Servi Car, Gob. Moyano and Bustillo.

Hospital Julio Roca 1487 (☎02902/491808 or 491001).

Internet Lago Digital, Libertador 1215, 1° piso (Mon–Sat 10am–1pm & 5pm–9pm).

Laundries $8 per basket: Lavadero, Libertador 1118; Cerro Cristal, Cte. Espora 95.

Pharmacy El Calafate, Libertador 1190.

Police Libertador 835 (☎02902/491077).

Post office, Libertador 1133 (☎02902/491012).

Remise taxis Buenos Aires, Campaña del Desierto (☎02902/491147); Calafate, Julio Roca s/n, by the bus terminal (☎02902/492005); $160 to Río Gallegos, $60 to Nibepo Aike; $80–100 to Perito Moreno glacier.

Telephone COOP Telefónica, Cmte. Tomás Espora 194 (incoming calls ☎02902/491882, fax 491300; open 8am–2am).

The Parque Nacional Los Glaciares

Declared a "Patrimony of Humanity" by UNESCO in 1981, the wild expanse of the **Parque Nacional Los Glaciares** encompasses environments which range from the enormous sterile glaciers that flow down from the heights of the Southern Continental Icecap, to thick, sub-Antarctic woodland of deciduous *lenga* and *ñire*, and evergreen *guindo* and *canelo*; from savage unclimbed crags where 5000mm of precipitation falls in a year, to billiard-table Patagonian *meseta* that receives little more than 100mm. A southern chunk of the park was ceded to Chile in 1999 after the dispute over borders in the area of the icecap, but it remains Argentina's largest.

The vast majority of this, nevertheless, is off limits to the public. Most will visit only the Fitz Roy sector for trekking in the north (see p.636) and the sightseeing area around the **Perito Moreno Glacier**, one of the world's most famous glaciers, as it plays push and shove with the lake it feeds. In this southern sector, there are three main destinations. Firstly there is the glacier itself. This lies in front of the **Península de Magallanes**, which is not a part of the park, apart from the fringe of land around the lake channels. The park's **main gate** is here, and the trees nearby are a favourite evening roost of the rabble-rousing austral parakeet (*cachaña*), the most southerly of the world's parrots. From here it is a forty-minute drive (a little more than 30km) past several campsites, picnic spots and one hotel to the boardwalks in front of the glacier. The *ripio* road is poor and very dusty in hot weather, but traversible by any family car. A second destination is **Puerto Bandera**, from where boat trips depart to Upsala and the other northern glaciers. Finally, the RP15 to the south leads to **Lago Roca** and the southern arm of Lago Argentino, the **Brazo Sur**.

Entrance to the park costs $5 per person and $3 per vehicle, which you must pay at the respective gates. Within the boundaries, be especially aware of the dangers of fire and extinguish any campfire with plenty of water (earth is not as effective) – an area of forest near Glaciar Spegazzini accidentally burnt in the 1930s (perhaps by Padre de Agostini himself) still hasn't even remotely recovered. **Mammals** in the park include the gato huiña wildcat, pumas and the endangered huemul, although you are highly unlikely to see any of these due to their scarcity and elusive nature. Instead, enjoy the flora, such as the *notro* bush, with its flaming red blooms in November and March, and birds such as the majestic black and red Magellanic woodpecker (*carpintero patagónico*).

Accommodation on the Península de Magallanes

The National Park authorities are trying gradually to withdraw facilities close to the glacier in order to reduce visual and aquatic pollution, so check at the gate or the park office which **campsites** are open. The first one after the gate is *Río Mitre* (though this is likely to close); *Bahía Escondida* (☎02902/493053; $4 per person, book in advance in Jan), 21km beyond the entrance, is just 8km from the snout of the glacier, and so gets extremely busy in high season, when the shower block is notably over-subscribed, and noise levels rise.

Currently, the only **hotel** close to the Moreno glacier (and with views of its left flank) is *Los Notros* (☎011/4814-3934, fax 815-7645, *notros@lastland.com*; ⑨; open mid-Sept to May), 22km from the park entrance. This is a tastefully designed and "rustic" wooden lodge built on private land, with an excellent if expensive restaurant that prepares regional specialities ($35 for three courses). It's much cheaper if you book in advance: check out the offers on two- to four-day all-inclusive packages with full board, excursions and pick-up from the airport. Since most of the Península de Magallanes is not a national park, it is conceivable – though not desirable – that other hotels will be built nearby to milk the cash cow.

The Perito Moreno Glacier

Argentina's two greatest natural wonders couldn't contrast more greatly: the sub-tropical waterfalls at Iguazú and the **Glaciar Perito Moreno** (also called Ventisquero Perito Moreno). At 30km, it's not the longest of Argentina's glaciers – nearby Glaciar Upsala is twice as long – and though the ice cliffs at its snout tower fifty to sixty metres high, the face of Glaciar Spegazzini in the same park can reach heights twice as great. However, such comparisons prove irrelevant when you stand on the boardwalks that face this monster. Moreno has a star quality that none of the others rival, performing for its public, who come to enjoy the spectacle of its titanic struggle with Lago Argentino as the glacier tries to reach the Península de Magallanes.

The glacier sweeps down off the icecap in a great motorway curve, a jagged mass of crevasses and towering, knife-edged obelisks of ice (seracs), almost unsullied by the streaks of dirty moraine that discolour many of its counterparts. When it collides with the southern arm of Lago Argentino, the show really begins. Vast blocks of ice, some weighing hundreds of tonnes, detonate off the face of the glacier with the report of a small cannon and come crashing down into the waters below. These frozen depth-charges then come surging back to the surface as icebergs, sending out a fairy ring of smaller lumps that form a protecting reef around the berg, which is left to float in a mirror-smooth pool of its own.

Along with the virtually inaccessible Pío XI in Chile, Moreno is one of only two **advancing glaciers** in South America, and one of the very few on the planet. Above all, the glacier became famous for the way it would periodically push right across the channel, forming a massive dyke of ice that cut the Brazo Rico and Brazo Sur off from the main body of Lago Argentino. Cut off from their natural outlet, the water in the *brazos* would build up against the flank of the glacier, flooding the surrounding area, until eventually the pressure forced open a passage into the Canal de los Témpanos (Iceberg Channel) once again. Happening over the course of several hours, such a rupture was, for those lucky enough to witness it, one of nature's most awesome spectacles – it's said that the roars of breaking ice could be heard in Calafate, 80km away. The glacier first reached the peninsula in 1917, having advanced some 750m in fifteen years, but the channel did not remain blocked for long and the phenomenon remained little known. This changed in 1939, when a vast area was flooded and planes made a futile attempt to break the glacier by bombing it. In 1950, water levels rose by 30m and the channel was closed for two years, whilst in 1966 levels reached an astonishing 32m above their normal level. The glacier then settled into a fairly regular cycle, completely blocking the channel approximately every three to seven years until the last time, in 1988. It's often said that the glacier is no longer advancing. This is not entirely the case: it does advance (at a rate of almost 2m a day in the centre), but not fast enough to block the channel. This rate equals that of wastage caused by contact with the lake, so its position has remained roughly constant in recent years.

Rather than bombs or ruptures, you'll have to content yourself with the thuds, cracks, creaks and grinding crunches that the glacier habitually makes, as well as the wonderful variety of colours of the ice: marbled in places with streaks of muddy grey and copper sulphate blue, whilst at the bottom the pressurized, de-oxygenated ice has a deep blue, waxy sheen – many people can while away hours in thrall to it, with some spending the whole day and returning the next to see it in different lights. The glacier tends to be more active in sunny weather and in the afternoon, but early morning can also be beautiful, as the light strikes the ice cliffs. Try also to arrive early or leave late to see it when the crowds have gone.

Many species of the park's native **flora** next to the boardwalks are handily labelled; look out, too, for the less nervous **fauna**, such as the crested rufous-collared sparrow (*chingolo*) and the brightly coloured Patagonian sierra finch (*fríngilo patagónico*), a little yellow and grey bird that has become semi-tame in the area.

Practicalities

Do not stray from the boardwalks: 32 people were killed by ice falls between 1968 and 1988, either being hit by lethal richocheting chunks of ice or swept off the rocks into the freezing water by the subsequent wave surge. In addition, it could hurt your purse, since *guardaparques* can give out spot fines of up to $500 if they catch you. A couple of **cafés** sell refreshments and snacks at a healthy mark-up, but you're free to use their toilet facilities whether you buy or not. **Boat trips** can be made from either Puerto Bandera or the much nearer Bahía Bajo de las Sombras (see below).

Hielo y Aventura, Libertador 935 (☎ & fax 02902/491053), organizes fun "Mini-trekking" excursions ($70) where you get **to walk on the glacier**. This is **ice-trekking**, not ice-*climbing* (try El Chaltén for that): you do not need to be some Goliath of a mountain man to do it. Bring sunglasses, suncream, gloves and a packed lunch, and wear warm, weatherproof clothes. As you will be issued crampons, company literature informs you that "high heel shoes are not advisable", but you could always give it a go. Leaving daily from Calafate at 8am, the bus takes you to the Bahía Bajo de Las Sombras near *Los Notros* hotel. A forty-seater launch leaves from here at about 10am, and approaches the glacier's snout to within about 200m, before dropping you off to walk to the glacier and begin a one-and-a-half to two-hour circuit on the ice, with an English-speaking guide. The bus brings you back to Calafate for about 6.30pm. In high season, another launch leaves the Bahía every hour from 11am–4pm for a thirty-minute trip close to the towering heights of the ice wall ($20), with minibus connections to and from the main boardwalk.

Upsala, Spegazzini and Onelli glaciers

Glaciar Upsala is the undisputed heavyweight of the park: between 5km and 7km wide, with a sixty-metre-high snout and a length of 60km. It's still South America's longest glacier, despite massive retrocession over the last four years, and covers a total area three times larger than that of metropolitan Buenos Aires. Upsala played an important role in consolidating Argentinian claims to its Antarctic territory – expedition teams used to acclimatize by living for months in a base on the glacier.

Navigating the **Upsala channel** is a highlight in itself. Apart from the wooded shores it could be Antarctica, as **icebergs** bob, grind and even turn occasional flips around you. As any good student of the *Titanic* will know, for every one part of iceberg above the surface, it has six to seven parts below, which gives an idea of the tremendous size of these blocks. Even in flat light, the icy blues shine as if lit by a neon strip light – an eerie, cerulean glow that you're likely to see in normal life only in the chemical blue bottles used for polystyrene chillboxes.

Glaciar Spegazzini is some people's favourite glacier, with an impressive ice cascade to the right and the most dizzying snout of all the glaciers in the park (80–135m high). The **Onelli** and **Agassiz glaciers** are less impressive – if still beautiful – and are reached by an easy eight-hundred-metre walk to **Laguna Onelli**, a chilly lake dotted with small bergs. The walk itself is likely to appeal only to those who haven't had the opportunity to see Patagonian forest elsewhere, since the beauty of these woodlands is not complemented by the presence of up to 300 day-trippers.

Practicalities

Boat trips to the Upsala, Spegazzini and Onelli glaciers are run as a park's concession from **Puerto Bandera** by Renée Fernández Campbell, using a fleet of modern catamarans and launches. There are various itineraries ($40–89), with trips running throughout the year except for June, and with daily departures on popular routes in high season. Prices are the same at all agencies, but if you buy direct from either Fernández Campbell, Libertador 867 (☎02902/491155 or fax 491154), or Sólo Patagonia, Libertador 963 (☎02902/491298, fax 491790), you may find special promotional extras are included. If the weather is fine, the excursions are definitely a memorable experience; if the weather's poor, they can be memorable for other reasons.

Dress in warm, waterproof and windproof clothing, and take spare film and food since prices on board are high. If badly affected by motion sickness, take precautionary seasickness tablets (*pastillas contra el mareo*) in windy weather: early summer is the worst for waves. Guides give a good commentary in English as well as Spanish. Before booking, remember that your scope for refunds is limited: the company fulfils its legal obligations if only one main part of the trip is completed. The weather has to be exceptionally foul for the trip to be cancelled entirely, and in windy weather especially, icebergs can block the channels, with Brazo Upsala being particularly prone. That said, the company is professional and tries hard to complete scheduled itineraries: in the event of **cancellation** you will be offered a refund or a passage the next day, and trips are not cancelled for reasons of low passenger numbers. Checking the Internet weather forecast may help, but the weather might be as cloudless as the Sahara in Calafate, whilst a miserable cloudy maelstrom broods over the icecap just 90km away.

The most popular trips, such as "Todos Glaciares" and "Ríos de Hielo" (better on even dates, when Glaciar Spegazzini is included), head up the Brazo Norte towards the Upsala area. The "Sólo Upsala" trip (Nov–March) is one of the few ways of gaining access to the central sector of the park, and involves several hours of walking in the windswept, desolate **Bahía Cristina** area (the isolated Estancia Cristina at the end of the bay was a favoured point of entry for explorers of the icecap, including Padre de

Agostini and Eric Shipton, the famous mountaineer and explorer of the 1960s). In addition, frequent sailings leave Puerto Bandera for the face of Glaciar Perito Moreno.

Lago Roca

Lago Roca, a branch of Lago Argentino, lies 52km from Calafate, and is much frequented by fishermen during the angling season (mid-Nov to March). It offers good horseriding and trekking possibilities in areas of open woodland and amongst the neighbouring hills of the Cordón de los Cristales, and has examples of rock art dating back 3000 years.

To get to Lago Roca, either take the day-trip offered by Leutz Turismo, 25 de Mayo 43 in Calafate (Tues, Thurs & Sun Sept–April; $35; ☎02902/492316) or rent a car or hitch. You may **camp** at the free *El Huala* site near the park gate (no services), or 3km further on at *Lago Roca* (☎02902/499500; $6 per person), an attractive lake-shore site sheltered by *lenga* and *ñire* trees. It has good showers plus the normal accoutrements of barbecues and a shop that sells fishing licences. The *Nibepo Aike* tourist estancia (see p.650) is another 4km beyond.

South from El Calafate

The zone to the southeast of El Calafate is one that you'll need to cross if heading to the deep south of Chile or across to the capital of Santa Cruz, Río Gallegos, and the RN3 along the Atlantic coast. It's not the most interesting of areas from a tourist's perspective, and much of it is blasted, flat steppe, although the southwestern area close to the Chilean border is richer in the way of grassland and has patches of dwarf southern beech woodland. You have several options in the way of horseriding, and the western reaches of the Río Gallegos offer some good fishing.

The RP5: Calafate to Río Gallegos

There are two main choices of routes from Calafate to Río Gallegos: one is more scenic and passes several crossing points into the deep south of Chile, while the other, taking the RP5, is quicker. The latter is the busiest of the roads that cross the deep south of Santa Cruz Province, since it's paved and relatively well maintained – whereas in the early twentieth century this journey took up to 45 days by ox-cart, you can now do it in less than four hours.

The RP5 is a continuation of the paved part of the RN40. They join where the (unpaved) RN40 turns off south, 94km southeast of Calafate. About 160km from Calafate, halfway to Gallegos, you can **refuel** at the optimistically named town of **Esperanza** ("Hope"). Take the RP7 here if you're heading from Río Gallegos to *Cancha Carrera* (see p.657). From Esperanza, the RP5 continues east to the *Güer Aike* tourist estancia (see p.617), some 30km west of Río Gallegos, next to the RN3 turn-off heading north.

Routes to Chile and the RN40 from Río Turbio to Río Gallegos

Where it links up with the paved RP5 heading on to Río Gallegos, 94km southeast of Calafate, the RN40 branches south to the Chilean border, reverting to its unpaved state as it crosses the dry, barren meseta. In the far distance, you catch your first views of the **Torres del Paine** massif in Chile.

At Tapi Aike, where the RP7 cuts across to Esperanza, there is little more than a **fuel** station and the tourist estancia *Tapi Aike* (☎02966/420092; ⑤ with breakfast;

Nov–April). Forty-five kilometres further on (175km from Calafate) you reach the steppe-land **border crossing** at **Cancha Carrera** (open 8am), the closest crossing to Torres del Paine National Park. Argentine border formalities are quite straightforward, but remember that meat, dairy products, fruit and fresh vegetables cannot be taken into Chile. You are likely to be searched when you get to the immigration post at **Cerro Castillo**, a tiny settlement with café and lodging, some 7km further on. You can hitch the 70km into Paine from here, but it's not a place you'd want to spend long in. On the Argentinian side, just to the south of the border post, is the tourist estancia *Cancha Carrera* (☎ & fax 02966/423063 or 424236; ⑨) ($300dbl) full board; Oct–March), with one of the most beautiful of the old *cascos antiguos* (main houses), in a typically Anglo-Patagonian style from the early twentieth century. Its rooms are elegantly furnished. Buses from Calafate to either *Cancha Carrera* or Río Turbio pass close by.

The Río Turbio area

The RN40 south runs parallel to the international border, passing through an enchanting valley with welcome copses of dwarf Patagonian woodland (keep a watch out for condors). This soothing scenery comes to an abrupt end 37km later, at the mining town of **RÍO TURBIO**, where you come face to face with the sorry scars left by Argentina's coal industry. The coal deposits at Río Turbio are the biggest in the country, but the industry has been hit by a severe depression. Colossal loading conveyor belts and massive hulks of dirty and abandoned works buildings line the valley from its sister town to the east, 28 de Noviembre, to Turbio itself. The coal is transported by rail to the new deep-water port near Río Gallegos. The train used to bask in the glory of being the most southerly in the world, but has been robbed of even this distinction since the construction of the upstart tourist train in Ushuaia. Of late, planners have been engaged in the manful task of brightening up this ugly place, making bold use of colourful roofs and turning some of the suburbs on the hillside into a low-cost toy-town.

If you need **accommodation**, there's *Nazo* in the centre, at Gob. Moyano 100 (☎02902/421800; ④ with breakfast). Turbio's main tourist attraction is in the attractive wooded hills 4km south of town: the winter-sports complex of **Valdelén**, where gentle downhill skiing is practised between June and August ($12 per hour with ski hire and lift pass). You can stay at the *Albergue Municipal* (☎02902/421950), which has hostel beds for $10 per person; or the three-star *Hostería de la Frontera* (☎02902/421979; ④), which lies a few hundred yards from the 24-hour **border crossing** of Paso Mina Uno. Chilean immigration is just the other side; from here it's a straightforward 26-kilometre run to **Puerto Natales** (see p.661).

Another **border crossing**, Paso Casas Viejas/La Laurita, lies to the south of Río Turbio, past the town of 28 de Noviembre. This is more convenient for those travelling between Puerto Natales and Río Gallegos. The RN40 continues eastwards after 28 de Noviembre for 250km of *ripio* road to Río Gallegos. After the first 20km, you come to the only recognized lodging on this route, the tourist **estancia** *Stag River* (☎02966/424410 or 422466; ⑧; Oct–May), where there's good trout fishing.

CHILE'S DEEP SOUTH: PUNTA ARENAS AND PUERTO NATALES

The great tourist lure in the south of mainland Patagonia is Chile's **Parque Nacional Torres del Paine**, a national park of awesome natural beauty that's famous as a trekking mecca. If you're planning to visit this park or if you're simply travelling overland between mainland Argentinian Patagonia and Tierra del Fuego (or vice versa), you

> The international dialling code for Chile from Argentina is ☎0056.

are almost certain to pass through the busting city of **Punta Arenas** and **Puerto Natales**, the latter a base for trips to the park. Chile is noticeably cheaper than Argentina, and it makes good sense to take advantage of its more economical postage and telecommunications rates. Entering Chile is straightforward, and you are given a ninety-day tourist card at the border, but citizens of Australia, the United States and Canada currently have to pay an entrance fee at the border ($30, $45 and $55 respectively), valid for multiple visits during one year. Everyone requires a passport that is valid for at least six months. No meat or dairy products may be brought into the country, nor any fresh fruit or vegetables. For a more detailed treatment of the region, refer to the *Rough Guide to Chile*.

Punta Arenas

PUNTA ARENAS is a bustling port, characterized by its engaging monuments and statues. It is the most venerable of southern Patagonia's towns, dating back to 1848, and for decades was the only substantial trading centre in the region. The town's golden age lasted from the late nineteenth century until World War I, an era of sheep-farming barons and merchants who made enormous profits from supplying the marine traffic around the Horn. The opulence of past times can be seen in the fine *belle epoque* buildings in the centre, with their mansard-roofs, European furnishings and urban luxury. Many have now been converted to banks, such as the ones around the attractive central plaza, the **Plaza Muñoz Gamero** – also known as the **Plaza de Armas** – with its mix of shady Chilean trees and its **statue of Magellan**, standing above a pair of native inhabitants, one Selk'nam (Ona) and one Aónik'enk Tehuelche. Ironically, the statue was donated by the family of José Menéndez, the most powerful of all the local landowning magnates. He was a prime suspect for bankrolling the bounty hunters responsible for the genocide of the Selk'nam in Tierra del Fuego (see p.692). Kissing the shiny bronze **big toe** of one of the well-muscled natives is reckoned to ensure you'll return to Punta Arenas, but if that sort of homage doesn't appeal, try rubbing it instead.

Arrival, information and orientation

The **airport** lies 20km to the north of town. Minibuses run from the offices of the main airlines in town to connect with flights ($3); a *remise* taxi to the centre will cost around $7, a regular taxi to the main square costs around $12. All **buses** connecting with Río Gallegos or Puerto Natales arrive and depart along Bulnes. There is no central bus terminal, so each company arrives at its own office in the centre, all within a few blocks of the main plaza. The Transbordadora Austral Broom **ferry** to and from **Porvenir** in Chilean Tierra del Fuego uses the port 5km to the north of town at Bulnes 05075. Taxis from here to the centre cost $4; alternatively you could take *colectivo* taxi #15 or #20, which will set you back around 200 Chilean pesos or US$0.40. Austral Broom also runs a useful, adventurous service to **Puerto Williams** (☎061/218100).

The most convenient **tourist office** (Mon–Fri 8am–7pm, Sat & Sun 10am–7pm; ☎061/221644) is the municipal one in the bandstand-like building in the Plaza Muñoz Gamero – a graceful wrought-iron and wooden structure that used to be a lookout tower on top of one of the city's more affluent town houses. The helpful staff will give you a copy of the Comapa town plan, the best of the free **maps** available. The regional **tourist office** is close by at Waldo Seguel 689 (March–Nov Mon–Fri 8.15am–12.45pm

& 2.30–6.45pm; Dec–Feb Mon–Fri 8.15am–8pm, Sat & Sun 10am–8pm; ☎ & fax 061/225385). The Comapa agency at Independencia 830, 2nd Floor (☎061/241437, fax 225804), sells passages on the luxury *Terra Australis* **cruise ship** for recommended seven-day trips to the majestic glaciers of the southern fjords and Beagle Channel as well as Ushuaia and Puerto Williams. It also acts as the agent for the **Navimag** from Puerto Natales to Puerto Montt.

The town's main north–south artery is **Avenida Bulnes**, which leads straight into the town centre from the north, before splitting into two parallel streets, Calle Bories (the principal shopping thoroughfare) and Calle Magallanes. These cross the wide, landscaped **Avenida Colón** – the main boulevard that runs westwards from the sea – before sandwiching the Plaza Muñoz Gamero two short blocks further on. Calle Lautaro Navarro, a busy commercial street lined with airline offices, travel agents and several accommodation options, runs parallel with Magallanes, one block to the east. North of the cemetery, Avenida Bulnes's street numbers are prefixed by an additional zero.

Accommodation

The nearest place for **camping** is the wooded, shoreline picnic area of Parque Chabunco, about 21km north of town (catch any bus heading to Puerto Natales). Though not strictly a campsite, you can normally pitch a tent here free from hassle, but there are no services provided.

Alojamiento Guisande, José Miguel Carrera 1270 (☎061/243295). A guesthouse that's much better on the inside than appearances might suggest, with a genuinely charming lady owner. ②.

Backpackers Paradise, Ignacio Carrera Pinto 1022 (☎061/249435). A lively, busy hostel, but now no longer a paradise, being sloppily maintained, with noisy rooms and primitive bathroom arrangements that lack privacy. It has a well-equipped Internet café in its basement, though, open to non-guests. ①.

Finis Terrae, Colón 766 (☎061/228200, fax 248124; *bwsudam@entelchile.net*). A comfortable, bright and modern hotel in the Best Western chain, with a fine bar upstairs. ⑧.

Hospedaje Huala, Maipú 851 (☎061/244244; *huala@ctcreuna.cl*). Relaxed and enjoyable hostel accommodation, run by hospitable, artistic owners. ①.

Hostal Calafate, Lautaro Navarro 850 (☎ & fax 061/ 248415 or 241281). A pleasant, meticulously clean town house, with a commodious living-room and personable owners who speak good English. Breakfast is included; but private bathrooms cost twenty percent extra. The same owners run a second hostel nearby with rooms for up to five people. ④ with bath, ③ without.

Hostal La Estancia, O'Higgins 765 (☎ & fax 061/249130). Homely accommodation with shared bathroom and breakfast. ③.

Hostal de la Patagonia, Croacia 970 (☎061/249970, fax 223670; *ecopatagonia@entelchile.net*). A snug, friendly home that offers welcoming, spruce rooms with beds that have good mattresses. Private bathrooms cost half as much again as the basic room price, but breakfast is included, and they offer hefty discounts from May to Oct. ③.

Hotel José Nogueira, (☎061/248840, fax 248832; *nogueira@chileaustral.com*). The most stylish hotel in town, in the Nogueira-Braun family residence, a national monument from the late nineteenth century. The old-world elegance and luxury is only slightly marred by the piped music in reception, and it has a restaurant, the exquisite *Pergola*, in the conservatory. ⑨.

Lodging "The King," Fagnano 589 (☎061/223924). A warm but rather dark family home, two blocks from main square, that has rooms with shared bathroom. Its owners are helpful and serve up hearty meals. ①.

Hotel Panamericana, Plaza Muñoz Gamero 1025 (☎061/242134, fax 229473; *hopanam@ctc-mundo.net*). The best value of the top-end hotels, with scenic views of the sea and main square from the fifth and third floor respectively. ⑥.

Turismo Manuel, O'Higgins 646 (☎ & fax 061/220567 or 245441). Recently renovated, and the least expensive decent hostel in town, offering clean, quiet, airy dorms and a good kitchen. It also has laundry, Internet and travel services. ①.

The Town

Within the town, the best museum is the Salesian religious order's eclectic **Museo Salesiano "Borgatello"** at Bulnes 374 seven blocks north of the main Plaza Muñoz Gamero (daily 10am–1pm & 3–6pm; $2.25). It has a Victorian-style assemblage of mounted specimens of the region's wildlife, heavily dusted with borax; as well as some superb ethnographic material, including a remarkable bark canoe made by the native Alacalufes, and an exquisite, rare cape made from cormorant skins. Just off the northeast corner of the main plaza, at Magallanes 949, is **Museo Braun Menéndez** (April–Oct Tues–Sun 11am–1pm; Nov–March Tues–Sun 11am–5pm; $1.80), a place of stiff European opulence, heavily influenced by nineteenth-century French tastes, with displays on the town's history, including some archeological relics from Sarmiento de Gamboa's settlement of San Felipe (Port Famine). The **Palacio de Sara Braun** ($2) is another of these noteworthy transplanted European mansions, found on the northwest corner of the same square. Charlie Milward – the great-uncle of Bruce Chatwin, and who figures prominently in *In Patagonia* (1977) – used to live in the sandstone Gothic house at Avenida España 959.

There is a fun open-air museum, the **Museo del Recuerdo** (Mon–Fri 9–11am & 2–6pm, Sat 9–11am; $2.25) at the excellent Instituto de la Patagonia, 4km north of town along Avenida Bulnes, with a variety of apocalyptic threshers, reapers and haymakers from a century ago, as well as rebuilt, typically Patagonian homes. Across the road from the Institute is the **duty-free** zone, the **Zona Franca** (Mon–Sat 9.30am–12.30pm & 3–8.30pm), which has supermarkets with cheap alcohol and some outlets with camping gear and film, but no astounding bargains.

Listings

Airlines DAP, O'Higgins 891 (☎061/223340, fax 221693); Lan, Lautaro Navarro 1155 (☎061/244544); Lan-Chile, Lautaro Navarro and Pedro Montt (☎061/241232).

Banks and exchange Banks are open Mon–Fri 9am–2pm. The best ones are grouped around the main plaza: Banco de Santiago, Citibank and Banco Edwards. *Casa de cambio* Gasic, at Roca 915 or Lautaro Navarro 1099 (Mon–Sat 9am–7pm), offers the best rates. Try Bus Sur when other places are closed (daily 9am–10pm).

Car rental América, José Menéndez 631 (☎ & fax 061/240852); Budget, O'Higgins 964 (☎061/241696).

Consulates Argentina, 21 de Mayo 1878 (☎061/261912); Denmark, Colón 819 (☎061/221488); Holland, Sarmiento 780 (☎061/248100); Norway, Independencia 830, 2nd Floor (☎061/241437); UK, Roca 924 (☎061/227221 or 244727).

Hospital Hospital Regional, Angamos 180 (☎061/244040); alternatively, there's a private clinic: Clínica Magallanes, Av. Bulnes and Kuzma Slavic (☎061/211527).

Internet Cybercafé Austrointernet, Bories 687, first floor; Backpacker's Paradise, Carrera Pinto 1022 (☎061/249435).

Pharmacies Salco, Bories 970; Estrella, Mejicana 716.

Photography Agfa at Bories 789 develops slides (a service not offered in the south of Argentina; $8 for 36 exposures, unmounted; 1 hour wait).

Police Carabineros, Waldo Seguel 653 (☎061/222295); emergencies ☎133.

Post office Bories 911 (Mon–Fri 9am–6.30pm & Sat 9am–12.30pm).

Taxis Sampaio (☎061/221818); Punta Arenas (☎061/226298).

Telephone Entel, Lautaro Navarro 931; CTC, José Nogueira 1116.

Travel agents Virtually all travel agencies offer afternoon tours to the Magellanic penguin colony 70km away on Seno Otway (Sept–March; departs 4pm; $7); and morning tours to the reconstructed fort, Fuerte Bulnes, on the site of Punta Arenas' original settlement, 60km to the south, combined with a visit to the site of Puerto Hambre (tours depart 9.30am; $11). Try Turismo Paliaike, Lautaro Navarro 1129 (☎ & fax 061/223301), or Eco Tour, Lautaro Navarro 1091 (☎ & fax 061/223670).

Torres del Paine and Puerto Natales

One of South America's most famous national parks, **Parque Nacional Torres del Paine** attracts visitors from all over the globe who come to enjoy the grandeur of its glaciers, lakes and, above all, its jagged mountain peaks. It is accessed from the unassuming little port town of **Puerto Natales**, which, with its mellow pace of life, makes an ideal base for trekkers.

Puerto Natales

PUERTO NATALES, attractively sited on the shores of Seno Ultima Esperanza (Last Hope Sound), has a contented small-town feel. Civic pride is expressed in characteristically modest manner with a jaunty train engine in the pretty central square, **Plaza Arturo Prat**, and fun painted rubbish bins welded into shapes such as a **milodón**, a giant ground sloth from the Pleistocene age that died out in the area some 10,000 years ago. Famously, rare freeze-dried remains of this creature were discovered in a cave, the **Cueva del Milodón** (daily: May–Sept 9am–5pm; Oct–April 8am–9pm; $4), which lies some 25km to the northeast of town and can be visited by taxi or on a tour. The story forms the background for Bruce Chatwin's *In Patagonia* (1977). Within town, the best sight is the commendable little **Museo Histórico** at Bulnes 285 (Mon–Fri 8.30am–12.30pm & 2.30–6pm, Sat & Sun 3–6pm; free), with lovingly presented displays on the region's history and wildlife.

Arrival, information and accommodation

Bus companies drop you at their respective offices in the centre. Finding your way around poses few problems, and everywhere you'll need is easily accessible on foot. The central artery and principal shopping street is **Avenida Manuel Bulnes**, which runs gently downhill to the seafront boulevard, **Avenida Pedro Montt**. The municipal **tourist office** (☎061/411263) is found in the same building as the Museo Histórico and has the same opening hours. Turn right at the foot of Bulnes to get to the scenically, if inconveniently, situated Sernatur **tourist office** on the seafront at Pedro Montt 19 (March–Nov 8.30am–1pm & 2.30–6.30pm; Dec–Feb daily 8.30am–8pm; ☎ & fax 061/412125); it has limited stocks of an excellent, free historical and touristic **map** of the region. The **port** lies a block to the left (south) of the foot of Avenida Bulnes, and is where the famous **Navimag** ro-ro ferry *Puerto Edén* sails for Puerto Montt; the ticket office is at Pedro Montt 380 (☎061/411421, fax 411642). Natales is connected with frequent buses to Punta Arenas 250km away.

Natales is blessed with numerous, value-for-money, cosy *casas de familia*. These fun budget guesthouses usually offer breakfast in the room price, store luggage, have kitchen facilities; and often provide a laundry service.

Alberto de Agostini, O'Higgins 632 (☎061/410060, fax 410070). A good-value four-star hotel, if lacking character. Some rooms have Jacuzzis. ⑥.

Concepto Indio, Ladrilleros 105 (☎061/413609, fax 410169; *indigo@entelchile.net*). A rather overpriced hostel but popular with a trendy young crowd. Its restaurant serves expensive but appetizing vegetarian food and juices; and the lively bar is open till 2am. Closed mid-March to Sept. ③.

Casa Cecilia, Tomás Rogers 60 (☎ & fax 061/411797 or 413875; *casacecilia@hotmail.com*). Modern rooms grouped around a covered central courtyard, and kept to a Swiss standard of hygiene, with crisp bed linen. English is spoken; and it has a book exchange, Internet, and good-quality bicycles and camping gear for rent. Breakfasts cost $2.25 extra. ①.

Casa Chila, Carrera Pinto 442 (☎061/413981). Great-value, sociable lodging with a marvellously hospitable, helpful family. It has a spacious kitchen and good shared bathrooms, but some squeaky beds. ①.

Casa Dixon, Bories 206 (☎ & fax 061/411218). A well-heated lodging house, with a large kitchen and good bathrooms. It offers a minibus service to Paine. ③.

Casa Lili, Bories 153 (☎061/414063). An excellent value, popular *casa de familia*. ①.

Casa Teresa Ruiz, Esmeralda 463 (☎061/410472). A bright and friendly place but without a guest kitchen. ①.

CostAustralis, Pedro Montt and Bulnes (☎061/412000, fax 411881). The most luxurious hotel in town, excellently sited on the seafront, and of international four-star comfort. It has modern, fully equipped rooms and a fine restaurant. Discounts available mid-April to mid-Sept. ⑦.

Hostal La Cumbre, Eberhard 533 (☎ & fax 061/412422). High-ceilinged rooms in an interesting and welcoming old mandarin-coloured home. No singles rates. ①.

Juan Ladrilleros, Pedro Montt 161 (☎061/411652, fax 412109). A hotel whose singles are expensive and rooms are rather small, but virtually all have views of Seno Ultima Esperanza. The restaurant is recommended for its affordable seafood. ⑥.

Residencial El Mundial, Bories 315 (☎061/412476; *monofortaleza@hotmail.com*). A rather crowded hostel, but run by a hard-working, friendly bunch. ①, ② with private bath.

Listings

Airlines Lan, Tomás Rogers 78 (☎061/ 411236).

Banks and exchange Banco de Santiago, Bulnes 436, and Banco de Chile, Bulnes 544, are both open Mon–Fri 9am–2pm. *Casas de cambio* Gasic, Bulnes 692, Andes Patagónicos, Bulnes 1053, and Cambio Sur, Eberhard 285 – the last is open Mon–Sat 10am–10pm.

Car rental Andes Patagónicos, Blanco Encalada 226 (☎ & fax 061/411594); Ultima Esperanza, Eberhard 19 (☎ & fax 061/ 410879).

Laundry Milodón, Baquedano 642; Servilaundry, Bulnes 513; Servimarie, Bories 20.

Photography Agfa, Bulnes 674 (slides developed).

Post office Eberhard 429 (Mon–Fri 8.30am–12.30pm & 2.30–6pm, Sat 9am–12.30pm).

Taxis Urban taxis cost $500 pesos within town; *colectivo* taxis cost $150 pesos. For longer trips, Fabian Oyarzo, O'Higgins 573 (☎061/ 412168), is recommended.

Telephone CTC, Blanco Encalada 169; Entel, Baquedano 270.

Torres del Paine

Some 150km to the north of Natales is the **Parque Nacional Torres del Paine** (pronounced "PAI-nei"), whose 2400 square kilometres were declared a UNESCO Biosphere reserve in 1978. The centrepiece of the park is the Paine massif, a prominent outcrop in the middle of the steppe that comprises several main mountain groups. These include the dramatic **Torres** ("Towers") themselves, which are incisor-shaped spires of smooth grey granite grouped around a central tarn; the **Cuernos** ("Horns") – jagged peaks of quite startling beauty, their dark upper caps of friable sedimentary rock contrasting with their pale igneous base; and **Cerro Paine Grande**, the tallest mountain of the park, at 3050m. Splayed around the foot of this massif are a collection of meltwater lakes of colours ranging from Prussian blue to bright turquoise; glaciers streaming off the Southern Patagonian Icecap; forests of *Nothofagus* southern beech; and semi-wooded pastureland that joins with boggy river meadows and arid steppe.

The main **park gate** is at Laguna Amarga (115km from Natales), from where several unsealed roads run further into the park. The principal route runs for 56km like a bent fishhook through the south of the park to the southern end of **Lago Grey**, which is fed by the enormous icecap **glacier** of the same name. On the way, this road passes a short detour to the pretty waterfalls of Salto Grande (24km from the gate); the exceptionally beautiful turquoise **Lago Pehoé** (27km), with its splendid views of the Cuernos del Paine and a beautiful **boat excursion**; and the main **park administration** and **information centre** at Lago del Toro (40km). Another road from Laguna Amarga gate runs 7km west to the *Hostería Las Torres*, which is the normal starting point for the classic treks of the park (see below); and a third runs north for a similar distance to the Cascada Paine, a low but impressively powerful waterfall in the gully of the Río Paine. The park is one of the best places to see guanaco up close, there's a healthy condor population, and you'll probably see semi-tame Patagonian grey foxes at the Lago Sarmiento park gate that most tour groups leave by.

The park is visited currently by over 60,000 visitors a year and, especially in high season (late Dec–Feb), you'll have to contend with some busy trails and coach tour groups at the major lowland sites of interest. Nevertheless, the park is extensive enough always to offer options for those who seek solitude. Although you can get a taste of the park on a day tour, you'll need seven to ten days really to get the most out of it. The best time to visit is from November – the best time for flowering plants – to early December, or in March and April – when it's less windy and the autumn leaves provide a stunning backdrop – and you stand your best chance of seeing an endangered huemul in winter when few people visit.

Practicalities

The three most common ways of getting to the park from Natales are by public bus, tour vehicle or taxi (arrange itinerary in advance). The cheapest option is by one of the regular public **buses**, which depart from their respective companies' offices. **Day tours** can be booked at most tourist agencies in Natales, stopping at all the major road-accessible spots in the park and visiting the Cueva del Milodón quickly on the way (leave at about 7.30am; 12hr; $32 per person, $40–45 in winter; park entrance not included). Baqueano Zamora at Eberhard 566 (☎ & fax 061/412911; *baqueano@entelchile.net*) has expert English-speaking guides, and offers a very professional bus service and tours, plus ones on horseback. Tours Mily, Blanco Encalada 266 (☎ & fax 061/411262 or 412748), is reliable and runs tours year round; Fortaleza Aventura, Arturo Prat 234 (☎061/414040, fax 410595), is owned by an active young crowd, and also offers a reliable, fun service; while Onas, Blanco Encalada 599 (☎ & fax 061/412707; *onas@chileaustral.com*), organizes interesting tours into the south of the park via the **Balmaceda Glacier** and **Río Serrano** ($66). Tomislav Goic Utrovicich at Bulnes 513 (☎ & fax 061/412869) is a private guide with an excellent knowledge of the park's wildlife and botany; and the taxi driver Fabian Oyarzo, O'Higgins 573 (☎061/412168; speaks no English), is also highly recommended.

Entrance to the park costs $7500 for foreign nationals (about US$16; payable at gate, and only in Chilean pesos), regardless of the length of stay. Fees for climbing are considerably higher, being in the region of $80 per person, and must be obtained ninety days before entering the park, from Chilean embassies or consulates in your country of origin. At the park gate, trekkers are required to register (bring your passport) and you will have your equipment checked. The **weather** in this area of the world is extremely temperamental. You can get caught in snow blizzards even in mid-summer, so it is vital that you come fully prepared even if you're just doing a day-hike. The place is also famous for its unremitting springtime **winds**, which can blow with such force that you may find yourself knocked off your feet, and such constancy that you can find yourself going mad. If you're just going for a day trip, it may be worth phoning the park administration (April–Sept 8.30am–6.30pm; Oct–March 8.30am–8pm; ☎061/691931) to check what the weather is like, as it can be very different to that in Natales. Administration will store excess luggage; and buses leave here for Natales between noon and 6.30pm in season (check off-season times in Natales).

You are strongly advised to invest in a decent **map** (especially if trekking), which are sold in numerous outlets in Natales: the best available is the *Mapas* series, #13 "Torres del Paine" ($7). It gives you plenty of information about the refuges and campsites in the park, which can be supplemented by chatting to fellow trekkers and the *guardaparques* to find out about the most recent conditions vis-à-vis litter, mice and trail conditions.

Accommodation in the park

The park is well served by a network of **campsites** and **refuges** as well as more luxurious hotel accommodation, which it is advisable to book in advance. The majority of places are run as short-term park concessions, and service varies depending on the concessionaire. Most refuges are currently run by Andescape, and you can reserve and pay for space in high season at their office in Natales, at Eberhard 599 or by email (☎ & fax 061/412592; *andescape@chileaustral.com*). These refuges are well-run, comfortable, thirty-bed outfits, and facilities include hot showers, kitchen, equipment rental, and a full meal service (dinner costs $10). Bunk-beds cost $17, but you'll need your own sleeping bag (or rent one at the refuge at $4 per night). You can also buy rather pricey groceries. Camping at these sites costs around $4 a night (hot showers $2 extra), but there are still some places in the park that are free, though usually poorly looked after. The free refuges, such as the one at Pudeto jetty on Lago Pehoé, are not particularly clean and are generally worth avoiding. In high season, some of the more popular campsites fill up with litter (Italiano is notorious for this) and, although there is no hantavirus in the park, mice have been known to chew through tents to get at food; to avoid them getting at yours, store your supplies in a plastic bag and tie it to a tree branch. Camping Pehoé ($20 per site for up to six people with free hot showers) is beautifully sited but gets extremely busy.

One of the major **hotel** options is *Hostería Las Torres*, an exclusive, privately owned estancia in the centre of the park, which runs its own tours and hires out horses (☎061/226054, fax 222641; *lastorres@chileaustral.com*; ⑧). On an island in Lago Pehoé is *Hostería Pehoé* (☎061/244506, fax 248052 for reservations; ⑦; closed May–Sept), reached by an idyllic bridge, but whose five-star setting overlooking the Cuernos is not matched by comfort – the rooms are very basic and the bathrooms run-down. Its restaurant gets very busy at lunchtime with tour groups. Just south of Lago Pehoé is the *Hotel Explora*, catering for luxury package tourists (☎ & fax 02/2066060; *explora@entelchile.net*; prices from $1040 per person for all inclusive three-day package); and at the southern end of Lago Grey is the recommended *Hostería Lago Grey*, with well-designed, airy cabins and attentive service (☎ & fax 061/410220; *hgrey@ctcreuna.cl*; ⑧).

Trekking in the park

Though there are hundreds of possible options for trekking in this extensive park, the two most popular ones are the "**Circuit**" and the "**W**" (so called for the pattern the trail marks on the map), both of which are physically challenging but not particularly technical routes. The Circuit is the classic Paine trek, which takes around five to seven days to complete, and loops – customarily undertaken anticlockwise – around the entire massif via the Refugio Dickson, the Paso John Garner (the highest point of the trail at 1241m) and Glaciar Grey. The first leg of the "W" takes you up to the Torres themselves, and this is the best option for those who only have time for a **day-hike**. You then retrace your steps and head up the next major valley to the west, the Valle Francés, as far as Campamento Británico, and complete the "W" by heading to Refugio Grey near the glacier. Pay particular attention at all times to responsible fire-lighting practices when camping; and, especially on the Circuit, be prepared for very boggy sections.

travel details

Buses

Out of season (Easter–Sept), some services do not operate, above all along and around the RN40, whilst others are severely curtailed.

Bajo Caracoles to: Posadas (2 weekly; 2hr).
Caleta Olivia to: Comodoro Rivadavia (hourly; 1hr); Puerto Deseado (3 daily; 3hr–3hr 30min); Río Gallegos (3 daily; 8–10hr).

Camarones to: Trelew (3 weekly; 3hr 30min).

Carmen de Patagones to: Bahía Blanca (6–8 daily; 3hr 30min); Buenos Aires (3 daily; 12hr); Comodoro Rivadavia (1 daily; 13hr); Mar del Plata (2 weekly; 9hr 30min); Puerto Madryn (1 daily; 6hr); Neuquén (1 daily; 10hr 15min); San Antonio (daily; 2hr 30min); Sierra Grande (1 daily; 4hr); Trelew (1 daily; 6hr 40min); Viedma (every 30min; 15min).

Comodoro Rivadavia to: Buenos Aires (4 daily; 26hr); Caleta Olivia (hourly; 1hr); Córdoba (daily; 25hr); Esquel (2 daily; 8hr 30min); Mendoza (daily; 28hr 30min); Puerto Madryn (4 daily; 6hr 15min); Río Gallegos (5 daily; 9–11hr); San Antonio (1 daily; 12hr); Sarmiento (5 daily; 2hr 15min); Trelew (10–12 daily; 5hr 15min).

Dolavon to: Gaiman (8–14 daily; 25–35min); Trelew (8–14 daily; 1hr–1hr 15min).

El Calafate to: Buenos Aires (daily; 40hr); El Chaltén (2 weekly to 6 daily; 4hr); Perito Moreno (3–7 weekly, 13hr); Río Gallegos (4 daily; 4hr); Río Turbio (daily; 4hr).

El Chaltén to: El Calafate (2 weekly to 6 daily; 4hr); Lago del Desierto (several daily; 50min); Perito Moreno (5–9 weekly; 13hr); Río Gallegos (2 weekly; 7–8hr).

Gaiman to: Dolavon (8–14 daily; 25–35min); Trelew (11–20 daily; 25–35min).

Las Grutas to: Bariloche (1 daily; 10hr 30min); Buenos Aires (3 daily; 14–15hr); Puerto Madryn (3 daily; 4hr); San Antonio Oeste (hourly; 20min); Sierra Grande (4 daily; 1hr 30min–2hr).

Los Antiguos to: El Chaltén (2 weekly; 13hr); Perito Moreno (5 daily; 50min).

Perito Moreno to: El Calafate (3–7 weekly; 13hr); El Chaltén (5–9 weekly; 13hr); Posadas (2 weekly; 4hr).

Piedra Buena to: Comodoro Rivadavia (3 daily; 6hr 30min–8hr); Río Gallegos (4 daily; 3hr); San Julián (4 daily; 1hr 30min–2hr).

Playa Unión to: Rawson (every 15–30min; 20min).

Posadas to: Bajo Caracoles (2 weekly; 2hr); Perito Moreno (2 weekly; 4hr).

Puerto Deseado to: Caleta Olivia (3 daily; 3hr–3hr 30min).

Puerto Madryn to: Buenos Aires (4 daily; 18–20hr); Comodoro Rivadavia (4 daily; 6hr 15min); Puerto Pirámides (2 weekly to 2 daily; 1hr 30min); Río Gallegos (3 daily; 15–17hr); Trelew (hourly; 1hr).

Puerto Natales to: Punta Arenas (6 daily; 3hr 30min).

Puerto Pirámides to: Puerto Madryn (2 weekly to 2 daily; 1hr 25min); Trelew (2 weekly to 1 daily; 2hr 45min).

Punta Arenas to: Puerto Natales (6 daily; 3hr 30min).

Rawson to: Playa Unión (every 15–30min; 20min); Trelew (every 15 min; 20min).

Río Gallegos to: Buenos Aires (4 daily; 36–38hr); Comodoro Rivadavia (5 daily; 9–11hr); El Calafate (4 daily; 4hr); El Chaltén (2 weekly; 8hr); Mendoza (daily; 41hr 30min); Puerto Madryn (3 daily; 15–17hr); San Julián (4 daily; 4hr 30min); Trelew (5 daily; 14–16hr).

Río Turbio to: El Calafate (1 daily; 4hr); Río Gallegos (4 daily; 5hr).

San Antonio Oeste to: Las Grutas (hourly; 20min).

San Julián to: Comodoro Rivadavia (4 daily; 5hr–6hr 30min); Piedra Buena (4 daily; 1hr 30min–2hr); Río Gallegos (4 daily; 4hr 30min); Trelew (4 daily; 10hr–11hr 30min).

Sarmiento to: Comodoro Rivadavia (5 daily; 2hr 15min).

Sierra Grande to: Buenos Aires (4 weekly; 16hr); Comodoro Rivadavia (1 daily; 8hr); Las Grutas (1 daily; 1hr 30min–2hr); Neuquén (1 daily; 8hr); Puerto Madryn (3–4 daily; 1hr 30min).

Trelew to: Bariloche (daily; 12hr 45min–13hr 30min); Buenos Aires (8–10 daily; 19–21hr); Camarones (3 weekly; 3hr 30min); Comodoro Rivadavia (10–12 daily; 5hr 15min); Córdoba (3 daily; 20hr); Dolavon (8–14 daily; 1hr–1hr 15min); Esquel (2–3 daily; 8hr 15min–8hr 30min); Gaiman (11–20 daily; 25–35min); Mendoza (2 daily; 24hr); Puerto Madryn (hourly; 1hr); Puerto Pirámides (2 weekly to 1 daily; 2hr 45min); Rawson (every 15min; 20min); Río Gallegos (5 daily; 14–16hr); San Julián (4 daily; 10hr–11hr 30min).

Tres Lagos to: El Calafate (7 daily; 2hr); El Chaltén (6 daily; 2hr); Perito Moreno (3–7 weekly; 10hr).

Viedma to: Carmen de Patagones (every 30min; 15min).

International Buses

Chile Chico to: Los Antiguos (2–10 daily; 40min).

El Calafate to: Puerto Natales (1–3 daily; 4hr 30min–5hr).

Los Antiguos to: Chile Chico (2–10 daily; 40min).

Río Gallegos to: Punta Arenas (1–2 daily; 4–5hr).

Río Turbio to: Puerto Natales (1–2 daily; 1hr).

Punta Arenas to: Río Gallegos (1–2 daily; 4–5hr); to Río Grande (Mon–Sat 1 daily; 8–10hr); Ushuaia (Mon–Sat 1 daily; 12–14hr).

Puerto Natales to: El Calafate (1–3 daily; 4–5hr); Río Turbio (1–2 daily; 1hr).

Train

Viedma to: Bariloche (Sun & Thurs 5pm; 16–17hr).

Ferries

Chile Chico to: Puerto Ibañez (3–7 weekly; 2hr 30min–3hr).

Puerto Natales to: Puerto Montt (1 weekly; 4 days).

Punta Arenas to: Porvenir (Tues–Sun 1 daily; 2hr 30min–3hr); Puerto Williams (Nov–March once every 8 days; 32–40hr).

Punta Delgada to: Crossing Magellan Straits (5–9 daily; 30min).

El Chaltén to: Helsingfors (daily; 2hr 15min–3hr 30min).

Helsingfors to: El Chaltén (daily; 2hr 15min–3hr 30min).

Domestic flights

El Calafate to: Buenos Aires (1–2 daily; 3hr); Río Gallegos (daily; 50min); Ushuaia (1 daily; 2hr 30min).

Comodoro Rivadavia to: Buenos Aires (1–3 daily; 2hr–3hr); Río Gallegos (daily; 1hr 15min); Trelew (daily; 45min).

Punta Arenas to: Puerto Williams (3–6 weekly; 45min).

Río Gallegos to: Buenos Aires (2–3 daily; 3hr); El Calafate (1 daily; 50min); Trelew (daily; 1hr 30min); Ushuaia (50min–3hr depending on routing).

Trelew to: Bariloche (2–3 weekly; 1hr–1hr 15min); Buenos Aires (3 daily; 1hr 50min); Esquel (2 weekly; 50min–1hr); Río Gallegos (1 daily; 1hr 30min); Ushuaia (1–2 daily; 2hr).

CHAPTER TEN

TIERRA DEL FUEGO

ierra del Fuego, the Land of Fire, is where South America finally funnels into the icy waters of the south: the end of the inhabited globe. Known to its erstwhile indigenous Selk'nam inhabitants as **Karunkinka**, it gets its Spanish name from the fires that these people lit when Magellan and his crew first sailed fearfully through the newly discovered straits. Strictly, it comprises the entire archipelago of southern Patagonia, but the term is more commonly applied to just the main island of the group, the **Isla Grande de Tierra del Fuego**, which is also known simply as **Isla Grande**. Roughly a third of the island (some 21,000 square kilometres) is Argentinian, the rest lies across the border in Chile. The region has three principal and strikingly distinct geographical zones – north, central, and southern – but only one principal tourist destination: **Ushuaia**, in the south. If at all possible, introduce yourself to the island with the stunning aerial views afforded by a **flight** down to Ushuaia.

Ushuaia is the base for visiting the tremendous **Canal Beagle** and the wild, forested mountain ranges of southern Tierra del Fuego. And with the **Parque Nacional Tierra del Fuego** just 12km to the west, you should aim to spend a week of so in the area to get the most out of your trip. **Estancia Harberton**, home to descendants of the Bridges family, is an easy day-trip from the city and you could also make a trip across the Beagle Channel to **Puerto Williams** on Chile's wild Isla Navarino.

The north of the island consists of windswept plains and scrubby *coirón* grassland, and you won't be missing much if you leave it to the sheep that thrive there. The main town here, **Río Grande**, is a bleak place, but nonetheless makes a useful overnight stop for travellers exploring the island's heartland, and for those heading south into the region overland. It's also popular with fly-fishermen, who come here from all over the world, hoping to outwit the sea-going brown trout of the Río Grande, the world's premiere river for catching that species. Central Tierra del Fuego spreads out from Río Grande to Paso Garibaldi 100km to the south, an area of considerably more interest than the north, and is centred on **Lago Fagnano** and the village of **Tolhuin**. Here, estancias nestle amongst patches of low, transitional, Fuegian woodland that looks as if it has been exposed to a tickertape parade of shredded rags, such is the prevalence of lichen beards hanging from the branches. Much of the area's beauty is only really accessible for those with their own transport: try the loop along the **RCf** and **RCh** or, better still, the **RCa**, which runs through some rugged scenery by the eastern coastline.

The southeastern chunk of the Tierra del Fuego, **Península Mitre**, is one of Argentina's least accessible regions. This triangle of land – which lies beyond the end of RCa and RCj – is only for the very few who are committed to slogging it out on foot, horseback, or perhaps a motorized quad bike across an intemperate boggy wilderness, with low scrub and next to no human habitation. You'll need a gaucho guide, good waterproof clothing, stamina, and a minimum of a week to spare. Finally, to the east of Península Mitre lies the **Isla de los Estados**, known in English as Staten Island. Almost perpetually swathed in mist and cloud, it is a land of deep fjords, swamps, scrubby subantarctic forests, and craggy peaks, and had a black reputation amongst mariners of past centuries for the fierce currents that surround it. There are currently plans to give this place protected status as a provincial nature reserve, but the only way

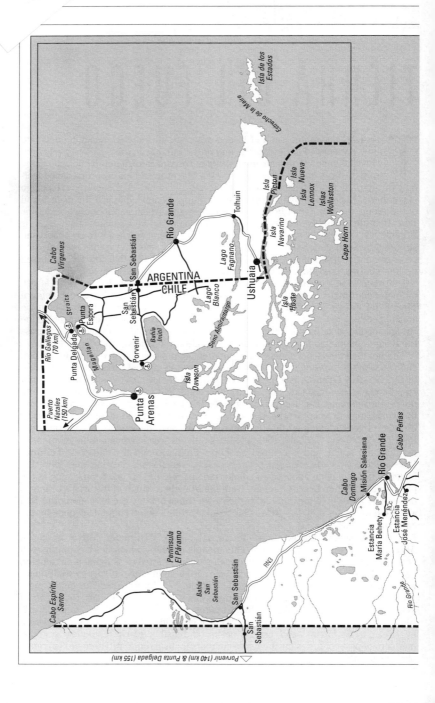

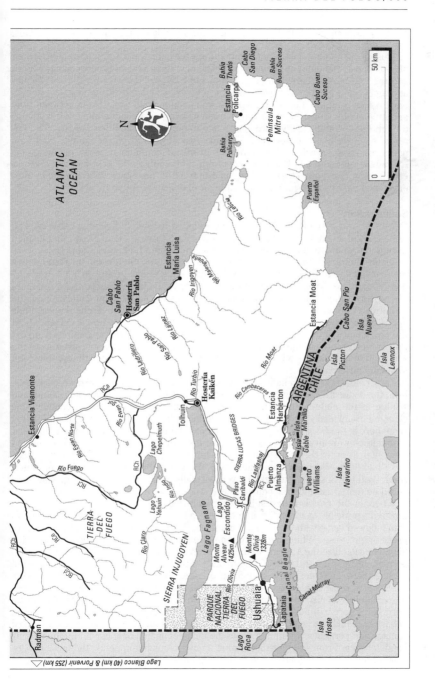

to visit at present is by extremely expensive chartered launch from Ushuaia; for details, ask at the tourist office or port.

Most people tend to visit Isla Grande during the summer months (Dec–Feb), when places such as Ushuaia can get very busy. The best **time to visit** is between late March and the end of April, when the mountains and hills are daubed with the spectacular autumnal colours of the *Nothofagus* southern beech woodland. Springtime (Oct to mid-Nov) is also beautiful. For **winter sports**, you need to head for Ushuaia between June and August: the area is good for cross-country skiing, especially around Sierra Alvear, though the downhill facilities are best suited to beginners and intermediates. The **climate** is generally not as severe as you may expect here given the latitude, and temperatures rarely reach the extremes of mainland continental areas of Patagonia. Average temperatures in Ushuaia range from 1°C in July, to 12°C in January, and you could easily find yourself sunbathing in balmy 20°C heat on a calm summer's day, enveloped not in some stuffy smog, but in air of delicious, Antarctic purity.

Some history

Cut off from the mainland, Isla Grande developed its own indigenous cultures. The first bands of nomadic hunter-gatherers crossed a temporary land bridge that formed during glacial fluctuations of the Pleistocene era, some 11,800 years ago. These were probably the direct antecedents of the **Mannekenk** and **Selk'nam** (or **Ona**) tribes that survived until the twentieth century. Later, indigenous groups living a predominantly maritime existence colonized the southern Fuegian channels: the forefathers of the Kawéskar (Alacaluf) who inhabited territory that is now Chilean; and the **Yámana** (Yahgans), the canoe people of the Beagle Channel. Archeological finds near Ushuaia attest to their presence from at least 4000 BC. No one is certain about the provenance of these people: new theories postulate seaborne migrations from the Pacific west; but current consensus still favours the idea that they evolved from the same ethnic base as the terrestrial groups, in spite of considerable ethnographic and linguistic differences.

Early contacts between indigenous groups and **European explorers** were sporadic from the sixteenth century onwards, even with the advent of commercial whaling and sealing in the eighteenth century. In the latter half of the nineteenth century, this changed dramatically, with tragic results for the indigenous population. When FitzRoy came here in the *Beagle* in the 1830s, an estimated three to four thousand Selk'nam and Mannekenk were living in Isla Grande, with some three thousand each of Yámana and Kawéskar living in the entire southern archipelago. A hundred years later, these cultures had been effectively annihilated, with the years 1870 to 1920 proving the watershed. By the 1930s, the Mannekenk were virtually extinct, and the other groups numbered no more than fifty individuals apiece.

Whereas the sophisticated subsistence cultures of indigenous groups developed through a principle of adaptation in the face of a hostile environment, the white settlers who followed came with the intent to dominate that environment, driven by motives of profit or progress. White settlement came in three phases. Anglican **missionaries** began to catechize the Yámana in the south, and Thomas Bridges established the first permanent mission on Ushuaia Bay in 1871. From the late 1880s, the Italian Roman Catholic Salesian Order began a similar process to the north of the Fuegian Andes, consolidated with the foundation of their first mission near the Río Grande river in 1893. Alluvial **gold** was discovered on the island in 1879, and soon thereafter the Rumanian-born adventurer, Julius Popper, established a fiefdom based around Bahía San Sebastián, which he ruled as a despot between 1887 and 1893, issuing his own gold coinage and periodically gunning down the indigenous inhabitants with the help of his bands of men. From the mid-1890s came a new colonizing impetus: the inauspicious-looking northern plains proved to be ideal **sheep-farming** territory, and vast *latifun-*

dias sprang up, owned by people such as José Menéndez. Croat, Scottish, Basque, Italian, Galician and Chilean immigrants arrived to work on the estancias and build up their own landholdings. Today, the sheep-farming industry is in crisis, with the price of wool at an all-time low, and the island's economy is more dependent on the production of petroleum and natural gas, fisheries, forestry and technological industries such as television assembly plants, which were attracted to the area by its status as a duty-free zone. Luxury items are comparatively cheap, but basic items such as food are much more expensive than in other parts of the country due to the huge distances involved in importing them. Hopes run high for the fast-expanding tourist industry centred on Ushuaia, and you'll find many people there who've relocated from Buenos Aires in search of a more relaxed style of life.

In 1991, the region gained full provincial status and is now known as the **Provincia de Tierra del Fuego, Antártida e Islas del Atlántico Sur**. Its jurisdiction is seen to extend over all territories of the south, including the Falklands Islands or Islas Malvinas (for more on this, see p.712), which lie 550km off the coast, and Argentinian Antarctica.

Ushuaia and around

USHUAIA, the hub of tourism in Tierra del Fuego, lies in the far south of the island. Dramatically located between the mountains – amongst them **Cerro Martial** and **Monte Olivia** – and the sea, the town tumbles down the hillside to the wide, encircling arm of land that protects its bay from the southwesterly winds and occasional thrashing storms of the icy **Beagle Channel**. In addition to having several of its own sites of interest, Ushuaia acts as a convenient base for exploring the rugged beauty of the lands that border this historically important sea channel. **Puerto Williams**, on the southern side of the straits is a boat trip away, and there are other trips, too: to **Estancia Harberton**, and on to Bahía Lapataia in the Parque Nacional Tierra del Fuego (see pp.681–686). In winter, good skiing can be had in the **Sierra Alvear** region north of town; this area, along with neighbouring Sierra Valdivieso and Chile's Isla Navarino (see p.680), are also the places to head for if you're looking for physically challenging **trekking**, some of it bushwhacking.

On June 21 of each year, the **Bajada de Las Antorchas** takes place, when the longest night of the year is celebrated with a torchlight ski descent of Cerro Martial's slopes that traditionally opens the season. Daylight lasts from about 9am till 4pm at this time of year. In mid-November, the town hosts the **Ushuaia Jazz Festival**, and between Christmas and New Year, the municipality organizes various events including live concerts, often with nationally famous bands.

Some history

In 1869, Reverend Stirling became Tierra del Fuego's first white settler when he founded his **Anglican mission** amongst the Yámana here; the city takes its name from the Yámana tongue, and means "bay penetrating westwards". Stirling stayed for six months, before being recalled to the Falklands Islands to be appointed Anglican bishop for South America. Thomas Bridges, his assisant, returned to take over the mission in 1871, after which time Ushuaia began to figure on mariners' charts as a place of refuge in the event of shipwreck. A modest **monument** to the achievements of the early missionaries can be found where the first mission stood, on the south side of Ushuaia Bay, and is reached by the modern causeway, southwest of the town centre.

In 1884, Augusto Lasserre raised the Argentine flag over Ushuaia for the first time, formally incorporating this area into the Argentine Republic. From 1896, in order to consolidate its sovereignty and open up the region to wider colonization, the

Camping Club Andino (1 km), ❶ (3 km) & ❷ (4 km)

Glaciar Martial (6 km), Aerosilla (4 km)

Ruta Nacional 3 (RN-3), Río Grande (232 km) & Lago Fagnano (98 km)

Parque Nacional (12 km), Lapataia (24 km), Camping Ushuaia Municipal (6 km) & Airport, Rugby Club (3 km), Camping Municipal (6 km) & Airport

CERRO MARTIAL

USHUAIA

0   250m

ACCOMMODATION

Hostería América	3	Residencial Linares	12
Casa de Familia Hilda Sánchez	11	Hostal Malvinas	9
Casa de Familia Silvia Casalaga	7	Refugio del Mochilero	10
Del Glaciar	2	La Posada	13
Las Hayas	1	Casa de Solari	6
Cabo de Hornos	14	Torre al Sur	4
Kaisken	5	Violeta de la Montaña	8

Argentinian State employed a popular nineteenth-century tactic and established a **penal colony** here. Forced convict labour was used for developing the diminutive town's infrastructure and for logging the local forests to build the town (by 1910, 25km of railway had been constructed for this purpose), but the prison had a reputation as the Siberia of Argentina and was eventually closed by Perón in 1947.

Nowadays Ushuaia has a quite different reputation: the most populous and popular town in Tierra del Fuego, it depends largely on its thriving tourist industry, capitalizing on the beauty of its natural setting. You'll soon catch on that this is the world's most southerly resort and you can gather claims to fame galore – golf on the world's most southerly course, a ride on the world's most southerly train – but do your best to ignore this irritatingly ubiquitous epithet. Ushuaia has plenty of sites worthy of a visit on their own merits not just for their fortuitous geographical circumstance.

Arrival and information

The new international **airport**, Malvinas Argentinas, is 4km southwest of town; there's no public transport to the city, and a **taxi** to the centre costs $5. **Buses** arrive and depart from their companies' respective offices: Líder, from Gobernador Paz 921 (☎02901/436421); Tolkeyen, from Maipú 237 (☎02901/427354); and Techni Austral outside its office at 25 de Mayo 50 in the morning, and outside the *Hotel Beagle* half a block away in the afternoon (☎02901/423396).

Avenida San Martín, the main commercial street, runs parallel to the seafront avenue, Avenida Maipú, one block back from it up the hill. At no. 674 you'll find the **tourist office** (Easter–Oct Mon–Fri 8am–9pm, Sat & Sun 9am–7pm; Nov–Easter Mon–Fri 8am–midnight, Sat & Sun 9am–11pm; ☎02901/432000, fax 424550; free local information line ☎0800/3331476; *muniush@tierradelfuego.ml.org*). Its well-informed, friendly staff speak English. They have an excellent free illustrated guide to the region that is of souvenir quality, a useful leaflet on walks in the area, and will help you find accommodation, even arranging to put you up with families where all else fails in high season. Two other small **information kiosks** operate in summer: one at the port, whose opening hours coincide with the arrival of cruise ships (Dec to mid-March); and another at the airport, opening when flights arrive (Oct–March only). The Tierra del Fuego National Park also has an office in town, at San Martín 1395 (Mon–Fri 8am–1pm), but it's unhelpful and offers little you can't get at the tourist office, with the exception of park **fishing licences**. Licences are also available from the Club de Caza y Pesca, at Maipú and 9 de Julio. For information on trekking and climbing, contact the **Club Andino Ushuaia**, Fadul 50 (3–10pm; ☎ & fax 02901/422335), who will also put you in touch with qualified guides, such as Luis Turi (☎02901/432642). Register here before embarking on any trek or climb, giving details of your planned route and the date of your return, and do not forget to inform the office that you have arrived back safely when you return.

Accommodation

Ushuaia has a good range of hotels and hostels, most of which are found along the first four streets parallel to the bay. Its two best luxury hotels are found up the mountainside on the road to Glaciar Martial. There are three useful **campsites**: the nearest to the centre is the well-equipped *Club Andino*, Alem 2873 (☎ & fax 02901/422335; $5 per person) at the base of the Club Andino skiing piste (free transfers from the site to the centre); on the way to the national park are the *Ushuaia Rugby Club*, by the Río Pipo, 5km from town (☎02901/435796; $5 per person), and the *Camping Municipal*, 8km from the centre, near the Tren del Fin del Mundo train station, which is basic (no showers) but free. From December to February, you are strongly advised to book **accommodation** in advance, even for hostels. Many hotels charge a ten percent surcharge on credit cards and travellers' cheques.

Hotel Cabo de Hornos, San Martín and Rosas (☎ & fax 02901/422313). A decent, very central mid-range hotel. Beds have firm mattresses, and some rooms have sea views. ⑤.

Casa de Familia Hilda Sánchez, Gob. Deloqui 395, 1° (☎02901/423622). Actually two separate hostels run by a chalk-and-cheese couple. The main house has a spacious kitchen and is run by a hard-talking, generous evangelical lady; whilst the second house run by her personable husband is better for party-people. ①.

La Casa de Familia Silvia Casalaga, Gob. Paz 1380 (☎02901/423202). A highly recommended, spotlessly clean B&B with fantastic views, and worth reserving in advance. Rooms have shared bathrooms. Closed May–Aug. ③.

Hotel Del Glaciar, Luis Martial 2355 (☎02901/430640, fax 430636). A large four-star hotel at the foot of the Glaciar Martial chair lift, 5km up the steep mountain from the city (free shuttle bus for guests). Choose between rooms with mountain or sea views; single rooms are expensive. ⑧.

Hostal Malvinas, Gob. Deloqui 615 (☎ & fax 02901/422626). A reliable option and well located. Beds have well-sprung mattresses; triple rooms are quite cramped. ⑤.

Hostería América, Gob. Paz 1665 (☎02901/423358 or fax 431362). A competitively priced mid-range hotel, but quite a walk from the centre. ④.

Hostal Kaisken, Gob. Paz 7 (☎02901/436756). A cheery, quiet hostel with rooms with shared bathroom for two to four people. Its owners are welcoming and helpful; and you can use the Internet ($6 per hr) and kitchen. Serves good breakfasts ($3). ①.

La Posada Hotel, San Martín 1299 (☎ & fax 02901/433330 or 433222). One of the best-value mid-range hotels, with bright rooms for two to four people, and panoramic views from the second floor. There's a ten percent surcharge on credit cards. ⑤.

Las Hayas Resort Hotel, Luis Martial 1650 (☎02901/430710, fax 430719). Ushuaia's only five-star hotel: luxurious, quiet, and high up, 4km from town on the road to the glacier. Most of its stylish, commodious rooms have views of the Beagle Channel; but singles are pricey and there are no triples. There's a health club and indoor swimming pool. An hourly shuttle bus runs from the port (9.30am–8.15pm). ⑧.

Refugio Club Andino Francisco Jerman, (☎02901/1560-3001). Ushuaia's cheapest accommodation, in a fun, no-frills mountain refuge by the Martial ski centre and chair lift. Bring your own sleeping bag (mattresses on the floor). There's a bar and they serve meals. It's a stiff hour's climb from the centre, or take the Pasarela bus (often free for refuge guests; otherwise $2). $3 per person.

Refugio del Mochilero, 25 de Mayo 241 (☎02901/436129, fax 431190). A cramped but cheap, fun and central hostel, with kitchen, laundry facilities and Internet access ($7 an hour, but free to send email). Other facilities include cable TV, and free coffee and *mate*. $13 per person.

Residencial Linares, Gob. Deloqui 1522 (☎02901/423594). An excellent B&B, in a cosy, split-level house with sterling views of the Beagle Channel. You can use the living-room after 4pm. ③.

Torre al Sur Hostel, Gob. Paz 1437 (☎02901/430745; *torresur@hostels.org.ar*). A popular, friendly YHA-affiliated hostel that gets extremely busy in summer, when it can be cramped and noisy. It has great views, a small kitchen, good-value meals, and Internet access ($1 for 10min). YHA-members $10, non-members ①.

Violeta de la Montaña Guest House, Belgrano 236 (☎02901/421884). Peaceful, clean and very welcoming hostel accommodation in a family home. One quadruple has a private bathroom. You can use the excellent, roomy kitchen, luggage store, and laundry facilities. $10 per person.

The Town

The best place to start wandering around town is down by the pier, the Muelle Turístico, where Lasserre joins the seafront avenue, Maipú. The 1920s **Provincial Legislature** overlooking the seafront here is one of the town's most stately buildings. It stands opposite the dwarf **obelisk** that commemorates Augusto Lasserre's ceremony to assert Argentine sovereignty in this area of the world.

Northeast of here at Maipú 175 is the small, recommended **Museo del Fin del Mundo** (April–Sept Mon–Sat 3–7pm; Oct–March daily 10am–1pm & 3–7.30pm; ☎02901/421863; $5), with exhibits on the region's history and wildlife. These include the serene polychrome figurehead of the *Duchess of Albany*, a ship wrecked on the eastern end of the island in 1893; a genuine one-gram gold coin minted by Julius Popper in 1889 at his mining base at El Páramo; and a rare example of the Selk'nam–Spanish dictionary written by the Salesian missionary, José María Beauvoir. Free half-hour guided tours are given in Spanish (Sat & Sun 11am & 5pm), and you can take photos. Stamps are on sale, and letters posted here are franked with an "End of the World" stamp, as is your passport if you bring it along.

You can visit the former **prison** to see the **Museo del Presidio**, also called Museo Marítimo (Nov–Easter daily 10am–1pm & 3–8pm; rest of year closed Mon; ☎02901/437481; $7), two blocks further along the front and two more inland, at Yaganes and Gobernador Paz. This houses a motley collection of exhibits, with the central draw being the sprawling prison building itself, whose wings radiate out like spokes from a half-wheel. The cells are complete with gory details of the serial killers and notorious criminals who occupied them, but the impact is diminished for those unable to read the detailed information boards, which are only in Spanish. The most celebrated prisoner was the early twentieth-century anarchist Simón Radowitzsky, whose miserable stay and subsequent brief escape in 1918, from this Argentinian Alcatraz, are recounted by Bruce Chatwin in *In Patagonia*. Those political prisoners who, unlike Radowitzsky, hadn't been incarcerated for violent crimes, lived with local families, and fought not the guards but

WINTER SPORTS IN THE USHUAIA AREA

To **ski** at the end of the world, you'll need to visit between late May and early September (June to August are the most reliable months). Ski equipment rental costs from $15 to $40 a day. The closest ski runs to town are the small Club Andino, 3km from town, and the more impressive one by the Glaciar Martial, 7km behind town. Otherwise, you have some excellent **cross-country** skiing (*esquí de fondo* or *esquí nórdico*) and several small downhill (*esquí alpino*) options in the Sierra Alvear, all of which are accessed from RN3 (see p.678). These include the modern Cerro Castor centre on the Cerro Krund mountain, 26km from town, with 15km of piste in runs up to 2km long. Most options are for beginners and intermediates, but a few black runs can be found. In addition, there are several winter-sports centres (*centros invernales*) where you can try out snowmobiles, snowshoes ($6 per hr), ice-skating and trips on dogsleds (*trineos de perros*).

boredom. A free guided **tour** of the museum's collections (Spanish only; daily 5pm) is the only time you're allowed to enter the otherwise locked scale-reconstruction of the former lighthouse on the Isla de los Estados, the inspiration for Jules Verne's *Lighthouse at the End of the World*. The best exhibits of all, however, are the painstakingly made scale models of famous **ships** from the island's history; and a much cruder, if equally painstaking, reconstruction of a Yámana canoe, complete with video of the archeologists' attempts to make it according to authentic techniques. Outside the museum is *La Coqueta*, a locomotive once used to transport the prisoners to their daily toil, logging the forests. If you just want a look at the prison interior without having to pay the entrance, have a coffee in the public **café-restaurant** in the main exercise hall (open till midnight).

A couple of other sites in town are worth visiting. These include the workshop of Renata Rafalak, in the centre of town at Piedrabuena 25. She makes some of the finest craft items in southern Patagonia, her specialities being reproductions of the bark masks worn by the Selk'nam and Yámana in their Hain and Kina initiation ceremonies. Another is the **Casa Beban**, at the southwestern end of the town centre at Maipú and Plüschow, which is a lovely pavillion-style place with steep roof and ornamented gabling that was prefabricated in Sweden in 1913. The Ushuaia Jazz Festival takes place here in November, and otherwise it hosts exhibitions of photos and artwork, as well as showing occasional films. Finally, for first-rate views of the Beagle Channel and the islands of Chile, you can head to the hanging **Glaciar Martial**, 7km behind the town; to get there, walk or take the Pasarela bus ($2) from the Muelle Turístico up to the *Hotel Del Glaciar*, and then climb or take the **chair lift** ($5) from behind the hotel. Take sun protection: the ozone hole affects these latitudes and solar radiation can be fierce. During the winter, Glaciar Martial offers the closest decent skiing to Ushuaia ($15 a day ski rental and $20 a day ski pass from the *Hotel Del Glaciar*; see also p.678).

Restaurants

Banana's, San Martín 273. A decent confitería and café on the main drag, with a lively buzz throughout the day.

Barracuda, Muelle Turístico. Champagne and *centolla* on board this sturdy launch. Shut your eyes, dress up (warm) and think of Monaco. Daily 7.30–10.30pm

Casa Tía, 12 de Octubre and Karukinka (☎02901/421273). Cheap snacks from $2, from an old Ushuaia favourite.

El Nono, Gob. Deloqui 429 (☎02901/423265). Local fast food in unfussy and friendly diner, serving giant hamburgers and snacks, but also a bargain *menú del día* for $5 with soft drink.

El Turco, San Martín 1440 (☎02901/424711). Sizeable, hearty portions of pizza, home-made pasta and meat dishes. Excellent $6.50 lunch menu; good-humoured service. Closed Sunday lunchtime.

SOUTHERN SHELLFISH

Do not collect your own shellfish in Tierra del Fuego, as it is occasionally affected by a deadly poisonous, colourless version of red tide (*marea roja*). Cooking only increases the virulence of red-tide toxins, and you do not build up tolerance by regularly eating seafood. Following a severe outbreak of red-tide related poisonings in the early 1970s, both Chilean and Argentinian authorities introduced strict shellfish controls. Testing is carried out on all seafood deemed to be a potential risk to ensure it is safe for consumption, so you can tuck in to the area's delicious mussels (*cholgas*) in shops and restaurants without fear.

Unaffected by red tide is the undisputed prince of the palate, the **centolla** (king crab). The crab's spindly legs can measure over a metre from tip to tip, but the meat comes from the body, with an average individual yielding some 300g. The less savoury practice of catching them with traps baited with dolphin or penguin meat has almost been stamped out by the imposition of hefty fines by both Chilean and Argentinian authorities, but despite controls on size limits, they are still subject to rampant over-fishing. Canned king crab is served off-season, but is bland and not worth the prices charged.

Ideal, San Martín 393 (☎02901/437860). Housed in one of Ushuaia's more venerable buildings, the *Ideal* seves king crab thermidor for $16; grilled trout is a more modest $10. Out of season, it serves a value-for-money *tenedor libre* (mid-March to Nov Mon–Fri; $7).

Las Hayas, in *Las Hayas Resort Hotel*. Serves *haute cuisine* but at *haute* prices (starters from $10; main courses from $18).

La Rueda, San Martín 193. One of the town centre's best options for carnivores, serving a full parrillada for $12.

Maximega, San Martín 131. A shop that sells everything from crossbows to a steak sandwich, and useful for snacks. Open round the clock.

Tía Elvira, Maipú 349 (☎02901/424725). Fine selection of fresh seafood, excellent mussels and a delicious *merluza negra a la Marquery* (black hake in a seafood sauce). Main courses from $10. Has a good list of Argentian wines.

Volver, Maipú 37 (☎02901/423977). An attractive building on the seafront, with intimate ambience and tango. Try the steaming *pescado en papillote* (fish baked in foil in a tomato and cheese sauce) for $15, a *centolla provençal* or one of their pastas. Closed Mon lunch.

Nightlife

Bar El Pueblo, a fun pub/bar with regular live music at weekends, although the *ranchera* night is full-on cheese. Monday tango classes.

Barnys, Antártida Argentina 173. A disco that is popular in high season, if none too sophisticated in its decor or choice of hybrid pop tunes.

Nautico, Maipú and Belgrano. A sit-down bar with fireplace and occasional live music for a more laid-back crowd who prefer chatting to dancing.

Sheik, Gob. Paz and Roca. Club playing a standard mix of mainstream pop tunes to a tourist crowd.

Listings

Airlines Aerolíneas, Roca 116 (☎02901/421228, fax 431291); Kaikén, San Martín 884, 1° (☎ & fax 02901/432963 or 432963); LADE, San Martín 542 (☎ & fax 02901/421123); Lan-Chile, Gob. Godoy 169 (☎ & fax 02901/431110); LAPA, 25 de Mayo (☎02901/432112, fax 432117).

Banks and exchanges There are ATMs at most banks. Try Banco Tierra del Fuego, San Martín 952, or Banco de la Nación, San Martín 190, which offer the best rates for all types of foreign cash. There's a *casa de cambio* at San Martín 877 (daily till 8pm; higher commissions for changing travellers' cheques at weekends) and a Western Union office at Gob. Paz 921 (☎02901/436683). All Patagonia, Juana Fadul 26 (☎02901/433622, fax 430707) is the American Express representative.

Bookshop Antorcha, San Martín 1154; World's End, San Martín 798 and 903.

Car rental Dollar, San Martín 955 (☎ & fax 02901/432134); Localiza, San Martín 1222 (☎ & fax 02901/430739); Seven, San Martín 802 (☎02901/437604); Visita, Maipú 13 (☎ & fax 02901/435181). Many companies do not permit you to take your rental car out of the Argentine part of the island, though Visita will for a surcharge. Either way, you should reserve two weeks in advance in the summer and note that roads are fairly reliable from October to early May; outside this period, carry snowchains and drive with caution.

Consulate Chilean, Jainén 50 (☎02901/430909 or 430910).

Hospital 12 de Octubre and Malvinas Argentinas (☎02901/422950). Emergencies ☎107.

Internet Foto Santamaría, San Martín 419 (send emails free; 9am–9pm); Locutorio del Sur, Laserre 124 ($1.50 for 15min).

Laundry Laverap Los Tres Angeles, Rosa 139.

Pharmacy Andina, San Martín 638. Open 24hr (☎02901/423431).

Police Emergencies ☎101.

Post office San Martín and Godoy (Mon–Fri 9am–4pm).

Taxis Asociación de Taxis, Maipú and Lasserre (☎02901/435995 or 422500); Julio Domínguez is a recommended driver (taxi #199; ☎02901/421077).

Telephone Locutorio del Sur, Laserre 124 (8am–midnight).

Travel agencies All Patagonia, Juana Fadul 26 (☎02901/433622, fax 430707) and Turismo de Campo, 25 de Mayo 70 (☎02901/437329, fax 432419), for tours to the national park and flights over the Beagle Channel plus general flights and services; Canal, Rivadavia 82 (☎ & fax 02901/437395) for 4WD trip to Lago Fagnano. For trips to Harberton and on the Beagle Channel, go to the Muelle Turístico and book direct.

Trips along the Beagle Channel

No trip to Ushuaia is complete without a trip on the **Beagle Channel**, the majestic, mountain-fringed sea passage to the south of the city. Most **boat trips** start and finish in Ushuaia, and you get the best views of town looking back at it from the straits. The standard trips visit Les Eclaireurs Lighthouse – sometimes erroneously called the Lighthouse at the End of the World; Isla de los Pájaros; and Isla de los Lobos. Boats depart from the pier, **Muelle Turístico**, where you'll find a huddle of agents' booking huts. Try the *Barracuda*, offering good-value three-hour tours (9.30am &

VISITING THE ANTARCTIC

Ushuaia lies 1000km to the north of Antarctica, but is still the closest port to the white continent – and most tourists pass through the town to make their journey across Drake's Passage, the wild stretch of ocean that separates the two continents. The grandeur of Anarctica's pack ice, rugged mountains, and phenomenal bird- and marine life will leave you breathless. Whales, elephant seals, albatrosses, and numerous species of penguins are just some of the rare wildlife you can hope to see, and you'll be shuttled to interesting sites by zodiac inflatables or even by helicopter.

Regular **cruise ships** depart from early November to late March and most cruises last between 8 and 22 days, some stopping at the **South Atlantic islands** (the Falklands, South Georgia, the South Orkneys, Elephant Island and the South Shetlands) en route. These trips are generally very expensive, but last-minute bargains can be snapped up in Ushuaia, with fares as low as $2500 for a nineteen-day trip to the Falklands, South Georgia and the Peninsula. Try contacting Zelfa Silva, the Argentinian agent for Quark Expeditions (☎011/4806-6326, fax 4804-9474; *zelfa@interar.com.ar*), who runs luxury cruises on Russian nuclear-powered icebreakers; Rumbo Sur (☎02901/422275, fax 430699; *rumbosur@satlink.com*), or Tolkeyen (☎02901/427354, fax 430532; *pretour@tierradelfuego.ml.org*).

3pm; $25); or Héctor Monsalve's trips for small groups on the quiet motorized sail-boat, *Tres Marías* (☎02901/421897; Nov–Easter 9.30am & 2.30pm; 4hr; $45), which includes a stop at Islas Bridges to see Yámana shell middens. Monsalve also arranges **diving** trips in the clear waters of the channel, as do Ushuaia Diver's (☎02901/423159, fax 444701; $100 a day).

Longer boat trips head further along the Beagle Channel: west to Lapataia in the National Park; east to Harberton and its Isla Martillo penguin colony, or to Puerto Williams on the Isla Navarino. Ideally, Lapataia options are best done as part of a combination tour, with one leg overland; and with a bit of ingenuity, you might be able to engineer something similar with Harberton. Tolkeyen's boat-only return trip to the **Isla Martillo penguin colony** includes an optional walking tour of Harberton (Tues, Thurs & Sat 2.30pm; 6hr; $75), but if Harberton is the main focus of your interest, you're better off taking the recommended Turismo Alvarez tour overland (☎02901/444043 or 15604230, fax 435729; 9.30am & 3pm; 6hr; $50), as your time at the estancia is less rushed and you still get a one-hour boat trip to Isla Martillo. Rumbo Sur, San Martín 342 (☎ & fax 02901/430699), operates a catamaran trip to Lapataia from Ushuaia by way of the lighthouse and islands, and variants of this that include return legs by land, where the bus tour of the national park is better value than the optional Tren del Fin del Mundo (see p.682). One other Beagle trip runs between Bahía Ensenada and Lapataia in the national park (see p.686).

On boat trips, look out for **seabirds** such as the black-browed albatross, the thick-set giant petrel, Magellanic penguin, and the South American tern; as well as **marine mammals** such as sea lions, Peale's dolphin (with a grey patch on its flank), the occasional minke whale, and just possibly even a killer whale (*orca*) or a southern right whale (*ballena franca austral*).

Ushuaia to Paso Garibaldi and the Sierra Alvear

The road from Ushuaia to Paso Garibaldi wends its way north and east through dramatic forested scenery, with great views of the valleys and savage mountain ranges that cross the southern part of the island, running diagonally northwest to southeast. Many activity centres and refuges have sprung up along the route, primarily to cater to **winter-sports** enthusiasts but which often also make excellent bases for adventurous **trekking** or horseriding. Above all, the rugged, serrated peaks of the **Sierra Valdivieso** and **Sierra Alvear ranges** make ideal bushwhacking territory. If rough-hiking independently, consult the helpful Club Andino (see p.673) in Ushuaia first, and do not underestimate the need for orienteering skills or the unpredictable nature of the weather: snow blizzards can hit at any time of year. You must also be prepared to get thoroughly soaked when crossing boggy ground and the ubiquitous streams, but you'll be rewarded by the sight of **beaver dams** up to two and a half metres high, as well, in all probability, as their destructive constructors.

Heading northeast from Ushuaia, the RN3 curls up around the foot of **Monte Olivia**, following the **Río Olivia** valley. To the right of the road, you can just catch a glimpse of the attractive **Velo de la Novia** (Bridal Veil Falls), peeping through the trees. The **Valle Carbajal** is bounded by the mountain ranges of the Sierra Valdivieso to south and the Cordón Vinciguerra to the north, the former with excellent rough-hiking opportunities. Further up the RN3, you enter the **Valle de Tierra Mayor**, the valley of the Río Lasifashaj. This is a popular area for winter sports and one of the first centres you come across heading this way is *Altos del Valle*, 18km out Ushuaia (☎ & fax 02901/422234 for reservations). This breeding centre for baying huskies (husky rides $20; or $60 for a day course) offers rustic *refugio*-style **accommodation** (bring sleeping bags; $10 per person plus $5 for breakfast). For **trekking** (guided or otherwise), there's a relatively clear trail to Laguna Esmeralda, and a challenging hike to Glaciar Alvear. A kilometre beyond this centre is the highly recommended refuge, *Nunatak* (☎02901/423240, fax 424108; *antartur@tierradelfuego.ml.org*; bring a sleeping bag; $10 with basic breakfast), which offers tremendous views across the peat flatlands of the valley floor and up to both the pyramidal peak of Cerro Bonete (1100m) and Cerro Alvear (1425m). The refuge is clean; it has showers, a kitchen, and even videos; and they serve meals ($6). Ask about their tough but fascinating guided trek up to Lago Ojo del Albino (10hr; $55 with guide, crampons and food included).

Estancia Harberton and the RCj

The unsealed **RCj** is one of the two most interesting branch roads on the island, offering spectacular views of the Beagle Channel and the chance to visit Patagonia's most historic estancia, Harberton. The turn-off for the RCj is 40km south of Ushuaia on the RN3. Twenty-five kilometres from the turn-off, you emerge from the forested route by a delightful lagoon fringed by the skeletons of *Nothofagus* beeches, and can look right across the Beagle Channel to the Chilean naval town of Puerto Williams. A few hundred metres beyond here, the road splits: take the left-hand fork heading eastwards across rolling open country and past a famous clump of **banner trees**, swept back in exaggerated quiffs by the unremitting wind.

Ten kilometres beyond the turn-off and 85km east of Ushuaia, is **Estancia Harberton** itself, an ordered assortment of whitewashed buildings on the shores of a sheltered bay (10am–4pm; ☎02901/422742, fax 422743). Though Harberton is assuredly scenic, it's the historical resonance of the place that fleshes out any visit: this farmstead – or more particularly the family that settled here – played a role out of all proportion to its size in the region's history. Apart from being a place where scientists and shipwrecked sailors would be assured assistance, Harberton developed into a place of voluntary refuge for groups of Yámana, Selk'nam and Mannekenk – somewhere where even the warlike Selk'nam would refrain from hostilities. It was built by the Reverend Thomas Bridges, the man who authored one of the two seminal Fuegian texts, the Yámana–English dictionary, and was the inspiration for Lucas Bridges' classic text, *Uttermost Part of the Earth*.

Today, the estancia is owned by Tommy Goodall, a great-grandson of Thomas Bridges, and his wife, Natalie, a renowned biologist who is currently trying to raise funds for a Marine Mammal Museum. Entrance to Harberton is by **guided tour** only (45min–1hr 30min; mid-Oct to mid-April 10am–7pm; last tour 5.30pm; $7). You will be shown the copse on the hill, where you learn about the properties of the island's plantlife, as well as see authentic reconstructions of indigenous Yámana dwellings, the family cemetery, and the old shearing shed. The *Mánacatush* **tearoom** is the only part of the main estancia building open to the public: here you can enjoy afternoon tea ($9), with large helpings of cake and delicious home-made jams, or – if you book two days in advance – a generous three-course lunch ($20). If at all possible, spend a night at one of the estancia's three **campsites**: all are free, but you must first register at the tearoom and obtain a permit. Choose between *Río Varela*, the closest site, 4km to the east, *Río Cambaceres*, 6km further east, and the beautiful *Río Lasifashaj*, 7km west of the estancia. All sites have abundant fresh water, but no other facilities.

Beyond Harberton, the RCj runs for forty spectacular kilometres to **Estancia Moat**, past the famous islands that guard the eastern mouth of the Beagle Channel: **Picton**, **Nueva** and **Lennox**. These rather barren-looking, uninhabited islands, have a controversial past, since both Chile and Argentina long claimed sovereignty over them. Simmering tension threatened to boil over between 1977 and 1979, when manoeuvres by the military regimes of both powers brought the two to the brink of war. Arbitration was left in the hands of the United Kingdom's Queen Elizabeth II, harking back to the days at the beginning of the century when the British Crown mediated a settlement along the countries' Andean frontier. This time, the Crown ruled in favour of Chile. Argentina refused to accept the judgement, but was eventually forced to cede sovereignty after a ruling by the Vatican in 1984. The track ends at a naval outpost. Beyond, the Península Mitre stretches to the far tip of Tierra del Fuego at Cabo San Diego.

Puerto Williams and Isla Navarino

Despite Ushuaia's pretentions to the title, Isla Navarino's **PUERTO WILLIAMS** really *is* the southernmost town in the world – a tiny place lying on the Beagle Channel, and set against a dramatic backdrop of the **Dientes de Navarino** mountains. It owes its existence to the Chilean Navy, for which it acts as a base, but though the first things you notice on your approach are likely to be the navy's sinister black gunboats, the town is an extremely relaxed, welcoming place. The small **Museo Martín Gusinde** in the west of town (Tues–Fri 10am–1pm & 3–6pm, Sat & Sun 3–6pm; $2.25), has some fascinating ethnographic and seafaring relics, and is the town's only real tourist site. If you have the time, you could make the easy two-kilometre stroll east to the hamlet com-

---

FUEGIAN FOREST UNDER THREAT

At the end of 1993, a US multinational company, Trillium Co., bought 2700 square kilometres of forest in the Chilean half of the Isla Grande de Tierra del Fuego, and followed this up with a purchase, in 1994, of almost a thousand square kilometres in the Argentinian half. Faced with ever tightening environmental legislation and well-organized pressure groups at home, Trillium seemed to have found easy pickings in Tierra del Fuego: vast swathes of ancient temperate hardwood forest in an area with a tiny population base and a young, emergent political structure. Their interest lay primarily in a wood ideal for the furniture industry: Patagonian *lenga* (high deciduous beech).

The issue had all the hallmarks of a neocolonial hit-and-run raid. No thorough, independent environmental impact studies had been carried out; no system had been elaborated for regular supervision of the company's logging practices; and no consideration had been given to the potential value of the forests as a future tourist resource. Envisaging a repeat of the disastrous rape of the temperate forests similar to that which has occurred in recent decades in mainland Chilean Patagonia, environmental groups **Defensores de los Bosques Chilenos** on the Chilean side, and **Finis Terrae**, based in Ushuaia, resolved not to let Trillium steamroller local concerns. The groups scored several legal victories along the way, despite woefully inadequate resources. In 1999, just after logging had started in Chile, permission to proceed with logging in Argentina was finally granted, despite petitions that demonstrated the remarkable degree of public concern about the issue on an island that depends heavily on tourism, but these decisions are being appealed against.

Environmental damage could well be catastrophic. Soil erosion is a great fear: topsoils on the island are very thin, winds are strong, and there's heavy rainfall. A diverse native forest ecosystem can absorb up to fifty times as much rainfall as agricultural land; with much of this felled, the purity of the island's lakes and streams would be affected by run-off and wood pulp. **Regeneration** takes at least thirty years, with most *lenga* trees taking over a hundred years to reach maturity. Naturally, environmental groups would like to see the cessation of all logging if possible, believing the value of the forests far exceeds the value of their timber. However, if logging is to continue, the groups aim to ensure that the local community benefits in some way, with wood being processed on the island for high-value manufactured items such as furniture parts, and not just exported as planks. Their campaign will focus on ensuring that the company is committed to sustainable practices, so that promised jobs and investment do indeed prove to be long term.

For more information on the campaign, contact Finis Terrae, Ap. Postal No. 22, C.P. 9410 Ushuaia ☎02901/434122, fax 433302).

munity of **UKIKA**, where you can buy reed baskets and replica canoes from families of Yámana descent (please do not intrude on family life, and ensure you respect these people's right not to be photographed). There are some excellent **hikes** on the island, such as the challenging five-day **trek** around the Dientes (or Colmillos) de Navarino, for which you'll need full outdoor gear.

The Tolkeyen **catamaran** *Mariana I* plies between Ushuaia and Puerto Williams (mid-March to April & June to mid-Oct Tues & Sat 9.30am; mid-Oct to mid-March Tues, Thurs & Sat 9.30am; returning same days, approximately 3.30pm; crossing time 2hr 15min–3hr; $40 one way, $60 return; ☎02901/422150 or 432920). Be prepared for a rough crossing, and expect some customs delays. Return tickets are open, but if you have got an important flight to catch, remember that departures can be delayed by poor weather. Austral Broom runs a useful freight and **ferry** service from Puerto Williams to Punta Arenas (☎061/218100; Nov–March weekly; $150 with bunk, $120 seat only; 32hr, but longer in high seas). For trekking information, ask at the **tourist office** (near the museum on Calle Ibañez) or at Turismo Sea and Ice and Mountains Adventures (see *Refugio Coirón* below), which offers other interesting tours around the island. Banco de Chile, Calle Yelcho, gives **cash advances** on Visa and changes US dollars but not Argentine pesos. To save time, day-trippers are advised to buy their Chilean pesos in Ushuaia. For **accommodation** in Puerto Williams, try the excellent *Refugio Coirón*, Maragaño 168 (☎ & fax 061/621150), which has shared **rooms** with bunks ($13 per person), a kitchen, and space for camping. *Restaurant Camblor*, Via 2 (☎ & fax 061/621033) offers accommodation with private bathroom ($16 per person with good breakfast; $33 full board) and is the best option for **food** (huge meals for $7.50). *Pensión Temuco*, Piloto Pardo 224 (☎ & fax 061/621113; $17.50 with breakfast) has decent rooms, and private bathrooms for a little extra, plus a $1 charge for use of the kitchen. The least expensive option is the *Pensión Flor Cañuñán*, Lewaia 107 (☎061/621163; $6.50), which has rooms in a rather basic, warm hut, with the bathroom in the main house. In the evening, head to the **Club de Yates Micalvi**, where you can board an ex-navy supply ship and drink or snack in an intimate, sociable bar, without worrying too much if your sea legs hold up.

Parque Nacional Tierra Del Fuego

The **PARQUE NACIONAL TIERRA DEL FUEGO** is the easiest to access of southern Argentina's national parks, situated a mere 12km west of Ushuaia. It protects 630 square kilometres of jagged mountains, intricate lakes, southern beech forest, swampy peat bog, subantarctic tundra, and verdant coastline. The park stretches along the frontier with Chile, from the Beagle Channel to the **Sierra de Injugoyen** (also called the Sierra de Beauvoir) north of Lago Fagnano, but only the southernmost quarter of this is open to the public, accessed by the RN3 from Ushuaia. Fortunately, this area contains much of the park's most beautiful scenery, if also some of the wettest, so bring your rain gear. It is broken down here into three main sectors: Bahía Ensenada and Río Pipo in the east, close to the station for the Tren del Fin del Mundo; Lago Roca further to the west; and the Lapataia area to the south of Lago Roca, which includes Lago Verde and, at the end of RN3, Bahía Lapataia on the Beagle Channel. You can get a good overview of the park in a day if you have your own transport or take a standard tour. Nevertheless, walkers will want to stay two to three days to appreciate the scenery and the **wildlife**, which includes birds such as Magellanic woodpeckers, condors, torrent ducks (*pato de los torrentes*), steamer ducks, upland geese, and buff-necked ibises; and mammals such as guanacos, the rare sea-otter or *nutria* **marina**, Patagonian grey foxes, and their larger, endangered cousin, the native Fuegian fox, once heavily hunted for its pelt.

The park is also one of southern Argentina's easiest to walk around, and offers several relatively unchallenging though beautiful **trails**, many of which are completed in minutes rather than hours or days. Recommended are the Senda Costera (Coastal Path) connecting Bahía Ensenada with Lago Roca or Bahía Lapataia; and the comparatively tough Cerro Guanaco climb from Lago Roca. Hardened trekkers looking for a stern physical challenge should lower their aspirations, as only a couple of trails are

---

EL TREN DEL FIN DEL MUNDO

El Tren del Fin del Mundo ($25 one way, plus $5 park entrance; ☎02901/431600) is one of Ushuaia's most publicized attractions, and can be used as a rather gimmicky means of entering or leaving the national park. It is the most southern of the world's railways, but offers nothing like the same experience as Argentina's other tourist railways. What it lacks is a sense of authenticity – the feeling that you may not be on anything other than a tourist toy train – and the price reflects the high investment outlay of the project rather than real value for money. Still, steam enthusiasts and youngsters will enjoy the 4.5-kilometre, forty-minute trip, which passes through woodland, meadows spiked with the stumps of logged trees and reconstructions of Yámana dwellings by the Río Pipo. Avoid going on cool, rainy days, as you won't see much, what with the mountains being in cloud, condensation on the windows, and the steam from the locomotive. The main station is 8km west of Ushuaia on the road to the national park (buses leave Ushuaia's Muelle Turístico; 4 daily; $4 return), and the other is just inside the national park's boundaries. In high season, there are at least four departures a day from each.

BIRDS OUT OF PLACE

Parrots and hummingbirds are the type of birds you associate more with the steamy, verdant jungles of the Amazon than the frigid extremes of Tierra del Fuego. Nevertheless, trust your eyes not your judgement, for you can see both in Ushuaia's Parque Nacional. The unmistakeably garrulous **austral parakeet** is the world's most southerly parrot, inhabiting these temperate forests year round. The Selk'nam christened this bird *Kerrhprrh*, in onomatopoeic imitation of its call. Once upon a time, according to their beliefs, all Fuegian trees had been evergreen, and *Kerrhprrh* it was who transformed some into deciduous forests, painting them autumnal reds with the feathers of his breast. The tiny **green-backed firecrown** is the planet's most southerly hummingbird, and has been glimpsed – albeit rarely – flickering about flowering shrubs in summer. Known to the Selk'nam by the graceful name of *Sinu K-Tam* (Daughter of the Wind), this diminutive creature was, strangely, believed by them to be the offspring of *Ohchin* the whale and *Sinu*, the wind.

demanding in this sense (for this, you'd do better looking to the Sierra Valdivieso and the Sierra Alvear, see p.678; or Isla Navarino, see p.680). Access is not authorized along the Sendero Lago Fagnano (marked on certain maps heading north from the Río Pipo waterfall), and you will be fined if caught here. Obey the signs warning you to refrain from collecting shellfish due to the possibility of red tide (see p.676), and light fires only in permitted campsites, extinguishing them with water, not earth.

Practicalities

There are three ways of **accessing the park**: by boat from Ushuaia to Lapataia; by train on the Tren del Fin del Mundo; or, by far the commonest and cheapest way, along the good dirt road from Ushuaia (sometimes cut off briefly by snowfalls, late May to early Oct). A $5 entrance fee must be paid at the main park gate. Virtually all travel agencies in Ushuaia offer **tours** of the park (around $25); most last four hours and stop at the major places of interest including Bahía Lapataia – be sure to book on a minibus and try to avoid the big tour buses. Several companies run regular public **buses** that stop at any point in the park between the entrance and Lago Roca or Lago Verde, but none goes as far as the end of the RN3 at Bahía Lapataia. Most leave from the Muelle Turístico or will pick you up from your hotel if arranged in advance. Bus tickets do not include the park entrance fee. A **remise** from Ushuaia to Lapataia, holding up to four people, costs $45, usually with a three-hour stay in the park, but arrange details before departing. You can also get to the park on a **boat trip** along the Beagle Channel from Ushuaia (see p.677) – services drop you at the jetty at Bahía Lapataia – or on the Tren del Fin del Mundo (see p.682), which drops you at the parks station, 2km from the main gate.

There are four main areas for **camping** in the park: Bahía Ensenada and Río Pipo are currently free, but you're better off heading to the paying sites of the Lago Roca and Lago Verde areas, which lie in the more exciting western zone of the park. Lago Verde has the two most beautiful campsites in the park, right next door to each other: on a grassy patch of land encircled by the Río Ovando is *Camping Lago Verde* (☎02901/421433; *lagunaverde@tierradelfuego.ml.org*; $2 per person), which has a tiny toilet block and sink, a shop, and rents tents ($10 a day, sleeping bags included); *Camping Los Cauquenes* (pay at *Lago Verde*; $2 per person) is just across the road, nearer the Archipiélago Cormoranes, and has lawn-like pitches tended by rabbits. Site no. 9 is the top spot, in an exquisite, reposeful setting on its own tiny bay.

If looking to contract a **private guide** to the national park, you may be lucky enough to hire the services of Graciela Ramacciotti, whose irrepressible good humour is matched only by her reserves of knowledge and love of the area (☎02901/434122, fax 433302). Claudio Giri is another good guide (☎02901/436835; $60 per day).

Bahía Ensenada and Río Pipo

To the north of the railway terminus is the pleasant wooded valley of Cañadón del Toro, through which runs the **Río Pipo**. A gentle four-kilometre walk along an unsealed road brings you to the Río Pipo **campsite** (free and with no services, although this status is likely to change), and a couple of hundred metres on you come to an attractive **cascade**. Although a route north from here through to Lago Fagnano is marked on some old maps, the area is now off limits and you will be fined if caught there. If you're heading from Río Pipo back south to Bahía Ensenada, take the **Senda Pampa Alta** trail, which is signposted off west on the way back to the crossroads. This offers 5km of fair-

---

THE YÁMANA: A LIFE AT SEA

The **Yámana** were a canoe-going people who lived in the channels of the Fuegian archipelago. The heartland of their territory was around the Beagle Channel, but they lived as far south as Cape Horn in the Wollaston Islands, and west as far as the Brecknock Peninsula, which formed a reasonably hermetic geographical divide between their people and the neighbouring canoe culture of the Kawéskar (Alacalufes) to the west.

Yámana society was based on tribal groups of extended families, each of which lived for long periods aboard their equivalent of a houseboat: a canoe fashioned of *lenga* bark that they even cooked and slept in. When not living aboard their canoes, the Yámana stayed in dwellings made of *guindo* evergreen beech branches, building conical huts in winter (to shed snow), and more aerodynamic dome-shaped ones in the summer (when strong winds blow). Favoured campsites were used over millennia, and, at these sites, **middens** of discarded shells would accumulate in the shape of a ring, since the door was constantly being shifted to face away from the wind.

The first Europeans to encounter the Yámana were a Dutch expedition that sailed near the Horn in 1624, but it was not until the era of the clipper ships, and especially the increase in sealing and whaling operations from the end of the eighteenth century, that contact became more frequent. These expeditions often resulted in suspicion, hatred and disease. Systematic contact only occurred once FitzRoy "discovered" the Beagle Channel, with the subsequent efforts of the Anglican South American Missionary Society to evangelize these "savages". Yámana culture, which depended on a finely tuned system of interaction with the environment developed over centuries, had few defences against these "civilizing" forces, even those forces which believed they were protecting the indigenous peoples. Civilization wiped out the Yámana as assuredly as a gun.

In 1884, the arrival of early settlers triggered a measles epidemic that killed approximately half of the estimated 1000 Yámana. However incomprehensible it would have seemed to Europeans, the Yámana certainly fared better in their pre-contact naked state. Damp, dirty clothing – European cast-offs given by well-meaning missionaries – actually increased the risk of disease, which spread fast in the mission communities where the Yámana were grouped. Missionaries promoted a shift to sedentary agriculture, but the consequent change of diet, from one high in animal fats to one more reliant on vegetables, reduced the Yámana's resistance to the cold, further increasing the likelihood of disease. Outbreaks of scrofula, pneumonia and tuberculosis meant that, by 1911, a total of perhaps only 100 Yámana remained. Well before the 1930s, commentators had written off their chances of survival, referring to them as one of the "races soon to be extinct". Abuela Rosa, the last of the Yámana to live in the manner of her ancestors, died in 1982. Nevertheless, a few Yámana descendants do still live near Puerto Williams. Bilingual, they can converse in a restricted version of their forefathers' tongue, and they conserve traditional crafts such as *möpi* reed basket-weaving, selling these items to visitors.

ly demanding walking and is a more interesting alternative to walking between the two by road, with fine views from a lookout over the Beagle Channel. It crosses the RN3 to Lapataia at a point 3km west of the station crossroads, and then drops sharply to the coast on a poor path through thick forest.

Bahía Ensenada, situated 2km south of the crossroads by the train station, is a small bay with little of intrinsic interest. It does, however, have the jetty for boats to Lapataia and the Isla Redonda, and is the trailhead for one of the most pleasant of the park's walks, the highly recommended **Senda Costera** (7km; 3hr). The route is not too strenuous and allows you to experience dense coastal forest of evergreen beech, Winter's bark, and *lenga*, whilst affording spectacular views from the Beagle Channel shoreline. On the way, you'll pass grass-covered mounds that are the ancient campsite **middens** of the Yámana. These mounds are protected archeological sites and should not be disturbed. In autumn, a confetti of evergreen beech leaves carpets the pathway, a phenomenon that has become more prevalent in recent years, and which some believe is linked to damage caused by the hole in the ozone layer. Along the route, you stand a healthy chance of seeing birds such as the powerful Magellanic woodpecker, and the flightless steamer duck (*quetro no volador* or *alacush*), an ash-grey bird with an orange bill that uses its wings in paddle-steaming fashion to hurry itself away from danger.

Lago Roca

Six kilometres from the railway station west, a turn-off to the right takes you across the lush meadows of the broad Río Lapataia, past the ruins of the burnt-out *Hostería Alakush* and, after a kilometre, to **Lago Roca** and its campsite. Just past the campsite buildings, there's a car park that looks out across Lago Roca, a lake that extends across the border into Chile. A gentle path hugs the northern shore of Lago Roca and heads through majestic *lenga* forest to the Chilean border at Hito XXIV (Boundary Marker XXIV), 5km away. Do not attempt to cross the border: it is under regular surveillance and you will be arrested if you attempt to do so.

A more spectacular but more tiring trek is the climb up **Cerro Guanaco** (970m; 8km; 3hr), the mountain ridge on the north side of Lago Roca. Remember that, at any time of the year, the weather can turn capricious with little warning, so bring adequate clothing even if you set out in glorious sunshine. Take the Hito XXIV path from the car park at Lago Roca and after ten minutes you'll cross a small bridge over a stream. Immediately afterwards, the path forks: left to Hito XXIV and right up the slope to the Cerro. The path up the forested mountainside crosses the Arroyo Guanaco at several points. It is not hazardous, but after rain, you're sure to encounter some slippery tree roots and muddy patches.

Above the tree line, the views are spectacular, but the path becomes increasingly difficult to follow in the boggy valley, especially after snowfalls. Cerro Guanaco itself is to the left on the ridge above you. Even if you can't make out the path, and as long as visibility is good, you can scramble your way to just about any point along the crest of the ridge with few problems. From the crest, the views of this angular landscape are superb: the swollen finger of Lago Roca, flanked by the spiky concertinaed ridge of Cerro Cóndor, with the jagged Cordillera Darwin beyond; eastwards lies Ushuaia and its airport; whilst behind you to the north, a vertiginous cliff plunges down to the Cañadón del Toro, and behind that rise the inhospitable Martial, Valdivieso and Vinciguerra ranges that obscure the view to Lago Fagnano. Best of all, however, are the views to the south: the tangle of islands and rivers of the Archipiélago Cormoránes, Lapataia's sinuous curves, the Isla Redonda in the Beagle Channel, and across to the Chilean islands, Hoste and Navarino, separated by the Murray Narrows. On a clear day, in the distance beyond the Narrows, you can make out the Islas Wollaston, the group of islands whose southernmost point is Cape Horn.

The Lapataia area

The Lapataia area of the park is accessed by way of the final four-kilometre stretch of the RN3, as it winds south from the Lago Roca junction, past **Lago Verde**, and on to **Lapataia** itself, on the bay of the same name. This is one of the most intriguing areas to explore: a kind of miniature "park within a park". Here, in the space of a few hours, you can take a network of short trails that enable you to see an incredible variety of scenery, which includes bogland, river islets, wooded knolls and sea coast. A few hundred metres past the Lago Roca junction, you cross the Río Lapataia over a bridge that's a favoured haunt of ringed kingfishers (*martín pescador grande*). Not far beyond the bridge the road passes through an area known as the **Archipiélago Cormoranes** (Cormorant Archipelago). Signposted left off the road here is a short (20min) circuit trail, the **Paseo de la Isla**, which heads through this scenery of tiny, enchanting humped islets that would not look out of place in a miniaturist Japanese garden, and which actually has more atmosphere in the drizzle. Just past the trail, to the right of the main road, is *Las Bandurrias* campsite, popular with fishermen ($2; pay at Lago Verde).

Next you pass Lago Verde, which is not a lake but actually a sumptuous, sweeping bend of the Río Ovando. Here you'll find *Camping Lago Verde* and *Camping Los Cauquenes*. From Lago Verde, it's only 2km to Lapataia. On the way, you pass several brief, easy nature trails that you can stroll along in twenty minutes or so, and which have signposts with ecological and botanical information in Spanish. Leaving the campsite, you cross the Río Ovando bridge, and a couple of hundred metres further on, you'll find the nature trail loop to **Laguna Negra**, a shallow pond fringed by a mulch of peat bog. Insectivorous sundew plants (*drosera*) grow by the lake shore, but sadly, few have taken to the area adjacent to the boardwalk that you must stick to. A little further along the RN3 – about 1km from Lago Verde – is a turn-off along Circuito Lenga, which takes you to a lookout over Lapataia Bay. This whole area to the left (east) of the RN3 is criss-crossed by trails through peat bog scenery, including the **Paseo del Turbal** (Peat-Bog Walk). Just past the Circuito Lenga turn-off along the RN3, is the start of the **Castorera** path, heading only a couple of hundred metres off the road to a **beaver dam**. You stand a good chance of spotting one of these goofy rodents (*castores*) if you time your arrival to coincide with early morning or dusk.

The RN3 comes to its scenic end – a mere 3063km from Buenos Aires, and marked by a much-photographed sign – at Lapataia on the **Bahía Lapataia**. Deriving its name from the Yámana for forested cove, it is a serenely beautiful bay studded with small islets. Near the car park here is the **jetty** for the boat trips to Bahía Ensenada and Ushuaia, and the adjacent grassy knolls are Yámana shell middens (see box on p.684). For the best, easy photo opportunity of the bay, it's worth taking the five-minute walk along the **Paseo Mirador**, which runs east from the carpark to the little wooded lookout hill at its head. A path on the western side of the bay crosses the meadows and reaches another beaver dam, but do not stray beyond here, as it's off limits.

Central and Northern Tierra del Fuego

The second largest town in Tierra del Fuego, **Río Grande** is also the only town of significance in the centre and north of the island. The sterile-looking plains that surround it and stretch to the north harbour fields of petroleum and natural gas that generate over $130 million of wealth annually, with over 1.5million cubic metres of gas a year exported by pipeline to Ushuaia and as far away as Buenos Aires and Río Negro. To the north of town, the RN3 runs through monotonous scenery towards San Sebastián, where you cross the border into Chile or continue north on a dead-end route to the mouth of the Magellan Straits at Cabo Espíritu Santo. Heading south of town towards

Tolhuin, the RN3 crosses the Río Grande, and soon enters the woodland scenery of the central region.

One of the region's principal tourist draws is its world-class **trout fishing**, especially for sea-running brown trout, which on occasion swell to weights in excess of 14kg. The Río Grande currently holds five of the fly-fishing world records for brown trout caught with various breaking strains of line. The mouths of the Río Fuego and Río Ewan can also be spectacularly fruitful; as can sections of the Malengüena, Leticia, Irigoyen, Indio, Claro and Turbio rivers; and lakes Yehuin and Fagnano.

Río Grande and around

RÍO GRANDE is a drab, sprawling city, which grew up on the river of the same name as a port for José Menéndez's sheep enterprises. The treacherous tides along this stretch of the coast, some of the highest in the world, can reach over fifteen metres at the spring equinox, and low tide exposes a vast shelf of mudflats that are better for seabirds than boats. The port therefore has virtually ceased to exist, having been superseded by the vastly superior one at Ushuaia. And in spite of the people's friendliness, the atmosphere here is as flat as the landscape: it's a place to pass through quickly, unless you're a trout fisherman, in which case it is a functional starting point for exploring the region's rivers.

The town does have one monument worth visiting: the **Candelaria Salesian Mission**, 11km to the north. There isn't much else to see, but if you're looking to kill time, you might consider taking a **city tour** ($22): a convenient way of visiting the town's scattered subsidiary sites that are otherwise awkward to reach, including the **Estancia María Behety**, 17km due west of town along the RCc, one of the island's largest and oldest sheep-farming establishments, dating from 1897.

Practicalities

Río Grande's **airport**, with daily services from Ushuaia and Río Gallegos, is 5km out of town. A **bus** connects it with Avenida San Martín in the town centre (every 15min; $1), or take a **taxi** ($5). The town's **bus terminal** lies on the seafront, at the junction of the seaside boulevard, El Cano (a continuation of RN3 from the north), and Avenida Belgrano, which heads inland for four blocks before crossing the town's major commercial artery, Avenida San Martín. The RN3 south runs parallel with Belgrano, ten blocks to the north, having dog-legged inland from the coast by the monument to the Falklands dead.

A block from the bus terminal you'll find the helpful provincial **tourist office**, the Instituto Fueguino de Turismo, at Belgrano 319 (Mon–Fri 10am–5pm; ☎ & fax 02964/422887; *infuerg@satlink.com*). They'll give you an excellent town map and can provide up-to-date information on flights, including the irregular, but extremely cheap $10 Aeronaval flight to Ushuaia. **Fishing licences** and information on fishing can be obtained from the Asociación de Pesca con Mosca at Montilla 1040. For **city tours**, contact Shelk'nam Turismo, Rosales 695 (☎ & fax 02964/426278; 2hr 30min–3hr; $22) or Kuanip Travel, Libertad 914 (☎ & fax 02964/427447; 2hr 30min–3hr; $22).

Accommodation in Río Grande is generally overpriced. The most comfortable option is the restful *Posada de los Sauces*, El Cano 839 (☎ & fax 02964/430672; ⑥), located across the road from the bus terminal, with a relaxed lounge bar and a high-quality *à la carte* restaurant. *Hotel Villa*, San Martín 277 (☎02964/422312; ③), is clean and central with en-suite bathrooms; while *hospedajes Noal*, Obligado 557 (☎02964/427516; ③, ① for single room with shared bathroom), and *Austral*, Moyano 397 (☎02964/421916; ②, ① for single room), are very basic, but the least expensive lodgings for single travellers on a tight budget. You can pitch a **tent** at the YPF fuel station opposite the bus terminal (ask permission at the administration first), but there is little shelter from the winds; or head for the Bomberos Voluntarios fire station on Libertad and Domingo Perón, a twenty-minute walk southeast of the bus terminal, where the volunteer firemen are happy to let you pitch your tent indoors in exchange for your travellers' tales. You can make use of their kitchen and hot showers, but beware the occasional night-time siren, which outdoes even your most hated alarm clock.

For **eating** in town, try the *Rotisería Carbel*, San Martín and Piedrabuena (an excellent-value set menu for $2). Otherwise, try the *tenedor libre* at *Cai*, Perito Moreno and 11 de Julio; or *Arauca's*, Rosales 566 (☎02964/425919; closed Mon), which serves excellent seafood dishes.

Misión Salesiana Nuestra Señora de la Candelaria

By the roadside, 11km north of the centre of Río Grande on the RN3, stands the **Misión Salesiana Nuestra Señora de la Candelaria**, a smart collection of whitewashed buildings grouped around a modest but elegant chapel. Río Grande's first mission, it was founded in 1893 by two of Patagonia's most influential Salesian fathers, Monseñor Fagnano and Padre Beauvoir, but their first township burnt down in 1896, and was relocated to its present site. Originally, it was built with the purpose of catechizing the island's Selk'nam, but in effect, it acted as part refuge and part prison, since local sheep magnates would round up the indigenous peoples on their land and pay the Salesians for their "conversion". In 1942, with virtually no Selk'nam remaining to administer to, the mission became an agricultural school, a role it has retained to this day. The **Museo Salesiano Monseñor Fagnano** (Mon–Sat 10am–noon & 3–7pm, Sun 3–7pm; $2; ☎02964/421642) is housed in the building to the left of the chapel as you enter the compound. Amongst homages to Don Bosco, the founder of the Salesian movement, you'll find some first-rate Fuegian indigenous items and a kerosene-lit projector that was used to entertain, and no doubt indoctrinate, the Selk'nam. Across the road is a fenced **cemetery** with some vandalized tombs of Salesian fathers and unmarked crosses indicating Selk'nam graves, symbolic testaments to a culture that had been completely depersonalized. To reach the mission from town, take the Línea B **bus** "Misión" from Avenida San Martín (hourly; 25min; $1).

North to San Sebastián and the Chilean border

North of the Misión Salesiano rears **Cabo Domingo**, and beyond that, the unforgiving plains of Patagonian shingle begin once again, dotted by shallow saline lagoons that sometimes host feeding flamingoes. The RN3 is paved as far as the **San Sebastián border post**, 82km north of Río Grande (April–Oct 8am–10pm; Nov–March 24hr; see box on p.689), on the bay of the same name. The bay itself is famous for its summer populations of migratory waders and shorebirds and is a vital part of the **Hemisphere Reserve for Shorebirds** that is designed to protect migratory birds along both the coasts and interior wetland sites of the Americas. Spare a thought for birds such as the Hudsonian godwit (*becasa de mar*) and the red knot (*playero rojizo*): they've travelled even further than you to get here – over 17,000km, from as far away as Alaska.

Tolhuin to Río Grande: RN3 and the rutas complementarias

The main route between Tolhuin and Río Grande is the fast, paved RN3, but if you have the time, the journey can be made more interesting by exploring one or more of the unsealed **rutas complementarias** (RC) that branch off it. These alphabetized roads provide access to the heartland of Argentinian Tierra del Fuego but are only really accessible to those with their own transport.

CHILEAN TIERRA DEL FUEGO

The Chilean border post of **San Sebastián** (April–Oct 8am–10pm; Nov–March open 24hr) lies 16km from its eponymous Argentinian counterpart. This is the only major land crossing between the two halves of the island – a much less significant one exists at Radman to the south. Formalities are straightforward, but you're not permitted to take any fresh fruit, meat or dairy products into Chile. Chilean time is one hour behind from March to October. By immigration there's a small kiosk that's a good place to lose any remaining Chilean pesos if crossing into Argentina.

There are two options for crossing the Magellan Straits by **ro-ro ferries**. The most frequently used is the one across the **Primera Angostura** (First Narrows) between Punta Espora on the south shore (also known as Bahía Azul) and **Punta Delgada** in the north (for exact times, phone Punta Arenas ☎061/218100; $2 per person, $16 vehicle). The ferry leaves from 8.30am to 10.30pm, making the thirty-minute crossing every ninety minutes, with delays at low tide and for bad weather. Punta Espora is connected to San Sebastián by means of a 150-kilometre dirt road, through the type of desolate scenery that saps morale.

The other ferry crossing is from **PORVENIR**, 147km west of San Sebastián (around 3hr by unsealed road). Set on a sheltered bay by the Magellan Straits, Porvenir is a well-kept little place whose optimistic name – meaning "future" – has failed to live up to expectations. It is the most important settlement in Chilean Tierra del Fuego but has little to see apart from the enjoyable little **Museo Provincial**, on Calle Jorge Schythe by the Plaza de Armas (Mon–Thurs 9am–5pm, Fri 9am–4pm, Sat & Sun 11am–4pm; $1), with exhibits about indigenous cultures and the gold-mining industry of the late nineteenth and early twentieth centuries. For **accommodation**, you have a choice of several family-run establishments, such as the cosy *Hotel Rosas* at Phillippi 296 (☎061/580088; ③ with breakfast); *Hostal Porvenir*, at Schythe 230 (☎ & fax 061/580371); or *Hotel España*, Croacia 698 (☎ & fax 061/580160; $11 per person). Telex Chile at Croatia 698 will change US dollars, Argentine pesos, and travellers' cheques, but the rates are poor: you're better off waiting till Punta Arenas if heading west. Change spare Chilean pesos here if heading towards Río Grande. Buses leave for Río Grande daily except Monday and cost $20: Pacheco (Tues, Thurs & Sat 12.30pm), and Techni Austral (Wed, Fri & Sun 12.30pm).

The **ferry** *Melinka* sails from Porvenir to Punta Arenas daily except Mondays (Tues, Thurs & Sat 2pm, Wed, Fri & Sun 5pm; reserve in advance for cars ☎061/580089; $7.50 per person, plus $40 per car). It departs from Bahía Chilota, 5km to the west of town on the north side of the bay (take a taxi or *colectivo* minibus). If arriving from Punta Arenas, you will be met by a variety of transport from taxis to *colectivos* to take you into town ($2). An alternative to the ferry is the twelve-minute **flight** across the Straits with DAP, whose office is at Manuel Señoret s/n (Mon–Sat, 8.30am & 5.20pm; $25 one way; ☎061/580089).

Rather than simply speeding up the RN3 to Río Grande, you can take a more scenic alternative route by travelling along the **RCh** (which branches off the RN3 22km north of Tolhuin) and the connecting **RCf**, which joins the RN3 some 10km south of the bridge over the Río Grande, just before the turn-off along the RCb. These two roads form a loop of 120km, and along the route you pass through undulating country of swathes of transitional Fuegian woodland and grassy pasture-meadows (*vegas*) populated by sheep. Along RCh you'll see the cone-shaped Mount Yakush and the pyramid-like Mount Atukoyak (950m) to the south. The RCh joins with the RCf by **Lago Yehuin**, a popular fishing spot. In the area, look out for guanacos and **condors**, which nest on Cerro Shenolsh between Lago Yehuin and its shallow neighbour, **Lago Chepelmuth**.

Some 38km north of Tolhuin, the most beautiful of the central *rutas complementarias*, the **RCa**, branches east. It heads east for the coast and the knobbly protrusion

---

AN EXTINCT RACE: THE MANNEKENK

Our knowledge of the **Mannekenk** (also known as the Haush or Aush), a relatively small ethnic group that was confined to the Península Mitre, is decidedly sketchy in comparison with other Fuegian tribes. Their culture was a mix of the Yámana and the Selk'nam ways, and intermarriage occurred with both these groups. Like the Yámana, they were heavily dependent on the sea for food, above all sea lion colonies, but they did not have canoe technology.

They were more similar, both physiologically and culturally, to the Selk'nam, of whom they too lived in fear, and it has been suggested that they were a related ancestral group, pushed into the less hospitable corner of the island by their more warlike cousins. And though their languages were unrelated, the Selk'nam adopted several Mannekenk terms in their sacred Hain ceremony, which may itself have derived in part from a Mannekenk initiation rite. "Haush" derives from a Yámana term meaning "seaweed-eaters", but Lucas Bridges tells us the Yámana called the Mannekenk "Etalum Ona", meaning "Eastern Ona", which suggests that the canoe-folk viewed them as a related race to the Selk'nam.

The first record we have of the Mannekenk came after a Spanish expedition in 1619. They were certainly acquainted with Europeans and their goods by the time Cook arrived, and he reported that they already had some Western trinkets at that time (possibly salvaged off shipwrecks). In the late nineteenth century, sealers and Eastern European gold miners made forays into their territory, bringing death through disease and sporadic skirmishing. Lucas Bridges, in 1890, estimated that there were only perhaps sixty left, a figure that had dropped to five by 1911. All that remains now is their shell middens.

---

of **Cabo San Pablo** through golden pastureland which is rimmed by flaming red *ñires* and less exuberant but nevertheless colourful *lengas* from the end of March. A wonderful panorama stretches out from the south side of Cabo San Pablo, encompassing an impressive beach and the wreck of the *Desdémona*, beached during a storm in the early 1980s. It is quite safe to walk out to the wreck at low tide. At the foot of the cape is the *Hostería San Pablo*, a brutal Stalinist construction from the 1960s, but magnificently sited on this wild coastline. If you can put up with cold showers, it offers **rooms** at budget prices ($10 per person). The Río San Pablo, like the Río Ladrillero just to the north, has some excellent **fishing** spots, which are best fished at high tide.

Beyond the cape, the road continues through wetland areas, burnt-out "tree cemeteries" and past the odd beaver dam. You're sure to glimpse troups of guanaco in the woodland, but will need a high-clearance 4WD to progress any further beyond the beautifully appointed *Estancia Fueguina*, 17km from the cape, and the public track eventually fizzles out at the *Estancia María Luisa*, 18km further on. Just beyond lie the famous fishing rivers, Irigoyen and Malengüena, but the rights are strictly private and only organized trips are allowed – contact Dan Pereira in Río Grande (☎02964/427487), or Mercedes Prada at the *Hotel Villa* in Río Grande, San Martín 277 (☎02964/422312; ③). This is the beginning of the **Península Mitre**, the bleak toe of land that forms the southeasterly extremity of Tierra del Fuego. This semi-wilderness – consisting primarily of swampy moorland and thickets, and fringed by rugged coastal scenery – was once the territory of the indigenous Mannekenk (see box, above), whose presence is attested to by old encampments marked by shell middens. Before the 1850s, the only white men who came ashore were sailors and scientists, such as FitzRoy and Darwin, and James Cook and Joseph Banks (in 1769), as well as shipwrecked unfortunates. The remains of many wrecks line the shore, including the late nineteenth-century *Duchess of Albany*, near **Bahía Policarpo**. The peninsula was subsequently colonized by groups of gold miners, petrified of attack by the Mannekenk; then by cattle farmers and sea lion hunters. Most farming establishments have been abandoned, and apart from a few ranging gauchos, the peninsula is now effectively uninhabited. To explore the area, you must seek permission at the *Estancia María Luisa* and plan it as an expedition, since the terrain is treacherous and the weather often foul. It is a three-day horseride to Policarpo, a journey that can also be made in stages by motorized quad bikes by taking advantage of the six- to eight-metre tides and using the beaches, but either way, you'll need a gaucho guide. For more information, contact the tourist office in Río Grande.

Heading north along the RN3 from the RCa turn-off, you pass **Estancia Viamonte** after some 37km. Established against the odds by Lucas Bridges with the help of his Selk'nam friends, this is one of the island's most historical farms and figures prominently in his epic work, *Uttermost Part of the Earth*. It is still run by his son, David Bridges, but is not open to the public. The section of the RN3 either side of Viamonte runs along the coastline: keep an eye open for flamingoes feeding in the sea pools. The scenery north of Viamonte also undergoes an abrupt transition, from scraggly clumps of Fuegian woodland to the forlorn, bald landscape of the northern steppe. South of the town of Río Grande, a few kilometres before you cross the Río Grande itself, you pass the turn-off for **RCb**, worth detouring along for 1km to see the tiny village of **Estancia José Menéndez**, whose shearing shed is emblazoned by the tremendous head of a prize ewe, its face obscured by an over-effusive wig of curls. The estancia was founded as Estancia Primera Argentina in 1896 by the powerful sheep magnate, Menéndez. The most notorious of its first managers was a hard-drinking Scotsman by the name of MacLennan, who earnt himself the sobriquet of "Red Pig" for taking pleasure in gunning down the Selk'nam. The RCb continues across the steppe for 70km to the Chilean frontier at **Radman**, where there's a little-used **border crossing** (Nov–March 8am–9pm), allowing access to Lago Blanco, an excellent fishing destination, as well as providing an alternative route west to Porvenir (see box on p.689).

Tolhuin and Lago Fagnano

TOLHUIN is a conscious creation of the 1970s, designed to provide a focus for the heartland of Isla Grande. A place of unassuming houses that hangs together with little focus of its own, it has an artificial commune-like feel, but makes a useful halfway point to break your journey if you're driving between Ushuaia and Río Grande. Heading south from the village you have a choice of two routes: the new RN3 bypass, or the more scenic old, unsealed RN3 route that cuts across the eastern end – or *cabecera* – of **Lago Fagnano**, 3km to the southwest of the village, along a splendid causeway. This impressive lake, also called Lago Kami from its Selk'nam name, is flanked by ranges of hills, and straddles the Chilean border at its westernmost extremity. Most of its 105km are inaccessible to visitors, apart from dedicated anglers who can afford to rent a good launch. The old RN3 rejoins the new route just past the causeway. Travelling along the RN3 as it parallels the southern shore of the lake, you'll see several sawmills, denoted by their squat, conical brick chimneys, which are used for burning bark. Further west, 50km from Tolhuin and roughly the same distance from Ushuaia, a four-kilometre road branches off to **Lago Escondido**, the last of the lowland lakes, situated at the base of the mountain pass, Paso Garibaldi.

Buses stop in Tolhuin at the *Panadería La Unión*, a bakery and restaurant that acts as the hub of village life. The *Hostal de la Cuesta*, at Angela Loij 696 in Tolhuin (☎02964/492037, fax 492049; ④, with breakfast), offers cosy, cabin-style **lodging** with views across to the mountains. For budget accommodation, head to the eastern end of Lago Fagnano to the *Hain del Lago Khami* (☎02964/425951), which has two types of **refugio** ($5 per person) and a **campsite** ($3 per person). Adjacent to this lies *Cabañas Khami* (☎02964/423031; $90 for up to seven people), with snug log cabins intended primarily for fishermen. A fresh wind sweeps straight off the lake in both places. At the

HUNTERS TURNED HUNTED: THE SELK'NAM

In 1580, Sarmiento de Gamboa became the first European to witness the Selk'nam themselves. He was impressed by these "Big People", with their powerful frames, guanaco robes, and conical *goöchilh* headgear. It was not long before their defiant nature became evident, and the bloody skirmish with a Dutch expedition in 1599 proved them to be superb warriors, a fact long known by the Yámana, who feared the people they called the **Ona**.

Selk'nam society revolved around the hunting of the **guanaco**, a species they used not just for meat: the skins were made into moccasins and capes; the bones were used for fashioning arrowheads, and the sinews for bowstrings. Hunting was done on foot, and they relied on stealth and teamwork to encircle guanacos, bringing them down with bow and arrow, a weapon with which they were expert. These proved to be of limited use, however, in preventing the invasion of white settlers at the end of the nineteenth century.

Selk'nam culture must bear some of the blame for its own demise. The tribe had always embraced violence to an extent, and the Selk'nam terrified other groups with their occasional sudden, devastating raids. Access to guns meant these conflicts became increasingly bitter and bloody. Later, when the Selk'nam realized the survival of their race was in jeopardy, a general truce was called, but not before it was too late. A covert campaign of **systematic genocide** began with the arrival of sheep-farming concerns. Hundreds of miles of wire fencing were erected, which the Selk'nam, unsurprisingly, resented, seeing it as an incursion into their ancestral hunting lands; however, they soon aquired a taste for hunting these slow, stupid animals which they referred to as **white guanaco**. For the settlers, this was an unpardonable crime and represented a drain on their investment. The Selk'nam were painted as "barbarous savages", who constituted an obstacle to settlement and progress. Soon, isolated incidents of attack and retaliation had escalated into bloody conflict. In a gruesome inversion of the contemporary white prejudice, it was the whites themselves who assumed the role of **headhunters**. Reliable sources point to prices being paid to bounty hunters on receipt of grisly invoices: a pair of severed ears (later to be modified to the whole head, after earless Selk'nam began to be seen roaming the countryside). Bonuses were paid for pregnant women. The headhunters were paid £1 sterling per "trophy" – the same price as for a puma – and some purchasers made a handsome profit, by selling the heads to Europe's museums. Sheep and whale carcasses were laced with strychnine to poison unsuspecting Selk'nam, and there were reports of hunting with trained dogs and even of injecting captured children with infectious diseases.

The assault on Selk'nam culture, too, was abrupt and devastating, led by the "civilizing" techniques of the Salesian missions, who were paid £5 sterling by landowners for each Selk'nam that they "rehoused" in one of their missions. In 1881, at the beginning of the colonizing phase of Tierra del Fuego's history, some 3500 Selk'nam lived on Isla Grande. Fifteen hundred were forced into the Salesian Candelaria mission in Río Grande in 1897, and many were then deported from their homeland to the mission on **Isla Dawson**, south of Punta Arenas. By 1911, an estimated 300 Selk'nam remained, but a measles epidemic in 1925 proved the effective death knell of the tribe. By the late 1920s, there were probably no indigenous Selk'nam living as their forefathers had done. The survivors had no alternative but acculturization. Lucas Bridges writes of the unparalleled skill of the Selk'nam as shepherds and shearers, but comments that: "Those Indians who avoided hard work soon became 'poor whites'." When pure-blooded Lola Kiepje and Esteban Yshton passed away in 1966 and 1969 respectively, Selk'nam culture died with them.

far end of the causeway, 7km from Tolhuin and just before the old RN3 links up with its successor, is the *Hostería Lago Kaikén* (☎02901/492208; ③), a lumpen building that commands fine views of the lake. This also has bungalows for rent ($60 for five guests) and a restaurant ($13 for a two-course meal). At Lago Escondido you can overnight in the *Hostería Petrel* (☎ & fax 02901/433569; ⑥, breakfast included), a **lodge** built in the typically heavy-handed, solid style of a 1960s ACA motel, but with soothing views of the lake.

travel details

Buses

Río Grande to: Tolhuín (11 daily; 1hr 30min); Ushuaia (6 daily; 3hr 30min–4hr).

Tolhuín to: Río Grande (11 daily; 1hr 30min); Ushuaia (6 daily; 2hr).

Ushuaia to: Río Grande (6 daily; 3hr 30min–4hr); Tolhuín (6 daily; 2hr).

International Buses

Río Grande to: Porvenir (Tues–Sun 1 daily; 5hr); Punta Arenas via Primera Angostura (Mon–Sat 1 daily; 8hr 30min–10hr 30min); Punta Arenas via Porvenir (Tues–Sun 1 daily; 8hr 30min–9hr).

Porvenir to: Río Grande (Tues–Sun 1 daily; 5hr).

Ushuaia to: Punta Arenas via Primera Angostura (Mon–Sat 1 daily; 12–14hr); Punta Arenas via Porvenir (Wed, Fri & Sun; 13hr).

Ferries

Porvenir to: Punta Arenas (Tues–Sun 1 daily; 2hr 30min–3hr).

Puerto Williams to: Punta Arenas (Nov–March approx 1 weekly; 32–40hr depending on weather); Ushuaia (2 weekly; 2hr 15min–3hr).

Punta Delgada: Crossing Magellan Straits at Primera Angostura (5–9 daily depending on tides; 30min).

Ushuaia to: Puerto Williams (2 weekly; 2hr 15min–3hr).

Domestic Flights

Porvenir to: Punta Arenas (Mon–Sat 2 daily; 15min).

Puerto Williams to: Punta Arenas (6 weekly in summer, 3 in winter; 45min).

Río Grande to: Río Gallegos (1 daily; 45min); Ushuaia (1 daily; 35min).

Ushuaia to: Buenos Aires (3 daily; 3hr 30min); El Calafate (1 daily; 2hr 15min–5hr); Río Gallegos (3 daily; 1hr); Río Grande (1 daily; 35min).

PART THREE

THE

CONTEXTS

HISTORY

The earliest records for human presence in territory that is now Argentina can be dated back 12,000 years, and at least 11,800 years ago the first nomadic groups reached as far as Tierra del Fuego. Over the millennia that preceded the arrival of Europeans, widely varying cultures developed. Some of these, such as those of the Pampas, the Patagonian plateau and the Chaco floodplains, were dependent on nomadic, terrestrial hunter-gathering. From at least 6000 years ago, distinct nomadic cultures like that of the Yámana (see p.684) emerged in the channels of the Fuegian archipelago, where canoe technology allowed the adoption of a marine-based life. Other groups, such as the Guaraní peoples of the subtropical northeast, evolved semi-nomadic lifestyles dependent on hunter-gathering and shifting, slash-and-burn agriculture, whereby they cultivated maize, manioc, beans and sweet potatoes while also producing cotton for textiles.

The most complex cultures emerged, however, in the **Andean northwest**, where sedentary agricultural practices developed from about 500 BC. Irrigation permitted the intensive cultivation of staple crops like maize, quinoa, squash and potatoes and this, combined with the domestication of animals like the llama, facilitated the growth of rich material cultures, as attested to by the archeological record. The most important early sedentary culture is the

Tafí one of the Tucumán region, whose people sculpted intriguing stone menhirs incised with geometric designs, feline shapes and human faces. This initial period saw the later development of Catamarca's **Condorhuasi** culture, renowned for its distinctive and beautifully patterned ceramics. From about 600 AD, metallurgical technologies developed, which saw the use of bronze for items as elaborate as ceremonial axes and chest-plates, as best witnessed in the **Aguada** civilization, whose territory also centred on Catamarca. From about 850 AD, the increasing organization of Andean groups is demonstrated by the appearance of fortified urban settlements, which, though relatively humble by the standards of the great civilizations further north, were nevertheless built in stone and had populations of up to a few thousand. Three important **Diaguita** cultures emerge: Sanagasta; Belén; and **Santa María**, whose overlapping zones of influence stretched from Salta through to San Juan, and which are notable for their elaborately painted ceramics, anthropomorphic funeral urns, superb metalwork, and the use of agricultural terracing. Further north, separate cultures develop in the Humahuaca region of Jujuy, including those of **Tilcara** and El Alfarcito, both of which have evidence of a marked use of hallucinogenic substances.

These Andean cultures engaged in trade with their counterparts on the Pacific side of the Andes and north into what is now Bolivia. Trade networks were vastly increased once the area came under the sway of pan-Andean empires: first that of Bolivia's great city, **Tiahuanaco**, which probably influenced Condorhuasi culture; and, from 1480, that of the **Incas**, who incorporated the area into Kollasuyo, their southernmost administrative region. Incredibly well-preserved finds, such as recent excavation of three **ritually sacrificed mummies** at the summit of 6739-metre Cerro Llulliallaco – the world's highest archeological discovery – are helping to reveal the extent of this influence in terms of customs, religion and dress.

In the early sixteenth century, before the arrival of Europeans, Argentina's **indigenous population** was probably in the region of 400,000, an estimated two-thirds of whom lived in the northwest – Andean groups such as the Diaguitas, the Omaguacas of Jujuy's

Humahuaca Valley, the Atacameños of the far northwestern puna, and the Tonocotés of Santiago del Estero. Other relatively densely settled areas included the central sierras of Córdoba and San Luis, where the **Comechingones** and the Sanavirones lived. The Cuyo region was home to semi-sedentary Huarpes; while to the south and east of them lived various Tehuelche tribes (see p.592), often referred to generically by the Spanish as Pampas Indians or, further south, Patagones. Tierra del Fuego was inhabited by Selk'nam and Mannekenk, as well as the Yámana sea-goers (see p.684). The Chaco region (see also p.361) was home to a bewildering variety of shifting nomadic groups, including Chiriguanos, the Lule-Vilela, Wichí, and groups of the Guaycurú nation, like the Abipone and Qom. The northeastern areas of El Litoral and Mesopotamia were inhabited by the Kaingang, the Charrúa and Guaraní groups.

The first group to encounter the Spanish were probably the nomadic **Querandí** of the Pampas region – the northernmost group of the wider Tehuelche culture. They lived in temporary shelters and hunted guanaco and rhea with bolas (*boleadores*): weighted thongs used to bring down their prey. Though they put up determined resistance to the Spanish for several decades, their culture was eliminated during the subsequent colonial period – a fate that was to be shared by many others.

EARLY SPANISH SETTLEMENT

In 1516, Juan Díaz de Solís, a Portuguese mariner in the employ of the Spanish Crown, led a small crew to the shores of the River Plate in the search of a trade route to the Far East. His dream ended here in failure, murdered by the Querandí or the cannibalistic Charrúa, who inhabited the eastern – or Uruguayan – bank. Another brief exploration into the region was made in 1520 by Ferdinand Magellan who continued his epic voyage south to discover the famous straits that now bear his name; while the next significant expedition to this part of the world was made by **Sebastian Cabot** who reached the River Plate in 1526 and built a small, short-lived fort near modern Rosario. Cabot misleadingly christened the river **El Río de la Plata** (the River of Silver), after finding bullion amongst the indigenous groups of Paraguay and believing there to be deposits nearby. This was not the case – ironically, this silver had probably been brought there by the Portuguese adventurer, Aleixo García. García, in 1524, traversed the continent as far as the eastern fringes of the Inca empire, but was murdered with his Andean booty on his return journey. The legends that Cabot's discoveries nourished after his return to Spain were to bring nothing but heartache for many that followed. Stories of a fabled civilization – variously called Trapalanda or the **City of the Cesars** – persisted well into the eighteenth century, tempting many into expeditions whose only return was hardship. Cabot's silver had its most lasting legacy in the word "**Argentina**" itself, which derives from the metal's Latin name, *argentum.* First used in a poem in 1602, it was adopted in the nineteenth century as the name of the Republic. A more immediate legacy was that, in 1535, Pedro de Mendoza was authorized by the Spanish Crown to colonize the River Plate in an effort to pre-empt Portuguese conquest. In February 1536, Mendoza founded Buenos Aires, originally named Puerto Nuestra Señora Santa María del Buen Ayre after the "good air" of the sweet-smelling river.

Mendoza's plans soon went awry: it proved impossible to subjugate the local nomadic Querandí, so as to use them for forced agricultural labour. Indeed, their aggression towards the Spanish invaders forced Mendoza to send Pedro de Ayolas upstream to find a more suitable site for settlement. In August 1537, Ayolas founded **Nuestra Señora de la Asunción del Paraguay** where the Spanish discovered a more amenable indigenous population in the semi-sedentary Guaraní. They received the Spaniards with gifts, including food and women, and, accustomed to agricultural work, they were more easily exploited for labour. Mendoza died at sea on a voyage to Spain and authority for the colony devolved to Domingo de Irala, who, after almost constant struggle with the Querandí, finally ordered the evacuation of Buenos Aires in 1541. By this time, Spanish interest in colonizing this area of the world had decreased significantly anyway, mainly as a result of **Pizarro**'s spectacular conquest, in 1535, of Inca Peru, with its vast reserves of bullion and a huge indigenous population that represented a tremendous labour resource to the conquerors.

From 1543, the new Viceroyalty of Peru, with its capital at Lima, was given authority over all of southern Spanish South America. The north-western Andean region of Argentina was first tentatively explored from the north in the mid 1530s, but the impulse for colonizing this region really came with the discovery, in 1545, of enormous **silver deposits** in **Potosí**, in Upper Peru (modern-day Bolivia). This led to the establishment of the **Governorship of Tucumán**, covering a region far larger than the modern province of that name, and embracing most of today's northwest. Conquistadors from Chile and Peru crossed the Andes seeking to press gang the locals into labour and find an overland route to the Potosí silver mines. Francisco de Aguirre founded Santiago del Estero in 1553, Argentina's earliest continually inhabited town, while other Spaniards established the settlements of Mendoza (1561), San Juan (1562), Córdoba (1573), Salta (1582), La Rioja (1591) and San Salvador de Jujuy (1593).

Meanwhile, the Spanish in Asunción sent an expedition of mainly mixed-blood *mestizos* under the command of Juan de Garay down the River Paraná, founding Santa Fé in 1573 and **resettling Buenos Aires** in 1580 – this time, for good. Buenos Aires was no longer dependent on having to secure its own indigenous labour force to avoid starvation, as it could be supplied from Asunción. Settlers also benefitted from one vital legacy of the Mendoza settlement – the feral **horses** and **cattle** that had multiplied incredibly in the area in the interim. Few then realized the significance these animals would have on most of Argentina's nomadic indigenous groups, who adopted the horse with alacrity and would round up the cattle for trade with Cordillera groups.

COLONIAL DEVELOPMENTS

Up until the late eighteenth century, the Governorship of the River Plate was largely overlooked by the Spanish Crown. Considered a remote and unproductive outpost of the empire, it had no mineral resources and no pliant indigenous populations. Direct trade with Spain from the River Plate was prohibited from 1554, and all imported and exported goods were meant to be traded via Lima, which restricted growth of the port, but encouraged **contraband** of cheap imported manufactured items. The governorship's agricultural potential was limited: there was no market in Europe at the time for agricultural produce, and indigenous populations were

relatively scattered and independently minded, so could not easily be yoked into the **encomienda** system of forced labour. *Encomienda* entailed the granting of land and custody of Amerindian populations to Spanish conquistadors and settlers. These *encomenderos* were, theoretically, responsible for the conversion and spiritual education of their native workforce in return for labour, but the system was openly abused and many *encomenderos*, concerned more with exploitation than evangelization, often treated their workforce no better than slaves.

More important than the River Plate at this period was the Governorship of Tucumán. The *encomienda* system was more effective here and in the central Córdoban sierras, as they were more densely settled. Though some trade from this area was directed towards Buenos Aires, the local economy was run so as to ensure that the all-important Potosí mine was provided with mules, sugar, cotton textiles and wheat.

More ruinous perhaps than the *encomienda* was the **mita**, originally an indigenous system of tribute labour used by the Incas for projects such as building roads, bridges and agricultural terracing. It was adopted and extended by the Spanish as the preferred system of labour for the mining industry and obliged indigenous peoples of the northwest and Upper Peru to toil for periods of the year in the silver mines of Potosí – a brutal undertaking that all too often led to deaths through malnutrition, mercury poisoning, psilicosis or rockfalls. Other tribute systems involved the entire relocation of communities to the agricultural areas of the northwest, to compensate for the demographic collapse caused by tribute labour and European diseases like smallpox. Indigenous resistance to the impositions of Spanish colonial society still erupted on occasion, as with the Diaguita rebellion of 1657, under the leadership of a Spanish rebel, Pedro Bohórquez. The rebellion was brutally crushed in 1659 and survivors were displaced from their decimated communities to be forcibly resettled on hacienda farms as a workforce.

By the second half of the eighteenth century demand for labour from both Potosí and the towns of Tucumán led to the importation of **black slave labour**. By 1778, it is estimated that around nine percent of Tucumán's regional population of 126,000 consisted of slaves, while well over a quarter were of pure indigenous blood. Racial divisions were strongly demarcated, and the rights of whites to control the best lands and political offices were reinforced by a dress code and a weapon ban for the non-white castes.

The economies of Buenos Aires, Santa Fé, Entre Ríos and Corrientes were not free from strife with nomadic native peoples either. Mounted raids by Chaqueñan indigenous tribes like the Abipone terrorized the littoral provinces well into the eighteenth century; whereas Buenos Aires, dependent on its round-ups of wild cattle (*vaquerías*) for its **hide** and **tallow industry**, frequently came into conflict both with Pampas groups of Tehuelches and, increasingly from the eighteenth century, Mapuche groups (Araucanians). These peoples relied on the same feral cattle and horses, driving vast herds of them to the northern Patagonian Andes for the purpose of trading with Chileans, both white settlers and other indigenous groups. The seventeenth and eighteenth centuries saw the emergence and apogee of the **gaucho**. These were nomadic horsemen, all too often of *mestizo* stock (mixed indigenous and criollo or black descent), who roamed in small bands and lived off the wild herds of livestock that roamed the plains. They were viewed as social outcasts, a motley collection that included vagrants, army deserters, fugitive criminals and escaped slaves. Their lives often involved incredible physical hardship but, nevertheless, in the late nineteenth century, they came to represent the same quintessential, romantic ideal of carefree liberty and freedom from authority as their North American counterpart, the "cowboy". This perception came about only when the state was extending its control over territory it claimed and the lives of those who lived there. The days of the true gauchos were already numbered by this time, but the image still exerts a powerful hold on modern Argentinian society and the popular imagination.

The seventeenth and eighteenth centuries also saw a developing feud between Spain and Portugal, focusing primarily on the River Plate region. Tension escalated after the Portuguese, in 1680, founded the town of **Colonia da Sacramento** on the **Banda Oriental** – the "east bank" of the Plate, in what is now Uruguay. Colonia became an entrepôt of contraband trade with Buenos Aires, and this encouraged increased traffic in illicit silver from Potosí. Violent struggles ensued between Spain and Portugal over control of Colonia, which changed hands several times in the eighteenth century. Spanish authorities were determined not to cede control of the River Plate and access to the Paraná. Settlements were established in other areas of the Banda Oriental to rival Colonia, the most important of which was **Montevideo**, founded in 1724. The wars were only settled in 1777 by the Treaty of Ildefonso, in which the entire Banda Oriental territory was ceded to the Spanish.

THE JESUIT MISSIONS

The Jesuits first arrived in the Paraná area during the late sixteenth century. Along with the official Church and other regular orders, they enjoyed favourable tax concessions and initially prospered under the protection of the Crown. The first **missions** to the **Guaraní** were established in the upper Paraná from 1609. Though the Jesuits were to try to evangelize other parts of the country, such as the Chaco and northern Patagonia, over the next 150 years, it was in the subtropical Upper Paraná where they had their greatest success. After raids in the region by roaming **Portuguese slavers** in the 1630s, the Jesuits established their own indigenous militias for protection. Thereafter, Jesuit activity thrived: there were as many as thirty missions here by the beginning of the eighteenth century, with a total indigenous population exceeding 50,000. The Guaraní who lived in the missions had the benefit of Jesuit education and skills, and were exempt from forced labour in silver mines, but this was no earthly paradise: coercion and violence were not unknown, and epidemics ravaged these densely populated communities on a periodic basis.

In the seventeenth century, the Crown revoked its tax concessions to the Jesuits and their communities were forced to enter the colonial economy. They did so with characteristic vigour, becoming exporters of **yerba mate**, sugar and tobacco. However, their success aroused jealousy. Some missions housed more than 4000 indigenous people and this **monopolization of labour**, together with the economic and political influence of the Jesuits in Córdoba, stirred the resentment of nearby settlers. In the 1720s, secular settlers rebelled, urging the Crown to curb the domination of the Jesuits. In and around Asunción and Corrientes, they subjected Jesuit communities to **raids**, kidnappings, massacres and starvation. Though it survived that threat, the mission experiment was to succumb soon afterwards, a victim of power politics in Europe, lobbying from landed interests bent on exploiting the native labour, and the Bourbon King, Charles III's perception that the existence of a powerful Jesuit community answerable to the pope was a threat to secular royal authority. In 1767, he ordered their **expulsion** from all Spanish territories – an order carried out the following year, as captured dramatically in the film, *The Mission*, starring Robert de Niro. The remaining communities were subsequently entrusted to the Franciscans, whose mismanagement and neglect led to them being plundered and to many Guaraní being led away to slavery.

THE NEW VICEROYALTY

By the late eighteenth century, the British controlled the Caribbean and were blocking the Lima sea routes, so it was vital that another route to the silver mines of Potosí be established. The River Plate seemed the logical choice, and the growing value of Buenos Aires both as a market and strategic post gained the recognition of the Crown when it was made the capital of the new **Viceroyalty of the River Plate**, created in 1776, and whose jurisdiction included Upper Peru (modern Bolivia), Paraguay, and the Governorship of Montevideo. With power concentrated in Buenos Aires, it came, increasingly, to dominate the interior. Commercial restrictions were gradually loosened, permitting trade with other ports in Spain and Spanish America, but the Crown still tried to hang on to its monopoly on colonial commerce and prohibited the sale of silver to foreign powers. Tension between **monopolist traders** and those who advocated liberal **free trade** was becoming more entrenched. During the European wars of the late eighteenth century, the mother country was unable to guarantee a steady supply of manufactures to its empire, and the Crown was forced to loosen its monopoly in 1797, allowing its colonies to trade with neutral countries. To the dismay of monopolist merchants, cheap European manufactures flowed freely into the city courtesy of contraband merchants using the cover of neutral ships

to import enemy goods. Monopolists trading on the traditional Cádiz route suffered from this, and exports to Spain dipped from millions of pesos to a mere 100,000 in 1798. However, once lifted, it became increasingly difficult to reinstate monopolist restrictions, and attempts to do so caused anger amongst those, such as the merchant **Manuel Belgrano**, who argued for free trade with all nations, but not rebellion against the Crown. although the progressive ideas of the French Revolution and the American Declaration of Independence circulated among the elites of Buenos Aires, there was not yet any significant form of revolutionary feeling against the Spanish authorities.

Other changes in the economy of Buenos Aires became increasingly apparent during the Viceroyalty. Rich merchants (*comerciantes*) helped to finance the growth of **estancia livestock farms** in the province: a shift away from the earlier practice of *vaquerías* – round-ups of wild cattle. By the end of the eighteenth century, these estancias had become highly profitable enterprises. Bolstered by immigration from peninsular Spaniards and Creole Spanish Americans from the interior, the city's population reached 42,540 by 1810 (up from less than 9000 in 1744). Despite the increased importance of the region, the territory that has come to be Argentina was still sparsely populated at this time, though, and, as late as 1810, half of its estimated 360,000 inhabitants were indigenous Amerindians.

THE BRITISH INVASIONS

The British had caught wind of the commercial tensions in Buenos Aires, mistakenly interpreting them as revolutionary. In **June 1806**, a force of 1600 men led by General William Beresford stormed into the city unchecked. Beresford hoped, ultimately, to assert British imperial control over the entire Viceroyalty and bring it into the British trading orbit. The Viceroy, the Marqués de Sobremonte, reacted to the news of the British landing by fleeing the city and the Spanish authorities grudgingly swore allegiance to the British Crown. Among the ordinary inhabitants, there were shouts of "treason" and a sense of offended honour at the way in which such a tiny force had been allowed to overrun the city's defences.

The people of Buenos Aires regrouped under their new commander-in-chief, the French-born

Santiago Liniers, and ousted their invaders during the **Reconquista** of August 12. Undaunted, the British captured Montevideo from where they launched a second assault on a better-prepared Buenos Aires in July 1807. This battle led to the surrender of the British and came to be known as **La Defensa**, a name imbued with the bravura of Liniers' hastily assembled militia, whose cannon- and musket-fire peppered the enemy, while women poured boiling oil from the tops of the city's buildings on the hapless British soldiers.

One consequence of the victory over the British was to make the people of Buenos Aires aware of the extent to which they could manage their own affairs and how little they could rely on either the viceregal authorities or the motherland. This was the first time that they had fought in unison against a foreign invader and the feeling of pride carried over into a stance of defiance in certain sectors against the monarchy as the Spanish Empire finally started to crumble.

THE MAY REVOLUTION

In 1808, events in Europe took a dramatic turn as **Napoleon Bonaparte** invaded the Iberian Peninsula. Napoleon forced the Spanish king, Charles IV, to **abdicate**, and installed his brother, Joseph Bonaparte, on the throne. These events had massive repercussions in the Latin American colonies, and ushered in a period of over a decade of upheaval in the viceroyalty.

A new viceroy, Viscount Balthasar de Cisneros arrived to replace the disgraced Sobremonte and relieve the pressure on Liniers. Cisneros scrapped most of the free-trade initiatives Liniers had issued in the interim, and the ban on trading in silver was reinstated. The Spanish administration still failed to grasp the importance of this issue and it was then that free-trade activists such as Belgrano began to plan a revolution. In 1810, news of the French capture of the last Spanish outpost, Seville, led to an extraordinary meeting of Buenos Aires notables. On May 25, the people of Buenos Aires gathered in front of the cabildo, proudly wearing rosettes made from sky-blue and white ribbons, the colours that were later to make up the Argentine flag. Inside, the Viceroy Cisneros was ousted after it was agreed that the Spanish administration in the motherland had effectively ceased to exist and the **Primera Junta** was sworn in to become the first independent government of the region. However, deposition of the Viceroy and the establishment of self-government did not necessarily mean advocating republicanism, and many proclaimed loyalty to Ferdinand VII, imprisoned heir to Charles IV. This heralded two decades of turbulence, involving **independence struggles** with Spain (led by the River Plate region – the first to declare its independence from the motherland – and supported by foreign powers like Britain) and **civil war** between Buenos Aires and the interior provinces of the old viceroyalty in the attempt to develop a new order to replace the old. It was not until the late 1820s, with the break-up of the viceroyalty, that the confederation that provided the nucleus of modern Argentina began to stabilize.

UNITARISM AND FEDERALISM: A PRELUDE TO CIVIL WAR

The Primera Junta was headed by Saavedra, who believed in sharing power with the provinces over the territory of the viceroyalty and insisted on proclaiming a token loyalty to the Spanish Crown. The other members of the Junta, which included Manuel Belgrano and Mariano Moreno, were less moderate free-trade enthusiasts, intent on bringing the rest of the territory under the control of Buenos Aires. Moreno's views came to represent what was to be the position of the **unitarists** (known as **Azules** – "Blues") who favoured centralism; while Saavedra's contained the first seeds of the ideas of later **Federalists** (the Colorados or Rojos – "Reds"), promoting the autonomy of the provinces within the framework of a loose confederation. This dispute was to dominate Argentine politics of the nineteenth century, causing bitter division and repeated civil war, and the tension between the provinces and Buenos Aires is still a feature of life in Argentina today.

While the Junta's internal disputes prevented unity in the capital, the May Revolution also failed to mark a clean break from the motherland. Royalists under the leadership of Alzaga continued to militate within Buenos Aires for the return of a Spanish Viceroyalty.

THE BREAK-UP OF THE VICEROYALTY

Authorities in Asunción, Upper Peru and Montevideo all rejected the authority of the Primera Junta. Having seen little of the benefit of free trade in the preceding years and having suffered heavy taxes from the viceregal capital, they were unwilling to submit to further domination from Buenos Aires. Like most of the interior provinces, they chose to declare their own forms of interim government. Thereafter, following complicated internal civil wars, struggles with Buenos Aires and independence battles with Spain, three new republics emerged from the old viceroyalty: **Paraguay** (1814); **Bolivia** (1825); and **Uruguay** (1828). The frontiers of these republics remained anything but fixed, but they do correspond, in essence, with the countries we know today. The most intractable struggle was the one that involved Uruguay, a region that had seen competing claims by the Spanish and Brazilian authorities during the colonial period, and where fighting involved various alliances between Portuguese, Spanish, local patriots led by the caudillo **Artigas**, and Buenos Aires and even the British, eager to protect trading interests. Eventually, in 1828, both Brazil and Buenos Aires agreed to the formation of a republic as a buffer nation between the two territories.

CIVIL WAR AND INDEPENDENCE: THE UNITED PROVINCES OF THE PLATE

The royalist factions in Buenos Aires had, by 1812, effectively been crushed, and a Creole front led by **José de San Martín** (see box on p.704), the Sociedad Patriótica, sought full emancipation from foreign powers. However, unitarist and Federalist interests continued to battle for control of the capital, and struggles with pro-royalist forces continued to flare up across the old viceroyalty. The struggles after 1810 saw the emergence in the interior of Federalist **caudillos**, powerful local warlords with their own militias and even their own self-declared independent "little republics" or *republiquetas*. They recruited – or, rather, press ganged – their rank and file from among the slaves, indigenous peoples and gauchos of the countryside. The most famous caudillos were Artigas in the Banda Oriental, Estanislao López in Santa Fé and Francisco Ramírez in Entre Ríos.

While the war with Spain raged on, two congresses were convened to discuss the future of the former viceroyalty on a pan-regional basis, but these were dominated by unitarists and failed to produce a plan for the country on which all sides could agree. In the second, held on **July 9, 1816** in the city of Tucumán, the inde-

pendence of the **United Provinces of the River Plate** was formally declared, a title first adopted by Buenos Aires in 1813. It was largely ignored by the caudillos but the date, July 9, has since come to be recognized as Argentina's official **independence day**.

Later that year, San Martín led a disciplined force of five thousand men across the Andes to attack the Spanish in Chile, in one of the defining moments of Latin America's struggle against its colonial rulers. During this time, he was assisted in the north by another hero of Argentinian Independence, **Martín Miguel de Güemes**, an anti-royalist, Federalist caudillo whose gaucho army eventually liberated Salta. Though caudillos such as Güemes were in favour of independence, many resented the heavy taxes imposed to fund the struggles, and tensions remained high. Men like López and Ramírez defeated the attempt to impose a unitarist constitution in 1819.

ROSAS – THE "CALIGULA OF THE RIVER PLATE"

The 1820s began with infighting amongst caudillo groups. In 1826, **Bernadino Rivadavia**, a unitarist admirer of European ideals and a proponent of foreign investment, became the first outright president of what was called the United Provinces of South America. He proposed a new constitution, but this was predictably rejected by the provinces, who objected to the call for dissolution of their militia and the concession of land to the national government. At the same time, the war with Brazil over the Banda Oriental led to a blockade of the River Plate and caused financial crisis in the city. These two issues brought Rivadavia's presidency to its knees by 1827. The bitter unitarist/Federalist fighting that ensued only ceased when a caudillo from Buenos Aires, **General Juan Manuel de Rosas**, emerged victorious. In 1829, he became governor of Buenos Aires, with dictatorial powers over the newly titled Confederation of the Río Plate or Argentine Confederation.

Rosas, one of the most polemic figures of Argentine history, was born into an influential cattle-ranching family, and identified himself as a leader of men, respected by his gauchos for his riding skills and reckless personal bravery. He was an avowed Federalist, but his own particular brand of Federalism had more to do with

SAN MARTÍN

It's impossible to stay for even a short time in Argentina without coming across the name of the national hero, **José de San Martín** – he's as ubiquitous as Washington in the United States or de Gaulle in France, and has countless streets, plazas, public buildings and even a mountain named after him, as well as innumerable statues in his honour. He's often simply referred to as **The Liberator** (*El Libertador*) and, appropriately given his surname, is treated with saint-like reverence. It's ironic, therefore, that he didn't even take part in the country's initial liberation from the Spanish Crown, that he actually helped to free Chile, Argentina's traditional rival, and that he spent the last 23 years of his life in self-imposed exile in France. Even this last fact is celebrated across the country by naming streets and whole barrios after Boulogne-sur-Mer, the French town where he died in 1850. A slightly larger-than-original replica of his Parisian mansion, Grand Bourg, built on the edge of leafy Palermo Chico, is now the Instituto Sanmartiniano, a library-cum-study-centre given over to research into the great man.

San Martín was born into a humble family – he was the son of a junior officer – in 1778 in the former Jesuit mission settlement of Yapeyú, Corrientes Province, where you can now visit his birthplace and a commemorative museum. He was packed off to the academy in Buenos Aires and then to military school in Spain, and later served in the royal army, taking part in the Spanish victories against the Napoleonic invasions in 1808–11. When he heard the news of Argentina's unilateral declaration of independence, he returned to his homeland, and assisted in training the rag-bag army that was trying to resist Spain's attempt to cling onto its South American empire. After having replaced Manuel Belgrano as leader of the independence forces in 1813, he became increasingly active in politics, as a pragmatic conservative, and attended the Tucumán Congress in 1816, at which a new state was officially declared. He then formed

opposing intellectual Unitarism, with its gravitation towards foreign, European influence, than it did in respecting provincial autonomy per se. As it turned out, his rule was more about centralizing power in his own province, Buenos Aires.

He left office at the end of his term in 1832 but returned as dictator in 1835 as the country teetered on the brink of fresh civil war after the assassination of an ally of his, the caudillo of La Rioja, **Juan "Facundo" Quiroga**. During the following seventeen years Rosas ruthlessly consolidated power using the army and his own brutal police force, the **Mazorca**. *Mazorca* means "the ear of wheat" and this symbol was used to promote an image of national unity just as Benito Mussolini used the Roman fasces to represent Italian unity in the twentieth century. The Mazorca used a network of spies and assassins to keep resistance in check, making sure the slogan "Long live the Federation! Death to the Unitarist savages!" was chanted in schools and meeting halls. On certain ceremonial days, they ensured that members of the public wore red, the colour of Rosas' Federalists. During this time, many opponents and intellectuals fled to Europe and Uruguay to escape the repression.

Continuing a **process of colonization** of the interior which had begun in colonial times, Rosas sought to improve his network of **patronage** through the expansion of territories available for farming in the Pampas. His **Desert Campaign** of 1833 against the indigenous peoples was the precursor to Roca's genocidal Conquest of the Desert of the late 1870s (see p.706). The vast landholdings that Rosas dealt out to "conquerors" ensured he retained a body of powerful allies. Rosas also tried to ingratiate himself with the Church, thereby assuring himself of the support of those provincial elites that had been appalled by the anti-clerical tone of Rivadavia's administration. The Church responded positively, with portraits of the dictator adorning the walls of its buildings.

Rosas managed to alienate many of the interior provinces by not permitting free trade along the Paraná, by increasing taxes on provincial trade, and by allowing the import of cheap foreign produce such as French wine into Buenos Aires which undercut provincial specialities. Though he quelled several uprisings, Rosas' bloody regime was brought to an end in 1852, in the battle of Caseros. Defeat came at the hands of a former ally, the powerful caudillo Governor of Entre Ríos, **Justo José de Urquiza**, since his own army, known popularly as the **Ejército de los Andes**, basing himself in Mendoza, where he was governor for several years, and in San Juan. From there he crossed the Andes and obliterated royalist troops at Chacabuco, thereby **freeing Chile** from the imperialistic yoke – though his friend and comrade-at-arms Bernardo O'Higgins got most of the credit – finally mopping up the remaining royalist resistence at Maipú in 1818, before moving on to Lima, Peru.

San Martín was not in the slightest bit interested in personal political power, but was in favour of setting up a constitutional monarchy in the newly emerging South American states. In 1821 he signed the so-called Punchanca agreement with the Viceroy of Peru to put a member of the Spanish royal family on the Peruvian throne, but the royalists did not respond and, ultimately, he unilaterally declared Peru's independence on July 12, 1821. Unable to hold the country together in the face of royalist resistance, he called upon **Simón Bolívar**, the liberator of Venezuela, to come to his assistance. The only meeting between the two giants of South American independence occurred in Guayaquil, Ecuador, in 1822. Bolívar's radical republican ideals clashed with San Martín's conservative mindset, so it seemed predestined that no compromise position would be found, and, though no one knows what exactly was said in this tantalizing encounter, San Martín opted to withdraw from Peru. Frustrated by an emerging Argentina that was neither the new-style kingdom he yearned for nor the democratic modern nation-state Bolívar had advocated but, instead, a patchwork of disunited provinces led by brutish caudillos every bit as power-hungry as the viceroys and governors they had replaced, San Martín took off to **France**. He was never to return to Argentina during his lifetime, and, in his self-imposed exile, he slipped into obscurity; all this changed after his death, however, and the national hero's bodily remains were repatriated later that century. He now lies buried in Buenos Aires' Metropolitan Cathedral, where his tomb is a national monument – a shrine to the "Grandfather of the Nation".

the huge cattle ranches of this state were deprived of their principal markets. Urquiza was backed by dissidents in Montevideo and a coalition of interests that desired free trade on the Paraná, including the Brazilians, British and French. After defeat, Rosas left for England to become a farmer in Southampton, where he died in 1877.

CONSOLIDATION OF THE NATION

The thirty years that followed the defeat of Rosas saw the foundations being laid for the **modern Argentinian state**. An important economic expansion and the triumph of Unitarism ensured the conditions for the boom that followed; Buenos Aires was finally to emerge supreme from its struggles with the provinces; and territorial conquest began in earnest, resulting in the subjugation of the most important of the unconquered indigenous groups: those of the south.

Urquiza's attempt to establish a unifying constitution sympathetic to Federalist interests foundered when Buenos Aires proved unwilling to renounce its privileged trading terms or submit to his rule. The province refused to approve the **1853 constitution**, which led to the creation of two separate republics: one in Buenos Aires and the other, the Argentine Confederation, centred on Entre Ríos and headed by Urquiza. This situation changed in 1861, when the governor of Buenos Aires, **Bartolomé Mitre**, eventually defeated Urquiza and his financially crippled republic. The 1853 constitution was, with a few significant amendments, ratified by Buenos Aires, and the basic structure of Argentine government was set. This established a bicameral federal legislature, an independent judiciary, and an executive president who would be elected for a fixed, nonrenewable six-year term. In 1862, Mitre was elected to the first presidency of the newly titled **Argentine Republic**. Other constitutional provisions included ending trade restrictions throughout the country and promoting the colonization of the interior, a result of which was the sponsorship of the small Welsh settlement in Patagonia (see p.597). Significantly, the president also held the right to dissolve provincial governments at will.

Mitre aimed for the rapid **modernization** of the country, focusing particularly on the capital. His achievements included promoting administrational efficiency, creating a national army, overseeing the expansion of a **railway network** and creating a national postal system. These initiatives were financed by foreign investment from Britain, which contributed the capital to build railroads, and greater export earnings as a result, particularly, of the important expanding trade in **wool**. A more integrated national infrastructure allowed a greater flow of trade and higher revenues in most of the interior. By the mid 1860s, therefore, much of the Federalist resistance had been stamped out and the term caudillo referred more to the election-riggers hired by the capital to control the interior.

The other significant event of Mitre's presidency was the **War of the Triple Alliance** (1865–70), a conflict that had its origins in the Federalist sympathies of Paraguay and disputes over navigation rights in the Paraná and River Plate. In it, Argentina allied with Uruguay and Brazil to defeat Mariscal Solano López of Paraguay. After this bitter campaign, Argentina secured control of the upper Paraná and the territory of Misiones.

The end of the war overlapped with the presidency of **Domingo Sarmiento**, the man who is most identified with the drive to "Europeanize" Argentina. Sarmiento was the arch opponent of *caudillismo* and was famous for pillorying the likes of Rosas, Quiroga, López and Ramírez in his literary works. Sarmiento believed that this age represented a "barbaric" era in Argentine history, its legacy holding the country back from contemporary North American and European notions of progress and civilization. These theories of progress were to impact heavily on the remaining indigenous populations of Argentina, as they sponsored those who believed in "civilizing the Indian", and helped to underpin the doctrine of the so-called "Generation of the Eighties" (the 1880s) who subscribed to imposing the nation state by force.

Sarmiento is also remembered for his highly ambitious **educational policy**, one element of which was the recruitment of North American teachers. He also encouraged European immigration on a grand scale (see opposite).

THE CONQUEST OF THE DESERT AND TERRITORIAL EXPANSION

With the near disappearance of wild herds of livestock and the inexorable movement of settlers further south into the Pampas, Mapuche and Tehuelche groups found it increasingly difficult to maintain their way of life. Indigenous raids – called **malones** – on estancias and white settlements became ever more frequent, and debate raged in the 1870s as to how to solve the "Indian Problem". Two main positions crystallized. The one propounded by Minister of War, **Alsina**, consisted of containment, using a line of forts and ditches, and aimed at a gradual integration of the indigenous tribes. The second, propounded by his successor, **General Julio Roca**, advocated uncompromising conquest and subjugation. An increasingly powerful and self-confident Argentina could, now the Paraguayan war had ended and the Federalist rebellions of the early 1870s had been stamped out, concentrate on territorial expansion to the south. Indeed, with the same clarity as the policy of Manifest Destiny in the United States, the likes of Roca viewed that herein lay the future of the Argentine nation.

Roca led an army south in 1879, and his brutal **Conquest of the Desert** was effectively over by the following year, leaving over 1300 indigenous dead and the whole of Patagonia effectively open to settlement. Roca was heralded as a hero, and swept to victory in the 1880 presidential election on the back of his success. He believed strongly in a highly centralized government and consolidated his power base by using the vast new tracts of land as a system of patronage. With the southern frontier secure, he could, from the mid-1880s, back campaigns to defeat indigenous groups in the **Chaco**, and thus stabilized the country's northern frontier with Paraguay.

SOCIAL AND ECONOMIC CHANGE: 1850–1914

Throughout the period, agriculture and infrastructure continued to expand, benefiting from massive British investment. The first **railway**, built in 1854, connected Buenos Aires to the farms and estancias in its vicinity. By 1880, the railway network carried over three million passengers and over one million tonnes of cargo, and between 1857 and 1890, nearly 10,000km of track were built. **Wool** production became such a strong sector of the economy in the second half of the nineteenth century that exports dwarfed those of hides, and sheep outnumbered people by thirty to one.

Sheep farms were small, privately owned or rented family concerns, in contrast to the huge impersonal estancias. This saw the growth of a strong middle-class group in the provinces. Also transforming the countryside was the boom in **export crops** such as wheat, oats and linseed. Another development of major importance was the invention of **refrigerator ships** in 1876, enabling Argentina to start exporting enormous quantities of meat to the urban centres of newly industrialized Britain and Europe.

The creation of farm colonies with European immigrants was part of a general policy of encouraging white immigration to the country. Significant numbers of French people arrived in the 1850s, followed later by groups of Italians, Swiss and Germans. As a consequence of this, Santa Fé saw a tenfold rise in population between 1858 and 1895. In Buenos Aires and other areas, the age of **latifundismo** had begun as huge tracts of land were bought up by Argentine speculators hoping to profit by their sale to railroad companies. In the meantime, they were rented out to sheep farmers and sharecroppers.

Between 1880 and World War I, an astounding six million **immigrants** came to Argentina. Half of these were Italians, a quarter Spaniards while other groups included French, Portuguese, Russians, Ottomans, Irish and Welsh. In 1895, foreigners represented nearly one-third of the population of the Buenos Aires city, which grew in size from 90,000 in 1869 to 670,000 in 1895. Many came in search of land but settled for work either as sharecroppers in estancias and *latifundios* or as shepherds, labourers and artisans. This convulsive influx caused occasional resentment among Argentines, particularly during periods of economic depression, which were usually sparked by events abroad. Growth depended largely on foreign investment and the country was susceptible to economic slumps like the one that affected Britain in the 1870s, prompting occasional debate about **protectionism**. Immigrant participation in the political life of the country was certainly not encouraged, and few took up Argentine citizenship on arrival, because citizens were obliged to perform military service. Generally, though, immigrants were welcomed as part of the drive towards economic expansion and colonization of the countryside.

POLITICAL REFORM AND THE AGE OF RADICALISM

As the twentieth century wore on, so the pressure for political change increased. Power still remained in the hands of a tiny minority of the landed and urban elite, leaving the professional and working classes of the rapidly expanding cities unrepresented. From 1890, a new party, the **Radical Civic Union** (Unión Cívica Radical or UCR), agitated for reform but was excluded from power. A sea change came with the introduction of **universal manhood suffrage** and secret balloting by the reformist conservative president, Roque Sáenz Peña, in 1912. This saw the victory of the first radical president, **Hipólito Yrigoyen**, in 1916, and ushered in thirteen unbroken years of radicalism, under him and his associate, Marcelo T. de Alvear. Soon after World War I, growth picked up again, with the expansion of manufacturing industry, but the benefits of economic growth were far from equally distributed. Serious confrontations between police and urban strikers in Buenos Aires led to numerous deaths in the **Semana Trágica** – or Tragic Week – of 1919. This was followed by the 1920–21 **rural workers' strikes** in southern Patagonia. Most strikers were immigrant peon farmhands from the impoverished Chilean island of Chiloe but there was also a handful of labour activists, Bolsheviks and anarchists. A first strike had taken place in 1920, sparked by the fact that peons had been unable to cash in or exchange the tokens with which they were paid by wealthy sheep barons – many of them British. The protest expanded to include a raft of other grievances concerning working rights and conditions, and radical factions latched onto what was, at root, a fairly conservative phenomenon. Shaken and surprised, the estancia owners promised to arrange payment, but when this was not forthcoming, a second strike was unleashed, this time releasing far more in the way of pent-up anger and frustration. Incidents of Luddite vandalism, rape and acts of **violent lawlessness** were used by opponents of the strike to panic the authorities, now better prepared, into **brutal repression**. The final tragedy came with the massacre in cold blood of 121 men by an army batallion, at Estancia La Anita. Later, the radicals introduced social security and pro-labour reforms.

By the end of the 1920s, Argentina was the **seventh richest nation** in the world, and confidence was sky high. Britain remained the country's major investor and market – as revealed in a confidential report by Sir Malcolm Robertson, Ambassador to Argentina, in 1929: "Argentina must be regarded as an essential part of the British Empire. We cannot get on without her, nor she without us." This was a nation that people predicted would challenge the United States in economic power. Within fifty years, however, Argentina had fallen to the status of a Third World power, and the loss of this golden dream of prosperity has haunted and perplexed the Argentine conscience ever since. This decline in status was not constant, but the world **depression** that followed the Wall Street Crash of 1929 marked one of the first serious blows. The effects of the crash and the collapse of export markets left the radical regime reeling and precipitated a **military takeover** in 1930 – an inauspicious omen of what was to come later in the century. The military restored power to the old, oligarchic elite, who ruled through a succession of coalition governments that gained a reputation for fraud and electoral corruption. Economic changes continued to shift away from the agrarian sector during this period, and by the late 1930s, the value of the manufacturing industry overtook that of agriculture for the first time. Immigration continued apace, with one important group being Jews, fleeing persecution in Germany.

RISE OF PERÓN

The first important real watershed of the twentieth century was the rise of **Juan Domingo Perón**, a charismatic military man of relatively modest origins who had risen through the ranks during the 1930s to attain the status of colonel. The outbreak of the **World War II** had repercussions in Argentina, though it chose to stay neutral. A split developed in the armed forces, with one faction favouring the Allies, and another larger one, the Axis powers. Not all who favoured an allegiance with the Axis were making a straightforward pro-Nazi endorsement, however: the motives of some, probably including Perón, were underpinned by a simmering anti-Americanism. Argentina had refused to join the Pan-American defensive alliance as a result of fiercely protectionist US trade restrictions, and its military had been enraged by the US selling arms to the country's old rival, Brazil.

Perón's involvement with politics intensified after a **military coup** in 1943, in which the army replaced a conservative coalition government that had come to be seen as self-serving and which was veering towards a declaration for support for the Allies. Perón's role was relatively minor at first, being appointed Secretary for Labour, but he used this post as a platform to cultivate links with trade unions. During an earlier spell as military attaché in Mussolini's Italy at the outbreak of war, he'd seen for himself the political momentum that could be generated by combining dynamic personal leadership with well-orchestrated mass rallies. The popularity of Perón alarmed his military superiors, who arrested him in 1945. However, this move backfired: Perón's wife, Evita, helped to organize the mass demonstrations that secured his release, generating the momentum that swept him to the **presidency** in the 1946 elections. His first term in government signalled a programme of radical social and political change, upon which the reputation and myths of the man largely rest.

Certainly, Perón's brand of fierce **nationalism** combined with an **authoritarian cult of the leader** bore many of the hallmarks of Fascism. Nevertheless, he assumed power by overwhelming democratic vote, and was seen by the poor as a saviour for the labour movement. Perón's scheme involved a type of "corporatism" that offered genuine improvements to the lives of the workers but, some would say, strengthened the ability to control them for the smooth running of the capitalist system. Perón saw strong **state intervention** as a way of melding the interests of labour and capital, and propounded the doctrine of **justicialismo**, or social justice, which soon began to be identified as **Peronism**. His administration passed a comprehensive programme of social welfare legislation that, amongst other things, granted workers a minimum wage, paid holidays and pension schemes, and established house-building programmes. These reforms could be paid for largely due to a healthy export trade of agricultural goods to a Europe still recovering from war. Popular support was mobilized through mighty trade unions like the General Confederation of Labour (CGT). He also supported **nationalization** and **industrialization**, in an attempt to render Argentina less dependent on foreign capital and less vulnerable to the depressions that periodically hit major European and American markets. One of the most significant acts of his administration was, in 1947, to nationalize the country's railway system, compensating its British owners to the tune of £150 million. In so doing, he also capitalized on a popular anti-British sentiment, which had been fostered over preceding generations by the disproportionate commercial influence wielded by the tiny class of British farming and industrial oligarchs. Nevertheless, some believe that he paid over the odds for outdated stock.

Controversy surrounds many other aspects of the regime too, and the man still has a great capacity to polarize opinion in Argentina. Dissident opinion had no place in his scheme: these years were marked by a **suppression** of the **free press**, increasingly heavy-handed control over institutions of higher education and the use of violent intimidation. He stifled political dissent by allowing only official unions, and inculcated a type of "industrial *caudillismo*", whereby strict loyalty to the party was the unwritten expectation for the gains apportioned to the masses. Though it is unclear to what extent he was personally involved, Perón's appar-

EVITA PERÓN

Evita Perón, in true rags-to-riches style, began life humbly. She was born María Eva Duarte in 1919, the fifth illegitimate child of Juana Ibarguren and Juan Duarte, a landowner in the rural interior of Buenos Aires. She was raised in poverty by her mother, Duarte abandoning the family before Evita reached 1. At the age of 15, she headed to the capital to pursue her dream of becoming an actress, and managed to scrape a living from several minor roles in radio and television before working her way into higher profile leading roles through the influence of well-connected lovers. Her life was to change dramatically, when, in 1944, she first met Juan Perón, then Secretary of Labour in the military government. She became his mistress and married him a year later, shortly before his election to the presidency.

As First Lady, Evita was in her element. She championed the rights of the working classes and underprivileged poor, who she named her **descamisados** ("shirtless ones"), immersed herself in populist politics and programmes of social aid. In person, she would receive petitions from individual members of the public, distributing favours on a massive scale through her powerful and wealthy instrument of patronage, the Social Aid Foundation. She played the feminine role of the devoted wife, but was, in many ways, a pioneering feminist of Argentine society, and has been credited with assuring that women were finally granted suffrage in 1947. She yearned to legitimize her political role through direct election, but resentment amongst the military forced her to pull out of running for the position of Vice President to her husband in the election of 1951.

Another role she revelled in was as glamorous **ambassador** for her country, captivating a star-struck press and public during her 1948 tour of postwar Europe, during which she was granted an audience with the pope. Hers was the international face of Argentina, which assuredly compounded the jealousy of Europhile upper-class women at home, as none of their number had ever been accorded such fame abroad. Evita was detested by the Argentine elite as a vulgar upstart who respected neither their rank nor customary protocol. They painted her as a whore and as someone who was more interested in feeding her own personality cult than assisting the *descamisados*. Evita, for her part, seemed to revel in antagonizing the oligarchic establishment, whipping up popular resentment towards an "anti-Argentine" class.

Stricken by **cancer** of the uterus, she died in 1952, at the age of only 33. Her death was greeted with the kind of mass outpourings of grief never seen in Argentina, before or since. Eight people were crushed to death in the crowds of mourners that gathered the next day, and over two thousand needed treatment for injuries. In death, Evita led an even more rarefied existence than she had in life. After the military coup of 1955, the military made decoy copies of her **embalmed corpse** and spirited the original away to Europe, all too aware of its power as an icon and focus for political dissent. There followed a truly bizarre series of burials, reburials and even allegations of necrophilia, before it was repatriated in 1974, during Perón's third administration and, later, afforded a decent burial in Recoleta Cemetery. This story is examined in Tomás Eloy Martínez's best-seller, *Santa Evita* (1995). To this day, Evita retains a saint-like status amongst many traditionalist, working-class Peronists, some of whom maintain altars to her in their homes. Protests and furiou0s graffiti greeted the casting of Madonna, fresh from a series of pornographic photoshoots, to portray her in the Alan Parker film musical, *Evita*. For many, this was sacrilege – an insult to the memory of the most important woman of Argentine history.

ent willingness to provide a haven for Nazi refugees has also cast a blemish on his, and his country's, reputation. Adolf Eichmann was one of the most notorious war criminals to find refuge here and, much more recently, Erich Priebke was extradited from Bariloche to Italy for atrocities committed in wartime Rome. A recent report has revealed that fewer Nazis actually fled to Argentina than the popular imagination suspects though, listing the number as 180, most of whom were Croats, not Germans.

PERÓN'S SECOND TERM

Perón, in 1949, secured a Constitutional amendment that allowed him to run for a **second term**. Though he won by a landslide in the elections of 1951, his position was severely weakened by the death of his wife, who had been one of his principal political assets. By this time, the cult of personality that had swept him to power and fed his reputation could no longer disguise the fact that his administration was losing political impetus. He faced dissent within the army, resentful at what they saw as the subordination of their role during Evita's lifetime. He had also incited the wrath of the powerful Catholic Church, whose privileges he had attacked. In addition, his successful wealth redistribution policies had alienated wealthy sectors of society whilst raising the expectations of the less well-off – expectations that he found increasingly difficult to fulfil, especially with declining agricultural revenues. Agriculture had been allowed to stagnate in preference to industrial development, and this helped cause a severe imbalance of payments, which caused inflation and precipitated economic recession.

THE MILITARY IN POLITICS: 1955-73

Against a background of strikes and civil unrest, factions within the military rebelled in 1955, with the tacit support of a broad coalition of those interests that Perón had alienated, including the Church and the oligarchy. In the **Revolución Libertadora**, or Revolution of Liberation, he was ousted from power and went into exile, to the delight of his enemies. The initial backlash against Peronism was swift and stinging: General Aramburu banned it as a political movement, Peronist iconography and statues were stripped from public places, and even

mention of his name was forbidden. There followed eighteen years of alternate military and short-lived civilian regimes like those of the Radicals Arturo Frondizi and Arturo Illia that lurched from one crisis to another with little in the way of effectual long-term policies. Civilian administrations were dependent on the backing of the military, which itself was unsure of how to align itself with the Peronist legacy and the trade unions. Much of the 1960s was characterized by economic stagnation, strikes, wage freezes and a growing disillusionment of the populace with the institutions of government. Throughout this time, Perón hovered in the background, in exile in Spain, cultivating dissidence amongst the trade unions, and providing a focus for opposition to the military.

In 1966, a **military coup** led by General Juan Carlos Onganía saw the imposition of austere measures to stabilize the economy, and repression to keep a tight reign on political dissent. This was not without consequences, and, in the city of radical politics, Córdoba, tension eventually exploded into violence in May 1969. In what has become known as the **Cordobazo**, left-wing student protesters and car-worker trade unionists sparked off a spree of general rioting that lasted for two days, left many people dead, and the authorities profoundly shaken. Onganía's position was becoming less and less tenable and, with unrest spreading throughout the country and an economic crisis that provoked devaluation, he was deposed by the army.

It was about this time that society saw the emergence of **guerrilla** organizations, which crystallized, over the course of the early 1970s, into two main groups: the People's Revolutionary Army (Ejército Revolucionario del Pueblo or **ERP**), which was a movement committed to radical international revolution in the style of Trotsky or Che Guevara; and the **Montoneros**, which was a more urban movement that espoused revolution on a more distinctly national model, extrapolated from left-wing traits within Peronism. Multinationals, landed oligarchies and the security forces were favoured Montonero targets.

THE RETURN OF PERÓN AND THE COLLAPSE OF DEMOCRACY

By 1973, the army seemed to have recognized that its efforts to engineer some sort of national unity had failed. The economy continued to splutter into recession, guerrilla violence was spreading and the incidence of military repression and torture was rising. army leader, General Lanusse, decided to risk calling an election, and in an attempt to heal the long-standing national divide, permitted the Peronist party – but not Perón himself – to stand. Perón, then living in Spain, nominated a proxy candidate, **Héctor Cámpora**, to stand in his place. Cámpora emerged victorious, but resigned almost immediately, which forced a reluctant military to allow Perón himself to return to stand in new elections.

By this time, Perón had come to represent all things to all men. Radical left-wing Montoneros saw themselves as true Peronists – the natural upholders of the type of Peronism that championed the rights of the *descamisados* and freedom from imperialist domination. Likewise, conservative landed groups saw him as a symbol of stability in the face of anarchy. Any illusion that Perón was going to be the cure-all balm for the nation's ills dissipated before touchdown at Ezeiza international airport. Like a group of unsuspecting wives assembled to greet a secret polygamist, his welcoming party dissolved into a violent melee, with rival groups in the crowd of 500,000 shooting at each other. No one is sure just how many people were killed in the melee, though the total is thought to be in three figures rather than the official figure of 25.

As his running mate, Perón chose a former actress from Venezuela – his third wife, María Estela Martínez de Perón, commonly known as **Isabelita**.

He was now 78, and his health was failing. Though he won the elections with ease, his third term was to last less than nine months, ending with his death in July 1974. Power devolved to Isabelita, who thus became the world's first woman premier. Isabel Perón managed to make a bitterly divided nation agree on at least one thing: that her regime was a catastrophic failure. Rudderless, out of her depth as regards policy, and with no bedrock of support, the unelected Isabelita clung increasingly desperately to the advice of José López Rega, a shadowy figure who became compared to Rasputin. Rega's prime notoriety stems from having founded the feared right-wing **death squads** (the Triple "A", or Alianza Argentina Anticomunista) that targeted left-wing intellectuals and guerrilla sympathizers. The only boom industry, it seemed, was corruption in govern-

ment, and with hyperinflation and spiralling violence, the country was gripped by paralysis.

TOTALITARIANISM, THE PROCESO AND THE DIRTY WAR

The long-expected **military coup** finally came in March of 1976, and so twentieth-century Argentine history entered its darkest phase. Under **General Jorge Videla**, a military junta initiated what it termed the Process of National Reorganization (usually known as the **Proceso**), which is more often referred to as the Guerra Sucia, or Dirty War.

In the minds of the military, there was only one response to guerrilla opposition: an iron fist. Any attempt to combat it through the normal judicial process was seen as superfluous and sure to result in failure. They therefore bypassed this and suspended the Constitution, unleashing a campaign of systematic violence with the full apparatus of the state at their disposal. In the language of chauvinistic patriotism, they invoked the Doctrine of National Security to justify what they saw as part of the war against international Communism. These events were set against the background of **Cold War** politics, and the generals received covert CIA support. Apart from guerrillas and anyone suspected of harbouring guerrilla sympathies, those who were targeted included liberal intellectuals, journalists, psychologists, Jews, Marxists, trade unionists, atheists and anyone who, in the words of Videla, "spreads ideas that are contrary to Western and Christian civilization".

The most notorious tactic was to send hit squads to make people "disappear". Once seized, these **desaparecidos** simply ceased to exist – no one knew who abducted them or where they were, and all writs of *habeas corpus* were ignored. In fact, the *desaparecidos* were taken to secret detention camps – places like the infamous Navy Mechanics School (ESMA) – where they were subjected to torture, rape and, usually, execution. Many victims were taken up in planes and thrown, drugged and weighted with concrete, into the River Plate. Most victims were aged between their late teens and thirties, but no one was exempt, including pregnant women and the handicapped. Jacobo Timerman, in *Prisoner Without a Name, Cell Without a Number* (1981), an account of his experiences in a torture centre, gives an insight into the mind of one of his interrogators, who

AN HISTORICAL DISPUTE: THE FALKLAND ISLANDS/ISLAS MALVINAS

Any British person travelling around Argentina is certain to become involved, at some point, in a discussion on the islands known to Brits as the **Falklands**, and to Argentines as **Las Malvinas**. The mere mention of British nationality brings up the mental association, and Brits are likely to hear the word several times a day. From the cradle – and with a fervour little short of indoctrination – Argentines are brought up being taught that the islands are Argentine. At every single point of entry to the country, visitors are greeted with a sign declaring *Las Malvinas Son Argentinas* – "the Malvinas are Argentine" – and, in 1999, a poll for the newspaper *Clarín* showed that only 14 percent of Argentines believe that solving the "Malvinas problem" is not important. In the vast majority of cases, these conversations are polite and usually very interesting. Only on extremely rare occasions is it raised in an antagonistic way: in these cases, it's best simply to avoid the subject and you won't have a problem. Come what may, it is always worth familiarizing yourself with the history of the islands and some of the resultant sovereignty issues.

The islands lie some 12,500km from Britain and 550km off the coast of Argentina. Disputes have raged as to who first discovered them, but the first verifiable sighting comes from the Dutch sailor, Seebald de Weert, who sailed past here in 1600. In 1690, Captain John Strong discovered the strait that divides the two major islands in the group, and christened the archipelago the "Falkland Islands", after Viscount Falkland, the Commissioner of the British Admiralty at the time.

French sailors from St Malo made numerous expeditions to the islands from 1698, naming them the Malouines after their home port, from which derives the Argentine toponomy of Islas Malvinas. The first serious attempt at settlement came with a French expedition sponsored by Louis de Bougainville, which established a base at a place they named Port St Louis in 1764. A year later, claiming ignorance of the French settlement, a small party of British sailors settled Port Egmont nearby, and claimed the islands for George III. The founding of this humble settlement was part of a wider strategy to break the Spanish monopoly over trade in the "Spanish Sea" – the Pacific – as it could act as a South Atlantic staging post for ships heading round the Horn. The Spanish, at this time, believed they had legal title to the area dating from the famous 1494 Treaty of Tordesillas, arranged by the papacy that divided the Americas between Spain and Portugal. (The British later claimed that this treaty was invalid as it rested on a papal authority they no longer recognized.) Though annoyed by the French settlement, Spain was reluctant to come to blows with an ally, and negotiated a settlement: Bougainville was paid off and, in 1767, St Louis was surrendered to a Spanish contingent. In 1770, the Spanish evicted the British

colony – an act that raised international tensions and caused the British to reassert their presence. In 1774, the British were persuaded to abandon their colony (although not, they would later maintain, their claims to sovereignty), at the same time that Spain agreed to cede control of Florida. The Spanish maintained a presence on the islands until 1811, when the garrison was withdrawn in order to combat pro-independence fighters in the mainland continental colonies.

In 1820, the newly independent Argentinian federation asserted what it viewed as the right to inherit the sovereign Spanish title to the islands. This was not, initially, contested by the British, but in the late 1820s Britain started to make noises again about reasserting its sovereignty claim: the desire to establish a marine base to carry out trade with its Australian colony as well as a need to prevent "piracy" and sealing/whaling rights being the driving forces. The self-appointed Argentine governor of the islands, **Luis Vernet**, had made attempts to impose restrictions on US and British sealers as regards the numbers of seals and wild cattle they culled and impounded three US sealing vessels. In response, in 1831, the US consul in Buenos Aires had sent a punitive expedition against him, and later, in 1833, the consul colluded with the British in the expulsion of the Argentine colony. The Argentinian federation, paralysed by internal disputes, was powerless to prevent the British from taking the islands. Britain established a base on the islands, and its colony developed significantly after the establishment, in 1851, of the Falkland Islands Company and with the beginnings of serious commercial exploitation: from the mid-1860s with the establishment of sheep farming and, as the century wore on, the boom in whaling and animal oil (elephant seal and penguin) industries. By 1871 there were already 800 people living in Port Stanley.

In April 1982, faced with severe domestic unrest, rampant inflation and high unemployment, Argentine General, Leopold Galtieri saw the opportunity to divert attention away from his junta's failed domestic policies by organizing a military crusade to liberate the islands. Far from noticing the signs of the impending invasion, the British actually contributed to Galtieri's mood of optimism by making preparations for the scrapping of HMS *Endurance*, the UK's only naval presence in the South Atlantic, an event interpreted by Galtieri as signalling that Britain was preparing to withdraw from the region. Galtieri, whose military regime was actively supported by the Reagan administration, believed he could count on US support: a miscalculation as it turned out. However, the most serious error of judgement was that he believed Britain would acquiesce in the face of an invasion. As far as the self-styled Iron Lady, Margaret Thatcher, was concerned, however, the invasion was a gift given her own domestic political problems at that time.

Following the arrival of the British Task Force, the conflict was mercifully short. The military struggle was unequal: poorly equipped, inadequately trained Argentine teenagers on military service, many from subtropical provinces like Corrientes and Misiones, were expected to combat hardened professional paratroopers more than capable of withstanding a harsh Pacific winter. The airforce was the only branch of the Argentine armed forces that was deemed to have acquitted itself well, sinking several British ships. However, the most significant ship to be sunk was an Argentinian one. In what proved the worst atrocity of the war, the *General Belgrano* was torpedoed outside the British-imposed naval exclusion zone, leading to the death of nearly four hundred Argentinian sailors. Whatever their position on the sovereignty issue and the validity of the war, this one event is still viewed with bitterness amongst Argentinians.

More than a thousand people perished in the 74-day war, and negotiations on the sovereignty issue were set back decades. At the time of the invasion, the islands were essentially a forgotten, far-off British colony that had long suffered economic stagnation and a dearth of infrastructure development. Indeed, what infrastructure projects there had been in the 1970s had been built by the Argentinians, including the airport. This process of gradual integration into the Argentinian economic sphere, encouraged by the British, stopped abruptly with the war.

The British Foreign Office's Shackleton Report of the late 1970s demonstrated that the islands were what they seemed: a monoculture colonial outpost that provided Britain with twice the value in wool exports of anything that it got in return. The report revealed a lamentable state of dependent tenant farming, with virtually non-existent opportunities for smallholders. The Falkland Islands Company owned half the land and half the sheep, employed a third of the workforce and was in control of all crucial sectors of the economy, including banking, shipping, wholesale and retail trade. Democratic institutions were highly paternalistic: the governor was appointed from Britain, the islanders had little say in the running of their own affairs, and only a third of the population were entitled to a full British passport. Foreign office documents from the 1930s show that Britain had secretly recognized that its legal claims to the islands were shaky, and there were attempts in the late 1960s to transfer sovereignty to Argentina. These had to be abandoned after plans were

leaked prematurely, but even as late as 1981, Thatcher's own government was seriously looking at the issue, analysing solutions such as a lease-back agreement similar to the one that existed with Hong Kong.

The monumental miscalculation that was the 1982 invasion ensured that much of the middle ground was lost. Whether Britain would like to engage in talks on sovereignty or not, the issue has been a non-starter since then, due to the oft-stated primacy of the islanders' desires to remain allied to Britain. However, the sovereignty issue will not simply disappear. Options have been put forward that attempt to bridge the gap between the islanders' right to determine their own future and Argentina's historical case for recognition of sovereignty. And, in many respects, the relationship between the islanders and the Argentines is getting closer. Economic treaties (which are definitely in the long-term interests of both the islands and the islanders) have been signed that pave the way for co-operation with regards to prospecting for suspected offshore oil deposits, and in the exploitation of fishing grounds (rich in krill, hake, cod and squid). The detention of Pinochet in Britain in 1998 was a twist that gave further impetus to bilateral talks, since crucial flight links between Chile and the islands were temporarily severed in protest at the arrest. In July 1999, Britain and Argentina signed an accord renewing flight links between Argentina and the islands and permitting Argentinian civilians to visit war graves without needing special permission. This provoked protest by certain radical groups on both sides. In August 1999, the first flight to come from Chile via Argentina caused much interest and controversy. The visitors were given a frosty reception by a group of islanders, but there were also many signs of a reconciliation, and the trip saw the return to the islands of the first Argentinian war veteran, who came this time in the capacity of a journalist. There are plans to dedicate some kind of war memorial to the Argentinian casualties of the conflict.

As yet, there is no change on the respective position of both countries as regards the issue of sovereignty, but both countries are determined that dialogue and co-operation, and not the politics of confrontation, should be the way forward. For too long, the islands have been used as a political football: a *cause célèbre* in Argentinian domestic politics that has frequently been abused for the sake of posturing, and an issue whose complexities have been clouded by ignorance on both sides.

Visiting the islands

To visit the islands, you have two principal options. First, some of the Antarctic cruise ships from Ushuaia stop here. A less expensive way, although by no means cheap, is to fly from Punta Arenas in Chile, or join at this service's once-monthly stopover in Río Gallegos (second Sat of the month, returns following Sat). Tourism on the island centres on vis-

its to the internationally important wildlife sites, where you'll see colonies of Magellanic, rockhopper and jackass penguins plus other abundant species of marine birds and mammals. For more details, contact the Falkland Islands Tourist Board, Falklands House, Broadway, London SW1 (☎020/7222-2542; *www.tourism.org.fk*).

told him: "Only God gives and takes life. But God is busy elsewhere, and we're the ones who must undertake this task in Argentina." Adolfo Pérez Esquivel, a practitioner of non-violence, was detained and tortured – which didn't do much for the military junta's PR, since he was awarded the Nobel Peace Prize in 1980 on issues unrelated to Argentina, and had already been a nominee when he was taken in.

In the midst of this, the armed forces had the opportunity to demonstrate the "success" of their regime to the world, by hosting the **1978 World Cup**. Though victory of the Argentine team in the final stoked nationalist pride, few observers were fooled into seeing this as a reflection of the achievements of the military. Indeed, the event backfired on the military in other ways. The vast expense of hosting the project (some $700 million – money sorely needed for other social development projects) exacerbated the national debt and compounded the regime's economic problems. In addition, it provided a forum for human-rights advocates, including a courageous new group called the **Madres de Plaza de Mayo**, to bring the issue of the *desaparecidos* to the attention of the international media. The Mothers of the Plaza de Mayo were one of the few groups to challenge the regime directly, organizing silent weekly demonstrations in Buenos Aires' historic central square demanding to know the whereabouts of their missing family members. Their protests have continued to the present day.

By the end of 1978, the most brutal phase of the violence had finished and the guerrilla movements had been effectively smashed, though the disappearances continued, and Argentina remained gripped by a climate of suspicion and fear. A slight softening of Videla's extremist stance came when **General Roberto Viola** took control of the army in 1978 and then the presidency of the junta in 1981. That same year, hardliners under **General Leopoldo Galtieri** forced him out. The military's grip on the country, by this time, was beginning to look increasingly shaky, with the economy in severe recession, skyrocketing interest rates, and the first mass demonstrations against the regime since its imposition in 1976. Galtieri, with no other cards left to play, chose this moment, April 2, 1982, to play his trump: an **invasion of the Falkland Islands**, or **Islas Malvinas** as they are known to the Argentines. Nothing

could have been more certain to bring a unified sense of purpose to the nation, and the population reacted with ecstatic delight. This, however, soon turned to dismay when people realized that the British government was prepared to go to war to reconquer the islands, and Argentine forces had been defeated by mid-June (see box, p.712). The military had proved incapable of mastering politics, they had proved disastrous stewards of the economy, and now they had suffered ignominious failure doing what they were supposed to be specialists at: fighting a foreign enemy. Perhaps the only positive thing to come out of this futile war was that it was the final spur for Argentines to throw off the shackles of their unwanted military regime.

While the junta prepared to hand over to civilian control, **General Reynaldo Bignone**, successor to Galtieri, issued a decree that pronounced an amnesty for all members of the armed forces for any alleged human-rights atrocity.

ALFONSÍN AND THE RESTORATION OF DEMOCRACY

Democracy was finally restored with the elections of October 1983, which were won by the radical, **Raúl Alfonsín** – the first time that the Peronist party had been defeated at the polls. Alfonsín, a lawyer much respected for his record on human rights, inherited a highly volatile and precarious political panorama. He faced two great challenges: the first, to attempt to build some sort of national concord after the bitter divisions of the 1970s; and the second, to restore a shattered economy, where inflation was running at over 400 percent and the foreign debt was over $40,000 million. In the midst of this, Alfonsín solved the politically sensitive border dispute with Chile over the three islands in the Beagle Channel – **Picton**, **Nueva** and **Lennox** – which had threatened to bring the two posturing military dictatorships to the brink of full-scale war in 1978. Papal arbitration had awarded the islands to Chile, but Alfonsín ensured, in 1984, that the mechanism for approving this was by public referendum.

The issue of prosecuting those responsible for crimes against humanity during the dictatorship proved an intractable one that Alfonsín, despite his skills of diplomatic compromise, had no chance of resolving to everyone's satisfaction. Alfonsín set up a **National Commission** on **Disappeared People** (CONADEP), under the presidency of the respected writer, Ernesto Sábato, to investigate the alleged atrocities. Their report, *Nunca Más* – or "Never Again" – documented 9000 cases of torture and disappearance, although it is generally accepted that the figure for the number of deaths during the Dirty War was actually closer to 30,000. In no uncertain terms, it recommended that those responsible be brought to trial. Those convicted in the first wave of **trials** after the report's initial findings included the reviled Videla, Viola, Galtieri, and Admiral Emilio Massera, one of the most despised figures of the junta. All were sentenced to life imprisonment.

Military sensibilities were offended by the proposed trials: defeat in the South Atlantic War had discredited them but, rather like a wounded dog, they could still pose considerable danger to the fragile, emergent democracy. While Alfonsín was willing to provoke a few growls, he felt he couldn't risk full confrontation. In 1986, he caved into militery pressure and passed "End Point" legislation (*Punto Final*), which put a final date for the submission of writs for human-rights crimes. However, in a window of two months, the courts were flooded with such writs, and, for the first time, the courts indicted officers who were still in active service. Several short-lived uprisings forced Alfonsín to pull back from pursuing widespread prosecutions. In 1987, the **Law of Due Obedience** (*Obediencia Debida*) was passed, granting an amnesty to all but the leaders for atrocities committed during the dictatorship. At a stroke, this reduced the number of people facing charges from 370 to less than 50. This incensed the victims relatives, who saw notorious torturers such as "The Angel of Death", Alfredo Astiz – the man who attained international notoriety through the brutal murder of the French nuns – escape prosecution.

As for the economy, Alfonsín managed to secure some respite from international creditors by restructuring the national debt and, in 1985, introducing a platform of stringent austerity measures, which were received with bitterness by many sectors of the population who had seen the restoration of democracy as a panacea for all their ills. These measures, named the **Plan Austral** in reference to the new currency that was to be introduced, were essential, however, with inflation running at well over a thousand

percent annually. The government continued to be crippled by **hyperinflation**, however, even after the introduction of a second raft of belt-tightening measures, the *Australito*, in 1987. The inflationary crisis turned to meltdown in 1989, when the World Bank suspended all loans: many shops remained closed, preferring to keep their stock rather than selling it for a currency whose value disappeared before their eyes. In supermarkets, purchasers would have to listen to the tannoy to hear the latest prices, which would often change in the time it took to take an item from the shelf to the checkout. Elections were called in 1989, but, with severe **civil unrest** breaking out across the country, Alfonsín called a state of siege and stood down early, handing control to his elected successor, **Carlos Saúl Menem**. This was the first time since 1928 that power had transferred, after a free election, from one civilian government to another.

MENEM'S FIRST TERM: 1989–95

The 1990s was a decade dominated by Carlos Menem – the son of Syrian immigrant parents – and was an era characterized by radical reforms and hefty doses of controversy. Menem had been governor of a relatively minor province in the interior of the country, La Rioja, at the outbreak of military rule in 1976 and, as a Peronist, he had spent most of the dictatorship in detention or under house arrest. His **Justicialist Party** (*Partido Justicialista* or PJ) was Peronist in name but – once elected in 1989 – not in nature, and he was to embark on a series of sweeping **neo-Liberal reforms** that reversed virtually all planks of traditional Peronism.

His most lauded achievement is that he finally slew one of Argentina's most persistent bugbears – **inflation**. This he achieved in 1991–92. With the backing of international finance organizations, Menem and his Finance Minister, **Domingo Cavallo**, introduced the **Convertibility Plan** (*Plan de Convertibilidad*). At the beginning of 1992, this pegged a **new currency** (the new Argentinian peso, worth 10,000 australes) at parity with the US dollar, and guaranteed its value by prohibiting the Central Bank from printing money that it couldn't cover at any one time with its federal reserves. Inflation, which at one point was running at 200 percent per month, had fallen to an annual rate of eight percent by 1993.

Throughout the 1990s, inflation remained in single figures.

The next stage of economic reform was one that horrified traditional Peronists: Menem's administration abandoned the principal of state ownership and the dogma of state intervention. The 1990s saw the **privatization** of all the major nationalized utilities and industries, many of which were moribund and a desperate drag on government finance. Electricity, gas, the telephone network, Aerolíneas Argentinas and even the profitable YPF, the state-owned petroleum company, were sold off, and this time, investment came primarily from Spanish, not British, corporations.

Free-market development policies also saw the cessation of all Federal railway subsidies in 1993 (a move that signalled the end of Argentina's love affair with the train); and the introduction of massive **public spending cuts**. In 1995, many regional trade barriers fell, as a consequence of the full implementation of the **Mercosur** trading agreement. This created a **free-trade block** of Southern Cone countries – Brazil, Argentina, Uruguay and Paraguay, with Chile developing close ties later on.

These economic readjustments caused seismic reverberations throughout Argentine society. Although people trusted the peso, huge numbers had none to spend. The downsizing of newly privatized industries and the removal of protective tariffs caused unemployment rates to rise to eighteen percent, but underemployment also became endemic, and acute financial hardship resulted in strikes and sporadic civil unrest, as more and more people fell beneath the poverty line.

One thing about Menem's Peronism that stayed faithful to Juan Perón's original was the style of government. A cavalier **populist**, Menem never stinted in trying to develop the "cult of the leader". He portrayed himself as a "man of the people", modelling his image on that of a provincial caudillo such as Facundo Quiroga, the famous La Riojan warlord of the 1830s. Not known for his modesty, he preached austerity at a time when he seemed to be developing a penchant for the life of a playboy.

The president increasingly became associated with trying to rule by **decree**. One of his most controversial aspects of this policy was the issuing of executive **amnesties** in 1989 to those guilty of atrocities during the 1970s.

Although the amnesty included ex-guerrillas, public outrage centred on the release of former members of the military junta, including all the leading generals. To Menem it was the pragmatic price to pay to secure cooperation of the military; to virtually the rest of the country, it was a flagrant moral capitulation.

In August 1994, he secured a **constitutional amendment** that allowed a sitting president to stand for a second term, although the mandate was reduced from six years to four. Voters, trusting Menem's economic record, elected him to a second term.

MENEM'S SECOND TERM

One of the hallmarks of Menem's second term as president was the increasing **venality** of an administration that had lost much of its earlier reforming impetus. In 1996, he sacked Domingo Cavallo – ostensibly for his unwillingness to counter greater state intervention in the economy, but some say because he saw his powerful minister of the economy as a potential rival. This move backfired to an extent, as Cavallo formed a new political party, the Acción por la República which, though never gaining much of a power base, served to bring the issue of corruption in government into higher public focus.

Human-rights issues continued to surface on the front-line agenda, despite Menem's attempts to stifle the issue. One of the most important developments was the start of a campaign to prosecute those guilty of having "**kidnapped**" **babies** of *desaparecidos* born in detention in order to give them up for adoption to childless military couples. This crime, not covered by the Punto Final legislation of Alfonsín's years, has resulted in the successful interrogation and detention of many of the leading members of the old junta, including Videla and Massera. Tension still simmers in minority factions of the military about this issue, although the armed forces in general are now very much subordinate to the civilian authorities. In the mid-1990s, the armed forces did, belatedly, acknowledge their role in the atrocities of the dictatorship, making a **public apology** – a symbolic act that was followed by similar repentance by the Catholic Church.

The economic situation remained on a knife-edge, with austerity measures seeming to apply to anyone not in government, and a foreign debt that continued to balloon. When, at the beginning of 1999, Brazil's currency lost fifty percent of its value, the government had to resist acute pressure to devalue the peso. Convertibility held, but Menem announced that Argentina ought seriously to consider the "**dollarization**" of the economy – an issue that would have severe ramifications on national pride. In the field of **foreign policy**, Menem proved himself able to rise above rhetoric. This included a significant *rapprochement* with Britain over the Falklands (see p.712); and in 1999, he finally secured ratification of a treaty with Chile conceding sovereignty over a disputed part of the Southern Patagonian Icecap in the southeast of the Parque Nacional Los Glaciares – the last of continental Argentina's **border disputes**.

As the end of his second term approached, the president indulged in an undignified display of political chicanery. This saw him moot the possibility of him running for a third consecutive term of office, by arguing that, although his own constitutional amendment of 1994 allowed a sitting president to stand for re-election only once, he had only enjoyed one full term of government since that amendment had been passed. The real issue here was not really whether he genuinely intended to stand or not – but that, it was widely felt, it was all bluster designed to alienate voters and to scupper the chances of fellow member of the Justicialist Party, Eduardo Duhalde, in the forthcoming election. Duhalde, as Governor of Buenos Aires Province, was the favoured candidate to replace the dead duck Menem and lead the election fight. However, Menem, who increasingly seems to treat the party as his own dynastic fief, apparently preferred the Justicialists to lose the election rather than see himself lose the position of party leader. This would then clear the way for himself to stand in the elections of 2003. The tactic certainly seemed to work: the shenanigans of the so-called *re-re-eleccionistas* alienated the populace from the Peronists still further, in the run up to the vote in 1999.

Fernando de la Rua, mayor of the city of Buenos Aires, won the candidacy of the **Alianza** (Alliance Party). The Alianza formed out of a coalition between the radicals (UCR), of which he was leader, and **FREPASO**, itself a coalition party of left-wingers and disaffected Peronists that rose to prominence in the 1995 election. A third coalition party involved in the elections was the National Action Party (PAN), led by ex-Minister of Finance, Domingo Cavallo, and running on a platform of fiscal responsibility, and, crucially, anti-corruption – the theme that dominated the election. With the desire for change palpable across the country, Fernando de la Rua, the candidate for the Alianza, won a clear mandate. Duhalde, embittered, vowed to continue what has become a personal vendetta against Menem.

THE CURRENT SITUATION

De la Rua's personality stands in complete contrast to that of the flamboyant Menem. He is known for his **steadiness** rather than his charisma and, in 1999, he seemed to represent the fiscal and moral probity that Argentines, tired of the excesses of Menem's administration in its later years, felt their country needed. Hopes for a complete overhaul of the political scenery were stifled by the fact that Carlos Ruckauf, ex-Vice President to Menem, won the governorship of the immensely influential and populous province of Buenos Aires. Though Ruckauf is no close personal ally of Menem's, it was evident that the Alianza would have to seek some pragmatic compromise with the Justicialistas in order to govern effectively.

Amid widespread rumours of a secret pact that assured political co-operation in return for not investigating him personally for corruption, Menem gave the Alianza his blessing, and handed over the burden of a colossal foreign debt.

At the beginning of the millennium, the immediate outlook is one not far removed from what came at the end of the last. Eager not to upset the money markets, the de la Rua administration has implemented austerity measures demanded by the IMF, cutting back hard on public workers' salaries. The spectre of **devaluation** is ever-present, although many argue that this might be exactly what the economy needs to kick-start economic growth. The high value of the peso means that it's a constant challenge to keep Argentinian exports competitively priced, which has become especially noticeable since its most important trading partner, Brazil, devalued its currency. Unemployment continues to be high, and violent social protests have hit provinces such as Neuquén, Salta and Corrientes. De la Rua's administration faces a stern test.

WILDLIFE AND THE ENVIRONMENT

Argentina's natural wonders are one of its chief joys. Its remarkable diversity of habitats, ranging from subtropical jungles to subantarctic icesheets, is complemented by an unexpected juxtaposition of species: parrots foraging alongside glaciers, or shocking-pink flamingos surviving bitter sub-zero temperatures on the stark Andean Altiplano. However, despite the protection afforded by a relatively well-managed national park system and several highly committed environmental pressure groups, many of the country's ecosystems are under threat.

Argentina is one of the world's leading destinations for ornithologists, with over a thousand species of **birds** – ten percent of the world's total – having been recorded here. It also has several destinations where you can reliably spot mammals and other fauna, notably the Esteros de Iberá swampland in Corrientes and the Península Valdés coastal reserve in Chubut, although for the most part you'll require patience and luck to see the country's more exotic denizens. Though the divisions are too complicated to list fully here, we've covered Argentina's most distinctive habitats below, along with the species of flora and fauna typical to each.

The country's precious environmental heritage is under threat on numerous fronts, however. Illegal hunting is often hard to control but, as ever, by far and away the most pressing issue is **habitat loss**. The chaco is a good case in point. Whereas environments such as the wet chaco have long felt the strain of population and land clearance, pressures have increased at an alarming rate in the dry chaco. Previously, the lack of water in the *Impenetrable* was the flora and fauna's best asset. Nowadays, climate change has seen rainfall levels increase, and irrigation projects are fast opening up areas of the *Impenetrable* to settlement and agriculture, with a continued, desperately poorly controlled exploitation of mature woodland for timber or charcoal and **land clearance** (*desmonte*) for crops such as cotton. This comes on top of a century of ruthlessly exploitive forestry by companies such as the British owned El Forestal, which completely transformed the habitat of entire provinces – Santiago del Estero, for example, saw the export of an estimated 240 million railway sleepers of *quebracho colorado* in the space of seventy years. Forestry in other areas of the country – notably in Misiones and Tierra del Fuego – is also giving cause for alarm. **Hydroelectric projects** in the northeast of the country have destroyed valuable habitats along the Urugua'í and Paraná rivers, and **overfishing** has severely depleted stocks in the latter and in the ocean, where controls are notoriously lax.

Fortunately, though, the outlook isn't completely bleak. Environmental consciousness is slowly gaining ground (especially amongst the younger generation); the national parks system is expanding with the help of international loans; and committed national and local pressure groups such as the Fundación de Vida Silvestre and Asociación Ornitológica del Plata (both based in Buenos Aires), Proyecto Lemú (based in Epuyén), Finis Terrae (based in Ushuaia) and Proyecto Orca (based in Puerto Madryn) are ensuring that ecological issues do not get ignored.

PAMPAS GRASSLANDS AND THE ESPINAL

The vast alluvial plain centred on Buenos Aires Province, and radiating out into eastern Córdoba, southern Santa Fé and the northeast of La Pampa Province, was originally pampas grassland, essentially treeless and famous for its clumps of brush-tailed *cortadera* pampas grass. However, its deep, extremely fertile soils has seen it become the agricultural heart of modern Argentina, and this habitat has almost entirely disappeared, transformed by cattle grazing and intensive arable farming, and by the planting of introduced trees such as eucalyptus. It's still possible to find a few vestiges of marshlands and grasslands, such as the area of tall *stipa* grassland around Médanos, to the southwest of Bahía Blanca.

Bordering the pampas grasslands to the north and west, across the centre of Corrientes, Entre Ríos, Santa Fé, Córdoba and San Luis provinces, is a semicircular fringe of **espinal woodland**, a type of open wooded "parkland" scenery. Common species of tree include **acacia** and, in the north, the ñandubay and **ceibo**, Argentina's national tree, which in spring produces a profusion of scarlet, chilli-pepper-like blooms. In the north, espinal scenery mixes in places with the swamps and marshes of Mesopotamia, and intermixes with Monte Desert in the south.

The only type of habitat endemic to Argentina is the narrow strip of so-called **monte scrub** that is found in the arid, sunny intermontane valleys that lie in the rainshadow of the central Andes. They run from northern Patagonia through the Cuyo region and northwards as far as Salta Province, where in some places they separate the humid yungas from the high-mountain *puna*. Monte scrub is characterized by thorny, chest-high *jarilla* bushes, which flower yellow in spring. In the Andean foothills and floodplains of the Mendoza region, much of this desert monte has been irrigated and replaced with vineyards. It's an interesting habitat from a wildlife point of view, for a high number of endemic bird species, such as the **carbonated sierra finch**, the **sandy gallito** – a wren-like bird with a pale eye-stripe – and the **cinammon warbling finch** (*moneterita canela*).

BIRDS AND ANIMALS

Once, these plains were the home of **pampas deer** (*venado de las pampas*), but habitat change and massive overhunting over the centuries has brought the species to the edge of extinction and today only a few hundred individuals survive, mainly in Samborombón and Campos del Tuyú in Buenos Aires Province. Standing 70cm at the shoulder, the deer has a short-haired, yellow-grey pelt, and is easily identified by its three-pronged antler.

The **coipu** (*coipo* or *falsa nutria*) is a large rodent commonly found in the region's wetlands, especially in the central east of Buenos Aires Province and the Paraná Delta, where it is farmed mainly for its fur but also for its edible meat. The great vizcacha dens (*vizcacheras*) described in the nineteenth century by the famous natural history writer, W.H. Hudson, have all but disappeared, but you may see an endemic bird named after the writer, Hudson's canastero, along with the **greater rheas, burrowing parrots** (*loro barranquero*), with their yellow rumps and browny-grey heads, and **ovenbirds** (*horneros*) that he so loved. Named after the domed, concrete-hard mud nests they build on posts, ovenbirds have always been held in great affection by the gauchos and country folk, who regularly refer to the species in human-sounding terms, with local names such as Juan Alonsito.

MESOPOTAMIAN GRASSLAND

Found across much of Corrientes and Entre Ríos provinces, and extending into southernmost Misiones, are the humid **Mesopotamian grasslands**. Here you will find *yatay* palm savannah and some of Argentina's most important **wetlands**, most notably the Esteros de Iberá and the Parque Nacional Mburucuyá, which make for some of Argentina's most productive **nature safaris**.

BIRDS AND ANIMALS

The wetlands have a remarkable diversity of birdlife, including numerous species of ducks, rails, ibises and herons. Some of the most distinctive species are the **wattled jacana** (*jacana*), which tiptoes delicately over floating vegetation; the **southern screamer** (*chajá*), a hulking great bird the size of a turkey, with a strident call like the cry of an oversized gull; the unmistakeable **scarlet-headed blackbird** (*federal*), which frequents reedbeds; filter-feeding **roseate spoonbills** (*espátula rosada*); the wonderful **rufescent tiger heron** (*hocó colorado*); and **jabirus** (*yabirú*), the largest variety of stork, measuring almost 1.5m tall, with a bald head, shoe-horn bill and red ruff around its neck. Up above fly **snail kites** (*caracoleros*), which use their sharp, curved bills to prize freshwater *caracoles* from their shells.

In the shallow swamps, amongst reedbeds and long grasses, you will find the **marsh deer** (*ciervo de los pantanos*), on the list of endangered species but still suffering from poaching. Standing 1.3m tall, it is South America's largest native deer, easily identifiable by its size and its multi-horned antlers that usually have five points. One of the most common wetland animals is the **capybara** (*carpincho*), the world's biggest rodent, weighing up to 50kg. Though most active at night, it is easy to see in the day, frequently half-submerged, as this grazer is a strong swimmer. In the past, it suffered heavily from hunting, as its skin makes a distinctive, soft, water-resistant leather, a demand now largely satisfied by commercial capybara ranches, though poaching continues. **Reptiles** include the **black cayman** (*yacaré negro* or *yacaré hocico angosto*), which grows up to 2.8m in length, and is the victim of illegal hunting; and snakes like the *lampalagua* **boa** (up to 5m in length) and the *curiyú* **yellow anaconda** (which can grow over 3m), both of which are non-poisonous, relying on constriction to kill their prey.

SUBTROPICAL PARANÁ FORESTS

Subtropical Paraná forest (*Selva Paranaense*) is Argentina's most biologically diverse ecosystem, a dense mass of vegetation that conforms with most people's idea of a jungle. The most frequently visited area of Paraná forest is the Parque Nacional Iguazú, but it is found in patches across lowland areas and upland hill ranges of the rest of Misiones, with small remnant areas in the northeast of Corrientes Province. It has over 200 tree species, amongst which figure the **palo rosa** (one of the highest canopy species, at up to 40m); the **strangler fig** (*higuerón bravo*); the **lapacho**, with its beautiful pink flowers that have made it a popular ornamental tree in cities; and the **Misiones cedar** (*cedro misionero*), a fine hardwood species that has suffered heavily from logging. Upland areas along the Brazilian border still preserve stands of **Paraná pine**, a type of rare araucaria monkey puzzle related to the more famous species found in northern Patagonia. Lower storeys of

vegetation include the wild **yerba mate** tree, first cultivated in plantations by the Jesuits in the seventeenth century; the **palmito** palm, whose edible core is exploited as palm heart; and endangered prehistoric **tree ferns**. Festooning the forest are lianas, mosses, ferns and epiphytes, including several hundred varieties of **orchid**.

BIRDS AND ANIMALS

More than five hundred species of bird inhabit the Paraná forest, and you stand a good chance of seeing the **toco toucan** (*tucán grande*), with its bright orange bill, along with other smaller members of the same family. Rarities include the magnificent **harpy eagle** (*harpía*), one of the world's most powerful and specialized avian predators, and the **bare-faced currasow** (*muitú*).

The fauna in this part of the world has also been hard-hit by habitat loss and hunting, although it's still one of the few places in Argentina where you might just see the highly endangered **jaguar** (*yaguareté* or *tigre*). Weighing up to 160kg, and more powerful than its African relation, the leopard, this beast is the continent's most fearsome predator. The beautiful spotted **ocelot** (*gato onza*) is similarly elusive and almost as endangered, having suffered massive hunting for its pelt during the 1970s.

THE WET CHACO

Found in the eastern third of Chaco and Formosa provinces and the northeast of Santa Fé is what is described as **wet chaco** habitat. It consists of small remnant patches of gallery forest (not unlike the Paraná forest), growing by rivers and ox-bow lakes; savannah grasslands studded with *caranday* palms and "islands" of mixed scrub woodland (*isletas de monte*); and wetland environments similar to those of the Mesopotamian grasslands. The key tree species is the **quebracho colorado chaqueño**, one of Argentina's four *quebracho* species, whose name means axe-breaker in Spanish, though it has always been valued more for its tannin than for its hard wood. It can reach heights of 24m, and the most venerable specimens can be anything from 300 to 500 years old. Other common tree species are the *urunday; timbó colorado; lapacho negro;* and the intriguing **crown of thorns** tree (*espina corona*), with clumps of dramatic spikes jutting out from its trunk. On the savannahs, the graceful **caranday** palms grow alone or in small groups (*palmares*) and reach heights of up to 15m. They are extremely resilient, surviving both periodic flooding and the regular burning of the grasslands in order to stimulate the growth of new shoots for cattle pasture: whereas most shrubs perish in the flames, the *caranday* seems to flourish.

The wetland swamps are often choked with rafts of **camalote**, a waterlily with a seductive lilac flower; or the large discs, some more than a metre in diameter, of another distinctive waterlily, the *flor de Irupé*, whose name comes from the Guaraní word for "plate on the water". *Pirí*, looking rather like papyrus horsetail, and *pehuajó*, with leaves like a banana palm, form large reed beds where the water is less deep.

BIRDS AND ANIMALS

The **birdlife** is similar to that in the swamps of Mesopotamia, and you're likely to see the **greater rhea** (called *suri* in this region more often than *ñandú*); the **fork-tailed flycatcher** (*tijereta*) with its unmistakeable, overlong tailfeathers; **monk parakeets** (*cotorras*), which build huge communal nests in *caranday* palms; the **red-legged seriema** (*chuña de patas rojas*), a long-legged roadrunner-type bird; and two birds that are trapped for the pet trade – the **red-crested cardinal** (*cardenal común*), and the **turquoise-fronted Amazon** (*loro hablador*), an accomplished ventriloquist parrot.

One of the most beautiful animals in the wet chaco is the solitary, nocturnal **maned wolf** (*aguará guazú* or *lobo de crin*), whose name means "big fox" in Guaraní, and which, to this day, is occasionally persecuted for fear that it's a werewolf (*lobizón*). This coppery auburn beast, standing almost a metre tall and weighing up to 25kg, actually eats birds' eggs, armadillos, small rodents and fruit. It is seriously endangered, with only an estimated 1500 remaining in Argentina.

One of the most curious-looking denizens of the region is the **giant anteater** (*oso hormiguero*, *oso bandera*, or *yurumí*), with its bushy tail and elongated face, gently curved like a shoehorn. Its astonishingly sensitive sense of smell is forty times better than humans', to make up for its poor eyesight. It breaks open rock-hard termite mounds with its exceptionally strong claws, and scours out thousands of termites a feed with its probing, sticky tongue. Much smaller is the **collared anteater** (*oso melero* or *tamanduá*), a perplexed-looking creature with a black and orange-yellow coat. Although it can often be found on the ground, it is ideally suited to clambering round in tree branches, making good use of its prehensile tail. So too do the region's primates: the **black howler monkey** (*carayá* or *mono aullador negro*), one of South America's biggest monkeys, weighing up to 7kg; the black-capped or **tufted capuchin** (*caí*); and the endangered **mirikiná** (*mono de noche*), Argentina's smallest primate (only 60–70cm long, including its tail), and the world's only nocturnal monkey.

THE DRY CHACO

The **dry chaco** refers to the parched plain of unruly thorn-scrub that covers most of central and western Chaco and Formosa provinces, northeastern Salta, and much of Santiago del Estero – where you'll find the best-preserved example of this ecosystem within the Parque Nacional Copo. This habitat was once more varied, but massive deforestation and the subsequent introduction of cattle has standardized the vegetation. There can be few places in the world where the cacti are not necessarily the spiniest of plants, as is the case here. Everything, it seems, is aggressively defensive: the *vinal* shrub, for instance, is dreaded by riders and horses alike for its brutal, reinforced spikes, up to twenty centimetres long. To the early explorers and settlers, much of the dry chaco was known simply as the *Impenetrable* for its lack of water and all species have adapted strategies to save water, about half of them losing their leaves during the winter drought. In places, a dense understorey of **chaguar** and **caraguatá** grow: robust, yucca-like plants which are processed by the Wichí to make the fibre for their *yica* bags. The *monte* scrub grows from ground level to a height of some four metres, and from this ragged tangle, trees liberate themselves once in a while.

The tallest trees in the dry chaco are the *quebrachos*, notably the **quebracho colorado santiagueño** (up to 24m tall and 1.5m diameter), exploited for tannin and by the timber industry; and the **quebracho blanco**, used extensively for firewood and whose bark – cracked into thick "scales", not dissimilar to cork-oak bark – has antimalarial properties. Its leaves resemble that of an olive tree, and its distinctive husk of a seed pod contains oval parchment-yellow flakes of seed.

Several other species can also reach imposing sizes, such as the two types of **carob tree**, the *algarrobo blanco* and *algarrobo negro*, both of which play an integral role in the life of the Wichí and other indigenous groups for the shade, firewood, edible beans and animal forage they provide. Regrettably, the species have been severely overexploited to provide a much-prized reddish wood for the furniture industry. The beautiful **guayacán**, with olive-green bark that flakes rather like a plane tree and leaves somewhat like a mimosa, is valued for its extremely hard wood, also used for furniture. Perhaps the hardest wood of all is that of the endangered, slow-growing **palo santo** (meaning "holy stick"). This tree, characteristically with a profusion of knobbly twigs and a host to many small, grey, octopus-like bromeliads, flowers in spring with tiny blooms the colour of lemon yoghurt. Its fragrant, green-tinged wood can be burnt as an insect repellent; though carvings are sold by the Wichí and Qom, export of the wood has been prohibited. Finally, the **palo borracho** (or *yuchán*) is the most distinctive tree of all, with a bulbous, porous trunk to store water; the tree protects itself, especially when young, with rhino-horned spikes, and it flowers with large yellow blooms from January to July, the seedpods producing a fluffy cotton-like fibre.

Creepers such as the famous medicinal **uña de gato** (or *garabato*) are quite common. **Cacti** are some of the very few plants here that grow straight: predominantly the candelabra *cardón* (a different species to that which grows in the Andes), which grows to the size of a tree; and its similar-looking cousin, the *ucle* (which has seven lobes per stem, compared with the *cardón*'s nine). These cacti are sometimes planted so as to grow into tightly knit hedges.

BIRDS AND ANIMALS

Commonly associated with dry-chaco habitat are birds like the **black-legged seriema** (*chuña de patas negras*), which is rather like an Argentinian roadrunner or secretary bird; and the **chaco chachalaca** (*charata*). A pair of *charatas* can make a cacophony to put a flock of geese to shame.

More excitingly, it holds forty percent of Argentina's mammal species (143 types). The edges of patches of woodland are usually the best places to see wildlife. A few **jaguars** hang on, despite trapping and trophy hunting, as do a handful of **ocelots**. Less threatened are the **puma** and the **Geoffroy's cat** (*gato montés*). One of three species of native Argentine wild pig, the famous **Chacoan peccary** (*chancho quimilero*), was thought to be extinct until rediscovered in Paraguay in 1975, and later in a few isolated areas of the Argentinian dry chaco.

Another high-profile living fossil is the nocturnal **giant armadillo** (*tatú carreta*). Up to 1.5m long and weighing as much as 60kg, a full-grown one is strong enough to carry a man, but its huge claws are no real defence against capture, as they're designed for digging, and impoverished *campesinos* know it makes good eating. Smaller but equally interesting are the **coatimundi** (*coati*) and the **crab-eating raccoon** (*aguará popé* or *osito lavador*). One of the most frequently sighted animals is the **brown brocket deer** (*corzuela pardo* or *guazuncho*).

Of the Chaco's numerous types of snake, the venomous (but generally unaggressive) **coral snake** (*coral*) and the innocuous **false coral snake** (*falsa coral*) are often confused. Both are similarly patterned in bands of red, black and white, and are best left alone. For the curious, the poisonous species has two white bands between a group of three black bands, and the imposter has only a single white band between two black bands. More dangerous are the **vipers**: the diamond-back rattlesnake (*cascabel*), the *yarará de la cruz*, and the *yarará común*, all of which have an extensive range in northern and central Argentina.

THE YUNGAS

The **yungas** is the term applied to the humid, subtropical band of the Argentinian northwest that's squeezed between the flat chaco to the east and the Andean pre-cordillera to the west, dropping south from the Bolivian border through Jujuy and Salta, Tucumán and into Catamarca. Abrupt changes of altitude in this band give rise to radical changes in the type of flora, creating wildly different ecosystems arranged in tiers. All are characterized by fairly high year-round precipitation, but have distinct seasons, with winter being the drier. The lowest altitudes are home to transitional woodland – no longer the thorn-scrub of the Chaco but retaining some varieties typical of the plains to the east – and lowland jungle (*selva pedemontana*), rising up to about 600m. Most of the trees and shrubs in these lower levels are deciduous and have showy blossoms: *jacarandá*, fuchsia, *pacará*, *palo blanco* and *amarillo*, *lapacho* (or *tabebuia*), *timbó colorado* (the black-eared tree), *palo borracho* (*chorisia* or *yuchán*), and Argentina's national flower, the **ceibo**. Much of this forest has been hard-hit by clearance for timber and agriculture, especially sugar-cane plantations.

Above 600m starts the most famous yungas habitat, the **montane cloudforests** (*selva montana* or *nuboselva*) – one of the country's most diverse and interesting ecosystems, and best seen in the national parks of Calilegua in Jujuy, and Baritú and El Rey in Salta. The *selva montana* is split into two categories: lower montane forest (*selva basal*), which rises to about 1000m; and true cloudforest, which is found as high as 2200m and depends for its moisture on winds blowing westwards from the Atlantic. These forests form a gloomy, impenetrable canopy of tall evergreens – dominated by laurels and acacia-like *tipas* at lower levels, and yunga cedars, *horco molle*, *nogal* and myrtles higher up – beneath which several varieties of cane and bamboo compete for the scarce, mottled sunlight. The tree trunks are covered in thick moss and lichen, lianas hang in a tangle, epiphytes and orchids flourish, while a variety of bromeliads, heliconias, parasites and succulents all add to the mysteriously dank atmosphere. On the tier above the cloudforest, you'll find typically single-species woods of alder, *nogal* or mountain pine form the *bosque montano* at 1500–2400m, where temperatures at night and in winter can be very low. Above this begins the pre-*puna* highland meadows (*prados*) of stunted *queñoa* trees, reeds and different sorts of *puna* grasses.

BIRDS AND ANIMALS

More than three hundred varieties of **bird** inhabit the yungas forests, with Calilegua having the richest supply of the national parks. Species include the **toco toucan** (the official symbol of Parque El Rey); the impressive and rare **black-and-chestnut eagle** (*águila poma*); the **king vulture** (*jote real* or *cuervo rey*), with a strikingly patterned orange head; dusky-legged and rare, red-faced **guans** (*pava de monte común* and *alisera* respectively); numerous varieties of **hummingbird**; **mitred**

and **green-cheeked parakeets** (*loro de cara roja* and *chiripepé de cabeza gris* respectively); and the **torrent duck** (*pato de los torrentes*) and **rufous-throated dipper** (*mirlo de aqua*), both found in fast-flowing streams. The morning chorus or cacophony is such that you'll wish you'd brought recording equipment as well as binoculars and a camera.

Like the flora, **fauna** in the yungas changes with altitude. Rich in fish and crustaceans, the crystalline streams are the favourite haunts of southern river **otters** and crab-eating **racoons** (called *mayuatos* here). Other mammals found close to the water include South America's largest native terrestrial mammal, the **Brazilian tapir** (*tapir*, *anta* or *mborevi*), a solid, Shetland pony-sized creature, with a trunk-like stump of a nose and which weighs up to 250kg in this part of the world. They are hard to see, however, being mainly active at night. The strange **tree-porcupine** (*coendú*) clambers around the canopy with the help of its prehensile tail, as do capuchins and black howler **monkeys**, while the **three-toed sloth** (*perezoso*), which virtually never descends from the trees, depends on its sabre-like claws for locomotion. Felines are represented by **jaguars**, **margays**, **pumas** and **Geoffroy's cats**. Of these shyer creatures, you will be very lucky to see anything other than tracks. This also applies to the most famous regional creature of all: the **taruca**, a stocky native Andean deer. Considered a delicacy, it was traditionally hunted by locals for Easter celebrations, but it was brought to the brink of extinction in Argentina and is now one of only three national animals protected by the status of Natural Monument – the other two being its Patagonian cousin, the **huemul**, and the southern right whale. It grazes in small herds just below the tree line in winter, and on high rocky pastures such as those above Calilegua in summer.

THE PUNA

The **prepuna** and higher **puna** of the Andean northwest encompass a range of extremely harsh, arid habitats that range from the *cardón* cactus valleys from Jujuy to La Rioja, to the highest bleak Altiplano vegetation below the permanent snow line. Everything that grows here must be able to cope with extremely impoverished soils, and a huge difference in day- and night-time temperatures. *Prepuna* habitat usually refers to the sparsely vegetated rocky gullies and highland meadows (*prados*) of the cordillera, and is found at altitudes of between 2000m and 3500m. You'll see bunch grasses, reeds and stunted *queñoa* trees, but the most distinctive *prepuna* plant is the candelabra **cardón cactus** (also called *pasakán*), which indigenous folklore holds to be the reincarnated form of their ancestors. These grow in a fairly restricted range centred on the Valle Calchaquíes, and take a century to reach their full height of 10m. Their beautiful yellow flowers produce a sweet fruit, and though they are now protected, their strong, light wood was used in the past as a building material.

The *puna* is found above 3400m, and is characterized by spongy wetlands (*bofedales*) around shallow high-mountain lagoons, and sun-scorched flat Altiplano pastures of tough, spiky grasses. On the higher slopes, you'll find **lichens** and a type of rock-hard cushion-shaped prehistoric moss called **yacreta** that grows incredibly slowly – perhaps a millimetre a year – but lives for hundreds of years. It has been heavily exploited – partly for making medicinal teas, but mainly because it is the only fuel to be found at these altitudes.

BIRDS AND ANIMALS

Of the fauna, birds are the most prolific: you can see all three varieties of **flamingo** wading or flying together in great pink flocks, especially on the banks of Laguno de Pozuelos. They are, in decreasing size, the Andean flamingo (*parina grande*; with yellow legs), Chilean flamingo (*flamenco austral*; with bluish-grey legs) and Puna or James' flamingo (*parina chica*; with red legs). The lesser rhea (*ñandú petizo, choique* or *suri*), a metre-high flightless bird, is shy here and will sprint away from you at incredible speeds. Binoculars can also be trained on **giant coots** (*gallareta gigante*) and it's extremely rare relative, the **horned coot** (*gallareta cornuda*), **Andean avocets**, **puna plovers** (*chorlito puñeno*), **Andean geese** (*guayata*), **Andean lapwings** (*tero serrano*), and all kinds of grebes, teals and other ducks. The most common bird you'll hear is the **grey-breasted seedsnipe**, but listen, too, for the modulated whistle of a wading bird called the **tawny-throated dotterel** – one of the most entrancing sounds to disturb the silence of the Altiplano.

The animals most people associate with the Andean *puna* are the four species of South American camelids, especially the **llama**, a domesticated species well adapted to harsh conditions, and which eats anything. The local people use llamas as beasts of burden, as well as for meat and their thick wool (shorn every other year, adults yield 4kg a time). The other domesticated camelid is the slightly smaller **alpaca**, which varies in colour from snow white to raven black, via a range of greys and browns. Alpacas produce much finer wool, and one thick fleece, harvested every two years, may weigh as much as 5kg. They're few and far between in Argentina, and you're only likely to see them in the Antofagasta de la Sierra area.

The two other South American camelids are both wild. The tawny-beige, short-haired antelope-like **guanaco** is found over a widespread area, stretching from the northwest *puna* to the mountains and steppe of Tierra del Fuego. Listen out for the eerie, rasping alarm call used to alert the troupe to possible danger. The guanaco population is still relatively healthy, although it is hunted for its meat and skin, despite being legally protected. The young, called *chulengos*, are easily approachable, unlike the adults. The guanaco's more diminutive cousin, the **vicuña**, is the most graceful, shy and – despite its delicate appearance – hardy of the four camelids, capable of living at the most extreme altitudes. It's usually found between 3500 and 4600m, as far south as the north of San Juan Province, although the biggest flocks are to be found in Catamarca Province. Like rodents they have incisors that continually grow, enabling them to munch away on the tough bunchgrasses, lichens and spiny Altiplano vegetation, but they're fussy eaters. After thousands were shot for their pelts during the 1950s and 60s, they faced extinction across their whole continental range, but national and international protection measures including a ban on trade in their skins has helped ensure that their numbers have risen back to safe levels. This has allowed a pilot project to begin in Jujuy's Valle Calchaquíes, whereby their valuable fur (the second finest natural fibre in the world after silk) is exploited on a strictly controlled, sustainable commercial level. Animals are rounded up once every three or four years – no mean feat considering that these animals can sprint at up to 60km per hour over short distances – and shorn, in a practice reminiscent of the days of the Incas. Then, only Inca noblemen could wear vicuña cloth, but nowadays you can buy one of the prestigious ponchos – weighing 1.3kg and requiring the wool of at least six animals – for $2000.

Other mammals spotted in the *puna* include the nearly extinct **royal chinchilla** and several varieties of armadillo. Mountain **vizcachas**, looking like large rabbits with curly, long tails, can often be seen nodding off in the sun near watering-places or heard making their distinctive whistle. You're unlikely to see the **puma**, silently prowling around the region but normally avoiding human contact.

THE PATAGONIAN STEPPE

Typified by its brush scrub and wiry grassland, the **Patagonian steppe** (*estepa*) covers the greatest extent of any Argentine ecosystem. This vast, grey-brown expanse of semi-desert lies to the south of the pampas grasslands, to the east of the Andean cordillera, and as far south as Tierra del Fuego, and includes areas of genuine desert and cracked, dessicated meseta. Vegetation is stunted by the poor, gravelly soils, high winds, and lack of water, except along the few river courses, where you find marshlands (*mallines*) and startlingly green willows (*sauces*). Just about the only trees apart from the willows are the trademark, non-native Lombardy poplars, planted to shelter estancias. The habitat itself can be broadly grouped into **brush steppe**, which frequently forms part of the brief transitional zone between the more barren lands to the east and the cordillera forests; and **grass steppe**, typified by tussocks of yellowy-brown *coirón* grass, usually closely cropped by sheep.

Much of the scrubby brush is composed of monochrome *mata negra*, but in places, you'll come across the resinous, perfumed *mata verde*, or the manicured ash-grey *mata guanaco*, which blooms with virulently orange flowers. You'll also see spiky **calafate** bushes, and the *duraznillo*, which has dark green, tapered leaves. One of the largest bushes is the **molle**, covered with thorns and parasitic galls. The adhesive qualities of *molle* sap was once utilized by indigenous peoples to fix arrowheads and scrapers to their wooden shafts, but nowadays the most common use for this bush is as firewood to prepare an aromatic *asado*. Smaller shrubs include the silver-grey *senecio miser*, compact, spiky *neneo* plants; and the *lengua de fuego*, a dull-grey shrub with bright-red flowers

when in bloom. In moister areas, you'll find the *colapiche*, whose name ("armadillos' tail") comes from the appearance of its smooth, leafless fronds.

BIRDS AND ANIMALS

Your best chance of sighting some of the key species of the steppe is in places such as Chubut's Peninsula Valdés and Punta Tombo. **Guanacos**, the graceful wild cousin of the llama, abound in these places. Look out too for the **mara** (Patagonian hare), the largest of Argentina's endemic mammals, and of the same family as the capybara. Sadly, this tremendous long-legged rodent, the size of a small dog, is becoming ever rarer, and its range has shrunk, thanks to competition from the ubiquitous European hare (*liebre*), introduced in the late nineteenth century.

The **zorro gris** (grey fox) is regularly to be found around national park gates, waiting for scraps thrown by tourists – try and resist. The only time you're likely to come across its larger, more elusive cousin, the **zorro colorado** (red fox), is on a barbed-wire fence – it having bitten something altogether less savoury, by way of poisoned bait or a bullet. Grey foxes regularly suffer the same fate at the hands of their foes, but are rather more astute at distinguishing friends.

Pichi and *peludo* **armadillos** are often seen scampering across the plains at surprising speed, like overwound clockwork toys. Even more regularly, they are spotted at the side of the road, forming the diet of a natty **southern crested caracara** (*carancho*) or a dusty-brown **chimango caracara** (*chimango*), the two most frequently sighted of Patagonia's scavenging birds.

Another characteristic bird of prey is the black-chested buzzard eagle (*águila mora*), a powerful flier with broad wings and splendid plumage. The classic bird of the steppe, though, is the **lesser** or **Darwin's rhea** (*ñandú petiso* or *choique*), best described in English by the seventeenth-century sea captain, Sir John Narborough, as "much like a great Turkey-cock . . . they cannot fly; have a long Neck, and a small Head, and [are] beaked like a goose". These ashy-grey birds lay their eggs in communal clutches, and in spring you'll see them with their broods of young.

The brightly coloured **Patagonian sierra finch** (*fríngilo patagónico*) is an attractive yellow and slate-grey bird which is often found in proximity to humans, as is the crested **rufous-collared sparrow** (*chingolo*). On lagoons and lakes of the steppe, you'll find the **black-necked swan** (*cisne de cuello negro*), a bird that suffered from severe overhunting in the early twentieth century to supply the demand from the European fashion industry for its feathers. Also look for **Chilean flamingos**; the beautiful, endangered **hooded grebe** (*macá tobiano*), only discovered in 1974 and endemic to Santa Cruz; the great grebe (*huala*); all four types of *chorlito* **seedsnipes**; upland **geese** (*cauquén* or *avutarda*), which migrate as far north as southern Buenos Aires Province and are shot for meat and sport; buff-necked **ibises** (*bandurrias*), who amble around in small bands, honking, as they probe wetland pastures with their curved bills; and the **southern lapwing** (*tero*), a bird that mates for life and whose eerie, plaintive cries and insistent warning shrieks are familiar to all trekkers.

THE PATAGONIAN CORDILLERA FORESTS

The eastern slopes of the Patagonian cordillera are cloaked, for most of their length, in forests dominated by the various species of **Nothofagus southern beech**. Two species run the length of the forests, from the northernmost forests of Neuquén to Tierra del Fuego: the **lenga** (upland beech); and the **ñire** (lowland or antarctic beech). Both deciduous, they frequently grow in close proximity, so telling them apart can be problematic at first. At lower altitudes, the *lenga* is by far the taller species, but closer to the tree line, the two intermingle as dwarf shrubs in impenetrably dense thickets. The *lenga*, capable of flourishing on incredibly thin topsoils, tends to form the tree line, reaching up to 1600m above sea level at the latitude of Neuquén. The *ñire*, which rarely grows more than 15m tall, tends to be found close to water; and whereas in autumn both species turn a remarkable variety of hues, it is the *ñire* that has the most vibrant palette, with astonishing garnets, golden yellows, rusty oranges, and pinks the colour of rosehip jelly. By comparing the leaves of the two species, you can always verify any preliminary identification: *lenga* leaves have lots of veins, with each band between the veins having a uniform double lobe on the edge; *ñire* leaves have far fewer veins, and each band has a less regular, crinkle-cut edge with several

lobes. Associated with *lenga* and *ñire* are three intriguing plant species: false mistletoe (*farolito chino*), a semi-parasitic plant that draws sap from its host as well as producing its own through photosynthesis; verdigris-coloured **lichen beards** (*barba del indio* or *toalla del indio*), which need unpolluted air to flourish; and the **llao llao** tree fungus, also called *pan de indio* ("Indian's bread"). When young, it does have a faintly sweet flavour, but is low on nutritional value. The *llao llao* produces the characteristic brain-like knots on trunks and branches that are so beloved of local artisans, who use them to craft animals and ashtrays.

Lenga and *ñire* are the only species that occur at all latitudes where you can find Patagonian Andean forest. The next most prominent tree species are two related evergreen beeches, the more northerly **coihue** and the **guindo** (or *coihue de Magallanes*), found mainly in Tierra del Fuego. Both have fairly smooth bark and distinctive laurel-green leaves that are small, shiny and tough, with a rounded shape and tiny serrations on the edge. Both trees grow only in damp zones near lakes or, in the case of Tierra del Fuego, by the shores of the Beagle Channel, where they reach 25–30m in height.

In central Neuquén, you find one of Argentina's most remarkable trees, the **araucaria monkey puzzle**, which grows on poor volcanic soils, in widely spaced pure forests or, more normally, mixed with species of Nothofagus. The forests of Parque Nacional Lanín contain two species of broad-leafed Nothofagus not found anywhere else: the **roble pellín** (named for its oak-like leaves), and the **raulí** (with more oval-shaped leaves), which together often form mixed, low-altitude woodlands. Also confined to the area is the **radal**, a shrubby tree with a creamy whitish flower and a greyish wood that is valued by craftsmen for its beautiful speckled vein, reminiscent of a sloughed snakeskin.

The most diverse type of forest in the region is the rare **Valdivian temperate rainforest** (*selva Valdiviana*), found in patches of the central Patagonian Andes from Lanín to Los Alerces, usually pressed up against the Chilean border around low passes where rainfall is at its heaviest. This verdant tangle requires extremely high precipitation (3000–4000mm annually) to flourish, and it is marked out from the rest of the forest by several distinguishing factors: different layers of canopy, thick roots breaking the surface of the soil, and both epiphytes and llianas. Two other tree species found only in the central Patagonian lake district are the scarce **arrayán** myrtle, always found next to water, and with a glorious, flaky, cinnamon-coloured bark; and the mighty **alerce**, or Patagonian cypress, which resembles a Californian redwood and is one of the world's oldest and grandest tree species.

The understorey of the forests is dominated in most places by dense thickets, up to six metres high, of a bamboo-like plant, **caña colihue**, a mixed Spanish and Mapudungun term that means "tree of the place of water". Every 7–12 years they flower, die and reproduce – a phenomenon that can spark a lemming-like plague of *colilargo* mice. The most stunning shrub, if you catch it in bloom (late spring or autumn), is the **notro firebush** (or *ciruelillo*), whose fiery flowers resemble miniature scarlet crowns. Another native to these parts, the **fuchsia**, has conquered the world as a garden favourite. Growing in Tierra del Fuego, and looking rather like a glossy rhododendron, the evergreen **canelo** takes its Spanish name from the fleeting cinnamon taste of its bark, a taste rapidly followed by a peppery tang. In English it is known as Winter's bark, after a certain Captain Winter of Francis Drake's expedition, who discovered that its leaves helped to treat and prevent scurvy. The native **wild holly** (*muérdago silvestre*) has glossy, dark-green leaves and, in spring, clusters of yellow-orange fairy-bell blooms the size of blackcurrants. Of forest flowers, some of the most brightly coloured are the **amancay**, a type of golden-orange lily that carpets glades in central Patagonia in midsummer; and the brilliant yellow flowers of the yellow **lady's slipper** (*zapatilla de la Virgen*), whose snapdragon blooms bob on their delicate stems in spring. **Lupins** (*lupinos*), introduced by the British to enliven estancia gardens, have spread like wildfire through parks like Lanín, and, though considered a plague, they do put on a glorious show from late December to January, when in bloom.

As you move away from the mountains towards the drier steppe, you'll often find a zone of **transitional woodland**, although the change from steppe to forest can be quite abrupt. In northern and central Patagonia, the woodland is normally composed of species like the mountain **cypress** (*ciprés de la cordillera*), or the autochthonous *retamo*, which flowers with pale-violet blooms.

Found on mountain-valley floors or just above the tree line are peaty **sphagnum moors** (*turbales*) and bogs (*mallines*). Here you'll find *chaura* prickly heath, and you can munch away on its waxy, pinky-red berries, which have a spongy texture and look like miniature Edam cheeses. The **creeping diddle dee** (*murtilla*) is a common upland plant; there are several types of berries that go under the local Spanish name of *mutilla*. On rocky soils, look out for the common blue perezia (*perezia azul*) whose diminutive, mauve flowers have a double rosette of elegant, spatula-shaped petals.

BIRDS AND ANIMALS

Many of the **birds** that inhabit the steppe are also found in the cordillera. Typical woodland species include the world's most southerly parrot, the **austral parakeet** (*cachaña* or *cotorra*); the **green-backed firecrown** (*picaflor rubí*), a type of tiny hummingbird; the curious and hyperactive **thorn-tailed rayadito**, a tiny chestnut-and-white bird with a prominent eye stripe, which flits about seeking insects in *Nothofagus* bark; two secretive ground birds, the chucao tapaculo and chestnut-throated huet-huet, with a piping call, are both more often heard than seen; and two birds that allow you to get surprisingly close – the powerful **Magellanic woodpecker** (*carpintero negro gigante*), and the hand-sized **austral pygmy owl** (*caburé*). Finally, if any bird has a claim to symbolizing the continent of South America, it is the **Andean condor**. With eyesight eight times better than that of man, and the longest wingspan of any bird of prey, (reaching up to 3.10m), it's the undisputed lord of the skies along the entire length of the Andean spine, from Venezuela to the tip of Tierra del Fuego. Until fairly recently, this imperious bird was relentlessly poisoned and shot, the victim of prejudice and macho posturing. Fortunately, it's now protected in Argentina and its population stable. Although you'll probably only glimpse a dot soaring far off in the sky, you may be treated to the sight of the ermine ruff of the adult bird or even the rush of the wind in its splayed wingtips as it sweeps past.

The principal predator of the cordillera mammals is the **puma**. Local farmers equate these cats with a dangerous drain on their finances: a female, teaching her growing youngsters how to kill, can slaughter more than fifty lambs in a night. The law confers protection on all pumas, but even conservationists recognize that this is hard to enforce outside the national parks: on private land they are seen as fair game, and the meat is considered a delicacy. Commonly known as *león* (lion) by country dwellers, this cat is no pussy either. Though the chances are that any puma will sight you and make itself scarce well before you sight it, there are extremely infrequent cases of attacks on humans, mainly by protective females with cubs, or old cats who can no longer catch more fleet-footed prey. In the highly unlikely event of being faced with a seemingly aggressive puma, do not run but make yourself appear as big as possible, and, facing it at all times, back off slowly, shouting loudly. A smaller feline, the **Geoffroy's cat** (*gato montés*), tends to run before you've even seen it.

Perhaps the most endangered creature is the **huemul**, a thick-set native deer whose antler has two prongs. It is a relative of the *taruca* of the northwestern Andes, and has likewise attained the status of National Natural Monument. Protected by this legislation, this docile animal may yet manage to survive; the chief threat to its survival is no longer hunting, nor even from diseases spread by cattle, but habitat loss and human encroachment. Almost as endangered is the **pudú**, the world's smallest deer, measuring a mere 40cm at the shoulder and weighing 10–12kg. It has small, single-pointed horns, and is devilishly difficult to see, as it inhabits the dense undergrowth of the central cordillera forests from Lanín to Los Alerces. Also hard to spot are the **opossum** (*comadreja común*) and another interesting marsupial of the humid forests of the Andes, the **monito de monte**. Localized and nocturnal, your best chance of seeing one is in Nahuel Huapi or the southern part of Lanín. The endangered *culebra valdiviana* is a poisonous (but not mortally) woodland **snake** that's confined pretty much to this range, too. Tierra del Fuego has no snakes at all.

In terms of mammals, you stand most chance of seeing **introduced species**. The European red deer (*ciervo colorado*) and European wild boar (*jabalí*) have reached plague proportions in some parts of the central lake district. The **beaver** (*castor*) was introduced from Canada to Tierra del Fuego in an attempt to start a fur-farming industry. Unfortunately, the species took to the Fuegian streams like the proverbial duck. The consequences for the Fuegian environment have been devastating. The rodents have run amok, chewing their way through valuable woodland and blocking streams with their dams, flooding mountain valleys, flatlands and pasture. To compound things, *ñire* and *lenga* trees are much slower-growing than the birches of the beavers' native Canada. To combat this public enemy, year-round, no-limits hunting has been permitted, with hunters being allowed to sell the furs. Yet the *castores* have proved that their skins are as thick as their pelts, and people now believe that indiscriminate hunting can actually increase beaver populations, since they respond by giving birth to larger broods. Other introduced fur species have had deleterious effects too: **muskrats** (*ratas almizcleras*) were introduced to the south of the island at the same time as the beaver; during the 1930s, **rabbits** (*conejos*) crossed into the northern plains from the Chilean half of the island, and invaded the southern region after escaping from a fur farm in Ushuaia in the 1950s; and, ominously, the destructive **mink** (*visón*) has also been around here for the last eight years.

THE ATLANTIC SEABOARD

Argentina has 4725km of Atlantic coastline, which comprises three main types of habitat. From the mouth of the estuary of the Río de la Plata to just beyond the southern limit of Buenos Aires Province, the shoreline is mainly flat, fringed by dunes, sandy beaches and pampa grass. South of Viedma begin the endless stretches of dessicated Patagonian cliffs (*barrancas*) such as those you see fronting Península Valdés, broken in places by gulfs and muddy or shingle river estuaries, but almost entirely devoid of vegetation. The most beautiful of these cliffs are the porphyry-coloured sandstone ones near Puerto Deseado. The third section of coastline is that found south of Tierra del Fuego's Río Grande, where you find, in succession, patches of woodland, the bleak moorland tundra of the Península Mitre, and the rich southern beech forests of the Beagle Channel, exemplified by those in the Parque Nacional Tierra del Fuego.

BIRDS AND ANIMALS

Several coastal areas, notably those of the Bahía Samborombón, Bahía San Antonio, and Bahía San Sebastián, have been integrated into the Hemisphere Reserve for Shorebirds, a network of reserves designed to protect migrant waders across the two American continents. Birds like the **Hudsonian godwit** (*becasa de mar*) and the **red knot** (*playero rojizo*) migrate from Alaska and as far as Tierra del Fuego – a distance of over 17,000km. Other typical coastal species are **Magellanic penguin** (*pingüino magellánico*, whose major continental breeding colony is Punta Tombo, but which is also found at Valdés, Puerto Deseado, San Julián and Cabo Vírgenes; **Chilean flamingos**; and the **South American tern** (*gaviotín sudamericano*). At Deseado, you can see all four different types of **cormorant** (*cormorán*) including the blue-eyed (*imperial*) and, most beautiful of all, the uncommon red-legged cormorant (*gris*). Look out for the curious, dove-like **snowy sheathbill** (*paloma antártica*); and several types of duck, including the **crested duck** (*pato juarjual* or *crestón*) and the flightless **steamer duck** (*quetro no volador* or *alacush*), an ash-grey bird with an orange bill that uses its wings in paddle-steaming fashion to hurry itself away from danger. On the open sea, especially in the far south, you stand a good chance of seeing the **black-browed albatross**, and the **giant petrel**, both superbly skilful fliers.

Península Valdés is the main destination for **marine fauna**, attracting more visitors per year than the Galápagos Islands. Its twin bays, Golfo Nuevo and Golfo San José (Latin America's first marine park), are where as much as a quarter of the world's population of **southern right whales** (*ballena franca austral*) breed annually. The peninsula is also host to a 40,000-strong and growing colony of **southern elephant seals** (*elefante marino*). Other sightings might be **sealions** (*lobos del mar*), which are found in colonies along the whole Atlantic coast, and possibly even a **killer whale** (*orca*). Further down the coast, at Cabo Dos Bahías, you can see the endangered **fur seal** (*lobo de dos pelos*); while Puerto Deseado and San Julián are fine places to catch the energetic, piebald **Commerson's dolphins** (*toninas overas*). Sea trips on the Beagle Channel offer a slim chance of seeing **Peale's dolphins**, a **minke whale**, or even perhaps an endangered **marine otter** (*nutria marina* or *chungungo*).

MUSIC

With the obvious exception of tango, the music of Argentina has a fairly low international profile. True to its image as the continent's "odd man out", the country has a tradition which doesn't quite fit the popular conception of "Latin American" music: there are none of the exhilarating tropical rhythms of say Brazil or Cuba, and very little of the Andean pan pipe sound popularized worldwide in the Seventies by Chilean group Inti-Illimani. Within Latin America, however, Argentina is famed for its rock music, known simply as "rock nacional" – a term which embraces a pretty eclectic bunch of groups and musicians from the heavy rock of Pappo, through the sweet poppy rock of Fito Páez to the ska and punk influenced Los Fabulosos Cadillacs. You'll hear "rock nacional" throughout Argentina and it's well worth checking out a concert – attended with a fervour similar to that provoked by football – if you can. Folk music, known as "folklore" in Argentina, is popular throughout the country and provides a predominantly rural counterpoint to the essentially urban tango. The genre has also produced two internationally renowned stars; Mercedes Sosa and Auhualpa Yupanqui.

TANGO

The great Argentinian writer Jorge Luis Borges was a tango enthusiast and something of a historian of the music. "My informants all agree on one fact," he wrote, "the Tango was born in the brothels." Borges's informants were a little presumptuous, perhaps, for nobody can exactly pinpoint tango's birthplace, but it certainly developed amongst the Porteños – the people of the port area of Buenos Aires – and its bordellos and bars. It was a definitively urban music: a product of the melting pot of European immigrants, criollos, blacks and natives, drawn together when the city became the capital of Argentina in 1880. Tango was thus forged from a range of musical influences that included Andalucían flamenco, southern Italian melodies, Cuban habanera, African candombé and percussion, European polkas and mazurkas, Spanish contradanse, and, closer to home, the milonga – the rural song of the Argentine gaucho. It was a music imbued with immigrant history.

In this early form, tango became associated with the bohemian life of bordello brawls and compadritos – knife-wielding, womanizing thugs. By 1914 there were over 100,000 more men than women in Buenos Aires, thus the high incidence of prostitution and the strong culture of bar-brothels. Machismo and violence were part of the culture and men would dance together in the low-life cafés and corner bars practising new steps and keeping in shape while waiting for their women, the minas of the bordellos. Their dances tended to have a showy yet threatening, predatory quality, often revolving around a possessive relationship between two men and one woman. In such a culture, the compadrito danced the tango into existence.

The original **tango ensembles** were trios of violin, guitar and flute, but around the end of the nineteenth century the **bandoneón**, the tango accordion, arrived from Germany, and the classic tango orchestra was born. The box-shaped button accordion, which is now inextricably linked with Argentine tango, was invented around 1860 in Germany to play religious music in organless churches. One Heinrich Band reworked an older portable instrument nicknamed the "asthmatic worm", which was used for funeral processions as well as lively regional dances, and gave his new instrument the name "Band-Union", a combination of his and his company's names. Mispronounced as it travelled the world, it became the bandoneón.

In Argentina, an early pioneer of the instrument was **Eduardo Arolas** – a man remembered as the "Tiger of the Bandoneón". He recognized its immediate affinity with the tango – indeed, he claimed it was an instrument made to play tango, with its deep melancholy feeling which suited the immigrants who enjoyed a sentimental tinge in their hard lives. It is not, however, an easy instrument, demanding a great deal of skill, with its seventy-odd buttons each producing one of two notes depending on whether the bellows are being compressed or expanded.

Vicente Greco (1888–1924) is credited as the first bandleader to standardize the form of a tango group, with his **Orquesta Típica Criolla** of two violins and two bandoneóns. There were some larger bands but basically the instrumentation remained virtually unchanged until the 1940s.

FIRST TANGO IN PARIS

Before long the tango was an intrinsic part of the popular culture of Buenos Aires, played on the streets by organ grinders and fairground carousels, and danced in tenement courtyards. Its association with the whorehouse and low-down porteño lifestyle, plus its saucy, some-times obscene and deeply fatalistic lyrics, didn't endear it to the aristocratic families of Buenos Aires, who did their best to protect their children from the corrupting new dance, but, like rock'n'roll in America, it was a losing battle.

A number of rich, upper-class playboys, such as poet and writer **Ricardo Guïraldes**, enjoyed mixing with the compadritos and emulating their lifestyle from a "debonair" distance. It was Guïraldes who, on a European grand tour in 1910, was responsible for the spread of the dance to Europe. In 1911 he wrote a famous homage, a poem called "Tango" in honour of the dance: "... hats tilted over sardonic sneers. The all-absorbing love of a tyrant, jealously guarding his dominion, over women who have surrended submissively, like obedient beasts ... ".

The following year Guïraldes gave an influential impromptu performance in a Paris salon to a fashionable audience for whom tango's risqué sexuality ("the vertical expression of horizontal desire" as one wag dubbed it) was deeply attractive. Despite the local archbishop's admonition that Christians should not in good conscience tango, they did, and in very large numbers. Tango was thus the first of the many Latin dance crazes to conquer Europe. And once it had been embraced in the salons of France its

credibility back home greatly increased. Back in Argentina, from bordello to ballroom, everyone was dancing the tango.

And then came **Rudolph Valentino**. The tango fitted his image to a T and Hollywood wasted no time in capitalizing on the charisma of the superstar, the magnetism of the tango and the attraction they both had on a huge public. Valentino and Tango! Tango and Valentino! The combination was irresistible to the moguls, who swiftly added a tango scene to the latest Valentino film, *The Four Horsemen of the Apocalypse* (1926). The fact that in the film Valentino was playing a gaucho (Argentinian cowboy) son of a rancher – and gauchos don't dance the tango – didn't deter them for a moment. Valentino was a special gaucho and this gaucho could dance the tango. And why not? The scene really was incredible: Valentino, dressed in the wide trousers and leather chaps of a gaucho in the middle of the pampa, holding a carnation between his lips, and a whip in his hand; his partner, a Spanish señorita, kitted out with headscarf and hair comb plus the strongest pair of heels this side of the Río de la Plata.

Predictably enough, the tango scene was the hit of the film and, travesty though it was, it meant the dance was now known all over the world. Tango classes and competitions were held in Paris, and tango teas in England, with young devotees togged up as Argentine gauchos. Even the greatest tango singer of all time, **Carlos Gardel**, when he became the darling of Parisian society, and later starred in films in Hollywood, was forced to perform his tangos dressed as a gaucho.

GARDEL AND TANGO'S GOLDEN AGE

Back in Argentina, in the 1920s, the tango moved out of the cantinas and bordellos into cabarets and theatres and entered a classic era under bandleaders like **Roberto Firpo**, **Julio de Caro** and **Francisco Canaro**. With their orquestas típicas they took the old line-up of Vicente Greco (two bandoneóns, two violins, a piano and flute) and substituted a double bass for the flute. This gave added sonority and depth, a combination which was to continue for the next twenty years, even in the larger ensembles common after the mid-1930s. It was during this period that some of the most famous of all tangos were written, including Uruguayan **Gerardo Hernán Matos Rodríguez's** *La*

Cumparsíta in 1917 – the most famous tango of all time. He took it to Firpo who was performing with his band in a Montevideo café: the rest as they say is history!

The first **tango-canción** (tango songs) used the language of the ghetto and celebrated the life of ruffians and pimps. **Angel Villoldo** and **Pascual Contursi** introduced the classic tango lyric of a male perspective, placing the blame for heartache firmly on the shoulders of a fickle woman, with Contursi putting lyrics to Samuel Castriota's "Lita": "Woman who left me, in the prime of my life, wounding my soul, and driving thorns into my heart ... Nothing can console me now, so I am drowning my sorrows, to try to forget your love ...". Typical of tango songs, male behaviour itself was beyond reproach, the man victim of women's capriciousness.

In its **dance**, tango consolidated its contradictory mix of earthy sensuality and middle-class kitsch. It depends on an almost violent and dangerous friction of bodies, colliding often in a passion which seems controlled by the dance itself. A glittering respectability hid darker undercurrents in the obvious macho domination of the male over the female in a series of intricate steps and in the close embraces, which were highly suggestive of the sexual act. The cut and thrust of intricate and interlacing fast leg movements between a couple imitated the movement of blades in a knife fight.

CARLOS GARDEL

The extraordinary figure of **Carlos Gardel** (1887–1935) was – and still is – a legend in Argentina, and he was a huge influence in spreading the popularity of tango round the world. He was actually born in Toulouse, France, but taken to Buenos Aires at the age of four by his single mother. He came to be seen as an icon of Arrabal culture, and a symbol of the fulfilment of the dreams of the poor porteño workers.

In Argentina, it was Gardel above all who transformed tango from an essentially low-down dance form to a song style popular among Argentines of widely differing social classes. His career coincided with the first period of tango's golden age and the development of tango-canción (tango song) in the 1920s and 30s. The advent of radio, recording and film all helped his career, but nothing helped him more than his own voice – a voice that was born to sing tango and which became the model for all future singers of the genre.

In the 1920s, like most tango singers, Gardel sang to guitar rather than orchestral accompaniment. Everything about Gardel, his voice, his image, his suavity, his posture, his arrogance and his natural machismo spelled tango. Interestingly enough he started out as a variety act singing traditional folk and country music in a duo with José Razzano. They enjoyed great success but Gardel's recording of Contursi's *Mi noche triste* (My Sorrowful Night) in 1917 was to change the course of his future.

During his career, Gardel recorded some nine hundred songs and starred in numerous films, notably *The Tango on Broadway* in 1934. He was tragically killed in an aircrash in Colombia at the height of his fame, and his legendary status was confirmed. His image is still everywhere in Buenos Aires, on plaques and huge murals, and in record-store windows, while admirers pay homage to his life-sized, bronze statue in the Chacarita cemetery, placing a lighted cigarette between his fingers or a red carnation in his buttonhole.

After Gardel the split between the **traditionalists** such as **Filiberto** and **D'Arienzo**, later Biagi and De Angelis, and those musicians called the evolutionists, such as **De Caro**, **Di Sarli**, **Troilo** and **Pugliese** became more pronounced. Bands, as elsewhere in the world during this period, became larger, in the mode of small orchestras, and a mass following for tango was enjoyed through dance halls, radio and recordings until the end of the golden age around 1950.

TANGO POLITICS

As an expression of the working classes, the fortunes of the tango have inevitably been linked with social and political developments in Argentina and the social classes they empowered. The music declined a little in the 1930s as the army took power and suppressed what was seen as a potentially subversive force. Even so, the figure of **Juan D'Arienzo**, violinist and bandleader, looms large from the 1930s on. With a sharp, staccato rhythm, and prominent piano, the Juan D'Arienzo orchestra was the flavour of those years. His recording of "La cumparsita" at the end of 1937 is a classic and considered one of the greatest of all time.

Tango fortunes revived again in the 1940s when a certain political freedom returned, and the music enjoyed a second golden age with the rise of Perón in 1946 and his emphasis on nationalism and popular culture to win mass support. This was the era of a new generation of bandleaders. At the top, alongside Juan D'Arienzo were **Osváldo Pugliese, Hector Varela** and the innovative **Aníbal Troilo**. Of all bandoneón players, it was Troilo who expressed most vividly, deeply and powerfully, and so tenderly, the nostalgic sound of what is now regarded as a noble instrument. When he died a few years ago half a million people followed his funeral procession to the cemetery.

Buenos Aires in the late 1940s was a city of five or six million and each barrio would have ten or fifteen amateur tango orchestras, while the established orchestras would play in the cabarets and nightclubs in the centre of the city. Somehow in this era, however, tango began to move away from working class to middle class and intellectual milieus. Tango became a sort of collective reminiscence of a world that no longer existed – essentially nostalgia. As a popular lyric, *Tango de otros tiempos* (Tango of Other Times), put it:

> *Tango, you were the king*
> *In one word, a friend*
> *Blossoming from the bandoneón music*
> *of Arólas*
> *Tango, the rot set in*
> *When you became sophisticated*
> *And with your airs and graces*
> *You quit the suburbs where you were born*
> *Tango, it saddens me to see*
> *How you've deserted the mean dirt-streets*
> *For a carpeted drawing-room*
> *In my soul I carry a small piece*
> *Of that happy past!*
> *But the good old times are over*
> *In Paris you've become Frenchified*
> *And today, thinking of what's happened*
> *A tear mars your song.*

In the 1950s, with the end of Peronism and the coming of rock'n'roll, tango slipped into the shadows once again.

ASTOR PIAZZOLLA AND TANGO NUEVO

Astor Piazzolla (see box on p.734) dominates the recent history of tango, much as Carlos Gardel was the key figure of its classic era. Born in Mar de Plata in 1921, Piazzolla spent his childhood in the Bronx, New York, where he was hired at age thirteen by Carlos Gardel to

play in the film *El día que me quieras* and booked for his Latin American tour. Luckily for Piazzolla he hadn't taken up the offer when the fatal aircrash in which Gardel died occurred. Back in Argentina, from 1937, Piazzolla played second bandoneón in the orchestra of Aníbal Troilo, where he developed his feel for arrangements. (While the first bandoneón takes the melody, it is the second bandoneón that gives the music its particular harmony and flavour.)

Troilo left Piazzolla his bandoneón when he died and Piazzolla went on to ensure that tango would never be the same again. In the 1950s he won a government scholarship to study with Nadia Boulanger in Paris (one of the most celebrated teachers of composition, who included Aaron Copland among her pupils). It was Boulanger who encouraged Piazzolla to develop the popular music of his heritage.

Piazzolla's idea was that tango could be a serious music to listen to, not just for dancing, and for many of the old guard it was a step too far. As he explained: "Musicians hated me. I was taking the old tango away from them. The old tango, the one they loved, was dying. And they hated me, they threatened my life hundreds of times. They waited for me outside my house, two or three of them, and gave me a good beating. They even put a gun at my head once. I was in a radio station doing an interview, and all of a sudden the door opens and in comes this tango singer with a gun. That's how it was."

In the 1970s Piazzolla was out of favour with Argentina's military regime and he and his family moved to Paris for their own safety, returning to Argentina only after the fall of the junta. His influence, however, had spread, and his experiments – and international success – opened the way for other radical transformations.

Chief among these, in 1970s Buenos Aires, was the fusion of **tango-rockero** – tango rock. This replaced the flexible combination of bandoneón, bass and no drums, as favoured by Piazzolla, with a rock-style rhythm section, electric guitars and synthesizers. It was pioneered by **Litto Nebbia**, whose own album, *Homage to Gardél and Le Péra*, is one of the most successful products of this fusion, retaining the melancholy of the traditional form in a rock format. Tango moved across to jazz, too, through groups such as the trio **Siglo XX** – Osvaldo Belmonte on piano, Narciso Saúl on

ASTOR PIAZZOLLA

Astor Piazzolla (1921–92) brought the tango a long way from when it was first danced in Buenos Aires a century ago by two pimps on a street corner. In his hands this backstreet dance acquired a modernist "art music" gloss.

Born in Mar de Plata, yet spending his childhood in New York, Piazzolla's controversial innovation came from his classical music studies in Paris with **Nadia Boulanger**, who thought his classical compositions lacked feeling – but upon hearing his tango *Triunfal* apparently caught him by the hands and said, "Don't ever abandon this. This is your music. This is Piazzolla."

Piazzolla returned to Mar de Plata in 1937, moving to Buenos Aires two years later, where he joined the seminal orchestra of **Anibal Troilo** as bandoneónista and arranger. In 1946 he formed his own first group and in 1960 his influential **Quinteto Nuevo Tango**. With this group, he experimented audaciously, turning tango inside out, introducing unexpected chords, chromatic harmony, differently emphasised rhythms, a sense of dissonance and openness. Traditional tango captures the dislocation of the immigrant, the disillusionment with the dream of a new life, transmuting these deep and raw emotions onto a personal plane of betrayal and triangular relationships. Piazzolla's genius comes from the fact that, within the many layers and changing moods and pace of his pieces, he never betrays this essence of tango – its sense of fate, its core of hopeless misery, its desperate sense of loss.

Piazzolla translated the philosophy expounded by tango poets like Enrique Santos Discépelo – who, in "El cambalache" (The Junkshop) concludes that the 20th-century world is an insolent display of blatant wickedness – onto the musical plane. A Piazzolla piece can shift from the personal to the epic so that a seeming cry from a violin or cello becomes a wailing city siren as if following a shift in landscape from personal misery and nostalgia to a larger, more menacing urban canvas.

In Piazzolla's tangos, passion and sensuality still walk side by side with sadness, but emotions, often drawn out to a level of almost unbearable intensity, are suddenly subsumed in a disquieting sense of inevitability. If you close your eyes while listening to his work, you can exploit the filmic dimension of the music: create your own music, walk Buenos Aires alone at Zero Hour, visit clubs and bars, pass through empty streets shadowed by the ghosts of a turbulent history. Piazzolla always said that he composed for the new generations of porteños, offering a music that allowed them to live an often dark and difficult present while absorbing their past.

Piazzolla's own ensembles turned tango into concert music. "For me," he said, "tango was always for the ear rather than the feet." This process escalated in the 1960s, when he started to work with poet **Horacio Ferrer**. Their first major work was a little opera called *María de Buenos Aires* (1967) but it was the seminal *Balada por un loco* (Ballad For A Madman) which pushed the borders of tango lyrics far from those of thwarted romance and broken dreams of traditional tango song. Surreal and witty, the ballad's lyrics reveal the tortured mental state and condition of a half-dancing, half-flying bowler-hatted apparition which appears on the streets of Buenos Aires. While it appalled traditional tangueros, the song inspired new aficionados at home and abroad, particularly among musicians.

Elected 'Distinguished Citizen of Buenos Aires' in 1985, Piazzolla's commitment to tango and its future was unequivocal. A prolific composer of over 750 works, including concertos, theatre and film scores, he created some atmospheric 'classical' pieces, including a 1979 concerto for bandoneón and orchestra, which combines the flavour of tango with a homage to Bach, and, in 1989, "Five Tango Sensations", a series of moody pieces for bandoneón and string quartet, commissioned by the Kronos Quartet. These are thrilling pieces, as indeed are all of his last 1980s concert performances released posthumously on CD.

guitars and Néstor Tomasini on saxophone, clarinet and percussion.

Meantime, the old guard had kept traditional tango alive, two key figures being Roberto Goyeneche and Osvaldo Pugliese. **Roberto "Polaco" Goyeneche**, born in 1926, had been vocalist for many orquestas tipicas before he followed in the footsteps of key singers Rivero and Fiorentino by singing with Troilo between

1955 and 1964. He then became a soloist working with various bands including **Hector Stamponi's** quartet, remaining a key interpreter until his death in 1994. He made more than one hundred records over his forty-year career. Pianist **Osvaldo Pugliese** remained one of the major tango musicians until his death in 1995 with many younger talented musicians serving their apprenticeships with him.

These days in Argentina, the tango scene is a pretty broad one, with rock and jazz important elements, along with the more traditional sound of acoustic groups. There is no shortage of good tangueros and they know each other well and jam together often. Nobody would think they had not been playing together in a band every night for years.

The big tango orchestras, however, are a thing of the past, and economic considerations mean that tango bands have returned to their roots, to an intimate era of trios, quartets and quintets, even a sextet is already serious business. Two of the best sextets, the **Sexteto Mayor** and **Sexteto Berlingieri**, joined together in the 1980s to play for the show *Tango Argentino*, and subsequent shows which revived an interest in tango across Europe and the USA, with each group going its own way in Buenos Aires. The Sexteto Mayor, founded in 1973 and starring the virtuoso bandoneonistas **José Libertella** and **Luís Stazo**, is one of the best tango ensembles playing in Argentina today. They can be seen periodically at El Viejo Almacén, Casa Blanca, and other tango places in Buenos Aires, when they are not on tour.

In a more modern idiom, singers like **Susana Rinaldi** and **Adriana Varela**, working with Litto Nebbia, are successfully renovating and re-creating tango, both at home and abroad, Varela particularly in Spain. They are names to look out for along with bandoneónistas **Osvaldo Piro**, **Carlos Buono** and **Walter Ríos** (Ríos is also working with the great "new song" singer Mercedes Sosa); violinist **Antonio Agri** who worked with Piazzolla and more recently with Paco de Lucía; bandoneonista, arranger and film-score composer **Nestór Marconi**; singer José Angel Trelles; pianist and composer **Gustavo Fedel**; and **Grupo Volpe Tango Contemporaneo**, led by Antonio Volpe.

Latterly tango is enjoying an upsurge of popularity in Argentina and other parts of the world – particularly Europe, where couple dancing seems right back in fashion. While there may be little discrepancy between the numbers of men and women looking for romance, flirtation and sex, modern pressures seem to prevent many people finding an ideal companion, making tango dancing – with its physical and emotional intensity, moments of courtship, male bravura and female aggression – a way of making contact and something of a wish-fulfillment.

According to choreographer Juan Carlos Copes, tango has responded to the viscitudes of contemporary gender values: "The tango is man and woman in search of each other. It is the search of an embrace, a way to be together, when the man feels that he is male and the woman feels that she is female, without machismo. She likes to be led; he likes to lead. The music arouses and torments, the dance is the coupling of two people defenceless against the world and powerless to change things."*

*Quoted in the definitive and beautifully illustrated book *¡Tango!* by Simon Collier (Thames & Hudson, 1995)

DISCOGRAPHY

Tango can increasingly be found in the world-music section of major record stores throughout the world; most commonly in collections of variable quality aimed at dancers, closely followed by the works of Carlos Gardel and Astor Piazzolla. An worldwide mail-order service is offered by the Buenos Aires' tango store, Zivals, accessed through their excellent Web site *www.zivals.com*.

The following recordings offer a good introduction to tango's major stars, both old and new.

The Rough Guide to Tango (World Music Network). With tracks from twenty of the greatest tango musicians – from Gardel and Piazzolla to contemporary artists such as Adriana Varela and Litto Nebbia – *The Rough Guide to Tango* is one of the best introductions to the genre.

Eladia Blásquez *La Mirada* (DBN). Recording from one of tango's finest modern singers and lyricists, including her first composition, the poetic *Sueño de Barrilete*.

Carlos Gardel *20 Grandes Éxitos* (EMI Odeon). One of the best of the innumerable collections of Gardel's finest recordings, packed with his unmistakeable renderings of iconic classics such as *El día me quieras*, *Volver*, *Caminito* and *Cuesta Abajo*.

Roberto Goyeneche *Maestros del Tango* (RCA). A superb compilation of hits from one of tango's most beloved characters, known affectionately as "El Polaco"; includes his classic interpretations of *Malena* (regarded as the definitive version of this tango), the seductive *Naranjo en Flor* and the wonderful *Sur*, an elegy to the atmospheric south of Buenos Aires, tango's true home. Another good compilation by Goyeneche is *El Disco de Oro* (RCA).

Tita Merello *La Merello* (EMI Odeon). Classic compilation by one of tango's early and most famous female stars, including her own composition, the bittersweet *Se dice de mí*.

Astor Piazzolla *Noches del Regina* (RCA). The master of modern tango interprets classics such as the polemical *Cambalache*, regarded as subversive by Argentina's military dictatorship as well as his inimitable and hugely popular *Balada para un loco*, telling the tale of a madman's wandering around the streets of Buenos Aires, with lyrics by Horacio Ferrer. For his most characteristic, avant-garde compositions, check out *Adios Nonino* (Trova) titled after perhaps his most famous composition, or *20 Éxitos* (BMG Entertainment) which also includes *Adios Nonino* as well as *Verano porteño*. Also look out for *Zero Hour* (Nonesuch), recorded in 1986, which Piazzolla himself thought was the finest set he ever made, with its evocative fusion of moments, emotions, situations distilled into moving form, charting the urban life of the individual in the city at Zero Hour, the time between midnight and dawn.

Osvaldo Pugliese *Tangos Famosos* (EMI Odeon). Classic recordings by the maestro of the "Generación del 40"; displaying his towering talent as both composer and pianist. There's also a multiple CD collection of his works, *Obras Completas*, also on EMI.

Susana Rinaldi *Cantando* (Polydor). One of tango's major contemporary female stars, noted for her powerful voice – occasionally a little strident but rich and expressive at its best. Includes classics such as *Cafetín de Buenos Aires*, *Madame Ivonne* and the gorgeous *María* by Cátulo Castillo.

Edmundo Rivero *En Lunfardo* (Polygram). The charismatic singer interprets classic tangos such as *El Chamuyo* and *Atentí, Pebeta*, infused with Buenos Aires' street slang, lunfardo.

Sexteto Mayor *Trottoirs de Buenos Aires* (World Network, Germany) Currently Argentina's premiere tango ensemble in the traditional style, the Sexteto Mayor is a shifting collection of virtuosi led by the two hugely experienced bendoneón players José Libertella and Luis Stazo, who started their vintage group in the early 1970s. This largely instrumental album of classic tangos is entirely thrilling, with Adriana Varela unleashing her deep, husky-

toned voice on four songs. Unashamedly emotional and utterly convincing.

Julio Sosa *El Varón del Tango* and *20 Grandes Éxitos* (both on Sony-Columbia). The self-styled "macho" of tango and last of the "old style" singers interprets classics such as *Sus ojos se cerraron* and the world famous *La Cumparsita*. Look out too for his version of *La Casita de mis viejos* for an insight into tango's almost mawkish attachment to the parental home – and in particular the mother.

Aníbal Troilo *Obra Completa* (RCA). Known affectionately as "pichuco", bandoneonista Aníbal Troilo led one of Argentina's most successful tango orchestras and composed many classics such as *Sur* and *Barrio de Tango*. His trademark *Che, bandoneón*, with lyrics by one of tango's great poets, Homero Manzi, is a sweet, sad elegy to the bandoneón itself.

Adriana Varela *Maquillaje* (Melopea). One of tango's most successful contemporary singers, offering a very distinctive, throaty interpretation of classic tangos and compositions by *rock nacional* superstars Fito Páez and Litto Nebbia.

Text courtesy of Jan Fairly, with a discography by Lucy Phillips.

ROCK NACIONAL

Listened to passionately throughout the country, Argentina's homegrown rock music – known simply as *rock nacional* – is something of an acquired taste, though amongst its numerous charismatic performers there's something for just about everyone.

Rock nacional first began to emerge in the 1960s with groups such as **Almendra**, one of whose members, **Luis Alberto Spinetta**, went on to a solo career and is still one of Argentina's most successful and original musicians and **Los Gatos**, who in 1967 had a massive hit with the eloquent *La Balsa* and two of whose members – Litto Nebbia and Pappo – went on to solo careers. From a sociological point of view, though, the significance of *rock nacional* really began to emerge under the military dictatorship of 1976–83, usually referred to simply as El Proceso. At the very beginning of the dictatorship, there was an upsurge in rock concerts, during which musicians such as **Charly García**, frontman of the hugely popular **Serú Girán** and now a soloist, provided a subtle form of resistance with song titles such as *No te dejes desanimar* (Don't Be Discouraged), which helped provoke a collective sense of opposition amongst rock fans. It wasn't long, however, before the military rulers clamped down on what it saw as the subversive atmosphere generated at rock concerts – one of the few opportunities for collective gatherings under the regime. In a famous 1976 speech, Admiral Massera referred to "suspect youths", whose immersion in the "secret society" of clothes, music and drugs associated with rock music made them potential guerrilla material. The clampdown began in 1977–78, with tear gas used at concerts, police repression and government-issued recommendations that stadium owners should not let their premises be used for rock concerts. Attempts to move the rock scene to smaller venues were equally repressed, and by the end of the 1970s many bands had split up or gone into exile.

In 1980 cracks began to appear in the regime: a growing recession saw powerful economic groups withdrawing their support, whilst the military leaders themselves were riven by internal conflict, and a subtle freeing up of the public sphere began, followed by the slow resurgence of rock concerts. In December 1980, a concert by Serú Girán attracted 60,000 fans to La Rural in Palermo: led by Charly García, the fans began to shout, in full view of the television cameras "no se banca más" (We won't put up with it anymore).

Without abandoning their previous repressive measures, the military regime, now under the leadership of General Viola, began to employ different tactics to deal with rock's subversive tendencies, producing its own, non-threatening rock magazine, and inaugurating a "musical train" which travelled around the country with some of Argentina's most famous rock musicians on board. Under Galtieri, however, there was a return to a more direct, authoritarian approach – though by now it was proving increasingly difficult to silence the opposition to the military. Rock concerts had begun to attract mass audiences again; together with religious pilgrimages to Luján, they provided the only significant gathering of young people during this dark period of Argentinian history. By 1982, the rock movement was a clearly cynical voice in society, creating massively popular songs such as **Fito Páez**'s self-explanatory *Tiempos difi-*

ciles (Difficult Times), Charly García's *Dinosaurios*, whose title is a clear reference to the military rulers and *Maribel* by Argentina's finest rock lyricist, Spinetta, dedicated to the Madres de Plaza de Mayo. When the Malvinas conflict broke out, **León Gieco**'s *Sólo le pido a Dios* clearly expressed antiwar sentiment and a commonly held suspicion of the government's motives in lines such as "I only ask of God/ not to be indifferent to war/ it's a giant monster and it stamps hard/ on the poor innocence of the people".

After the dictatorship ended, rock returned to a more apolitical role, typified by the lighthearted approach of 1984's most popular group, **Los Abuelos de la Nada**. However, one of the founding members of Los Abuelos, **Pappo**, went on to a solo career, making heavy rock and appealing to a predominantly working class section of society who felt that their lot had improved little with the coming of democracy; Pappo's music seemed to sum up their frustration with the system. One of the most popular groups of the 1980s was **Sumo**, fronted by the charismatic **Luca Prodán**, an Italian who had come to Argentina in an attempt to shake off his heroin addiction (an uncharacteristically sensitive recording of Sumo's is a version of the Velvet Underground's *Heroin*). Sumo made sometimes surreal, noisy, reggae-influenced tracks, expressing distaste for the frivolous attitudes of Buenos Aires' upper-middle-class youth on tracks such as *Rubia tarada* (Stupid Blonde). Luca Prodán died of a heroin overdose in 1987, but is still idolized by Argentinian rock fans. Like Sumo, the strangely named and massively popular **Patricio Rey y sus Redonditos de Ricota** (lit: Patricio Rey and the little balls of Ricotta) – who first began playing together in La Plata in the 1970s, though didn't record until the 1980s – made noisy, though slightly more serious, tracks with enigmatic titles such as *Aquella vaca solitaria cubana* (that solitary Cuban cow), often touching on the dissatisfactions felt by many young Argentines in the aftermath of the dictatorship. Another success story of the 1980s and 90s – albeit in a very different vein – was **Fito Páez**, whose 1992 album *El Amor después del amor*, with its sweet melodic tunes – one of them inspired by the film *Thelma and Louise* – sold millions throughout Latin America. Páez also made an anthemic recording *Dale alegría a mi corazón* (bring happiness to my heart), inspired by Diego Maradona. One of Argentina's most original bands also emerged in the 1980s – **Los Fabulosos Cadillacs**, with their diverse and often frenetic fusion of rock, ska, dub, punk and rap. An irreverent and ironic sense of humour often underlies their politicized lyrics, all belted out by their charismatic, astringently-voiced lead singer, Vincentico, and backed up with a tight horn section and driving Latin percussion. Their classic album is *El León* (1992), on which you'll find their most famous anthem, *Matador* (a savage indictment of the military dictatorship of the 1970s). Their follow-up, *Rey Azúcar* (1995), is also vibrant, including songs like *Mal Bicho* (Bad Critter), another with a guest appearance from Mick Jones, and a tongue-in-cheek Spanglish version of the Beatles' *Strawberry Fields Forever*, sung in duet with Debbie Harry.

Though countless new groups have sprung up in the last ten years or so, *rock nacional's* most enduring figures are still Charly García – whose wild exploits fill the pages of gossip magazines – Fito Paéz, Los Fabulosos Cadillacs, León Gieco, Luis Alberto Spinetta, Pappo and rosarino songsmith, **Litto Nebbia**, who has also made some excellent tango recordings.

CHAMAMÉ, CUARTETO AND FOLK

Tango aside, Argentine music is mostly rooted in the rural dance traditions of the countryside, an amalgam of Spanish and immigrant Central European styles with indigenous musics. Many of these dances – rancheras, milongas, *chacareras* and more – are shared with the neighbouring countries of Chile, Peru and Bolivia – while others, like chamamé are particularly Argentinian. This short article focuses on the urban musics of chamamé and cuarteto, and on rural folk music. Argentina, however, also has Amerindian roots, a music explored from the 1930s on by Atahualpa Yupanqui, which grew new shoots in the politicized *nueva canción* (new song) movement.

CHAMAMÉ

Chamamé is probably Argentina's most popular roots music. It has its origins in the rural culture of Corrientes in the northeast – an Amerindian area which attracted nineteenth-century settlers from Czechoslovakia, Poland, Austria and Germany, including many Jews. These immi-

grants brought with them middle-European waltzes, mazurkas and polkas which over time merged with music from the local Guaraní Amerindian traditions, and African rhythms from the music of the region's slaves. Thus emerged chamamé, a music of poor rural *mestizos*, many of whom looked more Indian or than European, and whose songs used both Spanish and the Indian Guaraní languages.

Chamamé's melodies have a touch of the melancholy attributed to the Guaraní, while its history charts the social, cultural and political relationships of *mestizo* migrants in a new environment. Until the 1950s, it was largely confined to its Corrientes home, but during that decade many rural migrants were moving into Buenos Aires to work in new industries, bringing their music and dances with them to local dance halls and cultural centres. Chamamé began to attract wider attention – in part, perhaps, because it was a rare folk dance in which people dance in cheek-to-cheek embrace.

The essential sound of chamamé comes from its key instrument – the large piano accordion (on occasion the bandoneón). It sweeps through tunes which marry contrasting rhythms, giving the music an immediate swing. Its African influences may have contributed to the music's accented weak beats so that bars blend and swing together. The distinctive percussive rhythms to the haunting, evocative melodies are the unique, compelling feature of this music.

Argentina's reigning King of Chamamé is *Raúl Barboza*, an artist who has had particular success in Europe in the 1990s. He followed in the footsteps of his Corrientes-born father Adolfo, who founded his first group in 1956. Barboza's conjunto features a typical chamamé line-up of one or two accordions, a guitar (occasionally two guitars whose main job is to mark the rhythm) and *guitarrón* (bass guitar).

CUARTETO

The Argentine dance style known as **cuarteto** first became popular in the 1940s. Named after the original **Cuarteto Leo** who played it, its line-up involved a solo singer, piano, accordion and violin, and its dance consisted of a huge circle, moving anticlockwise, to a rhythm called *tunga-tunga*. In the 1980s it underwent a resurgence of interest in the working-class "tropical" dancehalls of Buenos Aires, where it was adopted alongside Colombian *guarachas*, Dominican merengue and Latin salsa. It slowly climbed up the social ladder to reach a middle-class market, notching up big record sales. The most famous contemporary singer of cuarteto is **Carlos "La Mona" Jiménez**.

FOLKLORICA

In a movement aligned to nueva canción, dozens of folklorica singers and groups emerged in the 1960s and 1970s – their music character-ized by tight arrangements and four-part har-monies. Alongside nueva canción star **Mercedes Sosa** (see p.364), leading artists of these decades included the groups **Los Chalchaleros**, **Los Fronterizos** and **Los Hermanos Abalos**; and guitarists **Eduardo Falú**, **Ramón Ayala**, **Ariel Ramírez** (notable for his zambas and his Creole Mass), **Suma Paz** and **Jorge Cafrune**.

The 1980s saw the emergence of new folk composers including **Antonio Tarragó Ros** and **Peteco Carabajal**, while in more recent years groups have come through experiment-ing and re-evaluating the folk dance traditions of *zamba*, *chacareras*, *cuecas*, and the like, with a poetic emphasis. Among this new wave are **Los Trovadores**, **Los Huanca Hua**, **Cuarteto Zupuy**, **El Grupo Vocal Argentino** and **Opus 4**.

The best place to see folklorica music is at the annual **Cosquín national folklore festi-val**, which has been a fixture since the 1960s.

DISCOGRAPHY

Argentine: Musical Patrimony of the North-West Territories (Playasound). A compilation of the country music of this vast area: from *bagualas* to carnival dances.

Raúl Barboza *Raúl Barboza* (La Lichere). Born in Buenos Aires but absorbing the musical influ-ences of his father's Corrientes background,

Barboza is known as the King of Chamamé – a popular, deeply nostalgic music with percussive melodies. Barboza won the endorsement of Astor Piazzolla: "He's a fighter who deserves my respect and admiration." With guitar, bass, harp, percussion and second accordion, Barboza leads a compelling concert set of quintessential chamamé on this recording: typical rasguido dobles and polkas that sound like nothing you've ever heard in Europe.

Before The Tango: Argentina's Folk Trad-ition 1905–1936 (Harlequin). A fascinating col-lection of recordings which map the folk music of the country from the beginning of the twen-tieth century. It moves from improvising verses of payadores, through blind harpists to pasodobles, to *cuecas* and a Galician *muineras*: music from the interior of the country brought by immigrants from Spain, Italy and other parts of the world.

Chamamé (Iris Musique). A compilation featur-ing a number of small bands playing chamamé instrumentals and songs or poetic texts. Includes Los Zorzales del Litoral, Hector Ballario, Grupo Convicción and pick of the bunch, singer and accordionist Favio Salvagiot in a band with two dynamic accordions. However, none of the performances are equal to the recommended chamamé discs by Barboza and Flores.

Rudy and Nini Flores *Chamamé – Musique du Paraná* (Ocora). The Flores are two young brothers from Corrientes Province playing instrumental chamamé: Rudy (born 1961) on guitar and Nini (born 1966) on accordion. This superb collection of their work is an intimate disc of great artistry. A sharp, poignant and mis-chievous accordion sound that sustains the interest in nineteen chamamé duos.

Text courtesy of Jan Fairley

LITERATURE

Argentina's 95 percent literacy rate is one of the highest in the world and its many bookshops, especially the splendidly monumental ones in Buenos Aires, are a reflection of the considerable interest in what is written in both Argentina and the outside world. While Argentine nationals have won the Nobel prizes for chemistry, medicine and peace, none of the country's outstanding writers has ever been rewarded with the prize for literature – all the more galling for Argentines, given that two Chileans have been. Borges is the giant of Argentine literature, but he by no means dwarfs the country's other extremely original novelists and poets, many of whose works have been translated into English and make for highly readable companions during a visit to the country.

For much of the twentieth century Argentina's rich and varied literary production was dominated, for the outside world at least, by the country's greatest ever writer, **Jorge Luis Borges** (1899–1986). Borges is inextricably linked with Buenos Aires – a kind of anthropomorphic protagonist in much of his highly original prose and poetry. Like many of his compatriots, he was both fascinated and frustrated by the notion of the Argentine identity as a kind of extension of Europe, apparently incapable of throwing off the shackles of its immigrant past. Even now Argentine literature – mirroring general social concerns – often seems obsessed with the dichotomy between an archaic, thinly populated rural economy and one of the continent's biggest, most densely populated and modern cities, Buenos Aires. Ever since the country's independence in the early nineteenth

century, there has been an ongoing civil war of sorts, between the provinces seeking more and more decentralized power, led in the early days by General Rosas and later by Perón, and a sophisticated metropolis apparently more interested in what is going on in Paris, London and Madrid, or more recently in New York, Miami and San Francisco, than in its vast and seemingly primitive hinterland.

The writer who first seems to have grasped this phenomenon is nineteenth-century Renaissance man **Domingo Sarmiento** (1811–88), Rosas' arch enemy and president of Argentina from 1868 to 1874. A no-nonsense autodidact from San Juan, he was almost obsessed with the idea that Argentina was condemned to backwater status and economic ruin unless it invested in education, overthrew the Federalists like Rosas (which he helped to bring about) and introduced elements of North American society, including what he saw as a proper democracy. His classic *Facundo, or Civilization and Barbarism*, written while he was exiled in Chile in 1845, is a compendium of impressions about Argentina in the form of a romantic biography of a gaucho thug named Facundo Quiroga. A leitmotiv of the novel-cum-essay is the fact that Argentina's size is a curse rather than a blessing, hampering communications and making it possible for local strongmen like Quiroga (and Rosas) to flourish.

An even greater classic, regarded by many as Argentina's national literary work, is **José Hernández**'s *Martín Fierro* (1872), a novel in verse of epic proportions and traditionally learned by heart by many Argentines. Written as a protest against the corrupt authorities, it features a highly likeable gaucho outlaw on the run, who rails against the country's weak institutional structures and dictatorial rulers. One of the highlights is a lurid description of the hero's visit to an *encomienda*. Hernández (1834–86) published a second part, *The Return of Martín Fierro*, in 1879 but it lacked the drama of the earlier work. Written just before *Martín Fierro*, in 1870, is the equally gripping *A Visit to the Ranquel Indians*, by **Lucio Mansilla** (1831–1913). Taking the form of letters home to Buenos Aires, its anthropological descriptions are mingled with personal insights of a Porteño exposed for the first time to the realities of the country's far-flung outposts and indigenous peoples.

José Marmol's (1818–71) rambling *Amalia: a Romance of the Argentine* (Gordon Press, New York, 1977), written in exile, is a love story centred on the young heroine Amalia, while dealing with political intrigues under Rosas in the 1850s; while *The Slaughter House* (Las Américas, New York, 1959), was also written in exile and published posthumously in 1871 by an opponent of Rosas, the socialist poet **Esteban Echeverría** (1805–51) is a parable of the unspeakable brutality exacted by Rosas and his henchmen on a sensitive young man.

These preoccupations did not go away in the twentieth century. In 1926 **Ricardo Güiraldes** (1886–1927) was still writing about the gaucho way of life and the remoteness of rural Argentina in his elegiac *Don Segundo Sombra: Shadows on the Pampa*, whose eponymous hero is a guru-like figure and whose narrator is initiated in a range of manual and ethical skills to help him survive in the outback.

Argentina's Edgar Allen Poe, **Horacio Quiroga** (1878–1937), wrote some vivid and at times lurid short stories set in Misiones province – *The Decapitated Chicken and Other Stories* (University of Texas Press, 1976). More recent still is leading writer **Manuel Puig's** (1932–1990) *Heartbreak Tango: A Serial* (1982), a mordant anatomy of a provincial mind seduced by the apparent glamour of Buenos Aires, with more musings about living in Argentina's extensive flat wilderness. Puig is best known for his superb *Kiss of the Spiderwoman* (1984), a convincing albeit surreal portrait of a political militant sharing a prison cell with a homosexual obsessed with Hollywood starlets and romantic movies, itself turned into a brilliant film directed by Hector Babenco in 1985, starring William Hurt and Raúl Julia. Set during the military dictatorship of the 1970s, the novel shows how the two forge an ever-closer relationship, exploited ruthlessly by the thuggish authorities. **Juan José Saer** (born 1937) has written a number of modernist works set in and around his native Santa Fe, such as *The Event* (Serpent's Tail, 1998), in which the light and landscape condition the minds of his aimless characters.

By the beginning of the twentieth century the phenomenal urban explosion in the capital had sparked off some of Argentina's most intriguing and original fiction. Several writers vie for the accolade of the city's bard. **Leopoldo Marechal** (1900–70) self-consciously titled his mock epic of daily life in Porteño suburbia *Adán Buenosayres* (1948), with a gallery of bohemian poets and larger-than-life story-tellers as its cast. Until his tragically early death, **Roberto Arlt** (1900–42) captured the lot of the poor immigrant, with his gripping if idiosyncratic novels about anarchists, investors, whores and other marginal characters in the mean streets of 1920s Buenos Aires, most pleasingly portrayed in *The Seven Madmen* (1972). Published in 1933, *X-ray of the Pampa* by essayist and poet **Ezequiel Martínez Estrada** (1895–1964) again examines, in a quirky way, the mutual ignorance of the capital and the cattle-country stretching for hundreds of kilometres to the west. His contemporary **Eduardo Mallea** (1903–82) wrote somewhat ponderous fiction along similar lines, of which the best example is his 1941 novel *All Green Shall Perish*. Buenos Aires in the 1950s was conjured up poignantly by **Ernesto Sábato** (born 1911) a physicist by profession whose writings explore the city's nostalgia and feeling of utter alienation in three seminal works, *The Tunnel* (Cape, 1980), *On Heroes and Tombs* (Cape, 1982) and *The Angel of Darkness*, (Cape, 1992). **Julio Cortázar** (1914–84) spent much of his career in Europe, but his 1966 novel *Hopscotch*, albeit manifestly influenced by the French existentialist movement led by Sartre and Camus, features unmistakably Porteño characters; his later short stories, some of them collected as *Bestiary: Short Stories*, continue to dramatize the tense relationship between the Europe of Argentina's human origins and the construction of a new country on an alien continent – his stories are one of the highpoints of twentieth-century literature.

While Borges' friend, confidante and collaborator **Adolfo Bioy Casares** (1914–99) should not be overlooked – seek out his weird novella *The Invention of Morel* (1985) or the equally off-the-wall *The Diary of the War of the Pig* (1972) – it is Borges himself who put Argentine letters on the world map. Born in Buenos Aires, he spent his youth in Europe, mostly in Switzerland (where he died and is buried), and "rediscovered" Buenos Aires and its barrios upon his return in the 1920s. He started out as an avant-garde poet, translator, journalist and literary critic, but soon turned to quirky parables, with sardonic or provocative overtones and unexpected twists that had him described as a magic realist. His early poetry turns Buenos Aires and many of its sights – like La Recoleta cemetery and the Botanical Gardens – into semi-mythical beings, but his work as a whole sets up the city as a perplexing labyrinth. Another recurring theme is the idea of (national) identity as illusory, and he used his subtly allegorical style to criticize Perón's chauvinistic demagoguery – he had nothing but loathing for the president and the deified Evita. His teasing and certainly baffling *Fictions* and *The Aleph* are as good an introduction to his oeuvre as any; start with his own favourite story, *The South*.

BOOKS

There's a fair number of books on Argentina available in English, ranging from specialist academic publications to travelogues. Most major bookstores will have an historical work or two while secondhand bookstores are often a goldmine for finding quirky and obscure works by travellers in the nineteenth and early twentieth centuries.

The recent upsurge of interest in things Argentinian – thanks in part to the current tango craze and Alan Parker's movie *Evita* – has seen a concurrent small burst of new English translations and reissues of many of Argentina's classic novels. If your previous experience of Latin American fiction has been the classic "magic realism" of García Márquez or the works of Isabel Allende, then you'll find many surprises in Argentinian literature – from the dark urban narrative of Roberto Arlt, through Manuel Puig's idiosyncratic appropriation of the popular culture of soap operas and film, to the erudite yet absorbing works of the unique Jorge Luis Borges.

The books listed below have details of the UK publisher followed by those of the US publisher, where different. The term o/p denotes that a book is currently out of print, but is still generally available through secondhand bookstores.

TRAVEL

Bruce Chatwin, *In Patagonia* (Vintage/Penguin). For many travellers, *the* Argentine travel book; really a series of self-contained tales (most famously of the Argentinian adventures of Butch Cassidy and the Sundance Kid) strung together by their connection with Patagonia. An idiosyncratic book which has inspired a "Chatwin trail", though his rather cold style and literary embellishments on the region's history have their detractors too. Read it and make up your own mind.

Bruce Chatwin and Paul Theroux, *Patagonia Revisited* (Picador), published in the US as *Nowhere is a Place* (Sierra Club Books). The two doyens of Western travel writing combine to explore the literary associations of Patagonia. Wafer-thin and thoroughly enjoyable, this book throws more light on the myths of this far-flung land than it does on the place itself. With glorious photos by Jeff Grass.

Che Guevara, *The Motorcycle Diaries* (Verso, UK). A lively counterpoint to the weighty biographies of Argentina's greatest revolutionary, this is Che's own account of his epic motorcycle tour around Latin America, beginning in Buenos Aires and heading south to Patagonia and then up through Chile. Che undertook the tour when he was just 23 and the resulting diary is an intriguing blend of travel anecdotes and an insight into the mind of a nascent revolutionary.

Miranda France, *Bad Times in Buenos Aires* (Weidenfeld & Nicolson/Ecco). Despite the title and the often downbeat tone, this whimsical journal brings Porteños to life, and you can't help feeling the author secretly loves the place. Highlights include a near-miss encounter with Menem's toupée.

Eric Shipton, *Tierra del Fuego: the Fatal Lodestone* (o/p). An involved and passionate account of the discovery and exploration of the southernmost archipelago, recounted by a hardened adventurer and mountaineer who had more insight into these lands than most. A superb achievement that makes for a riveting read.

Paul Theroux, *The Old Patagonian Express* (Penguin/Cape Cod Scriveners Co). More tales about trains by the tireless cynic, but in the four chapters on Argentina, which he passed through just before the 1978 World Cup, he waxes lyrical about cathedral-like Retiro station and has a surreal dialogue with Borges.

www.amazon.co.uk (UK) and **www. amazon.com** (US) The world's major online bookstore, with hundreds of titles relating to Argentina, including many of those covered below.

Canning House Library, 2 Belgrave Square, London SW1X 8PH (☎020/7235 2303). A good selection of books on Argentina (and other Hispanic countries). Also produces a quarterly bulletin detailing new publications on Latin America.

Grant & Cutler Ltd, 55–57 Great Marlborough St, London W1V 2AY (☎020/7734 2012; *www.grant-c.demon.co.uk*). Major foreign-language bookstore, with a comprehensive range of Argentine literature in Spanish and English,

dictionaries and a small selection of history and travel. Also worldwide mail-order service.

Latin America Bureau, 1 Amwell St, London EC1R 1UL (☎020/7278 2829). Publishers of books on Latin America, which are available by mail order along with a wide selection of other publishers' titles. Also has an interesting library open by appointment.

South American Explorer's Club, 126 Indian Creek Rd, Ithaca, NY 14850, US (☎607/277-0488; *explorer@samexplo.org*). Among its mountain of resources on South America, this long-established organization produces a free catalogue containing a wide choice of books available by mail order, to members and non-members alike.

A.F. Tschiffely, *Tschiffely's Ride* (o/p). An account of an adventurous ride – described as the "longest and most arduous on record ever made by man and horse" – from Buenos Aires to Washington in the 1920s. The first forty pages deals with his trip up to the Bolivian border in Jujuy and, though his style is rather pedestrian, it provides an insight into rural Argentina of the time and includes a spot of grave robbing at the Tilcara ruins.

HISTORY, POLITICS AND SOCIETY

Lucas Bridges, *Uttermost Part of the Earth* (o/p). The classic text on pioneering life in Tierra del Fuego, related by the remarkable son of the famous missionary to the Yámana, Thomas Bridges. Its genius lies less in its literary attributes than in the extraordinary tales of an adventurous young man's relationship with the indigenous Selk'nam, and the invaluable ethnographic knowledge he imparts about a people whose culture was set to disappear within his lifetime. Well worth scouring secondhand bookstores to try to locate a copy.

Jimmy Burns, *The Hand of God* (Bloomsbury/Lyons Press), *The Land that Lost its Heroes* (o/p). *The Hand of God* is a compelling read in which Anglo-Argentine journalist Burns charts the rise and fall of Argentina's bad-boy hero of football, Maradona. *The Land that Lost its Heroes* is a considered and thoroughly researched account of the build-up to the Falklands/Malvinas conflict – and its aftermath. Burns was the only full-time British correspon-

dent (for the *Financial Times*) in Argentina during the conflict and his knowledge of both Argentina and Britain shines through.

Nick Caistor, *Argentina in Focus: a Guide to the People, Politics and Culture* (Latin America Bureau, UK). A highly accessible and concise introduction to the country, with chapters dedicated to the economy, culture, society, history and politics, and land and people.

Alicia Dujovne Ortiz, *Eva Perón: A Biography* (Warner/St Martin's Press). A biography of Argentina's most famous female icon from an Argentine author, who places her subject firmly within the context of national culture. A book which is as colourful as its subject, mixing fact, gossip and rumour to let you judge the woman for yourself.

Martin Honeywell and Jenny Pearce, *Falklands: Whose Crisis?* (o/p). A slim book, published in the immediate aftermath of the South Atlantic War, which takes the thorny issue of the Falklands/Malvinas by the scruff of the neck and strips it of the misinformation and propaganda that surrounds it. It savages both sides for jingoistic militarism, exposes shenanigans at the British Foreign Office and outlines potential solutions that haven't much changed since: essential reading for a background to the problem.

Daniel James, *Resistance and Integration. Peronism and the Argentine Working Class, 1946–1976* (Cambridge UP, UK). One of the most respected treatments of the complex subject of Perón's ambiguous relationship with the working class and the unions, examining the real improvements instigated by Perón, as well as his clampdown on dissent.

Simon Kuper, *Football Against the Enemy* (Orion/Trafalgar Square). A collection of essays on how politics is all too frequently the unwelcome bedfellow of football across the globe, including an entertaining and insightful chapter on the murky 1978 World Cup campaign in Argentina, with wonderful revelations about ex-president Menem's priorities in government: football comes first.

Richard Llewellyn, *Down Where the Moon is Small* (o/p). The concluding part of a trilogy that started with his famous *How Green Was My Valley*, this book examines the themes of faith, righteousness, exile and toil in the pioneering Welsh community of Trevelin around the end of the nineteenth century. Well-researched and evocative, it examines Chilean–Argentinian tension over the Andean border dispute, the failure of the early Welsh dream to be masters of their own land, the realities of incorporation into a nation state and the supplanting of the earlier indigenous culture. Although it over-romanticizes the local Mapuche, it offers a sympathetic insight into how these people – the real losers of the period – viewed the developments.

John Lynch, *Massacre in the Pampas, 1872: Britain and Argentina in the Age of Migration* (University of Oklahoma Press, US). A well-researched examination of nineteenth-century immigration to Argentina, and of its unsettling influence on sections of the criollo population, culminating in the bloody Tata Dios revolt in the town of Tandil.

Colin McEwan (ed), *Patagonia: Natural History, Prehistory and Ethnography at the Uttermost End of the Earth* (British Museum Press). A series of accessible, scholarly essays on aspects of Patagonian indigenous life and religion up to the disintegration of these cultures in the early twentieth century. It gives intriguing insights into the unwitting impact that these people had on developing key aspects of European thought such as Darwin's Theory of Evolution, and on the lack of real communication and understanding between dramatically distinct cultures. Released to coincide with a major exhibition, it is a beautifully illustrated volume that is the first port of call for anyone interested in the subject.

Greta MacKenzie, *Why Patagonia* (ISBN 0903960-12-5). A gentle and personal little work of social history, published by the author herself, tracing the emigration of Scottish crofters to Patagonia during the boom years of the early twentieth century. They came to work as shepherds or domestic servants and, though not as famous as the Welsh colony, many prospered in this harsh environment and put down roots.

Lucio V. Mansilla *A Visit to the Ranquel Indians* (University of Nebraska Press). An account of a military colonel's dealings with the Ranquel Mapuches in 1870, apporting much useful ethnographic material and giving insight into the Pampas frontier conflict. Though clouded in places by self-obsession and frustrated political ambition, it nevertheless provides an interesting contemporary counterpoint to the dominant theme of the day, the "Indian problem", questioning the assumptions that lay behind Sarmiento's narrow definition of civilization and inexorable progress. Eva Gillies' translation is excellent, with informative footnotes and a handy historical introduction.

Carlos Martínez Sarasola, *Nuestros Paisanos: Los Indios* (Emecé Editores S.A., Argentina). A sizeable and diverse volume, in Spanish, that aims to reassess the role of Argentina's indigenous populations throughout the region's history. Replete with maps and statistical charts, the book also contains a synthesis of indigenous issues in today's Argentina, and tries to dispel some of the ignorance that surrounds them, espousing the need for pluralism and tolerance.

Tony Mason, *Passion of the People? Football in South America* (Verso, UK). An analytical account of the developments and popularity of football in South America, largely concentrating on Brazil and Argentina. An interesting read that manages to interweave sport, culture and politics.

George Chaworth Musters, *At Home with the Patagonians* (o/p). The amazing 1869 journey of Musters as he rode with the Aónik'enk from southern Patagonia to Carmen de Patagones, becoming in the process the first outsider to be accepted into Tehuelche society and the first white man to traverse the region south to north. This book is our prime source for knowledge of the Tehuelche, and represents a snapshot of a nomadic culture that was about to be exterminated.

Alicia Partnoy, *The Little School: Tales of Disappearance and Survival in Argentina* (Virago, UK). A sometimes harrowing account of the time spent by the author in one of Argentina's most notorious detention centres during the 1970s. A bleak tale, though leavened by its portrayal of the ability of the human spirit to survive the greatest adversity.

Hernán Pisano Skarmeta, Alfredo Prieto, et al, *Patagonia: Introduction to Ethnographic Photography* (Patagonia Comunicaciones, Chile). A fine collection of early photographs of Patagonian and Fuegian indigenous groups, presented alongside bilingual text that examines the questionable motives and stereotypes of those who took the photos. Though the translation is sometimes weak, the subject and images are fascinating.

David Rock, *Argentina 1516–1987* (o/p). The seminal history work on Argentina in English; a vast and comprehensive book covering the country's development from the first European incursion until the end of the Alfonsín period. Rock attempts to tackle the eternal question of Argentina's failure to realize its potential, concentrating on political and economic issues.

Domingo F. Sarmiento, *Facundo, or Civilization and Barbarism* (Penguin Books). An often rambling, multilayered essay defining Argentina's cultural peculiarities and attacking the arbitrary, uncivilized rule of the provincial strongmen or *caudillos*.

Nicholas Shumway, *The Invention of Argentina* (University of California Press). A sterling treatment of nineteenth-century intellectual impulses behind the formation of the modern Argentine nation state and the development of a national identity, with analysis of key debates such as that between Unitarists and Federalists. Though the subject matter would seem weighty, the book reads extremely well, with rich cultural detail throughout, and is invaluable in shedding light on the country we see today.

Jacobo Timerman, *Prisoner Without A Name, Cell Without A Number* (Vintage). A gruelling tale of detention under the 1976–83 military dictatorship, as endured by Timerman, then the editor of leading liberal newspaper of the time, *La Opinión*. The author is Jewish, and his experiences lead to a wider consideration of antiSemitism and the nature of totalitarian regimes.

Horacio Verbitsky, *The Flight: Confessions of an Argentine Dirty Warrior* (New Press). A respected investigative journalist, Verbitsky tells the story of Francisco Silingo, a junior naval officer during the Dirty War, involved in the horrific practice of pushing drugged prisoners out of airplanes over the Atlantic Ocean and the River Plate. A meticulously researched account of a dark episode in Argentina's history, long common knowledge but only recently officially brought to light.

NATURE AND WILDLIFE

Charles Darwin, *The Voyage of the Beagle* (Penguin). Very readable account of Darwins' famous voyage, which takes him through Patagonia and the pampas. Filled with observations on the flora, fauna, landscape and people (including the dictator Rosas) that Darwin encounters, all described in the scientist's methodical yet evocative style.

Gerald Durrell, *Whispering Land* (Penguin/Viking Press). A lighthearted and wonderfully descriptive read detailing Durrell's antics and observations while animal collecting in Peninsula Valdés, the Patagonian steppe and the yungas. Enduring good-value, despite what now comes across as a colonial, expat tone: his capacity for making animals into characters is unsurpassed.

Gerald Durrell, *The Drunken Forest* (o/p). The accident-prone author strikes out in search of more unsuspecting wildlife. Essentially centering on a collecting trip in the 1950s to the Paraguayan chaco, but which could equally apply to the Argentinian chaco, with the same species involved, and with adventures in the estancias of the pampas.

Graham Harris, *A Guide to the Birds and Mammals of Coastal Patagonia* (Princeton University Press). An informative, slickly produced but somewhat expensive field guide that includes first-rate illustrations of Patagonian mammals. Stronger on Chubut Province than further south, especially as regards the birds and, for the purpose of identification, could do with illustrations of the cetaceans as you see them in the sea rather than just the whole animal.

W.H. Hudson, *Far Away and Long Ago* (The Lyons Press, US). A nostalgic and gently ambling portrait of childhood and rural tranquility on the Argentine pampas, this is a book where the background becomes the foreground and vice versa: politics and the "events" of civil war in Rosas' time recede, giving way to the little things of life, as noticed by a child with an intense, spiritual love of nature. An early environmentalist, the author regrets the expansion of agriculture and the destruction of habitat variety in the pampas in the course of his lifetime.

Martín R. de la Peña and Maurice Rumboll, *Collins Illustrated Checklist: Birds of Southern South America and Antarctica* (HarperCollins). The best field guide currently available on Argentinian ornithology, and a useful companion to even the non-specialist bird-watcher. It would benefit from some indication of frequency and an indexed list of local names, and there are some problems with certain plates as regards colouring and mixed scale, but overall can be thoroughly recommended.

Graciela Ramacciotti, *Flores and Frutos Silvestres Australes* (ISBN: 950-43-7293-7) Identification of the plants and flowers of Tierra del Fuego is made easy with this slim, lovingly-produced and bilingual (Spanish/English) photographic guide. It's also applicable to much of Patagonia; and there's a recipe section at the back. Published by the author.

THE ARTS

John King and Nissa Torrents (eds), *The Garden of Forking Paths: Argentine Cinema* (o/p). Authorative collection of essays on Argentine cinema, compiled by two experts in the field. An excellent introduction to Argentina's film industry.

Simon Collier (ed), *Tango! The Dance, the Song, the Story* (Thames & Hudson, UK). A glossy coffee-table book with a lively account of the history of tango and its key protagonists, well-illustrated with colour and black-and-white photos.

David Elliott (ed), *Art from Argentina: 1920–1994* (Museum of Modern Art, Oxford, UK). Comprehensive illustrated account of the development of twentieth-century Argentine art, composed of a series of focused essays and monographs of major figures. Indispensable to anyone with a serious interest in the subject.

FICTION

César Aira, *The Hare* (Serpent's Tail, UK). A witty novel about an English naturalist in nineteenth-century Argentina by Borges' literary heir, a truly prolific and original writer at the forefront of contemporary Argentine literature.

Roberto Arlt, *The Seven Madmen* (Serpent's Tail, UK). A new English translation of a classic novel by the incomparable Roberto Arlt, perhaps Argentina's first unmistakeably "modern" twentieth-century writer. Arlt weaves a dark and at times surreal tale of life on the margins of society in early twentieth-century Buenos Aires, filled with images of the frenetic and alienating pace of urban life as experienced by the novel's tormented protagonist, Remo Erdosain.

Jorge Luis Borges, *Labyrinths* (Penguin/W.W. Norton & Co). A good introduction to the short stories and essays of Argentina's most famous writer, with selections from various of his major collections, including the seminal *Ficciones*, first published in 1945. Includes many of his best known and most enigmatic tales, including the bizarre *Tlön, Uqbar, Orbis Tertius* – a typically scholarly incursion into an imagined culture; the archetypal Borgesian *Library of Babel*, an analogy of the world as a never-ending library; and *Death and the Compass*, an erudite detective story set in an unnamed city which Borges claimed to be his most successful attempt at capturing the essence of Buenos Aires. Borges is sometimes regarded as the founding father of magic realism, but his complex, highly original works are really in a class of their own.

Julio Cortázar, *Hopscotch* (Harvill Press/Pantheon). One of world literature's major twentieth-century works, published in Spanish in the 1960s as *Rayuela* and currently being reappraised as the first "hypertext" novel. In this fantastically complex work, Cortázar defies traditional narrative structure, inviting the reader to "hop" between chapters (hence the name), which recount the interweaving of lives of a group of friends in both Paris and London. Cortázar is also well regarded for his enigmatic short stories; try the collections *Bestiary: Selected Stories* (Harvill, UK) and *Blow Up and Other Stories* (Random House).

Tomás Eloy Martínez, *The Perón Novel* (Anchor/Vintage) and *Santa Evita* (Anchor/Vintage). In a compelling book which darts between fact and fiction, Tomás Eloy Martínez intersperses his account of the events surrounding Perón's return to Argentina in 1973 with anecdotes from his past. Perón emerges as a strange and manipulative figure, pragmatic in all his relationships and still irked by Evita's popularity 30 years after her death. The companion volume to *The Perón Novel*, recounting the fascinating, morbid and at times farcical true story of Evita's life and – more importantly – afterlife, during which her corpse is hidden, hijacked and smuggled abroad. Even after death, Evita continues to inspire devotion and obsession, most notably in her guardian, the anonymous Colonel.

Graham Greene, *The Honorary Consul* (Penguin/Simon & Schuster). A masterful account of a farcical kidnapping attempt which goes tragically wrong. Set in the litoral city of Corrientes and dedicted to Argentine literary doyenne Victoria Ocampo, with whom Greene spent time in San Isidro and Mar del Plata.

Ricardo Güiraldes, *Don Segundo Sombra* (University of Pittsburgh Press, US). A tender evocation of past life on the pampas, chronicling the relationship between a young boy and the novel's eponymous gaucho. A key text in the placing of the gaucho at the heart of Argentina's national identity.

Manuel Puig, *Kiss of the Spiderwoman* (Vintage, UK). Arguably the finest book by one of Argentina's most original twentieth-century writers, distinguished by a style that mixes film dialogue and popular culture with more traditional narrative. This is an absorbing tale of two cellmates, worlds apart on the outside but drawn ever closer together by gay protagonist Molina's recounting of films to his initially cynical companion, left-wing guerrilla Valentín.

Horacio Quiroga, *The Decapitated Chicken and Other Stories* (University of Texas Press, US). Wonderful, if sometimes disturbing gothic tales of love, madness and death. Includes the spine-chilling "Feather Pillow", in which the life is slowly sucked from a young bride by a hideous blood-sucking beast, found engorged after her death within her feather pillow.

Ernesto Sábato, *The Tunnel* (o/p). Existential angst, obsession and madness are the themes of this supremely accomplished novella which tells the story of tormented painter Castel's destructive fixation with the sad and beautiful María Iribarne.

Colm Toibin, *The Story of the Night* (Henry Holt). A moving tale of a young Anglo-Argentine trying to come to terms both with his sexuality and existential dilemmas in the wake of the South Atlantic conflict, and getting caught up in an undercover plot by the CIA to get Carlos Menem elected president.

Luisa Valenzuela, *Open Door* (Serpent's Tail, UK). A collection of short stories from one of Argentina's most talented writers. Written with a feminist and surrealistic slant, with a keen sense of Argentina's fascinating foibles and mordant black humour.

PAINTING AND SCULPTURE

The comprehensive catalogue published in 1994 for the exhibition of "Art from Argentina 1920–1994", held at the Museum of Modern Art, Oxford, claimed to be the first book on twentieth-century Argentine art ever to appear in Europe. The exhibition organizers put this down to the fact that, while Argentina is the Latin American country that appears to be most like Europe, the reality is more alien: that of a new, fast-growing but isolated nation, searching for a modern identity against a background of permanent insecurity, political violence, entrenched conservatism and generalized chaos. Surprisingly little has yet to be written in English-speaking countries, even the United States, about the plastic arts in Argentina, despite the country's massive, sometimes innovative and often fascinating production over two centuries of nationhood.

THE SEARCH FOR AN IDENTITY

It has been said that Argentina's artistic creativity was not decolonized until the **1920s**, when it finally ceased, albeit hesitantly, to draw its inspiration exclusively from France, Spain, Italy and other European countries. While a relatively progressive president, Marcelo T. de Alvear, was in power from 1922 to 1928, bringing about a relaxed climate of creativity and prosperity, key figures Xul Solar and Emilio Pettoruti came back to Argentina after long peregrinations in Europe, and the *Martín Fierro* magazine, a vaguely patriotic publication interested in criollo and neocriollo culture as a means of achieving a non-chauvinistic brand of "Argentinidad", in all fields of artistic creation, first went on sale in 1924; Borges was one of its contributors.

Of all the early "post-colonial" artists, **Xul Solar**, born Oscar Agustín Alejandro Schulz Solari (1887–1963), stands out, both technically and for his originality; he is one of the few artists in Argentina to have a museum all to himself, the fantastic – in both senses of the word – **Museo Xul Solar** in Recoleta, Buenos Aires. Solar was an eccentric polymath, born just outside Buenos Aires to a German-speaking Latvian father and a Genoese mother. After abandoning his architectural studies in the capital he set sail for Hong Kong but jumped ship in London, stayed in Europe for twelve years, and began working there as an artist. Back in Buenos Aires he experimented with new styles and influences but in 1939, fascinated in particular by astrology and Buddhism, he founded the **Pan Klub**, a group of artists and intellectuals sharing his Utopian pacifist credo. Some of his more disturbing pictures evoke the ruins left by World War II.

Xul Solar worked mainly with watercolour and tempera, preferring their fluidity and pastel colours to the relative rigidity of oils. While many influences are visible, his closest soulmate, both artistically and philosophically, is undoubtedly Klee, though artists as varied as Bosch, Braque, Chagall and Dalí evidently provided inspiration too. His beguiling paintings essentially work on two levels: a magical, almost infantile universe of fantasy, depicted in fresh, bright colours and immediately appealing forms, and a far more complex philosophy of erudite symbolism and allegory, in which the zodiac and cabalistic signs predominate, along with a repetition of snake and ladder motifs. His adopted name is not only a deformation of his real surnames but also "Lux" (light) backwards, while "solar" suggests his obsession with the planets. Octavio Paz's maxim "painting has one foot in architecture and the other in dreams" has often been quoted in his connection and the artist's early architectural training unmistakeably comes across in his paintings, in which buildings and futuristic urban plans predominate.

You can see a particularly fine watercolour, *Pupo*, one of Xul Solar's earlier works (1918), at Buenos Aires' **Museo Nacional de Bellas Artes** or MNBA, the country's biggest and richest collection of nineteenth- and twentieth-century painting and sculpture. In the same museum you can see a very fine painting – *Arlequín*, 1928 – by Solar's friend and contemporary, **Emilio Pettoruti** (1892–1971), whose major exhibition in 1924 sent ripples of scandal and excitement across the conservative capital. This event is widely interpreted as the beginning of the modern era in Argentine painting. Pettoruti transferred into painting and collage his personal and, for some, very Argentine vision of Cubism.

The MNBA not only houses a beautiful collection of art, but it also traces in a concrete form the very history of the country's painting and sculpture since independence in the early nineteenth century. In colonial times Argentina had relied on two main sources to satisfy the growing demand for artwork: the craftsmen of Peru and Bolivia, especially those of the **Cusco School**, who churned out mostly religious paintings and objects that added a *mestizo* touch to European baroque themes and styles; and artisans and artists from Brazil, whose slightly different techniques and inspiration provided some variety among the objects on offer. As a gaucho identity began to emerge and benefit from economic prosperity a more specific creativity appeared, in the form of mostly silver and leather *"motivos"* – *mate* vessels, saddles, knives, guns – of the kind displayed at museums right across the country. A major collection of these objects is housed at the **Museo Hernández**, in Palermo, Buenos Aires. But as a middle class and wealthy land-owning aristocracy became firmly established, they heaped scorn upon this "vulgar sub-culture" and would have nothing in their homes but fashionable European and European-style art. Not until 1799 did Buenos Aires have its own **art school**, the Escuela de Dibujo, but it was shut down upon the orders of King Carlos IV only three years later. After independence, an academy of fine art was founded, but all the teachers came from Europe and it too was closed down for lack of funding in the 1830s.

Carlos Morel (1813–94), one of the first recognized Argentine artists, had been trained there; firmly entrenched in the Romantic tradition of early nineteenth-century France, his oils of urban and rural scenes and military episodes were exquisitely executed and you can see a particularly fine example, *Carga de Caballería del Ejército Federal* (exact date unknown) on display at the MNBA.

ALL EYES ON EUROPE

Nearly all of the ground floor at the MNBA is taken up by paintings and sculpture from France (mostly), Italy, Holland and Spain, plus later works by artists from the United States – José de Ribera, Tiepolo, Toulouse-Lautrec, van Gogh, Sisley, Pollock and Rothko are all given pride of place. Virtually every Argentine artist worth his or her salt studied in Europe and slavishly imitated European styles, such as naturalism and Impressionism – and their work has been "relegated" to the upper floor. They include **Prilidiano**

Pueyrredón (1823–70), *Un alto en la pulpería* (c. 1860); **Eduardo Sívori** (1847–1918), *El despertar de la criada* (1887); **Martín Malharro** (1865–1911), *Las parvas* (1911); **Fernando Fader** (1882–1935), *Los mantones de Manila* (1914); and **Valentín Thibon de Libian** (1889–1931), *La fragua* (1916), all masterpieces in their way. One of the country's greatest-ever sculptors, realist **Rogelio Yrurtia** (1879–1950), heavily influenced by Rodin, was chosen to create a number of rather bombastic monuments across Buenos Aires, and his house in Belgrano is now a fascinating museum.

Apart from Xul Solar, who wanted South America to find its own artistic feet, the overwhelming majority of Argentina's artists continued to fix their gaze relentlessly on Europe throughout the 1930s – the so-called *"década infama"*, a period of political repression, economic depression, immigration controls and general melancholy – and increasingly on the United States, for inspiration, following trends and joining movements. Two of the greatest Argentine artists active in that period were **Antonio Berni** (1905–81), whose *Primeros pasos* (1937) is on display at the MNBA, and **Lino Enea Spilimbergo** (1896–1964) – seek out his *Figura* (1937) hanging nearby. Both were taught by the now much-overlooked French Surrealist André Lhôte, as shows clearly in their paintings, which aimed to depict the social reality of an Argentina in economic and political turmoil without espousing any political cause, whether left or right – Berni was hailed as the leader of the so-called *Arte Político*. His incredibly moving *La Torre Eiffel en la Pampa* (1930) singlehandedly seems to sum up the continuing dilemma among Argentine artists – are they nostalgic for Paris while in Argentina or for Buenos Aires and the pampas when in Europe?

BREAKING AWAY AND DRIFTING BACK

The big break came towards the end of World War II, for most of which Argentina had remained neutral, essentially because the politicians favoured Britain and the Allies while large sections of the armed forces sympathized with the Axis and its fascist philosophy. Argentina finally declared war on Germany in 1944, the year that *Arturo*, an abstract art review seen as a pioneer in world art circles, was first published. Argentine artists, many of whom were born in Europe, often in the Central and Eastern European countries most affected by both world wars, rejected what they saw as an unjustifiable hegemony, led from countries that had just indulged in such acts of barbarism that they could teach the New World no lessons, in politics or in art. **Abstract** forms were chosen as a way of protesting against reactionary politics in an indirect way, that could not be readily identified as subversion. Just after Perón came to power, a number of ground-breaking exhibitions were staged in Buenos Aires, including that of the Asociación Arte Concreto-Invención, in March 1946, and Arte Madí, in August of the same year. Three major art manifestos were published that year or the following, the relatively less influential Manifiesto Intervencionista (by Tomás Maldonado and his friends), the Manifiesto Madí, signed by Hungarian-born **Gyula Kosice** (born 1924) and his colleagues, and the Manifiesto Blanco issued by members of the Academia Altamira, which wanted to create a new art-form based on "matter, colour and sound in perpetual movement".

The last of the three was primarily instigated by **Lucio Fontana** (1899–1968), indisputably one of the twentieth century's key artists and founder of the Informalist movement. Fontana may have done most of his work, and died, in Italy – there is a foundation named after him in Milan – but he was born in Argentina, in Rosario de Santa Fe to be exact, the son of an Italian immigrant and an Argentine actress of Italian origin. For his education he was soon dispatched to Italy, where he studied architecture. A hero during World War I he returned to Argentina in 1940, after churning out a number of monuments for Mussolini's regime, though he never espoused fascism. In Argentina he worked for his father's firm sculpting funerary monuments, a job he quickly gave up for teaching art in the capital. A co-founder of both the Altamira School and the Escuela Libre de Artes Plásticos, on Avenida Alvear, Recoleta, he never recovered, either psychologically or in terms of his reputation in Argentina, from being runner-up in the competition to design the national flag monument in his native city. Perhaps a case of sour grapes, he later described those seven years spent in Rosario and Buenos Aires, as "una vita da coglione" (a shitty existence), and he decided to leave the country "as a more pos-

itive alternative to committing suicide". No wonder, perhaps, that Argentina has never gone out of its way to claim Fontana as its own. Back in Italy in 1947, he developed his own theory of art – enshrined in the **Spatialist Manifesto** issued that year – and his now unmistakeable style: a series of minimalistic monochrome canvases, slashed with one or more incisions or pierced with holes, apparently evocative of restrained violence or simply representing an "exploration of space". Known somewhat irreverently in the art world as "Lucio the Slasher" or "Lucio the Ripper", he has been the subject of a couple of major exhibitions in Buenos Aires in recent years, suggestive of a rehabilitation, but the rest of the world still thinks of him as an Italian creator. Nonetheless a couple of his works, including the somewhat unrepresentative *Concepto espacial*, are on prominent display inside the entrance to the MNBA.

Meanwhile in Argentina the other **avant-garde** artists seemed more intent on theory than practice, but nonetheless produced some work that is still regarded as significant to this day. Madí, probably a nonsense word like Dada, but sometimes said to be derived from "materialismo dialéctico", was decidedly political in its aims of creating a classless society, and reacted against Surrealism which it claimed was dominated by an elite. One of the movement's most radical ideas, cooked up in the 1970s, was to build a series of "Hydrospatial Cities" suspended in space over water, starting with the River Plate, where the urban environment would be so radically different from those previously created that there would be no need for art; this idea has yet to be put into practice. Back in 1946 Kosice produced a series of works using neon-lighting, thought to be the first of their kind, and he later experimented with glass, plexiglass, acrylic, cork, aluminium and bone – his intriguing *Dispersión del aire* (1967) at the MNBA is one such work. Kosice's articulated wooden sculpture *Röyi*, dating from 1944, is also regarded as revolutionary, as it is both abstract and lathed rather than "sculpted". Another member of the movement, Kosice's wife **Diyi Laañ** (born 1927), created works on a structured frame in an abstract, hollow shape such as her *Pintura sobre el marco recortado* (1948). **Rhod Rothfuss** (born 1920) was the Uruguayan leader of Madí, but his enamel paintings on wood, created in the 1940s were highly influential on that decade's art in Argentina.

Rivals of the Madí group, partly for personal reasons, the Asociación Arte Concreto-Invención or Intervencionistas, were far more radical politically, espousing solidarity with the Soviet Union largely as a means of protesting against growing US interference in Latin American affairs. Artistically they were more conventional than the Madí lot, and tended to produce paintings in traditionally shaped frames; they drew much of their inspiration from artists like Mondrian, Van Doesburg and Malevich. Members included the leading theorist **Tomás Maldonado** (born 1922), Claudio Girola, Lidy Prati and Gregorio Vardánega, but the most acclaimed artists in the movement are **Enio Iommi** (born 1926), **Alfredo Hlito** (1923–93) and **Raúl Lozza** (born 1911). The first of the three, Claudio Girola's brother Enio, is undoubtedly one of Argentina's greatest-ever artists and he stands out from the other Intervencionistas in part because he works in three dimensions. His exquisite sculptures in stainless steel – such as *Torsión de planos* (1964) at the MNBA – wood, bronze and aluminium, express his personal "spatialist" credo that in many ways links him more closely to Fontana. More recently Iommi underwent an about-turn and began producing objects with emphasis on the material, using wire, old boxes, industrial and household refuse including rusty nails – his 1977 Retiro exhibition significantly entitled *Adiós a una época* marked his switch to *arte povera*, after decades of using "noble" materials. Hlito, meanwhile, was a more "mainstream" Intervencionista, whose work displays the clear influences of people like Mondrian and Max Bill, and even surprisingly Seurat and Cézanne – though it was their use of colour and brushstrokes that most interested him. A very typical work, *Lineas tangentes* (1955), is on show at the MNBA. Lozza, on the other hand, became so obsessed with the problematics of colour, form and representation in art that he formed his own movement in 1949, called Perceptismo, according to which paintings must first be sketched obeying certain architectural rules before the colour can be filled in. His watershed work *Pintura Numero 153* (1948), executed just before he left the Intervencionistas, is on show at the MNBA and its geometric forms

against a bright orange background already point to this schism.

REACTIONARY POLITICS AND ARTISTIC REACTIONS

The 1950s and 60s were once again times of turmoil in Argentina; Peronism was replaced by democratic governments and military dictatorships that shared only one ruthless aim: eliminating Peronism. Perón himself returned to power briefly in the 1970s, before dying in office and transferring power to his third wife "Isabelita"; her disastrous period in charge resulted in another military backlash and the nightmarish Proceso. Since 1983, following the debacle of the South Atlantic conflict, Argentina has been unshakeably if imperfectly democratic. All of these ups and downs have been reflected in the country's postwar art as much as, if not more than in its literature, cinema and music. The reactionary politics of virtually everyone who held power in Argentina from 1944 to 1983 were either rebelled against by mainly leftist, *engagé* artists, or dictated by a more conservative approach, often based on mainstream artistic schools in Europe.

Raquel Forner (1902–87) came to the fore in the 1950s – even though she had begun to paint in the 1920s as a student of Spilimbergo – mainly because she was so unmistakeably influenced by Picasso. This comes through in her style – in which human figures are amalgamated with symbolic images – and subject matter. She painted two series of haunting oils about the Spanish Civil War and World War II: *España* (1937–39) and *El drama* (1939–46); the spine-chilling *Retablo de dolor* (1944), at the MNBA, which belongs to the second group, also reveals her interest in the religious paintings of El Greco. Sometimes likened to Karel Appel, a member of the CoBrA group – further proof that European comparisons remain legion in Argentina – she set herself apart in the 1960s by concentrating on the theme of the human conquest of space, as expemplified by her colourful 1968 masterpiece *Conquest of Moon Rock.*

Unusual sculptor **Libero Badii** (born 1916), some of whose work, including later paintings, is displayed at the Fundación Banco Francés, Belgrano, Buenos Aires, won a national prize in 1953 with a sensually organic marble figure,

Torrente, which can be seen at the MNBA. Arp and Brancusi are easily detectable influences on his earlier works.

From 1955 to 1963, **Jorge Romero Brest** was director of the MNBA; politics had its dictators and so did the art world, for this staunchly anti-Peronist guru of Argentine art then went on to direct the highly influential and virtually monopolistic Centro de Artes Visuales at the capital's wealthy Instituto Torcuato di Tella until 1970, and he had the power to make or break artists. Essentially a democrat, however, he staged increasingly subversive exhibitions by avant-garde artists after General Juan Onganía's mob seized totalitarian power in 1966, purportedly to combat Marxism and Peronism. President Onganía sent the police in to close an exhibition by minor artist Roberto Plate, which comprised a mock public lavatory in which visitors were encouraged to draw graffiti. In a famous interview Onganía said that he had taken such drastic steps because someone had outrageously drawn a penis and Argentina was not ready for that kind of thing; what really riled him, no doubt, was the fact that most of the graffiti consisted of political slogans and insults personally directed at him.

Romero Brest's most famous achievement while in charge of the MNBA was the discovery of four artists who went under the label of Otra figuración, after a ground-breaking joint exhibition of that name held in Buenos Aires in 1961. Part German-style Expressionism, part Dubuffet, part de Kooning and quite a lot of Rauschenberg, the young artists who had met in Paris dominated Argentine painting throughout the rest of the decade. **Ernesto Deira** (1928–86), **Jorge de la Vega** (1930–71), **Rómulo Macció** (born 1931) and **Luis Felipe Noé** (born 1933) all produced highly acclaimed work, though Vega is usually regarded as the most original. Deira's *Homenaje a Fernand Leger* (1963) at the MNBA speaks for itself; heavy neofigurative shades of Francis Bacon are easily detectable in Macció's *Vivir un poco cada día* (1963) also at the MNBA; while Noé's Ensoresque masterpiece *Introducción a la esperanza* (1963), at the same museum, illustrates his theory of "*cuadro dividido*", in which several paintings are chaotically assembled to make one work. Vega's *Intimidades de un tímido* (1960s) at the Museo Nacional is typical of his vast canvases, brimming with vitality but

largely mysterious in their imagery. Of all four group members, his work is hardest to pigeonhole. Similarly, while **Alberto Heredia** (born 1924), admirer of Marcel Duchamp and living up to his description as a "ramshackle artist", was closely related to the Otra figuración, he also has a lot in common with both Surrealism and Pop Art. His now famous *Camembert Boxes* (1961–63), filled with day-to-day flotsam and jetsam, are seen as a breakthrough in Argentine sculpture, while the gruesome later work *Los amordazamientos* (1972–74), displayed at the MNBA, is apocalyptic in its depiction of human despair.

Worldwide, the 1960s was marked by the new artistic phenomenon of Happenings, and what Argentine artists called Ambientaciones; despite their often massive scale and laborious preparations, they were by nature ephemeral events, and all we have left now are photographic documents. **Marta Minujín** (born 1941), whose colourful *Colchón* (1964) can be seen at the MNBA, has been a leading exponent. Her two key works in 1965, *La menesunda* and *El batacazo*, both staged at the Centro de Artes Visuales, were labyrinths meant to excite, delight, disturb and attack the visitor's five senses, and they caused both scandal and wonderment in Buenos Aires. She continued to perform into the 1970s, poking fun at national icons like Carlos Gardel and the ovenbird, Argentina's national bird; after creating *Obelisco acostado* in 1978, the following year she went to construct a 30-metre-high *Obelisco de pan dulce*, a half-scale model of Buenos Aires' famous phallic symbol clad with thousands of plastic-wrapped raisin breads, erected at the cattle-raisers' temple, the Sociedad Rural in Palermo. To celebrate the return to democracy in 1983, her *Partenón de libros* was a massive monument covered in books – many publications had been banned or even burned under the junta – also raised in the open air in the capital.

CONTEMPORARY ARGENTINE ART: BACK TO SQUARE ONE

The 1970s and early 1980s saw many Argentine artists leave the country, out of justifiable fear for their lives as dozens of artists disappeared during the brutal Proceso. Some preferred to stay, using indirect means of criticizing the Philistine barbarians who governed the country. In 1971 the Centro de Arte y

Comunicación was founded by art critic Jorge Glusman (now director of the MNBA), and took over where the disbanded Centro de Artes Visuales and Romero Brest had left off – though Glusman was less dictatorial in his approach. Two key figures stand out during this period: **Pablo Suárez** (born 1937) whose *La terraza* (1983) at the MNBA is typical of his black humour and anti-Argentinidad credo, being a sardonically cruel pastiche of the Sunday asado; and his contemporary **Víctor Grippo** (born 1936), whose *Analogía I* (1970–71) at the MNBA comprises forty potatoes in pigeonholes with electrodes attached, seen retrospectively as a horrific premonition of the military's torture chambers. Suárez had first had to rebel against his aristocratic *estanciero* family, which he did as an adolescent by fashioning erotic sculptures only to destroy them at once. Much of his later work is also sexually provocative, while poking fun at sacrosanct aspects of the Argentine way of life. His grotesque *Monumento a Mate* (1987) hits a raw nerve of the Argentine psyche, the national drink of *mate*, while his oyster-shaped sculpture *La Perla: retrato de un taxi-boy* (1992) depicts a naked adolescent reclining in the place of a pearl – taxi-boy is the Porteño term for a rent-boy, so-called because male prostitutes in the capital demand the "taxi-fare home" rather than payment for their services. As for Grippo, his most famous work is *Analogía IV* (1972), again featuring potatoes, highly symbolic as they are native to South America and successfully imported into North America, Europe and the rest of the world. In this seminal work a white table-top is laid with a china plate, metal cutlery and three potatoes, while another, black in colour, is laid with identical crockery and cutlery in transparent plastic – this mirror image of "real" and "fake" apparently represents military puppet President General Alejandro Lanusse's humiliating invitation to recall Perón from his Spanish exile in 1972. Another contemporary of theirs, **Antonio Seguí** (born 1934), is also out on an artistic limb: his comic-like paintings, such as the untitled acrylic (1987) on show at the MNBA, depict a somewhat sinister, behatted figure in countless different poses, representing urban alienation. Younger artist **Alfredo Prior** (born 1952) – whose *En cada sueño habita una pena*

(1985) at the MNBA, is one of the most horrific yet beautiful Argentine paintings produced in recent years – deliberately kept himself apart from artistic circles, rarely exhibiting his work. Minimalism and Japanese art are strong influences on his work along with Turner in his use of colour, as in *Paraíso* (1988). The style of **Ricardo Cinalli** (born 1948), who lives in London, has been described as postmodern Neoclassicism, and his *Blue Box* (1990) is a prime example of his original use of layers of tissue paper upon which he colours in pastel. **Mónica Giron** (born 1959) takes her inspiration from her native Patagonia and her environmental concerns to produce innovative works like *Trousseau for a Conqueror* (1993) which features a pullover specially knitted for a buff-necked ibis, putting her undeniably in the same school, despite her different style, as Marta Minujin.

Guillermo Kuitca (born 1961) is without a doubt Argentina's most successful contemporary artist – his paintings sell for over $100,000 at New York auctions – and in many ways he encapsulates what Argentine art has become, the way it has turned full circle. Argentina remains a country of mostly European immigrants and their descendants who, however hard they try, cannot sever the umbilical cord that links them culturally to their parents' and grandparents' homelands. Above all, Kuitca's work is highly original and makes no attempt to create something nationally Argentine – as witnessed by his beautiful painting at the MNBA, *La consagración de la primavera* (1983) – but it is no coincidence that his series of maps, such as those printed onto a triptych of mattresses (1989) are almost exclusively of Germany and central Europe where his own roots are. The 1986 novel *The Lost Language of Cranes*, by David Leavitt, in which the son's favourite pastime is drawing maps of non-existent places, was the main inspiration for this theme, while the choreography of German creator Pina Bausch is another source of ideas for the artist. Argentine artists seem finally to have given up trying to forge the Argentinidad that Borges and his colleagues were set on inventing in the 1920s, and have acknowledged instead that, in the global village of constant interaction, personal styles and talent are more important than an attempt to create an artificial national identity through art.

LANGUAGE

To get the most out of your trip to Argentina, you'll need to have a decent smattering of **Spanish**. Though you'll frequently come across English-speakers who'll be more than keen to try out their language skills on you, you can't rely on there always being someone there when you need them. In general, Argentinians are appreciative of visitors who make the effort to communicate in *castellano* – a great confidence booster for those whose language skills are limited. Any basic Spanish course will give you a good grounding before you go. A good pocket **dictionary**, such as Collins, is a vital accessory, while of the bigger dictionaries Collins, Oxford and Larousse are all good – make sure your choice covers Latin American usage. If you really want to refine your grasp of the subtleties of the language, a comprehensive grammar such as the excellent *A New Reference Grammar of Modern Spanish* by John

Butt and Carmen Benjamin (Edward Arnold, London 1988) is a good investment.

Argentinian Spanish is one of the most distinctive varieties of the language. Dominating the country's linguistic identity is the unmistakeable **Porteño accent**, a seductive blend of an expressive, almost drawling intonation, combined with colourful colloquialisms. Linguistically speaking, the capital's sphere of influence spreads out for several hundred kilometres around Buenos Aires; beyond this, subtle regional variations begin to take hold, though certain grammatical constructions and words hold for the whole country. If you've learnt Spanish in Spain, the most obvious difference you will encounter (true for the whole of Latin America) is the absence of the *th* sound for words like *cielo* (sky, pronounced SIE-lo in Argentina). In Buenos Aires, in particular, you will also be struck by the strong consonantal pronunciation of "y" and "ll", as in *yo* and *calle* (see pronunciation, opposite), a completely different sound to the weaker vowel-like sound used in Spain and much of Latin America. Another notable difference is the use of **vos** as the second-person pronoun, in place of *tú*, with correspondingly different verb endings (see box, below). As in the rest of Latin America, *ustedes* is used as the third-person pronoun instead of *vosotros*. In general, Latin American speech is slightly more formal than Spanish, and *usted* is used far more commonly. A good guideline is that *vos* is always used for children and usually between strangers under about 30; though within circles who regard themselves as politically progressive *vos* is used as a mark of shared values.

THE VOSEO

The use of *vos* as the second-person pronoun, a usage known as **the voseo**, is common to nearly the whole of Argentina. Though you will be understood perfectly if you use the *tú* form, you should familiarize yourself with the *vos* form, if only in order to understand what is being said to you.

Present-tense verb endings employed with *vos* correspond approximately to those used in European Spanish for the *vosotros* form. Thus, European *tú vienes* (you come) becomes Argentinian *vos venís*. Imperative forms are again derived from *vosotros*, though without the final "d": European *ven!* ("come here!") becomes Argentinian *vení!* Past, conditional, subjunctive and future forms used with *vos* are the same as the European *tú* forms.

Some examples

querés salir?	do you want to go out?	*tomá*	take (this)
hablás inglés?	do you speak English?	*comé*	eat
dónde vivís?	where do you live?	*seguí*	carry on

Argentinian **vocabulary** is often quite different to Spanish, too (see box on p.756) and the use of "*che*" (a vocative used when addressing someone, very loosely it approximates to something like "hey" or "mate" or "oi" in British English, used at the beginning of a phrase; *¿che, qué decís?* – "hey mate, how's it going?") in particular is so much identified with Argentina that some Latin Americans refer to Argentinians as "Los che". The word was, of course, most famously applied as a nickname to Ernesto Guevara, popularly known as Che Guevara.

PRONUNCIATION

The **Spanish pronunciation system** is remarkably straightforward and consistent, with only five, very pure vowel sounds (English has many more than this). Only a few sounds tend to cause problems for foreigners, most notably the rolled double R and the common R which, though not rolled, is pronounced in a subtly different way to its English counterpart. A general rule of thumb is to make sure you articulate words clearly and put more effort into pronunciation than you would in English: observation of native speakers will make you realize that speaking Spanish involves a much more obvious articulation of facial muscles than English, which often appears to foreigners to be mumbled through barely open lips. Another characteristic of Spanish is that there is no audible gap between words within a breathgroup; thus Buenos Aires is pronounced BWE-no-SAI-res and not BWE-nos-AI-res. Failure to observe this detail produces a very stilted Spanish.

A blessing for foreigners is the fact that Spanish is spelt exactly as it sounds – or sounds exactly as it is spelt. If this seems a minor point, imagine the problem for foreigners in working out the pronunciation of English words through, though, rough and slough.

VOWELS

Spanish vowel sounds do not exactly correspond to any sound in standard British or American English, though approximate sounds exist for all of them. In general, English vowel sounds are less "pure" than Spanish, tending to be formed by a combination of two vocalic sounds: English "close", for example, is really a combination of "o" and "w". Spanish has no such tendency, representing such sounds with two written vowels.

A is pronounced somewhere between the "a" of f**a**ther and that of b**a**ck.

E is similar to English g**e**t or t**e**n, pronounced with some of the openness of English d**ay** (though without the final "y" sound and much shorter).

I is similar to the sound in m**ee**t, though much shorter and without the final "y" sound.

O is a more open or rounded sound than English h**o**t, though shorter than d**o**se, and without the final "w" sound.

U is similar to the "u" of sch**oo**l, though again, much shorter and without the final "w" sound. A close equivalent is the French pronunciation of *coup*. In the combinations **gue** (as in *guerra* or war, pronounced GE-rra); **gui** (*guiso* or stew, pronounced GI-so); **que** (*queso* or cheese, prounced KE-so) and **qui** (Quito, pronounced KI-to), U is silent. A diaresis (like the German umlaut), preserves the U, producing a "w" sound in words such as *nicaragüense*, pronounced ni-ka-ra-GWEN-se.

DIPHTHONGS

A diphthong is basically a combination of two or more vocalic sounds (either the two "weak" vowels **i** or **u** or a "weak" and a "strong" vowel – **a**, **e** or **o**). Common diphthongs in Spanish include AU, as in *jaula* (cage), pronounced HAW-la and EI or EY as in *ley* (law) pronounced very like the English word lay. In general, once you have mastered the vowel sounds, diphthongs are entirely predictable and easy to pronounce. Only the rarer EU as in *Europa* (pronounced ew-RO-pa) and the very uncommon OU as in the *GOU* (Grupo de Oficiales Unidos, the group of officers from which Perón emerged in the 1940s, pronounced like English "go") take a bit of getting used to.

CONSONANTS

Consonants not covered below (eg CH, F, M, N) are, for all practical purposes, pronounced as in English.

B and V are pronounced identically in Spanish. At the beginning of a breathgroup (eg *Vino a casa* – he came to my house) or after **m** or **n** (eg *envidia*, envy) it is a hard sound, equivalent to English **b**ell. In all other positions, it is a much softer sound, pronounced by murmuring through barely open lips. There is no English equivalent, so the best way to learn the sound is by listening

ARGENTINIAN VOCABULARY

As well as the *voseo* and various different pronunciations, those who have learnt Spanish elsewhere (particularly in Spain) will need to become accustomed to some different **vocabulary** in Argentina. In general, Spanish terms are recognized but – as for all the other differences – a familiarity with Argentinian equivalents will smooth things along. Though few Spanish terms are not understood in Argentina, there is one major exception, which holds for much of Latin America. The verb *coger*, used in Spain for everything from "to pick up" to "to catch (a bus)" is never used in this way in Argentina, where it is the equivalent of "to fuck"). This catch-all verb is replaced in Argentina by terms such as *tomar* (to take) as in *tomar el colectivo* (to catch the bus) and *agarrar* (to take hold of or grab) as in *agarrá la llave* (take the key). Less likely to cause problems, but still one to watch is *concha*, which in Spain is a perfectly innocent word meaning shell, but in Argentina is usually used to refer to a woman's genitalia: Argentinians find the Spanish woman's name Conchita hilarious and the words *caracol* or *almeja* are used for shells.

Also note that some words which are feminine in Spanish are more often masculine in Argentinian; eg *vuelto* – change, *llamado* – (phone) call.

el almacén	grocery store	*la manteca*	butter
el auto	car	*las medias*	socks
la birome	biro	*el negocio*	shop (in general)
el boliche	nightclub; also sometimes shop in rural areas	*el nene/la nena*	child
		la palta	avocado
la cartera	handbag	*la papa*	potato
la carpa	tent	*la pollera*	skirt
chico/a	small (also boy/girl)	*el pomelo*	grapefruit
el colectivo	bus	*la remera*	T-shirt
el durazno	peach	*el suéter*	sweater
estacionar	park	*el tapado*	coat (usually woman's)
la lapicera	pen	*la vereda*	pavement
el living	living room	*la vidriera*	shop window

Colloquial speech and lunfardo

Colloquial speech in Argentina, particularly in Buenos Aires is extremely colourful and it's good fun to learn a bit of the local lingo. There's a clear Italian influence in some words. Many colloquial expressions and words also derive from a form of slang known as **lunfardo**, originally the language of the Buenos Aires underworld (hence the myriad terms in lunfardo proper for police, pimps and prostitutes). There's also a playful form of speech, known as **vesre**, in which words are pronounced backwards (*vesre* is *revés* – reverse, backwards) – a few of these words, such as *feca* (see opposite) have found their way into everyday speech. Though these sometimes very colloquial expressions will sound very odd coming from the mouth of a less than fluent foreigner, knowing a few of them will help you get the most out of what's being said around you. Lunfardo is also an important part of the repertoire of **tango lyrics**.

carefully to native pronunciation of phrases such as *soy de Buenos Aires* or *me gusta el vino*.

C has two pronunciations; before **e** and **i**, it is pronounced as an S, as in *cero* (zero, pronounced SE-ro). Before **a**, **o** and **u**, it is pronounced as an English "k".

D follows more or less the same pattern as B/V: at the beginning of a breathgroup or after **l** or **n**, it is a hard sound, similar to the English **d** of **d**og. In all other positions it is a soft sound, very similar to English **th**is. Between vowels and at the end of words it is pronounced very softly and

sometimes not at all (check out the cartoon strip *Inodoro Pereyra* on daily paper *Clarín*'s back pages for phonetic transcriptions of this tendency, associated in Argentina with the gaucho).

G follows a similar pattern to C: before **e** and **i** it is pronounced in a similar fashion as English **h**, though with a hint of a more guttural sound, rather like the **ch** in Scottish lo**ch** (note that this is much less strongly pronounced in Latin America than in Spain). Thus *general* is pronounced he-ne-RAL. Before **a**, **o** and **u**, G has two possible sounds: at the beginning of a

Words listed below that are marked with an asterisk (*) should be used with some caution; those marked with a double asterisk (**) are best avoided until you are really familiar with local customs and language.

afanar	to rob	
bancar	to put up with; *no me lo banco* "I can't stand it/him"	
bárbaro/a	great	
la barra brava	hardcore of football supporters; each club has its own *barra brava*	
la birra	beer	
el boludo/pelotudo	idiot**	
el bondi	bus	
la bronca	rage, as in *me da bronca*, "it makes me mad"	
el cana	police officer*	
canchero	sharp-witted, (over)confident	
el chabón	boy/lad	
el chamuyo	conversation/chat	
el chancho	ticket inspector*	
el chanta	braggart, unreliable person*	
el chorro	thief	
chupar	to drink (alcohol)*	
copado	cool, good	
el despelote	mess	
estar en pedo	to be drunk*	
el faso	cigarette	
el feca	coffee (from café)	
la fiaca	tiredness/laziness, eg *tengo fiaca*	
el forro	condom/idiot**	
el gil	idiot*	
la guita/la plata	money*	
el hinchapelotas	irritating person**	
laburar	to work	
el luca	one thousand (pesos)	
el mango	peso/monetary unit,	

	as in *no tengo un mango*, "I don't have a penny"
manyar	to eat
una maza	something cool, good, as in *es una maza*, "it's/he's/ she's really cool'.
el milico	member of the military*
la mina	woman/girl
morfar	to eat
onda	atmosphere/character, as in *tiene buena onda* "it's got a good atmosphere" or "she's good-natured"
el palo	one million (pesos); thus *un palo verde* is a million US dollars, in reference to the original colour of the bank notes.
la patota	gang
el pendejo	kid (also used derogatorily)*
petiso	small, thus also small person
el pibe	kid
pinta	"it looks good"
la pinta	appearance, as in *tiene pinta* or *tiene buena*
piola	cool, smart
el pucho	cigarette
el quilombo	mess*
el tacho	taxi (thus *tachero*, taxi driver)
el tano/la tana	Italian
el telo	short-stay hotel where couples go to have sex*
trucho	fake, phoney
la vieja/el viejo	mum/dad
zafar	to get away with*

breathgroup or after **n** (eg in tan**g**o), it is pronounced as in English **g**one. In other positions, G is pronounced as a soft fricative (meaning that the position of the tongue and throat are as for the hard G but that no closure takes place). As with soft B/V, there is no English equivalent, and this sound is best learnt through observation of words like *lago* (lake).

H is silent

J is pronounced in all positions in the same way as G before e and i.

L is pronounced as English **l**eaf. British speakers should avoid the tendency to produce a "w" sound at the end of words (imagine a cockney pronouncing the Mexican beer "Sol" and you'll get the idea): the Spanish L sound is always "clean".

LL is pronounced in Buenos Aires and much of the rest of the country rather like the j in French **j**our, or the g in be**i**ge, or sometimes as a softer sound, almost like "sh"; thus *calle* (street) is pronounced KA-je or KA-she. In parts of the country, notably the north, it is closer to the "y"

USEFUL GENERAL TERMS AND VOCABULARY

Basics

yes, no	*sí, no*	a little, a lot	*poco, mucho*
please, thank you	*por favor, gracias*	very	*muy*
where, when	*dónde, cuándo*	today, tomorrow,	*hoy, mañana, ayer*
what, how much	*qué, cuánto*	yesterday	
here, there	*acá, allá* or *aquí, allí* (the	someone	*alguien*
	former two are more	something	*algo*
	common in Argentina)	nothing, never	*nada, nunca*
this, that	*esto, eso* (when referring to	but	*pero*
	a general, unspecified	entrance, exit	*entrada, salida*
	thing; otherwise *este/esta*	pull, push	*tire, empuje*
	and *ese/esa* are used,	England	*Inglaterra*
	according to the gender	Great Britain/	*Gran Bretaña/Reino Unido*
	of the object referred to)	United Kingdom	
now, later	*ahora, más tarde/luego*	United States	*Estados Unidos*
open, closed	*abierto/a, cerrado/a*	Australia	*Australia*
with, without	*con, sin*	Canada	*Canadá*
good, bad	*buen(o)/a, mal(o)/a*	Ireland	*Irlanda*
big	*gran(de)*	Scotland	*Escocia*
small	*chico/a* or *pequeño/a*	Wales	*Gales*
more, less	*más, menos*	New Zealand	*Nueva Zelandia*

Greetings and responses

hello, goodbye	*hola, chau* (*adiós* is used		or, more informally
	too, but is more formal		*cómo andás?*
	and more final)	(very) well, thanks,	*(muy) bien gracias,*
good morning	*buen día*	and you?	*y vos/usted?*
good afternoon	*buenas tardes*	not at all/you're welcome	*de nada*
good night	*buenas noches*	excuse me	*(con) permiso*
see you later	*hasta luego*	sorry	*perdón, disculpe(me)*
how are you	*cómo está(s)?*	cheers!	*salud!*

Useful phrases and expressions

Note that when two verb forms are given, the first corresponds to the familiar *vos* form and the second to the formal *usted* form.

		. . . Canadian	*. . . canadiense*
		. . . Irish	*. . . irlandés(a)*
		. . . Scottish	*. . . escocés(a)*
		. . . Welsh	*. . . galés(a)*
I (don't) understand	*(no) entiendo*	. . . a New Zealander	*. . . neocelandés/a*
Do you speak	*Hablás inglés* or *(usted)*	What's the Spanish	*cómo se dice en*
English?	*habla inglés?*	for this?	*castellano?*
I (don't) speak	*(no) hablo castellano*	What did you say?	*qué dijiste/dijo?*
Spanish		I'm hungry	*tengo hambre*
My name is . . .	*me llamo . . .*	I'm thirsty	*tengo sed*
What's your name?	*cómo te llamás/cómo se*	I'm tired	*tengo sueño*
	llama (usted)?	I'm ill	*no me siento bien*
I'm English	*soy inglés(a)*	what's up?	*qué pasa?*
. . . American	*. . . estadounidense* or	I don't know	*no (lo) sé*
	norteamericano/a	It's hot/cold	*hace calor/frío*
. . . Australian	*. . . australiano/a*	what's the time?	*qué hora es?*

Hotels and transport

Is there a hotel/bank nearby?	*Hay un hotel/banco cerca (de aquí)?*	Turn left/right, on the left/right	*doblá/doble a la izquierda/derecha, a la izquierda/derecha*
How do I get to...?	*Cómo hago para llegar a...?*	Go straight on	*seguí/siga derecho*

one block/two blocks	*una cuadra, dos cuadras*	Do you know . . . ?	*¿sabe . . . ?*
Where is . . . ?	*¿Dónde está . . . ?*	Do you have . . . ?	*¿tenés/tiene . . . ?*
the bus station	*la terminal de omnibus*	a (single, double)	*una habitación*
the train station	*la estación de ferrocarril*	room	*(single/doble)*
the toilet	*el baño*	with two beds	*con dos camas*
I want a (return)	*Quiero un pasaje dos (de*	with a double bed	*con cama matrimonial*
ticket to . . .	*ida y vuelta) para . . .*	with a private	*con baño privado*
Where does the bus	*¿de dónde sale el*	bathroom	
for . . . leave from?	*micro para . . . ?*	with breakfast	*con desayuno*
What time does it	*¿a qué hora sale?*	it's for one person/	*es para una persona/*
leave?		one night/	*una noche/*
How long does it	*¿cuánto tarda?*	two weeks	*dos semanas*
take?		How much is it?	*¿cuánto es/cuánto sale?*
Do you go past . . . ?	*¿usted pasa por . . . ?*	it's fine	*está bien*
far, near	*lejos, cerca*	it's too expensive	*es demasiado caro*
slow, quick	*lento, rápido*	do you have anything	*¿hay algo más barato?*
I want/would like . . .	*quiero/quería . . .*	cheaper?	
there is (is there)?	*¿hay(?)(¿hay descuento para*	Is there a discount?	*¿hay descuento por pago*
	estudiantes?, is there	for cash	*en efectivo?*
	a discount for students?	fan, air conditioning,	*ventilador, aire a con-*
	or *hay agua caliente,*	heating	*dicionado, calefacción*
	hot water available)	Can you camp here?	*¿se puede acampar aquí?*

Numbers, days and months

0	*cero*	19	*diecinueve*	90	*noventa*
1	*uno/una*	20	*veinte*	100	*cien/ciento*
2	*dos*	21	*veintiuno/a*	101	*ciento uno/una*
3	*tres*	22	*veintidós*	200	*doscientos/as*
4	*cuatro*	23	*veintitrés*	300	*trescientos/as*
5	*cinco*	24	*veinticuatro*	400	*cuatrocientos/as*
6	*seis*	25	*veinticinco*	500	*quinientos/as*
7	*siete*	26	*veintiséis*	600	*seiscientos/as*
8	*ocho*	27	*veintisiete*	700	*setecientos/as*
9	*nueve*	28	*veintiocho*	800	*ochocientos/as*
10	*diez*	29	*veintinueve*	900	*novecientos/as*
11	*once*	30	*treinta*	1000	*mil*
12	*doce*	31	*treinta y uno/una*	1002	*mil dos*
13	*trece*	32	*treinta y dos*	100,000	*cien mil*
14	*catorce*	40	*cuarenta*	1000,000	*un millón*
15	*quince*	50	*cincuenta*	2000	*dos mil*
16	*dieciséis*	60	*sesenta*	2001	*dos mil un*
17	*diecisiete*	70	*setenta*	2002	*dos mil dos*
18	*dieciocho*	80	*ochenta*	2003	*dos mil tres*

The following **ordinal** numbers are invariably used in referring to the floors of high-rise buildings – useful when people ask you what floor you want in an elevator (*qué piso?*)

first	*primero/a*	sixth	*sexto/a*
second	*segundo/a*	seventh	*séptimo/a*
third	*tercero/a*	eighth	*octavo/a*
fourth	*cuarto/a*	ninth	*noveno/a*
fifth	*quinto/a*	tenth	*décimo/a*

Monday	*lunes*	Wednesday	*miércoles*	Friday	*viernes*	Sunday	*domingo*
Tuesday	*martes*	Thursday	*jueves*	Saturday	*sábado*		

January	*enero*	May	*mayo*	September	*se(p)tiembre*
February	*febrero*	June	*junio*	October	*octubre*
March	*marzo*	July	*julio*	November	*noviembre*
April	*abril*	August	*agosto*	December	*diciembre*

sound used in the rest of the continent. In Corrientes, it is often pronounced as a "ly" sound.

Ñ is a palatalized sound, pronounced with the tongue flat against the roof of the mouth. Try pronouncing an "n" followed very quickly by a "y", in a similar way to the "n" sound in the word "onion"; thus mañana is something like ma-NYA-na.

Q only occurs before ue and ui, and is pronounced like English K.

R is prounced in two ways; at the beginning of a word, and after **l**, **n** or **s** it is rolled as for RR, below. Between vowels, or at the end of a word it is a single "flapped" R, produced by a single tap of the tongue on the roof of the mouth immediately behind the teeth. This is actually quite difficult for English speakers to master; the tendency is to use a retroflex R (meaning that the tongue curls backwards), a very common sound in English. This pronunciation in words like *pero* and *cara* is probably the single biggest mark of a gringo accent.

RR Written "rr", or as "r" in the positions detailed above, the Spanish RR is a strongly trilled sound, produced in the same way as R, but with several rapid taps of the tongue. Some people (native Spanish speakers included) find it impossible to produce this sound, but it is important for differentiating words such as *pero* (but) and *perro* (dog), or the potentially embarrassing *foro* (forum) and *forro* (slang word for condom, or idiot). There are regional variations: in La Rioja, for example, it is commonly pronounced as a fricative, something similar to a heavy "s" sound: the speech of ex-president

Carlos Menem is a perfect example of this tendency.

S between vowels or at the beginning of a word is basically as in English **s**un. Before consonants it is commonly aspirated in Argentina; meaning that it sounds something like a soft English H: thus *las calles* (the streets) sounds like lah-KA-jes. You don't need to worry about replicating this sound yourself, but familiarizing yourself with this pronunciation will make it easier to understand what's being said around you. In some regions, S at the end of a word is weakened or even dropped.

Y between vowels; at the beginning of a word or after a consonant is pronounced as LL (see p.757). Otherwise it is pronounced as I (see p.755), as in *y*, the Spanish word for "and".

Z is pronounced as an S.

STRESS

Familiarizing yourself with Spanish **stress** rules will make it easy to work out where the stress falls when you are faced with an unfamiliar word. Basically, any vowel marked with an accent is stressed; thus *andén* (platform) is an-DEN; the Venezuelan Independence hero, Bolívar is bo-LI-var and María is ma-RI-a. If there is no written accent, then there are two possibilities. If the word **ends** in a **vowel**, **n** or **s**, it is stressed on the second to last syllable: thus *desayuno* (breakfast) is de-sa-JU-no, *comen* (they eat) is KO-men and *casas* (houses) is KA-sas. If the word ends in any consonant apart from n or s, then it is stressed on the last syllable: thus *ciudad* (city) is ciu-DAD, *comer* (to eat) is ko-MER and *Uruguay* is u-ru-GWAI.

GLOSSARY

ACA (Automóvil Club Argentino) National motoring organization (pronounced A-ka)
ACAMPAR To camp.
ADUANA Customs post.
AEROSILLA Chairlift.
AGRESTE Wild or rustic (often used to describe a campsite with very basic facilities).
ALERCE Giant, slow-growing Patagonian cypress, similar to the Californian redwood.
ALMACÉN Small grocery store, which in the past often functioned as a bar too.
ALTIPLANO High Andean plateau.
AÓNIK'ENK The Southern Group of Tehuelche (q.v), the last of whose descendants live in the province of Santa Cruz.
ARAUCARIA Monkey puzzle tree.
AROBA The @ sign on a computer keyboard.
ARROYO Stream or small river.
ASADO Barbecue (either on a parrilla or on the spit); *tira de asado* is beef ribs.
AUTOPISTA Motorway.
BACHE Pothole.
BAILANTA Dance club, where the predominant sound is *cumbia* (see overleaf).
BALNEARIO Bathing resort; also a complex of sunshades and small tents on the beach, often with a bar and shower facilities, for which users pay a daily, weekly or monthly rate.
BAÑADO A type of shallow marshland, often caused by a flooded river, and common in the Chaco region.
BANDA NEGATIVA Airline tariff bracket, where a percentage of seats are sold at heavily discounted rates.
BAQUEANO Mountain or wilderness guide.
BARRIO Neighbourhood.
BOFEDAL Spongey Altiplano wetland.
BOLEADORAS/BOLAS Traditional hunting implement, composed of stone balls connected by thick cord, thrown to entangle legs or neck of prey. Traditionally used by gauchos, who inherited it from Argentina's indigenous inhabitants.
BOLETERÍA Ticket office.
BOLETO Travel ticket.
BOMBACHA Wide-legged gaucho trousers.
BOMBILLA Straw-like implement, usually of metal, used for drinking *mate* from a gourd.
BONDI Colloquial term in Buenos Aires for a bus.
BOTIQUÍN Medicine kit.
C/ The abbreviation of *calle* (street); only rarely used.

CABILDO Colonial town hall; now replaced by Municipalidad.
CABINA TELEFÓNICA Phone booth.
CACIQUE Generic term for the head of a Latin American indigenous community or people, elected or hereditary.
CAJERO AUTOMÁTICO ATM, cashpoint machine.
CALAFATE Type of thorny Patagonian bush, famous for its blue berries.
CAMIONETA Pick-up truck.
CAMPESINO Country-dweller; sometimes used to refer to someone with indigenous roots.
CAMPO DE HIELO Ice cap or ice-field.
CAÑA COLIHUE Native Patagonian plant of the forest understorey, which strongly resembles bamboo.
CANCHA Football stadium.
CANTINA Traditional restaurant, usually Italian.
CARACTERÍSTICA Telephone code.
CARAGUATÁ Sisal-like fibre used by the Wichí for weaving *yica* bags.
CARPA Tent.
CARRETERA Route or highway.
CARTELERA Agency for buying discounted tickets for cinemas, theatres and concerts.
CASA DE TÉ Tearoom.
CASCO Main building of estancia; the homestead.
CATARATAS Waterfalls, usually used to refer specifically to Iguazú Falls.
CAUDILLO Regional military or political leader, usually with authoritarian overtones.
CEBAR MATE To brew *mate*.
CEIBO Tropical tree with a twisted trunk, whose bright-red or pink blossom is the national flower of Argentina, Uruguay and Paraguay.
CERRO Hill, mountain peak.
CHACO HÚMEDO Wet chaco habitat.
CHACO SECO Dry chaco habitat.
CHACRA Small farm.
CHAGUAR See *Caraguatá*.
CHAMAMÉ Folk music from the littoral region, specifically Corrientes Province.
CHANGO Common term in the northwest for a young boy; often used in the sense of "mate"/"buddy".
CHAQUEÑO Someone from the Chaco.
CHATA Slang term for pick-up truck.
CHE Ubiquitous, classically Argentinian term, tagged onto the end of numerous statements and generally meaning "mate" or "buddy". From the Mapuche for "person".

CHOIQUE Common term, deriving from Mapudungun, for the smaller, southern Darwin's rhea of Patagonia.

CHURRO Strip of fried dough, somewhat similar to a doughnut, often filled with *dulce de leche*.

COLECTIVO Urban bus.

COMBI Small minibus that runs urban bus routes.

COMPARSA Carnival "school".

CONFITERÍA Café and tearoom, often with patisserie attached.

CONVENTILLO Tenement building.

CORDILLERA Mountain range; usually used in Argentina to refer to the Andes.

CORTADERA Pampas grass.

COSTANERA Riverside avenue.

COUNTRY Term for exclusive out-of-town residential compound or sports and social club.

CRIOLLO Historically an Argentinian-born person of Spanish descent. Used today in two ways: as a general term for Argentinian (as in comida criolla, traditional Argentinian food) and used by indigenous people to refer to those of non-indigenous descent.

CUADRA The distance from one street corner to the next, usually 100 metres (see also *manzana*).

CUCHILLA Regional term for low hill in Entre Ríos.

CUESTA Slope or small hill.

CUMBIA Popular Argentinian "tropical" rhythm, inspired by Colombian cumbia.

DEPARTAMENTO Administrative district in a province; also an apartment.

DESCAMISADOS Term meaning "the shirtless ones," popularized by Juan and Evita Perón to refer to the working-class masses and dispossessed.

DESPENSA Shop (particularly in rural areas).

DÍA DE CAMPO Day spent at an estancia where traditional asado and empanadas are eaten and guests are usually given a display of gaucho skills.

DIQUE Dock; also dam.

E/ The abbreviation of *entre* (between), used in addresses.

EMPALME Junction of two highways.

ENCOMIENDA Package, parcel; also historical term for form of trusteeship bestowed on Spaniards after conquest, granting them rights over the native population.

ENTRADA Ticket (for football match, theatre etc).

ESTANCIA Argentinian farm, traditionally with huge areas of land.

ESTEPA Steppe.

ESTERO A shallow swampland, commonly found in El Litoral and Chaco areas.

FACÓN Gaucho knife, usually carried in a sheath.

FEDERALIST Nineteenth-century term for one in favour of autonomous power being given to the provinces; opponent of Unitarist (see p.764).

FERIA ARTESANAL/DE ARTESANÍAS Craft fair.

FERRETERÍA Hardware shop (often useful for camping equipment).

FERROCARRIL Railway.

FICHA Token.

FOGÓN Place for a barbecue or campfire; bonfire.

FONDA Simple restaurant.

GALERÍA Small shopping arcade.

GASEOSA Soft drink.

GAUCHO The typical Argentinian "cowboy", or rural estancia worker.

GENDARMERÍA Police station.

GOMERÍA Tyre repair centre.

GOMERO Rubber tree.

GRINGO Any white foreigner, though often specifically those from English-speaking countries; historically European immigrants to Argentina (as opposed to criollos), as in pampa gringa, the part of pampa settled by European immigrants.

GUANACO Wild camelid of the llama family.

GUARANÍ Indigenous people and language, found principally in Misiones, Corrientes and Paraguay.

GUARDAEQUIPAJE Left-luggage office.

GUARDAFAUNA Wildlife ranger.

GUARDAGANADO Cattle grid.

GUARDAPARQUE National park ranger.

GÜNÜNA'KÜNA The northern group of the Tehuelche (q.v.), now extinct.

HACER DEDO To hitchhike.

HUMEDAL Any wetland swampy area.

IGM (Instituto Geográfico Militar) The national military's cartographic institution.

IMPENETRABLE Term applied historically to the area of the dry chaco with the most inhospitable conditions for white settlement, due to lack of water; the name of a zone of northwestern Chaco Province.

INTENDENCIA Head office of a national park.

INTENDENTE Administrative chief of a national park.

INTERNO Telephone extension number.

ISLETA DE MONTE Clump of scrubby mixed woodland found in savannah or flat agricultural land, typically in the Chaco and the northeast of the country.

IVA (impuesto de valor agregado) Value-added tax or sales tax.

JACARANDÁ Tropical tree with trumpet-shaped mauvish blossom.

JUNTA Military government coalition.

KIOSKO Newspaper stand or small store selling cigarettes, confectionery and some food-stuffs.

KOLLA Andean indigenous group predominant in the northwestern provinces of Salta and Jujuy.

LANCHA Smallish motor boat.

LAPACHO Tropical tree typical of the littoral region and distinguished by bright-pink blossom.

LEÑA Firewood.

LENGA Type of *Nothofagus* southern beech common in Patagonian forests.

LICUADO Milkshake.

El LITORAL Littoral, shore – used to refer to the provinces of Entre Ríos, Corrientes, Misiones, Santa Fe and sometimes Eastern Chaco and Formosa.

LITORALEÑO Inhabitant of El Litoral (see above).

LOCUTORIO Call centre, where phone calls are made from cabins and the caller charged after the call is made.

LOMO DE BURRO Speed bump.

LONCO Head or *cacique* (see p.761) of a Mapuche community.

MADREJÓN A swampy ox-bow lake.

MALLÍN Swamp, particularly in upland moors.

MANZANA City block; the square bounded by four *cuadras* (see opposite).

MAPUCHE One of Argentina's largest indigenous groups, whose ancestors originally came from Chilean Patagonia and whose biggest communities are found in the provinces of Chubut, Río Negro and especially Neuquén.

MAPUDUNGUN The language of the Mapuches.

MARCHA Commercial dance music.

MATACO See Wichí.

MATE Strictly the *mate* gourd or receptacle, but used generally to describe the national "tea" drink.

MENÚ DEL DÍA Standard set menu.

MENÚ ECECUTIVO Set menu. More expensive than the *menú del día* (q.v.), though not always that executive.

MESOPOTAMIA The three provinces of Entre Ríos, Corrientes and Misiones, by analogy with the ancient region lying between the rivers Tigris and Euphrates, in modern-day Iraq.

MICRO Long-distance bus.

MICROCENTRO The area of a city comprising the central square and neighbouring streets.

MILONGA Style of folk-guitar music usually associated with the pampa region; also a tango dance and a subgenre of tango, more uptempo than tango proper.

MIRADOR Scenic lookout point or tower.

MONTE Scrubby woodland, often used to describe any uncultivated woodland area. Also used to refer to the desertified ecosystem that lies in the rainshadow of the central Andes around the Cuyo region.

MOZARABIC Spanish architectural style, originally dating from the ninth to thirteenth centuries and characterized by a fusion of Romanesque and Moorish styles.

MUELLE Pier or jetty.

MUNICIPALIDAD Municipality building or town hall.

ÑANDÚ A common name, derived from Guaraní, for the greater rhea, but also used to refer to its smaller cousin, the Darwin's rhea.

ÑIRE Type of *Nothofagus* southern beech tree common in Patagonian forests.

ÑOQUI Argentinian spelling of the Italian gnocchi, a small potato dumpling. Used to refer to phoney employees who appear on a company's payroll but don't actually work there; also slang for a punch.

NOTHOFAGUS Genus of Patagonian trees commonly called southern beech (includes *lenga* and *ñire* q.v.).

OMBÚ Large shade tree, originally from the Mesopotamic region and now associated with the pampa where it was introduced in the eighteenth century.

PAISANO Meaning "countryman"; sometimes loosely used as equivalent to gaucho and often used by people of indigenous descent to refer to themselves, thus avoiding the sometimes pejorative *indio* (Indian).

PALMAR Palm grove.

PALO BORRACHO Tree associated especially with the dry-chaco habitat of northern Argentina; its name (literally "drunken stick") is derived from its swollen trunk in which water is stored.

PALOMETA Piranha/piraña.

PAMPA The broad flat grasslands of central Argentina.

PARQUÍMETRO Parking meter.

PARRILLA Barbecue grill or restaurant.

PARRILLADA The meat cooked on a *parrilla*.

PASAJE Narrow street.

PASEAPERRO Professional dog walker.

PASTIZAL Grassland, often used for grazing.

PATO The Argentinian national sport; similar to handball on horseback.

PAYADA Traditional improvised musical style, often performed as a kind of dialogue between two singers (*payadores*) who accompany themselves on guitars.

PEAJE Road toll.

PEATONAL Pedestrianized street.

PEHUÉN Mapuche term for monkey puzzle tree.

PEÑA Circle or group (usually of artists or musicians); a *peña folklórica* is a folk-music club.

PEÓN Farmhand.

PICADA A roughly-marked path; also a plate of small snacks eaten before a meal, particularly cheese, ham or smoked meats.

PLANTA BAJA Ground floor (first floor, US).

PLAYA Beach.

PLAYA DE ESTACIONAMIENTO Parking lot; garage.

PLAZOLETA/PLAZUELA Small square.

PORTEÑO Someone from Buenos Aires city.

PREFECTURA Naval prefecture for controlling river and marine traffic.

PUESTO Small outpost or hut for shepherds or *guardaparques*.

PUKARÁ Pre-Colombian fortress.

PULPERÍA A type of traditional general-provisions store that doubles up as a bar and rural meeting point.

PUNA High Andean plateau (alternative term for *altiplano*, see p.761).

PUNTANO Someone from San Luis.

QUEBRADA Ravine, gully.

QUERANDÍ Original indigenous inhabitants of the pampa region.

QUINTA Suburban or country house with a small plot of land, where fruit and vegetables are often cultivated.

QOM An indigenous group, living principally in the east of Formosa and Chaco provinces. The word means "people" in their language.

RANCHO Simple countryside dwelling, typically constructed of adobe.

RASTRA Gaucho belt, typically ornamented with silver.

RC (Ruta Complementaria) Subsidiary, unsealed road in Tierra del Fuego.

RECARGO Surcharge on credit cards.

RECOVA Arcade around the exterior of a building or courtyard, typical of colonial-era buildings.

REDUCCIÓN Jesuit mission settlement.

REFUGIO Trekking refuge.

REMISE/REMÍS Taxi or chauffeur-driven rental car, booked through a central office.

REMISE COLECTIVO Shared cab that runs fixed interurban routes.

REPRESA Dam; also reservoir.

RÍO River.

RIPIO Gravel; usually used to describe an unsurfaced gravel road.

RN (Ruta Nacional) Major route, usually paved.

RP (Ruta Provincial) Provincial road, sometimes paved.

RUTA Route or road.

SALTO Waterfall.

SAPUCAY Bloodcurdling shriek characteristic of *chamamé* (see p.761).

SELK'NAM Nomadic, indigenous guanaco-hunters from Tierra del Fuego, whose last members died in the 1960s. Also called Ona, the Yámana (q.v.) name for them.

SENDERO Path or trail.

S/N Used in addresses to indicate that there's no house number (*sin número*).

SOROCHE Altitude sickness.

SORTIJA Display of gaucho skill in which the galloping rider must spear a small ring hung from a thread.

SUBTE Buenos Aires' underground railway.

TANGUERÍA Tango club.

TASA DE TERMINAL Terminal tax.

TAXÍMETRO Taxi meter.

TEHUELCHE Generic term for the different nomadic steppe tribes of Patagonia, who early European explorers named "Patagones".

TELEFÉRICO Gondola or cable car.

TENEDOR LIBRE Eat all you like buffet restaurant.

TERERÉ Common drink in the subtropical north of the country and Paraguay, composed of *yerba mate* served with wild herbs (*yuyos*) and ice-cold water or lemonade.

TERMINAL DE ÓMNIBUS Bus terminal.

TERRATENIENTE Landowner.

TIPA Acacia-like tree often found in northern yungas.

TOBA See Qom.

TRUCO Argentina's national card game, in which the ability to outbluff your opponents is of major importance.

UNITARISTS Nineteenth-century centralists, in favour of power being centralized in Buenos Aires; opponent of Federalist (see p.762).

VILLA Short for *villa miseria*, a shanty town.

WICHÍ Semi-nomadic indigenous group, living predominantly in the dry central and western areas of Chaco and Formosa provinces, and in the far east of Salta. Sometimes referred to pejoratively as Mataco.

YAHGANES See Yámana.

YÁMANA Nomadic indigenous canoe-going people who inhabited the channels to the south of Tierra del Fuego, and whose culture died out in Argentina in the early twentieth century. called Yahganes by later nineteenth-century missionaries.

YERBA MATE The leaves of the plant, used to brew *mate*.

YPF (YACIMIENTOS PETROLEROS FIS-CALES) The principal Argentinian petroleum company, now privatized. It is usually used to refer to the company's fuel stations.

ZONA FRANCA Duty-free zone.

INDEX

Stay in touch with us!

ROUGH*NEWS* **is Rough Guides' free newsletter.
In four issues a year we give you news, travel
issues, music reviews, readers' letters and the
latest dispatches from authors on the road.**

I would like to receive ROUGH*NEWS*: please put me on your free mailing list.

NAME . . . .

ADDRESS . . . .

Please clip or photocopy and send to: Rough Guides, 62–70 Shorts Gardens, London WC2H 9AH,
England or Rough Guides, 375 Hudson Street, New York, NY 10014, USA.

ROUGH GUIDES: Travel

Alaska
Amsterdam
Andalucia
Argentina
Australia
Austria

Bali & Lombok
Barcelona
Belgium &
  Luxembourg
Belize
Berlin
Brazil
Britain
Brittany &
  Normandy
Bulgaria
California
Canada
Central America
Chile
China
Corsica
Costa Rica
Crete
Croatia
Cuba
Cyprus
Czech & Slovak
  Republics

Dodecanese &
  the East Aegean
Devon &
  Cornwall
Dominican
  Republic
Dordogne & the
  Lot
Ecuador
Egypt
England
Europe
Florida
France
French Hotels &
  Restaurants
  1999
Germany
Goa
Greece
Greek Islands
Guatemala
Hawaii
Holland
Hong Kong &
  Macau
Hungary

Iceland
India
Indonesia
Ionian Islands
Ireland

Israel & the
  Palestinian
  Territories
Italy
Jamaica
Japan
Jordan
Kenya
Lake District
Languedoc &
  Roussillon
Laos
London
Los Angeles
Malaysia,
  Singapore &
  Brunei
Mallorca &
  Menorca
Maya World
Mexico
Morocco
Moscow
Nepal
New England
New York
New Zealand
Norway
Pacific
  Northwest
Paris
Peru
Poland
Portugal
Prague
Provence & the
  Côte d'Azur
The Pyrenees
Romania
St Petersburg
San Francisco

Sardinia
Scandinavia
Scotland
Scottish
  highlands and
  Islands
Sicily
Singapore
South Africa
South India
Southeast Asia
Southwest USA
Spain
Sweden
Switzerland
Syria

Thailand
Trinidad &
  Tobago
Tunisia
Turkey
Tuscany &
  Umbria
USA
Venice
Vienna
Vietnam
Wales
Washington DC
West Africa
Zimbabwe &
  Botswana

AVAILABLE AT ALL GOOD BOOKSHOPS